RISKY BUSINESS

RISKY BUSINESS

Rock in Film

R. Serge Denisoff
William D. Romanowski

Transaction Publishers
New Brunswick (U.S.A.) and London (U.K.)

Copyright © 1991 by Transaction Publishers,
New Brunswick, New Jersey 08903

Library of Congress Catalog Number: 90-10961
ISBN: 0-88738-843-4 Cloth
Printed in the United States of America

Library of Congress Cataloging-in-Publication Data

Denisoff, R. Serge.
  Risky business : rock in film / R. Serge Denisoff and William D. Romanowski.
    p. cm.
  Includes bibliographical references.
  ISBN 0-88738-843-4
  1. Rock films—United States—History and criticism.
I. Romanowski, William D. II. Title.
PN1995.9.M86D45 1990
791.43'657—dc20

                                        90-10961
                                          CIP

Contents

Preface

The name of the game in media can be summed up in one word: *exposure*. The days of, "Let's go to a movie!" or, "What's new?" asked at the record store are ancient history. Movie tickets at $7, albums listing at $9.98, and compact discs priced at $14.98 make consumers more discrete. There exist, also, competing and complementary means of using leisure time, such as radio, television, video cassettes, and, for some of us, books.

R. Serge Denisoff's *Solid Gold*, *Tarnished Gold*, and *Inside MTV* looked at the record industry and the media accessing its market. This volume is a reexamination and continuation of the previous works.

The role of motion pictures in giving exposure to pop, especially rock, music is highly significant. As Doherty, author of *Teenagers & Teenpics*, and the authors put forth, film was *the* medium in breaking rock 'n' roll.

Like others who developed innovations, the players were unaware of what they had wrought. Hollywood originally put Elvis behind a plow in a grade-B western. Bill Haley was reduced to mouthing lines such as, "See you later, alligator." Major labels, as the charts aptly demonstrate, had little knowledge of rock music in the 1950s and early 1960s. In 1962 Capitol Records reportedly turned down the Beatles, as it was believed a British group would fail Stateside; Veejay Records released the first Mop-Top album.

The merger of film with rock has been a long, messy process. *Saturday Night Fever*, the top-selling LP until *Thriller*, sparked interest; MTV's entrance into the arena enhanced the crosspollination of music and film.

Many attempted to codify the marketing strategy of soundtracks, benefitting both movie studios and record labels. Successful exceptions became the prototypes, despite the painful reality that most soundtracks were monumental stiffs.

ix

The success ratio of movie packages has presented a host of problems for the authors. Choosing selections such as *The Graduate*, *Easy Rider*, *American Graffiti*, *Saturday Night Fever*, *Help!*, and *Dirty Dancing* was easy. There are a plethora of productions, however, that are significant by their box office and record-store failures. The writers attempted to give equal time to these as well.

There is a methodological note the writers hope that reviewers, especially, will remember: Prior to *Fever*, films with rock music comprised a small percentage of motion-picture input. After 1983's *Flashdance* the situation drastically changed. In 1984, ten soundtracks, many in the pop/rock genre, were certified platinum. By the Orwellian year, it was clear that a full treatment of all rock scores would be an impossible task. The main criterion for inclusion became copies sold. The writers did, however, choose box office and record misadventures which seemed edifying, i.e., *9½ Weeks* or *Sid and Nancy*. Frankly, some of the films chosen occasionally reflected the bias of an author. (Denisoff loved *Streets of Fire*.)

Some may object to the brevity of the "rockumentary" section. Parales and Pat Romanoski asserted, "The best known and most important rock movies are the rock documentaries." The authors disagree. A vast majority of "rockumentaries" are little more than filmed concerts, adding another sensory dimension to "live" or concert recordings. Some— *Woodstock*, *Gimme Shelter*, *Don't Look Back*, *The Last Waltz*, and *Stop Making Sense*—have merit. In a majority of cases, including *U2: Rattle and Hum*, the album far outdistanced the film's earning power.

Acknowledgments

A book about the media is dependent on the assistance of many individuals. We'd particularly like to note the generous help of all the branches of MCA and Warner Brothers. Their home video people, particularly, were very helpful. At MCA Records, Andy McKaie and Jane Hoffman proved invaluable. Across the way, home-video publicists Georgia S. Cave and Jane Ayer provided material. In Burbank, Virginia Green and the record company publicists aided us. Honorable mention for press kits: Steve Rubin of Scotti Brothers Pictures, Orion Pictures, 20th Century Fox, Touchstone, HBO Home Video, Vicki Greenleaf of IVE, Media Home Entertainment, Kartes Video Communication, Geffen, RCA, Polygram, and Capitol Records, headed by Cary Baker, and Aurora Productions for *Eddie And The Cruisers*.

We express our warmest appreciation to Dave Schwarz and his assistants, especially Mitch Kaduboski of the Bowling Green State University Serials section and William Schurk of the Audio Library, for their invaluable assistance. The Popular Culture division of BGSU is, also, an oasis in a relative desert. Gary Burns and George Plasketes helped by sending CARE packages of photocopied articles.

Deb Fentress, Debbie Hill, and Deborah Schroeder created the final processed manuscript. No less a contribution, perhaps even a greater one, involved Christine E. Domme and Pamela L. Miller, who diligently typed first drafts. Kate Miller's, Jowell Weaver's and Shari Fiorino's contributions are equally appreciated. Thanks to all.

R.S.D.
W.D.R.

1

Rock Around The Clock: The Changing of Popular Music

In twenty years, when Junior has grown into a sedate married man, father and pillar of the community, he will remember "Ko Ko Mo" wistfully and be distressed no end by the songs his son admires. Only Tin Pan Alley will stay young with each new generation.
—Mitch Miller, Columbia Records executive

It's gotta be rock 'n' roll music
if you wanna dance with me.
—Chuck Berry, artist

. . . in the theatre, watching Blackboard Jungle, *they couldn't tell you to turn it down. I didn't care if Bill Haley was white or sincere . . . he was playing the Teen-Age National Anthem and it was so LOUD I was jumping up and down,* Blackboard Jungle, *not even considering the story line (which had the old people winning in the end), represented a strange sort of "endorsement" of the teen-age cause: "They have made a movie about us, therefore, we exist."*
—Frank Zappa, artist

The Fifties were a strange confluence of C. Wright Mills's Age of Somnabulism and Garry Marshall's *Happy Days*, mixed with technology seemingly run rampant. The decade was neither as tranquil as the ageless adolescent—Marshall—would portray nor as unconscious as the social gadfly Mills—the author of *Power Elite* (1956)—indicated. The fly in the

1

ointment was technology. In the form of audio/visual communications, drastically altered media would interactively reshape the world of adolescents.

With a fatherly war hero in the White House, the nation appeared fairly stable despite the Korean "police action" and the McCarthy "red scare." Appearances, as always, would prove deceiving.

Demographically and technologically, significant changes were taking place. The postwar birth rate augured ramifications for the social fabric.

The slumbering behemoth, television, was coming into its own. In 1952 one-third of American households were plugged into the tube, and the number continued to increase. The televisual home invader dichotomized life-styles and values along generational lines. The film industry was forced to redefine itself. Its massified notion of "family entertainment" was washed away by Ed Sullivan, Milton Berle, and Howdy Doody. New marketing, production, and distribution strategies became imperative. Old habits and notions, however, wither slowly.

The record industry, similarly, was being affected. The labels were run by an elite of A&R men (Mitch Miller, Ken Nelson and others) as powerful as the Meyers, Goldwyns, Cohns, and Warners had been in the 1930s. Their stable of swing-era remnants, however talented, lacked the universal appeal of earlier decades. Technology would accentuate the generational cleavage with the infamous "battle of the speeds."

At a 21 June 1948 press conference, Columbia Records (a division of CBS) president Edward Wallerstein introduced a "revolutionary new product" called the LP (long-playing) record. One side could play twenty-three minutes without interruption. The audio quality was excellent. Media people at the Waldorf-Astoria press gathering claimed the LP's sound quality surpassed that of the 78. RCA Victor, CBS's major competitor, was aware of the innovation but remained silent. CBS offered to share its engineering expertise with all of the labels; RCA's reticence, however, found Columbia with the only major-label 33⅓ product. The monopoly allowed the label to rack up 1.25 million in sales by the end of 1948.

The LP rapidly became a middle-class toy for upscale consumers. The new modality, according to inventor Peter Goldmark, was especially conducive to symphonic and operatic music. Jazz, unsuited to the confines of the 78, was showcased. Broadway musicals and "mood music" were strong sellers. All of these genres were aimed at adults.

RCA broke its silence in 1949 with the introduction of yet a third speed: 45 revolutions per minute (rpm). As with the LP, new hardware would accompany the seven-inch, vinylite disc. RCA advertised the product as having "the world's fastest changer." The sound and time quality of

RCA's entry was akin to that of the now-doomed 78. *Saturday Review* wisely noted that RCA had limited "itself to the convenience of one segment of the record public (the large mass market) and left the smaller, if more discriminating, public." The medium shortly would become the message.

The immediate public reaction was bewilderment. The industry itself, according to Schicke, "was utterly flabbergasted when the word of the third speed spread";[1] RCA's short-sighted decision to introduce a competing speed is best explained by the long-standing rivalry between the two recording giants. Gelatt describes consumer reaction to the myopic war of the speeds: "The postwar record boom had been turned into a bust." Retail sales dropped from a peak of $204 million in 1947 to less than $158 million the year RCA unveiled the short-playing record. Executive intransigence continued. CBS won the hearts and minds of adult record buyers in the speciality areas. Losing millions of dollars and faced with potential artist defections, RCA was reluctantly moving toward the LP.

"RCA would have probably continued to sustain financial losses to keep the fight alive, were it not for the fact that a number of Victor's most important artists threatened to quit"[2] wrote an observer. Upon hearing Bruno Walter on a CBS disc, the renowned conductor Arturo Toscanini became one of the discontented RCA artists.

The down side of the turntable *detente* was class and generational fragmentation. The LP until the Beatles, was a costly, upscale item—the product and hardware were aimed at adults.

Only a small number of rock 'n' rollers were deemed sufficiently commercially attractive to make albums. Elvis Presley's *Love Me Tender* soundtrack was released on a 45-rpm, extended-play disc (EP). The seven-inch EP, with four selections, priced at $1.49, was aimed at teens (c.1955, LPs listed at $3.98 and 45 singles were priced at $.89).

The lower-cost singles became the currency of the Top 40, rhythm and blues (R & B), and country consumers. Off the record, label executives would curse the high-profile, low-profit product. One executive said, "You know, the camel is a horse designed by a record company president."

CBS appeared to win the technology battle while losing the short-term market war. Radio stations that were tied to trade charts preferred cuing a one-song disc. Program directors felt AM hit-parade listeners were singles oriented, creating a self-fulfilling prophecy. Price-conscious buyers preferred the seven-inch disc. The key, however, proved to be the jukebox operators and their distributors, the "one-stops." Moving from 78s to smaller discs appealed to the machine operators. Thirty-three inchers, with many selections per side, were unacceptable to the hit-oriented merchandisers. One stops—independent distributors—sided with their best customers, the operators. The short-playing record became the modality for the youth music market. Unit numbers made the popular-music window the most profitable. LPs netted more per unit than their smaller counterparts; nonetheless, the volume was absent. Adults are low or moderate record buyers, regardless of price. Adolescents became a prime industry target.

A & R executives, when not shepherding a record or artist, were known to spend time with the latest issue of *Photoplay* in order to "psyche out the kids." Hagiographic stories about Marlon Brando (*The Wild One*) alerted the bizzers. Sam Phillips of Sun Records would utter the immortal phrase, "If I could find a white boy who could sing like a nigger, I could make a million dollars." Other executives politely kept the thought to themselves. In 1954, however, the record industry lacked a Brandoesque personality. Perry Como, Tony Bennett, Frank Sinatra, and even Eddie Fisher were voices out of the past.

The film industry, in dire straits, would probably have welcomed an "insignificant" quarrel over delivery equipment. Instead, film company lawyers were battling anti-trust suits that put the very substructure of the studios in jeopardy. Reeling from the *U.S. vs. Paramount et.al.* decision to divest chain-theater operations, and the unspeakable little glowing boxes placed prominently in the nation's living rooms, the film community was in a struggle for its very survival. Resorting to "big picture" spectaculars and enhanced technology proved uncertain, garnering diminishing returns. Million-dollar film budgets barely returned enough to keep the major studios afloat.

In simple statistical terms, television devastated filmdom. In 1949 there were one million television receivers. In a five-year span the number rose to thirty-two million. By the end of the Fifties, 90 percent of the American households owned at least one television set and 5,000 movie theaters had closed. The combined profits of the ten major movie studios plummeted from $121 million to $32 million despite a ticket price increase. A more telling comparison is that ninety million tickets were sold per week in 1949 but only forty-five million moved in 1956. The decline occurred although the U.S. population grew by nearly thirty million people during the 1950s. Employment in the film community was nearly halved, going from 24,000 in 1946 to 13,000 ten years later.

Like RCA Victor, the film industry adopted an ostrichlike posture, refusing to deal with the new medium. Television, desperate for film products, was denied the rental of studio vault material. Tied to the concept of "family entertainment," studios invested in mammoth super-screen technology. Cinerama and Twentieth Century Fox's Cinemascope were unveiled to lure young and old into the sparsely populated movie houses. Bankable names were signed to star in the wide-screen extravaganzas. Sound enhancement and abortive 3-D experiments were other ploys for increasing attendance at indoor showings. These innovations failed to aid most besieged exhibitors. A Sindlinger study found that during television's prime growth period, 1946 to 1953, 5,038 theaters folded. All but 334 drive-ins were "four-wallers." *Business Week* pointed to drive-ins, unaffected by Hollywood's new technology, as the "one shining exception" to the ravaged movie theaters.

Another study, vintage 1953, painted an even bleaker picture. The researchers found that 41 percent of indoor theaters were supported by their concession income, as opposed to 24 percent of drive-ins.[3] Hollywood's scarce resources, it appears, were going to the wrong exhibitors. Outdoor theaters were attracting entire families piled into the proverbial station wagons. John Durant noted, "It doesn't seem to make much of a difference what kind of pictures are shown, because drive-in fans are far less choosy."[4] The "junk" fare, in the words of a California outdoor exhibitor, would eventually drive Mom and Dad back to their glowing hearth while the drive-ins "gave way to teenage exploitation films."[5] As Jarvie nicely summarized the audience trends of the period, "The hard core is mainly the young and the unmarried who want to escape home and television."[6] The same description applied perfectly to "heavy" record buyers.

The time was not yet at hand for the studio community to realize the value of demographic analysis; instead the "great man" theory continued as film companies pursued a nebulous mass audience. The search for "hot" properties, producers, and personalities went on as usual. The expense of blockbusters soared. *My Fair Lady* (1952) cost $5.5 million, *The Robe* (1953) was made for $5 million, and another Biblical epic by C.B. DeMille, *The Ten Commandments* (1956), was delivered at $13.5 million. As the expenses mounted, the number of players inversely decreased. Financial backers demanded ironclad scripts and stars.

"With higher admission prices, the favored movies turned bigger profits," said Sklar. "The gold was there to be mined, only fewer people could share in it.[7] A back-to-basics approach was called for, and the smaller independent producers would pioneer the path. They were accustomed to Spartan conditions and being on the financial cutting edge. Russel Nye outlined the appeal of the so-called Grade Bs:

Safe returns lie in the low-budget pictures done for the drive-in, triple-feature trade, the films that titillate, enthrall, and amuse mass audiences at cheap prices just as the melodrama, vaudeville, farce, popular novel, and dime shocker always have. Out of Hollywood's total yearly production of films probably not more than one-quarter have ever been high-budget "A" films with well known stars. The rest have been routine bread-and-butter productions designed to fill in between "Spectaculars" and "Blockbusters," providing the night-to-night bills needed to keep the house partly filled on Tuesdays and Thursdays.

Great stars made only a limited number of films per year; the rest of the time screens were occupied by undistinguished movies with minor players. These routine "B" movies were the cinematic equivalents of the cheap novel on the newsstand, the sentimental melodrama in the tent show, the mass-produced magazine serial; they were and are stylized popular art aimed at nothing but transitory entertainment. They stayed with the trends, took no risks, disturbed nobody, raised no problems, simplified issues, and gave the public entertainment and not "art." Although they represent by far the majority of films produced over the years, their titles and the people who played in them are long forgotten, and appear in none of the many histories of the movies.[8]

Nye's point was supported by an MGM executive's comment, "It's not our business to promote the culture of the country, or to make art films. It's to make money.[9] Movie and music concerns lay in accessing, long before the term was popularized, the under-twenty-five segment of the population. Targeting for both media would be a new experience as massified raw numbers remained the dominant ideology. A German social philosopher once noted, however, that ideologies do change when economic necessity demands.

Rocking Blackboard Jungle

Even in the early Fifties cultural drift was in the air. The population explosion, to be termed the "Baby Boom," was beginning to filter into the consciousness of the entertainment media. The Ballad of "Davy Crockett" sold four million copies and created a craze; the $32-million sales of Silly Putty further illuminated the growing economic potential of this ill-defined, youthful demographic segment. The population transformation facilitating cultural change was on the horizon.

Radio, the dominant medium of music exposure, was flexing its corporate muscle. Airplay sold records. Gatekeepers have inherent interests. One was the result of a pre-war royalty dispute with the American Society of Composers, Authors and Publishers (ASCAP). Thriving in the white mainstream market, ASCAP refused to work with minority or specialty composers and performers. The result of the stalemate was the birth of Broadcasters Music, Inc. (BMI) as a competing licensing agent. (For a percentage of the mechanical fees, required for the use of copyrighted material, a licensing company serves as the collection agency for the composer/publisher.) Unable to contract mainstream lyricists and composers who resided at New York's legendary Brill Building on Tin Pan Alley BMI picked up the then less-saleable country, blues, and jazz artists.

"The work of many country and black musicians to whom ASCAP had refused admission regardless of prior publication," wrote Marc Hugunin, "provided a fertile field for BMI exploitation."[10] This structural change encouraged broadcasters to look more favorably upon so-called specialty material. Despite ASCAP claims, this was not done at the expense of established performers, but the perception that it did lingered. BMI merely provided a new, diversified source of music. As tastes began to change, BMI *did* benefit from the aesthetic shifts.

"The way for rock 'n' roll," suggested John Shepherd, "was undoubtedly prepared through broadcasts of country music and 'cover' versions of rhythm and blues. And since these broadcasts would not have been possible without the ASCAP-BMI dispute, that dispute is very important to the decline of Tin Pan Alley. Once the floodgates were open to non-ASCAP music, there was no looking back. For Tin Pan Alley, 'the ball was over.' "[11]

"Covering" simply refers to performer *Y* recording a release already recorded by artist *Z*. The practice goes back to the early days of vaudeville and sheet music. In the late 1940s, "covering" came to connote a mainstream act performing a specialty artist's success.

Country music was a prime choice for covers. During World War II thousands of enlistees and draftees were exposed—overwhelmed—by the likes of Roy Acuff, Bob Wills, and *Camel Caravan* troupers. Despite themselves, many came to like the country sound, or at least the softer version of the Nashville sound. Waylon Jennings once quipped that "City folks roll up their car windows when they play it." Middle-of-the-road artists legitimated the genre, albeit minus the twang. One post-war, Country and Western cover, "The Tennessee Waltz," sold four million copies. Other chart dwellers included "Cold, Cold Heart," "Doggie in the Window," "Your Cheatin' Heart," "Jambalaya," and "On Top of Old Smokey," a traditional folk song. Mitch Miller culled a number of hits for his Columbia Records stable of pop artists using country material by Hank Williams.

Black urban *a capella* or "doo-wop" groups occasionally found their songs put to luscious string arrangements, backing crooners. The Orioles' "Crying in the Chapel" was covered by at least three pop singers. BMI, representing the songwriters and publishers, was delighted.

The list of rock covers in the mid-1950s made "covering" synonymous with exploitation of blacks. Numerous writers have argued, as did Mike Gershman, that "the prevailing racism on white-owned radio stations could never permit a black blues artist the time to communicate his music to white audiences."[12] Racism in some instances *was* a factor. Profit was the dominant motive. The 1950s pop market was predominantly white. That's where the customers were. Using "name" mainstream acts to record a successful specialty number was an economic necessity. The lame renditions of "Sh-Boom" by the Crewcuts and "Ain't That A Shame" by Pat Boone made the triumph of Fats Domino and other authentic artists possible.

Postal worker Max E. Freedman, a sixty-three-year-old songwriter, was astutely aware of the changing market conditions. He expressed a desire to reach the increasingly younger 45 buyers with "jump" music. Although the ASCAP lyricist seemed an unlikely candidate, having written such compositions as "Liebestraum," "Blue Danube Waltz," "Song of India," and "Sioux City Sue," he joined "Jimmy DeKnight," *ne* James Myers, an East Coast music publisher to produce "Rock Around The Clock."

Bill Haley and Myers, especially the latter, have muddied up the history of the song. Myers, with Jack Howard, had started Cowboy Records in 1948. Howard, an ardent Country and Western fan, released some of Haley's original attempts at recording. Cowboy was essentially a vanity label, charging the artist for recording and pressing costs. (Many neophyte acts use vanities for demos, self-promotion, and sales at live appearances.) Haley's first single was issued on the Cowboy label: Hank Williams's "Too Many Parties, Too Many Pals" on the flip-side of "Four Leaf Clover Blues." As with most labels lacking distribution and promotion branches, the Cowboy enterprise failed. However, Howard remained Haley's informal manager until he launched the Arcade label in 1952.

Arcade specialized in country and novelty material. Nearly all of its artists were located in the Northeastern states. Haley, through the Howard connection and the Philadelphia country music scene, interacted regularly with "locals" involved in the company.

Howard recommended Haley to Dave Miller, the owner of Essex Records. Miller wanted a swing-sounding country act to cover a Sam Phillips-produced R & B number. Miller and Myers detested one another, however, and there was no way Miller would allow a Myers composition on the Essex label. The song was given to Howard. He chose Sonny Dae, whose main claim to fame was as a regular on the *Old Dominion Barn Dance* in Richmond, Virginia.

Sonny Dae and The Knights cut a jump-band interpretation. The exact date of the session is unclear but some rock historians date it as September

1952. The verifiable release date is March 1954. The "B" side was "Movin' Guitar" (Arcade 123). Lacking promotion and distribution the offering predictably stiffed. Although the beat-laden bottom of the reknowned Decca version was absent, Dae's version equalled a number of those by such rockers as Boyd Bennett. Freedman prematurely gave up on his song.

Impressed with Haley's live performances, Myers reasoned that the wrong act had recorded his and Freedman's masterpiece. From its inception, "Rock" proved to be remarkable resilient, due to Myers's dogged devotion to the potential moneymaker.

The chronology of the Dae record raises a number of questions best left to musicologists. In the summer of 1953 "Rock" was one of Haley's more popular club songs. This, it has been suggested, was the motivation for Arcade issuing the song. Less than a month after its street date, Haley would cut the song for Milt Gabler. An interesting question emerges, "Who was covering whom?" One plausible explanation is that Myers pitched the song to both artists.

Myers had provided the "novelty foxtrot" to cherubic bandleader Bill Haley. His club act, recently renamed the Comets from the original hillbilly-sounding Saddlemen, had enjoyed some recognition redoing R & B material. Haley's modest accomplishments included rearrangements of songs like Jackie Brenston's "Rocket 88," the first white cover of a song originally aimed at the black audience. "Rock the Joint" came from a Jimmy Preston cut issued by Gotham Records in 1949.

Only "Crazy, Man, Crazy" was an original. The song would be the first generic rock 'n' roll title in the trades, reaching number 15 on the *Billboard* chart. At Myers's behest Haley included "Rock" in the Comets' repertoire. The song generated an unusually spirited audience response. Myers saw the tune as a perfect followup to "Crazy, Man, Crazy." Haley agreed. David Miller, owner of Essex Records, dissented. Haley said, "I never could record it. I wanted to—had it rehearsed and all—but he just absolutely refused because of his dislike for Myers."[13] As the Essex contract neared completion, Myers set up a successful audition with Decca A & R man Milt Gabler. On 12 April 1954, Haley and the Comets cut "Thirteen Women" and "(We're Gonna) Rock Around The Clock" at the Pythian Temple Studio, the converted New York City dance hall that had been site of Louis Jordon's big hits sessions. Gabler used Jordon's back-beat arrangement with the Comets. A single was released in May with a full-page *Billboard* ad. Once again, the title failed to break, but Myers remained committed to the song.

Haley's next effort, another cover, "Shake, Rattle and Roll" reached the *Billboard* Hot 100 on 5 July 1954. This sanitized version of the Big Joe Turner rock song would sell a million copies. "Rock," reasoned Myers, should have earned a gold record. He commenced a blanket over-the-transom mailing: "I sent 200 copies of the song to Hollywood."[14] Myers's timing proved propitious as the studios were entering the context of synergy—without knowing it.

"Synergy," in the Fifties, was a technical term generally confined to biology and pharmacology. Practitioners used the concept to describe the interplay between organisms that increases their ability to achieve an effect of which each is individually incapable. More simply, synergy increases each component's effectiveness in reaching a mutually desirable goal.

Movie studios, reeling from television, began in mid-1954 a marketing technique called "two-way promotion." The "gimmick," as *Billboard's* June Bundy called it, was for a "top artist to record the title tune from a new movie to be used as a prologue to or background for the film." In turn "the diskery is expected to release the record at the very same time."[15] Movie production companies controlled the publishing rights to many film scores and soundtracks.

In 1954, middle-of-the-road (MOR) artists were used to crosspromote films and records. The Four Aces recorded "It's a Woman's World" for the picture of the same name. A year later, "Love Is a Many Splendid Thing" by the same quartet would become the first Number-1 single especially written as a film theme. Twentieth Century again used Frank Sinatra to sing "Three Coins in the Fountain" as a title song. "Hold My Hand" by Don Cornell was inserted throughout the Dick Powell and Debbie Reynolds vehicle *Susan Slept Here*. Other publisher-film tie-ins included *High Noon* and the Saulter-Finnegan instrumental for *The Moon is Blue*.

Vocalist-actress Doris Day started her own publishing firm, Arwin Productions. The concept behind the acquisition was to employ promotion people to hype songs to boast film attendance. *Young At Heart*, starring Day and Frank Sinatra, contained four songs belonging to her company. "Ole Blue Eyes," Sinatra, owned a piece of the title song, which was released by his record label, Capitol.

A precursory fly in the ointment appeared. Studios, anxious for the inexpensive exposure afforded by airplay, attempted to control artists' release dates. A & R people strongly objected to being influenced by film-opening dates. An artist with a charted hit did not need another title detracting from the original release. A record must "run its course" prior to a followup. Artists did not always appreciate the label's restriction. Pulled by large sums of money and the big lure of a chance to break into the picture business, even if only on the soundtrack, name artists would defy company wishes. In one case a studio actually changed the film title for a song. *Reno Brothers* was transformed into *Love Me Tender* to accommodate Elvis Presley.

Columbia Pictures and Mercury Records found themselves mired in a heated debate regarding Patti Page, one of the record industry's hot properties, and *Indiscretions of an American Wife* (1954). Columbia Pictures had commissioned a title song and four track selections from her and she was prominently featured in the "coming attractions" trailer. The studio assumed Mercury would release a single to coincide with the Jennifer Jones-Montgomery Cliff feature, but the label refused and a war of words commenced. The records did not materialize until long after the film was launched. This was one of the first skirmishes over street dates, which now have become endemic to the synergism process.

The basis of the dispute was not merely the attempt of one medium to maximize profits at the expense of the other. (Long-range planning, particularly in the record industry, is a rarity. Labels have no way of gauging the chart life of a record. This renders diskeries "reactive." Once a record is released, they respond to prevailing conditions. Release dates are thus fluid. The chart action of a preceding title has an effect on the next issuance.)

Studios only encounter the cluster problem during such peak street periods as early summer, back-to-school, and the holiday season. In 1984, a banner year, *Ghostbusters*, *Gremlins*, *Top Secret*, *Star Trek III*, and *Streets of Fire* opened within a seven-day period. One film, *Ghostbusters*, prevailed. The same year MGM shifted the opening date of a remake of *Blackboard Jungle* from the crowded Christmas season to what they, incorrectly, hoped would be a better month, October. Only with superstars can record labels manage to program in a similar manner.

Innocent optimists, the studios shrugged off the incident, production executives believed in successful title and theme songs. Myers introduced "Rock" into a colony of skeptics. Only director Richard Brooks believed the recording was sufficiently provocative to increase the film's desired "shock effect." Due to the director's insistence, MGM agreed to pay a licensing fee of $5,000. The entire song was available for $7,500. The studio declined. Instead of purchasing the rights to the song outright they decided to simply license.

There exist several accounts of the inclusion of "Rock" in the movie: that Myers was chosen as technical advisor due to the mood-invoking song, and, conversely, that in the capacity of technical advisor he suggested the use of "Rock" as the film's theme.[16] A common-sensical view is that Haley was chosen because of the popularity of "Shake, Rattle and Roll." In one of his few late-Seventies interviews, he recalled, "They wanted a song to fit the era of the teenagers, the high school . . . The producer had 'Crazy Man Crazy' and he remembered the kids jumping up and down with 'go go go go everybody,' and he said, 'We'll use a Bill Haley record.' They didn't want to use 'Shake, Rattle and Roll' because it was Number 1 and they felt it would go off the charts before the thing came out, and so they chose 'Rock Around The Clock.' They used it to open . . . and I think you know the answer from there."[17] The ASCAP song became an anthem of alienation for the youthful moviegoer. (Ironically, ASCAPers would charge that rock was a BMI plot foisted upon American youth.)

The association of the song with the Evan Hunter novel was "largely responsible for the record's extraordinary success," claimed art historian Carl Belz, because the "combination of the image of rebellious youth with the raucous and driving sound of rock spelled out an interpretation which was already implicit in the popular imagination: This was rebellious music." Arguably, the film did more to bestow the "deviant" label than did the song's harmless content. Pielke, perhaps, best captured the essence of the song, "Whether or not they were aware of it, when teenagers bought this 45, they were taking a stand against the established order." Sociologist Howard Becker wrote "deviance [rebellion] is in the eye of the beholder." As the New Orleans red light district tainted jazz, *Blackboard Jungle* cast rock into symbolic, if not real, rebellion. The influential author of the *Sound of the City* observed that *Blackboard* established "the connection between rock 'n' roll and teenage rebellion." Lillian Roxon termed "Rock" the "*Marseillaise* of the teenage revolution." "1954," recalled the then-boss of WABC-New York, Rick Sklar, "was the last year *without* a music generation gap."[18]

An old theatrical bromide from *Hamlet* states, "the play is the thing." For director Richard Brooks, *Blackboard Jungle* fit the description, as there was little doubt that the box office appeal was due to the best-selling Evan Hunter novel rather than a star cast. In fact, while the major roles were filled by competent, seasoned actors, none were guaranteed draws. The juvenile delinquents were played by relative unknowns.

The most recognizable member of the cast was Glenn Ford, who had just signed a five-year contract with MGM. A leading man who frequently did not get the girl, and who had performed in films ranging from *Gilda* (1946) to the *Big Heat*, Ford "had never been expected to carry a major feature on his own. He was essentially Mr. Nice Guy, the utility outfielder."[19] The harried, loyal wife was played by Anne Francis, whose major achievement at the time, had been as the sexy, half-dressed daughter of a scientist in *Forbidden Plane*. Cast members Louis Calhoun and Margaret Hayes were seasoned actors but the adolescent hoodlums-*qua*-students were neophytes to the big screen. For Rafael Campos, Danny Dennis, Jameel Farah (Jamie Farr) and Vic Morrow, *Blackboard* was the first big picture. Morrow would emerge as the "star" of the movie.

Reviewers generally agreed the casting was "exceptionally good." Most singled out the rowdy students. *New Yorker* critic John McCarten notes, "the best actors in *Blackboard Jungle* are the youngsters—a good many of them high school children (sic) who had never done any acting before." Poitier, however, was 31 and had several film credits. "Particularly good," indicated *Newsweek*, "are Ford as the embattled teacher, Vic Morrow as the enemy, and Sidney Poitier as the lonely Negro boy who becomes an ally." Bosley Crowther pointed to Morrow and Poitier as "superlatively realistic types," as were "the other 'Dead End' types." Another reviewer claimed "Morrow is brilliant as the leader of the pack of thugs."[20]

The high production qualities, underscoring the script, were praised. The four Academy Award nominations the project received involved the storyline and cinematography; even the soundtrack was enhanced to emphasize the narrative. Nevertheless, the film failed to win any Oscars.

The movie's soundtrack, according to producer Milt Gabler, was successful because *Blackboard Jungle* increased the decibel level to new highs. Roman Kozak reported, "Prior film soundtracks had a much deadlier sound, with the orchestra muted in the background. But here the heavily rhythmatic recording just jumped out at the audience."[21]

The Film

The opening frames fill the screen. A raucous, loud, infectious sound filled the theater. "One, two, three o'clock, four o'clock rock . . ." The raunchy music overlays a dingy, desolate, urban street, obviously on the wrong side of the elevated tracks. The camera comes to rest on North Manual Trades High School. Menacing youths move in the schoolyard behind a tall chain-link fence. "Rock," described as a "raspy jazz piece," introduces the strife-ridden vocational institution.

Richard Dadier (Glenn Ford), a Navy veteran, enters Evan Hunter's world with the belief, "Kids are people and most people are worthwhile." This premise is quickly put to the test as the literature teacher encounters the violence and despair rampant in the classrooms and hallways of the institution. After his initial meeting with the "wild one," Artie West (Vic Morrow), and his followers, played effectively by Sidney Poitier, Danny

Dennis, Dan Terranova and Rafael Campos, Ford asks resident cynic Mr. Murdock (Louis Calhern), "How do these boys graduate?" Murdock sarcastically snaps "Graduate! They just become eighteen," adding, "The only thing they know how to multiply is themselves." "Daddy-O," as the social misfits call him, is politely informed, "Don't be a hero and never turn your back to the class."

To illustrate the conditions prevalent in the stereotypical slum school, Dadier is confronted by the unruly class of rapidly evolving juvenile delinquents, "Did you ever try to fight thirty-five guys, Teach?" Motivated by military stubbornness and naive dedication, the English teacher perseveres.

The foreboding air of violence materializes as Miss Lois Hammond (Margaret Hayes), the faculty siren, is attacked in the library by a student. Asserting his Navy training, Ford thwarts the attempted rape and captures the youthful assailant. His heroics further alienate Dadier's charges. The rescued, not-so-innocent damsel becomes romantically attracted to the married newcomer. When rejected, she tells him her advances were due to occupational boredom, "teacher burnout" in 1989 jargon.

Dadier's situation is further complicated by his loving and pregnant wife (Anne Francis), who wants him to leave that garbage can of the educational system.

The most generationally divisive scene involves Dadier's overly motivated colleague Joshua Edwards (Richard Kiley). The sympathetic, misguided Edwards makes futile attempts to reach the students. In the belief that "music soothes the savage beast," he brings a valuable collection of 78s into class. The students become restless as he plays Bix Beiderbecke's "Jazz Me Blues." He tries something a bit more contemporary, Stan Kenton's "Invention for Guitar and Trumpet." As "I Can't Get Started" resounds, the Morrow-led pupils smash the valuable array of oldies. The shattered vinyl is symbolic of the destruction of Kiley's idealism.

On another level, music becomes the nexus of generational conflict. [Charlie] Gillett agreed the record-smashing scene "symbolized the mood of the film and its audience . . . the association of the film's violent content with rock 'n' roll music was part of the adult perception of the music as an expression of youth's violent attitude towards authority." The razing of the recordings, observed a reviewer, "is enough to make one want to kill the kid."[22]

Things worsen when Kiley and Ford are mugged upon leaving their after-work watering hole, and Anne (Ford's wife in the film), is revealed to be receiving poison pen letters and obscene phone calls accusing her spouse of infidelity with the amorous Miss Hammond. At this point, Dadier is close to resigning. He observes that household cooks and janitors earn more than the $2 an hour paid to beleaguered secondary school instructors.

Resolution occurs as Artie pulls the familiar switchblade on Dadier, wounding the teacher. Gregory Miller (Sidney Poitier) and a handful of the "unreachables" side with the bleeding pedagogue. A slow "problem" student grabs the flag stand and threatens the knife-yielding baddies with the golden eagle tip. The finale is predictable, as Dadier has "gotten through" to Miller, the informal leader, and at least some of his classmates. There may yet be hope for the black-leather-jacketed denizens of Manual Trades High. "Rock Around The Clock" returns for the close.

Reaction to the film was intense. What *Grapes of Wrath* did for Okie migrant workers, *Blackboard Jungle* did for besieged teachers.

Commonweal's Philip Hartung correctly outlined the irresistible social commentaries divined for the film and provided a negative analysis: The director, Richard Brooks, had selected "the more sordid details and piles them up in such a way that, though they may be true, they seem contrived." The *Nation* reasoned that "supposing that our schools—or at least some of our schools—are now only institutions of temporary confinement for armed and remorseless criminals, they are not going to be reformed into educational paradises by superman turned pedagogue." This position was contradicted by Otis Guernsey, Jr., who said, "The film as a whole pleads with such teachers to keep trying. Success is indicated, too—provided that an instructor, in a crisis, can disarm a husky, hopped-up teenager brandishing a whetted six-inch blade."

"While the film poses no easy answers," wrote Charlotte Speicher, "it insists with implacable urgency that answers must be sought with unremitting persistence." Critics, in the words of John McCarten, were too demanding, as "the dilemma presented by the twisted young characters in our schools has baffed all kinds of experts, and perhaps the movie men ought to be excused if their solution is no more convincing than any other." In a *New York Times* essay terming the film "social dynamite," Crowther went on to warn that "we suspect it may be challenged not only as responsible reporting but also as a desirable stimulant to spread before the young." *Variety*, with its usual box office concern, correctly predicted *Blackboard Jungle* was "a controversial blockbuster that should ride to an explosive exploitation box office before the pro and con ashes have time to settle."[23]

Sociological manifestos aside, critics found the movie provocative.

"Evan Hunter's novel published last year, has been made into a strong, effective film," offered Speicher, adding that it offered "another demonstration that ideas are not necessarily inimical to entertainment values."

The story line and production resulted in a film with "a melodramatic impact that hits hard at a contemporary problem," suggested *Variety*. Crowther found the film not a temperate "or restrained report on a state of affairs that is disturbing to educators and social workers today. It is a full-throated, all-out testimonial to the lurid headlines that appear from time to time, reporting acts of terrorism and violence by uncontrolled urban youths. It gives a blood-curdling, nightmarish picture of monstrous disorder in a public school. And it leaves one wondering wildly whether such out-of-hand horrors can be."[24]

Saturday Review and *The New Yorker* were more restrained. Guernsey praised Brooks. "Rowdy jazz [rock] and hard, bare silence are his sound effects, while the mocking adolescent face is the keynote in his visual scale. With such devices he has managed an earnest and gritty film in *Blackboard Jungle*, if not a sensitive one," he noted.

"While the film has a good many faults (the acting at times is a bit shaky and the conclusion is rather unbelievable), it nevertheless confronts its subject matter head on, and in the circumstances it is an unsettling piece of work," said McCarten.[25]

Less favorably, *Newsweek* noted that "The cumulative effect is too much for dramatic plausibility. But director Brook's insistence on realism is evident from an effective score to the performances of a carefully chosen cast." *The Nation*, more politically philosophical, rejected the film as "a sentimental melodrama masquerading as a social document, which in it own way is as dangerous a little gadget as a zip gun."[26]

Reviewers barely noticed the song, "jazz" or "novelty foxtrot," preferring to focus on the sociology of the feature. *Variety* did compliment the score for "theming the jazz beat that expresses the subject." "A raspy jazz piece," indicated Guernsey.[27] Unbeknownst to the sages of film, "Rock" was destined to become the centerpiece of the picture.

Bosley Crowther called *Blackboard Jungle* "social dynamite" upon its mid-March debut; the reference was to the simmering contradictions in urban working-class schools. The powerful but stereotypical film did little to correct the conditions of neglect in and incapacity of the system. The motion picture *did* present adolescents with an alternative lifestyle model. Although most, obviously, rejected the code of the switchblade, fashion, music and films would be dramatically affected.

In keeping with the McCarthy era, an hysterical overreaction to the film occurred in some quarters. Clare Booth Luce, ambassador to France, insisted the hoodlums-in-American-schools saga be withdrawn from the Venice Film Festival, and her request was heeded. Several cities, including Memphis—the home of Sun Records, banned exhibition of the movie.

MGM attempted to musically capitalize on the notoriety of *Blackboard Jungle*, producing a single titled "Rock Around The Clock" backed by the "Love Theme" from the movie, which was performed by the MGM Studio Orchestra. The 45 was aired by a few anti-R & B stations but attracted few teenage listeners.

However, teens, especially those who had seen the film, were enthralled by the Haley version of "Rock Around the Clock." There exist numerous explanations for its popularity. The most pervasive is that rock was simply awaiting discovery and *Blackboard Jungle*, simply was its vehicle. Frank Zappa and Milt Gabler seemed to have found the reason for the swing song's popularity: volume. White kids had never heard a back beat number quite that LOUD . . . if at all. Hearing the recording on a phonograph or radio missed the reverberations bouncing from one theater wall to the other.

Decca, totally unprepared, rushed the single back into production and promotion. The label's marketing plan was to capitalize on the free ink the controversial movie was receiving. The single finally appeared on the *Billboard* singles chart on May 4. It would remain there for a total of twenty-nine weeks.

On June 24, 1955 the LP rock album, *Shake, Rattle and Roll* entered the *Cashbox* listing. The ten-incher, described as "Fox Trots with Vocal Chorus by Bill Haley," experienced a nine-week run, hovering around the Number 15 slot. While it contained "Rock Around The Clock," no mention was made of *Blackboard Jungle*. Two EPs appeared for 45 buyers.

The releases coincided with a controversy swirling around R & B in the music medium.

On January 14, 1955, disc jockey Alan Freed put on the first Rock 'n' Roll Ball, at the St. Nicholas Arena in Harlem. Starring Joe Turner, Fats Domino, and a host of doo-wop, street-corner groups—The Clovers, The Moonglows, The Harptones—the two-night show attracted an overflow crowd.

Fifteen thousand patrons paid $2 per person to see the extravaganza. The $30,000 gross was "bigger than any jazz concert ever staged anywhere in New York," observed Herb Schoenfeld. The only casualties reported during the six-hour concert were several "cases of exhaustion brought on by mixtures of jitter-bugging and tippling . . . the cops and guards weeded the unrulier elements out of the crowd."[28]

Independent labels with R & B artists were elated. "It's good for the business because it sells records. And that's what counts," said Coral A & R man Bob Thiele. He added, "Every new release is like New Year's Eve . . . and it's just beginning to gain momentum."[29] The elation at specialty diskeries was not shared in the Brill Building, where ASCAP had its offices, or by big-band-oriented A & R personnel.

As the ASCAP licensees faded from the trade charts, *Variety* began a campaign attacking "rock 'n' roll." It was a curious exercise. In March Abel Green of *Variety* began a series of editorials condemning the genre. Interviews with Les Elgart, Irving Berlin, and deejay Bill Randle criticized R & B. The consensus was that rock was a dangerous fad capable of corrupting adolescents.

On February 23, 1955, five days prior to the release of *Blackboard Jungle*, *Variety* published a warning to the "music business." The crux of the message was that "leerics" were too sexually aggressive. "What are we talking about?" pontificated the writer. "We're talking about 'rock 'n' roll,' about 'hug,' and 'squeeze,' and kindred euphemisms which are attempting a total breakdown of all reticence about sex . . . Our teenagers are already setting something of a record in delinquency without this raw musical idiom to smell up the environment still more." Green concluded, "In short, chums, do it yourself or have it done for you. You're not going to get or have it done for you."[30]

Label executives partially dismissed this polemic on the basis that it was a thinly veiled attack on BMI. In the music industry, *Variety* was perceived as sympathic to Tin Pan Alley.

A follow-up editorial pointed to the specialty labels, who "neither know nor care about 'ethics' and 'concern about *potential* juvenile delinquency.' "[31] (emphasis added) Below the opinion piece appeared an interview with Cleveland rock 'n' roll deejay Bill Randle. Randle, who claims to have first brought Elvis Presley in to a major market, indicated rock and roll doesn't "cause delinquency—it just reflects it." He went on to explain that rock exhibited a "crude primitiveness" due to its origins. Because of this Jungian quality, rock has an earthly appeal.[32] Radio broadcasters were split on the issue. Battle lines were being drawn in music publishing and diskeries. The major labels, with new sound artists, and specialty labels as well welcomed increased sales. CBS's Mitch Miller dismissed the popularity of blues-derived material as a "fad."

The president of Fats Domino's record company replied to Green's charges:

> You are supposed to be an impartial newspaper. We made a living long before you started writing about rhythm and blues. In fact, if the major record companies and a few other people would stop jumping on our merchandise and use the ASCAP tunes that you constantly plug, I think it would be a much better

world. Why make an entire country conscious of suggestive lyrics when you would have to tear up 60% of the ASCAP tunes.

Lewis R. Chudd,
Imperial Records, Inc.[33]

"Most of the lyrics of the tunes offered aren't of an offensive nature," wrote a *Variety* reporter, "but instrumentalization and performer movements are at times suggestive." This was the description of Alan Freed's second Rock 'n' Roll Show at the Brooklyn Paramount Theatre. Three thousand patrons, mostly adolescents, packed the venue to see the likes of The Penguins, The Chuckles, The Moonglows, La Vern Baker, Eddie Fontaine, and others, who performed familiar hits.

The patrons were deemed a bit unruly.

"The kids were dancing in the aisles, clapping, clapping in time with the music and letting out shrills at a lively riff or just the announcement of an upcoming performer. At one point several youths hopped on the stage, but were soon ushered off."[34] One shoving match was reported. The Paramount replicated the activities of the jittering period when Benny Goodman coaxed fans into the aisles.

The April 18, 1955 issue of *Life*, was the first popular national magazine to address rock 'n' roll. Less than two months after the debut of *Blackboard Jungle*, a four-paragraph, three-page photo essay surfaced. In what would become normative, the piece attempted to circumvent facets of the new music. Rock was colored with shadings of St. Vitus Dance: "Rock 'n' roll is both music and dance. The music has a rhythm often heavily accented on the second and fourth beats. The dance combines the Lindy and Charleston, and almost anything else. In performing it, hollering helps and a boot banging the floor makes it even better. The overall result, frequently, is frenzy." According to the writer, adult authority figures misunderstood the genre. Teenagers, it appeared, were oblivious to the fuss, as "they all seemed to be bushily and blithely rockin' and rollin' around."[35]

Downbeat's Barry Ulanov took issue with the picture magazine's depiction of rock. In *Don't Knock the Rock*, the jazz chronicler insisted, "The current generation of hoppers and swingers and 'bug' is much better behaved on the dance floor than its counterparts of 20 years ago, the famous 'bobby-soxers' and 'jitterbugs' of the Goodman era, or those who first began to fit grimace and gesture to jazz beats in the cradle years of jazz in New Orleans, Chicago, the riverboats, and the towns along the levees." He went on to suggest the so-called "lewd" lyrics ascribed to R & B were in vogue but the purveyors were "third-rate beaters [crooners] who have become major box-office names because of their boudoir singing manners.'' Having zapped the Mitch Miller stable of ex-band vocalists, Ulanov concluded, ''What they are doing in their jazz dancing is open and aboveboard and even wholesome. It's their elders who get their kicks from songs and singers whose suggestiveness is just beneath the surface—hidden just enough to escape the censors—it's these not-so-'frenzied' folk who worry me.''[36]

The great rock 'n' roll controversy, as *Look* would label it, began as a tempest in a teapot. In April, 1955 New Haven, Connecticut police chief Francis McManus banned the musical style. June found Senator Estes Kefauver a one-man Senate investigating subcommittee, calling studio executives to testify in Hollywood, but the Tennessee legislator's credibility was questionable. He told Jack L. Warner that complaints had been made concerning *Rebel Without A Cause*. The veteran producer snapped, ''Whoever calls you must be working with radar. I haven't seen it myself.''

MGM's production head, Dory Schary, was also quizzed about *Blackboard Jungle*. When the senator pulled a clipping from a Nashville newspaper and read that a group of teenagers had set fire to a barn after seeing the film, Schary replied, ''There's no fire in the picture. They can't pin that on us.''[37]

As had been the case with the harangues of the junior senator from Wisconsin and the House UnAmerican Activities Committee in the past, there was little substance to allegations of youth corruption by movies or music. But for many, the perception became the reality.

The major conflict of 1955 took place on the trade charts and radio playlists. BMI and specialty labels were ravaging Tin Pan Alley and the major record companies. On November 12 *Billboard* buried on page 126 an item which properly should have been on the front page: ''Virtual Surrender 1955: The Year R & B Took Over the Pop Field.'' To add insult to injury, the article indicated R & B was gaining even more strength. ''The trend continues strong and despite covers by top pop artists, more and more original versions of tunes . . . are making it in all markets,'' it noted.[38]

Rocking the Headlines

> *Lord knows, I'll never make an Academy Award movie. But then I'm just as happy to get my achievement plaque from the bank every year.*
> —Sam Katzman, movie producer

*The kids are putting on the Seniors' Hop and
somehow they get all these great rock 'n' roll
stars to appear from out of nowhere and play
for them for nothing (oh sure, yeah) but the
parents and the school committee won't let
them put it on because it's bad or something
and somehow the big crisis is resolved and
near the end Bill Haley or somebody is playing
and the kids are all bopping away and the
parents are standing around watching, supervising, and the camera shifts to the parents'
feet and their toes are tapping, you know, and
they're snapping their fingers and their heads
are bobbing back and forth, looking at each
other and saying, "Gee, this music ain't so
bad after all, is it? Kinda catchy!"*
                                              —Michael Daly, writer

Picking up the *Los Angeles Times* and thumbing through *Variety*, veteran moviemaker Sam Katzman found his attention captured by youthful rowdies attending showings of *Blackboard Jungle*. He accepted the sporadic reports accusing a rebellious "new" sound of contributing to the disorders.

The disturbances that captured headlines were minor. A "feverish though harmless riot" was reported at Ivy League bastion Princeton University. The incident involved a student dormitory blasting Haley's hit all over Greek Row.

"Other phonographs joined in," according to *Billboard*, "making a medley which led to chanting and stamping by the staid Princetonians. At about midnight they gathered on the campus, set fire to a can of trash and paraded [thru] the streets until an assistant dean dampened their hilarity by pointing up the advantages of a more sedate mode of life."[39] The event could easily have been a product of the annual Spring Madness that gripped university campuses in May. Instead, Haley's record received the credit. Katzman, who excelled at cinematically exploiting a media event, would turn the rock 'n' roll brush fire into a full-blown prairie storm.

Despite the Brill Building inhabitants and major-label A&R men, rock music was an emerging reality. Skepticism abounded. Mitch Miller, the sharpest "ear" in the record business, accused broadcasters of abdicating their playlists "to the 8-to-14 year olds, to the preshave crowd that makes up 12 percent of the country's population and zero percent of it's buying power."[40] Many ill-timed obituaries were published: *Billboard*, on July 23, 1955, headlined "Death Certificate Premature: R&B Ain't Even Been Sick."

ASCAP's wishful thinking aside, the ill-defined hybrid genre was penetrating the trade charts, radio stations and suburban merchandisers. White kids, to the surprise of participants, were showing up at the stage shows of black artists. This was 1955. Rock, observe Jenkinson and Warner, "was creating a whole subculture based on its stars, followers, fashion and modes . . . [Haley] already [was] enjoying a small but growing cult following in the United States."[41]

Katzman possessed an intuitive quality broadcasters call "a golden gut." At a time in which studios maintained the "cherished fiction of service to a grand, broad-based public" the moviemaker was targeting a segment of the audience. This was long before the demographic, advertising term "teenybopper" entered the lexicon of the film colony.

The "juve" exploitation film, as employed by Katzman, in 1956 was a recognition of rock music as a psychographically defined generational boundary. *Clock* and *Don't Knock* were aimed directly at teenagers and voyeuristic adults. Excluding drive-ins, theatregoers were predominantly young and under twenty-five years of age. The lead caption on the *Rock Around The Clock* film poster promised "The Whole Story of Rock and Roll." Brooks's production had sold the Haley song; now Katzman would use the tune to exploit his picture.

Rock Around The Clock, with its instant name identification, proved a natural spinoff from Brooks's *exposé* of urban secondary education. [Brooks is well-known for the use of contemporary social issues as a cinematic setting. Prior to *Blackboard* he directed *Crisis* (1951), *Deadline U.S.A.* (1952), before doing the Elizabeth Taylor feature *The Last Time I Saw Paris* (1954).] Sam Katzman noted the possibilities. He told reporters, "I got a kind of feeling, a knack. Knock on wood—I've never been wrong. We don't get stories. We get titles and then write stories around them or fit them. I believe that if I produce films that are woven around yarns dealing with the latest recording hits, I'll be giving that segment [youth] of the public pictures they want to see." The Haley anthem would be one such title. After consulting with his "screening committee," comprised of his son, Jerry, and friends, Katzman was ready to do a rock 'n' roll film. "I spend six weeks in preparing such pictures on spot news and rush them right into work," he said.[42]

Katzman was the task master of the "fad-pic," a *Variety* term. Immediacy was the forte of "Jungle Sam," (so named because he had created the *Jungle Jim* serials). Katzman's theory, contend Ehrenstein and Reed, was that if "X-amount of kids would shell out so many dollars only to hear rock music on a movie's soundtrack, as with *Blackboard Jungle*, think how many more would be willing to pay not only to hear but to *see* the music performed on screen."[43]

The producer's experience with serials made contemporalia profitable. Even with a small budget and flimsy plot, he was able to make a movie with the proper "hook" in a matter of weeks. As with headlines, events overshadowed the players. Prior to *Clock* Katzman rarely, if ever, used bankable actors without the proverbial cast of thousands. The key was to have the movie in distribution before the news-grabbing phenomenon died. In the case of *Rock Around the Clock*, Richard Thompson noted, "He did not, of course, invent any of the musical rages. But he did take the fad from the contained universe of the radio/phono/jukebox and fuse it with an appropriately accurate yet romanticized lifestyle that perfectly filled out the dimensions of teenage movie watching."[44] The stars of the Katzman productions were the headlined fads.

Katzman commissioned "the whole story of rock and roll" from screenwriters Robert E. Kent and James B. Gordon, who appear to have dusted off yellowed scripts from the swing era. Their old, familiar storyline had a music bizzer discovering a band with a "new sound" and taking it to the "Big Time," where it became an overnight sensation.

Hollywood treated dance bands with "consistent inaccuracy," wrote big band critic George Simon. "Good taste and honesty were too often sacrificed for what a bunch of studio executives, most of whom had little feeling for the music, hoped would sell. (Twenty years later, writers would apply this thesis to rock musicals.)

"Without missing a beat, producers watered down plots and pushed the music forward,"[45] said Greil Marcus. The goal, of course, was to lure customers to the box office, *not* the record stores. Producers like Sam Katzman signed name artists with *established* hits to star in their films.

Marcus's assorted "never-weres and has-beens" proved to be extras to round out musical interludes. Some acts, as with *Rock, Rock, Rock*, involved package booking. Akin to concerts, the filmed jukeboxes were primarily addressing adolescent fans. The success of the rock exploiters rested on meeting expectations. Only Chuck Berry, Eddie Cochran and the irrepressible Little Richard substantially benefitted from the rocksploitation flicks.

Katzman's choice of Bill Haley was serendipitous, based on his son Jerry's remark, "Hey, you gotta get Bill Haley and do a movie." Since Katzman was acquainted with Jolly Joyce, Haley's booking agent, it was "simple as all that," recalled drummer Ralph Jones.[46]

Getting Bill Haley and the Comets was easy. The group lacked experienced management and had little idea of the economic machinations of the music world. Lord Jim Ferguson, misnamed the "con man's con man," the group's manager, proved easy pickings for Hollywood sharks. Haley and the band would receive $40,000 for six days work.

In addition, Boyd Bennett, a Haley clone with the minor hits "Seventeen" and "My Boy Flat Top," was signed.

The Platters, the only authentic R & B act to reach the Top 10 in 1955 also welcomed the opportunity to appear in a motion picture. So did Mercury Records. (Labels were happy to have the exposure even if the material was already off the charts. The fate of "Rock Around the Clock" after *Blackboard Jungle* did not escape their attention.) "Mr. Rock 'n' Roll," Alan Freed, was recruited to play himself.

Haley and the band were scheduled to lip-sync nine songs: "Rudy's Rock," "Mambo Rock," "Rock," "Rock-a-Beatin' Boggie," "Happy Baby," "See You Later Alligator," "Razzle Dazzle," "ABC Boogie," and the title selection. Four of the numbers were already on the *Shake, Rattle and Roll* album, and duplicating prereleased singles and LP selections mitigated against a soundtrack, although assuming the option had crossed the minds of Decca executives.

Boyd Bennett and the Bellhops would perform "Giddy Up, Ding Dong" and "We're Gonna Teach You to Rock," both of which had a strong visual component. Tony Martinez and his band provided a Latin flavor with "Mambo Capri" and "Cuero," among others.

The Platters, squeezed into mid-film, wailed with "The Great Pretender" and the best selling "Only You," a doo-wop classic.

Veteran double-feature leading man Johnny Johnston was teamed with newcomer Lisa Gaye for the romantic interest. Henry Slate was cast as Johnston's comic sidekick, with Alix Talton playing the conniving woman scorned. "A romantic triangle," observed Richard Staehling, "provides the necessary dead air between tunes."[47]

All of this came to pass after Katzman was able to raise a paltry $300,000 in 1955. Big-screen features usually cost at least five times that amount. The money men in the film community generally treated the proposed project as a high-risk venture, since the industry's flirtation with swing had proven a bust. Some argued that teenagers would not spend their allowances on free radio fare. However, Katzman's credits—his pictures had all returned their investments—prevailed. Columbia agreed to distribute *Rock Around the Clock*.

The last piece of the project was added when Fred F. Sears was assigned to direct. The Columbia staffer had thirty-two pictures to his credit— mostly vintage double-bill westerns, but also the Caryl Chessman "biopic" *Cell 2455, Death Row*, *Chicago Syndicate* and *Teen-Age Crime*

Wave. Production began in mid-January of 1956 and was completed by the opening week of February. Five weeks later it was ready for the streets.

On March 21, one year to the day after Crowther's "social dynamite" review, *Variety* analyzed *Clock's* launch. The film had previewed some nine days earlier with little of the predicted chaos, at least from teenagers.

The amount of vandalism and violence associated with the *film* appears to have been minimal. There were instances of misconduct, but most took place at live shows and record hops. Unfortunately, this distinction was rarely made. The fanfare *did* create a mystique for the movie, making it a boxoffice smash.

Columbia Pictures faced considerable exhibitor resistance based on the press accounts of the goings-on at the Paramount Theatre and various record hops. *Variety* reported:

> The juves didn't do anymore damage to the house than would be done in any concentrated period in which over $300,000 was registered. True, the youngsters ruined some seats with their overactivity in jumping, and a lot of them rested their feet against the walls, which will thus require some restoration. The kids also pockmarked the carpets with cigarette burns when ushers made them get rid of their weeds. However, with squads of Pinkerton and city police inside and outside the house, rowdiness was held down.
>
> That was seemingly left for their exit from the theatre. A group of the youngsters virtually wrecked a subway car after coming out of the theatre. They threw seats out the window, broke light bulbs and terrorized adult passengers until police apprehended several kids.[48]

This version of events also included the fact that the Paramount in Brooklyn took in "an all-time high" gross for Freed's ten shows. Theater men were caught in the middle. *Clock's* box office was undisputed, but newspapers, police and some community groups were vocal in their opposition to anything associated with the rock "craze."

In Hartford, E.M. Loew's Theatre postponed the debut of *Clock*. The Columbia promotion person, Joe Heidt, was told the film would run, but with no promotional "ballyhoo." In Baltimore, exhibitor Ray Rappaport also refused to run promotions because he didn't want any "trouble." A scheduled bus trip for Washington, D.C. high school students was cancelled when police objected to Columbia's transporting of moviegoers to see *Clock* at moviehouses in the nation's capital. *Variety* observed the "film opened quiet-like."[49]

Despite a few well publicized bannings, as in Bridgeport, Connecticut, the film debuted in most places with only minor disturbances, usually aggravated by "do-gooders." Columbia was hampered in promoting the film, but the media attention more than compensated.

Sociologist Ralph Turner suggested, years ago, that a different set of social norms can emerge in a setting in which participants feel that the rules of conduct that customarily guide behavior are inappropriate and some other form of action is permissible.[50] This description may be applicable to the movie theaters that exhibited *Rock Around the Clock.*

Most accounts of the "riotous" reaction of teenage patrons to the rhythms of Bill Haley, upon closer examination, indicate a general lack of anti-societal activity. (Dancing in dimly lit aisles can hardly be termed riotous.)

A large measure of the trouble that did occur was in response to the overreaction of theater operators.

"In cinemas where it *was* shown, dancing in the aisles was forbidden. In retaliation, seats were slashed open and ripped from their rows," noted Dave Rogers.[51] A Minneapolis record hop described as "Midnight Music Mania" in the local and national press displayed similar group dynamics. Intended as a teenagers' rock 'n' roll party, the affair came a cropper when part of the audience, including children twelve and thirteen years old, and even younger, staged a near riot. Police said that while rock 'n' roll records were played on the stage, the youngsters danced and whooped it up in the aisles and floor space down front. When ordered to return to their seats, the audience aimed a lusty chorus of boos at the squad of police that had been summoned. A hurled beer can narrowly missed one policeman.[52]

Press coverage of such events only fanned the flames of interest in *Clock.* Former Beatle John Lennon, then a quasi-member of Britain's subcultural youth group, the Teddy Boys, came back from a showing of *Blackboard Jungle* complaining that nothing uproarious had taken place. Exhibitors and promoters were on the horns of a dilemma. A not-too-sympathic *Variety* reporter aptly summarized the contradiction:

> Rock 'n' Roll—the most explosive showbiz phenomenon of the decade—may be getting too hot to handle. While its *moneymaking* potential has made it all but irresistible, its Svengali grip on teenagers has produced a staggering wave of *juvenile violence* and mayhem. Rock 'n' roll is now literal b.o. dynamite—not only a matter of profit, but a matter for the police.[53]

Theater owners were more than aware of the economic gains to be had from showing the Katzman rocker. They also demanded an unrealistic form of social conduct on the part of the adolescents. To avoid problems like that of the Paramount in New York, dancing was not permitted. When this petty rule was violated, the police or Pinkertons were summoned.

This mix was ideal for some form of deviant action. This was 1956, when permissiveness was akin to immorality, and crowd control came from the end of a baton. As in the swing era, the music was symbolic of generational conflict and shifting demographics; in the late 1930s, similar activity had received similar treatment. *New York Times* writer Jack Gould had portrayed jitterbugging as akin to "a chimpanzee suffering from delirium tremens."[54] Indeed, most objections to rock music—subversion, racial integration, juvenile delinquency—had been voiced during swing's hot era also.

The Film

Taking up where *Blackboard Jungle* left off, "Rock Around the Clock" (the song) reverberates through the opening credits of *Rock Around the Clock*, and gives way to the sweet strains of a Lombardoesque ballroom band led by George Hiller. The bandleader, disgusted with the sparsely populated dance floor, vents his frustration on Steve Hollis (Johnny Johnston). The manager replies that dancing is passe.

"You wait around for proof that the big-band business is dead," warns Hollis, "and you'll be paying the funeral expenses." He is fired. Bassist Corny LaSalle (Henry Slate), who agrees with Steve, joins him in a plan to return to New York. On the way, the duo lands in Strawberry Springs, population 1,472.

It's Saturday night and they are caught up in an excited parade of teenagers going to a dance at the "meetin' hall." Steve and Corny are surprised to find the venue packed with dancers foxtrotting to "See You Later, Alligator." Corny wants to know what the "young-ins" are dancing too.

"It's rock 'n' roll, brother, and we're rockin' tonight," is the shouted reply. The audience reaction interests Hollis, a band manager in search of a meal ticket.

He approaches Haley, wanting to know the name of the band.

"Hey guys," says the guitar-picking vocalist, "we got a couple of foreigners from the flatlands." Steve explains he's been ill. "Stick around alligator," Haley tells him, "Rockin' will cure anything you have." Following "Rock-A-Beatin' Boogie," Corny tries another ploy asking about the new sound.

Impressed with the combo's ability to get patrons on their feet, Hollis feels it has potential. He is equally struck by the brother-and-sister dance team of Jim (Earl Barton) and Lisa Johns (Lisa Gaye), especially the latter. He asks Bill if the rocker would like to make a fortune. Lisa, the aggregate's informal manager, questions Steve's offer to manage them for a 40 percent commission. She, uncharacteristically, cites 10 percent, a figure she read in *Variety*. Haley chimes in with, "We always get 100 percent of onions and turnips."

Steve decides to romance Lisa in order to sign the acts. They negotiate between kisses and seal the deal with another kiss.

Arriving in New York, Steve goes to see ex-flame Corinne Talbott (Alix Talton), the owner of the biggest agency in show business. They go to dinner to discuss the manager's new discoveries and listen to the mambo act, Tony Martinez and his band thus introducing two gimmicks repeated in countless backstager rock films: the club setting and the "other" woman. Operating on the assumption that Steve's revue will bomb, Corinne books the show into Mansfield School for Girls in Hartford, Connecticut, "the most exclusive in the country," for the senior prom. Martinez opens "with no exciting music" as "the professors have taken the *cha* out of *cha-cha*." Haley and combo appear with "Razzle Dazzle." Two chaperones are shocked. "Barbaric" and "infamous," they exclaim. As the Johns break the ice, the students begin clapping with the beat and filling the dance floor. The Bellboys, with Freddie Bell, follow with, appropriately, "We're Gonna Teach You to Rock." Catching the spirit, Martinez returns with an up-tempo number. Ms. Talbott Enterprises is even more determined to snare Hollis. "When Steve hates me enough, then he'll know he can't live without me," she tells assistant Mike (John Archer), who is in love with the haughty career woman. To anger Steve, she has the revue blackballed.

Later, when Steve and Corny are down to their last twelve dollars, Corny hears Alan Freed on remote from the West River Club. He recalls that "the king of rock 'n' roll" owes Steve a favor. Lisa and the manager go to the club just in time for the Platters "Only You," talk to Freed, and Haley is booked. He becomes the talk of the town, headlined in *Variety*.

Corinne offers Steve a three-year contract which he accepts. A clause is inserted prohibiting Lisa from marrying during the duration of the agreement. Hollis arranges the big show, "A Rock 'n' Roll Jamboree" at Hollywood Hall, to be telecast coast-to-coast. Emceed by Freed, the show opens with the Bellboys, trailed by the Platters's "Great Pretender."

"The thrill you've been all been waiting for" features the Comets performing "Rudy's Rock" highlighted by the acrobatics of the sax player and bassist. Lisa appears on stage to pass out plaudits ending with one to "my husband, Steve." They have outsmarted the cunning Corinne by wedding prior to the inception of the contract. "Clock" closes the film as musicians and patrons fill the dance floor . . . THE LIVING END.

Joel Friedman, in a *Billboard* "News Review," concurred.

"With the film scheduled to be booked in conjunction with a number of Alan Freed rock and roll personal appearances, the future augurs well for the disk market," he wrote.[55] Advertised as telling the story of rock, the Katzman project would itself become part of its history.

Several days after the debut of *Clock*, the Senate Subcommittee to Investigate Juvenile Delinquency issued its interm report on the impact of the film medium upon adolescents. Films, Kefauver's group indicated, were "trigger mechanisms" for teenage antisocial behavior. The conclusion was broader than the body of the report, which stated that movies could "initiate and provide for anti-social behavior on the part of emotionally disturbed children." This was a far-from-blanket indictment.[56]

Trade publications, including *Variety*, *Billboard*, and others, are addressed to industry insiders, and their review sections walk a fine line between aesthetics and commerce. Nearly all of the insider publications discuss the potential market as a sizeable number of readers are exhibitors and merchandisers. Trade critics err usually on the conservative side of the ledger. *Variety*, one of the few papers to review *Clock*, summarized it as a "bouncy musical drama with plenty of appeal to teenagers. Special handling can lure extra b.o. [box office] coin." It led with the obvious appeal of the movie to the "sweater-Levi trade." Having established that *Rock Around the Clock* was for teenagers, due to the music, the writer added "The talent's not all musical in this *good* Sam Katzman production" (emphasis added). A litany of compliments were then aimed at the screenwriters, the director, and the actors. The plot received one sentence: it "tells how a band manager finds the Haley Comets in the mountains and brings dancing back to ballrooms throughout the country."[57] Katzman, and particularly newcomer Lisa Gaye, "who could emerge from this teenage favorite," were delighted with the notice.

Several weeks after the review's appearance *Billboard* also ran a piece, with Joel Friedman asserting that *Clock* would gain a better-than-average reception from teenages and "the legion of fans who worship at the shrine of rock and roll." He further outlined the exposure value of the picture for record dealers.

"With more than 80 percent of the film's running time devoted to music" it would be the ideal showcase," he concluded.[58]

PTA Magazine ran a review from an "adult" perspective. The thrust was that "devotees are not likely to be bothered by the slim story and poor production values." Moreover, "Those not so young may have trouble distinguishing one number from another."[59] The Parent-Teacher Association gave the film a "poor" rating and suggested that those under fifteen not see *Clock*. This rating was not what Haley had in mind. He saw the film as a "chance to further demonstrate our music. Older people will go out of curiosity."

Once it was in general release, *Clock* garnered little if any, attention as a film. Instead, it was seen as a catalyst to adolescent anti-social behavior, generating a self-fulfilling prophecy. Some communities prohibited the screening of *Rock Around the Clock* because of the title; the city fathers never bothered to see the motion picture. The actual number of disturbances at showings was minute. The ensuing publicity more than made up for the lack of emotional contagion. "You can't buy that kind of publicity," the saying goes.

Stunned by *Brown v. The Board of Education (1954)*, segregationists attacked rock music as part of a Negro plot to subvert God-given values. For example, Asa E. Carter, self-appointed leader of the White Citizens Councils of Alabama, charged rock music was a plot inspired by the National Association for the Advancement of Colored People (NAACP). The corrupting sound, in his view, was "the basic heavy beat music of Negroes. It appeals to the base in man, brings out animalism and vulgarity." He targeted jukebox operators and record stores, threatening to post the names of businessmen failing to comply with a ban on rock. In response, one vendor called the demand "ridiculous," a vice president of a radio station in Birmingham said, "Carter's statement that the music is an attempt to destroy the morals of America's young people is absurd," and Roy Wilkins, NAACP president, said, "Some people in the South are blaming us for everything from measles to atomic fallout."[60]

Several months after the tumultuous release of *Clock*, Bill Haley told a *Downbeat* interviewer, "At the time that kids are out listening to music, they're not getting into trouble . . . in a crowd that large [7,000] somebody is sure to step on somebody else's toes." He continued, "I'm not saying that we'll never have any trouble . . . but as yet we've had none."[61]

Following the jazz magazine meeting, Haley embarked on a tour of the South. At an outdoor concert at Ponce de Leon Park outside Atlanta, five teenagers were arrested for fighting, but promoters claimed the ruckus was "no more than would occur at an ordinary sports event."[62]

Haley, the Pied Piper of rock 'n' roll, was picketed by the Asa Carter people in Birmingham. The White Citizens group was greeted by counter-demonstrators, a crowd of teenagers in favor of Haley.[63]

Moving on to San Antonio, the troupe earned $16,000 at the Municipal Auditorium on one night, surpassing Elvis's take of $14,000 for two dates. "There is plenty of money to be earned" on the road, Haley would say.

Sales figures for Haley's Decca product now totalled nine million and were climbing.

Reports of rock-related outbreaks of dancing and violence were usually confined to local and trade papers, but the summer of 1956 found the national news weeklies running the "horror" stories. Before Lear jets and Silver Eagle busses, the summer months were the peak touring time, as the often unrealistic routings cooked up by talent agents were reachable in clear weather. In addition school was out, making weekday and late-night concerts possible.

Media coverage only made a bad situation worse. The venue operators were increasingly uneasy, hiring more special police. These untrained peacekeepers heightened the tension.

"Something is happening here, but you don't know what it is, do you Mister Jones?" sang Bob Dylan years later. "Ballad of the Thin Man" was dedicated to a *Time* reporter. Fittingly, the Luce publication "introduced" its readers to rock music after a series of disorders and bannings occurred "in reaction" to film showings and stage shows. According to an unidentified staffer, rock was based on "Negro blues" and characterized by "an unrelenting, socking syncopation that sounds like a bull whip; a choleric saxophone honking mating-call sounds; an electric guitar turn up so loud that its sound shatters and splits; a vocal group that shudders and exercises violently to the beat while roughly chanting either a near-nonsense phrase or a moronic lyric in hillbilly idiom."[64] The article went on to suggest the sound was "not couth" and, "There is no denying that rock 'n' roll evokes a physical response from even its most reluctant listeners, for that giant pulse matches the rhythmical operations of the human body." To the writer's credit, the link between juvenile delinquency and rock was fudged, using quotes from a criminologist, Boston "banners," and Mitch Miller. Not all observers of rock 'n' roll were so restrained.

Time's weekly rival, *Newsweek* proffered a portrait of a Haley show at the National Guard Armory in the District of Columbia.

As 5,000 people, most teenagers, poured in for some rock 'n' roll, knives flashed and one young man was cut in the arm. Inside the auditorium, 25 special officers waited tensely for Bill Haley and the Comets to swing into the "big beat."

Haley gave the downbeat, the brasses blared, and the kids leaped into the aisles to dance, only to be chased back to their seats by the special cops. At 10:50, the Comets socked into their latest hit, "Hot Dog, Buddy, Buddy!" and the crowd flipped.

Some of the kids danced, some scuffled, fights broke out, a chair flew. William Warfield, 17, a high school junior, was hit. Suffering from a brain concussion and a severe cut over one eye, he was rushed to the hospital. "Before I knew it, everybody was pounding everybody," he said later. The fight overflowed into the street. A 19-year-old was struck over the head, and a 16-year-old was cut in the ear. Two cars were stoned and one exuberant teen-ager turned in a false alarm.

The Armory manager commented, "It's that jungle strain that gets 'em all worked up."

Newsweek concluded with a quote from an unidentified sociologist stating that "Rock 'n' roll fever is caused by the same virus which induces panty raids and goldfish swallowing. When kids run wild, any stimulus will do."[65] (This statement may have been derived from the works of Herbert Blumer or even LeBon, writers who, in the 1950s, were the definite word on riotous collective behavior.)

The *tour de force*, a fracas at the Palomar Ballroom in San Jose, California, occurred the weekend of July 7, 1956. The wire services spread the story from coast-to-coast. Many headlines screamed "Rock 'n' Roll Riot." A good deal of rumor and misinformation was published. Greg Shaw and Michael Ochs, conscientious mavens and journalists, offered the following account:

> Driven to a fever pitch by the rocking sounds (in combination with their own hoodlum tendencies and whatever contraband their fake IDs had purchased, of course), the audience of 2,500 broke loose into a riot . . . According to the police, the riot started when someone heaved a beer bottle into a group of dancers on the floor of the Palomar Gardens. In the mélee that followed, about 500 to 1,000 bottles were broken, furniture was torn down. Fats [Domino] and his band grabbed their instruments and ran for their lives. Charles Silva, owner of the place, reported "Everybody was at each other. Boys fought boys, and even girls. Girls were slugging boys and scratching one another." The police chief called it "the wildest riot in the history of our city." Fats must've found this a trifle disconcerting, coming in the midst of a set he'd played hundreds of times back in New Orleans."[66]

Most of this account was correct, except that Fats Domino wasn't playing or even on the bandstand when the riot broke out. A subsequent investigation cited the causes of the disturbance as the selling of beer in throwable bottles, the denial of 1,000 people entrance into the venue, and inadequate police power. Chief Ray Blackmore vindicated Domino and the combo of any wrongdoing.[67]

While *Time*, two weeks later, intimated that rock 'n' roll was responsible for eleven injured people and $3,000 in property damage at a San Jose dance hall, Silva told *Variety* that the damages were "about $1,000."[68] As these conflicting accounts evidence, the emotional contagion surrounding the Palomar riot was not confined to the ballroom.

Mayor Bernard J. Berry of Jersey City, New Jersey, prohibited a concert scheduled for the 24,000-seat Roosevelt Stadium, to be emceed by Paul Whiteman and star Bill Haley. "Rock 'n' Roll Under the Stars" was halted "in the interest of public safety." In frustration, Haley wrote a protest song, perhaps the first in rock history. "Teenager's Mother," the 'B' side to "Rip It Up," asked, "Are you right? Did you forget so soon? How much you liked to do the Charleston?" (perfect for *Don't Knock the Rock*).

The July 25 issue of *Variety* illustrated, once again, that inflammatory headlines had little to do with actual events. Although the headline read, "The Rocks Keep Rolling at R&R: Pittsburgh Is Latest Rioting Locale," the actual report indicated that "eight teenagers were arrested as they milled about the lawn of Soldiers and Sailors Memorial Hall after it *looked* as if a gang war might develop. Twin boys of 18 *turned up* at the concert drunk and were pinched *before* curtain time, and two 15-year-old girls were criminally attacked by four youths who picked them up *after* the performance."[69] On the basis of this account, promoter Robert Baltz's claim that rock music created no problems appears to be substantiated.

The summer's "troubles" were basically pseudo-events. Guardians of the public morality and special interest groups like ASCAP perceived a propitious opportunity to defeat the "perverts" of rock.

ASCAP and Teddys

The so-called "Rock 'n' Roll Riots," mostly noise and dancing in the aisles, and their spurious link to juvenile delinquency were creating considerable public concern. There appeared to be no end in sight. The *Billboard* charts clearly demonstrated that teenagers comprised the bulk of record buyers and they preferred "rock and roll and/or rhythm and blues . . . The Big Beat." By 1955 ASCAP's eight-to-two edge over BMI had been reversed. The culprit, Brill Building people were happy to tell any journalist willing to listen, was rock 'n' roll foisted upon adolescents by the broadcasters who "profited" from BMI.

Song Writers Protective Association (SPA) and former ASCAP president Otto Harbach charged, "It occurred to me that the greatest melodies of the past would never have had a chance to reach the public if they were written now instead of then. Would 'Smoke Gets In Your Eyes' be allowed by broadcasters to be heard instead of 'Be-Bop-A-Lula?' Could 'Indian Love Call' penetrate the airways which are flooded with 'Hound Dog?' "

In 1953, the SPA had brought a $150 million antitrust suit against BMI, charging the licensing company with conspiring to "dominate and control the market." The basis of the charge was that some broadcasters owned stock in BMI: listed co-conspirators included RCA Victor. As of the fall of 1956 nothing had come of the legal action.

The rock hysteria, on both generational sides, provided ASCAP with a propaganda tool. Russell Sanjek, vice president of BMI, outlined ASCAP's strategy to an assembly at the New School for Social Research. The executive suggested the public was intended to feel that "We never had rock 'n' roll before BMI. Rock 'n' roll is trash. Therefore, do away with BMI and you do away with rock 'n' roll."[70] This ploy had power, as many felt rock music was *so* bad there had to be a conspiracy to justify its popularity. This perception would be strengthened by the British reaction to Katzman's *Rock Around the Clock*.

Rock Britania

Headlines screaming "Rock 'n' Roll Riot," especially in the pages of *Variety*, rarely described more than disorderly conduct. The furor surrounding *Clock*, a self-fulfilling prophecy, palled in contrast to the movie's boisterous reception in the United Kingdom. The film would be the first visual exposure of rock 'n' roll in the shrinking British Empire. Its first fans would be the Teddy (Edwardian) Boys. The Teds, natives of London's East End working-class neighborhoods, were akin to Brandoesque bikers in the States, and their emergence coincided with the release of *The Wild One*. They aggressively flaunted wardrobes from the Edwardian era, including longcoats, suede shoes, velvet and moleskin collars, and string ties.[71] Their imitation of the finery of Britain's last glory days was a symbolic protest. George Melly described them as "profoundly anti-social: the dark van of popular culture dedicated to 'the giggle and kicks.' When rock 'n' roll cinematically entered British popular culture they were like a theatre audience, they were waiting for the curtain to go up, and like a rather old-fashioned theatre audience, they were formally dressed."[72]

American rockers, especially Haley, appealed to their working-class rebellion; English entrepreneurs serviced their whims and fancies but with restrictions. The Teds rebelled—lashed out—and tore the theaters to shreds.

Clock opened in London's West End without incident. Reportedly, the film was exhibited in 300 British theaters "scattered around the country (including such tough cities as Glasgow and Sheffield) without any trouble." But after a September 3 performance at the Trocadero cinema in

South London, several hundred teens sang and danced to "Mambo Rock," holding up traffic on the Tower Bridge. Some of revellers were arrested for "disorderly" conduct and one boy was fined a pound for kicking a policemen.[73]

This youthful exuberance was transformed by the *Daily Mirror* into a full-fledged riot involving 2,000 theatergoers. As in America, the press accounts fueled violence-prone adolescents like the Teds.

"A great deal of the trouble was obviously due to inflated publicity," wrote Mabley. "The publicity also introduced an element of competition between teenage gangs in different districts."[74]

At the time, a British teenager described the atmosphere after the *Mirror* story:

> Gangs filed in and filled up row after row. Unlike most of the films, this one had commanded an almost entirely adolescent audience. When the music started it was infectious—no one managed to keep still. It was the first time the gangs had been exposed to an animal rhythm that matched their behavior. Soon couples were in the aisles copying the jiving on the screen. The 'bouncers' ran down to stop them. The audience were mad. Chairs were pulled backwards and forwards, armrests uprooted, in an unprecedented orgy of vandalism.[75]

Fourteen seats were missing by the time the police arrived.

Such incidents increased, fanned by media reports. Events were "sensationalized in the Press, and—you might have guessed it—Teddy Boys were mixed up on all of it," wrote Dave Rogers.[76] One story passionately stated:

> Rhythm-crazed teenagers terrorized a city last night. Police had to radio for help to quell stampedes of Rock 'n' Roll Teddy Boys and their girlfriends. (*Daily Sketch*, 4 September 1956)

Teds were discovered by the British media, which "decided that they spelled full-scale revolution. For the first time (in the U.K.) the concept of 'teenager' was news, as a major selling point" Cohn observed.[77] The mounting hysteria in Britain became a vicious cycle. "As the papers hollered harder, the panic got greater, the circle kept spinning," Cohn continued. "Suddenly the generational war was open fact."[78]

Clock was banned in parts of London, Liverpool, Bristol, Brighton and Birmingham. One town received news space for *not* cancelling. Rank, Columbia's British distributor, refused to allow the running of the film on Sundays, the day of the Teds' night out.

Columbia Pictures protested, but not too strongly, blind bans of the film based strictly on "sensationalized" tabloid accounts. The company admitted, however, that the film was experiencing excellent box office and had broken attendance records in some venues.[79]

Heightening interest further was Queen Elizabeth's request for a private showing of *Clock* at her holiday castle in Balmoral, replacing a pre-release copy of *The Caine Mutiny*. The *Daily Mirror* headline read "THE QUEEN TO SEE THAT 'ROCK' FILM." Teenagers barred from viewing the Katzman project reportedly expressed considerable displeasure, claiming that this was obviously an unfair use of monarchal privilege.

In the States, meanwhile, rock and R&B were going strong and ASCAP insisted this was an abuse of monopolistic and corporate power. The demographic-technological-legal caldron came to a temporary boil on September 17 when Chairman Emanuel Celler (D-New York) gavelled the House Judiciary Antitrust Subcommittee to order in New York's Foley Square Courthouse. The subcommittee's hearings, called to probe the alleged monopoly hold of television networks, took a detour to review the SPA-BMI legal dispute.

At a recess press conference, held on federal property, SPA members held forth. A plaintiff, Arthur Schwartz ("Dancing in the Dark") told the assembled media "This investigation by Congress should be of great assistance to all writers and those who are engaged in a lawsuit against BMI and the networks should be benefited by the search light played on the evidence."[80]

What followed was an exercise in BMI bashing. The echoed refrain was that BMI, under the auspices of the audio-visual networks, had grabbed control of the bulk of singles buyers by foisting rock 'n' roll upon adolescents. The most commonly quoted testimony came from ASCAP's maverick librettist Billy Rose:

> Not only are most of the BMI songs junk, but in many cases they are obscene junk, pretty much on a level with dirty comic magazines. An ASCAP standard like 'Love Me and The World Is Mine' has been replaced by 'I Beeped When I Shoulda Bopped'. A lovely song like Irving Berlin's "Always' has been shunted aside for 'Bebopalula' I Love You' (sic). It is the current climate on radio and TV which makes Elvis Presley and his animal posturings possible.
>
> When ASCAP's songwriters were permitted to be heard, Al Jolson, Nora Bayes, and Eddie Cantor were all big salesmen of songs. Today it is a set of untalented twitchers and twisters whose appeal is largely to the zootsuiter and the juvenile delinquent.[81]

Singer Frank Sinatra added to the polemic, charging Columbia Records with giving him "many inferior songs, all, curiously, bearing the BMI label.'' Charges and rebuttals flew. The most factual response noted that of fifty-seven titles recorded by "Ole Blue Eyes," fifty-two were licensed by ASCAP. Eleven of those fifty-two were with Sinatra's own publishing house. Columbia's president Goddard Lieberson expressed bewilderment "as to what might have promoted the singer to make charges which are so contrary to the actual facts."[82] Observers also noted that Sinatra's only Top 40 hit at that time was "Young At Heart," a BMI tune.

Chairman Celler made little attempt to conceal his pro-ASCAP leanings. At the hearings and at media appearances, he denounced rock—the "Hound Dog" music—and the "people responsible."

At the very outset Celler warned broadcasters that they should divest themselves of BMI. In radio and television appearances, allegedly booked by SPA, the venerated legislator blasted rock music. His remarks could have been scripted at the Brill Building. He repeatedly insisted, "It caters to bad taste, like, for example, I may be accused unduly if I say this: nevertheless, I must say it. The bad taste that is exemplified by Elvis Presley's 'Hound Dog' music, with his animal gyrations, which are certainly most distasteful to me, are violative of all that I know to be in good taste." At another media opportunity, he said, "I am quite convinced that if BMI goes on we'll never hear serious and good music. We'll never get to hear the works of Kurt Weill or Deems Taylor . . . Those are the names to conjure with in American music, and not rock and roll and the songs that are sung with those animal gyrations and contortions by Pelvis—if I may call him Elvis the Pelvis." Moreover, he claimed, Elvis and Rock 'n' Roll were the "lowest denominators of bad taste."[83]

Harper's editorialized that "the juveniles may scream at Elvis today, Congressman, but they'll be voters tommorrow."[84]

Toward the close of the New York City hearings, Celler experienced a *tour de grace*. Appearing on Lester Wolff's Sunday afternoon *Between the Lines* on the Dumont Network, he was flanked by ASCAPers Oscar Hammerstein II and Arthur Schwartz and *Herald Tribune* scribe John Crosby, who had "described further evidences of suppression of songs by ASCAP composers coupled with a constant promotion of BMI songs,"[85] using testimony from the Celler hearings for supporting evidence.

On the television forum Celler "resolved" the pending court action, indicating that "better tastes would be satisfied" when the networks dropped BMI stock. The networks then owned 25.6 percent of the licensing company's paper. CBS reported its television arm aired 80 percent ASCAP material, while the radio networks played 74 percent Tin Pan Alley products.

In the *New York Times* Jack Gould asserted "It is not for the anti-trust sub-committee to choose the hit parade."[86]

Variety's Abel Green was clearly embarrassed by *Between the Lines*, condemning the lack of balance—"The evidence was loaded against BMI." He also attempted to distance himself and his publication from the controversy. Acknowledging charges that *Variety* was pro-ASCAP in it's reporting, he insisted, "News stories are not utilized for coloration; if the context of a story imparts a 'leeric' or a negative approach to the rock 'n' behaviorism, this is because it is a statement of news report."

Alan Freed disagreed. "About a year ago, they started a campaign against off-color lyrics in rock 'n' roll," he said. "Well, there are double meanings in popular songs, too, especially some of the more sophisticated ones. Now rock 'n' roll lyrics have been cleaned up.

"*Variety* is off on a campaign to link rock 'n' roll with riots. If a couple of kids dance in the aisles, they call it a riot. A couple of kids wrecked a subway car half an hour *after* seeing one of my rock 'n' roll shows. So all the well behaved teenagers get a black eye. It's guilt by association. And the daily press picks it up, too," concluded the deejay, "when they're looking around for sensational headlines."

When a *Look* reporter asked Green about these allegations, he replied, "Rock 'n' roll is just another story. Let the paper [*Variety*] speak for itself."[87]

Green's attempt to dissociate himself from the *Variety* rock pieces was somewhat disingenuous. Whatever the motive, the "leerics" stories were directed at BMI artists and labels. Headlines, written by editors, not reporters, frequently were unsupported by the text. Examples included "Blasts Seem To Make Rock 'n' Roll Only Get Hotter" (April 6, 1956), "Bix Big But So Are Kids' Riots" (April 11, 1956), "R & R Battered 'n' Badgered" (July 18, 1956), and "The Rocks Keep Rolling at R & R; Pittsburgh Is Latest Rioting Locale" (July 25, 1956). The word "riot" rarely accurately described the actual event related in the story. Imperial Records's Lew Chudd was correct: *Variety did* fuel ASCAP's propaganda machine.

Variety, in the context of the Fifties, should not be perceived as duplicitous or engaged in a conspiracy to ruin BMI or rock 'n' roll. The trade mirrored the adult view of the time. Rock, considered by many a fad, appeared to be hurting film and show venues. Green was accurate when he wrote in the famous "A Warning to the Music Business" op-ed piece that "A strong suspicion lingers within *Variety* that these business-men [labels] are too concerned with profit statements to take stock of what's causing some of their items to sell."[88] Having lived through the vaudeville "payola" period, Green knew all too well what "presidents" were all about. He was aware of artists like Al Jolson getting a "piece" of the song in exchange for performing it on stage.

In hindsight, *Variety* was walking the same thin line as many of its subscribers. Rock 'n' roll was for 45-buying teenagers. This was an economic fact of life.

Billboard, serving predominantly the record industry, was considerably more supportive. During the Celler tribunal the music publication head-lined on the front page, "Rock 'n' Roll in Disfavor." The two-paragraph piece said, in part, "With new experiences to their [theatre owners'] credit, such as calling riot squads, and with scars, such as damaged seats, for their buildings, some operators have turned thumbs down on any more rock 'n' roll. Some nix the whole idea. Some prohibit dancing but allow concerts. Some just hire the extra cops and let 'em go."[89]

The Subcommittee hearings ended October 6, with a finding promised by early the next year. Months dragged in dead silence, but portions of an interim report were leaked in late April 1957. The draft noted that it is "not clear that the BMI structure is illegal," but it did have the powerful opportunity "to exclude competing music on the air." The document recommended that the Justice Department investigate "all phases" of BMI's operations.[90]

A very watered-down report appeared June 10, with the Department of Justice urged to launch an "extensive investigation into all phases of the music field." Five members of the committee cautioned the finding should not influence the pending litigation. Dissident Kenneth Keating (R–New York) said, "Obviously we cannot and should not take any action or say anything which will in any way prejudice any party in that case."[91] This statement agreed with BMI's position. It's president, Carl Haverlin, testi-fied, "The court is in a much better position than the Committee to determine the merits of the charges made by ASCAP's members."[92] The polemic would resume in full force at the "payola" hearing years later.

ASCAP, however, was sledding on thin ice. The market split, due to the cost differential of the phonograph speeds, fragmented the audience. A spiraling number of teens preferred covers of country tunes, pouring millions into the coffers at BMI. These rearrangements led adolescents away from ASCAP material.

"None of them could write a rock 'n' roll number, so why kid them-selves?" said an unidentified BMI writer.[93] The individual was correct; Tin Pan Alley's public diminished in size. In addition, most ASCAP offerings— Broadway show tunes and "mood music"—were on long-playing albums.

"Rock Around the Clock," in the ASCAP catalogue, stiffed in its initial release as a single in 1954. Its surge to the top, as the opening and closing theme for *Blackboard Jungle* the following year, came despite broadcasters. Requests poured in and radio stations aired the record. Most of Haley's original material was licensed by ASCAP, but country—rock-a-billy—and R & B artists naturally affiliated with BMI. It was traditional.

This is not to suggest that BMI publishers were more insightful or virtuous than the tenants of the Brill Building. Stories abound, many verified, of country and blues music publishers, having recorded a specialty song, rushing the pre-release copy to Mitch Miller, hoping for crooner covers even at the expense of their own artists. Nashville insiders claim Acuff-Rose flew Hank Williams's newest release to Columbia before it hit the streets.[94]

Recalling the original resistance of broadcasters to authentic R & B and rock, it is very difficult to accept the argument that mainstream radio or television—despite Presley's limited appearances—foisted the genre upon the populace or any portion of it. Once more, it was easier to blame the messenger.

While the combatants were awaiting the Celler subcommittee recommendations, Fats Domino and his band ran into the third disruption of their touring year. It was the first to be quelled with the use of tear gas.

"It seems like the mix of the beat and the booze was too much and things just busted," related Duconge Wendell, the alto sax man. "Man, that tear gas was awful." Greensboro, North Carolina, police explained that when they were unable to penetrate a concert crowd, gas grenades were tossed into the ventilation system. This time news reports omitted the familiar description "riot."[95]

Rockin' The Blues

> You can call it rhythm and blues or rock 'n' roll . . .
> —Jumpin' George Oxford, deejay

Katzman's Grade-B pictures were popularized fluff, but within the idiom, they had merit. Teenage theatergoers got their money's worth. However, what came on the heels of *Clock* was an exploitation film in the negative sense.

Rockin' The Blues is omitted deservedly in most treatments of early rock-related motion pictures. Courageously, Ehrenstein and Reed list it in their annotated filmography. Their description is apt: "a primitive throwback to Forties filmed vaudeville."[96] Of interest to doo-wop mavens would be the one-hit Harptones performing three other numbers: "Mambo Boogie," "First and Only Girl" and "Oowee Baby," an exclamation cluttering many an R & B number. "Rock and Roll's The Last Fad," performed by Connie Carrol, was a precursor to the "will stay" songs to follow. The Harptones, with a Freed show to their credit and a minor hit, "Life Is But a Dream," were the only group with any visibility; the other eight acts in the film were virtually unknown outside the Apollo circuit.

Variety ran an impressionistic, but structurally accurate, account of the R & B effort:

> Here's a quickie, cheapie 70-minute catch-all designed to exploit the current rock 'n' roll music craze. With the disks rolling hot and the kids jumping, this all-Negro "Rockin' the Blues" has some special status in the current market. It may be compared to a filmed version of the talent roster at, say, the Apollo Theater in Harlem.
>
> The musical acts come on and off without any story line and with just a few interruptions coming from some comedic scenes supplied by Flournoy Miller and Manton Moreland and emcee intros by Hal Jackson, deejay on New York indie WLIB.
>
> It all adds up to an R & R overload that gets a bit wearisome. Neither the performers nor their musical repertoire have sustaining power. The producers should get the pic into the market fast to get any value from its marquee names.
>
> The producers obviously skimped on the budget outlay. Film is shot mostly as a stage presentation and when the camera wanders off it hits only stock sets. The sync job, too, leaves plenty to be desired. However, rock 'n' roll fans are notoriously easy to please.[97]

The effort, due to limited market appeal, poor distribution and a low budget, flopped. The black exploitation attempt would not be the only effort to stick "rock" into a title. In a matter of months Universal Pictures used the same gimmick.

You Can't Judge a Film by Its Title: Rock Pretty Baby

> *Cause we might get lucky—one never knows*
> *That's the way life is in rock 'n' roll*
> (c. 1987 Vera-Cruz Music Co. [ASCAP])

> *It's sure to be a smash with the youngsters . . .*
> *also has family appeal for it presents an inter-*
> *esting and wholesome glimpse of family life in*
> *suburbia.*
> *—Film Daily*

As the holidays rapidly approached, moviemovers were ready to service the lucrative Thanksgiving Day weekend and the Christmas/Hannukah break to follow. The motion picture colony was fully aware that Sam Katzman's rock "folly" would bring in more than a $1.2-million gross in U.S. revenues alone. Subtracting production and marketing expenses, *Rock Around the Clock* would easily net more than many of the so-called "big pictures."

Rock Pretty Baby (*RPB*) previewed in New York 15 November 1956. The score was inserted to sell the film; the title was gratuitous. One reviewer suggested that "Mineo and Saxon trying to pass themselves off as rock and rollers was enough to satisfy the females in the audience." The film, stated the *Variety* writer, should have been judged "for the purpose it was made—to cash in on the rock 'n' roll frenzy."[98]

Exploitation, the industry term for marketing and promotion, was an understatement when applied to Katzman. *Rockin' the Blues* can easily be translated to signify rhythm and blues; *RPB*, on the other hand, had little, if anything, to do with the rock genre or its culture.

Sal Mineo, an Oscar nominee for his misunderstood Plato in *Rebel Without a Cause*, was signed to headline *RPB* despite a supporting role. His identification with *Rebel* and *RPB* motivated Epic Records to sign the teen idol, and "Start Movin' " appeared in record shops five months after *RPB*'s debut. It reached the Top Ten the Spring of 1957.

Having begun his movie career with *Running Wild* (1955), John Saxon was the focus of the "rock" film. He, like Mineo, was typecast as a youth experiencing difficulties. Luana Patten, a former Disney child star, was cast as the level-headed romantic interest. Fay Wray of *King Kong* fame, in retirement since *Not a Ladies Man* (1942), played Saxon's mother. Shelley Fabares, who played Mary Stone on *The Donna Reed Show*, was also in the cast. Her song "Johnny Angel," issued by Columbia Pictures's record arm, Colpix, had peaked on the *Billboard* chart 7 April 1962 and stayed for two weeks. Throughout, Fabares maintained "I'm not a singer."

Music arrangers for the film included Henry Mancini, Rod McKuen, and Bobby Troup. None were remotely identified with the rock genre. Mancini, about to become the "most creative composer of theme music alive," was more jazz-oriented (as his *Peter Gunn* TV soundtrack would illustrate in 1958), and Troup's proclivities were similar. McKuen, destined to become something of a cult figure in the 1960s, was a poet who happened to write songs. (His claim to fame would, later, be the theme for *The Prime of Miss Jean Brodie*.) Rock 'n' roll was not their *forte*.

Rock Pretty Baby portrayed a Hollywood view of rock, not its reality.

In the film, Jimmy Daley (John Saxon) and his band, the Ding-A-Lings, have a gig at a college frat house. Wailing away, with Angelo "Nino" Barrato (Sal Mineo) on drums and the nicknamed sideman "Ox" (Rod McKuen), "Fingers" (John Wilder), "Sax" (Alan Reed, Jr.), and "Half-Note" (Bob Courtney), the group quickly discovers the hazards of Greek bookings. The college men want to party, not waste their energy on dancing. (At such affairs bands are merely human jukeboxes, providing background noise.) The frat men, their libidos frustrated, dismiss the combo. One of the foxtrotters, Joan Wright, (Luana Patten), wants to dance. When the music stops, she leaves with the bewildered musicians.

Joan, the daughter of a musician, hopes to follow the family tradition, and plans to attend the San Francisco Conservatory of Music. In the meantime, Saxon's band conveniently needs an arranger and Joan fills in. The musical collaboration, predictably, develops into "Young Love." (The Mancini composition in *RPB* should not be confused with the Carole Joyner/Ric Cartey tune recorded by Sonny James and covered successfully by Tab Hunter.)

In a Hillsdalian, upper-middle class environ, Jimmy is experiencing parental difficulties. His father, Dr. Thomas Daley (Edward C. Platt), frowns on Jimmy's musical aspirations, denying him a down payment for a $300 guitar. Mother Beth Daley (Fay Wray) sympathizes with her son but is powerless. Nino raises the money for Jimmy by borrowing from band members, arguing that it's a good investment for the group.

Jimmy gets his guitar, as well as Joan, but the Mineo character is troubled—he wants to date Claire Saunders (Carly Volkman), but she insists her twin sister come along. Thwarted, he goes on practicing with the group, waiting for the big chance.

Jimmy's group is set to compete in a talent contest hosted by disc jockey Johnny Grant, playing himself. (Grant, who months before had told *Variety*, "My show doesn't feature any R & B music because my listening audience doesn't request it," was an ideal choice for the film.) Just as things seem to be looking up, however, sinister rumblings of passion and lust emerge. Seeing Joan in a bathing suit excites the combo leader. Sensing the relationship is getting heavy, she withdraws, saying "we should see other people."

When Joan arrives at Jimmy's party with a date, a fight ensues. The upper-middle-class house becomes a war zone, the action spills over to the adjoining property, and the Continental in the driveway is damaged. Confused and humiliated, Joan leaves for the conservatory.

Compounding Jimmy's problems, Dr. Daley demands restitution for the harm inflicted on the yard next door and the car. Jimmy is forced to pawn his precious guitar and thinks things can't get worse.

Later, a remorseful father Daley coaxes Joan to forgive, forget, and return, and also gets his son's instrument out of hock. All that remains is to deliver the guitarist to the Johnny Grant contest. While racing to the broadcast site, father and son are stopped by the police, but the physician cons the officers into providing an escort. Jimmy arrives, but his group doesn't win the contest.

All is not lost, however. The Order of Bisons offers the combo a two-week gig at a summer camp, Jimmy reconciles with dad and Joan, and, as a final touch, Nino gets together with the elusive Claire.

Wedged into the eighty-nine minutes between the frat party and the televised talent show are a series of musical interludes. "Saxon and his colleagues have the opportunity to break out in song and instrumentals at the drop of a hat," noted an observer.

"Rock pretty baby, roll pretty baby . . ." opened the film. Vocalist Alan Copeland, a member of the restructured Modernnaires, did a jump version of Sonny Burke's title song. This was as close to the Haley sound as the entire score would come. Most of the instruments and a majority of the selections were straight out of the big-band era. The use of the word rock in "Jukebox Rock," "Big Band Rock and Roll," and other songs was gratuitous. The Ding-A-Lings were a mix of the Crewcuts, the Norman Petty Trio, and the jazz quartet, the Hi Los. Their sound on "Rockabye Lullaby Blues" was big-band harmonizing. Rod McKuen sang "Picnic by the Sea" and "Happy is a Boy Named Me." The tunes were prototypical McKuen—In 1956 he was as maudlin as his coffeehouse material some five years later. Throughout the film, the group's patter and monickers are difficult to accept. Rod McKuen as "Ox"? *National Parent-Teacher* reviewed the film as a "rock 'n' roll musical" in which the central characters' main interest was "jazz."[99] In this context, the description fits.

Three months after the movie's release, Decca produced a related sixteen-selection soundtrack album. The artists were listed as Jimmy Daley and the Ding-A-Lings. A closer look at the credits shows that of the six vocals, four were the Dings, with a solo by Copeland on the title song, and Rod McKuen on "Happy is a Boy Named Me." An instrumental of the Bill Haley tune "The Saints Rock 'n' Roll" was in the package. Mancini was responsible for the remaining instrumentals.

Rock Pretty Baby, the album, appeared on the *Cashbox* 25 best-seller list February 23, 1957 and stayed for eight weeks, peaking at Number 16. This was the second long-playing rock record to be advertised as "music from" a motion picture. (Chess's *Rock, Rock, Rock* (*RRR*) preceded it with a December 1956 street date. The Chicago-based label coordinated its album release with the film. Decca did not.)

These issues failed to establish any pattern; timing appeared inconsequential. *RRR*, linked to the film with familiar artists, failed to chart. (Trade "pop" charts prior to 1958 were misleading as applied to rock acts. Black artists frequently were listed in the non-pop sections as specialty performers. Consequently, it is impossible to determine just how well the album did.) Conversely *RPB*, with hardly a tie to the rock world, performed well, even when available only in the waning days of the film's first run. The reason for the differential performance is open to speculation, but the bottom line showed *Rock Pretty Baby* outselling its album competitor at the box office. The adage that movies sell records remained intact. On the North American continent *RPB* grossed $1,430,000.

Rock, Rock, Rock: Editing Out The Story

Rock, Rock, Rock, out the second week of December 1956, was advertised as "The Greatest Rock 'n' Roll Music Played by Biggest Rock 'n' Roll Groups This Side of Heaven" with "21 *New* Hit Songs (sic) 21." Truth in advertising was not the forte of theater sheets.

In the film, any hint of generational conflict or offensive "leerics" was excised. Male students wandered around in suits and ties. Tuesday Weld and her friends stepped off a page of a fashion magazine. Motorcycles, sideburns, leather jackets, and tight skirts were conspiciously absent.

The only remote point of conflict was that of teenage fiscal responsibility. Dad even sat down and watched Alan Freed. He, too, would swing and sway to the Big Beat.

Theatregoers were unconcerned. They ignored the intrusive scenes with trite characters and dialogue. The few nonmusical interludes allowed the patrons "a perfect opportunity to prowl the theatre, chat with friends and make dates for after the show. But when the music eclipsed the bubblegum story," noted Ehrenstein and Reed, "socializing ceased and the cheering began."[100]

If a patron was a minute late, he would have missed the opening song. Two sentences into the opening teenage foxtrot exhibition, Dori Graham (Tuesday Weld) lip syncs Connie Francis's "I Never Had a Sweetheart." At the close of the song the innocent, matter of factly, says, "That's how I feel."

The object of her affections, Tommy Rogers (Teddy Randazzo), appears, announcing he is a finalist in Alan Freed's Talent Contest. Filling out the key players, Gloria (Jacqueline Kerr), the new girl in town, interrupts, asking to be introduced. The stuck-up rich girl has her eye on Dori's beau. The principal players, performing a nonexistent plot, are identified two musical selections, and four minutes, into the motion picture.

Prior to the revelation of Dori's dilemma, she and Tommy meet in the park allowing him, yes, to sing a song. These totally unanticipated musical degressions complicate matters, as the viewer never knows if a line of dialogue or a vocal is coming.

Dori's father (Jack Collins), the only bona fide actor in the cast, becomes concerned with her spendthrift habits and promises to close the family charge accounts. Dori's need for money—in order to keep Tommy—is the remaining storyline.

In the movie, Dori's best friend Arabella (Fran Manfred) is babysitting at a posh country club, the local teenage hang-out. When her charge is asked, "What do you want?" Baby (Ivy Schulman) answers, "Baby Wants To Rock" with four unmiked male backups. She proves to be a New York Shirley Temple, singing "I don't want a lollipop, I just want to rock."

Returning home, Dori and Arabella join Dad in watching Alan Freed's *Rock 'n' Roll Party*. In rapid succession the deejay runs through numbers by the house band, Freddie Mitchell, and three Chess artists. Chuck Berry's "You Can't Catch Me" is the high point—duck walk and all. One cut away to the television viewers is provided. Tommy performs a Teddy Randazzo song and wins the contest.

Unaware that her credit line has been cancelled, Weld rushes down to the dress shop only to find Gloria. The threat for Tommy's affections materializes. Dori "just has to have" the strapless evening gown to wear at the prom with the rising pop singer.

The "desperate" teenager makes a deal with dad to raise the necessary money for a dress. In a convoluted scheme, during which Gloria black-mails Tommy into going to the prom with her, Dori prevails. She unmasks Gloria for the "no-goodnik" she really is and gets her blue dress.

Meanwhile, Tommy stops by the soda shop with the now-familiar announcement, "Alan Freed is coming to the prom and he's bringing his whole show." Freed "works cheap." Tommy then slips into "We're Gonna Rock Tonight." It's amazing: he doesn't move his lips while singing the song.

Discovering that Tommy is taking Gloria to the prom, Dori performs another Connie Francis overlay. She also exposes Gloria's machinations to win Tommy and goes to the prom. Alan Freed emcees, and the show begins with the Jimmy Cavall Houserockers repeating the title song. The Johnny Burnette Trio performs an infectious version of "Lonesome Train," one of the few animated moments in the film. After the Moonglows add another selection to the Chess album, Frankie Lymon and the Teenagers do a mini-set with the closing lyric, "It's easy to be good/It's hard to be bad/Stay out of trouble and you'll be glad," with hands poised as in prayer. The twinkle in Lymon's eye gives "I'm Not a Juvenile Delinquent" away. If *RRR* has a message, it's the title of this song.

During the show Tommy attempts to resume his relationship with Dori. He introduces his song with a dedication and performs "Give Me A Chance." She melts. "I'm sorry, I didn't *give you a chance*," she sings. As "Right Now" blasts, they share something resembling a kiss. THE END.

Katzman's original low-budget rockers, hardly profound, had a modicum of a plot, however thin. *RRR* was, however, another of the pasted-together stories writers could summarize in a sentence. The plot is about "a teenager who wants to get a strapless gown to wear to the high school prom and goes through all kinds of agonies to raise the necessary coin." Howard DeWitt: "Tuesday Weld played a teen-ager who lost her boyfriend, Teddy Randazzo, to the new girl in town.[101]

Given the nonexistent plot, *Variety* choose to rate the music performances. LaVern Baker, Chuck Berry, and Frankie Lymon were praised. "Talent runs out of class after that," wrote the reviewer. "Some of the turns are so incredibily bad there is even a Presley-aping guitar player named Johnny Burnette."[102] Hindsight can be a critic's nightmare. The revisionist consensus is that "While some of the performances are classics (Chuck Berry, Frankie Lymon and the Teenagers) and others offer rare glimpses of great but almost forgotten performers (Johnny Burnett, LaVern Baker, the Moonglows, and the Flamingos . . .), the majority are laughably old fashioned, offering convincing evidence that rock 'n' roll *had* to happen."[103] Pat Romanowski is correct, as in the Tin Pan Alley tradition, the other acts were either MOR or cover people.

With the opening credits almost exclusively music artists with label affiliation there is little doubt this was a teen-exploitation film *par excellence*. Characters break into song with a drop of a sentence or without a band being present. The music editing is sloppy, with numbers bleeding into the next scene. "Sound recording is unusually bad, many of the numbers being completely out of sync with the actor action. There's even a phony applause track thrown in," said *Variety*, which had to review the film.[104] The mass circulation magazines ignored it.

Freed shuts up and cues the songs with half-sentence introductions. Only the Burnett Trio, Frankie Lymon, and Chuck Berry, appropriately, garnered more than one-liners.

The film roster further indicated that *RRR* was promoting artists and records. Three listed acts were on Coral Records. As Pat Romanowski noted, "Not surprisingly, many of the lesser-knowns were signed to Coral Records, a label Freed was involved with, so you know they weren't included here because they were in any way important."[105] The writer seems to have forgotten Johnny Burnett was on Coral.

Chess Records equally manifested a Freed-related "coincidence of interest." The WINS platter spinner owned 50 percent of two songs on the soundtrack, "Sincerely" and "Maybellene." Berry stressed that Freed had nothing to do with the creation of "Maybellene," but the Freed estate still receives royalties from the song.

Even prior to August 5, 1957, when *American Bandstand* joined the ABC network, the musical jukebox vehicles were important visual exposure devices—*The Alan Freed Show* had briefly appeared on ABC-TV on May 4, 1957. (The premiere half-hour program included The Del-Vikings, Jay Hawkins, Martha Carson, The Clovers, June Valli, and Guy Mitchell. The program was quickly cancelled after Frankie Lymon was seen dancing with a white girl on camera.) They afforded rare opportunities for teens throughout the nation, to actually see their radio favorites.

Television variety shows, in the wake of the Elvis "The Pelvis" polemic, were definitely gun-shy. The presentation of black R'n'B artists was a violation of *de facto* network booking policies.

The importance of *RRR* was Chess Records's use of the movie to package three in-house artists on the long-playing album enscribed, "From The Motion Picture." This would be the first rock soundtrack album. The Chicago-based label turned the studio's strategy *camera obscura*. Instead of having the music promote the film, Chess used the film to justify an album.

Only four of the twelve album selections actually appeared in the film. The somewhat contradictory liner notes by co-producer Milton Subotsky correctly announced, "Here is the most exciting collection of rock 'n' roll music ever assembled—three of the greatest stars in this new, happy medium in an album that is delightfully different."

Chess promoted the track album as film-related, with additional greatest hits. Outside artists were absent and Jimmy Cavallo's title song was issued by Coral.

Fittingly, the first rock track showcase contained two-thirds filler. Eight of the hit songs had nothing to do with the film. This approach would become standard practice. Ironically, the Grade-B musical jukeboxes of the 1950s lent themselves to legitimate soundtrack efforts. Minus a plot, twelve representative tunes were, theoretically, available. In the early years of rock 'n' roll, however, labels guarded their rosters zealously.

RCA did exploit *Love Me Tender* as an extended play. The EP featured four new songs by Elvis. The fact that the music was more watered-down country than rock-a-billy did not bother consumers. Teenage shoplifters, according to a San Francisco department store clerk, loved the easily removable record with Elvis' picture on the cover. In 1956 anything Presley recorded was saleable, with or without a film. With *Loving You*, RCA did, however, release a long-play, with a "B" side of extraneous material.

Girl Can't Help It

One of the more thoughtful users of rock was Frank Tashlin. A veteran film director and writer, he made *The Girl Can't Help It* with "a certain cynicism" while participating in the very process he was satirizing. (The result would be the best overall rock picture until *A Hard Day's Night*.)

The film starts with a figure in evening clothes appearing in the center of the shrunken screen. The picture is black and white. As if introducing a symphonic recital, a narrator tells viewers that this is to be a story about music, but, first, "this was photographed in the grandeuer of Cinemascope and in gorgeous lifelike color by Deluxe," as the image expands and haltingly turns to color contrasts. The reference to *Rock Around the Clock* is unavoidable. ("And in sharp contrast," wrote Ehrenstein and Reed, "to the flat, backgroundless settings of those first few black and white rock films, the director unleashes all of Twentieth Century Fox's color and Cinemascope resources.")[106]

Tom Ewell, in tones reserved for Saturday afternoon opera broadcasts, informs the audience that the picture is about contemporary music, expressing "the culture, the refinement, and polite grace of the present day . . ." The camera pans to a garishly lit jukebox as Little Richard's title song, "The Girl Can't Help It," blares, drowning out the speaker's remarks.

The opener praises and mocks new conventions in one brief sequence. Deluxe color is great if it works—likewise popular music. Throughout the film, new versus old vis-a-vis values, lifestyles and music, is the undercurrent.

The story begins in a bistro with the ever-present musical accompaniment and the heavy-drinking agent Tim Miller (Tom Ewell). Tim, we'll discover, spends a lot of time in night spots listening to rock acts. He receives an invitation from Marty "Fats" Murdock (Edmond O'Brien) which he accepts, after finding his bar credit has been exhausted. Ex-mobster Fats is in a quandry. He misses his past notoriety, even mentions in the scandal magazines. In order to elevate himself into newsworthiness, Fats wants Ewell to make his girlfriend into a star. The agent refuses, until he bumps into Jerri Jordan (Jayne Mansfield), a tall, statuesque blonde in a skin-tight gown. Miller, still, protests that stardom takes time: "Rome wasn't built in a day." Murdock retorts "She ain't Rome. What we're talking about is already built." This is one of the first of many verbal and sight gags centered on Mansfield's physique. For example, Jerri tells Miller, "Nobody thinks I'm equipped to have kids," and Barry Gordon comments, "If she's a girl, then I don't know what my sister is." Some of these remarks are sexist by 1980's standards, but a few are harmless and funny. (Bosley Crowther took note of the stress placed on Mansfield: "Apparently, Mr. Tashlin (director) was so staggered by Ms. Mansfield's shape that he couldn't get his mind off the subject—nor the camera, nor even the picture's plot."[107]

Obtaining a $10,000 advance, Miller accepts Marty's challenge. He celebrates in another nightclub with a band blasting "Ain't Gonna Cry No More." After a bevy of sight gags stressing the Mansfield frame, the dejected agent discovers Jerri is uninterested in a musical career. She protests, "I'm domestic." Her life goals are cooking, keeping house, and having kids. This subtle dramatic twist is a bold departure from the hackneyed plots of the 1930s and, indeed, the Katzman rock projects. Tashlin and co-writer Herbert Baker cleverly turn the "rags-to-riches" formula *camera obscura*. They go through the motions, allowing the obligatory well staged musical interludes, all the while knowing that Jerri rejects fame and fortune. The price, marrying Fats, is too high.

As a marketing ploy, Miller escorts Jerri on a "nightclub crawl," displaying her to the bistro managers. Little Richard is seen performing "Ready, Ready," plus "She's Got It"; The Three Chuckles, featuring Teddy Randazzo, do "Lollipop Lies"; Eddie Fontaine performs "Rock Love"; and Abby Lincoln sings the gospel tune "Spread the Word." (In a '50s nightclub?) After the tour of various pitstops, Miller staggers back to his apartment to discover a vision of Julie London (a former love) singing "Cry Me A River." The haunting ceases with the music.

Fats, having hired Miller because he doesn't mess with clients, is becoming paranoid. The gangster provides the agent with an exhibition of his shooting skills. Miller argues that Jerri isn't interested in a career. Fats counters with a threat of violence and the agent retreats to a bar. "Cry Me A River" plays on the jukebox. A transparency materializes. It's Jerri Jordan. Miller's in love. The plot thickens.

Miller takes Jerri to a rehearsal hall. Beaux Arts provides more artist showcases. Gene Vincent and the Blue Caps provided a hellishly inspired visual of "Be-Bop-A-Lula." Biographer Britt Hagarty reports the most rousing portion of the on-film performance was cut: "The Caps all screamed at the end of the song, the framed portraits of Beethoven and Rachmaninoff hung on the wall behind them, suddenly fell to the floor with a BOOM!"[108] Trying to find Jerri's musical key, Miller discovers, much to their delight, that she has none. When she hits "mi" on the music scale, a light bulb shatters. They repeat the performance for Fats. The girl ain't got it vocally. Fats, however, is not dissuaded. He calls Jerri, demanding that she tune, immediately, to Channel 2.

Television host Peter Potter's image appears saying, "Ladies and gentlemen, Eddie Cochran, one of America's top rock 'n' rollers." The introduction was gratuitous, as Cochran's cameo in *Girl* was his first national exposure. Jerry Capehart, friend and temporary manager, discussed the significance of the film in Cochran's all-too-short career. "We went to Liberty," said Capehart, "on the strength of a song called 'Twenty Flight Rock' which was (to be used) in the film *The Girl Can't Help It*."

"With the two (label and studio) working together," wrote Lenny Kaye, "it was thought that Liberty would use the song from the movie, 'Twenty Flight Rock', as Eddie's first single. Liberty instead chose the John D. Loudermilk tune "Sittin' in The Balcony."[109] The film song was the "B" side. Unlike most movie, musical interludes, however compelling, Eddie Cochran's performance was central to the plot.

The rock-a-billy performance motivates the frustrated Murdock to demand a recording session as, *a la* Presley, the guy on TV "has a new sound." So does Jerri. Two light bulbs and a Cochran appearance later, Miller joins Fats to pick a suitable song from the gangster's prison-inspired compositions. O'Brien's character offers some novel titles. None would fit on a record label: "No Lights on the Christmas Tree Mother, They're Using the Electric Chair Tonight" or "I'll Get No Good Behavior Baby, If I Keep Thinking of You." They settle on "Rock Around The Rock Pile," a thinly disguised parody of the Haley song. "One rock-two rocks-three rocks-four rock . . ." was familiar to theatre goers and teenaged radio listeners. In a few scenes Tashlin zings Presley via the Cochran song— "Anyone Can Sing"—and the Katzman pics. Ray Anthony and band do the prison lyric "Rock, rock, rock around the rock pile . . ." Jerri inserts the piercing siren. (*Variety's* reviewer noted that the director "poked some fun at the current dance beat craze and the artists who deliver.")[110]

Miller goes to Chicago to pitch the song to a jukebox distributor. Upon arriving he calls Jerri, whose phone is tapped. They obviously are in love. Neither dares say so, for fear of Fats. Their conversation would give away the secret. Mousie (Henry Jones) splices the phone tapes, preventing Fats from catching on.

In the Windy City, the flustered agent auditions the tape, hoping the Wheeler Music Company will turn down the record. Instead the owner (John Emery) wants to sign Jerri.

"A voice like that will catch on," says Wheeler. "This girl will be a star." The jukebox king is interested in the songwriter also, because "He's got a feel for what people want today." Wheeler's cheerful attitude abruptly changes as he learns who Fats Murdock is.

Returning, bruised and beaten, Miller is told Wheeler is a former gangland rival of Murdock's; they fought over slot-machine routes. A resulting jukebox war result is an amusing parody of the 1930s Edward G. Robinson films. In Tashlin's picture, the music industry "is controlled from top to bottom by warring mobsters."[111]

As the aging mobsters recreate the Capone period, Fats plans a marriage. The climax occurs at the Rock 'n' Roll Jubilee Show. But first Fats Domino performs "Blue Monday," which reportedly premiered in the film. Mousie confronts Fats, asking the hoodlum boss to give up Jerri. Miller decides to leave. The distraught Jerri is scheduled to perform the now-famous scream with Ray Anthony. They affectionately—well almost—kiss. The Platters perform "You'll Never, Never Know." The segue is near perfect. Heartbroken Jerri, joining the Anthony group on stage, announces a change in the program, then breaks into a pop ballad reminiscent of "No Not Much" lifted from the Patti Page songbook. She *can* sing. Walking dejectedly to the parking lot, Miller encounters Fats. As the ganster shouts, "I'll be your best man," he is interrupted by Wheeler's band of assassins. Seeking safety in numbers, Fats gets on stage, performing a house-raising version of "Rock Around the Rock Pile." The teenagers flip. Wheeler tells his hoods, "Don't shoot! We'll sign him. That's talent up there, you jerk." The success of the song underscores, again, the rock audiences' lack of taste. Tim and Jerri marry and raise children with Fats as the family babysitter.

Unlike the preceding rock musicals, *The Girl Can't Help It* received coverage beyond the trades and *National Parent-Teacher*. *Time* and *Newsweek* published cryptic reviews.

"The underlying theory behind the enterprise seems to be that if Elvis could do it, so could anybody . . . little ado about nothing," said the *Time* writer. *Newsweek* barely indicated that the picture was a comedy starring Jayne Mansfield and Tom Ewell. This depiction jived with Fox's marketing approach, stressing the Monroe pastiche by Mansfield. "Rock 'n' roll comedy" was tucked away in the press kit. Bosley Crowther, whose last exposure to rock had been *Blackboard Jungle*, dismissed the female lead as merely "wiggling and squirming" throughout the picture. The scenery, the *Time's* man found, was "splashy and sporty," but still "the show is as meager and witless as a cheap pin-up magazine joke."[112]

Variety published a money review. *Girl* was, according to the critic, the first deluxe rock 'n' roll comedy.

"It is an hilarious comedy with a beat, and the younger set should take to it like a double chocolate malt with cheeseburger. Business prospects are first rate in regular situations."[113] The portrayal was the first unqualifiedly positive notice any rock-oriented film production had garnered. History would be much kinder than the film intellegensia of 1957.

Most post-Fifties writers followed *Variety's* model, which stated, the "Musical talent, most of the R & R variety, is tops in its field, the list reading like a special performance bash." In contrast, Crowther, who ignored the Haley theme in *Blackboard*, found the rock material as being "agonized." Future observers would prove supportive.

Greil Marcus termed the flick "first-rate." Gillett characterized the picture as a "remarkable collection of several of the best rock 'n' roll singers . . . and its strong story." Ehrenstein and Reed: "this delirious comedy presents some of the best looking rock-and-roll ever (before or since) on a movie screen."[114]

Cinematically, the film was a wide-screen spectacular, in contrast to most low-budget "teen exploitation" musicals. It exhibited an intelligent, perhaps too sophisticated plot, and was a box office success. It would gross $2.8 million domestically.

Jenkenson and Warner outlined the impact of *The Girl Can't Help It* on the esthetics and economics of the genre:

> The film moved rock into the gloss factory, away from poverty row . . . The film openly equated rock music with sex appeal and said so with dash. Although the teenage response was more subdued, the film quickly cleared its costs and reassured front office executives that rock could not only be contained, but could actually be assimilated by the production machine. This hint of "respectability" was to be a major incentive in a whole series of subrock "spinoffs."[115]

The motion picture perhaps did not provide the respectability the British authors claim, but it had the effect of legitimizing the idiom. *Girl* was unaccompanied by torn, slashed theater seats or outlandish behavior. In San Francisco, for example, the film ran at the deco Fox Theatre. It, attracted young and old and no reports of riotious behavior surfaced. The focus of moral entrepreneurs would soon shift to concerts, which were little more than "live" exploitation vehicles.

Albeit because of the Mansfield factor, the rock sequences, or a combination of the two, the film did good box office. Production costs were covered, and a pleasant profit margin resulted.

Talk of a possible soundtrack proved a waste of time. Although the assembled array of artists would have made an excellent soundtrack album, the differentiated labels, pre/post release dates, and legal territorality precluded a souvenir package. Grade-B production companies and a few majors were all vying for the same hot artists. Bill Haley, Chuck Berry, Little Richard, and Fats Domino were rapidly becoming fixtures in rock musicals, due primarily to their charting patterns. Appearing in films created a self-fulfilling prophecy: ergo, hit artist appears in a rock movie, gets exposure, and creates a hit. The Catch-22 involved was that film studios wanted established artists with familiar hits.

Katzman Replies: "Don't Knock the Rock"

Rock 'n' roll is really swing with a modern name . . . It's the rhythm that gets the kids. They are starved for music they can dance to, after all those years of crooners.
— Alan Freed, disjockey

Bill Haley was large and chubby and baby-faced. He had a kiss curl like a big C, slapped down on his forehead with grease and water, and he was paunchy. When he sang, he grinned hugely and endlessly, but his eyes didn't focus on anything. Besides, he was thirty, married, and the father of five children. Definitely, he was unlikely hero food. Just the same, he was the first boss of rock.
— Nick Cohn, writer

As box office reports filtered into the Columbia Pictures accounting offices, the ledgers clearly called for a follow-up. The theater disturbances, predominantly in the United Kingdom, the Freed Rock 'n' Roll shows' rowdiness, and the film bans were ideal for another Katzman "headline of the day" motion picture.

In the fall of 1956, the moviemaker reassembled the *Clock* production team for a film tentatively titled *Rhythm and Blues*. (As noted, R & B was the original culprit, "leer-ics," until the Katzman/Freed projects garnered press attention.)

"Don't Knock the Rock," the song, was written especially for the film by co-scripter Robert E. Kent and music supervisor Fred Karger. Due to

Kent's participation, the repeatedly heard number actually reflected the plot. The story line was easy to treat in song as "it has been wisely written so as not to get in the way of the music."

"Don't Knock" was scheduled to be released in conjunction with *Rumble On The Docks*. This film, borrowing heavily from the Brando portrayal in *On The Waterfront*, introduced James Darren as a leather-jacketed delinquent. One writer suggested *Rumble On The Docks*, which included Freddie Bell and His Bellboys, "only seemed to marry violence and rebellion to music."[116]

In the film, Arnie Haines (Alan Dale), a rock 'n' roll celebrity, is returning to Hometown U.S.A. only to discover author Thomas Wolfe was correct. Mayor Tom Everett (George Cisar) is waiting at the railroad station. The city official confronts the unsuspecting singer. In typical Yahoo fashion, he condemns the rock sound as corrupting the moral fabric of young America.

Reports of a Bill Haley rock jamboree increase the tension. The Haley show has ended in a melee. The city in which the performance occurred bans disruptive concerts.

Mayor Everett and most of the townspeople think a ban is a great idea. Throughout, comments are made such as, "Rock and roll is for morons" or, "Children should be seen and not heard." Censorship, however, is troublesome to the inhabitants of this middle-American town. The mayor encourages his daughter, Sunny (Jana Lund), to smuggle booze to discredit a teenage affair featuring the dreaded rock demon.

Dale, with the aid of agent Alan Freed, decides to demonstrate to the myopic folk that rock is a harmless outlet for today's youth. Haines, by now, has a ulterior motive. He is attracted to Francine MacLaine, whose mother (Fay Baker) is an "anti."

With Freed's guiding hand, local high schoolers plan "A Pageant of Art and Culture," another Andy Hardy "Let's-have-a-show" ending for social betterment. The pageant commences with arts and crafts displays followed by a series of folk dances. The resolution is provided by a terpsichoral demonstration of the sights and sounds of the Black Bottom and the Charleston. The small-town elders, realizing the connection of the Charleston to rock dancing, recant. One member of the audience admits to the kids, "You're right; we're really a bunch of narrow-minded fools." Freed, Dale, and the Comets have made middle America safe for rock 'n' roll. The fade-out resounds with "Don't Knock the Rock" and the slogan "Dig It Now" appears.

The scriptwriters could easily have picked up their finale from several *Variety* items dealing with Freed's "live" Rock 'n' Roll shows in New

York. The articles stressed "they are dancing in film theatres again," comparing the activities to the teen jitterbuggers of by-gone years.[117]

Variety, the bible of the film industry, fulfilled its mission and discussed *Don't Knock the Rock*. In usual fashion, the exhibitors were alerted that rock was on the wane. But, the "genre is still strong enough to insure a profitable return on the investment," the paper noted. The skimpy plot was covered in two sentences. A brief discussion of the sixteen titles and artists was followed by plaudits to some of the cast. From a commercial perspective it was a good, however condescending, review: "Top rock 'n' roll artists in tune-loaded juve story, probably destined for substantial box office response." The film earned $1.2 million in domestic distribution in 1957.

Live Rock

The film continued to be tied to live rock performance.

Washington's Birthday 1956 Alan Freed opened the Rock 'n' Roll Show at Manhattan's Paramount Theatre, blocked up traffic on Times Square, and made the front page of the *New York Times*.

During the Freed Broadway Paramount starfest, Bill Haley was performing in Glasgow, Scotland. On 10 March he was scheduled to appear on television's "Sunday Night At the London Palladium" to receive a gold record for selling over a million records in the United Kingdom; he was the first artist in history to achieve that number. Afterward he returned to the States in search of a hit record, but only produced, according to biographer John Swenson, "slick, empty adaptations of standards and trite novelty tunes."[118] A fading Haley would thus not be in the one headline grabbing event involving the picture. Rather, it was destined to be Alan Freed's showcase.

The Paramount crowd began assembling at 4 a.m. An estimated 5,000 blue-jeaned girls and lumber-jacketed males gathered near Times Square to catch the first film/stage show by Alan Freed in Manhattan. The theater admitted 3,650 at 8:15 a.m., some fifteen minutes late, while the throng milled about, pushing at police barriers and shouting obscenities at New York's famed mounted patrols. A glass restaurant door shattered. The theater ticket booth was damaged. The sound of breaking glass had a chilling effect on the crowd. This time when police reinforcements arrived they were cheered. By 10:30 a.m., traffic control was partially restored.

Inside, the balcony rafters seemed, to firemen, to be in danger as the audience stamped on the upper tier. Most of the second floor was evacuated while building inspectors rendered a verdict. At first, all but the bottom four rows were deemed usable. A half hour later the entire section was approved.

Covering the event for the *New York Times*, Edith Evans Asbury described dancing throughout the venue. Teens "screamed with delight as performers were announced, stamped their feet in time with the music and sang with the singers." She was impressed as the patrons "knew all the songs."[119]

The show featured *Don't Knock the Rock*, in its New York debut, twelve R & B and doo-wop groups, and a twenty-piece orchestra led by Alan Freed, the emcee. The film was overshadowed by the live acts and could barely be heard. "Screams of derision and boos" drowned out Mayor Everett's denouncation of rock 'n' roll.

"We expected a crowd, but not such a large one," said theater manager Robert Shapiro. "This is the largest opening crowd we have ever had." He reported that 15,220 individuals had attended the six stage presentations and seven film showings prior to 1 a.m. the next morning. The one-day gross was $29,000, an all-time record. [The three-day, nineteen-hour-run, however, grossed a disappointing $125,000 due to weather conditions. He did not repeat the $204,000 sum from the Brooklyn stands. Attendance at the Broadway Paramount dropped considerably after the holiday weekend of live entertainment. Shapiro indicated *Don't* was not expected to attract many patrons.]

Freed had a lucrative deal with Paramount. The house would receive $50,000 off the top, with 90 percent of subsequent earnings going to the disc jockey. Freed would pay the acts a total amount of $32,000. He claimed to have bought off some of the performers' conflicting bookings to facilitate their appearance in Manhattan. Some observers discounted this argument, contending Freed made arrangements with the acts recording companies and management.

If the record companies had underwritten the show, the results nevertheless upset some of them. Labels, particularly the specialty companies, did not appreciate a rehash of the "mass neurosis" notion posted by the guardians of public morality. The publicity attendent to the first day was viewed as counterproductive, even though little in the way of actual law breaking had actually occurred.

Don't Knock would be the first Grade-B rock musical the *Times* assigned for review. (*Girl Can't Help It* was a "big picture" by Hollywood standards.) H.T. Thompson was sent to critique the motion picture. He brought back a piece depicting the audience with a short paragraph addressed to the movie. "The dialogue couldn't even be heard above the restless din," he observed, noting:

A so-called "rock 'n' roll" musical program opened yesterday on the Paramount's screen and stage. The occasion (and the theatre experience of this reviewer's career) was a terrible little Columbia film called "Don't Knock the Rock," stringing together some musical sequences, and a stage bill that takes up exactly where the other leaves off.

What is "rock 'n' roll"? Well, to one comparatively middle-aged man who made the awful mistake of grabbing a seat down front, it goes thump, thump, thump, thump. The audience roared it right back, number for number, as it continued the scouting parties, up and down the aisles, the open warfare over seats and, of course, the aisle-dancing.

At 12:47 p.m., as Little Richard, who must be seen to be believed, cut loose with "Long, Tall Sally," this viewer, nudged by two young ladies tussling over a souvenir program, made a perfect three-point landing at the feet of two aisle-rocking bellies. "Ya mashin' my foot, ya square ya, square ya," suggested one.

Legging it up to the mezzanine for a crouching aisle position (on a giant wad of gum) this spectator watched the stage platform rise from the pit, as the entire, chanting audience mounted seats.

"Come on up here," offered a pig-tailed girl in dungarees. She extended a hand. "I didn't know you old folks went in for this stuff."

The stage portion, dominated by Alan Freed, again, and his orchestra, was obviously what the spectators had come for, and they thumped it on down with the whole performing gang. There the Platters, Ruth Brown, Jimmy Bowen, Nappy Brown, Frankie Lymon and the Teenagers, the Cadillacs (human) and even more.

And O-Daddy-O, those cats had it! Anybody above 30 who elects to brave the Paramount's new program may find himself amid a composite of a teen-age revival meeting and the Battle of the Bulge. And O-Daddy-O, with a slight case of St. Vitus Dance, compliments of the house—if it's still standing.[120]

Another writer in the crowd concurred. The show was characterized as a "boisterous community sing." *Variety* noted, "The kids buy the records, memorize 'em and come to the theatre to sing along with the performer. The noise can be deafening, but that's the way it now goes . . . the performers themselves can't be heard after the opening bars. Still, the leerics have disappeared and so have the off-key, wailing and the over abundance of suggestive gesturing."

The deportment of the patrons, however loud, was well received. An observer wrote that "except for an occasional delinquent who'd thrown a cigaret down from the balcony, most of the kids were even polite in the inevitable jostling."

The tumult at the Paramount did little to enhance Bill Haley's amorphous image. In the *Clock* sequel, the bandleader comes off as an anachronism in a milieu peopled by the likes of Little Richard. Some rock chroniclers point to Haley's acting in *Don't* as the downward point in his career. As early as 1969, Nick Cohn began the demystification, suggesting, "It was Haley's film, but he lost it; he had it torn right out of his hands by Little Richard . . . [he] was the real thing. Bill Haley wasn't. Haley kept grinning, but he sounded limp by comparison, looked downright foolish.[121] Nash and Ross, in capsulizing the film, noted, "It's Little Richard ripping through 'Long Tall Sally' and 'Tutti Fruitt' who shines, and makes this exploitation film worth watching."[122] Little Richard was in a league of his own. Haley's sound was infectious just months before, but the rock scene was instantaneously changing. Musically, *Don't* was vintage Haley. That was his problem. In 1954 there was no one with a major label to provide a comparison. "Rock Around the Clock" and "Shake Rattle and Roll" dwarfed the covers by Perry Como and other crooners trying to "rock" onto the charts.

The scripts given to Haley in the Katzman vehicles were "square" imitations of the music world. The constant use of "cat," "hot dog," and other exaggerated "jive" phrases made him into a creature of the past.

Big band leader Artie Shaw, when filming *Dancing Co-ed* (1941) declined to use scripted lines such as, "Swing cats and alligators, I'll dig ya," etc. Haley had no such qualms. In song titles and speech, he uttered, "See you later alligator," or "Hot dog buddy, buddy." He explained to *Down beat*, "Usually I try to use expressions that the kids can easily remember and repeat."[123] Haley did add a phrase connoting departure, still occasionally used, to the jargon—"See you later alligator!"

Don't Knock the Rock would be the last American motion picture to provide Haley with star billing. Despite confused protestions to the contrary, the Pied Piper of Rock lacked box office appeal west of the Atlantic, except as a bit of nostalgia.

In a 1977 Capital Radio interview with Roger Scott, Haley claimed, "We made eleven [films], but I don't think we made an impression with many of them. We did a film for Universal International called 'Round Up of Rhythm,' which has since been lost in the maze of many films." They must have been lost, as biographer John Swenson only mentions *Clock Don't Rock*.[124] Haley was the ignition for rock 'n' roll. He didn't invent the sound. He merely popularized it. Bill Haley had a brief, but magical moment, in the evolution of the genre, and in the myriad musicals that copied *Clock*.

Sam Katzman would not repeat the $3-million gross—domestic and international—of *Clock*. *Don't Knock* did poorly in the United States. Katzman refocused his attention on sci-fi and horror films, although in 1959 he made *Jukebox Rhythm* and jumped on a new sound with *Twist*

NOT BAD FOR A MIDDLE AGED, FAT MAN WITH A "C" CURL	
"Crazy, Man, Crazy"	First rock single on the Billboard chart
"Rock Around the Clock"	First rock single to reach #1 on the Billboard chart, July 9, 1955
	First rock theme in the musical score of *Blackboard Jungle*
Shake, Rattle and Roll	First rock album (10″)
Rock Around the Clock	First rock musical

Around the Clock (1961) and *Don't Knock the Twist* (1962). The storylines for the two Chubby Checker vehicles were identical to the Haley projects.

Bill Haley: An Appreciation

Haley and the middle-aged Comets were the ideal transition point from crooners—with or without a big band—to rock 'n' roll. The country swing "jump" band sound on "Crazy, Man, Crazy" was expanded by ex-Louis Jordan producer Milt Gabler. The result was "Rock Around the Clock" and the sanitized "Shake, Rattle and Roll." Decca Records termed the style "a novelty fox trot," and Haley also experienced difficulties defining what he was doing. "What I play and what I developed (sic) is a combination of Dixie, country and western, rhythm and blues and pop. I try to keep a little of each in the music," he said. On another occasion he said "We use country and western instruments, play rhythm and blues tunes and the result is pop music."[125] Haley neglected to mention that the original version of "Rock Around the Clock" was essentially a C & W jump tune. Charlie Gillett would call the genre "Northern Bank Rock 'n' Roll."

Nick Cohn, continuing with the demystification of Haley, wrote, "The moment Elvis cut 'Heartbreak Hotel,' Haley was lost. [He] didn't measure up . . . Elvis Presley did."[126] Myriad writers echoed this view. Comparing the two stars of 1956 exemplified the "apples-and-oranges" syllogism. Both were synthesizers; on stage they were absolute opposites.

Haley was in the right historical niche. In *Blackboard Jungle* the theme song is *symbolically* the antithesis of swing—Berigan, Kenton, and, ultimately, the crooners. Gillett insightfully noted, "The presence in [*Blackboard Jungle*] of the music of Bill Haley, rather than of Tony Bennett and Perry Como, helped to establish in the minds of both adolescents and adults the connection between rock 'n' roll and teenage rebellion."[127]

Musically, the process was not revolutionary, in Crane Brinton's use of the term, but evolutionary. Elvis, due to his charismatic persona, steeped in the shadow of *The Wild One*, and rock-a-billy strains, was able to wrest the title of "King" from Haley. The leader of the Comets was crowned by historical circumstance. He was the first, but Presley's palace coupe was engineered by the sheet brute force of sound and style.

Haley and Presley were rock 'n' roll artists. Even Haley's manager had problems grasping the fact.

"Some entertainers are selling sex, strictly sex," said Jim Ferguson. "That sort of thing has been going on in hillbilly for years. But moving the hips a little isn't rock 'n' roll."[128]

Musicologists, however, haven't done much better. Rock-a-billy is a marriage of country and blues with southern gospel—black and white—as the sacramental cement. Haley was a musical sponge, absorbing, unconsciously in some cases, numerous strains. Elvis was a synthesizer. The context and circumstances of the two suggest an evolutionary process rather than the simplistic view that Haley was an unworthy monarch, while Elvis was born for the position.

One essential ingredient of "*Rock Around the Clock*" is missing in *post factum* discussions. Prior to Presley, it was the music that appealed to teenagers. Outside the East Coast bar band circuit and publicity photos, properly posed, few music fans had any inkling of Haley's appearance. *Hit Parade* and other music publications of the period were total "fanzines." Haley's marital status and other personal matters were never mentioned. Indeed, few 1950s adolescents originally knew, or cared, about covers. Haley, The Crewcuts and, later, Pat Boone created the spin to R & B in major markets and clear-channel stations. These artists fueled the appetites of the ever-growing number of rock fans whom AM stations could not service. Millions of teenagers flocked to black specialty stations to quench their thirst for rock.

"Rock Around the Clock" has been trivialized through its countless appearances on shows like *Happy Days*. Yet the magic of hearing the song at the opening of *Blackboard Jungle* was an unforgetable experience in the Fifties. Frank Zappa, as always, captured the moment: "I didn't care if Bill Haley was white or sincere . . . he was playing the Teenage National Anthem and it was so LOUD I was jumping up and down. *Blackboard Jungle* represented a strange sort of 'endorsement' of the teenage cause: "They have made a movie about us, therefore we exist."[129] Adult reaction emphasized the sentiment. The emotional contagion would reemerge with the Katzman production. Haley was in the right place at the right time; unfortunately, he lacked the persona to sustain the moment. He spent the rest of his life drowning this fact in the alcohol which finally killed him.

Shake, Rattle and Rock, Not "Roll"

Shake, Rattle and Rock, not "Roll," was the title, even though Joe Turner was in the film. For some reason Big Joe would not perform his R & B hit song, which had been popularized on the Top 40 charts by Bill Haley. Several preview announcements used the song title, and one can only speculate on the title change.

Seven songs were featured. Fats Domino following his film debut in *The Girl Can't Help It*, continued to please. He performed the smashes "Ain't That A Shame" and "Honey Chile," and closed the picture with "I'm In Love Again." Joe Turner's big beat arrangements were "Lipstick, Powder and Paint" and "Feelin' Happy." Two unknown rock-a-billies, Tommy Charles and Anita Ray, included the Johnny Burnette favorite, "Sweet Love On My Mind." Despite the presence of Domino and Turner, the material lacked the punch of the Katzman efforts. Some suspected the sound was turned down on the film track. Milt Gabler argued that the success of "Rock Around the Clock" was partially based on letting the sound blast without "pinching the top and bottom of the spectrum of sound."

"When that sound hit the kids in the movie houses," he continued, "it revolutionized film recording."[130]

Using a topic similar to the Kent-Gordon collaboration on *Don't Knock*, Lou Rusoff had produced one of the best of the Grade-B, $125,000-budget scenarios. The American International (AIP) movie opened January 9, 1957 without much hoopla.

In the movie, *Rock, Roll and Shake* is a local television disc/dance show hosted by Gary Nelson (Mike "Touch" Connors), with a loyal, *very* clean-cut teenage following.

The community moral arbiters, SPRACAY (The Society for the Prevention of Rock and Roll Corruption of American Youth), is led by Eustrace (Douglas Dumbrille) with his dedicated and narrow-minded cohorts. His main supporters are the henpecked Horace (Raymond Hutton) and his very proper and snappish wife, Georgianna, marvelously played by the towering Margaret Dumont. The valuative vigilantes attack Nelson for purveying "vulgar, lewd rock 'n' roll," but, encouraged by girlfriend June (Lisa Gaye), the TV deejay plans a charity sock hop to underwrite a Teen Town clubhouse for the underprivileged.

The show, providing a musical opportunity featuring Domino and Turner, is spoiled by agent provacateurs Paul Duboy and Eddie Kafafian, inept gangsters who are of a mind to win back their reformed-delinquent prodigies. They ignite a series of brawls, disrupting the entertainers.

The local paper, *The Clarion*, notes "Teenage Rioters On Rampage," borrowing a headline from London's *Daily Mirror*. Its front-page story states that Nelson may be charged with "contributing." SPRACAY's membership, and especially Georgianna, are self-righteously delighted.

In an incredible set up, Nelson's trial is to be televised (in 1956?). The pro anti rock 'n' roll arguments are to be heard by a judge. (The first amendment somehow is lost.) The "blue-nose" contigent offers "evidence" of the roots of rock, exhibiting a *National Geographic* travel scene of dancing in an African Village.

"You see," Eustace tells the magistrate, "the disgusting source . . . for rock and roll."

Nelson counters with a visual of his own. He projects a picture of frenzied flappers doing the Black Bottom. Much to the astonishment of the morality brigade, there is Margaret Dumont performing a sinful variation of the fox trot.

(The footage was from a vintage Marx Brothers movie. Dumont, a tall, statuesque blonde, was frequently a humorous high-society matron in early 1930s films. She was the foil of Groucho's pranks. Now she was again playing a prototypical Boston book/music banner.)

The courtroom atmosphere changes drastically with the screen revelations. The antagonists rock along with the kids to "Yes, it's me and I'm in love again." The final credit flashes "The Most To Say The Least."

A synthesis of *Don't Knock* and *Shake* with a larger budget might have produced a stronger rocksploitation vehicle. In the double-feature idiom, Rusoff's storyline featured substance, a rare commodity. Dumont's character brought life into the abstract banners and burners. The Fat Man could have used a counterpoint with a Little Richard, an Eddie Cochran or even a Bill Haley.

Variety, one of the very few to cover the film, observed the "film fits handily into current r-r craze and comes up with a story to suit."[131] *Shake, Rattle and Rock* did fairly well, overshadowed by *Don't* publicity, in the drive-in circuit. *Clock*, however, remained the best worldwide money maker of the rock musicals.

The ethos of rock 'n' roll, established in *Blackboard Jungle*, continued to stress the beat and wild youth. The novelty value of rock were off as it was legitimized on Top 40 radio, and movie mogals went back to basics. Wayward youngsters were highlighted, with some R & B and Rock 'n' Roll sandwiched in or overlaid in a "juve" story.

Untamed Youth

Marilyn Monroe was *the* sex goddess of the 1950s. Her recurring contract disputes with Twentieth Century Fox took the star off the screen, but not the front pages. During one of Monroe's many self-imposed exiles, Fox touted Sheree North and Jane Mansfield as the next "blonde bomb-shells." North was substituted for Monroe in *How To Be Very Very Popular* (1955). The film presented the actress doing a tame bump-and-grind to a big band arrangement of "Shake, Rattle and Roll." The song was ideal for burlesque runway music.

Universal Pictures' answer to Twentieth Century's two new stars was Mamie van Doren and the "pyramid bra." Although married to band leader Ray Anthony and twenty-six-years old, van Doren was packaged as the sultry personification of "wild, rebellious youth." The title was also used, appropriately, for a juve exploiter marketed as *Untamed Youth*, in which she starred.

The offering borrowed heavily from Monroe's posturing, coupled with the "today's headlines" exposé. (Topicality was becoming a staple for drive-in quickies.) Sam Katzman's motto was "go with the trend" and in 1956 teenage unrest was definitely trendy. In *Untamed Youth*, the rebellion is justified, since it is directed at the corrupt chain-gang system.

In *Youth*, Penny Low (Mamie van Doren) and her sister Janey (Lori Nelson) are entertainers arrested and brought before Judge Steele's (Lurene Tuttle) court. They are unfairly tried and sentenced to a prison farm owned by the evil Mr. Tropp (John Russell), who is secretly married to the jurist. The judge's son, Bob (Don Burnett), spots Janey and signs on as a prison guard in the hope of starting a relationship. The sweaty, arduous task of picking cotton is filled with familiar scenes of exhaustion, dehydration, and correctional sadism. The coeducational prison farm also houses Bong (Eddie Cochran) as a hoboesque character who defiantly snaps his fingers singing, "No you ain't gonna make a cotton picker out of me . . ." The unaccompanied protest with Presley-like intonations is totally effective.

"The only bright spot during '57 was the release of *Untamed Youth*," wrote Lenny Kaye, for Eddie Cochran's career.[132] The film did not make cinematic history, but the "Cotton Picker" segment frequently is cited in rock chronologies.

As conditions deteriorate in the camp, Bob Steele is making points with Janey and van Doren finds time to gyrate and grind through four songs in the bunkhouse, all under the prominantly displayed SLEEP IN YOUR OWN BED sign. She performs "Go, Go Calypso" and "Salamander."

A crisis is reached when an inmate suffers a miscarriage and dies. The expected prisoner revolt takes place. The Steeles, minus Bob (who proves to be a decent sort), are brought to justice. Penny is given the opportunity to appear on national television and Bob and Janey get together. *Untamed*

Youth was one of many "wild youngsters in trouble" releases. Its claim to fame remains the Cochran song.

With a caveat—"some may supposed the moral tone isn't the best"—*Variety* generally applauded the Howard Koch production. The reviewer took note that the "driving beat of the music . . . holds the footage together moreso than the actual story development. Numbers are well staged within the plot framework, even though director Howard W. Koch tends to overflaunt Mamie van Doren's more prominent physical attributes and her bodily gestures."[133]

A. H. Weiler was less charitable. He saw the movie as "a mediocre melodrama of Mamie van Doren and rock 'n' roll routines." His short three paragraph analysis went down hill after the opening description, with the *PTA Magazine* finding "the antics of rock 'n' roll carried to an extreme."[134] The "blond sexpot" showcases by Tashlin and Koch used rock music effectively, moreso than the jukeboxers. The obvious reason was the plots. Whatever its flaw, the *Untamed Youth* storyline neatly accommodated the music. There was no rush to get to the next musical interlude.

Untamed Youth was an inexpensive dialectical blend of *The Wild One* ethos and the rocksploiters. The music was partially integrated into the plot. The film, while not a musical personality showcase *a la* Presley *per se*, contained a rocker in a supporting role. This was a variation on the use of singer as "himself" or "herself" in backstagers, which began with Katzman. The boundaries for teen exploiters became increasingly murky as the screen jukeboxes lost their "contemporalia status." Merely presenting clips of artists doing familiar hits lacked the box office magnetism of *Clock* or *Don't Knock The Rock*.

Notes

1. C.A. Schicke, *Revolution in Sound: A Biography of the Recording Industry* (Boston: Little, Brown and Company: 1974), 125; Also see Oliver Read & Walter L. Welch, *From Tin Foil to Stereo: Evolution of the Phonograph* (Indianapolis: Howard W. Sams and Company, 1976), 333–42.
2. Roland Gelatt, *The Fabulous Phonograph 1977–1977* (New York: Macmillan 1977), 295.
3. Cited in Bruce A. Austin, "The Development and Decline of the Drive-In Movie Theatre," in *Current Research in Film*, vol. 1, ed. B.A. Austin (Norwood:Ablex 1985), 67.
4. John Durant, "The Movies Take To the Pastures," *Saturday Evening Post* 14 (October 1950), 85.
5. Harley W. Lond, "Drive-In Operations: Still in the Game," *Boxoffice*, March 1982, 53.

6. I.C. Jarvie, *Movies and Society* (New York: Basic Books, 1970), 117.
7. Robert Sklar, "Hollywood's Collapse," in *American Mass Media: Industries and Issue*, ed. Robert Atwan, Barry Orton, and William Vesterman (New York: Random House 1978), 336.
8. Russel B. Nye, *The Unembarrassed Muse: The Popular Arts in America* (New York: Dial Press, 1970), 386.
9. Ibid., 389.
10. See Marc Hugunin, "ASCAP, BMI and the Democratization of American Popular Music" *Popular Music and Society* 7 (1) (1979), 12.
11. John Shepherd, *Tin Pan Alley* (London: Routledge & Kegan Paul, 1982), 135; also see Russell Sanjek, "The War on Rock" (unpublished paper, New School for Social Research, February 1971).
12. Mike Gershman, "The Blues, Once Black, Now a Shade Whiter" *Los Angeles Times*, 19 January 1969, 1-sec 6. The argument that broadcasters practiced *de facto* segregation is difficult to support. Mercury artists were knocked off the chart by the original version. Deejays refusing to air R & B after 1955 didn't last long. See R. Serge Denisoff, *Tarnished Gold* (New Brunswick, N.J.: Transaction Books 1986), 84–87.
13. Quoted in John Swenson, *Bill Haley: The Daddy of Rock and Roll* (New York: Stein and Day 1982), 45.
14. Ibid, 58.
15. June Bundy, "Title Tunes Cut for Picture and Disks," *Billboard*, 18 September 1954, 12, 18; "Pic Producers Get Hep to Deejay Power, Tune Pluggers Hit Road," *Variety*, 19 January 1955, 49.
16. Quoted in Dave Rogers, *Rock 'n' Roll* (London: Routledge and Kegan Paul 1982), 14. The difficulty with establishing the MGM-Myers connection is the publisher. Accounts of his relationship with Haley are questionable at best. Gabler is vague on the studio, which is typical of industry people. Every success has a thousand parents.
17. "Bill Haley Capital Interview: Part Two," *New Kommotion*, Spring 1977, 8.
18. Carl Belz, *The Story of Rock* (New York: Oxford University Press 1969), 36. Robert G. Pielke, *You Say You Want A Revolution: Rock Music in American Culture* (Chicago: Nelson-Hall 1986), 29. Charlie Gillett, *The Sound of The City: The Rise of Rock and Roll* (New York: Outerbridge and Dienstfrey 1970), 21. Lillian Roxon, *Rock Encyclopedia* (New York: Grosset and Dunlap 1978). Rick Sklar, *Rocking America: How the All-Hit Radio Stations Took Over* (New York: St. Martin's Press 1984), 41.
19. Rochelle Larkin, *Hail Columbia* (New Rochelle: Arlington House 1975), 161.
20. John McCarten, "The Current Cinema: Not to the Tune of a Hickory Stick," *New Yorker*, 26 March 1955, 121. "School for Savages," *Newsweek*, 28 March 1955, 94. Bosley Crowther, "Blackboard Jungle," *New York Times*, 21 March 1955.
21. Roman Kozak, "Bill Haley Was Rock Music's First Star," *Billboard*, 21 February 1981, 14. Unfortunately, it is not possible to ascertain just how this sound enhancement was accomplished. Obviously, the track would have to be cranked up to achieve the desired affect at all of the venues.
22. Charlie Gillett, "Just Let Me Hear Some of That Rock and Roll Music," *Urban Review*, December 1966, 12.
23. Philip T. Hartung, "Unstill Sits the Schoolhouse" *Commonweal*, 18 April

1955. "Blackboard Jungle," *The Nation*, 2 April 1955, 292. Otis Guernsey, "Tigers In the Classroom," *Saturday Review*, 2 April 1955, 31. Charlotte Bilkey Speicher, "Blackboard Jungle," *Library Journal*, 15 March 1955, 642. John McCarten, "The Current Cinema: Not to The Tune of a Hickory Stick," *The New Yorker*, 26 March 1955, 121. Bosley Crowther, "Blackboard Jungle," *New York Times*, 21 March 1955. "Brog," "Blackboard Jungle," *Variety*, 2 March 1955, 16.

24. Op cit.
25. Guernsey:32. McCarten:121.
26. "School for Savages," *Newsweek* 28 March 1955:94. "Blackboard Jungle," *Nation*: 295.
27. Brog and Guernsey: 31.
28. Herb Schoenfeld, "R & B big beat in pop music; Teenagers Like 'hot rod' tempo," *Variety*, 19 January 1955, 54.
29. "R & B Best Thing That's Happened in Disk Biz in Years: Bob Thiele," *Variety*, 23 February 1955, 43.
30. Abel Green, "A Warning To The Music Business," *Variety*, 23 February 1955, 2.
31. Abel Green, "Who Must Do The Cleanup?" *Variety*, 2 March 1955, 49.
32. "R & B May Not Cause Delinquency But It Reflects It: Bill Randle," *Variety*, 2 March 1955, 49–51.
33. Lewis R. Chudd, "Stop Jumping On Our R & B, Sez Indie Label," *Variety*, 23 March 1955, 46.
34. "They're Dancing Again In Pix Houses as B'klyn Par Shakes With 'Rock 'n' Roll'," *Variety*, 13 April 1955, 67.
35. "Rock 'n' Roll: A frenzied teen-age music craze kicks up a big fuss," *Life*, 18 April 1955, 166–68.
36. "Barry Ulanov," *Downbeat*, 1 June 1955, 23–24.
37. Quoted in Thomas M. Pryor, "Hollywood Test," *New York Times*, 26 June 1955.
38. "Virtual Surrender 1955: The Year R & B Took Over Pop Field," *Billboard*, 12 November 1955, 126.
39. " 'Rock Around' At Princeton," *Billboard*, 28 May 1955, 35.
40. Quoted in Ren Grevatt, "Pro's and Con's Have Their Say on Miller's K.C. Speech," *Billboard*, 24 March 1958, 14.
41. Philip Jenkinson and Alan Warner, *Celluloid Rock: Twenty Years of Movie Rock* (London: Lorrimer Publishing 1974), 9–10.
42. Quotes in "Jungle Sam," *Time*, 1 December 1952, 62; "Sam Katzman," *Variety*, 15 August 1973, 46; "5,600,000 Estimate For Katzman's 12–16 Columbia Pix Up to $6,200,000," *Variety* 6 March 1957, 5.
43. David Ehrenstein and Bill Reed, *Rock on Film* (New York: Delilah Books 1982), 15–16.
44. Richard Thompson, "Sam Katzman: Jungle Sam, Or, The Return of 'Poetic Justice, I'D Say," in *Kings of The Bs: Working Within The Hollywood System*, Todd McCarthy and Charles Flynn eds. (New York: E.P. Dutton 1975), 77–78.
45. George T. Simon, *The Big Bands* (New York: Macmillan 1967), 65; Greil Marcus, "Rock Films," in Jim Miller, ed., *The Rolling Stone, Illustrated History of Rock and Roll* (New York: Random House 1981), 390.
46. Quoted in Swenson, 72.

47. Richard Staehling, "From Rock Around The Clock To The Trip: The Truth About Teen Movies (1969)," in McCarthy and Flynn, 225.
48. "Alltime B'klyn 204G B.O. High On Rock 'n' Roll," *Variety*, 11 April 1956, 60.
49. "Col Finds Rowdy Reports Kick Back At 'Rock' Pic," *Variety*, 11 April 1956, 60.
50. Ralph H. Turner and Lewis M. Killian, *Collective Behavior*, 2nd ed. (Englewood Cliffs: Prentice-Hall 1972).
51. Dave Rogers, *Rock 'n' Roll* (London: Routledge and Kegan Paul 1982), 16.
52. " 'Midnight Music Mania Session'—Mpls Star," *Variety*, 11 April 1956, 60.
53. "Alltime," 60.
54. Cited in J. Fred MacDonald, "Hot Jazz, The Jitterbug, and Misunderstanding: The Generation Gap In Swing 1935–1945," *Popular Music and Society*, Fall 1972, 43–55.
55. Joel Friedman, " 'Rock' Seen Surefire With Teen Brigade," *Billboard*, 7 April 1956, 17, 21.
56. "Senate Unit Hits Violence in Films," *New York Times*, 27 March 1956.
57. *Variety*, 21 March 1956.
58. Friedman, 17.
59. "Rock Around the Clock," *National Parent-Teacher*, May 1956, 40.
60. Quoted in "White Council vs. Rock and Roll," *Newsweek*, 23 April 1956, 32; "Segregationists Would Ban All Rock and Roll Hits," *Billboard*, 7 April 1956, 46; and "Segregationists Wants Ban On Rock and Roll," *New York Times*, 30 March 1956, 39.
61. Quoted in Edith Schonberg, "You Can't Fool Public, Says Haley," *Downbeat*, 30 May 1956, 10.
62. "Teeners Figure In Haley Riots On Rock 'n' Roll," *Variety*, 30 May 1956, 46.
63. "Anti R & B," *Variety*, 30 May 1956, 46.
64. Quotes from "Yeh-Heh-Heh-Hes, Baby," *Time*, 18 June 1956, 54.
65. Quotes from "Rocking and Rolling," *Newsweek*, 18 June 1956, 42.
66. Liner notes *Fats Domino*, United Artists Records (UAS 9958).
67. Ralph J. Gleason, "Fats Domino: Not Responsible," *Downbeat*, 19 September 1956, 40.
68. "Rock 'n' Roll," *Time*, 23 July 1956 and "San Jose to Cool Off," *Variety*, 19 July 1956, 46.
69. "The Rocks Keep Rolling at R & B; Pittsburgh Is Latest Rioting Locale," *Variety*, 25 July 1956, 111.
70. Russell Sanjek, "The War on Rock," New York: New School for Social Research, 17 February 1971.
71. Dick Hebdige, *Subculture: The Meaning of Style* (London: Methuen, 1980), 50.
72. George Melly, *Revolt Into Style: The Top Arts* (Garden City: Anchor Books 1971), 31.
73. Ian Whitcomb, *After The Ball: Top Music From Rag to Rock* (New York: Simon and Schuster 1972), 226–27.
74. Richard Mably, *The Top Process* (London: Hutchinson Educational 1969), 46.
75. Colin Fletch, "Beat and Gangs on Merseyside," *New Society*, 20 February 1964.
76. Rogers, 16.

77. Cohn, 8.
78. Ibid, 9.
79. "Queen's Curiosity Aroused, Her Kingdom Much Upset by Rock 'n' Roll Film," *Variety*, 26 September 1956, 2.
80. Quoted in Herm Schoenfeld, "Celler Committee Hears ASCAP Blast vs. BMI and Broadcasters; Haverlin, Under Solons' Fire, Disputes Claims," *Variety*, 19 September 1956, 81.
81. This allegation in abbreviated form appeared in *Time*, *The Reporter*, and *Harper's*. The latter labelled it "nonsense." Rose's use of Al Jolson is interesting, as the songwriter gave the black-faced vaudevillian co-authorship for "Me and My Shadow," "That Old Gang of Mine," and "It's Only a Paper Moon" because "he had successfully plugged the song and it was a legal way to pay him off." Kenneth Aaron Kantor, *The Jews on Tin Pan Alley: The Jewish Contribution to American Popular Music 1883–1940* (New York: Ktav Publishing, 1982), 50.
82. "Sinatra's Bomb at Antitrust Probe: BMI Explosion or ASCAP Backfire?" *Variety*, 26 September 1956, 1, 44.
83. Quoted in Russell Sanjek, "The War on Rock," unpublished paper, New School for Social Research, 17 February 1971, 11–12.
84. "Sounds of the Times," *Harpers*, February 1957, 85.
85. Marya Mannes, "Who Decides What Songs Are Hits?" *The Reporter*, 10 January 1957, 37.
86. Jack Gould, "Long Standing Dispute Between BMI And Songwriters Flares Anew," *New York Times*, 7 October 1956, sec 2, 11.
87. Abel Green, "Strange 'Panel Show' " *Variety*, 3 October 1956, 63; "The Great Rock 'n' Roll Controversy," *Look*, 26 June 1956, 48. On other occasions Freed termed Green "a sensational headline seeker" and a "frustrated songwriter." See June Bundy, "Freed Replies to R & R Press Slurs," *Billboard*, 28 April 1956, 22.
88. Green, "A Warning . . .", 2.
89. "Rock 'n' Roll In Disfavor," *Billboard*, 22 September 1956, 1.
90. Quotes in Mildred Hall, "Celler Staff Report Sees BMI Power Opportunity," *Billboard*, 29 April 1957, 27, 57.
91. Quotes in Mildred Hall, "Celler Report Sparks Committee Dissension," *Billboard*, 10 June 1957, 20, 57.
92. "Sinatra's Bomb"
93. Quoted in Abel Green, "Tin Pan Alley's Blues," *Variety*, 6 March 1957, 16.
94. See R. Serge Denisoff, *Waylon: A Biography* (Knoxville: University of Tennessee Press 1983), 22; also Horowitz, "New Horizons for R & B Exploitation Upset Old Guard," *Billboard*, 4 February 1956, 55.
95. "Mix of Beat 'n' Booze' Blamed for Tear Gas, Etc., At Domino R 'n' R'er," *Variety*, 14 November 1956, 55.
96. Ehrenstein and Reed.
97. "Rockin' the Blues," *Variety*, 3 October 1956.
98. Ehrenstein: 45; "Rock Pretty Baby," *Variety*, 21 November 1956.
99. "Rock Pretty Baby," *National Parent Teacher*, February 1957, 30.
100. Ehrenstein & Reed, 34.
101. "Rock, Rock, Rock," *Variety*, 12 December 1956, and Howard DeWitt, *Chuck Berry: Rock 'n' Roll Music*, 2nd ed. (Ann Arbor: Pierian Press, 1985), 55.

102. RRR, *Variety*.
103. Patricia Romanowski in Michael Shore, *Music Video: A Consumer's Guide* (New York: Ballentine Books, 1987), 364.
104. RRR, *Variety*.
105. Romanowski, 364–65.
106. David Ehrenstein and Bill Reed, *Rock on Film* (New York: Delilah Books 1928), 18.
107. Bosley Crowther, "The Girl Can't Help It," *New York Times*, 9 February 1957, 12.
108. Quoted in Britt Hagarty, *The Day The World Turned Blue: A Biography of Gene Vincent* (Vancouver: Talonbooks 1983), 52.
109. Quoted in Adam Komorowski, "Three Steps to Heaven With . . . Eddie Cochran," *New Kommotion*, Summer 1977, 23.
110. Greil Marcus, "Rock Films" in Jim Miller, ed., *Rolling Stone Illustrated History of Rock 'n' Roll* (New York: Random House 1976), 391.
111. "The Girl Can't Help It," *Variety*, 19 December 1956.
112. "Bad Start," *Time*, 31 December 1956:61; and Crowther, 12.
113. *Variety*, "Girl"
114. Marcus:391. Charlie Gillett, *Sound of the City: The Rise of Rock and Roll* (New York: Pantheon Books 1983):206. Ehrenstein and Reed: 162.
115. Philip Jenkinson and Alan Warner, *Celluloid Rock: Twenty Years of Movie Rock* (London: Lorrimer Publishing 1974). Thomas Doherty, "Teenagers and Teenpics 1955–1957: A Study of Exploitation Filmmaking," in *Current Research in Film: Audience, Economics, and Law V. 2* Bruce A. Austin, ed., (Norwood, N.J.: Albex Publishing 1986), 53.
116. Lawrence N. Redd, *Rock is Rhythm & Blues (The Impact of Mass Media)* (East Lansing: Michigan State University Press, 1974), 55; Howard Thompson, "Don't Knock the Rock," *Variety*, 26 December 1956.
117. Ibid.
118. Swenson, 47.
119. Edith Evans Asbury, "Rock 'n' Roll Teenagers Tie Up the Times Square Area," *New York Times*, 23 February 1957, 1, 12.
120. Howard Thompson, "Don't Knock the Rock," *New York Times*, 23 February 1957, 13.
121. Cohn, 10.
122. *The Motion Picture Guide*, Jay R. Nash and Stanley R. Ross, eds., (Chicago: Cinebooks, Inc., 1985), 693.
123. Schonberg, 10.
124. "Haley Capitol", 9.
125. Quotes in Schonberg, 10; and Nick Toches, *The Unsung Heroes of Rock 'n' Roll* (New York: Charles Scribners 1984), 77.
126. Cohn, 11.
127. Gillett, 17.
128. Quoted in Al Portch, "Manager of Bill Haley Defends The Real Thing," *Downbeat*, 19 September 1956, 43.
129. Frank Zappa, "The Oracle Has It All Psyched Out," *Life*, 28 June 1968, 85.
130. Quoted in Ted Fox, *In the Groove: The People Behind The Music* (New York: St. Martin's Press, 1986), 92.
131. "Shake, Rattle and Rock!" *Variety*, 16 January 1957.

132. Lenny Kaye, *Eddie Cochran: Legendary Masters 4* (liner notes), United Artists UAS-9959.
133. "Untamed Youth," *Variety*, 27 March 1957.
134. A.H. Weiler, "Untamed Youth," *New York Times*, 11 May 1957, 24; and "Untamed Youth," *National Parent-Teacher* May 1957:37.

2

It's Only Make Believe (1958–1963)

The forbidden fruit of leer-ics, inflammatory newspaper items, Elvis from the waist up, gritty rhythms, and, most importantly, an emerging teenage subculture all fueled the Golden Age of Rock. Objectively, its lifespan was less than a scant three years. Its cinematic history began with *Blackboard Jungle* and closed with *Don't Knock the Rock* and includes flares of controversy as well as some untimely departures. Variety-show hosts found token rock 'n' rollers no longer bolstered ratings. Grade-B filmmakers, in the belief they owned the teen market, retreated into banality. Teens remained heavy filmgoers as television made little, if any, effort to court them. Hanging around the house, as the car culture (*a la American Graffiti*) was emerging, proved a drag. Viewing many of the movies at the drive-in was akin to watching submarine races. The under-eighteen-year-olds, with increasing spending power, were not to be ignored.

As Sam Katzman retreated into producing low-budget crime stories and other time-tested motifs, American International (AIP) entered the field of showcase rock. AIP purchased the movie rights to David P. Harmon's *The Little Guy*, originally telecast on NBC's *Jane Wyman Show*. The drama, a hybrid of *Petrified Forest* and *Time of Your Life*, was released as *Rock All Night*.

A thirty-year-old director, Roger Corman, was given the project. A simple remake of the half-hour-minus-ad-space teleplay was unmarketable, even for the double-feature circuit. Charles B. Griffith was brought in to do the screen adaptation. The screenwriter included a bar band and a singing ensemble for atmospheric as well as musical interludes. There was little doubt what the bawdy bistro music should be: rock 'n' roll. Mercury Records' promotional material exclaimed, "Hollywood movie studios are

73

hard pressed to find musical directors who 'dig' the present trend. It was inevitable (sic), therefore, that they discover Buck Ram.''

Predestination not withstanding, Ram, a white Los Angeles-based lawyer, songwriter and arranger, managed the Penguins (''Earth Angel'') and The Platters. He penned most of The Platters' original hits, beginning with ''Only You,'' featured in *Clock*.

His status as an ex-arranger for Glenn Miller and Count Basie, credentials in the rock fraternity, made Ram an ideal choice as a music supervisor. He, of course, used the opportunity to showcase ''the talents of the various artists shown in the picture whom he manages.''[1] Norma Hayes's versions of ''Only You'' and ''I Guess I Won't Hang Around Anymore'' were lip-synced by femme lead Abby Dalton. Ram sold Mercury Records on further hyping his clients on a soundtrack record.

Corman directed the entire picture in a mere five days—not an AIP landmark—and used a single set. A small, neighborhood, working-class bar with a stage for live entertainment was the locale for the entire sixty-two-minute project. The advertised ''Some Gotta Dance, Some Gotta Kill'' quickie was unveiled 24 April 1957, accompanied by Lou Rusoff's screen story *Dragstrip Girl*. Critics would find the ''leather-jacketed teens with hot rods'' a better product.

The story begins at the dingy Cloud Nine Club where Al (Robin Morse) is the presiding bartender. The Blockbusters and The Platters, featuring Tony Williams (''I'm Sorry'') and Zola Taylor (''He's Mine''), are the attractions. Following the *Girl Can't Help It*, the club setting allows the music to fit in with some level of credibility. The instrumentals, like ''Rock 'n' Roll Guitar-Parts I & II,'' prove more effective than the vocals.

The plot is carried by Dick Miller's portrayal of the 5'1" protagonist, the ''Shorty,'' who is constantly beseiged by real or imagined slights from ''big people.'' He exhibits a Richard Widmark attitude toward big men. After a series of scrapes, Shorty, along with the patrons, including the hero's favorite vocalist, June (Abby Dalton), are confronted by two fugitives fleeing a homicide charge. Shorty's barroom antagonists are cowed by the killers. In the process they reveal their innermost insecurities. Faced with the challenge, Miller is transformed into a ''little big man.'' He overcomes the goons, and his size, winning Dalton.

With the paid exception of Mercury's publicity people, the consensus view of *Rock All Night* was summed up in *Variety*. ''Lowgrade stuff attempts to copy a fast-buck ride on music fad.''[2] Only Miller's performance was positively reviewed.

Corman's five-day musical was correctly overshadowed by the hot rod pic that showed on the same bill, but it did produce the third rock soundtrack.

The soundtrack liner notes, including the hyperbole, are more entertaining than the film. For example, "The script was changed numerous times to avoid cutting away from the artists while performing and allow more time for music whenever possible which will surely send the movie audience away from the theatre humming the tunes."[3] ("In five days?," a cynic might ask.) To reach the average LP buyer, the anonymous scribe continued, "Although it will be classed as a 'rock 'n' roll' picture, all the music contained therein is of the highest caliber and can easily be classified in the 'pop' field as well." The crossover plea went unheeded. The album wound up in the R & B blues record bins and did not appear on the charts. The conventional industry wisdom, "Teens don't buy albums" was reinforced.

Another rocksploitation film, *Rock, Baby, Rock It*, was initiated by J.G. Tigar, a part-time talent agent who represented rock-a-billy artist Johnny Carroll. Tigar put Carroll into the Sellars studio in Dallas to cut four demo titles including "Rock It, Baby, Rock." Two offerings, "That's the Way I Love" and "I'll Wait," made the (Sam) Phillips International catalog and Decca picked up the singer. (Tigar, also a songwriter, was especially optimistic about "Hot Rock," which was to be the title theme to the film.) Norman Dudis was hired to do the "quickie" script. The screenplay became a clip-and-paste montage of all the previous low-budget jukers. The film was shot in Dallas using local talent and showcasing Johnny Carroll and the Hot Rocks. Tigar produced and M.D. Sporup directed. According to Tigar, the *Hot Rock* title was dropped due to exhibitor resistance. The Carroll rendition remained as the theme.

The film opens at the Texas Hot Rock Club, a teenage hangout.[4] The landlord is "Crackers" Louis, a sinister mobster. Crackers, acting on Syndicate instructions, tells Bob (Johnny Dobbs) and Marilyn (Linda Wheeler) that they are behind in their rent and serves them with an eviction notice. To preserve the meeting place they decide to stage a benefit. In Jane Mansfield/Tom Ewell fashion they club hop, allowing for the introduction of numerous musical acts. At one of the niteries they encounter dancer Kay Wheeler. She agrees to participate in the show. She also introduces them to her attorney who agrees to help. After the obligatory musical interludes, Bob and Marilyn finally arrive at Johnny Carroll's venue. Observing his energetic performance, they are delighted to have him appear at the benefit.

The mobsters are determined to stop the dance. Unbeknownst to the gangsters, the teens have discovered the location of a secret business ledger, "the illicit books." Wheeler's lawyer contacts the authorities. The resolution occurs at the Hot Rock Club as the underworld types attempt to dislodge the teenagers while Johnny Carroll entertains. A brawl develops as the local police arrive. Carroll breaks his guitar over Crackers's skull. The hoods are led away handcuffed.

Following protocol, the movie concludes with a show and dance. The finale features the entire musical cast: The Cell Block Seven, Preacher Smith and The Deacons, Don Coats and The Bon-Aires, and Johnny Carroll and His Hot Rocks.

Blair termed the movie "a very interesting, exciting and certainly enjoyable vintage rock and roll musical." Nash and Ross described the Tigar production as a minor cult film, "but you'll be better off if you skip it baby, skip it," they added.[5]

However Carroll, on the record, demonstrated a rock-a-billy flare which makes this film at least an interesting curiosity.

Decca, Carroll's label, refused use of its masters in the film. Carroll thus became one of many rock-a-billies buried in the catalogs of major labels.

After Elvis Presley made his film debut in *Love Me Tender* (1956), the major studios looked for a rockish personality. Pat Boone, who in a Chicago survey surpassed Elvis in popularity, was a natural choice. He, it was surmised, could transcend generational taste differences. In the 1950s, among teenagers, Boone was as controversial as Presley. The "white shoe" crowd exalted him. Rockers *qua* greasers or "bikers" in dress disliked the clean-cut collegiate crooner. However, Boone probably had turned more teens on to Fats Domino with his cover of "Ain't That a Shame" than Alan Freed's radio broadcasts had. Despite Alan Freed and other purists, Boone was partially correct in asserting, "Ninety percent of radio stations in America (1956–1957) wouldn't play R & B hits no matter how big they were. To get them on radio, other artists had to do them. I talked with Fats and Little Richard. There was a definite ceiling on how far they could go. When a white artist came along and sang their songs, they were introduced to audiences that they couldn't get to themselves."[6]

Boone was more than just another big band song stylist covering solid R & B titles. He, as Lillian Roxon suggested, was "often insipid, commercial and namby-pamby, but he *was* the answer to those who found it impossible to identify with a motorcycle hood like Elvis."[7] Boone was more Chet Atkins-Nashville Sound than Ames Brothers or Four Lads. By the spring of 1957, Boone had enjoyed five top-ten records with two Number 1s: "I Almost Lost My Mind" and "Don't Forbid Me."

20th Century Fox signed him to co-star with Terry Moore in *Bernadine*, a film originally designed to be a comedy. In light of Elvis's success with

Love Me Tender, three musical numbers were added to the script. Veteran Johnny Mercer wrote the title song and "Technique," a calypso ditty. "Love Letters in the Sand," which Boone had already recorded for Dot Records, was included. (Randy Wood would recut the song for the film and a third version was later released as the single.) A critic noted, "Boone does them all in winning style, a selling factor for the picture."[8] Three songs did not justify an EP, yet alone a long-playing album.

Boone's first film role was taken from the Broadway stage. Mary Chase's drama was rewritten for the screen by Theodore Reeves. As the *New York Times* reviewer was quick to note, the original play lost something in the film translation. The essence of the movie involves a clique of high school seniors who fantasize their ideal female. Beau (Pat Boone) is a member (He's the one who constantly says "gee."). The key member is Stanford Wilson (Richard Sargent). He discovers Jean (Terry Moore), a newly arrived telephone operator. She fits the fantasy description and Stanford falls in love with her. While Stanford studies for finals, Beau's brother (James Drury) steals the girl. This description, minus the dialogue, does not do the film justice, Thompson concluded. "The original cutting edge of 'Bernadine' is gone, but on the whole, you still couldn't find a nicer bunch of people," he said.[9]

Bernadine was traditional family entertainment, lacking the trappings of "juve" exploitation. "Love Letters in the Sand," a cover of Rudy Vallee and Bing Crosby efforts, was released prior to the film and was Number 1 as of 3 June 1957. It rested in the slot for five weeks. Even Boone was surprised.

"It's always been a mystery to me why it had universal appeal. There's nothing exciting about the arrangement or the way I sang it," he said.[10] Boone generally appealed to reviewers.

"It probably will not matter to his fans," said *Newsweek*, "that he can't act." A *Times'* critic wrote candidly, "Move over, Elvis Presley. And welcome Pat Boone, his exact antithesis. . . . Meet a singing teen-age idol—a sunny, clean-cut youth of many mien and fine voice—with a real screen future, in a wholesome, pleasant comedy about adolescence."[11]

The wholesome theme was replayed in one hundred theaters nationally on the lucrative Thanksgiving weekend. Boone's second film was *April Love*. Nick (Boone) is a big-city boy sent to Blue Grass country, where he meets and falls in for Liz Templeton (Shirley Jones) and takes up harness racing. After winning the all-important race, he also triumphs with Jones. When not adjusting to rural life and admiring horses, Boone, with Jones, manages to squeeze in a number of songs penned by ASCAPers Sammy Fain and Paul F. Webster. The Tin Pan Alley fare included "Give Me a

Gentle Girl," "Clover in the Meadow," and the title song. (Fain and Webster previously had succeeded with "Love Is a Many Splendored Thing" and "Secret Love.") "April Love" became a hit, topping the chart Christmas week. Boone voiced the reservation, "It didn't sound commercial." Once again an adaptation, *Home in Indiana* (1945), produced a chart-topping single for the "wholesome singer."

The musical did produce a soundtrack, which became available for Christmas week, nearly a month after the film's release. *Cashbox* listed it for fourteen weeks. *April Love* peaked at Number 9.

Newsweek repeated its cynicism.

"Boone threads his way through it all entirely relaxed, struggle or not. He does not have many changes of expression, but they are all inoffensive. He applies his mellifluous baritone to five songs. His fans may be interested to know that, as usual, he does not kiss the girl, but he does come very close to it," ran the review.[12]

Thompson would write, "Now what could be more apt on Thanksgiving Eve than a wholesome, pretty little family picture about a girl, a boy and a horse in the Blue Grass sector?" Moreover, he continued, *April Love* had it all over "the dark aroma of some recent trashy switch blade alley dramas. And let's not forget *Jailhouse Rock*, starring Mr. Boone's caterwauling rival, who shall be nameless."[13] The *Times* critic was joined by others who felt that Boone's persona, a good example for teens, justified some of his less-than-memorable acting attempts.

None of Boone's films can remotely be described as rock-oriented. They were marketed as direct opposites to Katzman's exploitation vehicles and, especially, the Presley offerings. The theater sheet—poster—for *April Love* announced:

> A LOVE STORY—For Mum
> RACE TRACK THRILLS AND SPILLS—For Dad
> IN FACT EVERYTHING—For Everybody . . .

Boone, in time, would demonstrate a knack for the movie musical. *Mardi Gras* surfaced for Thanksgiving 1958. The Jerry Wald production headlined Boone and Christine Carere with Tommy Sands and Sheree North co-starring. Fain and Webster provided the songs; Lionel Newman scored the project. The music was paramount; there was a simple story line. The tale is set during the *Mardi Gras* season in New Orleans. Four cadets accompany the Virginia Military Institute band to the festival. Pat Newell (Boone) meets Michelle Marton (Carere), not knowing she is a movie star and the queen of the *Mardi Gras*. Her studio publicist (Fred

Clark) thinks the relationship is great press and promotes the romance. Intertwined with a bevy of songs, the two actually fall in love. As *Variety* would comment, "Not much plot, but enough to hang some good songs and pleasant comedy on."

The trade-paper reviewer obviously enjoyed the musical offerings. "The Fain-Webster songs are diversified, jazz, ballad, and country-style, with a high hit potential," he said, adding, the compositions were major assets of the picture and "its promotion."[14] The musicals were hardly rock 'n' roll. These films and Boone's "born again" posture have glossed over his contribution to rock music as a cover artist, but in the context of the mid 1950s, "Ain't That a Shame" was pretty hot stuff to adolescents. Boone's assertion that his Dot recordings made it easier for the genuine articles to succeed probably has some merit. Popularizers have fared badly at the hands of rock historians.[15]

Another effort, *Carnival Rock*, resulted from the efforts of Joy Houck, who owned a string of theaters dotting the Southwest. Most were "Last Picture Show" operations complemented by drive-ins. As the supply of Grade-B double features declined in the 1950s, the New Orleans-based entrepreneur began financing projects for his movie houses. Ignoring the anti-trust rule, *U.S. v Paramount Pictures* (1948), he commissioned the king of the quickies, Roger Corman to make his second rocksploitation film.

Corman reused a standard motif. A barroom, again, would provide the backdrop for the characters and musical interludes.

Corman filmed the project at Kling Studios in Los Angeles in five days. It was released on 25 September 1957, paired with *Teen Age Thunder*.

Carnival Rock's theater life was nearly as brief as its production schedule. Outside of Houck's backwater venues in Texas and Louisiana, the film was short-lived. (Houck's geographical base may have been a factor in the choice of artists employed in the vehicle. David Houston and Bob Luman were country as well as rock-a-billy acts. Both would enjoy their later successes in Nashville.)

De ja vu, the picture begins in a night spot owned by Christy Kristakos (David J. Stewart), an ex-burlesque comic. The bistro is located on an amusement pier, therefore the film's title. Christy is in love with Natalie Cooke (Susan Cabot), who exploits this affection to further her singing career. The young vocalist is secretly attracted to a gambler named of Stanley (Brian Hutton). The triangle established, Cannon (Ed Nelson), an attorney, arrives, demanding Christy pay off his creditors. Threatened with foreclosure, the club owner is desperate. Things become worse when he discovers the relationship between Natalie and Stanley. Benny (Dick

Miller), Christy's friend, tells the club owner that things are bound to improve when "You have love in your heart."

Christy confronts Natalie ("You got your eyes open for every pair of pants that walks by."). Despite the recrimination, the club owner remains smitten. He unrealistically believes that saving the club will rescue his love life, and foolishly enters into a game of "high card draw" with Stanley, losing the club to the gambling man.

To be near Natalie, Christy returns to his old profession of comic, providing interludes between rock 'n' roll acts. Benny, the only realistic character, insists, "It's crazy. A baggy-pants comic. Can't you see they're only trying to hurt you? They'll laugh at you, and not because you're funny, but because you're pathetic!"

Christy goes from masochism to suicidal rage when Natalie and Stanley announce wedding plans. The singer, on her way to meet the gambler, is grabbed by the clown, who sets fire to the club to prevent the marriage. The club is symbolic of Christy's misplaced affection.

In the nick of time, Stanley arrives and drags Natalie and Christy from the burning building. Benny joins them. He is relieved to find the comic in one piece and proposes they move to Buffalo, where he has a relative with a television station. The title song blares. Benny and Christy walk off, in film *noir* fashion, leaving the pier, and hopefully the memory of Natalie, behind.

This film seems to operate at several levels. Either it is the ultimate exploitation flick or Corman is engaging in a subtle self-reflective parody. The "television will save the day" segment reflected a Glittertown reality in 1957. The career mobility theme is equally a mirror of previous rock musicals and industry mores.

Variety, in a word, found the picture "okay." Roger Corman did an okay job . . ." the okay musical break-ins." The not-so-hot summary termed *Carnival Rock* "satisfactory within its category," a hardly bankable review. Nash and Ross said the "only reason to watch is The Platters."[16]

John Blair, a rock musical aficionado and collector, flew 1,300 miles to see *Carnival Rock*. In *Goldmine* he reported:

> Although Cabot's songs in the movie were certainly connected with the plot, there wasn't any rhyme or reason given as to what Luman, Houston, or The Platters were doing there . . . this is probably the only late '50s rock musical that could undergo a title change, elimination of the three aforementioned artists, and have no bearing on rock and roll or little drawing power for the teenage audience.

He concluded, "Despite its shortcomings, *Carnival Rock* does have its moments, and despite its low-budget and two-bit acting, the film does not relevance both to the time in which it was made and to the music and audience which it sought to capitalize on."[17] This movie was the first tangible sign that the rock musical was reaching a saturation point. Its novelty and shock value were fading. The fall of 1957 would, however, witness more attempts in the idiom.

In mid-summer (1957) Presley and Boone were filling the theaters. Three-million-dollar-plus grosses were predicted. *Rock, Pretty Baby*, due to Sal Mineo, and *Don't Knock the Rock* were the only other rock-oriented pictures that appeared destined to earn over the magic million mark. Many attributed the success of the Katzman sequel to the Broadway Paramount flap reported nationally by the media.

The fall film releases, qualifying as rock musicals, were caught in a quandry. Rock 'n' roll was no longer a novelty. It had lost much of its irreverent status and was longer forbidden fruit. The exclusivity of the rocksploitation genre was being threatened and sanitized by television in the person of a little-known Philadelphia disk jockey, Dick Clark.

Prior to the appearance of *American Bandstand* on sixty-seven ABC-TV affiliates, the film exploitation medium enjoyed a visual-media monopoly on rock 'n' roll. Presley's short, infrequent visits on television variety shows were special events. Outside of New York City and well worn concert venues, rock was either aired on radio or exhibited at local movie houses and perhaps at drive-ins.

As Milt Gabler repeated, the "four-wall" sound system of movie theaters was made to order for rock music. The acoustics resonnated the large, powerful speakers. It was loud. No radio or television receiver, and small semi-speaker could possibly duplicate the resonnance of a cinema theater with three-to-four-foot speakers. This was an ideal setting for listening to recording artists.

Film provided flesh-and-blood images for voices emanating from the radio and record player. The audience involvement with the on-screen rock 'n' rollers compensated for the flood of hackneyed plots. Johnny Johnston had not drawn adolescents to see *Clock*; Haley and perhaps The Platters served as box office magnets. Quickly, the rock musicals had developed a performance-based star system. Little Richard, Fats Domino, Chuck Berry, and, due to *Girl Can't Help It*, Eddie Cochran became names associated with specific movies. The miserly allotments of Grade-Bs almost dictated inexpensive charismatic stage presence.

Filmdom's lock on rock was severely damaged 5 August 1957. Television had struck, it would seem, another blow. Monday at 3 p.m. (EST) a twenty-seven-year-old announcer stepped forward to the camera, smiling, and said, "Hi, I'm Dick Clark. Welcome to *American Bandstand*. You and I have got an hour and half to share together with some of my friends here, lots of good music, and our special guest stars. With us today is the 'I'm Gonna Sit Right Down and Write Myself A Letter' man, Billy Williams. The Chordettes will be here too. Right now, let's do a whole lotta shakin' with Jerry Lee Lewis."[18]

"Come on over, baby, whole lotta shakin' goin' on" echoed as the assembled teens jitterbugged to Lewis's record. (Exactly two weeks later the "Killer" would lip-sync the song in Clark's Philadelphia studio.) Clark was able to tap into the rock-artist pool. The first month of *American Bandstand* found Paul Anka, Gene Vincent, Sal Mineo, and Buddy Holly visiting with Clark.

In a matter of months, most of the names familiar to Top 40 listeners would be seen on *Bandstand*. Only Elvis Presley refused to appear; Colonel Parker complained about the fee, and Elvis didn't need the exposure. On 27 November Haley and the Comets acted out "You Hit the Wrong Note, Billygoat." An unfortunate choice of songs.

Clark was able to get the artists to perform for scale. He termed the celebrity visits promotional. Some acts, like Johnny and The Hurricanes, were forced to return their performance fees. With a lock on the after-school market, *American Bandstand* became a prime "exposure" venue, replacing Hollywood, where Grade-B film producers, operating on a minute profit margin, found it increasingly difficult, if not impossible, to produce bankable rock motion pictures.

For example, the film *Mr. Rock 'n' Roll*, "The Biggest of 'Em All," contained thirty tunes. The selections and roster allowed the studio to expand market size—assuming the ploy worked. Newspaper ads had pitched:

> That new music's not just for the young . . . it's for everyone! A new kind of American folk-music is sweeping the world—just as jazz and swing did before. And yet, here at home only the "younger generation" knows about it. Now a motion picture comes along that explains all about the exciting new rhythm— where it came from, why it's so popular, who are its biggest signing stars! So, young people—here's a chance to *show your adults* how terrific *your* music is! Take them to see this picture about *the honest musical expression of today's youth*! You'll find they'll love it just as much as you do!"[19]

Lionel Hampton reportedly was added to the cast to accommodate the stray adult accepting this slanted marketing attempt at demographic cross-over.

The theater sheet announced, "The whole rock 'n' roll story of the swingin' king of the cats—mister rock and roll." In the center was a head shot of Alan Freed superimposed on lead-sheet bars. A "bio pic," or docudrama of the life and times of the WINS radio personality, would have been *interesting*. (*American Hot Wax* [1978] did make an attempt.) Instead what appeared was an eighty-six-minute jukebox featuring exploitation favorites—Frankie Lymon, LaVerne Baker, Little Richard, Chuck Berry, Clyde McPhatter, Brook Benton, and country artist Ferlin Husky.

Mr. Rock 'n' Roll, scripted by James Blumgarten, was a loosely topical story, pulling bits and pieces from the public persona of Alan Freed. The screenwriter's synopsis *could* easily have come from June Bundy's *Billboard* piece, "Freed Replies to R & R Press Slurs." She wrote, "Freed claimed that many of the current press stories about rock and roll inciting riots are grossly exaggerated, including those circulated recently about his own shows at the Brooklyn Paramount and the State Theatre in Hartford, Connecticut."[20] One critic concurred, saying, "This pic runs off like an unadorned filmization of one of Freed's typical stage shows."[21]

In the film, reporter Carol Hendricks (Lois O'Brien) interviews rock star Teddy Randazzo. She returns to her paper and writes a piece praising the up-and-coming artist. The story is unusually kind to rock 'n' roll. Editor Joe Prentiss (Jay Harney), an avowed "anti," rewrites the article, accusing rock 'n' roll of fostering juvenile delinquency. Freed loudly objects. He protests on the air between cuts and "live" renditions by visiting music celebrities.

Using artists such as Lionel Hampton, LaVerne Baker, and Ferlin Husky, the deejay presents an oversimplified version of the evolution of American music up to the rock period. "It's just a harmless natural progression" was his thesis. Freed's film pulpit shifts to a theater stage, where he introduces acts and objects to aspersions against rock 'n' roll.

To add a Shakespearian touch, Teddy Randazzo romances Carol Hendricks, Prentiss's cub reporter. As a New York writer asked, "Where do we go from here?"[22] To more music and a positive verdict on the not-so-new sound.

In the film's resolution, Freed discussed a campaign to raise funds for the fight against neuphrosis, a childhood disease. Eleven thousand of his fans participated in the fund drive. The rock 'n' rollers, with the usual show, donate to the newspaper's heart fund. Rockers are good people.

Not since *Rockin' the Blues*, a cheapie even by Grade-B standards, was a film so blatantly scripted to accommodate the music; even additional song-plugging comedic scenes are sandwiched between song renditions.

The *New York Times* devoted two paragraphs to the project, as Freed was a subcultural institution in Gotham. The *Times* review began, "Suffice it to say that [the movie] the latest quickie film to capitalize on the metronomic musical craze, has more songs and less plot than any of its predecessors." Richard W. Nason was correct. "The plot isn't much and none of the leads could act their way out of a paper bag," observe Nash and Ross, "but with this much great music (over thirty songs!) in one film, such considerations fade into insignificance."[23]

The number of songs in the film is a bit overwhelming. Chuck Berry is welcome with the patented duck-walk on "Oh Baby Doll"; Little Richard blasts "Lucille," and "Keep a Knockin' "; and LaVerne Baker and Frankie Lymon and the Teenagers also liven up the atmosphere. With the glaring exception of Lionel Hampton, some of the other performances seem stale and too mechanical.

Another entry into the back-to-school film sweepstakes, 20th Century Fox's *Rockabilly Baby*, was a middle-class melodrama. Moreover its title constituted an exercise in misleading, if not false, advertising. No one at Sun Records, nor Gene Vincent, Bob Luman, or Eddie Cochran, was featured. The only recognizable music personality in the film was Les Brown—"for name lure among swing lovers." Although six songs by scorer Paul Dunlap were included, the vocalists were, and still are, unknowns. The title did, however, fit with the other part of the double feature, *Young and Dangerous*, a drama.

In *Rockabilly Baby*, Eleanor Carter (Virginia Field) is an ex-burlesque dancer and mother of two over-achieving high schoolers, Jimmy (Gary Vinson) and Cathy (Judy Busch). The Carters flee their town to escape the 1950s version of the Moral Majority, who consider ex-fan dancers immoral.

Relocated in a fresh-start community, the trio become active in school and community programs. Jimmy leads the school water-polo team to its first championship. Cathy starts a social club that competes with the "stuck-up" social climbers.

As the trials and tribulations of secondary school life are explored, Mrs. Carter develops a romantic link with high school principal Tom Griffith (Douglas Kennedy). Tom's ex-girlfriend discovers Eleanor's past and exposes it. Sound familiar? The expose fails as the townspeople rally around Carter, now a pillar of the community.

Variety's reviewer termed the film "bright and breezy. The movie will hit a responsive chord among teenagers especially and is refreshing fare for lower slot of program situation."[24] The writer singled out Marlen Willis, the teenage Linda, as exhibiting top form with "Is It Love?" and "I'd Rather Be." The film's remaining four songs, "We're on Our Way," "Why Can't I," "Teenage Cutie" and, for contemporalia, Dunlap's "My

Calypso Baby,'' did connect with the plot. There was no soundtrack, as the motion picture was not designed as a musical. It was a story with songs and teenagers in it. Despite *Variety's* characterization, *Rockabilly Baby* was outside of the genre.

Another teen rock film was released in mid-November, *Jamboree*, was produced by Max J. Rosenberg and Milton Subotsky, the team responsible for *Rock, Rock, Rock.* The project headlined seventeen recording artists performing twenty-one tunes, introduced by twenty-one disk jockeys. Somehow the eighty-five-minute movie was able to fit a "story" into the project.

The plot, what there is of it, involves two middle-of-the-road singers, Pete Porter (Paul Carr) and Honey Wynn (Freda Holloway), who "dig each other." When they are not squabbling, a strange love relationship between them emerges. The ogres of the piece are Pete's manager (Jean Martin) and her ex-husband (David King-Wood). These neurotics break up the odd couple, who are reunited by the end of the calvacade of stars. "That's not important," suggested Nash and Ross. "What is important is a chance to see Jerry Lee Lewis belt out 'Great Balls of Fire.' ''[25]

Lewis and Fats Domino were musical co-headliners in the film. The mercurial piano man had been recruited by Otis Blackwell, the composer of "Don't Be Cruel," who served as the film's musical director. Although Lewis lip-synced "Great Balls of Fire" for the film, he objected to the practice. Reportedly, director Ray Lockwood was so impressed with Lewis's cameo that he requested the song also be sung "live" for the picture's crew and staff. "Great Balls of Fire" was sung twice. Lewis, as the critics noted, stood out in the movie's crowded field despite a strained introduction from KIMN (Denver) Ray Perkins.

(When the film appeared, Lewis took a cousin to see a minute and forty-seven seconds of *Jamboree.* She had expected to see the entire film. The singer objected "You don't need to. There's nothing in it you'd wanna see. There ain't nothin' to it but my song, anyhow."[26] Film and music critics seem to agree.) Nevertheless, twenty-one deejays provided a marketing bonanza as each hyped the film, and frequently the song, on the air.

The film nicely competed with traveling road shows and Clark's afternoon televisuals, presenting Buddy Knox's "Hula Love," Fats Domino's "Wait and See," Charlie Gracie's "Cool Baby," Carl Perkins's "I'm Glad All Over," the Count Basie Orchestra's "One O'Clock Jump," and the blossoming *Bandstander* Frankie Avalon. Other acts of interest included Lewis Lymon and The Teenchords, Jodie Sands, and Jimmy Bowen. Connie Francis was used to overdub Holloway.

One significant aspect of *Jamboree* was the lack of established hits.

Basie, Domino, and Lewis did familiar songs, but "Cross Over," "Your Last Chance," and "Glad All Over" were hardly recognizable titles. This was thus the first overt jukeboxer to highlight the stars minus the Top 40 favorites. Many of the songs were penned specifically for the project. The use of Count Basie and Big Joe Williams, who belted out "Maleguena," varied from usual exploitation offerings; producers apparently were fishing around for some way to revitalize the rock film.

The *Variety* reviewer partially captured the ethos of the production, saying "Film is old-fashioned in concept, reminiscent of the early days of talking pictures when producers slapped a group of singing acts together." The writer went on, "Okay for program situations where young patrons like their vocalistics stylized, and particularly the jukebox trade."[27] It was a potpourri. Teens, however, wanted hits, not B-sides or selections by unknown artists.

The largest post-war increase in record industry grosses occurred in 1956, when the take increased a sizable 36.1 percent, rising from $277 million in 1955 to $377 million the following year. In 1957 the rate slowed, but not dramatically, to 22 percent. The climb would continue until 1960, boosted in large part by television exposure, especially *Bandstand*.

In 1957 the top *Billboard* song had been Pat Boone's "Love Letters in the Sand," and the Top 20 chart found several other film songs in position. "April Love" and "Jailhouse Rock", both products of the personality film, performed well.

In the film world, rock-oriented exploitation vehicles elicited a mixed response. Six rock films appeared in 1956, starting with *Clock*, as did one "personality pic." In North America *Love Me Tender* grossed $3.75 million in less than two months. The 1956 earnings for the first Katzman project in the U.S. and Canada were $1.1 million. None of the remaining offerings came near the million-dollar mark. Several released in the closing days of December spilled over into 1957.

Of interest is the fact that not one "rocksploitation" picture released in 1957 broke into the million-dollar club; all the high grossers were personality films. Of the thirteen rock-oriented movies to hit the street that year, four starred Presley and Boone. Two were well kept secrets imported from the United Kingdom: *Rock You Sinners*, which did not merit trade paper reviews and *The Tommy Steele Story*, Americanized and retitled *Rock Around the World*. Steele, frequently touted as England's version of Elvis Presley, was actually more in the Pat Boone tradition. Suffice it to say the "British Invasion" would have to wait another seven years, as both films fared poorly at the box office.

The beauty of the musicals, for their producers, was the gross/net ratio.

$1 Million Earners of 1957	
Love Me Tender (1956)	$4,500,000
April Love (1957)	$4,000,000
Jailhouse Rock (1957)	$4,000,000
Bernadine (1957)	$3,700,000
Loving You (1957)	$3,700,000
Girl Can't Help It (1956)	$2,800,000
Rock Pretty Baby (1956)	$1,430,000
Don't Knock the Rock (1956)	$1,200,000

Source: Variety "Top Grosses of 1957" 8 January 1958: 30.

Without international distribution Katzman would earn eight times his cost. The Corman quickies could gross $.5 million and be considered successes. As competition increased, however, costs increased. Increasing the number of artists and deejay personalities would soon make the rocksploitation vehicle economically prohibitive. The law of diminishing returns was at work. As a genre the rock film, by Christmas 1957, was rapidly fading. Studio accountants looked at their ledgers.

By contemporary standards, the studios' approach to the *Bandstand* challenge was an exercise in naïveté. The expansion of musical casts provided an opportunity for soundtrack recordings. Using *Rock, Rock, Rock* as a prototype, a cluster of acts from "hot" labels could have been used and film tie-ins would have benefited both industries. This packaging notion escaped the studios and the labels.

Instead, the filmmakers opted to expand the number of artists, many total unknowns, without any regard for ancillary record deals. This territorial myopia would hinder the interactive process for years to come.

By 1958, labels had little faith in film exposure as a marketing tool. Only the unique "Rock Around The Clock" showed any market movement, due to the success of *Blackboard Jungle*. "Twenty Flight Rock" could have been a hit if it had been released in conjunction with Tashlin's film, but Liberty Records choose another selection.

Both media are reactive in nature: Film studios desire box office draws and record labels need bankable artists. They had an inherent coincidence of interest, but, at the time, few executives were aware of it.

On Christmas Day, 1957, Alan Freed returned to the Broadway Paramount, where his Big Beat show grossed $24,000. Several days later 30,000 teenagers attempted to see the program and on 30 December the house record was broken with a take of $32,100. The first-week gross was a whopping $185,000. The deejay more than surpassed his costs of $148,000 during the show's twelve-day run; Freed grossed more than $300,000.[28] With box office receipts of this magnitude, Freed could pontificate on the money-making capabilities of rock. He would do just that in the pages of *Variety*.

In a New Year's summation Freed waxed enthusiastic regarding the union of rock and film. Noting that "the amount of monies being grossed by musicals featuring rock 'n' roll have been nothing short of fantastic," the deejay went on to suggest, "None of the rock 'n' roll musicals has been known to garner four-star critiques, it's true, but that too may come in time. One thing is sure—they do business at the box office."[29]

Freed's analysis may have been an exercise in selective perception. His examples were personality pictures. The original films produced by Katzman were unusual money makers. Some observers suggested *Don't Knock the Rock's* first run was rejuvenated by the disc jockey's widely publicized Times Square mob scenes. Some of the early low-budget movies did return their initial investments plus the usual profit margin. Two offerings would soon put the "B.O. Boffo" thesis to the test.

Sing, Boy Sing

Twentieth Century Fox, having hit paydirt with two "rock" personalities, Elvis and Boone, purchased the movie rights to Paul Monash's telescript, *The Singing Idol*. The teleplay, originally broadcast on NBC-TV *Kraft Theater* in January 1957, was loosely based on the rise of Elvis. For a time, there was a possibility the superstar himself might do the half-hour drama, but Presley withdrew. Instead, Tommy Sands, a southern country singer, was signed and became an overnight teen idol. Two songs were performed during the TV presentation: "Hep Dee Hootie" and "Teenage Crush," the latter going on to sell a million units.

The Fox deal called for Sands to recreate his television role, with minor adjustments for the longer script. The number of songs would be increased to twelve, the ideal number for an album. The script was scaled up from a mere indictment of the record industry to a morality play of sorts in which old-time religion completed with modernistic values. The *Times's* Thompson saw "two worlds meeting and colliding" in the film.[30]

The ninety-minute Harry Ephron film previewed in Hollywood the second week of 1958. For a "personality" presentation, *Sing, Boy, Sing* received surprisingly good West Coast reviews.

The picture opens with a down-home southern singer, Virgil Walker (Sands), being hustled into the caverns of Manhattan by a music industry manager aptly named Joseph Sharkey (Edmund O'Brien). Sharkey and press agent Fisher (Jerry Paris) are cynically priming the neophyte for their show biz blitz. They succeed and Sands, after a proper dose of musical interludes, is on the verge of earning $300,000 per year as a rock money-making machine. He appears to tolerate, if not condone the lack of ethics in the music industry. Sharkey, of course, epitomizes the worst aspects attributed to the rock world.

However, Virgil's fundamental socialization eventually begins to gnaw at the teen idol. He ponders the question, "What is the meaning of life?" C.K. Judd (Nick Adams), a "good ole boy," is hired as a companion and "gofer" to provide a touch of home.

Virgil's inner conflict is brought to the fore when he learns that his grandfather is critically ill. Returning to the land of Billy Sunday, the singer immediately visits the rapidly expiring minister (John McIntire). The reverend denounces the boy for living in sin. Caught up with guilt, Virgil succumbs to the demand that he join the ministry. Supported by local friend Leora Easton (Lili Gentle), he verbally rejects the bright lights and big city and pursues the task of saving souls. However, the preaching life does not ease the performer's existential despair. This spiritual conflict remains unresolved until Virgil's Aunt Caroline (Josephine Hutchinson) intervenes, convincing him that "one should always use God-given talents." Prior to Virgil's resumption of his old life, he does a roaring version of "Rock of Ages." With a new inner peace he returns to show biz.

Personality films, unlike their inexpensive rocksploitation counterparts, managed to get national exposure. *Time* compared Sands to The King "you know that here, in everything but name, is E..s P.....y." *The New York Times* was more supportive, but Thompson also noted the Presley contrast, saying Sands was "without the vulgarity" and "in between the slower ballads are nice and mellow. This lad, at least, is mellow." Of the movie's twelve selections, *Variety* predicted, the title tune was "a likely hit."[31]

The shadow of Elvis lingered, but Sands did well. Unlike Boone, reviewers felt, this one-hit wonder *could* act. "Sands is excellent, both as a singer and as a performer, handling himself with an ease and naturalness that gives the part credibility," said Thompson. Certainly not a rock fan, he admitted surprise at the "convincing performance by Sands." Nash and Ross later described the performance as "a successful screen debut."[32]

Capitol released the scout single, the title song, in the last week of January. On February 8 "Sing, Boy Sing" reached Number 58 on the *Cashbox* chart. It remained a brief three weeks. The soundtrack album, which appeared prior to *Sing, Boy Sing's* national movie distribution, did not make the charts. In the liner notes, Sands warns, "Don't get confused, though—I'm not *really* Virgil Walker and it's not the story of my life! Just remember when you see me up there on the screen that I'm acting—or at least trying to!"[33] The disavowal was curious. Sands had established himself as a credible actor, appearing in films such as *Mardi Gras* with Pat Boone, *Life in a Goldfish Bowl*, *Babes in Toyland*, and *The Longest Day*.

The Big Beat

Universal Pictures' *The Big Beat* emerged in 1958 as an upscale, color, and mainstream jazz backstager, demonstrating vestiges of "entertainment for the entire family."[34] Eighteen musical acts were billed; fifteen numbers appeared. Only three acts possessed rock credentials: Fats Domino, who did the title song, The Del Vikings, and The Diamonds. The Diamonds did perform some of their hit tunes, such as "I'm Walkin'," "Little Darlin' " and "Come Go With Me." The jazz entourage, less visable, was eager for exposure, and consequently was relatively inexpensive, in contrast to the name rockers.

Joseph Gershenson picked the musical roster and scored the film. Henry Mancini provided assistance with the jazz segments, which were of the big band and cocktail-lounge type, ranging from trumpeter Harry James to the George Shearing Quintet. This cafeteria-style musical approach frustrated many viewers and satisfied few. The film was released in the last week of January as a companion feature to *Summer Love*, the sequel to *Rock Pretty Baby*, which was the main attraction.

In *The Big Beat*, Joseph Randall (Bill Goodwin) is a record bizzer clinging to the old sounds. His son John (William Reynolds) urges a revitalization of the catalogue with rock music. The elder Randall (following in the tradition of Columbia Records) sets up a subsidiary label for rock releases, in order not to tarnish the good name of the parent company. This device, of course, allows artists to pop up in the film without notice. John finds a hit record and the Randalls are back on the charts and in the money. As real record executives know, there is more involved to success than production. John has neglected the distribution aspect of the business, and when his father returns from a business trip, he finds 350,000 unsold platters in the company warehouse. John promises to move the product. He conjures up a "revolutionary" marketing concept, selling records at supermarket check-out stands. The problem is solved.

Stylistically, *Big Beat* is a notch above most jukeboxers. As a *Variety* critic observed, "In the many musical numbers, Irving Glassberg's camera action manages to give freshness and interest to conventionally static sequences, aided by the Eastman color by Pathe." The Diamonds were singled out as the standout group in the musical smorgasbord. They, according to *Variety*, "score most heavily of the groups."[35]

Let's Rock With LaRosa?

Originally titled *Keep It Cool, Let's Rock* was another offering in the "something for every musical taste" sweepstakes. Hal Hackady's script is simplistic but accurate. Julius LaRosa, best known for being fired by Arthur Godfrey on the air, plays a ballad crooner resisting the forces of rock 'n' roll, represented by singing guests such as Danny and the Juniors, who do "At The Hop," and The Royal Teens, who perform "Short Shorts." Middle-of-the-road jump singers such as Roy Hamilton ("Here Comes Love," and "The Secret Path of Love") and Della Reese, who sings "Lonelyville," add something for the older audience. Paul Anka, in his film debut, performs "I'll Be Waiting for You." His presence went unnoticed by critics.

Crooner Tommy Andano (LaRosa) is a victim of rock 'n' roll. His ballads are not evoking wild applause or selling records; returns outnumber sales. His manager, Charlie (Conrad Janis), repeatedly urges the middle-of-the-roader to record a rock number. Andano resists, instead insisting on doing such Fisher-Sinatra numbers as "Two Perfect Strangers," "Casual," and "There Are Times." Kathy Abbott (Phyllis Newman), the romantic interest, isn't sure that sticking to big band arrangements is the road to fame and fortune. After much resistance, Andano agrees to record "Crazy, Crazy Party." The rock selection is a monster hit and he receives a gold record. His career is back on track, even if he has sold out.

The similarities to *Sing, Boy, Sing* are striking. The "what-price-fame" motif is an old one. (Two films about it in a matter of months may have been excessive.) The screenplay court both teenagers and older viewers. LaRosa, although attached to the pre-Haley -Presley sound, gives it a good shot, due to economic imperatives, and succeeds with the "new music."

Teen concerns were assuaged with the result—LaRosa had seen the proverbial light. The inclusion of Paul Anka, the Royal Teens, and Danny and the Juniors provided the *American Bandstand* flavor.

Following its predecessors, *Let's Rock* received very few press notices. *Variety* summarized the film as "slick rocker-'n'-roller for the juve crowd; Julius LaRosa's name should be top draw." The reviewer may have missed the essential point—unlike the story line, LaRosa's career was going nowhere. His standing in the rock world was below that of Pat Boone or

Perry Como. The trade reviewer's comments suggest a misreading of the teen audience. Following producer/director's Harry Foster's reasoning, the critic wrote, the "name of Julius LaRosa, who makes his film bow, should be a potent draw and lineup of name recording artist gueststars (that's *Variety*) further embellishes musical's possibilities in the particular younger market for which it patently is aimed."[36] "Misdirected" may have been a better description.

The studios' and the reviewers' perceptions mirrored a widely held view that putting the word "rock" in a title and trotting out several out-hit wonders would make a box office success. This was not the case in 1958, the first year to experience the "teen-scream cycle," which entails an internal shifting of the audience within a musical genre. It demonstrably lasted approximately three and a half years. The reason for this was quite simply demographics. The higher end of the teen market grew older, went to college or got jobs, and married. *New York Times* critic John S. Wilson made note of the fragmentation, but missed its direction. He argued:

> To some observers, the current adolescent swing toward simply stated ballads is an indication that art can be made to imitate life. According to these theories, the 13 and 14 year-olds who reached out so eagerly for the exciting beat of rock 'n' roll three years ago, are now 16 and 17 and romance has suddenly loomed up large on their horizons. They are now looking for something more than heavy beat in their music, and the idols they created are moving along with them.[37]

Wilson clearly outlined the conventional wisdom in the music industry. With age and maturity, rock 'n' rollers would discover "better" music. Entering the labor force, rockers could afford the upscale hardware and software of long-playing albums, "hi-fi" and the newly marketed stereo.

Stereophonics were made theoretically operable by A.D. Blumlein in 1931; but the system was not refined and made commercially available until the mid-1950s. Hardware manufacturers saw stereo as a major economic breakthrough as the equipment rendered "hi-fi" obsolete. More important, the new system required twin speakers and an amplification component. The original prices ranged from one to two thousand dollars. Stereo, if popularized, promised to become an economic bonanza. There were the nay-sayers, however, as this was a mere half decade after the advent of the LP. There was concern expressed that "it was too soon for another change." Some music had been only grudingly moving into the long-play modality, and record labels were less than supportive of that innovation. Catalog and vault material was almost exclusively on one-track, monaural records. Companies feared their stock "might soon be rendered worthless by the new multichannel recording technique."[38] These fears proved groundless, as most consumers preferred, or could only afford, the 45. In 1958 the styles that lent themselves to stereo were symphonies, jazz, and musicals, which appealed to older, more affluent listeners. Most rock-oriented albums would be recorded in mono until the mid-1960s.

Some of the first stereo works marketed were on Audio-Fidelity, a record company. They included titles such as *Bullring, Saint Saens' Third (Organ) Symphony* and the highly popular *Railroad Sounds*. The sound of trains running through a listening room, for some reason, appealed to those able to purchase the equipment. RCA Victor was the first major label to hit the streets with the "best" line albums, but by September 1958 all of the majors were participating. Two hundred titles were available in stereo; however, these were limited to mainstream styles and genres, hampering the spread of stereo in the specialty music fields.

The wait for adolescents to change their taste and economic status would prove to be a long one. The change from 45s to long plays, Haley to Sinatra, and high fidelity to stereo proved to be a slow trickle rather than a rush. While the 33⅓ and stereo, in time, did benefit, the taste change did not occur.

Wilson's teenagers failed to migrate to crooners or symphonic/operatic material. Taste alterations did take place in 1958; commercial folk music was the major beneficiary. Several days after the opening of *Let's Rock* there was some question as to "the future of live-performance rock 'n' roll—if not the disk and deejay versions." The *Variety* reporter could easily have added rocksploitation films to the litany. By mid-1958, rock music was mellowing, not necessarily improving. Dick Clark's *Bandstand* was akin to apple pie. Reports of rock riots were almost nil. Chuck Berry, Gene Vincent, and Jerry Lee Lewis, "The Killer", were the remnants of the so-called Golden Age of Rock 'n' Roll.

Berry and Lewis were packaged together by Alan Freed. March 28 witnessed the launch of Freed's "Big Beat" national tour. Beginning at New York's Paramount, the assembled troupe was destined to stage sixty-eight shows in thirty-seven venues. At least, that was the plan. Freed, on the basis of friendship and marketability, headlined the duck-walking Berry. Lewis strongly objected, telling his manager "I thought Alan Freed would've learned by now that I don't play second to no livin' human bean." Oscar David, Jerry's manager, countered, "The man's had a dozen hits in the Top 10, Jerry."[39] The Killer was unplaced.

To demonstrate his wrath, and his disappointment with Freed, Lewis set fire to a piano at one concert during "Great Balls of Fire." As Nick Tosches described the scene, "He drew a Coke bottle full of gasoline, and he doused the piano with one hand as the other hand banged out the songs; and struck a wooden match and he set the piano aflame, and his hands, like the hands of a madman, did not quit the blazing keys, but kept pounding, until all became unknown tongues and holiness and fire, and the kids went utterly, magically berserk with the frenzy of it all.'' Lewis would later explain, without a sign of remorse, ''Burned that piano to the ground. They forced me to do it, tellin' me I had to go on before Chuck.''[40] Throughout the tour Lewis became known for destroying grand pianos. It was expected. It was good box office and audience reaction was loud, but controlled.

Prior to the closing week, *the* problem of rioting crowds began in Fort Wayne. A crowd of 2,600 showed up at the Allen County Memorial Coliseum at 2 p.m. to see the Big Beat show. The program did not start until a half-hour later and the only big names to conclude the show were Lewis and Berry. The mix-up was blamed on the change to daylight saving time.[41]

Boston proved to be the Big Beat's waterloo, with the mayor banning the show after one ''riotous'' performance May 3, before 6,000 fans. Jerry Lee was scheduled to close the show. He was primed. ''Whole Lot of Shakin' '' and ''Great Balls of Fire'' brought the house down. The kids flowed into the aisles and toward the stage. Pockets of dancing were seen. A din of chants emanated from the crowd. The house lights glared overhead. The Boston Police entered the arena. Batons and clenched flashlights were clearly visible. Freed shouted into the microphone, ''I guess the police here in Boston don't want you kids to have a good time.''[42] The angry statement evoked choruses of catcalls and jeers aimed at the police. The law enforcers wisely withdrew.

Outside a throng had gathered in the hope that there would be another show. The police made matters worse by closing the box office. ''Rocks and bottles filled the air in front of the theater,'' recalled Myra Lewis. ''Clenched fists and claws, the protesters divided into factions and a melee of hand-to-hand combat jammed the metropolitan streets of Boston.''[43] The box office closing sparked the disturbance just as 6,000 excited teenagers exited. Fifteen people were either knifed, robbed, beaten, or raped outside the arena. A nineteen-year-old sailor was listed in critical condition with multiple stab wounds. A twenty-three-year-old woman was knocked to the ground and robbed by a gang of teenagers. A dozen police cars were called to reinforce the beseiged officers on the scene. As the crowd dispersed the action spread to other parts of the city. Gangs reportedly raced through the streets in the Roxbury and Bay sections. A gang of bikers attacked three men and took $50. (Some violence, attributed to the show, was arbitrarily associated with the "Big Beat".) Arena manager Paul Brown said another Freed show would be presented "over my dead body."[44]

Mayor John B. Hynes immediately banned rock shows. "As far as the City of Boston is concerned if the kids are hungry for this kind of music they'll starve for it," said the mayor, "until they learn to behave like citizens instead of hooligans. Boston will have no more rock 'n' roll."[45]

Freed was indicated on two counts, incitement to riot and unlawful destruction of real and personal property. Bail was set at $2,500. He told a reporter, "Juvenile delinquency is a major problem throughout America and the banning of rock 'n' roll won't cure it."[46] *Variety*, in an editorial, agreed with the rock entrepreneur. "The Pied Piper Muted" took a civil liberties posture and added a touch of the teen scream hypothesis. The writer rhetorically asked, "Isn't (Boston) going too far in pinning a deep-seated social phenomenon like juvenile delinquency on a passing musical fad like rock 'n' roll?" In what may have been an exercise in wishful thinking, the column closed with, "As the r 'n' r thing sags, (sic) a gent whose initials are Sol Hurok can't find enough longhair items to import and book in these United States." In an obvious reference to Freed's New Year's piece, it continued, "There's boffo b.o., too, in longhair as well as crewcut stuff. It is very heartening."[47]

In the wake of the Boston affair, Troy, New York, New Haven, Connecticut, and Newark, New Jersey cancelled Freed's scheduled appearances. Charges against Freed were dropped prior to the scheduled court date of 29 June 1959. The fates would not be as kind to the headliners of the Big Beat tour. Lewis, Berry, Freed and Holly would all experience the fickleness of fame. For Lewis, adversity would come in a matter of weeks. When his wife, Jane, was granted a divorce petition, the news barely garnered a back page gossip item.

High School Confidential

> *Don't tell me you never rode in a hot rod or*
> *had a late date in the balcony.*
> —Gwen Dulaine, hero's "aunt"

Albert Zugsmith, one of Hollywood's most versatile producers, arrived at MGM after completing a stint at Universal Pictures, where he produced *Written on the Wind* (1957) and *Tarnished Angels* (1958). At MGM Zugsmith was handed a screenplay by Lewis Meltzer and Robert Blees. The scenario dealt with the penetration of drugs into a middle-class high school. The topic was more like the Grade-B genre than MGM's usual "big picture" projects. Jack Arnold directed and a cast was assembled, but not before the first of *High School Confidential's* many censorship problems surfaced.

The Hays Office, Hollywood's censorship bureau, decided one of the film's characters (to be played by Mamie Van Doren) was a nymphomaniac and "completely unnecessary to the story." They wanted her expunged. Zugsmith and Arnold denied the request. Filming began. As this "wild youth" film had most of the trappings, a rock song, in MGM's *Blackboard Jungle* tradition, was deemed appropriate.

Jerry Lee Lewis was signed by director Arnold, to provide a title song and perform it in the film. (Ronald J. Hargrave actually wrote the song. Sun Records's Sam Phillips had pulled one of the industry's oldest ploys on the neophyte songsmith. "Jerry Lee would record the song for a piece of the song," the executive said. Established stars can, and do, get points and co-authorship credit for songs. Hargrave, hungry for a hit, agreed. He and Lewis copyrighted the tune January 28.) The Lewis Trio flew to Hollywood to act out the selection on a flat bed truck before a crowd of studio extras.

Lewis recorded "High School Confidential" 22 April in the Memphis Sun studios. It was designed to appear on extended and long-playing formats. The studio and Phillips discussed the possibility of a mutual street date for the single and the film; the last week of May was agreed upon.

Unbeknownst to the executives supervising *High School*, a significant new development had occurred. "On December 12, 1957 at 1:10 p.m., Jerry Lee Lewis, twenty-two, married Gale Brown, thirteen, in a wedding chapel at Hernando, Mississippi before the Reverend M.C. Whitten," ran the news. This marital tidbit would surface in May prior to the general release of the motion picture.[48]

One day after the film's Hollywood press preview, Jerry Lee and Gale arrived at London's Heathrow Airport. The *Daily Mail's* Paul Tanfield approached some of Jerry's entourage. Casually he asked their identity and relationship to the singer. This was background or color material. He asked Myra, "Who are you, miss?" "Jerry's wife," she answered quietly. The no-longer secret marriage rapidly filled the front pages of the British tabloids. The disclosure added more controversy to an already controversial film.

The effect of "child bride" stories was immeasurable. Concert dates were canceled. "High School Confidential" was blacklisted by many radio stations. "The record ain't sellin'," said Sam Phillips, "it ain't gettin' played. Oscar Davis, Lewis's manager, got a list of cancellations as long as my arm. I ain't spending' another cent on Jerry Lee Lewis till the slate's clean."[49] Rumors abounded that the Lewis connection was hurting *High School Confidential* at the box office. Ironically, the Lewis episode underscored MGM's publicity copy claiming that the film presented "the social ills of America's youth ripped from today's (and tomorrow's) headlines!" How the headlines played in the teen subculture is impossible to ascertain.

A look at the trade charts suggest that country music fans were more tolerant than their Top 40 counterparts. "High School Confidential" remained on the *Cashbox* listing for fourteen weeks. It peaked at Number 11, but rested in the Top 20 for eight weeks.

The pop rankings were less favorable. The song only reached Number 20 during an eight-week stay on the *Billboard* chart. Sam Phillips noted, "After hittin' number twenty-one, it dropped clean off the charts. Parents are callin' up the stations threatenin' to boycott sponsors' products if they don't quit playin' Jerry Lee Lewis."[50] Remarkably, the single nevertheless sold over a million units.

Mamie Van Doren and Jerry Lee Lewis provided all the sex, drugs, and rock 'n' roll publicity any studio needed—maybe more. Still, as Pielke argued, the teen *noir* of the period exhibited a contradictory duality. "This accord between music and narrative," he contended, "was no less superficial than the films themselves . . . the narrative lamented this deplorable situation and the threatened loss of American youth to demon rock and roll, the music was positively celebratory."[51] *High School Confidential* opened with such a dichotomy.

The Zugsmith production begins as a documentary. A stern narrator seated behind a barren desk, a member of the narcotics control board of the Los Angeles Medical Association, tells the viewer what is to follow is "not pleasant." This is the reality of high school drug abuse. He continues to suggest that viewers be on the alert for the depicted behavior in their local secondary schools.

As if to demonstrate the pervasiveness of the problem, the camera cuts to the Jerry Lee Lewis Trio belting and pumping out, "Boppin' (rockin') at the high school hop . . . Com on -ah- little baby let's rock a little bit tonight . . ." as a beat-up pickup truck creeps toward Santo Bello High. The students start an impromptu jitterbug, surrounding the vehicle. "Rocking the song as though in a life and death struggle with an invisible antagonist," wrote Gertrude Samuels, "was a tall thin, flaccid youth who pulled his stringy, blond hair over his eyes and down to his chin. He shook his torso about as the beat of the band seemingly goaded him on."[52] This contrast of the frenetic Lewis with the all-too-serious narcotics consultant apparently was added *after* the film was criticized for advocating the glamor of drug usage.

Into this maze arrives Tony Baker (Russ Tamblyn), a Chicago street kid who has flunked out of school three times. The transfer student's bad credentials are quickly established. Baker manages to put down the principal, come on to English teacher Arlene Wilson (Jan Sterling), and challenge the ultra-cool gangland leader of the Wheeler-Dealers, J.I. Coleridge (John Drew Barrymore). Coleridge loses not only the gang to Tony, but also his dope-smoking girl, Joan (Diane Jergens). She and Tony make a great couple. He carries a wad of greenbacks while she hides joints in her bra.

Tony's domicile is even more bizarre. He is staying with his married "aunt," Gwen Dulaine (Mamie Van Doren). Anything but a maiden aunt, Gwen parades around the house in super-tight sweaters carrying a half-empty whiskey glass. She obviously has more than maternal feelings for Tony. In a kitchen scene, she takes a bite out of his apple, whispering, "You looking for excitement?"

"Why not, I'm a citizen" comes the reply. Unrelenting, she blocks the door, insisting, "Stop treating me like a stranger . . . relatives should always kiss each other hello and goodbye, polite like."

"You getting paid for my room and board."

"But not enough." Tony's romantic interests, however, seem aimed, strangely, at the English teacher.

Through Joan, Baker is able to move up the drug chain. He offers J.I.'s ex-girl the money to buy pot if she introduces him to the pusher. A possible lead is classmate Doris (Jody Fair), a heroin addict. As Tony moves up the trail, Jukey Judlow (Burt Douglas) offers to connect him with the main man. J.I. is the next higher up. Attempting to get to Mr. Big (actually it's Mr. A, Jackie Coogan), Baker attends an auto race with Joan, who is "stoned on grass." Joan, in a smoke-induced buzz, manages to get the guys arrested. The police find Tony's stash of marijuana. Bix (Ray Anthony) bails Tony out and takes the youth to meet Mr. A Walking into the local hangout, Tony sees Doris writhing in pain. Mr. A. enters. He's the barroom piano player. The dealer demands that Doris to go into prostitution to pay for her habit. Suspicious of Tony, Mr. A wants reassurance. The test is Baker shot up with heroin. Tony fakes it with a small rubber ball cleverly concealed in the forearm. Until this point, Tony seems to be all he claims. The phony fix raises questions. "We get hints that Tony isn't the teenage punk his classmates think him to be; he drinks milk, turns down the sexual advances of his aunt, is civil to all-American boy Steve (Michael Langdon), refuses Joan's marijuana cigarette . . ." said one commentator.[53]

Thanks to Joan, again, the viewer's suspicions are confirmed. While waiting for her pot "fix," the dope smoker finds a tape of Tony's meeting with Mr. A. Tony refuses to explain, rushing out of the house for the heroin deal. He asks Ms. Williams to come and watch over Joan. Shortly after Tony's departure, J.I. and Jukey show up, extract Joan's secret, and warn Coogan. Tony—actually narc Mike Wilson—walks into a trap. Gun in hand, Mr. A plans to kill the undercover agent. Baker/Wilson throws the sinister white powder into the pusher's face as the police, with Steve and some clean-cut football players, pour into the back room. Subdued by judo, the drug kingpin is taken away. J.I., Jukey, Bix, and Mr. A are sentenced to correctional institutions.

In the closing scene Tony/Mike, Joan Jergens, and Arlene nestle in the front seat of his convertible while the reunited Dulaines kiss in the back. All is well as a voice announces "Joan only smokes ordinary cigarettes now." The relationship between Mike and Arlene continues unresolved.

Theater posters advertised: "Behind these 'nice' school walls . . . *A TEACHERS' NIGHTMARE! A TEEN-AGED JUNGLE!* Your own kids will never tell you, some won't . . . others *DARE NOT!*" Howard Thompson, rapidly becoming the *New York Times's* resident authority on rock/wild-youth movies, questioned the reality and intent of the Meltzer/ Blees screenplay. The motion picture, he wrote, supposedly was a "warning against narcotics traffic in high school." He cautioned that Tamblyn's portrayal of a teen hero was "going to be too much for a lot of people out front to take for so long." *Variety*, with qualifiers, praised the Zugsmith project, saying, "Although the presentation seems to 'exploit' to the fullest every facet of this evil situation, it does so skillfully and with compelling effect."[54]

Most *post factum* analyses of *High School Confidential* praised the presentation as a cult classic carrying on the tradition of *Reefer Madness* (1938). All of the writers discussed the title song performance of Jerry Lee Lewis.

In the preview critiques Lewis was ignored. The *Times* review sided with the Hays office, saying, "Why sandwich in, for instance, the extremely shapely Mamie Van Doren as Mr. Tamblyn's aunt . . . what exactly have her attempts at his seduction to do with the price of beans— or dope?"[55] The answer to the rhetorical question is obvious. Boxoffice.

Many countries banned the film, but it was released in the United Kingdom, as the *Young Hellions*, without incident. Zugsmith was correct in his statement, "A lot of people will hate this picture and not get the point.'' The producer was correct. Outside of the Presley films, only the *Girl Can't Help It* and *High School Confidential* enjoy contemporary currency.

Hot Rock Gang

Lou Rusoff, who had written *Shake Rattle and Rock*, penned and produced the first fast cars, teens, and rock 'n' roll project—*Hot Rod Gang*—also in 1958. American International and Allied would shortly unleash a bevy of these vehicles. A writer characterized the Rusoff production as being ''the type of entertainment which elicits sequels.'' The double feature specialist would take this advice to heart.

The drama repeated the *Untamed Youth* ploy of using a rock artist as an actor who would also provide the musical breaks. Gene Vincent, contracted to play the rock bandleader, nearly didn't make the start up date, having been arrested after a riotous performance in Globe, Arizona. He had to be bailed out to appear in Hollywood on schedule.

Vincent was joined by Eddie Cochran, who consented to do some background vocals, ''Dance in The Street'' and ''Git It.'' Other songs for the film included ''Baby Blue,'' ''Dance to the Bop,'' and ''Lonely Loretta.'' ''Git It'' was dropped from the soundtrack, an extended play which appeared in mid-April.

The film's release date was to be 2 July. *Variety* did not review it until a month and a half later, 22 August 1958.

In the film, John Abernathy III (John Ashley) is an upper-class heir in the guarded custody of prudish maiden aunts Anastasia (Dorothy Newman) and Abigail (Helen Spring). They stipulate that John must lead a highly respectable, conservative life if he is to receive his fortune.

John's interests, however, lie in hot rods, rock 'n' roll, and Lois Cavendish (Jody Fair), in that order. He organizes a hot rod club and with Gene Vincent, a rock band. (The group allows for inclusion of Vincent's songs and Ashley's attempts at swing versions of songs like ''Annie Laurie.'') The heir uses the group to earn money to build the ''ultimate racing machine'' for the Grand Nationals. He earns the money and goes on to the big meet. The moral is that even the privileged rich can succeed with racing and rock.

Gene Vincent and his group were excellent in this loosely plotted treatment of money, autos, and music. The rocker was allowed to use his favorite prop, the standup microphone. *Variety* termed the project ''okay'' as it offered ''a combo hot rod-rock 'n' roll backdrop to draw aficionados in both these fields.''[56]

Rock historians are fond of saying that Don McLean's line, "the day the music died" refers to 3 February 1959. Symbolically, the tragic deaths of Buddy Holly, The Big Bopper, and Ritchie Valens was the final scene in a costly drama effecting rock music. The ambience of Haley, Presley, and Little Richard was not repeated by those who followed. In a quirk of history, misfortune, accidents and the Selective Service decimated what, today, constitutes the Rock and Roll Hall of Fame. These unfortunate events are well documented, but two social forces are only mentioned in passing.

As many patrons of the Cavalcade of Stars tours went off to college, their younger siblings watched *Bandstand*. Dick Clark, for whatever reasons, had created a new batch of sanitized rock acts, some literally culled from the doorsteps of Philadelphia. Fabian fans were not Elvis supporters, or, more significantly, the reverse. Each musical generation does create it's own set of icons. At the same time, the so-called folk music revival fostered by the Kingston Trio's "Tom Dooley" fragmented the youth market along age, class and educational lines. Labels and studios misread the fragmentation. The rock/jazz mix in movies irritated one group or the other, in some cases both. (In addition, the Dave Brubeck era of "jazz goes to college" was fading with the introduction of soul jazz as played by Cannonball Adderley and cohorts fragmenting the jazz audience. Rock had a firmer base depending on the style and artist.)

In the past, the strength of the "personality" films had involved unconscious targetting. As record sales demonstrated, Presley, Boone, and a few others had loyal followings. While Elvis could, and did, make movies universally dismissed by film and records critics as trash, his films made money.

The Grade-Bs, until the Twist craze, were "teen exploitation" vehicles. The problem was that teens were no longer a neatly defined, homogeneous unit. In response, *Billboard* wisely merged its "Hot 100" chart, including R & B, MOR, C&W and other categories, as record sales declined.

Stereo, designed for the older up-scale music consumer, could not have arrived at a more propitious time for ASCAP. The licensing agency was reeling from a second Congressional rebuff.

Early in 1958, George Smathers, a conservative Democratic senator from Florida, had introduced a bill prohibiting broadcasters from engaging in the manufacture, publishing, or sale of sheet or recorded music. (The targets of the proposed legislation were the 624 broadcasters with BMI stock.) Thirteen days of hearings, spread over several months, were chaired by John Pastore (D.-Rhode Island). The sessions were reminiscent of the Celler probe. From the beginning it was generally acknowledged, even by the disinterested sponsor, that the divestiture bill had little chance of clearing the Commerce Sub-Committee on Communications, let along reaching the full Senate. As with the "Foley Square Follies," the hearings generated considerably more heat than light.

The hearing opened 11 March with Smather supporters testifying in the opening five sessions. Oscar Hammerstein III and Arthur Schwartz repeated their accusations of discrimination against ASCAP writers. Schwartz contended that the gatekeeping disc jockeys "naturally favored the boss' music." Hammerstein, the composer of *South Pacific*, objected that "unworthy" music was crowding his material off the airwaves.[57]

Vance Packard, author of the best selling *Hidden Persuaders* (1957) and a consultant to SPA, made headlines by accusing BMI and broadcasters of foisting rock music on "passive" teenagers. The gatekeepers, he urged, manipulated playlists in order to keep "cheap music" on the air. Asked what constituted cheap music, Packard replied, "hillbilly, Latin, R & B or rock 'n' roll." These genres were "cheaply obtained and easy to record," he said. Several senators loudly objected to the slur on country and western music. Chairman Pastore insisted that Packard and other witnesses supply "exhaustive statistics to prove this thing one way or the other."[58] Unlike Congressman Celler, Pastore frequently dismissed unsubstantiated claims.

At the hearings, California attorney Seymour Lazar added "payola" to ASCAP's charges. He told a surprised chairman that deejays were earning $300 to $500 a week in gratuities for playing BMI products. This corruption, he continued, was being used to "suppress ASCAP music. To keep ASCAP royalty prices down for broadcasters." He singled out the Los Angeles market as a hotbed of rampant payola. Questioned by Pastore, Lazar conceded that the majors, in most instances, used ASCAP titles but cautioned that there was a "potential danger" they would follow the lead of the independents.[59]

Deejays were quick to respond. KLAC's Peter Potter insisted, "It's a damn lie except in three isolated cases, 97 percent of the deejays here are honest." Over at KFWB, "Color Radio," Al Jarvis and Chuck Blore quickly expressed their resentment. Blore told a reporter, "I do . . . resent his (Lazar's) blatant generalizations and rise to the defense for the deejays at KFWB . . . who to a man, regard an attempt at payola as a personal affront." One executive cited by Lazar, dismissed the accusations saying his artists "perform more ASCAP than BMI material because ASCAP has a vastly larger repertoire of highly popular standards than BMI."[60] Within a year, Lazar's payola charge would be resurrected.

(ASCAP and SPA had not proven their case, and some ASCAPers were uncomfortable with the tone of the allegations. An ally would prove to be an unexpected embarrassment to them. At the 44th Annual ASCAP dinner, Congressman Emanuel Celler had delivered a blistering address aimed at broadcasters who promoted "pelvic contortionists." Noting the presence of some key network executives at the dinner, he threatened "you will feel my sting." He reportedly received an ovation, but several members of ASCAPs board said, "We didn't like it at all."[61]

The anti-divestiture witnesses reiterated the argument that there was no conspiracy. Imperial's Lewis Chudd testified that there was not "the slightest evidence that any broadcaster, program director or disc jockey had any interest in whether a song was licensed by ASCAP or BMI."[62]

Paramount Pictures's vice president, Paul Railbourne, agreed, adding that the film industry needed to be involved with music as "many a motion picture has been helped to success just because of the popularity of a song." "To Each His Own" and "Golden Earrings" as singles, had aided box office receipts, the executive noted.

As the hearings dragged on, it became apparent the committee would not be able to report on the bill during the 1958 legislative year. Pastore put the final nail in the Smathers' legislation when he told reporters there was no evidence to support the "compulsion" thesis put forth by supporters.

In August, *Variety* editorialized that "ASCAP failed to make the kind of clear-cut case against BMI that would win if justice were the only yardstick in Washington. The other shoe dropped in October with the issuance of the committee's 1,237-page report. "I am certain that no one here has any idea of destroying either BMI or ASCAP," said Smathers. "We need them both. The objective is the serving of the public interest. If that cannot be done, if the public interest will not be served by the legislation, why then of course, the bill should not be adopted." ASCAP lost the battle and, eventually, the war. SPA's $150-million suit failed. As a popular song of the time indicated, rock 'n' roll was here to stay. Its prominence on the silver screen was another matter.

Go, Johnny Go, But Where?

The rock music audience has never been monolithic or homogeneous. In the so-called Golden Age (1955–1958) there existed minor fissures. The Pat Boone, Top 40 crowd was socially removed from the ducktailed "greasers" immersed in rock-a-billy and R & B. There was, of course, some crossover, particularly by the Boone contingent. Most significant, the "juves" were identified by age. By 1959, this was no longer the case.

That year saw the first fragmentation in the rock audience. Record and tape sales jumped 18 percent to $603 million, spent on a plethora of teen idols and specialty artists. The annual *Billboard* Top 10 included three country crossovers, two R & B derivatives, songs by Frankie Avalon, Paul Anka and Bobby Darin, and Ritchie Valens' "Donna." Stylistically, only the Valens product could claim allegiance to the roots of the Golden Age. A *Rolling Stone* writer best summarized the dissolution: " 'Real' rock 'n' roll music began to take a back seat to divergent forms of pop music which were influenced by rock 'n' roll and which, in turn, would influence rock 'n' roll."[63]

Generational shifting and external events equally played a hand in this development. Rock demi-gods were growing in short supply. Buddy Holly, Little Richard, Chuck Berry, Jerry Lee Lewis, Carl Perkins and Elvis Presley were removed from the scene. Perkins' career was stalled by a car accident, Presley was drafted into the Army, Berry was convicted under the Mann Act for bringing a minor across state lines for immoral purposes.

The R & B market was looking inward. Berry Gordy borrowed $700 from his family to produce "Come to Me" by Marv Johnson, which climbed to Number 6 on the specialty chart in March 1959. The Miracles released "Bad Girl," with "I Love You Baby" on the flip side, in September. R & B was moving in one direction, and *Bandstand* and Top 40 another.

The payola scandals also cast a pall on radio playlists. (Alan Freed and Dick Clark were both affected. Freed was ruined; Clark divested enough to walk away unscathed with millions.) Targeting an unsettled market was difficult for movie makers as well. Only two film offerings actually fit the genre: *Go Johnny Go*, a typical jukeboxer, and Fabian's *Hound Dog Man*. The rest comprised a potpourri of rock sandwiched into "wild youth" vehicles and even a documentary, *Jazz on A Summer's Day*, which included Chuck Berry performing "Sweet Little Sixteen." (In technique and format, *Summer's Day* would be the precursor to the rockumentary concerts of the late 1960s.) The film did poorly. As Bowsley Crowther suggested, "For those who like jazz, it should be perfect—perhaps not even enough. But for those who can take that stuff or leave it, it is likely to be too much."[64] The excellent effort was doomed by limited distribution and market appeal. Jazz fans constitute less than 5 percent of the music market.

Meanwhile Sam Katzman presented *Juke Box Rhythm* to the Grade-B outlets. The script has Princess Ann (Jo Morrow) and Aunt Margaret (Frieda Inescort) slipping into the Big Apple to purchase a coronation wardrobe. Vocalist Riff Manton (Jack Jones), whose father George (Brian

Donleavy) is the producer of "Juke Box Jamboree," encounters the royal duo during their shopping spree. To aid a friend, ex-junkman-turned-designer Brodine (Hans Conreid), the younger Manton attempts to steer them to Brodine. Needless to say, Conreid clothes royalty and Jones wins the princess' hand.

This rehash of a Broadway show includes four songs that are vintage middle-of-the-road: Jo Morrow sings "Let's Fall in Love," Jones sings the title song, "The Freeze," and "Make Room For Joy," and veteran juke boxers The Treniers act out "Get Out of the Car." The one memorable song in the film is John Otis's "Willie and the Hand Jive." Of the remaining acts, the Earl Grant Trio is the only recognizable name. This was a true "quickie" and Katzman's box office record remained unbroken.

Juke Box Rhythm, unlike most of Katzman's "little musicals," had no sense of audience direction. Having a vaudeville anachronism, George Jessel, singing "Spring Is the Time for Remembering" defied any notion of audience targeting. Tongue in cheek, *Variety* noted the "name of George Jessel—in as guest star—may spark it [the film] exploitationwise in some situations."[65]

Further exploitation occurred in the film *Daddy-O*, starring accordionist Dick Contino, known mostly for a tussle with the Selective Service and "Lady of Spain." In this forgettable film, Contino plays a would-be rock singer conned by mobsters into driving a getaway car. Released on probation, he wages war on the bad guys between performing "rockers" such as "Rock Candy Baby." Nash and Ross describe the AIP film as "good for a laugh."[66] Also issued under the title *Out on Probation*, the film received little attention. An undissuaded Contino would later appear in Albert Zugsmith's second Van Doren epic, *Girls' Town*.

Mamie Van Doren, by 1950s' mores, was kinky. In *Untamed Youth* and *High School Confidential* all sorts of sexual deviations on her part were implied. *Girls' Town*, also released as *The Innocent and the Damned*, went further. "The screenplay of the film is as flimsy as a G-string, and designed for somewhat the same purpose," said *Variety*. "It includes all the staples of the exploitation film—a drag race, a necking party, the flip and shallow conversation of a segment of youth, the slight and unconvincing nod to conventional morality at the ending." *Variety* reviewers generally avoided the "moral" implication of movies, but in this instance the critic cautioned that *Girls' Town* "cannot help but be ammunition for the opposition [censors] . . . there is not a mitigating ounce of artistry or the pretense of it."[67]

As the title suggests, Silver Morgan (Mamie Van Doren), falsely accused of causing the death of a young man, is sent to a Catholic reformatory.

There she confronts a typical inmate power struggle, while coping with the nuns in charge of the elegant mansion. In time, Silver is made to see the error of her sinful life and is deemed worthy of returning to society. A number of music people appear in the film: Mel Torme, Ray Anthony, Cathy Crosby, Dick Cantino, The Platters, and Paul Anka. The Platters sing "Wish It Were Me"; Anka performs his hit "Lonely Boy" and "Ava Maria," a rendition that was akin to Frankie Lymon's treatment of "I'm Not A Juvenile Delinquent."

Months prior to his fall from grace in 1959, Alan Freed had decided to finance a quasi-backstage musical jukebox. The rock entrepreneur reasoned that with the right acts, the previous teen exploiters could be eclipsed aesthetically and economically. *Go, Johnny Go*, based on a refrain from "Johnny B. Goode," paralleled preceding films in many ways. In the central role Freed cast young Jimmy Clanton, who had had one hit song, "Just A Dream." The romantic interest was Sandy Steward, best remembered for her appearances on the *Eddie Fisher* and *Ernie Kovacs* television shows.

The film opens as the camera pans to the brightly lit Loew's State marquee. Alan Freed is staging a Big Beat cavalcade starring Johnny Melody (Jimmy Clanton). As Melody performs a nondescript number to the adulation of the crowd, Chuck Berry stands with Freed in the wings. Johnny is followed by The Flamingos, who perform "Jumping At The Break of Day," then returns to do "Angel Face" (in a doo-wop style totally inappropriate for his voice).

Berry triggers the film's flashback scenes by asking Freed about Johnny Melody. The viewer is transported to a choir rehearsal with Johnny, the orphanage kid, singing lead.

Mr. Martin (Milton Frome), the choirmaster, congratulates the clean-cut kid for his fine performance and also manages to knock the rock. "Let's hope it will be gone by the time you're a man," he tells Johnny. Thinking the "square" is gone, Johnny and the choir break into a rock-oriented "Ship On A Stormy Sea." Mr. Martin overhears. Johnny is dismissed from the choir. The ex-choir boy is determined to become a rock 'n' roll star.

Freed, meanwhile, is fronting a bill at the New York Paramount. Harvey Fuqua opens. (He should have stayed with the Moonglows.) Johnny turns up as an usher. A Brenda Lee/Theresa Brewer soundalike does, "Momma Can I Go Out," which is definitely not *Hit Parade* material. Johnny, however, is rocking right along when the head usher enters and tells him, "This is your farewell performance." Totally unperturbed, the discharged usher meekly asks if he can remain until the end of the show. Freed announces, "As of now, I'm looking for a boy with a beat. A youngster who will go straight to the top with a one-record smash." "When I find him, I'm going to call him 'Johnny Melody' and start him spinning to the top, too." There is no doubt *who that* is going to be. The question, during the rest of the movie, is "when?"

After the show Johnny literally bumps into Julie Arnold (Sandy Stewart), his friend from the orphanage, who is now the adopted daughter of a wealthy ad man. Johnny, the aspiring singer, also corners Freed. Impatiently, the deejay suggests that Johnny stay in school and admits the "Melody" campaign is a gimmick.

Apparently, nobody else agrees. Freed's office is deluged with hundreds of letters from people wanting to be the next name rock star.

Julie and Johnny meet again at a recording studio. She offers to sing background on Clanton's song "My Love Is Strong." The ballad is the singer's strongest offering. The chemistry between the orphaned kids heats up.

Johnny sends the demo to Freed. Berry and his manager, Herb Vigran (Bill Barnett), flip over the record. The Clanton character tries to get a reaction from Freed in vain, however. The remaining storyline will focus on Freed and Johnny connecting after a few detours and more songs.

At one point, Johnny, Julie, and Julie's parents go to the Krazy Kuffee Kup, a night spot, where Freed, Vigran, and Berry just happen to be listening to Jackie Wilson and The Cadillacs. Johnny misses Freed who, now, badly wants to find the singer of "My Love is Strong." He airs the song on his show every fifteen minutes. When, during intermission, Freed offers to book "Johnny Melody" into the Loew, Julie breaks out in the song, "Heavenly Father." (All of film's other musical numbers are included realistically—sort of—on stage, in a studio, or in a rehearsal.) She rushes off to find Freed and finds him playing drums for Berry at another club; Harry's Hideaway, where Ritchie Valens is in the audience.

Freed and company find Johnny as he is about to steal a gold pin for Julie from a swank shop. Freed gallantly saves him. All ends well as Johnny performs, Mr. Martin applauds, and Freed proudly states that Clanton is going to be "quite a singer." Julie chimes in, "and quite a husband."

Go, Johnny Go had an engaging, if not complex, plot. The musical interludes toward the close became a distraction, however. Valens's song, "Ooh My Head," is ill placed and shabbily treated. Only Eddie Cochran and Chuck Berry provide satisfying musical moments. Technically, the film was better written and acted than earlier attempts, but as a whole it didn't work and received little notice at the time of its release. *Variety* did not review it. Rock historians cite its significance as being due to Ritchie Valens's appearance.

Only Berry performed familiar songs (Clanton's hits "Just A Dream," was absent). Sandy Stewart's "Playmate" demo was an above-average presentation. The versatile Cadillacs, with "Jay Walker," did one of their patented skits, but it worked. Some of the other performances are best left unmentioned.

Go, Johnny, Go was the last of the rock exploitation films of the 1950s. (Katzman's "twist" pictures several years later were not aimed exclusively at teens.) It was another fading film artifact of the post-Golden Age of Rock. The jukeboxers would be shelved, but the personality showcases marched on.

Who's The Real Hound Dog Man?

Lillian Roxon captured the common-sense view of the late 1950s when she wrote "When Elvis still seemed like just another fabulous freak, anybody with an eye to a bank balance was trying to reproduce the phenomenal formula. Get a good-looking boy, teach him to sing like Elvis, to move like Elvis, and wowee, a fortune." Bob Marcucci and Peter de Angelis, owners of the Philadelphia-based Chancellor Records, were advocates of this philosophy. In 1958 they applied it to Frankie Avalon and it worked, with the aid of *American Bandstand*. When Avalon told his manager, Marcucci, about a kid who looked "like a cross between Elvis and Ricky Nelson," they tried again. Fabian Forte was hardly a vocalist, but "I figured he was a natural," recalled Marcucci. "It's true he couldn't sing. He knew it and I knew it. But I was pretty sure he could be taught something about singing." Chancellor and talent agents underwrote singing lessons for Fabian. With the assistance of an echo chamber their "discovery" would sneak by. His visual personae was considered "dynamite."[68]

Fabian's first offering, "Lillie Lou," became a local hit and prompted Clark to use him on *Bandstand*. The dance-party format, and Fabian's later films proved ideal for the artist, as they were lip synced.

On 12 December, Fabian reappeared on the Clark program "reeling like a top, snapping his fingers and jerking his eyeballs, with hair something Medusa had sent back, and a voice that has enormously improved by total unintelligibility," said John Crosby.[69] "I'm A Man" was released several weeks later but despite a heavy promotion on *Bandstand*, it did not crack the charts. Fabian was, however, viewed as a "rising star." His "Turn Me Loose" previewed on *Bandstand* in March climbed to Number 9 on the

Billboard chart, quickly followed up by Fabian's signature song, "Tiger," which reached Number 3. On the basis of that song, producer Jerry Wald and director Don Seigel screentested the Philly rocker. He was cast in *Hound Dog Man* (a highly misleading title as the film had nothing to do with rock or Elvis). The film poster read, "The Fabulous Fabian in His First Motion Picture . . . With That 'Blue Denim' Girl!" Its graphics were reminiscent of *Love Me Tender*. Beginning 27 October 1959 theatergoers discovered there was little comparison between Fabian and the King.

"Starring the singing teenage idol, Fabian and the unlikely title, 'Hound Dog Man,' the movie turns out to be a delightful surprise," wrote Philip T. Hartung.[70] The surprise was the title applied to the role played by Stuart Whitman. He is a free-spirited hunter with a pack of hounds.

In the film, Clint McKinney (Fabian), accompanied by younger brother Spud (Dennis Holmes), joins Blackie Scantling (Stuart Whitman) for a two-day trip in the country, amid luscious southern greenery, rolling hills, and sparkling streams. Hunting and fishing allow them to escape from the everyday drudgery of family chores. Blackie, called "the Hound Dog Man," is a hard-drinking master of avoiding responsibility, a strong contrast to their hard working, proper and dull parents (well played by Arthur O'Connell and Betty Field). The boys idolize him.

During this respite in the lazy, hazy summer of 1912, Clint learns about the opposite sex from Blackie, whose interest in Dony (Carol Lynley) does not include traveling the love-and-marriage route. Clint's romantic interest is in Nina (Dodie Stevens).

The backwoods romp is cut short when the trio discovers an injured man, a harsh reminder of the realities of everyday life in rural small town America.

Saturday night a barn dance allows Fabian and the thirteen-year-old Dodie Stevens (of "Pink Shoe Laces" fame) to do some folk-country style vocalizing, such as "Hay Foot, Straw Foot." Blackie, with some of the local "good old boys," does some serious drinking, arousing the ire of the townsfolk when he leaves the dance with a married lady.

The resolution to the mellow film has Whitman and Lynley settling down with a mutually agreeable arrangement. She promises, noted Stanley Kauffmann, "as women will, not to hackle him."[71] Seeing his role model "domesticated," Clint realizes that's the way things are destined to work out. With this insight, he accepts his father as his real hero. Given the pastoral milieu of the film, any other conclusion would be implausible.

The rustic setting, in Deluxe color, seems to have tranquilized the critics. More than the number that usually reviewed films starring a rock teen-idol paid attention to *Hound Dog Man*.

A near consensus was reached regarding the placement of the musical material in the movie. In *Variety*, director Dan Siegal was credited with staging "the singing numbers so they are a part of the film, and involve others than the principals chiefly known for song, Fabian and young Dodie Stevens." Philip T. Hartung concurred, saying, "Fabian (who's not too Presley) sings every now and then, and the songs are well integrated into the picture's themes, especially those sung at the barn dance." Stanley Kauffmann, whose disdain for youth pictures would get worse, found the star "behaving himself agreeably and refrains from singing too much." "There are no Presley-like contortions here: during the course of the film he sings a couple of *appropriately* Western-style ballads in an appropriately modest and modulated voice and style," observed Arthur Knight. Howard Thompson of the *Times* put aside his anomosity towards rock 'n' rollers, saying, "The best tune of Fabian is a nice ballad called 'Friendly World.' And in 'Hound Dog Man'—why not?—it sure is."[72]

Fabian and the picture received exceptionally laudatory notices. Knight called *Hound Dog Man* a "modest, heart-warming, and thoroughly honest little film." *Variety* put it best; calling the movie "a good example of how to use a singing personality in a theatrical film, displaying the star to favorable advantage and at the same time making a picture with general appeal."[73]

The plot, as Thompson had correctly suggested, did not amount to much. The acting was solid and the cinematography outstanding. As an overall package it worked. To paraphrase Leo Marx, it took the machine out of the garden.

The Wald production gave birth to a two-sided hit. "Hound Dog Man" reached Number 9 in *Billboard*, it was followed by the "B" side, "This Friendly World," which hit Number 12. Chancellor, a singles label, did not issue a soundtrack album. The double-barrelled single would be Fabian's last visit to the singles chart. His acting career seemed to be on the ascendent with roles in *High Times* (1960) with Bing Crosby, and John Wayne in *North To Alaska*. But as the teen idol's status faded, so did his "big picture" roles. "It very nearly worked," wrote Roxon, "but in the end Fabian never did become a rock star."[74]

Hound Dog Man's gross did not reach the $1-million first-run club, while Presley's and Boone's maiden efforts had doubled or tripled the figure. Fabian's receipts failed to meet studio expectations.

Beginning with *Blackboard Jungle* through the last month of the 1950s, there were approximately thirty-three rock-oriented films released. Eight were personality showcases starring Elvis, Pat Boone, Tommy Sands, and Fabian. Five were "wild youth" projects with rock in the soundtrack or artists used in the picture. *The Girl Can't Help It* was the one major motion picture with a jukebox affect. The remaining titles were "juve exploitation" films. (Jerry Lewis, and also Abbott and Costello comedies with rock in the title are omitted).

The latter part of the Fifties produced eight soundtrack albums. Five came from the personality pictures and three—*Rock, Rock, Rock, Rock All Night*, and *Rock, Pretty Baby*—were jukeboxers. Various collectors claim that *somewhere* a Johnny Carroll *Rock, Baby, Rock It* album exists. There are no listings of such a product.

In nearly all of these cases the film popularized the record. Artists such as Elvis Presley merely needed to record the product for it to reach gold. The film industry *did* use hits and recording acts as a lure to teenagers, but after the fact. The ploy was simply, "Come see your favorite singing artist," or "See and hear your favorite hit." Filmmakers operated under the assumption that rock stars sold tickets.

Twist Around The Clock

The Twist craze of the early 1960s established the discotheque as a setting for dance in movies with rock music. "The Twist" was originally written and recorded by a Detroit R & B group, Hank Ballard and The Midnighters, best known for "Work With Me Annie," an R & B hit that was banned by many radio stations in the early 1950s. (Ballard wrote "The Twist" after seeing teenagers doing the dance in Tampa, Florida.) The song was put on the B-side of "Teardrops on Your Letter," which became a Top 10 R & B hit in 1959. Disc jockeys began flipping the record over and Dick Clark noticed that teenagers loved dancing to "The Twist." The rock entrepreneur booked The Midnighters on *American Bandstand*, but for some reason the group failed to appear. Clark suggested that another artist also record a twist song, and Chubby Checker was recruited. Cameo-Parkway records did little to promote the single, but Checker was determined to succeed, so much so that he lost thirty pounds doing the Twist on television shows and in live appearances. His single reached Number 1 on the *Billboard* charts in September 1960.

Like dance fads before it—the jitterbug and the Charleston, for example—the Twist was denounced as barbaric, overtly sexual, and physically damaging to young teenage bodies. *Time* described the dance as "a replica of some ancient tribal puberty rite."

> The dancers scarcely ever touch each other or move their feet. Everything else, however, moves. The upper body sways forward and backward and the hips and

shoulders twirl erotically, while the arms thrust in, out, up and down with the pistonlike motions of baffled bird keepers fighting off a flock of attack blue jays.[75]

One Munich psychiatrist considered the dance a byproduct of the cold war. "The twist craze," he said, "can be attributed to *Atomangst*."[76] American Studies professor Marshall Fishwick went even further, identifying the Twist as "a valid manifestation of the anguish, frustration, and uncertainty of the 1960s, an effort to release some of the tension which, if suppressed and buried, could warp and destroy."[77]

The Twist touched off a national craze, first among teenagers and then adults, that would not be paralleled until disco in the late 1970s. Chubby Checker was at the center of it all. His fee for a performance jumped from $100 to $2,500 a show. The Twist phenomenon was a merchandiser's dream come true. A full-page $6,000 ad in the *New York Times* announced:

MANUFACTURERS ATTENTION: A new nationwide name to presell your product . . . The Twist with Chubby Checker (the king of the twist) who created the greatest nationwide dance craze in years!!!
LICENSES AVAILABLE! . . . "BIG NAMES MEAN BIG BUSINESS"[78]

Checker's agent, Harold Bell, was flooded with requests from manufacturers and hoped to duplicate the Elvis Presley craze (At its peak, forty-two manufacturers sold $30 million worth of Elvis products in three months).[79]

The Twist craze faded for a while, but Checker continued to score Top 10 hits with "Pony Time," "Let's Twist Again," "The Fly," "Slow Twistin'," and "Limbo Rock." Then adults began to get dance fever. The Twist debuted at the Peppermint Lounge in New York in October 1961. Overnight, the Manhattan club became all the rage as celebrities and aristocrats showed up to try the Twist. The attendant publicity quickly rejuvenated the Twist as an international phenomenon, spreading it to England, France and Germany. An appearance by Chubby Checker singing "The Twist" on Ed Sullivan's show in late October inspired a re-release of that single. An ad in *Billboard* proclaimed: " 'The Twist' dance rage explodes into the adult world!" The song returned to the top of the Hot 100 for two weeks in January 1962, earning it the distinction of being the only record to reach Number 1 on the pop charts two different times.

Film companies scrambled to be the first to exploit the Twist craze. American International Pictures won the race with *Twist All Night* (also known as *The Continental Twist* and *The Young and the Cool*) opening in theaters in December 1961, just fifteen days before Katzman's Columbia release, *Twist Around the Clock*. Both of these films had flimsy plots built around outbursts of people doing the Twist. *The Motion Picture Guide* called *Twist All Night* "an idiotic mess that smacked of ripoff."[80] Its plot centers on Louis Prima, a nightclub owner whose business is going under because a group of loitering teenagers frequent the club but never spend any money. Prima discovers it is all a plot by the owner of an art gallery on the floor above who wants Prima out of business. Prima exposes the man as an art thief and has him arrested. The film ends with a twist block party and the club back on the road to success.

Sam Katzman, dubbed by *Variety* "filmdom's fastest man with a fad," jumped on the Twist craze while it was still hot.[81] History repeated itself. The king of the Bs duplicated his exploitation formula for the Twist craze. In *Twist Around the Clock*, unemployed promoter John Cronin discovers the new dance and tries to promote it nationally. His problem is that the owner of a large talent agency, who could catapault the twist to fame, has a daughter who is in love with Cronin. Cronin, however, has fallen for a dancer. Predictably, it is all resolved in the end.

Chubby Checker appeared as himself in the movie and singers Dion and Vicki Spencer performed several songs to further entice teens into the theaters. *Variety* considered Katzman's formula successful again, calling the production "attractively and resourcefully mounted and endowed with a reasonable sense of dramatic content and concern for characterization." The reviewer also noted that "Man's face may be more beautiful than his backside . . . but Gordon Avil's bottoms-up photography does not exactly adhere to this view. Most of the choreographic action is regarded from below-the-belt, which, of course, is where the Twist really comes on strong.[82]

Chubby Checker repeated his starring role in Katzman's sequel, *Don't Knock the Twist*, released in April 1962. The slim plot of this film revolved around attempts to produce a television special on the Twist and help a summer camp for orphans. A love triangle provided occasion for musical numbers and plenty of dancing. Reviews were not favorable.

In between the Katzman offerings, Paramount got in on the action, with its *(Hey) Let's Twist* reaching theaters in February 1962. The film was shot in fifteen days with the cast working eighteen hours a day, and Paramount's $500,000 advertising budget exceeded production costs. Joey Dee and The Starliters, Jo-Ann Campbell, Teddy Randazzo, and Kay Armen starred in this "authentic" Twister (as producer Harry Romm called it).[83] In this movie, Dino di Luce wants his two sons to get college educations, but they are more concerned with turning his Italian restaurant into a Twist lounge. In the end, the boys come to their senses and find profit and fame. Scenes were shot at the Peppermint Lounge and The Starliters and the Peppermint Loungers appeared in the movie. The *Times* called it "a wobbly little mess concerned with the rise, decline and present glory of the New York night spot called the Peppermint Lounge, it rates a ripe raspberry."[84]

"Hey gang, let's go down to the beach and hang ten!"

In 1938, a small resort town in Florida with a high percentage of retired people invited college students to a "swimming forum." That invitation began an annual trek for collegiates fleeing the cold weather of the north for the sunny beaches of Fort Lauderdale. Twenty years later, *Time* reported that 20,000 students had invaded the town, practicing the same spring-break ritual as their predecessors over the last two decades—"they grilled themselves medium-rare all day, beach-boozed all night, and blew the foam off the early hours by decanting sand sharks and alligators into local swimming pools."[85] When one co-ed was asked why she made the springtime migration she replied, "This is where the boys are." Her comment inspired a novel by Glendon Swarthout which was quickly adapted for the screen by George Wills. The MGM comedy-romance gave Fort Lauderdale the dubious reputation as the favorite destination of college students in the spring.

The 1961 MGM production was aimed at teenagers and young adults. As Ehrenstein and Reed pointed out, "What was new about *Where The Boys Are* was that this material was being given the full MGM gloss, and being pitched at the largest possible audience."[86] MGM spent $3 million on this youth-oriented beach film. To help ensure the film's success, company executives cast their hottest female singer, Connie Francis, in the picture.

After a slow start, Francis had scored big with a string of hit singles, beginning with "Who's Sorry Now?" in 1958. In 1960, she had back-to-back Number 1 singles with "Everybody's Somebody's Fool" and "My Heart Has a Mind of Its Own." For seven consecutive years she was voted *Billboard*'s Top Female Singer. From 1959 to 1964, *Cashbox* named her the Most Programmed Female Vocalist. On the basis of her recording success, MGM cast her in *Where The Boys Are*.

Francis convinced film executives to allow New York songwriters Howard Greenfield and Neil Sedaka, who had penned several of her earlier hits, to compose the title song. In four days they wrote two songs titled "Where The Boys Are." Although MGM producer Joe Pasternak chose the one the songwriters hated, the song became Number 1 in fifteen countries and nine different languages. It reached Number 4 on the

Billboard charts. "Where the Boys Are" was the tenth consecutive million-selling singles for Francis.

The singing star appeared in three other MGM movies during the 1960s: *Follow the Boys* (1963), *Looking for Love* (1964), and *When the Boys Meet the Girls* (1965), singing the title songs, which were released as singles. MGM soundtracks accompanied all three of the other films, but not *Where the Boys Are*.

Where The Boys Are was a sanitized version of collegiate exploits in the sun during spring vacation. *Time* described the movie as "a corny, phony, raucous outburst of fraternity humor, sorority sex talk and house-mother homilies that nevertheless warms two hours of winter with a travel-poster panorama of fresh young faces, firm young bodies and good old Florida sunshine."[87]

The film opens with a panorama of Florida's sunny beaches, green grass, palm trees, and ocean views. A narrator explains the two-week Easter vacation phenomenon:

> The students swarm to these peaceful shores in droves 20,000 strong. They turn night into day and a small corner of heaven into a sizeable chunk of bedlam. The boys come to soak up the sun and a few carloads of beer. The girls come, very simply, because this is where the boys are.

Connie Francis sings the title song, a schmaltzy ballad that can hardly be considered rock music. The scene shifts to a wintry blizzard at a Midwestern college where four co-eds are nursing colds. Merit (Dolores Hart) is sent to the dean's office for speaking out about "backseat bingo" in a sex education class. She joins three friends—Mel (Yvette Mimieux), Tuggle (Paula Prentiss), and Angie (Connie Francis)—for an Easter pilgrimage "to meet boys" in Fort Lauderdale.

When the girls arrive they quickly join in the ritual of the great American dating game. The four co-eds search for husbands, but the boys just want to separate the "girls from the Girl Scouts." Three girls remain chaste and win the men of their dreams. Only Mel takes the backseat bingo route. She allows herself to be seduced by several men and winds up in the hospital after a suicide attempt. The message was clear and the censors were pleased. The film ends with Merit and her new-found love (George Hamilton) strolling the beach, with "Where The Boys Are" playing in the background.

Most critics treated the MGM production as light-hearted entertainment. "This breezy comedy-romance about college kids on the loose in Florida presents a lot of new faces in an old-fashioned story that clearly feels only the scantiest obligation to make sense," wrote *Newsweek*. The picture did, however, probe the serious subjects of teenage alcoholism, sexual ethics, and even rape, if only in the form of a conventional morality tale. A writer in *America* noted the film's overly simplistic depiction of the contemporary dating system. "Its real trouble is that it is too realistic to be dismissed as a modern fairy tale," the reviewer said, "yet at the same time it is a dangerously romanticized and uncritical look at an alarming present-day phenomenon."[88]

The popularity of MGM's sandbox teenpic was not lost on other film companies. The beach provided an ideal setting for teenage exploitation films: a paradise of eternal summer, teenage antics, and bikini-clad bodies jiggling to rock music.

Get ready for the next beach blast . . .

Executives at American International Pictures had been quick to react to the growing teen market for films. Between 1954 and 1967 AIP produced more than one hundred and thirty low-budget features, grossing some $250 million. The company targeted the teen-age passion-pit crowd with such titles as *The Day the World Ended*, *It Conquered the World*, *The Undead*, *The Brain Eaters*, and *The Bucket of Blood*. Its classic *I Was a Teenage Werewolf* was filmed for under $125,000, grossed $2 million, and caused traffic jams at drive-in theaters. It was followed by *I Was a Teenage Frankenstein* and *Teenage Caveman*.

The success of AIP's teenage and topical *Dragstrip Girl* spawned *Reform School Girl*, *Sorority Girl*, and *Cat Girl*. The independent film company also produced a series of biblicals—*Goliath and the Barbarians*, *Goliath and the Dragon*, *Goliath and the Vampires*, and *Goliath and the Sins of Babylon*—along with eight Edgar Allan Poe pictures including *The House of Usher*, *The Pit and the Pendulum*, and *The Masque of the Red Death*. The time lag between conception and national release was a short four months.

In 1963, Sam Arkoff and James Nicholson teamed up with William Asher, a successful television director who won Emmys for *I Love Lucy* and the *Dinah Shore Show* to make movies about "the marvelous moment just after adolescence and just before facing responsibility," Asher said. "I wanted to deal with kids who take that moment and make it last as long as three years. After that, you become a bum," he added.[89] AIP began a series of beach party movies that *Newsweek* aptly described as "one long round of beach bunnies undulating to rock 'n' roll."[90] Nicholson, Arkoff, and Asher assembled a cinematic package that captured the fantasies and spirit of teenage culture in the early 1960s. The bikini movies were perfect fare for the drive-in theater crowd.

In all probability the film company's intent was to create cheap versions of *Where The Boys Are*. AIP transported the action from Fort Lauderdale to Malibu. The studio's beach films became the equivalent of a television series for the drive-in crowd, based on the MGM production as a pilot. "We take the same teenagers and put them into a slightly different experience in each picture," Asher explained. "The plot may change but the faces stay the same."[91] AIP produced ten sandpics beginning in the fall of 1963. The films ended with trailers advertising the next offering in the series, i.e., "Get ready for the next beach blast . . . *How to Stuff a Wild Bikini.*"

Where The Boys Are was filmed primarily in Hollywood studios, AIP cut costs by shooting their sand-and-surf features at a public beach. Scripts were usually used for one-third to one-half of the movie, with the rest filled by improvisation. The AIP series starred rock idol Frankie Avalon as "Frankie" and ex-Mouseketeer Annette Funicello as his girlfriend "Dee Dee." (Avalon's recording career had been launched when "Venus" rocketed to the top of the charts in 1959, the first of seven Top 10 singles for the Philadelphia singer that year.)

Avalon developed his acting career with roles in Alan Ladd's *Guns of the Timberland* and *The Alamo* with John Wayne. In 1962 he appeared in an AIP picture, *Panic in the Year Zero!*, and had worked with his manager, agent, and the screenwriter of *Panic* to develop the idea for the beach party films.[92] Funicello's success on the *The Mickey Mouse Club* (1955–59) led to parts in the Disney films *The Shaggy Dog* (1959) and *Babes in Toyland* (1961). She had also scored Top 10 hits with "Tall Paul" in 1959 and "O Dio Mio" the following year. Funicello remained under full contract to Walt Disney (who reportedly told her, "I don't mind you wearing a two-piece, but I would prefer you not showing the navel")[93] throughout her beach film career.

The beach films were a mixture of comedy, music, romance, and satire, resembling Mack Sennett's bathing-beauty silents and Keystone Kop classics. Though enormously popular, AIP's bikini pictures were characterized by their sameness; plots were formulaic and predictable. The stories were created for the passion-pit crowd, who were very likely too preoccupied with other matters to pay much attention to the screen anyway. What narrative there was generally revolved around a romantic mix-up. Frankie was smitten by some gorgeous body in a two-piece bathing suit. Dee Dee became jealous and contrived to win him back. The relationship between Frankie and Dee Dee epitomized young love. Circumstances in each film tested their faithfulness. In the inevitable happy ending, everyone found true love.

Frankie and Dee Dee were joined by a gang of beachniks with vigorous young bodies, few inhibitions, and even fewer brains. Among the regulars were Jody McCrea, John Ashley, Donna Loren, and Dolores Wells. The only cloud in the sky of Coppertone paradise was Eric Von Zipper (Harvey Lembeck) and his motorcycle gang, the Rats. Von Zipper, as a slapstick parody of Brando in *The Wild One*, provided much of the humor. The "carbon-monoxide commandos" were a black-leather-jacketed gang that acted like the Three Stooges. The bumbling bikers hung out at a pool hall and stood in stark opposition to the clean-cut, nonsmoking surfers.

There were plenty of opportunities in each film for Frankie, Dee Dee, and other members of the cast to break into songs, providing musical interludes in the inane plots. Guy Hemric and Jerry Styner composed most of the songs for the AIP pictures, Les Baxter was responsible for many of the scores, and Beach Boy Brian Wilson co-wrote several songs for *Muscle Beach Party* with Roger Christian and Gary Usher. (Wilson also appeared as a background player in that film, *Beach Party* and *How to Stuff a Wild Bikini*.)

Music Appeal

Though rock groups could enhance box office appeal, AIP seldom featured big-name musical acts in the bikini pics. Presumably this was to keep costs at a minimum. Two Motown acts, however, were spotlighted: *Muscle Beach Party* introduced Little Stevie Wonder, who also sang "Fingertips" in *Bikini Beach*; The Supremes sang the title song for *Dr. Goldfoot and the Bikini Machine*. Nancy Sinatra performed in *Ghost in the Invisible Bikini*. James Brown sang in *Ski Party*. Songs were also performed by a number of lesser groups, including Dick Dale and The Deltones, The Exciters, The Pyramids, The Hondells, and The Kingsmen.

A true movie soundtrack was never released with any AIP beach pic. Albums identified with the movies included a few songs from the film and other surfin' songs as filler. Several regulars in the AIP features released singles and/or LPs, none of which were successful. Annette Funicello recorded three albums featuring songs from AIP films—*Pajama Party*, *Beach Party*, and *Muscle Beach Party*—and a collection, *Annette Sings Golden Surfin' Hits*. Avalon also released a separate *Muscle Beach Party* LP. Donna Loren's *Beach Blanket Bingo* appeared on Capitol, with liner notes identifying the record with the film. Candy Johnson did an album with The Exciters, *The Candy Johnson Show at Bikini Beach,* on the local Canjo label.

Other film companies used rock groups more prominently than AIP. Jan and Dean scored a Top 20 hit with the theme song from Columbia's *Ride the Wild Surf.* Bruce Brown's critically acclaimed *Endless Summer* featured music by The Sandals. The Gentrys, The Toys, The Animals ("We Gotta Get Out of This Place"), and the Castaways all performed in Trans-American Pictures's *It's a Bikini World.* Paramount's *Beach Ball* was advertised as "A Beachload of bouncy tunes and talent!" The talent included The Four Seasons, The Hondells, The Righteous Brothers, and The Supremes singing the title song. *Girls on the Beach* (1965) featured music by The Beach Boys, The Crickets, and Lesley Gore. Surprisingly, though the Beach Boys popularized the image of California beaches as a surfing utopia, this was the only beach film in which the group was featured.

Beach Party Films 1961–1967

Movie	Film Company	Soundtrack
Beach Ball (1965)	Paramount	—
*Beach Blanket Bingo (1965)	AIP	Capitol
*Beach Party (1963)	AIP	Buena Vista
*Bikini Beach (1964)	AIP	Buena Vista
Dr. Goldfoot and the Bikini Machine (1965)	AIP	—
Dr. Goldfoot and the Girl Bombs (1966)	AIP	Tower
Endless Summer (1966)	Columbia	World Pacific
For Those Who Think Young (1964)	United Artists	—
Ghost in the Invisible Bikini (1966)	AIP	—
Girls on the Beach (1965)	Paramount	—
The Horror of Beach Party (1963)	20th Century Fox	—
*How to Stuff a Wild Bikini (1965)	AIP	Wand
It's a Bikini World (1967)	Trans. American Pictures	—
*Muscle Beach Party (1964)	AIP	Buena Vista
Pajama Party (1964)	AIP	Buena Vista
Ride the Wild Surf (1964)	Columbia	Liberty
Ski Party (1965)	AIP	—
Surf Party (1964)	Twentieth Century Fox	20th Century Fox
Where The Boys Are (1961)	MGM	—

*denotes films that featured Frankie and Dee Dee.

The bikini films were jam-packed with the latest fads, which offered some variety and excitement. "We never depend on one fad," explained Nicholson. "What we're really doing at American International," added Arkoff, "is stuffing bananas with bananas."[94] The teen crazes included surfing behind a speedboat, bodybuilding, drag racing, karate, Zen Buddhism, volleyball, and skydiving.

An endless list of guest stars and zany characters spiced up the formulaic plots. Bob Cummings was an anthropologist studying teenage sexual habits through a telescope in *Beach Party*. Linda Evans was featured as a budding singer named Sugar Kane in *Beach Blanket Bingo*; Paul Lynde acted the part of her enterprising manager. Don Rickles made his film debut in *Muscle Beach Party*.[95] He later appeared as the operator of a teenage hangout in *Bikini Beach* and as Big Drop, the owner of a skydiving school, in *Beach Blanket Bingo*. Candy Johnson, whose snappy hips could cause traffic accidents, appeared in several films as Miss Perpetual Motion. Buster Keaton can be seen in three films: The silent screen star played himself in *Beach Blanket Bingo*, a deranged Chief Rotten Eagle in *Pajama Party*, and the tipsy Tahitian witch doctor Bwana in *How to Stuff a Wild Bikini* (Elizabeth Montgomery made a one-shot appearance as Bwana's witch daughter.)

In *Pajama Party*, former Disney star Tommy Kirk played a Martian scout sent to check out the Earth as a possible invasion site. Kirk also starred with Deborah Walley in *Ghost in the Invisible Bikini*. The list goes on to include Mickey Rooney (as a promoter named Peachy Keane in *How to Stuff a Wild Bikini*), Boris Karloff, Buddy Hackett, Morey Amsterdam, Basil Rathbone, and Susan Hart.

In a new slant on the beach cycle, Norman Taurog directed a beach parody of the James Bond series, *Dr. Goldfoot and the Bikini Machine*. Vincent Price starred as Dr. Goldfoot, a mad scientist who planned to take over the world with a troupe of bikini-clad robots. In the sequel, *Dr. Goldfoot and the Girl Bombs*, Dr. Goldfoot undertook a scheme to ignite a war between the United States and the Soviet Union. Rock idol Fabian tried to foil the plot. Goldfoot's exploding girl robots tried to seduce NATO officers. The mad scientist "places the detonation device in their navels (!) so when a lusty general attempts to make love—kaboom!" quipped *The Motion Picture Guide*.[96]

AIP advertising lured the young audience with peek-a-boo promises on a grand scale: "BIKINI BEACH, WHERE BARE-AS-YOU-DARE IS THE RULE!" "WHAT HAPPENS WHEN 10,000 KIDS MEET ON 5,000 BEACH BLANKETS!" "WHEN 10,000 BICEPS GO AROUND 5,000 BIKINIS . . . YOU *KNOW* WHAT'S GONNA HAPPEN!" These tan-and-turf flicks had the goods, but never delivered anything beyond handholding or a kiss behind a surfboard. A *Times* reviewer noted of *Beach Party* that the film producers "kept the proceedings flat, contrived and neatly and serenely suggestive."[97] Echoing the moral of *Where The Boys Are*, Dee Dee's message to the girls in the audience was: "A girl needs a ring before she can swing."[98] "The key to these pictures is lots of flesh but no sex," explained the director. "It's all good clean fun. No hearts are broken and virginity prevails."[99] Asher never strayed from the rules. During the filming of *How to Stuff a Wild Bikini*, Funicello was pregnant and totally covered. To make up for her, four *Playboy* playmates appeared as beach girls. As Ehrenstein and Reed correctly observed, "the constant display of nubile flesh twisting and frugging to the big rock beat more than compensates for the erotic constraints of the script."[100]

Critics complained about AIP's lowbrow, low-budget productions, calling them "pure, dull junk" and "horrible juvenile comedy." Reviews were of little concern to AIP cinemologists, who stayed tuned to reports on teen fads received from twenty-eight offices in the United States. Arkoff concluded that teenagers wanted "pure escapism, a never-never land without parents, without adults, without authorities. Kids get lectures from their parents all the time. They don't want to hear them from us."[101] Consequently, the serious issues of predecessor *Where The Boys Are* were completely absent in AIP pics. Societal fears about juvenile delinquency aroused by youth-oriented Fifties' biker films were doused by Von Zipper's gang. Rock music became a harmless soundtrack for innocent teenage frolicking in the sun or handholding on the beach beneath the starry sky at night.

The AIP chairman knew how important teenagers were at the box office. From a decade of research into the teen market, AIP developed a marketing strategy called the "Peter Pan Syndrome:"

1. A younger child will watch anything that an older one will watch.
2. An older child will not watch anything a younger child will watch.
3. A girl will watch anything a boy will watch.
4. A boy will not watch anything a girl will watch.
5. In order to catch your greatest audience, you zero in on a nineteen-year-old male.[102]

In 1965, the U.S. Bureau of Census reported that half of the nation's population was under twenty-five. An AIP sales director said, "We'd like to make nice family pictures, but we're in this for the money. If the kids think it's a good picture and the adults don't, that's all right. Seventy-five percent of the drive-in audiences are under 25, and 70 percent of our gross comes from drive-in theaters. God bless the whole 5,000 of them."[103]

The sand-and-sex pictures were both loved and ridiculed, but most of all they were box office bonanzas for AIP. Most were produced for under $200,000 and several grossed more than $2 million.

By 1965, AIP's phenomenal commercial success attracted both publicity and competition. Film companies that previously ridiculed bikini beach productions now flooded the market with beach pictures modeled after the AIP offerings. "Teenage tastes are exerting a tyranny over our industry," complained one film studio executive in 1965. "It's getting so show business is just one big puberty rite."[104] Twentieth Century-Fox combined a typical AIP double feature into one movie, *The Horror of Beach Party* (1963), hailed as "the first horror monster musical." The next year *Surf Party* starred Bobby Vinton. Paramount climbed on the bandwagon with *Beach Ball*, starring Ed "Kookie" Brynes and Chris Noel, in 1964, and *Girls on the Beach* the following year. Trans American Pictures entered the game late with *It's a Bikini World* in 1967. The film starred Tommy Kirk and Deborah Walley.

Arkoff lamented that all the publicity his film studio received was costing the company money. Production people, he said, "have read so much about how much money American International Pictures is making that they've started asking for higher salaries." Nicholson echoed the same concern. "The success of our whole operation depends on our ability to bring in pictures on modest budgets," he said. That's become almost impossible now." AIP spent more than $1 million on *Doctor Goldfoot and the Bikini Machine*, with little to show for it at the box office. "The bikini beach cycle has had it," Arkoff admitted in 1965. "We've had some real bombs lately."[105]

(The beach genre was revived in the 1980s with *Gidget's Summer Reunion*, *The Beach Girls*, and Alan Carr's remake of *Where The Boys Are*. Carr offered Connie Francis a part in the 1984 remake, but she refused after reading the script. In 1987, Frankie Avalon and Annette Funicello starred in a $9-million Paramount production, *Back to the Beach*. Frankie and Dee Dee finally went all the way; now they are married with kids and living in Ohio.)

The sand-and-surf cycle reflected the youthful innocence and bouyant optimism of the early 1960s, before political assassinations and draft calls for the Vietnam War. The beach films also caught a wave in the teen market during a period of low inventiveness in the recording industry. The induction of Elvis into the Army, the payola scandals, and the deaths of several rock artists (in what singer Don McLean later dubbed "the day the music died'' in his hit ''American Pie'') had taken their toll. The Beach Boys had surfaced during this musical void with what Jim Miller labeled ''their own variant on the American Dream, painting a dazzling picture of beaches, parties and endless summers, a paradise of escape into private as often as shared pleasures . . . it was the suburban myth transported to the Pacific Ocean, but rendered heroic.''[106] The saga of Frankie and Dee Dee thrived in that atmosphere, but it was not to last forever. The appearance of The Beatles on Ed Sullivan's show in February 1964 proved a watershed moment in rock music history. The beach pics succombed to the British Invasion. In *Bikini Beach*, Frankie portrayed an English singer named Potato Bug. A sorority trying to raise money falsely assumed they'd booked The Beatles for a fundraising concert in Paramount's *Girls on the Beach*. The Beach Boys substituted.

The importance of the beach party series should not be underestimated. The characters, content, and zany antics of the beach films established patterns for the teen offerings that followed, including George Lucas's *American Grafitti*. By the mid-1960s, however, the sandbox features had run aground while the Beatles took rock music and teen exploitation films in a new direction.

Notes

1. Liner Notes, *Rock All Night*, Mercury Records Mc 20293.
2. ''Neal,'' ''Rock All Night,'' *Variety*, 1 May 1957.
3. John Blair, a maven and collector, dissents: ''The music was secondary to the plot.'' ''A Focus on Carnival Rock,'' *Goldmine*, December 1980, 170.
4. This entire discussion of *Rock, Baby, Rock It* is based on John Blair's ''Rock and Roll Cinema: A Focus on 'Rock, Baby, Rock It','' *Goldmine*, October 1979, 9. The film escaped the attention of the trades and folded in a matter of days. Blair's invaluable account unfortunately lacks the niceties of identifying the actors. The authors, with the aid of some secondary information, have *assumed* protagonists Bob and Marilyn are played by Johnny Dobbs and Linda Wheeler. The antagonist, ''Crackers'' Louie, the mob figure, remains a mystery.
5. Ibid; Nash and Ross, 2650.
6. Fred Bronson, *The Billboard Book of Number One Hits* (New York: Billboard Publications, Inc. 1988), 22.
7. Roxon, 61.
8. ''Bernardine,'' *Variety*, 20 July 1957.
9. H.H. Thompson, ''Bernardine,'' *New York Times*, 25 July 1957, 28.
10. Bronson, 22.
11. ''And Pat Boone Sings,'' *Newsweek*, 5 August 1957, 94; Thompson, 28.
12. '' 'Delinquent' With A Song,'' *Newsweek*, 2 December 1957, 91; Thompson, 28.

13. H.H. Thompson, "April Love," *New York Times*, 28 November 1957, 57.
14. "Mardi Gras," *Variety*, 19 November 1958, 6.
15. Boone's role in the evolution of popularized rock in the mid-1950s is entirely beyond the scope of this volume. It should be noted, however, that even on a cursory level the preppish singer was a force in the mechanics of the new sound. He was overshadowed by Elvis, quite rightly, but he does deserve a better historical fate than that proffered as of this writing.
16. "Carnival Rock," *Variety*, 25 1957, Nash and Ross, 362.
17. John Blair, "A Focus on Carnival Rock," *Goldmine*, December 1980, 170–71.
18. Quoted in Michael Shore with Dick Clark, *The History of American Bandstand* (New York: Ballatine Books 1985), 17.
19. Quoted in John Blair, "Early Rock Cinema 1956–1960," *Goldmine*, September 1979, 10A.
20. June Bundy, "Freed Replies to R&B Press Slurs," *Billboard*, 28 April 1956, 19, 22.
21. "Mr. Rock and Roll," *Variety*, 23 October 1957.
22. Richard W. Nason, "Mr. Rock and Roll," *New York Times*, 17 October 1957, 42.
23. Nason, 42. Nash and Ross, "Mr. Rock and Roll," 1989.
24. "Rockabilly Baby," *Variety*, 23 October 1957.
25. Nash and Ross, 1455.
26. Quoted in Nick Tosches, *Hellfire: The Jerry Lee Lewis Story* (New York: Dell Books 1983): 33–34; and Myra Lewis with Murray Silver, *Great Balls of Fire: The Uncensored Story of Jerry Lee Lewis* (New York: Quill 1982), 112.
27. "Jamboree," *Variety*, 12 November 1957.
28. "Alan Freed's Big Beat Rocking New York Paramount to Whammo 1850 Gross," *Variety*, 1 January 1958, 1, 47.
29. Alan Freed, "One things for sure, rock 'n' roll is boffo B.O.," *Variety*, 8 January 1958, 214.
30. Howard Thompson, "Sing, Boy, Sing," *New York Times*, 22 February 1958, 9.
31. "Why, It's E...s P.....y!" *Time*, 3 February 1958, 87; Thompson; and "Sing, Boy, Sing," *Variety*, 15 January 1958.
32. "Sing" *Variety*; Thompson; Nash and Ross: 2934–35.
33. "Howard Cook 'Sing, Boy, Sing' Tommy Sands Does," *Billboard*, 24 February 1958, 7.
34. Doherty: 48–49.
35. "The Big Beat," *Variety*, 5 February 1958.
36. "Let's Rock," *Variety* 7 May 1958.
37. John S. Wilson, "What Makes 'Pop' Music Popular," *New York Magazine*, 8 December 1957, 28; also see R. Serge Denisoff "Psychographics and MTV: An Interview with Marshall Cohen," *Popular Music & Society*, Fall 1987, 33.
38. Schicke: 149–51.
39. Quoted in Myra Lewis with Murray Silver, *Great Balls of Fire: The Uncensored Story of Jerry Lee Lewis* (New York: Quill 1982): 148.
40. Nick Tosches: 145–46.
41. "Stay Away, Freed," *Variety*, 7 May 1958, 58.
42. "Background on Boston," *Variety*, 7 May 1958, 58.
43. *Great Balls of Fire*, 151–52.

44. "Boston Common to Hoot Mon Belt They Rock 'n' Riot Out of This Velt," *Variety*, 7 May 1958, 58.
45. Ibid.
46. "Hub DA to Freed: Better Show Up; D.J.'s 'VIP Atty.'," *Variety*, 14 May 1958, 46.
47. "The Pied Piper Muted," *Variety*, 14 May 1958, 2.
48. Ibid.
49. Ibid, 180.
50. Ibid, 180.
51. Robert Pielke, *You Say You Want A Revolution: Rock Music in American Culture* (Chicago: Nelson-Hall 1986), 99.
52. This description is from a *Big Beat* show, and fits the opening scene to a tee. Gertrude Samuels, "Why They Rock 'n' Roll—And Should They?" *New York Times Magazine*, 12 June 1958, 18.
53. Danny Peary, *Cult Movies 2* (New York: Dell Publishing 1983), 71.
54. Howard Thompson, "High School Confidential," *New York Times*, 31 May 1958, 6; "High School Confidential," *Variety*, 28 May 1958.
55. Thompson, 6.
56. "Hot Rod Gang," *Variety*, 22 August 1958.
57. Quoted in Mildred Hall, "Songwriters Blast BMI Before Senate Hearing," *Billboard*, 17 March 1958, 9.
58. Quoted in "Delinquency R & R, Deejays Get Into Act," *Billboard*, 17 March 1958, 6, 9.
59. Quoted in Mildred Hall, " 'Payola' Hit at BMI Inquiry: Chairman Calls for Proof," *Billboard*, 24 March 1958, 2, 12.
60. "Jocks, Publishers Hit 'Payola' Charge," *Billboard*, 24 March 1958, 2, 8.
61. Quoted in "Celler Sounds Off at ASCAP Dinner," *Billboard*, 7 April 1958, 10; and Abel Green, "Celler Blasts BMI at ASCAP Dinner Where Web Execs Are Honor Guests," *Variety*, 9 April 1958, 97.
62. Quoted in "Imperial's Chudd Smacks Smathers Bill, ASCAP: Bevy of Others on Stand in D.C. to Voice Pro-BMI Sentiment," *Variety*, 7 May 1958, 55–56.
63. *Rolling Stone Rock Almanac*, 43.
64. Bosley Crowther, "Jazz on a Summer Day," *New York Times*, 29 May 1960, 46.
65. "Jukebox Rhythm," *Variety*, 25 March 1959.
66. Nash and Ross, 543.
67. "Girls Town," *Variety*, 25 September 1959.
68. Roxon: 175. Quoted in Ren Grevatt, "On The Beat," *Billboard*, 10 November 1958, 6.
69. Quoted in Arnold Shaw, *Rockin' '50s* (New York: Hawthorn Books 1974), 256.
70. Philip T. Hartung, "The Screen: It's So Beautiful in the Country," *Commonweal*, 4 December 1959, 289.
71. Stanley Kauffmann, "Black Orpheus, White Nimrod," *New Republic*, 4 January 1960, 21.
72. "Hound Dog Man," *Variety*, 4 November 1959; Hartung, 290; Arthur Knight, "Of Boats, Boys and Bedrooms," *Saturday Review*, 21 November 1959, 37; and Howard Thompson, "Hound Dog Man," *New York Times*, 28 April 1960, 29.

73. Knight, 37; *Variety*, "Hound Dog."
74. Roxon, 176.
75. "Instant Fad," *Time* 20 October 1961, 54.
76. Quoted in "Der Liszt Tvist," *Time*, 16 February 1962, 28.
77. Marshall Fishwick, "The Twist: Brave New World," *Saturday Review*, 3 March 1962, 8.
78. Quoted in "The Sacrolili-act," *Newsweek*, 4 November 1961, 80.
79. Ibid.
80. *The Motion Picture Guide*, Vol. 2 Jay R. Nash and Stanley R. Ross, eds., (Chicago: Cinebooks, Inc., 1985), 3582.
81. *Variety*, 11 April 1962, 26.
82. *Variety*, 27 December 1961, 6.
83. Quoted in "Fastest, Firstest in Scramble of 'Twist' Features," *Variety*, 29 November 1961, 1.
84. Howard Thompson, " 'The Errand Boy' and 'Hey, Let's Twist' on Neighborhood Bill," *New York Times*, 8 February 1962, 25.
85. "Beer & the Beach," *Time*, 13 April 1959, 54.
86. David Ehrenstein and Bill Reed, *Rock On Film* (New York: Deliah Books 1982), 48.
87. "The New Comedies," *Time*, 20 January 1961, 72.
88. "The Faces Are Fresh," *Newsweek*, 23 January 1961, 84; Review of 'Where The Boys Are,' *America*, 4 February 1961, 605.
89. Quoted in Alan Levy, "Peekaboo Sex, or How To Fill a Drive-in," *Life*, 16 July 1965, 85.
90. "Z as in Zzzz, or Zowie," *Newsweek*, 5 May 1967, 61.
91. Quoted in Peter Bart, "Hollywood Beach Bonanza," *New York Times*, 13 December 1964, sec. 2, 9.
92. Fred Bronson, *The Billboard Book of Number One Hits*, rev. ed. (New York: Billboard Publications 1988), 62.
93. Quoted in Rob Burt, *Surf City Drag City* (New York: Blandford Press 1986), 94.
94. Quoted in Alan Levy, 83.
95. Of note, Peter Lorre made a final unbilled film appearance in *Muscle Beach Party*. The closing credits announced, "The producers extend special thanks to Mr. Peter Lorre for his contribution to this film as 'Mr. Strangdour.' Soon to be seen in BIKINI BEACH." Lorre died before the next film went into production.
96. Nash and Ross, *The Motion Picture Guide* (Chicago: Cinebooks 1985), 2, 675.
97. "Screen: 'Beach Party,' *New York Times*, 26 September 1963, 40.
98. Alan Levy, 83.
99. Quoted in Peter Bart, 25.
100. Ehrenstein and Reed, 50.
101. Quoted in "Z as in Zzzz, or Zowie," 61.
102. Quoted in Alan Levy, 82.
103. Quoted in "Z as in Zzzz, or Zowie," 61.
104. Quoted in Peter Bart, "Hollywood Finds Gold on Beaches," *New York Times*, 22 June 1965, 25.

105. Quoted in "Film Company Seeks a New Locale for Its Teen-Age Movies," *New York Times*, 6 November 1965, 18.
106. Jim Miller, "The Beach Boys," in *The Rolling Stone Illustrated History of Rock & Roll*, ed. Jim Miller (New York: A Random House/Rolling Stone Press Book, 1976, 1980), 162.

3

Help! I Need Somebody

The fact remains that A Hard Days Night *has turned out to be the* Citizen Kane *of juke box musicals.* . . .
—Andrew Sarris, *Village Voice*

A man went looking for America.
And couldn't find it anywhere.
—Advertisements for *Easy Rider*

. . . American Graffiti *became the boom generation's* Roots *and one of the biggest money-makers of all time. Combining rock with the movies was the consummate baby-boom ploy.*
—Landon Y. Jones, *Great Expectations*

During the 1960s, movie attendance continued to drop severely, but a small number of movies attracted larger numbers at the box office than ever before. With higher ticket prices, that meant larger profits for these films. Hollywood studios began investing enormous sums of money into single productions, joining established formulas with proven draws, hoping for a box office bonanza. The collapse of the vertically integrated studio system put producers in a position of high risk on any one production; the financial stability of the studios often rested on the success or flop of one multi-million dollar picture, as a continuous decline in revenues weakened motion picture studios. A number of film studios—Paramount, Warner Brothers, United Artists, Universal—were easily acquired by large conglomerates.

Conservative Hollywood continued its attempts to reach a mass audience, but increasingly fewer films were successful. The postwar Baby

Boom generation, the first of whom reached the college years during the Sixties, was a huge untapped audience for movies. The first generation of "TV babies" was a young audience already familiar with visual media. As Robert Sklar asserted, "The challenge to Hollywood was to come up with offerings of its own to please this potential new audience."[1] The problem was that most filmmakers were too old to understand the new sensibilities of the young and too conservative to change their marketing philosophies. Rock music was simply noise to most Hollywood executives. Throughout the decade, film and record companies both continued to operate on the assumption that soundtracks would not sell. The Beatles would demonstrate otherwise.

When United Artists executive George "Bud" Orenstein first approached film producer Walter Shenson in 1963 about producing a film with The Beatles, Shenson asked, "Who are The Beatles?" The producer agreed to make the movie on the condition that he could make "a comedy, not a popular musical."[2] In October of that year Beatles manager Brian Epstein met with Orenstein and Shenson. Epstein was easily induced by the prospect of his group following Elvis into the movies. During the negotiations, he clearly underestimated The Beatles' potential as a pop music phenomenon. Unaware that UA was willing to go as high as 25 percent, Epstein inked a deal for 25,000 British pounds and 7.5 percent of the film's profits. The three-picture contract included a clause reverting all rights to the movie back to Shenson after fifteen years.

The film company was more than happy with the arrangement. As Beatle biographers Peter Brown and Steven Gaines noted, "UA was less interested in making the movie than they were in releasing the soundtrack album; even if the movie was a flop, United Artists would almost certainly make a profit from record sales."[3] EMI and Capitol, the Beatles' record distributors, neglected to include soundtrack rights in the original contract negotiated with Epstein. In an unprecedented twist, United Artists employed the film to sell records. This was a lesson that would not be lost in the future by record companies such as MCA, RSO, and others with film studio connections.

The impact of The Beatles on the international pop music scene in the mid-1960s was staggering. On 1 February 1964, the quartet's first U.S. single reached the top of *Billboard*'s Hot 100 and stayed there for seven weeks. "I Want to Hold Your Hand" remains the largest-selling British single of all time, with international sales around fifteen million. Next to Bill Haley's revolutionary "(We're Gonna) Rock Around the Clock," Fred Bronson considered "I Want to Hold Your Hand" as "the most significant single of the rock era, permanently changing the course of music."[4] In an unprecedented feat, the Beatles held down the top five positions on the *Billboard* Hot 100 on March 31. Sales of the British group's singles grossed $17.5 million. In a six-month period ending June 1964, The Beatles placed an incredible twenty songs on the U.S. charts. As The Beatles were international stars, Epstein could have renegotiated their contract with United Artists, but, ever the British gentleman, he stood by his agreement.

Richard Lester Meets The Beatles

Prior to *A Hard Day's Night*, British pop stars Cliff Richards, Tommy Steele, and Billy Fury competed for the title of the "British Elvis" with cheap exploitation flicks. To add U.S. appeal, American performers such as Gene Vincent, Ray Charles, and Jerry Lee Lewis were usually included in these films. The Beatles were adamant that they did not want to make a cheap, moronic rock musical. "We won't do a rags-to-riches story," they maintained. "Nor the one about the record being smuggled into the studio in the last reel and put on by mistake and . . . ," another added. "Yeah, we've seen that one," they all concurred.[5] Under the direction of Richard Lester, both *A Hard Day's Night* and *Help!* became more than showcase films for a rock group.

Lester was a successful U.S. television director with CBS when he settled in England to work in live television and commercials. He became known for a 1959 Peter Sellers short, *The Running, Jumping and Standing Still Film*. Lester directed, edited, scored, and acted in the film. The Sellers picture, which was made for seventy pounds with a 16mm camera, garnered Lester an Oscar nomination.

Producer Milton Subotsky had seen Lester's debut film and his thirty-minute pilot, *Have Jazz, Will Travel*, that included modern jazz music. Subotsky, in the habit of giving new directors a break, hired Lester as director/producer of *It's Trad, Dad!* (1962), a jazz imitation of the 1950s teenpics. Subotsky wrote the screenplay, which *Variety* termed "as slim as a chorine's waist."[6] Craig Douglas and British teen vocalist Helen Shapiro starred as two teenagers frustrated by their small town's negative reaction to their jazz activities. When the town mayor revokes a cafe's license for having a jukebox, the young people fight back. They enlist the aid of some top disc jockeys to help them stage a jazz festival. The host of Dixieland bands and singers featured included Mr. Acker Bilk and His Paramount Jazz Band, Kenny Ball and His Jazzmen, Bob Wallis and His Storyville Jazzmen, and Terry Lightfoot and His New Orleans Jazz Band. Americans Chubby Checker, Gary "U.S." Bonds, and Gene Vincent made special appearances.

The difficulty for Lester was how to cram twenty-six songs in the film's hour-and-fifteen-minute length. He accomplished this by having several cameras simultaneously capture each musical number from different angles. Shooting was completed in three weeks with production costs at 50,000 pounds. A Twist dance scene was shot in New York at the director's own expense. Columbia released a soundtrack album.

The film achieved critical success. The *London Times* noted "Lester's immoderate interest in technical tricks—speeded-up action, multiple exposures, eccentric angles, tricky masking and so on," but concluded that "it is all done with such frank enjoyment and at such a determined pace that criticism is disarmed."[7] *Variety* saw the Columbia Pictures production for what it was, "a single showcase for introducing a parade of pop performers." Lester's slick directorial technique, however, could not be overlooked.

> Most interesting aspect of this bright little film is the direction of Dick Lester, a comparative newcomer to the feature film scene. He has worked out some witty and unexpected camera angles . . . And he keeps the screen alive through pace and shrewd cutting by Bill Lenny.[8]

It's Trad, Dad! (aka *Ring-A-Ding Rhythm*) is clearly a period piece set in the British pop music scene of the early 1960s. The film revealed Lester's cynicism about the pop music business and his disenchantment with stardom. He was also preoccupied with the brewing generational conflict and the exploitation of youth, especially by the media. These same themes, and Lester's cinematic techniques, would be used again in the Beatle productions.

Lester's surrealist humor and ability to film musical numbers made him Shenson's choice as director of *A Hard Day's Night*. The two had already worked together on *The Mouse on the Moon* (1963) for United Artists. The Beatles' EMI producer, George Martin, was an obvious choice to score the quartet's first feature film. Epstein suggested Alun Owens as scriptwriter. Owens, who had written several TV dramas . . . (most notably a British television film *No Trains to Lime Street*) was Liverpudlian himself and had an ear for the accent. He traveled with the Beatles for several days before writing the script. Shenson and Owens agreed on several rules for the script:

> There must be no romance. . . . No Beatle must go unrecognized in the story, because it is impossible in real life here and would immediately strike the fans as absurd. Each Beatle must have a solo scene, partly because the fans have

their favorites but also because Shenson wants to make use of the fact that the four have clearly defined personalities.[9]

Under Lester's direction, the first two Beatle films captured the atmosphere of "Swingin' London" and the burgeoning youth revolution. In the early 1960s, Britain was marked by political and economic turmoil. The Profumo scandal in 1963 had tarnished the image of the power structure. In the general election the following year, the thirteen-year reign of the Conservative Party was replaced by the Labour government of Harold Wilson, who promised that a technological revolution would transform British society. The Wilson Era is remembered, however, as a period of frivolity and extravagance while the country teetered on the edge of economic ruin.[10]

Against that background, the British youth culture thrived in the early Sixties. Swingin' London, as the press tagged it, was a kind of working-class laugh at the aristocracy—antipathetic to anything remotely conventional. A modest background was revered. Sex was "free" and talked about openly. Scandalous miniskirts and long hair for men (attributed to the Beatles) were the fashion rage. Pop Art and Op Art were celebrated. Richard Lester's mid-Sixties' films, Neil Sinyard wrote, "came in on the wave of that mood, expressing the cockiness and confidence of a new generation that was no longer intimidated by class and no longer awed by society's symbols of authority and power."[11]

It's Been a Hard Days Night

Production of their first full-length feature film began just two weeks after the Beatles' successful U.S. appearance on "The Ed Sullivan Show" in February 1964. Shooting was completed in six weeks, just in time for The Beatles to depart for a tour of Europe and the Far East. Shenson brought the film in for $560,000, although United Artists had been willing to double the production budget, in light of the Beatles' explosive popularity following their U.S. trip.

The film was shot on location in England amid hysterical crowds that often delayed production. The final television-special scene was shot at the Scala Theater in Soho before a live audience that screamed at the mere sight of a Beatle. Though being under the same roof as The Beatles was enough, these overexcited extras were paid $11 a day and given a free lunch. To avoid mobs, Shenson hired a train for a week to film in during its daily run from 8 a.m. to 6 p.m. through rural England. British Railways reluctantly allowed the producer to use a minor London station on a

Sunday morning for one scene. "They've had enough trouble with Beatle crowds in real life," Shenson said.[12]

On one occasion, Lester just let the cameras roll when a mob of girls converged on The Beatles' limousine at the end of a day of shooting. The scene, which occurs after The Beatles are in the train station, was edited and put in the picture. A close look reveals that The Beatles are wearing one set of clothes on the train and another set in the car. For the playing-field scene Lester explained that he

> wanted that sequence to contrast with the claustrophobic feeling you get in all those trains, hotels, studios, cars. We taught the boys three games, told them to go ahead and play them any way they liked. Then we shot the scene from different angles—a helicopter one day, varied distances the next.[13]

Lester made silent film techniques into Sixties Pop Art. Film analyst Robert B. Ray noted that the director "seemed to have worked out a perfect commercial synthesis of all the new formal elements in recent European films: *cinema-verite*, jump cutting, hand-held cameras, delirious tracking shots, rapid kaleidoscopic editing."[14] Lester's visual style was perfect for rock music; his influence can still be seen in today's videos. *A Hard Day's Night* and *Help!* are direct ancestors of today's music videos.

In semidocumentary style, the camera merely follows The Beatles around during a thirty-six-hour, behind-the-scenes adventure in *A Hard Day's Night*. The film was originally titled *Beatlemania*, but was later changed to a favorite Ringo phrase. Owen's script is filled with witty remarks, funny antics, disguises, mistaken identities, and comedic situations that made The Beatles look like modern Marx Brothers. Actually, Shenson thought he was in a Marx Brothers picture when he first met The Beatles. "They have a marvelous quality of disrespect," he said.[15]

Shot in black and white, the film begins with the familiar opening chords of "A Hard Day's Night." The Beatles run for their lives from a frenzied crowd of mostly female fans. The foursome escape on a train bound for London, where they are to do a live television show. Backstage scenes, rehearsals, and the final show provide ample opportunities for The Beatles to perform. Musical numbers were brilliantly worked into the story to enhance and carry the plot forward.

In the film, Lester used Beatlemania as a thematic framework for his critique of British society in the early 1960s. Four working-class youth are suddenly catapulted to fame and fortune not for their pursuit of art, literature or science, but for singing rock'n'roll—yeah, yeah, yeah. The director expressed this theme by unveiling the response from different quarters of British society to the Beatles as a popular culture phenomenon.

The hysteria of Beatlemania is shown from the perspective of the Beatles. "The film was based on their life living in small boxes, as prisoners of their own success," Lester explained. The concept came from Lennon's description of a trip the Beatles made to Stockholm: "You get off the plane, they push you into a car, you're delivered to a hotel, have cocktails and those godawful cheese sandwiches, get into another car, drive to your performance, then back to the airport, fly home." The director said, "That became our signal of how to do *A Hard Day's Night.*"[16]

The Beatles' fame prevents them from leading normal lives. Road manager Norm (Norman Rossington) acts like a teacher, making the "boys" stay in to answer fan mail as though it were a homework assignment. When they skip out and go to a dance club, Norm and his assistant Shake (John Junkin) round them up like disobedient children and send them back to their hotel rooms. Advances toward women are frustrated by the confines of stardom or the relentless manager. On the train, The Beatles play "I Should Have Known Better" in a cage surrounded by adoring fans, metaphorically imprisoned by their own popularity. A writer in *Newsweek* later described the portrayal of the Beatles "not as triumphant superstars but as ironic kids trapped in their huge success and scheming to escape like four musketeers trying to evade the cardinal's evil cohorts."[17]

Several scenes demonstrate the conflicts among classes and generations, and the new confidence of the youth revolution. A rather impolite British gentleman reading the *Financial Times* on the train is disturbed by the music George Harrison is listening to. He reaches over and turns off the tape player, arguing for his rights. "We have rights, too," the brazen Beatles assert. "I fought the war for your sort," the man says. A Beatle retorts, "Bet you're sorry you won." Ironically, The Beatles' success gave the British economy a needed shot in the arm.

At a press conference, reporters eat their fill while The Beatles cannot get a hold of a bite—a clever metaphor for the press feeding off The Beatles as news. The Beatles score a verbal victory over the condescention of the press; their satirical style was strongly reminiscent of the Marx Brothers. "How did you find America?" a reporter asks. John Lennon answers, "Turn left at Greenland." Ringo is asked if he is "a Mod or a Rocker?" "I'm a mocker," he replies. "What would you call that hairstyle you're wearing?" "Arthur," Harrison says. The foursome sneak out of the room, the press totally unaware.

In a moment of mistaken identity, Harrison is ushered into the office of a clothing designer named Simon (Kenneth Haigh). Simon, constantly on the look for youthful fashion trends to exploit, co-opts the young's vocabulary, turning words into sales tools. His encounter with Harrison reveals his contempt for the youth culture by which he profits. Harrison confounds the designer. "You don't think he's a new phenomenon do you?" Simon asks, unaware that Harrison is a Beatle. His secretary puts it in marketing terms: "You mean an early clue to a new direction?"

In one of the most memorable scenes from the movie, The Beatles escape from their hotel and romp around, playing games in an open field. "Can't Buy Me Love" plays in the background. The youthful frivolity and fresh air of the field stand in sharp contrast to the enclosed world of trains, cars, stuffy hotel rooms, and TV studio tunnels. Up until this point, life has been a mad dash, but this scene is an exhilarating burst of energy. As the song ends, an adult authority figure, with hands on his hips, says, "I suppose you know this is private property." Harrison's satirical response is, "Sorry we hurt your field, Mister." "The irony is that the status of the Beatles as *public* property is the thing that has driven them into this field," Sinyard noted. "In the full context of Lester's sixties' films, it is an ominous moment."[18]

The turning point comes when Paul's mischievous, but "very clean," grandfather (Wilfred Brambell) convinces Ringo that he is being taken advantage of and not living life. Ringo abandons the group, leaving the studio just before their final rehearsal for the show. With only about an hour before showtime, the television director (Victor Spinetti) is frantic. The Beatle drummer goes parading through the streets (in disguise of course), photographing everything. Wandering around, accompanied by the instrumental "Ringo's Theme (This Boy)," Ringo meets a young boy who gives him a lecture on the importance of loyalty to friends.

"Real" life does not work out very well for the prodigal Beatle. He gets arrested as a "nasty troublemaker." At the jail he meets Paul's grandfather (who is "a trouble maker and a mixer"), hauled in for his own good when he gets mobbed peddling fake autographed Beatle stills. The cynical old man escapes to inform the other Beatles of the lost drummer's whereabouts. Ringo is rescued in a high-speed, Keystone-Kop chase scene with the British police. Eventually, The Beatles play several songs on stage before an audience of screaming girls. Immediately after the show, the Beatle entourage boards a helicopter. In a touch reminiscent of Fellini, they fly off, with grandpa's pictures of The Beatles floating down from the aircraft.

Because another cheap exploitation musical had been expected, the spontaneity and wit of *A Hard Day's Night* caught everyone by surprise. As writer Greil Marcus noted, "The film, probably more than their music, took the Beatles across social barriers, won them an audience among the intelligentsia, and broadened their hardcore base from teenage girls to rock and roll fans of every description."[19] Lester's and The Beatles' cynicism struck a chord with young viewers in the mid-Sixties. As film analyst Robert B. Ray observed, the Beatles "provided an ideal symbol for an American audience developing an ironic attitude toward an ideology it wished to retain."[20]

Critics praised the film. *Variety* raved about it. *Time* called it "one of the smoothest, freshest, funniest films ever made solely for the purposes of exploitation." "The legitimacy of the Beatles phenomenon is finally inescapable," wrote *Newsweek*. "With all the ill will in the world, one sits there, watching and listening—and feels one's intelligence dissolving in a pool of approbation and participation." Much to his own surprise, *Times* critic Bosley Crowther called it "a whale of a comedy." He wrote:

> It's a fine conglomeration of madcap clowning in the old Marx Brothers' style, and it is done with such a dazzling use of camera that it tickles the intellect and electrifies the nerves.
>
> This is the major distinction of this commercially sure-fire film: It is much more sophisticated in theme and technique than its seemingly frivolous subject matter promises.

In a spectacular review, *Village Voice* film critic Andrew Sarris called the film "the *Citizen Kane* of juke box musicals, the brilliant crystallization of such diverse cultural particles as the pop movie, rock'n'roll, cinema-verite, the nouvelle vague, free cinema, the affectedly hand-held camera, frenzied cutting, the cult of the sexless sub-adolescent, the semi-documentary and studied spontaneity."[21]

The film had an unprecedented global order of between 1,500 and 1,800 prints. Its royal premiere in England, in July 1964 at the Pavilion Theatre was attended by Princess Margaret and her husband, the Earl of Snowden. *A Hard Day's Night* opened in five hundred theaters in the U.S. in August 1964. In one week the film earned a colossal $1.3 million in U.S. box office rentals.

The roar of screaming in theaters rivaled that in live concert appearances. The Beatles' first U.S. tour, which included twenty-four cities, coincided with the opening of the film. (Their first visit, in February 1964, with appearances on "The Ed Sullivan Show" and concerts at the Washington Coliseum and Carnegie Hall, was really a publicity trip to promote U.S. single releases.)

By October 1964, *A Hard Days' Night* has grossed $5.8 million in U.S. rentals. The tour brought in another $1 million. The Beatles had sold ten million records, including three million-selling singles. Their British record company, EMI, announced a 12 percent sales increase. Their U.S. distributor, Capitol Records, reported a 17 percent increase. EMI chairman Joseph Lockwood cited "the outstanding success everywhere of the Beatles" as largely responsible for the rise in revenues.[22] It was estimated that the Beatles earned an unbelievable $56 million in one year, giving a boost to the flagging British economy.[23] The film eventually grossed more than $13.5 million; United Artists received $6,165,377 from domestic rentals. The picture received two Academy Award nominations, one for Owen's script and the other for Martin's musical direction.

The Beatles were responsible for many musical innovations in the mid-1960s. They lured adolescents away from Top 40 singles and introduced them to the viability and economy of albums. Each Beatle album was like a package of hit singles. It is no surprise that The Beatles created the bridge that made the union between the movie and record industries possible. Up until that time, soundtracks usually consisted of an expanded theme song and instrumental fillers. *A Hard Day's Night* and *Help!* changed that; both albums spawned multiple hit singles.

A Hard Day's Night's soundtrack was the first album composed of songs entirely by John Lennon and Paul McCartney. It became one of the fastest selling albums in the history of the recording industry. The soundtrack was released in July 1964 on EMI's Parlophone label in Britain and by United Artists in the U.S., with advance orders of 250,000 in Britain and one million in the United States. By October, it topped sales of one million in the U.S. and 600,000 in Britain. The soundtrack held down the Number 1 slot for fourteen weeks in the U.S. and twenty-one weeks in Britain.

The single "A Hard Day's Night" topped the charts and sold more than one million copies in both the U.S. (Capitol) and Britain (Parlophone). The film's title song earned The Beatles a Grammy Award for Best Performance by a Vocal Group. Capitol also released "And I Love Her," which reached Number 12, and "I'll Cry Instead," which peaked at Number 25.

Until *Sergeant Pepper's Lonely Hearts Club Band* appeared in 1967, different versions of Beatle albums were released in the United Kingdom and the United States. The British albums always contained more material than their American counterparts. The additional tracks from the U.K. versions were used to create interim American releases. The soundtrack from *A Hard Day's Night* followed this pattern. The British EMI-Parlophone LP included all of the new songs from the film along, with five titles written for the movie but not included in the soundtrack. United Artists, which had acquired the exclusive rights to the movie soundtrack in the

U.S. released only eight new numbers from the film, plus instrumental versions of Beatle songs arranged and orchestrated by producer George Martin.

Capitol, which owned non-movie Beatles rights, soon released *Something New* as "the third great Beatles album for Capitol." The liner notes made it clear that the album contained "five hit vocals from that movie, United Artists' *A Hard Day's Night*." Three of the additional cuts from the British version were also included, along with three filler tracks. *Something New* sold more than one million copies.

Help!

Help! was a Walter Shenson-Subafilms Production released through United Artists. Production began in the winter of 1965. Because of the remarkable success of their first outing, there were no budget constraints on The Beatles' second feature. Originally entitled *Eight Arms to Hold You*, this second film cost $1.5 million—triple the budget of *A Hard Day's Night*. It fared almost as well as The Beatles' first celluloid feature; domestic rentals brought United Artists more than $5.4 million.

The film was shot on location in London and Salzbury, Austria. Several scenes were filmed in the Bahamas as part of an attempt to establish a company there, as a shelter against high British taxes. "That was why we shot part of *Help!* in the Bahamas," Shenson said. "It was a goodwill exercise to persuade the Bahamian authorities we were an asset to their business community."[24]

By their own admission, The Beatles smoked marijuana constantly during the making of *Help!*. "They were high all the time we were shooting," Lester said. "But there was no harm in it then. It was a happy high."[25] Lester had control in this second feature. Lennon complained that the Beatles were "guest stars in their own film."

> *Help!* was a drag, because we didn't know what was happening. In fact Lester was a bit ahead of his time with the Batman thing, but we were on pot by then and all the best stuff is on the cutting-room floor, with us breaking up and falling all over the place.[26]

The Beatles were not at all pleased with Lester's second effort. They thought it had nothing to do with The Beatles and objected to their being presented as contemporary Marx Brothers, whose films they had to study in preparation for their roles in *Help!*.

Biographer Philip Norman rightly described *Help!* as "Swinging London personified—part music, part color supplement travelogue, part Pop-Art strip cartoon.[27] The plot again revolved around The Beatles' lives, this time elevated to the realm of fantasy. The Beatles appear as four charming lads. "Adoration hasn't gone to their heads one jolt," a neighborhood woman says as The Beatles enter a building through four separate doors that lead to one huge communal apartment.

The opening scene shows an Eastern religious cult preparing to make a sacrifice to the goddess Kali. Each day, a new victim must be chosen for Kali. The ceremony is interrupted when high-priest Clang (Leo McKern) discovers the female sacrifice is not wearing the sacrificial ring. "Where is the ring?" he asks. The camera cuts to the huge jewel on Ringo's hand as he plays the drums in the title track. Ringo had received the ring in a fan letter from an Eastern woman; with it stuck on his finger, his life is in jeopardy.

Trying to duplicate the success of The Beatles' first offering, screenwriters Marc Behm and Charles Wood penned a James Bond-type parody. Familiar Bondesque music accompanies a myriad of spy-like episodes involving trap doors, wild inventions, disguises, poison gas, flamethrowers, sci-fi weapons, and chase scenes. The Swamee Clang, his assistant, Ahme (Eleanor Bron), and their henchmen travel to London and conspire to retrieve the sacred ring. Several slapstick attempts are bungled, mostly because Ahme saves The Beatles. At one point she informs the audience, "I'm not what I seem." It can be assumed Ahme, whose sister was to be sacrificed that day, mailed the sacred band to Ringo.

The Beatles unsuccessfully consult an Oriental and then a jeweler, whose tools break trying to cut off the ring. They visit a scientist, Foot (Victor Spinetti), and his bumbling aide, Algernon (Roy Kinnear). Foot is amazed when his invention fails to change the molecular structure of the ring. He decides that with the ring he can rule the world. "If he can get a government grant," his assistant jokes.

The Beatles head to the Austrian Alps for safety; both the bloodthirsty Swami and the fiendish scientists follow in pursuit. Returning to London, they request that Scotland Yard provide protection during their recording session the next day. A play on The Beatles' fame begins: "So this is the famous Beatles," the superintendent says. "How long do you think you'll last?"

The recording session takes place in the middle of an open field near Stonehenge, with The Beatles surrounded by what appears to be the entire British army in camouflaged tanks. They perform "I Need You" and "The Night Before." Meanwhile, Clang and his cohorts tunnel beneath the field to plant explosives under the group. Ahme foils the scheme, but the explosion ignites a farcical battle. A hit on the tank carrying The Beatles is celebrated with *The 1812 Overture*. They escape to a "well known palace" (Buckingham Palace), but are assailed by the crazy scientists masquerading as palace guards.

The Beatles seek refuge in the Bahamas. The Eastern cult group follows in the Goodyear Blimp, the scientists in a specially equipped sail boat. Clang has the whole temple transported from the East for Ringo's sacrifice. The Beatles have a chance to escape on bicycles, but decide to "go back and get 'em," with a John Phillip Sousa-type version of "I'm Happy Just to Dance With You" in the soundtrack.

The Scotland Yard inspector concocts a "famous" plan to trap Clang's horde with the help of the Bahamian police. Meanwhile, Ringo is kidnapped by Foot, then escapes to be captured by Clang. As the Beatle drummer is about to be sacrificed on the beach in front of a statue of Kali, the ring slips off his finger. More comical fighting ensues with the title song ending the film. With typical Beatles humor, the film was "respectfully dedicated to the memory of Mrs. Elias Howe, who in 1846, invented the sewing machine."

Critics considered *Help!* inferior to The Beatles' first offering. The *Film Quarterly* called it "Plop art. . . . It's cotton candy, and in wide-screen Technicolor." *Newsweek* thought the foursome left something to be desired as actors, but noted the highly professional production, cinematography, and editing. *The New Yorker* applauded Lester's work, considering the movie not "such an effortless-seeming feat of spontaneous combustion as 'A Hard Day's Night,' it's still wonderful enough for all impractical purposes." *Variety* and the *Times* both gave it mild reviews, the latter calling it "90 crowded minutes of good, clean insanity." Sarris thought this second Beatles' offering was a "distinct disappointment" in comparison to the first, noting the weaker soundtrack as well as the failure of the James Bond parody and Marx Brothers' resemblance.[28]

As is often the case, audiences ignored the critics. The Beatles' enormous popularity overshadowed any artistic deficiency at the time. The *Time*'s critic reported receiving piles of letters from irate Beatlemanes for his less-than-rave review. He printed a number of responses, concluding, "How can a critic persist in protesting the limitations of the Beatles to their adoring fans?"[29]

Though the film still mirrored the "irreverence and uninhibitedness of youth," as one critic observed, it lacked "a satiric pattern or even a tangible theme."[30] *Help!* did not have the sarcastic edge, or thematic unity that held scenes together, of *A Hard Day's Night*. Still, there is evidence of Lester's critical vision. The movie is filled with derisive references to

Britain's national heritage, icons, and personalities. Mocking Wilson's technological revolution, British technology is shown throughout as inferior to that of other countries. British plugs fail to work; a car won't start. When an English revolver won't fire, the scientist mumbles, "If I had a Luger." Much of the keen social wit of *A Hard Day's Night*, however, was replaced with a bizarre plot and slapstick comedy in *Help!*. Also, while The Beatles' first outing spotlighted thirteen songs (with some repeated), *Help!* featured only six.

"Help!" was released as a single and entered *Billboard*'s Hot 100 on 7 August 1965, just two weeks before the film opened in New York. The single became the Beatles' ninth Number 1 hit in America, topping the chart on September 4. Earlier, "Ticket to Ride" had reached Number 1 on 22 May. The credits prematurely announced it was "from the United Artists Release *Eight Arms to Hold You*."

The *Help!* soundtrack demonstrated the influence of Bob Dylan in Lennon's "You've Got to Hide Your Love Away." Harrison contributed two songs, "You Like Me Too Much" and "I Need You." Paul's "Yesterday" appeared only on the Parlophone version of the soundtrack, but Capitol released it as a single in the United States in October 1965. It rocketed to Number 1, selling more than one million copies in ten days, with global sales exceeding 2.5 million. "Yesterday" became the most recorded song ever, with over 2,500 versions by 1980.

George Martin produced all of The Beatles' recordings for *Help!*, but because of a dispute with Lester during *A Hard Day's Night*, the Beatles' producer was "included out" as musical director. Ken Thorne, a friend of the director, scored the Beatles' second film.

The U.S. and British releases of *Help!*, like *A Hard Day's Night*, differed. The Capitol version of the *Help!* soundtrack included the seven Beatles songs from the film and music from Ken Thorne's score. Six of the songs were Lennon/McCartney compositions; "I Need You" was by Harrison. The British Parlophone label issued a disc with the seven Beatle songs on Side One and an equal number on the second side. These included the Lennon/McCartney songs "It's Only Love," "Tell Me What You See," "I've Just Seen a Face," and "Yesterday"; Harrison's "You Like Me Too Much"; and covers of "Act Naturally" and "Dizzy Miss Lizzy."

Help! was the first album in the history of the recording industry to have a pre-release order of more than one million in the United States. It became The Beatles' ninth million-selling LP in the U.S.

Help! was a commercial success, but it did not meet the expectations set by *A Hard Day's Night*. If *A Hard Day's Night* was characterized by its innocence, *Help!* marked the end of it. Lennon thought the recording of "Help!" was done too fast for commercial purposes, but he still considered it one of the best songs he wrote. "I meant it—it's real," he said. "It was just me singing 'Help!' and I mean it."[31]

The times they were a'changin. The Beatles established rock as a musical form. Dylan was strongly impressed when he first heard The Beatles on the radio in 1964. "They were doing things nobody was doing," Dyland said.

> Their chords were outrageous, just outrageous, and their harmonies made it all valid. . . . Everybody else thought they were for the teenyboppers, that they were gonna pass right away. But it was obvious to me that they had staying power. I knew they were pointing to the direction where music had to go.[32]

While The Beatles were still singing love songs to hysterical teen crowds, The Byrds and Bob Dylan were infusing rock with the poetry and social awareness of folk music. The folk-rock style was launched when The Byrds scored a Number 1 hit in June 1965 with a rock version of Dylan's "Mister Tambourine Man." Dylan's now-famous appearance at the Newport Folk Festival that year, where he sang "Like a Rolling Stone" and other songs accompanied by the Paul Butterfield Blues Band using electric instruments, solidified the trend.

The Beatles' next album demonstrated that inspiration was a two-way street. On *Rubber Soul* (1965), which biographer Geoffrey Stokes considered a watershed album, The Beatles absorbed and advanced the folk-rock hybrid, giving "a depth and texture that had long been missing from pop sensibility.[33]

Magical Mystery Flop

Biographer Philip Norman later called *Magical Mystery Tour* "a glorified and progressively irritating home movie.[34] After Brian Epstein's sudden death, Paul asserted his leadership of the group. *Magical Mystery Tour* was his idea for The Beatles' first Apple Films project. The concept was inspired by the cross-country travels of Ken Kesey and his Merry Pranksters, a band of hippies who rode around in a psychedelic painted bus touting the dubious delights of LSD. (Their journey was chronicled in Tom Wolfe's *Electric Kool-Aid Acid Test*.) The Beatles' version was a play on the "mystery tours" advertised by British travel agents.

The idea was to create a one-hour television special. Biographers described it as "a kind of *Sergeant Pepper* with pictures."[35] This time there would be no outside producer or director to interfere with The Beatles' own artistic vision. They would have complete control over the project as writers, producers, directors, and editors. "I knew we were in trouble then," John said later. "I didn't have any misconceptions about our ability to do anything other than play music, and I was scared."[36]

The Beatles' mystery tour was filmed in the fall of 1968, less than a month after Epstein's death. Their former manager's attention to detail was sorely missed. Brown and Gaines called the whole affair "a mess."[37] Hotel and film studio arrangements were not confirmed in advance. On one occasion, The Beatles expected George Martin to get a forty-piece orchestra for a recording session the following evening. The tour was hounded by the press and fans. Money was squandered. One scene, in which Paul sings "The Fool on the Hill," was shot in Nice, France at the cost of 4,000 British pounds. Production costs for the fifty-minute film went over $90,000; Lennon derided it as "the most expensive home movie ever."[38]

A cast and crew of forty-three people boarded a bus painted yellow and blue, with rainbow-colored letters spelling "Magical Mystery Tour" on the side. The entourage left London headed for a still unknown destination somewhere in the English countryside. Most of the filming was done with a hand-held camera. The script was never actually written, but improvised during production. A press release described the story thus: Away in the sky, beyond the clouds, live 4 or 5 musicians. By casting wonderful spells they turn the most Ordinary Coach Trip into a Magical Mystery Tour.[39] The film opens with the title song. Ringo and his Auntie Jessie are bickering over petty things as they board the bus. The driver, Jolly Jimmy Johnson, welcomes this strange group of passengers and introduces the tour hostess, "The Delightful Wendy Winters."

What follows is a hodgepodge of unrelated scenes that have no sense of theme or direction. While sitting on the bus, Paul has a daydream of romping on the French Riviera to the tune of "The Fool on the Hill." A carnival organ plays "She Loves You" at an absurd fair that turns into a Mack Sennett-styled speedy race. Scenes show The Beatles as Merlin-like magicians monitoring the bus and talking about casting wonderful spells. An instrumental "All My Lovin' " serenades the old Mr. Buster Blood-vessel and Ringo's Auntie Jessie as they dance on a beach.

Along the way the tour meets The Recruiting Sergeant (Victor Spinetti, by now a regular in Beatles' films). Dressed in brightly colored outfits, and then the animal costumes on the album cover, The Beatles perform Lennon's "I Am the Walrus." The tour is treated to a private showing of a film with a mystical George sitting Indian-style in a smoke-filled room singing "Blue Jay Way." Maggie the Lovely Starlet entertains the patrons at a striptease club. The finale, "Your Mother Should Know," is a Busby Berkeley-inspired scene with The Beatles dressed in white tuxedos descending a staircase amidst a chorus of dancers.

Eleven weeks of editing was hampered by each Beatle re-editing the other's work. When *Magical Mystery Tour* was finally completed, the BBC purchased the rights and aired it on 26 December 1967. The lack of professional production and direction was obvious. The British press hated the film, calling it "tasteless nonsense," "blatant rubbish," and "a great big bore."[40] The press seemed eager for a chance to criticize the Beatles. The *Daily Express* wrote, "The whole boring saga confirmed a long-held suspicion that the Beatles are four rather pleasant young men who have made so much money that they can apparently afford to be contemptuous of the public."[41] In a report on television abroad, *Time* quipped, "Paul directed, Ringo mugged, John did imitations, George danced a bit and, when the show hit the BBC last week, the audience gagged.[42] While admitting failure, Paul responded to the bad press in his typically witty fashion, saying, "Aren't we entitled to have a flop? Was the film really so bad compared with the rest of the Christmas TV? You could hardly call the Queen's speech a gasser."[43] The Beatles' million dollar American television deal with NBC was canceled as a result of the critical battering it received, but *Magical Mystery Tour* was later released in foreign markets, including the United States. All told the film earned more than $3 million from overseas markets, a testimony to the remarkable popularity of The Beatles.

The soundtrack album salvaged the whole fiasco. Within ten days of its release, the *Magical Mystery Tour* album earned $8 million in the U.S. EMI's Parlophone label released a double-disc EP version which went to Number 2 in England. Global sales of both topped three million copies.

The album included six songs from the film: "Magical Mystery Tour," "Your Mother Should Know," "I Am the Walrus," "The Fool on the Hill," "Flying," an instrumental credited to the entire quartet, and a Harrison number, "Blue Jay Way." Some of the best material on the album, however, was not included in the television special: "Hello, Goodbye," "Penny Lane," "Strawberry Fields Forever," "All You Need Is Love," and "Baby, You're a Rich Man."

"Penny Lane" and "Strawberry Fields" were released as Side A and B of a single that sold well over two million copies internationally. "Penny Lane" topped the U.S. singles charts and reached Number 2 in Britain. "Strawberry Fields" made the Top 10. "Hello, Goodbye," backed by "I

Am the Walrus," went to Number 1 in both the United States and Britain and also sold over two million copies.

We All Live in a Yellow Submarine

The Beatles were obligated to do a third film for United Artists, but they could not agree with Shenson on a script. It was suggested they do a Western based on Richard Condon's novel *A Talent for Loving*, play the Three Musketeers, or be four facets of the same personality. A script was finally commissioned entitled *Up Against It* which outrageously portrayed the Beatles as "anarchists, adulterers and urban guerrillas.[44] It was rejected without comment.

The original idea for a full-length, animated cartoon came from Al Brodax, head of the Television and Motion Pictures Division of King Features Syndicate, an American firm known for *The Flintstones* cartoon series. The company also handled the syndication rights of The Beatles' comic strip. Brodax had produced more than 500 animated shorts at King Features, including the half-hour Beatle cartoon series for ABC. He thought of combining Beatles themes into a full-feature cartoon along the lines of Disney's 1940 masterpiece *Fantasia*, a landmark in the advancement of animation. King Features, Subafilms, and The Beatles' Apple Films thus produced *Yellow Submarine*, a full-length animated cartoon distributed by United Artists. *Magill's Survey of Cinema* called it "a triumph of animation and a splendid union of music and pictures."[45]

Before his death in 1967, Epstein had begun the arrangements for this third UA project which was given to a little-known director George Dunning, who produced mostly commercials and sponsored films. The director considered *Yellow Submarine* an experimental film. He assembled a very creative group of writers, designers, cinematographers, animation directors and special-effects people into what he called "a gathering of talents, an explosion."[46] Together they developed an overall framework for *Yellow Submarine*, furnishing a visual interpretation for each song. With considerable imagination, Dunning and company wove together an endless stream of Beatles' songs, ingenious special effects, and bizarre supporting characters.

The creative team turned eclecticism into a style of animation for this fantasy extravaganza. *"Yellow Submarine* combines every trick and treat of film animation with a dazzle of takeoffs on schools and styles of art," *Time* reported.

> Picassoesque monsters compete with gentle grotesques from Dr. Seussland. Graham Sutherlandish plants burst in and out of bloom. Plump Edwardians

wander with suave decadence out of Aubrey Beardsley's world, and creatures consume themselves with Steinbergian detachment. There are silk screens from Warholville and numbers from Indiana. Psychedelia explodes and art nouveau swirls in the most unexpected places. Corridor doors are open on surrealist nightmares, Freudian symbolism and early movies—all combined in a swiveting, swirling splurge of phantasmagoria, puns, pastiches and visual non sequiturs.[47]

German graphic artist Heinz Edelmann was the main creator behind the stylized designs of The Beatles and other human characters, as well as most of the backgrounds. Edelmann studied *A Hard Days' Night* to get The Beatles' characteristic walks. The Chief Blue Meanie was modeled after Hitler's movements in old newsreels. The Snapping Turtle Turks were inspired by an "indigestible Turkish meal" once forced upon Edelmann. The Flying Glove became the symbol of evil because "gloves are worn by criminals and therefore stand for action in a secret, malevolent way."[48] More than forty animators and 140 technical artists turned Edelmann's sketches into half a million drawings.

The screenplay, based on an original story by Lee Minoff, is credited to Minoff, Al Brodax, Jack Mendelsohn, and Erich Segal. The musical score was written by Beatles' producer George Martin. *Yellow Submarine* was completed in one year—less than half the time of a Disney full-length, animated feature. Martin composed the musical score while the animation was in progress.

The plot was constructed around the themes of a dozen Beatle songs, especially "All You Need Is Love." "Once upon a time, or maybe twice, there was an unearthly paradise called Pepperland." Eighty-thousand leagues beneath the sea, Pepperland is a kingdom of music, love, celebration, and colorful splendor.

The inhabitants of Pepperland are besieged by the Blue Meanies, who attack this "tickle of joy on the blue belly of the universe" with missiles that drain the color out of everyone and everything. A blue bubble envelops the Sergeant Pepper Band, smothering their life-giving sound. As the invasion continues, top-hatted men with stiltlike legs bonk people on the head with green apples (the Apple Corp. logo). Snapping Turtle Turks have shark jaws protruding from their bellies. The ultimate weapon, the Dreadful Flying Glove, smashes anything that still moves.

Newly appointed Lord Admiral Fred escapes, in a yellow submarine, to seek help. "Eleanor Rigby" plays over scenes of London as the yellow submarine arrives and follows Ringo home. He rounds up the other Beatles and they sail off on a fantastic voyage through seas of green to save Pepperland from the Blue Meanies. Along the way they sail through the Sea of Time ("When I'm Sixty-Four"), the Sea of Science ("Only a

Northern Song''), and the Sea of Monsters. They encounter a consumer Vacuum Monster who eventually sucks himself up his own trumpet-like snout. Jeremy the Nowhere Man goes round and round in circles as though caught in the groove of a record. Finally, The Beatles fall through the "holy sea," the Sea of Holes (there are enough to fill the Albert Hall), and end up in Pepperland.

The Beatles find the original Sergeant Pepper Band's uniforms and instruments. Playing "Sergeant Pepper's Lonely Hearts Club Band," they restore life and color to the people of Pepperland. The Chief Blue Meanie and his Dreadful Flying Glove are defeated by "All You Need is Love." Ringo uses a hole in his pocket, which he took from the Sea of Holes, to let the air out of the blue bubble that had silenced the original Sergeant Pepper Band. The Beatles make a brief appearance at the end to introduce "All Together Now."

Their contract gave the film's producer permission to use about twelve old Beatle songs, but also obligated the quartet to supply four new titles. By this time, The Beatles were suspicious of anything that was not their own invention. They had no enthusiasm for the project. Even the voices behind their cartoon characters were provided by actors using a moderate version of the Liverpudlian accent. The foursome generated four mediocre songs with the attitude "Right, that's good enough for the film. Let them have that." George Martin said *Yellow Submarine* "scraped the bottom of the Beatle music barrel as far as new material was concerned."[49] The four new songs and eight previously recorded tracks were included in the film. Several Lennon/McCartney songs that were used in the film were not included on the soundtrack album: "Sergeant Pepper's Lonely Hearts Club Band," "Eleanor Rigby," "Lucy in the Sky with Diamonds," "Nowhere Man," "Baby, You're a Rich Man," and "When I'm Sixty-Four."

Initially, The Beatles wanted to release an EP containing their four-song contribution to the film on their own. The film producers decided to put together a separate LP that would tell the *Yellow Submarine* story with Martin's score, voices, and narration from the film. Suddenly, the Beatles "changed their collective mind," according to Martin. "What they had realized, of course, was that EPs didn't sell in America, while LPs did. What's more, they probably realized by then that, in spite of their lack of interest or co-operation, the film was likely to be the success it eventually proved to be."[50] The soundtrack LP featured two new Lennon-McCartney compositions, "All Together Now" and "Hey, Bulldog," and two Harrison numbers, "Only a Northern Song" and "It's All Too Much." Reissues of "Yellow Submarine" and "All You Need Is Love" completed the first side. George Martin's musical score filled Side 2 with orchestrated arrangements "Pepperland," "Sea of Time & Sea of Holes," "Sea of Monsters," March of the Meanies," and "Pepperland Laid Waste." The musical director also arranged the Lennon and McCartney song "Yellow Submarine in Pepperland."

The album was released in Britain in December 1968 and in the United States in January 1969. It reached Number 3 in England and Number 2 in the U.S., selling more than one million copies globally.

Yellow Submarine premiered in mid-July 1968. Reviewers raved about its imaginative animation and music, but one faulted the storyline as being like "one of John Lennon's semiliterate Joycean pastiches." *Variety* said, "Dunning has brought to the screen a vivid and highly enjoyable film, bristling with ideas, psychedelic sound and color and novelty fun, though it tends to sag towards the end." Sarris, on the other hand, thought "only the songs make the movie at all bearable." Other critics commented on the aesthetic influence of marijuana. "If the result seems less a coherent story than a two-hour pot high," said *Time*, "*Submarine* is still a break-through combination of the feature film and art's intimacy with the unconscious." *New York Times* critic Renata Adler very discreetly suggested that viewers might want to see *Yellow Submarine* while stoned:

> That sense of perception washed clean . . . is certainly accessible to people who are not high, but in an overstimulated urban environment, probably rarely. There is certainly no point in seeing "Yellow Submarine," or anything else that is good, drunk. But the best music has been most accessible to an occasional high for a long time, and movies as it turns out more and more, are such an intensely musical form.

Noting the high-powered merchandising in conjunction with the movie, Pauline Kael wrote, "Wasn't all this supposed to be what the Beatles were *against*? The way attacks on the consumer society become products to be consumed is, to put it delicately, discouraging."[51]

Nevertheless, The Beatles' remarkable success led the way for the British Invasion of the U.S. market. Other English groups followed the Fab Four into the theaters. Lester's cinematic style set the standard, but most films about British pop groups more closely resembled the pre-Beatle teen exploitation movies of Sam Katzman and AIP. With the exception of a few, they were largely unsuccessful. Richard Staehling pointed out that although The Beatles "were certainly a new trend, there was little a Hollywood huckster could do to cash in on them; they were simply too unique to be exploited."[52] Imitations plainly lacked the wit, social satire, sophistication, and originality of Lester and The Beatles. In anticipation of other British pop groups following "in the Beatles' cinematic foot-steps," one critic moaned, "this new vogue may well be the most depressing thing to happen in darkened theaters since Follow-the-Bouncing-Ball."[53]

British Rockers Invade U.S. Theaters'

In the wake of The Beatles' first screen success, United Artists tried to mine the roster at NEMS Enterprises. Another Liverpool group, Gerry and the Pacemakers, was signed to star in *Ferry Cross the Mersey* (1964). Cilla Black and The Fourmost, also represented by NEMS, were featured, along with The Blackwells, The Black Knights, and Earl Royce and The Olympics. Epstein was listed as co-producer. The United Artists release was an unabashed copy of Lester's first Beatle production, with Mack Sennett-styled chase scenes and frenzied fans in pursuit of the British pop group. "The world isn't ready for more Beatles," wrote a *Times* critic.[54] UA released the soundtrack in the United States and the title song reached the Top 10.

Guest performances by The Dave Clark Five and The Animals were featured in MGM's *Get Yourself a College Girl* (1964), produced by Sam Katzman. In this film, an Ivy League co-ed using a pseudonym is writing hit pop songs with "modern viewpoints concerning women." When the Board of Trustees finds out, they threaten to expel her. The college founder's son is a senator seeking the youth vote to help his bid for re-election. A grand finale rock show helps his cause and the female song-writer.

MGM signed The Dave Clark Five to star in *Having a Wild Weekend*, made in 1965 as *Catch Us If You Can*. The film was about the "swinging London scene," but lacked any of the power of Antonioni's *Blow-Up*. John Boorman, who later directed *Deliverance*, made his feature film directorial debut here. Eight songs by the quintet appeared in the movie; the title song became a Top 10 hit. This cult film received little exposure in the United States until 1967, when it was sold to a distribution chain.

In 1965, Herman's Hermits starred with Shelley Fabares in another Katzman production, *Hold On*.[55] The MGM picture looked like a cross between *A Hard Day's Night* and the AIP beach films. It's inane plot has a NASA official investigating the Hermits during a U.S. tour because Gemini astronauts want to name their spacecraft after the group. The Hermits performed eight songs in the movie; two singles, "A Must To Avoid" and "Leaning on the Lamp Post," both reached the Top 10.

The Hermits scored another Top 10 hit with "Listen People" from

MGM's *When the Boys Meet the Girls* (starring Connie Francis) in 1965, but things got worse for the Hermits. A 1968 offering produced by Allen Klein (who later managed The Beatles for a short period) had the boys taking a bus to London for the dog races in *Mrs. Brown You've Got a Lovely Daughter.*

Freddie and the Dreamers were featured in *Seaside Swingers* (1964) (aka *Every Day's a Holiday* in England) and *Cuckoo Patrol* (1965).

Antonioni's Blow-Up

The swinging London scene was also used as the setting for Michaelangelo Antonioni's *Blow-Up* (1966). The Italian director already enjoyed a prestigious international reputation when MGM signed him. The screenplay was an Antonioni, Tonino Guerra, and Edward Bond collaboration based on a story by Julio Cortazar, author of *All Fires The Fire*. During the filming of *Blow-Up*, which was Antonioni's first picture in English, the director said:

> The young people among whom my film is situated are all aimless, without any other drive but to reach that aimless freedom. Freedom that for them means marijuana, sexual perversion, anything. . . . What you get at the end doesn't interest me. . . . It's that conquest of freedom that matters. The pursuit of freedom gives man his most exciting moments. Once it's conquered, once all discipline is discarded, then it's decadence. Decadence without any visible future.[56]

William J. Palmer strongly argued that the movie's central theme was human impotence—physical, moral, aesthetic, and existential.[57]

In the film, a trendy London fashion photographer (David Hemmings) casually photographs two lovers in a park; inadvertently, he has captured a murder on film. Driven to uncover its meaning, the photographer continually enlarges the film, but to what end is left unclear. The protagonist grows to doubt his own perceptions; the quest for meaning and understanding disintegrates in the decadent lifestyle of swinging London. The film featured music by The Yardbirds, who performed "Stroll On" in a rock cellar-club in one scene, ending with a guitar smashing *a la* The Who.

Blow-Up was the first film to be refused approval by the Motion Picture Association of America (MPAA) since the adoption of the new liberalized Production Code in 1966. The Production Code office objected to one scene showing sexual intercourse and another of the photographer frolicking on his studio floor with two nude teenage girls. The film studio stood by Antonioni; an MGM subsidiary distributed the film without the MPAA

Seal of Approval. It opened in New York in December 1966. MGM executives were surprised by the critical and commercial success of *Blow-Up*, which placed fourteenth on *Variety*'s year-end chart. The distributor earned $6.3 million in domestic rentals.

Hey, Hey We're the Monkees

Inspired by The Beatles' phenomenal success, the recording industry and television joined forces behind an American made-for-television rock group modeled after the British Fab Four. Bob Rafelson and Bert Schneider were working at Screen Gems, a television subsidiary of Columbia Pictures, when they concocted the idea for a TV comedy series about a pop group. Originally, the two TV producers considered building the program around an established band, The Lovin' Spoonful, as an American counterpart to The Beatles. Instead, the co-producers decided they could have more control if they created their own made-for-TV rock group. So, *Time* gibed, the "wily promoters ran the Beatles through a Xerox machine and came up with the Monkees."[58] An ad appeared in the *Daily Variety* and the *Hollywood Reporter* in September 1965:

> Wanted: Four insane boys, aged 17 to 21, to form a group for a TV show. The program will reflect the adventures of an unknown, young, long-haired, modern-dressed band, and their dreams on the way to fame and fortune.[59]

The list of "insane" performers who applied but were rejected has become legendary. Stephen Stills, songwriter Paul Williams, Paul Petersen (formerly of *The Donna Reed Show*), and Danny Hutton of Three Dog Night are listed among the 437 candidates. The four chosen to become the Monkees—Mickey Dolenz, Peter Tork, Mike Nesmith, and Davy Jones—were not selected for their musical abilities, but their screen presence and the chemistry of their personalities. They each had a certain level of proficiency at singing and/or the guitar, but there was no time to mold them into a rock group. Instead, Screen Gems marketed an image. Executives considered it too risky to even allow the quartet to play their own instruments in recording sessions. "This isn't a rock 'n' roll group," Jones admitted. "It's an act."[60]

Screen Gems allocated $225,000 for a sample pilot film in 1965. In five days, Rafelson and Schneider (whose father was president of Columbia Pictures) filmed a half-hour TV version of *A Hard Day's Night*. "It all went great," Rafelson said. "NBC bought the series twenty-four hours after it saw the pilot and sold it to two sponsors seventy-two hours later."[61]

The whole Monkee enterprise was kept under the Screen Gems umbrella which included Colgems, a newly formed record label, and the Columbia Music Publishing Company. Screen Gems filmed the series. Colgem president Don Kirshner ("The Man with the Golden Ear")[62] found material for The Monkees from his roster of talented songwriters under exclusive contract at the Screen Gems publishing company: Tommy Boyce-Bobby Hart, Neil Diamond, Gerry Goffin-Carole King, Neil Sedaka, and Monkee Mike Nesmith penned several hits during the run of the show from 1966 to 1968. Kirshner acted as music supervisor for the early sessions. The co-producers inked a deal with RCA to manufacture and distribute The Monkees' records. The recording company also contributed $100,000 in promotion.

The show's improvisational format was modeled after The Beatles' movies, with jump-cut editing, speedy chase sequences and silent comedy antics. "Buster Keaton, Harold Lloyd, Charlie Chaplin. I'd say the biggest influence was the Marx Brothers," series producer Rafelson said. "They weren't silent, of course (except for Harpo), but it was group comedy— absurd group comedy."[63] Unfortunately, though each *Monkee* episode was like a mini-Beatle movie, the show lacked the comedic flair exhibited by Richard Lester. In post-MTV retrospect, it appears that each episode contained a video promotional clip for songs by The Monkees. Rafelson has been referred to as "the godfather of rock video,"[64] but the title more properly belongs to Lester.

The Monkees' success rivaled that of the Beatles. During the course of the TV series' run, they had six Top 10 singles, with three topping the charts. The first, "Last Train to Clarksville" by Boyce and Hart, was issued on the Colgems label on 16 August 1966, almost four weeks before the official premiere of NBC show. TV exposure sent the single to the top of the *Billboard* pop charts. A million copies were sold within a month, with sales eventually topping three million. Hart actually got the idea for the song when he heard The Beatles' "Paperback Writer" on the radio and misunderstood the words, thinking they were singing about a "last train" to somewhere. The Monkees' first album was Number 1 for fifteen weeks. The self-titled record outpaced The Beatles' start, selling more than three million copies in less than three months to become the top-selling LP that year.

Their second single, "I'm a Believer," written by Neil Diamond, coincided with the debut of the television series in the British market. Both were a tremendous success, launching The Monkees as international stars. Colgems' manufacturer and distributor, RCA, received an advance order of 1 million for the single; previously only Elvis Presley records generated orders that large. The song was released on 26 November 1966. "I'm a Believer" sold more than three million copies in the U.S. in two months and 750,000 in Britain. International sales have been estimated at an incredible ten million. The second LP, *More of the Monkees*, had an advance sale of one-and-a-half million, unprecedented for a vocal album. Issued on 1 February 1967, *More* was Number 1 for eighteen weeks in the U.S. and two weeks in Britain.

Eventually The Monkee musical facade caused a disruption between Screen Gems executives and the band. The Monkees, (especially Mike Nesmith), grew increasingly frustrated with their lack of creative control and mounting criticism over their failure to play their own instruments. The controversy exploded in the press. The group was given more creative control beginning with their third album *Headquarters*, which topped sales of two million copies in 1967. Kirshner was removed from the project; he went on to The Archies. *Pisces, Aquarius, Capricorn and Jones*, a fourth album, was certified platinum in 1967. The group scored a Number 1 hit with "Daydream Believer" in December of that year. The follow-up, "Valeri," reached Number 3 in March 1968, marking the end of The Monkee's Top 10 appearances. After fifty-nine episodes, NBC cancelled the show after the 1967-68 season. Album sales for their remaining projects reflected the group's waning popularity.

After the TV series ended, Rafelson teamed with actor Jack Nicholson to write a script for a movie starring The Monkees. Nicholson had earlier written *The Trip* (1967). (The project began a long working relation between the two; Rafelson later directed the actor in three films, *Easy Rider*, *Five Easy Pieces*, and *The Postman Always Rings Twice*.) Nicholson and Rafelson co-produced the movie, Rafelson directed, Bert Schneider served as executive producer, and Columbia distributed the production, which was budgeted at a moderate $750,000.

Head was a series of largely unrelated surrealistic vignettes. *Variety* described it as "a mind-blowing collage of intercuts and mixed media that moves along at a rapid pace with little sense of direction, a plotless script and a free-for-all freakout of rock music and psychedelic splash of color."[65] The film begins and ends at a ribbon-cutting ceremony for a new bridge. Mickey Dolenz breaks the ribbon like the finish line of a race and then leaps off the bridge into the San Francisco Bay, in a symbolic suicide of The Monkees' image. After performing an underwater ballet to "The Porpoise Song," mermaids come to the rescue. A collage of *avant garde* fantasies ensues, including parodies of Hollywood genres—Westerns, Eastern desert adventures, and war films. In numerous scenes, The Monkees mock commercialism and ridicule their own manufactured image.

Footage from classic Hollywood films and newsreel shots of Vietnam are included. Annette Funicello, Frank Zappa, Sonny Liston, Carol Doda, and Victor Mature make guest appearances.

Critics were not impressed. The *Times*'s Renata Adler suggested *Head* "might be a film to see if you have been smoking grass or if you like to scream at the Monkees, or if you are interested in what interests drifting heads and hysteric high-school girls." Pauline Kael walked out.[66]

Head was just too confusing for The Monkees' pre-teen audience. The movie flopped at the box office. The soundtrack contained six songs from the film and bits of dialogue as filler. "The Porpoise Song" and "As We Go Along" were released as singles, but failed to chart in *Billboard*. Album sales were disappointing. The Monkees' movie did, however, launch Rafelson's film career.

AIP Revisited

As the British Invasion reached the U.S. cinematic shores, the flood of beach-blanket films was drying up. The research staff at AIP stayed plugged into trends in the youth culture. Arkoff and Nicholson decided to change direction in the late 1960s by "reflecting the exciting social changes, crises, rationalizations and adjustments of society in our time." The AIP philosophy, like Katzman's, was rapid production of youth-oriented films reflecting immediate concerns. The social and political turmoil late in the decade made the bikini features seem like a never-never land of the past. "Burning issues is what we're after," Arkoff said. "How else are we going to get the young people?" Asked about a Vietnam picture, he replied, "Too controversial. Besides, if peace breaks out, you're dead."[67] A.I.P. churned out a stream of low-budget features exploiting the counterculture, the hippie phenomenon and the drug scene with several scoring at the boxoffice.

Roger Corman produced and directed the company's first "protest film," *The Wild Angels* (1966). Corman made the film, which was originally titled *All the Fallen Angels*, to take advantage of the media attention the California motorcycle gang Hell's Angels was receiving at the time. (California's attorney general had initiated an offensive against organized motorcycle gangs the year before). The script was based on stories the Angels had told Corman and screenwriter Chuck Griffith. Hell's Angels themselves played gang members. State police followed the production with warrants for the arrest of most of the biker extras. The film was made in seventeen days on a limited budget.

"Wild youth" was an image for the juvenile delinquent in the 1950s;

Corman reshaped it into an icon of the rebellious counterculture in the late Sixties. The bikers in *The Wild Angels* "are past the age where they can be called juvenile delinquents," film historians Seth Cagin and Philip Dray noted. "They are not the sons and daughters of Brando and Dean so much as they are Brando and Dean ten years later: the fifties rebels have grown up to become a disciplined army of hardened outlaws, systematically alienated from every value held dear by the surrounding society."[68] "Their credo is violence . . . Their God is hate and they call themselves THE WILD ANGELS," an advertisement read.[69] Corman indicts society for producing the menacing Angels. Images of urban decay, and especially a hospital's cold clinical treatment of a wounded gang member, are combined with an unapologetic portrait of biker culture.

The Wild Angels starred Peter Fonda, Nancy Sinatra, and Bruce Dern. The lead role was originally given to George Chakiris, who had played the Puerto Rican gang leader in *West Side Story*. When Chakiris refused to ride a motorcycle, Fonda moved into the lead as Heavenly Blues, the leader of a biker gang that terrorizes west coast towns, an early version of "Captain America" in *Easy Rider*. Mike (Sinatra) is his girlfriend. When a rival gang steals Loser's (Bruce Dern) motorcycle, they rumble. Loser is wounded by police in the brawl. The Angels "rescue" him from a hospital while also raping a nurse on duty. Without proper treatment, Loser eventually dies. The Angels arrive at the church to pay their last respects. Heavenly Blue tells the minister, "We don't want nobody telling us what to do. We don't want nobody pushing us around. We want to be free. Free to ride without being hassled by the man, we want to . . . have a good time." In total sacrilege, they tie up the minister, wreck the church, and rape the deceased's girlfriend in an orgy that includes homosexual activities in the background. With Loser's body wrapped in a Nazi flag, the gang takes him to the cemetery, where local citizens attack the Angels. The biker's flee, leaving their leader at the grave murmuring, "There's no place to go."

The Wild Angels was greeted "with some astonishment and moral disapproval by industry officials," the *Times* reported.[70] The film's appearance at the Venice Film Festival in August 1966 outraged critics. In a review of the film's December opening in New York, the *Times*'s Crowther wrote:

> This is the brutal little picture about a California motorcycle gang and its violent depredations that was shown at the Venice festival as an American entry (by invitation) and caused quite a few diplomats to mop their brows.
>
> It is an embarrassment all right—a vicious account of the boozing, fighting, "pot"-smoking, vandalizing and raping done by a gang of "sickle riders" who

are obviously drawn to represent the swastika-wearing Hell's Angels . . . And despite an implausible ending and some rather amateurish acting . . . it gives a pretty good picture of what these militant motorcycle-cult gangs are.

Mr. Corman has shot the whole thing in color and in a cinema verite style that makes it resemble a documentary.[71]

Corman's chopper flick was a critical disaster. Not surprisingly, the controversy the film generated and Fonda's name on the marquee fueled movie attendance. In an unprecedented merchandizing strategy, AIP arranged for displays of posters and soundtrack albums in movie theater lobbies. The film's opening coincided with Fonda's arrest for possession of marijuana. The enormous press coverage helped established him as a pop icon of the young, rebellious generation. A poster of the anti-hero on a motorcycle became a best-seller. Fonda's version, though exaggerated at points, shows the whirlwind of events that spurred the picture's success and created the countercultural image he would maximize in *Easy Rider*:

Now, as all this was going on, my trial in Los Angeles began. The film did $16 million in drive-ins alone, eventually making over $25 million. It only cost something like $360,000 to make. Simultaneously, I was in the front pages of newspapers being arrested for possession. It was a very strange chain of events. Roger put me on the screen as a cult hero. AIP then marketed posters of me worldwide showing me on my cycle taking a toke. And the Los Angeles police put me in the headlines, causing all the disenfranchised youth of the country, who were all popping their zits at that time, to notice me.[72]

The Wild Angels became the most successful picture in AIP history; box office receipts captured an impressive $7 million for the distributor.

After the film was released, the Hell's Angels brought a lawsuit against Corman for defamation of character. Corman told an interviewer, "A television news broadcaster laughingly reported that the Venice and San Bernardino chapters of the Hell's Angels sued Roger Corman and New World Pictures for defamation of character because they were portrayed in the picture as an outlaw and motorcycle gang whereas in reality they were a social organization dedicated to spreading technical information about motorcycles."[73] The $2-million suit dragged on for some three years; it was finally settled for $2,000.

The movie's soundtrack was issued on the Tower label. The theme song, "Blue's Theme," by Davie Allan and The Arrows, reached Number 37 on 23 September 1967. As was typical of AIP features, however, the music was primarily background to the action. This style became the pattern for the wave of motorcycle movies that followed, including *Thunder Alley*,

The Devil's Angels, *Hell's Angels on Wheels* (all 1967), and *Angels from Hell* (1968).

In 1967, American International released twenty-one features. Sam Katzman produced *Riot on Sunset Strip* (1967), based on the police riots in Hollywood when the strip was a hangout for protesting hippies. In true form, Katzman got this exploitation flick into the theaters within six weeks of the actual occurrence of the riots. In the film, Lt. Walt Lorimer (Aldo Ray) is a divorced cop who tries to maintain law and order on the strip. The police lieutenant is caught between the businesses operating there and his own belief that the hippies have rights. Then Lorimer's daughter returns to Los Angeles after living for years with his alcoholic former wife. At a party she attends, LSD is put into her drink; she is brutally gang raped and taken to a hospital emergency room. Her father goes on a personal rampage for revenge. Actual newsreel footage was included. Issued on the Tower label, the movie's soundtrack featured music by The Chocolate Watch Band and The Standells.

The burgeoning drug culture became the next subject for Corman to mine in the AIP classic *The Trip* (1967). The controversial film was shot in fifteen days with production costs around $450,000. The director wanted "to make an honest film about the drug scene and specifically LSD."[74] Corman, who assembled a cast "connected with this movement," tried LSD himself before making the picture. Actor Jack Nicholson penned a script that supported hallucinogenic drugs as a force for both personal and social transformation. In the movie, Paul Groves (Peter Fonda) is a director of television commercials who is distressed over the emptiness of his professional and personal life; his marriage to Sally (Susan Strasberg) is falling apart. Friend John (Bruce Dern) introduces him to a hippie pusher (Dennis Hopper) who turns him on to LSD. The movie is a montage of unrelated, rapidly cut scenes attempting to duplicate a hallucinogenic drug trip on film. Kaleidoscopic fun turns to horror as images of Groves's sexual guilt and anxiety haunt him. Bergman and Fellini symbols are sprinkled throughout these psychedelic religious visions. Groves awakens the next morning in bed with Glenn (Salli Sachse) and reborn from the drug experience.

Much to Corman's regret, AIP added a voiceover prologue denouncing LSD usage. The film company also altered the film's ending. Corman had left the final scene ambiguous regarding the results of the trip. "AIP superimposed a sheet of broken glass over Peter's face at the end, implying that the trip would have dire consequences on his life," Corman said. "My only solace is that I don't think anyone knew what the damned glass was doing up there. All AIP did was mess up the end of the picture."[75] AIP's editing eventually led Corman to start his own production and distribution company, New World Pictures, in 1970. His final picture with AIP was *Gas-s-s-s* in 1969, an unsuccessful, surreal comedy about the young ruling the world when a nerve-gas leak kills everyone over twenty-five.

Despite AIP's precautions, *The Trip*'s glamorization of the drug culture stirred controversy. The National Association of Broadcasters sent a memorandum to more than 396 member stations advising them not to use a commercial spot for *The Trip* that included two nude scenes and references to LSD. The association considered the promotion an affront to "good taste, community attitudes and responsibility to children," citing restrictions in its code regarding commercials about hallucinogenic drugs that "glamorize or excite interest in the subject." AIP sent a re-edited version of the commercials with the questionable scenes and language deleted.[76]

Critical reactions varied. "Roger Corman's psychedelic Pilgrim's Progress is dull enough to drive kids back to Disney," *Newsweek* quipped. In trying to visualize Fonda's LSD trip, "Roger Corman has simply resorted to a long succession of familiar cinematic images, accompanied by weird music and sounds," said Crowther in the *Times*. "And I would warn you that all you are likely to take away from [the picture] is a painful case of eye-strain and perhaps a detached retina." An angered Judith Crist called it an "hour-and-a-half commercial for LSD." *Variety* recognized its appeal. "As a far-out, free-floating LSD freak-out, 'The Trip' should provide enough psychedelic jolts, sex-sational scenes and mind-blowing montages and optical effects to prove a boxoffice magnet for the youth market," it noted.[77]

AIP scored again with *The Trip*, earning $5.5 million in theater rentals. The Sidewalk soundtrack featured music by Mike Bloomfield and The Electric Flag. (In an interview, Fonda claimed he put up $7,500 to get the music produced, but Corman denied this.)[78]

The Corman Connection

The significance of Roger Corman in the history of American film should not be underestimated; Corman was a Hollywood phenomenon. Almost all of his films were box office successes. While he exhibited great imagination and creativity at moments, he also produced some of the worst schlock ever seen on the screen. The independent filmmaker remains virtually unknown to the general public, but Corman was the progenitor of a new wave of young American filmmakers in the late Sixties. Francis Ford Coppola, Peter Bogdanovich, Martin Scorsese, and later George

Lucas and Gary Kurtz (*American Graffiti* and *Star Wars*) were among the talented film students eager to work under Corman just for the experience. Corman let his proteges work in every aspect of filmmaking—budgeting, scheduling, editing, and shooting. The students acquired invaluable experience working on the nonunion, low-budget features that Corman produced. Their inexpensive labor also helped keep production budgets down. AIP provided an easy outlet for Corman's pictures. "He [Corman] ran what amounted to a film school at AIP," Kurtz said about the period from 1962 to 1966. "When I first met him he had a deal with AIP as a producer wherein they would accept films that he gave them as long as they met AIP's technical requirements—which, I believe, meant that they had to run 90 minutes. Even if the films didn't make it as theatrical releases, AIP would take them, selling them directly to television."[79]

Experience with Corman productions oriented these young filmmakers to the youth market, trained them in the art of making movies on a limited budget, and made them familiar with the use of rock music in movies. Many of them went on to use rock music with great effectiveness in film productions: Lucas in *American Graffiti* (1973), Scorsese in the powerful portrait of New York's Little Italy *Mean Streets* (1973), and Coppola in his Vietnam saga *Apocalypse Now* (1979). Scorsese was also co-supervising editor of *Woodstock* (1970) and director of The Band's farewell concert film, *The Last Waltz* (1978).

Your Sons and Daughters Are Beyond Your Command

Barry Shear was hired to direct *Wild in the Streets* (1968), AIP's version of *Privilege*, a British film about a rock singer who is almost made into a messiah by business executives. Arkoff and Nicholson produced this Orwellian picture about a liberal California senator (Hal Holbrook) who elicits the support of overnight pop sensation Max Frost (Christopher Jones) to capture the youth vote. When he wins, the senator keeps his campaign promise and the voting age is lowered to fifteen and a generational civil war erupts. The young riot and dump LSD into the water supply, forcing Congress to amend the Constitution and lower the presidential eligibility age to fourteen. The pop star turns politician and is elected president. Mandatory retirement is set at thirty-five, at which time the old folks are sent to "rehabilitation camps" where they are given a regular diet of LSD. In the end, the youth revolution comes full circle. President Frost is beset by contentious children who assert that "Everybody over ten ought to be put out of business."

Renata Adler called *Wild in the Streets* "a kind of instant classic, a revved-up *La Chinoise* or *Privilege* for the drive-ins in summertime." AIP scored at the box office again, with $5.5 million in domestic rentals against production costs of almost $1 million. While the plot was absurd, the explosive population of people under-twenty five in the United States and the turmoil on university campuses and in the streets in 1968 gave the theme a kind of prophetic significance. A *Newsweek* reviewer considered the exploitation pic from AIP "a witch's brew prepared in the pressure cooker of commerce," yet concluded that the movie was "nothing substantial and everything urgent." Writing in *Life*, Richard Schickel argued that the current mass alienation, politicalization, and growing anarchy of American youth were not subjects to be carelessly exploited in film. "What is unusual here," he said with some alarm, "is that normally cultivated people have so lost their cool over recent events that they are looking at *Wild in the Streets* not for what it is—mindless commercial exploitation—but for what they would like it to be—an authentic exploration of our current agony."[80]

The soundtrack featured a compilation of unknowns. The successful songwriting team Barry Mann and Cynthia Weil composed five songs that were worked into the film. One, "Shape of Things to Come" by Max Frost and The Troopers, reached Number 22 on the trade charts in September 1968. Les Baxter did the score.

Lester and the Beatles had created new possibilities for rock music in movies, but AIP production people were principally filmmakers; they used rock as a secondary element that enhanced the setting of youth-oriented pictures. Soundtrack sales were a bonus. AIP features seldom explored innovations in the integration of popular music with the story. Exceptions were Corman's *The Trip* and Richard Rush's striking portrait of San Francisco's hippie culture, *Psych-Out* (1968).

AIP distributed this Dick Clark Production (originally titled *Love Children*) about a young girl, Jennie (Susan Strasberg), who goes to San Francisco in search of her lost brother Steve (Bruce Dern). Steve is an artist who has dropped out of society and is living in the wild world of Haight-Ashbury. Jennie, deaf from a childhood trauma, meets Stoney (Jack Nicholson), who leads a rock band. Stoney and friends join in the search, which takes them through a series of incidents related to the world of freaked-out hippie culture, including hallucinogenic drug experiences. Rush's portrait of San Francisco hippies was realistic and balanced, showing love, dope, and "Be-In's" alongside the seemy aspects of STP overdoses, gang rapes, violence, and filth.

Variety reviewed the film positively, considering Rush's direction "quite exceptional . . . Were he a foreigner—Canadian, British or French, per the

vogue—he might be greeted by 'auteur! auteur!' cries.'' The *Times*' Renata
Adler said it had "considerable elan," noting how the structure of the
classic Western was superimposed onto hippie culture.[81]

Psych-Out dramatically employed music of The Strawberry Alarm Clock
and The Seeds, including performances by those rock groups in the film.
The Sidewalk soundtrack included the Alarm Clock's 1967 chart-topper
"Incense and Peppermints." Rush's other 1968 production, the biker film
The Savage Seven, effectively utilized music by Iron Butterfly and Cream.
Rush also directed Nicholson and Adam Roarke in the 1967 Fanfare
production *Hell's Angels on Wheels*. In 1969, a United Artists picture,
Revolution, featured music by The Quicksilver Messenger Service, The
Steve Miller Band, and Mother Earth in its treatment of the hippie
community in San Francisco's Haight-Ashbury district.

The fact that low-budget pictures reflecting the issues of the counterculture were drawing huge audiences of Baby Boomers to the theaters was
not lost on film studio executives. In the midst of Hollywood's cheap
exploitation of the youth counterculture, several films came from the
mainstream that tracked the postwar generation's challenge to the meaning
of the American Dream. Loss of social consensus and fragmentation
became topical fare for the majors at the end of the Sixties.

Warren Beatty's *Bonnie and Clyde* (1967) was a clear break with
traditional Hollywood. The film's glamorization of violence and unconven-
tional treatment of sex forced film critics to draw battle lines over the film,
which became a popular-culture phenomenon that year. Stanley Kubrick's
2001: A Space Odyssey likewise drew critical fire, but became a major box
office attraction in 1968. Older critics found themselves out of touch with
the sensibilities of the under-thirty moviegoing audience. These films,
along with *The Graduate* and *Easy Rider*, generated the first upswing in
box office attendance since the late 1940s. *The Graduate* "has taken aim,
satirically, at the very establishment that produces most of our movies,
mocked the morals and values it has long lived by," one reviewer observed. "It is a final irony that it has thereby gained the large young
audience it has been seeking and has been rewarded by a shower of
gold."[82]

Hollywood Graduates

Embassy Pictures financed *The Graduate* at $3 million. The film was
distributed in the international market by United Artists. The screenplay,
by Calder Willingham and Buck Henry (who appeared in the film as the
hotel clerk), was based on the Charles Webb novel of the same title.

(Published in 1963, the book had sold a respectable 20,000 copies, attracting the attention of Hollywood executives eager for material on the youth culture.) Producer Lawrence Turman recommended the project to Mike Nichols, who found the story's "pertinence to the present scene" appealing. The director was intrigued with Benjamin's basic dilemma: a wealthy young man living in present-day America "who has every desirable object he could want—a young man who has just obtained an excellent education without knowing its purpose."[83] (Nichols had begun his career as a director of Broadway hits including *The Odd Couple* and *Barefoot in the Park*. He directed his first feature film in 1966. *Who's Afraid of Virginia Woolf?* won critical acclaim and captured Academy Awards for Elizabeth Taylor for Best Actress and Sandy Dennis for Best Supporting Actress.)

To the surprise of many, Nichols cast an unknown actor, Dustin Hoffman, who appeared in a number of off-Broadway plays, in the lead. Hoffman's ordinary looks (he was described as resembling "a swarthy Pinocchio")[84] made him an unlikely choice for the part, but the director thought Hoffman understood the struggles of the character. "He had a kind of pole-axed quality with life," Nichols said, "but great vitality underneath."[85] As it turned out, Hoffman's first movie performance became a *tour de force* for the young actor.

The Graduate is set in an affluent Los Angeles suburb. The protagonist, Benjamin Braddock (Dustin Hoffman), is a stellar athlete and student, not at all the kind of political agitator (as a Berkeley landlord calls him) associated with the Sixties' generational conflict. Even straight-laced Benjamin is "very confused," and as a result falls short of his parents' expectations. The film begins with Ben arriving at the Los Angeles International Airport. Simon and Garfunkel sing "Sounds of Silence" during the opening credits while Ben rides a moving sidewalk through the airport; the scene is juxtaposed with his suitcase on a conveyor belt. The song ends with a close-up of Ben in front of an aquarium. The college graduate is worried about his future, wanting to be different from his parents but unsure of which direction to take.

Hoffman's character is the quintessential upper-middle-class Baby Boomer. *The Graduate* embodied all of the themes burning among the young generation in the late Sixties: adult hypocrisy, antimaterialism, and natural love over mechanical sex. Reared in an affluent family, he grew up taking for granted a world of sleek cars and swimming pools. Presumably, his parents, raised during the Depression and Second World War, had experienced a harder life. The high value they place on material success appears shallow, even crass, to this member of the postwar generation. The material-oriented values of the affluent society do not satisfy his thirst for meaning, but Benjamin does not know where to turn. A friend of the family corners Ben at his graduation party. He offers the secret to success—"Plastics . . . there's a great future in plastics." "That line is embedded in the collective memory of the baby-boom generation," wrote Landon Jones.[86] The word summed up all that the baby boomers thought was wrong with the adult generation—sterility, artificiality, dishonesty, and fraud.

At the party, Ben escapes to his room. Mrs. Robinson (Anne Bancroft) the wife of his father's longtime business partner, talks him into driving her home. A neurotic alcoholic, Mrs. Robinson is extremely confident of her sexual wiles. She tries unsuccessfully to seduce Ben and gives him a standing offer to have an affair with her. Ironically, her husband advises the young man to take it easy for awhile and "sow a few wild oats."

Ben quickly begins to suffocate in the environment of the affluent American family. (Nichols explained the film's shots through the fishbowl and scuba diving in the pool as conveying the image of drowning.) For his twenty-first birthday, Ben's parents give him a full scuba diving outfit; he is expected to perform for his parents' friends in the backyard swimming pool. The camera puts the audience inside the scuba suit with Ben looking out the mask and hearing only breathing and splashing water. Ben lies on the bottom of the pool like a fish in an aquarium.

Ben is awkward and ill at ease in his parents' world, though he is unable to articulate the reason. He accepts Mrs. Robinson's sexual invitation. The older woman is cold, direct, and manipulative in her seduction of Ben. She uses him for the sexual excitement lacking in her own marriage. Ben is awkward (this may be his first time). He calls Mrs. Robinson "the most attractive of all my parents' friends." After the affair is consummated, "Sounds of Silence" fills the soundtrack. "April Comes She Will" carries the plot through months of Ben wallowing time away floating in the pool and sleeping with Mrs. Robinson. He and his lover have nothing in common except sex. The affair continues out of sheer boredom; it is the one thing he has to look forward to, he says. His parents try to confront him about his lethargy and nights away from home, but Ben is aimlessly drifting through life.

That changes when Ben, at the insistence of his parents, goes out with Elaine Robinson. A notable weakness in the film is the failure to explore the character and motivation of Mrs. Robinson, especially regarding the Freudian overtones of the love triangle between mother, daughter, and Benjamin. Ben wrongly assumes Mrs. R. does not consider him good enough for her daughter. The film suggests otherwise. The lead-in to mother warning Ben to stay away from her daughter is a discussion about the abandoned dreams Mrs. Robinson had of being an artist. The unexpected pregnancy which led her to marriage also ended her artistic pursuits. The scene suggests that Mrs. Robinson has mixed emotions of resentment toward Elaine and jealousy over her youthful beauty, sexuality, and potential in life.

The film is vague about both Ben's and Elaine's motivations, their attraction to each other, and their future goals. It is clear the two share a kindred spirit; both are trying to escape the lives their parents have designed for them. Furious with Ben, Mrs. Robinson exposes the illicit affair to prevent him from seeing her daughter. "Scarborough Fair" weaves in and out of the story as Elaine leaves for school in Berkeley: "She once was a true love of mine." Ben follows, determined to marry Elaine.

The Robinsons hastily put together a wedding for Elaine and "All-American" med student Carl Smith. Fraternity brothers refer to Smith as "the old make-out king." Their unseemly talk degrades Elaine, especially in comparison to Ben's feelings for her. Nichols breaks Hollywood tradition with Ben arriving at the church just as the ceremony ends. Suddenly the marriage ritual and the past affair do not matter; they are merely the machinations of the plastic adult world. What *does* matter is the natural love between Ben and Elaine. In a highly dramatic scene, Ben pounds on a glass wall of the church balcony crying, "Elaine!" Jump-cutting shows the Robinsons' rage. Ben's determination, and the hostility that surrounds her, is an epiphany for Elaine. She screams, "Ben!" and runs down the aisle. A fight ensues. Mrs. Robinson slaps Elaine saying, "It's too late." The daughter responds, "Not for me." In a highly symbolic moment, Ben fights off Mr. Robinson and wedding guests with a cross and uses it to lock the doors of the church, trapping them all inside. The couple hop on a bus full of old people staring at them. Triumphantly, they sit in the backseat, Elaine in her wedding gown, with "Sounds of Silence" in the background.

The ending is left ambiguous, which bothered some critics. The nagging question about what Ben will do with his life is only partly answered by his love for Elaine. Nichols's strong reliance on the love-conquers-all convention for a resolution was a disappointment.

For the most part, *The Graduate* received rapturous reviews. *Variety* applauded the film, calling it "a delightful, satirical comedy-drama." *Time* said Nichols "moves easily from lacerating social satire to brittle neurotic comedy to surreal lyricism, and his work is greatly enhanced by Robert Surtees's photography and a superb score written and sung by Simon and Garfunkel." "Funny, outrageous and touching, *The Graduate* is a sophisticated film that puts Mr. Nichols and his associates on a level with any of the best satirists working abroad today," wrote the *Times*'s Crowther. His colleague Renata Adler was critical of some elements of the plot, but concluded that the film was "the most brilliant, if rather unstable, movie in quite some time." Only *Newsweek* was not impressed with Nichols's effort, calling it "a victim of the sophomore jinx."[87]

The Graduate was nominated for seven Academy Awards; Mike Nichols won the Oscar for Best Director. He also picked up the New York Film Critics award for Best Director that year. Simon and Garfunkel won three Grammy Awards: Record of the Year, Best Contemporary Pop Performance for "Mrs. Robinson," and Best Original Score (Paul Simon).

The Graduate was a landmark picture, elevating the integration of story and rock music. Director Mike Nichols used Simon and Garfunkel songs to reveal the main character's inner struggles. As Ehrenstein and Reed pointed out, "*The Graduate* turned song into a form of interior monologue *cum* Greek chorus commentary."[88] It has been argued, as *Film Quarterly* reviewers did, that the music "pumped poetic and intellectual content into *The Graduate*."

> Because the songs . . . are so concise, lyrical, eloquent, we're tempted to believe that the film contains their insights and that Ben understands them. We're supposed to assume that Ben shares Paul Simon's perceptions of 'people talking without speaking, people hearing without listening' in a world whose 'words of the prophet are written on the subway walls,' but in truth Ben couldn't *begin* putting the world in that kind of order.[89]

A better view is that the music functions on an aesthetic level of its own in the film, contributing to the audience's understanding of characters and the meaning of events. Where Ben might be confused and inarticulate, Simon and Garfunkel songs provide a musical commentary that allows the viewer to see through the protagonist's disorientation with a certain attitude toward him and the society in which he lives.

Four of the songs on the soundtrack were previously released tracks from Simon/Garfunkel albums, *Sounds of Silence* and *Parsley, Sage, Rosemary and Thyme*, both from 1966. "Sounds of Silence" topped the singles charts that year. "While I was writing a whole score for the film," Paul Simon explained, "Mike Nichols was using existing material to fill in the places where the score was supposed to be, and the more he lived with it, the more he decided that that material was absolutely appropriate, so the only new song that made it into there was 'Mrs. Robinson.' "[90] Two other singles were released during the film's run.: 'Scarborough Fair/Canticle" reached Number 11 on 16 March 1968 and "Mrs. Robinson" was Number 1 on 4 May 1968. The version of the latter hit single issued, however, was not from the movie soundtrack, but from the duet's *Book-ends* LP, released months later.

Columbia scored big in 1968. Three Simon and Garfunkel albums with songs from *The Graduate* finished in the Top 10 that year. *The Graduate*, *Parsley, Sage, Rosemary and Thyme*, and *Bookends* each sold more than one million copies.

The Graduate reached theaters in December 1967. Despite a limited run in only 350 theaters in the United States, the Embassy Picture reaped more than $35 million at the box office by July 1968. World net rental was estimated at more than $85 million by January 1971.[91] The film remains in the Top 100 of *Variety*'s all-time film rentals. The trade publication lists the distributor's gross at slightly more than $44 million.

In its initial run, *The Graduate* became the third top-grossing movie of all time, behind *The Sound of Music* (1965) and *Gone With the Wind* (1939). Writers contrasted *The Graduate* with the top-grossing film, as, despite some overlap, two entirely different audiences accounted for the enormous success of both. The Julie Andrews picture attracted the over-thirty-five crowd; *The Graduate* generated repeated viewings by young people aged seventeen to twenty-five. Young viewers returned again and again, watching for nuances or hidden meanings they might have missed.

Nineteen sixty-eight was the first year that entire college graduating classes consisted of Baby Boomers. It was also the year that graduate-student draft deferment was annulled. Protests against the Vietnam war heightened. *The Graduate* was playing in theaters while major events were taking place outside: the Tet Offensive, the Mai Lai massacre, police riots at the Democratic Convention in Chicago, and the assassination of Martin Luther King and Robert Kennedy.

The young audience at the time strongly identified with the confusion and alienation of Ben, along with the film's satire of middle-class values. Benjamin's honesty and idealism appeared to triumph over the shallow, materialistic values of the corrupt adult middle class. Benjamin articulated the feelings of a generation. Nichols later related a story about a meeting with one of the leaders of the Columbia University student uprising. He and his confederates loved *The Graduate*. "In a way, it was what the strike was all about," the student told the director. "Those kids had the nerve, they felt the necessity, to break the rules," Nichols said.[92]

Getcher Motor Runnin'

Easy Rider was a seminal film that brought the proclivities of low-budget exploitation flicks into mainstream Hollywood. (The first genuine motorcycle movie was *The Wild One* in 1954. Brando's role as the gang leader linked sexuality, rebellion, and the motorcycle together in the popular imagination. AIP's *The Wild Angels* was so closely modeled after the Brando picture that the producers feared charges of plagiarism.) In 1963, avantgarde filmmaker Kenneth Anger released an underground film on the biker culture. *Scorpio Rising* was the first dramatic film to incorporate rock music; its soundtrack contained eleven rock songs. One reviewer said the bikers were "drenched in earsplitting canonical rock'n'roll."[93] Though highly influential, it remained an "underground" classic. Each of these chopper flicks contributed to the design of *Easy Rider*.

Anger was a leader in the underground cinema. His films indulged in violence, mysticism, the occult, and lechery. In *Scorpio Rising*, the director explored the violence, homosexuality, and rituals of a motorcycle gang. The film revealed his fascination with the dress and initiation rites of black-leather-jacket youth who were alienated from society. Anger's editing and direction invited insistent comparisons with the *Hitlerjunge* of the 1930s. "All of this Anger sets forth with incredible and intoxicating intensity, and with a camera delicately attuned to each nuance of their shocking rites," wrote one critic. "Anger's film probes an increasingly malignant sector of our society."[94]

Scorpio Rising opened on the West Coast. Critics liked the film, but the Los Angeles police considered Anger's portrait beyond the limits of contemporary standards. When the film was shown at a Los Angeles art theater, the manager was arrested and the run cancelled. Ironically, a few days later the Ford Foundation selected Anger as a recipient of a fellowship award for creative filmmaking.

Scorpio Rising became an influential underground classic. The film made a number of sporadic appearances on college campuses and in film societies and then resurfaced for a run in New York in 1966. A newly formed *avant garde* film group, The Film-Maker's Distribution Center, screened Anger's portrait of the outlaw biker culture as part of its public debut. A critic for *The New Yorker* called it "by far the best of the so-called underground movies." *Variety* labelled it "a brilliantly executed, frighteningly serious film." "*Scorpio Rising* is the jewel of the avant-garde's surrealist school, a narcotic-high spin through the world of the motorcycle fetishists," wrote *Newsweek*. "Director Kenneth Anger orchestrates a relentlessly thumping pop soundtrack, psychedelically brilliant color and zig-zag cutting into a symphony of the senses."[95] The movie's songs included "I Will Follow Him" (Little Peggy March), "Hit the Road Jack" (Ray Charles), "Wipe Out" (The Sufaris), "My Boyfriend's Back" (The Angels), "Fools Rush In" (Kris Jensen), "Blue Velvet" (Bobby Vinton),

and material by Elvis Presley, The Rondells, The Crystals, Gene Mc-
Daniels, and Claudine Clark.

The Wild Angels + The Trip = Easy Rider

Easy Rider is an ironic portrayal of American individualism and freedom, a countercultural reversal of the Hollywood classic western. American society is depicted as malevolent; the random murder of the two biker
hippies shows that it has become dangerous. This countercultural vision
of a reborn America had at its core "another metaphorical frontier, an
image of new possibilities derived from drugs, sexual freedom, and a vague
spirituality," observed film analyst Robert B. Ray. "Above all, drugs
stood for the new uncharted territory, as dangerous as the real frontier
and, for the adventurous, equally tempting."[96]

Corman said that he conceived the bikers in *The Wild Angels* "to be to
a certain extent latter-day cowboys roaming free, on motorcycles rather
than horses."[97] The protagonists of *Easy Rider* are a synthesis of Corman's
biker sociopaths and the LSD hipsters of *The Trip*. "Those two films were
like classes for me," Peter Fonda explained.[98] Heavenly Blues acted out of
a simple desire to be free; the more intelligent Paul Groves sought answers
in LSD. The two are combined in *Easy Rider*.

The rock soundtrack for the film was treated as an integral part of it.
Songs were carefully placed as a musical commentary throughout the
picture, especially during the cross-country rides. In this sense, *Easy
Rider* went beyond AIP pictures. (*Scorpio Rising* and *The Graduate* had
both anticipated this use of rock music as an artistic statement complementing the plot and visual images in film.) The Dunhill soundtrack, which
featured music (some previously released) by Steppenwolf, Jimi Hendrix
Experience, The Byrds, The Band, and The Electric Prunes, was certified
gold in January 1970. (The Byrds and Steppenwolf were also featured on
the soundtrack for *Candy* in 1969.) Steppenwolf's "Rock Me" reached
Number 10 in March.

Stars Peter Fonda and Dennis Hopper had met at Hopper's wedding to
Brooke Hayward in 1961; the Hayward family were longtime friends of the
Fondas. By then they were both considered "Hollywood hippies," Cagin
and Dray noted, "who perceived themselves as full-fledged guerrillas in
the cultural revolution sweeping America."[99]

Ironically, the idea for *Easy Rider* was inspired by a Jack Valenti speech.
While the MPAA president was arguing for more pictures like *Doctor
Doolittle* (which was an enormous flop), Fonda defiantly resolved to make
a drug and motorcycle epic. *Easy Rider* was conceived as a variation of

the AIP motorcycle sagas. Fonda came up with the idea from a still photo of him and Bruce Dern on bikes in *The Wild Angels*. He quickly formulated the basic plot: "So I thought, 'These two guys, they score dope, sell everything and split L.A. for Florida: retired—great American dream to retire in Florida . . . they go across the country, they'll come face to face with themselves in all sorts of different situations'."[100] Together he and Hopper elaborated on the central storyline. The final screenplay is credited to Terry Southern, Fonda, and Hopper, though there was a reported dispute after the film was released about the degree of Southern's involvement.[101]

Easy Rider began at AIP. Executives were reluctant to give the erratic Hopper directorial control. They wanted a clause in the contract permitting them to replace Hopper if the film ran over budget. Fonda would not agree. He and Hopper took a twelve-page synopsis of the project to Bob Rafelson and Jack Nicholson, who were writing the script for *Head* at the time. After a dispute with Arkoff, who thought the biker pics had run their course, Rafelson took a second mortgage on his home and financed *Easy Rider* himself for a modest $385,000. Another $180,000 was spent on postproduction work. The film was made in seven weeks, but took another twelve months to edit the footage because of Hopper's resistance to cutting anything out of it.

Hopper's eccentric style and temper tantrums intensified when his wife left him during the production. The director became impossible to work with; Fonda reportedly hired a bodyguard. Nicholson was called in to salvage the deteriorated situation. When Rip Torn walked out, Nicholson took over the part of lawyer George Hanson, if only because he happened to be there. Nicholson eventually stole the show as the alcoholic ACLU lawyer who joins the trip for a brief time. Critics raved about his performance. The role landed Nicholson, formerly a "B" actor, an Oscar nomination as Best Supporting Actor, putting him on the road to stardom.

When the picture was complete, Rafelson managed a screening at Columbia, perhaps only because Bert Schneider's father was chairman of the board. By the time the final credits rolled, not a Columbia executive was left. "We can't distribute a picture like this," Rafelson recalled executives saying. "The people are ugly and have long hair and smoke dope; it's immoral, it's this, it's that." The director took *Easy Rider* to the Cannes Film Festival where it was a surprise hit, winning him the award for Best New Director. Columbia reconsidered the Pando Company-Raybert Productions film. "I charged them triple," Rafelson said.[102]

Peter Fonda and Dennis Hopper star in *Easy Rider* as two hippie bikers traveling from Los Angeles to the *Mardi Gras* in New Orleans. Wyatt

(Fonda) is "Captain America." His helmet, black-leather jacket, and motorcycle are decorated with the stars and stripes. His maniac sidekick, Billy (Hopper), wears frontier buckskins. The allusion to the traditional West of Wyatt Earp and Buffalo Bill (or is it Billy the Kid?) is unmistakable. In one scene, a camera shot shows them in a barn repairing a flat tire on Wyatt's cycle while farmers are outside shoeing a horse. While camping, Billy jokes that they are "out here in the wilderness fighting Indians and cowboys on every side." They are like young American trailblazers, modern variation of the classical frontier heroes, crossing vast stretches of land in search of the next frontier. "If instead of a white Stetson he [Wyatt] wears a red-white-and-blue crash helmet," one reviewer said, "this chiefly indicates a change in forms of locomotion."[103] The magnificent landscape of the Southwest and ribbons of highway—images of movement and freedom—give the picture an epic quality. Cinematographer Laszlo Kovacs, who like the others involved in *Easy Rider* came from under Corman's tutelage, contributed to the improvisational visual style of the film, which proved highly influential.

The film opens with the two making a cocaine purchase in Mexico. In the next scene, they rendezvous with a drug pusher under the landing approach at the Los Angeles airport, trading the white powder for cold, hard cash. Commercial airliners roar overhead as the transaction takes place. In the film's terms, drug dealing is acceptable as a means to pay for the freedom quest, but the soundtrack is filled with Steppenwolf's singing commentary, "God damn the pusher," suggesting something else. Wyatt stuffs the cash into a clear plastic tube, then inserts it into the teardrop gas tank on his motorcycle, which is painted with the Stars and Stripes. Hopper and Fonda mount their bikes like countercultural horsemen about to ride through the American mythic West of so many cowboy movies. Wyatt holds up his gold watch, then throws the timepiece to the ground. Just as they rev up their cycles, Steppenwolf's "Born to Be Wild" blasts in the soundtrack: "Getcher motor runnin'/Head out on that highway." The titles appear as the hippie cowboys begin their great adventure.

The film is a chronicle of the bikers' encounters with society as they travel across America. (From the outset, Wyatt is quietly observant, in search of something.) Their first night on the road they are refused a room at a motel. From that point on they camp alongside the road, smoking dope and philosophizing around an open fire.

On their journey Wyatt and Billy meet others who have found a measure of freedom in different ways, but none of them appeal to Wyatt and Billy. When they stop to fix a flat tire, a Southwestern farmer invites them to stay for dinner. He tells them he was once headed for California, "but you know how it is." Wyatt responds, "You've got a nice place. It's not every man can live off the land, ya know. You do your own thing in your own time. You should be proud."

The scene shifts to the two bikers winding through a forest, with "Wasn't Born to Follow" by The Byrds playing in the background. The music fads into the roar of the motorcycles as they stop for gas. When Wyatt and Billy are back on the road, The Band's "The Weight" accompanies panoramic shots of the wide-open Southwest. The duo delivers a hitchhiker to his home on a commune, where members all live a very simple, earthy existence—city kids struggle to grow crops in the arid climate and sandy soil. The leader suggests that the commune might be the right place for Wyatt and Billy, but Wyatt responds, "I just gotta go."

Each day, as they head further East, their encounters become more volatile and the American dream becomes a nightmare. When they join a small-town parade on their bikes, they are arrested for parading without a license. In jail they meet ACLU lawyer George Hanson (Jack Nicholson) who is sleeping off a hangover. Hansen offers his services and gets the boys out for a $25 fine. (Hopper described Nicholson's character as symbolizing "trapped America, killing itself.")[104] The southern lawyer dons an old football helmet and joins them on the trip to New Orleans to visit Madame Tinkerton's famed bordello. "If You Want to Be a Bird" plays as the three ride down the highway. That night they introduce Hanson to marijuana. Billy thinks he sees a UFO, which sends the lawyer off on a hilarious tale about aliens from advanced technological civilizations who are already in contact with government officials. He says Venusians are mating with people on earth from every walk of life so that "man will have the chance to transcend and evolve with some equality for all." Wyatt and Billy have a vague idea about freedom, but seem unable to express anything more than a desire to live free of societal strictures; Hanson is clearly the most articulate.

The next day the threesome enters a small-town restaurant. A group of young girls flirt with them in one booth, but the trio is surrounded by local rednecks and law officers who taunt them: "Looks like refugees from some gorilla love-in . . . We ought to mate 'em up with . . . black wenches. That's as low as you can git." Refused service and sensing possible trouble, they leave. That night Hanson says, "This used to be a hell of a good country. I can't understand what's gone wrong with it." He explains to Wyatt and Billy how the country has changed and why people refused service to them.

> GEORGE: Oh, they're not scared of you. They're scared of what you represent to them.

BILLY: Hey, man. All we represent to them, man, is somebody needs a haircut.
GEORGE: What you represent to them is freedom.
BILLY: What the hell's wrong with freedom, man. That's what it's all about.
GEORGE: Oh, yeah; that's right—that's what it's all about, all right. But talking about it and being it—that's two different things. I mean, it's real hard to be free when you're bought and sold in the marketplace. 'Course, don't ever tell anybody they're not free, 'cause they're gonna get real busy killin' and maimin' just to prove to you that they are. Oh, yeah—they're gonna talk to you, and talk to you, and talk to you about individual freedom, but they see a free individual, it's gonna scare 'em.
BILLY: Mmmm, well, that don't make 'em runnin' scared.
GEORGE: No. It makes 'em dangerous.

Hanson's speech anticipates the next scene. Locals beat the trio with bats while they're in their sleeping rolls, and Hansen is killed. The remainder of the film suffers from his absence. The Electric Prunes' "Kyrie Eleison-Mardi Gras" plays as Wyatt and Billy dine at a restaurant in New Orleans (before visiting the brothel because "he would have wanted us to.") Madame Tinkerton's place is decorated with religious images. Wyatt has a premonition of the tragedy to come. He and Billy pick up two prostitutes (Karen Black and Toni Basil) and embark on an LSD trip in a nearby cemetery. (The scene was shot in 16mm and then blown up for effect.) Jimi Hendrix's "If 6 Were 9" provides the accompaniment. The premonition is repeated.

As they leave New Orleans enroute to retirement in Florida, Billy says, "We're rich. We did it . . . that's what it's all about, man. You go for the big money and then you're free. Ya dig?" Wyatt is despondent. "We blew it," he responds cryptically.

"From the perspective of the 1980s, with the idealism of the counterculture long since tarnished, it's fairly obvious that Billy and Wyatt have 'blown it' by selling out," commented Cagin and Dray. "They are neither communal nor idealistic; they are, finally, just greedy."[105] The search for America ends with the realization of their own corruption—they too are part of the system.

The movie ends with the senseless violence that has come to characterize much of the Sixties. Two rednecks in a pickup truck caught Billy, pointing a shotgun at him: "Want me to blow your brains out? Why don't you get a haircut?" The biker flips him the finger. A shotgun blast wounds him. Wyatt circles back to help his friend. He heads off for medical help. In the meantime the truck makes a U-turn, presumably to eliminate any witnesses. Wyatt and his motorcycle are blown off the road in slow-motion. The film ends with an aerial shot of the burning bike on the side of the highway as Roger McGuinn sings the "Ballad of Easy Rider."

Though critics found some fault with the film, reviews were generally strong. It was the *phenomenon* of *Easy Rider*, its merger of artistic statement with topics and production styles associated with cheap youth exploitation flicks, that fascinated film critics. *Newsweek* noted how the film transcended its cheap predecessors. " 'Easy Rider' has the immediacy of these earlier movies, but it uses violence sparingly, to devastating effect," Morgenstern wrote. "And it develops its single, strong idea through flashes of brilliant writing and performance that more than make up for the foolishness, and through dazzling photography . . . that reminds us of how ravishingly beautiful parts of the nation remain." *Time* considered it a "major movie." "Like other films directed to—and by—youth, *Easy Rider* could have settled for catcalls and rebellion," the reviewer wrote. "Instead the film has refurbished the classic romantic gospel of the outcast wanderer. Walt Whitman might not have recognized the bikes— but he would have understood the message." *Variety*, too, commended most aspects of the production, saying, "It is far above the usual films on this subject." Even Canby, who offered only a mild review, was impressed by the impact *Easy Rider* and several other low-budget films with unknown or relatively unknown casts might have on the film industry. He said, "The most exciting thing about *Easy Rider* is neither content nor style nor statement, but the fact that it was made for less than $500,000 (less than the cost of one set for some super-productions), by young men working outside the moviemaking establishment, and that it is apparently reaching a large audience." A reviewer in *Film Quarterly* called the film "honest, almost always convincing, beautiful, and engrossing."[106]

Easy Rider eventually grossed more than $60 million. Columbia earned $19 million in domestic theatrical rentals. Fonda reportedly owned 22 percent.[107] The film's stars did not fare as well afterwards as others involved in the project. Hopper faded from the movie scene after the disappointing *The Last Movie* in 1971, but made a successful comeback beginning with *Hoosiers* and *Blue Velvet*, both in 1986. Fonda never made it as a director, but continued to act throughout the Seventies, even though he was overshadowed by his sister Jane. Nicholson obviously went on to extraordinary achievement, with numerous Oscar nominations and awards, including Best Actor for his performance in *One Flew Over the Cuckoo's Nest* (1975). After the surprise success of *Easy Rider*, Columbia signed BBS Productions (Schneider, Rafelson, and Steve Blumer) to a multipicture deal, giving the independent company complete artistic control. Relying on BBS to make inroads into the youth market, Columbia agreed to finance and distribute six films with budget ceilings at $1 million. Two of the six, *Five Easy Pieces* (1970) and *The Last Picture Show* (1971), were both critical and commercial successes. (The latter was directed by Corman apprentice Peter Bogdanovich.)

Hollywood discovered the youth market in the surprising triumph of *The Graduate, Easy Rider, Bonnie and Clyde*, and *2001: A Space Odyssey*. As Cagin and Dray noted, "The overwhelming success of *Easy Rider* suggested a future of Hollywood movies that would involve a small risk yet would yield an enormous profit, that would be relevant and artistic and popular, that would revitalize Hollywood at the same time it acknowledged Hollywood tradition."[108] Seeking to reverse the long trend of declining revenues, the major studios jumped on the juvenile bandwagon. Hollywood began to court the Baby Boom generation. Topics once relegated to the low-grade exploitation films were now acceptable for the majors as they targeted the under-thirty audience.

Antonioni revisited the youth uprising in 1970 with *Zabriskie Point*, a lesser achievement than his first successful probe of the youth culture, *Blow-Up*. For this second MGM production the director moved the action to the American West. While Antonioni captured the ambience of West Coast Pop Art, the drama and dialogue left something to be desired. In the film Mark sees a policeman kill a surrendering black militant during a campus riot in Los Angeles. He draws his own gun just as someone else shoots the cop. Mark escapes, steals a plane, and flies to the desert, where he meets Daria, a gorgeous hippie secretary on assignment with her real-estate supervisor. The two tramp around a barren, deserted area called Zabriskie Point. They criticize the system, make love, and paint the plane with psychedelic colors. Daria goes on to her conference; Mark flies back to Los Angeles, where he is killed by police when he refuses to stop the plane.

Zabriskie Point shows the tensions in the American youth revolution. The film begins with real radical politics. The scenes in the desert are concerned with reactions to political events. Daria's apolitical cultural rebellion is juxtaposed with Mark's frustration over the slow progress of political action. His death symbolizes the failure of do-your-own-thing politics isolated from a mass base, particularly the working class. From his European Marxist perspective, Antonioni "finds both aspects of the youth scene somewhat frivolous," one reviewer pointed out. "The movement of the picture is *away from* Mark and Daria's original states: toward death in his case, and toward involvement, or at any rate a recognition that some things may be terrible after all, in hers."[109]

Pink Floyd pioneered the synthesized rock score for *Zabriskie Point*. Numbers by The Rolling Stones, The Grateful Dead, and Pink Floyd backed many of the scenes. Much of the music from the movie, however, was not included in the MGM soundtrack.

Zabriskie Point was one of several 1970 films with rock soundtracks that dealt with radicalism among American university students. One, Columbia's *Getting Straight* which starred Elliot Gould and Candice Bergen, included songs by The New Establishment and P.K. Limited. Another, MGM's *The Strawberry Statement*, based on the novel by James Simon Kunen, featured music by Crosby, Stills, Nash and Young. Also in 1970, Melanie was featured in the soundtrack for *RPM*, which starred Anthony Quinn and Ann-Margret. Following Hollywood conventions, however, these films all tended to trivialize their sensational subject matter by reducing political activism to sex. The major issue of student protest, the Vietnam War, was essentially ignored. Consequently these pictures never probed their subject deeply enough. These films appear superficial in comparison with the real-life campus unrest and violence at colleges and universities sweeping across the country in the late Sixties, most notably at Columbia, Berkeley, Harvard, Kent State, and Jackson State.

Also in 1970, Paramount released *Been Down So Long It Looks Like Up To Me*, based on the Richard Farina novel, whose soundtrack included music by The Five Satins, The Platters, and The Four Lads. Rolling Stone Mick Jagger appeared in the violent *Performance*, a Warner Brothers picture co-directed by Nicholas Roeg and Donald Cammell.

A problem for filmmakers examining the youth revolution at that time was determining the genuineness of the movement. "There was always a chasm between sixties rhetoric and sixties action, a difference that was only exaggerated by an acute sensitivity to mass media on the part of would-be revolutionaries," Cagin and Dray pointed out. "Most sympathetic filmmakers were well aware that their footage not only failed to bridge the chasm but actually widened it by providing a vicarious substitute for the very revolution it sought to promote."[110]

Entering the "Me Decade"

If there is a pivotal film bridging the revolutionary Sixties and the complacent 1970s Me Decade, it is *American Graffiti* (1973). This movie about the end of the Eisenhower Era played in theaters at the end of the Vietnam Era; rapid cultural change made the yesterday of a decade earlier seem like textbook history. One reviewer noted the film's "weird, unnerving distillation of future shock."[111] On the one hand, *Graffiti* was "designed primarily for fun, to be *entertaining*, a warm movie about what it's like to be a teenager," director George Lucas explained, adding:

But it's also about the end of a political era, a sociological era and a rock era. You have three eras coming to an end, and people have to change and the country has to change. You have to go from a warm, secure, uninvolved life into the later sixties, which was involvement, anti-war stuff, revolution, and a different kind of rock'n'roll. Now we're changing again. You can't fight change on any level. I guess that's the only statement I was making in the film. A lot of people might say it's simpleminded, but for lot of kids, it's one of the hardest things to do in life, to plunge into something new.[112]

The young filmmaker had decided to make an optimistic film during a period of cynicism in America. The movie is set in the optimistic era of Kennedy and Martin Luther King—pre-Vietnam, pre-Watts, pre-Watergate. It embodies the American ideals that Lucas found to be true during his own experience breaking into filmmaking.

Though *American Graffiti* was drawn from the director's personal background, the film communicates the universal experience of American adolescence. It is, as one critic observed, "a *rediscovery* of the past."[113] For the Baby Boom audience that made this picture a smash hit in 1973, *American Graffiti* was like seeing their whole teenage experience compressed into one summer night in southern California.

Where were you in '62?

George Lucas merged his own adolescence and interests in *American Graffiti*. The film is about those high school "cruisin' " years in Modesto, what he called the "endless parade of kids in flamed, lowered and customed machines who rumble down the one-way street, through the seemingly adultless, heat-drugged little town."[114] Most of the incidents in the film came from Lucas's experience, but they were glamorized for the movie. "I spent four years of my life cruising the main street of my home town, Modesto, California," Lucas said. "I went through all that stuff, drove the cars, bought liquor, chased girls. . . . I think a lot of people do, which is the whole idea behind the title—a very American experience."[115] Lucas actually saw himself as a composite of the main characters. "I started out as Terry the Toad, but then I went on to be John Milner, the local drag-race champion, and then I became Curt Henderson, the intellectual who goes off to college," he explained. "They were all composite characters, based on my life, and on the lives of friends of mine. Some were killed in Vietnam, and quite a number were killed in auto accidents."[116]

Beyond its autobiographical nature, *Graffiti* showed the filmmaker's interest in anthropology and the social sciences. "I was always interested in America and why it is what it is," he said. "I was always fascinated by the cultural phenomenon of cruising, that whole teenage mating ritual. It's really more interesting than primitive Africa or ancient New Guinea—and much, much weirder."[117]

Lucas was a shy teenager who "barely squeaked through high school," by his own admission.[118] Engrossed in comic books and fanatical about his souped-up Fiat, he spent nights blaring rock music on the radio while cruising Modesto's, 10th Street. Three days before his high school graduation he was nearly killed in a car crash; he spent four months recuperating. After that he left cars behind, his dreams of becoming a car racer crushed. He spent two years at Modesto Junior College as a social science major, during which time he developed an obsession with movies. His interest in becoming a filmmaker was encouraged by noted cinematographer Haskell Wexler. When he left Modesto to enter film school, Lucas laughed, "Everybody thought I'd end up as a ticket-taker at Disneyland."[119]

Ignoring warnings that he could not get into the film business, Lucas came into his own at the prestigious Cinema School of the University of Southern California. His futuristic sci-fi short, *THX-1138:4E*, won first prize at the Third National Student Film festival in 1965 and a six-month scholarship to observe production at Warner Brothers, where he was assigned to *Finian's Rainbow*, directed by Francis Ford Coppola, who took an immediate interest in Lucas. After Lucas graduated in 1966, Coppola hired him as a production assistant and allowed him to make a documentary about the production of Coppola's *The Rain People*. (Lucas also worked as a cameraman on the Rolling Stones documentary *Gimme Shelter*.) Coppola's influence got Lucas a contract with Warners to develop his sci-fi short into a feature film, *THX 1138* (1971). The grim portrait of the twenty-fifth century fared well with the critics and eventually drew a cult following, but was a commercial flop.

After *THX 1138*, Lucas labored unsuccessfully on *Apocalypse Now* for four years before Francis Ford Coppola finally bought the property back. The pressure was on the young filmmaker.

Lucas wrote the script for *American Graffiti* in collaboration with Gloria Katz and her husband Willard Huyck, whom he had met at USC. The couple heightened the script's fantasy element and added humor to Lucas's more realistic portrait. Lucas and producer Gary Kurtz pitched the project to United Artists with a tape recording of period songs playing to establish the atmosphere. UA commissioned a screenplay, but after seeing several drafts still considered the project too risky because of its impressionistic dependence on the aura of the period instead of a dramatic storyline. This was before the Fifties nostalgia craze, and UA dropped the project. In the meantime, Lucas refused several other projects offered to him while he peddled the script for *Graffiti* around town for another year. Every major studio turned down what would become one of the top-three-grossing pictures of 1973.

Eventually Universal reconsidered. Vice president Ned Tanen agreed to finance the project if a bankable name could be attached to the property. Someone, Kurtz explained, "who would in himself represent a salable commodity. From their point of view, we had nobody. *THX 1138* had done fairly well critically but was playing on the bottom half of a double bill with a Warner's flop. My track record was not encouraging, and we had no names for the cast. It was at that point we went to Francis [Coppola] and asked him if he would come into the project.[120]

A more bankable name could not be found at the time; Coppola had recently finished his magnificent directorial work on *The Godfather* for Paramount. The 1972 picture became the top-grossing film in the industry's history, giving Coppola enormous influence. Coppola actually served in a nominal capacity as producer of *American Graffiti*, with Kurtz as co-producer. Lucas and Kurtz naively submitted an "honest" budget of $800,000. Standard operations were that producers inflated the budget in order to deal with the film studio; Universal countered with $650,000. The parties compromised on a minimal $715,000 budget.

Graffiti was filmed with an extremely talented cast of relatively unknowns including Richard Dreyfuss, Ron Howard, Paul Le Mat, Charlie Martin Smith, Cindy Williams, Candy Clark, MacKenzie Phillips, and Harrison Ford; for most of them the Lucas film proved an important career stepping stone. Disc jockey Wolfman Jack was hired for a minimal fee. (The weirdo DJ had a kind of omnipresence in the southern California youth culture in the early 1960s. While FCC regulations limited radio stations to 50,000 watts, the Wolfman Jack's program was transmitted from Tijuana using 250,000 watts.) "He has an ethereal presence in the lives of young people," explained Kurtz, "and it was that quality we wanted and obtained in the picture."[121] Lucas had listened to disc jockey Wolfman Jack during his cruising days.

> I was always very interested in the relationship between teenagers and radio . . .
> For teenagers the person closest to them is a fantasy character. That's the disc
> jockey . . . a lot of teenagers have a make-believe friend in a disc jockey, but
> he's much more real because he talks to them, he jokes around. Especially a
> really excellent disc jockey like Wolfman Jack. He's part of the family. You
> listen to him every day, you're very close to him, you share your most intimate
> moments with him.[122]

Lucas mined the techniques and conventions of early AIP pictures. In fact, the director wanted the film to look "like a 1962 'Hot Rods to Hell' jukebox."[123] His old friend Haskell Wexler was brought in as "visual consultant" to overcome the difficulties of shooting the entire film at night. (The cameraman had to fly every evening from Los Angeles, where he shot commercials during the day, to the film's location just north of San Francisco to shoot at night.) "I wanted the film to look sort of like a Sam Katzman beach-party movie, all yellow and red and orange," explained Lucas. "And Haskell figured out how to do it. . . . The movie looked exactly the way I wanted it to look—very much like a carnival."[124]

The film was shot for a minuscule $780,000; Lucas ended up borrowing and investing his own money in this project about the last day of summer for the Class of '62. Shot with a crew of about forty people and a short, twenty-eight-day shooting schedule, the production was a grueling affair with cold temperatures hampering the odd working schedule. Lucas said, "*American Graffiti* was unpleasant because of the fact that there was no money, no time and I was compromising myself to death. But I could rationalize it because of the fact that, well, it is just a $700,000 picture— it's Roger Corman—and what do you expect, you can't expect everything to be right for making a little cheesy, low-budget movie.[125]

After the film was completed Universal remained reluctant to release it; executives considered it instead for a TV movie. Only after Coppola offered to buy the film back from the studio did Universal reconsider.

American Graffiti is a nostalgic look at four high schoolers on the last night of summer 1962—the next morning, two of the friends are scheduled to leave for college in the East. It seems an entire year of comic, frightening, and romantic escapades occurs in one night as the storylines of the four main characters crisscross in a dusk-to-dawn adventure. Mel's Burger City Drive-in is the hub for bored teenagers who cruise endlessly around the block in a small American city. The automobile is the focus of Lucas's scrupulous ethnographic portrait of teen culture at that time. Though the year is 1962, the cars and outfits, sock hop and drive-in restaurant, references to James Dean and Sandra Dee, and music make it appear more like the Land of Father Knows Best in a time-frozen Fifties.

The film does not actually have a conventional storyline, but is a series of vignettes sewn together by nonstop rock soundtrack. *Graffiti* opens with Haley's "Rock Around the Clock," a clear identification with *Blackboard Jungle* and the beginning of the rock film era. The song's title is also an appropriate metaphor for this around-the-clock, teen rite of passage. Lucas does not sentimentalize or exploit the teen culture of the tranquil period before assassinations and draft calls. Instead, he explores the feelings and associations people had while trying to remember and make sense of it. The characters are unaware of the earthshaking events destined to alter the American landscape in the next few years and destroy their innocence forever. Though the four main characters were built on composites, each goes beyond traditional stereotypes.

Class president Steve (Ron Howard) begins his supposedly final night in the nest confident about leaving for college. He breaks up with steady girlfriend and head cheerleader Laurie (Cindy Williams) because he wants to date other girls while he is away at school. Laurie reluctantly agrees, but schemes all night to keep him from leaving. In the end, Steve decides his life in the small town is too valuable to leave behind for a new one. He and Laurie are reunited at dawn.

Steve had allowed "Terry the Toad" (Charlie Martin Smith) to take care of his car while he's away at college. In his newly acquired wheels, Terry picks up Debbie (Candy Clark), who wears her hair in a bouffant, thinking she looks like Sandra Dee. Terry stumbles through a series of comical situations including getting liquor without an I.D., having the car stolen, and getting "sicker than a dog" from drinking.

Local drag-strip king John Milner (Paul Le Mat) ends up driving thirteen-year-old Carol (Mackenzie Phillips) around for most of the night while avoiding a challenge by newcomer Bob Falfa (Harrison Ford). Milner has been number one on the strip for a long time, but realizes the crown will not be his forever. He makes several references to the dying teen utopia. "The whole strip is shrinking," he complains. "Five or six years ago it used to take a couple of hours and a whole tankful of gas just to make one circuit." Later he denounces the Beach Boys' surfing sound: "Rock 'n' roll's been going downhill ever since Buddy Holly died," he says. Finally, Milner and Falfa race. The king beats Falfa, but only because the challenger loses control of his car and crashes.

Only Curt (Richard Dreyfuss) is able to venture beyond the small town's borders, although he is unsure about leaving, wondering if he is "the competitive type" who can survive at an Eastern college. Throughout the night he pursues a beautiful, mysterious blonde (Suzanne Sommers), who drives around in a '56 Thunderbird. A local gang, the Pharoahs (Bo Hopkins plays the leader), "abducts" Curt for sitting on one of their cars. They put him through an initiation to become a gang member, which shows Curt that he has more courage than he thought.

Desperate to link up with the blonde in the Thunderbird, Curt goes to the radio station outside of town in search of Wolfman Jack, a demigod-like disc jockey. The mysterious Wolfman appears as a kind of Wizard-of-Oz-DJ, omnipresent over the airwaves. He claims he can "make all your dreams come true'' and Callers make requests for songs that will save broken relationships. At the station, Curt finds a kind but obscure man eating popsicles. He is Wolfman, who vainly tries to conceal his identity while encouraging Curt to pursue his dreams and experience the world. ''This encounter clinches Curt's decision to leave his childhood wonderland,'' observed one reviewer. ''At last he knows that the emerald city is a mirage.''[126] The DJ makes Curt's plea for the blonde to call him over the airwaves but the two never get together. Curt leaves for college the next morning. From the plane he sees the white Thunderbird driving down the highway. The film ends with yearbook photos and inscriptions telling the fate of the four friends:

Steve Bolander is an insurance agent in Modesto, California.

Terry Fields was reported missing in action in Vietnam.

John Milner was killed by a drunk driver in December 1964.

Curt Henderson is a writer living in Canada.

Critics responded to *Graffiti* with great enthusiasm. ''Few films have shown quite so well the eagerness, the sadness, the ambitions and small defeats of a generation of young Americans,'' wrote *Time*'s Jay Cocks. ''Bitchin', as they said back then. Superfine.'' *Variety* said, ''Lucas has done a truly masterful job.'' A reviewer writing in the *Atlantic Monthly* dubbed the movie ''one of the best American films about adolescence ever made.'' *American Graffiti* ''is a rock & roll movie deep down in its soul,'' wrote Jon Landau in *Rolling Stone*. ''It is a brilliantly original conception of not just the nature of the past, but the roots of the present—a very immediate past and present that readers of this particular magazine should find extraordinarily significant and moving.'' *Times* critic Stephen Farber (filling in for vacationing Vincent Canby) hyped *American Graffiti* as another *Bonnie and Clyde* and *Five Easy Pieces*. ''The nostalgia boom has finally produced a lasting work of art,'' he wrote. ''Lucas has brought the past alive, with sympathy, affection, and thorough understanding . . . at 28 he is already one of the world's master directors.'' When Canby returned, he qualified his associate's hyperbole. ''*American Graffiti*'' he wrote, ''is such a funny, accurate movie, so controlled and efficient in its narrative, that it stands to be overpraised to the point where seeing it will be an anticlimax.''[127]

Lucas's paean to the Modesto car culture of 1962 featured a continuous background of golden oldies. The material for the soundtrack was drawn from a list of some two hundred songs that Lucas and Kurtz put together from the director's huge collection of 78- and 45-rpm rock records from his teen years. The low production budget, however, meant sacrifice in the music department. A desired Presley number was deemed too expensive. The anticipated fifty songs from the pre-Beatle period were reduced to forty-one. Lucas spent between $75 and $80,000 to purchase the music rights for the film's soundtrack. The songs were so integral to the plot that they were actually written into the script. Walter Murch blended the unending stream of rock oldies together into a collage of sound. Murch and Lucas found it easy to make substitutions when a song was too expensive or unavailable:

> You'd put a song down on one scene, and you'd find all kinds of parallels. And you could take another song and put it down there, and it would still seem as if the song had been written for that scene. All good rock and roll is classic teenage stuff, and all the scenes were such classic teenage scenes that they just sort of meshed, no matter how you threw them together. Sometimes even the words were identical.[128]

Kim Fowley produced two original recordings for the film that were performed by Flash Cadillac and The Continental Kids as a local rock band at the sock hop.

The chatter of Wolfman Jack and the host of hit singles he spins over the radio are not just atmosphere in *Graffiti*; they are like characters in this kaleidoscope of Fifties teenage culture. *Times* critic Stephen Farber described the effectiveness of the music in the film:

> The soundtrack has a special importance. A nonstop stream of fifties music, punctuated with fragments of a disk jockey's crazy freeform monologue, accompanies all the action. The radio is these kids' lifeline, and by keeping it in the background of almost every scene, Lucas mesmerizes us right along with the characters. The music releases our own memories, and gives an emotional charge to everything on screen.[129]

Lucas turned the forms and rhythms of rock music into a cinematic technique, one reviewer observed. "*American Graffiti* has no traditional structure," he wrote,

> . . . because it works the way pop music does: it depends on pace, energy, and the selection of images that will set up resonance with its audience. Its shots are often like rock lyrics—simple, hard, and filled with implications. It's a new, loose way of working in movies and the success of *American Graffiti* may well encourage others to try it.[130]

The *American Graffiti* soundtrack of classic oldies sold a tidy 2.5 million copies.

ABC later brought the nostalgia generated by *Graffiti* to television: Ron Howard of the *Graffiti* cast starred in *Happy Days*, which became a top-rated show; behind *Happy Days* in the ratings was *Laverne and Shirley*, with *Graffiti*'s Cindy Williams as co-star.

Some critics have charged Lucas with fueling the complacency of the young after the social upheaval of the previous decade. "Well, the main thing I would say is that there is going to be complacency whether I encourage it or not," the director replied. "That's because kids in the last ten years have been beating their heads against the wall, and their brains and their blood are all over the pavement."[131] Lucas argued that *Graffiti* was a film about change that operated on a number of levels. "It's about the change in rock and roll, it's about the change in a young person's life at 18 when he leaves home and goes off to college; and it's also about the cultural change that took place when the fifties turned into the sixties— when we went from a country of apathy and non-involvement to a country of radical involvement," he said. "The film is saying that you have to go forward. You have to be Curt, you have to go into the sixties. The fifties can't live."[132]

American Graffiti became the surprise hit of 1973, and the largest-grossing film made for under $1 million. All told the film returned $145 million worldwide against Universal's $780,000 investment.[133] United Artists received $55 million from domestic theatrical rentals alone. *Graffiti* remains on *Variety*'s list of the Top 100 All-Time Film Rental Champs. The overwhelming success of his nostalgic venture gave Lucas the leverage he needed to negotiate a deal with Twentieth Century-Fox for his next project, *Star Wars*.

More American Graffiti?

George Lucas' own independent production company, Lucasfilm, produced the sequel, *More American Graffiti* which was written and directed by B. W. L. Norton and produced by Howard Kazanjian. Lucas served only as executive producer. Only Richard Dreyfuss is absent from the original principal cast; Wolfman Jack is once again heard on the soundtrack and Harrison Ford makes an uncredited appearance as a police officer.

The plot suffered from the ending of *American Graffiti*, which robbed the sequel of dramatic surprise by revealing the fate of the four main characters. The movie jumps around during the turbulent years 1964–67. John Milner is still drag-racing his car, Terry the Toad and Little Joe are in Vietnam, Debbie and Carol are flower children in San Francisco, Steve and Laurie have twin sons and marital problems, and the Dreyfuss character Curt is replaced by Andy (Will Seltzer), a draft-card-burning college student. Unlike in the original, the anthology of music in this film seems incidental to the plot. Period pieces simply established the time. Norton and Kazanjian utilized split-screen techniques and a jigsaw puzzle of the period to show the fragmentation of the characters' lives. The attempt was "daring, but ultimately pointless," said *Variety*. The *Times*'s Janet Maslin said the film was "grotesquely misconceived, so much so that it nearly eradicates fond memories of the original."[134]

The *More American Graffiti* LP had a twofold marketing impact—it was both a soundtrack and a nostalgia album. MCA hoped it would reach both the twelve-to-twenty-five-year-olds and an older audience. Marketing director Sam Passamano explained the rationale:

> In a soundtrack like *More*, where the songs were chosen because of their sequencing in the movie, the soundtrack in the first place was marketed to enhance the success of the movie, not just as nostalgia, since filmgoers were predicted to be a younger audience for whom the music would not be nostalgia. We tied in very heavily with the Universal people in going after that younger audience."[135]

The strategy did not work; the MCA soundtrack sold poorly. The film also flopped. Universal saw a return of only $8 million in domestic rentals. Audiences in Carter's 1979 America were not ready to revisit the Sixties.

Keep On Rockin'

In the years 1971–77, *American Graffiti* and *Tommy* were the only rock soundtrack albums to appear in the year-end Top 10 best-seller lists. In that period, Scorsese's *Mean Streets* (1973) had featured The Rolling Stones and The Ronettes. The director used jump-cutting techniques pioneered by Richard Lester. Despite critical acclaim, the movie and its soundtrack both flopped. The nostalgia film *That'll Be the Day* (1973) spawned a Top 10 hit for David Essex, "Rock On." It's songs included a host of oldies by the Big Bopper, Dion, The Everly Brothers, Jerry Lee Lewis, Little Richard, and The Platters, among others, and Ringo Starr and The Who's Keith Moon were among the cast. Warners *Flame* (1974) was a showcase for the British rock group Slade.

The Rocky Horror Picture Show first appeared in 1973 in London as a play by Richard O'Brien. American entertainment executive Lou Adler purchased the U.S. rights and brought the play to the Roxy, a rock club on Sunset Strip in Los Angeles, where the show had a successful run for ten months in 1974. Adler closed it to allow cast members Tim Curry and

Meatloaf to work on the film version, but an original Roxy cast album was released in 1974 on Adler's Ode Records.

The film was shot in eight weeks; Twentieth Century Fox invested about $1 million in the production. (Adler had mounted a Broadway version of the play in the spring of 1975. It bombed, closing after only forty-five performances.) The Lou Adler/Michael White film opened in Los Angeles in September 1975 with very little fanfare. Fox executives were apprehensive about the picture and it consequently got few bookings or reviews. "It was a secret release," an employee at Adler's firm said. "Twentieth keep the film secret by sending out only seven prints of the film. It's no wonder there weren't many reviews."[136]

A year and a half after *Rocky Horror* opened, the film company was ready to bury it, having received only $400,000 from rentals. Word of mouth, however, turned *Rocky Horror* into a midnight moneymaker. The story about two naive young lovers who stumble upon the castle of transvestite scientist Dr. Frank N. Furter developed a cult following in the midnight circuit normally reserved for films like *Night of the Living Dead* and other classic monster movies. *Rocky Horror* became *the* late night cult film. A report in the *Times* described the theater experience as "a cross between sitting ringside at a Las Vegas floor show and ogling the crowd at a punk-rock concert, perhaps the biggest audience-participation movie ever made."[137] A decade after its original opening *Rocky Horror* became "a sleeper hit for insomniacs," grossing over $60 million from Friday and Saturday midnight showings in scattered theaters across the country.[138] The film starred Tim Curry as the bi-sexual scientist with Barry Bostwick and Susan Sarandon as the recently engaged couple, Brad and Janet. Rock singer Meat Loaf made an appearance as biker Eddie.

A&M distributed the film's 1975 soundtrack album on Ode Records. The Ode release is really an original cast recording, including Rockyite favorites: Frank N. Furter's "Sweet Transvestite," Janet singing "Toucha, Toucha, Touch Me," and the theater-aisle dance number "Time Warp" by Riff Raff, Columbia, Magenta, the Narrator, and the Transylvanians. Meatloaf is noticeably absent. The LP entered the *Billboard* charts on 15 April 1978. It spent fifty-eight weeks on the charts, reaching Number 49. Gold certification was awarded in April 1978.

In 1978, *Times* critic Janet Maslin observed that rock itself had become an appropriate subject for Hollywood treatment, noting several movies that were "offering a crash course in the history of rock and roll."[139] For example, *American Hot Wax*, *I Wanna Hold Your Hand*, *FM*, and Scorsese's *The Last Waltz* each explored different phases of the rock era. They all flopped at the box office. One writer noted, "If the movie industry recognizes rock's commercial potential, it has yet to grasp either its actual subject matter or its audience's tastes, which may explain why the LP packages prove generally more satisfying than the films they're drawn from.''[140] That critic was only partially correct. With the exception of *FM*, the soundtracks mentioned all failed to generate significant sales. Stigwood's *Fever* and *Grease* aside, *Thank God It's Friday*, *The Rose*, and rockumentary *The Kids Are Alright* were the only rock soundtracks certified platinum in 1978–79. The success of *The Rose*, with quasi-rock music, can be attributed to the outstanding debut performance of Bette Midler, and, to a lesser degree, the Top-10 title track. Other films in the rock exploitation genre all bombed at the box office and in the record stores. (One important reason was that RSO's dance musicals were stealing the show with an unprecedented strategy for the synergism of rock music and movies (see Chapter 4).)

Freed's In Hot Wax

American Hot Wax (1978) was Paramount's follow-up to the Stigwood productions *Saturday Night Fever* and *Grease*. Produced by Art Linson, who also did *Car Wash*, the semibiographical plot involved a week in the life of legendary disc jockey Alan Freed (Tim McIntire). Freed pioneered black rhythm and blues among the white teenage audience in the Fifties. In the mold of its rock-musical ancestors, the plot of *American Hot Wax* builds to a big rock'n'roll show finale at the Brooklyn Paramount (It was actually shot at the Wiltern Theatre in Los Angeles).

As critics noted, performances by veteran Fifties' rockers Chuck Berry, Jerry Lee Lewis, and Screamin' Jay Hawkins provided the film's only exciting moments. The thin plot also lacked credibility, as it sentimentalized the rebel DJ as a martyr for rock 'n' roll and a prophet among the moral guardians of American society. Andrew Sarris called it a "glossy deification of Alan Freed."[141] Screenwriter John Kaye defended the film, saying, "It's not a documentary, but the spirit, the authenticity are there. We're trying to capture the naive excitement of a certain time, when rock'n'roll was being born."[142]

Consequently, Freed's indictment in the payola scandals, as well as his poor health, were mentioned only in passing. The feud between rock legends Berry and Lewis was also omitted.

Trying to repeat the Stigwood strategy, Paramount produced a one-hour TV variety show, *Thank You, Rock'n'Roll*, to generate enthusiasm for *American Hot Wax*. The television special was scheduled to air the week before the movie began its mid-March run in 600 theaters.[143] The promotional effort could not make up for the lackluster story.

Critics were disappointed. David Ansen said, "*American Hot Wax* seems less like a finished film than a 90-minute trailer for itself."[144] Both the film and the soundtrack flopped. Paramount captured only $5.5 million in domestic rentals.

I Want to Hold Your Glands?

Robert Zemeckis and Bob Gale were employed at Universal as television scriptwriters when they came up with the idea for a feature film about Beatlemania. The two proteges of Steven Spielberg sold the project to Warner Brothers on the basis of a one-sentence synopsis, but their final script was rejected. Zemeckis and Gale contacted Spielberg, who had enormous clout after the huge success of *Jaws* (1975) and *Close Encounters of the Third Kind* (1977). In a replay of Coppola's role in providing help for Lucas with *American Graffiti*, Spielberg persuaded Universal to purchase the property on the promise that he would be executive producer. Zemeckis was signed as director. Universal took little risk, setting the production budget at $2.5 to $3 million. Shot on a thirty-eight-day schedule, the film came in at $2.7 million, a paltry figure for a major studio production. The title was changed to *I Wanna Hold Your Hand* after the Broadway show *Beatlemania* opened.

The film is a lighthearted comedy about four New Jersey teenage girls attempting to get into The Beatles' hotel room on the day they appear on The Ed Sullivan Show in February 1964. (Actual news footage of the British group's arrival in New York and Sullivan performance adds to the nostalgic account.) Rosie (Wendie Jo Sperber) worships Paul and teams up with nerdy Ringo fanatic Richard "Ringo" Klaus (Eddie Deezen). Grace (Theresa Saldana) is an attractive high school photographer in search of exclusive pictures of The Beatles for which she almost sacrifices her virginity, to launch her career. Janice (Susan Kendall Newman) is a committed folkie who wants to make a public statement in protest of The Beatles because they "undermine artistic integrity." Initially more interested in her body than her beliefs, Tony (Bobby DiCicco) helps her. Pam (Nancy Allen) is supposed to elope the next day, but comes along for a last fling with her girlfriends. Larry (Marc McClure) "borrows" his undertaker father's limousine to drive them all to New York.

Comical events occur as the subplots crisscross. Pam manages to get into The Beatles' suite under the tablecloth of a room service cart. After a lascivious moment with the band's instruments, she hides under a bed when The Beatles return. Two of the others manage to get tickets to The Ed Sullivan Show, while the fourth ends up driving The Beatles away in the borrowed limousine afterwards.

The film received mild reviews. The *Times*'s Janet Maslin called it "an A-plus B-movie, but it's a B-movie just the same." Richard Corliss referred to it as "a seventies version of a Sam Katzman picture."[145] Although it was a smart teenage comedy, it failed at the box office. The credits listed seventeen pre-February-1964 Beatle songs, courtesy of EMI. Understandably, no soundtrack was released of The Beatles' material.

Rock'n'Roll High School: A Katzman Rerun

Roger Corman's New World Pictures came out with the sophomoric *Rock'n'Roll High School*, featuring New Wave band The Ramones, in 1979. Corman served as executive producer, with Allan Arkush as director. Arkush chose the New York group because they were "very present-day."[146] *Rock'n'Roll High School* cost a mere $300,000 to make. It was an uninspiring combination of the low-budget rock musicals and teen exploitation films that came before it. (During production Arkush discovered the high school he was filming at, the former Mount Carmel High School in Los Angeles, was in fact the location for Katzman's legendary *Rock Around the Clock*.)

The movie's plot pits Ramone groupie Riff Randell (P. J. Soles, who appeared in *Halloween* and *Carrie*) against the new principal of Vince Lombardi High School, Miss Togar (Mary Woronov, a New World regular and former Andy Warhol model), who is made up like something out of an AIP vampire movie. The record-burning administrator plans on carrying out her duty "with an iron hand." The high schoolers have gone crazy over rock'n'roll, music which lowers young people to a "shameless display of adolescent abandon," she says. As in previous rock musicals, the music is shown as a positive force in teenagers' lives. Togar concludes the opposite after conducting "scientific" experiments with rock music on mice.

A Ramones concert becomes the focus of the battle between the administrator and Riff for control of the student body. The rock 'n' roller is determined to get to the concert in hopes she will get the New Wave group to consider songs she has written for them. Togar and two hall monitors dressed as Hitler Youth try to prevent Riff and her friend Kate (Dey Young) from going to the show, to set an example for the whole student body. When the principal fails, her "final solution" is a bonfire of rock records. The students riot, taking over the school as The Ramones arrive.

That night they destroy the school's records and torch the place while The Ramones sing Riff's composition "Rock'n'Roll High School." A local radio personality calls the riot "a classic confrontation between mindless authority and the rebellious nature of youth."

The film, pitched at fifteen- and sixteen-year-olds for its initial run in April 1979, flopped. In an attempt to salvage it, New World released the picture with much less promotion in San Francisco and Chicago. Although the movie managed to attract some older teens and New Wave fans, it never generated a great following, even as a cult film. Some exhibitors refused to show it because of the ending.

The Sire soundtrack also bombed. It contained seven Ramone songs, including two new ones—the title track and "I Want You Around." Additional filler material came from Chuck Berry, Nick Lowe, The Velvet Underground, Devo, Alice Cooper, Brian Eno, MC5, Todd Rundgren, and others. Dave Marsh reviewed the soundtrack in *Rolling Stone*. The title track, was ". . . razor sharp," he wrote. "In the great tradition of schlocky rock soundtracks (*The Wild Angels, Blow-Up*), it's all downhill from there."[147]

The Who's Adolescent Wasteland

Based on the success of *Tommy*, Polygram financed another Who rock opera *Quadrophenia*, in 1979, which cost $3 million. The movie was loosely based on The Who's 1973 album of the same title. The album on the MCA label went to Number 2 in both Britain and the U.S. in 1973, selling triple platinum. Co-producer Roy Baird suggested that was the reason the film project was backed by Polygram. "Americans make movies like *Mean Streets* and *Saturday Night Fever* all the time," he said, "but I can assure you that *Quadrophenia* would never have been financed—I repeat, *never*—except that it was based on a hit album."[148] MCA had passed on the soundtrack rights in light of the enormous sales of the 1973 disc, but Polygram grabbed international rights to the soundtrack, which featured new material by The Who along with remixed tracks from the MCA album. The double LP also included period pieces by The Kingsmen, Booker T and the MGs, James Brown, The Chiffons, The Crystals, Marvin Gaye, Manfred Mann, The Ronettes, and The Supremes, among others.

Major American film studios were not confident about the production's potential in the U.S. market. Paramount and Universal offered to distribute the film but release it in a single New York theater. The film's producers signed a deal with an independent distributor World- Northal instead, on the promise of a national release.

Set in Britain circa 1963, the movie centers on a young man (Phil Daniels) struggling through adolescence. In search of identity, he joins the Mods, who are engaged in a violent clash at seaside resorts with a rival group, the Rockers. Sting (formerly of The Police) is featured as one of the Mods. (Sting also appeared as a gas-station attendant obsessed with guitarist Eddie Cochran in *Radio On* (1979).) None of The Who appear in the film, but posters of the group hang on walls, their music plays at parties, and the hero watches the band perform on television.

Released several months after The Who rockumentary *The Kids Are Alright*, *Quadrophenia* was a big hit in the U.K. but failed in the U.S. market. Critics greeted it unenthusiastically. Though the movie purportedly dealt with the "universal adolescent dilemma," as Who manager and film co-producer Bill Curbishley put it, American audiences did not relate to the British youth subcultures treated in the film nor heavy accents of the actors.[149] Soundtrack sales were also disappointing.

Some Say Love It Is a Flower

Bette Midler made her cinematic debut in *The Rose*, a Twentieth Century Fox film. Aaron Russo (Midler's manager until 1979) co-produced the $8.5-million saga, which was loosely based on the life of Janis Joplin. Midler had originally turned down the script, then called *Pearl*, shortly after Joplin died. "I didn't know Janis, but I thought she was treated irreverently," she said. "It wasn't that it was a bad script; it was just the idea of not letting this person alone, especially so soon after she died."[150]

However, the energetic pop singer had been unable to duplicate the success of her smash album *The Divine Miss M* (1972). Though Midler was eager to get into films, Hollywood saw her as a risky venture. Midler reconsidered the *Rose* script, and some changes were made, making it strongly resemble Midler's own story, including the rocky relationship with her manager. In the end, the producers contended it was a composite story of tragic Sixties rock figures including Joplin, Jimi Hendrix, and Jim Morrison.

Thirteen songs were carefully and effectively worked into the story. Midler is not a blues singer or rocker, but her outstanding performance made the audience (but not the critics) forget this. Although set in the late Sixties, the film has the look and feel of the time when it was produced.

Midler plays "the Rose," a self-destructive rock singer struggling with sex, drugs, and the never-ending road life of a live entertainer. She is quick-tempered, vulgar, and bawdy. The overworked rock star suffers under the thumb of tyrannical manager Rudge (Alan Bates), who is more concerned about $3 million worth of concert dates than the wellbeing of his tired artist. There is a child-like dependency in the Rose, stemming from her own self-hatred and anguish. She is haunted by the sexual exploitation in her past, including bisexuality and a gang bang with the high school football team.

Despite her destructive lifestyle, the Rose sings her heart out night after night, putting on a show charged with energy that drives crowds to a frenzy. The film's concert footage sparkles. Rose falls in love with chauffeur Houston Dyer (Frederic Forrest) who is an AWOL Army sergeant. She loves him, she says, because he does not care about what she did before or what she is now, but *who* she is.

Several scenes show the increasingly volatile state the rock singer is reaching, reflecting both her past and present conditions. She incites a fight at a redneck truck stop, gets on stage at a homosexual nightclub (with three male impersonators in drag doing the Rose, Barbra Streisand, and Diana Ross), marches through a men's bathhouse in search of Dyer, and is nearly seduced by a former gay lover.

The story leads to a final confrontation with her jaded past at a concert in her hometown. She drives around town the day of the show longing to be recognized as the star she is, but seen only as what she was. When the singer presses her manager for a year off after this show, he threatens to cancel the concert and end their business relationship. In one of the film's most powerful scenes, the Rose enters a telephone booth at the high school football stadium just before the concert. On the verge of a breakdown, she washes down a handful of pills with some whiskey and calls Rudge to come and get her. While waiting for him to arrive she calls her parents, talking to them like a little girl. After the conversation, she shoots herself up with more drugs.

A helicopter takes her to the packed stadium for the concert. On stage she talks with an enthusiastic hometown crowd, asking forgiveness for being late. "I forgive you, too," she tells them. The Rose puts all the life she has left in her into one final song, "Stay With Me," then collapses on stage. The title track begins to play as the credits roll.

Critics frequently compared Midler in *The Rose* with Barbra Streisand in *Funny Girl* and Diana Ross in *Lady Sings the Blues*. Based primarily on Midler's performance, *The Rose* received glowing reviews. "Bette Midler's star is born," said a *Village Voice* critic. *The Rose* is "a fevered, fearless portrait of a tormented, gifted, homely, sexy child- woman who sang her heart out until it exploded," Jack Kroll wrote in *Newsweek*, adding, "Midler's performance is an event to be experienced." Janet Maslin's review in the *Times* was somewhat prophetic—"She may even be a better actress than a singer, on the evidence of her first film role."[151] Midler, nominated for an Oscar for this debut performance, began a successful acting career that has included *Down and Out in Beverly Hills*, *Ruthless People*, and *Beaches*.

The Rose had a limited opening in forty-four theaters in November 1979. Early box office statistics were impressive, and another 360 bookings were added 21 December to capitalize on the Christmas rush. The Atlantic soundtrack was not released until December 1979. (Given the depressed state of the recording industry, Atlantic feared competition with Midler's other 1979 release, *Thighs and Whispers*.) The album spent three weeks at Number 12 (23 February to 8 March 1980), coinciding with the first single released from it, "When a Man Loves a Woman," which stalled at Number 35. The LP then dropped out of the Top 40 the first week in April, but the single "The Rose" entered the Top 40 on *Billboard*'s Hot 100 April 26. The popularity of the second single turned album sales around; the LP began to climb again, reaching Number 14 for two weeks in July, just after the title track peaked for three weeks at Number 3. The music had a clear impact on movie attendance; weekly box office figures fluctuated with the charting of the album and singles. The soundtrack was certified platinum in June of 1980. Twentieth Century Fox eventually earned $19 million in domestic rentals.

Notes

1. Robert Sklar, *Movie-Made America: A Social History of American Movies* (New York: Random House 1975), 301.
2. Peter Bart, "Keeper of the Beatles," *New York Times*, 5 September 1965, sec. 2: 7. Earlier the Beatles did a concert film for British television titled *Around the Beatles*. Two American independent filmmakers, Albert and David Maysles, made a 55-minute documentary about the Beatles New York arrival called *What's Happening!: The Beatles in the U.S.A.* It was shown on British television, but was not released in the United States.
3. Peter Brown and Steven Gaines, *The Love You Make: An Insider's Story of The Beatles* (New York: McGraw-Hill Book Company 1983), 133.
4. Fred Bronson, *The Billboard Book of Number One Hits*, rev. ed. (New York: Billboard Publications 1988), 143.
5. Quoted in Stephen Watts, "The Beatles' 'Hard Day's Night'," *New York Times*, 26 April 1964, sec. 2: 13.
6. *Variety*, 2 May 1962, 6.
7. Quoted in Neil Sinyard, *The Films of Richard Lester* (London and Sydney: Croom Helm 1985), 5.
8. *Variety*, 2 May 1962, 6.
9. Stephen Watts, "The Beatles'', 13.
10. Sinyard, 18, 19.

11. Ibid., 19.
12. Quoted in Stephen Watts, "The Beatles", 13.
13. Quoted in George Bluestone, "Lunch with Lester," *Film Quarterly*, 19, (Summer 1966), 14.
14. Robert B. Ray, *A Certain Tendency of the Hollywood Cinema* (Princeton, New Jersey: Princeton University Press 1985), 270–71.
15. Quoted in "George, Paul, Ringo, and John," *Newsweek*, 24 February 1964, 57.
16. Richard Lester is quoted here in Ray Coleman, *Lennon* (New York: McGraw-Hill 1984), 229. This version of the Lennon quote is from George Bluestone, "Lunch," 14–15.
17. Jack Kroll, "Strawberry Fields Forever," *Newsweek*, 22 December 1980, 43.
18. Sinyard, 26.
19. Greil Marcus, "Rock Films," in *The Rolling Stone Illustrated History of Rock & Roll*, rev. version, ed. Jim Miller (New York: A Random House/Rolling Stone Press Book, 1976, 1980), 393. At least one critic thought the Beatles' films contributed greatly to the longevity of the British group. See Peter Bart, "Keeper," 7.
20. Robert B. Ray, 270.
21. *Variety*, 15 July 1964, 6; "Yeah? Yeah. Yeah!" *Time*, 14 August 1964, 67; "Yeah Indeed," *Newsweek*, 24 August 1967, 79; Bosley Crowther, "Screen: The Four Beatles in 'A Hard Day's Night'," *New York Times*, 12 August 1964, 41; Andrew Sarris, "Bravo Beatles!" *Village Voice*, 27 August 1964, 13.
22. Quoted in "The Beatle Business," *Time*, 2 October 1964, 112.
23. Ibid.
24. Quoted in Philip Norman, *Shout!: The Beatles in Their Generation* (New York: Simon and Schuster, A Fireside Book 1981), 318. The enterprise ended in financial loss. See also Brown and Gaines, 170.
25. Quoted in Philip Norman, 244.
26. Quoted in Sinyard: 33 and *Beatles In Their Own Words*, Barry Miles, ed., (New York: Music Sales Corporation; Quick Fox, 1978), 111; See also Hunter Davies, *The Beatles*, 2nd rev. ed. (New York: McGraw-Hill 1985), 337.
27. Philip Norman, *Shout!*, 248.
28. John Seelye, "Help!," *Film Quarterly* 19, Fall 1965, 57; "Chase & Superchase," *Newsweek*, 3 September 1965, 84; Brendan Gill, "The Current Cinema: Hit or Miss," *The New Yorker*, 28 August 1965, 101; *Variety*, 4 August 1965, 7; Bosley Crowther, "Screen: Beatles Star in 'Help!', Film of the Absurd," *New York Times*, 24 August 1965, 25; Andrew Sarris, "Films," *Village Voice*, 9 September 1965, 15.
29. Bosley Crowther, "The Other Check To the Beatles," *New York Times*, 12 September 1965, sec. 2, 1.
30. Bosley Crowther, "Pop Go The Beatles," *New York Times*, 29 August 1965, sec. 2, 1.
31. Quoted in Barry Miles, 80.
32. Quoted in Geoffrey Stokes, *The Beatles* (New York: Times Books, a division of Quadrangle; A Rolling Stone Press Book, 1980), 117, 121.
33. Ibid., 154.
34. Norman, 316.
35. Brown and Gaines, 276.

36. *Ibid.*, 276.
37. Ibid., 276.
38. Quoted in Ray Coleman, 321–22.
39. Brown and Gaines, 276.
40. Quoted in "TV Abroad: Fab? Chaos," *Time*, 5 January 1968, 61.
41. Ibid.
42. Ibid., 60.
43. *Ibid.*, 61.
44. Norman, 278.
45. Judith A. Williams, "Yellow Submarine," in *Magill's Survey of Cinema* Series II, V.6 (Englewood Cliffs, New Jersey: Salem Press 1981), 2730.
46. Ibid.
47. "New Magic in Animation," *Time*, 27 December 1968, 42.
48. Ibid., 47.
49. George Martin with Jeremy Hornsby, *All You Need Is Ears* (New York: St. Martin's Press 1979), 226.
50. Ibid., 230.
51. "Bad Trip," *Time*, 22 November 1968, 80; *Variety*, 24 July 1968, 6; Andrew Sarris, "Films," *Village Voice*, 14 November 1968, 45; "New Magic in Animation," *Time* 27 December 1968, 42; Renata Adler, "Beatles, Comic Strip Style," *New York Times*, 17 November 1968, Sec. 2, 14; Pauline Kael, "The Current Cinema: Metamorphosis of the Beatles," *The New Yorker*, 30 November 1968, 153. See also Paul D. Zimmerman, "Beatles in Pepperland," *Newsweek*, 25 November 1968, 108; "Bad Trip," *Time*, 22 November 1968, 78.
52. Richard Staehling, "From Rock Around the Clock to The Trip: The Truth About Teen Movies," in *Kings of the Bs*, Todd McCarthy and Charles Flynn, eds., (New York: E.P. Dutton & Co., 1975): 238.
53. "Follow-the-Leader," *Time*, 3 September 1965, 84.
54. Eugene Archer, "The Screen: 'Ferry Cross the Mersey'," *New York Times*, 20 February 1965, 16.
55. Shelley Fabares appeared in several movies during the 1950s—*Never Say Goodbye, Rock, Pretty Baby*, and *Summer Love*—before landing the role of Donna Reed's daughter on the popular family television sitcom *The Donna Reed Show*. In 1962, she recorded a single, "Johnny Angel." Exposure on the TV show sent the single to the top of the *Billboard* pop charts. After *Donna Reed*, she also starred in three Elvis movies and *Ride the Wild Surf* with Fabian in 1964.
56. Quoted in Nadine Liber, "Antonioni Talks About His Work: 'First I Must Isolate Myself,' " *Life*, 27 January 1967, 65.
57. See William J. Palmer, *The Films of the Seventies: A Social History* (Metuchen, N.J. and London: The Scarecrow Press, 1987), 83–98.
58. "Rock'n'Roll: Evolution," *Time* 17 February 1967, 70.
59. Bob Gilbert and Gary Theroux, *The Top Ten: 1956-Present* (New York: Simon and Schuster; A Fireside Book, 1982), 125.
60. Quoted in "Romp! Romp!" *Newsweek* 24 October 1966: 102.
61. Quoted in "Monkee Do," *Time*, 11 November 1966, 84.
62. Betty Rollin, "TV's Swinging Monkees," *Look*, 27 December 1966, 96.

63. Quoted in Frank Lovece, "Bob Rafelson: An Offbeat Director's Unpredictable Career," *Video*, August 1987, 60.
64. Ibid.
65. *Variety*, 13 November 1968, 6.
66. Renata Adler, "The Screen: 'Head,' Monkees Movie for a Turned-On Audience," *New York Times*, 7 November 1968, 51; Pauline Kael, "The Current Cinema: Muddling Through," *The New Yorker*, 23 November 1968, 202.
67. Quoted in "Z as in Zzzz, or Zowie," *Time*, 5 May 1967, 61–62.
68. Seth Cagin and Philip Dray, *Hollywood Films of the Seventies: Sex, Drugs, Violence, Rock'n'Roll & Politics* (New York: Harper & Row 1984), 57.
69. J. Philip di France, ed., *The Movie World of Roger Corman* (New York: Chelsea House Publishers, 1979), 119.
70. "Venice To Show 'The Wild Angels'," *New York Times*, 20 August 1966, 10.
71. Bosley Crowther, review of 'The Wild Angels', *New York Times*, 22 December 1966, 40.
72. Quoted in Ed Naha, *The Films of Roger Corman: Brilliance on a Budget* (New York: Arco Publishing 1982), 64.
73. Quoted in *The Movie World of Roger Corman*, J. Philip di Franco, ed., (New York: Chelsea House Publishers, 1979), 45.
74. Ibid., 48.
75. Quoted in Ed Naha, 65.
76. See "TV Stations Warned On Using a Nude Ad For Movie on LSD," *New York Times*, 20 August 1967, 26.
77. Joseph Morgenstern, "Trip of Fools," *Newsweek*, 11 September 1967, 100; Bosley Crowther, "Screen: 'The Trip' on view at 2 Houses," *New York Times*, 24 August 1967, 43; Judith Crist is quoted in Ed Naha, 188; *Variety*, 16 August 1967, 6.
78. Rex Reed, "Holden Caulfield at 27," *Esquire*, February 1968, 75.
79. Quoted in Ed Naha, 85–86.
80. Renata Adler, "Screen: Blunt Philosophy With Dual Exhausts and a Celar Logic," *New York Times*, 30 May 1968, 21; Joseph Morgenstern, "Kiddie Coup," *Newsweek*, 3 June 1968, 104; Richard Schickel, "Overpraised Quickie on a Vital Theme," *Life*, 26 July 1968, 10.
81. *Variety*, 13 March 1968, 6; Renata Adler, "Screen: 'Psych-Out' Draws a Bead on the Hippies," *New York Times*, 28 March 1968, 52.
82. Hollis Alpert, " 'The Graduate' Makes Out," *Saturday Review* 6, July 1968, 32.
83. Quoted in Peter Bart, "Mike Nichols, Moviemaniac," *New York Times*, 1 January 1967, sec. 2, 7.
84. Quoted in David Zeitlin, "The Graduate," *Life*, 24 November 1967, 112, 114.
85. Ibid., 112.
86. Landon Y. Jones, *Great Expectations: America and the Baby Boom Generation* (New York: Ballantine Books 1980), 136.
87. *Variety*, 20 December 1968, 6; Joseph Morgenstern, "A Boy's Best Friend," *Time*, 1 January 1968, 63; Bosley Crowther, "Film: Tales Out of School," *New York Times*, 22 December 1967, 44; Renata Adler, "A Brilliant Breakdown," *New York Times*, 11 February 1968, sec. 2, 1, 13; "The Graduate," *Newsweek*, 29 December 1967, 55. See also Andrew Sarris, "Films," *Village Voice*, 28 December 1967, 33. The extraordinary success of the film prompted

an unusually lengthy analysis in *The New Yorker.* See Jacob Brackman, "Onward and Upward with the Arts: 'The Graduate'," *The New Yorker*, 27 July 1968, 34–66.

88. David Ehrenstein and Bill Reed, *Rock on Film* (New York: Deliah Books 1982): 66–67.

89. Stephen Farber and Estelle Changas, revision of 'The Graduate,' *Film Quarterly*, Spring 1968, 38.

90. Quoted in Fred Bronson, 241.

91. Joseph Murrels, *Million Selling Records From the 1900s to the 1980s: An Illustrated Directory* (New York: Arco Publishing 1984), 270.

92. Quoted in Hollis Alpert, " 'The Graduate' Makes Out," *Saturday Review* 6, July 1968, 32.

93. Brendan Gill, "The Current Cinema: Easeful Death," *The New Yorker*, 23 April 1966, 131.

94. Arthur Knight, "The Creative Artist and the Cops," *Saturday Review*, 11 April 1964, 42.

95. Brendan Gill, "Easeful Death," 131; "Scorpio Rising," *Variety*, 25 May 1966, 6; "Up From Underground," *Newsweek*, 25 April 1966, 91.

96. Robert B. Ray, 255–56.

97. Quoted in J. Philip di Franco, 119.

98. Quoted in Ed Naha, 89.

99. Cagin and Dray, 45.

100. *Ibid.*, 62.

101. Cagin and Dray, 62–63.

102. Quoted in Frank Lovece, "Bob Rafelson: An Offbeat Director's Unpredictable Career," *Video*, August 1987, 107. It should be noted there was only one other film competing in the category of best picture by a new director.

103. Ironically, the evil and violence come from the established society of the East instead of the primitive West. Harriet R. Polt, "Review of 'Easy Rider'," *Film Quarterly*, Fall 1969, 24.

104. Beverly Walker, "The Bird Is On His Own," *Film Comment* 21, May-June 1985, 53.

105. Cagin and Dray, 73.

106. Joseph Morgenstern, "On the Road," *Newsweek,* 21 July 1969, 95; "New Movies," *Time*, 25 July 1969, 73–74; *Variety* 14 May 1969: 6; Vincent Canby, " 'Easy Rider': A Statement on Film," *New York Times*, 15 July 1969, 32 and "For Neo-Adults Only," *New York Times*, 27 July 1969, sec. 2, 16. See also Harriet R. Polt, "Review of 'Easy Rider'," *Film Quarterly*, Fall 1969, 22 and Jacob Brackman, "Films," *Esquire* September 1969, 12–18.

107. Jack Barth and Trey Ellis, " 'Easy Rider' Revisited," *Premier*, May 1989, 88.

108. Cagin and Dray, 66.

109. Ernest Callenbach, "Review of 'Zabriskie Point,' " *Film Quarterly*, Spring 1970, 36.

110. Cagin and Dray, 104.

111. Michael Dempsey, "Review of 'American Graffiti,' " *Film Quarterly*, Fall 1973, 59.

112. Quoted in Judy Klemesrud, " 'Graffiti' Is the Story of His Life," *New York Times*, 7 October 1973, sec. 2, 13.

113. Stephen Farber, " 'Graffiti' Ranks With 'Bonnie and Clyde,' " *New York Times*, 5 August 1973, sec. 2, 6.
114. Quoted in John Culhane, "George Lucas: Mastermind of the *Star Wars* Family," *Families*, March 1982, 50.
115. Quoted in Judy Klemesrud, " 'Graffiti' Is the Story," 1.
116. Ibid.
117. Quoted in Stephen Farber, "George Lucas: The Stinky Kid Hits the Big Time," *Film Quarterly*, Summer 1974, 6.
118. Quoted in Judy Klemesrud, " 'Graffiti' Is the Story," 13.
119. Quoted in Paul Gardner, " 'Graffiti' Reflects Its Director's Youth," *New York Times*, 19 September 1973, 40.
120. Quoted in Hollis Alpert, "The Year Before," 41.
121. Ibid.
122. Quoted in Stephen Farber, "George Lucas," 6.
123. Quoted in Judy Klemesrud, " 'Graffiti' Is the Story," 13.
124. Quoted in Stephen Farber, "George Lucas," 7.
125. Quoted in Paul Scanlon, "The Force Behind George Lucas," *Rolling Stone*, 25 August 1977, 44.
126. Stephen Farber, " 'Graffiti' Ranks," 1.
127. Jay Cocks, "Fabulous '50s," *Time*, 20 August 1973, 58; *Variety*, 20 June 1973, 20; Joseph Kanon, "Movies: On the Strip," *Atlantic Monthly*, October 1973; 125; Jon Landau, " 'American Graffiti': A Sixties Novella," *Rolling Stone*, 13 September 1973, 72; Stephen Farber, " 'Graffiti' Ranks": 1; Vincent Canby, " 'Heavy Traffic' and 'American Graffiti'—Two of the Best," *New York Times*, 16 September 1973, sec. 2, 3. Only Sarris was not enthused about the film, deeming it "okay, but hardly oy vay." See Andrew Sarris, "Dusk to dawn on the drag strip," *Village Voice*, 23 August 1973, 63.
128. Quoted in Stephen Farber, "George Lucas," 6–7.
129. Stephen Farber, " 'Graffiti' Ranks," 1.
130. Joseph Kanon, "Movies: On The Strip," 127.
131. Quoted in Stephen Farber, "George Lucas," 8.
132. Ibid.
133. *Time*, 23 May 1983, 66.
134. *Variety*, 25 July 1979, 16; Janet Maslin, "Screen: 'More American Graffiti' Covers '64 to '67," *New York Times*, 17 August 1979, C14. See also Veronica Geng, "The Current Cinema: Have a Nice Day," *The New Yorker*, 20 August 1979, 91.
135. Quoted in Susan Peterson, "Key label executives analyze their approach to the marketing of movie music," *Billboard* October 6, 1979, ST-6.
136. Quoted in Kenneth Von Gunden, "The RH Factor," *Film Comment* September-October 1979, 55.
137. Anna Quindlen, "Midnights at 'Rocky Horror'," *New York Times*, 9 March 1979, C1; Richard Corliss, "Across the Land: The Voice of *Rocky Horror*," *Time*, 9 December 1985, 22.
138. Ibid.
139. Janet Maslin, "The Rock Era Seen as History," *New York Times*, 30 April 1978, 15.
140. Sam Sutherland, "Rock soundtracks: American Hot Wax, The Last Waltz, FM," *High Fidelity*, July 1978, 126.

141. Andrew Sarris, "Now Let Us Praise Nice Movies," *Village Voice*, 27 March 1978, 38.

142. Quoted in Tom Nolan, "America Waxes Hot," *Village Voice*, 20 March 1978, 42.

143. See "Borrow 'Fever' Tactics To Hype 'American Hot Wax' Via Tube," *Variety*, 1 March 1978, 5.

144. David Ansen, "Platter Chatter," *Newsweek*, 27 March 1978, 96. For other reviews see Richard Corliss, "It's Only Rock & Reel," *New Times*, 15 May 1978, 81; Frank Rich, "Rock Follies," *Time*, 27 March 1978, 77; Janet Maslin, "Screen: 'American Hot Wax,' " *New York Times*, 17 March 1978, C13; Molly Haskell, "Profiteer With Honor," *New York*, 3 April 1978, 67; Pauline Kael, "The Current Cinema: Shrivers," *The New Yorker*, 20 March 1978, 122; *Variety*, 15 March 1978, 21.

145. Janet Maslin, "Screen: Recapturing Day of the Beatles," *New York Times*, 21 April 1978, C11; Richard Corliss, "It's Only Rock & Reel," *New Times*, 15 May 1978, 81. For other reviews see *Variety*, 19 April 1979, 26; David Ansen, "Yeah! Yeah! Yeah!" *Newsweek*, 1 May 1978, 91; Frank Rich, "Teen Dreams," *Time*, 8 March 1978, 70.

146. Quoted in Lloyd Sachs, "The Making of 'Rock'n'Roll High School'," *Rolling Stone*, 12 July 1979, 25.

147. Dave Marsh, review of 'Rock'n'Roll High School,' *Rolling Stone*, 12 July 1979, 72. For other reviews see John Rockwell, "Film: 'Rock'n'Roll High School' with the Ramones 'Punk' Band," *New York Times*, 4 August 1979, 10; J. Hoberman, "Blitzkrieg Bop Bingo," *Village Voice*, 13 August 1979, 49; *Variety*, 25 April 1979, 19.

148. Quoted in Stuart Byron, "Rules of the Game," *Village Voice*, 22 October 1979, 60.

149. Quoted in "15 Yrs. Of Mayhem, Today's Adolescent Dilemma Told In The Who Theatricals," *Variety*, 14 March 1979, 4.

150. Quoted in Timothy White, "The Homecoming," *Rolling Stone* 13, December 1979, 63.

151. Tom Allen, "Bette's Best," *Village Voice*, 12 November 1979, 47; Jack Kroll, "Hippie-Freak Queen," *Newsweek*, 12 November 1979, 107; Janet Maslin, "Film: Bette Midler in 'The Rose,' " *New York Times*, 7 November 1979, sec. 3, 23. See also Vincent Canby, "Show-Biz as Subject, Again," *New York Times*, 25 November 1979, sec. 2, 11; *Variety*, 10 October 1979, 20; Frank Rich, "Flashy Trash," *Time*, 12 November 1979, 122; Renata Adler, "The Current Cinema: Straits," *The New Yorker*, 12 November 1979, 97.

4

Shake That Moneymaker

Disease: Saturday Night Fever. *Symptoms:*
Spends lavishly on three-piece white suits,
clingy black shirts and gold neck chains.
Crowds his school locker with hair brushes and
blow driers. Shows a tendency to break into
the Spanish hustle on elevators.

—Newsweek

Arch your back. Go. It's all in the hips: Bring
them back and thrust them out. Now really let
go. You are dirty dancing.

—Life

The dance musical is one of Hollywood's most enduring genres. Wedding familiar faces and predictable plots with the latest technology, the magic of Hollywood musicals has captured the public's imagination with fantasies that appear more real than life. Enormously popular, dance films proved to be a reliable box office formula until the late 1950s. The genre could not keep up with changes in public taste that were effecting the film industry at that time.

The movie musical has its roots in vaudeville, the musical hall, and the theater, and emerged in the late 1920s with the advent of "talkies." (While debating the merits of sound in motion pictures, Harry Warner is reported to have said, "Who the hell wants to hear actors talk? The music—that's the big plus about this.")[1] Warner's first production with synchronized sound, *The Jazz Singer,* grossed an unprecedented $3 million despite a limited showing because of the small number of theaters equipped to handle sound at that time. Conceived of as a novelty to change the fortunes of the film company, *The Jazz Singer,* in 1927, began a new era in film.

In 1929, *The Broadway Melody* became the first true musical. Advertised as "all talking—all singing—all dancing," MGM's first sound film was one of the early "backstage" musicals. The Broadway stage provided a setting with plenty of reasons for singing and dancing: auditions, rehearsals, and the final performance. *The Broadway Melody* was the first movie musical to win the Academy Award for Best Picture, and MGM earned $4 million against its $280,000 production costs. The title song drew considerable attention as an effective tool in marketing the film.

"Repeated performances for such songs, on stage, records, and over the radio, was a rich source of free publicity for the movie in question," explained writer David Ewen,[2] so theme songs were ordered for musical and nonmusical pictures alike. Of the 335 talkies produced that year, fifty-seven were musicals and ninety others had songs in them.

The box office success of *The Broadway Melody* confirmed the appeal of musicals, and filmmakers set out to fine tune the formula. The genre evolved in the 1930s with the Busby Berkeley extravaganzas, most notably *42nd Street* and *Gold Diggers of 1933*. In the late Thirties, the Fred Astaire-Ginger Rogers vehicles, particularly *Top Hat* (1935), *Follow the Fleet* (1935), *Swing Time* (1936) and *Shall We Dance?* (1937), raised the genre to its classic stage. During the following decade, the formulation of the "integrated" musical occurred. John Russell Taylor and Arthur Jackson described the concept:

> The idea, briefly, is that the musical should aspire towards the condition of opera by integrating dialogue, song, dance and incidental music in such a way that the whole work 'flows,' each constituent element serving to forward the story in its own fashion, with no obvious breaks, cues for song or excuses to drag in a musical number by its hair.[3]

Employing this model, the Hollywood musical flourished during the 1940s and 1950s under the leadership of Arthur Freed. Freed's MGM unit was composed of a host of talented film and music directors, choreographers, and dancers. Together they assembled the glittery MGM musicals of the 1940s and early 1950s, beginning with *The Wizard of Oz* and *Babes in Arms* in 1939 and culminating with *Singing in the Rain* (1952) and *The Band Wagon* (1953).

The glorious musicals had faded in popularity by the end of the Eisenhower era. Those that *were* successful were adaptations of already popular theatrical productions like *Oklahoma!* and *South Pacific*. Leonard Bernstein's score for *West Side Story* in 1961, renewed public interest, which climaxed with *Mary Poppins* in 1964 and *The Sound of Music* the following year. Barbra Streisand scored with *Funny Girl* in 1968, but many other musicals were commercially unsuccessful. The Hollywood musical seemed to have lost its box office magic.

The most important factor in that trend was the dramatic shift in audience demographics and musical tastes. By the mid-1960s, it was clear that young people bought records and rock 'n' roll was here to stay. People under twenty-five were also the primary movie-going audience. The striking success of *The Graduate* and *Easy Rider* took the industry by surprise.

Hollywood remained cautious in courting the youth market. The rock-music audience appeared unpredictable, and therefore financially unreliable. Filmmakers were also uncertain about how to utilize rock in a musical; rock music was difficult to adapt to film narrative. While the melodic songs of Tin Pan Alley easily melted into plots, the strong rhythmic-based rock made breaks between songs and narrative awkward and disruptive. Dances that accompanied rock music in the Sixties did not lend themselves to splashy choreography. Also, Hollywood writers had difficulty finding plots, themes, and settings that allowed characters to burst into song. British rock entrepreneur Robert Stigwood, however, recognized the potential power of a merger of rock music and movies. As RSO Group President Freddie Gershon said, "Bob Stigwood understood better than anyone else that you could take a musical vehicle and build on it by promoting the music so that it got better known than the play or movie."[4] More than anyone else at the time, Stigwood recognized that the synergism of rock music and movies, beyond aesthetic possibilities, had incredible potential as a marketing phenomenon. His productions combining rock and film began in the early seventies and culminated with the blockbuster *Saturday Night Fever* and *Grease* later in the decade.

The Reign of RSO

In the early 1970s, *Jesus Christ Superstar* was an unprecedented multi-media event. *Superstar* began as a 45-rpm single and blossomed into a double album, a Broadway musical, original cast recording, and full-length feature film. The "rock opera" was written by two young British writers, lyricist Tim Rice and composer Andrew Lloyd Webber. (The two had a successful collaboration on *Joseph and His Amazing Technicolored Dreamcoat,* based on the biblical story of Joseph. After their musical rendition of Richard the Lion-Hearted, *Come Back, Richard* flopped, they returned to the Bible for a musical about Jesus.)

Lloyd Webber and Rice peddled their idea to many English labels, all of which were not interested. MCA-Decca however, was not only interested, but eager (MCA had purchased Universal Studios and Decca Records in 1959. Decca had a history of packaging movie soundtracks for leasing to television stations. When the MCA record label released *Oklahoma!*, the company was on the vanguard of a new trend establishing Decca as a leader in Broadway musical cast albums. By 1968, Broadway producers were putting pressure on record companies to invest in productions in order to release the original cast albums.) Decca at the time was a catalog company with a number of successful country artists and only one rock group with notable record sales—The Who, whose rock opera, *Tommy*, had just been released. Meanwhile, executives were scouting for new talent in the hope of improving their status in the rock-dominated record market.

The Lloyd Webber and Rice's idea for a rock opera matched Decca's specialization. Executives decided to take a gamble on the as-yet-unwritten opera, but not without first testing the waters. The British division was given the go-ahead to record one song, to be released as a 45-rpm single. Lloyd Webber and Rice received $20,000 toward the single and the early stages of the album.[5] The song, "Jesus Christ, Superstar," sung by Murray Head with the Trinidad Singers, brought mixed reactions from MCA board members. "We're crazy if we put it out!" "The whole thing must be handled in good taste." "Every churchman in the country will stone us." "The stations aren't going to play it." "We could use a little controversy."[6] MCA was desperate. In all likelihood, the flagrancy of *"Superstar"* would engender an audience for the picture, resulting in increased box office revenues.[7]

"Superstar" was released on the Decca label, which identified the song with the forthcoming production: "from the rock opera *Jesus Christ Superstar,* now in preparation." The single, shipped to distributors and radio stations on 1 December 1969, drowned in the flood of Christmas products. Some excitement, mostly controversy, was generated by the song and more stations began airing it. Decca was deluged with letters, both pro and con. One radio station in Arkansas banned "Superstar," along with all Decca records. Decca publicity people responded to letters by sending a record and press kit. "The kit contained pro comments from clergymen and favorable reviews," said a publicity manager.

> As I look back it seems to me that we went to a great deal of trouble to hide the fact that *Superstar* was not your traditional biblical fare—that it was rather unconventional. The rock opera itself was certainly no *King of Kings* or *Greatest Story Ever Told*—in no way! As a matter of fact, the rock opera turned out to be more successful than those two movies combined![8]

Eventually the single would sell more than a million copies, but by May 1970 it still had sold only 100,000 and made a poor showing on the *Billboard* pop singles chart. "Superstar" entered the Hot 100 the last week of January 1970 at Number 99; in four weeks it crept only to Number 74. Three weeks later it was off the chart. This was a major disappointment, considering the gamble Decca had taken on it. Still, "Superstar" generated enough publicity for Decca to move ahead with the Lloyd Webber/Rice production. A second single, Yvonne Elliman's "I Don't Know How to Love Him," did better, reaching Number 28 in June 1971. A 1971 cover version by Helen Reddy surpassed the original, peaking at Number 13.

The rock opera was a Rice/Lloyd Webber version of the last seven days of Christ's life, told through the eyes of Judas.

"We thought it was a superb story," Rice explained. "We approached Christ as a man—the human angle—rather than as a God."[9] Though primarily rock music, the opera reflected Lloyd Webber's eclectic taste and included classical, vaudevillian, and electronic compositions. (Early rumors had surfaced that former Beatle John Lennon would play the part of Christ and his wife Yoko Ono would play Mary Magdalene, but MCA production people felt that Lennon's own superstar status would detract from the part itself.) Deep Purple lead singer Ian Gillan got the role of Jesus and Yvonne Elliman played Mary Magdalene. Murray Head, who had appeared in the cast of *Hair,* appeared as Judas. None of the artists anticipated the success of the *Superstar* album. In fact, Elliman had even declined a percentage and received a flat fee of 100 pounds [about $240]. Of all the singers, only Murray Head opted for royalties.

Decca put continuing pressure on its British division for a September release in order to reach retail outlets in time for Christmas. However, the project was bogged down in long and costly recording sessions. An eighty-five piece orchestra was used, along with British rock musicians, eleven primary singers, sixteen chorus singers, and three choirs. The final count was sixty recording sessions—400 hours of recording time—at a total cost of $65,000, a figure considered extravagant for British productions at the time.[10] Finally a single, "Heaven on Their Minds," was released in America. The 45 failed to draw critical attention despite press information citing the single as "from the opera *Jesus Christ Superstar.*"

Decca executives were careful to market the rock opera with a certain dignity, to make it attractive to both consumers and radio programmers. "Weve got to give the public the first-class presentation it has a right to expect," MCA vice-president Ned Tanner told *Variety.* "Even the merchandising activities must be very discreet. We can't permit trash merchandising, and we won't do it ourselves. The show's material, though handled in a contemporary manner, is sacred to millions of people."[11] The British version of the album cover did not fit the bill. Ellis Nassour described it in his book about the making of *Superstar:*

> The cover was made up of a yellow ball (the sun or center of the universe) with red and white tints. At the top of the ball the title was printed in a biblical script. On the back were four pointed flaps that opened into a silver star and revealed a back panel of sixteen colorful paintings of Christ from art books and four by London schoolchildren.[12]

The British version was considered "ugly, awkward, and impractical."[13] Delays in the British production of the LP cover forced an American edition which was eventually adopted by all MCA licensees, including Britain. The U.S. version was designed to be more fitting for an opera, with a logo combining angels in prayer with the title. In a first for Decca, the design appeared both on the LP cover and the record label.

Two weeks before the New York preview, the Big Apple's top underground radio stations—WNEW-FM, WABC-FM (later WPLJ), and WCBS-FM—were invited to an exclusive prerelease playing of the LP. All three stations were enthusiastic and wanted to be the first to air the entire album, uninterrupted by commercials. WNEW was given permission by MCA'S marketing executive, Tony Martell, but WABC-FM aired an English version of the album two days earlier than WNEW.

Decca's new A & R executive, Tom Morgan, secured St. Peter's Lutheran Church for the New York preview of *Jesus Christ Superstar* on 27 October 1971. "The setting would lend the proper listening atmosphere," he said. "We will not instigate any salesmanship or do anything crassly commercial. ... The event will be handled with impeccable taste. The writers will be coming in from England and will add dignity to the occasion."[14] Morgan convinced the church staff to allow Decca to use both the sanctuary for the preview and the reception hall for a party afterwards. Decca paid only $400 for use of the facility, but there was one drawback. Church bylaws forbid the serving of alcoholic beverages. "What! No booze at a record party?" said Rice. "That's like barring reporters from bars."[15] Decca's publicity campaign included national radio buys and ads in trade and consumer publications, as well as posters, calendars, and buttons. The campaign was so extensive that one reporter said it "could elect a president."[16]

Despite the promotional campaign, the turnout for the preview was disappointing, although reviewers from *Rolling Stone, Time, The Village Voice, Billboard, Cashbox,* and other publications did attend. The fifty-six-minute program included a shortened version of the rock opera and a slide presentation of religious paintings, backed by Lloyd Webber/Rice compositions.

Following the preview, Lloyd Webber and Rice were flooded with requests for interviews from trade publications and major news magazines. Calls and letters from concert promoters and Broadway producers, including one from British entepreneur Robert Stigwood, poured in. The LP was given an incredible amount of coverage in newspapers and magazines and heralded by critics as nothing less than a masterpiece. Albums sales soared. *Jesus Christ Superstar* topped the *Billboard, Cashbox,* and *Record World* charts in February 1971.

The Robert Stigwood Connection

Robert Stigwood's career reads like a classic rags-to-riches story. In the late 1950s Stigwood left Australia, at the age of twenty-three, and arrived in England with virtually no money. He worked at a theatrical agency before forming his own firm in 1962.

Stigwood's first move into cross-promotion began with an independent record production. "Commercial television had just started in London," he explained. "The big agents were ignoring it. In the space of a few years, I suppose I was handling half the casting for all English commercials. Then I found I was handling some good, legitimate talent. My first break was with John Leyton."[17] (Leyton was a television actor Stigwood represented.) At that time, three major British record companies dominated distribution in Britain—EMI, Decca, and Pye. Stigwood did an independent distribution of Leyton singing the U.S. hit, "Tell Laura I Love Her." The single was released by Top Rank. The song began to sell, but Top Rank was bought up by EMI, who owned the original version, and Leyton's rendition was put on the shelf.

Stigwood then played a hunch. He recorded another Leyton song, "Johnny Remember Me," and got him a part as a pop idol in a television series. Stigwood, confident that national exposure of the song on Leyton's television show would make it a smash hit, convinced the show's producer to have Leyton sing the song on the show. Due to that exposure, EMI agreed to distribute the song. Stigwood's gamble paid off. The song reached Number 1 in Britain and sold a million copies. Stigwood became a leader in British independent record production. "Suddenly, I had five records in the Top 50," he recalled, "completely from left field." His flamboyant lifestyle, however, led him to bankruptcy. By March 1965, he had to liquidate his company. Reportedly he had acquired a debt of 39,000 British pounds.[18]

There were some hard years, but early in 1967, Stigwood joined forces with Brian Epstein, whose NEMS company managed The Beatles. According to Beatles' biographer Philip Norman, "Stigwood provided what Brian had been looking for—a chance to be rid of NEMS enterprises altogether . . . Stigwood became joint managing director, pending his acquisition of a majority shareholding."[19] Stigwood was offered controlling interest for a trifling 500,000 pounds; two years earlier Epstein had rejected a $20-million bid. The Fab Four were unaware that Epstein had offered Stigwood control of NEMS, and after Epstein's sudden death The Beatles opposed a Stigwood takeover. Stigwood yielded and left NEMS in 1968 with 500,000 British pounds and about half the artist roster, including The Bee Gees and Cream.

Backed by Polygram, he formed the Robert Stigwood Organization (RSO), which went public in 1970; shares plummeted. Then, however, he launched the biggest coup of his career, striking a new deal with Polygram Records. The label purchased all of RSO's stock at $1 a share (slightly above market price) and set up a new company in the United States with Stigwood in charge. Stigwood received $1.5 million of the $8 million the deal cost Polygram. The rock tycoon now had a partner in *Fortune*'s global Top 20. The German-Dutch conglomerate financed his entertainment adventures for the next decade. The Stigwood Group opened offices in New York in mid-1976; Stigwood eventually became a director of Polygram.[20]

With such sound financial backing, Stigwood broadened his interests. He secured British rights to several American plays and brought *Hair, Oh, Calcutta,* and *The Dirtiest Show in Town* to the London stage. The purchase of a small talent agency moved him into television, and his new clients included the writers of the BBC television series *Till Death Do Us Part* and *Steptoe and Son,* which became the models for the CBS hit series *All in the Family* and *Sanford and Son.*

Stigwood, who had earlier turned down *Superstar,* now recognized its commercial possibilities. While everyone else wanted a piece of the action, Stigwood coveted the whole bag—the rock opera and its composers. He courted Lloyd Webber and Rice royally, with expensive dinners, entertainment, and limousines.

In the meantime, the Lloyd Webber and Rice relationship with MCA-Decca had turned sour. Their manager, David Land, was urging Decca to renegotiate their contract in light of the success of the *Superstar* LP. Contract negotiations with MCA Records's new president, Mike Maitland, were difficult. By the time Maitland became company president everyone involved in the U.S. packaging of *Superstar,* with the exception of executive vice president Jack Loetz, had been fired or resigned. Maitland detested Lloyd Webber, who was accustomed to getting his own way. The composers' original contract was eventually adjusted but with great reluctance by Decca executives.

Despite the financial success of *Superstar,* Decca treated it like any other property. They considered the writers' expenses extravagant and questioned whether Decca should foot the bills. For Land, Lloyd Webber, and Rice, Decca paled in light of Stigwood's treatment. MCA owned the *Superstar* album, but the company had overlooked the performing rights. Stigwood acquired them by purchasing Land's London management agency, New Talent Ventures. Land kept part ownership in Lloyd Webber and Rice, along with their creations, and became a partner in the Robert Stigwood Organization as head of Superstar Ventures. MCA now had to deal with both Land and the shrewd Stigwood. "Robert had more foresight than the entire battery of MCA executives and lawyers," said former RSO executive Peter Brown. "He walked into the black tower and turned things around. He got a very favorable deal, where this enormous organization had to match everything we did."[21] Stigwood invested millions, making *Jesus Christ Superstar* into a multi-faceted cross-promotion event: the album selling tickets to the theatrical show, the show selling albums, the albums selling movie tickets, the movie in turn selling albums. One writer called it "a cybernetic spiral of cross-selling that wrings a property of every last drop of profit."[22]

In July 1971, *Jesus Christ Superstar* made its theatrical debut before an enthusiastic audience in the Pittsburgh's Civic Arena. *Superstar* earned $2 million in its first eight weeks on the road. (Two more traveling companies were added later.) At the same time, Stigwood spent $598,000 in the lawsuits to protect the performing rights of *Superstar* from being violated by unauthorized productions. In 1978 it was reported that the live performances earned $40 million.[23]

By the time *Jesus Christ Superstar* opened on Broadway, MCA had netted $16.5 million from the sale of more than two million albums and 600,000 tapes in the United States and Canada. Profits were also reaped from extensive sales of sheet music.[24] Riding on the success of the album, the Broadway production captured enormous amounts of publicity, which generated unprecedented advance ticket sales.

The Broadway production was "conceived for the stage and directed by Tom O'Horgan," Stigwood's choice over Broadway producer Frank Corsaro. Corsaro had worked extensively on the production without a contract, but while he was hospitalized after an auto accident, he was quietly replaced by O'Horgan. The Broadway production cost $750,000.[25] *Jesus Christ Superstar* opened on Broadway on 12 October 1971. In the *Daily News,* Bob Sylvester wrote, "Every few years a piece of theater comes along which is more than a show and it somehow becomes an event . . . Such was the case with *Jesus Christ Superstar.*"[26] On one side of West Fifty-first Street celebrities arrived in a fleet of limousines. Across the street, picketers chanted and carried signs denouncing the play as an unfair depiction of Jesus Christ. Inside the Mark Hellinger Theater, the musical came off smoothly, with the audience responding enthusiastically.

The cast party that followed the Broadway opening inaugurated a Stigwood tradition. Media people, plus 1,000 guests were invited to the $25,000 extravaganza, which included a live rock band, an assortment of hors d'oeuvres, a buffet table, and (unlike at Decca's album preview party) champagne and wine. The celebration lasted throughout the night, but was spoiled in the morning by reviews. Only *Daily News* critic Douglas Watt hailed *Superstar* as "a triumph." The important *New York Times'* reviewer, Clive Barnes, thought different. "Nothing could convince me that any show that had sold two-and-one-half million copies of its album before the opening night is anything like all bad," he wrote. "But I must also confess to experiencing some disappointment when *Jesus Christ Superstar* opened. . . . It all resembled one's first sight of the Empire State Building— not at all uninteresting, but somewhat unsurprising and of minimal artistic value."[27] To make matters worse, the American Jewish Committee and the Anti-Defamation League of B'nai B'rith announced concern over the stereotypical depiction of the Jewish priesthood as Christ killers in *Superstar.* "But what made it all bearable," wrote Nassour, "was that huge, huge advance sale and the avalanche of publicity that *Jesus Christ Superstar* was receiving with every move it made."[28]

Despite hostile reviews and criticism from the religious community, there were long lines at the box office the day after the opening. Riding on the success of the album, the Broadway play was a hit even before it opened; more than $2 million in ticket sales guaranteed a successful run. At the time of the Broadway opening, the single "Superstar" had sold more than one million copies. Album and tapes sales had reached three and a half million, grossing $40 million.[29]

MCA followed its tradition of producing an original cast album, this one recorded at the Columbia Records studio in New York the Sunday following the play's New York opening. This is customary on Broadway since traditionally there are no performances on Sunday. Ironically, the original cast album was a recording of a Broadway show that was based on a recording.

There are specialty markets for original cast recordings in New York and Los Angeles but outside of those markets, sales are usually not good. Consequently, economic factors are imperative in production considerations, especially since Sunday work means overtime pay for everyone. MCA's East Coast A & R director, Tom Morgan, was coordinator of the project and Rice and Lloyd Webber were producers. Morgan had a reputation for bringing in a good quality cast album cheaply; however, Lloyd Webber's outlandish demands made the production difficult. Costs skyrocketed to more than $70,000—more than the original recording, which had been done over a six-month period. Since the original Decca release had sold so well, the label decided to release a one-record cast album to keep the price down. It had initial sales of $150,000.

The Broadway show ran strongly on its advance sales for about eight months before business began to fade in the spring of 1972. Tickets for a Broadway show were too expensive for the potentially large younger audience who wanted to see *Superstar*. Stigwood took his rock opera to Hollywood. Production of the *Superstar* movie began in August. Norman Jewison was selected by Stigwood and MCA, who owned the motion picture rights, to direct. (Jewison had received an Oscar nomination for *In the Heat of the Night* and had recently edited the movie version of *Fiddler on the Roof*.)

It was Jewison's idea to film in Israel, an attractive location because the government was anxious to attract foreign moviemakers. Monies invested in a film made in Israel received a 20-to-25 percent rebate, according to the size of the film's budget from the government. This meant that MCA and Stigwood would be responsible for $2.6 of the $3.5 million projected budget for *Superstar,* with the Israeli government covering the balance.[30]

Despite economic promise, there was angry debate among Israeli government officials about cooperation with the production of a movie about Jesus. As one Parliament member said, "It might be difficult for some people to understand but Jesus Christ is still rather unpopular here." A diplomat with the Israeli Mission in New York remarked, "On the one hand you can call it developing an industry and on the other you can call it selling yourself down the river." A Tel Aviv policeman remarked, "We already had one Jesus here and he gave us more than enough trouble."[31]

Rice and Lloyd Webber had been far from satisfied with O'Horgan's stage presented of their rock opera, and the composers were anxious to be involved in the film version. *"Jesus Christ Superstar* on the screen will not be anything like the Broadway production," Jewison claimed. "It will have a uniqueness—an originality—all its own. Author Tim Rice and composer Andrew Webber will personally supervise every frame of the film.''[32] Nevertheless, while Jewison was attentive to suggestions from Lloyd Webber and Rice, he carried on with his own vision for the movie.

The setting for the film was a combination of first and twentieth centuries: Israeli Phantom jets soar through the sky and tanks stalk Judas over sand dunes. Costumes combined Biblical-looking garb with contemporary styles. Mary Magadalene's sackcloth dress had a low neckline. Roman soldiers carried machine guns and wore Israeli Army fatigues and boots. Herod wore tennis shorts and granny glasses. In the opening scene, the cast arrived in a bus, framing the action as a show within a show. Two understudies from the Broadway production captured leading roles in the film version: Ted Neeley as Jesus and Carl Anderson as Judas. Yvonne Elliman, Barry Dennen, and Bob Bingham retained their parts for the film. The fifteen weeks of shooting began in August 1972; the film was completed on schedule in December.

Andrew Previn arranged and scored the music for the soundtrack recording, which was done in London prior to shooting the film. Lloyd Webber and Rice added one new song, ''Then We Are Decided.'' The soundtrack was released simultaneously with the film. It stalled just short of the Top 20, but still sold one and a half million copies worldwide.

The release of the film in the summer of 1973 renewed the religious controversy over its content. Christian groups criticized it as sacrilegious for not portraying Jesus as divine. Jewish groups attacked the film for anti-Semitic depictions of Jews as ''Christ-killers.'' Black spokesmen objected to the casting of a black man as Judas. The National Jewish Community Relations Advisory Council released a vehement statement condemning the Universal picture as an ''insidious work'' damaging to Christian-Jewish relations and provoking racial hostility. Jewish leaders charged the film perpetuated ''anti-Semitic racial stereotypes'' for a whole new generation that responded to rock music. One Jewish leader wrote to Universal president H. H. Martin with documentation that ''the classic 'Christ-killer' canard has been used against the Jews as a religious justification by reactionary elements for their exploitation of anti-Semitism for ideological purposes.''[33] The Israeli government issued a statement disassociating itself from the movie.

The outburst of criticism coincided with the film's opening in several key cities. Universal executives refused to discuss the film with religious groups. Instead, the film company released a statement explaining that *Jesus Christ Superstar* was a ''rock opera, a musical entertainment, not a religious tract.'' The statement continued:

> With every respect for the sincerity and concern expressed, we do not believe their views to be supported by the content of the film or shared by the many

millions who have listened to the music or viewed the concert and stage presentations throughout the world since 1970.[34]

Critics were also displeased. A *New York Times* reviewer wrote "The mod-pop glitter, the musical frenzy and the neon tubing of this super-hot stage bonanza encasing the Greatest Story are now painfully magnified, laid bare and ultimately parched beneath the blue, majestic Israeli sky, as if by a natural judgement." *Rolling Stone*'s Jon Landau agreed, *"Jesus Christ Superstar,"* he said "is intellectually as vacuous as the Tim Rice and Andrew Lloyd Webber rock opera it so faithfully follows, visually as barren as the Israeli desert it was photographed in, and religiously as authentic as Sunday morning services at the White House." Actors Carl Anderson and Yvonne Elliman received critical praise, but Ted Neeley's interpretation of Jesus was disappointing to reviewers. Landau called Neeley's portrayal of Jesus "the biggest gaping hole in the center of a movie since Ali McGraw's turn in *The Getaway*."[35]

The *Superstar* phenomenon seemed immune to criticism; its multimedia success was stagging at the time. The rock opera was staged in almost every country in the world. By August 1972 earnings from stage productions in the United States alone reached $62 million. The film version did just over $13 million in domestic box office rentals. The original album became the best-selling two-record set of all time, with sales reported to be 5.5 million copies in 1975. The whole affair—albums, stage productions, the film—were estimated to have earned approximately $125 million. MCA's Lew Wasserman said: "It's not a record, it's an industry!"[36]

The success of *Superstar* was followed by some lean years for Stigwood, however. A musical, *Rachel Lily Rosenbloom,* closed before its Broadway opening. Though under no obligation, Stigwood returned $650,000 to investors. The careers of several rock artists he managed, The Bee Gees and Eric Clapton in particular, were faltering. Another rock opera, The Who's *Tommy,* would eventually turn things around.

Tommy Can You See Me?

During the 1960's, The Who was the only rock group on the MCA-Decca label that had any commercial or artistic clout. Specializing in original Broadway musical soundtracks, the company's executives had little understanding of how to market a British rock group in the United States. As a result, the label's U.S. packaging of The Who was shabby, and promotion was poor. The group earned their reputation in the U.S. as a touring band, and had created a sensation by smashing their instruments at the end of their performance at the Monterey Pop Festival in 1967.

In 1969, Decca released The Who's magnum opus, *Tommy,* with much fanfare, saying it was the first rock opera. *Tommy* was greeted with critical praise and was considered by many a landmark in rock music. Rock critic Albert Goldman called it "a triumphantly successful ROCK OPERA!" and praised The Who for "the amazing breakthrough they had scored, the opening they had blasted out of the dreary, dying world of traditional rock into the exhilarating, intoxicating atmosphere of the future," *High Fidelity* dubbed it "superlative rock-and-roll." An estimated four million copies of *Tommy* were sold.[37]

Pete Townshend's original idea for *Tommy* came after a heavy dose of Herman Hesse novels and a religious experience with an Indian guru Mehere Baba. "I can talk for hours about Meher Baba the God Man who describes creation," Townshend explained. "But ultimately, I realize that I see it all through these two little slits labeled R&R."[38] In the end, *Tommy* was an eccentric combination of eastern mysticism, portentous art, and simple rock 'n' roll. Though the album guaranteed the British rock group a place in Rock 'n' Roll Heaven, it bordered on the pretentious. Music critic Dave Marsh rightly observed that The Who's rock opera "veered between crackpot genius and plain farce, spiritual message and ludicrous conceit."[39] Composer and librettist Townshend actually considered the album just a series of singles, several of which were written before the allegorical story was conceived. In retrospect, The Who's creative leader said, "As a gag, when we were working on it, we started to call it a rock opera knowing full well it wasn't a true opera at all. I didn't need the music critics to tell me it wasn't an opera. I've probably listened to as much straight opera as many of them. But the tag stuck and we realized it was maybe a bit fanciful, but in spite of that we quite liked the idea."[40] The Who premiered their work at London's Coliseum and New York's Metropolitan Opera House in 1969. *Time* called the latter "an appearance that was less an honor than a shrewd piece of promotion."[41] The two shows in New York grossed $55,000, according to one estimate.[42] Excerpts from the opera were included in The Who's 1969 tour, which climaxed with a week of performances at the Fillmore East in New York in October.

Several stage renditions followed, including a ballet by Les Grands Ballets Canadiens in 1971. A London stage version featured the London Symphony Orchestra and Chamber Choir and a host of rock performers including Rod Stewart as the Pinball Wizard, Merry Clayton as the Acid Queen, Steve Winwood, Ringo Starr, and The Who. Ode Records released a version with the London Symphony Orchestra in 1972. An estimated ten million copies of the two versions were sold.[43]

Members of The Who were reluctant to see their "masterpiece" turned into a film, but Stigwood's success with *Superstar* and Ken Russell's reputation as an imaginative director convinced the band to sell the film rights to Stigwood. The project had been refused by every major studio in Hollywood, but Stigwood eventually found backing from Columbia Pictures, which helped with the financing and distribution of the film. The project, budgeted at $3.5 million, took just over three months to film in 1974.[44]

The movie was as bizarre as the combination of director Russell and composer Townshend. (Russell had a passion for classical music, and when he first heard *Tommy,* he responded with one word: "Rubbish."[45] The director preferred making biographical films about artists with a surrealistic Freudian interpretation. Aside from a 1969 screen adaptation of the D. H. Lawrence novel, *Women in Love,* all his films had been commercial flops.) Russell and Townshend spent a year working together on the script. "The chasm between the original record album and the film is a great one," Pete Townshend said after the film was completed, "but everything Ken Russell has done with the story and the music has my full blessing.[46]

The film was shot entirely in England. The movie soundtrack was snared by Polydor Records for a reported $1 million.[47] The double album listed for $9.98. Townshend wrote four new songs (expanding the length of the movie soundtrack by thirty-five minutes to a feature-length 110 minutes): "Champagne," "I.V. Studio," "Mother and Son," and "Bernie's Holiday Camp." All of the songs were recorded in quintaphonic sound before shooting began. Performers lip-synced their parts. The actors, who included Oliver Reed, Jack Nicholson, Ann-Margret, and seasoned rockers Elton John, Eric Clapton, Tina Turner, all did their own vocals. When asked about his singing ability, Jack Nicholson replied, "The voice is incomparable."[48] Quintaphonic sound demanded an equivalent reproduction system, a step above quadrophonic with a fifth speaker behind the screen carrying the vocal tracks. Stigwood and Polydor saw to it that several large theaters in major cities were equipped with such a system for the movie's launch.

While planning the marketing strategy for *Tommy,* publicity people at Columbia Pictures discovered that it's senior executives had never heard of the rock opera. With more than $4 million invested in the project, Stigwood and the studio decided to test the public waters. Beverly Hills publicists Rogers and Cowan were hired as consultants. An elaborate plan was devised built around what one writer termed the *"That's Entertainment* thesis!"

The adults who grew up on the musical numbers spliced together into *That's Entertainment* urged their children to see the picture, and the young people who are growing up with rock would urge their parents to reciprocate by seeing *Tommy*. To promote *Tommy* was to educate the adult market (including exhibitors) about contemporary music and film.[49]

Rogers and Cowan convinced Columbia executives that although the film studio was not involved financially with Polydor's soundtrack, the sucesss of each was dependent on the other. Radio airplay was essential exposure, they said. By November 1974 a list of responsibilities was drawn up; Columbia's included distributing press kits to radio and print media and helping determine AM/FM stations for promotion.

As a second facet of the marketing operation, Columbia employed a New York research firm, E. J. Wolf Associates, to conduct a "five-market inquiry" to determine the advertising and promotional campagin for the film. As reported in *Variety*, the survey revealed a great awareness of The Who's six-year-old rock opera among the twenty to twenty-four age group. Younger teens, the report concluded, could be enticed into the theaters through disk jockey promotions. "These kids are easily impressed by their immediate elders," the marketing data indicated, "and form the backbone of Elton John's phenomenal success. Building enthusiasm among this group is an obvious marketing objective, and one not difficult to achieve."[50] The survey also showed that the cast of rock artists in the film had a wide appeal for the radio audience: The Who and Eric Clapton were played regularly on AOR (Album-Oriented Rock) FM. Elton John had several Top 40 hits and some appeal in the R&B market, as did Tina Turner.

Surprisingly, the data showed rock stars were "more critical to the film's promotion" than the movie stars in the cast, including the award-winning Nicholson. Still there was evidence that adults would be drawn to the theaters to see these films stars, and Russell's cult-like followers would be interested in his latest production.[51]

Plans were made for extensive advertising on Top 40 and FM rock radio to reach the twenty- to twenty-four-year-old audience. The promotional package included interviews, music from the soundtrack, the album, and movie-ticket giveaways. Interviews and behind-the-scenes documentary footage was supplied to rock-oriented television shows like *Don Kirschner's Rock Concert*, NBC's *Midnight Special*, and *Soul Train*. Ads appeared in *Rolling Stone, Crawdaddy, Creem*, the *Village Voice*, and underground and college newspapers. A Columbia Pictures advertisement was pure hype: *"Tommy* is greater than any painting, opera, piece of

music, ballet or dramatic work that this century has produced.'' Director
Ken Russell commented, ''they get carried away, you know. I think what
I actually said was that *Tommy* was the best modern opera since Berg's
Wozzeck.''[52]

Promotional expenses included $25,000 for Hollywood publicitiy parties,
and opening-night parties in New York, Chicago and Los Angeles cost a
total of $100,000. *Tommy* opened in New York in March 1975, with
Stigwood rented out the mezzanine of Manhattan's Fifty-seventh Street
subway station for the opening-night party. Seven hundred guests, including pop artist Andy Warhol and actor Anthony Perkins, were treated to an
extraordinary smorgasbord:

> 50 lbs. of octopus flown in from the Bahamas, 50 dozen oysters from Virginia,
> five 30-lb. lobsters from Nova Scotia, a 20-lb. Alaskan king crab, 100-lb. rounds
> of roast beef from Omaha and pastry fantasies as arcane as Ken Russell's own
> visions. By the subway entrances sat an 8-ft.-long *Tommy* sign fashioned from
> 3,000 tomatoes, radishes, cauliflowers and broccoli.[53]

The happening cost Columbia Pictures about $35,000; the lobsters alone
was $14,000. Townshend was a bit upset by the whole affair. While looking
over the crowd he said, ''I just hope none of 'em turn up at any Who
concerts.''[54]

As in its predecessor *Jesus Christ Superstar,* there was no spoken
dialogue in *Tommy*. The movie was a surrealistic collage of psychedelic
images backed with an assault of music blaring in quintaphonic sound.
One reviewer described the ''experience'' as ''benumbing.''[55] *Newsweek*
dubbed it a ''phantasmagorical nightmare,'' saying Russell's excessive
visual imagination met The Who's rock opera to produce ''a roller-coaster
ride through the wasteland of post-World War II civilization.''[56] The film
satirized every issue on the Sixties' countercultural agenda: hypocritical
parents, greedy materialism, organized religion, and, on the whole, a
generally corrupt society.

Tommy is about a blind deaf-mute who becomes a pinball wizard and
then a countercultural messiah. ''It's meant to be multileveled,'' Townshend explained. ''Tommy is a fantasy messiah—a phony one. He's deaf,
dumb and blind because we're deaf, dumb and blind to spiritual potential
that's within us.''[57]

In the film, Tommy (Roger Daltry) is the son of Nora Walker (Ann-
Margaret). Nora's husband is a Captain in the British Air Force whose
plane was shot down in World War II and was reported missing in action.
Apparently, however, he survived and returns home, but after Nora has

already remarried. Tommy wakes up one night and witnesses the murder of his father (a reversal of the album plot) by his stepfather, Uncle Frank (Oliver Reed). The Freudian connotations are obvious. Nora and Uncle Frank admonish him, "You didn't hear it. You didn't see it. You won't say nothing to no one ever in your life." Traumatized by the event, he is struck deaf, mute, and blind.

Tommy grows up in a world of exploitation and abuse. He is tortured by his sadistic cousin Kevin and sexually molested by his perverted Uncle Ernie. Tommy's mother and stepfather subject him to a series of cures. They take him to a guitar-playing Preacher (Eric Clapton) at the temple of celluloid goddess Marilyn Monroe. On the altar is a milk-white statue of Marilyn with her skirt blowing up in her famous *Seven Year Itch* pose. The statue's supposed healing powers have no effect on Tommy. Uncle Frank introduces him to a Gypsy Acid Queen (Tina Turner) who sends the boy on a horrifying LSD trip.

Using only his sense of touch, Tommy becomes pinball champion of the world by dethroning the reigning Pinball Wizard, played by Elton John. Now a cult hero, Tommy is catapulted to fame and fortune. Nora and Frank take him to a Harley Street quack (Jack Nicholson), who fails to restore Tommy's senses. In frustration Nora accidently throws Tommy through a mirror. He lands in a pool of water on the other side. Miraculously cured, he runs wild, singing "I'm Free."

A self-proclaimed messiah, Tommy attracts a throng of followers, whom he forces to wear dark glasses and ear plugs, and to place corks in their mouths, while practicing pinball at Tommy Holiday Camps all over the world.

The cult members rebel and kill Tommy's parents. Destroying his pinball machines, the killers sing, "We're Not Gonna Take It." The film ends with blatant religious symbolism: Tommy walks away from the ruins, he is cleansed under a waterfall (a symbolic baptism), and climbs to the mountaintop where his parents first pledged their love, symbolically reclaiming his own innocence. The Who's "See Me, Feel Me," plays in the background. Tommy returns to an inner solitary confinement.

For the most part, the film received lukewarm-to-favorable reviews. *Variety* called it "spectacular in nearly every way."[58] Jay Cocks wrote in *Time*, "*Tommy* stirs a memory of a lyric from an old Jerry Lee Lewis song: it shakes your nerves and it rattles your brain." Its reviewer thought director Ken Russell's "unceasing imagination gives the movie an exhilarating boldness, a rush of excitement," concluding that "the movie ultimately fails . . . because all of Russell's invention exposes but does not defeat the daffy banality of *Tommy* itself."[59]

The entire production was overblown, but in some sense it was appropriate for the time. A defender of Russell's bold imaginative visual style admitted, "In *Tommy* Russell has turned into exactly what his detractors always said he was: a vulgar Barnum who sacrifices everything to flash and gimmickry."[60] There was a loss of distinction between fantasy and reality in *Tommy*. Russell's flamboyant visuals mixed with Townshend's newly acquired mysticism made *Tommy* a feeble story, especially when combined with The Who's adolescent egomania. " 'Tommy' is not the sort of movie you may ever want to see again," *New York Times* critic Vincent Canby wrote, "but it's an unforgettable souvenir of a time in our history when the only adequate dose was an overdose."[61]

The *Tommy* soundtrack album was released in conjunction with the opening of the film in March 1975 and was certified platinum in November of that year. The film's distributors received $17.7 million in domestic rentals. Though *Tommy* was only a mild success, *Rolling Stone* summarized the film's greater significance:

> It brings together, for the first time really, the two main camps of contemporary entertainment, rock music and film, and utilizes the talents of the top figures of each. So the result is a kind of artistic detente, with the likes of Jack Nicholson, Oliver Reed and Ann-Margret acting as ambassadors from one nation, and the Who, Elton John and Eric Clapton standing up for the youthful and lusty land of rock & roll.[62]

In that sense, *Tommy* marked a beginning. Traditionally, Hollywood looked to Broadway shows for movie musicals. When rock took over the record industry, Hollywood viewed it as a threat, as television had been in the 1950s. During the Vietnam years, rock was seen as a symbol of the youthful countercultural rebellion and experimental lifestyles. Hollywood steered clear for fear of a box office drought. There were some glaring exceptions: *The Graduate* and *Easy Rider* in the late Sixties and *Superstar* and *Tommy* in the Seventies. With the Vietnam war over, the student protest movement expired, and Nixon out of the White House, however, the 1970s were a new ball game. The political revolt of the Sixties was replaced by the self-fulfillment and self-gratification of the Me Decade. Rebellious rock stars were now celebrities, and much of the recording business was now centered in Los Angeles. Film and record executives crossed paths along Sunset Strip.

Disco Inferno: Saturday Night Fever

Robert Stigwood, not unlike his predecessor Sam Katzman, watched carefully for the next trend to exploit as a multimedia enterprise. A story by Nik Cohen that appeared in the June 7, 1976 issue of *New York* magazine caught his attention. The story, entitled "Tribal Rites of the New Saturday Night," concerned New York's disco subculture. "When I read it," Stigwood said, "I thought it would be a perfect film, particularly with the disco craze starting to sweep the country. I felt sure that was going to build."[63] Within twenty-four hours Stigwood had struck a deal with Cohen's agent.

Disco had grown up around the cynicism of the post-Watergate era. Survival was a dominant theme in the music. In trying to explain its immense popularity, one writer said, "Disco transformed the passive, frustrated television audience of the Watergate Hearings into performers . . . Disco celebrated the fact that we had survived Nixon."[64] One of the first disco albums was recorded by Shirley and Company in 1975, *Shame, Shame*. The cover featured a drawing of Shirley shaking her finger at Richard Nixon.

Disco, dubbed by critics as "rhythm without the blues," danced its way out of New York's black, Hispanic and gay ghettos in the early 1970s. The music was a fusion of Motown and soul: the smooth sounds of TSOP (The Sound of Philadelphia) created by Philadelphia International Records producers Kenneth Gamble and Leon Huff wedded to the funky R&B of Isaac Hayes ("Theme from *Shaft*") and Curtis Mayfield (soundtrack from *Superfly*) can be heard in it.[65] "Rock the Boat," by the Hues Corporation, a Las Vegas lounge band, marked the beginning of a series of dance songs that became hits through radio exposure. The song was initially a hit in dance clubs, then sailed to the top of the *Billboard* singles chart in July 1974, selling more than two million copies. George McCrae's "Rock Your Baby," written and produced by Harry Wayne Casey and Richard Finch, replaced it the following week. That duo went on to form K.C. and the Sunshine Band, who scored with a series of dance songs beginning with "Get Down Tonight," a Number 1 hit in August 1975. Almost three months later, "That's the Way [a-ha, a-ha] (I Like It)" topped the charts. In September 1976, "(Shake, Shake, Shake) Shake Your Booty" reached Number 1. In June 1977, the group's "Miami Sound" gave them another Number 1 hit with "I'm Your Boogie Man."

In the meantime, Van McCoy and the Soul City Symphony had topped the charts in July 1975 with "The Hustle," a Latin-flavored cut from the album *Disco Baby*. A hustle dance craze followed the song, which won a Grammy Award for Best Pop Instrumental. When the German Group Silver Convention reached Number 1 on *Billboard*'s Hot 100 with "Fly, Robin, Fly" (which won a Grammy Award for Best Rhythm and Blues Instrumental Performance) the Eurodisco sound was launched.

The most prominent producer of Eurodisco was Giorgio Moroder, who did "Love To Love You Baby," which featured Donna Summer's orgasmic moans. The song was a smash disco hit in Europe in 1976. Moroder brought the record to Casablanca Records founder Neil Bogart, who suggested he make a longer version. Moroder extended the song to twenty minutes, and a sixteen-minute, fifty-second version became the rage in Manhattan discos. It reached Number 2 in February 1976. The song established Casablanca Records as a major disco label and changed the commercial format for disco records: The longer, twelve-inch single replaced the seven-inch with disc jockeys and eventually was sold in record stores.

By 1975, airplay began to expand the disco audience. Upscale white singles, especially in urban markets, were intrigued. Within a year, 10,000 discos were operating in the country compared with 1,500 in 1974. Still, this was perceived as an underground phenomenon until the reemergence of The Bee Gees.

The Bee Gees had signed with Stigwood's agency in 1967 and had a string of hits beginning with "New York Mining Disaster 1941," and including "To Love Somebody," "Holiday," "Words," "I Started a Joke," "Lonely Days" and "How Can You Mend a Broken Heart." The Gibb brothers then went through a low period in the early part of the 1970s.

Their sensational comeback began in 1975 with the release of the album *Main Course* on Stigwood's RSO Records label. Two songs from the LP, "Jive Talkin' " and "Nights on Broadway," had a disco style appealing to the dance market.[66] The English group was so far out of the limelight that there was barely a chance that radio stations would get excited about anything they released. Promos leaving the artists unidentified, a scheme that had been used to promote "New York Mining Disaster 1941," worked a second time. "Jive Talkin' " went to Number 1 on the *Billboard* chart and "Nights on Broadway" reached the Top 10. A third single, "Fanny (Be Tender With My Love)" reached Number 12. The album was certified gold.

A 1976 release, *Children of the World*, was certified platinum that year and gave the Bee Gees their third Number 1 single, "You Should Be Dancing." The song followed the formula from *Main Course*, keeping the disco style and falsetto harmonies that had become distinctive parts of The Bee Gees' sound. In 1977, the trio had just begun laying tracks for another album when Stigwood put them to work on the music for the *Saturday Night Fever* soundtrack. They took about two and a half weeks to write five original songs for the film. ("If I Can't Have You" had already been recorded for the aborted album project.) Four more were written at Stigwood's request.

Bee Gee Maurice Gibb noted three important elements in the phenomenal success of *Fever:* "It was a triangle of Robert Stigwood making the film to start with, having John [Travolta] as the lead, which was a damned good choice, and us writing the music."[67]

Stigwood had no trouble finding a distributor for *Saturday Night Fever.* Paramount president Michael Eisner and chairman Barry Diller were both in their mid-thirties and had grown up on rock music. "They knew The Bee Gees," explained on Simpson, then vice-president of production at Paramount. "So they went after it as if it were *The Godfather.*"[68] Stigwood negotiated with Paramount for 45 percent of the gross theatrical rentals of *Saturday Night Fever.* According to director John Badham, Paramount completely misjudged the success of *Fever;* executives estimated the company would earn only $20 million from domestic box office rentals.[69]

The film company had no interest in Polygram's soundtrack; the rule of thumb in the film industry was that soundtracks just didn't sell. If a movie was a smash at the box office, a package of songs from the score was thrown together with the hope that a few copies might sell. That was before *Saturday Night Fever.* RSO Films head Bill Oakes said that during the filming of *Saturday Night Fever* in 1976, Paramount "wasn't even remotely interested in even participating on the album in terms of being a royalty earner."[70] Stigwood cleaned up on the revenues from the soundtrack.

The rock tycoon commissioned Norman Wexler, who had written the screenplays for *Joe* and *Serpico,* to pen the script for *Saturday Night Fever.* John Avildsen, the original director for *Saturday Night Fever,* was fired the very day he was nominated for an Academy Award for Rocky: Stigwood feared Avildsen was turning the disco drama into a "dancing Rocky."[71] (Ironically, that is exactly what happened in the sequel, *Stayin' Alive,* under the direction of Sylvester Stallone.) John Badham *(The Bingo Long Travelling All-Stars and Motor Kings)* replaced Avildsen.

Originally, Badham thought he was working with an ordinary drama. "I read the script," Badham explains, "and I'm reading this story of a young kid growing up in Brooklyn who goes to a discotheque, a story about a guy who's a fish out of water . . . I get on a plane to go to New York, I'm reading the script again the next day, and it's only then that I realize, 'Oh my god, it's a *major musical.*' "[72] Bedham received a cassette tape from Stigwood with five Bee Gees songs on it. The challenge for Bedham was to integrate the music into the film, which was difficult at times. One Bee Gee song had been recorded at a different tempo than the original demo used when the dance scene was shot and the sound and visuals kept falling out of sync until finally a device was found that could alter the tempo of the recording without raising the pitch. In addition, some songs had to be remixed and some dance routines changed.

Stigwood thought the movie should be called *Saturday Night,* and wanted The Bee Gees to retitle ''Stayin' Alive,'' but The Bee Gees remained adamant. They wouldn't change the title, Maurice Gibb said, ''because there are so many bloody records out called 'Saturday Night.' It's corny; it's a terrible title.'' Barry Gibb added, ''We said, 'Either it's 'Stayin' Alive' or we'll keep the song.' '' The debate continued. The Bee Gees had already written ''Night Fever.'' ''We told him we didn't like the title *Saturday Night* for the film, and he said he didn't want to call the movie just *Night Fever.* So he thought it over for awhile, called us back, and said, 'O.K., let's compromise. Let's call it *Saturday Night Fever.*' ''[73]

While The Bee Gees were in France writing the material for *Fever,* Travolta was in the United States putting together dance routines. He choreographed a dance to The Bee Gees' ''You Should Be Dancing'' and refused to rework the routine for another song in the movie. ''He didn't want to rehearse to another number, didn't want to start doing the same dance routine to a different song,'' explained Maurice Gibb. ''It was supposed to be 'Night Fever' in that scene, but we didn't mind, and Robert didn't mind. It was an old hit of ours, but he made the song come alive again for us with that dance routine.''[74]

Stigwood wanted the Bee Gees to write a song eight minutes long for the climatic scene with Travolta and Stephanie in the dance contest. ''It would have a nice dance tempo, then a romantic interlude, and all hell breaking loose at the end,'' explained Barry Gibb.[75] Stigwood's group thought he was crazy; a song with rhythmic breaks would have little hope as a single. The film was changed.

Stigwood confidently signed John Travolta to a three-picture contract. (Ironically, years earlier he had auditioned for a part in the Broadway production of *Jesus Christ Superstar,* but Stigwood considered him too young in comparison with the rest of the cast.) Travolta was already identified as having great appeal to the teen audience. He had been cast in a prime supporting role in Brian DePalma's high school horror film, *Carrie,* at the same time he landed the part of ''Sweathog'' Vinnie Barbarino, on the ABC television series *Welcome Back, Kotter,* which he stole the show from star Gabe Kaplan. Travolta had quickly became a teen heartthrob, receiving 10,000 fan letters each week, and his popularity led to a recording contract with Midsong International. His first album, entitled *John Travolta,* yielded a Ten 10 hit, ''Let Her In.'' Travolta was voted *Billboard*'s new pop male vocalist of the year. "Slow Dancing," a single from a second LP, *Can't Let You Go,* also charted. Travolta was making $1,500 a week doing *Kotter* when Stigwood offered him a $1 million contract.

Travolta was marketed as a sex symbol. "We were making a heroic, or quasi-mythic, sort of image with him," Badham explained. The idea was to market an attractive man to please the female audience. "Its been effective," Badham continued. "Most of our repeat viewers were women, and they're not going back to see my work, I can assure you. They're going back to look at Travolta."[76] In preparation for the role of Tony Manero in *Saturday Night Fever,* Travolta took dance lessons and dropped twenty pounds working with the same trainer Sylvester Stallone had used for *Rocky*.

Travolta and scriptwriter Norman Wexler did on-sight research at Brooklyn discos. "A lot of what I put on the screen came from guys I met," Travolta explained. "They were extreme in their personalities. I'd see where their values were—where women and dancing stood in their lives. They all had one thing in common—they wanted to get out of Brooklyn."[77] Many of the regulars in Brooklyn discos were used as extras in the film; several invited Travolta home to meet their families and that gave him material for his role. "A lotta the stuff in the scenes at home," Travolta explained, "at the dinner table, and the ones with my brother in the picture, who's leaving the priesthood—I got the feel of those moments from those Brooklyn dinners."[78]

Before *Saturday Night Fever,* the strategy for marketing soundtracks was simply to release the soundtrack album at the same time as the movie premiered. *Saturday Night Fever* changed that, becoming the prototype of synergism between the film and record industries. Exposure was the key. "We have less than sixty people employed in this company," explained RSO Records president Al Coury, "and more than half of them are in promotion. Because I realized a long time ago that promotion people working close with radio stations create demand. I can't sell any record unless people hear it."[79]

Stigwood had learned the art of cross promotion through *Jesus Christ Superstar* and *Tommy*. Timing was essential for success and RSO had a strict schedule for *Saturday Night Fever*. In September, a thirty-second trailer played in 150 theaters across the nation. Travolta strutted down the city sidewalk with The Bee Gees' "Stayin' Alive" pounding in the background. The song had not been released as a single and the soundtrack was still not available. The trailer created immediate interest demand. "There was tremendous feedback from people coming into the theaters," said RSO president Al Coury. "Radio people and retailers got back to us expressing interest in 'Staying' Alive.' When the soundtrack album came out, they jumped on it immediately, playing both that song and 'How Deep Is Your Love.' ''[80]

Paramount employed a three-minute trailer that included music by The Bee Gees, Tavares, and Yvonne Elliman. This had the dual effect of plugging both the movie and the soundtrack. The trailer ended with a shot of the opened album cover and a voice-over letting the audience know the soundtrack containing all the songs from the movie was available. Audiences in a theater in Washington, D.C. applauded the trailer.[81]

Coury pioneered a strategy for staggering the release of singles to maximize exposure for both the album and the movie. As one single neared the top of the charts, another was released. This procedure kept cuts from the soundtrack in constant airplay over an extended length of time, coinciding with the run of the film.

Thirty days before the issue of the soundtrack album, the Bee Gees "How Deep Is Your Love" was released as a single to provide exposure for the upcoming LP. The song appeared on *Billboard*'s Hot 100 at Number 83 on 24 September 1977. It reached Number 1 on December 24 and remained in the Top 10 for seventeen weeks, making it the longest-running single in the history of the Hot 100. On 10 December, just before "How Deep Is Your Love" reached Number 1, another Bee Gees' single, "Stayin' Alive," was released, coinciding with the film's street date. It entered the charts at Number 65 and reached Number 1 February 4, 1978. With "Stayin' Alive" on top of the charts and "How Deep Is Your Love" still in the Top 10, "Night Fever" was released, entering the Hot 100 at Number 76 on February 4. This third single from the *Saturday Night Fever* soundtrack quickly joined the other two in the Top 10. The same week "Night Fever" reached Number 1, "Stayin' Alive" fell to Number 2.

The Bee Gees became the first group to hold down the top two slots on *Billboard*'s Hot 100 since the Beatles in 1964. Yvonne Elliman's "If I Can't Have You," written by the Bee Gees, was yet another single to top the Hot 100. It entered the charts at Number 89 on 28 January 1978, hitting the top position fifteen weeks later on 13 May. This marked four Number 1 singles from the soundtrack, an unprecedented feat that has yet to be repeated.

Several other records were shattered by The Bee Gees' performance. Their four consecutive songs to reach Number 1 surpassed the Lennon and McCartney record of three in 1964. Six consecutive Number 1 singles for RSO Records was four more than for any other label. In April 1978, RSO Records president Al Coury said The three Bee Gees singles had sold

Figure 4.1. Saturday Night Fever

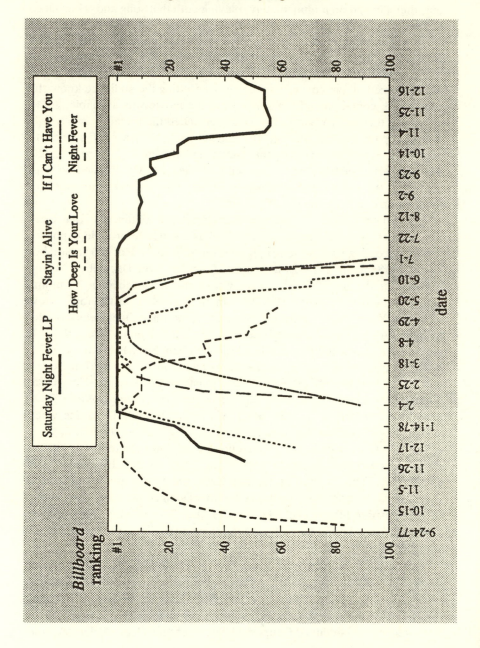

6.6 million units: "How Deep Is Your Love" (1.8 million), "Stayin' Alive" (2.8 million), and "Night Fever" (2 million).[82]

Polygram distributed the RSO soundtrack, which was released in the United States in November 1977. The double-disc album sold in retail stores for $12.98. One million copies were shipped to retail outlets with another 750,000 stored in the RSO warehouse. According to RSO Records president Al Coury, the soundtrack sold 850,000 copies before the film was released on 16 December 1977. "Then we converted the campaign to selling the soundtrack, and piggybacked onto the success of the film," Coury explained. "Ten days after the movie was out, we felt the impact of the film. We sold 750,000 copies of the album in four days between Christmas and New Year's."[83]

In ten weeks the soundtrack was at the top of *Billboard*'s Top Pop Albums; it held that spot for twenty-five straight weeks. The album also crossed over onto the R&B and Album Oriented Radio (AOR) charts as well. In less than six months, *Fever* became the largest-selling album in history. At its peak, the soundtrack sold two million copies in the first two weeks of February alone. After that the LP sold at the rate of about 500,000 copies per week.

The appeal of *Saturday Night Fever* reached beyond the prime record-buying audience to include the aging Baby Boom market, now the eighteen-to-thirty-four age group. Demographer Landon Y. Jones explained the phenomenon:

> Demographic studies showed it was most favored by single and divorced people living in the coldly urban world of strangers. Their jobs were depressing and their prospects worse. The lyrics spoke not of teenage passions and high school, as songs during the fifties and sixties, but rather of boring jobs and adult lust. The common lyrical theme . . . was *survival*. In a deteriorating world in which all institutions were crumbing, disco offered a way out.[84]

The observations of retail store owners supported Jones's statement. "The demographics are amazing," said one Los Angeles retailer. "We get kids, the Beverly Hills type, all age groups." Record store owners were ecstatic. "We're getting a lot of elderly people from the condominiums who say they love to hustle," said one retailer. "People come up with Beethoven in one hand and ask for the 'Saturday Night' album, almost embarrassedly," said another. Some were enticed by Bee Gees' singles they heard on the radio, while others were "not record buyers," one store owner observed, "but they've obviously seen the movie and liked it."[85]

The soundtrack also fueled sales of anything at all related to the project—the Bee Gees' catalog, records by other artists on the soundtrack, disco products, and anything with the RSO label on it. Spin-off sales increased by 50 percent, according to one estimate.[86]

People in the record and film industries were boggled. Soundtracks and collections by various artists (this one with several re-releases) were traditionally not very lucrative investments. *Saturday Night Fever* was a glaring exception. Along with the Bee Gees numbers, several of its other artists placed songs on the trade charts: K. C. and the Sunshine Band's "Boogie Shoes" reached Number 35, Tavares's version of "More Than a Woman" was a minor hit, and The Trammps' fiery rendition of "Disco Inferno" reached Number 11 on the *Billboard* pop charts and Number 9 on the R&B listings. Walter Murphy's "A Fifth of Beethoven," a synthesized disco interpretation of Beethoven's *Symphony No. 5 in C Minor,* had already achieved Number 1 status back in October 1976, but was reissued. Kool and the Gang, Ralph MacDonald, M.F. S.B., and David Shire (who scored the music for the film) all provided additional cuts for the soundtrack.

When *Saturday Night Fever* opened in 504 theaters in mid-December 1977, "How Deep Is Your Love" was a Number 1 hit. RSO executives claimed that the music enticed moviegoers into the theater "Every time the deejay announced 'Stayin' Alive,' he said, 'that's from the movie *Saturday Night Fever* starring John Travolta,' " explained RSO president Al Coury. "It was millions and millions of dollars of free publicity."[87]

The movie begins with Tony Manero (John Travolta) swinging a can of paint and strutting confidently down a city street in the Bay Ridge section of Brooklyn. His steps are in time with the pounding disco beat of the Bee Gees' song "Stayin' Alive." Disco is like the rhythm of his life, the pulse of Brooklyn's night life. Only the lyrics to the song hint at his dilemma: "Ain't goin' nowhere, somebody help me." Manero wants to get out of this urban wasteland, but first has to come to a realization of this himself.

Manero is a nineteen-year-old working-class Italian. Posters of Al Pacino as Serpico and Sylvester Stallone as Rocky decorate his small, crowded room. Tony's life is constantly divided into seemingly irreconcilable worlds. Women are either nice girls or whores. "Spics," "fags," and "niggers," ironically the racial and ethnic subcultures imitated in the disco phenomenon, inhabit the world outside his circle of friends. Members of his gang are brutal, insensitive, and unimaginative.

Tony lives in a dead-end workaday world Monday through Friday. His Italian-Catholic family, one reviewer noted, "resembles a Progresso commercial invaded by the Three Stooges."[88] The family is being torn apart by the effects of a sick economy and changing urban values. The father is an unemployed blue-collar worker whose dignity has been destroyed.

Older brother Frank is disillusioned with the priesthood, giving yet another blow to his devout Catholic mother whose faith no longer seems to be enough to help her cope with the harsh realities of life.

Only the exciting world of the disco provides a temporary escape from the boredom of blue-collar, ethnic life. At the disco Tony comes to life—he transcends the world of boredom, a meaningless job, and Catholic guilt that exists outside the walls of 2001 Odyssey. Fantasy and reality merges on the dance floor in a moment of self-realization. "How come we never talk about the way we feel when we're dancing?" Tony asks his partner, Stephanie Mangano. Referring to dancing, he says, "I would like to get that high someplace else in my life." When Tony bursts through the doors at 2001, people part like the Red Sea did for Moses. Tony is the king of the disco. People clear the lighted dance floor to make room for his solos (and fall in line for Lester Wilson's choreographed dance numbers).

But the tension between the two worlds had become too great for Tony. Even the hedonistic world of the disco holds little promise. The greatest aspirations are shallow at best—revengeful gang fights, backseat sexual encounters, and primping at the disco. Tony eventually sees where he is headed—selling paint at a hardware store for the rest of his life. In desperation, he seeks a way out.

Stephanie Mangano (Karen Lynn Gorney) comes from the same world as Tony, but she is going somewhere. She has landed a job as a secretary at an advertising agency and is moving to Manhattan. Around Tony and his friends, she puts on a sophisticated air, drinking tea with lemon instead of coffee, and dropping names of all the "interesting people" she meets at work. Tony is attracted to her because she's "different." She is breaking out of Tony's world and challenges his values and his lack of ambition. All that holds them together is an agreement to be dance partners in the $1,000 dance contest at 2001.

The Verrazano-Narrows Bridge is an apt symbol of Tony's avenue of escape from his dead-end life in Brooklyn to the promise of Manhattan: it is dangerous. In one scene, Tony and his friends play a sick joke on Annette, a 2001 regular, pretending to fall from the bridge. This foreshadows a young member's suicidal fall. In one scene Tony demonstrates that he knows every detail about the bridge.

The disco prince has to get up the courage to move into a new and different situation. To make the transition, Tony must first change his attitude toward family, friends, women, and traditional values. In the final dance contest at 2001, Tony and Stephanie discover their feelings for each other. Their emotions take precedence over the dance. Their routine, to Bee Gees' "More Than A Woman," is disappointing, considering the amount of time they spent rehearsing. Still, Tony and Stephanie are the winners, but only because of racism and favoritism for the hometown boy: a Latino couple is clearly better. Tony realizes the whole thing is a sham. He gives the trophy and prize money to the Latinos, at the same time rejecting Bay Ridge, his friends, and his life in the paint store.

In frustration, Tony tries to force himself sexually upon Stephanie, but is rejected. He sits quietly in a car's front seat while his friends gang rape Annette. At the Verrazano Bridge, Michael's suicidal fall shows just how miserable the world the friends inhabit really is. Tony spends a soul-searching night riding in subway cars. In the morning he goes to Stephanie's Manhattan apartment. He plans to move to Manhattan, and promises to try to be "friends" with Stephanie. In the final, ambiguous scene they are embracing.

Critics were impressed with Travolta, who received an Oscar nomination for Best Actor. *Newsweek*'s David Ansen called his performance "a triumphant starring debut . . . The man can boogie!" "John Travolta is a revelation," said *Time*'s Frank Rich. "At once mean-looking and pretty, he conveys the kind of threatening sexuality that floors an audience." A *New York Times* report said Travolta has "the supply line and magnetic vitality that could make him the Astaire or Kelly of the new dancing style."[89]

Lester Wilson's choreographed dance sequences were applauded by the critics. Pauline Kael said they were "among the most hypnotically beautiful pop dance scenes ever filmed." "The disco dance scenes are brilliantly executed," a review from *Cineaste* maintained, "the camera dollying, zooming and panning from every angle, with multicolored filters and flashing lights evoking the electricity of the whole scene." Another reviewer said the dance scenes "explode with an energy that is skillfully channelled by the well-paced direction, camerawork, cutting, and choreography into a highly charged cinematic experience."[90]

Most critics were disappointed with Norman Wexler's clumsy screenplay. The "hackneyed subplots borrowed from other movies," as *Newsweek* put it, were weak and unnecessary. *Time,* too, lamented that Wexler filled "the script with a series of stagy and unconvincing plot incidents: a suicide, a gang rumble, a gang bang."[91] Tony's brother leaving the priesthood and the arbitrary gang war distracted from the main action instead of enhancing it. One subplot *was* a successful backdrop to Tony's inner struggle: Michael's relentless pursuit of advice on how to deal with his guilt and pregnant Catholic girlfriend leads to his suicidal fall from the Verrazano Bridge. This subplot illustrated the illusion of friendship in the struggle for survival.

Variety compared *Saturday Night Fever* to Sam Katzman's rock films of the 1950s, considering the Stigwood production to be a "more shrill, more vulgar, more trifling, more superficial and more pretentious exploitation film." The reviewer concluded: " 'Saturday Night Fever,' which seemed to promise a sight-and-sound collage of the disco world and its people, is a major disappointment in that the topical disco milieu is a slapdash backdrop to the worst in teenage exploitation rehash." [92]

In the first twenty-four days of its release (December 16 through January 9), *Saturday Night Fever* average $1.1 million daily at the box office. In the first three months of 1978, the picture was pulling in an average $600,000 daily in domestic box office receipts, which *Variety* called "just terrific." The month of May 1978 showed a continued strong daily average of $300,000. *Saturday Night Fever* played in 14,000 theaters in the United States and Canada in the first year of its release. By the end of 1978 the domestic gross in film rentals was over $71 million. [93]

In anticipation of television broadcasts and airline usage, a PG-version of *Saturday Night Fever* was shot simultaneously with the originally released R-rated version. Paramount's vice president for technical operations, Mike Policare, explained, "Paramount's policy is to try to get the television version of a movie ready simultaneously with the theatrical film, before the actors are off the payroll. We like to have the original director do it because he has the feel of the picture, the mood. John Badham worked very closely on the PG version of 'Saturday Night Fever.' " [94] About seven minutes were cut deleting much of the graphic sexually and obscenity of the R-rated version. When the time came to release the PG-version, Paramount people had an even better reason for putting it in theaters.

Paramount executives considered running the two versions simultaneously and submitted a proposal to the MPAA. Upon reconsideration they withdrew the proposal before the MPAA committee reviewed it. Paramount's senior domestic vice president, Frank Mancuso, said, "We realized the film was performing too strongly to risk limiting the momentum of the R version by bringing in a PG. With that in mind, we consciously accelerated our distribution plan to extract the maximum from the original before going ahead with the PG." [95]

In January 1979 the R-rated prints were withdrawn from distribution. The MPAA waived its ninety-day rule to allow Paramount to release the PG version within sixty days of the withdrawal of the R version. A $2-million advertising campaign accompanied the release of the PG version. It was first introduced in the southern and Midwestern markets in March and reached the rest of the country in April. The emphasis of the advertising push was on the under-seventeen audience—a large segment of the potential audience for the film that had been kept away by the R rating. Paramount executives banked on the popularity of the Bee Gee's music and Travolta to insure a successful run of the milder version. Paramount chairman Barry Diller said, "We felt a lot of people who would enjoy the film were excluded from seeing it. Why shouldn't we let them see it and make ourselves some money? Young people knew and responded to the music. We would not be doing this without the immense appeal of the Bee Gees' music."[96]

Saturday Night Fever catapulted John Travolta to superstardom. The Bee Gees became the hottest group in the recording industry. The *Fever* movie and soundtrack gave new life to the dying disco subculture. Al Coury, who was president of RSO Records then, said the *Saturday Night Fever* soundtrack "kind of took disco out of the closet."[97]

The *Fever* phenomenon turned disco into an overnight sensation. Men were trading in their blue jeans for gold neck chains, polyester shirts, and white three-piece suits. Suddenly more than 20,000 discos arose across the country; they were visited by an estimated thirty-six million people in 1978 alone. Studio 54, dubbed "the mother church of international nightlife chic,"[98] opened in April 1977. The Manhattan disco was originally a theater and then was converted into a television sound stage before becoming the disco of the celebrities. San Francisco's legendary Fillmore West was just one of numerous rock palaces converted into discos. Around two hundred radio stations changed to all-disco formats—New York's WKTU was one of the most noted. "It's the most phenomenal thing since the Beatles," exclaimed a Washington, D.C. rock promoter. "You can't run away from that music."[99]

There were disco proms, disco cruises, and disco rollerskating rinks. Twenty of *Billboard*'s Top 100 in 1978 were disco songs and disco records captured eight of fourteen Grammy Awards that year. *Newsweek* called disco "one of the biggest entertainment phenomena of the '70s."[100] Any song or musical style could be adapted to disco's 125-beats-per-minute formula. Former rockers jumped on the disco bandwagon. The Rolling Stones, Rod Stewart, The Beach Boys, and Cher recorded disco songs. *Disco Mickey Mouse* featured disco versions of Disney favorites, like "Chim Chim Cher-see" and "Zip-a-Dee-Doo-Dah." "We're in a period of the McDonalds of music, where it's mass-marketed like junk food," said singer Melba Moore, who had a Top 40 disco hit with "You Stepped Into My Life." Disco quickly became an industry that generated four billion dollars annually.[101]

The two-disc *Fever* soundtrack sold a staggering twenty-five million copies worldwide; twelve million in the United States. Sales figures for the album were estimated at about $285 million.[102] *Saturday Night Fever* shattered previous records and remained the largest-selling album of all time until Michael Jackson's *Thriller* surpassed it in 1984. The film remains on *Variety*'s Top 100 All-Time Film Rental Champs, with domestic rentals totaling $74.1 million. The profit was incredible, considering that production costs were a mere $4.5 million.[103] "And that's the way it goes," *Forbes* concluded of Stigwood's marketing successes. "The music hypes the movie, the movie hypes the music. Everybody gets rich. Especially Bob Stigwood."[104]

By conservative estimates, the Bee Gees earned about $50 million from *Saturday Night Fever*.[105] The trio won five Grammy Awards for the *Saturday Night Fever* LP: as artists for Album of the Year, as producers for Album of the Year, Best Pop vocal Performance by a Duo, Group or Chorus, Best Arrangement for Voices (for "Stayin' Alive"), and Producers of the Year. "How Deep Is Your Love" had won as Best Pop Vocal Performance by a Duo, Group or Chorus in 1977. Despite the incredible impact the album had, Hollywood ignored the Bee Gees' achievement. *Saturday Night Fever* was not even nominated for an Academy Award, although as noted, Travolta was nominated. Stigwood boycotted the ceremonies.

Saturday Night Fever managed to capture the spirit of the late 1970s. Writer Albert Goldman noted, "Outside the entrance to every discotheque should be erected a statue to the presiding deity: Narcissus."[106] *Saturday Night Fever* was a cinematic depiction of historian Christopher Lasch's "culture of narcissism."[107] The film was set in a period of diminishing expectations, when the ethic of self-preservation was replacing the Protestant work ethic. The characters were obsessed with personal preoccupations and living for the passion of the moment. They seemed ignorant of the social upheaval of the Sixties—Vietnam, student protest, race riots, Watergate—implying a retreat from politics and an acceptance of the American middle-class values and way of life. Pauline Kael rightly observed: "These boys are part of the post-Watergate, working-class generation with no heroes *except* in TV-show-biz land: they had a historical span of twenty-three weeks, with repeats at Christmas."[108]

Fever documented the assimilation of the youthful Sixties counterculture into mainstream American life. Historian Peter N. Carroll observed that the movie "reinforced a conservative message of conformity, expensive dress, and self-discipline. Only by embracing these traditional American values could the youthful ethnic hero . . . hope to attain the upward mobility implied in leaving his working-class origins in Brooklyn for a new life in Manhattan.''[109]

Part of Lasch's theory was that "The media give substance to and thus intensify narcissistic dreams of fame and glory, encourage the common man to identify himself with the stars and to hate the 'herd,' and make it more and more difficult for him to accept the banality of everyday existence.''[110] That was at least part of the impact of *Saturday Night Fever*. *Time*'s Frank Rich asserted:

> Under the strobe lights, with the throb of the Bee Gees' music engulfing him, Tony can be a prince, a star. And being a star appeals to millions of young people who, like Tony, fear that anonymity and dull routine of adult responsibilities. If Tony can find escape and glory in dancing, perhaps millions of his peers can too. *Saturday Night Fever* suggests that anyone, no matter how trapped by life's trying circumstances, can be a hero. As one recent graduate of a Washington, D.C., high school explains: '*Saturday Night Fever* is my life. It says that if you dance well and look great, you're on top, even if you work pumping gas.'[111]

Disco artist and composer Barry White agreed. "At a disco, the record buyer can be the rock star," he said. "People can dress up in the baddest fashions and look like they're in somebody's group. The hippest mother gets a shot at stardom at the disco.''[112] The disco was reparation for a mundane job and a life lacking substantial meaning.

Grease Is The Word

Stigwood's next box office bonanza, was ointment for what Landon Jones called "the arthritis of the baby boom"—nostalgia.[113]

Grease rode the crest of a wave of nostalgia that swept the entertainment media in the late 1970s. George Lucas's *American Graffiti* had started it all in 1973 and the television shows *Laverne and Shirley* and *Happy Days* continued the trend.

Grease was a Robert Stigwood-Allan Carr collaboration. Carr had entered the entertainment world as personal manager for Ann-Margret, Peter Sellers, Nancy Walker, Marvin Hamlisch, and Stockard Channing. Stigwood, had previously joined with him to produce the exploitation movie *Survive,* an $800,000 film about cannibalism among survivors of a plane crash in Chile. (A sensationalist promotional campaign had said, "Warning! Scenes of cannibalism may be too vivid for certain moviegoers.") The low-grade picture grossed $13 million. Carr had also teamed up with Stigwood as creative consultant in the marketing and promotion of *Tommy*.

The musical *Grease* opened in New York in 1972 to indifferent reviews, but its appeal to Baby Boomers was obvious. The show moved to Broadway where it began a record run of 3,388 performances lasting, until 1980. *Grease* became temporarily the longest-running Broadway show in history. By the time the film opened, the Broadway show and touring companies had grossed an estimated $50 million profit.[114]

Carr had sold Stigwood a half interest in the movie rights to *Grease;* he had originally intended to cast Ann-Margret and Elvis Presley in the leading roles. Failing, he offered the lead to Henry Winkler of *Happy Days,* who turned down the part because it was identical to his television character, the Fonz. Carr was in a bind when he tuned into friend Gabe Kaplan's TV show and "out came this charismatic kid, this wonder, John Travolta."[115] Stigwood agreed. (Earlier in his career, Travolta (then eighteen) had been cast in *Grease* in a supporting role and as understudy to the lead in a touring company and on Broadway.

Grease would have been the first film starring Travolta, but production was held up and in the meantime Travolta was cast in *Saturday Night Fever.* His success greatly benefited *Grease.* (The Broadway producers of *Grease,* Kenneth Waissman and Maxine Fox , had thought the film would shorten the stage production's run and reduce their profits. They held up film production for almost a year before a release date was established through arbitration. As part of the settlement, Paramount had to run a thirty-second commercial for the Broadway show at theaters within a 125-mile radius of New York City.)

Grease was in rehearsal and Carr still had not found a woman to play opposite Travolta. Marie Osmond looked too much like Travolta's sister. Susan Dey, former star of the television series *The Partridge Family,* refused it hoping to change her image by playing more mature and sexy roles.

Carr then met Olivia Newton-John at a party hosted by singer Helen Reddy. He was "knocked out" by the Australian beauty and immediately offered her the leading role in *Grease.* Newton-John was already a singing star in her own right. During the early 1970s, the country and pop vocalist had charted four singles and four albums that all went platinum. Her CMA Award nearly caused a revolution in Nashville. She was less successful on the screen. In 1970, she starred in a British science-fiction musical, *Toomorrow.* The film, a tremendous flop, was never released in the United States. "It was such a disaster, I was quite nervous about getting into any more movies," confessed Newton-John.

I had had offers but nothing concrete. When I saw 'Grease' on the stage in London, for example, I loved it but never thought of it as a film I might do someday. What sold me later on was that the part of Sandy is not too far away from myself in reality, and though in the end the character does change, I thought it was close enough to my own experience.[116]

Nevertheless, Carr was sure he had found the right person to play the innocent Sandy. After a successful screen test, which Newton-John insisted upon, she was given a reported $125,000 just for signing and it was agreed she would get equal billing with John Travolta. For *Grease,* Olivia Newton-John's American film debut, she reportedly earned $10 million.[117]

The two media entrepreneurs assembled an inexperienced team for their first co-production. *Grease* was Carr's first shot at producing. It was also director Randal Kleiser's feature-film debut. He had previously worked with Travolta on TV's *The Boy in the Plastic Bubble* and received acclaim for his work on *The Gathering,* a 1977 Christmas show starring Ed Asner and Maureen Stapleton. Choreographer Patricia Birch was a four-time Tony nominee—one for her choreography of *Grease.* She had choreographed several other Broadway musicals, including *A Little Night Music, Candide, Pacific Overtures,* and *Happy End,* but her only experience choreographing for the screen before *Grease* was the film version of *A Little Night Music.* Only cinematographer Bill Butler, who already had *Jaws* and *One Flew Over the Cuckoo's Nest* to his credit, could claim any significant film experience.

The Robert Stigwood-Allan Carr production began filming in June 1977. It was shot at Paramount Studios and on location at several high schools in sunny southern California—the oasis of teenage mythology. The film was produced for $6 million and Paramount reportedly spent another $3 million on promotion. "This is a salesmanship business," Carr said. "We have to be more than packagers. You wouldn't find people in Detroit making a car and then not selling it."[118]

Paramount launched a two-prong marketing strategy. While *Grease* was still in production, the film company established a tie-in with stores around the country. Various drawings, screen tests, and beauty and dance contests were held at stores, with winners appearing in the movie. Gimbel's in New York claimed 60,000 entries. Transportation (via American Airlines) and hotel rooms were provided through Paramount tie-ins.

The forty contest winners (twenty-five girls and fifteen boys) arrived in Los Angeles in late August for a three-day Hollywood adventure. The group was treated to a tour of Paramount Studios and a party at producer Allan Carr's, with brief appearances by *Grease* stars Sid Caesar, Eve Arden, Stockard Channing, Olivia Newton-John, and John Travolta. Kleiser managed to cram all forty "Be A Star" winners into one split-second appearance. "I devised a new transition," he proudly explained, "in which you hear a bell ring, then see the kids bursting out of school, yelling and shouting; afterward, you cut to other kids entering the carnival. It will probably end up in the picture. And we were able to use all of them in one shot."[119] For a mere $10,000, Paramount captured an incredible amount of publicity. Film crews recorded the extras' every move and sent photos and footage to their hometown newspapers and television stations.[120]

When the film opened in theaters, *Grease* cast members made personal appearances at the stores that had the biggest promotional campaigns. A tie-in with Pepsi involved a $2.5 million promotional blitz that included radio, television, and newspaper advertisements along with point-of-purchase displays tied to a two-for-one coupon ticket scheme. Paramount asked exhibitors to honor the coupon tickets at the same that time the company announced the availability of a fifteen-minute short free of charge to exhibitors playing *Grease*. The short, sponsored by Pepsi, featured rock group Lynyrd Skynyrd. Research done by the soft-drink company showed the youth market was eager for clips showcasing bands as long as they accompanied films that emphasized their soundtracks.[121] This was three years prior to MTV.

In 1978 RSO dominated the trade charts. Stigwood's label had a song at the top of the *Billboard* Hot 100 for thirty-one weeks. RSO Records received more platinum single awards in 1978 than the entire recording industry collected the previous year. *Saturday Night Fever* was still Number 1 when the soundtrack from *Grease* was released. The two albums spent much of the summer together in the Top 10. Freddie Gershon, president of the Stigwood Group, predicted revenues for 1978 of between $300 and $500 million.[122]

During negotiations for the film rights, musical director Bill Oakes made sure a clause was put in his contract allowing him to spice up the music. Oakes used several songs from the original score, but added a number of Golden Oldies and some new compositions. Barry Gibb wrote the title song for *Grease* without having seen the Broadway play or the screenplay. RSO's vice president of music publishing said:

> The first line of the chorus 'Grease Is The Word' is so efficient that it is being used as the core slogan of the film and soundtrack advertising campaigns with 'Grease is the Music' the slogan that has been adapted for use by our music publishing division. This use just further illustrates the important role music plays; and in this particular case, it's a lyric.[123]

Olivia Newton-John's musical director, John Farrar, contributed the dreamy ballad "Hopelessly Devoted to You" and the energetic finale,

Figure 4.2. Saturday Night Fever/Grease

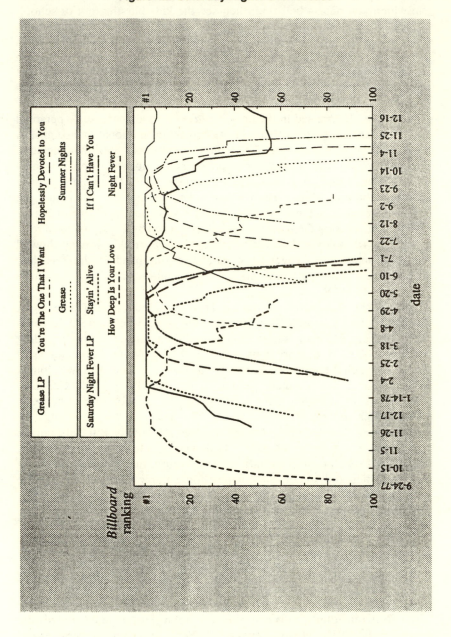

"You're the One That I Want." Louis St. Louis teamed with Scott J. Simon for "Sandy," a clever Fifties spoof on love lost at the drive-in.

As in previous RSO multimedia productions, the soundtrack album was strategically released before the opening of the film. It sold at an even faster pace than *Saturday Night Fever,* selling five million copies in four months. Disc jockeys were sent switchblade combs to encourage airplay for songs from the soundtrack.

"You're the One That I Want" was the first of four singles released from the soundtrack to sell more than one million copies, performing that feat in the first week of its release; and in twelve days it was certified gold. It entered *Billboard*'s Hot 100 at Number 65 on June 10 and reached Number 1 in ten weeks. Frankie Valli's "Grease" topped the *Billboard* chart in the last week in August and sold more than three million copies. (The title song featured Peter Frampton playing lead guitar.) Olivia Newton-John's "Hopelessly Devoted to You" (also written and produced by Farrar) and Travolta/Newton-John Duet, "Summer Nights," both reached the Top 5. RSO had the rights to Travolta/Newton-John duets, "You're the One That I Want" and "Summer Nights" and Frankie Valli's "Grease." MCA claimed the rights to solos by Newton-John and Midsong International retained rights to Travolta solos.

The *Grease* soundtrack was Number 1 on the *Billboard* pop album charts three different times, for a total of twelve weeks, from July to October. The album eventually sold twenty-four million copies internationally, following *Saturday Night Fever* as the second-biggest-selling soundtrack of all time.

On its opening weekend, June 16 to 18, *Grease,* as well as Universal's *Jaws 2,* shattered previous records, reaching what *Variety* called "stratospheric weekend box office heights."[124] *Grease* opened in 902 domestic market theaters and tallied more than $9 million for the weekend. The musical grossed more than $100 million in domestic box office receipts in 1978, surpassing *The Godfather* as Paramount's leading box office hit. (*Saturday Night Fever* was third.) Its revenues from motion pictures in the 1978 totaled $287 million for Paramount shattering the company's previous record for domestic film rentals, which had been set in 1975. According to the annual report of parent company Gulf + Western, the film studio came within $1 million of the industry's all-time high.[125] *Grease* eventually grossed $150 million and became the most financially successful movie musical ever made.[126] It remains in the Top 20 of *Variety*'s Top 100 All-Time Film-Rental Champs with domestic rentals exceeding $96 million.

In the meantime, the runaway success of the film benefited the original Broadway musical. Ticket sales receipts ran 10 to 15 percent ahead of the corresponding period the previous summer. Paramount's media hype and the stage production's own beefed-up advertising to capitalize on the film's release were cited as additional factors. Paramount reportedly contributed $53,000 to the stage production for advertising time on television. Producers Ken Waissman and Maxine Fox increased the show's budget for television spots from $6,000 to $11,000 a week just before the film opened. "We realized that we had to make sure the public knew that the show was still playing," explained producer Maxine Fox, "and we made a conscious effort to separate the show from the film in the public's mind."[127]

Usually there is a delay of several years after the closing of a Broadway show before the film opens. Confident that *Grease* would still be running, Waissman and Fox were reluctant to give Paramount a summer 1978 release. The Stigwood/Carr version however, differed significantly from the Broadway production. The film included about half of the original score and was oriented to a much younger audience. The Broadway producers were "relieved that the film is different. Audiences can attend the show and not feel they're seeing a carbon copy. We know from the box office treasurers that people who've seen the movie are coming right over to the show."[128]

While the ambiance for *Grease* is the 1950s teenage culture, the film transcends the characters, costumes, and music of the period to become a timeless tale about youth. The story is the simplistic formula of boy-meets-girl, boy-loses-girl, boy-gets-back-girl. Danny Zuko (John Travolta) and Sandy Olsson (Olivia Newton-John) fall in love at the beach during the summer. The film's opening scene shows them parting with "Love Is a Many Splendored Thing" blaring above the roar of ocean waves. At the end of the summer, Sandy's family suddenly moves from Sydney, Australia to the United States. That fall Sandy is enrolled at Bobby Rydell High School where (surpise!) Danny is a duck-tailed greaser. When blonde, pony-tailed Sandy shows up as Danny's ballyhooed summer fling, Danny's tough guy image is tarnished.

A rocky relationship ensues, hinging on the possibility of reconciliation between the two sides of teenage culture in the 1950s. Innocent, bobby-soxed Sandy sings "Hopelessly Devoted to You" as she pines after leather-jacketed Danny. The macho-hoodlum imagine Zuko must maintain as leader of the T-Bird gang prevents them from getting together at first, but eventually they do. Several sparkling songs and marvelous dance scenes take them through a semester in High School U.S.A. Stockard Channing plays Rizzo, leader of the Pink Ladies girl gang and the school trollop. She does a beautiful paraody of clean-cut Sandy ("Look At Me, I'm Sandra Dee") at a girl's pajama party; Rizzo is Sandy's social opposite. Channing's commentary on sexual double standards, "There Are Worse Things I Could Do," is a strong ballad that nicely changes the tempo of the film. Travolta's ode to "Sandy" while he's "stranded at the drive-in" is a piquant play on 1950s passion pits.

At the nationally televised high school dance, Sha Na Na renditions of Fifties classics spiced with the sounds of the Seventies provides the music for some electric choreography: Several of *Grease*'s dance sequences are like those of Busby Berkeley musicals. (Frankie Avalon's cameo appearance as a teen angel singing "Beauty School Dropout" and the auto repair shop number, "Greased Lightning," stand out.) For the "Summer Nights" scene, choreographer Patricia Birch said, "We had John and Olivia dance as though they were in an old MGM musical."[129]

There is a big car race scene with the gang from across town, a la *Rebel Without A Cause*. Guest appearances make the film a panorama of Hollywood nostalgia. Eve Arden plays the high school principal, Dody Goodman is her assistant, Sid Caesar is Coach Calhoun, Joan Blondell is the malt shop waitress, and Ed "Kookie" Byrnes makes a brief appearance as host of National Bandstand.

Finally, at the carnival graduation celebration, Sandy gives up her virginal "Sandra Dee' image for a black-leather jacket, skintight satin pants, red high heels, and vampish makeup. She and Danny fly off together in a '57 Chevy. Interestingly, the ending of the film foreshadowed Newton-John's career. After *Grease,* she shed her girl-next-door image in two platinum-selling albums, *Totally Hot* and *Physical*.

There were two voices among critics concerning *Grease*. One group applauded the film for its artistic merits; for a movie musical, it was considered spectacular. *The New York Times*'s Vincent Canby saw *Grease* as "a contemporary fantasy about a 1950's teenage musical—a larger, funnier, wittier and more imaginative-than- Hollywood movie with a life that is all its own." Canby applauded Bronte Woodward's screenplay, Patricia Birch's choreography, and the performances of Travolta, Newton-John, and Channing. Two days after seeing the film Canby went to see the Broadway production for a comparison. Despite some hesitations about the conventions of movie musicals, he remained enthusiastic about the film. "*Grease*," he said, "Is nothing but fun. It's pop entertainment of an extremely clever, energetic sort, sung and danced with style by its two stars, Travolta and Miss Newton-John." *Variety* also raved about the film. "*Grease* has got it," the viewer said, "from the outstanding animated titles of John Wilson all the way through the rousing finale as John Travolta and Olivia Newton-John ride off into pre-Vietnam era teenage happiness."[130]

It was the "pre-Vietnam era teenage happiness" that brought less favorable reviews from other critics, who looked at the film as an expression of the cultural landscape in the late 1970s. These reviewers concentrated on thematic differences between the Broadway and film versions. *Time*'s Richard Schickel thought the movie paled in comparison to the Broadway play, and blamed Kleiser's direction, saying:

[Kleiser] has no feel for the times when kids were trying to resolve the contradictions between an inherited style of surviving adolescence and the radically different, new possibilities . . . for a while in the '50s, two ways of being a teen-ager existed side by side. The poignancy of *Grease* derived from the juxtaposition: Can sweet Sandy, representing the Sandra Dee side of the coin, find happiness with dangerous Danny, the dark, flip side of it? Kleiser simply flattens out this conflict.[131]

For this group of critics, the absence of class conflict undermined the social tensions of the period and left, Schickel said, "a large black hole at the center of the film, into which, finally, an entire made-up universe disappears."[132] In this context, the characterizations, stylized dance numbers, and plot appeared as absurd. "Beneath Danny's black leather jacket is most likely a gray flannel suit," wrote one reviewer. Sandy's transformation "becomes more a question of trying to get Danny's senior ring than some lovin.' " Instead, Rizzo, "with her black calf-length skirts, cinch belt, unreciprocated love for Danny, and false pregnancy, is the only character in GREASE who even suggests that the problems of adolescence might be a bit weightier than whether or not it will rain on Prom night."[133]

Grease was a superb musical that fulfilled the nostalgic yearnings of Baby Boomers in the late 1970s. Southern California kids with Brooklyn accents is not exactly realism, but neither is teenagers breaking out into song and dance in the high school cafeteria. The conventions of the musical allow for such suspension of disbelief.

Grease is revisionist history in popular film. "It lets us remember things not as they were, but as we would have them be," said Marjorie Rosen, author of *Popcorn Venus: Women, Movies, and the American Dream.*[134] The film's flash-from-the-past portrait arrests any of the social elements that were just below the surface of Eisenhower's supposedly tranquil era—elements that when fused together became the explosive mixture of the Sixties' countercultural rebellion.

The Paramount release met the criteria for success in the post- Watergate era that Tom Wolfe had aptly dubbed the "Me Decade." It was a good tonic for the homesickness of the Baby Boomers, longing for the innocence they had before the social upheaval caused by Vietnam and the

Civil Rights Movement and the cynicism left behind by Watergate. "A society that has made 'nostalgia' a marketable commodity on the cultural exchange quickly repudiates the suggestion that life in the past was in any important way better than life today," wrote Christopher Lasch. "Having trivialized the past by equating it with outmoded styles of consumption, discarded fashions and attitudes, people today resent anyone who draws on the past in serious discussions of contemporary conditions or attempts to use the past as a standard by which to judge the present."[135] (The phenomenon would be repeated again on the 1980s with a flood of films trying to refight the Vietnam War.)

In retrospect, the RSO soundtrack proved to be a temporary grasp by the recording industry at the Baby Boom market, whose unprecedented size had contributed greatly to the spectacular growth the industry had witnessed since the mid-Fifties. *Saturday Night Fever* and *Grease* sold forty-two million copies combined in 1978. *Billboard* and *The Wall Street Journal* partially blamed the music industry depression, which began in 1979, on RSO's successes. Writing in the *Journal,* Stephen Grover said:

> It was also this success that led to the industry's slump earlier this year [1979]. What happened is that record companies, impressed by the sales of the leading albums, rushed into distribution a number of recordings of lesser note in the hope that they would also sell like hot cakes. They didn't, and the record companies were stuck with them.[136]

The stunning success of *Fever* and *Grease* at both the box office and record stores created great enthusiasm for film projects with rock soundtracks. Together they launched what Vincent Canby called "a new era of movie musicals."[137]

Sergeant Pepper's Lonely Hearts Club Band

The resounding success of *Saturday Night Fever* and *Grease* was followed by just as big a flop. *Sgt. Pepper's Lonely Hearts Club Band* seemed to have everything needed to make it three in a row for Stigwood. The rock mogul called his $12- million-dollar production "my ultimate musical."[138] The movie was based on The Beatles' legendary rock album *Sgt. Pepper's Lonely Hearts Club Band,* which was first released in 1967. (Stigwood had purchased the rights to twenty-nine Beatles songs, primarily from the *Sgt. Pepper* and *Abbey Road* LPs.) Beatle producer George Martin signed on as musical director.

The combination of The Beatles' music with The Bee Gees popularity and the RSO promotion machine seemed like a sure box office winner. Rock star Peter Frampton, still riding the crest of his *Frampton Comes Alive!* LP, which sold ten million copies, was signed. A 1976 tour in support of the album grossed $70 million. The Stigwood organization was entirely optimistic. "It could make 'Saturday Night Fever' look like a punk album," Coury said of the *Sgt. Pepper* LP, "like a test run for the main event."[139]

Sgt. Pepper began shooting in October 1977 while the *Saturday Night Fever* phenomenon was exploding. Stigwood had again gambled on an inexperienced team: Director Michael Schultz had never made a musical, and it was Henry Edwards's debut as a screenwriter. For Frampton and The Bee Gees, this was their first feature film. Veteran George Martin, who produced all of The Beatles' albums, assumed the duty of recording the music for the movie.

The *Sgt. Pepper* soundtrack LP was distributed in the United States by RSO and in the United Kingdom by A&M Records. A&M had rights to Peter Frampton singles, Columbia to the Earth, Wind & Fire and Aerosmith solos, Warner Brothers to the Steve Martin and Alice Cooper songs, and RSO had "everything else."[140] An unprecedented three million copies of the soundtrack were shipped in order to accommodate advance orders. Pressing plants across the country were working twenty-four hour shifts in what was referred to as the "greatest manufacturing task ever undertaken."[141] According to Steve Bedell, vice president of music at Paramount, this extravagant shipment was partly to blame for the failure of the project. "During the days after *Saturday Night Fever* and *Grease,* there were a whole slew of movies out with soundtracks, not all of which were bad," Bedell explained.[142] The law of diminishing returns was becoming operative.

The LP listed at an unprecedented $15.98; the price was driven up by high royalties and an extravagant album cover. RSO calculated its own profit on the album with a $14.98 list price to be about 65 cents per album. By including a poster, centerfold, and additional color on the embossed album sleeve, the price was raised and RSO could make what Coury called "a normal profit."[143]

The RSO promotional campaign for the soundtrack cost more than $1 million. A tie-in with Dr. Pepper was included. Three singles were released in conjunction with the *Sgt. Pepper* soundtrack. The most successful, Earth, Wind & Fire's "Got To Get You Into My Life," sold a million copies and cracked the Top 10. Robin Gibb's "Oh, Darling" reached Number 15; Aerosmith's version of "Come Together" stalled at Number

23. Of note, the EW&F and Aerosmith numbers were released on the Columbia label and included on separate LPs.

Incredibly, the RSO *Sgt. Pepper* soundtrack debuted on the *Billboard* Top Pop Album chart at Number 7 in August. The following week the album rose to Number 5, where it remained for six straight weeks. The album initially received an enormous amount of pre-sale airplay, which trailed off as radio programmers became cautious. *Sgt. Pepper* began to drop in the ranking and within a short eleven weeks fell out of the Top 100 Albums.

The problem, according to RSO president Al Coury, was timing:

> With 'Fever' and 'Grease' the timing of the release of the album (five to six weeks before the film), the timing of the release of the singles (before, during and after the album's release) were what we laid out, what proved to be a successful format. But when we got into the situation with 'Pepper' we did not have the luxury of that kind of planning, because everything was pushed up to an early date. The film was originally scheduled to come out Christmas of 1978, but Universal wanted the film out in the summertime, so the production schedule was really rushed. We got the album out four or five days before the picture came out, so consequently we did not have a chance to use the music of "Sgt. Pepper" to presell the motion picture.
>
> In looking back, when we released the album, we had absolutely unbelievable acceptance on radio. Every major station from coast to coast put the album on immediately and played almost the entire album the minute they got their hands on it. Then, a few days later, the picture came out and got terrible reviews, and immediately radio backed off. If we had done it the way we had before, giving the record an eight-to-10 week lead, we wouldn't have had the motion picture to be compared to. The music would have had a much greater chance to saturate the marketplace, and it would have guaranteed a greater opening for the motion picture.
>
> Of course, it couldn't guarantee the picture would be a great success over a long period of time, but a healthier opening. Now it could very well be that if we did everything right, it still would have wound up being a disaster. I can't say that. All I can tell you is the timing is of the utmost importance.[144]

There was another issue. *Sgt. Pepper* was the third double album RSO released at a list price of $12.98 or more. The three albums drained the marketplace.

Ironically, *Sgt. Pepper* created a demand for Capitol's Beatles catalog; three Beatle albums made a showing on *Billboard*'s Top LP and Tape chart. To profit from the surge of interest generated by the Stigwood production, Capitol released a picture disk of The Beatles' *Sgt. Pepper* album along with three color vinyl albums: The Beatles' album and two double-album Beatle anthologies.[145]

Sgt. Pepper opened in theaters in the United States in July 1978. Stigwood launched the musical with an enormous $6-million promotional campaign that included hot-air "Pepper" balloons and a "Pepper" celebration at Studio 54. Despite all the hoopla, the film failed miserably. Domestic rentals total $11.4 million against costs exceeding $18 million. The multiplatinum soundtrack sales, however, covered the production's losses.

Paul McCartney expressed his own doubts about making the album into a film because of the difficulty of representing fantasy in visual form. "I thought at the time of *Sgt. Pepper* that they couldn't make a film of it," the former Beatle said. "And we just thought, you just can't capture it: once it gets to be a film, it's always going to be a bit plodding compared to the album. Those days it was a fantasy thing, it all took place in your mind, and it would really be harder than anything to capture that feeling. And I think from what I've heard of the Stigwood thing, it doesn't seem to have captured it."[146] Stigwood had stipulated to scriptwriter Edwards that there be as little dialogue as possible. The idea was to create a cinematic rock fantasy, and the burden of creating that fantasy was put on set designer Brian Eatwell. Eatwell filled the screen with giant toys, including an elongated limousine, a seven-story balloon, and a gigantic hamburger. "With no dialogue, you have to keep coming up with a visual *tour de force*," he said in frustration.[147]

The pitiful plot centers on Frampton and The Bee Gees as Billy Shears and his band, who reside in a fairy-tale place called Heartland. ("The whole focus of the movie is on Peter [Frampton]," Robin Gibb said with some dismay. "We're always running around saving him from something."[148]) For some fifty years the original Sergeant Pepper and his Lonely Hearts Club Band played the music that made the world dance, but the band leader had died in 1958. Heartland major and narrator Mr. Kite (George Burns) explains that the quartet's instruments "have the power to make dreams come true and as long as they remain in Heartland's care humanity would live happily forever after."

Sergeant Pepper's nephew, Billy Shears (Peter Frampton), forms a new Sergeant Pepper's band with his three best friends (The Bee Gees). Brother Dougie Shears (Paul Nicholas) appoints himself their manager. The band is offered a recording contract by a Hollywood record company. Billy says farewell to his true love, Strawberry Fields (San Farina), and the band goes off to L.A. in a hot-air balloon. B. D. Records' head B. D. Brockhurst (Donald Pleasence) seduces the boys with promiscuous women, drugs, and wild parties. They sign on the dotted line, record an album and begin the climb to stardom, filling B. D.'s office with bags of money.

Meanwhile, back in Heartland, a villianous real estate agent, Mean

Mister Mustard (Frankie Howerd) receives orders from the mysterious, "F.V.B." to steal the band's instruments. As commanded, Mustard takes the cornet to Dr. Maxwell (Steve Martin), a crazed and corrupt dentist. Father Sun (Alice Cooper), a media specialist brainwashing kids to form an army for F. V. B. to conquer the world, receives the tuba. Mustard is allowed to keep the drum for himself; the saxophone goes to F.V.B.

The absence of the instruments sends Heartland in to its darkest hour. Mustard buys up real estate and turns the former utopia into Sodom and Gormorrah. In desperation, Strawberry Fields takes a bus to L.A., with Mustard in pursuit. In a fantasy she sees Shears and the band fall prey to the temptation of Lucy in the Sky with Diamonds (Dianne Steinberg). Strawberry informs the boys about Heartland's plight. They take Mustard's computerized van and return to save Heartland from ruin. Three of the four instruments are retrieved before the real estate agent's computer explodes.

Heartland is desperate; B. B. is losing money on cancelled concerts. Dougie gets the idea for a benefit concert in Heartland. While Earth, Wind & Fire perform "Got to Get You Into My Life," Mustard kidnaps Strawberry Fields and heads for "F.V.B. Central with the instruments where the evil genius would surpress the magical instruments and make the world safe for his corrupt legions," explains the narrator. "It was the end of decency unless the band could get there in time to stop them." Billy Shears and the boys follow in the hot-air balloon. F.V.B. stands for "Future Villian Band" (Aerosmith), whose motto is "Hate Joy. Hate Love. Love money." The Sgt. Pepper band defeats F.V.B. in hand-to-hand combat, but in the struggle Strawberry Fields falls to her death.

The instruments are safely returned to Heartland, but the whole town mourns the loss of Strawberry Fields. All is not lost, however. The Sgt. Pepper wind vane (Billy Preston) comes alive, singing "Get Back." With a pointed finger he zaps Heartland "back to where you once belong," and resurrects Strawberry Fields. In the final scene, a star-studded crowd of townspeople sing a lively rendition of "Sgt. Pepper's Lonely Hearts Club Band" (Reprise). The Heartland guest list of seventy-two musical groups and performers includes George Benson, Stephen Bishop, Curtis Mayfield, Robert Palmer, Wilson Pickett, Helen Reddy, Johnny Rivers, Carol Channing, Donovan, Sha-Na-Na, Del Shannon, Seals and Crofts, Connie Stevens, Tina Turner, and Wolfman Jack.

In addition to Frampton, The Bee Gees, and numerous cast members, Alice Cooper, Aerosmith, Billy Preston, and Earth, Wind & Fire perform.

Critics panned the movie and the soundtrack. "It is a film with a dangerous resemblance to wallpaper," wrote *Newsweek*'s David Ansen, "perfectly designed for extended forays to the popcorn counter." *Rolling Stone* said Stigwood "not only produced one of the worst movies ever made . . . but also managed to trash whatever rock and roll reputations such Seventies artists as Peter Frampton and the Bee Gees had before this excremental soundtrack was released."[149]

Ironically, The Bee Gees' rise and fall both came with a Stigwood production. Their distinctive sound was everywhere in the late 1970s. During the first week of March 1978, the British trio was responsible for half of the Top 10 on *Billboard*'s Hot 100 Singles. They penned hits for younger brother Andy Gibb ("I Just Want to Be Your Everything," "(Love is) Thicker Than Water," and "Shadow Dancing"), Samantha Sang ("Emotion"), and Frankie Valli (the title song from *Grease*). RSO had so many hit artists in its stable that it was difficult to keep them from competing with each other on the charts. Executives had to time the release of singles and albums from The Bee Gees, Andy Gibb, Samantha Sang, and Eric Clapton, along with movie soundtracks. "Nobody smokes," Al Coury said. "Everybody wants to live till the end of the year to find out how many weeks we're Number One."[150]

Production trio Barry Gibb, Albhy Galuten, and Karl Richardson had put together a string of seven Number 1 hit singles in six months, shattering the record of four in the same period of time set by Beatles producer George Martin in 1964. Barry Gibb had also produced Barbara Streisand's *Guilty* LP, which sold more than 20 million copies worldwide, making it her largest-selling album. A Streisand/Barry Gibb duet, "Woman in Love" reached Number 1 in October 1980 and earned the pair a Grammy for Best Pop Performance by a Duo or Group with Vocal.

The Bee Gees were successful throughout the 1970s. Under extreme pressure to duplicate their success with *Fever,* the trio recorded *Spirits Having Flown* in 1978. Three singles from the album topped the *Billboard* Hot 100 in 1979: "Too Much Heaven," "Tragedy," and "Love You Inside Out." This marked nine Number 1 singles for the Bee Gees. They tied The Beatles with six consecutive Number 1 hits, becoming the first group to have three consecutive chart-topping singles from two successive albums. In 1979, The Bee Gees embarked on a fifty-show tour in thirty-eight cities, playing before crowds ranging from 10,000 to 50,000.

The *Sgt. Pepper*'s debacle seemed to mark the end of The Bee Gee's eminence, however. Their biggest hit in the Eighties was "The Woman In You" which reached Number 24 on the *Billboard* listing. The song was from the soundtrack of *Stayin' Alive,* the 1983 sequel to *Saturday Night Fever.*

In October 1980, The Bee Gees filed an over-$200-million lawsuit against

Stigwood and parent company PolyGram. As reported in *Rolling Stone,* the suit sought $75 million from both Stigwood and the PolyGram Group (co-owner of the Stigwood companies), $50 million in punitive damages, millions in back royalties, the return of all the Bee Gees' master recordings and copyrights, and releases from all contractual obligations to Stigwood.[151] The Australian brothers claimed an independent audit revealed that Stigwood owed them millions in back royalties; they charged that Stigwood had mismanaged them to his own advantage. Stigwood Group president Freddie Gershon called the lawsuit "revolting" and maintained that the audit showed only $300,000 in unpaid royalties, which RSO promptly paid to the Gibb brothers. Gershon saw the whole affair as contract negotiations through the press. Stigwood himself called the suit "an ill-advised stunt."[152] The parties settled out of court in May 1981 with public apologies. Gershon saw it as a Stigwood victory. "If you've been in the business long enough," he said, "you know that all artists go through periods of temporary insanity."[153] Reportedly, The Bee Gees received $70 million.

The Gibbs issued their last album with RSO *Living Eyes,* in 1982. After a six-year hiatus, they released an album with Warner Brothers, *E.S.P.,* which flopped. Some felt the failure was because the Gibbs could not escape their disco image; radio programmers were reluctant to play the new material and listeners were not anxious to buy it. "The Bee Gees got tagged with that whole disco thing, but what they were essentially making was dance music," explained Gary Borman, co-manager of the group (with Harriet Sternberg), "but getting swept up in the *Saturday Night Fever* thing, being branded with that and having that much success sometimes creates a certain backlash. So one of the reasons they laid off for six years was just to let it go away."[154]

Thank God It's Friday

There *was* life after *Saturday Night Fever,* as several disco artists proved—at least for a while longer. Donna Summer was really the only "star" to emerge from the disco trend, but she quickly abandoned the genre for mainstream rock. Her first Number 1 hit, in November 1978, was her disco version of Jimmy Webb's "MacArthur Park." The single was edited from an eight-minute, twenty-seven second version on her 1978 double album, *Live and More.* "Hot Stuff," the first single released from her *Bad Girls* LP in 1979, reached Number 1, was bumped by The Bee Gees' "Love You Inside Out," then returned to the top position for another two weeks. While "Hot Stuff" was still Number 1, Casablanca released a second single, "Bad Girls," which also reached the Number 1 spot, in July 1979.

The disco queen starred in one of the few profitable disco films released during the reign of RSO. Columbia Pictures tried to ride the disco wave *Saturday Night Fever* had created with a 1978 release, *Thank God It's Friday,* a teen exploitation flick. The low budgeted, $2.2-million production could not compare with Stigwood's blockbuster.

The film, produced by Motown and Casablanca record companies, was ultimately a showcase for their artists using the form of previous films *Car Wash, Nashville,* and *SNF.* "This movie wasn't photographed," wrote *Times* critic Vincent Canby. "It was pressed—by Motown and Casablanca Records, who co-produced it."[155] The soundtrack included thirty-two songs from the two labels' vaults, with appearances in the film by Donna Summer and The Commodores.

There was no prerelease screening of *TGIF* for critics. "This is definitely *not* a critics' film," Casablanca president Neil Bogart explained. "I don't think we made a critics' pictures, therefore there was nothing to gain by screening it for the critics."[156] The film opened in New York theaters on 19 May 1978 with a $3-million promotional campaign. A full-page ad appeared in *Billboard* boasted the "campaign that will make everyone say and see 'Thank God It's Friday.' " The list of media events included an unprecedented six and one-half hours of national television: a special two-part *Merv Griffin Show* (18 and 19 May) celebrating disco night life, an *American Bandstand* tribute to Disco (27 May), a *Midnight Special* Disco salute (May 26), and a nationally syndicated half-hour television program about the making of the movie. All of the shows highlighted *TGIF* cast members and music. National radio promotions in 200 key markets featured tie-ins with dance contests and theater openings. Cast members spent a month on a national tour of high schools and colleges. *TGIF* store displays, T-shirts, and bumper stickers flooded department stores, and other tie-ins were made with commercial sponsors. A special three-record soundtrack album was released with the movie.

Donna Summer made her film debut in *TGIF* as an aspiring disco singer whose determined quest to get a break into stardom is only one of several subplots that are glued together by a nonstop soundtrack. The whole story takes place one Friday evening at the Zoo, a Los Angeles discotheque. The characters are complete stereotypes and the series of events is entirely predictable. Two teenage girls in platform shoes sneak into the disco in hope of winning $200 in a dance contest so that they can buy tickets to a KISS concert (another Casablanca act). A straight-laced, middle-class couple find, at the Zoo, some needed excitement. There are also a philandering club owner (Jeff Goldblum), a computer-matched odd couple, a Mexican-American who is obsessed with dancing, and plenty of extras looking for some cheap thrills. Debra Winger, a relative newcomer at that time, played an innocent woman who stumbles on Mr. Right. Predictably, everything comes together at the big dance contest.

The problem with the film was that the producers tried to make a dance musical out of a situation comedy. The monotonous disco soundtrack serves primarily as Muzak behind the scattered subplots. Donna Summer's sultry "Last Dance" stood out, but this only pointed out the potential that was never exploited in the film. The Commodores' performance at the dance-contest finale was disappointing. Despite the continual build-up throughout the film, the contest itself is an uneventful let down.

Unlike *Saturday Night Fever, TGIF* failed to integrate the essential elements of disco culture, music and dance, with the plot in any effective way. In *Fever,* the music was central to the action; dance sequences carried the plot along. In *TGIF,* almost all of the dancing consisted of sporadic snapshots of the crowded Zoo dance floor. There was one exception: Marv Gomez (Chick Vennera) did an acrobatic disco dance on the car tops in the Zoo's parking lot. The number is energetic and reminiscent of Gene Kelly, but the scene is cut short. The producers should have minded Vennera's adage, "Dancing—everything else is bullshit."

Critics panned the film as a chaotic collage of music and story; director Robert Klane never allowed either one to develop. *Rolling Stone* dubbed the Columbia release "Saturday Night Earache." A *Village Voice* reviewer summed it up as a "pinball movie: how to richochet more than two dozen caricatures . . . through the gaudy, tinhorn microcosm of a discotheque."[157]

TGIF broke no records at the box office; the film earned only $7.8 million for the distributors. Veering from Stigwood's usual strategy, the soundtrack and several singles were released in April to coincide with the movie's premiere. "Our intention is to have at least five in the Top-10 disco records by the time the movie opens, and I hope two or three Top 10 singles," Bogart said.[158] Casablanca's president was overly optimistic. The *TGIF* soundtrack stalled at Number 11 on the *Billboard* charts in late July and then dropped quickly in the rankings. It still sold more than one and a half million copies.

Can't Stop The Music

Can't Stop The Music featured The Village People in a predictable love story about a top model (Valerie Perrine) trying to help an ambitious disco composer (Steve Guttenberg). The outrageous disco group had had a series of hits from 1977 through 1979. Producer Jacques Morali invented the concept for the group, a parody of popular gay fantasy characters, as "a protest against Anita Bryant," and co-wrote their material.[159] Tom Smucker described them as "gay goofs to those who got the joke, and disco novelties to those who didn't."[160]

The Village People had six gold and four platinum records, and their 1979 tour sold out in forty-five cities. The Sha Na Na of disco, they sold more than twenty million singles and eighteen million albums internationally. Their Top 5 hits in 1978 and 1979 included "Macho Man," "Y.M.C.A.," and "In the Navy," described by *Rolling Stone* as "a mock recruiting song with a John Philip Sousa best and an S&M subtext." Reportedly, the Navy decided not to sue over the gay intimations in the song, but instead took an option to use "In the Navy" for recruiting purposes.[161]

Allan Carr produced the Village-People vehicle and teamed with Bronte Woodard to write the screenplay. Jacques Morali and Henri Belolo composed most of the music. Advertisements prematurely called it "the musical event of the '80s." (Actually, the group's machomania had already fizzled in the anti-disco backlash after 1979.) Carr squandered $20 million on the project, including $8 million on promotion. Commercial tie-ins were established with Toyota, Minolta, the National Dairy Association, and Baskin-Robbins.

Variety gave it a somewhat favorable review and regarded its boxoffice appeal as promising.[162] The film flopped, however, and proved a last gasp for disco. Casablanca was not too disappointed. The soundtrack managed a ranking of Number 47 on *Billboard*'s pop album chart and reportedly sold two million copies worldwide by March 1981.[163]

Roller Disco in Kubla Khan's Palace: Xanadu

Xanadu was just not a great musical. Universal executives knew it. At the last moment, they cancelled the critics' screening. "Tsk, tsk for such faint-of-heart," quipped *Variety*. "After all, who else this summer has Olivia Newton-John starring as a roller-skating lightbulb?"[164]

The film unsuccessfully attempted to rejuvenate and update the Hollywood movie musical, casting Gene Kelly with Olivia Newton-John in a story that fused music and dance of the 1940s and 1980s. Gene Kelly was, of course, a bankable dancer, director, and choreographer from the heyday of Hollywood musicals. Newton-John had some dancing experience from *Grease,* but the other male lead, Michael Beck, had no training. It showed.

The dance scenes seemed amateurish. Kelly was a saving presence, but limited by his partner. Newton-John was not nearly as smooth as Kelly, and the tight Army dress she wore for their dance number inhibited her movements.

Universal producer Joel Silver hired Greenberg Associates, a company that specialized in graphic animation and special optical effects, to handle the extensive special effects in the movie.[165] Silver considered the special sequences an essential part of the production, and special effects people were involved during the pre-production stage. In an opening scene, The Electric Light Orchestra's (ELO) "I'm Alive" brings the muses to life as they dance out of a wall painting and are beamed away in colorful streaks of light.

The soundtrack featured songs by Jeff Lynn of ELO and John Farrar, Newton-John's producer/songwriter. All the songs were performed by the Electric Light Orchestra and Olivia Newton-John, who also sang a duet with Cliff Richard on Farrar's "Suddenly."

The album yielded five Top 20 hits. Prior to the release of the soundtrack album, Olivia Newton-John's single "Magic" entered *Billboard*'s Hot 100 on May 24 and climbed to Number 1 in August. The MCA soundtrack debuted on *Billboard*'s charts at Number 79 during the week of 12 July and peaked at Number 4 in October. The week the soundtrack was released ELO's "I'm Alive" reached Number 16 and "All Over the World" began its climb into the Top 20. The title track, "Xanadu," performed by Newton-John and ELO, was next enroute to the Top 10, and "Suddenly" debuted on the singles chart in November and reached the Top 20 in January 1981.

Xanadu was billed as "a musical fantasy of all time to transport you beyond your dreams." Olivia Newton-John plays a Muse, one of nine daughters of Zeus whose job is to make the dreams of mere mortals come true. Actually, the Universal pictures was an updated version of a 1947 film *Down to Earth* that starred Rita Hayworth as Terpsichore, who helped Larry Parks stage a Broadway show.

For the Eighties' version the writers invented a Muse and named her Kira. Kira's (Newton-John) assignment is to encourage struggling artist Sonny Malone (Michael Beck), who is looking for a "meaningful" project. Kira teams him up with Danny McGuire (Gene Kelly), a millionaire in the construction business. McGuire is a former clarinet player who loves big band music. Flashbacks reveal that he had been wooed by the same muse in the 1940s, but he does not recognize her now in cotton dress, leg warmers, and roller skates.

McGuire, who had played with Glenn Miller, dreams of opening a club like one he had in New York in 1945. "Maybe his dream is big enough for the both of you," Kira tells Malone. McGuire and Malone fuse their dreams, as well as the dance and music of their respective generations. Together they build a huge, deco roller-disco palace. The Muse suggests a name from the fabulous stories of the Far East: "In Xanadu did Kubla Khan a stately pleasure dome decree." There are numerous costume changes and dancing and roller-skating numbers that are accentuated with special lighting effects, and, in one scene, there is an animation sequence.

Meanwhile, the Muse falls in love with the mortal Malone (forbidden by the laws of Zeus) and returns to Mount Olympus. Malone follows her by crashing through the painting of the nine sisters. The artist confronts Mr. and Mrs. Zeus and daughter Kira is allowed to attend the grand opening of the rock palace. Xanadu's clientele look like leftovers from a nuclear holocaust, in weird costumes and fluorescent-colored hair. In a flurry of costume changes, Olivia sings and dances through a medley of songs with her Muse sisters. When the show is over, the Muses are beamed back up to Mount Olympus and all seems lost for the lovesick Malone. Then a waitress who looks exactly like Kira offers him a drink. THE END.

"It's a pity 'Xanadu' hasn't more real pizazz," wrote Janet Maslin in the *Times*. *Variety* said it was "truly a stupendously bad film whose only salvage is the music."[166] Its distributors reaped only $10.9 million in domestic rentals. The soundtrack fared much better, selling double platinum.

Times Square: Hear the Movie, See the Album

At its peak in the late 1970s, the Robert Stigwood Organization had twenty-nine divisions, including everything from personal management, records, theater, television, film, and music publishing. In 1977, Stigwood's organization earned more than $100 million in U.S. revenues. Estimates for 1978 were $300 million.[167] With *Times Square* in 1980, Stigwood lost his Midas touch. The $20-million production was a financial disaster.

Times Square was shot on location in New York. The movie is about two girls—one rich, one poor—who meet in a psychiatric hospital. They escape and, in a sanitized version of New York City's legendary Times Square, are transformed into a punk rock duo, The Sleaze Sisters. Johnny LaGuardia, a disc jockey played by Tim Curry of *Rocky Horror Picture Show* fame, gives them their big break with a guest appearance on his show. The film climaxes with an unbelievable pseudo-punk concert on top of a Times Square theater marquee.

Bill Oakes, who was associate producer of the film, compiled the soundtrack. The double album (by now a trademark in RSO soundtracks) featured twenty songs, mostly by British and American New Wave groups. Original music by the Pretenders, Roxy Music, Garland Jeffreys, Suzie Quatro, XTC, and Joe Jackson was combined with classic tracks by a number of artists, including Lou Reed, Patti Smith, Talking Heads, and The Ramones. RSO released the package six weeks before the film premiered in November. It reached Number 37 on *Billboard*'s Pop Album chart.

In September, Associated Film Distributors, the U.S. distributor of the film, held an unusually large number of major screenings at theaters in twenty-five cities. The aim was to convince exhibitors of the potential of the film among fifteen-to-twenty-five-year-olds.[168] Promotional plans included $6 million in television and radio spots and print advertisements, with almost half spent in the first week of the film's release, to coincide with an RSO soundtrack push.

The critics panned it. *"Times Square* rips so many things off that it shreds itself to tatters in the process," wrote *Newsweek*'s David Ansen. "You could look at it as the visual liner notes for the sound-track album." Writing in *New York,* David Denby called the film a "true atrocity . . . This evil, lying little fantasy has been photographed in ugly color, and a mess of mediocre rock music has been draped across it like mozzarella on lasagna." The *Village Voice* mocked Stigwood's success formula: "Robert Stigwood's recipe for a blockbuster is to season liberally a young-and-the-restless script with top-of-the-pops music, dish up and serve . . . Hear the movie, see the album is Stigwood's operative principle."[169]

Greasier

Robert Stigwood and Allan Carr tried their hand at a sequel to their recording-breaking *Grease,* but with little success. The absence of John Travolta and Olivia Newton-John in the sequel no doubt hurt the film's chances at the box office. There were a few carry-overs from the original movie version. Eve Arden, Sid Caesar, and Dody Goodman revived their roles and Connie Stevens and Tab Hunter were added to the Rydell High faculty. Didi Conn returned as Frenchy. Patricia Birch served as both choreographer and director of the sequel.

Ken Finkleman's script was built around a sexual role reversal. Michael Carrington (Maxwell Caulfield), the Australian cousin of Newton'John's character Sandy, is at Rydell High as an exchange student. Stephanie

Zinone (Michelle Pfeiffer), leader of Rydell's Pink Ladies, takes over the Travolta part.

The story is right out of the comic books. It's 1961 and JFK is in the White House. Michael is smitten at first glance by Stephanie, a gum-chewing biker's lady who works pumping gas. Teen social law allows Stephanie, only as a Pink Lady, to date T-Birds. Besides, the British bookworm is far from her idea of a dreamboat biker who is "hell on wheels." Determined to win her love, Michael writes essays for the T-Birds to earn money for a motorcycle. The Clark Kent of Rydell High is transformed into Superbiker, a combination of comic book heroes Super-man and the Lone Ranger (Who was that masked biker?). After several mysterious appearances, the Lone Biker saves the high school Hawaiian luau from destruction by a rival motorcycle gang. Predictably, Michael is unmasked and made an honorary member of the T-Birds. He and Ste-phanie are united.

There were some dance highlights amidst the horrible plot. The opening "Back to School" number was an energetic scene demonstrating Birch's unmistakable Broadway-style choreography. An evening at the bowling lanes—"Let's Bowl, Let's Bowl, Let's Rock'n'Roll"—was cleverly done. (It included the sexual innuendo, "We're gonna score tonight"). A biology class on "Reproduction" explodes into a lesson on teenage passions. There were, however, no really memorable songs among the Louis St. Louis compositions.

Grease 2 drowned in the flood of summertime movies released in 1982. Among them were the all-time box office champion, *E.T. The Extra-Terrestrial, Rocky III, Poltergeist,* and Paramount's other summer picture, *Star Trek II.* The *Grease* sequel didn't have much of a chance. More important, Stigwood's sequel lacked the chemistry of *Grease.* The male and female leads fell short of the dynamism of Travolta and Newton-John and couldn't match the singing and dancing of the original film.

New York Times critic Janet Maslin said *Grease 2* was "less a sequel than a retread" and *Newsweek* suggested it be titled "Greasier." *Time*'s Richard Schickel rightly observed that "the whole movie seems to be nothing more than an excuse for a sound track album."[170]

The sequel earned a paltry $6.5 million in domestic rentals; the sound-track struggled to Number 71 on *Billboard*'s Top Pop Album charts.

Breakin' . . . They All Rap Happily Every After

Flashdance and *Footloose* gave a nod to the exploding urban dance style, "break dancing," in the early 1980s. Several film groups had tried to capitalize on the music and dance trends popular among urban black and Latino teenagers, but these low-budget pictures represented the ultimate in mainstream co-option of their style. The ghettos were defused with dance and music, beautifying broken lives and providing healthy alternatives to crime, drugs, gang warfare, and discontent. The mythical American melting pot was kept alive in urban centers; "breakin' " was portrayed as a way city kids could make the American Dream come true for themselves. As a *Village Voice* reviewer observed, "These films testify that the romantic imagination can prevail over a grim, quotidian social order, that—in America at least—one can still sing and dance (or paint), one's way to the top."[171]

Rap music, breakdancing, and graffiti art were born in the streets of Harlem and the South Bronx in the late 1970s. The music became trendy in Manhattan discos before it attracted the attention of Madison Avenue and Hollywood entrepreneurs. Charles Ahearn, a kind of anthropological filmmaker, considered the whole urban style a dramatic expression of social discontent. U.S. sources were not interested in the project, but with practically one phone call Ahearn acquired the necessary funding from London's Channel 4 and Germany's ZDF. The low-budget documentary film cost about $250,000.

Ahearn spent three years in New York's Lower East Side, putting together a film and soundtrack which *High Fidelity* called "the best raw evocation of the origins of rap."[172] The film was centered on South Bronx street culture with a cast of rappers, breakdancers, and graffiti artists recruited from the streets. The plot grew out of this setting, revolving around a reporter in search of a story and a graffiti artist on a quest for self-expression. The director played down the image of the city as chaotic and decaying, emphasizing instead what critic David Denby called "neighborhood democracy."[173] "I didn't want to make an exploitation picture of the evils and perils of the ghetto," Ahearn said. "Sure there was a lot of violence, hold-ups, and all, but it never touched us. People knew exactly why we were there . . . and they welcomed us in."[174] His concern was to show how the makers of this street culture had developed an aesthetic through self-expression, a "wild style" the director labeled "kinetic cubism."[175] Ahearn's 1983 documentary, *Wild Style,* drew attention to the urban culture of New York City and became a model for subsequent films.

Breakin' was the first commercial feature film to exploit the inner-city dance craze. Cannon Films had taken a page from Katzman's book and rushed the breakdancing fad to the screen in May 1984. *Breakin'* was filmed and in the theaters in four months, getting the jump on rival Orion Pictures' *Beat Street* by a month.

Breakin' was indebted to both *Flashdance* and *Stayin' Alive* for elements of its plot, which was wedged between rap numbers. In the film, Kelly (Lucinda Dickey) is a part-time waitress and aspiring dancer who is introduced to the breakdancing subculture by a gay black friend. Frustrated by the serious dance world, this rich white girl needs "a whole new life" and finds it in the hip-hop street world. (Hip-hop is a collective term for the urban culture of rap music, breakdancing, and graffiti art.) A song in the movie described breakin' as "the sound, the culture, the style, the street." Hip-hop provides an ideal setting for a musical. Dance and music flow naturally from boogie boxes in the streets and disc jockeys at dance halls, transforming mundane urban life into something exciting.

The street culture, overflowing with energy and life, is pitted against the snobbish, elite dance world. "Street dancing belongs in the street. It won't get you to Broadway," Kelly's agent tells her. (*Flashdance* revisited.) Kelly forms a dance group with Hispanic and black street dancers Ozone and Turbo. A sympathetic manager gets them a professional audition and they land starring roles in a Broadway musical *Street Jazz*. The climatic stage production number parallels the finale of *Stayin' Alive*.

Despite its low-budget, critics enjoyed the film. *Variety* called it "quite satisfactory and breezily entertaining on its own terms." As a reflection of the political climate in 1984, the *Village Voice* observed that the dance trio "conjure up a black-Hispanic-female rainbow coalition that would conceivably defeat Ronald Reagan."[176]

Breakin' was the most commercially successful of the hip-hop films, earning MGM/UA distributors more than $15.7 million from domestic rentals. The soundtrack sold triple platinum and spawned a Top 10 single, "Breakin' . . . There's No Stopping Us," by Ollie and Jerry. Other artists appearing on the soundtrack included the Bar-Kays, Fire Fox, Carol Lynn Townes, Re-Flex, Rufus, and Chaka Khan. The Polydor soundtrack climbed to Number 8 on *Billboard*'s Top Pop album chart and Number 2 on the Black Album chart.

Close behind *Breakin'* was the Orion release *Beat Street,* which *Variety* called "an impressively produced, music-loaded panorama of ghetto-derived contempo culture."[177] The storyline was minimal and moved along between musical numbers. Atlantic Records vice president Dave Glew described this urban fable about the trek to fame and fortune as "nothing but music."[178] As in previous films, the hip-hop community is an American melting pot. Kenny (Guy Davis) and younger brother Lee (Robert Taylor) have aspirations to be a rapping deejay and breakdancer, respectively. Lee meets Tracy (Rae Dawn Chong), a college music major who admires their talent and falls for the older brother. Meanwhile Puerto Rican friend

Ramon (John Chardiet) is a graffiti artist trying to support his wife and child, but some unknown person is defacing his work. The film emphasized hip-hop culture as a positive alternative in the city when it was revealed that Kenny's older brother was killed in the urban gang wars in the 1970s.

Atlantic's Glew was optimistic that the music on the two soundtrack albums had the potential to "cross over. Like Michael Jackson, this can cover all the different formats."[179] Artists on the albums included Grandmaster Melle Mel and The Furious Five, The System, Jenny Burton and Patrick Jude, Soulsonic Force, and Celia Cruz. A massive promotional campaign included tie-ins with independent record companies who released twelve-inch singles, Puma sneakers, Magnavox, and several clothing companies. To avoid price resistance from the young black audience, Atlantic decided two soundtrack albums would be released instead of a double album.

The album, *Beat Street,* entered the *Billboard* charts just prior to the opening of the film in early June 1984. The album reached Number 14 on the Top Pop album chart and Number 10 on the Black Album chart. It was certified gold. *Beat Street II* was released in September; the second LP never cracked the Top 100 on the Pop Albums chart and reached only Number 47 on the Black Album chart. *Beat Street* earned more than $7.5 in domestic rentals. It was certainly not a bonanza, but it was enough for Orion to reap a profit, considering the company's small investment.

Special K, Ozone, and Turbo were back on the screen before the breakin' trend could run dry. Tri-Star Pictures released *Breakin' 2: Electric Boogaloo* in December 1984. Kelly, now an established stage dancer, is offered a leading role in a dance musical in Paris. Ozone and Turbo are teaching kids to dance in a rundown community center they've named Miracles. A corrupt politician wants to tear down the building to make room for a shopping mall. City officials give the breakers thirty days to raise $200,000 to renovate the building. Kelly forsakes her dance career to help. Under Ozone's leadership they put on a show to raise the money. "And there you have it," said The *Times*'s Janet Maslin. "A plot no teen-movie enthusiast could fail to recognize. Be it break-dancing or drag-racing or surfing, some things never change." The fund-raising show afforded more group choreography, but, as *Variety* noted, "This is at least the fourth time around in film for the hip-hop culture and the whole business is starting to look a bit dated."[180]

The Cannon Group sequel was disappointing, with only $5 million in domestic rentals, though still profitable. Several new artists were included in the sequel soundtrack—George Kantz, Steve Donn, Midway, Mark Scott, and Rags & Riches—along with a number who appeared on the first, but the soundtrack also sold poorly. It fizzled at Number 52 on the Pop Album chart and Number 25 on the black Album chart.

Warner Brothers tried to exploit the popularity of urban rap music with *Krush Groove,* a 1985 release. Departing from previous rap films, *Rappin'* and *Beat Street, Krush Groove* was more a showcase for rap artists Run-D.M.C., Kurtis Blow, and the Fat Boys.

The whole project was put together in about six months. Shooting was completed in just twenty-six days on location in Manhattan, Queens, and the Bronx. "I wanted to prove that you could do a good picture in New York, working with good crews and all, for under $5 million," said director and co-producer Michael Schultz, whose credits included *Car Wash* (1979) and Motown's *The Last Dragon* (1984). Schultz brought *Krush Groove* in for about $3 million, a "very low budget for a musical."[181]

An opening scene at the car wash pays homage to Schultz's earlier picture. The story traces the trek of unknown street kids in New York City from washing cars to stardom, where, *Variety* quipped, "They all rap happily ever after."[182] Krush Groove is the name of an independent recording studio in New York. The script, written by Ralph Farquhar, was based on events in the life of Russell Simmons (played by Russell Wright) who, in real life, manages several rap groups, including Run-D.M.C. and Kurtis Blow. Several scenes were drawn from incidents that actually happened to the artists featured in the film.

Schultz was careful about "crafting a soundtrack that wasn't all rap music . . . so we'd have some variety and movement."[183] The Warner soundtrack included cuts by Debbie Harry, Chaka Khan, Sheila E. (Prince's protegee), and The Gap Band in order to generate interest in the album beyond the black teenage rap audience. Co-producer Russell Simmons publicly voiced his disapproval.

Krush Groove earned $5.1 million in domestic rentals in 1985. The soundtrack sold over one million units. A *Times* reviewer considered the screenplay weighed down in conventional subplots: "Rap music is infinitely more original than these creaky devices, and it deserves something better." *Time* rendered a rappin' review: "Like I say, this ain't art like you find in the Louvre. But If you wanna go deaf you oughta rush to *Krush Groove.*[184]

Dirty Dancing All the Way to the Bank

Dirty Dancing rivaled the success of *Saturday Night Fever.* The Vestron/RCA collaboration showed that films with rock soundtracks could work two ways: While the Bee Gees' music had drawn record buyers into the theaters to see *Fever,* the Dirty Dancing movie sold its soundtrack.

Dirty Dancing was the first national theatrical release for Vestron Pictures, the film production arm of Vestron, Inc., the nation's largest independent video retailer. Anticipating a shrinking supply of videos, Vestron raised $185 million over two years and established its own television and film production company (and foreign sales division) in January 1986. The company's strategy was to produce features with a $6-million ceiling on production costs. It produced and screened several films on a regional basis, including the Australian comedy *Malcolm,* Ken Russell's horror drama *Gothic,* and a ribald comedy, *Personal Services.*

In 1986, the company's earnings dropped 64 percent, and employment cutbacks accompanied a first-half loss of $8.6 million.[185] To make matters worse, Vestron was tied up in a prolonged lawsuit with Hemdale Film Corporation over the videocassette distribution rights to *Platoon* and *Hoosiers.* It was estimated that Vestron could receive as much as $10 million in revenues from the videocassette release of those films and $6 million in pre-tax profits as well as access to retail outlets for other Vestron titles.[186] Vestron was counting on the Hemdale deal for financial recovery.

In spite of it all, Vestron president Bill Quigley insisted that the company was free from debt and financially sound, with $100 million in cash assets. Revenue declines were blamed on "a flattening of the video explosion and increased taste for 'A' titles at the expense of exploitation and made-for-video fare."[187]

The stunning success of *Dirty Dancing* gave Vestron and the soundtrack label, RCA, both in uneasy financial situations, "a critical market credibility."[188] *Dirty Dancing* was produced for under $6 million. As Vestron's vice president for producton Michael Cannold explained, "At Vestron we've been fighting the understandable skepticism that we could make a studio-quality picture, get theaters and market a film. *Dirty Dancing* deals with that head-on."[189] In its first ten days, *Dirty Dancing* captured $10 million in box office receipts and Vestron shares soared 60 percent.

Dirty Dancing began in the late 1950s and early '60s, when its scriptwriter, Eleanor Bergstein, competed in "dirty dancing" contests and worked her way through college as an Arthur Murray dance teacher. Bergstein wrote the screenplay and co-produced *Dirty Dancing.* "I meant *Dirty Dancing* to be a celebration of the time of your life when you could believe that a kind of earnest, liberal action could remake the world in your own image," she said in a *Times* interview, adding:

> The film couldn't have been set a few months earlier or later . . . It was the summer of the Peace Corps and the summer of the "I Have a Dream" speech.

It was like the last summer of liberalism. Because two months after the movie is over, J.F.K. is assassinated. And two months after that the Beatles are on the "Ed Sullivan Show." And after that, it's radical action.[190]

The different styles of music in the movie anticipated the cultural differences emerging in the U.S. Bergstein, who maintained an unusual amount of control over the production, divided musical selections into three groups: Latin mambo for Kellerman's dance floor, clean teen pop for the Houseman cabin, and erotic rock and soul for the resort's staff quarters. "I tried to choose the harshest music I could find, the music that would be most sexually shocking to a young woman who'd never heard it before," Bergstein explained. "Because I imagined that in Baby's bedroom at home there'd be early Joan Baez, the Weavers, maybe Harry Belafonte."[191]

Dirty Dancing was director Emile Ardolino's first feature film. (He had won a 1984 Oscar for a documentary, *He Makes Me Feel Like Dancin'*, and produced and directed several programs in the Peabody Award-winning PBS series *Dance in America*. He also had directed a number of television productions, including *Baryshnikov at the White House*.) "I do love dance. I do love music," Ardolino said. The script for *Dirty Dancing* offered a perfect package that contained drama, comedy, music, and dance.

It was a script in which the dance was used to move the plot along, to reveal character, and the story didn't stop; in addition to which, I saw a subtext of body language throughout. So I related to all that immediately. I also related to the music. The music and the dances were the lifeblood of the script. It was the music I grew up with. I was like, 19, in 1963.[192]

Patrick Swayze was both a professionally trained dancer and an experienced actor. He had worked with the Joffrey and Harkness ballet companies, was a principal dancer with the Elliot Feld Dance Company, and also had danced in several Broadway musicals, including *West Side Story* and the lead role in *Grease,* replacing John Travolta. Critics had compared him to Travolta and Valentino after his appearance in the teen pic *Skatetown, U.S.A.* Swayze had appeared in a number of other films, including Francis Ford Coppola's *The Outsiders,* Randall Kleiser's *Grandview U.S.A.*, John Milius's *Red Dawn, Uncommon Valor,* and *Youngblood.* He also had starred in the successful television miniseries, *North and South* and *North and South, Book II.*

Unlike Swayze, co-star Jennifer Grey had no prior dance experience, except for a part in a Dr. Pepper commercial. A third-generation performer, Grey was considered a kind of ugly duckling. "I was too Jewish for 'Flashdance,' " she said. "I didn't even make it in to see Zeffirelli for *Endless Love*. His assistant said, 'Sorry,we're looking for a beautiful girl.' But the one that killed me was *Down and Out in Beverly Hills*. I thought, if I can't play Bette Midler's daughter and Richard Dreyfuss's daughter, why am I in this business?"[193] Grey *did* land a minor teen part in *Reckless* and then was cast in Coppola's *Cotton Club, Red Dawn* with Swayze, and John Badham's *American Flyers*. Her break came as the bratty young sister in the 1986 summer smash *Ferris Bueller's Day Off*. After her alluring performance in *Dirty Dancing*, Hollywood "reclassified her as a swan."[194]

Cynthia Rhodes was a veteran dancer and performer who had appeared in *Xanadu* and Coppola's musical *One From the Heart*. In 1983, Rhodes left her mark on moviegoers with dance scenes in both *Flashdance* and *Staying Alive*. Her duet with Frank Stallone on the *Staying Alive* soundtrack was a Top 20 hit.

Choreographer Kenny Ortega began in feature films as assistant choreographer for *The Rose* in 1979. He had choreographed music videos and dance numbers for a number of rock stars, including Madonna, Cher, Billy Joel, Rod Stewart, and The Pointer Sisters. In 1980, he co-choreographed the musical *Xanadu* and won an MTV Award for Best Choreography for Madonna's "Material Girl" video. Ortega had arranged special dance sequences in John Hughes's *Pretty in Pink* and the "Twist and Shout" scene in *Ferris Bueller's Day Off*.

The "dirty" dance from which the film drew its title was a manifestation of the old adage that dancing is "vertical expression of horizontal desires." The dance itself is a kind of anachronism, a 1980s version of the Twist. *Life* described it:

> The first thing you do is get close. Real close. No closer. Look into each other's eyes. Slowly push your hips forward. And back. Feel the music. Now press against your partner. Faster. That's it. Arch your back. Go. It's all in the hips: Bring them back and thrust them out. Now really let go. You are dirty dancing.[195]

The story behind the making of the *Dirty Dancing* soundtrack was described as "one of wheeling and dealing and trading on old friendships."[196] It centers around Jimmy Ienner, a producer and musical consultant at Vestron who liked "to walk the tightrope between the creative process and the guys with suits and cigars."[197] He was involved in the production of several gold and platinum albums with numerous artists, including The Raspberries, Grand Funk Railroad, The Bay City Rollers, anbd Three Dog Night. He also owned publishing companies and his own Millennium Records label. A shrewd producer, Ienner observed the increasing use of rock music tied to movie scripts before coming up with a model for a successful musical:

> The movie *Back to the Future* grossed $150 [sic] million and had a No. 1 single with Huey Lewis, the soundtrack album only sold 600,000 copies. That's because the music was "wallpapered" into the movie, and the songs were not an essential part of the emotional experience. For a soundtrack to be really successful—like *Top Gun* or *The Big Chill*—you have to hear what you see. And to make that happen, the director usually has to shoot scenes using either the actual music in the film or something that's very similar.[198]

Ienner established a reputation within the industry through his involvement in several soundtracks, including Fellini's *The Clowns, Amarcord,* and *You Gotta Walk It Like You Talk It*. He signed with Vestron as a music consultant when the company launched its film production division in 1986.

Normal budgets for soundtracks range from $300,000 to $800,000. Vestron budgeted $350,000 for new material and music rights with another $250,000 for the movie's score. Danny Goldberg, who managed rock artists Belinda Carlisle, Steve Jones, and Bonnie Raitt, was hired by Vestron to find new material and acquire rights from record companies for us of songs in the movie and soundtrack. Goldberg was largely unsuccessful, and eventually left the project, but his name appears in the credits as music supervisor.

When Ienner inherited the project, less than $200,000 was left in the budget, not one song pleased the producers, and three important scenes, including an almost seven-minute finale, needed music. He began a frantic search for material. "It was not an easy sell," he later explained. "It was a dance movie with a silly name and a small budget. That did not encourage people to rush out and write songs."[199]

Ienner asked Franke Previte, who was once the frontman for The Knockouts, who had a Top 10 hit in 1981 on Ienner's former Millennium Records label, to submit material for the movie. The songwriter collaborated with friends John DeNicola and Donald Markowitz to write the movie's theme song, "(I've Had) The Time of My Life." Ienner chose the Previte composition from almost 100 songs submitted for that sequence in the film. Previte and DeNicola also wrote "Hungry Eyes," which was performed by Eric Carmen, another artist Ienner produced at Arista Records.

Ienner bought out a deal Goldberg had struck with Motown Records and began shopping around for a record contract. Vestron suggested Polygram, but executives there turned the project down. Ienner turned to friends at

RCA Records. A talent scout and consultant at RCA, Bob Feiden, immediately recognize the potential for music in the *Dirty Dancing* script. "It involved youth, dancing, and coming of age," he said. "I thought every teen-age girl would identify with the Cinderella aspect of the story."[200] Feiden recommended the script to RCA president Bob Buziak, who was a longtime friend of both Vestron president Jon Peisinger and Ienner. The RCA deal gave Ienner another $210,000 to work with. The six new songs were expensive, because they needed two versions of each. "(I've Had) The Time of My Life" cost close to $70,000; the others cost between $20,000 and $30,000 apiece. "We needed different mixes for the film and record," Ienner recalled. "For example, the guitars were dropped way down for the film because guitars weren't a dominant instrument back then; saxophones were. We took out most of the synthesized stuff and replaced it with organ in the film versions. In some cases we used completely different solos to accommodate dialogue and some of the dancing.[201]

As a result, when Ienner began negotiating for rights to oldies for the project, he was working with a "used-Schwinn budget—which was a problem, because lots of these guys had gotten used to getting paid Rolls-Royce prices for their songs," he said.[202]

Producer Bergstein demanded Ienner get permission for three songs: "Big Girls Don't Cry" (The Four Seasons), "Be My Baby" (The Ronettes), and "Will You Love Me Tomrrow' (The Shirelles). Ienner begged, called in favors, and made promises in order to get the rights to fourteen old songs, along with the production of six new ones for $400,000. "I did a lot of horse-trading," he recalled.[203]

Ienner wanted the title tune to have a period feel and was set on getting Sixties soul singer Bill Medley to sing it. The former Righteous Brother was reluctant, as his duet with Gladys Knight, "Loving on Borrowed Time," for the soundtrack of Stallone's *Cobra* had flopped. "I thought a Stallone movie couldn't miss," he said. "With a hit movie, the title song has a real good shot to make it. When the movie flopped, that took the heart out of me. I wasn't that eager to do another soundtrack song, especially for a small movie with an unknown cast. Odds were against this movie becoming a hit."[204] Ienner offered to move the record session from New York to Los Angeles so that Medley could be close to his pregnant wife, and Medley reconsidered.

Jennifer Warnes, selected as his partner, was already known for her successful "Right Time of the Night." She had achieved status in the business, with three more theme songs to her credit: "It Goes Like It Goes" from *Norma Rae* (1979), "One More Hour" from *Ragtime* (1981), and a Number 1 hit in 1982 with Joe Cocker, "Up Where We Belong" from *An Officer and a Gentleman*. All three songs received Academy Award nominations for Best Song from a Motion Picture; "It Goes Like It Goes" and "Up Where We Belong" both won. Ienner thought the singer's blend of the earthy and the pristine approximated the images of the young lovers."[205] "(I've Had) The Time of My Life" became Medley's third Number 1 single (Warnes's second) and marked the longest span between Number 1 hits for an artist—twenty-two years and ten months. The song captured both Grammy and Academy Awards that year.

The film used an 80 to 20 percent balance of oldies and new material. For the soundtrack album, six new songs were recorded and combined with an equal number of oldies. Period pieces included "Be My Baby" (The Ronettes), "Stay" (Maurice Williams and The Zodiacs), "You Don't Own Me" (The Blow Monkeys), "Hey Baby" (Bruce Channel), "Love Is Strange" (Mickey and Sylvia), and "In the Still of the Night" (The Five Satins).

The success of the *Dirty Dancing* soundtrack surprised everyone. The album topped the charts for nine weeks during the Christmas season outranking competition from superstars Michael Jackson, George Michael, Bruce Springsteen, and Whitney Houston. It was the first multiartist soundtrack to hold down the Number 1 slot for that length of time since *Footloose* in 1984. All this was, *Rolling Stone* noted, "without star power."[206]

RCA president Bob Buziak cited the "emotional windows" in the Vestron film as crucial to the soundtrack's success. "The emotional scenes are the element that make the difference," he said. "People wanted to relive the movie with the music."[207] Ienner concurred. "The movie simply hit an emotional chord," he explained. "The music, the dance, and the fantasy all worked."[208] RCA Records executive vice president Rick Dobbis noted the importance of the album's three singles as contributors to the LP's success. He also pointed out that it was the movie itself which generated large initial sales.[209] Retailers agreed. "People would see the movie and come straight in for the soundtrack without going home," observed one buyer for a record store chain.[210]

The activity of the album and singles on the *Billboard* charts supported this contention. RCA released "(I've Had) The Time of My Life" in June 1987, anticipating the opening of the movie one month later. Vestron, however, decided to postpone the movie's opening from late July to late August in order to avoid competition from *La Bamba* and other popular summer pictures. Without the promotion of the movie, there was nothing to generate enthusiasm among radio programmers and listeners for the

Medley/Warnes duet. The single stiffed. "It was a major crevice that put us into 'code blue' situation," Ienner said. "But once the movie was out, people started walking out of the theater and asking for the record."[211]

When *Dirty Dancing* reached theaters in late August, album sales began to soar; within five weeks the soundtrack had sold one million copies. RCA had hoped for sales of 300,000 to 500,000; an initial press of 50,000 created stock problems for retailers. The *Dirty Dancing* LP sold at an incredible pace. The album was certified gold and platinum simultaneously in October 1987, double and triple platinum in December, and reached sales of five million in February 1988.

The *Dirty Dancing* soundtrack debuted at Number 77 on *Billboard*'s Pop Album chart on 9 September 1987. "(I've Had) The Time of My Life" entered the singles charts the following week at Number 73. Both the album and the single rocketed to the top of the charts. The album reached Number 1 the week ending 14 November; the Medley/Warnes duet hit the top 2 weeks later. *Dirty Dancing* held down the top spot for nine consecutive weeks before being bumped by George Michael's *Faith* and returned to the top position 3 March 1988 for another nine weeks. Its eighteen-week total at Number 1 was topped only by the *Saturday Night Fever* soundtrack, which had lasted twenty-four weeks.

Following Al Coury's staggered-release strategy, when the first single entered the Top 10 a second was released. (Both singles were backed with videos on VH-1.) Eric Carmen's "Hungry Eyes" debuted on the Pop Singles chart at Number 88 on 7 November 1987 and climbed to Number 4 the week ending 13 February 1988. "She's Like the Wind," written by Patrick Swayze and Stacey Widelitz and performed by Swayze, followed, peaking at Number 3 for three weeks. Merry Clayton's "Yes" was not nearly as successful, stalling at Number 45.

Record-store owners noticed that the soundtrack, like *Saturday Night Fever, Flashdance,* and *Top Gun,* appealed to a wide audience. "There are grandmothers and little kids buying *Dirty Dancing*," said a Chicago retailer. "Those same people aren't buying Springsteen, Jackson, or Whitesnake."[212] The album drew the over-forty crowd into the record stores as well as the traditional twenty-to-twenty-five-year-olds, though the younger group was "strongly female, or guys buying for a girl."[213] Several reasons were cited as attributing to the broad appeal of the album, including the blend of oldies and new tracks, the strong media campaign, strong airplay for singles, and simple word of mouth.

The movie itself was start-to-finish music. Behind the opening credits, the Ronettes sing their hit "Be My Baby." It is 1963, the summer of

Camelot—that moment between the Cuban Missile Crisis and the Kennedy assassination; between the Peace Corps and the counterculture.

In the film, Francis "Baby" Houseman (Jennifer Grey) and her family are vacationing at Kellerman's Resort in the Catskill Mountains. Her father (Jerry Orbach) is a liberal-minded physician, her mother (Kelly Bishop) a silent, suburban housewife. Baby is a high school senior who firmly believes in the liberal values her upper-middle-class Jewish parents have taught her. She plans to major in the "economics of underdeveloped countries" in college before joining the Peace Corps. Her father tells resort owner Max Kellerman (Jack Weston) "Baby's gonna change the world." In contrast, her nerdy sister Lisa (Jane Brucker), a somewhat jealous sibling with a fully developed body, will merely "decorate" the world.

During her first evening at the main lodge, Baby gets a dose of the resort's behind-the-scenes class conflict. She overhears Kellerman instructing the Ivy League waiters to "keep your fingers out of the water, your hair out of the soup, and show the goddamn daughters a good time." Enter maverick dance instructor Johnny Castle (Patrick Swayze) and the working-class help, who are not part of the waiters' clique. The resort owner gives them strict orders to stay uninvolved with the wealthy customers: Dance with them, but "keep your hands off!" Baby is smitten.

Bored by the stifling social atmosphere at the guest lodge, Baby wanders the camp grounds, meeting a friend from the staff who reluctantly takes her to a dance party in the staff quarters. Baby steps into a room full of sweating bodies "dirty dancing" to The Contours' R&B classic, "Do You Love Me?" Johnny and his dance partner, Penny Johnson (Cynthia Rhodes), stand out among the sensual and exhilarating dancers. Somewhat mockingly, Castle takes Baby onto the dance floor and introduces her to the bodily freedom of the dance.

Baby has been taught to see beyond class distinctions. Though sincere and well intentioned, her actions do not go over well with the staff. Naive and altruistic, she tries to resolve the problem of Penny's pregnancy. "Go back to your playplen, Baby," Penny tells her. Baby confronts the father, waiter Robbie Gould (Max Cantor), but the Yale medical student refuses to fund an abortion. "Some people count, some people don't," he replies. Determined, Baby gets a loan from her father to "help someone in trouble." "It takes a real saint to ask Daddy," Castle says sarcastically. Still, Penny accepts the money. The illegal abortion is scheduled at the same time as an important appearance the dance duo must keep at the nearby Sheldrake Hotel; Baby fills in for Penny.

The rehearsal scenes that follow are given power by Eric Carman's "Hungry Eyes." The development of Baby's dancing talent parallels her sexual maturation and growing social awareness: The young woman is sickened by the artificiality and arrogance of the lodge's guests and introduced to the real dilemmas of the working class. The hours of dancing with Baby gradually break down Johnny's toughness, revealing a warm vulnerability. Variations on the movie's theme song fill some tender moments.

The Sheldrake appearance is a success even though Baby is nervous and stiff and fails to perform the lift. When she and Johnny return they find Penny seriously ill after the back-alley abortion. Baby gets her father to help Penny. He completely misunderstands the situation, assuming Castle is the father and that Baby will be his next victim.

Later Baby returns to Johnny's room to apologize for her father's attitude toward the dancer. Johnny expresses his admiration of her courage and commitment. The young girl is attracted to the dancer's abandon, sensuality, and genuineness. After a slow-moving dance to "Cry to Me," they make love.

Baby's boldness and determination to live out her ideals alienates her father. "You're not the person I thought you were, Baby," he tells her after caring for Penny. "I'm not sure who you are." Ironically, the doctor approves of the relationship between Lisa and playboy Robbie, who only interest in a woman is as a sexual score.

The film moves toward a climax when Johnny rejects the proposition of a wealthy guest who, the next morning, sees Baby leaving the instructor's cabin. Embittered, she frames Johnny as a thief. Johnny claims he was in his room reading. Rather than see him lose his job, Baby confesses to being with him the entire night. Her parents are shocked. Though not entirely proud of herself, Baby confronts her dismayed father about his own shallow, elitist philosophy, saying "You told me everyone was alike and deserved a fair break, but you meant everyone who was like you. You told me you wanted me to change the world, make it better, but you meant by becoming a lawyer or an economist and marrying someone from Harvard." Johnny is acquitted but fired for sleeping with a guest's daughter. Baby's actions on his behalf stir the dancer's own self-esteem and Johnny begins to believe that he can become more than society would allow. He leaves, driving off with "She's Like the Wind" in the background.

The plot lines come together during the choral finale of the season-end talent show. Dr. Houseman discovers that Robbie was the responsible party in the "Penny situation." Dressed in black, Johnny returns, looking like a combination of Brando and Gene Kelly. He escorts Baby to the stage and announces he will do the last dance of the season with special partner "Frances" Houseman. "(I've Had) The Time of My Life" plays as the two perform their Sheldrake mamba spiced with some dirty dancing. The staff joins in some solid choreography. This time Frances performs the lift, in the center aisle.

Guests and workers mingle on the dance floor. Houseman admits he was wrong and father and daughter are reunited. In the final moment, dancing in each others arms, Johnny sings to his young love, "I've had the time of my life and I owe it to you." The music fades with the visual. Merry Clayton's "Yes" rocks the theater as the credits roll.

In general, critics thought the music and dance compensated for weaknesses in the plot. *Time*'s Richard Schickel said, "If the ending of Eleanor Bergstein's script is too neat and inspirational, the rough energy of the film's song and dance does carry one along, past the whispered doubts of better judgment." Writing in *Newsweek,* David Ansen said *Dirty Dancing* "integrates dance and drama better than any movie since 'Saturday Night Fever.' " *Times* critic Vincent Canby called it "an engaging pop-movie romance of somewhat more substance than one usually finds in summer movies designed for the young." The dancing, Canby said, "has a drive and a pulse that give the film real excitement."[214]

Dirty Dancing was at its best when it focused on the youthful rite of passage symbolized by the "dirty dancing." The plot was cluttered by the collage, of thematic undercurrent—adult hypocrisy, politics, class barriers, and the generation gap. Canby rightly observed that Bergstein "seems to want *Dirty Dancing* to be seen as a fond goodbye to a comfortable, *liberal* American way of life before the country was radicalized by the assassination of President Kennedy and by the increasingly bitter anti-Vietnam War movement." He added, "That's loading a small movie with rather more than it can carry without a lot of highly detailed program notes."[215]

At a screening of the film, *New York* critic David Denby spotted the beginning of the *Dirty Dancing* phenomenon. "As I was sitting in the screening room muttering to myself about what a piece of cheese the movie was, women all around me were smiling at the screen. They may have also thought it was junk," he said, "but they were enjoying it."[216] Strong repeat business fueled *Dirty Dancing*'s box office prowess, which in turn generated sales for the soundtrack album. Woman returned to the theaters endlessly turning a low-budget summer flick into a multimedia bonanza. Some women reportedly saw the film 10, 25, 50, even 125 times! *Newsweek* described one repeater as "clearly in a state of Dirty Denial. She needs the help of a support group, perhaps Women Who Love Patrick Swayze Too Much."[217] Fans quoted from the film, "When I'm wrong, I say I'm wrong," and "No one puts Baby in a corner." A Patrick Swayze poster quickly sold out at 25 thousand copies. Vestron considered the reaction to the film "more than a little spooky."[218]

Several erotic scenes with Swayze and Jennifer Grey were left on the cutting-room floor in order to receive a PG-13 rating. "The movie isn't about bumping and grinding," Swayze insisted. "It's about connecting with someone. It's like the Fred Astaire movies with great dancing and a good story."[219] It didn't matter. One freelance writer argued, "It's the only girls' porno movie that's ever been made. It has a plot that slowly unfolds, and [Swayze] is another Baryshnikov—he sort of explodes."[220] Reviewers agreed. *Variety* called it a "skin-deep but inoffensive teen-throb pic designed to titillate teenage girls." David Denby referred to *Dirty Dancing* as a "female wet dream."[221]

In January 1988, RCA's executive vice president, Rick Dobbis, speculated that the "cross-marketing opportunities [on *Dirty Dancing*] will continue through next summer."[222] That same month, Vestron shipped 280,000 units of *Dirty Dancing* videocassette at a suggested list price of $89.98. A commercial tie-in was established with Nestle Food Corporation and its Alpine White chocolate candy bar. A "Sweet Dreams" thirty-second ad appeared at the beginning of the *Dirty Dancing* videocassette; executives anticipated ad exposure to about fifty-two million people via rentals of the Vestron movie. Though details of the Vestron-Nestle contract were not disclosed, *Variety* reported "it was not a mere exchange of Nestle's promo support for the 30-second *Dirty Dancing* spot."[223]

Unlike in the Paramount Home Video deal with Pepsi for a Diet Pepsi ad in *Top Gun,* the Nestle pact did not reduce *Dirty Dancing's* list price. "What it will bring the vid industry is a cross-promotional campaign Vestron is hoping will lengthen the title's period of peak rental demand far beyond what most releases enjoy," reported *Variety.* "That would mean more rentals for each tape a vidstore buys, and the ability to stock more copies of the film and still make money on each copy."[224]

Using the *Dirty Dancing* theme, Nestle launched a national consumer sweepstakes in February 1988, with prizes to contestants including a New York or Los Angeles vacation, videocassettes, and posters. The campaign involved point-of-purchase materials at outlets that sold Nestle's candy, advertisements in *USA Today,* and promotion centered on an Aspen ski contest. The *Dirty Dancing* videocassette was one of four titles that broke the 300,000 barrier, selling more than 360,000 copies by Feburary 1988. Suppliers credit the marketing efforts tied to the January releases as essential to the unprecedented success of the films in the video market.[225]

RCA received 3,000 letters from fans wanting to hear the rest of the songs in the movie. A soundtrack sequel, titled *More Dirty Dancing* in order to avoid conflict with a *Dirty Dancing II* film, was released in March 1988 to coincide with the premier of *Dirty Dancing* on cable television. "This is much more than a marketing endeavor to milk more money," said Ienner. "This is truly dealing with demand, which makes it a whole other ballgame."[226]

The initial orders of 600,000 units exceeded RCA's expectations. The LP included eight additional Sixties hits, seven instrumentals written for the movie, and an extended version of "(I've Had) The Time of My Life." Both *Dirty Dancing* albums were in the Top 10 at the same time—a recording industry first. *More Dirty Dancing* becme the most commercially successful soundtrack sequel on the *Billboard* album charts. (The only other sequel to crack the Top 10 was *Woodstock 2,* which reached Number 7 in May 1971. Others barely charted. *More American Graffiti* and *More Songs From The Big Chill* reached number 84 and 85 respectively. *Urban Cowboy II* and *Beat Street, Volume 2* never made it into the Top 100.) The *Dirty Dancing* soundtrack topped eight million in domestic sales and *More Dirty Dancing* sold another three million copies. The combined domestic sales of the two albums tied the record set by the *Saturday Night Fever* soundtrack in 1978. Together the *Dirty Dancing* LP's sold twenty-two million copies worldwide.

In May, RCA Records joined Rowe Video Jukebox to promote *Dirty Dancing: The Concert Tour.* Across the country, Rowe's video jukeboxes aired *Dirty Dancing* videos and provided local *Dirty Dancing* concert tour information. "We're working very closely with RCA on this project," Rowe's director of video operations said. "This is very exciting because we're creating something and making it available in a way that has never been done before."[227]

A special Oprah Winfrey show helped launch the concert tour: The Contours and Merry Clayton performed their respective hits from the soundtrack and dancers demonstrated as Kenny Ortega gave dancing lessons. "It's like having sex with your clothes on, only you don't feel guilty afterwards," the choreographer said. "Hungry Eyes" provided music for a dirty dancing contest.

The 100-city tour opened in May 1988 in the Catskills (the film's setting) and lasted through July. The show featured Bill Medley, Eric Carmen, Merry Clayton, and The Contours (whose "Do You Love Me?" hit was included in the *More Dirty Dancing* LP), along with eleven musicians, the Original Dirty Dancers, and a $1-million set. *Rolling Stone* called the show "a hokey but often entertaining smorgasbord of song and dance."[228]

CBS launched a prime-time television series based on the movie with a one-hour premier in November 1988. Critics were not impressed. The risque movie subplots were deleted for the TV audience, robbing the show of the emotional conflicts that brewed over political and social conflicts in the screen version. Michael Lloyd was hired as music supervisor and Kenny Ortega repeated as choreographer. Despite a story that was "squeaky clean to the point of boredom," the prime-time version offered "dance sequences that make the big-screen version's seem as tame as a grade-school square dance," quipped *Variety*.[229] The show was canceled in its first season.

In March 1989, RCA released a third record project as a spin-off from the touring show: *Dirty Dancing—Live In Concert*. The album was recorded live at the Greek Theater in Los Angeles in August 1988. Ienner served as executive producer. The tour soundtrack was mostly a live version of material already offered on the previous albums. Merry Clayton, The Contours, Eric Carmen, and Bill Medley were each featured on a side of the double LP. A duet between Eric Carmen and Merry Clayton, "Almost paradise," was released as a single and video clip. Vestron also cashed in on the tour's success with a videocassette, *Dirty Dancing: The Concert Tour,* released for distribution simultaneously with the concert LP.

According to a *Business Week* report, RCA's share of the multimedia success of *Dirty Dancing* alone reached an astounding $105 million by June 1988. The soundtrack albums accounted for about one quarter of the record label's domestic revenues. The Vestron picture grossed more than $100 million; $25 million in domestic rentals. The entire *Dirty Dancing* enterprise—the film, soundtrack albums, videocassette, touring company, and television series—grossed about $350 million by August 1988.[230] Vestron plans for a sequel to reach theaters in late 1989 never materialized.

A host of dance musicals, from *Saturday Night Fever* to *Dirty Dancing,* has given new life to the genre. Filmmakers continue to fuse contemporary music and dance with advanced cinematic techniques. The enduring success of these films shows that the universal magic of musicals can be acclimatized to new social and cultural settings and still spark the public imagination.

Notes

1. Quoted in William R. Meyer, *Warner Brothers Directors: The Hard-Boiled, the Comic, and the Weepers* (New Rochelle, New York: Arlington House 1978), 69. There are a large number of volumes on the Hollywood musical. For more detail see Jane Feuer, *The Hollywood Musical* (Bloomington:

Indiana University Press 1982); John Kobal, *Gotta Sing Gotta Dance: A Pictorial History of Film Musicals* (New York: Exeter Books 1983); Ethan Mordden, *The Hollywood Musical* (New York: St. Martin's Press 1981); John Russell Taylor and Arthur Jackson, *The Hollywood Musical* (New York: McGraw-Hill 1971).

2. David Ewen, *The Life and Death of Tin Pan Alley* (New York: Funk and Wagnalls 1964): 314.

3. John Russell Taylor and Arthur Jackson, *The Hollywood Musical* (New York: McGraw-Hill Book Company 1971), 20.

4. "Supermogul In The Land Of Opportunity," *Forbes,* 10 July 1978, 42.

5. "Super profits from 'Superstar,' " *Business Week,* 11 September 1971, 46.

6. Quoted in Ellis Nassour and Richard Broderick, *Rock Opera: The Creation of Jesus Christ Superstar from Record Album to Broadway Show and Motion Picture* (New York: Hawthorn Books 1973): 13-14. Much of the following discussion of *Superstar* relies on this work.

7. *Ibid.,*

8. *Ibid.,* 34.

9. Quoted in Jack Kroll, review of 'Jesus Christ Superstar,' *Newsweek,* 25 October 1971, 84.

10. Nassour and Broderick, 62.

11. *Ibid.,* 201.

12. *Ibid.,* 66.

13. *Ibid.*

14. *Ibid.,* 67-68.

15. *Ibid.,* 71.

16. *Ibid.,* 67.

17. Quoted in Anthony Haden-Guest, "Robert Stigwood Has the Stomach," *New York,* 30 January 1978, 52.

18. *Ibid.*

19. Philip Norman, *Shout!: The Beatles In Their Generation* (New York: Simon and Schuster 1981): 285-86. See Peter Brown and Steven Gaines, *The Love You Make: An Insider's Story of The Beatles* (New York: McGraw-Hill 1983), 237-8; Anthony Haden-Guest, "Robert Stigwood Has the Stomach," 52.

20. Tony Schwartz with Martin Kasindorf, "Stigwood's Midas Touch," *Newsweek,* 23 January 1978, 40; Anthony Haden-Guest, "Robert Stigwood Has the Stomach," 53.

21. Quoted in Anthony Haden-Guest, "Robert Stigwood Has the Stomach," 53.

22. David Ansen, et al., "Rock Tycoon Robert Stigwood," *Newsweek* 31 July 1978, 41.

23. See Anthony Haden-Guest, "Robert Stigwood Has the Stomach," 53; "Super profits from 'Superstar,' " 46; Tony Schwartz with Martin Kasindorf; 50.

24 "Super profits from 'Superstar,' "46; Nassour and Broderick, 1971.

25. Nassour and Broderick, 178. According to Nassour, there were rumors that the show actually cost over $1 million, with Stigwood's treasury making up the difference.

26. *Ibid.,* 137.

27. *Ibid.,* 173 and 174.

28. *Ibid.,* 175.

29. Jack Kroll, review of 'Jesus Christ Superstar,' 84.

30. See Nassour and Broderick, 224.
31. *Ibid.*, 226.
32. *Ibid.*, 216.
33. Quoted in Sanka Knox, "Jewish Group Charges Anti-Semitism in Movie," *New York Times,* 9 August 1973, 28. See also "Jewish Charge: Jewison Worsened Objectionable Stage Angles of 'J.C.'; Catholics, Protestants Less Upset," *Variety,* 27 June 1973, 4; Irving Spiegel, "Jewish Unit Calls Movie 'Insidious,' " *New York Times,* 24 June 1973, 44; Terence Smith, "Israeli Government Moves to Dissociate Itself From 'Jesus Christ Superstar,' " *New York Times,* July 1973, 19.
34. Quoted in Linda Greenhouse, " 'Superstar' Film Renews Disputes," *New York Times,* 8 August 1973, 24.
35. Howard Thompson, "Mod-Pop 'Superstar' Comes to Sreen," *New York Times,* 9 August 1973, 28; Jon Landau, "Jesus Christ, Star of Stage, Screen & 'Hullaballoo,' " *Rolling Stone* 2, August 1973, 54.
36. Quoted in Nassour and Broderick, 192. See Joseph Murrells, *Million Selling Records From the 1900s to the 1980s* (New York: Arco Publishing 1984), 298.
37. Albert Goldman, " 'Tommy': The Red Dawn of Revolt?" *New York times,* 30 June 1969, D30. In another review Goldman wrote, "This pinball opera, all slamming jolts and gidget chatter, [is] the heaviest score of the rock Generation." Albert Goldman, "A Grand Opera in Rock," *Life,* 17 October 1969, 20. See also John Gabree, "And Now a Rock Opera!" *High Fidelity,* September 1969, 80; "Super profits from 'Superstar,' " *Business Week,* 11 September 1971, 46.
38. Quoted in Dave Marsh, "The Who," in *The Rolling Stone Illustrated History of Rock & Roll,* ed. Jim Miller (New York: Random House/Rolling Stone Press Book 1976, 1980), 290.
39. *Ibid.*
40. Quoted in "What's Deaf, Dumb & Blind and Costs $3.5 Million?" *Rolling Stone,* 10 April 1975, 44.
41. Jay Cocks, "Tommy Rocks In," *Time,* 31 March 1975, 56.
42. Joseph Murrells, 295.
43. John Leverence, "Promoting *Tommy,*" *Journal of Popular Culture* 8:3 Winter 1974, 466.
44. Jay Cocks, "Tommy Rocks In," 57; "What's Deaf, Dumb & Blind and Costs $3.5 Million?," 44.
45. Jay Cocks, "Tommy Rocks In," 56.
46. Quoted in "What's Deaf, Dumb & Blind and Cost $3.5 Million?", 44.
47. Joseph Murrels, 393.
48. Quoted in "What's Deaf, Dumb & Blind and Costs $3.5 Million?," 44.
49. John Leverence, 471.
50. "Market Study Maps Safeway Path to 'Tommy'; Lure of Ann-Margret, Jack N., Reed?" *Variety,* 26 February 1975, 4. For a full summary of the details of this survey see John Leverence: 470-71.
51. *Ibid.*
52. Quoted in "What's Deaf, Dumb & Blind and Costs $3.5 Million?," 44.
53. "The Bash," *Time,* 31 March 1975, 57.
54. *Ibid.*, 57.

55. Judith Crist, "Opera on the Rocks, With a Twist," *New York,* 7 April 1975, 64.
56. Charles Michener, "The New Movie Musicals," *Newsweek,* 24 March 1975, 59.
57. Quoted in Bob Gilbert and Gary Theroux, *The Top Ten: 1956–Present* (New York: Simon and Schuster 1982), 159.
58. *Variety,* 12 March 1975, 18.
59. Jay Cocks, "Tommy Rocks In," 56.
60. Stephen Farber, "Russellmania," *Film Comment,* November–December 1975, 44.
61. Vincent Canby, "When Too Much Is Just About Right," *New York Times,* 30 March 1975, sec. 2, 13.
62. "What's Deaf, Dumb & Blind and Costs $3.5 Million?", 44.
63. Quoted in David Leaf, *Bee Gees: The Authorized Biography* (Los Angeles: Pinnacle Books 1979), 128.
64. Jim Curtis, *Rock Eras: Interpretations of Music and Society, 1954-1984* (Bowling Green, Ohio: Bowling Green State University Popular Press 1987), 299–300.
65. See Stephen Holden, "The evolution of a dance craze," *Rolling Stone,* 19 April 1979, 29; Michael Bane, *White Boy Singin' The Blues* (New York: Penguin Books 1982): 234–39.
66. "'Jive Talkin' '" was inspired by the sound Barry's car tires made when crossing railroad tracks. One night his wife said, "Hey, listen to that noise . . . It's our drive talking." See Fred Bronson, *The Billboard book of Number One Hits,* rev. ed. (New York: Billboard Publications 1988), 412.
67. Quoted in David Leaf, 132–33.
68. Quoted in Ben Fong-Torres, "Rock on Reels," *Rolling Stone* 20 April 1978, 47.
69. Eric Breitbart, "Lost in the Hustle: An Interview with John Badham," *Cineaste,* Winter 1978–79, 3.
70. Quoted in Debby Miller, "Rock is Money to Hollywood Ears," *Rolling Stone,* October 27, 1983, 103.
71. David Ansen, et al., "Rock Tycoon Robert Stigwood," *Newsweek,* July 31, 1978, 45; Tony Schwartz with Martin Kasindorf, "Stigwood's Midas Touch," 40.
72. Quoted in Steve Pond, "Night Fever, Ten Years After,' *Premiere,* December 1987, 97.
73. Quoted in David Leaf, 130–31; Gary Theroux and Bob Gilbert, 277.
74. Quoted in David Leaf, 131–32.
75. Quoted in Gary Theroux and Bob Gilbert, 275.
76. Eric Breitbart, "Lost in the Hustle," 4.
77. Quoted in Maureen Orth, "From Sweathog to Disco King," *Newsweek,* 19 December 1977, 63. See also Judson Klinger, "TV's Teen Idol Comes Down With Adult Movie 'Fever,' " *New York Times,* 11 December 1977, sec. 2, 32.
78. Quoted in Tom Burke, "Struttin' His Stuff," *Rolling Stone,* 15 June 1978, 77.
79. Quoted in Ben Fong-Torres, "Al Coury Owns Number One," *Rolling Stone,* 5 October 1978, 44.
80. Quoted in Todd Everett, "Trailers, Teasers Vs. 'Screen Clutter,' " *Variety,* 7 December 1977, 72.

81. *Ibid.*
82. Paul Grein, " 'Fever' Sells At White Hot Pace Setting New Record," *Billboard,* 22 April 1978, 3.
83. Quoted in Ben Fong-Torres, " 'Saturday Night' Bumps 'Rumours,' *Rolling Stone,* 9 March 1978, 12.
84. Landon Y. Jones, *Great Expectations: America and the Baby Boom Generation* (New York: Ballantine Books 1980), 316. See also pages 327–28.
85. Quoted in Dick Nusser, "Dealers Say 'Fever' Igniting Other Sales," *Billboard,* 6 May 1978, 92.
86. *Ibid.*
87. Quoted in David Ansen, et al., "Rock Tycoon Robert Stigwood," 41.
88. Al Auster and Leonard Quart, review of 'Saturday Night Fever,' *Cineaste* 8:4, 36.
89. David Ansen, "The Boogie Man," *Newsweek* 19 December 1977, 65; Frank Rich, "Discomania," *Time,* 19 December 1977, 69; Hugh Fordin and Robin Chase, "Hollywood Puts on Its Dancing Shoes Again," *New York Times,* 25, June 1978, sec. 2, 8.
90. Pauline Kael, "The Current Cinema: Nirvana," *New Yorker,* 26 December 1977, 59; Al Auster and Leonard Quart, review of 'Saturday Night Fever,' *Cineaste* 8:4 1978, 36; Marsha Kinder, review of 'Saturday Night Fever,' *Film Quarterly,* Spring 1978, 40.
91. David Ansen, "The Boggie Man," *Newsweek* 19 December 1977, 65; Frank Rich, "Discomania," *Time* 19 December 1977, 69.
92. Rev. of 'Saturday Night Fever,' *Variety,* 14 December 1977, 12.
93. See David Ansen, et al., "Rock Tycoon Robert Stigwood," 45; "Sleeper of '78, 'Sat. Nite Fever' Hits 600G Daily," *Variety,* 19 April 1978, 140; Paramount's 'Fever' Passes $100,000,000," *Variety,* 7 June 1978, 3; "7 Mins. Verbal, Sexual Cuts Sends 'Fever' into 500-Print PG Cycle March 2; Par's New Campaign," *Variety,* 17 January 1979, 50.
94. Quoted in Aljean Harmetz, " 'Fever' Redone for PG Rating," *New York Times,* 11 January 1979, C15.
95. Quoted in "7 mins. Verbal, Sexual Cuts Sends 'Fever,' " 7.
96. Quoted in Aljean Harmetz, " 'Fever' Redone for PG Rating," C15.
97. Quoted in Steve Pond, "Night Fever, Ten Years After," 98.
98. Nathan Fain, "Discomania and the beat goes on!" *Dance Magazine,* March 1979, 90.
99. Quoted in Susan Cheever Cowley, "The Travolta Hustle," *Newsweek,* 29 May 1978, 97.
100. Maureen Orth et al., "Get Up And Boogie!" *Newsweek,* 8 November 1976, 94.
101. Estimates vary. Three sources reported the $4 billion figure. See Jesse Kornbluth, "Merchandizing Disco For The Masses," *New York Times Magazine,* 18 February 1979, 22; "The feverish hustle for big disco profits," *Business Week,* 26 June 1978, 42; Herschel Johnson, "The Discotheque Scene," *Ebony,* February 1977, 60. Two other sources estimated the industry at $8 billion annually by the end of the decade. See Landon Y. Jones, *Great Expectations,* 315; Stephen Holden, "The evolution of a dance craze," 30.
102. David Ansen, et al., "Rock Tycoon Robert Stigwood," 40.
103. See David Leaf, 138; Steve Pond, "Night Fever, Ten Years After," 97.

104. "Supermogul In The Land Of Opportunity," 42.
105. Steve Pond, "Night Fever, Ten Years After," 98.
106. Albert Goldman, "The Disco Style: Love Thyself," *Esquire,* 20 June 1978, 77.
107. See Christoher Lasch, *The Culture of Narcissism: American Life in an Age of Diminishing Expectations* (New York: W. W. Norton 1978).
108. Pauline Kael, "The Current Cinema: Nirvana," *New Yorker,* 26 December 1977, 60.
109. Peter N. Carroll, *It Seemed Like Nothing Happened: The Tragedy and Promise of America in the 1970s* (New York: Holt, Rinehart and Winston 1982), 266.
110. Lasch, 21.
111. Frank Rich, "The Year of John Travolta," *Seventeen,* November 1978, 113.
112. Maureen Orth et al., "Get Up And Boogie!" 95.
113. Landon Y. Jones, 280.
114. Richard Hummler, " 'Grease' Film Spurs B.O. For B'way Original," *Variety,* 19 July 1978, 107.
115. Quoted in Gary Theroux and Bob Gilbert, 269.
116. Quoted in Jim Waters, "Olivia Newton-John: Not Really the 'Girl Next Door,' " *New York Times,* 11 June 1988, sec. 2, 35.
117. *Ibid.* See also Gary Theroux and Bob Gilbert, 269.
118. Quoted in "Merchants Tied to 'Grease' Pic; "Win A Role' Pitch For Youths," *Variety,'* 8 June 1977, 5. For production figures see "Supermogul In The Land of Opportunity," 42. The $3-million production figure in this report is low; $6 million is the accepted amount. See "Par Bid-Asking As To 'Grease' Carries a 'Free' Pepsi-Cola Sell," *Variety,* 15 March 1988, 40; Marjorie Rosen, "Musical Grease," *American Film,* February 1978, 10.
119. Quoted in Marjorie Rosen, 'Musical Greease," 16.
120. "Old Time Bally: Bring In Youths, For 'Grease' Role," *Variety,* 31 August 1977, 32; "Merchants Tied to 'Grease' Pic; "Win A Role' Pitch For Youths," *Variety,* 8 June 1977, 5.
121. "Par Bid-Asking As To 'Grease' Carries A 'Free' Pepsi-Cola Sell," 40.
122. David Ansen, et al., "Rock Tycoon Robert Stigwood," 46.
123. Quoted in "*Billboard* Salutes the Bee Gees," *Billboard* sec. 2, 2 September 1978, 40.
124. A.D. Murphy, " 'Jaws 2,' 'Grease' Set New B.O. Records," *Variety,* 21 June 1978, 1.
125. See "Inside Gulf + Western: Gulf + Western Industries, Inc. 1978 Annual Report," Special Section, *Time* 5 February 1979: G + W 8.
126. *The Rolling Stone Encyclopedia of Rock & Roll* Jon Pareles and Patricia Romanowski, ed., (New York: Rolling Stone Press/Summit Books 1983), 394.
127. Quoted in Richard Hummler, " 'Grease' Film Spurs B.O. for B'way Original," 107.
128. *Ibid.*
129. Quoted in Marjorie Rosen, "Musical Grease," 17.
130. Vincent Canby, "Screen: A Slick Version of 'Grease,' " *New York Times,* 16 June 1978, C10; Vincent Canby, "Having Fun With the 50's," *New York Times,* 25 June 1978, sec. 2, 17; review of 'Grease,' *Variety,* 7 July 1978, 28.
131. Richard Schickel, "Black Hole," *Time,* 19 June 1978, 78.

132. *Ibid.*
133. Al Auster, review of 'Grease,' *Cineaste* 9:1, 42.
134. Marjorie Rosen, "Musical Grease," 17.
135. Lasch, xvii.
136. Stephen Grover, "Record Industry May Be in Groove Again (sic) After One of Worst Slumps in Its History," *Wall Street Journal,* 5 September 1979, 10. See also David Lieberman, "Pressuring a Soft Economy," *Billboard,* 27 October 1979, 22.
137. Vincent Canby, "Having Fun With the 50's," *New York Times,* 25 June 1978, sec. 2, 17.
138. Quoted in David Ansen, et al., "Rock Tycoon Robert Stigwood," 40.
139. Quoted in Paul Grein, " 'Fever Sells At White Hot Pace," 77.
140. *Ibid.*
141. Quoted in Ed Harrison, " 'Pepper' Sets Production Records," *Billboard,* 29 July 1978, 1.
142. Quoted in Ralph Kisiel, "Soundtrack Fever," *The Toledo Blade,* 26 May 1985, e1.
143. Quoted in Ben Fong-Torres, "Al Coury Owns Number One," 44.
144. Quoted in Susan Peterson, "Key label executives analyze their approach to the marketing of movie music," *Billboard* 6 October 1979, ST-2.
145. See Adam White, "The Beatles Rise Again Thanks to 'Pepper' Film," *Billboard,* 26 August 1978, 3; Jim McCullaugh, "Cap's Beatles,' 'Pepper' Pic LP Joins Movie," *Billboard,* 29 July 1978, 3.
146. Quoted in Paul Gambaccini, "A Conversation With Paul McCartney," *Rolling Stone,* 12 July 1979, 45.
147. Quoted in "The Yellow Brick Road to Profit," *Time,* 23 January 1978, 80.
148. Quoted in "The Bee Gees: They Make You Feel Like Dancing," *Time,* 3 April 1978, 88.
149. David Ansen, "Stigwood's Home Movie," *Newsweek,* 31 July 1978, 42; Paul Nelson, " ' Sgt. Pepper' gets busted, " *Rolling Stone,* 5 October 1978, 71.
150. Quoted in Ben Fong-Torres, "Al Coury Owns Number One," 44.
151. Marc Kirkeby, "Bee Gees Sue Stigwood, Charge Mismanagement," *Rolling Stone,* 13 November 1980, 23.
152. Quoted in Richard M. Nusser,"'Stigwood Slams Gibb Suit," *Billboard,* 18 October 1980, 1.
153. Quoted in Steve Pond, "Bee Gees Say They're Sorry," *Rolling Stone,* 25 June 1981, 13.
154. Quoted in Steve Gett, "Bee Gees Ready To Win Again," *Billboard,* 12 September 1987, 21.
155. Vincent Canby, "Films To Break—or Make—A Vacationer's Summer Doldrums," *New York Times,* 11 June 1978, sec. 2, 21.
156. Quoted in Ben Fong-Torres, " 'Friday': disco drone on film," *Rolling Stone,* 13 July 1978, 11.
157. *Ibid.;* Tom Allen, "Portents of Underdevelopment," *Village Voice,* 22 May 1978, 46.
158. Quoted in Fong-Torres, "Rock on Reels,' 47.
159. Quoted in Babara Graustark, et al., "Disco Takes Over," *Newsweek,* 2 April 1979, 64.
160. Tom Smucker, "Disco," in *The Rolling Stone Illustrated History of Rock &*

Roll, ed. Jim Miller (New York: Random House/Rolling Stone Press 1976, 1980), 428.

161. Quoted in Stephen Holden, "The best goes on—and on, and on," *Rolling Stone,* 14 June 1979, 95. See Michael Musto, "The Village People boogie from disco to the mainstream," *US* 26 June 1979, 18; Barbara Graustrak, et al., "Disco Takes Over," *Newsweek,* April 1979, 64.
162. *Variety,* 4 June 1980, 20.
163. Joseph Murrells, 486.
164. *Variety,* 13 August 1980, 26.
165. For an explanation of special effects in *Xanadu* see R. Greenberg, "Building Unique Special Effects for 'Xanadu,' " *American Cinematographer,* August 1980, 820-25.
166. Janet Maslin, "Movie: Miss Newton-John in 'Xanadu,' " *New York Times,* 9 August 1980, 10; review of 'Xanadu,' *Variety,* 13 August 1980, 24. See also David Ansen, "Oh, Shut Up, Muse," *Newsweek,* 18 August 1980, 85.
167. Tony Schwartz with Martin Kasindorf, "Stigwood's Midas Touch," 40; "Supermogul In The Land Of Opportunity," 42.
168. Quoted in "AFD Hands Exhibs 25-City 'Sneak' for 'Times Square,' Bow," *Variety* 10 September 1980: 3 and 50.
169. David Ansen, "Pied Pipers of Punk," *Newsweek,* 3 November 1980, 92; David Denby, "Desert Song," *New York,* 3 November 1980, 84; Carrie Rickey, "Soft Corps on 42nd Street,' *Village Voice,* 15 October 1980, 50.
170. Janet Maslin, "Screen: More 'Grease,' " *New York Times,* 11 June 1982, C10; David Ansen, "Return to Rydell High," *Newsweek,* 14 June 1982, 88; Richard Schickel, "Teeny Bombers," *Time,* 21 June 1982, 74.
171. J. Hoberman, "Their Big Break," *Village Voice,* 19 June 1984, 53.
172. Crispin Cioe, "The Real Jam Masters," *High Fidelity,* June 1984, 78.
173. David Denby, "Movies: The Entertainers," *New York,* 12 December 1983, 90.
174. Quoted in Karen Jaehne, "Charles Ahearn: *Wild Style," Film Quarterly,* Summer 1984, 2.
175. Quoted in Harlan Jacobson, "Wild Style (interview with Charles Ahearn)," *Film Comment* May–June 1983, 66.
176. *Variety,* 9 May 1984, 526; J. Hoberman, "Alphabet Soup," *Village Voice,* 15 May 1984, 56.
177. *Variety,* 23 May 1984, 26.
178. Quoted in "Crossover Eyed for 'Beat Street,' " *Billboard,* 7 April 1984, 66.
179. *Ibid.*
180. Janet Maslin, "Screen: 'Breakin' 2,' " *New York Times,* 19 December 1984, C-22; *Variety,* 19 December 1984, 19.
181. Quoted in Phil DiMauro, "Schultz Lensed 'Groove' In 26 Days For $3,000,000," *Variety,* 6 November 1985, 7.
182. *Variety,* 30 October 1985, 22.
183. Quoted in Phil DiMauro, "Schultz Lensed 'Groove', 38.
184. Janet Maslin, "Film: 'Krush Groove,' By Michael Schultz," *New York Times,* 25 October 1985, C8; *Time,* 18 November 1985, 94.
185. Gretchen Morgenson, "Fancy Dancing," *Forbes,* 21 September 1987, 194.
186. William Harris, "Lights, camera, lawyers!" *Forbes,* 10 August 1987, 33. The case with Hemdale dragged through 1987 and was finally settled out of court

in January 1988. Vestron reportedly received $15.7 million from Hemdale and rights to the production company's *Bestseller;* Time Inc.'s Home Box Office was given videocassette distribution rights for *Platoon* and *Hoosiers.* See "Time's HBO Settles Suit Over Video Cassette Sales," *Wall Street Journal,* 18 January 1988, 20.

187. James Greenberg, " 'Dancing' No Dirty Word At Vestron; First Hit Fuels More," *Variety,* 16 September 1987, 6.
188. Stephen Holden, "The Pop Life," *New York Times,* 9 December 1987, C33. Subsequent Vestron offerings were not nearly as successful as *Dirty Dancing.* As a result, Vestron shut down its filmmaking division in 1989. Harriet Johnson Brackey, "Big losses star in Vestron script," *USA Today,* 22 August 1989, 3B.
189. Quoted in Gretchen Morgenson, "Fancy Dancing," *Forbes,* 21 September 1987, 194.
190. Quoted in Samuel G. Freeman, " 'Dirty Dancing' Rocks to an Innocent Beat," *New York Times,* 16 August 1987, sec. 2, 19.
191. *Ibid.,* 20.
192. Quoted in Lawrence Van Gelder, "At the Movies," *New York Times,* 21 August 1987, C6.
193. Quoted in Aljean Harmetz, "Moving Up To 'Pretty' Roles," *New York Times,* 28 August 1987, C14.
194. *Ibid.*
195. "Erotic Floorplay," *Life,* October 1987, 6.
196. Jon Bowermaster, "The 'Dirty Dancing' Music Man," *Premiere,* August 1988, 90.
197. *Ibid.,* 92.
198. Quoted in Stephen Holden, "The Pop Life," *New York Times,* 9 December 1987, C33.
199. Quoted in Jon Bowermaster, 91.
200. Quoted in Stephen Holden, "The Pop Life," C33.
201. Quoted in Jon Bowermaster, 91.
202. Quoted in Jon Bowermaster, 92.
203. *Ibid.*
204. Quoted in Fred Bronson, 683.
205. Stephen Holden, "The Pop Life," C33.
206. Adam White, " 'Dirty Dancing' sountrack proves a left-field hit," *Rolling Stone,* 25 February 1988, 15.
207. Quoted in Jean Rosenbluth, "Sounstracks," *Billboard,* 16 July 1988, S1.
208. Quoted in Jon Bowermaster, 92.
209. Quoted in Ken Terry, " 'Dirty Dancing': Giant Killer Still Has Legs," *Billboard,* 16 January 1988, 3.
210. Quoted in Adam White, " 'Dirty Dancing' soundtrack," 15.
211. Quoted in Stephen Holden, "The Pop Life," C33.
212. Quoted in Ken Terry, " 'Dirty Dancing': Giant Killer," 67.
213. *Ibid.*
214. Richard Schickel, "Teenage Turmoil," *Time,* 14 September 1987, 77; David Ansen, "An August Heat Wave," *Newsweek,* 24 August 1987, 60; Vincent Canby, "Film: 'Dirty Dancing,' A Catskills Romance in 1963," *New York Times,* 21 August 1987, C3.

215. Vincent Canby, "Film: 'Dirty Dancing,' ", C3.
216. David Denby, "The Princess and the Peon," *New York,* 7 September 1987, 60.
217. Charles Leerhsen with Tessa Namuth, "Getting Down and Dirty," *Newsweek,* 21 December 1987, 63.
218. *Ibid.*
219. *Ibid.*
220. *Ibid.*
221. *Variety,* 20 May 1987, 104; David Denby, "The Princess and the Peon," 61.
222. Quoted in Ken Terry, " 'Dirty Dancing': Giant Killer," 3.
223. Tom Bierbaum, "Nestle To Have Upfront Ad Spot In Vestron's 'Dirty Dancing,' Vid," *Variety,* 30 December 1987, 21.
224. *Ibid. Dirty Dancing* was one of seventeen titles Vestron discounted at $24.98 in August 1988. See Stephen Advokat, " 'Cinderella' joins the discount list," *Channels: The Beacon Journal's TV Magazine,* 21–27 August 1988, 25.
225. The other three titles were *Platoon, Robocop,* and *Predator.* See Tom Bierbaum, "Four Homevid Titles in January Outperfomed Any 1987 Release," *Variety,* 17 February 1988, 165; Al Stewart, "Video Suppliers In Clover," *Billboard,* 13 February 1988, 1, 80.
226. Quoted in Bruce Haring, "RCA Releases 'More Dirty Dancing,' " *Billboard,* 12 March 1988, 67.
227. RCA Records Press Release, 23 May 1988.
228. David Wild, " 'Dirty Dancing,' spin-off tour opens in Catskills," *Rolling Stone* 18–28 July 1988, 30.
229. *Variety,* 9 November 1988, 43.
230. David Lieberman, "Now Playing: The Sound of Money," *Business Week,* 15 August 1988, 86.

5

Post-Fever Blues

After Saturday Night Fever *there was a flira-
tion with the music business. But there was a
series of flops. And, by the early '80s, the
movie business had pretty much decided that
we were all a waste of time.*
— Danny Goldberg, music supervisor

By the 1980s, the record industry's days of wine and roses were over.
Columbia Records' Robert Altshuler observed, "Everything was bigger
and better for 20 years. Now, the day of reckoning has come."[1] Thanks to
RSO, 1978 was the industry's peak, with shipments of 726.2 million units
and a gross of $4.13 billion. A year later, the unit figure dipped to 701
million, with a cash intake of $3.68 billion. While it was still surpassing
competitors in the quest for discretionary media dollars, the music industry was uneasy. Disco failed to dent the hardcore rock market. *SNF*,
according to observers, was a unique event appealling to one-time record
buyers. "Disco sucks" banners proliferated in 1979, as Dire Straits and
Rickie Lee Jones replaced The Village People and Evelyn "Champagne"
King as *Billboard*'s "Newcomer champs." Paul Grein described 1979 as
"the year of change in popular music,"[2] an understatement, as unit sales
would drop by twenty-five million copies.

In summer 1980, *Billboard* labelled the decade opener the "Year of the
Soundtrack." The sheer volume of entries, around forty titles, appeared
to lend support to the hyperbole.

One Casablanca executive predicted a glut. "It looks like there's going
to be two or three real big ones," said Bruce Bird.[3] He proved prophetic
as only four platinum certifications were awarded to soundtrack albums.
Honeysuckle Rose and *Urban Cowboy* were crossover, or progressive

country. *Xanadu* and *The Rose* (1979) at best gave a nod to the pop/rock genre. (*Fame*, a 1980 product, would be certified in 1981). *American Gigolo*, buoyed by Blondie's Number One single, "Call Me," and *The Empire Strikes Back* both exceeded the 500,000 sales required for a gold plaque. Nineteen-eighty may have been labelled, *vis a vis* soundtracks, "The Year of Great Expectation"—and shattered dreams.

Hustling the Rich and Famous: American Gigolo

Paul Schrader, the writer of *Taxi Driver*, presented the screenplay *American Gigolo* to Paramount (with John Travolta scheduled to star) in 1978. The studio agreed to a $10 million budget. Travolta chickened out. "John liked the title, liked the clothes, liked the posters, but he was afraid he would fall on his face," the director said. "When *Moment by Moment* failed, he was just too damned scared it would happen again."[4]

Richard Gere, who had appeared in *Looking For Mr. Goodbar* (1977) accepted the role. "I had enough offers to play Italian crazies for the next fifteen years," the actor said. "The bastards want to put you in a box with a label on it and crush it. If you have any hope of growing, of being taken seriously, you have to control the vultures."[5] The film was shot in some of the most posh milieus in Lotusland, including Palm Springs, choice property in Malibu, and the Beverly Hills Hilton.

Giorgio Moroder (*Midnight Express*) was signed to do the score. Moroder originally pitched the opening theme to Stevie Nicks; when she declined he sought out Deborah Harry. The result was "Call Me" put to Moroder's instrumental.

Harry's theme deviated from the traditional Blondie sound. "We really tried to vary our music and we really tried not to mimic ourselves," she explained. "Once you sort of establish a formula, (some people) stick with it because it's safe and people know and like it. We tried to be a little daring.[6] The result was a chart topper. Record industry observers would later say that the film should have been titled "Call Me" as the disk reportedly out-performed the film.

In some instances the backstage machinations involving *Gigolo* surpassed the project's storyline. Finding a singer to do the opening theme was a problem. The marketing strategy was uncertain and unorthodox. Director Schrader objected to the "terrible" trailers (The print was made from uncut negatives, out of sync with the soundtrack) and he was given an additional $15,000 for a new coming attractions bite.

Release dates became a problem. The production was originally set to debut in a New York City art house, but Paramount later decided on a blanket national release. Veteran Leo Greenfield, formerly of Warner's and MGM, told *Variety* that Frank Mancuso "figured that the adult audience would be *starving* for a new picture by the beginning of February, and that he'd be the only one in there. It was risky, it was daring, and it worked."[7]

The studio played heavily on Richard Gere as sex object. Eddie Kalish, Paramount marketing vice president, said, "we went heavily on soaps and game shows with our spots, which isn't done very often nowadays. The common belief is that men make movie-going decisions and that there's no longer a 'women's market' per se. But our audience surveys show we were right. Women come in groups to *Gigolo*."[8] The marketing ploys were not as fruitful as anticipated. As the studio's returns sagged, projection fees were raised to the dismay of exhibitors.

Blondie's "Call Me" charted at Number 80 two weeks after the film debut. The same week, *Billboard* described the single as a "sizzling theme song [that] rates as one of Blondie's better efforts. Deborah Harry's sultry vocal is pitted against the band's harmonies and a pulsating backbeat."[9]

The album was recognized in the trades two weeks after the film's release. *Billboard* gave the offering a polite, but indecisive endorsement. "Call Me" is one of Blondie's best yet.[10] The Polydor package charted at Number 112 on March 1.

The film opened on more than 500 screens nationally the first day of February, following an old adage in the film industry, "when unsure of a movie, shotgun it before word-of-mouth begins."

The Jerry Bruckheimer production opens with Julian Kay (Richard Gere) racing his black Mercedes 450SL down a picturesque Southern California highway. Blondie's "Call Me" reverberates in the background. The self-styled "translator, guide, and chauffeur," actually a high-priced male stud for bored upper-class matrons, commences his tour of the haunts of the rich and the famous. His appointments become a travelogue, ranging from Malibu to Rodeo Drive, from Chansen's to the Polo Lounge—"where the famous people go"—to Westwood to Palm Springs, where the story, however shallow, finally begins. "The plot, such as it is, takes a long time developing, and the hard-core audience for this kind of come-on may grow restive," Sarris understated. Canby was more direct: "The early part of the movie is a lot like thumbing through a magazine at the barbershop."[11]

At the Polo Lounge, Julian encounters Michelle Stratton (Lauren Hutton) who slowly comes on to him—"There's an international language." Uncharacteristically, he declines.

Leon James, a pimp, asks Julian to service a wealthy Palm Springs client as a special favor. The drive into the desert provides Moroder with another syntho-instrumental opportunity. (Synthesized music, in this movie, accompanies Julian's every road trip.) The client, Judy Rheiman (Patti Carr), and her voyeuristic spouse are into S & M—"rough trade." Kay complies despite his assertion that he doesn't do "kinky sex."

Returning to his *Playboy* like apartment and *GQ*-type wardrobe, the hustler finds the persistent Michelle ringing the doorbell. They make love. The next day Julian finds Judy's picture in the paper—she had been raped and murdered. Back at the Polo Lounge, Detective Sunday (Hector Elizondo), a disheveled Columbo type, questions Julian. The hustler offers a phony alibi. Things begin to unravel as Michelle proves to be the disenchanted wife of a prominent California politician and Sunday chooses Julian as his prime suspect in the Rheiman homicide. Julian seeks to discover who is trying to frame him. Only Michelle, growing fond of the hustler, believes he is innocent.

Searching for an alibi, Julian travels to Los Angeles's seamier side to find Leon in a "rough trade" gay bar. Cheryl Barnes's "Love and Passion" resounds. (This sequence could easily have been clipped from Schrader's *Hardcore* (1979).) In return for the exclusive use of his "services," Leon suggests that he might help.

Later, Julian sees Leon's gay lover in his garage. Transforming his apartment into an expensive pile of rubble, Julian locates Mrs. Rheiman's incriminating jewelry obviously planted, to more "Night Driving" music. He confronts Leon with the gems. "Nobody cared about you," answers the procurer, "you were frameable." Leon, despite Julian's futile attempt to prevent it, falls to the cement below. (The reason for this episode is never made clear.) Julian is arrested and charged. At this juncture, suggests McCarthy, "audience sympathy diminishes in inverse ratio to [the] extent [the] plot forces emotional investment in the character's destiny."[12]

"He surfaces behind bars a changed man after Hutton provides a scandalous alibi that frees him of the murder rap," summarized the *Film Journal* review. "It took so long to come to you," confesses Julian. "It's assumed they'll live happily or at least make love frequently every after," according to the *Journal* contributor. Schickel also objected to the conclusion. "Having spent almost two hours getting Julian into a tight corner, Schrader cannot bear to leave him there," he wrote. "The picture ends with a cockamamie implication that love will conquer all—even the false, but seemingly air tight, murder rap,"[13]

Reviewers found myriad blemishes in the film. The pacing, plot, direction, and star, Richard Gere, were all fair game. "We aren't supposed to identify with *American Gigolo*," noted Sterritt. "Rather we are supposed to keep our distance, to think about the story, not be seduced by it. That's why the plot moves so slowly, and the leading actors do so little acting.'' Champlin characterized the picture as ''an improbable tissue of fantasies and dime-novel borrowings that from moment to moment it seems to be making fun of itself, although the joke is disguised perfectly.'' ''The film is about the guilty obsessions of a filmmaker who seems incapable of giving pleasure to an audience,'' contended Ansen.[14]

Gere, without much of a role, took a number of shots. Schickel called him ''essentially a boring actor.'' Ansen considered him ''a 'star' with a fatal lack of personality.'' Canby said, ''Mr. Gere stands in front of the camera, but when the film is developed, the essential image has vanished.''[15]

Negative media barely dented the first week's box office. Playing in more than 500 theaters, *Gigolo* returned $1.8 million to the studio. By its third week, the figure had increased to $4.4 million. The final count was $11.5 million and a lucrative $6-million, exclusive deal with ABC-TV. The success of the movie was credited to its popularity among women. David Denby, with the aid of market research, understood the demographic impact. ''Men are angry,'' he wrote, ''precisely because the whole media culture tells them that they should be attentive to women, sexually pleasing to women, and so on, and in fact they don't know what to do with women a lot of the time.''[16] Julian Kay fulfilled the fantasies of many neglected spouses and aspirants.

Gigolo's modest box office achievement had little connection with the single, released February 1, or the album, issued a month later. The package's gold status can be attributed to the album's value as a souvenir of the movie. Had Gigolo been labeled ''Call Me'' perhaps the connection would have been made.

''Are Your Sure Stigwood Done It This Way?'': Roadie

Robert Stigwood proved a rock entrepreneur could earn megabucks with motion pictures even if the movies were box office disasters. *Sgt. Pepper* failed to return its costs, but the soundtrack more than made up for that. Irving Azoff, repeated the feat with *FM*, and Shep Gordon's Alive Enterprises, with clients such as Alice Cooper and Deborah Harry, entered the sweepstakes, hoping to replicate the success of *SNF* or at least *FM* with *Roadie*. ''The *Roadie* soundtrack was put together,'' said Gordon, ''. . . to exist independently from the film and independently from the single.''[17] *Footloose*'s Dean Pitchford would later observe, ''In the period between *Fever* and the present there was a whole spate of what I call sound-tracks-in-search-of-movies, where a lot of songs are gathered together, like *Roadie*, which had no reason for its existence except for the fact it showcased a number of rock performers: Alice Cooper, Meat Loaf, Blondie.''[18]

Alive Enterprises chose a short story by journalist Big Boy Medlin that concerned the trials and tribulations of life on a cross-country rock tour. Medlin collaborated with film critic Michael Ventura (*L.A. Weekly*) on the screenplay for *Roadie*. ''We realized we were making a film, the backdrop of which was the life we knew—rock'n'roll. All of our lives at Alive have dealt with life on the road. That's what we know. So the backdrop, usually just a toss-away, became really important, and the credibility of it became really important,'' noted Gordon.[19] Carolyn Pfeiffer of Alive Enterprises would produce and Alan Rudolph (*Welcome to L.A.* and *Remember My Name*) who had good notices despite disappointing box office, was given the director's chair.

Roadie is a direct descendent of Frank Tashlin's satire, *The Girl Can't Help It* (1956). Tashlin's showcase found Tom Ewell portraying a talent agent wandering from nightclub to rehearsal hall and visiting recording studios in order to promote a reluctant client, Jayne Mansfield. At each stop rock artists perform their biggest hits. In *Roadie*, Meat Loaf is the unifying thread, showcasing Alive Enterprises' clients. Deborah Harry covers Johnny Cash's ''Ring of Fire'' and Alice Cooper is highlighted at Madison Square Garden. The project is more style than substance reminiscent of the black-and-white Grade-Bs of the 1950s, in which Sam Katzman and Roger Corman employed wafer-thin plots to provide musical interludes.

Award-winning record producer Bones Howe was signed in August 1979, two months prior to the 20 October starting date. He would later explain, ''By bringing me into the film, they have created another station in the production nucleus. I just wish I had been there six months earlier, when they were still writing the script.''[20] This statement, made several months prior to the film's release, would be clarified by the media.

Meat Loaf, born Marvin Lee Aday, was contracted for the title role. Many observers were surprised by the selection. The 260-pound singer was best known for the platinum album *Bat Out of Hell*. He had, however, a long list of acting credits, ranging from off-Broadway's *Rainbow in New York* to the spacey biker in *The Rocky Horror Show*. In *Roadie*, Kaki Hunter was employed as Meat Loaf's star-struck romantic foil. The $5-million production was scheduled for a nine-week shoot in New York, Los Angeles, and Austin, Texas.

In the post-production phase the sixteen-song, two-record soundtrack was compiled, with Howe as musical supervisor.

Gordon, Howe, and Steve Wax decided against the golden-oldie, superstar format. "As we started to package the album," recalled Gordon, "we realized it was really a series of major superstars. We decided we needed something fresh. I played Alan Rudolph a bunch of new groups Steve Wax and I liked. Alan liked Sue Saad and the Next and "Double Yellow Line" was written for a specific scene on the highway."

"Pat Benatar was very different," Gordon continued. "We needed a source song. Everybody here in our office really believed in Pat Benatar. Chrysalis was very anxious for her to participate in the film . . . Freshness gives it that edge, as do the magical combinations we went for." Gordon prophetically observed, "There are great possibilities for magical duets to do soundtracks."[21] This was two years before *An Officer and a Gentleman.*

Warner Brothers distributed the package. The movie's scout single arrived at radio stations in mid-May entering the *Billboard* Hot 100 at Number 88 the week of 24 May. The film's street date was to be 13 June. The trade reviews emerged a week prior to the cinematic debut. *Billboard* greeted the offering with a qualified endorsement: "The diverse array of talent gives the package a potpourri feel with no unifying thread tying it together. Yet the performances are quite good and the mixed bag of rock and progressive country keeps the music stimulating." Gordon later admitted, "In sequencing the album, it became almost four distinct albums."[22] The label ran full-page color ads, using a line from the movie: "Bands Make It Rock, but the Roadies Make it Roll."

The film opened with Cheap Trick's "Everything Works If You Let It" playing as three armadillos scurry across a deserted Texas highway, emphasizing the rural roots of "Good ole boy" Travis W. Redfish (Meat Loaf) who shares a cabin with his backwoods, tinker-inventor father, Corpus C. (Art Carney). (Corpus has invented, among other things, a train which delivers drinks.) Travis has inherited the family capacity for mechanical innovation; he can repair anything.

This ability propels him into the zany world of rock tours, as he is summoned to repair a van containing Hank Williams, Jr.'s concert equipment. A devoted C&W fan, Travis is delighted. He connects with sixteen-year-old Lola Bouilliabase (Kaki Hunter), an aspiring groupie who is saving her Twiggy-like frame for Alice Cooper. (One of the few memorable exchanges in the movie is Travis's reaction to Alice. "Isn't she one of Charlie's Angels?" he asks. Lola snaps, "I can't believe you ain't never heard of Alice Cooper! Don't you read T-shirts!")

Infatuated with the teenager, Travis drives her to the Rock'n'Roll

Circus, whose equipment is also on the blink. (Throughout the film, millions of dollars in state-of-the-art electronic gear is in a constant state of disrepair. This is the backdrop of road life. Mr. Fix-It always comes to the rescue.) Promoter Mohammed Johnson (Don Cornelius of *Solid Gold*), seeing Travis as a portable repair shop, offers him a job as a driver-gofer-handyman, *ergo*, roadie. To accommodate Lola, Travis commits himself to the Circus and begins the cross-country migration to Pat Benatar's "You Better Run," Eddie Rabbitt's "Drivin' My Life Away" and Sue Saad and the Next's "Double Yellow Line." Although these songs are hardly in the same league with those Steppenwolf or the Byrds used in *Easy Rider,* the intent is the same. The film provides detours for barroom brawls and high speed chases; Austins' main traffic artery provides a drag strip. Corliss described these diversions as "live action *Road Runner* cartoons and the added exuberant bad taste of Russ Meyer's redneck sex movies."[23]

Travis's attempts to bed Lola are frustrated because "she's saving herself for Alice." The rock version of Home Handyman eventually encounters Alice, who is having—naturally—equipment malfunctions. Travis arranges a *quid pro quo* with Cooper: For a bus ticket back to Texas, plus the satisfying of Lola's sexual fantasy, the concert will go on. As the tour ends, Lola experiences reality, shedding her aspirations, and her dreams of Alice. At heart, she's a good ole girl and Travis is a good ole boy.

The sparse number of print reviews were contradictory. *Variety*'s preview assessment indicated the film had limited appeal, but "it should please enough teens and music fans to perform solidly during the summer months." *Time*'s Corliss concurred: "*Roadie* is still the weirdest, funniest movie of the summer, with the genuine energy of good pop music." Tom Allen insisted, "Roadie is one of the true comic surprises of the year."[24]

However, many reviewers dissented. "*Roadie* is supposed to be funny, or at least lively, or a least 'way out front in the rock-and-roll vanguard. It succeeds on none of these scores," wrote Maslin, who dubbed the sound-track "an ear-splitting, but otherwise unremarkable musical backdrop." Tom Mline objected to the treatment of rock 'n' roll "in such a crude and conventionally exploitative manner." "Like the Redfish family motto, 'It'll work if you let it,' we wished that we could or that it [the film] did," reported Keneas.[25] The *Film Journal*'s Perchaluk, among others, lamented, "*Roadie* might have amounted to something more than an advertisement for a soundtrack." It didn't. Sterritt found the movie as "Just a teaser for that all-important record," which was precisely what it was.[25]

Roadie opened in mid-June in ninety-two theaters. The first week it returned a meager $395,709. By its third, and last, week it was on sixteen screens with only $569,377 in studio earnings. By July 9, *Roadie* had completed its first run.

The film was reissued in August with a wider distribution, but its year-end return was a disappointing $1.4 million. The second run did nothing for the album—it found little favor with critics or record buyers. The album did poorly, climbing to Number 108. Its chart life was twice that of the film. The singles by Cheap Trick plus Orbison/Harris did better, and remained on the charts longer than the film remained in theaters. The scout, "Everything Works If You Let It," peaked at Number 44. "That Lovin' You Feelin' Again," issued June 28, reached Number 55, but went on to win a Grammy in the C&W category.

Steve Wax told an interviewer, "For *Roadie*, we used more pop-rock style which appeals to a broader audience."[27] *Rolling Stone* found the attempt to court "a broader audience" resulted in a "rotten" collection. Steve Holden, especially, objected to the inclusion of Alive client Alice Cooper. "Indicative of the filmmakers' stupidity," he wrote, "is their decision that Cooper, whose grand style of purile *Grand Guignol* has been passe for years, be trotted out as a rock icon, comic or otherwise." Holden did not pull any punches. "*Roadie* is just a hodgepodge—rock & roll, country music, a little R&B—that's weakest where it should be strongest."[28] *Roadie*'s fatal flaw was its attempt to reach a broad audience, throwing targeting aside. (Most rock music fans prefer certain substreams within the genre.) The consensus rockers, the superstars, were notably absent from the compilation.

The introduction of country music into the mix further complicated matters. The prominence of Deborah Harry's version of "Ring of Fire" in the film turned off country fans. Rockers no doubt were not thrilled with Eddie Rabbitt. The occasional C&W maven stumbling into the theater would have a hard time with Alice Cooper's "Pain."

The entire cross-cultural premise of the movie and the album, whichever came first, just didn't work. *Fever* and *FM* were marketed to specific demographic units—the disco and AOR audiences. *Fever*'s crossover was an unexpected bonus; *FM*'s title virtually guaranteed the package AOR exposure. Alive Enterprises appears to have missed these lessons.

A $37-Million Mission From God: The Blues Brothers

John Belushi and Dan Aykroyd, more equal than others on *Saturday Night Live*, introduced the characters Jake and Elwood Blues on the show. The comic team had independent versions of their creation: Belushi claimed to have discovered Chicago and Memphis soul while on location filming *Animal House*; Aykroyd insisted he converted brother Jake's ears with a rendition of James Cotton's "Rocket 88." (The song, generally attributed to Jackie Brenston, was later covered by Bill Haley and The Saddlemen).

The Blues Brothers were inserted into *SNL* and earned highly appreciative reactions to their material, such as Floyd Dickson's "Hey Bartender." In the late summer of 1978, the duo served as the warm-up act for Steve Martin at the Universal amphitheater. Reviews and word-of-mouth were uniformly positive, and the duo's manager pitched them to Universal Pictures.

As Universal's Sean Daniel recalled, "Those guys were bloody meat in shark-infested water. . . . we wasted no time in making a deal." The decision appeared sound, as the Blues Brothers' LP *Briefcase of Blues* sold two million copies. Aykroyd then delivered a 324-page movie script to director John Landis. The material was "pared" down into a "clean, streamlined" storyline.

In August 1979, Landis, actors, and crew invaded Chicago. Abe Peck of the *Chicago Sun Times* described the filming as akin to the way "Sherman went through Georgia."[29] With the picture half-finished in October, Landis had spent $10 million of the $12 million originally budgeted.

The situation was further complicated by the box office performance of Steven Spielberg's *1941*, which starred Aykroyd, Belushi, and Ned Beatty. Critics lambasted the movie. Universal-Columbia Pictures, despite a massive publicity campaign, failed to recoup their $27 million investment. The joint venture provided a $23.4-million split. Displeased with *1941*, Universal began to pressure Landis, who told Abe Peck, "I think a lot of it is that I am twenty-nine. That *Animal House* came from nowhere and was a huge success. That John Belushi is a major star and doesn't go on the Johnny Carson show. Everything you've heard about Hollywood is true. People are basically petty and jealous." The director defended his $30-million expenditure. "The $30 million that *Apocalypse* cost two years ago is now $50 million," he said. "It's a reality."[30] Landis's inflationary rate was disputed. Moreover, comparing *Blues Brothers* to the Coppola epic was a bit much.

Universal's Sean Daniel attempted to put the best face on the cost overruns. "When you have an army this size," he said, "every overage is multiplied a hundred-fold." Furthermore, "It really and truly was not out of control," he maintained. "It's not a situation in which everyone had the impression that they were making a small movie and came up with a giant, endless movie.[31] The costs were sizable. Band members and guest artists earned unheard-of salaries of over $70,000 each. "Each cost us 120 grand," noted executive producer Bernie Brillstein, "and when do you hear that for a musician making his first film?"[32] The stars shared a more than $10 million advance, based on a verbal agreement.

The two-hour, thirty-nine minute film was deemed "endless" by bookers and exhibitors. Landis, forced to trim it to 133 minutes, cut a gas-station explosion and yet another car crash.

Promotion for the project ran into difficulties. In March 1980 Universal announced plans for a lavish Chicago premiere in Mid-June. Some twenty-five film critics were to be junketed into the Windy City for a week of hype, interviews, screenings, and *La Dolce Vita*. Universal's costs were estimated at $200,000. The last week of May, Universal abruptly cancelled the affair, as things were getting out of hand; the studio announced a $50,000 donation to Chicago charities instead. Brillstein believed there was more to the cancellation than mere confusion. Universal executives, he contended, "did not understand the movie." He commended Sean Daniel for being the only studio person who understood. "He made that film happen," Brillstein said. "Notice you didn't see them [Universal executives] at the premiere," he told *Billboard*.[33]

Record company support proved minimal. The scout single entered the *Billboard* listing at Number 81 two weeks before the film's debut: "Gimme Some Love" was a Stevie Winwood piece popularized by The Spencer Davis Group in 1966. The album was spotlighted June 21, *after* the picture's first weekend. A reviewer said, "With a film tie-in like this, the second Blues Brothers LP may probably do as well as the first, which made it to the top of the charts." It also went double platinum. "This LP can stand on its own, even without the new film," concluded the notice. Atlantic Records and Universal Pictures did little to coordinate their promotional efforts, as the first album promised some follow-up sales (and there was always *SNL* in constant reruns.) Still, as Brillstein noted, "Three million people buying a Blues Brothers' LP is not enough to make a $27-million movie work."[34]

The film appeared June 20 and earned $4.66 million in three days. The amount jumped to $13 million for its first ten days.

The film begins with a helicopter pan shot of the Illinois State Penitentiary. Guard dogs bark. An American flag is raised, topping a barbed-wire, chain-link fence. This is the release date of "Joliet" Jake (John Belushi). Elwood (Dan Aykroyd) awaits his brother in the Bluesmobile, a 1974 Dodge Monaco 440. "My own brother picks me up in a police car," objects Jake. "She Caught the Katy" greets the freed convict as a glowing white light surrounds the prison.

The brothers reunite with sadistic Sister Mary Stigmata, "The Penguin" (Kathleen Freeman), who needs $5,000 to save her orphanage. Due to their "bad attitudes" she whips them, literally, out of the shabby building. They then begin their tour of musical opportunities, first visiting with Cab Calloway, the building superintendent, who had first turned the brothers on to blues. The brothers encounter the "jive-assed preacher" Cleophus James (James Brown). As James rants, Jake, uncomfortable, stares at his watch. Brown moves the assembled congregation with a stirring "The Old Landmark" (an obvious showcase device). The worshippers move to the music in a highly choreographed number. Jake is possessed; Elwood follows. Divine light embraces the church. "I'm on a mission from God," exclaims Jake. His euphoria is interrupted by Sam and Dave's "Soul Man." Inspired, Jake becomes determined to reunite his old blues band. However, Elwood's abysmal driving record finds the duo escaping from the law, beginning a series of interminable auto-chase sequences that culminate in the destruction of a shopping mall. It is tiresome, though many teenagers who were unaware of the *French Connection* thought the action "neat." "It destroys more real property than any other event since the bombing of Dresden," wrote Champlin, "all by itself it solves Detroit's inventory problem by totaling enough automobiles to transport four Army divisions and the cast of *Ben Hur*." "If all the cars that were trashed in this movie were Chryslers, the company wouldn't need a Federal loan," indicated Ansen. *Time*'s Corliss saw the highway carnage as symbolic of the entire production. "More noise, more car crashes," he wrote. "Alas, more is less, and *The Blues Brothers* ends up totaling itself." Sarris concurred. "All the 'energy' has gone into the car crashes, and all of the talent has gone into musical numbers. The rest is undeveloped drivel." *The Nation* saw the car pursuits as "A parody of a parody, being yet another point of gargantuan destruction that for some time has been Hollywood's way of commenting on its own taste for violence."[35] Assuring the audience that this is only the beginning, a frustrated state trooper promises, "I'll catch that sucker if that's the last thing I ever do."

The plot thickens as the duo attempts to reassemble their band. A mystery woman (Carrie Fischer), an old flame, attempts to waste Jake (to the brief, misplaced strains of "The Peter Gunn Theme.") The L train passes as the lady attempts to blow up the siblings.

In the quest to find ex-band members, various antagonists (and skits) are introduced. Neo-Nazis led by Sommerlier (Henry Gibson) are confronted by the dynamic duo. A brief encounter with legendary bluesman John Lee Hooker follows. They manage to find Aretha Franklin, officially described as "the soul-food cafe owner," who belts out "Think," *the* memorable song from the motion picture. (Aretha's short-order cook is an ex-band member.) The growing ensemble then invades a pawnshop owned by Ray Charles. A band member sets up *the* scene: Commenting on a piano, he says, "There's no action left in this key." Faster than one can say "Shake Your Tailfeather," Charles is pounding the keyboard doing the song. The mystery woman reappears to fire-blast the band. Naturally, they escape.

The Blues Brothers arrive at their first gig. "Your Cheating Heart" greets the band as they enter Bob's Country Bunker, a prototypical redneck bar. "This has to be some kind of mistake," someone says. "What kind of music do you have here?" Elwood asks the bartender. "We have both kinds," answers the man, "country and western." The room fills. The blues notes coming from behind the stage's chicken wire are met with flying bottles. The band switch to "Rawhide" and then Tammy Wynette's "Stand By Your Man." The off-key rendition is welcomed with thunderous applause, suggesting C&W fans have no taste. (The slight goes further when the Good Ole Boys, a Nashville band, are presented in the most negative of terms. The country musicians, armed, pursue the transplanted bluesman. The highway patrol joins in—"That shitbox Dodge, again.")

The end is close at hand as Landis injects an Andy-Hardy type finale: "Let's have a show." The event is to be staged at the Palace Hotel Ballroom. On the way, to heighten what little suspense there is, the Dodge runs out of gas.

To the shouts of "We want Soul," Cab Calloway fills in with a rousing "Minnie the Moucher," his signature song. (It is, of course, a production number.) Meanwhile, the pursued duo sneaks into the ballroom. They are met with silence, a setup for the closer. "Everybody Needs Somebody To Love" brings the house down. Jimmy Reed's "Sweet Home Chicago" evokes a similar reaction. Having their $5,000 fee in hand, the twosome exits, only to be greeted by their accumulated antagonists.

The mad woman confronts Jake with an M-16, screaming, "I remained celibate for you!" They reconcile as law-enforcement people, rednecks, C&W artists, Nazis, soldiers, and others appear. A superfluous and cliched car chase ensues. (Many of the freeway scenes were blatant lifts from *The French Connection*.) Only the amount of damage distinguishes this sequence from its predecessors. At this point the sight gags grow wearisome. All is well that ends well? Not quite. The actors, director, and studio officials were yet to be subjected to the press.

The good news came from *Billboard* and the *New York Post*. The music trade's Chris McGowan praised the film. "Belushi and Aykroyd display a

hilarious comedic presence, the script (by Landis and Aykroyd) is unremittingly funny and the music makes you want to get up and dance." "Let
me be frank," wrote Winsten, *"The Blues Brothers* is practically a
religious experience."[36] So much for the good news.

Remaining reviewers found little plot, meaning, or even civility in the
Landis project. The $30-million price tag brought the ire of several writers.
"What did all that money buy?" asked Maslin. "Scores of car chases. Too
many extras. Overstaged dance numbers. And a hollowness that certainly
didn't come cheap." Eva Zibart in *The Washington Post* also asked how
the stars could "have stretched an outworn *Saturday Night Live* into a
two and a half-hour, $30-million movie that earns its tantalizing R-rating
with a splattering of extraneous four-letter words?" Her answer was
"brass aplenty." Todd McCarthy observed the combined works of Laurel
and Hardy, Abott and Costello and The Marx Brothers cost less than *The
Blues Brothers*. A theme running through many critiques stressed the
notion that "less was better" without mentioning production costs.[37]

Several scribes made note of the similarity of the glossy production with
a hackneyed plot borrowed from the Andy Hardy and Katzman films.
Keneas: "The plot, of course, is an imitation of '40s Hollywood musicals
and '50s rock and roll B movies and no less silly as spoof." Graphically,
Paul Taylor described the motion picture as akin to "some expensively
pedigreed shaggy dog (meandering) through 70s/80s American cinema and
50s/60s American rock, cocking its leg happily at every popular landmark
on the way."[38]

A recurrent theme throughout most of the reviews, the most painful to
Belushi and Aykroyd, was that the artists were exploiting the blues and its
exponents. The argument is an old one, having surfaced in the Swing era
and the dawn of rock 'n' roll. Mick Jagger was roundly criticized for
covering Muddy Waters. John Hammond, Jr. and The Butterfield Blues
Band became the center of the "Can-a-white-man-sing-the-blues?" polemic.

One response was that visible white performers helped expose R&B and
blues to a market the authentic artists were unable to reach. The Crewcuts
and Pat Boone *did* help the integration of Fats Domino and *a cappella*
groups into the mainstream pop music charts. Hammond and others
opened up the folk music circuit to John Lee Hooker, Mance Lipscomb,
John Hurt, and Lightning Hopkins. Still, the argument has never been
resolved to anyone's satisfaction.

Pauline Kael found Landis's use of black artists "somewhat patronizing." Following this path, Denby wrote, "The Blues Brothers routine has
inhabited an uneasy region between parody and put-on." Others were

even less tolerant. The film, in a *Jump Cut* analysis, was "a reflection of the filters, distortions and censures that bourgeois ideology and bourgeois demands place[d] on blacks."[39]

Music writer Dave Marsh, long a foe of blue-eyed soul, objected that "The Blues Brothers pander to both nostalgia and the ignorant assumption that black popular culture is some sort of joke." He maintained, "Using black people to betray and exploit themselves isn't exactly a noble endeavor." A spokesperson for Alligator Records, the blues specialty label located in Chicago, characterized their artists' reaction as, "It's just another white band trying to rip off our music." Mindy Giles added, "The live thing really works. They've said from the stage, 'If you like us, go out and buy Muddy Waters,' and that's admirable."[40]

Belushi said he was "very bummed out. . . . made me think of something besides acting and being a celebrity." "Sure it [the criticism] bothers me," added Aykroyd. "It's too bad that they aren't buying Fenton Robinson and John Lee Hooker." But, "we haven't ripped anybody off. Everybody's been compensated. Actually we don't do a strict blues number. It's as bluesy as Wayne Cochran."[41] The controversy failed to harm or help the movie. For most filmgoers, the Blues Brothers' credentials in the music scene were deemed insignificant.

The film returned $32 million to Universal exceeding the box office take for *1941*. The break-even point had been projected to be $50 million. The personality vehicle, with outlandish production costs, unintentionally proved the Katzman philosophy—keep it cheap and simple—valid.

The RSO Backlash

Anticipating the nearly forty soundtracks due in the summer and fall of 1980, *Billboard*'s Paul Grein explained that the record industry, admittedly flat, saw the film studios as a much-needed source of marketing capital for the duration of "the tight money" situation. RSO's experience with *Fever* and *Grease*, neither of which garnered much AOR exposure, reminded the labels that double-record souvenir items were highly competitive titles. "Record companies," asserted Stephen Holden, "have found that they can reap huge profits with these inferior-quality packages because they have a ready-made merchandising tie-in." Casablanca Records president, Bruce Bird, disagreed. "There's a lot better music—it's definite—a helluva lot better music these days in motion pictures than before. The record companies are more involved in putting the artists on the soundtracks, and movie producers realize that they can make extra revenue by putting good artists and good songs in the movie, and that the record companies are going to get behind it and push it even harder.

The executive acknowledged that the studios' huge promotional budgets, by record-label standards, were welcome. "You're getting the expectation of a film that might have a $4-million budget for advertising alone. A $4-million budget for a record company to spend on an album—you'd be out of business quick. But for a soundtrack they [film studios] can do it."[42]

The motion picture studios are conservative to a fault. They frequently point to "big pictures" (those that were profitable) to justify a project; generic failures are ignored. For example, the Stigwood productions, musically driven, were justifications for more of the same, as were *The Electric Horseman* which grossed some $31 million and *Coal Miner's Daughter*, the Loretta Lynn bio, which returned $10 million more and earned gold certification. (Hit C&W albums rarely exceed 500,000 copies.)

As Robert Mercer of EMI Films, said, "If there's conjunctive promotion of films and albums, the result adds up to more than the sum of the parts.[43]

Al Coury, RSO Records chief, cautioned that timing was essential. He pointed to the disastrous *Sgt. Pepper's Lonely Hearts Club Band* (1978), whose record package had appeared four days before the Universal film. "The movie came out four days later," complained the record executive, "and died a horrible death, and the LP was dropped like it had leprosy. If I'd had the soundtrack six or seven weeks beforehand, it would have gotten great play and the people would have anticipated a great movie. The music would have helped the box office."

Irving Azoff, savoring the success of *FM*'s soundtrack even as the movie flopped, partially dissented. "It takes some time for people to get familiar with the songs, and six weeks seems about right for that," he said. "*But* you don't want the soundtrack to be old hat by the time the movie comes out."[44]

Neither executive challenged the RSO formula; both stressed the significance of timing and release dates. Warner/Elektra/Atlantic (WEA) International's late president, Nesuhi Ertegun, outlined the marketing strategy. "Essentially our New York office develops a general plan of all possible promotional tie-ins, often involving varied divisions of Warner Communications," he said. This plan, he went on, "is then discussed with the film distributor's foreign regional coordinators in terms of allocating responsibility and sharing costs.

"After this, our New York office sends a refined plan out to all concerned affiliates," he added. This approach, designed for global usage, was equally suitable for domestic service. Ertegun indicated that the ideal strategy was to release a scout single, followed by the album and then the movie. On paper, the blueprint appeared promising. Ten WEA titles would soon test the formula.[45]

David Sterritt pointed to the flaw in the blueprint. "Do the tactics of Top-40 radio have a happy effect on Hollywood?" he asked. "Clearly not. For proof, look at this season's musicals, which are a sorry lot by almost any standard."[46] Two of the filmwriter's main offenders were WEA productions, *The Blues Brothers* and *Roadie*.

Sterritt was correct. Those assembled soundtracks had little to do with their films' content. *Roadie*, a rock film, featured a soundtrack in which the most memorable titles were "That Lovin' You Feelin' Again" by Roy Orbison and Emmylou Harris and "Drivin' My Life Away" by Eddie Rabbitt.

Music critic Stephen Holden joined in the fray. The *New York Times* contributor agreed with Sterritt, but from a musical aesthetic. "Most of these soundtracks lack a conceptual center and instead rely on one or two hits surrounded by lots of filler," he wrote.[47]

With record sales falling, labels viewed these packages as outperforming a sluggish marketplace. Filmmakers remained silent on the issue of soundtracks. "In the old days," as Sterritt was quick to note, "a movie studio might try to earn extra money by marketing an album of soundtrack music. Nowadays, the process works in reverse."[48]

Fever and *Grease* had a profound impact on both media. The recession in the music industry was fueled by Christgau's Disco Disaster. With AOR stations retreating, en masse, from the musical sons and daughters of *Fever*, the labels lacked an alternative vehicle of exposure. They were left with the dwindling Top 40 audience.

The studios, wishing to hedge their corporate box office bets, found rock artists on soundtracks to be an insurance policy against theatrical flops. Film executives, however, had little awareness of their record-business counterparts. "The film companies have made rock the messiah," said Shep Gordon. "A movie like *Saturday Night Fever*," observed Danny Goldberg, "was the exception that proved the rule. There a record made people go see a movie. A unique case." Having seen *Can't Stop the Music* stall at Number 49 on the chart, Bird concurred, "I don't think we'll see a *Saturday Night Fever* again . . . for quite awhile."[49] The *SNF* model bordered on gospel in the film community. Labels were more than willing to exploit this conventional wisdom.

Acting on this perception, filmmakers increasingly sought out contemporary soundtracks. With few exceptions, most knew little about the uses of rock in cinema. They were, however, dissatisfied in the knowledge that albums frequently earned more than their pictures. This gave rise to a poorly specified occupational role: a liaison to bridge the gap between the two giant media. Most of the pioneers—Danny Goldberg, Becky Shargo, David Franco, John Brown, Shep Gordon, Irving Azoff, and Bones Howe—were music-business alumni. Howe, who produced the Association and The Fifth Dimension and worked on *Roadie*, acknowledged the murkiness of the new position. "In the vernacular of the record business, I'd be a producer," he said, "but I think we're going to have to invent a title. Music director, music producer, music supervisor, music coordinator—none of them is quite right. I'm defining this job as I do it." For *Roadie*, Howe was charged with obtaining clearances, music placements, and integrating rock into the movie.[50]

David Franco, calling himself "a movie music specialist," founded International Music Productions in fall 1979. His first assignment was *The Island* (1980), described as an "absolutely awful thriller" about a reporter investigating strange happenings in the Caribbean Islands.

Franco, formerly A&R director at RCA and WEA, perceived his role as putting together the correct film with the proper talent for the right price. "If a producer wants to spend $50,000 for music I'll set up a $50,000 package," he said.[51] Goldberg's duties were similar, but he called himself a consultant. Film and record people used the title "music supervisor." As rock soundtracks became legitimized in the 1980s, music supervisors developed loyalties to those who signed their checks. Most consultants were, at best, however, emotionally tied to the industry from which they came—music. The result was predictable. A number of artist with no FM exposure were included in films and soundtracks, and rejects from name artists also began to surface in movies.

The consultants were not entirely at fault, however. Studio heads longed for a repeat of *Fever* and were reinforced by some music writers. "Soundtrack Sales Good Despite LP Slump." This claim was spurious. Of the top 100 *Billboard* albums, only five were soundtracks. Six offerings received R.I.A.A. recognition. Two selections, *Fame* and *Urban Cowboy*, went platinum. *American Gigolo*, propelled by Blonde's Number-One single "Call Me," Bette Midler's Joplinesque *The Rose*, and *Coal Miner's Daughter* (country), and *The Empire Strikes Back* (symphonic) earned gold plaques.

Merchandisers resented soundtrack albums. "Every soundtrack that comes out is the next *Saturday Night Fever*," complained Flip-Side Records Carl Rosenbaum. "A lot of us were victims of a super-hype on the *Urban Cowboy* soundtrack."[52] The plethora of film packages merely took up valuable shelf space, the dealers asserted. Even successful soundtrack albums were seen as "one-shot" sales by very marginal product buyers. "At every garage sale, you'll find at least one copy of *Saturday Night Fever*," one dealer quipped, "and not much else."

One Trick Pony

As the "battle of the speeds" had illustrated, CBS played hardball with its major competitors. The rivalry between CBS and RCA Victor had spanned nearly half a century. By the mid-1970s, Warners had became CBS's chief antagonist. Warner Communications, Inc. (WCI) had temporarily lured Bob Dylan away from the Columbia label. In turn, James Taylor switched from Warners to CBS. In another CBS coup, Mick Jagger reportedly signed for $17 million. (The Stones' lead vocalist was previously distributed by WEA.)

A disgruntled Paul Simon was also up on the auction block in 1978. His divorce from CBS had hardly been amiable, and he sued the company for back royalties. The diskery was willing to let Simon go, as he had failed to produce an album since *Still Crazy After All These Years*, released in 1975. The departure cost Simon $1.5 million in back royalties. Simon's score for *The Graduate* had proved to be a highly successful first cinematic effort, and nearly a decade later Woody Allen had provided the songster with an acting debut, in *Annie Hall* (1978). (A cameo role followed in *All You Need is Cash* (1978), a Beatles' satire about a group called The Rutles.) "I wanted to do something other than just record an album," explained Simon. "I felt my choices were either to write a broadway show or a movie. I chose the movie because I thought it would be closer to the process of recording. . . . Also, I could still record and use the movie as a score."[53] Warner financed *One-Trick Pony* at $8 million. In light of *Roadie*'s box office, it was widely assumed the conglomerate was buying the soundtrack in the tradition of *A Hard Day's Night*.

A scout single, "Late in the Evening," surfaced in early August, almost two months before the film's appearnace. It reached a respectable Number 6 on *Billboard*'s Hot 100, enjoying a sixteen-week tenure. The title song, "One-Trick Pony," appeared the week of the film's debut. It would not rise beyond Number 40.

A six-week concert tour with a thirteen-piece band, was scheduled to promote the film. Simon acknowledged the tour was "virtually sold out and way in the red." The "red," was estimated to be around $300,000. As Dave Marsh observed, it was "not exactly economic good sense."[54]

The film experienced preview problems: Denver and New Haven found the original close confusing. (The initial version had the Simon character reconciling with his ex-wife, but retaining his mobile life style.) A new ending was filmed in fall 1979.

Savoring its roster addition, Warner's announced in bold print 30 August, "Paul Simon's First Album on Warner Bros. Records." Almost as an afterthought, in much smaller type the forthcoming film was mentioned. *Billboard* hailed the studio album as possessing "A dynamic and enriching rhythmic sound."[55]

One Trick Pony is introduced with "Late in the Evening," the scout single, with flashbacks to the 1968 Eugene McCarthy bid for the presidency. Jonah Levin (Paul Simon) is performing at a fund-raising benefit. Jonah is obviously a child of the 1960s, a point perhaps overstated throughout the film.

The storyline segues to Cleveland's Hopkins Airport and a $14.95-per-room Budget Motel, hardly up to high-rolling, record-industry standards. To further illustrate Jonah's decline, his band is playing at Cleveland's Agora, a hard-rock night club. They perform the title song to polite applause. Levin appears locked in a time warp, which provides the essential theme of the movie. "Every Rocker's Elvis Obsession seems to be the key to One-Trick Pony," observed Dave Marsh. "Certainly, it explains the character of Jonah Levin better than anything in the film."[56]

Having bedded a Janis Joplinesque groupie—"Rock'n'Roll is my life," she says—Jonah, the musical nomad, wanders the streets to the sounds of "Heart Approaches." He phones his estranged wife, Marion, insisting, sardonically, "I'm not dead. I'm in Cleveland." Marion (Blair Brown) underscores the vehicle's main thesis. As Maslin correctly observed, the "Domestic episodes run into trouble." Moreover, the picture "seems infinitely more comfortable when it confines itself to the foibles of the music world."[57]

The Brown character emphasizes, by inference, Jonah's 1960s fixation (she adopts an Earth Mother posture, talking to house plants.) She berates the musician for experiencing the "longest adolescence I've ever seen," charging that he had "gone straight from adolescence to middle age" and become a "grown man in a kids world." The *Kramer Vs. Kramer* aspect of the film, while occasionally charming—father and son baseball—begins to detract from the plot. Simon's early mid-life crisis (he's thirty-four) is unpersuasive.

The basic storyline resumes when Jonah faces record-label president Walter Fox (Rip Torn) and promo man Cal Van Damp (Allen Goorwitz). The label's motto is: "Twenty years of AM music," but Levin's material is hardly Top-40 fare. His "Ace in the Hole" is auditioned to less-than-enthusiastic executives: Fox politely responds, "It's pretty, but Top 40 is getting much more sophisticated for a ballad to make it." Having bragged about his credentials, Van Damp lectures, "If you don't have a hook, you're at an incredible disadvantage these days in Top 40." Defending his song, Jonah alludes to Albert Schweitzer. Cal asks, "What label was he on?"

To further underline the generation gap, the band engages in a trivia game of "dead rocker," differentiating between "fallen stars" and those who overdosed.

At this juncture the film becomes repetitive. Jonah, symbolically, finds the first club "I ever played in" defunct. He is invited to a *Radio and Record* convention to join Sam and Dave, "Soul Man," the reunited Lovin' Spoonful, and Tiny Tim for a 1960s revival. Simon performs "Soft Parachute," an antiwar tune unfortunately absent from the album.

Fox assigns Steve Kunelian (Lou Reed) to produce Jonah as Kunelian has "A good sense of Top 40." The producer "sweetens" "Long, Long, Day," with a string section. The company president is excited. This is "the most commercial thing you've cut in a long time," he tells Jonah. To complicate matters, Jonah's road band is excluded from the studio sessions.

A tame resolution closes the picture. The Simon character steals the tape and destroys it. One critic described the close as being basically an "Adolescent gesture," which aptly describes the film's "adult-in-a-kid's-music-world—motif." The ending is unconvincing. Afterall, having experienced a 1968 folk-rock hit, Jonah must have learned *something* about the record industry.

The conclusion, that record labels are commercially motivated makers of plasticware, is obvious. Simon candidly admitted his character was "out there hustling a buck, and I'm not."[58] As he had just paid CBS more than $1 million for a contract release in February 1979, Simon's distress seemed justified, but barely convincing.

There are neophyte artists in the music business who only desire to play their music. After several years, those same individuals will complain to anyone willing to listen that the record company ripped them off. By the late 1970s, artist management was evolving into a highly specialized profession. Given those facts, Jonah's lack of a manager defies credibility. Was the singer actually an adolescent in the corporate confines of the music community?

Ironies abound when one considers *One-Trick Pony* in a historical context: Simon and Garfunkel's later double album, *Concert in Central Park* (1982), would be their first record certified gold since *Still Crazy*. The cablecast concert was a "live" golden oldies package.

Overall, the film received good reviews when viewed as a treatment of the music industry. The *Christian Science Monitor*'s Sterritt, for example, said that the film was "the most grown up movie ever made on the subject of rock-and-roll." There was dissent. *Variety* said, "While pic would ordinarily seem to have solid trappings of a success, recent flops of such inside-the-biz tunners as 'Honeysuckle Rose' and 'Roadie' necessarily cast some doubt on genre's general appeal, no matter what the quality of individual film." " 'One-Trick Pony' isn't a movie at all," objected Ansen, "but a long commercial for the soundtrack album."[59] The album contained ony ten songs, as opposed to the eleven in the movie. B-52's material, Tiny Tim, and the Lovin' Spoonful, as well as "Soft Parachute," segments of which appeared in the film, were overtly absent.

The film's marketing campaign succeeded in moving vinyl, not celluloid. On 9 September the "solo" album entered Number 25 pushing to Number 13. It remained on the charts for twenty-three weeks easily outperforming the motion picture. *One-Trick Pony* opened in twelve theatres the first week of October, returning a flat $122,000. By 12 November, with $283,305 going to the studio, the first run was over. Dave Marsh's prediction that the movie was "a chancy proposition . . . in a season when such projects are generally on the wave," proved correct.[60]

1981:The Year of the Soundtrack Drought

1981 was not a stellar year for the film and record industries. Ticket sales had inched slightly upward to 1.027 from 1.022 billion in 1980 (a year described by *Variety* as nothing "to brag about." *Variety*'s A.D. Murphy observed, "Given this domestic b.o. environment, one can call it either 'stagnant' or 'stable.' A pessimist might prefer the 'stagnant' label, looking only at the sterile statistics vis-a-vis growing population, gross national product, disposable income, etc., and smoking that very expensive stuff called Columbian homevideo."[61] Most observers agreed that *Raiders of the Lost Ark* and *Superman II* had saved the industry from a downward spiral. The movie studios' 8.3-percent income rise was entirely due to inflation and increased ticket prices.

The record industry, in 1981, was down nearly 8.5 percent in shipments. (In 1980, 649 million units went to retailers. A year later the figure was 549. RIAA revised these figures in 1983. According to the new numbers, unit shipments in 1981 totalled 635.4 million, the lowest since the year of *Saturday Night Fever* (1977).)[62]

Rock soundtracks were hard hit. Only *Heavy Metal*, the Azoff compilation, and *This Is Elvis*, a rockumentary, received certifications. The two soundtracks that attracted the most attention were *Metal* and the econom-ically unsuccessful *American Pop*. *Metal* reached platinum, but *Pop* had failed to chart. (For a discussion of *Heavy Metal*, see Chapter VI).

American Pop (1981): Pogrom to Punkitude

Ralph Bakshi, considered by many to be an iconoclastic animator extraordinaire, had planned a multi-generational epic of *Godfather* propor-tions. The creator of *Fritz the Cat, Heavy Traffic*, and *Lord of the Rings* envisioned the "most complex story ever attempted in animation. Char-acters grow up and get older and die. They go off to wars and get killed. They have children. They travel cross country. It's a massive experiment in animation."

Peddling the concept to Columbia Pictures, major film executive David Melnick urged that it be tied into the American popular music scene. As Bakshi would later tell *American Film*, "I was going to lay the background music in anyhow. All Danny did was push the music forward. It was a great suggestion."

Ronni Kern, who was approached to write the screenplay, especially appreciated the title, *American Pop*, as "it's not just about music—it's about the popular culture and also about father-son relationships." "Pop," in this context, had two meanings, familial and musical.

Lee Holdridge arranged and placed the forty-one-song score, the most ambitious undertaking since Lucas's *American Graffiti*. Spanning some seventy years, the selections ranged from Scott Joplin's "Maple Leaf Rag" to Fabian's "Turn Me Loose" to Bob Seger's "Night Moves." *American Pop*'s treatment of rock, soon to come under severe criticism, was somewhat opinionated. "Though it's never said, there's a certain selfishness and egomania to all the characters [in the film]," Holdridge said. "Egomania is an essential ingredient in rock—and there is certainly the implication that all these great songs that have come down through the years were written under questionable circumstances. The pop music world is still very much a street business, and Ralph brings this out in the film."[63] Music arranger Holdridge and music supervisor John Beug were faced with monumental obstacles.

Having to negotiate through seventy-five-year's worth of copyrights and licensing claims made the difficulties experienced by the makers of *Easy Rider* and *Graffiti* seem easy in comparison. (Raybert Productions had reportedly spent nineteen months securing the rights to the *Rider* sound-track, and Capitol had refused to grant rights to The Band's song "The

Weight." *American Graffiti* had proved easier, since many of its oldies were simply gathering dust in 1973).

By 1980, with the proliferation of soundtracks, it was definitely a seller's market, and Lee Holdridge ran into a legal maze which would severely hamper the structure of the film. Licensing problems placed Bakshi in the position of excluding the likes of Elvis Presley, The Beatles, and Bruce Springsteen from a historical epic addressing popular music. Numerous critics would jump on this omission. "Elvis, incidentally, never appears; the ad image is an Elvis clone from a background," wrote Jon Pareles. "It was a matter of rights and artists' availability," indicated Benson. "It's a pity. Bob Seger is good, Bruce Springsteen is great," he continued.[64]

The movie's accompanying soundtrack was equally problematic. In *Easy Rider* and *American Graffiti*, the music reflected a specific period. Bakshi, however, was forced to use, or, conversely, exclude songs that were identified with given periods. He partially recouped by including songs by Scott Joplin, Benny Goodman, Dave Brubeck, and Jimi Hendrix.

The record label releasing a soundtrack from *American Pop* was faced with a dilemma—few consumers have eclectic enough tastes to want to listen to the panorama of styles and genres presented in the motion picture. MCA Records' ten-cut soundtrack was thus more a reflection of *Graffiti* than *American Pop*. Of the selections, seven were by Sixties artists such as The Doors, Hendrix, and Big Brother and The Holding Company. However, including superstars' familiar hits does little to stimulate sales, and the fate of the soundtrack was totally contingent upon the public's response to the film, which opened 13 February 1981.

This dark tale of four generations of Bolinskis opens in Tzarist Russia as Rabbi Jaacov Bolinski is praying to the background sounds of a Ukrainian religious chant. Cossacks interrupt the prayer and the rabbi becomes another bloody pogrom victim while defending the *Torah*.

His wife and ten-year-old son, Zalmie, escape, immigrate to America, and pass through the portals of Ellis Island to find a home in New York's Lower East Side. Mrs. Bolinski finds work in a garment-district sweat shop, the Triangle Shirtwaist Company, which goes up in flames. Zalmie, orphaned, finds employment at Minsky's, a New York night club encountering a showgirl, Bella, who introduces him to manhood. They marry, producing a son, Benny, before Bella dies. (As Sheila Benson noted, "It doesn't pay to be a woman in this saga: they're killed or lost at a great rate.")[65] Zalmie enters the gangland world of the 1930s and his son Benny becomes a piano player in a Harlem band, the only white in the ensemble. To solidify his underworld position, Zalmie asks Benny to wed the daughter of underworld czar Nicky Palumbo. They marry and she becomes pregnant. World War II breaks out; Benny enlists. He reappears in the ruins of a European village, where he spies a piano. Unable to resist, he sits down and begins to pick out "As Time Goes By." A Nazi trooper emerges from the rubble. Startled, the American shifts to "Lili Marlene." When Benny is finished, the German politely says "Danke," and then murders him.

The plot picks up with Benny's son, Tony, who is the third-generation Bolinski. Apparently for story line reasons, the 1950s Beat culture and the late sixties world of psychedelia are merged together in Tony's life. A denizen of Greenwich Village, he basks in Allen Ginsberg's *Howl*, until he sees grandfather Zalmie testify, on television, against his former underword associates. Disillusioned, Tony hits the road in a stolen car. At a Kansas truck stop he beds a blonde waitress to the strains of Sam Cooke's "You Send Me" before continuing on to Haight-Ashbury. There Frankie, an apparent Grace Slick-Janis Joplin composite, introduces him to sex, drugs, and rock'n'roll. (The movie's ploy of having Tony in a 1960s band is ideal, as it allows him to compose "Somebody to Love," "People are Strange," and "Don't Think Twice.") Living through the turbulent Sixties, Frankie and Tony become drug addicts.

On tour with Hendrix, they encounter "Little Pete"—the product of Tony's long-forgotten, one-night stand, in Kansas. Pete accompanies the band to New York, where Frankie overdoses to "Waiting For My Man." Pete becomes his father's drug supplier, hustling while Tony barricades himself at the Chelsea Hotel—when Pete discovers that Tony has pawned his son's guitar, he leaves. Remorseful, Tony sends his offspring the pawn ticket along with a bag of narcotics. The dope provides Pete with an entry into the music world, as people in that industry come to depend on him for their supplies. He uses this leverage to gain a recording contract and attain punk stardom. As one critic summarized, "Before you know it, it's fame, fortune and gold-record time, with every iron intact. A family line that began as a rich ethnic vein ends with a rich, bitter, friendless bastard—in the most literal sense of the word."[66] The theme of the motion picture could easily have been "from pogrom to punkdom," highlighted by the repeated and closing use of the opening religious hymn.

The ninety-five-minute Rotoscoed production proved to be a reviewers dream despite a dismal box office and an MCA ten-song soundtrack that failed to chart. Nearly all of the reviews used such terms as "too ambitious," "a bleak sociological vision," "Bakshi's ears hear only the downbeats," or "an unremitting bummer." Some writers, while agreeing with those assessments, nevertheless found the work to have value. *Variety*'s Ginsberg concluded that the film "represents something quite different from the array of recent studio efforts. That in itself probably makes it worth seeing."[67]

American Pop's ambitious title focused attention on popular music from ragtime to rock. While reviews were mixed, they tended toward the negative. The music, contended Sterritt, weakened some segments: "Just when we need a burst of energy, we get a watery Bob Seger song with no explanation: a 1950s classic is used to illustrate the 1980s punk scene."

The film's use of music emerged as a major problem for reviewers. "Jamming everything from Scott Joplin to Bob Seger in a short history of America, Bakshi has time to press only the obvious buttons," asserted Ansen. *Time*'s Corliss focused on structure, likening the feature to a "series of melodramatic scenes from late-night movies with commercials every ten minutes for Greatest Hits LPs." *Billboard*'s Cary Darling found the first half of the film "effective," but "from there, the film falls flat on its face as it pushed into the psychedelic 1960s and the punked-out 1970s and 1980s, the critic added, ending with, "There is no soundtrack album."[68]

Michael Sragow added insult to injury in the pages of *Rolling Stone*, saying, "Bakshi's most convincing proof of the degradation of pop culture will come if *American Pop* is a hit."[69] It wasn't.

Nineteen eighty-one was a drought year for rock-oriented film packages. It was popularly assumed the target demographic was busy in the arcades trying to master Pac Man and Donkey Kong. More knowledgeable observers suggest another view, that 1980, misnamed the "year of the soundtrack," could not have replicated the successes of 1977, or even 1979, as motion picture projects are in gestation for over a year, adding that the poor showing of 1980 rock scores precluded a continuance of these projects for 1981. The year signaled to the media that new strategies needed to be developed in order to lure young people away from their joy sticks, out of the arcades, and into the population of movie patrons and record buyers.

Notes

1. Quoted in Harold R. Kennedy, "Record Makers' Drive to Rev Up Sagging Sales," *Billboard*, 14 December 1981, 39.
2. Paul Grein, "1979: The Great Rock/Disco Title Bout," *Billboard*, 22 December 1979, TIA-3.
3. Quoted in Ed Ochs, "Mining Gold From The Silver Screen," *Billboard*, 2 August 1980, M-3.
4. Quoted in Michael Segell, "Heartbreaker: The Hard Times and High Hopes of Richard Gere," *Rolling Stone*, 6 March 1980, 58.

5. Quoted in Seqell, 59.
6. Quoted in Fred Bronson, 524.
7. "Schrader Deep in 'Gigolo' Ad Plan," *Variety*, 27 February 1980, 44.
8. Quoted in "Schrader," 44.
9. *Billboard*, 16 February 1980, 92.
10. Ibid., 91.
11. Andrew Sarris, "Different Strokes," *Village Voice*, 4 February 1980, 43; Vincent Canby, " 'American Gigolo,' a southern California Melodrama," *New York Times*, February 1980, C14.
12. Todd McCarthy, "American Gigolo," *Variety*, 30 January 1980, 28.
13. "American Gigolo," *Film Journal*, 9 March 1980, 9; Richard Schickel, "Pinkeye," *Time*, 11 February 1981, 95.
14. David Sterritt, "American Gigolo," *Christian Science Monitor*, 22 February 1980; 19; Charles Champlin, "American Gigolo," *Los Angeles Times*, 1 February 1980, 1; David Ansen, "Movies," *Newsweek*, 11 February 1980, 82.
15. Schickel, 95; Ansen, 82; Canby, C14.
16. David Denby, "Laid Back," *New York*, 4 February 1980, 63.
17. Quoted in Ed Ochs, "Mining Gold," M3.
18. Quoted in Peter Occhiogrosso, "Reelin' and Rockin'," *American Film*, April 1984, 47.
19. Ibid.
20. "Film and Contempo Music Join To Create New Type 'Producer,' " *Variety*, 13 February 1980, 219.
21. Quoted in Ochs, "Mining Gold," M12.
22. Ochs, "Mining Gold," M3.
23. Richard Corliss, "A Great Rock'n'Roll Caravan," *Time*, 7 July 1980, 44.
24. Todd McCarthy, "Roadie," *Variety*, 11 June 1980, 20-21; Richard Corliss, "A Great Rock'n'Roll Caravan," 44; Tom Allen, "Roadrunner Cowboy," *Village Voice*, 23 June 1980, 44.
25. Janet Maslin, " 'Roadie' Shows How Rock Keeps Rolling," *New York Times*, 13 June 1980, C8; Tom Mline, 'Roadie," *Monthly Film Bulletin*, June 1981, 119; Alex Keneas, "Roadie," *Newsday* 13 June 1980, 7.
26. E. Perchaluk, "Roadie," *Film Journal*, July 1980, 8; David Sterritt, "Sorting Through the Summer Slump," *Christian Science Monitor*, 24 July 1980, 19.
27. Quoted in Cary Darling, "Rock Movies Grow Up," *Billboard*, 2 August 1980, M-4.
28. Steve Holden, "Roadie," *Rolling Stone*, 21 August 1980, 50.
29. Quotes in Abe Peck, "The Blues Brothers Ask the $32 Million Question," *Rolling Stone*, 7 August 1980, 29.
30. Op cit.
31. Op cit.
32. Quoted in Roman Kozak, " 'Blues Bros.' Movie a $27 Million Laugh," *Billboard*, 28 June 1980, 79.
33. Ibid.
34. Quoted in *Billboard*, 21 June 1980, 94; Kozak, 79.
35. Charles Champlin, "Blues Brothers," *Los Angeles Times*, 20 June 1980, 1; David Ansen, "Up From Hunger," *Newsweek*, 30 June 1980, 62; Richard Corliss, "A Great Rock'n'Roll Caravan," *Time*, 7 July 1980, 44; Andrew Sarris,

"Can't Stop The Blues Brothers," *Village Voice*, 2 July 1980, 33; Robert Hatch, "Films," *Nation* 12-26, July 1980, 93.

36. Chris McGowan, "Blues Brother Hilarious," *Billboard*, 28 June 1980, 79; Archer Winsten, "Blues Brothers," *New York Post*, 20 June 1980, 33.

37. Janet Maslin, "Blues Brothers—Belushi and Aykroyd," *New York Times*, 20 June 1980, C16; Eva Zibert, "Belushi & Aykroyd Turn Their 'Blues' Into Blahs," *Washington Post*, 27 June 1980, 19; Todd McCarthy, "The Blues Brothers," *Variety*, 18 June 1980, 22.

38. Alex Keneas, "The Blues Brothers," *Newsday*, 20 June 1980, 7; Paul Taylor, "The Blues Brothers," *Monthly Film Bulletin*, October 1980, 187.

39. Pauline Kael, "Muckrackers & Saints," *New Yorker*, 7 July 1980, 97; David Denby, "Two-Faced Blues," *New York*, 30 June 1980, 54; Doug Eisenstark, "The Blues Brothers; Bad Boys Make Movie," *Jump Cut*, October 1980, 66.

40. Dave Marsh, "The Blues Brothers Original Soundtrack," *Rolling Stone*, 4 September 1980, 51; Giles quoted in Abe Peck, "But can they really sing the blues?" *Rolling Stone*, 7 August 1980, 30.

41. Quoted in Peck, "But can they," 30.

42. Paul Grein, "Large Surge In Record and Film Tie-Ins," *Billboard*, 31 May 1980, 1,33,42; Stephen Holden, "Movies, Music and Money: Who's On First?" *Hi-Fi*, 30 October 1980, 108; Ed Ochs, "Mining Gold," *Billboard*, 2 August 1980: M1, M3.

43. Quoted in Grein, "Large," 33.

44. Quoted in Marc Kirkeby, "Soundtrack Sales Good Despite LP Slump," *Rolling Stone*, 4 September 1980, 24.

45. Adam White, "WEA Worldwide System Aids Soundtracks," *Billboard*, 30 August 1980, 3.

46. David Sterritt, "Sorting Through the Summer Slump," *Christian Science Monitor*, 24 July 1980, 19.

47. Holden, "Movies," 108.

48. Sterritt, "Sorting," 19.

49. Quoted in Donald Lyons, "Music Videos Give New Eyes to Hollywood," *Rock Video*, September 1984, 63; Ochs, "Mining Gold," M12.

50. Quoted in "Film and Contempt Music Join To Create New Type 'Producer,' " *Variety*, 13 February 1980, 219.

51. Quoted in George Kopp, "Soundtrack Specialists Proliferate," *Billboard* 19 July 1980, 73.

52. Quoted in Alan Penchansky, "Dull Product Extending Slump," *Billboard*, 30 August 1980, 15.

53. Quoted in Dave Marsh, "What Do You Do When You're Not A Kid Anymore And You Still Want To Rock & Roll?" *Rolling Stone*, 30 October 1980, 45.

54. Op cit.

55. *Billboard*, 30 August 1980, 30.

56. Marsh, "What Do," 44.

57. Janet Maslin, " 'One-Trick Pony' of Paul Simon," *New York Times*, 3 October 1980, C14.

58. Marsh, "What Do," 45.

59. David Sterritt, "One-Trick Pony," *Christian Science Monitor*, 16 October 1980, 19; Todd McCarthy, "One Trick Pony," *Variety*, 1 October 1980, 20; David Ansen, "Sour Simon," *Newsweek*, 20 October 1980, 84.

60. Marsh, "What Do," 43.
61. A.D. Murphy, "Inflation Cues '81 Film B.O. Record," *Variety*, 6 January 1982, 1, 34.
62. See Horowitz, "Label Shipments Off 8.5% In 1981," *Billboard*, 10 April 1982, 1, 78. See R. Serge Denisoff, *Tarnished Gold* (New Brunswick: Transaction Books 1986) for a discussion of these statistical machinations.
63. Quotes in Rex McGee, "All That Jazz . . . Swing . . . Pop . . . And Rock," *American Film*, July-August 1980, 24, 29, 30.
64. Jon Pareles, "Pop and Son," *Village Voice*, 18 February 1981, 48; and Sheila Benson, "American Pop," *Los Angeles Times*, 13 February 1981, 1.
65. Benson, 1.
66. Ibid.
67. Ginsberg, "American Pop," *Variety*, 11 February 1981, 20.
68. David Sterritt, "American Pop," *Christian Science Monitor*, 26 February 1981, 18: David Ansen, "Movies," *Newsweek*, 16 March 1981, 94; Richard Corliss, *Time*, 6 April 1981, 71; Cary Darling, "Animated 'American Pop' Falls On Its Cliched Face," *Billboard*, 7 March 1981, 48.
69. Michael Sragow, " 'American Pop' Flops," *Rolling Stone* 2 April 1981, 49.

6

It Was the Year That Wasn't: 1982

In 1982, *Variety* enthusiastically noted that box office sales were up by 9 percent from the previous year. 1.165 billion "ducets" (tickets) were sold, contrasted to 1.067 billion in 1981. The dollar amounts, some 16 percent, were misleading, however, due to ticket price inflation.

The record industry, in the same year, experienced a 17.9-percent decline in units shipped, 576 million in 1982, as opposed to 701 million in 1979. RIAA President Stanley Gortikov said, "These figures dramatically portray the troubled economic circumstances of our industry."

Record labels had little to celebrate in 1982; the lack of success of movie soundtracks mirrored the overall state of the industry. The soundtrack of *Annie* a Broadway transplant, did sell a million, and that of *E.T.*, the highest grosser in movie box office, did earn a gold certification (with a score by the always reliable John Williams.) The poor record performance was not due to a lack of promotion. Films such as *Conan, Ragtime, Tron, Victor/Victoria*, and Burt Reynolds's *Sharky's Machine* all featured soundtracks, but none of those had broken into the top half of the *Billboard* 200 ranking. In 1982 gold was scarce.

Hanging Out, Male Bonding at the Diner

> Ever get the feeling that there's something going on we don't know about?
> —Fenwick, college drop-out, 1959

United Artists, before its merger with MGM, botched the *Idolmaker* (1980) advertising by attempting a return to mass marketing. In 1982, it appeared likely that the film *Diner*, directed by neophyte Barry Levinson, would suffer a similar fate.

Levinson, a Baltimore native, was a product of television and the American University. "I would do the morning news, then take a class, then run back to the station and do a kiddie show," he said. "It was a great learning experience. Television was still young in the sense that you could play around with a lot of things. I learned by trial and error."[1]

After graduating, he moved to Southern California and worked at The Comedy Store with actor Craig T. Nelson, which led to writing for *The Tim Conway Show* and *Carol Burnett*, earning three Emmys.

Mel Brooks then hired the writer. "Doing *Silent Movie* and *High Anxiety* with Mel was worth about three years of school," stated Levinson who, with his wife also wrote *And Justice For All*.[2]

While working with Brooks, Levinson mused over his boyhood and adolescence in Baltimore in the late 1950s. Brooks felt that "This could make a good kind of first film—something like *I Vitelloni* (1953). "I realized that underlying most of my anecdotes was one idea," Levinson explained, "Boys play with boys until they're twelve or thirteen. Then they start talking about girls. Then they date, which is like stealing someone from another tribe and then returning to your tribe to talk about it. But after you're twenty-one or twenty-two, you're supposed to go back to your own tribe!"[3] The tribal gathering place in his film was the prototypical Hillcrest Diner, "a jukebox with seats instead of records inside."

MGM/UA picked up the project, allowing Levinson to direct and setting the budget at $5 million. After auditioning five hundred actors, the director settled on three newcomers for starring roles, with other little-knowns filling out the rest of the cast.

The film was originally test marketed in four cities and did poorly. The Phoenix test was disastrous. Levinson complained, "Because it's about young people, they thought of it as a teenage movie. They hyped it as a rock-and-roll kind of film, and when we went into Phoenix with it, the kids didn't like it; they expected something else. It was horrendous. I thought well, I've spent 19 months on a movie, and it will disappear in Phoenix."[4] Talking to the *Film Journal*, he elaborated. "My impression is that they [MGM/UA] saw *Diner* and said, 'Another youth movie! Its not as funny as *Animal House* but then it does have a few good laughs, and there's plenty of 50's rock music.' They also figured that New Yorkers wouldn't go for it, and it was more of a rural audience. In other words, I don't think they really had a good fix on what kind of movie it was. So they said, 'Let's sell it as a 'kids' movie, a rock 'n' roll type of thing.'"

The studio's marketing chief responded, "We never considered it to be a rock 'n' roll movie. We opened it in a variety of techniques which I think is, the only way to put a film like *Diner* across, which isn't an easy film to market, no matter how you look at it."[5]

The debate continued. Levinson told one writer, "Well, I just wish the studio had given us some ads. I mean, there was nothing. It was very tough."[6] He objected that the film's Washington D.C. opening had been ineffectual. "*Diner* had an ad in the *Washington Post* but no decent review quotes to go with it. The only movie playing in that town was just *sitting there* at the Dupont Circle Theatre! And people wonder why doesn't somebody like it enough to give it a good quote," he said.

He further complained, "We never asked MGM/UA to go with a big radio and television campaign. We knew a big all-media break wouldn't work. All we wanted was a small, carefully-constructed release pattern. But what they've done now is rob the film of its strength, and I can't figure out why no one seems to be willing to answer that question."

Nathaniel Kwit, the studio marketing head, was quick to reply, "What we've done repeatedly with films similar to *Diner*, and with considerable success, is to take things slowly, market-by-market, and plan the campaign very carefully, which is what we're doing. This is the *only* way a film of this type has any chance at all, and it isn't easy. It takes tremendous energy and a tremendous commitment, because you're dealing with literally hundreds of markets."[7]

Marketing the movie was further complicated by Elektra Records. A film-supported two-record soundtrack, in the *American Graffiti* tradition, was not released until mid-April, more than a month after the film. *Billboard* raved about the package saying, "What a great collection of classics from the late '50s and early '60s.[8] The laudatory notice did little to boast wholesale buys; the album failed to chart.

Aesthetically, the twenty-song product captured the period, but it's fate was inextricably linked with the motion picture's box office. Moreover, MGM, by withholding the film from the New York market, was essentially ignoring the media center of the nation.

As with *The Idolmaker*, an authentic historical work was dismissed as a teen film. Levinson said, "*Diner*, ultimately, is the sort of film that confuses people because it combines a lot of things together." *Diner* was *not* a teen pic, but the studio was ambivalent.

Kwit, in a *Film Journal* interview, described the marketing confusion. He told Jeffery Wells, "The problem with movies like this, which have youthful actors and also, one hopes, will evoke nostalgic memories, is that if you use a media saturation campaign, in the sense of spending a lot of money on TV and print ads, you're basically expecting a quick sell, which we weren't with *Diner*. The easiest way, is to make up 1,000 prints, spend

$5 or $6 million on advertising,'' he went on, ''push the button and if it hits the first weekend, you're OK. It it doesn't, then forget it.''

The result was that *Diner* became fundamentally a specialty—''Cult''—film which depended on word of mouth. The film created its own momentum with selected showings. Levinson said, ''They're basically expecting a quick sell, which we weren't with *Diner*.[9] He stressed that twenty-four-to-forty-five-year-olds should have been targeted. The film eventually opened in the Boston, Washington, Chicago, Pittsburgh, and Baltimore, grossing a little under $4 million. A gala New York opening was planned for 14 April.

Diner, in the tradition of *American Graffiti*, employs numerous subplots with the unifying thread of men returning ''habitually to some hangout or restaurant . . . while talking constantly about sex, to the tune of a incessant parade of hit records.[10] Levinson's film was set in 1959, when ''the Eisenhower years are over, in a sense, but the Sixties haven't begun yet. In the Fifties, you stayed at home until you were married.'' ''The guys in *Diner* are the second generation of Americans,'' he added. ''Their fathers had only one option—to go to work. The guys in the next generation had the freedom to say 'I don't know what I want to do.' '' ''The diner is their temple away from the temple.''[11]

Vincent Canby eloquently summarized the plot:

> Young men in their early 20's, a couple of years out of high school, in college or dropping out, working at boring jobs, one married too soon, another about to be, having no clear goals and only vaguely aware that something important is missing. Though its mood is deceptively lighthearted, ''Diner,'' which is set in Baltimore in 1959, is far more like Federico Fellini's classic ''I Vitelloni'' than George Lucas's ''American Graffiti.'' The characters in ''American Graffiti'' still had several years to go before experiencing the angst that hangs over the young men in ''Diner'' like not entirely unpleasant, greasy griddle smoke.
>
> The principal characters are Fenwick (Kevin Bacon), a good-looking waspy young man who has dropped out of college, drives a neat red sports car, lives on a $100 a month trust fund and, in all likelihood, will be an alcoholic by the time he's 30; Shrevie (Daniel Stern), who sells TV sets, married his high school sweetheart and, because they have nothing to talk about, spends most of his off-hours with his old gang at the diner; Eddie (Steve Guttenberg), an obsessed Baltimore Colts fan, who's engaged to marry Elyse—whom we never see-but only if she passes a sports trivia test he has made up for her. Eddie doesn't want to make Shrevie's mistake. He wants to be sure that he and Elyse will have something to talk about when they are thrown together.
>
> There are also Modell (Paul Reiser), a young man who cannot commit himself to anything, even to the asking of a direct question; Bill (Timothy Daly), who's in graduate school and wants to marry the girl he's made pregnant, though she

turns him down, and, the most interesting of the lot, Boogie (Mickey Rourke), who works as a hairdresser by day, is deeply in debt to the bookies, and pretends to be studying law by night, in this way to neutralize some of the more unpleasant associations that attach to the reputation of male hairdressers.

One of the ways in which "Diner" does recall "American Graffiti" is the ease with which Mr. Levinson handles these six, more or less co-equal characters, each being immediately indentifiable and different yet, one can believe, best friends.

The propelling central situation is Eddie's forthcoming marriage which in various ways, prompts minor crises of one sort and another for each of the others, to say nothing of Elyse, who remains offscreen cramming for the multiple-choice, true-false test that will decide whether or not she'll be Eddie's bride.

As the writer-director of "Diner," Mr. Levinson has successfully disciplined himself, his material and his actors. The film is episodic in form but the episodes fit together so tightly, with little or no waste space in between, that "Diner" manages to move forward with the kind of pacing one ordinarily associates with a far more plotty film. Though it's full of artifacts of the era, especially the music, "Diner" is no ride down Memory Lane. It possesses a number of moments of true sentiment without ever slopping over into sentimentality. There are not tears clouding its vision.

Especially moving—and bleak—are the sequences featuring Shrevie and Beth, his valentine-faced wife, played by Ellen Barkin with just the right amount of stubborn stupidity and helplessness. Shrevie and Beth are incapable of furnishing their Blue Heaven with anything but records, appliances, misunderstandings and arguments. Though the film tries to suggest at the end that Shrevie and Beth are on their way to growing up, it's clear that they'll be in some cut-rate divorce lawyers' pockets before the next year is out.[12]

Diner was a critical success. Some writers compared the film to a "thinking man's *Porky's*" (which had been released around the same time). David Denby called the vehicle "a small American classic."[13]

Most writers made a comparison to *American Graffiti*. "*Diner* is another replay of *American Graffiti* set in Baltimore during the Christmas season of 1959," wrote the *Christian Science Monitor's* David Sterritt. "It's vulgar language and preoccupation with sex reflect the lingering adolescence of its characters, who are poised on the brink of adulthood and can't quite find the courage to plunge in." David Ansen said, "*Diner* bears certain obvious similarities to George Lucas's *American Graffiti*. It's about a group of young men perched apprehensively on the brink of adult responsibilities, clinging for security to their comfortable camaraderie, which is symbolized for them by happy bull sessions at Fells Point Diner, where the specialty is gravy-drenched potatoes, and the talk is of sex, the Colts, marriage and sex." Asahina noted the "girl on the horse:" "There is even a fantasy girl who intermittently appears riding a horse, evidently the Maryland version of the white T-Bird that carried Suzanne Sommers along California highways in Lucas' first popular excursion into nostalgia." *American Graffiti* and *Diner* were characterized as "affectionate and exquisitely cast with actors who will—or already have—gone on to impressive works," said Benson.[14]

Micky Rourke, singled out as the "new" Jack Nicholson, received plaudits. Ironically, Corliss suggested that "He could have trouble finding a movie that offers him as sexy a role."[15] (*9 ½ Weeks* had yet to be contracted.)

In the diner, the jukebox and the dialogue focus on period music; a major debate is whether Frank Sinatra or Johnny Mathis provide the best background for sex. "Chances Are" wins.

One character, Shrevie (Daniel Stern), has a passion in rock music and berates his wife Beth (Ellen Barkin) when she fails to memorize the B-sides of hit records and misfiles his record collection. ("How *could* you file my James Brown record under J?" he demands.)

The musical score is integrated with the plot. (The *New Statesman's* Coleman would note, "The music's right." but the film's poor box office precluded an appreciation of the oldies package.[16] Nevertheless, *Diner*, earned critical acclaim and grossed more than $12.5 million returning to the studio $5.5 million. Michael Shore in the excellent *Music Video* work, praised the movie as containing an, "outstanding golden oldies musical soundtrack," continuing, "*Diner* is one magnificant must-see of a movie."[17] (The double-record soundtrack stiffed.)

The failure of the soundtrack, one of many, was due to oversaturation in the marketplace and the focus of the motion picture. Moreover, some of the movie's most memorable tunes, like Elvis's "Don't Be Cruel," were absent from the record.

Still, more movie soundtracks kept coming.

Irving Azoff Visits Ridgemont High and Fails

> *Awesome! Totally Awesome!*
> —Jeff Spicoli, student

Robert Stigwood's golden touch died with Sgt. Pepper, remembered as an "attempt to link songs from the Beatles classic album into some sort of storyline that just doesn't work; sequences range from tolerable to embarrassing. As to the Bee Gees' acting talent, if you can't say something nice . . ."

Stigwood's heir apparent was Irving Azoff, a twenty-year veteran of the music industry. Beginning in artist management, he had worked with the powerful Geffen-Roberts organization before forming Front Line, whose clients included The Eagles, Dan Fogelberg, REO Speedwagon, Stevie Nicks, Steely Dan, Jimmy Buffett, and Boz Scaggs.

Because of Front Line's highly visible roster, Azoff was brought in as executive producer for Universal Pictures' *FM* (1978). Azoff withdrew from the project after screening the rough cut, two months before its 28 April release date. The film was "not an authentic representation of the music business," he said. "It's an AM movie made about FM radio," he told *Rolling Stone*, "When shooting started, the very first day, Cleavon Little (portraying a deejay) had on a three-piece suit and tie when it's supposed to be six in the morning. I knew I had trouble." Azoff was bitter. "I think they wanted me for the soundtrack," he complained, "I feel like the music financed the movie. It was like minimizing our risk."

The *FM* album arrived at the *Billboard* offices the week of 22 April (as did the *Last Waltz*), carrying the claim that it represented a continuation of the *Saturday Night Fever* success. "Tie-ins between hot-grossing rock-oriented films and their soundtrack counterpart are reaching incredible sales plateaus," said *Billboard*. Dealers were told the "film and the soundtrack should be huge grossers."

The movie opened on ninety-six screens a week later, earning a very uninspiring $348,200. A single from the record, Linda Ronstadt's "Tumbling Dice," entered the chart at number 60. By the third week the number of exhibitors was down to thirty-three. The rentals at that juncture totaled a meagre $642,675; year-end studio earnings were $2.9 million.

The album, conversely, spent twenty-eight weeks on the charts, peaking at a very respectable number 5, and going on to multiplatinum status, provided MCA with an estimated $24 million gross. Dave Marsh noted "the profits ought to be substantial enough to help amortize the film's nose-dive.[18] Critic Peter Occhiogrosso characterized *FM* as a "shameless excuse to string together songs for the sake of a sound track album." The movie was merely "an advertisement for is own soundtrack album," echoes Ansen. Music writer Mitch Cohen joined in. The songs, he noted, "seem chosen more with a best-selling two-LP set (that is, naturally, getting heavy play on the new FM radio) in mind than with thoughts of a first-rate film score." "*FM* is frankly an exploitation film in the very sleaziest sense of the word," he concluded. *Variety's* Pollock agreed, saying, "The album's better than the film." In the *Village Voice*, Georgia Christgau characterized *FM* as "pretty boring and pretty sexist."[19]

One of the few positive statements emanated from the pages of the *New*

York Times, in which Maslin argued, "The look of the film is convincing, and its soundtrack very well-chosen."[20] Three million consumers agreed.

The phenomenal success of the *FM* soundtrack hooked Azoff; he knew the music business and its people, and belie certainly could do as well. Taking another page out of Stigwood's playbook, he created *Urban Cowboy*, a virtual replay of Stigwood's *Saturday Night Fever*. Like *SNF*, the film was based on a magazine story, this one from *Esquire*. Azoff paid an incredible $250,000 to *Esquire* and Mickey Gilley for the film rights to the short story about Gilley's Texas nightclub.[21] Gilley's western palace replaced the 2001 Odyssey of *Fever*. Aaron Latham, who had written the *Esquire* piece, teamed with director James Brides (*The China Syndrome*) to construct the screenplay. This all occurred before Azoff approached Paramount with the project.

Urban Cowboy would become the third double-album soundtrack linked to a film starring John Travolta. (The highly publicized failure of *Moment by Moment* had made the screen star cautious, but he was immediately attracted to *Urban Cowboy*). After reading the script, "I wanted to check out Gilley's and the bull," he said. "It seemed like something new to me, with a rough element that made it exciting. The bull riding, the dancing, the dangerous atmosphere—it had all the right elements."[22]

As he had done for the Tony Manero role in *Fever*, Travolta spent weeks in preparation for *Urban Cowboy*, learning to ride the mechanical bull, acquiring a Texas drawl, and dancing the Western two-step. He hung out at Gilleys, following the "cowboy" clientele around to study their behavior.

"Irving saw from the beginning," recalled music supervisor Becky Shargo, "that it would be a fantastic display of music."[23] Acting as an executive producer, Azoff was determined to create the most popular $15.95 package possible. While using Front Line artists—"Naturally I'm partial to my own people"—he wanted original material, as "Who wants to buy an album of greatest hits?"

"*FM* sold well," Azoff noted, "but I'm sure the sales would have been stronger if there had been more new songs on it.[24] Sixteen songs in the album were written especially for the *Urban Cowboy* film. "This way there's a much bigger financial upside," he explained.

Becky Shargo added, "We did a lot of songs very quickly, too; many were recorded in a day." Minimizing buy outs, the music production costs totaled less than $100,000.[25]

For the use of five CBS acts, a shaky *quid pro quo* was negotiated: In exchange for the use of The Charlie Daniels Band, Mickey Gilley, Boz

Scaggs, J.D. Souther, and Dan Fogelberg on Azoff's Full Moon label, CBS would receive the pressing and taping franchise.

The country and western flavor of the storyline was a further consideration; the sound would be "progressive country." Willie Nelson and Waylon Jennings, Texas demigods, were rumored to be signed for the production. "We wanted to create a much more contemporary mood than might be expected in a movie heavily involved with country music," commented Ms. Shargo. "One way to do that was to have contemporary artists doing country songs. We wanted to pretty much update them and get them in a crossover situation so they could have more appeal." Many of the tunes were more Southern California than Nashville or Austin, as the songsmiths and producers were only remotely "country." "A good portion of *Urban Cowboy's* music is Los Angeles-oriented" observed critic Stephen Holden.[26]

The album's supervisor agreed, saying, "There was a lot more leaning toward a pop audience in that first album . . . A lot of that was added toward the end of the film, after it was completely shot, when we were adding source music. Those were the songs that were brought to us by Irving and the things that he wanted for the album." Much of this post-production material came from Front Line clients.

Travolta was featured prominently on the album cover to assure identification with his past successes. Ads featured Travolta and Debra Winger "dancing together in provocative pose, which calls to mind photos used on two previous Travolta blockbuster, 'Saturday Night Fever' and 'Grease'," noted *Variety's* Todd McCarthy.[27]

Billboard received the fourteen-artist anthology 3 May, a month before the film's 5 June release date. The spotlighted album was associated with Travolta's role which "could be enough to sell the album," said *Billboard*, which went on to stress the crossover motif, noting "the LP makes a neat gift that will serve as an introduction to rockers not quite familiar with artists such as Kenny Rogers, Gilley and others and to fans of the latter who may be hearing Bob Seger and Joe Walsh for the first time. In any event, there's plenty of music for a wide audience."[28] Two weeks following the album's appearance, Joe Walsh's quasi-rockbilly song, "All Night Long" reached number 74 on the "Hot 100."; it later peaked at number 19.

Lacking a title song that promoted identification with the film, Azoff and Front Line vice president Larry Solters embarked on a media campaign, focusing on five major markets. Nevertheless the film and the soundtrack both experienced sluggish openings. Azoff told *Variety*, "There might have been consumer reluctance in the beginning."[29] In fact, the album failed to break into the top ten until July 12. This was hardly a replay of *SNF* certified platinum within a month.

In the movie, Bud Davis (John Travolta) drives his black pickup truck to Houston to find work in an oil refinery. His Uncle Bob introduces him to night life at Gilley's, "the biggest honky tonk in the world . . . three-and-a-half acres of concrete prairie." Gilley's giant saloon is a frontier fantasy world of hot-headed, macho urban cowboys who try to authenticate their manhood in beer, brawls, dancing, and fake frontier amusements. *Variety* described the movie's cowgirls as "Texas lovelies just now learning the first news of feminism while still accustomed to accepting a good clout from the old man for being late with dinner."[30]

Bud quickly becomes a regular at Gilley's, where he meets Sissy (Debra Winger). They are married (at Gilley's, of course), but tensions continue to build between them (The rambunctious bride even threatens Bud's masculinity by riding the new mechanical bull at Gilley's.) Their premature marriage falls apart when Bud, suspecting she's been unfaithful, throws Sissy out of their trailer. Sissy moves in with Wes (Scott Glenn), a "real cowboy" and rodeo rider who turns out to be a paroled convict who abuses her. Bud is courted by Pam (Madolyn Smith) an uptown girl whose daddy is a Texas oilman—"Daddy does oil and all that that implies," she says.

Most of the action takes place at Gilley's; at the center of it all is a mechanical bull, "a steel and leather contrivance that behaves like a cross between an eggbeater, a seesaw and a merry-go-round horse." Riding El Toro is a barroom rite of passage. The conflict between Bud and Wes climaxes at the mechanical bull rodeo contest at Gilley's—a substitute shootout. Bud is victorious. Wes, who was counting on the huge cash prize to finance his getaway, tries to rob Gilley's instead. Bud unknowingly foils the plan, saving Gilley's. Wes is put back behind bars and Bud and Sissy get back together.

At the box office, the movie only earned $1.7 million during the opening week playing in 183 theaters. Part of the problem was competition from *The Empire Strikes Back* and the premiere of the widely publicized *Blues Brothers* production. Critical reaction was decidedly negative.

Variety's opening review, making no mention of the score, contended that "city slick teenagers in the audience may grow a bit bored with all the bull ridings, along with all the other trappings at Gilley's. Certainly, the dancing that goes on there is mainly a variation on the old two-step and while Travolta does it well, it's nothing to equal the flash of 'Fever' or 'Grease.' "

On opening day the *Los Angeles Times*'s Charles Champlin wrote, "It's fascinating unless you've got no eyes for Texas at all, and no ears for the sleeked-up country music—*bankhouse disco* is what it is—that co-producer Azoff has assembled for the film.'' He went on to say, "Anyone who can't respond to the Daniels Band doing 'The Devil Went Down to Georgia' needs a complete medical checkup.''[31] As reviewers posted notices it appeared that numerous visits to doctor's offices would be needed. *Time's* Schickel commented, "*Urban Cowboy* is one of those movies that are all packaging and no execution.'' The film, commented Sarris, "never really *says* anything.'' He charged that the motion picture bastardized Latham's short story. Asahina made a comparison: "Unlike *Saturday Night Fever*, the film it is self-consciously styled after, *Urban Cowboy* has little dramatic movement.'' "It's bull, all right,'' concluded Denby. The *New York Post* said, "If you're looking for a great picture, forget it.''[32]

The film's story—boy meets girl, loses girl due to "other woman," boy regain's girl—is hardly original. But Gilley's provided the setting for appropriate musical showcases.

The movie's similarity to *Fever* focused attention on its soundtrack. "The music, which is the heart of both phenomena, serves *Cowboy* mainly as a banal background,'' said Schickel. Ansen claimed the production was well served by the "seductive score, masterminded by co-producer Irving Azoff, which ranges from Charlie Daniel's C and W to the mellow L.A. sounds of Boz Scaggs.'' The *New Leader* found the music "enjoyable'' while wondering about the "inexplicably absent'' Nelson and Jennings.[33] Gelmis candidly asserted that the music was featured "to promote the movie and to merchandise for ancillary income''[34] and he was absolutely correct. (Soundtracks, since *SNF*, were offsetting losses or adding to studio profile margins, and record labels were delighted to go along for the ride.) The production cost for Azoff—a mere $100,000—was a bargain. The album climbed to number 3 by September, but Gilley's single stalled at number 22 in August. The second single released, Kenny Rogers's "Love The World Away,'' bypassed the first and peaked at number 14 at about the same time. Johnny Lee's "Lookin' for Love'' came next and reached number 5. It was followed by Boz Scaggs's "Look What You've Done To Me,'' which made it to number 14. Anne Murray's "Could I Have This Dance,'' the fifth single from the album, fizzled at number 33 as the soundtrack LP was falling off the charts. "The more important sales figures indicated the anthology certified triple platinum with estimates of a possible two more million. Seven singles, a la Stigwood, were charted. Azoff was surprised, calling the situation "pretty preposterous.''[35]

An added bonus was to be found on the Country charts, on which

Urban Cowboy ranked number 1. "Lookin' For Love" was well on its way to selling a million; this was more than hillbilly heaven, it was crossover bliss. A *Rolling Stone* critic noted the package "is a lot stronger, and is doing better commercially, than the movie."[36] *Variety* led with "Soundtrack Pulls In Many To See 'Urban Cowboy.' "

By September 1980, *Urban Cowboy* had grabbed about $42 million at the box office. Looking at the receipts, Azoff said, "The reason it has stabilized is the album keeps the people coming in."[37] The audience for *Cowboy* was generally over eighteen. "We're not getting the youth," said Paramount's senior marketing vice president, Eddie Kalish. "The campaign has been based on the quality of the film so far. We've used reviews, and this has appealed to older audiences."[38]

The movie and album generated a country-western revival, but it was not nearly of the magnitude of disco fever. By the end of September 1980, four Los Angeles radio stations had switched to country formats, hoping to be on the fore front of a new trend. Overnight, former discotheques were coverted into clubs modeled after Gilley's. Urban cowpunchers tested their rodeo skills on a herd of about 400 mechanical bulls spread across the country. One New York saloon manager said, "It's like having the only Hula-Hoop in Manhattan."[39]

A sequel LP, *Urban Cowboy 2* was released in December 1980. The album included songs by Charlie Daniels, Johnny Lee, J.D. Souther, The Bayou City Beats, and Mickey Gilley. It first appeared on the *Billboard* charts in January 1981, but peaked at number 128 with a brief stay of seven weeks. It did better on the country charts, peaking at number 30.

Latham had centered his *Esquire* piece on two regulars at Gilley's whose love story sounded like a Country and Western ballad.

> Dew met Betty at Gilley's, *twang-twang*. Dew fell in love with Betty at Gilley's, *twang-twang*. They had their wedding reception at Gilley's, *twang-twang*. But they quarreled over the bull at Gilley's, *twang-twang*. And then Dew met somebody new at Gilley's, *twaaaang*.[40]

Urban Cowboy failed to popularize country music, but it did rate triple platinum. Studios with risky or marginal youth-oriented films clamored for Azoff's services as an executive producer. In the wake of *Cowboy*, Columbia signed Azoff for *Heavy Metal*, produced by Ivan Reitman. His central task was acquiring artists and songs for the soundtrack album, predictably a two-record set. Azoff was literally becoming an insurance policy for film projects.

Leonard Mogel, co-founder of National Lampoon, Inc., basking in the success of *Animal House* decided to make a movie based on *Heavy Metal*, an adult sci-fi magazine. Seven segments would be featured in the animated film, with nearly 1,000 artists from seventeen countries providing graphics. An eleven-week production schedule was arranged. The target audience was twenty-two-year-olds, allowing an "R" rating. Numerous critics would later note the film's appeal was predominantly "under fifteen and male."

Columbia Pictures signed onto the film's distribution for $8 million, exceeding their $7.5 million. The studio earmarked a $6-million marketing war chest, most to be spent on television time on youth-oriented programs.

Multi-media connects were scheduled, including a one-hour radio show and a 128-page book, *The Art of Heavy Metal*. A 7 August opening date was scheduled for 600 theaters to accommodate back-to-school mall traffic.

Full Moon/Asylum took out full page ads in living color announcing:

> HEAVY METAL
> means
> HEAVY BUSINESS
> Why bother with expensive lightweight imitations?
> Now you have the real thing within your grasp,
> HEAVY METAL . . .
> Go for the HEAVY METAL
> and put a steel edge on your business!

Billboard's reviewer shared the enthusiasm, writing, "There is enough metal here even to give the most devout metallurgists more than their share. For those who prefer something quieter, there are contributions from Donald Fagen, Don Felder, Stevie Nicks and Devo. Their inclusion may become clearer after viewing the animated film (based on the famous *Heavy Metal* illustrated magazine). This soundtrack has instant AOR appeal and all of the songs here are new so this should generate more interest than some recent soundtracks which used already available material."[41]

As with *Urban Cowboy*, the album title was misleading. "People shouldn't take the title too literally," noted Azoff. "Just as every cut on *Urban Cowboy* wasn't country, every cut here isn't heavy metal."

"We didn't want heavy metal fans to think they were getting ripped off, yet we didn't want to turn off the mainstream pop audience," said compiler Bob Destocki. The title did reflect the magazine, but hardly the music.

"You couldn't just take some pound'em, rock'em, sock'em heavy metal music and have it work straight through the film," explained Azoff.

"Besides, as used in the movie, the title comes from *Heavy Metal* magazine, not heavy metal music."[42]

The compilation proved a classic example of record label wheeling and dealing: For the rights to three CBS Group Artists Azoff again relinquished international distribution and pressing rights, as he did with *FM*, and included an unknown act from the Columbia roster, Trust.

"They wanted a shot at trying to establish Trust here," he said. "It was also to help the album internationally: Trust is a very big French act." Continuing to discuss his relationship with Columbia, Azoff added, "The Journey and Blue Oyster Cult cuts are going to appear on albums in the near future. That's because Walter's (Yetnikoff) tougher than anybody else." Yetnikoff did allow Full Moon to release the Cheap Trick single "Reach Out" as "we don't have an album to sell right now." This would be the final collaboration between Azoff and CBS. The manager felt he was being jerked around. The CBS/Records Group president responded, "Irving doesn't pay enough to artist and record companies. I've questioned some accounting we've gotten on previous material he used."[43] This would be one of the many salvos between the record label and soundtrack editors.

Don Felder's "Heavy Metal (Takin' A Ride)" was the scout single. It entered the Hot 100 25 July 1981 at number 85 and failed to climb beyond number 50 during a nine-week stay. Azoff was correct in saying, "I don't anticipate with this type of music as great singles penetration." "Heavy Metal" did receive considerable AOR exposure.

Heavy Metal was a somewhat mindless, adolescent, animate fantasy set to rock music, but critical response began on a positive note. Klain in *Variety*, predicted strong youth appeal, saying a particularly strong marketing plus will be a bevy of hard rock groups (Black Sabbath, Blue Oyster Cult, Cheap Trick, etc.) as both patron lure and soundtrack tie-in fodder." Janet Maslin provided another up-beat notice, saying, "*Heavy Metal* has been animated with great verve, and scored very well with music much less ear-splitting than the title would suggest." She did caution that "Animated or not, this isn't a movie to take children to, unless you'd like them to develop an early interest in bondage." The ensuing euphoria at Columbia Pictures was short lived, as later reviews were uniformly negative."[44]

Bob Browning said the film's "R" rating excluded "the very audience for which it was intended" and Sheila Benson, in Los Angeles, concluded, "It may or may not beat getting hit by lightning in the kidneys." Andrew Sarris indicated that "the ideal audience for *Heavy Metal* might just as well come from another planet." Richard Harrington, in the *Washington*

Post, called the film "one of the worst ideas ever to be translated into a movie." The *Christian Science Monitor* portrayed the ninety-minute cartoon as a "piece of trash on every level." The movie was, according to Coleman, "conceived for those who breathe heavily while reading comics with their fingers."[45]

Azoff's album also earned the wrath of the scribes. Ansen characterized it as "schlock acid rock" targeted at "horny adolescent boys." "Surrounding sound that passes for music," offered the *New York Post*. Azoff's most formidable critics were at the *Washington Post*. "The soundtrack is junked up with snatches of rock melodies that will constitute a best-selling soundtrack that has nothing to do with the film," wrote Harrington. Browning found "the greatest failure of the movie is the criminally negligent use of the soundtrack." The writer went on to call the songs gratituous, as "it's only for four or five bars at best."[46] Azoff's creation, as with *FM* and *Urban Cowboy*, was an insurance policy for the movie. The practice of joining rock music to films regardless of appropriateness was rapidly taking hold.

However, the music failed to regenerate a failed picture. The studios return was a mere $9.3 million; post-production costs were not covered. The album, easily outdistancing the movie, spent seven months on the trade charts near the top and became certified platinum. Azoff's track record remained intact, despite the two box office flops.

Fast Times

Cameron Crowe, the *wunderkid* of rock journalism, had published features in *Rolling Stone* at the age of eighteen. Reportedly, he was the protype for *Rich and Famous*. In 1979, the youthful writer undertook the massive project of "going undercover" in a Southern California high school—Redondo Beach—to study teen culture. He remained for a year. The result was the novel *Fast Times At Ridgemont High*, which Azoff decided to make into a film. Producer/writer Art Linson, of *Where The Buffalo Roam*, was enlisted, and Azoff's would co-produce. Linson applauded Crowe's published account, saying, "It wasn't a look at the way older people think teenagers act. It was approached from the teenagers' perspective . . . Cameron's approach is special because it's what it is. This is what's happening. The intent of this was to make a movie about kids by people who are young."

Azoff called Crowe the "culture expert in this movie. He really understood it, knew it and lived it. It's about relationships and growing up fast. The time goes by so fast for kids today who are out on their own much earlier then in the past. They learn how to deal with their independence.'' Linson noted that the director Amy Heckerling and Crowe were ''both very young. They are comfortable with the subject matter . . . they understand the youth view of sex and comedy and rock 'n' roll.''

Crowe, in a press release, said ''It is true to the humor of the kids. It's not a teen exploitation picture. It's the way they live. The anguish and adolescent turmoil is important but the humor is also important. The kids have fun.

''The contemporary kids also lead adult lives at younger and younger ages,'' he went on. ''For instance, making money is important to them. They feel that an allowance from parents is humiliating. The economy has affected them more than people know.

''Adolescence is faster than it was in the past,'' he continued. ''The other meaning is that it captures the whole fast-food system that these kids are involved in today. Kids are working and leading adult lives. They cram much more into a limited time before going out into the work world.'' It was time for the film world to translate these concepts onto the screen.

Azoff's success with the teen market, while declining, was impressive: A double soundtrack, regardless of box office, would more than offset distributor losses. MCA would underwrite this Eighties version of *American Graffiti*.

The eight-week production took place in the Los Angeles Area, in the affluent Sherman Oaks Galleria Mall and Van Nuys High School. The inexpensive film—under $10 million—starred relative unknowns Sean Penn, Jennifer Jason Leigh, and Judge Reinhold.

Azoff supervised the soundtrack, assembling ''a super star collection of entertainers writing all new, original material for there will be a few new acts on it also because I always do that since I feel an obligation to expose some new talent.'' Of the nineteen acts included on the double album, there were only three new artists: Jackson Browne, individual members of the disintegrating Eagles, Sammy Hager, Billy Squier, The Go Go's, Quartermaster, Graham Nash, Jimmy Buffet, Stevie Nicks, and The Cars were familiar names to rock fans; Oingo Boingo and The Ravyns were new. Front Line was more than adequately represented.

Azoff severed relations with CBS. He explained, ''Universal demands more rights than any other picture company, and CBS grants less rights than any other record company. Their business affairs departments were basically incompatible and I had a deadline. We would have been negotiating three years from now trying to figure out the formula for payment on videocassettes. Because of business complications on the *Heavy Metal* and *Urban Cowboy* projects, I've decided life is too short to try and mix

Warners and CBS artists." Azoff's attitude was widely held in the film industry. CBS was "difficult" in the arena of video and "other back-end rights."[47]

The film and the album both hit the streets on 13 August.

Billboard greeted the record's arrival by making note of Azoff's previous successes. "While the novel inspiring the movie slanted its music to heavy rock by Led Zeppelin and Rainbow, among others, this sampling of 18 acts edges toward a softer, more varied array of styles that should allow mainstream pop as well as AOR acceptance," it noted.[48] The album debuted on the charts two weeks later at number 74.

Jackson Browne's scout single, "Somebody's Baby," surfaced at number 73 on the singles charts during the first week of August. (The choice was questionable as Browne was an AOR artist.) The Ravyns' "Raised on Radio" was scheduled for release a week later. The title song was withheld.

Bob Destocki, a "co-compiler," complained, "Some acts don't understand what the soundtrack business is all about. Artists don't make a giant amount of money off soundtracks."[49] This view was not universally shared. Visions of substantial *SNF* royalty payments to virtual unknowns lingered in the folklore of the music industry.

Fast Times was squarely in the tradition of beach party films. These pictures, as Cagin and Dray indicate, stressed "tribal rites that identify and define youth culture."[50] *Ridgemont* is replete with the Southern California surfing-and-mall-cruising teen culture. Director Heckerling would later say, "We had to settle between what is the cool thing to wear and reality."

The movie has a series of subplots centering around The Ridgemont Mall. The ninety-two-minute film opens at the complex's entry as the Go-Go's "We Got The Beat" introduces the central characters. Scalper Mike Damone (Robert Romanus) is hustling concert tickets outside of Perry's Pizza where the temporarily virginal, fifteen-year-old Stacy Hamilton (Jennifer Jason Leigh) and her "sophisticated" pal, Linda Barrett (Phoebe Cates), a waitress. Across from the pizza parlor is the movie theater employing Mark "Rat" Ratner (Brian Backer), who develops a slight interest in Stacy. At the All-American Burger joint is Stacy's older brother, Brad (Judge Reinhold), applying a dress code to super surfer Jeff Spicoli (Sean Penn) whose "been stoned since the third grade."

These adolescents have one common interest—sex. Linda urges her inexperienced friend to date a twenty-six-year-old customer, Ron Johnson (D.W. Brown). "Stacy, what are you waiting for? You're fifteen years old," she asks. Prior to the covert liason, using a carrot, Stacy is shown the mechanics of oral intercourse. At "The Point," the baseball stadium, Stacy loses her virginity as Jackson Browne's "She's Got to Be Somebody's Baby" echoes.

Brad, conversely, can't get his "steady," for two years, to "The Point." Instead, he lavishes tender loving care on an aging Buick sedan to the tune of "Raised on Radio" by Baltimore's The Ravyns. The vehicle becomes his security after he loses his mall job and girlfriend, who "wants to be just friends."

The Rat, with Mike's coaching—"on a date put on side one of *Led Zeppelin IV*"—goes out with the newly liberated Stacy. She overwhelms the shy youth, who flees.

Jeff, the spaced out, irresponsible surfing bum, appears to lack an overactive libido, preferring to vex history teach Mr. Hand (Ray Walston) and "party." As *Variety's* Harwood noted, "his role has no particular plot importance." Penn's character, suggested Kevin Thomas, was "one of the most hilarious presences to hit the screen since the late John Belushi in *Animal House*—especially when he comes against astringent history professor Ray Walston, for whom he defines the Constitution of the United States as a 'cool set of rules.' "[51]

Stacy, Mike, Brad, and Linda become involved in a series of sexual misadventures. Mike's fumbling attempt at intercourse impregnates Stacy; he is proven more inept by refusing to pay for the ensuing $150 abortion. Rat, learning of the operation, feels betrayed. (This episode finds Stevie Nicks and The Go-Go's ineffectually providing background.)

The influence of *American Graffiti* is highlighted when Brad spies the blonde "Beautiful Girl in the Car" (Nancy Wilson replacing Susan Sommers), to the strains of The Cars' "Moving in Stereo," and abandons Capt. Hook's Fish and Chips. Louise Goffin's "Uptown Boys" overlays the rebellion.

In the tradition of Sam Katzman and Roger Corman, the teenpic nears its conclusion with the big finals-week dance. On stage, joined by Beach-Boy-attired Spicoli, Reeves Nevo and The Cinch sing "Life in the Fast Lane" and the California party favorite, "Wooly Bully." Deviating from the norm for teen films, the gala resolves little. Only Mike and Mark are reconciled.

The following day at the mall a chastened Stacy reveals, "I don't want sex. I want a relationship," beckoning to Rat. A coda, as with *American Graffiti*, provides resolution, but only after Brad heroically subdues a convenience-store robber, allowing Spicoli to exclaim the immortal phrase "Awesome! Totally, awesome."

Lotusland critics dissented. The *Los Angeles Times* said it was "ridiculous" to assume teenagers "never have anything on their minds but sex." Harwood dismissed the project as not offering "a lot beyond the Sophomore class."[52]

New York writers were a bit more generous. "A jumbled but appealing teenage comedy with something of a fresh perspective on the subject," offered Maslin. Pauline Kael said, "It's certainly likable." In *New York*, Denby praised "A fresh, funny exploration of adolescent anxieties and confusions." Azoff's negative assessment of the East Coast Market appeared flawed until *Newsday* and *The Voice* hit the newstands. Gelmis characterized *Fast Times* as cruder than it needed to be to make its points. *Fast Times* appeared to the *Voice* reviewer as "something of a marketing wet dream: you can read the movie, listen to the book, and see the soundtrack album. Moreover, it's a curiously empty movie."[53]

The national news magazines were equally divided. *Newsweek* asked, "Looking for a sleeper for 1982? Try *Fast Times*." *Time*'s Corliss viewed the film as "laced with decal cliches on the screen" in the structure of *American Graffiti* and "its 467 imitators."[54]

Predictably, most writers placed *Fast Times* in the *American Graffiti*, beach-party genre. One reviewer asserted, "Compressed to fundamentals, the high school characters of the 1980's aren't that different from the 1950's."[55]

Structurally, Crowe's protrayal of Valley adolescents evolved from the mild youth vehicles of the 1950s. The story flaw was its time frame. Teens of the 1980s were a different breed than those of the Seventies, when Crowe's "undercover" work took place. (Paul Brickman's dark *Risky Business* would perhaps be a more adequate representation of Reagan era highschoolers.)

Azoff's use of music received mixed reviews. Pauline Kael was positive. "The music isn't obstreperous; it doesn't underline things—it's just always there when it's needed," she wrote. Conversely, Maslin stated, "The music, which ought to be one of the movie's bigger selling points, is for the most part thrown away." Moreover, she added, the songs "seem to drift in and out of the movie distractingly instead of helping to propel it along."[56]

Other reviewers fell somewhere in between. *Monthly Film Bulletin* described the score as "the U.S. marketing hook." Corliss called it a "requisite two-record album of last year's hits (sic) that function as the music track." "The music of Spicoli and his pals sometimes conveys that dispirited 'no future' anomie," noted the *Village Voice*, "But more often than not the soundtrack pulses with the *artificially* upbeat." (emphasis added)[57] The score lacked a "hook" tune.

The record entered the weekly charts in August and peaked at number 48. Despite a four-month stay, the anthology failed to garner an RIAA certification by the year's end. "It ended the feeling that you could put any kind of collection of rock-star tracks on and the public would buy this compilation without regard for its connection to the film," said Danny Goldberg of *No Nukes*.[58] The independent "music supervisor" was partially correct as synergy would become the misused word in the following years.

The disappointing showing of the album, attributed to the song placement, may have mirrored the sagging state of the record industry in 1982. *Fast Times*'s album managed to rank number 9 on *Billboard's* year-end soundtrack chart, but didn't earn a gold plaque.

The product's performance, in part, brought into question the viability of a rock album insuring a studio's investment. The success of the film was due to many factors. As Carrie Rickey of the *Village Voice* said, "The largest cohort of the movie audiences is under 30: nab them and you've got a hit." Doherty insightfully described the crossover aspect of the film as "unmistakably, emphatically adult." The picture's "R" rating—unenforceable—underlined its dual appeal.

The film returned $16 million to Universal, surpassing *Heavy Metal*, but failing to match *Urban Cowboy's* $24 million.

Ridgemont ended Azoff's reign as Stigwood's successor as it failed to garner an RIAA certification. Although Azoff soon would become head of MCA Records, the prominent soundtrack label, a contender was emerging: Taylor Hackford. Hackford would get off to a slow start with the film *The Idolmaker*, but learned quickly. By the early Eighties his films would earn several Best Song Oscars and RIAA plaques.

Taylor Hackford's American Dream: Idolmaker & Officer

I wanted to be Pygmalion
—Bob Marcucci, Chancellor Records

Bob Marcucci, a legend in the music industry, created two successive teen idols, Frankie Avalon and Fabian, in the heyday to *American Bandstand*.

Having founded Chancellor Records with Pete DeAngelis in 1957, Marcucci was determined to find artists with "the look" for the label. "We need some idols," he would tell his partner. DeAngelis knew a trumpet player in the Philadelphia area—Frankie Avalon. When he was auditioning a singer in Avalon's ensemble, Marcucci discovered that the horn player could sing. Frankie objected, "I'm not a singer," he said, to which the entreprenuer responded, "You're great. You got personality." His first single bombed.

Marcucci, at the time, was cultivating Dick Clark by sending him gifts when Chancellor products were aired on *Bandstand*. "Dick Clark was the only way to get your artist to be seen throughout the country in the matter of one day" he informed Joe Smith.[59] Avalon appeared on the show 18 September 1957, but was not particularly memorable. Later, however, the label owners found a suitable song for the ex-trumpeter: "DeDeDinah" was issued December 5. Avalon lip-synced the tune on *Bandstand* seven days later. According to Marcucci, "it was a smash."

This success only fueled Marcucci's desire to find a new start. Avalon "didn't have *that look*," he said. But Fabian Forte, a goodlooking fifteen-year-old, did.

Fabian, who had no entertainment experience, accepted Marcucci's offer to make him an idol strictly for money. He recalled:

> The strategy was for me to be a male teen performer, but the big problem was songs. They put me together with Doc Pomus and Mort Shuman, and they gave me "I'm a Man," which was a medium hit. Got me on the charts. After that I had "Turn Me Loose," and that one did a lot better.

> Performing terrified me. People were screaming, and I had no idea why. Bob would say, "Move this way, move that way,' until it became second nature. Bob was the guru. The only thing he couldn't do anything about was my face. I had my face. Bob always wanted to be a star himself. He kind of lived through Frankie and me.

There was, of course, more than mere vicarious gratification.

> "Disc jockeys treated me well, too. We all washed one another's hands. The standing joke in the business was, "Of course payola exists. How else would a man like this make it?" I am afraid that is part of my legacy."[60]

In 1964 Marcucci, who had lost his proteges, faded from the music scene. In the mid-1970s he re-emerged to work on a film documenting the *American Bandstand* scene. At the time, Dick Clark was planning a similar project.

In the wake of *Grease*, nostalgia-laced projects were the vogue and *Bandstand*, an artifact of the 1950s, was a natural for film exploitation.

Marcucci peddled his project to producer Gene Kirkwood, who liked the concept as, he said, it contained "a *Rocky*-like story that is very American. He's part of the American dream. A young man's drive, wanting to succeed."[61]

Kirkwood's partner, Howard Koch, Jr. the son of the former Paramount Pictures president and legendary director, appreciated the rock-oriented plot. (In 1964 he had worked for British talent agent Harold Davison as a tour manager, crossing the country with The Dave Clark Five and other acts.) Kirkwood and Koch assigned the script to two-time Emmy-winner Edward Dihorenzo. Taylor Hackford was hired to direct. Hackford was an ideal choice, a self-described "child of Rock 'n' Roll."

"My grammar school years were infused with Elvis Presley, Little Richard, Chuck Berry, Big Joe Turner, and those people that kind of define that kind of music. It was my music of choice," he said. "Rock 'n' roll was the popular music of my genreation. I love it. And if I hadn't gone in one direction, in school politics and so forth, I would have probably been a rock 'n' roll singer. I had a group of friends and we sang and we did things they went out and had bands. If I score my life to music and I think in terms of songs in different periods of my life, why shouldn't the characters in my films do the same . . . I love music and I've tried to infuse music in my films in a dramatic way." Hackford was delighted with the opportunity. "I would literally have done anything to get that shot," he recalled.

In a *Films in Review* interview, he admitted a good deal of dramatic license came into play during the filming. "I was interested in making it more of a morality play about the individual wanting to be a performer himself, and not making the Frankie Avalon and Fabian story," he said. "To me that—certainly musically—wasn't very interesting. I was interested in doing an original musical with new music." This interest would prove disastrous.

The plot also jived with the director's working-class origins. "I came out of the working class. I grew up in Santa Barbara, which is a nice place. My mother's yearly income was about $6,000 a year, so the fact is I relate to working-class situations," he told an interviewer. He rejected law school in order to join the Peace Corps and served in Bolivia. Returning, he went to work for Los Angeles's PBS affiliate, KCET. "I liked their programming and thought that with my social concerns that it would be a better place for me to go than commerical television," he said. Eventually he supervised documentaries and rockumentaries, producing and directing the award-winning film *Teenage Father*, "the *boy's* view in a teenage pregnancy."

Neophyte actors Paul Land and Peter Gallagher were signed to star.

The $4.5-million production was shot in New York and Los Angeles. Hundreds of teenage extras were recruited and the concert sequences were filmed at the Fox Wilshire in Beverly Hills during Easter break.

Rolling Stone would later comment, "Hackford stages his mock-Fabian concert scenes with all-stops-out bravura."[62]

In the meantime, Dick Clark had abandoned his film project.

United Artists, in anticipation of an early November release date, targeted seventeen markets and 150 theaters; 100,000 posters appeared, proclaiming "Caesare Is Coming" or "Tommy Dee Is Coming." There was no mention of a film.

Hy Smith, advertising and publicity vice president, devised an ad proclaiming "He's got the look. He's got the talent. He's got the *Idolmaker*." The rationale for the campaign was, again, demographic cross-over.

"It's being aimed at the teenagers and the teenyboppers, so we're not playing on *The Idolmaker*," Smith explained, "but at the same time in that copy approach we're saying there is an *Idolmaker* that may be of more interest to the *older* audiences. The same guy who rooted for Rocky Balboa . . . can see this ad and think, 'Hey, if I go see this movie I can see how an idolmaker could make me an idol.' It was just one more way of personalizing the TV spots and trailer."

UA was in fact reinventing the wheel. "One of the exciting things for us with this film was signing two young kids who we would promote as teen idols," said Koch. "We taught them to [sing and perform] for the movie. Then in the movie they're taught and promoted as stars. And now that the movie is being released we're promoting them [both as themselves and as their characters] it's like a manual of how to make a teen idol."[63] The studio would not replicate Marcucci's success despite a media blitz including the syndicated *Merv Griffin Show* and a New York sneak preview to which WABC and WCBS-FM offered 2,500 free passes.

A&M Records reportedly was to participate in the campaign by passing out coupons, for a dollar discount on the soundtrack, in theater lobbys. There was, however, "very bad coordination."

Cashbox included *Idolmaker* at number 162 December 13. A week later *Billboard* had the title in the number 172 slot.[64]

Jeff Barry's score was doomed from its inception. "We didn't want to do another film with the oldies but goodies. It's been done with *American Hot Wax* and *American Graffiti*," Koch said, "and we felt that today's music going back to the simpler sounds of the late '50s and early '60s, but with more sophisticated instrumentation."

"It's surprising," he went on, "when people come up and say, 'Boy, you really captured the late '50s and early '60s sound,' and other people say 'You really cheated because that's today's sound.' I think we did a good job of it because people who don't really know that period are assuming it's today's sound, but people who remember that period say, 'Yeah, I remember songs like that.' It's only a nostalgia movie to those of us over 20.''[65]

The difficulty arose as most filmgoers, especially for rock-oriented backstagers, were under twenty-five and the radio program directors in major markets were older. *Variety's* McBride quickly grasped the contradiction, saying that the cuts "often have too contemporary a sound, a decision that may have been calculated to appeal to today's teen audience rather than to express the period with accuracy. Too bad, since the film is otherwise faithful to details.[66] Radio programmers shared this opinion. Some six years later Hackford would tell an interviewer, "I discovered at that point that there really needed to be some involvement in planning the music and its release in coordination with the film."[67] The backstager opened two weeks before the overcrowded Thanksgiving weekend.

The Sage?

In the film, Vincent Vacarri (Ray Sharkey) is presented as a twenty-seven-year-old songwriter, working as a waiter, who dreams of succeeding in the recording industry. Early on, he points to the covers of fan magazines, claiming that Elvis, Rock Hudson and others "got *it* all right there." "It" is the teen-idol "look."

Visiting an Italian nitery, he encounters a Johnny and the Hurricanes ("Red River Rock") soundalike band. A blonde lead singer performs "Jenny" to a polite response, but the ethnic saxophonist has the crowd roaring. (Avalon played trumpet). The audience response validates Vinnie's belief that "women don't want blonde singing idols. They want dark hair." He approaches the saxophone player, repeating, "You got *it*. What's it gonna be, pizza or caviar?"

"What's caviar?" inquires the recruit, Tommy Dee.

Dee rehearses ceaselessly until every move, gesture, and note to "Here Is My Love" is automatic. With his robotized product polished, Vacarri obtains financing from his shady but "connected" absentee father. With $10,000 and Dee in tow, he hits the record-hop circuit. Predictably, "Here Is My Love" is greeted by screaming teenyboppers as Vinnie cues every motion from the wings. The deejay hosting the dance is noncommittal until some "presidents" (dollars) are provided. This is one of the movies few references to payola, which some say was a standard music business practice in the late 1950s.

Courting the media, the manager approaches *Teen Scene* editor Brenda Roberts (Tovah Feldshuh). She agrees to a mention on time, but Vinnie insists, "I want the cover." He prevails, but not until the editor receives 50 percent of merchandising—"pictures, posters, souvenirs, the works." This arrangement by which gatekeepers received a percentage of a song or artist in return for exposure, would come to be known as "Clarkola."

With his face on the cover of *Teen Scene*, Tommy appears on "National Bandstand," hosted by Ed Sharp (Michael Mislove). Again, the response is frantic. The formula is working. "The kid's a gold mine," says Brenda. Vinnie, however, is becoming disillusioned with his creation.

As Tommy is enjoying the star trip, Vinnie has a second protege literally stumbling into the equation. Unlike his predecessor, Guido, now Caesare, can't carry a tune. His debut, due to stage fright, is a disaster. Undaunted, Vinnie insists the discovery will be bigger than Presley. A poster campaign is mounted—"Caesare Is Here," and an engineered single, "I Know Where You're Goin'," amplified and echoes to minimize Caesare's vocal shortcomings, is issued. Appearing, finally, before an audience, Caesare is mobbed. After a retreat he returns and performs a dirgelike chant, "Baby." The recitation evokes pandemonium. Caesare's persona is more reminiscent of *Grease's* John Travolta than Fabian.

Realizing the limitations of his "new find," Vinnie shelters Caesare, and the press labels the new idol "the rock hermit." However, Caesare later meets with a female *Teen Scene* reporter, not for an interview, and also is arrested for drunk driving. Vinnie is furious, but the artificial star, who has been Number 1 for twenty-five weeks, insists on a tour. The idolmaker books his student into Memphis. The decision is greeted by the local media as "Carpet Baggers Invade Elvis Country" and signs reading "Caesare Go Home."

The invasion of Elvis's milieu culminates with a strobe light production number, "However Dark the Night." The performer brags that he deserves his celebrity. Vinnie objects. "When you were up on that stage it was *me*. Every note you sing it was *me*! Every move you make it was *me*!" he yells. Angered, Caesare destroys the dressing room mirror; the "look" and Vinnie's fantasy are destroyed.

The discovery-of-self theme of the film violates the Avalon-Fabian aspects of the sage, but film's devotion to history has often been deficient.

As a backstager, *Idolmaker* worked when stressing the "hype" involved in idolmaking. Marcucci insisted the tyrant was exaggerated. "I was the essence of the character, but Sharkey made it also a second person, who was maybe more arrogant than I was," he said. "I don't think I was as hateful as he turned out to be. But I did believe in what I was doing. I wanted to be Pygmalion."[68]

The Marcucci role may have been gentler, but still the buying of exposure was downplayed in the film. *Idolmaker* presented a business-as-usual characterization. How Tommy Dee reached "National Bandstand" is ignored. Indeed, Marcucci's relationship with Dick Clark was overtly ignored.

Following the marketing strategy of "covering both generational audiences," scorer Jerry Barry impressed neither. Critical response to Barry's musical material was uniformly negative. "Music is very important to a movie like this," wrote Maslin, "and the music in *Idolmaker* is awful. In a hugely misguided attempt to spin contemporary hit singles out of a period film, Jeff Barry concocts a score that's neither here nor there." "While the imposition of strong, contemporary-beat music may have been a conscious departure, presumably for marketing reasons, it nevertheless strikes a false note, and undermines the authenticity of the (otherwise brilliantly evoked) reactions of hysterical high school fans," stated *Monthly Film Bulletin*. Asahina said the songs sound "more like disco tunes than rock and roll." Corliss added that the selections "sound as if they came from Broadway rather than Broad Street." "Nursery rhymes for berserk adolescents," insisted Kael.[69]

The cast ties and similarities to *Grease* no doubt contributed to the confusion. One critic suggested the film, set in an Italian section of New York City, "Offers two semi-Travoltas for the price of one real thing." "Peter Gallagher as Caesare is too Travolta for words (he's yet another *Grease* graduate)," stated Rickey.[70]

As for the music, Barry's compositions, while an aesthetic improvement, with the exception of "Baby," just did not fit the film, and soundtrack sales reflected that. Reaching the charts in mid-December, the album lingered at Number 124, falling off after a nine-week stay. Taylor Hackford would learn a bitter lesson about "bad coordination." "The record came out three weeks after the movie," he recalled, "and by that time the movie was gone. I discovered at that point there really needed to be some involvement in planning the music and its release in coordination with the film."[71]

Idolmaker debuted in early November in sixty-eight theaters in eight markets and earned a disappointing $295,500. (The all-important first week netted a mere $43,000.) By mid-December it peaked on eighty screens nationally, with a $1 million studio return. A week later, exhausted, the film was playing in thirteen theaters.

Hackford's *Idolmaker* was a depiction of the rags-to-riches American Dream. Since *Rocky*, upward mobility had become fashionable, and the pugilistic story, was definitely in vogue in the early 1980s.

In search of a follow-up production, Hackford was given a script by Douglas Day Stewart. The storyline, essentially, concerned two people trying to improve themselves in a military setting. *An Officer And A Gentlemen* was absolutely in the self-reflective genre of filmmaking: it mirrored the director's Peace Corps experience and Santa Barbara upbringing in a work-a-day, blue-collar world.

The film, he said, "was interesting to me as a project, not because of its military basis. But because of the working-class nature of its characters, these were not people who had all the options of middle-class life available to them. That's why they gravitated to the military. It was a ticket."

He told an interviewer that *Officer* and *Idolmaker* were both "about people who are trying to discover something about themselves. Maybe they're not even trying but the essence of the film (*Officer*) is to show them going through the process of self-discovery. In both instances they're about people who are shut off and are forced to confront themselves and change. Which I think all of us are dealing with every day of our lives. Debra Winger starts out as a small-town girl who is hot to trot and in the course of the film discovers a certain amount about herself, makes some choices for her personal integrity. So I think that there's something in both films about people growing. I like to make films that have some sort of positive statement."

The script required polishing. "It was a script I admired," said the director, "and I came in and made changes." With the rewrites, the Paramount studio people approached the Department of the Navy. "The Navy refused to cooperate. They thought the film was blasphemous. They hated it," said Hackford. DOD cited the language in the film and the lack of military equipment as the reasons. The studio executives replied the picture was about a "guy who changes his life and becomes a positive human through the military experience." The Navy did not relent. (Later, the Pentagon would express regret over the decision.)

The MPAA ratings committee gave *Officer* an "X" rating until the Winger/Gere love scene was reshot.

Reminiscent of the marketing of Hackford's maiden effort, Paramount Pictures was not sure how the film should be launched. The movie originally slated for an October release (when old moviegoers emerge), but Frank Mancuso, the studio's vice-president of advertising, recalled a New Orleans sneak preview that created doubts. Response in the city, "a mid-American, blue-collar market," was favorable.

"A month later," he told the *New York Times*, the same response was duplicated in Toronto, an upscale market of movie buffs. So in March we decided to take a shot at the summer. We were sure that people who went to see *An Officer And A Gentleman* would like the film. The challenge was to get people in to see it in the first place.''

To facilitate a word-of-mouth drive the film was screened in June and July "for librarians, cab drivers, beauticians, women's clubs, museum groups," said Mansuco, "for anyone who'd be likely to talk about it.''

The graphics campaign was old-fashioned "with the stars embracing and beneath them the trainees running." Some Paramount executives objected, wanting to sell it as a military film, but Mancuso and Mark dissented. The theater sheets and newspaper ads were only marginally effective, Mansuco admitted. "If word-of-mouth hadn't been terrific, everything we did made up a very bad plan," he acknowledged.[72] "Promotions can buy us a couple weeks' business and after that it has to be word-of-mouth," commented Fox's John Friedkin. "If the picture is bad, you might as well shoot everybody coming out of the theater—they will quickly enough kill any film."[73] With *Officer* the reverse occurred.

Having endured *Idolmaker*, Hackford switched record labels. Island replaced A&M. He also selected established contemporary writers and artists. The director appeared oblivious to Stigwood's staggered-release strategy. The signature tune, "Up Where We Belong," was written by lyricist Will Jennings, folksinger Buffy Sainte Marie, and her husband Jack Nitzsche during one weekend. (The tune was recorded some thirty days before the film's release.) Artists were chosen carefully. Jennifer Warnes had won an Oscar for "It Goes Like It Goes" in *Norma Rae* (1979), and Joe Cocker, seemed an ideal counterpoint. The single surfaced at number 89 on 21 August; by November it placed at the top *Billboard* slot, maintaining its dominance for three weeks.

Hackford's song placement paralleled that of *The Graduate*. As Ronald Bowers noted, "In a scene reminiscent of *Norma Rae*, Zack dashingly swoops Paula up in his arms, kisses her, and marches out." All the while "Where We Belong" underscores the uplifting event.[74]

The song was fundamentally an up-tempo adult contemporary offering; its presentation in the movie was memorable and effective.

The movie's storyline can be briefly summarized as featuring a Navy abused brat attempting to find respectability at a Naval Aviation Officers Candidate School. His thirteen weeks of hell are complicated by antagonist Drill Instructor Sgt. Emil Foley (Louis Gossett, Jr.) and his love interest, Paula Pokrikfi (Debra Winger), a paper-bag factory worker in search of an "MRS." with a naval aviator. The most revealing dialogue in the movie is Gere's confrontation with the D.I., in which Gossett demands a DOR (Drop Out on Request) and Gere responds, "I got nowhere to go. I got nothing else."

Reactions to the motion picture were mixed. Steven Jenkins, in the *Monthly Film Bulletin*, backhandedly noted that *Officer* was "an old fashioned, regressive, right-wing fantasy designed to appeal to all age groups." Schickel called the film "a Big Mac of a movie, junk food that somehow reaches the chortling soul." "In a season in which most American films are aimed at subteenagers," wrote Kissel, "it is enormously invigorating to come across a movie with adult characters whose problems are probed with such power and compassion."[75]

Frank Mancuso had told a writer that if *Officer* earned $2 million the first weekend, everything would be "just fine." The earnings exceeded $9.8 million. By the year's end, the $7-million production would gross more than $115.2 million.

This ticket action was not due to a song. Rather, the Cocker/Warnes single and the subsequent album, released 23 October were film driven. *Billboard* greeted the album by saying "The film 'An Officer And A Gentleman' is turning out to be big news at the box office while the theme 'Up Where We Belong' is a smash hit single. With these two credits, this soundtrack should do very well. However, there is more to this soundtrack than one song. Also included are Dire Straits' 'Tunnel of Love,' Pat Benatar's 'Treat Me Right,' Z.Z. Tops' 'Tush,' Sir Douglas Quintet's 'Be Real,' and Lee Ritenour's 'Love Theme.' A varied and worthwhile collection."[76]

The Island Record offering outpaced *Idolmaker*, attaining a number 31 slot as the high point of a twenty-one-week tenure on the charts. Despite a top-ranked single, however, it failed to earn a gold plaque.

Overall, 1982 was a severe disappointment to record companies. Unit shipments dropped from a peak of 344 million albums in 1977 to approximately 244 million. Rock-music purchases were at an all-time low of 34 percent. The year-end soundtrack listing reflected the downturn: only three of the Top 10 were rock-oriented: *Heavy Metal*, *Ridgemont High*, and *Rocky III*. The bottom, apparently, was falling out of the rock-and-reel union.

Notes

1. Stephen Farber, "He Drew His Boyhood To Make 'Diner,' " *New York Times*, 18 April 1982, 18.
2. "My Diner with Barry," *American Film*, June 1982, 35.
3. Michael Sragow, " 'Diner' Guy Makes Good," *Rolling Stone*, 13 May 1982, 39–40.
4. Chris Chase, "How 'Diner' Finally Made It To New York," *New York Times*, 2 April 1982, C8.

5. Quoted in Jeffrey Wells, "How To Market A Mixed Bag: Kwit vs. Levinson Over 'Diner,' " *Film Journal*, 12 April 1982, 13.

6. Chase, C8.

7. Wells, 13.

8. *Billboard*, 17 April 1982, 56.

9. Wells, 13.

10. Janet Maslin, "Nostalgic Visit To The 50s in 'Diner,' " *New York Times*, 2 April 1982, C3.

11. Quoted in " 'Diner' Buy," 40.

12. Vincent Canby, "A Feast of Interesting, Original New Work," *New York Times*, 11 April 1982, 1, sec. 2.

13. David Denby, "Eat Here and Get Laughs," *New York*, 5 April 1982, 58.

14. David Sterritt, "Diner," *Christian Science Monitor*, 29 April 1982, 19; David Ansen, "If At First You Do Succeed," *Newsweek*, 19 April 1982, 96; Robert Asahina, "Sex Three Ways," *News Leader*, 3 May 1982, 19; and Sheila Benson, "Diner," *Los Angeles Times*, 7 May 1982, 1.

15. Richard Corliss, "Five Friends," *Time*, 19 April 1982, 85.

16. John Coleman, "Gang Show," *New Statesman*, 26 November 1982, 32.

17. Michael Shore, *Music Video* (New York: Ballentine Books 1987), 118.

18. *Billboard* 22 April 1978: 88. The downfall of the film, release date not withstanding, was the 1960ish plot of a "hip" Los Angeles FMer refusing to "sell out" by airing U.S. Army jingles. The unbelievable deejays stage a sit-in, refusing to leave the premises. The outcome is totally predictable. See Janet Maslin, "Mr. Smith Goes to L.A.," *New York Times*, 28 April 1978, C12. Quoted in Ben Fong-Torres, "Rock on Reels," *Rolling Stone*, 20 April 1978, 48; Dave Marsh, *Unfortunate Son* (New York: Random House 1985), 154.

19. Peter Occhiogrosso, "Reelin' and Rockin'," *American Film*, April 1984, 47; Mitch Cohen, "FM," *Phonograph Record Magazine*, May 1 1978, 15; D. Pollock, "FM," *Variety*, 3 May 1978, 27; David Ansen, "Dippy Hipsters," *Newsweek*, 22 May 1978, 73; and Georgia Christgau, "FM—The Soundtrack," *Village Voice*, 8 May 1978, 54.

20. Maslin, "Mr. Smith," C12.

21. Quoted in Lane Maloney, "Azoff Says Soundtrack Pull In Many To See 'Urban Cowboy'," *Variety*, 16 September 1980, 73.

22. Quoted in Timothy White, "True-Grit Tenderfoot," *Rolling Stone*, 10 July 1980, 35.

23. Quoted in Rick Forrest, "In Search of the Celluloid Singing Cowboy," *Billboard*, 2 August 1980, M10; and Naomi Glauberman, "Ripped From the Headlines," *American Film*, March 1984, 50–56.

24. Quoted in Paul Grein, " 'Urban Cowboy' LP in 2 Parts," *Billboard*, 12 April 1980, 4.

25. Mark Hunter, "Hitching Discs To Flicks," *Mother Jones*, May 1981, 56.

26. Forrest, 10; and Stephen Holden, "Urban Cowboy," *Rolling Stone,* 10 July 1980, 54.

27. Todd McCarthy, "Is 'Western' Plot Now a B.O. Liability?" *Variety*, 25 June 1980, 28.

28. "Urban Cowboy," *Billboard*, 3 May 1980, 50.

29. Maloney, 73.

30. *Variety*, 4 June 1980, 20.

31. J. Harwood, "Urban Cowboy," *Variety*, 4 June 1980, 22; Charles Champlin, "Urban Cowboy," *Los Angeles Times*, 11 June 1980, 1 sec. VI.

32. Richard Schickel, "Sunbelt Saturday Night: 'Urban Cowboy,' " *Time*, 9 June 1980, 74; Robert Asahina, "Urban Cowboy," *New Leader*, 14 July 1980, 20; David Denby, "Throwing the Bull," *New York*, 16 June 1980, 55; and Archer Winsten, "Urban Cowboy," *New York Post*, 11 June 1980, 45.

33. Schickel; David Ansen, "John Travolta: Back On Track," *Newsweek*, 9 June 1980, 84; and Asahina.

34. Joseph Gelmis, "Urban Cowboy," *Newsday*, 11 June 1981, 68.

35. Maloney, 73.

36. Stephen Holden, "Movies, Music, and Money," *Hi Fi* October 1980: 106.

37. Maloney, 73.

38. McCarthy, "Is 'Western' Plot Now a B.O. Liability?" 28.

39. Quoted in Diane McWhorter, "Night Spots Turn Bullish On Cowboy Club Theme," *New York Times*, 8 October 1980, A20.

40. Aaron Latham, "The Ballad of the Urban Cowboy: America's Search for True Grit," *Esquire*, 12 September, 1978: 22.

41. *Billboard*, 25 July 1981, 66.

42. Quoted in Paul Grein, "Azoff Unleashes 'Metal' Track," *Billboard*, 1 August 1981, 4.

43. Quoted in Paul Grein, " 'Fast Times' LP Features Front Line Clients, Friends," *Billboard*, 7 August 1982, 8.

44. S. Klain, "Heavy Metal," *Variety*, 5 August 1981, 18; and Janet Maslin, " 'Heavy Metal' Animated Cartoon," *New York Times*, 7 August 1981, C14.

45. Bob Browning, " 'Heavy Metal:' Zap the Orb," *Washington Post*, 7 August 1981, 17; Sheila Benson, "Heavy Metal," *Los Angeles Times*, 7 August 1981, 9, (Calender); Andrew Sarris, " 'Heavy Metal' in a Time Warp," *Village Voice*, 5 August 1981, 35; Richard Harrington, " 'Heavy' Going," *Washington Post*, 8 August 1982, C10; and David Sterritt, "Heavy Metal," *Christian Science Monitor*, 10 September 1981, 19.

46. Browning, 17; Harrington, C10.

47. Grein, " 'Fast Times.' "

48. *Billboard*, 4 August 1982.

49. Quoted in Grein " 'Fast Times,' " 64.

50. Seth Gagin and Phillip Dray, *Hollywood Films of the Seventies: Sex, Drugs, Violence, Rock 'n' Roll and Politics* (New York: Harper and Row 1984), 195.

51. J. Harwood, "Fast Times at Ridgemont High," *Variety* 11 August 1982, 20; and Kevin Thomas, "Fast Times at Ridgemont," *Los Angeles Times*, 13 August 1982, 16 (*Calender*).

52. Thomas, 16; and Harwood, 20.

53. Janet Maslin, "Ridgemont High," *New York Times*, 3 September 1982, C6; Pauline Kael, "Rice Krispies," *New Yorker*, 22 December 1982, 146; Joseph Gelmis, "Fast Times," *Newsday*, 3 September 1982, 11 (Part II); and Carrie Rickey, "High School Confidential," *Village Voice*, 14 September 1982, 48.

54. Richard Corliss, "School Daze," *Time*, 13 September 1982, 87; Jack Kroll, "The Right Kid Stuff," *Newsweek*, 20 September 1982, 92.

55. J. Harwood, "Fast Times at Ridgemont High," *Variety*, 11 August 1982, 20.

56. Kael, 146; Maslin, C6.

57. Rickey, 48.

58. Quoted in Rob Tannenbaum, "Soundtracks Thrived in Summer of '85," *Rolling Stone*, 21 November 1985, 15.
59. Quotes in Joe Smith, *Off The Record* (New York: Warner Books 1988), 141.
60. Smith: 142–43.
61. Quoted in Ralph Kaminsky, "UA's 'Idolmaker' Gearing up for Wide Thanksgiving Break," *Boxoffice*, 26 May 1980, 3.
62. Quotes from Michael Sragow, "Small Triumphs Over the Formula," *Rolling Stone*, 5 February 1981, 37; John Calhoun, "Taylor Hackford," *Films in Review,* November 1982, 539–44.
63. Quotes in Jimmy Summers, "UA Promo Borrows From Film," *Boxoffice*, November 1980, 8.
64. Quoted in Chris Morris, "Early Music-Film Ties Best," *Billboard*, 6 December 1986, 77.
65. Summers, 8.
66. J. McBride, "Idolmaker," *Variety*, 5 November 1980, 22.
67. Morris, 77.
68. Quoted in Roman Kozak, "Marcucci Sees His Career In A Movie," *Billboard*, 22 November 1980, 72.
69. Janet Maslin, " 'Idolmaker' Creates a Teen Star," *New York Times*, 11 November 1980, C8; Jo Imeson, "Idolmaker," *Monthly Film Bulletin*, April 1981, 68; Robert Aschina, "Out-Acting the Script," *New Leader*, 1 December 1980, 19; Richard Corliss, "The Idolmaker," *Time*, 10 November 1980, 65; and Pauline Kael, "Poses," *New Yorker*, 8 December 1980, 100.
70. Carrie Rickey, "I'm Forever Blowing Bubblegum," *Village Voice*, 18 November 1980, 56.
71. Morris, 77.
72. Quotes from Aljean Harmetz, "How A Gamble Paid Off For Premiere of 'Officer'," *New York Times*, 17 August 1982, C7; Calhoun, 539–44.
73. Quoted in David Anthony Daly, *A Comparison of Exhibition and Distribution Patterns in Three Recent Feature Motion Pictures* (New York: Arno Press 1980), 90.
74. Ronald Bowers, "An Officer And A Gentleman," *Magills,* 248.
75. Steven Jenkins, "Officer," *Monthly Film Bulletin* March 1983, 74; Richard Schickel, "Big Mac," *Time*, 9 August 1982, 58; and Howard Kissel, "Officer . . . ," *Women's Wear Daily*, 27 July 1982, 28.
76. *Billboard*, 23 October 1982, 76.

ELVIS PRESLEY (courtesy of Alfred Werthheimer)

LITTLE RICHARD AND HIS BAND (courtesy BGSU Archives)

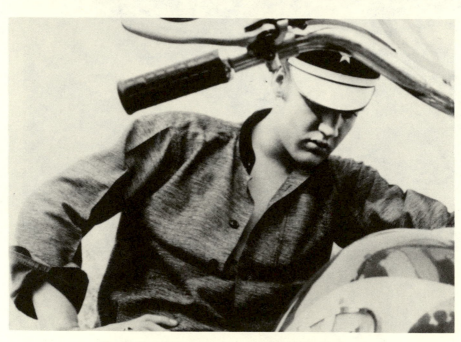

ELVIS PRESLEY (courtesy of Alfred Werthheimer)

THE BEACH BOYS (courtesy of Capitol Records)

THE BEATLES (courtesy of Capitol Records)

THE MONKEES (courtesy of NBC-TV)

THE BEE GEES (courtesy of RSO Records)

THE BAND (courtesy of Warner Brothers Records)

DONNA SUMMER (courtesy of Geffen Records/Tony Viramontes)

THE RAMONES (courtesy of Sire Records)

PAUL SIMON (courtesy of Warner Bros./Gary Heery)

ALICE COOPER (courtesy of Warner/Reprise)

SEAN PENN (courtesy of MCA Home Video)

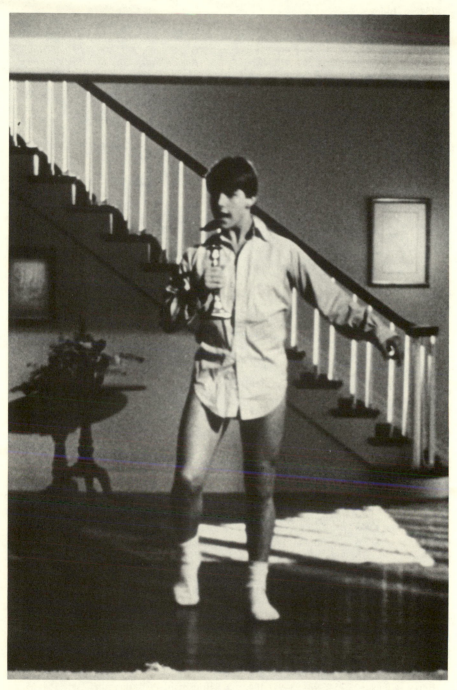

Tom Cruise (courtesy of Warner Bros./MCA Home Video)

PRINCE (courtesy of Water Productions/Warner Bros.)

RAY PARKER JR. (courtesy of David Geffen Co./Veronica Sim)

SPINAL TAP (courtesy of Polygram Records)

MADONNA (courtesy of Warner Bros.)

CAST OF *THE BREAKFAST CLUB* (left to right) ALLY SHEEDY,
JUDD NELSON, ANTHONY MICHAEL HALL, EMILIO ESTEVEZ,
AND MOLLY RINGWALD
(courtesy of MCA Home Video/Annie Leibovitz Ltd.)

DIRTY DANCING CASTMEMBERS (left to right) CYNTHIA RHODES, JENNIFER GREY, AND PATRICK SWAYZE (courtesy of Vestron Pictures)

DAVID LEE ROTH (courtesy of Warner Bros./Neil Zlozower)

PLATOON STARS (left to right) WILLEM DAFOE, CHARLIE SHEEN, AND TOM BERENGER (courtesy HBO Home Video)

SMOKEY ROBINSON (courtesy of Motown Records)

MEL GIBSON, STAR OF *LETHAL WEAPON* (courtesy of Capitol Records)

CHUCK BERRY (courtesy MCA Home Video)

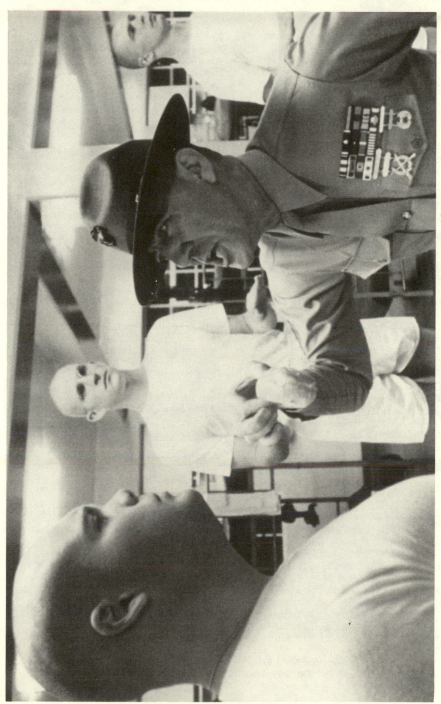

FULL METAL JACKET STARS (from left to right) VINCENT D'ONOFRIO, MATHEW MODINE, LEE ERMEY (courtesy of Warner Bros.)

GOOD MORNING VIETNAM STAR ROBIN WILLIAMS
(courtesy Touchstone Pictures)

JOE COCKER (courtesy of Capitol Records/Abe Frajndlich)

JERRY LEE LEWIS (left) AND DENNIS QUAID WHO PLAYED LEWIS IN THE FILM *GREAT BALLS OF FIRE* (courtesy of Orion Home Video/Mark Lawson Shepard)

7

Movie + Soundtrack + Video = $$$!!!

Tom Shales, television writer for the *Washington Post*, contends that technology and especially computers turned the Eighties into the "Re Decade," a "replay of every decade."

"People think the Eighties have no texture, no style, no tone of their own. They don't," he wrote. "They have the texture and style and tone of all the other decades, at least those that were recorded on film or tape, because the 'Re Decade' is everything that preceded it thrown into one big electronic revue. The Re Decade is the decade of replay, recycle, recall, retrieve, reprocess, and rerun.'[1]

The Re Decade encompassed "oldies but goodies" in music, print advertising, television commercials, CDs, movies and videos. Many of its films, for example, are throwbacks to those with John Wayne singlehand-

345

edly winning World War II. Reviewing the Clint Eastwood movie *Heartbreak Ridge* (1986), Vincent Canby wrote "To describe 'Heartbreak Ridge' as a 'Green Berets' for the 1980s is to overstate the obvious." The *Green Berets* (1968) was described by reviewers as a "cliche-ridden throw-back to the battlefield potboilers of World War II." More precisely, *Life's* critic Richard Schickel wrote, "Mr. Wayne is still fighting the same battles he waged 20 to 30 years ago." Nearly twenty years later, *USA Today* said of *Rambo* (1985), "Waving a machine gun and fighting for his country, Stallone's become a more modern John Wayne."[2] *Miami Vice*, a Florida-based cop show, was prototypical of the Re Decade. "*Miami Vice* isn't about Miami; it's about its punch-drunk and image-besotted self," wrote John Leonard, "a savage cartoon of the way we see and feel."[3]

Another innovation, music video, was called by programmer Rick Skler, "the second British Invasion." The fare and format of music television are the product of the "cutting-edge visual sophisticates as opposed to well read renaissance types," he said. Appearing on *Nightline*, MTV executive vice president Robert Pittman said, "What we've introduced with MTV is a nonnarrative form. As opposed to conventional television, where you rely on plot and continuity, we rely on mood and emotion. We make you feel a certain way as opposed to you walking away with any particular knowledge." He added, ". . . the advent of a *Flashdance*, even *Footloose*, to a certain extent, the story is really subordinate to the music, and the music is the umbrella on which everything else in the movie hangs."[4]

"The visual media have moved away from the traditional linear mode," Pittman told the American Newspaper Publishers Association convention, "In movies, images shift abruptly from one whole scene to another, and the transitions are left to the eye of the beholder . . . if older viewers find this quick-edit communication motif disjointed or disorienting, the TV babies find it exciting and even stimulating. It's even possible to have movies in which images and sounds have taken the foreground and made words almost irrelevant."[5] Friends and foes alike would concur with Toby Goldstein, who called Pittman "a man who says he learns about the news from skimming headlines and is proud that his attention span is so brief as to render him incapable of reading a publication like the *New Yorker*."[6] The blueprint for MTV, however, had roots in radio and other media, especially Album Oriented Rock (AOR) radio programming, in which deejays create an unstructured, free-form, or "underground," atmosphere.

The most retrospective aspect of MTV lies in the format, which fits the "Re Do" mode: The weekend *Top 20 Video Countdown* is a throwback to *Hit Parade* broadcasts and the music network exhibits a number of other properties borrowed from the age of Top 40. The blossoming of MTV no doubt will be treated as the chronological milestone for the Re Decade.

MTV entered the New York-Los Angeles television markets in 1983. That year witnessed films such as *Flashdance* and *Eddie & The Cruisers* addressed to both teens and Yuppies, and *Staying Alive*, an attempt to rekindle the glory days of disco. The title of one 1983 film, a nostalgia Sixties movie, would be used by pollsters such as Pat Caddell to designate a generational life-style: *The Big Chillers*. Many of these had been made prior to MTV's acsendence. For example, *Flashdance*'s steamy dance segments were aimed at people who frequented dance or disco clubs, not the executives at Warner-Amex. Trade analyses of *Flashdance*'s success, however incorrect, influenced future marketing strategies, which were directly aimed at the Music Television Channel so that film critics could legitimately compare a motion picture to a ninety-six-minute music video clip, or "closet musical."

Music Vision

MTV is the epitome of the Re Decade, a "twenty-four-hour-a-day reprocessing center." Videoclip directors can transform the past into the present: Madonna in "Material Girl" is Marilyn Monroe lipsyncing "Diamonds Are a Girl's Best Friend" in *Gentlemen Prefer Blondes*.

"MTV in particular blurs distinct separations and boundaries between past and present," wrote Kaplan. MTV, according to then CEO Robert Pittman, was "the hub of it all," the "all" being the popular culture of the Eighties. MTV both reflected and influenced popular fashion, television styles, films, and music.

The origins of music television cannot be credited to music producers; rather MTV is the indirect progeny of the giant conglomerates American Express and the Warner Cable Corporation (WCC). The concept in fact, was developed long before the two *Fortune* 400s agreed to a merger in September of 1979.

Satori Productions produced a taped hour rock music program, "Video Concert Hall," in November 1979, two years before MTV's fall 1981 debut. Aired on sixty East Coast cable systems, it featured promotional film footage provided by record companies. Artists included Queen, Rod Stewart, and Emerson, Lake and Palmer (ELP). *Billboard* labeled the weekly show "A Novel Disk Promo Vehicle."[7] The experiment was short lived. As Warner's Jo Bergman said, "I don't think that it was something we thought was well done at all. Which it really wasn't."

Few music mavens or journalists appreciate their favorite song, album, or artist being treated as a "product," a term universally employed by entertainment companies. However, aesthetics have little to do with the music economy: Art is a byproduct of the corporate process. Music video, given the monetary stakes involved, was an industrial risk: A quirk of fate and a need for money set the wheels in motion for the eventual creation of MTV.

James Robinson III, chairman of American Express (Amex), was in the enviable position of having an excess cash flow. He felt a communications revolution was on the horizon and after several unsuccessful media bids struck an arrangement with Warner Communication, Inc. (WCI). Amex acquired a 50 percent share in WCI's cable subsidiary, Warner Cable Communications (WCC), for $175 million. A delighted Robinson, eyeing the potential of the interactive, two-way, QUBE cable system, said the investment allowed for "entry into the fast-growing, at-home consumer and entertainment industry." His WCI counterpart, Steven Ross, also believed the merger would aid in realizing "the huge potential of the cable industry."[8]

November 9 Warner Amex announced the formation of an entertainment/distribution company to service WCC, the Warner Amex Satellite Entertainment Company (WASEC), headed by ex-CBS-TV president John A. Schneider.

"We intend to define and develop our understanding of the marketplace and develop the organization to participate fully in that marketplace," Schneider told the *New York Times*.[9]

One executive of the new company, John Lack, had preceded Schneider in the journey from CBS to WCI, where as vice president of programming and marketing, his responsibilities included the QUBE operation in Columbus, Ohio, the neophyte Nickelodeon children's channel, the all-movie Star Channel (which would shortly become the Movie Channel), and Warner's 140 cable systems. Lack, instrumental in the early development of the Movie Channel, also lobbied for his "brainchild" a music television outlet to be named MTV, while Schneider was toying with a possible "shopping service and games channel." Lack's view prevailed. Schneider said, "We were looking for opportunities, windows, blank spots on the spectrum. . . . MTV was the easiest to do because it was the cheapest and we could get it going quicker. There were [three-minute promotional] videos available . . . a body of work that had never been exploited."[10] Lack commissioned a series of half-hour "visual-radio" clips for Nickelodeon from the newly formed Pacific Arts, sired by Mike Nesmith, who had entered the video market to promote his records.

"We want to promote software. We want to be your radio stations," asserted John Lack at the opening session of *Billboard's* First International Video Music Conference, insisting that cable television could be an "exposure" medium for video music as significant as radio had been. He urged cooperation from record labels: Warner Amex needed "service"—promotional clips—provided by the record companies.[11] Lack later recalled, "It was the first time that we may have talked to the Hollywood community, or the record community, that loud about it. Of course, Sidney Sheinberg [MCA president] destroyed me that day . . . 'No way you're going to get these clips.' "

After a short tenure, Nesmith's *Popclips* series on Nickelodeon expired. Only one executive objected—Robert Warren Pittman, a highly regarded radio programmer hired to acquire films and supervise scheduling on the Movie Channel.

Bob Pittman, a college dropout but "quick study," had used research data to successfully compete in the Pittsburgh, Chicago, and New York markets. Much to the surprise of his colleagues at WNBC-AM (New York) and the executives at the NBC-TV-affiliate-serviced *Album Tracks*, Pittman left for the fledgling WASEC Movie Channel (at that time) directly in competition with Time Inc.'s pioneer Home Box Office (HBO), as director of the Pay-TV division.

Lack's motive for creating a music television channel was remarkably simple. "It made good economic sense," he said. "Record companies were having a very difficult time breaking in new music." Album-oriented rock-stations, once the main vehicle for album exposure, were avoiding new acts in favor of established acts like Led Zeppelin. Additionally, advertisers, Lack reasoned, were experiencing little youth-market response to products advertised on television. In fact, attempts by the networks to court teenagers and young adults had been ineffective since the days of *American Bandstand*. Two decades had passed since adolescents raced home from school to watch Fabian, Paul Anka, Frankie Avalon, and Bobby Rydell lipsync the words to their latest releases.

Lack's final argument was that cable programming was stagnating: "Cable operators had no new programming." The statement was valid. Besides Ted Turner's Atlanta "Super Station," the all-sports ESPN, Cable News Network (CNN), a host of televangelistic outlets, and pay movie channels, the infant cable industry was dormant. Lack felt the development of "visual radio" was, therefore, a natural. He had enlisted Pittman to transform the idea for MTV into a reality.

Lack, and then Pittman, were bombarded with the same question: "What makes WASEC think you can succeed where all others have failed?" Pittman explained, "It dawned on us that the reason rock music never worked on TV was that the forms were inconsistent. The live concerts, the talk shows, the dance shows, they looked out of place no matter how good the group was. So we shifted our emphasis. We realized we needed a new form.''[12]

In December 1980 WASEC assembled a team to study the feasibility of music television. It included Schneider, Lack, Pittman, Bob McGroarty (senior vice president for marketing and sales), technological wiz Andy Setos, and chief research analyst Marshall Cohen. Cohen provided the financial rationale for the station and outlined its subsequent day-to-day operation. (The massive reams of financial data, however, also facilitated the rationalization of some questionable programming decisions.)

At the *Billboard* Video Music Conference, Robert Pittman repeated the advantages of audience targeting via cable TV as opposed to the increasing conservativism of FM radio. "Radio stations' objectives are not the same as record companies' objectives," he emphasized, citing the Disco Disaster of 1979 and the ensuing sales decline, and concluding that the cable industry could deliver the audience the record companies were seeking.

At a strategy meeting in January 1981, the top brass from WCI and American Express "asked if I really understood the appeal of the channel," recalled Schneider. "I said, 'Yeah I do.' "[13] As Lack noted, "The American Express people asked a bunch of questions. 'Would it reach the audience effectively? What would it cost? Did we have enough clips?' " Eventually, $20 million for the operation was approved.

A month after that gathering, *Billboard's* George Kopp wrote that record companies, with the possible exception of the giants, were unprepared for the "voracious appetite" of the cable medium in general. John A. Lack responded, "Imagine a radio station visually—that's the idea behind our twenty-four-hour channel. It will be both promotional and entertainment for its own sake, with clips, personalities, and commercials." Lack went on to repeat the pitch presented at the First Video Music conference, i.e., "If we can do the same job, then [record labels] will increase their presence in the video marketplace. The record companies will be one of the sources for our programming."At the time the closing sentence was more wishful thinking, than reality.

Even Warner Brother's Jo Bergman had reservations. "There's no way to prove that TV or video actually sell records, or what great a part it plays in the sales of records," Bergman said.[14] Other promotion people were equally unconvinced. Some objected to the "narrowcasting" of cable channels. Record label executives still thought in terms of "big hits" with universal appeal. They were still leary of programming to appeal to differing audience characteristics, while the visual media was already toying with VALS (values and lifestyle) typology and psychographics, namely targeting a market according to lifestyle and not just demographic factors like age, sex, or race.

To introduce MTV, WASEC launched a full-court press with Lack, Schneider, and Pittman handling the reporters. Lack told *Los Angeles Times* reporter David Crook that the project would "have a strong appeal to young adults," noting, "There's no paucity of product at this point" as record companies were then producing fifteen to twenty video clips a month for the foreign market.

Schneider spoke with *Variety's* Jack Loftus. After outlining the proposed format, he made noted that MTV expected labels and artists to provide broadcast material "free of charge—much the same way radio stations operate."[15]

Billboard carried a lengthy front-page story focusing on the benefits that "MTV: The Music Channel" could offer the record industry. Robert Pittman was quoted as saying, "It will be as important to people as radio, but more importantly, we are targeting to the record buyer. And we will be putting more of an emphasis on new music than radio does. We will take extra pains, in fact, to sell new music. We will also explain who the new artist is. What we will do is expose a whole new genre of artists and we will give them familiarity and break them. Radio will then have new artists to draw from. A music radio station will benefit from having this service in their market."[16] The record industry, reeling from the Disco Disaster and its aftermath, welcomed these sentiments.

At the Television Academy Luncheon in New York, he repeated that MTV's primary audience would be "record buyers" adding, "It's more like radio than TV: It catches their ear and they can come in and out of the room to watch. And the advantage of this age group is that we don't have to worry about diverse tastes in music as we would with the forty-year-old age range."[17]

While record companies were needed to provide "building blocks," as promotional clips were tagged, advertisers and cable operators were equally essential to the neophyte enterprise. However, advertisers and record companies were at first hesitant to participate.

"At first, advertisers thought we were crazy, a bunch of guys working out of a phone booth. We finally persuaded thirteen hardy souls to come with us," said Bob McGroarty.[18] The thirteen buyers were big youth market players: the Gap Stores, Warner-Lambert (Listermint and chewing gums), Jovan, Pepsi Co., 7-Up, Dolby Laboratories, Atco-Embassy, Filmways, United Artists, Universal Pictures, Warner Brothers, the United

States Navy, and Atari. Only 30 percent of MTV's ad slots were sold when the channel first aired.

Record executives, meanwhile, resisted providing "free service." Polygram and MCA Records originally insisted on payment for the videoclips it had supplied for free to programmers abroad. MTV executives downplayed the resistance. As John Sykes diplomatically recalled, "There will always be nonbelievers at the start of anything . . . At that point there were probably some companies that were taking the wait-and-see attitude."

Several months after the initial press campaign Lack and Pittman again spoke with the *Los Angeles Times*, considered a must-read by the music industry. Pittman repeated his thesis that "with the music channel, you can watch or listen as you do other things. Stations are becoming more conservative in their programming and people are beginning to look for something fresh," he told reporter Bob Hilburn. John Lack added, "We're not trying to be all things to all people. We're going after the rock audience that grew up on television and music, the one we feel will respond most to this concept."[19]

Pittman later did a lengthy interview with *Variety's* Richard Gold at a meeting of the National Cable Television Association (NCTA). Much of the material covered familiar ground. "Radio is now targeting the twenty-five to fifty-four age group. New groups can't get exposure," he said, adding, "We've developed a mutually beneficial relationship with the labels. It's going to be much easier for them to get something on here than on radio." The programming head also fleshed out the format, outlining such categories as "Power Oldies," "Oldie," "Power Current," and "Current," in rotations that would mirror radio's cycle of three-, six- and eight-hour plays. Contests would play a significant role, as they did at WNBC-AM (New York). For example, "We might rent a Lear jet and fly four contest winners to Japan for a concert," he said.[20] (One of the first contests on MTV did just that for the New Age Asia tour.)

As cable operators are the cultural gatekeepers in the industry, the NCTA Convention provided an opportunity to promote the recently formed channel to 15,525 exhibitors, delegates, and other assorted conventioneers. Lack, Pittman, and McGroaty, conveyed their message, relying heavily on four of Marshal Cohen's psychographical profiles of MTV's anticipated audience. Lack compared the twelve to thirty-four-year-olds to *Saturday Night Live's* audience, which had transcended this age group with fully 40 percent of its audience over thirty-five years of age. Reiterating the "need for building blocks" from the labels Lack added that if they were not provided, "we'll go direct to the artist or to independent video producers."[21] (Lack and Pittman never did resort to this tactic although Tom Petty's management once provided videos when MCA refused.)

Despite Cohen's research, MTV was an untried commodity. The uncertainty fueled the creative juices of the staff, who threw caution to the winds. "Freedom's just another word for nothing left to lose," says a Kris Kristofferson lyric. At MTV, freedom involved risk taking, which frequently was successful.

July 31, while Manhattan was gearing up for the dog days of August, MTV executives were preparing for the midnight take-off of MTV. A caravan of limos, buses, and autos made the trip to The Loft, a Fort Lee, New Jersey, restaurant, for a party for assembled 150 staffers and guests. Few print people attended, although Robert Hilburn covered the event for the *Los Angeles Times*.

For John Lack, the midnight debut represented the culmination of seemingly endless frustrations:

> We were all there. But that night I decided I was going to say the first words on the channel, and I introduced it that night with 'Ladies and gentlemen, rock and roll!' Then we went into 'Video Killed the Radio Star' . . . I had always wanted to run a contemporary radio station. And I never did. I ran news radio stations for CBS. The great joy for me was being able to say at the beginning of the first rock and roll television network 'Ladies and Gentlemen, Rock and Roll.' The rocket ship went up and the first clip went on.
>
> All of my dreams at that age in my life had been reached. I had a dream, I got someone to fund it. I hired the people to do it and it happened. I mean it was as great a thrill as one could have. It's something that you care about. That you believe in. That's important it happened.

"It was an incredible moment," echoed veejay (video jockey) Martha Quinn.[22]

A multi-media, audiovisual followed the appearance of MTV's logo. Russell Mulcahy's 1979 video filled the glowing screens to The Buggles' Trevor Horn's high-decibel, "Do you remember back in 1962 . . ." *bleeding, superimpositions, cuts, zooms* . . . The title chorus, "Video killed the Radio Star," exploded to the cheers of on-lookers. Horn segued, "pictures came and broke your heart . . ." As one critic later recalled, "TV sets erupted through a floor to displace a mountain of old thirties-style radio sets to the cranked-up refrain . . ."[23] The vidclip highlighted the MTV campaign to minimize the exposure value of AOR.

The debut was a success, but MTV had a long row to hoe. "One thing for sure," Lack joked to Bob Hilburn, "When you start out in the basement in Fort Lee, N.J., you can only go up."[24] Pittman, however, did not like what had appeared on The Loft's TV sets. He thought that "mood and emotion" was absent; the opening hour was too much like traditional television. (The set, lighting, and other mood creating fixtures were thus drastically altered—the result was a highly structured environment which appeared casually thrown together.) The veejays were also a problem, Pittman said. The stares of the veejays on camera reminded him of the prowlers in *Night of the Living Dead* and he ordered their teleprompters yanked. The veejays were told to ad-lib. (In time, when this failed, the veejays would be taped and introductions segued in at the appropriate time). The overhaul eventually cost $2.5 million.

Madison Avenue remained leery. Network television was already considered a poor time buy; cable remained untested.

On the networks, *Saturday Night Live* was one of the few shows to capture the fourteen-to-thirty-five-year-old audience. Memories of the unsuccessful *Midnight Special, In Concert, Shindig,* and other music shows lingered. In addition, the youth market was aging, and TV clients frequently feared that rock 'n' roll could hurt their corporate images. Additionally MTV's time-sales people were perceived as aloof and arrogant.

Following the announcement of MTV, advertising giant BBDO's media director, Arnie Semsky, told *The Wall Street Journal*, "The concept is excellent and there already is a lot of music programming on the air. But the execution will determine how well it is received."[25]

Critics liked MTV's opening execution, but most of the reviews were confined to the trades. Susan Spillman of *Advertising Age* wrote an overview of the channel, using quotes from executives at MTV and record companies. *Billboard's* Laura Foti did a similar piece with Pittman and John Lack quoted extensively. Foti ended with Lack's observation, "It's in our best interest that everybody prospers." (In industry jargon, that's a "money review.") "We welcome MTV to cable's fold," wrote Robert Titsch, "and wish it every success." Robert DiMatteo stated, "The channel is a bold example of the cable industry's move toward specialized audience programming (in this case the 12-to-34-year old record buying market)." The 10 October issue of *Billboard's* front page read, "MTV Cable Spurs Disk Sales of Artists."[26]

Favorable analyses of industry trends are normative in trade publications, so *Rolling Stone's* negative review of cablecasting rock, with the main culprits being USA's *Night Flight* and MTV, roused the ire of Bob Pittman.[27] (Reviewer Marc Kirkeby had pointed to MTV's willingness to play new artists as a technique to obtain promo clips and stated the obvious: Many areas of the United States were without cable.) However, it had little effect. To the contrary, *Fortune* magazine selected MTV as providing one of the significant new "products of the year." Andrew C. Brown recognized the value of cablecasting because of "its ability to serve up specific audiences for advertisers, much as specialized magazines do . . . the purist example to date is Music Television from WASEC."[28] MTV ended 1981 with a promising public profile, even though its five-month earnings were $515,000 after the Warner-Amex investment of nearly $20 million. As Lack had observed, "You can only go up."

MTV ushered in 1982 with:

"Live! From New York City! Be with us as the New Year rolls across America! The party starts . . .

Karla DeVito, Bow Wow Wow, and ex-New York Doll David Johansen entertained the revellers at a televised New Year's party. It was estimated that "120 percent" of those invited attended. Word of mouth was helping the fledgling channel, yet the station remained unavailable in the New York area, the hub of the broadcast industry. Jack Schneider was anxious to break through Manhattan Cable's resistance. The absence of MTV in the Los Angeles market was also a problem, since most of the record companies were headquartered in Southern California. Jo Bergman of Warner Brothers observed, "It's one thing to have reports coming from the field. It's another to go home at night and put it on in your bedroom." Having "ears" in the record industry has little to do with radio's Arbitron (ARB) rating system or Nielsen numbers, so Schneider, Pittman, and Lack set about expanding their base. This was, partially, a structural problem: The cable industry was a transmission system based in nonurban areas.

Cablecasting, however, had become more viable, and by the early 1980's had seriously eroded the network's stranglehold on television viewing, although syndicated sitcoms and old motion pictures dominated the screen. Even MTV, from the offset, ran reprocessed material: videoclips had been produced by artists with commercial potential, including established artists and newcomers with observable momentum. (Abroad this involved airplay on the British Broadcasting Company (BBC) and TV services on the Continent.) The neophyte acts telecast on MTV were virtual unknowns in the U.S. except in New Wave and synthesized New Music circles. This partially accounted for the innovative aspect of MTV: The availability of clips. To fill a round-the-clock channel avant-garde material was used.

To demonstrate the "exposure value" of music video, MTV had to penetrate the major urban markets. The "I Want My MTV" advertising campaign on network TV was part of the effort. Pete Townshend's commercial bite, "Call you cable operator now! Call him and say 'I Want My MTV!' " was widely aired. He was joined by a galaxy of rock artists including Adam Ant, Pat Benatar, Stevie Nicks, Sting, Mick Jagger and Peter Wolf, who worked free of charge for the "exposure."

The campaign worked. Retailers throughout the country found teenagers walking into their places of business and asking for unheard-of artists and in some cases nonexistent—in the U.S.—albums. A merchandiser in Seattle told *Billboard*, "While the MTV universe is small, it's heavy in record buyers." In Buffalo, one retailer said, "It seems to spur sales of obscure groups, and it helps because radio stations won't play new artists." "A lot of New Wave and obscure stuff is selling, that I'm sure wouldn't sell otherwise," said an Ohio record store owner.[29] Record labels, while not convinced, did respond somewhat by increasing their video output. RCA's Jack Chudnoff summed up a growing industry view that "MTV does sell records. Video has definitely become more important to artists."[30] Robert Pittman would confidently tell the *Philadelphia Enquirer*, "At MTV, we don't shoot for the 14-year-olds—we own them. We will reach 90 percent of them."[31]

Cable operators were deluged by cards, letters, and phone calls urging the inclusion of the music channel in their packages. Denise Bozi, public relations of Manhattan Cable, indicated that the "I-Want-My-MTV" campaign highlighted potential audience interest and established the channel as "very viable," and by fall 1982 MTV was available in the southern portion of Manhattan. January 1983 witnessed the Los Angeles and the remaining New York City markets opening up to MTV. *Billboard,* "The Bible of the music industry," included MTV's programs.

The Lack-Pittman game plan was showing results. MTV's profitability rose as increasing numbers of cable companies signed on the dotted line. Advertising had grown to around 100 sponsors with more than 200 products.

In contrast to the commercial networks, MTV was considered a good "time buy." "Commercial television costs can be very prohibitive," said Frank McDonald of Cunningham & Walsh. "I think it's great, it's super," explained Bob Daubenspeck of Foote, Cone & Belding. "As a cable venture, that was an obvious one. That audience is hard to reach through normal broadcast channels. There aren't many shows devoted to that audience segment." Doyle, Dane & Bernbach's Jay James said, "This is the most concentrated teen audience we can find, and that is terrific advertising for a cable programmer."[32] MTV's access to the youth market and its relatively inexpensive rates attracted many advertisers.

As MTV's credibility rose, competitors for its advertisers emerged. *Night Tracks* on TBS (Turner Broadcasting System) and NBC's *Friday Night Videos* appeared. *Night Flight*, which had aired several months prior to MTV, continued. The contenders did fairly well, but, as *Night Flight's* producer Cynthia Friedland said, "When people talk about music television or music videos, they mean MTV." Although it lacked WTBS's or NBC's household penetration, MTV had the advantage of being on the air twenty-four-hours, seven days a week, a point many advertisers mentioned. MTV's success was not lost on movie studios, which were becoming aware of its potential as a total-exposure platform.

Hollywood Wants Its MTV

When MTV first aired, five film studios were advertisers. Music videos, not to mention the viewers in the twelve-to-twenty-five-year-old age group, held obvious appeal for Hollywood marketing departments, especially after its appearance in the New York and Southern California markets.

Music video provided an effective medium for promoting films and records by allowing their potential audience to both hear and see the musical acts. As Al Teller, president of CBS Records, said, "The key marketing aspect has been the video trend. It can't be overestimated. Unlike records, which the public can sample over the airwaves, with movies you either see them or you don't. With the cost of advertising being what it is, the chance to put segments of films on the air (via music video) is an important break from that limitation.[33]

Throughout the entertainment industry there is a consensus that the burgeoning teen audience that MTV has captured is identical to the moviegoers and record buyers the film and record industries hope to reach—the crucial twelve-to-twenty-five-year-old market. MTV's Pittman *did* claim ownership of the youth market.[34] For films with rock soundtracks, "video spinoffs represent a new bonanza of free advertising and promotion," said *Variety's* Richard Gold.[35]

Flashdance Sets the Tempo

The movie *Flashdance* demonstrated just how powerful music television could be as a marketing device for movies with a rock soundtrack.[36]

Flashdance, described as "pure glitz" or "airheaded," "a nonmovie," appeared as millions of Americans were filling their annual 1040's. Many, particularly young women, appear to have kept enough change to lavishly support the Paramount Pictures scenario. The movie album, fashions, and related paraphenalia prospered.

In nearly one voice critics panned the dance film. Word of mouth and video material fueled interest in the maligned project.

Director Adrian Lyne's storyline was a thinly disguised *Rocky*esque fantasy of Alex Owens' (Jennifer Beals) Cinderella-like transformation from a blue collar factory worker into an aspiring ballerina at the prestigious Pittsburgh Conservatory. "The plot could barely fill a short form video without Ms. Beals, or the unbilled French dancer [Marine Jahan] by night," wrote Michael Sragow, "She soaks up her inspirations from the jive moments of side-walk 'break' dancers and rhythmic traffic cops—it's 'Symphony of the Street,' circa 1983."[37]

The runway of a working class neighborhood bar provides the setting for Alex's "sexy, high-tech floor show." The performers are accompanied by Michael Sembello's "Maniac" and other *Fever*ish selections. The displays, also, network with John Travolta's white suit disco stage shows. "One after another," opined *Time* "lithe stunners display terrific muscle tone in discreet rock-'n'-roll stripteases."[38]

The reaction to the "nonmovie" was remarkable. Several weeks following the release, Paramount's Gordon Weaver indicated "It's too early to call *Flashdance* another *Saturday Night Fever* but it looks as if it might become that kind of phenomenon."[39] *Billboard's* "Top Album Picks" (May 7, 1983) announced:

> This album explodes on the pop chart this week, leaping from 166 to 29. That's a spectacular jump, but it perhaps shouldn't be too surprising . . . Most of the music on the album is trendy, urban dance rock [disco] though there are also a few ballads . . . the most interesting facet of the album is that it mixes cuts by dance queen Donna Summer and aspirants to the throne Irene Cara and Laura Brannigan.

In two weeks *Flashdance* raked in $11.3 million more than covering the film production costs, which some attributed to the fact that time buys on the music channel were the initial exposure.

The Marketing of Flashdance

"It was a film that, without the music in it, didn't add up to much" recalled RSO film head Bill Oakes. "A lot of people call it an extended MTV clip."[40] *Variety's* reviewer did just that. *Flashdance* was compared to "looking at MTV for 96 minutes."[41] The Don Simpson - Jerry Bruckheimer production was universally lambasted as a femme version of *Rocky* or *SNF* without emotion, significant dialogue or an engrossing plot. Critics qualified their collective disapprovals with a *cavaat* the vehicle has box office potential. After several weeks of distribution *Rolling Stone's* Michael Sragow would write "This film's commercial success is a true Triumph of the Swill."

"It was not designed to be a video movie," said Paramount's Dawn Steel. "It happened to have a modular structure—the modules were interchangeable—they were even moved around in the editing—and that's what made the movie adaptable to MTV."[42]

This was one example of Paramount's decision to structure the film in such a way as to make it acceptable to dance-club audiences. Word-of-mouth, they reasoned, might promote the movie.

Michael Sembello's famous "Maniac" videoclip, highlighting the movie's erotic dance sequences appeared on the music channel the week of May 11. (The film had premiered nearly a month *earlier*.) By the second week of May, the picture had grossed $20.3 million and the album was in platinium numbers. The only crosspromotional activity so far had been the release of Irene Cara's single, "Flashdance . . . What a Feeling." *Flashdance* lacked a title in the heady environ of the top ten, but Paramount innovatively used two-minute segments on MTV, specially edited for the cable network's commercial slots. A sizeable amount of the $2.9 million promotion budget—"invisible marketing"—went to visual media. Bragged Jack Schneider, "Paramount gives MTV credit for the success of *Flashdance*." "The MTV audience likes music, movement, dancing," explained the studio's vice president, Gordon Weaver, "We hoped the movie and MTV would make a happy marriage. And it happened." In another interview he observed, "We incorporated the music into all our radio and TV spots . . . like crosspollination." He said of the youth market served by MTV. "It's a godsend. The demographics are so perfect with music video."[43] Music consultant Danny Goldberg suggested that videos could help a film a great deal more than the record industry could. "The opening weekend for a movie is all important for volume of business," he told *Rock Video*, "and MTV can clinch a big opening weekend QED."[44]

Flashdance's marketing strategy was widely and incorrectly reported as due to crosspromotion. In time, the perception became the reality. " 'Flashdance' was the picture that brought all the studios into the music video field," claimed MTV's Les Garland.[45]

The success of *Flashdance*, as Jay Cocks suggested, was "a confluence of good commercial instincts and some savvy guesswork, and now . . . Hollywood has found a new formula."[46] Radio, record, and print executives, as of this writing, are loathe to admit that Paramount's placement of short-form videos, derived from the film, helped establish *Flashdance's* 1980s unparalleled popularity. Yet one rival marketing executive conceded, "Paramount didn't know what they had, but they knew where to sell it. The MTV buys allowed them to aim a shotgun directly at their target, instead of scattering buckshot through a general TV approach."[47] In the case of *Flashdance,* MTV's role was significant in prolonging the longevity of interest. The cable channel would repeat this feat with Michael Jackson's *Thriller.*

Prior to airing of the fourteen-minute-long videoclip "Thriller," its album sales were down to a quarter of a million per week.

"The first week MTV played it," said Robert Pittman, "sales jumped from 250,000 to 657,000 copies, next week to a million, and the third week in excess of a million."[48] "Maniac" and "Thriller" both rejuvenated and sustained momentum, but did not create the original impetus. Some observers felt the heavy airplay given these clips were free commercials.

The trade and popular media took note of the crosspromotion of *Flashdance*. Gary LeMel told *Variety*, "Hollywood sees a way to get a lot of advertising and marketing for its target audience. The target audience for MTV is the same [as the] target for pictures. You need the twelve to twenty-five demographic."[49] "If you have a really hot soundtrack," added Lenny Goldberg, "and you can get MTV playing it all day long, you're in business."[50] Once the audits were completed, the "little picture" had grossed $185 million, the soundtrack enjoyed profits from 17 million sales, and video cassette sales were more than $8 million.

The entire entertainment industry took notice. "It started with *Flashdance*," said Danny Goldberg. "*Flashdance* was like watching MTV, but that was actually its glory—and that was what made it a hit." He told another writer the film was "synergy—a natural marriage of consciousness."[51]

However, several critics questioned the transference of MTV's mood or ambiance to the big screen. "We make you feel a certain way, as opposed to you walking away with any particular knowledge," explained Robert Pittman on a segment of *Nightline*. *Chicago Tribune* critic Gene Siskel retorted, "You just sit there glued, transfixed, and the images just hit your face, as opposed to leaning forward, engaging the film . . . I think that a lot of what Bob had to say is poppycock. I mean, I think that this whole genre—and I even hate to use a fancy word on such junk—is just that, junk." Kenneth Turan, less passionately, suggested: "Had *Flashdance*, for instance, been made in the Thirties or Forties, what took its director and writers an hour and half to tell would have taken up perhaps twenty minutes of screen time: the picture would have really started when Jennifer

Beals's character entered that snooty ballet school and faced the challenges of an alien world . . . Today's video-influenced filmmakers want to dazzle the eye to the exclusion of every thing else."[52] Bizzers found *Flashdance's* profit margin more persuasive than aesthetic dissents.

Tryin' To Stay Alive

I know it's true
Oh so true
'Cause I saw it on TV
—© 1984 Wenaha Music Co. ASCAP

The publicity surrounding *Blackboard Jungle* (1954) motivated Sam Katzman to paste together *Rock Around the Clock* (1955). The July 2nd ads for *Staying Alive* boldly headlined "The Best Selling Album of All Time Now Has A Sequel." "And the Bee Gees' smash hit, 'The Woman in You' is only the first of what is sure to be a long list [sic] of hit singles to emerge from this monumental album," the copy emphasized.

In two industries obsessed with the notion of "imitation is the best road to profitability," *Staying Alive* was a "natural." Under the supervision of RSO's William Oakes the sequel to *SNF* was directed by actor Sylvester Stallone, hot from the *Rocky* films. The Bee Gees had produced five songs for the soundtrack. All of the *Fever* machinery was primed to synergize the project billed as "The Fever Still Burns." The fate of the "momentum-creating" title song, the Bee Gee's "The Woman in You," augered the negative reactions to come. "Woman" just didn't have it "in the grooves."

"The Woman In You" appeared on the *Billboard* list at 49 for week ending May 21. MTV began running a videoclip nearly a month later, 15 June. Its televisual life was short, ending July 6 when Frank Stallone's "Far From Over" arrived on the cablecast screen.

The Australian trio enjoyed a special relationship with Stigwood (they were original clients) and Polygram. A unique contract stipulated that a Bee Gees song be the first single release from the movie. They also commanded one side of the album, despite sequencing problems. "The Woman In You" lacked the infectiousness of "How Deep Is Your Love." Reissuing "Staying Alive," despite the remix, as a single appeared too risky.

The poor showing of "Woman" motivated the label to rush release Frank Stallone's "Far From Over" as a follow-up. Television time-buys shifted to the "hotter" vehicle, which featured John Travolta's rehearsal scene in the film with infrequent cutaways to Frank Stallone. Reviewing

Staying Alive, Richard Corliss singled out this segment as the high point: "With the exception of one rehearsal sequence, feverishly edited to Brother Frank Stallone's catchy "Far From Over," the movie brings neither kick nor context to its song track."[53] Director Sylvester Stallone provided the ideal vehicle for his sibling. Asked about his near disappearance in the clip, he explained, somewhat disingenuously, "In the video, something happened to my hair. It got caught in an eggbeater or something. And I have a headband on, so I look like an Italian Arapaho. It's ridiculous."[54] Polygram allied with Paramount Pictures to foot the bill, as both desired a music video promoting the album and the struggling film, but the entire campaign flopped. The more successful "Far From Over" had peaked at Number 10 position on 1 October 1983. The MTV clip ran for two-and-a-half months.

As with Stigwood's *Sergeant Pepper*, the LP charisma was missing. On 2 July *Billboard* selected *Staying Alive* as the feature album pick. The anonymous reviewer said, "The fever continues with this single-disk compilation of music targeted at pop, black and dance formats." The writer cautioned, however, "The music market has changed a lot in the past six years, but the key songs here should find a wide audience, especially if the film does well."[55]

The album lacked the meteoric magnetism of the *Fever* package, or even *Flashdance*. "I think the score for *Flashdance* was far superior to the score for *Staying Alive*," observed Lenny Goldberg. "Had the quality of the scores been reversed, *Flashdance* wouldn't have done nearly as well and *Staying Alive* would have done much better."[56] The critics, in destroying the film, did not spare the soundtrack, including the Bee Gees and the director's brother.

Writing in *New York*, David Denby said, "The five new Bee Gee songs are only mediocre, but the Bee Gee's music is like Gershwin compared with the Vegas showroom junk composed by Frank Stallone, the director's brother. And that stuff never shuts up."[57] "Unfortunately, the music score of the film is a distinct disappointment," stated *Variety*. "The five new tunes turned out by the Bee Gees would seem to have none of the chart-busting potential of their 'Saturday Night Fever' collection, and the other numbers, many of which were co-written and performed by Frank Stallone, are none too catchy." *Time's* Corliss labelled "Far From Over" "catchy." Stallone concurred, and implied that "Far From Over," in light of its chart success, should have been the first single, "but that's what the Bee Gees wanted, and that's what they got."[58] Despite the airplay on MTV, however, the soundtrack sold only one-tenth as much as its predecessor. (The one compensation was that *Staying Alive* went platinium.)

If film critics killed *Flashdance*, *Staying Alive* was a chainsaw massacre. Using *auteur* to the ultimate, *Fever* and *Flashdance* were utilized as models to dismember Stallone and his misdirected follow-up. Few sequels measure up to the original (a notable exception was Coppola's *Godfather II*), however, the *Staying Alive* endeavor was based on the advertising slogan, "The fever still burns." Norman Wexler disagreed, calling the screenplay "a cliche-ridden, teeny bopper picture."

"It's less a story than an epilogue," wrote Vincent Canby, "a completely out-of-character one that's been inflated to feature length."[59]

In the film, six years after *Fever*, Tony Manero (Travolta) is uprooted from Bay Ridge to Manhattan. Here, in *Flashdance* style, he pursues a Broadway career. As David Denby suggests, "Tony, the outsider, the Brooklyn palooka, is going to triumph over all the snobs and hardnoses of New York and make it as a dancer."[60] Manero auditions at a "cattle call" for *Satan's Alley*, described as a "rock musical comedy version of *Dante's Inferno*."[61] As a member of the dance chorus he becomes enamored of the show's star, Laura (Finola Hughes). A turbulent, unsatisfactory, but predictably bittersweet relationship ensues. As the script would have it, the opening night finds Tony confronting Laura. The original leading man conveniently fades out and the Travolta character replaces him. The stage is set. The opening bell strikes. One critic, mindful of the three *Rocky* episodes, wrote, "They dance fifteen rounds, and Travolta gets the decision on points. He throws her around, and she claws at him, drawing blood at the temple, yet he outdances her . . ."[62] Savoring triumph, he tells his dedicated female companion, "You know what I wanna do? You know what I wanna do? Strut." He singularly "struts" away to the sounds of "Stayin' Alive" (shades of *Fever*).

Film critics showed little mercy; *Newsweek's* David Ansen took careful aim at the consensus villain Sylvester Stallone, saying "Many filmmakers fall back on cliches; Stallone lusts after them with awesome indiscrimination . . . Taking to its absurd limit the style that was marvelous in 'All That Jazz' and merely flashy in 'Flashdance,' Stallone smashes dancing into tiny fragments: leaps that don't land, a wriggling shoulder here, a thrusting crotch there. This is madness: a movie that celebrates a dancer but doesn't trust the audience's ability to sit through a pas de deux."[63]

At *Time*, Corliss wrote, "*Staying Alive* doesn't make it anywhere: not as character study, not as an ersatz *Chorus Line*, not even as a canny exploitation of the good will engendered by *Saturday Night Fever*. This is no ordinary terrible movie; it's a vision of the end . . . As you watch it, the idea of what a movie is—an idea that has lasted more than a half-century—crumbles before your eyes . . . Stallone shoots dance the way he shoots boxing—in fragments, close up, with bodies whizzing by and lots of sweat and pounding flesh."[64]

The kindest review, not surprisingly, came from *Variety*. The subhead read "Travolta's hot, but Rocky's not."[65]

Nearly all of the reviewers alluded to *Flashdance* in their columns. Some suggested overt copycatism, but this was not the case. *Alive* and *Flashdance* were filmed during the same time period at Paramount Pictures. Given the general adverse reaction to dance (aka/disco) music in the industry, the possibility of targeting night clubs could have influenced both. Synergyism was RSO's strategy. Nonetheless, the comparisons permeated the press. *Variety*, again, wrote, "the dance and music-dominated feature doesn't generate the heat and sense of style that have made Paramount's own *Flashdance* such an unexpected sensation."

"Like *Flashdance*," added Denby, "it's a movie for people who need nothing but a beat blasting into their ear all day long."[66]

Frank Stallone told *Rolling Stone*: "I was watching how people reacted in the movie theaters—how they reacted was more important than how the critics reacted—and they really seemed to like it. They want entertainment."[67]

The reported $10-million marketing budget produced a highly uneven result: The singles failed to duplicate the *Fever* hits and the soundtrack outdistanced both .45s, partially due to Polygram's "Take The Movie With You" souveneir ad campaign. Harry Losk, the record label's marketing vice president, admitted, "We realize that it's not a great movie," while Paramount's Weaver credited the soundtrack for the relatively adequate summer season.[68] The maligned movie earned $58.3 million at the box office.

Synergy was tarnished, but far from discredited. Most observers agreed that a mediocre package had fared better than expected due to multimedia marketing. The three significant motion pictures that appeared in the waning months of the summer—*Risky Business, Eddie and The Cruisers* and *The Big Chill*—all paid lip service to synergy.

Easy Rider in Reagan's American: Risky Business

> *I deal in human fulfillment.*
> *I made $8,000 in one night.*
> —Joel Goodsen, high school student

Paul Brickman, author of the well received screenplay for *Handle With Care* (1982), made his directorial debut with *Risky Business*. His innovative spirit found its way into the structuring of the musical score as well as the film.

Brickman and John Avent, who co-produced the film with Steve Tisch, picked the tracks to *Risky Business* prior to filming, a radical departure from the standard practice of postproduction scoring. Outside of New Age instruments by Tangerine Dream, a German group, the material was vintage AOR rock. "Jeff Beck's 'The Pump' is not modern music," said Avent, "but it caught the feeling of cruising and being an adolescent and being hot—that restless energy looking for a place to go."[69]

While their novel approach to scoring seemed logical and efficient, Brinkman and Avent appear to have overlooked the problem of clearances. Obtaining rights to pre-recorded material is simple—for theater exhibition. Labels charge a flat fee; on occasion "points," or a percentage of the box office gross, are demanded. Videos, soundtracks, and "buy-outs" can become a filmmaker's nightmare. Even lawyers considered this aspect of usage a "legal no-man's land." By preselecting musical material the filmmakers abdicated a strong bargaining posture. Brinkman, without discussing the specifics, told an interviewer, "It's getting more difficult all the time . . . it's getting very expensive *if* they'll let the tune go at all."[70] The eventual soundtrack very much reflected the legal and marketing misadventures brought about by that early commitment.

Risky Business debuted the first weekend in August. The ninety-six-minute-film received an "R" rating—a double-edged sword for the under-twenty-five audience. Mostly, the fate of the picture was left to word-of-mouth transmission, but Geffen Pictures purchased some ad time on MTV.

Organization Man's Habitat Revisited:

> . . . in the harmonious organization one has most of the material rewards necessary for the good life, and none of the gnawing pains of the old kind of striving.
> —William H. Whyte, Jr., *Organization Man*

In 1955 William H. Whyte, Jr. published *Organization Man*. The best seller chronicled the residents of Glencoe, Illinois, an upper-middle-class Chicago suburb. Nearly thirty years later, Paul Brickman cinematically visited the same territory in *Risky Business*.

In the film, Joel Goodsen (Tom Cruise) is a seventeen-year-old, average, virginal, high school senior preoccupied with sex and entry into the Ivy League.

In one of Joel's fantasies, a naked girl is showering. He stares as she seductively invites the shy teenager to wash her back. As he approaches, the steamy bathroom lengthens: "I keep losing her." He is thrust into the in-progress SAT exams with only two minutes remaining: "I'll never get to college. My life is ruined." The fantasy becomes a nightmare. Robert Asahina described this scene as a "clever interweaving of adolescent anxieties regarding sex and success."[71] The sequence does set up the story.

Joel's perfectionist and proper parents (Nicholas Pryor and Janet Carroll) leave to visit an aunt. Alone in the house, he ineffectually attempts to manage. He is unable to defrost a TV dinner, but can lipsync and play a mean air guitar.

The musical highlight of Risky Business came from a mere line in the shooting script: "Joel dances in underwear through the house." The one-minute scene had Cruise using a candlestick as a rock star's microphone, cranking up the stereo, prancing, and cavorting to the sounds of a Bob Seger number, "Old Time Rock 'n' Roll." "He kicked off a memorable one-minute sequence of sexy air-guitar strutting and mock-macho hilarity that endeared Cruise to film audiences," wrote a *Rolling Stone* contributor. "Imagining himself a rock star dancing," observed Pauline Kael, "he's a charmingly clunky dynamo." Peter Occhiogrosso captured the significance of the short scene saying, "The invocation of 'Old Time Rock 'n' Roll' itself unleashes a slew of associations having to do with the knockdown of parental authority and the sexual awakening that will soon follow." The *Voice* critic went on to link the Seger song to the same generational rebellion conjured up by "Rock Around the Clock" in *Blackboard Jungle*,[72] but Joel's high school is light years and several social classes apart from Evan Hunter's ghettoized institution. The rebelliousness of the scene thus has little to do with the conformist thrust of the movie. At lunching in the neat cafeteria, the topic of heated discussion is upward mobility. "Harvard MBAs begin at $40,000," offers one student. Another counters, "Veterinarians start at $60,000." As universities and salaries are mentioned, Joel asks, "Doesn't anyone want to accomplish anything or just make money?" "Make money" comes the answer, as the questioner is pelleted with pieces of bread. The organization-man ethic is alive and well at Joel's school.

Later in the film Miles (Curtis Armstrong), a conniving companion, answers a personal ad using Joel's name and address. A black transvestite, Jackie (Bruce Young), appears. With diplomacy, and $75, Joel extricates himself from the situation. Jackie graciously provides the would-be Lothario with a phone number to "get what he wants." Lana answers.

Lana (Rebecca DeMornay) enters Joel's moonlit house as her client mentally conjures pictures of a police raid and the destruction of his future. Lana whispers, "Are you ready for me?" Joel's fantasies are fulfilled. The bliss fades, temporarily, when Lana deserts her procurer, Guido (Joe Pantoliano). Joel accidentally allows dad's prized platinum Porsche to roll into Lake Michigan. (The sportscar had been off-limits.) For dallying at home and cutting classes, he is suspended for a week. Worse, he is expelled from Future Enterprisers (a version of Junior Achievement). With nothing left to lose, he succumbs to Lana's desire to transform his home into a bordello for one lucrative night. With Muddy Waters's "Mannish Boy" providing background music, customers, teenage Johns with $300, descend on the house. A voiceover explains:

> Just the sheerist pursuit of immediate material gratification. What a capitalist. She told me I can make more money in one night than I can make all year. Enough to pay for my father's car.
>
> She told me she'd be my girlfriend. She told me a lot of things. I believe in all of them.
>
> So she introduced me to her friends (pause) and I introduced her to mine. Then we'd bury our treasure.
>
> Lana concentrated on production. I concentrated on sales.

"I'm an M-A-N, child" fades as a line of parked cars overflows on Joel's tree-lined street. Joel, cigarette dangling from his lips, cheap black sunglasses, is now a free-enterprising pimp.

The moral denouement occurs when Bill Rutherford, the Princeton University admissions officer, appears in the midst of the horny teen revellers. Joel's chances to enter the prestigious Ivy League university are now in jeopardy. Innovative entrepreneurship prevails; the interviewer spends time with the ladies of the night. Joel earns more than enough to pay for repairing the water-logged sportscar. Even Guido's revenge, stealing the Goodsen's furniture, is remedied. Rutherford decides, "Princeton can use a guy like Joel." Joel and Lana are "going to make it big."

The finale finds Joel saying, "I deal in human fulfillment. I grossed $8,000 in one night." As John Simon observed, "With Lana and Princeton for mentors, he will end up worldly, wealthy, and wise,"[73] and a mirror image of Glencoe's adult population.

Several reviewers compared *Risky Business* to the classic *The Graduate* (1967). *Variety's* McCarthy said, "This is as close to a contemp(orary) *The Graduate* as has come along in a while."[74] Another writer paralleled Joel's concern with the future as "not unlike the older Benjamin in *The Graduate*."[75] Can Lana's predatory nature be contrasted to Mrs. Robinson? Is

Joel's future to be *in*, or merely plastic? Is prostitution an exercise in supply-side economics? Brinkman's story seems to answer in the affirmative. Joel "surmounts his sex and career anxieties by turning himself into a pimp,"[76] said *New York* magazine's David Denby. Its conclusion has merit, as Joel is unscathed by the excesses of fulfillment. "Patiently, the world of *Risky Business* is anything but risky," noted Geduld. "It's a place in which there are no serious consequences, in which everyone (more or less) gets what he or she wants . . ."[77]

"Long live wealth, success, status, and the best lay that money can buy," concluded Sarris.[78]

The implicit analogy in the film is that selling and procuring are on the same plateau: It is all free enterprise.

Christopher Connelly labelled the Brickman project the *"Easy Rider* (1969) of the MTV generation." *Risky Business* denied the *Zeitgeist* of what was termed "a cultural civil war" in which "innocence is crowded out, exterminated, like the buffalo."[79] Joel Goodsen and classmates would never say, "This used to be a helluva good country; I can't understand what's wrong with it."

The self-gratification of upper-middle-class materialism in *Risky Business* was manifest to a majority of critics. The film, one writer suggested, "ultimately endorses its perported target."[80] *Variety* said, "Ultimately, the picture seems to endorse the bottom line, going for the big buck above all other considerations."[81]

"This is presented, without irony or a hint of criticism, as a triumph of free enterprise," said Denby.[82]

Several reviewers targeted the sexism of the film's shallow portrayal of women as prostitutes with enchanting sexual appeal. Pauline Kael said, "The picture is centered on this tiresome lie, which appears to satisfy some deep vanity in men." A review in the *Humanist* was less restrained, calling the film a "blatantly irresponsible sexploitation" vehicle.[83]

Remaining analyses ranged from David Ansen's—"this summer's one genuine sleeper"—to Stanley Kauffman's lamention on the state of teen-oriented movies.[84]

The only critical consensus was in favor of Rebecca DeMornay's characterization of Lana. The actress was universally acclaimed for the portrayal and was favorable compared to sultry Veronica Lake of the film *noirs* of the 1940s. Andrew Sarris said she made "a stunning debut as the luscious young hooker with the kind of calculating mind that belongs in the boardroom of IBM."[85]

The controversial soundtrack received barely a mention by most film journalists. Kael and Maslin described New Age pioneer Tangerine

Dream's sound as "jangling electronic mood music" or "electronic incidental music." Two reviewers took note of the air-guitar scene. Rock critics remained silent.[86]

While the under-twenty-five-year-olds flocked to the movie, bestowing "big summer-hit" status upon *Risky Business*, Brickman and record labels were still maneuvering over legal rights. Three selections were pivotal to the movie: Bob Seger's "Old Time Rock 'n' Roll," the Muddy Waters urban-blues classic, "Mannis Boy," and Phil Collins's "In the Air Tonight." The centerpiece was the Seger composition. "Old Time Rock 'n' Roll" had been filler on Seger's 1980 release, *Stranger in Town*, and Capitol withheld permission to use the song on a soundtrack album or as a scout single. Nearly three months after the opening of *Risky Business*, Capitol ran a front-page ad in *Billboard*. Under a color photo of Tom Cruise holding the candlestick imaginary microphone, stripped down to a buttoned-down shirt and BVDs, the copy asked merchandisers:

> Did the song make the movie a smash or did the movie make the song a smash? What's the difference? BOB SEGER'S OLD TIME ROCK & ROLL is a hit and so is RISKY BUSINESS, the movie it comes from. And there's only two places your customer can get it. That's the single, or better yet, inside BOB SEGER'S STRANGER IN TOWN album. The one we've just stuck a special sticker on. Look for it. You can be sure everyone who loves to rock and roll will. On Capitol.[87]

As Brickman and Avent had chosen songs for the film prior to the shooting, there was no record or video support until after the original theater run.

The videoclip of "Old Time Rock 'n' Roll" followed a month after the single was issued. The record charted 17 September. The lateness of the release was due to legal complications and inner cuts to Bob Seger that were included in the trailer video. John Sykes said, "We're not looking for a straight-ahead trailer."[88] The MTV Acquisitions Committee had a rule of thumb—at least half of a film-based clip had to be original footage. This proved to be a problem for both Geffen Pictures and Capitol. "First, we couldn't get any live footage of Seger," said Capitol's Michelle Peacock, "but Geffen Company wanted to give MTV something, so we put together a trailer-type video with footage of Seger, but then we had to edit out the appearance of a half-nude girl and a Budweiser bottle."[89] The beer bottle violated another MTV standard rule, "no commercial products," especially alcoholic beverages, in videoclips. Capitol, having served MTV for several years, was aware of the restrictions. Warner was not. Seger's management company provided live footage, Geffen edited the clip, and Capitol paid for the re-editing and distribution. The video of Cruise's "performance" to "Old Time Rock 'n' Roll" was cablecast the week of 26 October 1983. It remained for a month; the single peaked at a disappointing Number 50 and fell off the chart after eleven weeks. The video cassette appeared in time for the Christmas shopping season.

The album, minus "Every Breath You Take" (Police), "Swamp" (Talking Heads), and Bruce Springsteen's "Hungry Heart," appeared in the United Kingdom in January 1984 and in American stores the following month. Said Rick Lawler of Jem, the distribution company, "It sold very well through May. Then it had slowed down, and we figured it was spent. In the beginning of August, HBO started to show it, and the album went crazy. We've probably sold more albums in August than during the preceding six months."[90]

Warner's advertising vice president, Joel Wayne, told *Boxoffice*, "We tend to put our trailers on music video shows instead of specially produced material. If a trailer is good enough to put in theatres then we don't have to make something different to communicate to television."[91] He denied that *Risky Business*, the film, was hampered by the lack of a supporting music video. Domestically, the picture would come in twelfth for 1983 studio grosses, with $28.5 million.

Wayne's not so subtle belief was fueled by the box office *Risky Business* enjoyed during the summer. Having more than amply recouped production costs, Warner was content to let Virgin and Capitol worry about record sales and the accompanying videoclip. Wayne's perception was common among marketing executives in the movie and record industries. Synergism *did* work when the parties involved transcended traditional territorial boundaries. In this instance, however, the marketing was only partially a success.

Because of its import status, final sales figures for the soundtrack are unavailable. The trades did not chart the album. Seger's single stayed in the lower half of the Hot 100 for eleven weeks; had the marketing been handled differently, it might have earned a platinum, or at least a gold, record. In light of the film's final theatrical gross of $65 million, the Seger material, by exposure alone, should have been a hit.

"On The Dark Side": Eddie & The Cruisers

> An overnight success created by the press
> But they'll eat you up if you show them any
> stress.
> —© 1984 Slam Dun Music Fate Music, ASCAP

*Eddie Wilson was a step ahead of us and
I don't think we've caught up with him yet.*
—Maggie Foley, reporter,
Eddie & The Cruisers

Aurora Productions, flush after a successful public partnership offering of $16 million in December 1982 announced the acquisition of a "music-themed" property titled *Eddie & The Cruisers*. Joe Brooks (*You Light Up My Life*, 1977) would produce and score the film. Martin Davidson, best known for *Lords of Flatbush* (1974) and co-author of the *Eddie* script, was given the directorial position.

The movie was based on P.R. Kluge's novel about a visionary 1950s rock singer with the desire to synthesize black and white music into a lasting new musical form. The singer dies in a car wreck after a recording session. The story was seemingly a perfect vehicle for the ten-to-eighteen-year-old market. It equally bode well for a viable soundtrack.

Both executives had experience with musical scores. Davidson's *Lords* had produced an obscure ABC Records track anthology. Better known was Brooks's *Light Up My Life*. A faceless jingle singer, Kacey Cisyk, originally recorded the title song when Debbie Boone overdubbed the lyrics, it won an Oscar for Best Original Song, and stayed at Number 1 on the *Billboard* chart for an impressive ten weeks.

Brooks was hoping for a repeat success with the new project. Eight "pure rock 'n' roll" songs were planned for it. He hoped to create a tune "that would be a hit in '62 that would still appeal to today's young audience." If successful, "a hit soundtrack could take care of $2 million of the budget."[92]

The project, originally budgeted at $4.8 million, was scheduled to begin filming in New Jersey and New York 15 March 1982. Davidson had yet to assemble a cast. (While tensions over the score were mounting, he chose a relatively unknown actor, Michael Paré, for the title role.) Brooks and Davidson found themselves in an unresolvable concept struggle. Footing the scheduled $5 million outlay, Aurora supported Davidson.

Brooks became a symbolic figurehead as a co-producer. Davidson attempted to coax Southside Johnny to compose the score. The Asbury Park artist declined. John Cafferty eventually got the job.

When the production was in the filming phase Aurora began to hype the film in the industry trades. Full-page ads occasionally appeared in *Variety* portraying The Cruisers gathered around a '57 Chevy with the New Jersey license plate P4C-295. Black sax player Mike "Tunes" Antunes sat apart on road equipment. The Springsteen-Clemons analogy was born.

As rough cuts became available, Lorimar, with international distribution rights, outlined the marketing game plan. Larry Sugar, international president, targeted thirteen-to-nineteen-year-olds, who were expressing interest in the Sixties. "Paré, as Eddie, plays a principled protagonist. He refuses to 'sell out' to the music establishment," said Sugar. "Youth audiences will be able to identify with Eddie's dilemma." The Lorimar division head promised a "full international marketing approach."[93]

In August 1983, three video clips from the motion picture were being readied for telecasting. The soundtrack album was promised in the record bins by "late August." Both, wrote Maitland McDonagh, "will help introduce The Cruisers' music before the film opens."[94] The projected release date had been pushed back from Brooks's original prediction of an album "two months prior to the picture with all the cuts pushed hard as singles."

The film was previewed by the media in New York City September 4. No coinciding records or videos appeared. Journalists at Loews Showplace 2 saw, for ninety-two minutes a "poorly scripted rock music nostalgia drama" with a "strong soundtrack."[95] Davidson, however, described it as a "multi-layered story about a search, a romance, and what it was like to be part of a band in the heyday of rock 'n' roll."[96]

As the film begins, "Eddie, Eddie, Eddie" echoes, overwhelming the noise generated by an off-camera crowd. A roar welcomes the perspiration-drenched, Matt Dillon-John Cougar Mellencamp look-a-like. Eddie Wilson (Michael Paré), eyes glazed, poignantly mouths, "Dark side is coming . . . nothing is real." A band kicks in following the opening piano triplets, "She'll never know just how I feel . . ." The volume cranks up. "On the dark side . . . OOOH YEAH . . . ON THE DARK SIDE." Panning the camera focuses on the word SPRING—the beginning.

The performer fades from a wide-screen television as *Media Magazine* reporter Maggie Foley (Ellen Barkin) pitches a story to the assembled staff. Following a stormy recording session, Eddie Wilson had left the studio, never to be seen again. Maggie tied the disappearance to the shadowy French poet Rimbaud, noting the tentative title for the tapes was "Season in Hell." The "rejected" concept album tracks had been unexplicably removed from the vaults the day after the rock artist drove a sky-blue '57 Chevy convertible off a local levy. The body was not recovered.

The quest for the tapes, and perhaps the vanished singer, provides the foundation for the storyline. "March 16, 1964 . . . somebody checked them out . . . the day after Eddie supposedly died."

The tone-setting scene was reminiscent of *Citizen Kane*, but director Davidson resisted the comparison saying, "It's amazing how many people have given me credit for the subtle brilliance in that shot, but it's coincidence."[97] Another critical consensus was that Barkin had "the film's most awkwardly written role." This proved to be the movie's undoing. As *Film Journal's* Maitland McDonagh noted, "Although the investigative report is the link that connects the first flashbacks and the present-day story, the film's narrative is not completely straightforward. Some of the story emerges through the reporter's interviews while other scenes develop out of conversations between the people involved, with the result that no one character ever finds out everything," including Maggie Foley.[98]

Davidson shrugged off this criticism. "A lot of people were worried that people won't know where they are, and I thought they would. And if they're not sure I think they'll catch on real quick. I'd rather be ahead of them five seconds than behind them one second," he said. Echoing Bob Pittman, the director was banking on the nonlinear impressionism of the targeted thirteen-to-nineteen-year-old audience.

Screening in thirty markets indicated that Davidson was on the correct track. "The audience gets it and they loved the flashbacks," he reported. "Did they get the ending? Do they want to be hit over the head harder, and if they don't get it, do they mind not being sure? What we found was that those who got the ending liked it, and those who weren't sure liked not being sure."[99] Writers of the linear school *did* object.

Davidson's nonlinear film confronts this very issue in stressing Eddie's relationship with Frank "The Wordman" Ridgeway (Tom Berenger), the first interviewee on Foley's list. A songwriter turned high school teacher, Ridgeway mentally returns to a club on the Jersey Shore in Summer 1962, with Del Shannon's "Runaway" playing. ("Runaway" and Santo and Johnny's "Sleep Walk," while highly effective numbers, for some reason were excluded from the soundtrack album.) Joann Carlino (Helen Schneider) walks into the club, leans on the bar as if in a western, and silently stares at Ridgeway, who is sweeping up. Wilson menacingly joins her. The Cruisers enter; an uneasy Frank asks, "Can I help you guys?" After a dramatic pause, Sal Amato, the consumate rocker, breaks the silence. "Tell Tony Eddie and The Cruisers are here!" The theme of culture conflict is established: The college kid meets the wild ones.

The struggle recurs the next day during band rehearsal. "Betty Lou's Got a New Pair of Shoes" lifelessly emanates from the small stage. Eddie stops in the middle of the riff. "Wait a minute! Where you racing, where's the fire?" Sal retorts "No fire, that's the way the song was written; it goes that way. Up beat. What's the problem?" The battle of the musical wills begins.

EDDIE: The problem is the same words. You've got to give me a little room, so
    people know that I'm singing.
SAL: Hey, you lose the beat, people lose a step. We want 'em to dance.
EDDIE: They miss a step. What are you, a moron?
SAL: Can you believe this guy?

The argument drags on. The bassist expresses his subordinate position
in the discussion: "I don't know anything? Everyone you being in this
band is an expert, but Sally. Sally's a dumb guinea." Eddie, in frustration,
turns to Ridgeway, who is cleaning the tavern.

EDDIE: What do you think?
FRANKIE: I think he's [Eddie] right; it needs a *sans souci*.
EDDIE: See my way . . . with a *Caesarean*.
SAL: A What!
EDDIE: Tell 'em, Frankie.
FRANKIE: *Sans souci* . . . that's a timely pause, kind of a strategic silence.
EDDIE: That's exactly right!

Frankie pulls out a Rimbaud paperback and reads. "Sounds like shit,
right!" Eddie says with pride. Hearing the same passage with the proper
diction, Eddie gloats, "Now that's got class." On the basis of his recitation, the "preppie" Ridgeway is accepted.
    This interchange underscored a recurrent theme in the movie. Eddie is
torn between his working-class mentality and the desire to pioneer new
vistas. Frankie, inducted into the band after Joann learns of his writing
skills, represents a means to rise to a new height. Eddie Wilson is both
afraid and eager to try the untested waters.
    The Paré-Berenger interaction is interrupted by a series of disjointed
events that attempt to refocus the initial plot. Ridgeway finds his mobile
home ransacked. Doc Robbins, ex-Cruiser manager, now a deejay, wants
to reassemble the remaining Cruisers. Ridgeway dismisses the notion. In
the interim he discovers that the ex-manager's trailer has also been torn
apart: "Looks like we have the same decorator." As he muses over the
break-ins, the missing "Season in Hell" tapes are reintroduced.
    The story segues to a Holiday Inn, the graveyard of aspiring and
disillusioned musicians, where Sal heads a nostalgia ensemble. A tuxedoed
emcee introduces a fifties band of "New Jersey boys that really made
good." The pale comparison to the Cruisers is heightened by "Betty Lou"
resounding minus the *sans souci*. Ridgeway shuffles into the crowd, only
to be greeted by the persevering Maggie Foley. They agree to a drink after
Sal's show. (The motel-lounge scenes are remarkably realistic. "Some of
the details ring uncannily true," wrote Janet Maslin, "like the slick 'oldies'

nightclub act that one of the Cruisers is still doing nearly twenty years after Eddie's supposed death.''[100]

Sitting at the bar, Ridgeway recalls becoming a Cruiser and the creation of their hit single. ''Joann was telling me you write music,'' said Eddie. ''Thinks you might be good. We'll give you a try. What I want is songs that *echo*.'' At this point Eddie Wilson halfheartedly opens up saying, ''That stuff we're doing now is like someone's sheets . . . There are songs I want to be able to fold ourselves up in 'em, wrap 'em, you understand. That's the most you'll ever get out of me, Wordman, ever.''

Practicing ''On the Dark Side'' as a ballad, Doc and the group members chuckled and ridiculed Frank's effort. Eddie intervened saying, ''He's got something we need, words and music . . . words and music.'' The heckling stopped. ''All right, let's get on with the music,'' he said. The tentative bond was established. Eddie's arrangement transforms the melody. Instantaneously, a final version is performed on the motel balcony. Eddie's rock 'n' roll odyssey has been launched providing the transition to ''Season in Hell.''

The Wordman's attention is transported back to the reality of the Holiday Inn. Sal closes the set with ''Oldies but Goodies Remind Me of You'' and an *a cappella* tribute to Eddie. In part, he says, ''Never a day passes I think he's around somewhere out in the street, around the corner, he's not far away at all.'' Backstage, Sal laments the disappointments Eddie's disappearance has caused.

The culture-conflict theme finally reappears. The Cruisers accept a booking at Benton College, apparently a prestigious institution, at Frank's insistence. (It was his *alma mater*.) Towing a U-Haul trailer, their slick Chevy pulls onto the campus, with strains of ''Sleep Walk'' providing background. The band's working-class roots immediately resurface. ''This is a mistake, we don't belong here,'' they observe.

A disjointed sequence finds Frank visiting former drummer Kenny Hopkins (David Wilson) on the Atlantic City Boardwalk; Kenny now deals blackjack. The scene partially underlines Frank's naivete regarding street life. He discovers that sax player Wendell Newton (Michael ''Tunes'' Antunes) did not die of a heart attack, but overdosed. The scene then segues into Joann's reemergence into the film.

Eddie's ex-girl is reunited with Frank. She tells him of receiving a series of anonymous phone calls, which they agree are connected with the ''old tapes.'' They reconstruct the last recording session, which preceded Eddie's disappearance. All of the film's tensions merge in this retrospective sequence.

Strains from ''Season in Hell'' fill the recording studio. Eddie paces while some band members sip beers and others stare blankly. An argument is erupting between Doc and a record executive. Abruptly the music stops. Eddie, followed by the group, storms into the control booth and overhears a heated exchange. Satin Records executive Lew Eisen (producer Kenny Vance) rants, "This is a disaster . . . You wanna be a poet, try Greenwich Village . . ." Eddie joins the shouting match. "Hey, I put up ten grand," exclaims Eisen. "I expect something for my money. This is what I've been waiting for? A bunch of jerkoffs makin' weird sounds . . . you're not going to see a red penny."

Bass player Sal tells Eddie, "You're wrong, you're wrong. They want 'On the Dark Side.' What we're giving them is some damned opera. I don't know what you're after." Eddie explains, "I wanna do something *nobody's ever done before. Somethin' great.*" Sal disagrees. "We ain't great. We're just some guys from Jersey," he says.

"If we can't be great, then there's no sense in ever playing music again" is Eddie's exit line. He storms out of the building, with Joann in close pursuit. She catches up with him in the car. They drive off to a psychedelic junkyard, the Palace Depression, a modern art piece constructed by a recluse who believed "he could build a castle out of a bunch of junk." Eddie calls it "a monument to nothing . . . Here's to nothing." Dropping Joann at her car, Eddie races off.

Meanwhile, back at the cocktail lounge, Joann finally admits she knows the location of the tapes. She was the *someone* who took them. They have been hidden for two decades. "Eventually she finds the tapes," wrote Peter Occhiogrosso, "preserved intact after all that time in a wooden box ridden outdoors in a junkyard . . . (no wonder record companies have been going broke—wasting all that money on *storage vaults*.)"[101]

Having retrieved the tapes, Joann drives Frank to her home. On the way, Eddie's phantom '57 Chevy, supposedly destroyed, appears. Inside, the dreaded phone calls resume, with "Tender Years" playing on the other end. Joann believes the caller is Eddie, whose convertible then pulls into her driveway. The lights blink their old signal. Frankie, having hidden his vehicle, jumps out of the bushes, dragging a leather-jacketed figure out of the Chevy. "You, You, You," screams Joann, hitting Doc Robbins repeatedly.

Doc cries, "I'd have it made for once in my life. I'd bring home a winner." Joann hands Doc the cherished tapes. Frank nods approval. There is a majestic loose end left in the film: Eddie Wilson's watery demise.

The footage screened by the *Media Magazine* staffers reappears. This time the set is in an appliance storefront. A thin crowd gathers. Maggie's voice begins:

> The essence of the fifties was over and so was rock 'n' roll as we knew it. We were entering a new age. An age of confusion, an age of passion, of commitment. Eddie Wilson saw it coming. "Season in Hell" is a total innovation for its time. It was a signal of greatness yet to come.
>
> Eddie Wilson was a step ahead of us and I don't think we've caught up with him yet. Eddie's been dead for almost eighteen years, but his music is as alive today as the day he recorded it. To me and to everyone that listens to music Eddie Wilson lives and always will.

Black and white stills flash on the TV screen. A bearded Eddie Wilson, clad in a leather jacket and jeans, stares at his television image. The opening chant, "Eddie, Eddie . . .," resumes. As the credits role, the rocker fades into the darkness of the night.

Many critics suggested this outcome was the films glaring flaw. *Variety* typified the response, saying the "Film takes a disastrous turn when Frank is reunited with the group's beautiful femme singer Joann. Amidst howler lines that belabor the obvious ('What's going on?,' 'Where are the tapes?'), picture segues into the structure (but minus the thrills) of a 'he's returned years after' horror film leading to a stupid anti-climax."[102]

The parts of *Eddie & The Cruisers* proved more significant and satisfying than the motion picture as a whole, but even these components came under attack.

"What I was looking for was a combination of three different rock stars that I'd loved through the years, from 1953 to 1983—for the life of rock and roll," explained the director. The first model for the composite was Dion of Dion and the Belmonts, a doo-wop group that introduced Davidson to rock music, he said. "Then," he continued, "I jumped ten years later, to Jim Morrison and the Doors, because Morrison wrote poetry and had charisma, a sense of danger and a dark side." The third archetype was Bruce Springsteen because "he went back to basic rifts, the joy of early rock 'n' roll, without losing any of the lyrics. So somewhere in there was my vision of Eddie Wilson . . . What I really wanted was to create someone fresh and new who could give me the thirty years of rock 'n' roll that I wanted Eddie to encapsulate."[103]

Southside Johnny (Lyon) and the Asbury Jukes appeared to fit the musical bill. The ten-piece group had a bluesy R&B sound with a touch of the Jersey shore. This eclecticism fit two-thirds of Davidson's requirements. The director had asked Lyon to write songs for the film. He declined, but worked on the project as a technical advisor, coaching the actors. (Reportedly the task involved hours of instruction.) The end product, especially Michael Paré's performance, received favorable comments. Peter Occhiogrosso of the *Village Voice* called Paré "surprisingly nifty as the conglomerate rocker." *Variety* noted that Paré lip-synced "very well and is dynamic in his sketchy (flashbacks only) role." *Times* critic Janet Maslin equally praised the portrayal as "a fine debut; he captures the manner of a hot-blooded young rocker with conviction, and his lip-syncing is almost perfect."[104]

While Paré got high grades for *Eddie*, Davidson's overall effort was roundly criticized. For example, only Wilson, in the final cut, appears to have aged; members of The Cruisers seem ageless. Several reviewers took note of the time warp. "Unfortunately, with the conspicious exception of Michael Paré, all of the actors are really too old to play their characters in 1963; it is a little ridiculous when Eddie calls Frankie 'kid' since Berenger looks every inch of the 40ish English teacher he plays in the present-day scenes," observed McDonagh.[105] "On the Dark Side" and several other cuts would hardly have been "the rage in 1963," he added.

The Asbury Park Backlash

You don't tug on Superman's cape . . .
—© 1971 Blendingwell Music, Inc. [ASCAP]

Rock music's pantheon has housed a handful of deities and a host of demigods. The gods—Elvis, The Beatles, Led Zeppelin—were allowed disciples: rock-a-billies, heavy metalers, and "British Invaders." Bruce Springsteen's coming, however, was a singular event. No interlopers allowed.

Rock fans, at least the carriers of the True Faith, embraced and championed the messiah of the 1980s. Having lost Led Zeppelin, the wearers of "Disco Sucks" pins allowed no pretenders to Springsteen's throne. The artists with the misfortune of honing their skills in the Jersey shore niteries or the New England frat-bar circuit were perceived as sacrilegious exploiters of The Boss.

Many Springsteen loyalists forgot his lengthy struggle to escape the "New Dylan" label, originally applied by *Crawdaddy's* Peter Knobler and encouraged by CBS's publicity department. (In the wake of *Born to Run*, The Boss also had been compared to Elvis and other legends.) Still, the fans resented artists with a link, however tenuous, to the Jersey mega-star. The first interloper was Johnny Lyon. "I went through that Springsteen comparison thing," he told a writer. "All you can do is keep playing." Springsteen, asked about the comparisons, said, "It's here today and it's gone tomorrow. It's only there to sell a newspaper for a day or two. . . . Go home and write some good music, play some good shows, and that's how you redefine yourself. You make people deal with you."[106]

Dave Marsh, The Boss's biographer, avoided labels. Discussing the Juke, he wrote, "because they're from Asbury Park, New Jersey, are produced by Miami Steve Van Zandt of the E Street Band, and have recorded several of Bruce Springsteen's songs . . . have been identified with Springsteen's musical style. This is far from an apt comparison: Springsteen's antecedents are much broader than this combination of doo-wop and Stax/New Orleans rhythm and blues."[107]

Southside Johnny and his band had fortunately escaped from the Stone Pony club scene with *I Don't Want to Go Home*, released less than a year after *Born to Run*. (While dominating the covers of *Time* and *Newsweek* within a twenty-four-hour period in 1975, Springsteen, "the future of rock 'n' roll" had not yet achieved musical god-status.[108]

By 1983, Springsteen was the only rock Olympian remaining. (*Thriller* was perceived as irrelevant by die-hard rockers, an aberration confined to Michael Jackson fans. Into this environment entered director Davidson, whose "Eddie Wilson" in dress and musical direction, mirrors the Eighties' king of rock, Springsteen. (Neither Jim Morrison nor Dion Di Mucci exert a comparable influence on the character.)

Prompted by the Springsteen angle, the director's casting plans also included a black sax player. "I was kind of thinking Clarence Clemons," he confessed.[109] Kenny Vance, the former member of Jay and The Americans who worked as music supervisor of the film, recalled seeing a possible candidate in Michael "Tunes' Antunes of Beaver Brown, an East Coast bar band. (The group had performed at the Other End in Greenwich Village in the late 1970s; Vance attended one performance. As its leader, John Cafferty, later mused, "There's an old show biz saying, 'You gotta be great every night, because you never know who's in the audience.' Well, that's how we got the movie deal. Kenny Vance was in the audience . . . one night about six years ago. He never introduced himself; I never talked to him until . . .''

Lyon was aware of Beaver Brown, having shared the bill with them at several Shore clubs. He, Springsteen, and Cafferty had occasionally jammed together on "Twistin' the Night Away" and "Raise Your Hand" in Jersey bistros. "Bruce and Southside Johnny would come up on stage," said Cafferty of the Asbury Park gigs, "and sing with us."[110] Davidson and Vance flew to Rhode Island, the home base of Beaver Brown.

Beaver Brown apparently was ideal for the *Eddie* model. Davidson reportedly was "knocked out." He and Vance approached Cafferty with the script. "There were no record companies interested at the time . . . Marty Davidson and Kenny Vance came along and said they believed in what I was doing," said Cafferty who, on another occasion, noted, "A band has to keep making progress, and the film project seemed like the way to do it."[111] Cafferty was offered the opportunity to write original material for the film; band members were on both original and cover material. Vance performed the lead vocals on two fifties-era doo-wop numbers, "Betty Lou" and "The Oldies But Goodies."

Cafferty wrote three more original pieces after "On the Dark Side." Two of his previously recorded songs were added. Cafferty was uneasy with the latter inclusion. He told Steve Pond, "It's really hard for me to deal with the fact that 'Tender Years,' my most important song, is in a film and somebody else is lip-syncing it. But I had to face the fact that nobody would give that song a life."[112] Kenny Vance produced the material at the RCA studios in New York.

Beaver Brown's decision had merit, as record companies weren't looking anxiously for new acts. One CBS executive said, "The economy doesn't let us speculate much on our signings." At RCA, Joe Galente agreed, saying, "There were acts who used to get signed to major label deals who won't make it today."[113] Under normal circumstances, Cafferty and Co could have done better, but 1981 and 1982 were stagnation in the music industry.

Once the soundtrack was on a master, Davidson needed a record label. ABC Records, The *Lords of Flatbush's* outlet, was nonexistent, but he did know of Scotti Brothers through Sylvester Stallone, who had debuted in *Lords*. Tony Scotti had successfully pitched *Survivor* to Stallone. "They saw the movie," said John Musso, president of Scotti record division, "and came up with 'Eye of the Tiger.' " The single sold five million copies and the album was certified double platinum.

An arrangement was reached with Scotti Records to "work" *Eddie and The Cruiser's* Johnny Musso. "When we release a record, all of our efforts are focused on that record's success," Musso said.[114] John Cafferty and Beaver Brown finally landed a recording contract. CBS would do the promotion and distribution. Reviewers were not impressed. *Rolling Stone* led with " 'Eddie and The Cruisers': Hollywood rips off Bruce." Steve Pond ravaged the film with, "Isn't it a little early to make *The Bruce Springsteen Story?*" The Cafferty songs "are the closest thing to Springsteen this side of *The River*," or "music sounds uncannily like, and slightly inferior to, Springsteen's." Retreating somewhat, "Once you get past the

Springsteen similarities, much of the music can stand on its own."
"Sounds a lot like Springsteen," decided Janet Maslin.

With "On the Dark Side" the scout release, Cafferty could hardly
disavow the comparison. Moreover, Davidson was muddling up the situation with comments like, "I don't think he's a gun for hire," *but* if The
Boss had wanted to do the script, "there's a good chance we would have
talked business."[115] Cafferty declined to discuss the film publicly, acknowledging that it had provided his big break.

The Asbury Park influence was undeniable, and Springsteen had helped
with songwriting tips. He had sat in with Beaver Brown, The Cats, and
other bands at Shore bars, especially the Stone Pony. Upon signing Beaver
Brown, Scotti Records set the wheels in motion to convince people of
Eddie Wilson's true identity. After the all-important holiday season, Scotti
Brothers' record division president Johnny Musso complained, "We're
trying *now* to establish that Eddie and The Cruisers are John Cafferty and
his band.[116] "Eddie Wilson lives in Beaver Brown." Despite the adverse
publicity the album sold 175,000 copies. The film failed to return its original
investment, grossing only $4.7 million, $100,000 less than the original
budget. Aurora and Embassy began to plan postrelease marketing with
home video and the increasingly lucrative "pay" cable services.

Eddie and The Cruisers was not an impressive movie or an interesting
failure. In addition, it was poorly timed and promoted. The project illustrated the need for an *exposure* game plan.

The timing problem was further underscored by the release of *The Big
Chill* days after *Eddie*. Both packages were aimed at the twelve-plus age
group, though the older Baby Boomers were more aggressively courted by
the *Big Chill*. ("They made a movie about us, therefore, we exist," Frank
Zappa had said of *Blackboard Jungle* (1954). The description would be
applied, again, to *The Big Chill*.) "Once upon a time, in a mythical decade
called the '60s," said David Ansen, "there lived a colorful collective beast
called 'us.' As in Us-versus-Them. As in 'We Shall Overcome.' "[117]
"Eddie's" commercial fate was in the hands of the lower portion of the
youth market. "It was the eight to twenty-one-year-olds who watch cable
who responded to the film and the soundtrack as substitutes for an era
they never knew," said. The MTV audience saw Michael Paré's video clip
in October through December.

A major difficulty in promotion was the lack of a flesh-and-blood artist
to facilitate a marketing campaign. Paré, busy acting in *Streets of Fire*,
was unavailable; Cafferty remained in the background. Outside the East
Coast tour route, potential record buyers were generally unaware of the
confusing Cafferty/Paré identity. Potential record buyers asking for Paré

or Cafferty's "new record" frequently received strange glances from the store clerk. Trailers from *Eddie* consisted merely of the "Dark Side" video. Paré's uncanny ability to lip-sync had convinced many MTV viewers that the actor was the *actual* singer.

Reviewers and filmgoers with the patience to sit through the credits knew the score was John Cafferty's. The *Village Voice* informed readers, "The soundtrack was composed and played, as you probably know by now, by John Cafferty, a longtime Jersey-bar-band leader and Springsteen protegé."[118]

The film's release strategy was perplexing. The movie opened at 225 showcase theaters nationwide the first week of October, facing the likes of *Risky Business*, *Revenge of the Ninja*, *The Return of the Jedi*, and *National Lampoon's Vacation*.[119] All were teen favorites. The market was crowded. The Davidson film appeared on the *Variety* chart October 5 with a gross of $680,962. The "On the Dark Side" single, listed as performed by "Eddie and The Cruisers," charted at Number 94 8 October, remaining on the "Hot 100" until 10 December 1983. The title barely reached Number 66.

The videoclip featured Michael Paré. (Recalling the balcony scene, Cafferty labeled the song "a vehicle for actors."[120]) It first appeared in MTV's "light" rotation 5 October (A light listing refers to two or more plays per twenty-four-hour period). Its tenure exceeded a month; but the exposure was still modest.

The soundtrack album entered the *Billboard* chart at Number 70 15 October 1983 and peaked at Number 55. It continued on the bottom half of the chart until year's end.

Cashbox originally charted the album 16 October; in six weeks *Eddie* reached Number 37. After a slow decline for another twelve weeks the title exited. The LP was charted for a total of four and one half months.

A cursory examination of film reviews of the top-selling "rock" soundtrack albums of 1983 and *Eddie* demonstrate that the rock mystery, especially its performances and music, outdistanced *Flashdance* and *Staying Alive*. Aesthetics, however, do not sell records. Attempts to cross-promote *Eddie* failed. The 1983 run grossed a disappointing $1.76 million in North America.

The record release dates were delayed. The ancillary single, album, and video coincided with film's distribution. Consequently, the album reached the bins as the holiday issues were beginning to flood the market. Timing, in the film and music industries, is essential. *Eddie* got lost in the shuffle.

Eddie's Encore—One Year Later

Footloose, street wisdom suggested, basically reaffirmed the synergistic formula of profitability: record + MTV rotation + film debut + album.

The stagger- or cluster-record release methods functioned, depending on the release and distribution in the two media. Once the picture had run its course, the soundtrack album became yesterday's press handout.

Scotti Brothers Records, having signed John Cafferty and Beaver Brown, was faced with the delicate task of breaking a "new act." Michael Paré *was* Eddie Wilson. The video clip of "On the Dark Side" reinforced this perception. Cafferty, outside of the East Coast circuit, remained merely a name on the credits as the theater emptied.

Aurora Productions and Marty Davidson did little to alter the popular misconception; consequently, the "Dark Side" videoclip featured Paré and the movie "band." The Scotti organization brought out only the soundtrack, believing that the film would sell the album. The faceless odd man out was John Cafferty. His signing with Scotti reprioritized the equation. The indie label had the unenviable job of practicing a variant of "doublespeak." Marketing Paré as the movie Eddie Wilson and Cafferty as the audio version was no simple assignment, especially in the video idiom, which blended the two media. With a master tape in the box, ready for release, the spotlight needed to be focused on Cafferty.

July Fourth 1984 came and went with the obligatory appearance of presidential aspirants. More significantly meanwhile, the Jacksons were preparing for the Friday, 6 July, launch of their Victory Tour at Arrowhead Stadium, Kansas. The proposed road show was still embroiled in controversy over the ticket plan. Springsteen was comfortably atop the album charts with *Born In The USA*. *Purple Rain* entered the chart at Number 11 immediately, posing a threat to The Boss's dominance. (The much publicized Prince movie would not appear until later in the month.) The listing of *Eddie and the Cruisers* in television logs, 7 July, under the HBO and TMC logos, paled in contrast. Box office disasters never die; they just keep insomniacs company.

Eddie showcased Saturday morning, the day after the Jacksons' opening, on HBO. The channel would rotate twenty viewing "ops" (opportunities) in July. In mid-1984 the top ranked pay service enjoyed 13.5 million subscribers. The Movie Channel, with 3.1 million households, cablecast the "rock 'n' roll mystery" a week later. The thirteen showings ended August 6.

The response to the saturation thirty-three showings startled the record industry. Within one week of the HBO launch, the cable exposure had generated orders for an additional 25,000 albums. The number doubled within the next week. The 152-store Record Bar chain reported an increase of sales from 12 per business week to 4,581. The escalation occurred in a month's period.

The surge caught merchandisers unprepared. "Everyone missed this one," observed Bob Varcho of the 151-store Camelot chain. Norman Hunter conceded that more attention needed to be paid to cable titles, saying "Cable exposure of movies has the potential to sell more soundtracks than theater exposure. It presents an easy opportunity for more people to see a film in a month than see it in a year in theaters." Another album buyer for National Record Mart agreed, noting, "with HBO and Showtime, all a view has to do is hit a button."[121]

The CBS Group began to dust off publicity and promotional material for the soundtrack. There was a problem. Scotti Brothers wanted the promo campaign addressed to Cafferty not the celluloid version of Eddie Wilson.

On the road, John Cafferty and the band were performing in New Haven at Toad's Place, working at bar-band wages. The group's manager came backstage and asked, "Do you know you've sold 30,000 copies of the soundtrack this week, and you're back on the charts?" Having given up on the "big break," Cafferty recalled, "I just couldn't believe it."[122] Lead guitarist Gary Gramolini, with resignation, said, "We're still juggling salaries to pay for groceries . . . It's like 'What's wrong with this picture?' I mean we're in the Top 10, but here I am still playing at Toad's Place."[123]

The Paré/Cafferty dilemma continued unresolved when *Eddie* returned to the *Billboard* chart at Number 13 on 11 August. Temporarily lodged at Number 30 on 1 September, the Rhode Island band was, at last, identified as "Eddie and the Cruisers," and credited with the longevity of the album, whose life was listed at seventeen weeks, including the 1983 stay of thirteen weeks.

Music video outlets were provided with a Cafferty and Beaver Brown performance videoclip shot in a Boston club. Unfortunately, it lacked the dynamism of the movie-based clip. MTV cablecast *both* versions of "Dark Side" in the heavy rotation.

By 27 August the soundtrack was certified gold—502,000 copies—on its way to the one million, platinum mark.

A Scotti Brothers press release celebrated, "People learn the name 'Eddie and the Cruisers.' People start to learn the name JOHN CAFFERTY AND THE BEAVER BROWN BAND . . ."

The CBS ad campaign in mass music publications read: GIVE CREDIT WHERE CREDIT IS DUE: JOHN CAFFERTY AND THE BEAVER BROWN BAND *ARE* "EDDIE AND THE CRUISERS." A photo of the group was backed by a ghostly album-cover shot of Michael Paré. The ad copy promised the reader, "You'll be hearing a lot more . . . A lot more. And soon." The bottom line was that *Eddie* broke because of HBO and "word of mouth" rather than any machinations by marketing people.

Premium cable channels became an important generator of a "second life" for soundtracks after their film had been exhibited in traditional movie houses, particularly if the film had been a flop. Film producers, while not as enthusiastic, found some value in home video exposure. *Apocalypse Now* (1979) a staple on Showtime, The Movie Channel, and Cinemax, was re-released in selected markets in 1987 due to cable exposure.

Predictions of planned summer rentals to pay cable outlets abounded. The summer was ideal, as *Rolling Stone's* Chris Connelly noted, "when the kids are at home, bored and ready to spend."[124] Synergism, the total media saturation approach, added another variable into the mix.[125]

The unanticipated boomlet for *Eddie* on HBO highlighted a recurrent issue between studios and labels. The contentious hook was a legal mechanism called the "video buy-out." This referred to a stipulation giving a studio all future rights after a movie's consignment to cable television and home video. Paul Brickman, having been burned by the soundtrack hassles surrounding *Risky Business*, said, "It's getting very expensive," a reference to Bob Seger's "Old Time Rock 'n' Roll."

"And I'm hearing horror stories about video rights, where you have the rights for the movie [theatre run] but not for videocassettes or cable—or even foreign rights. So when the film comes out on HBO or is sold to home video, you have to go and pick new songs and redub the reels."[126] Becky Shargo told several writers CBS was most difficult in the buyout field. Buyouts involved, in 1984, $10,000 to $15,000 per song title. (Director Peter Bogdanovich had convinced Bruce Springsteen to grant permission to have three compositions in *Mask*. Given the stature of the artist, Universal offered $200,000. CBS Records countered with a demand for $500,000 and 25 percent of cable and home-video grosses. Bob Seger's material was inserted instead.)

Record labels justified their position, claiming that soundtracks sell cinema. Therefore, diskeries reasoned, they should share in post-theatrical profits. An article in *ASCAP in Action* reported that hit songs "boost the boxoffice and extend the commercial lives of movies."[127] Company spokespersons pointed to title songs such as Phil Collins's "Against All Odds," and Vangeli's "Chariots of Fire."

Filmmakers objected, suggesting some hit soundtrack albums and singles did little to promote films. *Two of a Kind* and *Hard to Hold* were major box office disappointments whose soundtracks had been awarded platinum albums. Don Simpson, a major practioneer, offered, "Soundtracks don't have that much impact on the success of a picture."[128]

Eddie supports the film industry view. Director Marty Davidson's conceptualization, and the commissioning of the material from an unsigned artist, John Cafferty, made the platinum album possible. Few established recording acts would have risked changing their sound to fit three music periods. CBS and the Scotti Brothers omitted mentioning John Cafferty and Beaver on the album label. This, however, does not negate Universal Studios president Frank Price's view, "There's no question that music as a promotional tool for pictures is going to be around indefinitely."[129]

Gary LeMel's concept of an "organic thread" can be viewed as a form of biological symbiosis, "the living together of two dissimilar organisms, especially when this association is mutually beneficial."[130] In 1984, the biological analogy should have been Darwinian rather than functional. Even the megahit *Purple Rain* would have its territorial disputes.

In the more "civil" climate of 1988, Aurora Productions had been consulting with Michael Paré, a co-star of the CBS-TV police series *Houston Knights*, concerning a sequel to *Eddie*. A spokesperson said the project "is planned though no production date has been set as of this time." Still, as Danny Goldberg indicated, "there is a delicate detente between the two worlds of cinema and music. It's a tricky thing."[131]

"You Can't Always Get What You Want": The Big Chill

> *It's a cold world out there*
> —Nick, drug dealer

> *Sometimes I feel as if*
> *I'm getting a little frosty myself*
> —Meg, real estate lawyer

Director Lawrence Kasdan, hot from the success of the noir *Body Heat* (1982), co-wrote *The Big Chill* with Barbara Benedek. The script addressed the aging of the protesters of the Sixties.

The Ladd Company, which had distributed *Body Heat*, had first rights to Kasdan's project, but declined. Producer Michael Shamberg experienced problems peddling the property. Studios, said Shamberg, "thought it was 'too old'—that is, its characters are older than the prime moviegoing audience . . . I don't think we're going to get twelve- to seventeen-year-olds because it's an R-rated film anyway . . . Larry [Kasdan] was trying to reach the large segment of the public that's alienated from films."[132] With the exception of Columbia Pictures, all of the "majors" passed on the project.

The film was filmed on location in Beaufort, South Carolina, after a month's rehearsal, in fifty-four days for $8 million. The marketing budget equalled the production expenses.

The studio's music division, Colpix Music Group, was assigned the task of obtaining a record deal. The selling of *Chill's* musical overlay proved difficult because the material was, again, "too old."

"Rock songs with emotional impact," said Meg Kasdan, wife of the director and *The Big Chill's* music consultant, describing songs used in the film. Most were the Kasdans' favorites from their undergraduate days at the University of Michigan—five Motown classics and only a handful of selections identified with the counterculture. (Kasdan admitted a distaste for acid rock and the socially significant, folk-rock genres.) Beatle material was deemed too expensive.

"The '60s were an explosion, an incredibly varied explosion of pop music," Kasdan explained. "For a lot of people in my generation, rock 'n' roll hasn't since equalled that period in terms of richness or emotional impact. The songs really spoke to us, spoke to a lot of our concerns. Even if it were just the fact that we were living vividly, these songs spoke to those emotions in a very strong way."

Columbia Pictures was uneasy with the memory-lane selections. (*Flashdance*, dotting the trades, had fresh material.) Oldies might fit the time frame in *Chill*, but the choices precluded the airplay vital to the crosspromotion process. Robert Holmes, senior vice president of Colpix Music Group, encountered a considerable amount of resistance from the studio and record company. "A lot of people were pushing for the use of a contemporary song in the film," he said. The Kasdans, aided by producer Michael Shamberg, prevailed. "There was a fear that we would not be able to acquire sufficient [album] cuts at the royalty [fee] we had to acquire them at. It went down absolutely to the wire," said Holmes. In the end, thirteen song clearances were obtained for the first soundtrack. Notably absent were three of the most memorable overlays from the picture. The tone-setting Rolling Stones number, "You Can't Always Get What You Want," was unavailable for record release. Capitol Records repeated its *Easy Rider* decision to refuse the rights to The Band's "The Weight" and "Bad Moon Rising" could not be cleared in time for the film's opening. (Both would appear on the *More* sequel album.)

The Kasdans' choice of soul classics and Holmes's previous Motown Records affiliation made the label a natural choice, however. Jay Lasker, the flamboyant Motown head, was originally lukewarm to the soundtrack. Few oldies packages since *American Graffiti* had done well in the marketplace and consequently "I didn't look at this," recalled Lasker, "as it's gotta be a smash."

The label's hesitancy was understandable. AOR stations rarely air oldies, especially by 1960s Motown artists. "AOR programmers would say this music doesn't fit their demographic" said Lasker, "but the people going to see this movie are basically the same people they say are their demographics." He defined the target audience as "white, upper-middle-class college kids and alumni." To offset the resistance, Motown purchased sixty-second spots on 100 FM stations nationally. Urban Contemporary outlets were generally ignored, as "Black radio plays Marvin Gaye and The Temptations all year long as oldies."

Motown's fears were allayed when reviews of the film appeared. "As soon as people started to see the picture they would walk into the stores and ask for the soundtrack," Lasker said, noting that sales appeared to be especially strong everywhere the picture was a hit. The souvenir aspect of the record anthology appealed to its consumers.

" 'American Graffiti' is the only other soundtrack I can recall that was big without a new hit single in it," said Lasker, "where a bunch of older hits from an era got this kind of reaction."[133]

Belatedly, Columbia Pictures commissioned a video for Marvin Gaye's "I Heard It through the Grapevine." Larry Kasdan approved the material to be merged with Gaye's footage. The clip was "too old" for MTV, but would appeal in local music video showcases and dance clubs.

The Movie: Existential Despair

Cars enter a dirt parking lot as well-dressed individuals, singularly or paired, gravitate to a rural chapel. Seven University of Michigan alumni gather to mourn Alex, who has inexplicably committed suicide. Alex's demise brings the old friends together to ponder their lost Sixties past and the reality of the Reagan Eighties.

A jaded minister eulogizes a man he did not know: "Where did our hopes go? Aren't the satisfactions of being a good man among our common men enough anymore?" Apparently not. "Karen (Jo Beth Williams) will play one of Alex's favorite songs," closes the preacher. She sits down at the organ and the overdub of a Rolling Stones classic filters through.

"You Can't Always Get What You Want" accompanies the casket from the rustic church to its final resting place. "In this scene, as in many others, the choice of 60s music not only contributes a nostalgic backdrop to the proceedings, but wittingly comments on them," wrote Wendy Weinstein.[134]

The film's use of the track to underscore themes is apparent. Pat Caddell, the political pollster, has repeatedly stressed appreciation of the

Jagger song as a psychographic determinant. *Variety's* McCarthy observed that "contemporaries of the characters will find plenty to 'relate' to."

"The moment depends on the shared history," echoed David Ansen, "between audience and characters."[135] Music will be significant in the introspective weekend reunion.

Harold (Kevin Kline) and Sarah's (Glenn Close) oceanside house provides the center stage. Director Lawrence Kasdan uses the ex-"revolutionaries" to explore vanished dreams juxataposed with contemporary realities. "Larry's intention is to be affectionate toward this group of people coming of age," said Michael Shamberg, "who had such high hopes, and not to say because they've failed in their vision they've failed as people."[136] At the ensuing reception, the characters are fleshed out.

Harold and Sarah host the weekend gathering. A hip capitalist with a twenty-seven-store sportswear chain, Harold is most financially successful of the seven. He worries more about SEC regulations than global issues, but does manifest some ties to the 1960s. (As he centers an album on Harold's hi-tech stereo equipment, Michael (Jeff Goldblum), the urban sophisticate, asks, "You mean you still listen to that music?" Harold snaps back, "There is no other music." So much for New Music.)

Sarah, a pediatrician, is nearly the prototype, post-Sixties professional spouse. One writer described her as "glowing with generosity and nurturing warmth." She is the most affected by Alex's death—They had an affair five years earlier. Clinging to her memories of the progressive Ann Arbor scene, she finds the notion of "selling out" vaguely distressing. "I hate to think," she says in a moment of self doubt, "it was all just fashion." "What?" someone asks. "Our commitment," she responds. Isidore Silver captured the entire group's ambiance when he wrote, "They seem to have achieved great (even remarkable) world success without much effort and commitment (even to money)."[137]

Sam (Tom Berenger) is the title character in the action television show, *J.T. Lancer*, (which has a strong resemblance to Tom Selleck's "Magnum P.I."). Uncomfortable with the success of the series, he rationalizes to Karen, "At least once every show I *try* to put in something of value." However, his clumsy attempt at repeating Lancer's arobatic car jump underlines Sam's lack of import in the production.

Richard (Don Galloway), Karen's husband, epitomizes the once-dreaded "Establishment." The solid corporation executive says, "You set your priorities and that's the way life is. Nobody said it was going to be fun—at least not me . . . Alex couldn't live with it." (Unfortunately, the needs of the script remove the antagonist, allowing Karen a soul-searching liaison with Sam. Richard's smug, "I-told-you-so!" attitude would have been an interesting catalyst.)

Mary Kay Place, best known for *Mary Hartman, Mary Hartman*, played Meg, the lawyer. She ruefully departed Legal Aid where she defended "scum," for real-estate law; her clients merely "*rape* the land." Her goal, an important subplot, is bearing a child: "The only thing I've always known I really wanted." Having given up on men "as a long term investment," and realizing that her "biological timeclock is ticking," Meg decides to have one of her college chums impregnate her. Her quest for a suitable partner dominates the last half of the picture. Sarah eventually convinces Harold to perform the stud service.

Meg's first candidate was Nick (William Hurt). With one foot firmly planted in the 1960s, he's a drug dealer who drifts aimlessly in a vintage black Porsche. In one scene, Nick conducts a retrospective interview with himself, recalling his tenure as a call-in pop psychologist on San Francisco's KSFO. He sees the Sixties as akin to the fleeting callers to the advice show. "A long time ago, we knew each other for a short period." Nick, in the closing, decides to finish where Alex left off with Chloe (Meg Tilly), the deceased's live-in lover. Perhaps she can reverse his impotency—cause unknown.

Chloe is not a *Big Chiller*. A "space cadet," she is "completely unconcerned by the spectre of time passing that haunts the rest.[138] Chloe eloquently represents the younger generation. She cautions Nick, "I don't like talking about my past as much as you guys do."

Comparing success stories, Harold mentions his twenty-seven chain stores. Sam quips, "Who'd ever thought we'd make so much bread . . . two revolutionaries." While a good deal is made of the career successes the players have achieved, few specific references are introduced dealing with their roles in The Movement. A *Nation* writer complained, "A little political frankness would have helped *The Big Chill* a lot." Another critic agreed that the script "goes to extraordinary lengths to avoid recalling just what the program of the Movement was. So there is no yardstick to measure just how far these characters have departed from their original goals." The script, said Denby, didn't "risk alienating any of the audience by spelling out what they did." There are a few clues: Sam's "big rally speech" in Ann Arbor, Michael's "all-nighter" at a Washington March, and the admission of being "revolutionary" all suggest some issue-oriented commitment. The name of Harold's footwear line is a play on Marxist-New Left jargon, "Running Dog." Sarris said, "Indeed, most of these one-time idealists have spent their after-school years jogging alongside the 'running dog' of American capitalism."[139] The six "sell outs," in

Sixties terminology, are likeable, decent people. The song "You Can't Always Get What You Want" rings true.

There's A Bad Moon Rising: The Critics

Critics loved *The Big Chill* or hated it. Andrew Sarris, who was excluded from the prerelease press screening, assessed his colleagues' reviews, saying, "Curiously, the pans of *The Big Chill* are running neck-and-neck with raves."[140]

The mix was inordinately tilted by the number of political observers entering the fray. Vincent Canby found the motion picture to represent "the best of mainstream American film making. A reminder that Hollywood is loaded with talent."[141] *Film Journal* called it "an entertaining and intelligent film." "The weekend is fun for us despite the chill," said Judith Crist.[142] However, "The film will therefore seem rather mild and light-weighted," cautioned *Variety*, "to those who aren't enjoying seeing so many aspects of themselves up on the screen."[143]

Newsweeks' David Ansen said, "*The Big Chill* is masterly, entertaining, in many ways irresistible. But, perhaps, it's time someone asked new and tougher questions about what happened to us."[144]

"*The Big Chill* may be nostalgic for the late Sixties," wrote Denby in a charitable moment, "but it's been shrewdly designed for the Reagan eighties."[145]

Not surprisingly, *Commentary* noted, "The 'soft' Left, however, is alive and well, and *The Big Chill*, almost a walking embodiment of the Soft Left in its present phase, is one of the biggest hits of the fall season."[146]

Silver said, "The movie affirms a sneaking suspicion I have always harbored that the Sixties generation was better at proclaiming than at achieving such values as sensitivity, mutual caring, and emotional closeness"[147] the neoconservatives rallied at the self delusions of the "soft Left." The relatively candid *Nation* printed, "Underneath the we-all-loved-each-other-so-much nostalgia is a phony cynicism."[148]

Reviewers may have differed regarding the social significance of *Big Chill*, but the nostalgic soundtrack was applauded almost unanimously.

In 1983 film critics, when they could, tended to downplay soundtracks. (*Staying Alive* and *Eddie* did garner attention.) The positive comments directed at *The Big Chill's* background music stressed its uplifting underscoring of the action. That Ann Arbor existed in the shadow of Motown established the credibility of the songs. (Outside of Procol Harem's "Whiter Shade of Pale," Credence Clearwater Revival's "Bad Moon

Rising,'' and The Band's ''The Weight,'' few ''underground'' staples are included.)

Chill's forte was conversation. Here, music can be intrusive or disjointed. ''You Can't Always Get What You Want'' worked as the mourners left the church and motored to the cemetery. ''I Heard It Through The Grapevine,'' preceeding the Stones rendition, was less suitable. The Marvin Gaye song was utilized to highlight the summoning of friends to the funeral of their soul mate. Peter Occhiogrosso failed to see the relevance of ''Grapevine.'' ''It's simply in poor taste,'' he wrote.

Procol Harem's popular seller, like Martha Reeves' ''Body Heat,'' was repeatedly used to overlay scenes. ''A movie with 'A Whiter Shade of Pale' on the soundtrack,'' noted Joe Klein, ''has two strikes against it.''

Naturally, economics are an important, if not overriding, factor in the choice of material used in a film. Labels are inclined to use their own artists or vault tapes, enhancing their catalogue exposure and profits. Davidson and Kasdan, however, choose sounds that they personally enjoyed. Davidson's vision, however flawed, was more appropriate to the film than that of Kasdan. ''The role of rock as an energizing force for the sixties generation is here trivialized,'' said Silver.[149]

Some critics and more than a million record buyers thought otherwise. At least two reviewers applauded the soundtrack. Denby said, ''Kasdan doesn't stint on the sixties music, which still gives off a powerful charge and certainly won't send anyone home hungry.''[150] *Variety* suggested that the soundtrack, with its familiar late-1960s pop tunes, would ''bring pleasant smiles of recognition to the faces of the intended audience.''[151]

Jim Thompson of the North Carolina-based Record Bar chain reported, ''A lot of people were apparently affected by the film . . . Demand was outstripping supply and we were out of stock for at least two weeks.'' Motown Records, preoccupied with Lionel Ritchie's *Can't Slow Down*, was surprised at the demand, he claimed, adding, ''They didn't expect 'The Big Chill' to do anything.''

Eight weeks following the film's box office release it had grossed $16.8 million; the soundtrack had sold 750,000 copies. ''Everywhere that the picture is a hit,'' said Motown president Jay Lasker, the souvenir album had sold.[152] This was with little or no radioplay and minimal video exposure.

Billboard's year-end cumulative chart found three rock-oriented soundtracks in the Top 10. To nobody's surprise *Flashdance* easily topped the list, followed by *Staying Alive*. *Officer and A Gentleman* (1982) scored Number 4.

The box office grosses for these films was equally impressive. *Flash-*

dance ranked sixth, followed by *Staying Alive*, on *Variety's* "Big Rental Films of 1983." Both grossed more than $30 million.

Fueled by the audio-visual successes of even critically panned films, the media began looking more closely at crosspromotion, or "synergy." Awareness of the process was one thing; implementing the concept, however, was another. Yet 1984 would be the film industry's banner year, and record companies also would hit a new peak of profitability.

Notes

1. Tom Shales, "The ReDecade," *Esquire*, March, 1986, 67.
2. See Karen A. Peterson, "Stallone As 'Rambo' Gets Blood Boiling," *USA Today*, 7 June 1985, 2A; Susan Jeffords, "The New Vietnam Films: Is the Movie Over?" *Journal of Popular Film & Television* 13, Winter 1986, 186–94.
3. John Leonard, "Evil Under The Sun," *New York*, 8 October 1984, 80.
4. "Music Video," *Nightline*, 14 September 1984.
5. Toby Goldstein, "Doing the Perpetual Bop at a Flick of the (Cable) Dial," *Creem*, April 1982, 38.
6. Quoted in M.L. Stein, "The MTV Generation," *Editor and Publisher*, 10 May 1986, 16.
7. Jim McCullaugh, "First National Cable Vidshow," *Billboard*, 3 March 1980, 1, 38. Also see Pat Anfderheide, "Music Videos: The Look of the Sound," *Journal of Communication* 36;1 Winter 1986, 71–73.
8. Quotes in "Amexco Buys Half of Warner Cable: Expansion Planned," *Broadcasting*, 17 September 1979, 30.
9. Quoted in Leonard Sloane, "A Network Man Moves to Cable," *New York Times*, 13 November 1979, D2; and "Cable-TV Joint Venture Will Launch Company to Distribute Programs," *Wall Street Journal*, 9 November 1979, 35.
10. R. Serge Denisoff, *Inside MTV* (New Brunswick: Transaction Books 1988), 27, 29.
11. "Billboard's First International Video Music Conference," *Billboard*, 15 December 1979, 47–48.
12. Quoted in David Fricke, "The Shape of Things to Come?" *Melody Maker*, 27 March 1982, 31.
13. Quoted in Robert Hilburn, "MTV: The Birth of A Rock Sensation," *Los Angeles Times*, 21 August 1983, 81. Also, Bernice Kanner, "Can't Stop the Music Channel," *New York*, 11 October 1982, 20.
14. Bergman would later explain that MTV's credibility problem was caused by its novelty and the lack of exposure it received in the two main media markets, New York City and Los Angeles County. See Arnold Mitchell, *The Nine American Lifestyles* (New York: Warner's Books 1983).
15. Jack Loftus, "Warner/Amex Preps All-Music Cable Channel," *Variety*, 4 March 1981, 1, 108.
16. Jim McCullough, "Cable Channel Seen Helping Record Sales," *Billboard*, 14 March 1981, 80.

17. Clarke Taylor, " 'TV Generation' Key to Cable Success," *Los Angeles Times*, 18 April 1981, 2–8.
18. Quoted in Bernice Kanner, "Can't Stop the Music Channel," *New York*, 11 October 1982, 20.
19. Robert Hilburn, "TV Goes FM: Rock Around the Clock," *Los Angeles Times Calendar* (SEC), 17 May 1981, 6.
20. Richard Gold, "Wamex Music Channel Acquires Library of 400 Promo Videos; Requires Stereo Transmission," *Variety*, 27 May 1981, 89,91.
21. Sam Sutherland, "Extensive Research Behind New Stereo Music Channel," *Billboard*, 13 June 1981, 6, 15; "Music Programming Lags Within Cable TV Industry," *Billboard*, 13 June 1981, 5, 76.
22. Quoted in Howard Polskin, "MTV at Five: There's a Flip Side to Its Success," *TV Guide*, 23 August 1986, 38.
23. Michael Shore, *The Rolling Stone Book of Rock Video* (New York: Quill Books 1984), 262.
24. Robert Hilburn, "Music TV: Hope Rocks Fort Lee," *Los Angeles Times*, 4 August 1981, sec IV, 3.
25. Quoted in John E. Cooney, "Cable TV Will Bet All Music Channel Running 24 Hours," *Wall Street Journal*, 4 March 1981, 56.
26. In order of appearance the reviews discussed are: Susan Spillman, "MTV Kicks Off; All Ears Watching," *Ad Age*, 10 August 1981, 11–12; Laura Foti, "MTV Cable Channel Exposing New Acts," *Billboard*, 15 August 1981, 3, 58; Robert Titsch, "Music For the Eyes," *Cablevision*, 17 August 1981, 6; Robert D. Matteo, "Cablevision Reviews," *Cablevision,* 24 August 1981, 34; James P. Forkan, "Things Upbeat at Music TV," *Ad Age*, 14 September 1981, 71; Jim McCullaugh, "MTV Cable Spurs Disk Sales of Artists Aired," *Billboard*, 10 October 1981, 1, 68.
27. March Kirkeby, "MTV, 'Night Flight' Leads Cable-TV Rock Invasion," *Rolling Stone*, 10 December 1981, 64, 66.
28. Andrew C. Brown, "Music to Particular Fans," *Fortune*, 28 December 1981, 66.
29. Quotes in "Survey Finds MTV Strongly Affecting Record Sales," *Billboard*, 11 September 1982, 3, 60.
30. Quoted in Laura Foti, "Labels Hike Video Clip Production," *Billboard*, 24 July 1982, 29.
31. Christian Williams, "MTV Is Rock Around the Clock," *Philadelphia Enquirer*, 3 November 1982, D1.
32. Quoted in Ed Levine, "TV Rocks With Music," *New York Times Magazine*, 8 May 1983, 44.
33. Sam Sutherland "Labels Studios Get Closer On Soundtrack's" *Billboard* 30 June 1984: 62. Sutherland, 3.
34. Quoted in Williams, "MTV Is Rock Around The Clock," D1.
35. Quoted in Richard Gold, "Hollywood Majors Spinoff Videos From Youth Pix," *Variety*, 22 February 1984, 1.
36. Quoted in Jay Cocks, "Sing a Song of Seeing," 63. Richard M. Levine accurately describes *Flashdance* as a "nonmovie." He explained, "A nonmovie is really a multimedia collage in which a variety of trendy pop phenomena—graphic looks, fashion styles, dance steps, musical sounds, even personality "stances"—that are about to go public in a big way are strung together

on a pretext of a storyline . . . A nonmovie is a kind of journalism, an up-to-the-minute report on the audiovisual environment." See Richard M. Levine, "Life After *Flashdance*," *Esquire*, January 1984, vol. 101, no. 1, 85–6.

37. Michael Sragow, " 'Flashdance:' Last Go-Go in Pittsburgh," *Rolling Stone*, 26 May 1983, 64.
38. Richard Corliss, "Manufacturing a Multimedia Hit," *Time*, 9 May 1983, 80.
39. Corliss, 80.
40. Quoted in Debby Miller, "Rock is Money to Hollywood Ears," *Rolling Stone*, 27 October 1983, 102.
41. "Flashdance," *Variety*, 20 April 1983, 12.
42. Sragow, 64; Cocks, 63.
43. Quotes from Fred Gardner, "MTV: Everybody Wants It," *Marketing and Media Decisions*, August 1987, 67; Richard Corliss, "Manufacturing a Multimedia Hit," *Time*, 9 May 1983, 80; Richard Gold, " 'Flashdance' Film, LP Feeding Off Other," *Variety*, 11 May 1983, 3, 46; "Growth Pains Greet Studio Video Boom," *Billboard*, 28 January 1984, 70.
44. Quoted in Donald Lyons, "Music Videos Give New Eyes to Hollywood," *Rock Video*, September 1984, 62.
45. Quoted in Richard Gold, "H'wood Majors Spinoff Videos From Youth Pix," *Variety*, 22 February 1984, 108.
46. Cocks, 63.
47. Quoted in Gregg Kilday, "Nineth Annual Grosses Gloss," *Film Comment*, 20, 2, March–April 1984, 63.
48. Quoted in Victor Livingston, "Whole Lot of Shakin'," *Cablevision*, 30 April 1984, 32.
49. Richard Gold, "H'wood Majors Spinoff", 108.
50. Miller, 102.
51. Quotes in Rob Tannenbaum, "Soundtracks Thrives in Summer of '85," *Rolling Stone*, 21 November 1985, 15.
52. "Music Videos: Art of Fluff?" *Nightline*, ABC-TV, 14 September 1984; Kenneth Turan, "The Art of Revolution: Video Is Taking Over Popular Culture," *Rolling Stone Year Book*, 1984, 134.
53. Richard Corliss, "42nd Street Meets Flashdance," *Time*, 18 July 1983, 63.
54. Miller, 103.
55. "Top Album Picks," *Billboard*, 2 July, 1983.
56. Miller, 103.
57. David Denby, "Invasion of the Movie Snatchers," *New York*, 1 August 1983, 55.
58. Miller, 105; Ray Loynd, "Wexler Roasts Stallone, Travolta For Distorting His 'Alive' Script," *Variety*, 27 July 1983, 3.
59. Vincent Canby, " 'Staying Alive' Succumbs to a Host of Missteps," *New York Times*, 24 July 1983, 15.
60. Denby, 54.
61. Corliss, 63.
62. Denby, 55.
63. David Ansen, "Monday Morning Blahs," *Newsweek*, 25 July 1983, 75.
64. Corliss, 63; Denby, 54–5.
65. "Staying Alive," *Variety*, 13 July 1983, 15.
66. Ibid.; and Denby, 55.

67. Miller, 105.
68. Quoted in Richard Gold, " 'Staying Alive' Soundtrack Album . . . ," *Variety*, 10 August 1983, 36.
69. Quoted in Debby Miller, "Rock is Money to Hollywood Ears," *Rolling Stone*, 27 October 1983, 104.
70. Quoted in Peter Occhiogrosso, "The Beat Goes On . . . ," *American Film*, April 1984, 48.
71. Robert Asahina, "Hyping Mediocrity," *The New Leader*, 19 September 1983, 19.
72. Quotes from Miller, 84; Christopher Connelly, *Rolling Stone*, 19 June 1986, 38; Pauline Kael, "Sex and Politics," *New Yorker*, 5 September 1983, 109; Occhiogrosso, 47.
73. John Simon, "Simple but not good," *National Review*, 14 October 1983, 1296.
74. Todd McCarthy, *Variety*, 27 July 1983, 21.
75. Robert Asahina, "Hyping Mediocrity," *The New Leader*, 19 September 1983, 19.
76. David Denby, "Supply-side Hero," *New York*, 22 August 1983, 62.
77. Harry M. Geduld, "Prodigal Business," *The Humanist*, Nov/Dec 1983, 41.
78. Andrew Sarris, "A requiem for Fassbinder," *Village Voice*, 16 August 1983, 49.
79. Frederic Tuten, "Introduction to Easy Rider," in *Easy Rider* (New York: Signet Books 1969), 37.
80. Asahina, 20.
81. *Variety*, 21.
82. Denby, 62.
83. Geduld, 20.
84. David Ansen, "Love For Sale," *Newsweek*, 15 August 1983, 64; Stanley Kauffmann, "Flash and Fraud," *New Republic*, 19 and 26 September 1983, 22.
85. Sarris, 49.
86. Kael, "Sex and Politics," 109; Janet Maslin, "Film: Paul Brickman's 'Risky Business,' " *New York Times*, 5 August 1983, C13.
87. *Billboard*, 26 October 1983, 1.
88. Quoted in Becky Sue Epstein, "Music Video—The Hot New Way To Sell New Movies," *Boxoffice*, July 1984, 16.
89. "Growth Pains Greet Studio Vidclip Boom," *Billboard*, 28 January 1984, 70.
90. Quoted in "Pay Cable Films Boost Track Albums," *Billboard*, 1 September 1984, 58.
91. Quoted in Epstein, 16.
92. Quoted in Jim Robbins, "Aurora Preps 'Eddie and Cruisers' For N.Y. and Jersey Production," *Variety*, 17 February 1982, 36, 41.
93. Quoted in Judith McGuinn, "Eddie and The Cruisers: A Direct Hit On the Youth Market," *American Premiere*, March 1983, 12, 14.
94. Maitland McDonagh, " 'Eddie and the Cruisers' Tracks Rock Era," *Film Journal*, 19 August 1983, 74.
95. Lawrence Cohn, "Eddie and The Cruisers," *Variety*, 7 September 1983, 16.
96. Quoted in Judith McGuinn, "Eddie and the Cruisers: A Direct Hit on the Youth Market," *American Premiere*, March 1983, 12.

97. Quoted in Steve Pond, " 'Eddie and The Cruisers:' Hollywood rips off Bruce," *Rolling Stone*, 29 September 1983, 62.
98. Maitland McDonagh, "Eddie and The Cruisers," *The Film Journal*, 23 September 1983, 22.
99. Quoted in Maitland McDonagh, " 'Eddie and The Cruisers' Tracks Rock Era," *Film Journal*, 19 August 1983, 8.
100. Janet Maslin, "Eddie and The Cruisers," *New York Times*, 23 September 1983, C8.
101. Peter Occhiogross, "Eddie and The Abusers," *Village Voice*, 4 October 1983, 94.
102. Cohn, "Eddie and The Cruisers," *Variety*, 7 September 1983, 16.
103. "Tracks Rock Era," 74.
104. Maslin, C8.
105. McDonagh, 22.
106. Quoted in Pond, 63; "Tunnel of Love," MTV, 30 April 1988.
107. Dave Marsh, "Southside Johnny: The Asbury Jukes," *The New Rolling Stone Record Guide* (New York: Random House 1983), 476.
108. See Andrew M. Greeley, "The Catholic Imagination of Bruce Springsteen," *America*, 2 February 1988, 110–15.
109. Quoted in Pond, 62.
110. Quoted in Geoffrey Himes, "The Rise of the Rhode Island Rockers," *Washington Post*, 21 October 1984; also Pond, 58.
111. Pond, 59.
112. Pond, 59.
113. Quoted in Kip Kirby, "Label Executives Are Cautious," *Billboard*, 15 January 1983, 35, 38.
114. Quoted in "Releasing The Tiger in Scotti Brothers Records," *Billboard*, 21 January 1984, SB24.
115. Quoted in Pond, 62.
116. Quoted in "Releasing The Tiger," SB6, 24.
117. David Ansen, "You Can't Go Home Again," *Newsweek*, 26 September 1983, 90.
118. Occhiogross, 94.
119. For the release pattern, see Alexander Auerbach, "Stretching Bucks To Make 'Eddie,' " *Boxoffice*, October 1983, 12.
120. Quoted in Christopher Connelly, "Cable TV gives 'Eddie and The Cruisers' new life," *Rolling Stone*, 11 October 1984, 38.
121. Quotes from Fred Goodman and Sam Sutherland, "Pay Cable Films Boost Track Albums," *Billboard*, 11 October 1984, 1, 58.
122. Connelly, 38.
123. Quoted in Geoffrey Himes, "The Rise of the Rhode Island Rocker," *Washington Post*, 21 October 1984.
124. Connelly, 38.
125. R. Serge Denisoff, "Cafferty band fuels 'dream factory'," *Sentinel Tribune*, 27 December 1984, 11.
126. Occhiogrosso, 48.
127. Ian Dove, "Soundtracks Score with Rock 'n' Roll," *ASCAP In Action*, Spring, 1986, 35.

128. Quoted in Rob Tannenbaum, "Soundtracks Thrived in Summer of '85," *Rolling Stone*, 21 November 1985, 15.
129. Quoted in Cathleen McGuigan, "Rock Music Goes Hollywood," *Newsweek*, 11 March 1985, 78; Gary Burns, "Film and Popular Music" in Gary Edgerton, ed., *Film and the Arts in Symbiosis*, (Westport, Conn.: Greenwood Press 1988).
130. Neil Hickey, "The Verdict on VCRs (So Far)," *TV Guide*, 19 March 1988, 14.
131. Quoted in David Lyons, "Music Video Give New Eyes to Hollywood," *Rock Video*, September 1984, 64.
132. Quoted in Wendy Weinstein, " 'The Big Chill' 60s Generation Comes of Age," *Film Journal*, 23 September 1983, 6.
133. Quotes from Richard Gold, "Motown's 'Big Chill' Was Nearly Big Nothing . . . ," *Variety*, 30 November 1983, 2, 99.
134. Wendy Weinstein, "The Big Chill," *Film Journal*, 23 September 1983, 21.
135. T. McCarthy, "The Big Chill," *Variety*, 7 September 1983, 16.
136. Weinstein, "60s Generation," 6.
137. Isidore Silver, "Big Chill, Big Deal," *Society*, March/April 1984, 91.
138. David Ansen, "You Can't Go Home Again," *Newsweek*, 26 September 1983, 90.
139. Andrew Sarris, "Art, Politics, and Oh Yes, Talent," *Village Voice*, 11 October 1983, 48.
140. Sarris, 47.
141. Vincent Canby, "The Big Chill," *New York Times*, 23 September 1983, C14, 21.
142. Judith Crist, "Heat and Chill," *Saturday Review,* September/October 1983, 37.
143. McCarthy, 16.
144. Ansen, 90.
145. David Denby, "A Small Circle of Friends," *New York*, 26 September 1983, 92.
146. Richard Grenier, "The Hard Left and The Soft," *Commentary*, January 1984, 59.
147. Silver, 90.
148. Katha Pollitt, "The Big Chill," *The Nation*, 22 October 1983, 380.
149. Occhiogrosso, 47; Joe Klein, "You Can't Get There From Here," *American Film*, October 1983, 43; Silver, 91.
150. Denby, 92.
151. McCarthy, 16.
152. Quoted in Gold "Motown's," 99.

8

Synergizing 1984?

In a Hollywood Studio Far, Far Away
It's Filmmakers vs. Music Supervisors
In Soundtrack Wars. . . .
—Kate Bales, *Billboard*

In 1984, the closest the nation had come to Big Brother was the re-election of the "Great Communicator," Ronald Reagan. In the music business, "Turntables spun, gold chains jingled, cash registers beeped," summarized Jon Pareles, who could have added the industry's "Disco Disaster" was over.[1] Artists such as Prince, Huey Lewis, Van Halen, Bruce Springsteen, Cyndi Lauper, the Jackson family, Tina Turner, and John Cougar Mellencamp had all contributed significantly to the record industry's then-banner $4.5 billion gross. Ten movie soundtracks sold over a million copies each. Orwell had dreaded the year; industry moguls welcomed it.

The music television channel made money for the first time. By the year's end, MTV had penetrated 25.4 million households, a 38 percent rise from 1983. The cultural significance of the channel was immeasurable, as it influenced fashion, music, advertising, and movies. MTV's income, still primarily derived from Madison Avenue, jumped an impressive 175 percent to $72.9 million, in contrast to $26.5 million the previous year. Robert Pittman was able to brag, without fear of contradiction, "we're the hub of it all."

The ten soundtracks platinum certifications doubled the number compiled in the golden year of 1978, when *Saturday Night Fever, Grease, FM, Thank God It's Friday,* and *Sgt. Pepper's Lonely Hearts Club Band* were million-or-more sellers. RIAA's market research committee explained the upsurge as a reflection of the country's stronger economy, heavy sales by superstars, and multiple hits from individual albums. Many of these multiple hits had originated on film scores: *Footloose* alone had generated six Top 40 titles; seven film singles were Number 1 on the *Billboard* chart. Prince's artist management company partner said, "The music business and the film business are closer than at any time in history and are about to crash into each other."[2]

Danny Goldberg was popularizing the term "synergy" in the trades, but it was not a clear-cut term that set out specific steps needed for profitable marketing campaigns. In fact, some of the platinum earners had deviated considerably from conventional wisdom and individual "synergized" campaigns expanded upon the formula. *Eddie and The Cruisers* and *Hard to Hold* could credit HBO, the Movie Channel, and MTV for their successful album sales. *Against All Odds* did much better than its reviews indicated it should have, due to the title-track song tacked onto the closing credits of the film. Only *Purple Rain* and *Footloose* followed the classic Stigwood, prerelease marketing strategy carefully, and these two titles dominated the *Billboard* and *Cashbox* album charts for nearly six months.

By 1984 the rock soundtrack was established as an intrinsic aspect of film *and* record marketing. Rock was no longer a mere novelty or tied to nostalgic flashbacks to the Fifties and Sixties. Danny and The Juniors had been right, "Rock 'n' Roll was Here to Stay," although with the Hollywood caveat, "Handle With Care," promising both profits and pitfalls.

"Let's Hear It For The Boy": Footloose

Paramount, with the Stigwood dance productions and the prototypical *Flashdance*, was becoming the MGM of the Eighties. Their marketing approach, pioneered by Robert Stigwood, had created multimedia successes admired by corporate readers of the trade press.

Because *Staying Alive*, despite being devastated by critics, had enjoyed a respectable bottom line, Paramount Pictures (in association with CBS Records) tested its formula again, with modifications, in promoting *Footloose*. Al Teller, then senior vice-president and general manager of CBS, altered the Stigwood cycle. "If we had followed the conventional staggered release pattern, we could put out singles for a year,"[3] he said. Instead, the issuance pattern was correlated with the film's initial sixteen-week run. The film's success, it was anticipated, would carry the musical product.

Released in early February 1984, *Footloose* epitomized the "Re Decade." The project was yet another "old-fashioned film made for young people." It employed every cliche from Grade-B rock pictures of the

Fifties. For example, in a game of "chicken" *a la Rebel Without a Cause*, two farm tractors raced toward each other while Bonnie Tyler's "Holding Out for a Hero" plays in the background. Kevin Bacon's shoelace became tangled around a pedal, and he couldn't leap off the tractor. His opponent, forced to jump, ends up crawling out of a stream of water.

The remarkable success of *Footloose* was a triumph of synergism in marketing, or, in Al Teller's more colorful terminology, "a critical mass of airplay."[4] The formula worked to perfection despite a shaky start for the project.

Dean Pitchford, fortunately, had his first *Footloose* screenplay ready just as he was nominated for an Academy Award for his work in *Fame*. "I knew that if anything was to come of it, it would have to be when people were willing to see me," he recalled. "People are never more willing to see you than when you're up for an Oscar."[5] Producers Craig Zadan and David Melnick picked up the musical, Melnick made a deal with Paramount Pictures, and Herbert Ross was hired as director.

Ross used music to create mood behind the scenes as well as in the soundtrack. Bob Seger's "Old Time Rock 'n' Roll" was used on the set, although Sammy Hager's "The Girl Gets Around" was heard by consumers. Ross, having immersed himself in MTV as the filming went on, desired a realistic set. "One of Herbert Ross's most difficult tasks has been to take trained dancers and make them look as if they aren't trained," said Melnick. Ross added, "The movement is dictated by the area."[6] The attempt failed, nearly all of the reviewers agreed. "The kids in Beaumont have been denied dancing for five years, yet they are as slick as the regulars on *Soul Train*," said one.[7]

Upon completion of the $8-million film, Pitchford collaborated with a number of songwriters. The score was, he said, "a rock video in reverse. The idea was to mold the music to fit the visual images. . . . There's a difference between doing a conventional score, a song compilation, and something as thought-out as this. I wanted the songs to be a subtext for the film," he continued. "I didn't want tracks that had been left off of old albums, and I didn't want 'trunk songs' that had been lying around."[8]

Coproducer Zadan agreed, but in more pragmatic terms. "We want to write songs specifically for the needs of the moment, as close as possible to the release of the album," he said. "The soundtrack business changed a lot of things. The success of *Saturday Night Fever*, *Fame*, and *Flashdance* forced a rethinking and made us realize the need to plan a marketing campaign around the music very early."[9] CBS's Al Teller partially viewed this approach as exhibiting a greater "sophistication" on the part of Hollywood producers.

Pitchford and music supervisor Becky Shargo found themselves with myriad songwriting arrangements and limitations. The music budget was pegged at $30,000 per song, plus royalties. This excluded artists such as John Cougar Mellencamp and Pat Benatar, who reportedly were asking $100,000 for a song. They were equally hampered by their desire to use Kenny Loggins on their soundtrack, as CBS allowed its artists only one cut for an outside label. "Walter Yetnikoff (label president) is very guarded about using his artists for other soundtracks," noted Shargo. Loggins was the focus of the deal. "It felt to me he was like the voice of the country, America," said Pitchford. "It felt raucous and joyous and there was a hopefulness in what he was doing."

Paramount, over budget on the score, requested and got an advance of $250,000 from Columbia Records that included the proviso that Paramount "deliver two outside artists of gold level." Moving Pictures, Shalamar, and Sammy Hagar became the external performers; the remainder were on the CBS label, which badly wanted to penetrate the rock-soundtrack arena. With *Footloose*, the opportunity was there, but as Shargo indicated, "they were hesitant about putting up too much money *on the basis of the script.*" From forty-seven possibilities, nine cuts were finally selected.

Teller rejected the scout-staggered format. "We wanted the singles to be out while the movie was out," he said. Film executives were thinking more in terms of serial release than of Teller's clustering, however. "We are releasing the 'Footloose' record in January," Zadan told *Esquire*. "The film doesn't come out until February. By that time we would have at least one Top 10 hit." Teller had also wanted "to create pre-release enthusiasm" for the soundtrack and film."[10] The predictions fell some twelve rankings short the week of the film's nationwide debut. Bonnie Tyler's "Holding Out For a Hero" entered the marketplace at Number 84 the week of 25 February 1984. The album appeared on the *Billboard* and *Cashbox* charts a week earlier.

The all-important *Footloose* video appeared on MTV as the Loggins single surfaced in record stores and on radio playlists. The videoclip was in "heavy rotation" (four plays per day) the week of the film's general distribution. Teller was pleased as, "with the cost of advertising being what it is, the chance to put segments of films on the air (via music video) is an important break."[11] Film trailers, or ads, were frequently intermixed into the video, with occasional cutaways to the vocalist. Providing this interface was a problem, as MTV insisted that 50 percent of the footage focus on the singer.

Shalamar's "Dancing in the Sheets" reached the Black Singles listing the final week of February at Number 70. (It would later crossover on the basis of the film's popularity.)

Footloose's box office performance was astounding. Opening in 1,340 theaters, the musical was the top-grossing film during its initial three weeks of exposure. Production costs were recouped in one weekend. The popularity of the movie aided sales of the accompanying record releases, encouraging CBS to cluster rather than issue the singles in a staggered manner.

An informal survey of Top-40 program directors by *Variety* found that the motion picture was pushing the titles. Todd Chase (WHTX-FM Pittsburgh) indicated that the film was the key factor in "add-ons" on his playlist. In New York, WPLJ-FM's Larry Berger said that the cluster-release influenced his rotation of soundtrack cuts, saying, "radio forced them (the label) into releasing the Williams tune although CBS was pushing Tyler and Shalamar." "Let's Hear It For The Boy," as opposed to "Dancing" or the Tyler offering, was showcased in the film.

In June, six *Footloose* singles enjoyed chart status, two as Number 1. *Footloose*, the album, displaced Michael Jackson's *Thriller* and remained Number 1 for two-and-a-half months. The soundtrack would eventually sell over 9 million copies. The film grossed $80 million, ten times its cost, although, as with *Flashdance*, critics roundly panned its shallow, contradictory story.

An apt description of the film was provided by Marianne Meyer, who wrote, "*Footloose* was, quite simply, a hit record with pictures. The starts were cute, the story's mild-mannered rebellion appealed to teens, and the dance-and-romp sequences were modeled after the fare on MTV."

"The soundtrack to *Footloose* is so calculated to follow in the goldplated footsteps of *Flashdance* that it can't fail," wrote *Rolling Stone's* Don Shewey. Ironically, Pitchford had criticized films such as *FM* and *Thank God It's Friday* as "shameless excuses to string together songs for the sake of soundtrack albums."[12]

Footloose opened with a contrived trailer for Kenny Loggins's title song. As Corliss described the moment: "Here are a couple of dozen happy feet moving irresistibly to a pounding Kenny Loggins raver that finds its inspiration in every let's-rock anthem from 'Rebel Rouser' to 'Devil with the Blue Dress On.' 'You can fly if you'll only cut loose,/Footloose,/Kick off your Sunday shoes.' Any viewer with a pulse rate above 25 will be bound to do the same."[13]

The action begins with a yellow Volkswagen bug entering the community of Beaumont, or, in David Ansen's terminology, "Moral Majorityland, 1984."[14]

A voiceover segues to a frantic minister, Reverend Shaw Moore (John Lithgow), booming, in cadence, a tirade against modernity: "If our Lord wasn't testing us, how do you account, these days, of this obscene rock 'n' roll music . . . with its gospel of easy sexuality and relaxed morality. If our Lord wasn't testing us, why He could take all these pornographic books and albums and turn them into one big fiery cinder."

Into this environment comes Ren McCormack (Kevin Bacon), a teenage Chicagoan. While not the leader of the pack, he does preordain a conflict between teens who want to dance and their elders who forbid it.

The prototypical fire-and-brimstone preacher conveniently has a confused daughter, Ariel (Lori Singer), who is more rebellious than Ren (who merely wants the right to dance). Ariel's costumes alone cause dissension, as does her dancing at the drive-in. The good reverend just happens to arrive as daughter Ariel is displaying *Solid Gold* dance moves.

The rock-menace motif is reinforced as Ariel apologizes to her prudish parent, who is listening to classical music. She asks him, "What's that music?" He answers, "Oh, it's Haydn chamber music." Ariel asks, "And . . . that kinda' music's okay?" "It's uplifting. It doesn't confuse people's minds and bodies," asserts Moore. To further underscore the musical bigotry, Ren is stopped by the local police for violating the noise ordinance by playing rock 'n' roll by Quiet Riot.

Interspersed with dance sequences, the story unfolds. Five years ealier, the minister's son was killed in a car accident while on the way home from a dance club that featured rock music. By association, the whole town identified rock and dancing with uncontrollable youth and tragedy. This explains the dance ban. As Ariel says, "Father went off the deep end."

The subplots continue, "with motifs on book burning, mid-life crises, AWOL parents, fast car crashes, drug enforcement, and Bible Belt vigilantism," explained Corliss.[15]

The turning point occurs at a City Council meeting when Ren confronts Rev. Moore and the city fathers. He requests a high school *dance*. Dismissing the petition as illegal, the Lithgrow character cautions that dancing is fraught with peril, adding, "The thing that distresses me even more is the spiritual corruption."

With Ariel's assistance in using Biblical references, Ren quotes the *Psalms* and *Ecclesiastes*. "Praise thy Lord," he recites, "sing unto the Lord a new song. Let them praise His name in the dance."

"It was King David," he says, as the crowd chants "Amen," ". . . David *danced* before the Lord with all His might . . . leaping and *dancing*."

A closing spectacular choreographical sequence, the dance, follows after the teens receive the benign acquiescence of Reverend Moore. Nothing has actually been resolved. A jurisdictional loophole made the dance possible, and community attitudes remain in place. The dance is pyrrhic.

A *Rolling Stone* contributor characterized *Footloose's* plot as "screw-loose."

"Totally unbelievable," added *Rock 'n' Roll Confidential*, "and the music sucks."[16]

Film in Review, albeit using more diplomatic terminology, concurred, saying, "Contrary to one of the promotional blurbs, the music is *not*, unfortunately, on Ren McCormick's side. The choice of soundtrack, co-written by Pitchford, is inappropriate and lame at points. In the film, Ren discussed his favorite bands with Willard, mentioning The Police and Men at Work—two popular New Wave bands. Yet, we never hear songs from these bands or anything that could even remotely pass as New Wave."[17] The reviewers were correct. Ren's musical tastes and dress were certainly not New Waveish.

Footloose, the album, moved five million copies domestically. Foreign sales totalled four million.

For many film critics, the music was the film's only redeeming feature. Describing *Footloose* as toe-tapping "big-screen reminders of what's hot today in music video," *Variety*, as usual, fashion set the tone.[18] Andrew Sarris of the *Voice* said, "I did tap my foot to some of the music, and that may mean something commercially. My own gut instinct is that there are too many long stretches in which nothing happens."[19] "The music and dialogue collide instead of merging in a pop apotheosis," maintained Corliss. "It might more wisely have obeyed a simple musical imperative: Let's dance!" This sentiment dominated numerous reviews; i.e., Corliss said it was "a jolt of disposable but pleasant energy that makes you want to roll back the rug and boogie." Maslin added, "Have fun and keep on dancing." *Time* ended with, "Let's dance!"[20]

That suggestion was taken quite seriously in studio boardrooms, where executives and filmmakers desired to follow in the footsteps of *Flashdance* and *Footloose*. However, that desire was difficult to translate into marketing strategy, although Taylor Hackford had grasped the basic nuances of a scout-single prerelease to hype *Against All Odds*, and Universal Pictures created a platinum album from a box office disaster, *Hard to Hold*.

Against All Odds

Several weeks after the opening of *Footloose*, a film *noir* (a genre gleaned from 1940s detective-action vehicles) titled *Against All Odds* appeared. Taylor Hackford, having showcased "Up Where We Belong" in *Officer and a Gentleman*, harbored big musical plans for *Odds*. He had in the past combined an interest in rock music with movie projects when he had directed *Idolmaker*, 1980. Pleased with Atlantic's promotion of *Officer*, Hackford signed with the label. They provided an artists' roster. Phil Collins was chosen, Hackford said, because "there was a distinctive quality in his voice. I go after people with signatures in their vocal style, particularly with ballads that sell films."[21] The singer/drummer was on the road with Genesis; in order to accommodate the tour, the sweetening—strings and piano—was done in New York, while producer Arif Mardin cut the vocal and drums in Los Angeles.

"Against All Odds (Take a Look at Me Now)" was created expressly for the movie. As director Hackford said, it was a "textbook case of *designing* a song to reflect what the film is, having the title of the song be the title of the film—and when it went out into the marketplace, I think it decidedly helped the film. People heard it and like the song, they identified it with the film and they came to see the film." (emphasis added)[22]

Danny Goldberg agreed on the impact of the tune on *Odds's* box office. "It made millions after no reviews, and largely because there is a passion in the Phil Collins vocal in the video which implies a passion in the movie, where in fact there is, I think, little real passion."[23] Aesthetics aside, Gary LeMel at Columbia felt that the Collins contribution was worth at least $5 million in additional box office receipts because "a *title* song, like 'Against All Odds,' has much more impact." Specifically, "We saw when the record went top five, about five weeks into the run of the movie, the movie actually increased a little bit—which is really unusual."[24]

The Collins composition had had the signature of the film inserted so that the result read "Against All Odds (Take a Look at Me Now)." This gimmick had assured the studio that the film would be identified each time the scout was aired or cablecast. The title song was *not* the theme—flip the album to Side 2, and the first cut is "The Search (Main Title Theme From Against All Odds)," which also opens the motion picture. The average listener, or viewer of MTV, would naturally assume that the Collins vocal is prominent in the film. It's not. In fact, in the movie, only Kid Creole and The Coconuts provide night-club atmospheric footage, with a segment of "My Male Curiosity" that was designed to be an inexpensive video. (Savvy directors had rapidly learned that "in-picture" performances meet with MTV approval.)

Columbia Pictures paid Hackford $20,000 for a finished Collins video-clip, "Against All Odds," which emerged, accompanied by the single, the last week of February. The single, starting at Number 67, slowly climbed the "Hot 100," reaching its peak for two weeks at Number 1 the week of

21 April. The long, gradual ascent was a definite bonus for the film and the soundtrack; its long chart duration more than compensated for the late release date. (The single had appeared a mere week prior to the film's March 2 debut.)

The Odds Are All Odds: The Film

An aging, high-salaried, professional wide receiver, cut by the Los Angeles Outlaws, finds himself down and out on the Mexican resort island of Cozumel. While picture-postcard scenes of Yucatan beaches flash by, Terry Brogan (Jeff Bridges) searches for a wayward, mixed-up heiress, Terry Wyler (Rachel Ward). Terry is being sought by a mob-connected ex-lover, Jake Wise (James Brooks), and independently by her socialite mother (Jane Greer). Mrs. Wyler is, among other things, the owner of the Los Angeles Outlaws.

Tired from running up to the natives and asking, "Have you seen this woman before?" Terry orders a cold beer. An explanatory flashback ensues.

Due to a knee injury, the athlete had been considered expendable in the minds of the Outlaws' management. A Tom Landryish head coach harrasses Terry, despite the humane interventions of trainer Hank Sully (Alex Karras). Terry is let go because the team wants "more profit, less talent."

An angry Brogan approaches his former agent, Steven Kirsh (Saul Rubinek), for help. The legal flesh-peddler, who has grown rich on football innocents (plus inside-betting information), is now hyping Mrs. Wyler's land speculations under the supervision of wheeler-dealer Ben Caxton (Richard Widmark). Kirsh politely tries to avoid the alienated football player, pleading that he must attend a corporate office party, where there will be important Southern California politicians.

Jake summons Brogan. Their wild lifestyle is established when they engage in a sportscar chase, pitting a Porsche against a Ferrari. The auto maneuvering, according to Canby, was symbolic of "lives lived speeding down the wrong side of the road around blind curves."[25]

Jake offers the unemployed wide receiver a job as a "celebrity bartender," which the "destitute" former Outlaw refuses. Jake makes another proposal: find Jessie Wyler, whom he accuses of stealing $50,000 from him. A $20,000 finders fee—plus expenses out front—is the deal. Still anxious to return to the gridiron, Terry declines, choosing instead to visit Mrs. Wyler. The businesswoman also, however, desires Jessie's return. Terry holds out, saying, 'I'm not going to spy on her for you or Jack Wise."

A cat-and-mouse game ensues. Jessie gets the best of the jock. He is taken with the beautiful, spoiled rich girl. In a subsequent encounter, he stomps off, swearing. Without any apparent reason, she invites him to the "prettiest place on the island." A love affair flourishes. (In the film, the romantic interlude drags on.) Exhibiting her smoldering neuroses, Jessie distances herself from the increasingly committed Terry. "Can't anyone love me without it being a matter of life or death?" she asks. In a carefully crafted scene, they make love in the stone-cold gaze of Mayan idols, only to be interrupted by the Alex Karras character.

Sully's appearance is far-fetched. As Pauline Kael noted, "When Karras casually trots in and just stands there, we're probably meant to think important thoughts, such as, 'There's no place for lovers to escape to in this corrupt world.' But a hoot or a giggle is more to the point." Karras, she added, was completely lost; "He's outclassed by these burnished love wrestlers and the fancy electronic zhooms and vroops on the track."[26] The trainer has been sent by Wise to retrieve Brogan and Wyler. A struggle results. Jessie kills Sully. In a prolonged death scene, Sully says, incorrectly, that he too is a victim of the decayed system.

The killing is the denouement. Terry says, "It's not something we can run away from."

"You just don't understand do you," Jessie snaps before she flees to Beverly Hills. Terry follows her.

At the Century City Plaza the story ends. In the parting moments, Terry is signed by the Miami Dolphins. "Against All Odds (Take a Look at Me Now)" makes its appearance as the closing credits roll.

"The ending is a muddle of sweet and sour, neither upbeat enough for the masses, nor downbeat enough for the mandarins," wrote Sarris. "*Against All Odds*, like *True Confession* and *Chinatown*, is at heart a political film, though Mr. Hackford and his associates probably would prefer it not be labelled as such," noted Canby. "It doesn't preach in any fashion, but its view of life in the once-promised land is dark indeed." *Variety's* Harwood simply concluded that *Odds* "simply ends oddly."[27]

Film reviewers, overall, ignored the score, but Kael liked it. *Film in Review's* Marcia Magill, however, characterized the music as, "intrusive, often downright bizarre."[28]

Critically, *Odds* was in trouble by the day Eric Hughes completed the screenplay. Based on the 1947 film *noir* classic *Out of the Past*, Hackford's project ran directly into a comparison with that film by Andrew Sarris. In the *Village Voice*, Sarris resurrected James Agee's *National* review of *Past*. Predictably, when measured against that standard, *Odds* was found wanting. Sarris said *Odds* found "itself becalmed in the more relaxed decadence of the '80's in California and a very touristy Mexico, came too easily in this milieu to generate the obsessive yearning of money, sex, drugs, 40's noir."[29] *Time's* Richard Schickel and *Newsweek's* David Ansen concurred. Schickel said the film "inexplicably leave[s] out everything that was interesting and memorable in the original." Ansen advised wise viewers, "For the price of two movie tickets to *Odds*, rent a video cassette of *Out of the Past*." All of the reviewers referred to *Past*, although some did like Hackford's film in part. The film "is dazzling entertainment for half of its running time," wrote Magill. "Mr. Hackford's brand of glossy, romantic escapism," noted Maslin, "doesn't have to work as a homage. It has a vitality of its own."[30]

Against All Odds enjoyed a fourteen-week first run, grossing $7.7 million during this period. The soundtrack spent eleven weeks above Number 40 on album chart, for a total stay of eight-and-a-half months. This put Atlantic in the black as albums, rather than singles, are the key to profitability. The film's scout single accomplished its mission, garnering attention for both the film and the album, although Hackford's marketing ploy helped the album more than the motion picture.

Hackford, Kasdan, Simpson-Bruckheimer, Davidson, and other young directors appreciated rock music. They had grown up with it. "I put music in my films because popular music is important in my life," Hackford told the *Washington Post*.[31] By contrast, many of the power people in Hollywood, while attempting to reach the twelve-to-twenty-five-year-olds, were woefully ignorant about the music and its performers. The Academy Awards "Collins incident" of 1985 is illustrative.

In late February, the Academy had announced the nominees for Best Original Song and Score. The list included Prince, Ray Parker, Jr., Kris Kristofferson, Kenny Loggins, Stevie Wonder, and Phil Collins. Wonder, Deneice Williams, and Ray Parker, Jr. were approached to perform on the 25 March network telecast. Collins, who had cleared his European tour dates to appear, was not invited. Atlantic's vice president, Paul Cooper, complained to Larry Gelbart, co-producer of the show. Gelbard replied, "Thank you for your note regarding Phil *Cooper*. I'm afraid the spots have already been filled." Later, a CBS publicist speaking to Oscar producer Gregory Peck, found that the actor "didn't seem to know who Phil Collins was."[32] *Variety* learned that Cher had been approached to perform "Against All Odds" at the ceremony, but had declined due to commitments for her film *Mask*.

Gary LeMel, the studio rocker, expressed "shock" at the Academy's actions. "Why don't they want to use the real thing? I can only imagine they don't understand who Phil Collins is, how big he is. The producers of the show are all older guys . . ." he said.[33] Hackford said he was "dumbfounded. It's a terrible mistake . . . as the original composer and a fabulous performer, I think it's only fitting he do the song." Despite the director's feelings, Ann Reinking lip-synced the song during her dance routine on the telecast. Collins had a three-word response, "It was awful."

Gregory Peck finally commented, "It's just that we decided early on that we would not be using five recording artists . . . it's pure showmanship. We wanted variety."[34] The myopia of established film people would play directly into the hands of the record industry. Hollywood moguls, though sophisticated in film production, obviously were hayseeds when it came to rock. The inevitable happened: a lot of schlock was incorporated into film scores. Taylor Hackford noted, "When you are successful and you get a Number 1 song and people in the Hollywood community see it, they immediately start running around with a big fat checkbook saying 'I want a hit song for my movie . . .' "[35]

The unexpected successes of otherwise shallow dance films piqued media interest in soundtracks. CBS Records Bob Biniaz commented, "Obviously everyone is going to want to have their own *Flashdance* and *Footloose*."

"Movie producers today are trying to get a soundtrack attached to everything," repeated Becky Shargo.[36] As *Against All Odds* climbed the record charts, promoting a weak film, soundtracks became perceived as important.

Film executives were in for a rude awakening when they ordered, "Get me Springsteen!" Record labels were willing to go along with Hollywood, for a *price*. "We're in the business of selling records, not films," was frequently heard at record companies. Synergizing a campaign was no simple feat. A major difficulty at film and record companies was coordinating internal divisions, much less working with an external entity. "These are two different businesses," wrote West Coast general manager and vice president for Polygram Records, Jeffery M. Sydney. "Filmmakers and studios use soundtracks to sell records and develop artists' careers." More specifically, the timing of a scout single is important to the label and the studio. Filmmakers want attention for the about-to-be-released motion picture; diskeries desire publicity for their albums. A coincidence of interest exists. Recurring hit singles keep the released film in the public arena. However, record labels earn most of their money from albums. Sydney correctly noted, "singles and videos are important only as tools to sell those albums."[37] The Stigwood and Teller release strategies accommodated both media. Simultaneous releases work *if* the products are relatively balanced. Jerry Bruckheimer noted that successful products tend to "regenerate one another."[38]

The ideal, in 1984, was *Purple Rain*. "When Doves Cry," the movie's scout single, climbed to Number 1 on the charts. The album went platinum the day it was released. With this prerelease momentum, Warner's film division reluctantly supported the movie, which it originally considered only marginal.

Synergism works when two or three separate components work toward a mutual goal. Paramount, MCA, Polydor, and the CBS Record Group were models. For them, the commercial potential of musical material became central to the selection process. Marketing people, who were usually handed a project as a *fait accompli*, were integrated into the take-off stage. Steve Bedell, Paramount's vice president for music, explained, "We try to keep them informed as we're selecting music, as to the kind of music we are involved with, what the potential is in terms of record albums, and when the album is scheduled for release. We also discuss videos, marketing campaigns for the record as it relates to the film . . . we try to put the marketing department of Paramount in touch with the marketing department of the record label we may be dealing with." Glen Lajeski suggested that MCA's advertising arm appreciated the greater participation. Universal Pictures, he said, "didn't just put [*Streets of Fire*] together and just hand it to us. We're actively trying to work much closer with each other."[39] (The result was the inclusion of MCA's The Fixx in *Streets*, at the expense of an Epic act.)

Under the tutelage of Al Teller, CBS quickly got the knack. "Record companies have become more sophisticated in their dealings with studios," Teller said, "and are becoming involved with pictures at an earlier stage in the creative process."[40] Teller's "early stage involvement" frequently translated into pushing CBS artists onto the album lineup with an attractive (or token) artist from the outside—the inclusion was to boost the album or, in the worst case, avoid antitrust laws. Regardless of the motives, defining mutually beneficial interest at the start is essential.

Synergism, in this sense, is designed to function regardless of corporate relationships, as intraconglomerate networking is not necessarily more effective than intercorporate cooperation. One area in which financial structure is important is artist availability, which is greatly influenced by label affiliation to the studio. Warner Pictures can easily include artists from the WEA stable. The same studio would encounter days, if not months, of negotiations to obtain rights to CBS, Capitol, or RCA Victor's acts. Becky Shargo, recalling the *Footloose* score, said, "CBS let us use the Quiet Riot song [exclusively in the film] only because we're doing the album with them.'' Album producer Spencer Proffer included several CBS Group artists, including Ian Hunter and Cheap Trick, on the *Up the Creek* (1984) soundtrack, released by Pasha Records. The small label was affiliated with CBS, and Proffer enjoyed an ''ease of access'' to their artists.[41]

Up the Creek, despite a solid soundtrack with CBS name artists, was a financial failure. *Billboard* picked the album as one of the better of the soundtracks, but the reviewer must have missed the movie. Starring Tim Mathesen, it was a transparent take-off on *Deliverance* (1973). Described as a ''sophomoric white-water competition between inept students and ruthless preppies,'' the vehicle was, indeed, swallow and inept. The album became the best-kept secret in the summer sweepstakes of 1984.

Interconglomerate cooperation (i.e., MCA and Warner) facilitates lower costs for music titles. Up-front payments of ''video buyout'' rights are dictated by creative corporate accounting rather than overt profiteering. Robert Gustafson provided a glimpse of the internal workings in Burbank when he said, ''Many films released by Warner Brothers are financed internally by WCI, which makes loans to its film company for an eighteen-month period, during which Warner can use these funds as it sees fit.'' Thus, he continues, ''the financing of Warner Brothers productions by WCI tends to seal capital within the corporate divisions and gives the film [record] company the advantages of on-the-spot repayment flexibility.''[42] One Burbank executive commented, ''we do have to live together.'' Similar statements can be heard down the freeway in Universal City.

Relations between cinema and music have been colored by the ''video buyout.'' In 1984, labels were increasingly concerned with the infant, but growing, videocassette market, and cable. Over several years, cable ''pay'' services appeared; they were desperate for new titles and willing to purchase exclusive film rights for hundreds of millions of dollars. Studios benefitted. By 1987, film companies were using up-front (prepaid) home video and cable money to underwrite new projects.

Record labels demanded a piece of lucrative residuals. (The days of nearly ''giving'' movie rights away ended with *Saturday Night Fever*.) Diskery lawyers demanded soundtrack royalties, and some of the prices quoted to film companies were excessive. The 1984 soundtrack mania created a seller's market—the $200,000 for one title asked by a label was equivalent to the entire music budget for most films prior to *Footloose*. That musical had been allotted $30,000 per song; *Up the Creek's* track cost $190,000.

To cope with soaring music costs, studios created ''contemporary music consultants,'' was akin to the ''house hippies'' employed by record labels in the 1960s. The new role was fundamentally a bridge between the studio and the record/video industries. "It's a new and innovative job that involves interfacing between the two proud arts," wrote David Lyons in *Rock Video*.[43] The Goldbergs, Shargos, LeMels, and some others did little to ease the frustration of filmmakers. They explained the nature of the recording beast, but producers and directors remained unhappy with the situation.

Synergism is designed to preclude one component from profiting at the expense of the other part. Still, labels and studios, even those under the same corporate logo, spend a good deal of energy advancing their respective divisional turfs. A campaign becomes problematic as the diskery and the studio "rogue elephant" a project, or in other words, they look after their own interest (the album or the film) without regard for the success of the other. *Eddie and the Cruisers'* theater run demonstrated the folly of the film promotion negating a solid soundtrack album.

There are few documented cases of a soundtrack hurting a film's box office, but there is little question that in their zeal to reach the teen market with singles and MTV videos, producers sometimes would choose inappropriate songs that detracted from the film. Frequently, studio executives were more impressed with an artist's selling ability than the music. In contrast, Hackford's use of a Phil Collins song may have been gratuitous, but it did attract attention to the film without interfering with the storyline.

Joe Jackson's *Mike's Murder* score is a frequently cited illustration. The A&M artist used an already recorded final cut upon which the soundtrack was based. Market testing of *Murder* indicated that sample audiences disliked the violence in scenes tied to the songs. The "offensive" material was removed. A&M released the soundtrack album, but "didn't have a film to go with the soundtrack," explained Jackson.[44] The buyout advance covered only the session costs. On the other hand, little was left of the film score. Both flopped.

Grumbling about costs and buyouts is commonplace in studio boardrooms and commissaries. There are the omnipresent rumors and allegations. One of the more prevalent is the "package deal." "You can have artist X *if* Y and Z *also* appear on the album," is the demand. The implication is that inappropriate musical material is being forced upon a film as a *quid pro quo*. There exists no concrete evidence that any studio actually succumbed to such an offer. In fact, only a handful of contemporary scripts are structured in a manner that would accommodate such a request. Few, if any, labels have the breadth of artists on contract to do so. Nevertheless, a lack of musical sophistication can create problems.

Period pieces set in the Fifties and Sixties could lend themselves to "packaging"; however, in the wake of previous unsuccessful golden-oldies tracks, most labels would be uninterested. However, the *Big Chill*, in the Eighties, successfully showcased "oldies but goodies," as did *Good Morning, Vietnam* (1987).

A more plausible scenario suggests itself when an artist signed to an outside label performs five to six songs in a movie. Filler is required to make up a record package. Under these circumstances, the issuing label utilizes its negotiating leverage to push its roster. In *Billboard's* editorial page, Danny Goldberg commented, "Soundtracks have made people money. They have been perceived by the rock business primarily as an ancillary scam in the same general category as K-tel packages and 'Greatest Hits' albums. They've been a haven for outtakes and a pastime for record executives between jobs. And they've gained an Irish Sweepstakes aura by all those stories of artists who made a million dollars from one song on 'Saturday Night Fever.' "[45]

This is Spinal Tap

I turn within to see the forces that created me
—1983 EmbCom Music Publishing [ASCAP]

The rock music world is a dual entity. Economic considerations, first and foremost, power it. Aesthetics, frequently a by-product of commerce, represent the opposite side. All too frequently the two are in conflict. A senior officer at a record label candidly said, "Good is what sells." This kind of honesty is rare in an industry inhabited by entrepreneurs as impresarios, artists as farsighted sages, and salespeople posing as "friends." The dualism of the rock community deserves a sceptical look. (The Beatles partially poked satire at the foibles of the British rock scene in *A Hard Days Night*. The Ruttles were basic ersatz.) Rock interviews are replete with banal statements filled with self-aggrandizement. Rock may be the soundtrack of American culture, and anything that significant cries out for parody and satire. *Spinal Tap*, Rob Reiner's outrageous parody of the world of Heavy Metal bands, provided it.

A chance conversation at the Chateau Mammont Hotel on the Sunset Strip, a Hollywood layover for rockers, had actuated the film's Nigel Tufnes character. Christopher Guest overheard a "duncelike" dialogue between a rock bassist and his road manager:

MANAGER: All right, well, we'll take our instruments up the room.
ROCKER: Don't know where my bass is.
MANAGER: I beg your pardon.
ROCKER: I don't know where the bass is.

MANAGER: Where is is?
ROCKER: I think it's at the airport.
MANAGER: You have to get back there, don't you?
ROCKER: I don't know, do I?
MANAGER: I think you better.
ROCKER: Where's my bass?
MANAGER: It's at the airport."[46]

Regardless of the authenticity of the dialogue, Guest did capture the ambiance of some rock musicians from the United Kingdom, especially punkers and some metalers, imitating John Lennon—at his worst. Some of it may be a product of chemicals, jet lag, and the insidious Eleven Plus, a repressive British high school examination. This was music to a satirist's ear. Guest tucked the Nigel character away for future reference.

In 1978, the rock bassist was resurrected. Joining Michael McKean, Rob Reiner, and Harry Shearer for the taping of an ABC-TV special, Guest became one of three "heavy metalers" to spoof *The Midnight Special.* "We were shooting a takeoff on 'Midnight Special,' recalled Shearer, "just lying on the ground waiting for the machine that was supposed to make the fog effect to stop dripping hot oil on us—and to relieve the tension of that moment, we started ad-libbing these characters."[47] Spinal Tap emerged, performing "Rock 'n' Roll Nightmare." Rob Reiner portrayed Wolfman Jack. ABC-TV didn't find the debunking TV show suitable family fare and buried it at 11:30 p.m.

Several years later, the quartet gathered to make a twenty-minute demonstration film financed by Marble Arch. (The firm went out of business before the project was pitched to various studios.) "We literally walked from one lot to the next, with a can of film under our arms," remembered Reiner. Nothing happened. Reiner was then called by Embassy Pictures to possibly direct a project. He showed the studio executive the movie demo. The response was, "never mind my idea. I want *Spinal Tap.*" (Norman Lear and Jerry Perenchio had meanwhile bought the film company. Reiner would say, "Norman is responsible for the two greatest things in my life. 'All in the Family' and 'Spinal Tap.' "[48]) The project was budgeted at $2.2 million.

The film was shot in five weeks in the Los Angeles area. In one club-date scene, *Spinal Tap* was the warm-up act for the temporarily reassembled Iron Butterfly. "We were louder than they were; actually, we had to be. No one knew who we were. They took us at face value as a new British band trying to make its mark on L.A.," said Shearer. At another club, he continued, they opened for Killer Pussy, "which gives you an idea of what that gig was like."[49]

The script was improvised. Said Reiner, "The first time, I'd just turn on the camera and see what happened. The second time, we added things or changed focus. The third time was to get variations, and the fourth time was to get cutaway shots." Karen Murphy, the producer, gave a documentary flavor to the plot. Peter Smolker of *Gimme Shelter* did the camera work. Both added authenticity to the "mockumentary." A 16-millimeter hand-held camera was used and the film was later enlarged to the more usual 35-millimeter size. The movie was marketed in major cities and then "rolled out," or spread, to outlying or secondary areas.

Spinal Tap, like *Eddie*, was spared the "buyout" problem as the fictitious made-for-visuals band consigned rights to Embassy. Polygram received a finished product, as they would have from a genuine act. All ancillary rights belonged to the moviemakers. Unlike in *Eddie*, what the viewer saw on the screen was available on the album.

Tongue-in-cheek, the Polygram marketing people went through the motions of a real promo campaign. Beginning with the album graphics, the *Spinal Tap* promotion outdistanced those of most legitimate artists. As with "greatest hits" anthologies, each song listed had a recording date and source, (i.e. " 'Heavy Duty' (4:26) From the LP *Bent for the Rent*, (1976).") Prominently placed on the back of the jacket is the band's biography and discography "reprinted" from the *Rocklopedia Brittanicus* (p. 743). It closes, "Though neither a critic's nor a public favorite, Spinal Tap continues to fill a much needed void."

MTV aired Tap's video, "Hell Hole," a week before the film's opening in New York 2 March. Although it was relegated to the light rotation for much of March, this was better than many legitimate recording artists could do. Television exposure included Shearer's old haunt, *Saturday Night Live*. *Spinal Tap* appeared at CBGB's, the famed New York punk-rock club. *Newsweek's* Cathleen McGuigan would later write, "Now these three grown men spend half their time thinking that they *are* Spinal Tap."[50]

There was no real attempt to synergize the parody, despite the tongue-in-cheek campaign. A television ad, in K-tel style, offered an anthology of the group's *Greatest Hits*. The announcer read, "a treasury of seventeen years of nerve-damaging music." The label gave a press party at which the band was awarded a platinum record for one million "returns." This was followed by their holiday cassette, "Christmas with the Devil." Media people received a tour T-shirt accompanied by an iron-on "cancelled" decal.

Media people, accustomed to intense hype, enjoyed the spoof campaign. *Rolling Stone* ran a three-page spread on the band. Feature pieces appeared in *Newsweek* and the *Village Voice*. Excellent coverage for a fictitious quintet.

The title album, *This Is Spinal Tap*, was reviewed in *Billboard*. The critic found the "seasoned, doggedly obscure rock quintet flexes a host of metal cliches (and a few from earlier eras as well); it's endearing for the band's determination, if not originality. That's the premise behind the screen satire, which apes rock documentary form and hits its rock target dead center, and the ersatz band's music follows."[51] Predictably, the album remained at the lower end of the trade charts. One deejay observed, "I wonder how they would have done if it wasn't a put-on."

Hard to Hold had been unintentionally funny. *Spinal Tap* provided many more laughs and insights into the world of rock 'n' roll.

Rock and Roll Creation: The Film

> And the people stood and stared
> Loved us more than we had dared to—
> In America
> —© 1983 EmbCom Music Publishing [ASCAP]

A seventeen-year old British rock band arrives in America to revive its fledgling career by promoting a new album, *Smell the Glove*, with a tour. This is no ordinary trek across the country, as noted film director Martin DiBergi (Rob Reiner) plans a "rockumentary" of the cross-country show. The project is spurred by the belief that the evolved heavy-metal *Spinal Tap* has, with fifteen albums, "redefined rock 'n' roll."

Interviewing lead guitarist David St. Hubbins (Michael McKean), lead guitarist Nigel Tufnes (Christopher Guest), and nondescript bassist Derek Smalls (Harry Shearer), the film director traces their roots back to the Liverpool Sound. An aged black-and-white kinescope from the *Pop, Look and Listen* show appears. The Merseyish "Gimme' Some Money" is performed by the mop-tops.

The history of the band reveals that a series of its drummer's have died suddenly, under strange circumstances. Peter James Bond "blew up on stage," literally. Another choked on vomit—"Not his own" offers the verbose Nigel.

At the New York-tour opening party, Polymar Record executives surface in the midst of a radical chic crowd. Label president Sir Denis Eton-Hogg (Patrick MacNee) and super-publicist Bobbi Flekman, delightfully acted by Fran Drescher, orchestrate the proceedings.

On the road, the band lives up their billing, performing screaming riffs while dressed in skintight Spandex pants: the sights and sounds of heavy metal. "Big Bottom" blasts "Drive me out of my mind. How can I leave this behind?"

The lads are once again mired in a sea of blue suits at the Record Industry Convention. The executives express growing concern regarding the delayed release of the tour-supported album. David complains, "It's hard to promote something that doesn't exist." Ian Faith (Tony Hendra), the prototypical manager, hoping to hasten the street date, approaches the record label's publicist Ms. Flexman. After some verbal sparring, she says that the label brass have found the album's art work "very offensive, very sexist." She informs Ian that Sears and K-Mart refuse to stock material depicting a greased naked woman on her hands and knees with a dog collar around her neck and a leash with a man's arm holding it, pushing a black glove in her face. Nigel innocently inquires, "What's wrong with being sexy?" Persisting, the band's manager rationalizes, "You should have seen the cover *they* wanted to do." The answer is short and to the point: "Money talks, bullshit walks." In keeping the industry tradition, the graphics will be changed.

In keeping with the *verite* genre, DiBergi reads fictitious reviews to the band. "They are treading water in a sea of retarded sexuality." "Nitpicking, isn't it," replies the dense, but opinionated Nigel.

Date cancellations and relegation to smaller venues increase. DiBergi asks Ian whether the band's popularity is on the wane. "No, no, no . . . their appeal is becoming more *selective*," he answers in a typical managerial response. The band harkens back to a time when the "world's ear" was tuned to "(Listen to the) Flower People," a psychedelic video easily culled from the days of *Shindig* or *Hullabaloo*.

Conditions deteriorate when astrology nut Jeanine Pettibone (June Cadwick) enters the picture. She's St. Hubbins' lady. Minutes after her arrival, the "Black Album" is released—a portent of things to come? Derek is trapped inside a glass bubble as "Rock 'n' Roll Creation" is performed.

Paul Schaffer portrays Artie Funkie, a Chicago label representative. (Promotion people, as the Rolling Stone's song suggested, are viewed charitably as a necessary evil. A deejay once observed, "they come on like they're my long, lost friend when they want something.")

Funkie sets up an autograph party to hype the finally released LP. Nobody comes. Berating the store owner, Artie yells, "I thought we had a relationship." David says, "We were told massive radio support."

Spinal Tap's fortunes continue to plunge. Cleveland appears promising. A large crowd assembles there, but the band loses its direction in the underground labyrinth of the arena.

Hoping to end the downward slide, the band decides to highlight "Stonehenge" with a lavish production number. Nigel draws a blueprint of the ancient site, confusing inch symbols with feet. The backdrop set arrives eighteen inches in height; Ian hires dwarfs to parade around it. The mood is destroyed. St. Hubbins is enraged and confronts the manager. An argument follows, with Ian quitting when Jeanine decides to co-manage the group, using an astrological chart.

The bickering between the lead guitarists continues. The stoic Derek Small explains to the Reiner character, "like Byron and Shelley, we have two visionaries in the band. They are like fire and ice." He's in the middle, "like lukewarm water."

Following signs from the stars, Jeanine books the group into Seattle's Lindbergh Air Force Base for the At-Ease festivities. The bands blaring music causes the hangar to empty. Clean-cut military personnel reject the metalists to the tune of "Sex Farm Woman." Nigel stomps off stage. The tour mercifully ends.

As everything seems bleak, Nigel returns with an offer for a reunion tour in Japan, following in the footsteps of Deep Purple, Dylan, and Asia. David refuses, but then changes his mind. They do a successful tour of Japan, now the career-revitalization mecca designation of the world. Together again the band runs on to pursue the goals of sex, drugs, and rock 'n' roll.

The storyline is the tour, with neatly arranged scenes providing rock-scene vignettes. Some are probing and insightful. Others merely highlight the ineptitude of the band with sight gags. The publicist Flekman and the Chicago promo jerk, Funkie, are gems, easily holding their own with the zany members of Spinal Tap. The manager, played by ex-*National Lampooner* Hendra, is more than believable.

This Is Spinal Tap says more about the industry in a short eighty-two minutes than many "serious" films and rockumentaries. A good time was had by all, especially people observing the music business.

Media people, constantly exposed to the foibles of the entertainment world, almost unanimously praised the film. *Film in Review's* John Nangle praised "this witty mock-documentary that takes the *cinema verite* approach to a subject long overdue for parody." Michael Goldberg noted the film "takes the rock 'n' roll world in all its pompous glory and manages to poke fun at almost every aspect of it." Admitting ignorance of rock music, Stanley Kauffmann joined the chorus, saying the movie was "clever throughout, is especially sharp as a satiric comment on youth-enforced cultural change." Robert Christgau, in a mild departure from his music critic role, with Carola Dibbell applauded the film. "It's fitting that this unlikely candidate for music's finest fiction film should pay ambiguous tribute to the mediocrities who are also part of its glory,'' he wrote. ''This is surely the funniest movie ever made about rock 'n' roll, and one of the funniest things about it is that it may also be one of the most accurate,'' observed David Ansen in *Newsweek*.[52]

Even Vincent Canby, a frequent critic of the intrusiveness of rock scores, congratulated the creators of *Spinal Tap*. They, he suggested, ''have made one of the season's most satisfying comedies, as well as the rock-concert-tour film that tops all the others.''[53]

Spinal Tap's critical acclaim would be its Achilles' heel. Recalling a test screening in a Dallas shopping mall, the film's director said, ''A small section of the audience laughed. The rest asked why we would make a serious documentary about a terrible band they had never heard of.'' ''It's like reality is calling our bluff at every stop along the way,'' noted Shearer.[54] Maslin captured the bottom line, saying, ''There's an in-joke quality to the film, one that will make it all the more hilarious to anyone at all knowledgeable about either the esthetic or business aspects of pop music.''[55]

This Is Spinal Tap enjoyed an eleven-week maiden run, grossing $1.8 million. It quickly reached the status of a ''cult'' classic, with $2 million in box office.

The entire package, so carefully crafted, did appeal to insiders, but transcended conventional wisdom. Only a journalist in pursuit of an interview would totally appreciate Howard Hessman's line, ''Listen, we'd love to stand around and chat, but we've got to sit down in the lobby and wait for the limo.'' It's better than the usual brush-off, ''No! Hope you enjoy the show.''

As the summer of 1984 rolled around, *Spinal Tap* was a critical success. Only *Time's* Richard Corliss dismissed the move, saying, ''It plays like *Scenes from a Marriage* translated from Gibberish.''[56]

Odds had flirted with rock as background. *Spinal Tap* affectionately spoofed it. In a slightly more than $2-million project, Rob Reiner *et al* produced an adult movie filled with iconoclastic barbs sharply focused on the pretentiousness of segments of the music industry.

Hard to Grasp: The Rick Springfield Movie

> *Bob 'til you drop/in the hot city*
> *Keep on working day and night*
> *Don't stop 'til you get what you want*
> —© 1984 Vogue Music (BMI)

One case caught in the ebb tide of intercorporate maneuvering was Universal Pictures' *Hard to Hold*. The Rick Springfield "personality" picture was conceived at the MCA-owned studio. The actor/singer was an RCA recording artist. Casting the soap-opera star as the film's lead meant producing an outside track, as RCA would never consider allowing a six-song contribution to a competitor. Part of the filler on the album, such as Graham Parker's "When the Lights Go Out," came from RCA people. RCA conceptualized the album as a singular entity—Paul Atkinson, RCA's West Coast vice president of artists and repertoire, maintained that its promotion and marketing should operate independently of the movie. "A big hit single is not going to save a movie at the box office, and a hit movie won't save a record. I don't think we can market films, and I don't think [studios] can sell records," he said.[57] To the A & R man, *Hard to Hold* was a solo project.

RCA Victor's original promotion did accommodate Universal Pictures. "Love Somebody" surfaced on *Billboard's* Hot 100 a month before the movie was released. It entered at Number 49. The album's shipping date coincided with the film's debut. The label ignored Al Teller's clustering strategy in favor of staggered releases. "Don't Walk Away" came out May 26, almost two weeks after the movie's original run. As Atkinson had suggested, the *Hard* campaign was to promote the record.

Secure in his heartthrob status on ABC-TV's *General Hospital*, with several hit records, Rick Springfield was shopping for a feature film. Marty Davidson had passed on him for the Eddie Wilson role in *Eddie and the Cruisers*, as the director wanted an unknown for the part. "Rick Springfield," he reasoned, "would have been Rick Springfield. And he might have been great, and we might have opened strong and had an album that went platinum, but he wouldn't have spanned the history."[58] Springfield had been originally cast to star in the *Buddy Holly Story*, but Gary Busey eventually played the rock-a-billy from Lubbock, Texas.

Springfield's career was not totally ill fated. He was signed by Capitol Records in 1972 on the basis of a hit single, "Down Under." His "Speak to the Sky" peaked on the *Billboard* chart in the Top 20, but the accompanying publicity campaign stigmatized him. "I came over here and people said, 'Here's another cute face.' To me it was all just publicity. I would do these long interviews with teen magazines about my music and it would come out, 'Rick Springfield is too tall to love?' . . . I had to do something so I went to acting school."[59] Ironically, this attempt to escape the stereotypical image would serve to reinforce it.

Ten years later, the thirty-three-year-old soap-opera physician was under contract to Universal Pictures. Larry Pierce chose him to headline in a project playing a rock star. The film was not designed as a personality vehicle *per se*. Rick Springfield was perceived as a teen idol, but his discography showed few indications of superstardom. He was an actor with several hit singles, "Jessie's Girl," "I've Done Everything For You," and "Don't Talk to Strangers" to his credit, and two platinum albums.

Besides *General Hospital*, he had done guest television appearances on the *Rockford Files, The Six Million Dollar Man*, and *Wonder Woman*. Springfield's acting abilities were adequate, and portraying a rock musician appeared to be a natural. However, the movie's heavy-handed direction even of the concert footage, would require him to use considerable ability to play James Roberts.

Hard to Hold opened with James "Jamie" Roberts (Springfield) racing to his dressing room, as a concert crowd roars its approval. He encores with "Love Somebody," one of two on-stage renditions of the song. (The imagination is strained to see a jaded San Francisco audience responding positively to the contrived Jaggersque performance.) Retreating to a hot shower, the rocker, implausibly, is locked out the dressing area and finds himself pursued by overzealous fans. Clad only in a wrap-around towel, he flees. The attempt at slapstick continues as Jamie borrows a roadie's oversized trousers as well as his car. He literally runs into Diana Larsons's (Janet Eilber) automobile. (Any resemblance to *A Hard Day's Night* is purely coincidental.) The rock star offers to buy Larson a new car. "Your insurance will do," she snaps. Disoriented, he remarks, "I don't take care of that kind of thing!" Jamie's improbable romantic pursuit of Diana, a child psychologist, commences.

She rebuffs several of his overtures, including the gift of a new Volvo. A "chance" encounter in the Fairmont Hotel lounge sets up the undercurrent. "Stop hassling me . . ." she insists. "I know who you are. You're a rock person . . . I don't like your music. It's bubblegum." Failing to interrupt her accusations, Jamie finally asks, "What kind of music *do* you like?"

DIANA: Tony Bennett.
JAMIE: Jesus!
DIANA: No, Tony Bennett.
JAMIE: TONY BENNETT!!!

If musical tastes are a gauge of psychographic preferences, a clash of lifestyles is promised. Can a child psychologist and a rock star find happiness in "Bagdad By the Bay?"

With a few unresolved subplots—Jamie's writing block and Diana's uneasy tie with her father Johnny Larson (Albert Salmi)—the story centers on the shallow interaction between the Springfield and Eilber characters. "To commit or not to commit," that is the storyline. The outcome is predictable.

Jamie continues the chase. He appears outside of Diana's Pacific Heights apartment with a Tony Bennett imitator, who performs, "I Left My Heart in San Francisco."

Diana wakes her suitor, saying, "Time for you to go home." Barely awake, Jamie protests, "We just made love." "No, we didn't," she objects. "We just had sex." The union came about for no apparent reason. "No matter that the couple has barely had a civil conversation to this point," noted *Variety*.[60]

The duo engage in a tiresome "love" match. Diana tells Jamie, "You're the kind of guy a girl could take home to Dad." Jamie is the perfect example of an outlandish, yet respectable, teen idol. Once, as the couple embraces in the back seat of a taxi, the cabbie asks, "Mr. Roberts, can I have your autograph?"

In a scene reminiscent of *Risky Business*, Diana imitates a *Solid Gold* dancer, prancing around her office to one of Springfield's tunes; her secretary joking shouts, "Slut."

The writing block worsens. "The words don't come anymore," he says. "It just don't work." If Diana's responsible for the malady, it is unclear. (Although changing costumes and visiting the tourist traps of San Francisco with her can be distractions.) Without developing this subplot, the story quickly returns to the "hot-cold-hot . . ." relationship. "I don't want your autograph, I want 'you,' " Diana tells him. One revealing line is Diana's comment, "Isn't life nuts?" This summarizes her feelings and the thrust of the movie. (A profound statement from a psychologist.)

Following the death of her father, Diana decides to leave for London. Jamie cannot intervene, as he must satisfy his fans. "Love Somebody" is the grand finale, as the crowd repeats the closing line of the chorus "one night, one night . . ."

Triumphantly, the rocker races to the loading ramp. "Give me the keys to the car," he commands. "Oh man, not again," mumbles the roadie. Jamie intercepts Diana at the airport. She breaks down, sobbing, "I was scared, I was scared . . ." They run off hand in hand, presumably into the world of rock 'n' roll.

An astute reviewer suggested that *Hard* might make up one short-form MTV clip. He was being gracious. The roster of cardboard characters, a schizoid attempt at comedic romance—"I really, really, really, really care about you"—and a Gray Line tour of San Francisco do not make a video.

Hard to Hold is as advertised. Outside of the overly slick concert scenes, the film slips away.

There is an unspoken rule among newspeople: bad records, concerts, and films by "name" performers are fair game, but lackluster showings by insignificant artists are ignored. "Don't waste the space" is a cardinal consideration. *Hard to Hold's* reviews nationally numbered less than ten. Even some film journals overlooked it. The national news magazines were silent. The only exposure the film received came from "Love Somebody" and other cuts on radio and video.

The handful of trade critics discussing *Hard* ravaged it. *Variety's* Greenfield dissected the film as a "skin-deep romance wrapped around a forgettable rock score. Even Springfield's primarily preteen audiences may find *Hard to Hold's* high gloss hard to catch . . . Springfield is too good to be true."[61] When the "Bible of cinema" pans a film, things are bound to get worse. They did. Alan Karp, one of the less opinionated reviewers, wrote, "*Hard to Hold* contains about enough worthwhile material for one MTV video." More specifically, "Although thirteen-year-old Rick Springfield fans might like it, it's hard to think of anything else positive to say about this embarrassing trifle of a love story. Springfield's motion picture debut is marred by an incredibly hackneyed script, shoddy acting, and a complete lack of credibility." Maitland McDonagh, while kinder to Springfield, suggested that the singer could not transcend the script's "poorly constructed narrative, and the film's often truly awful dialogue defeats him at every turn."

Several writers, mindful of Hedley's screenplay for *Flashdance*, pointed out that *Hard* lacked the nonstop movement of the dance film and, as one noted, the "relentless music of the soundtrack."[62]

Janet Maslin, no stranger to the rock world, caught the essence of the film. She wrote:

> *Hard to Hold* is a movie for anyone who thinks this sounds like real behind-the-scenes rock-and-roll ambiance and for anyone who thinks Rick Springfield is a real rock star. It's not a movie for anyone else, except perhaps film students who will find that Larry Pierce has included more weak transitions, conversational cliches, unflattering camera angles and ethnic restaurant scenes in this films mere 93 minutes than some director's manage in an entire career.[63]

Fortunately, teenyboppers do not read trade reviews or the august *New York Times*. Otherwise, the film would have disappeared as rapidly as an unsuccessful Broadway offering or *Heaven's Gate* (1980). However, it ran just over a month nevertheless.

The Springfield showcase had it in the music, but not on the screen. In the heyday of MTV, this was a significant drawback. Comparing the motion picture to the video found the Pierce production wanting. *Hard to Hold* was an endeavor in which the high points were the musical interludes, not the dramatic scenes. The movie set up the videos and the songs; this was hardly a balanced presentation. The one-dimensionality of the movie magnified the stage scenes. Theatergoers preferred watching the video and buying the album to sitting through the movie.

Billboard staffer Jim Bessman added insult to injury when he indicated that the movie spoiled Springfield's video. He wrote in *Rock Video*

> Springfield—or the video director—cleverly integrates the movie footage into the movie video by setting up a scenario where he is singing the song while editing his own movie, quite dramatically at times. The integration of the film clips into the video clip is no problem—after all, this type of music video is meant to promote the movie rather than the song. Unfortunately, and unintentionally, the opposite effect is achieved, since the *Hard to Hold* footage which Springfield (and we) are watching is truly wretched. I mean, having seen the movie video, I wouldn't go near the movie.[64]

Hard to Hold, the film, grossed barely over a million dollars the first week of exhibition. Its theater run lasted a mere 5 weeks, earning $1.9 million. By contrast *Purple Rain*, somewhat similar in genre, grossed $7.7 million its first weekend. *Hard* finally amassed $5 million in North America.

A *Rolling Stone* contributor insisted that the movie's platinum album and two videos, "Someone to Love," and "Bop 'Til You Drop," with special effects by George Lucas's Industrial Light and Magic, "were superior to the film."[65] Critics found many villains in the production, but the major culprit mentioned was director Larry Peerce, with writer Tom Hedley (*Flashdance*) a close second. *Boxoffice* noted that the director "apparently subscribes to the theory if your characters spend a lot of time laughing at their own actions, this will somehow rub off on the audience."[66]

"All the moving about, pretty people and nice sets," Greenberg wrote, "don't pump any life into any of the characters . . . A nighttime view of S.F. from the top of the Fairmont Hotel looks good only if there is nothing going on in front of it," wrote another critic.[67]

MTV, according to Fred Bronson, was an ideal vehicle for the Australian-born singer. "His television exposure on ABC-TV's 'General Hospital' made him a perfect candidate for the new visual art," he wrote.[68] Paul Justman directed "Don't Talk to Strangers," which was one of the first "rejected-voyeuristic-ex-boyfriend" videos. This ploy allowed the camera to cut between the singer and the storyline. "Affair of the Heart" was yet another excellent video featuring Springfield. RCA made good use of the photogenic artist in hyping MTV. They did the video; Universal Pictures released a soundtrack-dominated movie. The album, on RCA not MCA, was successful, due to RCA's heavy promotion on radio and MTV. The staggered-release strategy worked independent of the short-lived film. (The key to synergism is having the two entities enjoying success in their individual efforts. As the bottom line indicated, RCA prevailed in its mission, but the film flopped.) By midsummer, the movie was being peddled to cable outlets. HBO and Movie Channel exposure helped keep the soundtrack on the charts for eight months.

Hard to Hold, supposedly a "backstage" movie, provided few insights into the machinations of the rock world. Lines such as, "The music's changing . . . We gotta' change with it," had little basis in reality. If Springfield had possessed a roadmap to the future, perhaps he would not have made *Hard to Hold*.

Hard to Hold appeared prior to the summer onslaught of youth-oriented films which are, economically, highly significant to the entertainment media. Only television generally undergoes a slump. In the book, record, and film markets, profits are to be made, but the competition is fierce.

In film-industry jargon, potential theatergoers are most accessible on the Memorial Day and Thanksgiving Day weekends. (Memorial Day 1988 had set a record high of $65 million with *Crocodile Dundee II* and *Rambo III* combining for a gross of $41.2 million. In 1984, *Indiana Jones and the Temple of Doom* pulled in a record Memorial Day $33.9 million. Two significant rock soundtrack offerings had quickly followed. *Streets of Fire* and *Ghostbusters* hit the circuit in June.) While the entire summer is attractive, June and July are premiere release months—school's out. The summer—Memorial Day through 1 September—accounts for 40 percent of gross annual box office.

Summer release is fraught with pitfalls even for good pictures. An independent distributor outlined the 1984 situation when three potential hits would hit the streets: *Ghostbusters*, *Gremlins*, and *Top Secret*. "We know we can't go June 8," observed Stuart Strutin, "and if every one of those pictures is successful and holds, it's going to be tough."[69] *Streets of Fire* would surface the same day as *Star Trek III*.

"Tonight Is What It Means To Be Young": Streets of Fire

> *I'm wandering, a loser down these tracks . . .*
> *I walk with angels that have no place*
> *Streets of fire.*
> —© 1978 Bruce Springsteen [ASCAP]

"A lot of young directors and screenwriters who are making movies are of the generation that grew up with rock music," A & M Record's David Anderle observed. "When they're writing their scripts," he continued, "there's a lot of rock music involved. In addition, filmmakers obviously want to take advantage of the teen audience through music and the record companies want to give their acts some exposure through films."[70] Marty Davidson, Taylor Hackford, Larry Kasdan, and Walter Hill personified the new filmmakers. Hill added *Streets of Fire* to the list of rock-supported serious films. (Described as the top directorial practioner of "sheer visceral expertise," Hill had become a highly desirable property after Paramount released his *48 Hours*, which grossed $108 million and catapulted *Saturday Night Live's* Eddie Murphy to Hollywood stardom. The film also had provided MTV with a video, The Bus Boys' "The Boys are Back.")

Universal's president Robert Rehme received the script on a Friday. In two days, a production deal, originally costing $14.5 million was negotiated and signed. Hill's "rock 'n' roll fable where the Leader of the Pack steals the Queen of the Hop and Soldier Boy comes home to do something about it" appeared a natural for the multifaceted MCA.[71] The film company was delighted to lure "a team that delivers a hit." The potential intrigued Irving Azoff, MCA Records head, who, upon joining the entertainment conglomerate in May 1983, had contended, "Obviously, the picture company has been more successful than the record company; I need them to help me build a record company." MCA Records had enjoyed a string of soundtrack successes: *American Graffiti*, *Jesus Christ Superstar*, and *Tommy*. "Now I've got these two great big companies to marry," Azoff went on, "not just an individual picture here and there. My efforts in the feature area will be restricted to those activities that can help spawn hit records."[72] With the departure of Elton John and The Who to WCI, *Streets of Fire* appeared a promising acquisition.

For Hill, *Streets* was a regression. "I tried to make what I would have thought was a perfect movie when I was in my teens," he recalled. "I put in all the things I thought were great then . . . custom cars, kissing in the rain, neon trains in the night, head-speed pursuit, rumbles, rock stars, motorcycles, jokes in tough situations, leather jackets, and questions of honor."[73] In two words, *film noir*, a genre alien to the twelve- to twenty-five-year old audience. Still, Hill argued, "This is a good movie for high school kids—maybe it'll stir them up in a good way."[74]

One reviewer would later suggest that Hill's attempt failed because the director "has to struggle even harder (and in the end, fruitlessly) to recapture the zest of immaturity," or "he hasn't decided for himself whether he wants audiences to hoot at his comic book dialogue and mock heroic postures or to cheer his cardboard hero in earnest. He's too good and too young to be playing these cheerless self-referential games.''[75]

To achieve the "ancient light of magic," Hill employed a promising ensemble. Michael Paré and Diane Lane (*Rumblefish*) headlined. Supporting roles included Rick Moranis, *SCTV's* McKenzie brother, and William Dafoe as the "wild one." Choreographer Jeffrey Hornaday and dancer Marin Jahan, who had been the *real* stars of *Flashdance*, once again joined forces. Peter Occhiogrosso described the cast as an "unbeatable combination of sex, violence, rock 'n' roll, and box-office clout.''[76]

The futuristic setting, "a seedy version of the fifties"—mostly filmed in East Los Angeles with one sequence in downtown Chicago—featured a "grubby and desolate city of rain-soaked, sullen streets, empty cafes, and junk-filled factory yards.''[77] In this milieu Paré and Dafoe acted out their comic-book, cliched characters.

Record producer Jimmy Iovine supervised the song selections utilizing such established songwriters as Tom Petty, Stevie Nicks, and Jim Steinman. He had originally intended to incorporate Bruce Springsteen's "Streets of Fire" and a CBS group, Face to Face. As the filming progressed, the musical score was proving difficult. The main obstacle was Springsteen. The title song was supposed to come from his *Darkness at the Edge of Town* album, but the Boss hesitated to approve a cover version by a girl singer. Jim Steinman wrote "Tonight Is What It Means To Be Young" for the upbeat finale. Problems of an undisclosed nature with Face to Face found MCA's The Fixx being added to the final track.

Universal was not terribly disappointed as the now-$17-million picture needed music videos for MTV and home cassette consumption. Some of the *Street*-generated videos included footage absent from the motion picture.

The synergistic marketing campaign surfaced in late April, with the release of Dan Hartman's scout single "I Can Dream About You." The song climbed to the high 30s on the *Billboard* chart, remaining for several months and eventually reaching the Top 10. To coincide with the single's release, co-producer Joel Silver spoke with *Billboard's* Ethlie Ann Vare. "Walter and I were the first movie company to really utilize video. We cut a clip from *48 Hours* of the Bus Boys and put it on MTV," he said. Silver went on to discuss the multimedia approach. "In the movie there's even a sequence that shows a video on-screen. We shot it on film, cut it on tape, and then transferred the tape back to film," he explained. His goal was "a hit record, a hit video, and a hit movie—that gets the most exposure possible. It becomes a part of popular culture.''[78] With considerably more understatement, music supervisor Jimmy Iovine said, "The music in this movie is all valid. There's a reason for every song to be there; it's not a bunch of B sides strung together. And the videos are valid, because there's actually a band in the movie, and the song are actually performed in the movie. It's not just a song running behind an advertisement." The producer was correct. The *a capella* Sorals and the rock-a-billy Blasters *do* perform original material, Lane's backup band was comprised of known session musicians, and Ry Cooder arranged the overlays. (Only one of his selections was to be found on the album, however—"Hold That Snake.") Link Wray's "Rumble" and other slide-guitar pieces were confined to the film track.

More confusing were the dubs for the kidnapped rock singer, portrayed by Diane Lane. Session singers Laurie Sargent, Holly Sherwood, and Rory Dodd had their vocals mixed—"a collage of vocals"—to overdub the on-screen performance. Stevie Nick's powerful composition "Sorcerer" was performed by Marilyn Martin on the soundtrack album only. Lane, a vocalist in her own right, was precluded from duplicating any of the film material. This mishmash created a severe marketing problem, in that "Sorcerer" and the opening and closing numbers were the strongest cuts on the album. The days of billing "by the cast of" had vanished. This maze of sound crippled the audio promotion, creating a total reliance on the visuals.[79]

In May, MCA announced a massive media-saturation program, including prereleases of four videos for network and cable TV. The ten-song soundtrack was charted two weeks after the film debuted 1 June. The album entered in the mid-100s in *Billboard* and *Cashbox*. The Hartman video was aired on MTV, in the medium category (guaranteed three views per day) for several months. However, as one of the more insightful observers of the rock soundtrack phenomena wrote, "Between constant showings of 'I can Dream About You,' (in which white singer Dan Hartman's off-camera voice competed for recognition with on-screen black performance group, the Sorals), and the repeated commercial trailers, the marketing was as subtle as the film's sledgehammer showdown."[80]

A major target was the VCR market. MCA Home Video promised to ship a cassette with several long-form, six- to seven-minute selections, and a "featurette," "Inside 'Streets of Fire.' " Fashioned after 'Making Michael Jackson's, Thriller," the promo-vid was priced at $19.95 (quite reasonable in 1984). Suzie Peterson, director of new product development, admitted the effort was behind schedule, but, she said, "There was just no way to get out sooner."[81] MCA hoped that the twenty-six-minute videocassette would promote the album and the movie. Despite the quality of the album and a good-faith promotional effort, only 300,000 copies were sold.

The overall project seemed star-crossed. Even the opening date, as scheduled, presented obstacles.

The Film

Streets of Fire went on exhibition June 1 nationally in 1,150 theaters. In a matter of days it was in direct competition with *Indiana Jones and The Temple of Doom* and *Star Trek III: The Search for Spock*. The hope of capturing the youth market rapidly evaporated. In its first ten days of exhibition, *Streets* grossed a meager $4.5 million, in contrast to the *Star Trek* sequel, which earned $34.8 million.

The rock 'n' roll fable happens in "another time, another place," a mythical milieu where bikers, rock-world denizens, cops, and the protagonists coexist. The setting, reminiscent of that of *Escape From New York*, consists of steam jets, neon lights, rain-slicked streets, junk-filled lots, and elevated subway platforms. This urban never-never land has "undeniable texture."

To a throng of New Wave admirers, rock star Ellen Aim (Diane Lane) lip-syncs "Nowhere Fast." Her concert is interrupted by a gang of black-leather-jacketed motorcycle marauders. The Joan Jettish vocalist is swept from the stage by the bikers' leader, Raven (William Defoe), and spirited away to the Bombers' headquarters at Torchie's Bar.

A soldier of fortune, gun-for-hire, and comic book hero, Tom Cody (Michael Paré), Ellen's old flame, is summoned to the rescue. Prior to embarking on his odyssey across, or under, the tracks to The Battery, Cody befriends McCoy (Amy Madigan). The worldly McCoy has one of the few memorable lines in the film. "Some people never talk about their feelings because they ain't got any."

Cody's rescue efforts are sweetened by Ellen's sleazy manager, Billy Fish (Rick Moranis), who offers a $10,000 reward for her return.

Torchie's proves to be a rock club. The Blasters wail on "One Bad Stud" as Marine Jahan performs an erotic strip tease on the bar *a la Flashdance*. It is in The Battery, amid the trash, fog, smoke, and sound, that the action really occurs.

Tom brings Ellen back to the Richmond, their turf. While exercising his heroics, Cody manages to burn "half the place down" including the Bombers' bikes. This sets up the ultimate showdown with the punk (as in rock) leader of the gang.

To the accompaniment of "Rumble" and a cop's admonition, "Let's see how well you can do . . . kick his ass," Cody defeats Raven in a sledgehammer duel. *High Noon* it's not.

In a fleeting subplot, Tom and Ellen reconcile until the concert finale. There, Ellen begins "Tonight is What it Means to Be Young." Fisher, standing in the wings, turns to a stagehand, bragging, "Yuh know something Waldo, we're gonna' be rich."

"Yeah, along with rock 'n' roll," is the response. The wall of sound intensifies in the strobe-lit, smoke-filled auditorium. The *denouement* comes with Cody's departure. "If you ever need me for something, I'll be there," he tells Ellen.

Paré walks down the shadowy wet street, barely lit by neon reflections. McCoy picks him up in a 1950 Mercury, and they ride off into the darkness.

The surrealistic attempt to mold a comic-book orientation, a mock-epic, a movie heroic, and cowboy-cliche dialogue into a whole film elicited varied critical responses. Hill compounded the reviewers' difficulties by using the Borges scripture, "a different sort of order rules them, one based not on reason . . ."[82]

Boxoffice's Alan Karp was a "voice crying in the wilderness" in applauding this bizarre mix. He called it "a strange blend to be sure, but say what you will, this unorthodox romp is one of the best rock 'n' roll movies since *A Hard Day's Night*."[83]

At the opposite end of the spectrum, J. Hoberman questioned Hill's entire conceptualization. "Maybe he saw it as the super rock video to end rock videos. But whatever the concept, the result is so utterly inferior to the average MTV promo that the only riots to greet this dud should be teenagers storming the box-office for a refund," he wrote.[84]

Most writers concurred. "This movie's unusual narrative may not appeal to all tastes" and, juxtaposed Janet Maslin, "the gap between the visual effects and their narrative idiocy is enough to make you weep."[85]

A consensus, of sorts, emerged. The film was successful *noir* visually, but an aimless "story."

The score garnered considerable attention. Ironically, several songs were pounced on for functioning in Hill's scheme of things, thus, adding to the confusion.

The critics were decidedly split on the musical merits of *Streets*. The initial *Variety* commentary praised the soundtrack as "terrific," saying, "musically the movie is continually hot, with lyrics charting the concerns of the narrative line, simplistic as it is." Karp labelled the score "top notch."[86]

Conversely, in a film context, Maslin found "most of the music does more harm than good."

"The rock 'n' roll is undistinguished," said Ansen. Hoberman noted "Ry Cooder's obtrusively banal score." With more gusto, he attacked the closing concert, writing that "Tonight" sounded "like Meat Loaf fronted by Debbie Boone."[87]

A more in-depth analysis was provided by Los Angeles media writer David Chute. He objected to the use of Jim Steinman's "Tonight" as opposed to the original Springsteen number, saying, "the upshot is . . . that the rocker whose work gave *Streets* its title and (presumably) its emotional focus is not represented on the music track. It's hard not to feel that an imprimatur has been withdrawn." The critic further objected that the essence of rock, blue-collar youth alienation, was absent from the film. "The problem with *Streets of Fire* . . . is that it's not *enough* like MTV; it abandons the experiment too soon," he wrote. Ending this provocative and worthwhile piece, Chute suggested that Springsteen's recently released *Born in the U.S.A.* "may stir people up in spite of themselves. I wish I could say the same for *Streets of Fire.*"[88]

The Springsteen comparison, however it applied to *Eddie and The Cruisers*, was somewhat shaky with *Streets*, although it is difficult to determine whether the alternative song would have worked. Most rock films close with the music being cranked up. In the context of the film, "Tonight" seemed appropriate.

Despite what some conservatives say in diatribes against the media, film critics rarely influence viewing habits. They bring attention to the product, but rarely influence it. *Flashdance, Footloose*, and *Staying Alive* would have folded in days had the critics exercised their so-called power. The teen subculture rarely acts on the dictates of *The New York Times* or *Variety*; word-of-mouth prevails. As *Star Trek* and *Indiana Jones* dominated the market, *Streets* ironically got lost in the comic-book world of sci-fi.

On September 28 MCA Home Video announced the release of *Streets* as a video cassette. With *Streets* everything that could malfunction did. Synergism, to work, has to be put in operation, not merely discussed in trade publications. "Working" a vehicle is different from "promoting" it.

"Who You Gonna' Call"/Ghostbusters

> . . . *[the title song] added another $20 million to the box office.*
> —Gary LeMel, Warner Brothers

Former *Saturday Night Live* player, Dan Aykroyd had written a script reuniting him with John Belushi. After Belushi's death in 1982, the project was revived with Harold Ramis and Bill Murray almost a year later. The seventy-five-page working script, due to the film-community rumor mill, rapidly became a hot property. *SNL* alumni were highly marketable. (Murray, however, had another project planned. With John Byrum, he was developing a remake of *The Razor's Edge*. Studios were leery of a serious adaptation by a comedian. "Well," suggested Akroyd, "tell 'em they [Columbia Pictures] can have *Ghostbusters* if they do the *Razor's Edge*."[89] The deal was consumated in less than an hour. Bernie Brillstein would co-produce with Ivan Reitman (*Meatballs, Stripes*) directing. Aykroyd/Ramis wrote the loose final version of the screenplay, based on *The Sentinel* (1977).

The technological innovations in the film transcended the usual "annual summer giggle" of the *SNL* mavens, according to Richard Schickel.[90] Richard Edlund, whose special effects credits included *Star Wars, Return of the Jedi, Raiders of the Lost Ark*, and the cinematography of Laszlo Kovacs's *Easy Rider*, created an impressible visual milieu. The picture started production in October 1983 and was completed in April.

Midway through the filming, an ectoplasmic character appeared on Sunset Boulevard billboards. The ghostly logo was captioned, "Coming to Save the World." No mention of the film was made. Ads were placed in major market newspapers *away* from the film pages. The ad was black with a white ghost encased in a red "prohibited" circle. The "no-ghosts-allowed" symbol seemed to appear everywhere. TV spots were purchased in fifteen-second bites during prime time. Still no mention of the feature film was made. Columbia Pictures' Ashley Boone, vice president of distribution and marketing, said, "Very few people knew what we were talking about, but they thought it was cute, interesting and memorable. For a movie campaign, it was minute in its frequency, but highly memorable."[91] The key in this ad drive was "word-of-mouth, which costs you nothing." In this respect, Columbia did more to hype the film and the album than the record company's promotion people. Both, obviously, would benefit from the campaign.

Columbia Pictures signed the soundtrack agreement with Arista Records. (The label, as Bell Records, had at one time been affiliated with the studio.) Ray Parker, Jr., on Arista in 1984, was called in to screen the picture. Executives told him they had sixty submissions for the title song, "but we don't like any of them." The composer of "Jack and Jill" and "The Other Woman" was asked to try his hand at a theme. The song needed to have a "hook," an attention-getting sound, and to include the film's name. "It's hard to write a song where your main objective is to use the word 'ghostbusters,' " Parker would say later. "I figured the best thing to do was to have somebody shout, 'Ghostbusters!' In order for that to work, I had to have something before it or after it. That's when I came up with the line, 'Who you gonna' call?' I wanted to make a simple, easy song people could sing along with and not have to think about.''[92] In two days, reportedly, the song was written and on the master tape.

Some observers questioned the song's creation. It was compared to Huey Lewis's "I Want a New Drug." The leader of The News saw "remarkable similarities" between his hit and the Parker effort. Lewis's manager "freaked" when he heard "Ghostbusters."[93] Multi-Oscar winner Elmer Bernstein did the scoring.

Director Ivan Reitman filmed a video, with MTV definitely in mind. A dance segment was set up, with Murray, Aykroyd, and Ramis leading a contingent of recognizable celebrities down a Manhattan street. The "names" included John Candy, Chevy Chase, Danny Devito, Peter Falk, Melissa Gilbert, and Carly Simon. MTV premiered the clip as an exclusive on the day of the picture's debut. A number of viewers believed the video participants were in the theater offering.

The effort was variously described as "wildly funny," "delightfully silly," and "a jumbled, unstable mix of media parody, satirical observation of social types, wild slapstick, and sneaky-dirty sex."[94]

Ghostbusters proved to be a success despite its $30 to $32-million price tag. ("Big picture" attempts at comedy in the Eighties were, deservedly, box office and aesthetic disasters. *The Blues Brothers* (1980) was overwhelmed by special effects—chases and other superfluous distractions. *1941* (1981) provoked laughter, but in all the wrong places. Both exploited *Saturday Night Live*, forgetting the centerpieces of the television show were the actors. *Ghostbusters* was a return, sort of, to roots.)

Manhattan—The Exorcism

In *Ghostbusters*, scared by flying index cards and books, a New York librarian needs help. Ray Parker's refrain echoes.

Three zany parapsychologists from Columbia University answer the distress call, only to be overwhelmed by the poltergeist. Their troubles escalate as the educational bastion cancels their ESP-related grant and unceremoniously expels them from their cluttered university quarters. Having been labelled an "academic disgrace," Dr. Peter Venkman (Bill Murray) rationalizes that the expulsion was an act of destiny. Drs. Stantz (Dan Aykroyd) and Spengler (Harold Remis) join him and start a new enterprise designed to counter supernatural forces. Their base of operations is an old Greenwich Village fire house. Their transportation is a used Cadillac hearse.

Dana Barrett (Sigourney Weaver) is a symphony musician living in the penthouse suite of a New York high-rise. Strange things are happening in the apartment, especially in the refrigerator. Eggs fry on the kitchen counter and when Barrett opens the fridge, a dragonlike miniature creature growls, "Zuul." Questioning her sanity, Dana sees a late-night television spot for "all your supernatural elimination needs." She contacts the ghosthunters.

Murray is more interested in Weaver than in what's happening in her kitchen. "I'll take her back to her apartment and check her out," he says quickly correcting himself to add, "er . . . check *it* out." Finding nothing mysterious, he comes on to Dana. She rejects him, underscoring his lack of supernatural expertise. "We both have the same problem," she says. "You."

A legitimate job offer comes as bits of "Cleanin' Up the Town" play. Weighted down with "Nuclear Accelerators," the ghostbusters manage to capture a green spirit, "full-floating vapor," while destroying most of a hotel ballroom and one entire floor. The flustered manager is presented a bill for $5,000.

Conveniently, a wave of ghost sightings occur in Manhattan. Headlines scream, "Ghost Fever Grips N.Y." The disoriented heroes' business soars. Murray tells a reporter, "No job is too big. No fee is too big." Winston Zeddmore (Ernie Hudson) joins the erstwhile ghost chasers as the supernatural mania persists. The quartet is now ready to confront the evil Zuul, who they discover is a 6,000-year-old Summarian demon. Dana asks, "What's he doing in my ice box?"

A subplot develops as the Environmental Protection Agency (EPA) descends upon the ghost fighters. In the person of Walter Peck (William Atherton), the EPA needs to know the monster's "impact on the environment." Venkman, using bureaucratese, refuses to cooperate.

Dana's apartment building, Spook Central, becomes the focus of the story. The gargoyles on the roof come to life. The monsters/demons inhabit the bodies of Dana and her neighbor, Louis Tully (Rick Moranis). In the film's terminology, she is the Gatekeeper, and he is the Keymaster. Possessed, Dana is transformed into a seductress. Venkman arrives for a date. Dana tells the flustered psychologist, "I want you inside of me." Venkman, sizing up the situation, replies, "Sounds like you already have two in there, honey."

Peck, doggedly pursuing the demon fighters, invades the fire station, has them arrested, and foolishly releases the captured spirits. The building explodes spectacularly, polluting the New York skyline. Spirit sightings plague Gotham. In desperation, the mayor frees the ghostbusters. They convince the politician he will have saved the lives of millions of *registered* voters if they can combat the forces of Zuul.

With apocalyptic pronouncements heralding the end of the world, the four media heroes climb to Dana's apartment. Stantz asks Venkman in a typical exchange, "Where do these stairs go?"

"They go up," is the response. Zuul's domain atop the building is reminiscent of Demille's Biblical epochs.

From Stantz's mind, Zuul conjures up a Godzilla-like, building-tall Marshmallow Man, who looks like a dangerous reject from a Thanksgiving Day Parade. The creature does battle with the stalwart ghostbusters. After a huge explosion, in which plaster, debris, and marshmallow parts rain down on New York City, the ghostbusters prevail. Louis, returned to a nerdish state, comments, "Boy, the superintendent is going to be pissed." Up come the closing theme and "Clean Up This Town" by The Bus Boys.

Reviews of the blockbuster movie were mixed. *Time* lavished praise on "everyone connected with *Ghostbusters* for thinking on a grandly comic scale and delivering the goofy goods, neatly timed and perfectly packaged."

"Everyone," said *Newsweek*, "seems to be working toward the same goal of relaxed insanity." Recognizing the big-picture comedic flops, *Boxoffice* noted, "It's probably the first time for this generation of comics that a big budget hasn't worked against the laughs."[95]

There was little neutral ground concerning *Ghostbusters*. Coleman, in the *New Statesman*, said "what rubbish is expensively spread before us." Kopkind added, "Too bad it is about to take over the world," a reference to the movie, not Zuul. "With all this going on, there is more attention to the special effects than to humor," suggested Maslin. The *New York Times* writer liked Murray and parts of the movie, but not the end product. Surprisingly, the *Variety* assessment was negatively cautious. Cohen warned that the movie "looks too good, but not fantastic results in the summer box office sweepstakes."[96] The opening weekend, in 1,339 theaters, the film grossed a record-setting $14 million. It also stole the thunder from *Streets of Fire* and other pictures.

Musically, only the Parker and Bus Boys compositions had any ties to the screen action. Elmer Bernstein wrote a credible score, but one device, totally unnecessary, was having Aykroyd tell his passenger, "Let's hear some music." On came an album cut. It was totally gratuitous.

Arista made no effort to scout the Top 40 market. The Parker single's entry level, at Number 68, occurred several days after the film's release. The video appeared at the same time. The album was issued a month after the film, video, and single, July 7, and enjoyed a slow but steady climb.

By 11 August, *Ghostbusters* could be found on the top of the *Billboard* singles chart, dislodging "When Doves Cry." It was also in MTV heavy rotation, exceeding the minimum four plays per day. Both trade charts recorded the album's nine-month stay. It would be certified platinum by year's end.

Arista got the better of the deal with four acts on the album. Although Parker and The Bus Boys were heard in the movie, The Thompson Twins plus Air Supply went along for the royalty ride.

The *Saturday Night Live* connection probably assisted most in the promotion of the film, and then the album. The exposure on MTV was significant. Airplay, in this instance, appears to have been typical for a hot rotation in its persuasive impact. The only remarkable aspect in the electronic promo campaign had been the attention-getting video. Polygram's bogus *Spinal Tap* marketing push easily surpassed that of *Ghostbusters*. As Jay Lasker observed, a blockbuster movie does sell product.

Another movie spoofing "creature" films was exhibited the same week as the Reitman project. *Gremlins*, a Steven Spielberg production, was aptly described as excellent monsters, not-so-hot story, and also a little mean-spirited: The reviewer was referring to Chris Walas's special effects. The relationship of the movie to its rock mini-album can cynically be described as covering all the bases. Michael Sambello of "Maniac," did the title song, "Mega Madness," with Peter Gabriel's "Out Out." Quarterflash's "Make It Shine," from the *Take Another Picture* album, filled out the rock music portion of the preadolescent vehicle.

Jerry Goldsmith, the seasoned scorer, composed the remainder of the album. Unfortunately, as Neil Portnow, EMI-America vice president, commented, "The tendency is that once there's a little success, everybody does it. And it doesn't mean that everybody can do it well."[97]

The Spielberg imprimatur provided sufficient bait to lure patrons into 1,511 moviehouses. The picture grossed $12.5 million during its first three days, $1.5 million less than the box office-smashing *Ghostbusters*.

"Baby I'm a Star:" Prince

Hey! Look me over
Tell me do u like what u see
—© 1984 Contemporary Music [ASCAP]

The leader of a pack in a brave new world
without rules or categories
—Ariel Swartley, media critic

Purple Rain spotlighted Prince, a personality uniformly described as an "enigma wrapped in a mystery." Other characterizations presented the lead as a murky, uncertain, self-enveloped star. Part truth/part fiction, or a mere publicity-generating device? "When he did talk," wrote Debby Miller, "he often contradicted himself. Rumors started to spread, and now his silence feeds them."[98] Prince rationalized, "I used to tease a lot of journalists early on because I wanted them to concentrate on the music and not so much on me . . . What was important was what came out of my system that particular day."[99] In the wake of this admission, Prince Rogers Nelson's background, central to the *Purple Rain* storyline, remains nebulous.

The Minneapolis-born son of jazz pianist John Nelson and singer Mattie Shaw grew up on the North Side. His parents were divorced in 1968 when Prince was ten years old. Self-taught on several instruments (numbers range from three—piano, guitar, and drums—to a "couple of dozen,") he formed Grand Central with Andre Anderson and Morris Day—at the age of thirteen. Between shuttling between domiciles, Prince led the teenage group in various musical competitions. (One opponent was Flyte Time, later renamed The Time, featuring Morris Day). At the age of sixteen, Prince wrote songs in Anderson's basement, three to four a day. They were "sexual songs," as Prince described them. Disgusted with the Minneapolis scene, Prince moved to New York. Through his sister, an "agent" entered the picture. Danielle was connected to the music industry in some unspecified manner: "She wanted me to sell my publishing for like $380 or something like that," Prince said. He returned to Minneapolis, where a part-time promoter/advertising executive, Owen Husney, became his manager. Warner Brothers, A&M, and CBS were contacted.

Prince claimed, "They [Warners] made me do a demo tape. So I did it, and then they said, 'that's pretty good,' and so I did another one. Then they said, 'Okay, we can produce your album.' "[100]

Lenny Waronker, now Warner president, later expanded upon Prince's version of these happenings. "I met him when we first signed him," he said. "Russ Titelman [producer] and I took him into the studio one day, much to his chagrin. So we said, 'Play the drums,' and he played the drums and put a bass part on, a guitar part. And we just said, 'Yeah, fine that's not good enough.' "[101] The important audition was to determine if the artist was capable of producing, as he was already signed. It was Husney who began the image manipulation. Prince became a teenage *wunderkind*—he was twenty in 1978—endowed with a monarchial name. (He actually was named after his father's jazz trio, Prince Rogers.) Allegedly, Prince was a one-man band on the demo tape, although he said,

"Well, on the demo tapes I didn't play too many instruments."[102] The "musical genius" from the Land of 10,000 Lakes, however, enthusiastically went along with the ruse. After supposedly being signed for "well over a million," an album, *For You*, was released. The title, which ran $40,000 over budget, stiffed.

Bob Cavallo, Joe Ruffalo, and Steve Fargnoli (CRF) signed the mercurial, multifaceted performer in 1979. The management team also represented Weather Report, Earth, Wind and Fire, and Ray Parker, Jr. Prince's management change paid off. A self-titled album, *Dirty Mind*, and *Controversy* each were certified gold. The original efforts stressed Hendrix-style guitar riffs, with *a cappella*, gospel, and Motown mixed in. *Dirty Mind* established Prince's new trademark, licentious journeys into Freud with a touch of Kraft-Ebbing. One writer tagged him, "a raunchy prophet of porn."[103] Critic Stephen Holden observed, "On *Dirty Mind*, Prince exalted brother-sister incest, oral sex and lesbianism, among other carnal delights. *Controversy* moved beyond sex to religion and politics. Though the rhetoric was naive, the music was hotter than ever—a heavily synthesized pop-funk lava through which Prince's gasps and whines cut a sharp swath."[104]

The double album *1999* established Prince as a *bona fide* crossover star. The multiplatinum effort contained hits such as "Delirious," "1999," and "Little Red Corvette." The metaphorical "Corvette" was heavily rotated on MTV, unusual at the time for a black artist. This visual success, and an equally successful tour, motivated the "monumental chutzpah," according to Kurt Loder, for Prince to covet a feature-film role based on his brief life.[105] As egoistic as the request sounded, Prince's instincts had merit. Many in the music industry agreed with Jo Bergman's assessment, "Prince pretty much directs his own videos."[106] On screen, there was a charisma absent from most rockers *qua* actors. As Elvis Presley had painfully discovered, electronically lit runways are quite different from intriguing plots and correct camera angles. Prince needed a vehicle to showcase his persona. "I feel that I'm going to have to do exactly what's on my mind and be exactly the way I am," he told an interviewer. "I just want to do what I'm really about."[107] (This was two months prior to filming *Rain*.) He expressed that wish to Steve Fargnoli, who took some of the musician's vague jottings and ideas to film studios. "A lot of laughs" was the collective reaction.

His management team, aware of Prince's economic importance, agreed to finance a project which could easily have become a multimillion dollar, narcissistic home movie. They didn't have a script or specific concept.

CRF approached William Blinn, executive producer of the highly acclaimed television series *Fame*. Rumors abounded that the show would not be renewed for a third season. Under the circumstances, Blinn, who had scripted *Brian's Song*, was receptive to writing a movie. He was, however, unfamiliar with Prince.

After several meetings with the rock artist, Blinn began to write *Dreams*. The story involved The Kid (Prince), whose parents died in a murder-suicide. A girl, Vanity, enters The Kid's music world in Minneapolis and fills the emotional void created by his father's rage. One trait of Blinn's fictional Kid was, "music was a womb."

Fame was, however, picked up for a third season. Blinn departed, leaving behind a roughly drafted script and an unfilled demand that "purple" be in the film's title. He would remain as coauthor.

CRF stumbled upon Al Magnoli, whose main credit was as film editor of *Reckless*. He had had no experience overseeing a feature film. After several conversations with Cavallo and Prince, Magnoli agreed to direct. Upon spending a month in Minneapolis, especially the First Avenue Club, and soaking up the milieu, Magnoli rewrote Blinn's draft. It became the final, "nearly autobiographical" storyline. "We [Magnoli] used parts of my past and present to make the story pop more," said Prince, "but it was a *story*."[108]

Location shooting was scheduled to begin 1 November 1983. Most of the songs, "Computer Blues," "I Would Die For U," and "Let's Get Crazy," were cut prior to the filming. Prince's improbable "home movie" was finished in the frosty atmosphere of the Twin Cities within seven weeks, to avoid winter, at a relatively modest cost of $7 million. Reportedly, Warner had appropriated an additional $2 million to promote the "accompanying album." As late as June 1984 Warner Record executives were publicly distancing themselves from the uncertain film project.

While utilizing the fluid-synergism approach, Warner Brothers Records preferred to bank on Prince as a solo artist. *1999*, a two-record set, was platinum. Consequently, as the label's president of sales, Lou Dennis, indicated, "The album is *not* quite a soundtrack; it's music from the movie, but the material that The Time and Appollonia 6 perform in the movie isn't included. To us, this would still be a Prince album, without the movie."[109] Ruffalo emphasized the separation in *Variety*, saying, "It's our belief that this project was sold to Warner Brothers as an excellent film." He continued to suggest that a "synergistic marketing of the record and film" remained on the drawing board."[110]

One of the main tasks of any artist's management team is to obtain company support. Cavallo, *et al.*, easily pitched Prince's musical material from the film to Warner Brothers Records as a follow-up to *1999*. Getting the label behind a platinum-selling artist required little effort. Persuading the film division required considerable more energy.

A rock star's box office appeal, in 1984, was highly questionable. Movies starring Mick Jagger, The Bee Gees, David Bowie, and other recording names had drowned in seas of red ink. Musical charisma does not always translate onto the big screen; many singers are poor actors. In addition, a platinum-selling act's fan pool is easily exhausted on a summer weekend. Film executives were highly conscious of these pitfalls. Prince's project required outside momentum to convince the studio to give the film a high marketing priority.

Cavallo, Ruffalo, and Fargnoli used a tired, but useful, marketing strategy. The trade press blitz began in May. Ruffalo told *Variety* of the artist's crossover appeal to the fourteen- to twenty-five-year-old audience. "We believe Prince has much greater name value than the number of records that he's sold," Bob Cavallo informed *Billboard*. "There's something about Prince that piques people's interest a little more than some other artists. People don't know a lot about him; he's a little mysterious and has a controversial image." Fargnoli added, "The studios had to be educated as to who Prince was, what he meant, and whether he had the potential to be an actor on a screen."[111] The support material was designed to sell records and heighten studio support for *Purple Rain*. Then Prince's desire to be *more* than a mere rock star would be satisfied.

The ice-breaking scout single was scheduled for 16 May release. "When Doves Cry," a post-filming selection, was chosen. It entered the *Billboard* chart at Number 57 2 June 1984. The trade chose the selection as their top pick, characterizing the performance as "direct and emotional," with the production being "daringly spare." It was destined to become the Number 1 single of 1984. As the record steadily climbed the chart, MTV aired the video incessantly, or so it seemed.

Prince was a natural for videoclips. His concert and performance clips were drenched with sensual magnetism. One writer noted, "He can stare down the camera like nobody's business, and that's all he has to do to make the screen smolder."[112] This presence, many insiders felt, was the key to *1999*'s three-million-copy sales. Warners was to capitalize on the success of these clips by issuing "When Doves Cry," a mix of film and concept footage, and "Let's Go Crazy," from the opening sequence of the movie.

"Let's Go Crazy" appeared in *Billboard* the week of 4 August at Number 45. It was the second single from the film and reached the top spot for a two-week stay on 29 September 1984. Remarkably, two more singles were culled from the album.

The album hit the streets 29 June. Warners claimed that the record sold 1.3-million copies "out of the box." Lou Dennis said, "I don't know what you can compare it with. As we shipped the album, 'When Doves Cry' was the No. 1 black, pop and dance single. By the time the film opens, we will have an album that went crazy . . . *Purple Rain* is one of the most exciting records I've ever worked on, and I've been here for a lot of records."[113] The fact that Michael Jackson's *Victory* album appeared almost the same day no doubt added to Dennis's excitement.

Kurt Loder did the four-star *Rolling Stone* record review, saying that "the spirit of Jimi Hendrix must surely smile down on Prince Rogers Nelson," and ending, "anyone partial to great creators should own this record."[114] The album would persist, according to Robert Palmer, long after "the Jackson and Springsteen albums are packed away . . . as an enduring rock classic."[115]

In retrospect, the game plan worked. Jeff Ayeroff, Warners marketing vice president, noted that the record division had delivered, as promised, a top-charted single and album, and MTV heavy rotation, prior to the film's release. Ayeroff's game plan, he said, was to capture the urban-contemporary window with airplay, as the "black market is not cablized."

To continue the momentum, Warner Brothers made a deal with MTV. The *quid pro quo* involved awarding the music channel exclusive rights to the movie's Hollywood premiere party July 26 and the underwriting of MTV's production costs for cablecasting the gathering.[116] In return, MTV did spots for the arranged "special," thus continuing the momentum for the synergized project. This type of an arrangement is fairly common for MTV. Specials, by their very nature, promote the product *and* the channel.

In Prince's case, the rotation status of the videoclips was unaffected. The chart positioning of the recorded material guaranteed cableplay. (In other instances, rotations have been known to be, as one insider said, "political.")

The promo party worked well for all involved, as Lionel Richie, John Cougar Mellencamp, Stevie Nicks, and Little Richard attended, joined by members of Kiss, Quiet Riot, Devo, Talking Heads, and others.

Based on the success of "Doves," the single, the videoclip, and other spots, *Purple Rain's* five sneak previews were sellouts. In San Diego, 1,000 tickets were sold in fifteen minutes. The result, according to Joe Ruffalo, was, "a national commitment from them [the film studio] for the film's release, which is planned for 700 theaters and could go higher."[117] The national opening occurred in 917 theaters.

Film exhibitors are decidedly conservative; they like established, saleable properties. The Stallones, Eastwoods, and a handful of proven bankable attractions are exhibited by the picture renters *en masse*. Prince was beyond the comprehension of these film retailers. The fact that *1999* was triple platinum, and the soundtrack was rapidly approaching that figure, was insignificant to mall chain-theater operators. Bob Cavallo correctly described the mind set of exhibitors: "If Prince has two million record fans, you can swallow them up in a Saturday."[118] Only a bandwagon effect will influence theater owners. *Purple Rain* lived up to the hype surrounding it. It was Prince's picture, with all the ambiguity of the character highlighted under Magnoli's tutelage.

Purple Rain

"Ladies and Gentlemen, The Revolution" overlayed the Warner logo. Centerstage is The Kid (Prince), situated in his natural habitat, The First Avenue Club and Seventh Street Entry, awash in a strobe-drenched, purple haze, repeating, "Hang on children, He's coming. He's coming. He's coming." Interspersed in the sequence are quick cuts introducing the central players, especially the arrival of Apollonia (Patty Kotero) into the Minneapolis music world. The intercuts established "more in pantomime than any of the subsequent dialogue sequences," opined Lally.[119] The patrons appear to enhance the performer and the song, but not in the usual showcase structure. The club becomes the central backdrop for the tensions, antagonisms and revelations to follow. Morris (Day) and The Time follow The Kid, accompanied by the ever-present comedic foil Jerome (Benton).

The Kid, Morris, Apollonia and Revolution—especially Wendy and Lisa—are the denizens of the egomaniacal dream factory. Apollonia's sneaking into First Street and Morris's constantly primed "zoot-suited, concert-stage persona" highlight the desirability of the night life.

The visual interchange between the Kid and Apollonia, without a word being spoken, suggests the magnetic power of stardom and belonging. "They look at each other," said Pauline Kael, "and that's all there is."[120]

The introductory club scenes set up the film's juxtaposition of the light and dark sides of The Kid. Leaving the glamor of the music world, the Prince character is thrust into the "real" world of domestic verbal and physical violence. He finds his father (Clarence Williams III) assaulting the mother character (played by Olga Karlatos). When he attempts to intervene, the father's rage becomes focused on The Kid, whom he knocks on the floor. (Rock star Prince, when asked about his music, said, "All fantasies, yeah. Because I didn't have anything around me . . . there were no people.")[121]

The "autobiographical" story is complicated by Morris, the villainous rival, who schemes to destroy the Kid's escape route through the fantasy avenue of music. The street conversation between Morris and the club owner, Billy Sparks, emphasize these elements:

MORRIS: You need to get rid of him . . . he's just playing a lot of shit nobody wants to hear/
BILLY: Just like his old man, Francis L.
MORRIS: Now the Kid's doing the same shit!

Morris continues to suggest that he is forming a girl group which could be The Kid's replacement at First Avenue.

The predictable romantic link between The Kid and Apollonia evolves as Prince practices a form of misogyny, reflecting his parental role model, by tricking her into stripping and plunging into a chilled lake.

Morris and Jerome again muddy up the situation as they plot to entice Appollonia into the female trio, and Day's bedroom. In the process, they enact one of their comedy routines, reminiscent of the famous Abbott and Costello sketch, "Who's on First?" They perform a street rap version of "The Password is What?" "What's the password?" Morris Day's comedy makes him a likeable, although nefarious, character.

The Kid's quest for stardom is also distorted by the feminine members of Revolution, again hinting at misogyny. Wendy (Melvoin) and Lisa (Coleman) pitch their demo tape at The Kid. He ignores them. Wendy, angered, lashes out, saying, "You know, you can really hurt people. Doesn't that mean anything to you? Doesn't that make you feel like shit?"

The tape provides a traditional teaser throughout. Prince starts it on several occasions and tinkers with the opening bars on the basement piano. As Ken Terry wrote, "Although we don't hear the entire song until Prince's performance of it at the climax, the premonitary exposures of the tune serve as a unifying thread."[122]

Apollonia's musical ambitions, trivialized by The Kid, are encouraged by Morris, who invites her to join his proposed group. She protests that The Kid will help her. Morris responds "He's never done anything in his whole life for anyone but himself."

Returning to The Kid's basement, the setting for their previous sensuous love scene, Apollonia presents him with a white guitar. Then, when she announces that she is joining Morris's group, The Kid knocks her to the floor. Domestic violence is reenacted. "The Kid sees his father's madness infecting both his music and his own life, and he tries burying himself even deeper in his music, with negative results to both," wrote Kirk.[123]

The kid's tenure at First Avenue is further jeopardized with the emergence of Apollonia 6. Billy summons The Kid. "One of you has got to go," he says. Prince ponders, as "When Doves Cry" plays, "Maybe I'm just like my father, too bold." There is an innercut to the ever-present quarreling. "Maybe you're just like my mother, she's never satisfied . . ." Apollonia is seen. "Why do we scream at each other? . . ."

The father figure retreats into his deepening, depressive self-pity, telling his son, "Never get married." The domestic situation is deteriorating.

The Kid lashes out from his pulpit, the stage, upon spying Apollonia with Morris. "I knew a girl named Nikki/I guess you could say she was a sex fiend . . ." He glares, points, grinds, and writhes on stage. She flees. Increasingly, with the exception of "When Doves Cry," the musical performances appear to be moving the storyline forward.

In a scene unsuccessfully devised to manifest Prince's frustration and rage, Billy appears to restate, "The stage is no place for your personal shit, man . . . Your music makes no sense to no one but yourself."

The plot has heightened to the point of resolution, but it's time for Apollonia 6's debut of "Sex Shooter" at the up-town club, The Taste. Musically, this is the low point of the film. The piece is contrived and reminiscent of the stage scenes in 1950s Grade-Bs. Following the show, Morris drunkenly escorts "new star" Apollonia to his limo. Astride his huge purple motorcycle, The Kid menacingly appears, snatching up the girl. "Long-hair faggot," shouts Morris.

Another disjointed scene finds the singers quarreling under a freeway ramp. The Kid raises his fist, but stops, for some unexplained reason. She willfully tosses his gift of jewelry to the ground, indicating it's over. Some might contend that it never really started. Vincent Canby said, "Mr. Magnoli, whose first theatrical film this is, has seen to it that the movie is so efficiently edited that the story ends sometime before the movie does."[124]

Returning to his domestic purgatory, The Kid melodramatically flips a light switch, a split cinematic second before a gun is discharged. Francis's failed suicide attempt creates the emotional catharsis as the Prince character flashes visions of himself hanging.

Self-realization is expanded when he finds the sheet music written by his comatose father. Francis once told The Kid about music, "It's all up here," pointing, "in my head." He is the son of the father. Redemption is on the way.

The climax occurs where it all began, the First Avenue stage. With smoke bellowing and lights flashing, Prince's presence dominates, as he stands holding the white guitar. Haltingly he says, "I'd like to dedicate this to my father . . . this is a song two girls in the band wrote, Lisa and

Wendy . . ." The now-familiar opening triplets resound: "I never meant to cause you any sorrow/I never meant to cause you any pain . . . I only want to see you laughing in the purple rain." The gathering throng explodes into arm-waving motions intermixed with applause. Triumphantly, The Kid marches backstage. Removing his elegant jacket, he races to his massive bike. Apollonia is waiting with an "all-is-forgiven" attitude. Reinforced, The Kid returns for an encore. He appears oblivious to the applause and cheers. A defiant, self-congratulatory smirk crosses his face. "I Would Die For You" is the finale, again, intercut with solutions to all of the problems presented in the film. As director Magnoli would later note, "We wanted to say: life's a bitch but *wow*, if you can just get it together . . ."[125]

Music critic Robert Palmer wrote, in *The New York Times*, "what the film critics will make of all this remains to be seen, but the album *Purple Rain* is a winner, creatively and commercially." The writer did not have to wait long. *Times* writer Vincent Canby found the film "the flashiest album cover ever to be released as a movie . . . though sometimes arresting to look at [it] is a cardboard come-on to the record it contains." The film critic, aware of the *a priori* successes of the audio, added that the movie "may become a hit, but of a different caliber." Janet Maslin complemented Canby, suggesting, "The musical sequences have a way of lending credence, or at least interest, to the rest of what happens."[126] At the *Times*, it was the music that drove the movie.

Other critics applauded Prince, the persona and the performer, but had reservations about the storyline and the production. Candidly, Andrew Kopkind wrote, "Prince's greatest commercial triumph is his movie, but it is not the perfect vehicle for his talents." David Denby contended that the movie was not very good, but it was "a rock star's mixed-up confession and self-glorifying fantasy." The *Film Journal* commented, "Prince's charismatic performance in *Purple Rain* should turn this flawed film into a popular success." Pauline Kael added, "He learns to reach out and touch somebody's hand, and that frees him to be a star."

"As a rock star, he's outrageous, but plausible. As a movie star, he's unprecedented," wrote *Newsweek's* Ansen. Even Carol Cooper, who tore the film's structure to shreds, admitted to reason the film worked was due to the strength of the peculiarly "charismatic gestalt" of Prince.[127]

These "money quotes" were beyond any publicist's wildest dream. Some writers went so far as to compare *Purple Rain* to *Woodstock, The Last Waltz, A Hard Day's Night,* and, by Sarris's, implication *Citizen Kane.* The *Los Angeles Herald Examiner* led with "Prince delivers the *best* rock film *ever* made" (emphasis added). Only Chu and Cafritz, incorrectly, labelled *Rain* as a "boring rock video" urging, "Spend your time and money elsewhere." In a more tranquil moment, Canby, Cooper, and Denby captured the ethos of the vehicle by indicating that the enigmatic Prince exhibited both strengths and weaknesses. "His screen presence," observed Canby, "is a pale reflection of the dynamic recording personality."[128] While not remotely akin to *Hard Day* (or *Citizen Kane*), *Purple Rain* easily transcended *Flashdance, Footloose* and other performance films by its striking, if egocentric, uniqueness.

Rain grossed $7.7 million its opening weekend. The production costs were recovered in three days. At the end of its monumentally successful run, this "home video" earned more than $100 million.

By the close of 1984, the album was purchased by ten million consumers. Two singles, "When Doves Cry" and "Let's Go Crazy," charted at Number 1. The Times' "Jungle Love" and "The Bird" broke past the Top 40. The home video, budget priced for a feature film at $29.95, was a hit. D. Barry Reardon of Warner Distribution summed up the project as an "ideally balanced campaign between Warner Brothers Records, MTV, and our film division."[129] Synergism, temporarily at least, was vindicated.

Following in the footsteps of *Making Michael Jackson's Thriller, Purple Rain* furthered the synergism between film and music. Warner Home Video released the video cassette several weeks prior to the 1984 Christmas rush. The initial shipment of 400,000 copies was followed, according to the company, by 70,000 reorders. These numbers augured a spot in sales surpassed only by the highly touted *Thriller* video. According to *Billboard*, *Purple Rain* was penetrating the record/tape merchandising market. Camelot's video buyer said, "We will probably put 50 music video titles into 96 of our stores next week . . . the potential for music video is there."

"This is a very important item for Christmas," Record Bar's Steve Bennett indicated. "We only got into the Michael Jackson in a kind of limited way." He planned to rack more cassettes. Chamber, however, wisely cautioned, "Prince is not the norm."[130]

Purple Rain began a trend by demonstrating that blockbuster soundtrack films could be marketed to young VCR users. A 1988 AGB Television Research study of 986 VCR households had reported that people under eighteen are heavy viewers, and prerecorded cassettes account for 87 percent of machine viewing. Moreover, the under-eighteen age group spent 61 percent more time than adults with prerecorded tapes.[131] Cognizant of this phenomenon, advertisers began including lead-in spots on videos such as *Top Gun*, the first, *Platoon*, and *E.T.*

Woman in Red: Moliere Goes Top 10

> *Oh everyone has got a weakness in life*
> *Girl, you just happen to be mine.*
> —© 1984 Jobete Music Co. [ASCAP]

Mel Brooks and Gene Wilder are Yuppie cult figures. They, however, have managed, with certain vehicles like *Blazing Saddles* and *The Producers*, to access a wider audience. Wilder had set out to make *Woman in Red*, a remake of a sex farce of the late 1970s. (The seven-year itch theme has been the grist for the movie makers since silents.) To shore up the adult market and perhaps reach the younger theatergoers, Jack Frost Sanders, the producer, toyed with using Dionne Warwick for a musical theme. The singer, best known as the voice of Burt Bacharach and Hal David, had had considerable adult contemporary success with the themes from *The Valley of the Dolls* and *Alfie*. She, however, recommended Stevie Wonder.

Wonder, a notoriously slow songsmith, agreed to do the score. Orion Pictures held up the final prints to accommodate the composer's work habits. Motown, naturally, produced the album.

Jay Lasker, savoring his unexpected success with *The Big Chill*, became concerned about the project upon hearing Wonder's original efforts. The label president also wanted the long-awaited and promised solo album. "When he first presented it [the soundtrack] to me, I really tried to discourage his doing the soundtrack," Lasker recalled, "because he was just about ready to deliver his new LP which he had been working on for four years . . . I didn't think the three songs he had sung were very good. So he went back and did some more songs, of which 'I Just Called to Say I Love You' was one. This is the record I picked and said I want out as a single."[132]

The score was considerably more "commercial" than Wonder's usual hi-tech fare. The Lasker pick was an ideal scout record, even though Wonder's tardiness prevented an early prerelease. Adult Contemporary (AC) stations hotly rotated the song.

As the film opens, the camera pans the San Francisco skyline, setting on a hotel-building ledge. A lone figure, Theodore "Teddy" Pierce (Gene Wilder), a public relations executive, is precariously perched on the outcropping. "How the hell did I get up here?" he asks.

(Critic Jimmy Summer's warning immediately comes to mind. Those adverse to mid-life sexual crises *a la* Moliere are "going to be driven up the wall" by this movie," he wrote.[133]

Wilder's adaptation of *Pardon Mon Affaire* (1977) finds the muddled protagonist struck with awe at the sight of the long-legged Charlotte (Kelly Le Brock) in a Marilyn Monroe-esque scene literally lifted from *Seven Year Itch*. This time the dress is red.

Obsessed by the vision, Teddy begins his middle-aged "crisis." He spies the model in an outer office of the advertising agency. In a twist common to French films, he reaches the office wallflower, lonely Ms. Milner (Gilda Radner), and mistakenly invites her to dinner, thinking, of course, that he's talking to the beautiful Charlotte. Doggedly, he continues his pursuit.

The planned rendezvous is aborted after Didi Pierce (Judith Ivey), his unbelievably loyal wife, empathizes with disillusioned wives. "I'm really a very jealous woman," she asserts, condemning philandering husbands. In one of the movie's few funny scenes, she accidentally discharges a revolver into an open bedroom drawer. A pair of Teddy's shorts are blown away. This symbolic castration is highlighted as she sits, complaining, with her plotting spouse. All the while, she is loosely holding a handgun pointed at his private parts. He skips the dinner date with Ms. Radner.

In scenes reminiscent of *Tin Men*, the homely office worker retaliates by vandalizing Teddy's car. Gilda Radner does the best she can with a shallow role as Wilder's vexation. The mistaken-identity gag continues throughout the film, as do Pierce's predicaments.

Despite one idiotic setback after another, Teddy persists in his Walter Mittyish chase. Just when Wilder's credibility is nearly spent, he plots to fly to Los Angeles to meet the woman of his dreams. The flight is diverted to San Diego. Stranded at the airport, he gloats, "I have adventure in my life"—two women are waiting in different cities. Nothing seems to affect the ad man's self-delusion.

Finally arranging a date, Teddy takes Charlotte to a birthday meeting with his grandmother. It turns out to be a surprise party. Didi and the two children are present. Teddy's buddies come to the rescue. John spirits Charlotte out of the party. Unmasked, the pursuit now should be over, but, as befits a hidden persuader, Teddy is whisked to a meeting with the model. Arriving at her luxurious hotel room, the once cool and aloof woman suspends reality and joins in Wilder's fantasy. "I want you more than I have wanted any other man," she says, as the disrobing begins. They awkwardly undress and climb onto the waterbed. In a totally uncharacteristic line, she purrs to Teddy, "Come and get it, cowboy." The buzzer interrupts. "My husband's downstairs," she says. Reenacting a scene from Grade-B farces, Teddy climbs onto the ledge overlooking a courtyard some 100 feet below. Rescue crews and television cameras descend on the hotel. The Pierce family dutifully watches the proceedings.

Promising never to sin again—impure thoughts—Teddy jumps into the safety net. While suspended in midair, he spies a comely female reporter. To be continued?

American film critics seem in awe of comedies with a French connection. *Woman In Red* benefitted from this. *Time's* Schickel, in a two-paragraph review, called the film one of "this summer's more pungent pleasures, a well made sex farce of classical proportions."

"Lusty comedy should have late-summer success," offered *Variety*. Maslin said, "Most of the film is more appealing than its premise."[134]

A few writers politely dissented. Cautiously, *Boxoffice* called it "a good adaptation of a French sex farce, but *only* if one likes that sort of filmmaking." The movie, following in the path of *10*, once again illustrated that "to be a sexually aggressive person in contemporary American movies is to be a clown and a loser," commented Denby. David Palmieri was more direct: "There's a sad, restrained unoriginality to Wilder's comedy . . . as if his desire to fashion his own narratives has hampered his understanding of why he was funny, most memorably in *The Producers* and *Young Frankenstein*." Edelstein described Wilder as a "weirdly schizo director cruelly insensitive one moment and maudlin the next. His films can be amusing for a second and then ghastly."[135]

As with *Purple Rain*, the Motown contribution was the album. Stevie Wonder's last album had appeared in 1980. The package very likely would have gone platinum without a film or Dionne Warwick's duets. A few complaints were voiced concerning her inclusion in the package.

Rolling Stone infrequently runs soundtrack reviews, but Christopher Connelly did write up *Woman In Red*. Predictably, the writer mentioned the promised in-progress album and turned his attention to his single. " 'I Just Call,' " he wrote, "sounds as inventive as a Wurlitzer on automatic: The song doesn't build or climax . . .

"The rest of the material," he went on, "is dreary, if amiable, adult-contemporary fodder, further dragged down by Dionne Warwick's narcoticizing presence on three cuts. Perhaps Wonder didn't want his music to overshadow the movie it accompanies."[136] Most film critics paid scant attention to the scoring, focusing on Wilder.

Motown Records was the big winner. Lasker was able, finally, to get an album from the label superstar. A bonus was the Number 1 single. (Since the mid-Seventies, Wonder has become a predominantly crossover album performer.)

Woman In Red enjoyed a respectable eleven-week opening theater run. The original ticket gross totaled $12.5 million. The hit single probably sold more tickets than the film farce itself.

Misunderstanding: Teachers

Teachers, moved up from its originally scheduled Christmas debut to the "back-to-school" early October period, was advertised as a social commentary on America's secondary school system. Instead, what appeared was a cross between *Ridgemont High* and *Blackboard Jungle*. The film raised many issues and answered none except, perhaps, that outpatients from Riverdale Mental Hospital can make meritorious high school teachers.

Director Arthur Hiller (*The Americanization of Emily, Love Story*), admitted, "I would like to do films of social relevance. But somehow, I get caught up in comedy role." *Teachers*, he said, unlike *Blackboard Jungle*, became a "black comedy about teaching, about the problems of teachers, students, administrators, school boards, and parents. It doesn't offer solutions, but it does say that you have to face the problem and do something about it, not just give up . . . that's a terribly important message."[137] This point frequently was lost in the comedy skits throughout the film. The most positive review ended, "It celebrates the victory of caring."[138]

As the film begins, a uniformed officer unlocks the door to John F. Kennedy High as the student body crushes in. The characters are introduced in the principal's office, under the familiar sign, "Know Thy Self." Lisa (JoBeth Williams), a crusading attorney, appears to take depositions in the *Calvin Case*. (John Calvin had graduated without learning to read.) Incidents document the chaotic conditions. The teachers have a 10-percent daily absentee tally. The school psychologist flips when a teacher mimeographs his *daily* examinations. Nicknamed "Ditto" (Royal Dano), he has won three teaching awards for running "an orderly class." In one of the funnier scenes, Ditto dies, and students parade in and out of the classroom without noticing. When the ambulance attendants finally find the Dano character, he is pronounced dead. An instructor asks, "How can you tell?" In the office, a teacher checks her .38 pistol.

To fill the classrooms, substitutes are called. Herbert (Richard Mulligan), a mental patient, responds. Throwing the text out of the window, he wins the hearts and minds of the students by performing in costumes of historical characters, ranging from Lincoln to Custer.

The Calvin suit is stonewalled by the school administration, lead by superintendent Dr. Burke (Lee Grant) and vice principal Roger (Judd Hirsch), who plot a cover-up. The major protagonist in this educational maze is Alex Jural (Nick Nolte), a Sixties burnout, who has given up on the system and is willing to go along with the administration. He feels the primary motive in education is money. Roger rationalizes the bottom line, drunkenly saying, "We're the last stand of civilization, if we fail—ANARCHY."

The plot is further complicated with the introduction of Eddie (Ralph Macchio), a problem student. He, too, is illiterate. Alex is assigned to counsel the youth. Lisa, a former student of Alex's, is having trouble with a deposition. The principal answers all of the questions with, "I don't know." Totally afraid of making decisions, he really is uninformed. Her frustration showing, Lisa laments, "It's not a school anymore; it's a lonely bin." To which Alex replies, "It's not about education; it's about money."

The Nolte character, rarely teaching, discusses the case in class. The negative responses of the students prompt an assignment in "communication." Eddie excels by stealing a camera and photographing conditions in the building. The photos are run in the school paper. Roger is furious.

The next crisis involves one of Alex's students, Diane (Laura Dern), impregnated by a gym coach, the last of three. Eddie steers her to the social studies teacher. Driving back with Alex, in a throwaway line, she says, "I just had an abortion. I'm old enough to smoke," asking for a cigarette.

A fellow instructor, Carl Rosenberg, confesses that the school's policy is to graduate everyone, despite evidence of achievement. Roger sides with the administration.

Eddie printed a photo of an undercover agent in the school with a sign reading "NARC." When a raid ensues, all of the drugs in the building are found in the narcotics officer's locker. Reese, a mentally unstable student, panics, grabbing the weapon stolen from the pistol-packing teacher. The police needlessly shoot him.

The Riverdale attendants catch up with Herbert, dressed appropriately as General Custer. The students boo as he is led away. In the hall, he tells Jural, with pride, "I am a teacher!"

The death of Reese resurrects Nolte's idealism. He will support Rosenberg's testimony. Lisa is shocked to discover her firm has settled out of court for $50,000. "We're just a business," says her boss. She realizes Alex was correct. The economic imperative prevails.

Alex's resignation is requested. After unsuccessful appeals to his "friend" Roger and others, the teacher gives in. As he is packing his things, Lisa and the students, accompanied by Joe Cocker's "Edge of Night," intervene. In a once again totally unnecessary scene, Lisa performs Alex's dictum that the key to understanding JFK High is to "walk naked" through the halls. She does, interrupted by a false fire alarm. Students mill in front of the evacuated building. Jural confronts Dr. Burke, announcing he is remaining because, quoting Herbert, "I'm a teacher." "Understand" by Bob Seger resounds.

Despite the rousing close, most critics did not accept the screenwriter's intent. The consensus was that the W.R. McKinney script was "unwieldy, unsteady, fragmented," or a raft "set adrift, looking for a logical line to which their bedraggled characters might cling." David Ansen wrote, "Was there no one on the set who could tell the good ideas from the bad?"

"No matter what the actors do—and they do try everything—the script finally gets the best of them," noted *Boxoffice*. *Commonweal*'s O'Brien said, "The plot is saddled with too many other relationships and absurdities to make a serious, and finally, even intelligible, statement about the problems of teaching or teachers." The movie is "not as thematically effective as *'Up The Down Staircase'* (1967) or *'Blackboard Jungle'* (1955)," wrote Loynd, "because it lacks cohesion." Maslin charged the script with alternating "believable episodes with several that are anything but."[139]

Nearly all of the reviewers praised specific skits and performances. Richard Mulligan and Ralph Macchio (*The Karate Kid*) received considerable plaudits.

The motion picture was interesting, but it did not venture beyond the sum of its parts. Had the screenwriter made a black comedy or a straight social commentary, it could have worked. As it was, it turned out to be a miasma of enticing scenes without a serious conclusion.

Teachers did add a synergistic wrinkle. The credits began with "soundtrack produced by Aaron Russo . . . on Capitol Records." The credit may have partially worked as some film reviewers actually referred to the rock-based score. (Production notes in press kits include score and song credits.)

Treatments of the music stressed its marketing appeal. "The movie's soundtrack is made up exclusively of music by pop performers, so apparently the producers are trying to appeal to young people" observed *Boxoffice*. *Variety* billed it as "a box office asset but song placement in the narrative doesn't propel the plot as it might."[140] The musical inserts, while uneven, did function. Joe Cocker's "Edge of a Dream" was superfluous to the "stay Alex" scene, but overall the positioning of the songs was above average: somewhere between *Ghostbusters* and *Woman In Red*.

Teachers presented a strong musical lineup. Capitol's resident artists Bob Seger, Joe Cocker, 38 Special, and The Motels were joined by Z.Z. Top, Ian Hunter, and Queen's Freddie Mercury. The scout single, "Teacher Teacher" by .38 Special, while not "Rock Around The Clock," had promise. The strongest cut was Z.Z. Top's "Cheap Sunglasses," the concert version. The act, however, was contracted to Warner Records, and as a previously recorded song lacks film identification, it is not likely to stir Top-40 program directors. The album did garner some AOR action.

The synergy process was followed. "Teacher Teacher" was an MTV add-on the final week of September. Simultaneously, the single was shipped, six weeks before the film's release. In mid-October the theme, not the title song, "Edge of a Dream" by Joe Cocker, entered the "Hot 100" at Number 83. Seger's "Understanding" was the AOR follow-up. The album appeared in merchandiser's bins several weeks after the effort was showing in theaters.

The formula was adhered to in textbook fashion. *Teachers* was hardly a box office phenomenon, but did a respectable $7 million its first week, equalling *Hard to Hold*. By the year's end, the gross amounted to $9.5 million. The album lasted over five months on the charts without breaking Number 50. (To be successful, an album has to reach and remain in the Top 10 for several weeks.)

One unforeseen factor was the unrelenting staying power of Prince, Springsteen, The Cars, Madonna, Tina Turner, and Huey Lewis in the Top 10. The only soundtracks to penetrate this closely guarded turn were *Eddie* and *Woman In Red*. Timing is a perennial problem in scheduling record releases. Without a top ranked single, the soundtrack package was D.O.A. (dead on arrival).

Teachers was wisely scheduled for the first week of October. An onslaught of rock-flavored films would commence in a matter of weeks. In mid-October, three rock-oriented films debuted in four days. Two had performance or concert motifs while *Thief of Hearts* followed in the Jimmy Page, *Death Wish II* genre.

Thief of Hearts, Not Minds

Thief of Hearts is the movie that Simpson/Burkheimer press bios neglect. The producers of *Flashdance*, *Beverly Hills Cop* (I and II) and *Top Gun* had followed Stigwood/Coury as proclaimed "masters" of the synergizing of movies and music.

The film and its soundtrack and its selections are strong candidates for Trivial Pursuit: Both were ignoble flops. Still, as a *Life* writer noted, "in Hollywood, three out of four makes them hotter than Malibu beach at high noon."[141]

Paramount producers pride themselves on "breaking" new directors. "It gives us an even bigger thrill," says Burkheimer, "to take directors who maybe haven't had their big successes yet and give them an opportunity." *Flashdance's* Adrian Lyne was the first. Douglas Day Stewart, screenwriter for *An Officer and a Gentleman* (1982), brought the *Hearts* project to the studio.

Thief of Hearts, originally conceptualized as a *noir* psychodrama, passed through two studios before landing on Simpson/Burkheimer's production schedule. The script underwent twenty-seven complete rewrites in four years. "The problem was that the film is a funky genre, working with elements of romance, film noir, 1940's mood and a European feel," Stewart observed. "The key was to make the audience like each character, but in early drafts, they remained unsympathetic."[142] Some critics felt he failed. All the characters, especially the burglar, were ill-defined neurotics.

The film, having completed a nine-week production for $9 million, was scored after the final cut. "You don't really concentrate on music until after a picture is made," said Simpson.[143] Harold Faltermeyer did the score. Giorgio Moroder contributed the title song. Casablanca Records signed the soundtrack, with Polygram promoting and distributing.

In the film, the camera interrupts a burglary in progress as Scott Muller (Steven Bauer) neatly chose items to steal. In the living-room safe, the thief finds several hardcover ledgers. Without opening them, Scott takes the "valuable" books. The volumes are kept by Mickey Davis (Barbara Williams), an interior designer. Finding their home looted, her husband, Ray Davis, realistically portrayed by John Getz, nonchalantly accepts the obvious saying, "we're insured." Mickey is overtly distraught. She, according to the stolen diaries, has a dual psychic life, one of proper wife and one as the fantasized libertine, Michelle.

Scott, thumbing through the passages of Mickey's inner existence— "my secret garden"—is turned on. "Water is sexual . . . his tongue moves down my skin," he reads.

Posing as a wealthy playboy, he approaches Mickey to decorate his barnlike apartment. Using the ill-gotten information extracted from the journals, his seduction begins.

The psychological interplay commences with an "accidental" meeting at the supermarket and moves to his apartment and sailboat. Aware of Mickey's fantasies, Scott acts out portions written in the books. The conquest occurs in a psuedo-Freudian manner. As McCarthy cleverly noted, "Gun enthusiasts may also find here their favorite Hollywood picture since 'Red Dawn,' as Bauer finally seduces Williams as she tries out his pistol at his home practice range."[144]

The affair, hardly torrid, flourishes while the husband, a prosperous author of children's books, starts to see beyond his typewriter. The plot, in quasi-*noir* fashion, begins to coalesce with an interesting twist for the finale.

In 1984 *Hearts's* opening received little press attention. Perhaps the October deluge of films contributed to the oversight. Taking note of the patented Paramount overuse of "trendy trappings," *Variety's* McCarthy objected that they "often work against the grain of what might have been a penetrating psychological study of two hopelessly mismatched but magnetically attracted people." The *Film Journal* analysis found the film flawed with clutter: "Who notices the patches of smooth pavement on a street chock-full of potholes?" Vincent Canby put a positive spin on the effort, judging it "as good a romantic suspense film as 'Body Heat,' although a few important plot twists don't stand careful scrutiny."[145]

The yet-to-be-released soundtrack attracted some attention. "A throbbing synthesizer score, complete with one Giorgio Moroder tune," observed *Variety*. Conversely, *Film Journal* provided a cliched reaction: "the music is barrenly intrusive."[146]

As trade publications were dotted with soundtrack pieces, the "Thief of Hearts" single by Melissa Manchester was, finally, shipped over a month *after* the feature debuted. The Moroder/Faltermeyer composition began the chart sweepstakes at Number 88. At the time of the album's release 22 December the single was stationed at the absolute chart bottom. Somebody had forgotten Zoetrope's head Robert Spiotta's admonition, "We didn't bring the music out as an album before the picture was released;" consequently, the film failed.[147]

The album languished on the lower half of the listings, barely crossing the 150 mark. It remained for eleven weeks. MTV's rotation list made no mention of a *Heart* videoclip.

The missing synergy campaign suggests S&B were occupied with other matters—*Beverly Hills Cop*. In light of their previous kudos to MTV, *vis a vis Flashdance*, it is difficult to justify the absence of a video to promote the picture, or the late record releases.

Hearts, after a five-week run, grossed $3.2 million. The final domestic tally was a meager $5 million. (*Flashdance* had earned $270 million.) Stewart returned to Twentieth Century to write and direct a World War II prison camp drama. October had been, overall, an unhealthy month for soundtracks, even for rock 'n' roll's elite.

Bored Street: A Day In The Life

> Anyone can make films. you don't have to do
> all this messing around with . . . scripts
> worked out to the last word.
> —George Harrison, musician

Some twelve years after the release of *Let It Be* in the United Kingdom, Paul McCartney wanted to do a film. He approached several playwrights, including Willy Russell and Gene Roddenberry, to no avail; all were busy with other projects. He decided to have a go at screenwriting. At a press conference, he discussed the difficulties of the task. "I had to just get down pure information; there was no style necessary," he said.[148] Many script writers would disagree.

The lack of style was manifested in other areas. A first-time screenwriter with a neophyte director (Peter Webb) and $9 million dollars to work with can create mischief. One critic would write of his film, "The real shame is that the sluggish plot detracts from the music."[149]

Give My Regards to Broad Street took two years to finish. The movie would debut in the United States in mid-October 1984. McCartney's new label, CBS, released the soundtrack.

Little attention was paid to the record release dates. For an ex-Beatle, prerelease publicity was deemed insignificant. As a Capitol Records executive once said, "All we had to do was announce the Beatles had a new album, and that was it." The same attitude appears to have been applied to *Broad Street*. The video gleaned from the motion picture, "No More Lonely Nights," was the opening and closing theme. The singer/composer attended the New York premiere.

Gridlocked in London traffic, rock superstar Paul McCartney daydreams. The master tape he is delivering disappears, and a greenmail artist threatens to take over his music firm. This is the essential plot. An ex-convict, Harry (Ian Hastings), is accused of having made off with the precious tape for a shady investor who is ready to claim the company by midnight. This deadline is designed to create suspense, as Paul spends most of the film rushing from one musical situation to another. The nonchalant McCartney begins by entering the studio, joined by Ringo Starr, on drums, plus George Martin behind the glass, and performing a medley of Beatle oldies—"Yesterday" and "Here, There and Everywhere." Only Martin's presence adds any semblance of authenticity to the session. After a brief superficial flashback to Harry, (remember him?) a lavish production number is staged. The keyboard player is Linda McCartney. "Silly Love Songs," with the required multicolored lighting and smoke, is a sequence overly designed for the MTV Acquisitions Committee. Cuts from one video to the next obscure the flimsy plot. Paul suspects that Harry is innocent, but, first performs a radio interview and segment for the B.B.C.

The film's "Eleanor Rigby" sequence is a long-form video set in Dickensian London with its contrast of upper- and working-class lifestyles. It is difficult to believe that George Martin produced this musical remake of this Beatles classic.

Driving back to the company, Wings' "Band on the Run" resounds; every auto scene has musical backup.

"No More Lonely Nights," the theme, provides the interesting, *noir* video with mandatory rain-drenched streets. Meanwhile, Paul discovers the missing masters and Harry, who has accidently locked himself in a riverfront shack. Does Paul get the tapes to the company in time? His dream ends and "No More Lonely Nights" plays over the credits.

Broad Street was hardly a critical success. "McCartney plays one emotion throughout—bemusement—and awkwardly at that," wrote Connelly. Edelstein added that in "McCartney's paean to his own sunny temperament, the ex-Beatle sprinkles fairy dust over all who cross his path."

"McCartney moves through it all as if he didn't have a care in the world," said *Variety*. He is supposed to be concerned with finding the missing matter and saving his company. Maslin excused "what is, at least to some extent, a home movie on an amazing scale," since the ex-Beatle "elicits the kind of deference befitting rock royalty."[150]

With the exception of the *New York Times* review, the film received a "thumbs-down" treatment. "It's all embarrassingly innocuous," said *Variety*. The *Village Voice* commented, "No, Paul, it isn't wrong to fill the world with silly love songs, but it's better if you don't sing them into a mirror." A *Rolling Stone* writer quoted a McCartney line to conclude " 'What good is art when it hurts your head?' " Shore wrote "The seemingly total lack of any direction makes this movie drag."[151]

The *Miami Vice*-like video, "No More Lonely Nights," was on MTV's heavy rotation the first week of October. The single surfaced on the trade charts several days later. On 13 October *Billboard* listed the song at Number 48. The film opened in New York City two weeks later; McCartney traveled to Gotham for a press conference at the Plaza. The CBS album was released several weeks later. LP buyers were told, "Longer versions exist on cassette and compact disc."

The film generated little box office. The $9-million home movie grossed $612,072, playing at eighteen major-market theaters for an original run of three weeks.

The album and video easily surpassed the movie. *Broad Street*, while not a Top-10 title, did manage to remain on the trade album charts for over half a year. The song predictably reached the first percentile on the singles listing.

As with Stevie Wonder, the ex-Beatle revisited the high-chart planes *despite* the short-lived motion picture. McCartney, once again, illustrated that rock stardom is not necessarily bankable in the movies.

Broad Street legitimated previous "backstage" rock efforts. Presented as a "daydream," the music is presented in a cloud of unreality. This may have worked previously, but the theatergoers of the Eighties were significantly more sophisticated than the consumers of Sam Katzman's musical jukeboxes. *Spinal Tap* easily had been *the* rock-business offering of 1984. *Hard to Hold* touched on some aspects of the scene absent from McCartney's wanderings. The world's wealthiest rocker (estimated at a $200-million net worth), surely does not function as chaotically as portrayed in the film.

Paul McCartney, who has had the most Number-1 singles in history, reaffirmed that "personality" films by a rock star are not *ex post factum* box office sensations. The formula had worked for Elvis Presley, but the times had changed.

With Presley, Colonel Parker had religiously guarded The King from overexposure. The snake-oil peddler turned manager carefully controlled Presley's accessibility. Following his Army stint, the superstar's appearances were confined to the big screen. The tactic boosted box office and record sales.

In 1984, it was doubtful the Colonel's strategy could have worked. Music videos demanded availability, *albeit* on the tube. Even the reclusive Bob Dylan made videos. To be successful, a star-oriented film required more than a decent soundtrack.

Ironically in McCartney's case, The Beatles were generally credited with the audiences' changing expectations. *A Hard Days Night* raised the aesthetic level of rock musicals. Singers needed to be actors, and films required storylines tying musical interludes into the whole. *Purple Rain* was the quintessential backstager. *Eddie and The Cruisers*, "the rock mystery," exhibited a plot significantly superior to *Broad Street*'s. Eddie Wilson's missing tapes are the movie's glue. Maggie, Doc, and other characters emphasize the import of the recorded material. McCartney appears indifferent and totally blasé throughout. His character is unconcerned. The viewer has little reason to become involved, especially as his or her attention is repeatedly refocused on the next production number.

Musically, *Broad Street* lacked freshness. Nine of the twelve scored songs were remakes of Beatles and Wings material. Only "Yesterday" stood up to the originals: The street-corner-busker version was one of the musical highlights of the film.

The theme single was a hit—with or without the movie. As Presley, The Beatles, and Prince had demonstrated, new material in a backstage movie is a definite asset. Nostalgic oldies usually work only in concert settings—it's expected—and film biographies, such as the Williams, Lynn, Holly, and Valens docudramas.

Banner Year

Ten soundtracks were certified platinum in 1984, four more than in the three previous years: 1981, *Jazz Singer* and *Fame*; *Annie* and *Chariots of Fire* in 1982; *Flashdance* and *Staying Alive* the following year. Only 2 of these (*Flashdance* and *Stayin' Alive*) could loosely be classified as "rock" in juxtaposition to "dance music," as disco was labelled in the Eighties.

Of the ten 1984 platinums, more than half were "straight-ahead" rockers—*Purple Rain, Footloose, Eddie and The Cruisers, Hard to Hold, The Big Chill,* and *Ghostbusters.* The others—*The Woman in Red, Two of a Kind, Yentl,* and *Breakin'*—were in the adult, or urban contemporary, categories. Three of the rockers emanated from films set in the music scene. *Footloose,* and *The Big Chill* particularly reflected the atmosphere of a particular period. *Ghostbusters* and *The Woman in Red* did not require scores except to make the films more accessible to teenagers. ("Accessibility" would shortly become the "in" term at studio project-marketing conferences.)

Scout singles performed admirably. Seven placed Number 1 on *Billboard*'s "Hot 100." Prince's "When Doves Cry" was the top single of the year. Four compositions were all-important title songs. Only one, *Ghostbusters,* was recorded by a marginally known artist (Ray Parker, Jr.). The star-studded videoclip more than compensated for this shortcoming. At the time, Phil Collins lacked a high Q-Profile, but his name was familiar to Genesis fans and rock-media consumers. *Footloose*'s cluster strategy worked, as six cuts reached the all-important Top-40 slots. (Only *Urban Cowboy* (1980) had previously accomplished this feat. The Gilley's backgrounder was a two-record set.)

The conventional wisdom on marketing rock soundtracks eroded, replaced by the "accessibility" and "synergism" concepts. Films, the argument went, must be relevant to twelve- to twenty-five-year olds and competitive in the music-video and radio media. The rush to synergize would later create some strange pairing of rock and reels. As Russ Regan, Polydor's chief soundtrack player, subtly suggested, "The new generation of filmmakers aren't intimidated by music. They realize that pop can enhance a film rather than threaten it.''

In the entertainment media, trends, or even eras, can be measured in months or years. Rock-a-billy, acid, and folk rock enjoyed the spotlight for a few short years. The Grade-B rock jukebox films of the Katzman school nearly vanished from the drive-in circuit after a profitable three-year time span. The years 1983 and 1984 were characterized by naivete in establishing guidelines for the usage, structuring, and marketing of movie scores. The ambiance at MTV in the first year and a half allowed an atmosphere of "anything can happen here," and occasionally it did. Several insiders at the channel frankly echoed Kris Kristofferson's line, "Freedom's just another word for nothing left to loose." Concretizing a concept precludes innovation; the rigidity of the process terminates creativity and risk taking.

Many of the rock soundtracks of the mid-1980s were based more on instinct than computer printouts and trade-magazine charts. Davidson, Brickman, Kasdan, Hackford, Simpson/Bruckheimer, and others choose artists and songs on the basis of personal preference rather than hit-single potential. Davidson and Kasdan were attempting to recreate portions of their pasts. Brinkman and the Paramount duo picked the material and artists they liked, or at least felt sounded right. In some cases, their efforts succeeded. The trail-blazers did create paths that others would follow. But many, lacking music industry savvy, blindly plunged into soundtracks with disastrous consequences.

Danny Goldberg's popularization of "synergy" provided a vague road map to marketing soundtracks, at least from a moviemaker's perspective. The facade of demographic sophistication frequently collapsed, due to shortsightedness and parochialism. The early Eighties had witnessed a story union of music and film—the shotgun wedding and honeymoon were rapidly fading as the cold light of the economic dawn appeared. The interfacing of box office and album sales, the bottom line, required a cooperation that was rarely provided willingly. Different marketing strategies and goals clashed. Prince's management team was on the mark when it claimed that the two media were on the verge of "a collision." The increasingly significant auxiliary sources of profitability—cable, home videos, and theater reissues—promised to heighten territorial anxiety levels.

Only a handful of directors, like Simpson/Burkheimer, Hackford, and Mann, and studio executives, such as Danny Goldberg, Gary LeMel, and Becky Shargo, appeared to have grasped the nuances of synergy. (Even Simpson and Burkheimer would improvise with *Beverly Hills Cop*.)

Once again, industry creativity flourished amid a state of despair. Reaching youth was an imperative. Rock music, regardless of its appropriateness, became central to film. Stumbling around the mine-filled rock field, hitherto ignored artists like John Cafferty and Marilyn Martin garnered exposure. The "Seger-thing" scene in *Risky Business* made Tom Cruise a star. The contrived use of contemporary rock was sometimes embarrassing. Some users, however, were blinded by greed encased in musical ignorance. A cardinal dictum in the record industry has been "give the people what they want, not what you like." Becky Shargo claimed that a "musical subtexture" is vital to a film. She explained, "I just read a script from a top studio about a corporate business falling apart, and they wanted a rock 'n' roll soundtrack." Filmmakers are not especially interested in album sales. Still, the score must have a thematic base, regardless of serial synergy.

As the clock signaled the end of 1984, the industry needed to change. A rock-music score could no longer be used to sell a motion picture. (Specialty rock films were those treating the creation of the sound, artists, or the industry. *This is Spinal Tap* and *Eddie and The Cruisers* qualified as rock films, as did *Streets of Fire*. The repeated use of musical performances legitimated that motion picture as a "rock 'n' roll fable.") The rock-music designation in 1984 was no longer viable—if it ever had been. *Against All Odds* was in the *noir* genre with a rock New Age orientation. The questions, for 1985 and after, would be, "Is rock music enhancing or merely marketing a film?"

Notes

1. Jon Pareles "Work Hard, Play Hard" *Rolling Stone*, 20 December 1984, 14.
2. Quoted in Paul Grein, "Unorthodox 'Prince' of a Film," *Billboard*, 16 June 1984, 57.
3. Quoted in Richard Gold "Labels Bunch Singles Releases . . ." *Variety*, 16 May 1984, 6.
4. Quoted in Anthony DeCurtis " 'Top Gun' A Victory for the Marketing Men," *Rolling Stone*, 25 September 1986, 21.
5. S. Graham, "Inside Moves," *Esquire*, February, 1984, 94.
6. Quotes in David Kehr, "Can't Stop the Musicals," *American Film*, May 1984, 35.
7. Richard Corliss, "Rebel Without a Cause," *Time*, 20 February 1984, 82.
8. Quoted in Marianne Meyer, "Rock Movideo," *The Rolling Stone Review 1985* Ira Robbins, ed., (New York: Charles Scribners and Sons 1985), 168; and Paul Grein " 'Footloose' Forges New Movie—Music Tie," *Billboard*, 11 February 1984, 82.
9. Quoted in Kehr: 35.

10. The "success" of the title song reportedly convinced Paramount to stick with Pitchford's collection of cuts. Prior to that time, they were at the verge of dropping seven of the nine selections. Ian Dove "Soundtracks Score With Rock 'n' Roll" *ASCAP IN ACTION* Spring, 1986, 35; also "Inside Moves," 94; Quotes in Richard Gold "Labels Bunch Singles Releases in New Film-Related Strategy," *Variety*, 16 May 1984, 128.

11. Quoted in Sam Sutherland, "Labels, Studios Get Closer On Soundtracks," *Billboard*, 30 June 1984, 3.

12. Don Shewey, "Footloose: Original Motion Picture Soundtrack," *Rolling Stone*, 29 March 1984, 73; Meyer, 168.

13. Corliss, 82.

14. David Ansen, "Boogieing in the Bible Belt," *Newsweek*, 20 February 1984, 78.

15. Corliss, 82.

16. Meyer, 168; and Dave Marsh, et. al. *Rock 'n' Roll Confidential Report* (New York: Pantheon Books 1985), 235.

17. Louise Stanton and P.C. Noble, "Footloose," *Film in Review*, April 1984, 236–37.

18. J. Harwood, "Footloose," *Variety*, 15 February 1984, 24.

19. Andrew Sarris, "Bill Forsyth: Humanist and Humorist," *Village Voice*, 26 February 1984, 49.

20. Ansen; Corliss; Maslin, "Footloose, Story of Dancing on the Farm," *New York Times*, 17 February 1984, C12.

21. Quoted in Richard Harrington, "The Saga of the Soundtracks," *Washington Post*, 12 January 1984, K11.

22. Ibid.

23. Quoted in Donald Lyons, "Music Videos Give New Eyes to Hollywood," *Rock Video*, September 1984, 64.

24. Quoted in Rob Tannenbaum, "Soundtracks Thrived in Summer of '85," *Rolling Stone*, 21 November 1985, 16; Dave DiMartino, "The Big Score of '87," *Billboard*, 3 May 1987, S6.

25. Vincent Canby, "French Words for a California Condition," *New York Times*, 11 March 1984, sec. 2, 18.

26. Pauline Kael, "King Candy," *New Yorker*, 19 March 1984, 129.

27. Andrew Sarris "ou sont les film noirs d'antan," *Village Voice*, 13 March 1984, 41; Canby "French," 17; "Har," "Against All Odds," *Variety*, 15 February 1984, 24.

28. Marcia Magill, "Against All Odds," *Films In Review*, April 1984, 238.

29. Sarris, 41.

30. Richard Schickel, "Of Hotels, Hoods and a Mermaid," *Time*, 19 March 1984, 91; David Ansen, "Love in the Ruins," *Newsweek*, 5 March 1984, 82; Magill; Janet Maslin, "Against All Odds," *New York Times*, 2 March 1984, C14.

31. Quoted in Harrington, K11.

32. Quoted in Bronson, 586.

33. Quoted in "Academy Causes Flap By Not Asking Collins To Sing," *Variety*, 13 March 1985, 109.

34. Bronson, 586.

35. Harrington, K11.

36. Quoted in Richard Gold, "Studios and Labels Pan Soundtrack," *Variety*, 18

April 1984, 216; Cathleen McGuigan, "Rock Music Goes Hollywood," *Newsweek*, 11 March 1985, 78.

37. Jeffrey M. Sidney, "Putting Soundtrack on a Sound Basis," *Billboard*, 14 February 1987, 9.

38. Quoted in Paul Grein, "Music Means a Lot to 'Cop' Producers," *Billboard*, 27 July 1985, 37.

39. Quotes in Ian Dove, "Soundtracks Score With Rock 'n' Roll," *ASCAP In Action*, Spring 1986, 35; Meyer, 170.

40. Quoted in Sam Sutherland, "Labels, Studios Get Closer on Soundtracks," *Billboard*, 30 June 1984, 3.

41. Quoted in Gold, "Studios," 216.

42. Robert Gustafson, " 'What's Happened to Our Pix Biz?' From Warners Brothers to Warner Communications, Inc.," in *The American Film Industry*, Tino Balio, ed., (Madison: University of Wisconsin Press 1985), 581.

43. Quoted in Donald Lyons, "Music Videos Give New Eyes to Hollywood," *Rock Video*, September 1984, 62.

44. Quoted in Gold, 216.

45. Danny Goldberg, "Tracking the Hip Ingredient," *Billboard* 25, February 1984, 10.

46. Quoted in Michael Goldberg, " 'Spinal Tap': The Comics Behind The Funniest Rock Movie Ever," *Rolling Stone*, 24 March 1984, 38. If the hotel's name sounds familiar, it's because it was the site of John Belushi's death.

47. Quoted in Peter Occhiogrosso, "Shearer on Tap," *Village Voice*, 6 March 1984, 54.

48. Quoted in Goldberg, 39; Aljean Harmetz, "Reiner Has Last Laugh With His Rock Spoof," *New York Times*, 25 April 1984, C20.

49. Occhiogrosso, 54.

50. Cathleen McGuigan, "A Spinal Tap for Your Health," *Newsweek*, 14 May 1984, 69.

51. "Album Review," *Billboard*, 7 April 1984, 64.

52. Quotes from John Nangle "This Is Spinal Tap," *Film in Review*, May 1984, 308–9; Goldberg, 38; Stanley Kauffman, "Playing Around With Facts," *New Republic*, 21 May 1984, 24; Robert Christgau, and Carola Dibbell, "The Man in the Band," *Village Voice*, 6 March 1984, 52; David Ansen "Rocky Road," *Newsweek*, 5 March 1984, 82.

53. Vincent Canby, " 'Spinal Tap' Draws Laughter From Rock," *New York Times*, 18 March 1984, 18.

54. Occhiogrosso, 54.

55. Janet Maslin, "This Is Spinal Tap," *New York Times*, 2 March 1984, C6.

56. Richard Corliss, "Cold Metal," *Time*, 6 March 1984, 86.

57. Quoted in Sam Sutherland, "Labels, Studios Get Closer on Soundtracks," *Billboard*, 30 June 1984, 62.

58. Quoted in Maitland McDonagh " 'Eddie and The Cruisers' Tracks Rock Era" *Film Journal* 19 August 1983, 74.

59. Quoted in Cary Darling "Springfield Doubling As a Singer and Actor" *Billboard* 27 June 1981, 51.

60. J. Greenberg, "Hard to Hold" *Variety* 11 April 1984, 16.

61. Ibid.

62. Alan Karp "Hard to Hold" *Boxoffice* June, 1984, R75; Maitland McDonagh "Hard to Hold" *Film Journal* May, 1984, 25.

63. Janet Maslin "Hard to Hold" *New York Times* 6 April 1984, C16.

64. Jim Bessman "Video Lowdown" *Rock Video* August 1984, 5.

65. Meyer, 170.

66. Karp, R75.

67. Greenberg, 16.

68. Bronson, 546; and Lenny Kaye "About His Videos: Rick Springfield" *Rock Video* October, 1985, 29.

69. Quoted in Alan Karp "Majors, Indies, Go for Gold" *Boxoffice* May, 1984, 16.

70. Quoted in Ivan Dove "Soundtracks Score with Rock 'n' Roll" *ASCAP In Action* Spring 1984, 35.

71. Liner notes *Streets of Fire* (MCA 5492).

72. Quoted in Paul Grein "Azoff Looking Beyond Records" *Billboard* 7 May 1983, 1, 66.

73. Liner notes.

74. Quoted in Michael Shargon, "Hill's Street Blues," *American Film*, June 1984, 42.

75. David Chute, "Dead End Streets," *Film Comment*, July/August 1984, 74.

76. Occhiogrosso, 50.

77. David Denby, "Lost in The Thrill Machine," *New York*, 4 June 1984, 74.

78. Quoted in Ethlie Ann Vare, "Four Clips Taken From 'Streets of Fire' Movie," *Billboard*, 5 May 1984, 28.

79. Quoted in Tony Seideman, "Three-Pronged Promo For 'Streets of Fire' Package," *Billboard*, 9 June 1984, 43.

80. Meyer.

81. Seideman, 43.

82. *Streets of Fire* (liners) MCA Records 5492.

83. Alan Karp, "Streets of Fire," *Boxoffice*, August 1984, 97.

84. J. Hoberman, "White Boys," *Village Voice*, 5 June 1984, 63.

85. Janet Maslin, "Streets of Fire," *New York Times*, 1 June 1984, C8.

86. *Variety*, 14; Karp, R97.

87. Maslin, C8; Ansen, "A Rocky Horror Show," *Newsweek*, 11 June 1984, 81; Hoberman, 63.

88. David Chute, "Dead End Streets," *Film Comment*, July/August 1984, 55–58.

89. Timothy Crouse, "The Rolling Stone Interview: Bill Murray," *Rolling Stone*, 16 August 1984, 46, 48.

90. Richard Schickel, "Exercise for Exorcists," *Time*, 11 June 1984, 83.

91. Quoted in "Columbia's Ghost Is a Smash, Too," *New York Times*, 29 September 1984, 31.

92. Bronson, 592.

93. Quoted in Michael Goldberg, "Ray Parker, Jr. from Sideman to Lady's Man," *Rolling Stone*, 27 September 1984, 71.

94. Quoted from Jimmy Summers, "Ghostbusters," *Boxoffice*, August 1984, R92; David Ansen, "Got a Demon in Your Icebox?" *Newsweek*, 11 June 1984, 80; David Denby, " 'Oh Zuul You Nut!' " *New York,* 11 June 1984, 66.

95. Schickel, 83; Ansen, 80; Jimmy Summers, "Ghostbusters," *Boxoffice*, August 1984, R92–93.

96. J. Coleman, "Things From Outer Space," *New Statesman*, 7 December 1984,

35–36; Andrew Kopkind, "Ghostbusters," *Nation*, 21 July 1984, 23; Janet Maslin, "Ghostbusters," *New York Times*, 8 June 1984, C5; and L. Cohn, "Ghostbusters," *Variety*, 6 June 1984, 20.

97. Quoted in David D. Martino, 5–6.
98.. Debby Miller, "Prince: The Secret Life of America's Sexiest One-Man Band," *Rolling Stone*, 28 April 1983, 20. Miller, a reliable journalist, has been contradicted on numerous occasions by the subject of the piece. Emboldened by later revelations, the authors have attempted, with a grain of salt, to present a composite, however short, biography. *Purple Rain* has to be seen in the context of Prince's background, as murky as it may be.
99. Neal Karlen, "Prince Talks," *Rolling Stone*, 12 September 1985, 26.
100. Barbara Graustack, "Prince: Strange Tales from Andre's Basement," *Musician*, September 1983, 62.
101. Miller, 20.
102. Graustack, 62.
103. Ibid, 56.
104. Stephen Holden, "Prince," in *The New Rolling Stone Record Guide*, Dave Marsh and John Swenson, eds., (New York: Random House 1983), 401.
105. Kurt Loder, "Prince Reigns," *Rolling Stone*, 30 August 1984, 21.
106. Quoted in Michael Shore, *The Rolling Stone Book of Rock Video*, (New York: Quill 1984), 298.
107. Karlen. This dictum about poor scripts was demonstrated in Prince's second acting role, *Under the Cherry Moon*. The film was a deserved flop.
108. Karlen, 26.
109. Quoted in Sam Sutherland, "Labels, Studios Get Closer on Soundtrack," *Billboard*, 30 June 1984, 62.
110. Quoted in Richard Gold, "WB Records To Release 'Rain' Single 3 Months Ahead of Film," *Variety*, 16 May 1984, 107.
111. Quoted in Paul Grein, "Unorthodox 'Prince' of a Film," *Billboard*, 16 June 1984, 57.
112. Shore, 298.
113. Quoted in Richard Gold, " 'Purple Rain' Sells Rock at Boxoffice," *Variety*, 1 August 1984, 29.
114. Kurt Loder, "Purple Rain" [album review], *Rolling Stone*, 2 August 1984, 102.
115. Robert Palmer, "Prince Creates a Winner with 'Purple Rain,' " *New York Times*, 22 July 1984, 2–23.
116. Gold, "Sells Rock," 29.
117. Ibid.
118. Grein, 57.
119. K. Lally, "Purple Rain," *Film Journal*, September, 1984, 60.
120. Pauline Kael, "The Current Cinema," *New Yorker*, 20 August 1984, 87.
121. Barbara Graustark, "Prince: Strange Tales from Andre's Basement," *Musician*, September 1983, 58.
122. Ken Terry, " 'Purple Rain' Seen As Forerunner of New Longform Genre," *Variety*, 5 September 1984, 80.
123. C. Kirk, "Purple Rain," *Variety*, 4 July 1984, 16.
124. Vincent Canby, " 'Purple Rain' With Prince," *New York Times*, 27 July 1984, C5.

125. Kurt Loder, "Prince Reigns," *Rolling Stone*, 30 August 1984, 21.
126. Palmer, 23; Canby, C5; Janet Maslin, "Movies For Every Teenager's Wish," *New York Times*, 12 August 1984, sec. 2, 17.
127. Andrew Kopkind, "Purple Rain," *Nation*, 22 September 1984, 253; David Denby, "Dr. Feelgood," *New York*, 13 August 1984, 50; Lally, 60; Kael, 60; David Ansen, "The New Prince of Hollywood," *Newsweek*, 23 July 1984, 65; Carol Cooper, "Oh Bondage, Up Yours," *Village Voice*, 31 July 1984, 55.
128. Canby.
129. Gold, " 'Purple,' " 29.
130. Grein, 57.
131. AGB Television Research Report 1988.
132. Bronson, 596.
133. Jimmy Summers, "The Woman in Red," *Boxoffice*, October 1984, R122.
134. Richard Schickel, "A Woman in Red," *Time*, 27 August 1984, 64; J. Harwood, "The Woman in Red," *Variety*, 15 August 1984, 14; Janet Maslin, "Woman in Red," *New York Times*, 15 August 1984, C24.
135. Summers, R122; David Denby, "Adrift in the City," *New York Times*, 3 September 1984, 57; David Palmeri, "Woman in Red," *Film Journal*, September 1984, 27; David Edelstein, "August is the Crudist Month," *Village Voice*, 28 August 1984, 52.
136. Christopher Connelly, "The Woman in Red," (record review) *Rolling Stone*, 8 November 1984, 73.
137. Quoted in Wendy Weinstein, "Hiller's 'Teachers' Does For Ed What 'Hospital' Did For Med," *Film Journal*, September 1984, 12.
138. Wendy Weinstein, "Teachers," *Film Journal*, November 1984, 54.
139. Richard Schickel, "Teachers," *Time*, 5 November 1984, 81; David Ansen, The ABC's of Survival, *Newsweek*, 8 October 1984, 87; T. O'Brien, "All of Them," *Commonweal*, 30 November 1984, 60; R. Loynd, "Teachers," *Variety*, 3 October 1984, 16; Janet Maslin, "Teachers," *New York Times*, 5 October 1984, C10.
140. Loynd, 16.
141. Margot Dougherty, "1 + 1 = \$935 Million," *Life*, April 1987, 97.
142. "Five Young Men, Stewart's Next Pic, To Roll for 20th Fox in '86," *Variety*, 31 October 1984, 30.
143. Quoted in Ken Terry, " 'Beverly Hills Cop' Illustrates Synergy of Film Record Tie-In," *Variety*, 26 June 1985, 87.
144. T. McCarthy, "Thief of Hearts," *Variety*, 17 October 1984, 30.
145. McCarthy, 30; J. Lener, "Thief of Hearts," *Film Journal*, November 1984, 14; Vincent Canby, " 'Thief of Hearts' Finds Secrets," *New York Times*, 19 October 1984, C17.
146. McCarthy, 30; Lener, 14.
147. Quoted in Jeffrey Chown, *"Hollywood Auteur: Francis Coppola* (New York: Praeger 1988), 160.
148. Quoted in Wendy Weinstein "McCartney Scales the Legend Down to Size," *Film Journal*, December 1984, 8.
149. David Shilren, "Give My Regards to Broad Street," *Film Journal*, November 1984, 51.
150. Christopher Connelly, "Broad Street, Paul's Dead End," *Rolling Stone*, 6 December 1984, 57; David Edelstein "That Obscene Object of Desire,"

Village Voice, 6 November 1984, 69; T. McCarthy, "Give My Regards to Broad Street," *Variety*, 31 October 1984, 24; Janet Maslin, "Paul McCartney Stars in 'Broad Street,' " *New York Times*, 26 October 1984, C14.
151. Edelstein, 69; Connelly, 57; Shore.

9

Soundtrack Wars

> *The* Footloose *album sold a cool million cop-*
> *ies, so in the next year you can be sure there'll*
> *be more soundtracks with themes designed for*
> *all-hit radio, not to mention video clips that*
> *double as coming-attractions trailers.*
> —Jon Parles, music critic

> *It's very important that film companies walk*
> *that delicate line of not oversaturating the*
> *marketplace.*
> —Steve Bedell, vice president,
> Paramount Pictures

Shep Gordon, president of Alive Enterprises, prophetically said, when discussing *Roadie* (1980), "Freshness gives it that edge, as do the magical combinations we went for. What we tried to do was really what we knew best—to take a piece of product that has credibility and something about it that was interesting and magical.[1]

Synergy Appeal

Before the term "synergism" entered the industry lexicon, the key terms for marketing were "freshness" and "interesting." By 1985, "innovative" or "new" soundtracks were fading. *Saturday Night Fever, Flashdance, Footloose, Eddie and The Cruisers* and *Purple Rain* had been attempts at exploiting rock. Title songs, back-stagers, unrelenting instrumental scores, and staggering had been tried with mixed results. The key to success in 1985 was basic—creativity. In May alone, twelve albums had appeared that promoted and capitalized on summer box office offerings. In this field,

Beverly Hills Cop, *The Breakfast Club*, *Back To The Future* and *St. Elmo's Fire* would be standouts among the host "of the barely mentioned."

The Mean Streets of Beverly Hills

Beverly Hills Cop, the ninth biggest-grossing picture in filmdom, was conceptualized in the mid-1970s. Considering the euphoria of *Flashdance's* unanticipated success, Paramount Pictures head Michael Eisner had assigned the Danilo Bach story to Simpson and Bruckheimer Productions. Bruckheimer recruited Dan Petrie, Jr. to pen the screenplay. After one rewrite, the script was accepted.

The lead was offered to Sylvester Stallone who immediately agreed, desiring to escape the prizefighter stereotype, but who also "asked to do a rewrite on his character. After all, he's Stallone. He came back with what was virtually a new script and it was extraordinary . . . it was, however, different." Stallone was wedded to his changes and a standoff resulted. (In the film industry this type of conflict is euphemistically called "creative differences.") Jeffery Katzenberg, then Simpson's assistant, suggested that Eddie Murphy be cast in the lead. *Saturday Night Live* star Murphy, who had had success with *48 Hours* and *Trading Places*, and the project was rushed into production.

Production pressures precluded synergistic marketing strategy. "The time period between when it was actually given a 'go,' " Simpson said, "and when we actually shot it was short, so that we had to pay attention to the making of the movie . . ." He told another writer, "We pay attention to the script first. The movie is everything. The. music comes not only secondarily, but way down the line."[2] The line proved to be a long one, as the script was in a constant state of flux. "There were seven versions of the script that were cut," remembers Michael Brest, the film's director. Brest, "pasted and rewritten before each scene. We were reshaping the material every day . . . That the film turned out to be coherent is a miracle." David Ansen, like most reviewers, described the plot as "merely perfunctory."[3]

The post-production scoring phase was a compact four weeks. (Only one selection, The Pointer Sisters' "Neutron Dance," was tied to a filmed segment. It was used as "temp" music for the patrol car, truck-chase scene to tempt or direct the audience's attention to the song.)

MCA Records was contracted. Kathy Nelson, director of film music at MCA, noted at the time that the film studio "didn't have a specific idea of what artists they wanted, but they knew what kind of music they wanted.[4]

The desired sound was the all-too-familiar, "up," foot-tapping dance genre.

Nelson scheduled a screening for potential contributors, "including MCA artists." Overall, the producers and Brest sorted through some 450 song possibilities. Harold Faltermeyer (*Thief of Hearts*) and Keith Forsey (*Flashdance*) were commissioned to write, as well as produce, some material. The duo wrote "The Heat Is On" for MCA artist Glenn Frey. At the behest of Irving Azoff, label president, Patti LaBelle, who recorded for Philadelphia International, was brought in for two selections. One, "Stir It Up," was produced by Faltermeyer and Forsey. "Axel F" was a Faltermeyer creation.

Variety's Ken Terry asked Simpson about the criteria for song selection. "We looked at every song for hit potential [but some] didn't fit the movie," Simpson said.[5] An album package containing ten cuts, with a strong dance-disco flavor, was finalized. (S/B, since *Flashdance*, had demonstrated a strong affinity for this genre. The Melissa Manchester title for *Thief of Hearts* had received its primary chart life on the dance track. The producers' original Polygram albums had done considerably better with the dance-music stalwarts than with rock-music mavens. Some material did cross-over, but the music can be best characterized as *Fever*-oriented, adult contemporary.)

Kathy Nelson and Larry Solter, another MCA executive, mapped the MCA media campaign. They chose the best known MCA artist, Frey, to promote the album, as the ex-Eagle had considerably more AOR appeal than either LaBelle or The Pointer Sisters.

RCA, hoping to push the Pointers' *Break Out* into double platinum, initiated the exposure drive, releasing the "Neutron Dance" single and video during the 24 November 1984 charting period. It appeared on the Hot 100 at Number 73. MTV provided a "breakout" slot.

Glenn Frey's "The Heat Is On" single listed at Number 81 two weeks later. The issuance coincided with the film's release. The picture grossed $2 million the day it opened, playing in 1,532 theaters. A video would not air on MTV, in the medium rotation, until the last week of January. MCA timed the Frey clip wisely, as "Neutron" was slipping on the music channel.

The soundtrack album hit the bins during Christmas week. It began a crawl up the charts; six months and two million copies later it was ranked Number 1. It would sell another million during its chart run.

The $14-million film begins in the bombed-out squalor of Motown's inner city. Glenn Frey's "Heat Is On" underscores the scene as the camera rests on a sign reading, "You're in Detroit."

Axel Foley (Eddie Murphy) is loudly negotiating the price of a truckload of cigarettes—"Read my lips . . . $5,000"—as several patrol cars pull up. A high-speed chase ensues, with the required vegetables littering the street with produce. "Neutron Dance" accompanies the chase. The sequence proves to be for naught as it's a bad bust, but does establish the perils of survival on the mean streets of Detroit.

Having been properly berated by Police Inspector Todd (Gilbert Hill), but not chastened, Axel returns to his apartment to find paroled high school chum Mikey Tandino (James Russo). Mikey is working in Beverly Hills as a security guard. As they reminisce about adolescent high jinks, Mikey reveals a cache of negotiable German bonds. Shortly thereafter, Mikey is murdered by Mob types led by the sadistic Jack (Jonathan Banks) as Foley is knocked unconscious.

Axel is determined to apprehend the killers, but Todd refuses to assign him to the case. Transparently, the detective demands vacation time which Todd approves, warning it could be the "longest vacation you ever heard of . . . if you butt into this case." (The off-duty rogue cop, disobeying orders, is a well worn motif in action films.) Petrie's storyline is built on this premise, while incorporating some of John Hughes's (*Breakfast Club*, *Sixteen Candles*) philosophy—adult authority figures are stupid and inept.

Arriving in Hollywood driving a "crappy blue Chevy Nova," Murphy seems oblivious to the posh surroundings as LaBelle's "Stir It Up" predicts the cultural collision that is about to occur. The tensions follow, whatever direction the volatile Murphy pursues. (It's *Saturday Night Live* visiting the capital of conspicuous consumption and the rigid, hi-tech law enforcer assigned to protect it.)

Without any sense of purpose, Axel stumbles into an expensive hotel, The Beverly Palm (actually the Biltmore) which is booked to capacity. He loudly tells the receptionist he is in town to do a story on Michael Jackson for *Rolling Stone*. The clerk insists that there is no room. When the would-be journalist complains about swank hotels denying admission to blacks, the manager installs Axel in a suite for the price of a single room.

Foley strolls to the art gallery of Tandino's employer, finding another childhood friend, Jenny Summers (Lisa Eilbacher), in his employ. She directs Axel to the offices of Victor Maitland (Steven Berkoff), a character easily taken from a World War II Bogart picture. "Detroit is a very violent place," he tells Foley, upon being informed that Mikey is dead. The villainous entrepreneur has the transplanted copy thrown out of the building. Tossed through a window, Foley is unceremoniously greeted by the local law. "You guys arresting me for getting thrown out of a f—king window. What's the charge for being thrown out of a moving car—jaywalking?'' snaps Murphy.

On the way to the police station, Axel is taken with the cruiser. "You know this is the cleanest and nicest police car I've ever been in, in all my life. Nicer than my apartment," he says. Murphy's arrest and the ride downtown underline the foreignness of the Beverly Hills Police Department to a black, street-wise cop. ("In fact," wrote David Edelstein, "the real Beverly Hills cops are more nervous than the baddies at the thought of this wiry black officer snooping around town—suppose he upsets the residents?")[6] Foley's nemesis, Lieutenant Bogomill (Ronny Cox), would tell him, "We don't get around search warrants in Beverly Hills." This, of course, does not hamper the Detroit detective from slipping into Maitland's warehouse, where he is caught by security people. Flashing his badge, Foley feigns being a U.S. Customs Inspector and orders the entire staff to find manifests. The ruse works. Repeatedly, Foley demonstrates that skullduggery is functional while orthodox, hi-tech methodology is cumbersome and counterproductive. Luring his foils, Sgt. Taggart (John Ashton) and Det. Billy Rosewood (Judge Reinhold), into a strip joint, Axel stops a robbery. The officers are docked three days' pay. By the film's close the policemen learn the error of their ways and fabricate a delightful tale for the benefit of the chief. Murphy stands silent, smiling and nodding approval.

This approach can easily be lifted from John Hughes's scriptbook. The producer/director's thesis in *Sixteen Candles* and *The Breakfast Club* is simply, "The young are often subject to absurd, arbitrary, and unthinking exercises of power."

"In Beverly Hills Cop," asserted Michael Sprinkler, "the 'let's put one over on them' theme is blended with the more serious moments of confrontation with real evil."[7]

Following a second encounter with Maitland and Zack, Axel is rearrested and ordered out of the city. Rosewood is assigned to escort him. Foley cons the young detective into returning to the warehouse. Jenny insists on coming along. Foley and Summers are caught by Maitland and the gang. Roseland, suspecting something is amiss, agonizes over a course of action. This all leads to the final shootout, in the process of which Axel's *modus operandi* is vindicated and part of the Beverly Hills Police Department converted. Murphy suggests a sequel, threatening, "I may start my own private investigator company in Beverly Hills." "Stir It Up" closes the film as Taggert, Rosewood, and Foley agree to meet for drinks. "Trust me," says Murphy with a wide grin.

The crime/action portion of the 105-minute production could easily have been reduced to a Sonny Crockett adventure on *Miami Vice*. Eddie Murphy's three-quarters of an hour, a critical consensus says, were put to good use. Sprinkler suggested that "good-hearted youngsters make light of the various incarnations of authority (teachers, cops, parents) and emerge from their antics virtually unscathed."

"Foley is a well intentioned troublemaker, whose talent for cracking crimes shares equal time with his disregard for police department rules," wrote Weinstein. Vincent Canby said that *Beverly Hills Cop* "may not be a great film, though it is a perfect showcase for the young actor's discreetly raffish comic abilities."

"Murphy is the audience's surrogate id," observed Ansen. "The good bad boy who breaks all the rules and ends up the teacher's pet." Over at *Time*, Corliss found "the film's only function is to provide Murphy with the opportunity to work a dozen or so variations on his familiar and oddly endearing routine: top Whitey."

"Many of Murphy's encounters have the eerie magic of habitants of two planets getting to know one another," stated Denby. Overall, the reviewers agreed that *Beverly Hills Cop* was Murphy's showcase.[8]

Few critics bothered to mention *Cops*'s musical material. *Newsday's* Leo Seligsohn remembered that "hard-rock vibes" thundered during the opening. *Variety* devoted a short paragraph to the music. The producers, noted the critic, "deftly hit the soundtrack button again with a terrific score from Harold Faltermeyer and solid contributing numbers from such off-screen artists as The Pointer Sisters and Patti LaBelle, among others."[9] By 1984, rock soundtracks were becoming commonplace, and frequently mediocre.

Despite talk of collaborative soundtracks, the labels were playing to the studios' desire to reach the youth market. The artists on scores, more often than not, were the second or third choices of filmmakers. Springsteen, always the *desired* artist, reportedly was being replaced by other less expensive performers. Rock stars *could* be used only if the studio was willing to settle for outtakes deemed unworthy for an album. Some producers proved willing victims. The result, normally, was that albums served predominantly as souvenir packages. "Take the memory with you" was a valid slogan, as the records could not pass muster without the films. Two writers, arguing the merits of a soundtrack, once ended their polemic with, "You saw the movie. I didn't."

At the close of 1984, ticket buyers had spent $100 million to see Murphy fight crime on the mean streets of Beverly Hills. The project was well on its way to a final gross of $350 million. It proved to be Murphy's signature film and the blockbuster of a rather tame year. David Ansen predicted for summer 1985 "an eternity of teen fantasies. Lots of hormones and little risk."[10] Part of the statement was right. The music package was awarded platinum.

Heaven Help Us

Producer Dan Wigutow, who had retreated to New York from Los Angeles in search of a fresh property, found an NYU Film School dropout, Charles Purpura, who had a rough screenplay entitled *Catholic Boys*.

The coming-of-age-in-parochial-school tale went through a series of sporadic rewrites over a four-year span. Wigutow unsuccessfully pitched the project at the studios. Fox liked the idea, but objected to Michael Dinner, a neophyte director picked by Wigutow. (The Dinner choice would eventually prove to be a wise one.)

Dinner accidently met the head of Silver Screen, HBO's new production company, which, anxious for projects, signed the story. Heartthrob Matt Dillon's younger brother Kevin was the only actor signed who had marquee recognition. Tri-Star pictures, the distributor, demanded and received a title change to *Heaven Help Us*. "The title doesn't reflect the movie," Dinner told *Esquire*. Critics agreed. *Variety* and Rex Reed found the original title "uncommercial, but more descriptive."[11] A more appropriate title could have been *Catholic Graffiti*, combining the George Lucas, California-teen film with *The Trouble With Angels*.

Silver Screen signed a soundtrack deal with EMI-America, a Capitol Records subsidiary. Of the seventeen titles credited in the film, ten appeared on record or tape. Six were Motown licensees, following the *Big Chill* tradition. Otis Reddings' centerpiece composition was included. The Roches' "Hallelujah Chorus" as the opening theme and Presley's version of "Blue Suede Shoes" were omitted, as was Bobby Vinton's "Blue Velvet." The songs, especially the Redding compositions, were well placed in the film. The Indian-raga score proved another matter.

The soundtrack package failed to chart. It lacked substance beyond the film, unlike those from *Graffiti* or *Chill*. John Coleman, for one, called the track "tarnished pop."[12] The film opened 8 February nationally in 1,003 theaters.

The forces of change affecting the adolescents of America in the 1960s seemed light-years away inside the halls of Catholic elementary and secondary education. Charles Purpura provided a glimpse into an urban high school, St. Basil's, located in Brooklyn, New York.

The film commences as a priest celebrates Communion before a sea of uniformed, blue-blazered male students. Monks patrol the aisles. The repressive atmosphere is strengthened as the high schoolers file past the statue of St. Basil on their way to class.

Michael Dunn (Andrew McCarthy), a transfer student from Boston, is thrust into Brother Constance's (Jay Patterson) class. The monk proves to be a sadistic headbanger as he berates a teen egghead who has visions of attending Harvard med school, Caesar (Malcolm Daivare), and the troublemaking Rooney (Kevin Dillon). The next day, Dunn is caught up in a Rooney-inspired prank as Brother Constance, in a *Caine Mutiny*-like scene, demands to know "who took the screws" from Caesar's chair. Dunn is brutalized, but wins Rooney's friendship for remaining silent.

Across the street from St. Basil's is the all-too-familiar soda- fountain refuge, run by worldly dropout Danni (Mary Stuart Masterson). She tolerates the immature high jinks of the customers, which are interrupted by occasional raids by the robed monks. After one incursion, Dunn remains to help clean up the rubble left by the fleeing high schoolers. "You're not like those other jerks are you?" says Danni.

Dunn, introspectively battling the demands of his grandparents that he enter the priesthood and his emerging sexuality, is the epitome of "troubled youth." He is searching. Highlighting the quest for self are the constant reminders of the rigid, religious environment. A gym teacher warns that the Communists are fierce fighters bent on killing Catholics. Classmate Williams (Stephen Geoffreys) is dissuaded from revealing his penchant for masturbating "—5.6 times a day"—at Confession. The *tour de force* is Father Abruzzi's (Wallace Shawn) dire, predance, lust lecture. "There is a beast living within each one of you," he says, teeth bared, "a filthy beast whose name is LUST . . . have a nice time. Enjoy the dance." The aftermath of the chaperoned, "eight inches apart," dance finds Rooney attempting to make it with Janine (Dana Barron). His seduction strategy is foiled when she vomits from an overabundance of whiskey. Moreover, the borrowed family Lincoln is caught in the jaws of a drawbridge as Bobby Vinton's "Blue Velvet" emanates from the car radio. ". . . through my tears." The ramifications of Rooney's misadventure are not explored.

He, Dunn, Caesar, and the rest of the clique quickly run afoul of Brother Constance. They sneak off to see Elvis Presley's *Blue Hawaii* as the school applauds the touring Pope John—to the strains of Italian opera. They are assigned to clean pigeon droppings off St. Basil on Sunday.

Danni stirs Dunn's inner self as they visit a "weird, fantastic planet," Coney Island in the desolation of early spring. *Newsday's* Joseph Gelmis noted, "The scene is filmed in a tavern opening onto the boardwalk. Walls of windows look out over the ceiling and walls are bordered by rows of softly colored lights. They define and set off this space from the rest of the world.''[13] In this special place, they slow dance to Otis Redding's ''I've Been Loving You Too Long.'' As the melody continues, Michael Dunn experiences sexuality under the boardwalk.

The soda fountain is revisited by the monks. Danni blocks their entrance by locking the doors and pulling down the shades. All the while, Caesar attempts to explain *David Copperfield* to Rooney, who is buried in a Classic Comic. Brother Constance demands that the soda shop be closed for encouraging delinquency. Danni and her depressive parent are taken away by the welfare people. Rooney and cohorts decapitate St. Basil. They are discovered by—whom else?—Brother Constance, who locks them in a closet with Dunn, as the now persistent, jangling raga music filters throughout the school. ''There were times when I thought St. Basil's might be a coverup for the Hare Krishna movement,'' observed Rex Reed.[14] The resolution occurs as the sadistic monk takes the five boys into the gym for a thrashing. Corbet (Patrick Dempsey) and Williams are brought to tears. Caesar's pleas for mercy are ignored. Yelling, ''You leave him alone,'' Michael knocks the brother off his feet and flees. Brother Constance chases him into the auditorium, where an assembly is taking place. The desperate student decks his pursuer to the cheers of the gathered student body. The five are suspended for two weeks. The mean-spirited monk is transferred ''away from students.'' Elvis Presley's ''Blue Suede Shoes'' overlays Kevin Dillon's narration, ''Dunn and Danni got together at Woodstock . . .''

With one eye on the screen and the other on the boxoffice, film pundits were ambiguous. Lally's *Film Journal* posting was typical: ''Michael Dinner, making his feature directing debut after the TV film *Miss Lonelyhearts*, successfully evokes the Catholic school setting, but fails to set a consistent tone for the film. *Heaven Help Us* may need some divine intervention to attract more than a marginal teen following.'' Reviewer Alan Karp joined in, pointing to a ''lack of central focus.'' In backhanded fashion he wrote ''The filmmakers have provided their audience with more substance than is generally found in most teen-oriented comedies.'' Never one to restrain his observations, Rex Reed wrote ''This is no smut-and-pimples orgy for kids.''

''You don't want to overpraise 'Heaven Help Us' just because of its competition's shabbiness,'' added the *Los Angeles Times*. With the exception of Reed, most critics danced around the issue of the picture being too substantial in the age of *Porky's*. Only David Denby, surprisingly, dismissed the film, calling it ''timid, and all but worthless.''[15]

McCarthy, et al, received plaudits, as did Dinner. Janet Maslin appreciated such "well observed moments" as the boardwalk sequence. Kroll wrote, "This is a reasonably engaging kids' flick that is given humor and heartbreak by director Michael Dinner and a cast of splendidly scruffy young players."

Heaven Help Us earned Andrew McCarthy some notices. "Wary, sensitive and alert" was *Variety's* description. Overall, the youth ensemble was well treated in the print media, unlike at the box office.

The opening weekend saw the motion picture return $2.2 million. The year-end take was an unimpressive $2.7 million in domestic box office only. The album failed to chart. This outcome was predictable, as the titles were all oldies, minus a focus. Only the Otis Redding piece stood out in the film.

Ego Quest

Executive producers Jon Peters and Peter Guber had purchased the film rights to the highly praised Terry Davis novel *Vision Quest*. Harold Becker was signed to direct. (Becker had done two Joseph Wambaugh screen adaptations, including *The Onion Field*. He was best known for *Taps* 1981), a film generally damned by the "name" critics. *Time's* Schickel, saying "its big guns are loaded with nothing more lethal than Hollywood nerve gas," was joined by *Newsweek's* Ansen, who wrote, "How many teenagers do you know who would sacrifice their lives for a *military school*?" A lone writer accused reviewers of knee-jerk antimilitary feelings.[17] Despite aesthetics, *Taps* returned an unexpected 20.5 million dollars and the designation of being the first "brat pack" ensemble pix.)

In *Taps*, Becker had chosen Timothy Hutton (prior to *Ordinary People's* release), Sean Penn, and rookie actor Tom Cruise for major roles. Cruise was elevated from a minor part after the director observed him working out with the Valley Forge Military school cadets. Becker said of the cast, "Since the kids don't go to see names it means one is free to cast the best people available, not merely bankable names that studios approve."

Becker also had been taught a marketing lesson at 20th Century Fox. "Stanley Jaffe and I had approved a poster and campaign for *Taps* picturing Hutton in a Hamlet pose with copy stressing his crisis of conscience," he said. "We showed the finished film to Norman Levy at Fox and afterwards he said, 'I know how to sell the picture.' " The director continued, "Levy came back with a poster of Hutton flanked in the background by kids holding automatic weapons, dramatizing their takeover of the school at gunpoint. This was a campaign to get a visceral audience response."[18] The youth rebellion motif worked, even though it missed the point of the film cadets rising up to *save*, not overthrow, the military academy. A similar ploy would be utilized in the film itself to Peters's credit, music would be an integral part of the targeting.

Joel Sill, Warner Brothers Pictures music vice president, was assigned the task of molding a soundtrack. Lyricist John Bettis, who had written several Carpenters' songs, including "Top of the World," and the theme to "Growing Pains," was contacted by Warners Pictures' music director. The studio executive was looking for songs suitable for the *Vision Quest* project. "In reading the script, the scene I wanted to write a song for was the first time that the two main characters dance together," said Bettis. Co-writer Jon Lind found a title, "Crazy For You" which "was really descriptive of the scene in the film." Their collaboration was sent to Sill. Phil Ramone, a *Flashdance* and *Yentl* graduate, wanted the tune in the film sung by the highly visible Madonna.

Bettis and Lind harbored reservations over the choice of artist. "Jon and I were surprised at the choice of artist, if you want to know the truth," Bettis told Fred Bronson. The duo attended a recording session of the song, where their misgivings were reinforced. "Jon and I were depressed about the way the song came out," he added.[19] They feared Sill would reject "Crazy For You." The Warners vice president's views on soundtrack material were well known. "The film must be served first, but if you can expand a scene to include music, and a video clip, it always makes sense," he had said.[20] Rob Mounsey, brought in to rearrange the song, added the all-important back-up vocals. (Bettis credits Mounsey with making a hit record out of the selection.) "Crazy For You" became the breakout song. Madonna, a WCI performer, was the least of Sill's problems.

Jon Peters and Peter Guber wanted the CBS act Journey for the film. Sill was more than aware of the label's reputation as expensive and a "leader in putting in onerous clauses."[21] In the *Vision Quest* deal, CBS lived up to that reputation.

Billboard spotlighted *Vision Quest* in its "Album Picks" section. Suggesting a strong "commercial outlook" to merchandisers, the writer went on to say that "The movie itself has been described by one insider as 'Rocky Meets the Karate Kid' and the selections here suggest the same sort of commercial activity: John Waite, Madonna, and Don Henley all make timely appearances, with strong performances to boot."[22] *Vision Quest* advertising stressed the romantic sub-plot rather than the central focus on high school wrestling. The film was sneak-previewed at some 300 theaters nationally in the hope of stimulating word-of-mouth advertising among the under-twenty-five-year-old population. Trailers with Madonna were scheduled as videoclips for MTV and other stations a month before the film's 15 February release date.

Warner Brothers Pictures purchased eighty spots on MTV. The thirty-to-ninety-second commercials paralleled those of *Flashdance*. The advertising focus was in total disarray, vacillating between the male lead and the love angle. The album cover featured both.

As the film begins, the narrative introduces a muscular athlete skipping rope to Journey's "Only the Young." "My name is Louden . . . last week I turned eighteen and I wasn't ready for it as I haven't done nothing yet . . ." But he plans to, telling the wrestling coach (Charles Hallahan) that he (Matthew Modine) is going to change weight divisions in order to challenge the "baddest" wrestler in the state, Shute (Frank Jasper). He jogs as "Only the Young" resounds. The opening credits roll. The basic storyline and rock "workout music" are instantaneously established—*Rocky* and *Flashdance* visit secondary school athletics.

When not exercising to overlayed rock music, Louden is a bellboy in the local hotel where Elmo (J.C. Quinn) is the short-order cook and spiritual advisor. Kuch (Michael Schoeffling), Londen's Mohawked high school buddy, gossips while claiming Native ancestry. He is responsible for suggesting the vision-quest concept—the discovery of self—to which Louden naively replies, "I just wanna wrestle Shute." His collegiate scholarship will be on the line. Even at this early stage, the outcome of this "impossible" confrontation is hardly in doubt, that is, until the arrival of the dark-haired, hardened vixen Carla (Linda Fiorentino).

On her way to attend art school in San Francisco, Carla somehow becomes stranded in Spokane. The young swain is immediately infatuated with Carla despite his Dad's warning, "She's been around the block a few times." (Cox's description omits the somewhat puzzling characterization of a street-smart Jerseyite whose musical preferences run to Vivaldi's *Four Seasons* rather than to Springsteen.) She, of course, will be Louden's other quest. Louden scouts Shute, a high school version of Conan, as he carries a telephone pole trunk up the stadium stairs. All the while, the would-be champion is on a starvation diet. The competitive pursuit becomes more *Rockyish*.

In one of many segues the youthful wrestler drops in at the local tavern, where Madonna is singing "Gambler," only to encounter Carla. "What are you doing here?" he asks. A good question for both individuals. They dance to "Crazy For You" with very brief cutaways to the singer.

As the plot slowly works its way toward the climax, exercise or travelling—jogging, driving—are ideal rock-track opportunities to play "Shout

To The Top," Don Henley's "She's On A Zoom," and the omnipresent "Crazy For You."

The plot development is thin as Carla, the tough chick, objects to wrestling as a "macho-violence trip" until our hero illustrates the sport is "balance more than strength." The film's stress, however, is on power, not balance.

Louden and Carla verbally spar about his sexuality: "Intercourse burns up 200 calories" is but one illustration.

Finally, on a trip to visit Grandpa Swain in the picturesque Northwest, Carla matter-of-factly seduces Modine. Having gotten the unexplained intimacy out of the way, the Big Match between Shute's Hoover High and Swain's Thompson "Warriors" looms.

To his credit, director Howard Becker makes the preordained contest interesting. The last forty-seven seconds are slow motion, like a *Miami Vice* scene, to heighten the suspense. Having completed the quest, Louden has discovered that one must live for the present, since "there is no other way." Journey returns. Several reviewers dismissed using "vision quest" as the feature's title. The point was well taken, as the concept as defined by the Mohawked Kuch—"finding your place in the circle"—is only toyed with. The introductory narrative had set up the initiation with the information that Louden has turned eighteen, having done nothing—but "this is the year I make my mark." He does. Still, the cosmic aspect of a "vision quest," along with the closing narrative, is hardly demonstrated by wrestling and the loss of virginity.

Vision Quest opened 15 February in 993 theaters. It attracted a disappointing $2.7 million in box office. (*Breakfast Club* deservedly was draining the target audience.) The film also failed to titillate critics. Only the *Los Angeles Times*'s Kevin Thomas and Jack Kroll praised the Peters-Guber production.

Matthew Modine was generally praised by Establishment critics. Vincent Canby compared Modine's "boyish charm" to that of a youthful Gary Cooper. Several writers found the actor's work to be the only redeeming feature in the film.[23] Coming-of-age vehicles directed at the teen market had been monopolizing the nation's screens. In this context, many reviewers found *Vision Quest* to be a cliche within a cliche.

Variety's Greenberg signaled the assault. The picture, he contended, was "a virtual catalog of cliches from recent teen hits without a true heart of center of its own." Noble saw the film as patterned after the producers' successful dance film, saying, "After all, bits and pieces of *Flashdance* dominated Videoville for most of 1983. Here, in *Vision Quest*, there are enough scenes of muscular young men lifting weights and practicing drills to turn out a brief and appropriately shallow exercise cassette." Edelstein provided the finishing blow: "The hack commercial producers, Jon Peters and Peter Guber, and the director, Harold Becker (*Taps*), have squeezed the story into a *Footloose/Flashdance* package, complete with Journey and Foreigner pumping up the soundtrack." The *Voice* writer concluded, "It's a rich irony that a textbook teen pic is thoroughly unqualified to handle real teen crises."[24]

Although the soundtrack was released by Geffen Records, the recognizable stamp of Al Teller's "clustering" strategy was apparent. Journey, a CBS act, provided the scout single, "Only the Young." Released several weeks prior to the film on 26 January, it charted at a respectable Number 43. There was no video, as the group's management felt clips were too expensive. CBS Records reportedly received an enormous $200,000 fee for the use of what was essentially a song of B-side quality. Taylor Hackford, a director with an impeccable soundtrack record, complained that *Vision Quest* paid "Journey an astronomical amount of money for an outtake, in my opinion. It was a good song but inappropriate for the film. That's unconscionable. At the same time it poisons the well for everybody else."[25] The song did reach the *Billboard* Top Ten, at Number 9 23 March and immediately began a downward spiral.

John Waite's "Change" followed in February as an MTV add-on. It joined the artist's "Reckless Heart," which had spent five weeks on the music channel's power rotation. "Change" lasted for over a month. Chrysalis Records released the single several weeks later, 2 March—the same date as Madonna's "Crazy For You." The Waite song lingered in the midsection of the chart.

"Crazy For You" was the musical breakout. Retrospectively, John Koladner, vice president of Geffen Records, mused that "*Vision Quest*, a relatively successful movie, really should have been retitled 'Crazy For You' to coordinate with Madonna's song and video. The two million records that were sold certainly couldn't have hurt the film."[26]

The video aired 23 January accompanied by "The Gambler," also from the movie. The two *Vision Quest* videoclips joined Madonna's "Like a Virgin" still on MTV after three months. "Crazy For You" started in the power rotation. The title's four month stay ended 30 April in the heavy category.

John Bettis, the lyricist, was in for a pleasant answer to his question about Madonna, "Can she sing a song like this?" It peaked at the Number 1 slot 11 May 1985 only to be bumped by the *Breakfast Club* opener by Simple Minds. (Madonna had easily outperformed the non-WEA acts.) Jimmy Summers outlined the problem in *Boxoffice*, saying, "The inclusion of a dozen or so new rock songs might help attract attention for the movie. But most of them, especially a number ["Gambler"] performed on screen by singer Madonna, seem jammed into the movie with a plunger and with little thought to appropriateness. The Madonna number is especially awkward since no one else from the movie appears on screen with her, suggesting her scene was filmed months later and shoved into the movie to capitalize on her current popularity." *Variety*'s Greenberg felt that the exploitation was mishandled, and P.C. Noble wrote that the cutaways marred Madonna's appearance: "Although her song 'Crazy For You,' plays at least three different times on the soundtrack, Madonna herself is only visible for about a minute and a half, in a sequence not even long enough to be lifted out as a video." (The videoclip proved to be better than the movie.) *Variety's* Greenberg concurred, labeling the score "heavy and intrusive." He perceived that the material by Tangerine Dream, Journey and Madonna was going in "too many directions at once. Try as it might," he concluded, "this picture goes nowhere."[27] The album went well, but the year-end studio receipts totalled only $5.2 million.

Detention at Sherimer High: The Breakfast Club

Located in Charlie Chaplin's old studio lot, A&M Records is unique in the music industry. A small, closely knit operation, it has repeatedly parlayed artist development into chartbusters. In the mid-1980s, the Alpert-Moss union remains the one significant record label unblemished by a corporate takeover.

In 1983 the company's head, Gil Friesen, an industry veteran, desired diversification. "We started this," explained executive vice president Andy Meyer about forming A&M films, "because it's something Gil really wanted to do and he felt it would be the way for us to expand A&M in a very creative way, doing what we do best, this finding and discovering new talent. That's what A&M has done well in the record business and we thought we could apply the same skills to films."

The application of the disk-marketing formula involved picking a small number of strong characters like Herb Alpert and The Tijuana Brass, Cat Stevens, Joe Cocker, The Flying Burrito Brothers, and Joe Jackson. Friesen and Meyer had felt that Alan Parker's *Birdy* (1984) followed in the tradition. It flopped, as did the first releases of The Carpenters, Humble Pie, and Peter Frampton.

A&M Films was strictly a production company. "We're independent and proud of it," said Meyer. "We act as executive producers, but we're in the development side."[28] In synergistic fashion, A&M owned ancillary record rights plus 50 percent of video proceeds; the distribution company, such as Tri-Star or Universal Pictures, received the other half. The company's second project would be Chicago-based writer/director John Hughes teen pic *The Breakfast Club*.

John Hughes, an ex-*National Lampoon* editor, established screenplay credentials with his adaptation of "Vacation '58" (a special issue of *National Lampoon*) into the successful *National Lampoon's Vacation*, and also *Mr. Mom*, (both in summer 1983). His directorial debut, in 1984, was *Sixteen Candles*. The $6.5-million production garnered mixed reviews, but earned a respectable $20 million at the box office.

In Sixteen Candles, set in a Chicago suburb, Samantha (Molly Ringwald) plays a middle-class princess whose all-important sixteenth birthday is ignored, due to her sister's wedding. To make her existence even more unbearable, the "love of her life," Jake, is going with the prom queen. Further complicating matters is The Geek (Anthony Michael Hall), described by *New York*'s David Denby as "a skinny freshman with braces— a brilliant, infuriating nonstop talker and con artist" who has a crush on the insecure girl. The picture received mixed notices. Edelstein noted, "What ruins it, for me, is that he (Hughes) ends up endorsing that (caste system), along with its stupidest stereotypes: afraid that kids will get restless; and he never hints that some lower-rung denizens of his slapstick universe might be less than comfortable with their station." The director/ writer, according to Denby, "knows that high-school romance is largely a matter of kids trying to act out a certain image of themselves . . . watching *Sixteen Candles* is like finding a couple of cans of champagne in a six-pack of Schlitz." (Product placement in a review?)[29]

Jim Cahill was Universal's director of video production, in the studio's production division as opposed to marketing. "I like to think of these things," (referring to videos) he said, "as pieces of art rather than marketing. We're treating them as a creative vehicle to help movies." Cahill assigned *Hard To Hold*, *Streets of Fire*, and *Sixteen Candles* for video treatment.

Kanew-Deuton Video was brought in to do the clip for Hughes's directorial debut, using "Hang Up The Phone" as the leader. (The televisual firm had edited *Risky Business* and *Streets of Fire* for television and closed-circuit mall viewing.) Howie Deutch, in keeping with Cahill's approach, employed an "integrating device" of a final shot of the cast dancing on a cake with the film title boldly iced on the object. "I wanted to do something different based on the energy and attitude of the song," Deutch told Jim Bessman, "that will in turn help the film, more than a video that is not done in the spirit of the film. *Sixteen Candles* is a very pretty movie, done in great taste, and to have made the video any other way would have been as productive for the film.''[30] The originality of the clip, more expensive than a trailer, helped, as the Annie Gold vocal and lyric were built on the structure of the Supremes 1966 success "You Can't Hurry Love."

The Deutch video appeared on MTV several weeks before *Candles* was released on 4 May 1984. The single emerged at the same time, but failed to chart. The album suffered a similar fate.

The soundtrack album contained five songs. The title was a cover of The Crests version by the rock-a-billy Stray Cats. Patti Smith redid Them's "Gloria." The Golden offering, also, was a remake. "If You Were Here" by The Thompson Twins and Ira Newborn's "Geek Boogie," written for the film, filled out the roster. The 12-inch EP was a commercial disappointment.

The Breakfast Club revisited the land of *Ordinary People*, *Risky Business*, and *Candles*, creating what some writers labeled "The Little Chill." The film site was a vacant high school in Des Plaines, Illinois. The gymnasium was the sound stage for the library set and Mr. Vernon's office.

The cast consisted of two *Candles* alums, Molly Ringwald and Anthony Michael Hall, and the fast-rising Emilio Estevez, Ally Sheedy, and Judd Nelson. ("They're just kids" was co-producer Michelle Manning's characterization.) Several would become charter members of David Blum's "Brat Pack," a group of young Hollywood starlites. *All My Children's* Paul Gleason portrayed the antagonistic school administrator.

John Hughes is a strong proponent of the soundtrack. *American Graffiti*, to which *The Breakfast Club* would be compared, and *Animal House* were models for the director. They showed how the score can "heighten the visual effect of the scene and the intellectual effect of the dialogue with the emotional effect of the music." The script was penned during what Hughes called his "Clash-Elvis Costello period."[31] (Both CBS artists were absent from the A&M album.) The synergy strategy was patterned on the Universal/MCA Records approach to *Sixteen Candles*.

Hughes utilized Keith Forsey to produce and compose the original material. Forsey, co-writer and producer of "The Heat Is On," penned "Don't You (Forget About Me)", the opening and closing theme. He tailored the song for Bryan Ferry, who declined.

There was an alternative, as musician-writer Kenn Lowy suggested that, Simple Minds lead singer Jim Kerr "sounds just like Bryan Ferry." Unaccustomed to doing others' material, that band also refused. With dogged persistence, however, Forsey talked the band into viewing a screening of Hughes's effort. Afterward he pitched the song. "If you don't like what we've got, then change [the song], make it work for you,'' he told them. Kerr returned several days later and indicated no changes were necessary, as "I love it."[32]

A&M continued its practice using a video for initial exposure. Simple Minds, "Don't You (Forget About Me)," directed by Danny Kleinman, and "Hyperactive," a Thomas Dolby clip, debuted on MTV's medium rotation the week of 16 January. The release date of the film was 5 February. The single and the album became available after 23 February 1985. The album, described as "pop/rock/dance" by *Billboard*, hit the bins along with Pat Matheny's *Falcon and the Snowman* score, the dance-oriented *Into The Night*, and Maurice Jarre's *A Passage To India*.

The Keith Forsey composition was well served by the video. Singer Jim Kerr is presented in the midst of television monitors, showing segments from *The Breakfast Club*, childhood toys, and a Seeburg jukebox. *Rock Video* applauded, saying, "The video for 'Don't You' shows a band first beginning to become that which they were always meant to be."[33] The single spent twenty-two weeks on the charts, climbing to the coveted Number 1 spot 18 May. The album was certified gold, with a thirty-one-week stay on the trade scale. The video promoted the song and the film. The Hughes production aided an aesthetically rather weak album.

Simple Minds' "Don't You (Forget About Me)" plays over the film's opening credits, coming to rest on a verse from David Bowie: "They're quite aware of what they're going through . . ." It's a cold March morning at Shermer High School as four very distinctive vehicles—a BMW, a Cadillac Seville, a sedan, and a van—each disgorge a student for a 7 a.m. Saturday detention. A fifth arrives shortly after. A voiceover from Brian Johnson (Anthony Michael Hall) introduces the diverse quintet that makes up the conscripted breakfast club. "A brain, an athlete, a basket case, a princess, a criminal" encompass the labels ascribed to them in the milieu of an upwardly mobile suburban, secondary school.

They assemble in a modernistic library to be confronted by an overbearing adult authority figure, Mr. Vernon (Paul Gleason). He instructs them not to talk or move; they are required to write a 1,000 word essay on "Who You Think You Are." (This will serve as the thrust of the film.)

John Bender (Judd Nelson), the resident "wise-ass" greaser, quickly establishes his role; he becomes cruel and cutting. When not aggravating Claire Standish (Molly Ringwald) over her elitism and confused sexuality or wrestling jock Andrew Clark (Emilio Estevez), Bender hums the opening to "Sunshine of Your Love." The verbal status game introduces Brian Johnson, the over-achieving *A* student, and, by her silence, Allison Reynolds (Ally Sheedy), a withdrawn, Sixtyish space cadet. Most of the morning is spent exchanging insults pertaining to stereotypes. Bender, never at a loss for words, mocks Andy's sport, wrestling, as a bunch of guys with lobotomies and tights. Richard Vernon wanders in, occasionally, to berate and threaten his charges, with little effect.

The Gleason character is an overdrawn adult buffoon. As he commiserates with the janitor, the eyes and ears of the school, a few fleeting clues to the bored teacher are exposed. When he complains of the current class of students, the janitor, Carl (John Kapelos) responds, "If you were sixteen, what would you think of you?" No answer was given.

Lunch is announced. Going for Cokes, Allison expresses her choice of another beverage, vodka. This is her first intelligible utterance. The midday meal is another exercise in social stratification. Claire's sushi contrasts with Brian's well balanced, all-American package of peanut butter and jelly with a container of soup. The jock opens a virtual grocery store of food, and Allison constructs a sandwich of Captain Crunch and salt between bread slices. Bender comes empty-handed. The post-lunch sequences intensify status divisions and roles with talk of autos, food, and fashions. The overt tension is between Bender and the world, especially the seemingly petty institutional symbol, Vernon.

Lunch has energized the detainees, who creep off to Bender's locker, where a stash of marijuana is retrieved. Vernon, having spilled coffee over his clothes, is also prowling the halls. The students race down the halls to escape detection as Wang Chung's "Fire In the Twilight" is heard. The song is awkwardly placed. Bender decoys the administrator as the others find safety in the library. For his sacrifice Bender is locked in a supply closet. He escapes. The Catalytic dope-smoking, to the instrumental "I'm a Dude," ensues. The self-searching revelations commence. One student proffers, "Home life is unsatisfying," to which Andy knowingly snaps, "Everyone's is." Allison complains, "They ignore me." The statement is greeted with recognition. The wrestler and the academic "dork" confess that they are overachievers due to the demands of parents. The pressure to excel has landed them in Saturday detention. Allison admits she's present because "I didn't have anything better to do." Andy rhetorically ponders, "Are we going to be like our parents?"

"It's inevitable," Allison states with pessimism, "when you grow up your heart dies."

Brian raises a more immediate concern—Monday. The student bonding will be short-lived, responds the prom queen, as Allison, Brian, and Bender are not "friends with the same kind of people." Pausing, she notes "the pressure they can put on you." The others object, half-heartedly, that they will overcome the peer-applied caste system. As if to celebrate,

Karla DeVito's "We Are Not Alone" fills the library as the ensemble gyrates to the beat. (The dance scene doesn't fit; it appears to be created for MTV consumption.) Richard Corliss labelled the rite "only one *Footloose* dance initiation." Another writer asked, "What is a rock music record doing in the school archives?"[34] The nine-hour detention is over. Claire has partially conned Brian as "you're the smartest," into writing a collective essay, which he signs "The Breakfast Club."

Leaving the deserted school, Alan and the transformed Ms. Weirdo embrace, auguring a happy future. A similar show of affection, including a kiss, between the leader of the pack and the teen queen lacks any commitment. Bender leaves with a souvenir, Claire's diamond earring, and Allison with a new persona, due to Claire's make-up skills. Perhaps the belle of Shermer was deeper than the facade she exhibited.

Breakfast Club works *if* role suspension is akin to discarding an overcoat on a hot day or Allison's flowering with a new face and hair style. Can an intense group dynamic triumph over years of parental and peer pressure? Hughes, as other playwrights and screenwriters, appears to advocate this outcome. Only the complex Claire seems to symbolize role suspension as situational, and her lapse is momentary—paid for by one diamond trinket.

The release date for *Breakfast Club* proved, ironically, to be a bonus. In the valley of the blind, the one-eyed man is king; a large number of critics utilized this thesis as the lead-in to their pieces about the Hughes picture. Edelstein and Corliss, particularly, spent a good deal of space examining the teen pics. "What's the matter with kids' movies today? There are too damn many of them, that's what, and they are all about the same damn thing," objected the *Time* reviewer. "The glandular convulsions of adolescence are just not interesting or complex enough to sustain the plots of half a hundred Hollywood films each year." Corliss went on to explain the filmmakers' fixation on reaching the youth market. "More than half the U.S. movie audience is in the 12-to-24 age group, so Hollywood keeps grinding out these smudged, cracked funhouse mirrors of teendom. It matters not that most megahits cast their nets over broader demographics. Teenpixs come close to guaranteeing a decent return on a modest financial and creative investment. They will keep coming until Chip and Wendy Q. Public weary of seeing their screen doubles lose their virginity for the zillionth time to an MTV beat," he wrote. He concluded his piece by praising Hughes for demonstrating that "there is a life form after teenpix." Most critics echoed the sentiment that *Breakfast Club* was flawed, *but* "it is one of the better teen films among the rash of recent competitors," wrote Stanton.[35]

Press notices focused on the director/writer and the acting ensemble.

Kevin Lally wrote that the director had "an empathy and respect for young people that may be unmatched in movies today," while Fleischmann said, "Teendom may just have its first major-league amateur." Ansen, Corliss, Edelstein, and others applauded the contribution of the "gifted ensemble." Denby enjoyed the group with the exception of Judd Nelson, whom he described as going too far with "jeering sarcasm."[36]

The Breakfast Club had a small band of detractors. *Variety* led the attack with, "John Hughes has come up with a wondrous message: No matter what is wrong with the individual youth of today, it is the parents' fault . . . it may be. But not unless the brain has already started to rot with films like this." Even an advocate of the project like Lally took note of the generational bashing, writing, that the film "may be too unremittingly critical of adult authority figures . . ."[37]

Universal's marketing focus on videoclips recognized the statistical reality that 68 percent of music video viewers chose a movie to see as a result of cable exposure. Music trailers *did* serve as ideal scouts for teen-oriented film and music makers. "They're targeting the same market—for films and MTV" said then-vice president John Sykes. Al Newman, MGM/UA publicity vice president, concurred, saying, "The audience that pays attention to music videos pretty much parallels the core of movie-goers."[38] Radio, even with a title song, was less effective in promoting a film.

One strength of video was found in its ability to highlight bankable, instantly recognizable young stars and singers. Images of Molly Ringwald or Judd Nelson did stir interest in the Simple Minds song and *The Breakfast Club*.

The slight differential in impact was offset by cost. A support video became economically viable when some product or box office action was in evidence. Hughes's teen pics were ideal for MTV's audience. Annie Golden and Simple Minds had had very low rock Q-profiles, if any. Strong videoclips could generate radio and box office activity, resulting in album sales. Universal Pictures had re-used the *Flashdance* formula and purchased more than fifty thirty-second inserts on MTV.

The Breakfast Club enjoyed the high visibility of the S.E. Hinton adaptations *Tex* and *The Outsiders*, Emilo Estevez, and *Candles*'s Ringwald, and Hall. Their presence enhanced the video, song, and film.

The prolonged interval between the screening of the video and the release of the musical product was curious. A&M appears to have chosen to stress the outcome of the motion picture, hoping for a ripple effect on vinyl. The ploy worked as the film earned $5.1 million in four days at 1,071 theaters. The year-end box office total was $34 million. After theater, cable, and syndication exposure, the soundtrack tally was 750,000 copies.

Which Came First?

> *"Power of Love"* is number one, but I don't
> believe it added any money to the box office,
> because most people don't even know it's from
> a movie.
> —Gary LeMel, Columbia Pictures

> The greatest *Leave It To Beaver* episode ever
> produced.
> —Steven Spielberg, producer

In mid-1985, Rockbill's founder and president, Jay Coleman, defined synergy as "each division feeding off others."[39] The "feeding" process was rapidly becoming more a question of the survival of the fittest. It was fairly clear that each project was a gamble. Strong films *did* rack up souvenir sales when the soundtrack was properly integrated into the movie. Infectious soundtracks, as *Vision Quest*, could outstrip a carrier film's longevity and profitability. The biological analogy was one of minnows feeding off the sharks, but the question was, which medium was the minnow? Studio people unhesitatingly pointed to the music industry.

Producers were rapidly learning terms such as "sync rights," "performance fees," "master-use," and "buyouts." Synchronization rights involve the song publisher's permission to correlate the music scenes in the film. Performance fees are payments to the publisher to exhibit the material in the United States. Master-use rights, permission to use a particular song in a film, are paid to the record company. Buyouts are a one-time payment to a label for the use of a song on video cassette. One studio executive said, "Oh, it's terrible. Our music budgets have gone way up. Three minutes of music used to be like $3,000 ten years ago. The publishers want an arm and a leg for the use of these songs. They are raking in the money like you wouldn't believe." A *Premiere* contributor wrote that the music companies were in the dominant position: "It's a seller's market, and they know it."[40]

Studio protestations had merit, on the surface. In the supply-and-demand world of Hollywood, producers in search of reaching the youth market were lining up for music rights. Prices soared. Even relatively low-budget vehicles were paying more than $200,000 for rights. Masters for especially attractive tunes could run as high as $60,000.

Taylor Hackford, possibly the ultimate practitioner of synergy, sees both industries as too greedy. "Producers will pay anything now," he noted, "just to get a hit song in their new movie. It's a creeping monster." Record labels, he suggested, were more than willing to exploit this naivete. "They think some big producer will come around and buy one [anything]. 'It wasn't good enough to go on our album but what the hell do the producers know? They want a hit song by us, and they will pay us a lot of money.' Too often," he continued, "they are tracks that did not have the integrity to make it on the LP."[41]

The costs partially explain the curious mix of songs actually heard in movies, those listed in the closing credits, and the selections finally appearing on vinyl. *Beverly Hills Cop* featured material by Frey, Junior, The Pointer Sisters, and Patti LaBelle's "Stir It Up." The latter, prominently used throughout the movie, was listed on the credits with Vanity's "Nasty Girl." Vanity, Warner Brothers artist, was absent from the track and the album. The MCA album contained ten songs. Some selections fit the ambiance; some represent contractual *quid pro quos* between the studio and the label.

Producers, however, were not total innocents begin ravaged by greedy record bizzers. Stories abound, as with *Risky Business*, of filmmakers insisting on a certain song performed by a name artist. One observer suggested, "No negotiating factor is more important than how badly the producer wants to use the song."[42]

The avalanche of teen pictures in 1985 and the blossoming home-video market strengthened the position of publishers and labels.

Rock was being legitimized as a staple for motion pictures, especially the flood of youth-targeted films. In 1985, as in 1958, the novelty of rock soundtracks was fading. The stakes, for filmmakers and labels, were increasing, but so were the risks.

The formulas of the *SNF, Flashdance*, and *Footloose* years were giving way to the tried, and not-so-true, "golden-gut" approach to scoring. As costs escalated, filmmakers *partially* retreated to the studio system. Composers and record producers, such as Faltermeyer, Cooder, Bones Howe, and others, could be hired to create or cover material for the film, reducing studio costs. This variation was particularly appealing to Universal and Warner Brothers, who had record labels under the same corporate logo. The ultimate proceeds went into the same stockholders report.

There was, of course, a down side. Scored material did not fit the scout formula of marketing. As Ry Cooder explained, "It's music freed from the constraints of the four-minute song, freed from the horrors of 'How do we sell it?' "[43]

Teaching Chuck Berry "Johnny B. Goode"

Steven Spielberg's production of *Back To The Future*, the largest domestic grosser of 1985, demonstrated a successful 50/50 split between name rockers and film scoring.

Bob Gale, with screenwriting partner Robert Zemeckis, was working on *Used Cars*, a 1982 tale of the exorbitant means salesman will resort to in the pursuit of money. During his free moments Gale perused his father's University Hills High School *Yearbook.*" He found his parent's photo captioned "Senior Class Vice President." This serendipitous encounter spawned the film, *Back to the Future*.

"I thought to myself," he remembered, " 'Geez, could I ever have been friendly with the type of guy who ran for class office?' " He approached Zemeckis with the rhetorical question. Zemeckis told the *New York Times*, "We wondered if we would be their pals, if we would've hung out with them. We couldn't answer that question. It's impossible. They would always be our parents. That could never change through time." The existential query resulted in the storyboard for *Back To The Future*. The working scenario was, "A kid goes back in time, meets his parents, interferes with their lives, and affects their future." The writing duo wanted to avoid creating cliched, time-travel picture, instead opting for the socio-psychological interplay in and between generations. "This movie is about people," they would say.[44]

The project was written with the use of 3″ x 5″ cards pinned on a bulletin board. "We'd pull a card off the wall and act out the scene, sketch out the action and try to fill in what dialogue would work and what props we would need to make our point," said Zemeckis.[45] Each sequence would stress the collision of historical subcultures. Some of the most lingering impressions of the film are from these exchanges.

Like Tom Cruise's air-guitar scene, the most frequently cited segment of *Risky Business*, the "Johnny B. Goode" bit was *Back To The Future's* contribution to rock in film trivia. Loynd wrote, "The most rousing and audience-grabbing scene of culture shock comes when Fox mounts the '55 high school stage, says he's going to play an oldie, and digs into Chuck's 'Johnny B. Goode' at the dawn of rock 'n' roll."

"This white '80s teenager must teach black '50's musicians the finer points of rock 'n' roll," said Corliss. "Out-rageous!"[46] The execution of the sequence is nearly perfect.

In order to facilitate the bonding of Marty McFly's (Michael J. Fox) future parents, he must sit in for injured Starlighter guitarist Marvin Berry (Harry Waters, Jr.). Having accomplished the feat, assuring his survival,

Marty is asked to undertake an unfulfilled dream. "Do something that really cooks," says a Starlighter. Addressing the microphone, Fox says "This is an oldie . . ." The now-familiar ringing introduction fills the auditorium. The teenagers instinctively jive to the sound. "Marty becomes so immersed in his performance that he begins to play like a 1985 heavy metal musician," asserted Blake Lucas, "causing stunned silence in the audience and among the musicians before he stops. Sliding across the stage on his knees, duck walking, and kicking speakers."[47] As all of this is happening, the sidelined leader telephones his cousin. "Chuck, Chuck!," he shouts into the receiver. "This is your cousin Marvin Berry. You know that new sound you've been lookin' for! Well listen to this . . ." Several critics took exception to this perceived racial slight. They missed the point. Finishing, Marty, looking at the stunned audience, says, "I guess you guys aren't ready for that yet. But your kids are gonna love it." The musical fare of the period was already established with prerock favorites like "Mr. Sandman" and "The Ballad of Davy Crockett." Scenes such as this give the film a substance appealing across generations.

With a working script, Spielberg and Zemeckis wanted teen-throb Michael J. Fox *Family Ties* as the time traveling McFly. The producer of the sit-com, Gary David Goldberg, refused to release Fox for the movie. Based on his performance in *Mask* and a screen test, Eric Stoltz was chosen for the part. In order to meet a summer release date, shooting began in December 1984. Six weeks and $4 million into the filming the actor was dismissed.

Stoltz's exit created a minor controversy. Reportedly, Stoltz was let go because his performance "wasn't consistent with the original concept" or he was "too intense for the mood of the film." The actor's agent, Helen Sugland, told a reporter the decision came "as a complete surprise . . . totally out of left field" as they had "heard only positive things." Producer Spielberg attempted to put the best spin on the situation. "I'm still miserable—not about the decision, which was right, but what I should have done, which was allow Bob Zemeckis and Gale to wait until the first of the year, when Michael was available," remembered the filmmaker. "I should have waited, and yet I wanted the film out for the summer."[48] With seven episodes of the television series yet to shoot, Fox worked on both productions for nearly two months in order to make the time-warp movie. "For six weeks Michael would work all day on 'Family Ties,' " remembered the director. "Then he'd work with us from 6 o'clock until midnight, go home and go to sleep."[49] The final production and distribution costs were estimated at $22 million, less than *1941*, but more than *Goonies*, which was brought in for $15 million.

Steven Spielberg, with an uncanny ability to understand and exploit the icons of youth culture, exhibited little if any interest in the music of preadults. *Gremlins*, a $78-million box office smash, generated few soundtrack sales. *Goonies*, early in the production stage, seemed destined for a similar fate. This was despite the fact that it contained all of the ingredients for a successful synergy campaign. The film promised good box office, and its performing artists included Cyndi Lauper with a title song, "The Goonies 'R' Good Enough," which had a heavy-rotation MTV clip and CBS Record Group production. Leonard Petze, a senior manager at Epic A&R, anticipated three to four singles from the album, reminiscent of *Footloose*.

"Once we got involved in the project," recalled the executive, "we realized we were fighting a real uphill battle with Spielberg as far as the music goes, because none of his movies have featured music." Petz cited the fate of Arthur Baker's "Goon Squad—Eight Arms to Hold You" in *Goonies*. The scene with the song was cut. "So you can go to the theatre and watch *Goonies* and won't hear it," Petze explained. REO's "Wherever You're Going" (It's Alright)" also got lost in the editing. Lauper's scout single *did* break into the Top 10, promoting the flim but doing little for the album. Gary LeMel discounted CBS's explanation for the dismal performance of the album, saying "You can talk about promotion money and all that stuff, but if it's not in the grooves, it's not going to happen."[50] This industry cliche is valid; however, had the producer cooperated with the label, the result may have been different.

Spielberg's indifference was utilized to advantage by music supervisor Bones Howe, a veteran producer and session man who had worked with The Association and The Fifth Dimension, among others. Using the script's songs, artists were integrated into period pieces over the thirty-year time span. "I went home," he recalled, "and did my music research, which really wasn't that difficult, because I was in the music industry in 1955."

Spielberg, Zemeckis, and Gale were insistent on featuring Huey Lewis on the soundtrack. "I Want a New Drug" was employed as a temporary track during the shooting; the singer was not yet signed. He did agree, telling the filmmakers "In the Nick of Time" was just right for the project. "Oh, that's wonderful" was the reaction. Negotiations with Lewis's management dragged on. The wonderful song finally went to the Richard Pryor vehicle, *Brewster's Millions*, and Patti LaBelle performed the song for the closing theme of *Back to the Future*. "Everybody was really upset about it," said Howe. Lewis reassured the worried executives "Don't worry, I'm writing a great song for the end of the picture called 'Back In Time.' It'll work great."

"Power of Love" bumped up against the deadline. The music supervisor asserted, "We went right up to a couple of days before the final mix of the movie before we had the finished version."[51] "Back In Time" was favored by the studio people as the feature song; Howe believed in "Power" and prevailed. The single was utilized to overlay Fox's skateboarding adventures. It was the only place possible, according to Zemeckis.

The resultant album had ten selections, oldies and contemporary cuts. The two Lewis numbers were added to Eric Clapton's "Heaven Is One Step Away" and Lindsey Buckingham's "Time Bomb Town." Both were WEA artists, barely noticed in the film score. The tunes central to the storyline—"Earth Angel (Will You Be Mine)" and the memorable "Johnny B. Goode"—were produced by Howe for the movie. Harry Waters, Jr. sang the "Marvin Berry" rendition of The Penguins' classic. Mark Campbell's cover would be lip-synced by McFly on "Johnny B. Goode." Tim May did the frantic guitar solo.

The Howe productions, prominently placed in the film, were the highlights of the album. Taking a page from *Rock, Pretty Baby* (1956) and *You Light Up My Life* (1977), Howe managed to have five songs on the album cut by session people, a considerable savings to the MCA accounting office, thus allowing for the use of recognizable artists like Lewis and Clapton. The Johnny Ace classic "Pledging My Love," which filtered out to the high school parking lot, was not included on the disk. The final MCA package, aesthetically, worked well only as a souvenir album.

The Enchantment-Under-the-Sea-segment of the film is central to the plot. The director wisely used cover versions of familiar Fifties rockers. (Having the "Starlighters" or Marty lip-sync the originals would have destroyed the credibility of the scenes and one of the more provocative lines in the movie.) The performances were more than sufficient musically, while retaining the believability of a high school dance.

Back To The Future, film and album, were scheduled for a 3 July release. Both products enjoyed some prerelease momentum. The imprimatur of Steven Spielberg on the picture aided exhibition. Using Huey Lewis's "Power of Love" as a scout single, while it was not an immediate blockbuster, proved a wise move. (Lewis was a beneficiary of consumer largess in 1984 with the album, *Sports*. The LP was multiplatinum, selling nine million copies, and produced five Top-20 singles.) *Billboard* predicted *Back to the Future* (film and album) would be the "summer's biggest" offerings.[52] MCA Records, anxious to repeat its *Beverly Hills Cop* experience, ran full-page ads announcing, "THE FUTURE IS NOW." The copy stressed the inclusion of Huey Lewis and The News, Eric Clapton, and Lindsey Buckingham. The three were all with other labels.

Back was entering a crowded field of youth-oriented summer films. Yoram Globus of Cannon action films, retrospectively described the summer of 1985 thus: "Teenage movies about weird science, science this, science, science, science. Nobody wanted to see them."

"Too many people," agreed Samuel Z. Arkoff, "jumped on the youth bandwagon." *Village Voice* critic David Edelstein noted, "The marketing guys ordered more and more teen pix—'We've got 'em by the balls!' they cried. But the audience's boredom was swift and deadly. . . ."[53] The summer of the Brat Pack was not a propitious time for a high-tech, teenage saga.

Many of the brat-pack films had featured soundtrack albums. The 4 May issue of *Billboard* announced, "Soundtracks Dominate May Release List." The trade magazine counted a dozen titles. Half carried the MCA logo. A majority of the films and their companion albums stiffed.

Fifteen top-selling soundtracks were listed by *Billboard* at the year's end, but only three summer releases earned a place on the year-end chart. (*A View to A Kill*, a James Bond thriller, included a title track by Duran Duran, but cannot be classified as a rock-oriented film.) The Memorial Day-through-Labor Day season did not appear hospitable to a Michael J. Fox showcase.

The Chrysalis Records single, "Power of Love," landed on the Hot 100 at Number 46 a week prior to the film and album release. The scout thus had little time to aid the movie. "Power of Love," noted Gary LeMel, did little for *Back To The Future* "because most people don't even know it's from a movie."[54] The song did have an unusually long stay on the charts. A month later, three weeks after the film's opening 24 July, MTV added the song's videoclip to its heavy-rotation category.

The 4 July weekend found *Future* in ninety-nine movie theaters. The gross was $1 million, second only to *Rambo II*. *Boxoffice*, an exhibitor's trade paper, termed it the "strongest" of the summer season.

Back To the Re Decade?

Back to the Future commences, fittingly, with a host of clocks ticking away the remaining minutes until 8 a.m., 10 November 1985. The emphasis on time and place augurs an examination of the present in a relative framework, which requires a past. The film provides a chronological contrast, and what better place than the workplace of eccentric inventor

"Doc" Emmett Brown (Christopher Lloyd), "a real nut case," with a mutt appropriately named Einstein?

"Take Einstein's theory of relativity, add Freud's Oedipus complex, sprinkle with several episodes of 'Leave It To Beaver,' " read *Newsweek's* introduction to the film.[55]

Into this laboratory *qua* Rube-Goldberg assembly line enters protagonist Marty McFly (Michael J. Fox), a harmless, Hill Valley High student with adolescent aspirations of becoming a rock star.

Arriving late for class after skateboarding to school to the strains of "Power of Love," Marty is berated by a teacher for behaving "just like your father." McFly quips, "Human history is going to change."

At the audition for the school talent show, Marty does a visual Van Halen with a Lewis instrumental and is told, "You're just too darn (damned?) loud" by a bespectacled judge (cameoed by Huey Lewis).

The dejected youth is comforted by girlfriend Jennifer Parker (Claudia Wells) as they plan a weekend together, again to the sound of "Power." Marty's super-straight parents wouldn't approve, as Lorraine McFly (Lea Thompson) was "born a nun."

The weekend sojourn appears thwarted upon Marty's return home. The getaway car has been wrecked by the overbearing, aggressive Biff (Thomas Wilson). Mr. McFly (Chrispin Glover), a wimpish weakling, is incapable of coping. The Caspar Milquetoast admits that he's "not very good at confrontations."

Lorraine McFly, a wasted, middle-class haus frau, shows Puritan attitudes—"Terrible, girls chasing boys." Her descriptions of growing up in the Fifties would categorize *Happy Days* as a "wild youth" series. The generational barbs hint that Shales's repetitive-decade thesis may be incorrect, despite Spielberg's calling the picture "the greatest *Leave It To Beaver* episode ever produced." *The Wonder Years's* family is downright decadent when contrasted to the McFlys. (Although Mom does display an affinity for an extended happy hour.) Lorraine's seemingly disjointed reminiscences regarding her past—"night of that terrible thunderstorm"— serve as a future reference.

Marty escapes the humdrum bickering of home life by joining Doc Brown in the inventor's madcap pursuits. Arriving at the deserted Twin Pine Mall, he witnesses, emerging from a stream of blue smoke, a gull-winged steel gray DeLorean. The machine is for time travel. At eighty-eight miles per hour, Einstein's theory works. Doc's moment of glory is interrupted by an unhappy group of Libyan terrorists from whom Doc had stolen the DeLorean's power source. Seeing the scientist felled, Marty finds himself transported to 10 November 1955.

His fuel exhausted, Marty walks by a vacant lot, Lyon Estates, where his home would later be built. Entering a small village, he is greeted by the Four Aces cover of "Mr. Sandman" emanating from a record shop bearing a sign proudly announcing the arrival of "The Ballad of Davy Crockett." He glances at the marquee of the Hill Valley theater, which advertises *Cattle Queen of Montana*, headlining Ronald Reagan and Barbara Stanwyck.

He wanders into a soda shop, down vest and all, in search of a phone book. This is the first of many dialogues highlighting the culture shock awaiting the time traveler:

SODA JERK: Hey kid, what did you do, jump ship?
          What's with the life preserver?

The nonplussed Marty is told to order something to drink.

MARTY: Gimme a Tab.
SODA JERK: I can't give you a tab unless you order something.
MARTY: OK, give me a Pepsi Free.
SODA JERK: If you want a Pepsi you're gonna have to pay for it.

He settles for coffee.

Coincidentally, our hero himself is sitting on the stool next to the very, very square George McFly. Biff naturally stops by to bully the timid teen. Marty follows his father, minus thirty years, home only to discover his future parent is a voyeur. Marty saves George from being hit by a car, reversing history. Stunned by the accident, he is cared for by Lorraine Baines. "You're my . . . you're so thin," stumbles Marty when he sees her.

Totally confused by events and his feelings, Marty flees to an "old friend, Doc." Already a bit quirky, the young wiz questions Marty as to the identity of the 1985 President of the United States. To Marty's answer, he sardonically says "Ronald Reagan the actor? And who's vice president, Jerry Lewis?" Fleeing, he shouts "And I suppose Jane Wyman is the First Lady!" Doc resumes the role of father-confessor. He cautions the visitor not to cause repercussions for future events. The damage has, of course, been done, as Lorraine thinks Marty's a "dreamboat" and George is a total wimp. "You interfered with your parents," says Doc. "Doc, are you trying to tell me my mother has the hots for me?" Before one can say Oedipus Rex, Doc answers, "Precisely." Marty must now reset history before he can return to his time. Otherwise, he and his siblings will never materialize.

The resolution to the McFly union, predictably after a plethora of detours, occurs at the Enchantment Dance, with the fateful kiss of George and Lorraine to the chords of "Earth Angel." Marty's wish to rock is fulfilled. Departing, he tells the happy couple, "Hey, if you guys ever have kids and one of them, when he's eight years old, accidentally sets fire to the living room rug, go easy on him, will ya?"

Marty is restored to the Eighties, where several surprises await him. The twists and turns of the journey are masterful, better seen than summarized.

Unlike *The Way We Were* and *The Big Chill*, *Back to the Future* suggests another dimension beyond mere replication and reproduction. The Zemeckis/Gale story indicates the similarities between teens that spans three decades. The differences are equally striking. The 1950s adolescents were far more sensual than the Cleaver and *Father Knows Best* episodes portray. Moreover, as Steve Gould wrote, "No wonder extraterrestrials don't visit Earth; even English-speaking humans, given a few years' time span, can't communicate."[56] The soda fountain and the "Johnny B. Goode" scenes are but two illustrations. Shales's thesis is valid only when the mirror pastiche is added. Redoing the 1950s is seeing the decade through the eyes of the present.

The writers' 3″ x 5″ cards, the Freudian hook, and the time machine worked. Most critics penned "money reviews," notices with quotable one-liners. David Denby's close epitomized the critical consensus: "In its goony way, *Back to the Future* gets at some things we have all felt about our town, our parents and ourselves. It's probably the wittiest and most heartfelt dumb movie ever made."[57]

Rex Reed and Shelia Benson objected to the premise and the execution of the production. Reed found little "offensive" about the film "if all you crave for your money is brainless juvenile escapism."

"Big, cartoonish and empty" wrote Benson in the *Los Angeles Times*."[58] In the summer of 1985, critics over the age of consent were justified in dismissing teen pics. However, *Back To The Future* was considerably more sophisticated than the average offering.

Several writers noted the crossover draw of the movie. "It suggests a way of attracting older audiences to a fantasy aimed largely at youngsters," wrote the *Monitor's* David Sterritt. Tom O'Brien labelled it "this summer's best family picture."[59] Venue lines supported these observations.

"Johnny B. Goode" by Marty McFly and the Starlighters was featured in MTV's light-rotation 1 August. The Michael J. Fox video ran for four weeks.

In late August, "Power of Love" climbed to the peak of the chart and MCA Records issued "Johnny B. Goode" by Marty McFly with the Starlighters. *Billboard* described the 24 August release as "the zillionth cover version." It failed to chart.

The logic for the record was simply that "Power of Love" was being carried by the hottest film of the summer. "Johnny B. Goode," like "Good Time Rock 'n' Roll," was *the* central song in the movie. The only flaw appears to have been that the Berry composition did appeal to the single-buying consumer.

As Huey Lewis, the first American to reach Number 1 since Madonna sang "Crazy for You," played king of the mountain, John Parr's "St. Elmo's Fire" was second. The following week (September 7) the positions were reversed. Tina Turner's "We Don't Need Another Hero" from *Beyond Thunderdome* was third. Paul Grein reported, "This week marks the first time in the rock era that the three top positions on the pop singles chart are all held by film themes."[60]

Three months after its debut, the *Back To The Future* album received gold certification. In light of the film's tremendous box office, plus a Number-1 single, the figure was unimpressive. During the first go-round on the charts it remained with a large black dot—an indication of 500,000 copies sold. With cable exposure the LP eventually reached platinum.

The movie was the top domestic grosser of 1985, surpassing *Rambo II*, earning $94 million, contrasted to Stallone's $80 million. In a press release (March 3, 1986) MCA boasted a $200 million take. The video surpassed Tri-Star's *Rambo* sequel, with five-hundred thousand prerelease orders.

The success of *Back To The Future* was determined in the theaters. "Well, this reviewer attended a recruited high school screening, and the fifteen-year-old girl next to me was on the edge of her seat, hanging on every word in those '1955' scenes," wrote Steve Gould. Marvin Antonowski, Universal's marketing president, captured the secret of the success, saying, "We've had a lot of product this year that's played to older audiences and a lot of product that's played very young, but we haven't had a lot of cross over product that's played to both and that's where you get bit hits."[61]

Post Collegiate Chill: St. Elmo's Fire

> Lots of hormones and little risk
> —David Ansen, *Newsweek*

Lawrence Kasdan's Sixties reunion film had not only contributed a new category to Madison Avenue's psychographic lexicon—"Big Chillers"—

but also provided a prototype for other film makers. "Its idea of camaraderie—the notion of the all-star, upscale clique—is lending itself to inexhaustible recycling," observed Janet Maslin. "It is more saleable than ever
when geared to the younger set."[62] *Breakfast Club* was a descendent.
Some called the Hughes picture "the little chill."

Screenwriter/director Joel Schumacher was comfortable with the clique-
ensemble structure; he had used the device in *Car Wash* and *D.C. Cab*.
His coming-of-age hook was, "all the important things in my life, fights,
reconciliations, good times, had been played out in public places." The
proposed characters were to be recent college graduates facing the demands and responsibilities of life in the Establishment. "For *St. Elmo's*, I
felt that there are too many things going on in life after college, too many
factions to cover with just two or three characters," recalled Schumacher.
"I think life's like that; many things are going on all at once, which
interrelate." A bistro in the shadow of Georgetown University would serve
as the watering hole and focus for his ensemble of players. Columbia,
distributor of *The Big Chill*, as the studio which "understood the screenplay the best and were going to make the movie," was the director's
choice of studios.

Casting the roles was not a matter of recruiting the Brat Pack. (The term
would not surface in *New York* magazine until June 1985.) "Though
hindsight disguises the fact, the actors were not all that well known and
four of the ultimate leads in the picture had to do screen tests," claimed
the director.[63] Most of the leads were graduates of such Brat Pack spawning
pictures as Coppola's *The Outsiders* (1983) and Hughes's *The Breakfast
Club*. Jeffery Chown, in an excellent bio-filmography of Coppola, writes
of the *Outsiders*, "The casting seems very inspired, and many of the
supporting characters have gone on to major roles in subsequent films,
reminiscent of the way *American Graffiti* launched a generation of young
actors."[64] Coppola's cast included Tom Cruise, Ralph Macchio, Diane
Lane, Patrick Swayze, Rob Lowe, and Emilio Estevez. Several would
become founding Brat Packers and key players in youth-oriented movies.
(Estevez quite realistically told a reporter, "If a studio's making a film and
it wants a young actor who has a certain recognizability, it's gonna go to
one of eight guys."[65] This fact did not escape Columbia Pictures when
Lowe and Estevez were cast. They, particularly Lowe, were bankable.)

Writer David Blum coined the Brat Pack designation with a piece entitled
"Hollywood's Brat Pack." It was a play on the Rat Pack of the 1960s,
which included Frank Sinatra, Sammy Davis, Jr., Dean Martin, Peter
Lawford, Shirley Maclaine and, occasionally, Joey Bishop. The mid-
Eighties version was headed by Emilio Estevez and a handful of young

actors. Most commonly cited are Rob Lowe, Sean Penn, Tom Cruise, Judd Nelson, and Timothy Hutton. Membership is as clear and concise as Blum's definition: "They make major movies with big directors and get fat contracts and limousines. They have top agents and protective P.R. people. They have legions of fans who buy them drinks and follow them home. And, most importantly, they sell movie tickets."[66] Schumacher's *St. Elmo's Fire* would quickly test Blum's definition, where it counted, at the box office.

A youth-oriented project, *St. Elmo* was a natural for market accessing. Teen idols, MTV clips, and a hit single were all part of the exposure campaign. Two of those elements were the forte of then-Columbia Pictures music head Gary LeMel.

LeMel was a confirmed advocate of the film-name-*qua*-song-title school. A good title song, even when tacked onto the credits, was perceived as worth several million dollars in revenue. When the studio signed on the project, this belief was drilled into the screenwriter/director.

David Foster was recruited as the music supervisor and scorer for *St. Elmo*. A seasoned lyricist and composer, he contributed to Alice Cooper, Tom Petty, Boz Scaggs, Kenny Loggins, Chicago with Peter Cetera, and others. The film track promised to be a routine assignment until the studio brass decided to hasten the release date of the project by a month. The picture was rescheduled to coincide with summer vacation, mid-June. "Now we're going out into slaughter alley," observed Schumacher. This put pressure on Foster to select the songs for the film in a hurry.

The songsmith was impressed by John Parr's "Naughty, Naughty." He was added to the A-list for the title song. "There was resistance from Columbia," said Parr, "because I was virtually unknown to them. It was really David who said he wanted to work with me."

The date acceleration necessitated a one-to-two-day session between Parr and Foster. "We only had one day to write it . . . the first song we came up with was called 'Dirty Pictures.' That didn't work for the picture at all," said Foster. Director Joel Schumacher approved of the lyrics, but, true to the LeMel rule, said, "Can't you get the title *St. Elmos' Fire* in there somewhere?" In the process, Foster recalled, his co-written "From the Inside." "In ten minutes the final piece was written," he said. "Man In Motion," coupled with the film title, was approved. It was a loose fit—Parr admits this was the case, saying, "We were vague enough with the lyrics that the people involved with *St. Elmo's Fire* thought it was about the movie."[67] The actual film theme, a Foster instrumental, was more effective. It lacked CHR (Contemporary Hits Radio) appeal. "St. Elmo's Fire (Man In Motion)" became the designated scout release.

The videoclip received initial exposure in MTV's light rotation 12 June 1985. Video writer Jim Bessman noted, "In the case of this coming-of-age indulgence, the clip is the film."[68]

The single appeared on the trade charts ten days later at Number 90.

The Atlantic Records album coincided with the film's debut. *Billboard* listed *St. Elmo's Fire* as a "pop pick." The anonymous reviewer lauded the contributions of Billy Squier, Fee Waybill, and Jon Anderson, and noted, "This is a soundtrack that could fly without a successful film, but will definitely be aided by a box office hit."[69] Hardly a glowing endorsement. After 26 weeks on the LP listing the title had a gold certification.

The production, with a $10 million cost, promised a respectable box office, due to the presence of the Brat Pack. Veteran actor Terence Stamp, connecting on the ensemble's bankability, said, "Kids want to see kids. Cinema is for children now, isn't it?" Schickel predicted that *St. Elmos'* stars' following "could amount to a large audience."[70] The question for Columbia Pictures was, how large?

The film opens with a septet of Georgetown University graduates, still in regalia, running toward the camera. The surge is interrupted by the sound of a large crash. This is the introduction to a fantasy world somewhere between *The Breakfast Club* and *The Big Chill*. The motion picture is essentially a series of soap-opera vignettes, barely held together by the thesis of the conflict between the high jinks of college and the demands of material survival.

St. Elmo's Bar is the base of operation and regeneration. Toward the close of the film, Billy Hixx (Rob Lowe) indicates that the film's title is more than a communal watering hole; it is rather an illusion, an "electric flash of light that appears in dark skies out of nowhere." Sailors, the irresponsible saxophonist goes on, were guided for entire journeys by the nonexistent radiance. "There wasn't even a St. Elmo. They made it up . . . to keep them going when things got tough," he explains. Breaking away from societal and self-induced illusion appears to be the theme that writers Carl Kurlander and Joel Schumacher, also the director, had tried to convey. The illusionary St. Elmo's fire allows for each character to stumble into various misadventures, many of which are more selfishly comic than self-exploratory.

John Parr's title song introduces the upscale saloon, centrally located in the Georgetown University grid, where aspiring Yuppies gather after having bailed Billy out of jail. The hedonists are oblivious to the charge that he has endangered Wendy (Mare Winningham) and totalled her car. Indeed, St. Elmo's Bar serves as a pit stop for group reinforcement for each of the seven young people as they pursue their egoistic quests, no matter how ill defined or incomprehensible.

Kirby Kager's (Emilio Estevez) obsessive romantic chase of medical intern Dale Biberman (Andie MacDonald) is but one of many sit-com sub-plots. The "waiter studying to be a lawyer" recognizes his freshman theater date at the hospital, where Billy is treated for bruises incurred while driving under the influence. Kirby falls in love. He invites Dale to lunch at a very posh eatery—"Money is no object"—but before they are served she is called back to the hospital. Undaunted, he continues to stalk her. In a driving rain Kirby follows her to a night club. Face pressed against the window, reminiscent of a child at a candy store, he watches the formally dressed partyers.

Kager stumbles into the black-tie affair, dripping water. Dale takes him home and expresses a concern about the economic aspect of medicine. Kirby is immediately convinced that the way to the intern's heart is through money. The means to finance the chase are hardly explored, except to suggest that he is now out of law school and working for the shady Mr. Kim (Mario Machado), a notorious Korean lobbyist. While Kim is away on business, Kirby throws a party in his expensive digs for Dale. She instead goes on a skiing weekend with a male friend. In anger, Kirby follows, only to be trapped in the snow. After managing one wet kiss and a photograph, it's over (as if the relationship actually had begun. The *Cyrano*-like subplot would have made more sense in a junior high school setting.) David Denby described the character as "meant to be a youthful romantic, [who] comes off instead as a close equivalent to John Hinckley."[71]

Billy's escapades equally transcend credibility. He proves to be an itinerant twenty-two-year-old horn player with a wife and baby who is living off the largesse of the other Georgetown graduates. Although he manages to embarrass, humiliate, and sponge off of the group, especially the vulnerable Wendy, he retains his membership at St. Elmo's. After an enlightening dialogue with Jules (Demi Moore), the saxophonist leaves for New York to find fame and fortune in the music business. Blowing a mean sax is about all that Billy has going for him. "He drinks. He won't work," noted Janet Maslin. "He chases women and neglects his wife and baby. He doesn't have a war wound, as William Hurt did in *The Big Chill*, but his failures are almost as awkwardly documented. In these films, the notions of closeness and happiness are so artificial that actual failure need not even rear its ugly head."[72]

Julianna "Jules" Van Patten is one of the more believable neurotics in the ensemble. Jules presents herself as the ultimate, chic, Yuppie party girl, sniffing coke, living in ultra-modern digs. Her life appears to be one huge, nonstop, out-of-control party. She is living St. Elmo's Fire. Billy, in an uncharacteristic moment of insight, tells her, "You're making up all of this!"

"It's our time. Time on the edge," she says, explaining, "I'm so tired. I never thought I'd be so tired at twenty-two. I just don't know who to be anymore." She is living a self-indulgent existence to gain favor with her significant others. In the closing scene of the film she resumes her tall tales to a half-hearted "boo" from the group. The audience never really knows if she's reverted, or is on the road to self-actualization.

Any tale of Yuppie mobility must have a sex angle. Kevin Dolenz (Andrew McCarthy), Leslie Humphries (Ally Sheedy), and Alec Newberry (Judd Nelson) provide a *menage a trois*. Alec is a philandering political operative "moving up." He switches allegiance from a Democratic congressman to a conservative Republican senator because "It pays a lot more than working for a Democrat." His materialism is tempered by his longing for stability in a relationship with Leslie. He loves her, but he can't resist other women.

Kevin is an obituary writer, on "the death squad," for a Washington newspaper. The stereotypical hard-drinking and disillusioned scribe claims to be contemptuous of love, as "it's all an illusion." Secretly he pines for Leslie, his best friend's girl. Opportunity strikes when Alec announces a June wedding date without Les's approval. She snaps, "What about your extra curricular love life?" Alec attacks Kevin, thinking he was betrayed, and shouts at Leslie, telling her to move out. In a sequence befitting *Porky's*, Leslie and Kevin make love. Alec shows up the next morning to apologize to Kevin. He is prepared to leave when Les pops out from the bedroom to confront him. To complicate matters, Kevin wants to set up housekeeping with Leslie. Overwhelmed, she objects, "I just wish everything could be like it used to be . . . just friends." Kevin's offer is rejected.

The denouncement is end-of-the-week soap opera with, as David Edelstein suggested, a Pirandelloish twist. Jules attempts to freeze to death, bolting shut the doors and windows. The rescue attempt is pure slapstick comedy, followed by the expository dialogue between Billy and Jules.

The film concludes with Leslie's statement, "I'm going to try life without miracles for a while." They agree to meet for a Sunday brunch—not at St. Elmo's bar. Not surprisingly, a number of writers agreed with video critic Jim Bessman, who wrote, "All the pseudo-intellectual, meaning-of-life talk in the world, however, can't mask the fact that no one in this movie has anything to say."[73] Barring the Jules/Billy exchange on St. Elmo's Fire, he's 98 percent correct.

Most critics centered their *St. Elmo's* discussions around the utilization of the Brat Pack to address the youth-film market. *Variety's* Harwood signaled the approach suggesting that although the players weren't interacting, "it probably won't bother those who like the film." Maslin, on a more positive note, concluded that the film could be placed in a time capsule to illustrate "what and *whom* young viewers want, and how eager Hollywood is to give it to them. Denby wrote, "Perhaps it's silly to get upset, for *St. Elmo's Fire* is less a movie than a pretentious teen product—Guess? Jeans on celluloid."[74]

Newsweek's Kroll liked the production, saying, "You can feel the high voltage of friendship crackling between these kids." Over at the other national news magazine, Schickel wrote "One can think of adolescent fads a lot less cute than (Rob) Lowe and his friends." The *Film Journal* provided the money, or quotable, review: "The film features ensemble work by a cluster of talented young actors, matched by a clever—never condescending—script, and firm well paced director." Kelleher applauded David Foster's "evocative score." He would be the only opening reviewer to characterize the soundtrack.[75]

The Brat Pack, individually and as a group, received mixed credits. Kelleher praised, "this is top drawer ensemble playing by some of the screen world's brightest newcomers."

In between the polarities, "Although the cast performs admirably in well chosen roles, none of the characters is remotely interesting, let alone attractive, although all are beautiful," wrote Bessman. Reed added, "These seven 'Brat Pact' members make lively, heroic paramedics, but their's is dead on arrival."[76]

On 7 September, John Parr's "St. Elmo's Fire" reached the top of the Hot 100, pushing the Huey Lewis entry aside. Gary LeMel attributed this CHR achievement as causing a 48-percent infusion at the boxoffice. The movie, he noted, "was losing steam by mid-summer at $25 million in box office revenues. But when the single hit top five, it took the movie along with it. *St. Elmo's Fire* ended up with revenues at around $38 million."[77] The album barely reached gold certification.

Aesthetically, the Foster package, hastily assembled, had its high points, like the instrumental love theme, but suffered in contrast to *Risky Business*, *The Breakfast Club*, and LeMel's overlooked *Against All Odds*. A plethora of tunes could have been overlayed at the bistro. Rob Lowe's bongo scene, to the lyrics of Aretha Franklin's "R-E-S-P-E-C-T," is absent. (The song came from Atlantic's catalogue.) Foster's "Love Theme" appeared on the *Billboard* singles chart 24 August. The mood-setting instrumental remained for twenty-two weeks, peaking at Number

15 in November. LeMel had the title song reach Number 1, but Atlantic's album sales were disappointing in light of the single's chart life and the publicity surrounding the *St. Elmo's* thespians.

Say You Say Me: Hackford's White Nights

An Officer and A Gentleman (1982) had been a significant learning experience, but the training occurred off the set. Gordon Weaver and Steve Ross, the marketing gurus behind *Flashdance*, schooled *Officer's* flamboyant director Taylor Hackford in the intricacies of reaching target groups, and media relations. In *Officer's* post-production period it was Hackford's decision to recruit Will Jennings to write "Up Where We Belong." He chose Joe Cocker to sing with Jennifer Warnes. The selection met with considerable studio opposition.

"The head of the company said, 'This will never be a hit.' The chairman of the board said, 'Forget it.' We called another prominent record executive who said, 'Forget it. Jennifer Warnes has never had a hit song and Joe Cocker's a has-been,' " said Hackford. Paramount brought in another artist to do the segment. The performer told the studio brass, "Hey, I can write something, but it's not going to work as well as the song you've got." As the release date neared, the duet remained in the film. "It proved," said Hackford, "that a good song in a good film can be successful."[78]

"Up Where We Belong," followed by Phil Collins's "Against All Odds," certified Hackford as a soundtrack pioneer. He told the *Washington Post*, "I certainly wasn't the first person to use contemporary music in film, but in recent years I have pioneered the use of contemporary music in nonmusical films. I always do it with an eye to fitting the emotional and dramatic content of my movies." Beyond the film itself, "contemporary," or rock music, appeals to youth, he said. "Don't forget," he insisted, "young people score their lives to radio and tapes. Guys take out girls and play a song in the car on their first date."[79] With two Number 1's, the director more than appreciated the box office value of successful title and score songs. Several studio executives attributed, in part, the staying power of *Against All Odds* to the Collins hit.

During the film of *Officer*, Hackford had received commitments from two top dancers for a future film. Ballet star Mikhail Baryshnikov would be teamed with Broadway sensation Gregory Hines in a project. Finding the proper vehicle was no simple task, as "*Rocky*-goes-ballet" had already been exploited in *Flashdance*.

James Goldman, inspired perhaps by the Soviet downing of the KAL

Tokyo flight, wrote the basic storyline and the original screenplay. Orion, followed by Paramount, passed on the concept. Columbia Pictures, after several rewrites, agreed to distribute. The title, *White Nights*, referred to Siberian days with twenty-four hours of sunshine. Using contemporary music—rock and dance—in a Soviet setting starring a ballet star was no simple feat.

"I was moving towards designing the music to be more than background," said Hackford, "more than to score dramatic situations, to actually use it as a catalyst for the characters and the story." The catalytic prop is the Russian dancer's collection of American pop tunes, which he carries in a tape recorder. The director explained, "It's really set up by Hines being out not just of American, but of Western popular, culture for 10 years. He's been shut off from that whole evolution and when Baryshnikov drops out of the sky and has this electric group of tapes, it is in fact a discovery for Hines. It's the catalyst by which they dance, but it also allows him to rethink his decision [to defect to the USSR] and rediscover his cultural roots." Having found a device to cinematically integrate rock into the picture, the director needed a hook tune. He approached Steven Bishop, who had contributed the title song for *Animal House* and a cut to *Tootsie*. Bishop found the concept "interesting; "Separate Lives" was the result. In the interim, Hackford was still studio shopping for the project. Bishop ended up giving the evocative tune to Phil Collins. Collins, of course, had successfully cut "Against All Odds" and Atlantic Records was Hackford's choice for the soundtrack. Marilyn Martin, a background vocalist on Loggin's "Footloose," also was with the WCI subsidiary. The label's president Doug Morris, with visions of another "Up Where We Belong," pitched Martin to Collins. Arif Mardin produced the duet. The result was a prototypical soundtrack cut with a recognizable hook. A title song, a LeMel requirement, was still to be found.

Lionel Ritchie, a very hot crossover star, screened the film and agreed to write a title song. Ken Kragen, the singer's manager, called LeMel, saying, "Look, he can't seem to write anything called 'White Nights,' but he's written something that he thinks is one of the better things he's written and it fits the picture perfectly." LeMel and Hackford concurred. Another skirmish in the soundtrack-war saga materialized.

Motown, Ritchie's record label, recalls LeMel, "would not allow us to have 'Say You, Say Me' on the soundtrack, but they agreed to release it as a single in time to promote the picture." Hackford would provide the video for the song. For Lasker's company and the studio this was a beneficial arrangement, as "the movie didn't suffer," according to LeMel. Still, the album would have sold more had the song been there.[80] Hackford, a master at synergy, was in the same position as Lasker when the central songs from *The Big Chill* were withheld. *White Nights'* love theme, "Separate Lives," consequently would serve as the campaign scout.

Following the Hughes' model, the video appeared 25 September on MTV's medium rotation. The single surfaced two weeks later at Number 45 on the Hot 100. *Billboard* featured the album 19 October. The trade described the "pop pick" as "classy with commercial clout . . . stylistic breadth (pure pop, tough rock, dance) and an imposing cast of recording artists."[81] Merchandisers and broadcasters would be required to wait several more weeks prior to the album's shipment. The film was showcased at the Chicago Film Festival 9 November. Two months of electronic media exposure later, *White Nights* opened in the major markets.

The Hackford video for the Motown single reached MTV the week of the Chicago premiere. It would join "Separate Lives" in the medium-rotation slot. An accompanying single entered the CHR chart at Number 40. The week of the film's national release, the love theme rested at Number 3, with the so-called "title song" at Number 22, with a bullet.

Having reviewed the film in late October, *Variety*'s McCarthy wrote a mixed notice. "The Columbia release possesses the stellar cultural components to establish it as a major, serious year-end entry," he wrote, "but business prospects appear just okay." He continued, "Director Taylor Hackford has made a film with good looks, but no style." The reviewer complained about the "assorted modern stuff in blatant music video contexts."[82] (Since *Flashdance*, critics had been highly conscious of MTV setups.)

With the musical momentum going, Hackford received another bit of news. Several big holiday features were postponed, thus providing the $20-million film with almost clear sailing—except for *Rocky IV*—as the "big holiday pic."

White Nights opens with the camera riveted on the facial features of Nikolai "Kolya" Rodchenko (Mikhail Baryshnikov), who is about to glide into a ballet sequence with Florence Faure. They perform Roland Petit's "Le Jeune Homme et la Mort" for a London audience as the extended credits roll. As we listen to the symphonic accompaniment by Bach, a credit citation reads, "Title song by Lionel Ritchie." The ballet performance completed, Kolya and manager Anne Wyatt (Geraldine Page) board a British Orient flight to Tokyo for the next stop of the tour. The flight is interrupted by electrical problems over Siberia, forcing a landing at the top-secret Norilsk Soviet Air Defense Base. Four passengers die; twenty are injured. One of the injured is Kolya. In a transparent scene, the dancer feigns French citizenship, only to be greeted by a sinister KGB Colonel Chaiko (Jerry Skolimowki) who says, "Welcome home, Nikolai."

On a weather-beaten community center in Olney Island, Raymond Greenwood (Gregory Hines) taps out the role of Sportin' Life in a ragtag version of *Porgy and Bess*. Colonel Chaiko appears to praise the American defector and enlist his aid with Kolya. Disgusted with singing "There's a Boat That's Leaving for New York" to baffled Russian peasants, Ray agrees. He is to be the keeper, guard, and handler of the politically volatile prize.

Greenwood and his Russian wife Darya (Isabella Rossellini) occupy a dingy home in Taimyr. When Kolya arrives, Ray protests that he is a "selector, not a defector" who was disaffected by life in the South Bronx and the cruelities of the war in Viet Nam.

A tenuous relationship begins between Kolya and Ray as they move to the ballet star's luxurious apartment in Leningrad, blocks away from the Kirov Ballet. At the world-famous theater Ray attempts to coax Koyla into practicing. For some mysterious reason "I don't feel like dancing," Kolya says, turning on his boom box. "My Love Is Chemical" by ex-Velvet underground member Lou Reed fills the rehearsal hall. "What's that?" asks Greenwood, a Marvin Gaye fan. "That's dangerous stuff," is the reply. The reluctant dancer violates his house arrest in a bungled attempt to visit ex-lover Galina (Helen Mirren). The KGB takes Darya Greenwood away. The Hines character appears to be taken aback by his adopted country. In an interlude, Baryshnikov performs on the Kirov stage to the raspy voice of the late Soviet dissident Vladimir Vysotsky. "The Horses," in the empty theater, is a powerful statement. "It is a burning and indelible moment of humanism," wrote Shelia Benson, "shatteringly moving since it is touched with our knowledge of Baryshnikov's own defection."[83] In the wings Galina stands weeping—women cry nonstop in this movie—and plans a meeting with the American Embassy. Kolya, appearing to cooperate, induces the KGB to return Darya. The reunion with Ray injects "Separate Lives" onto the soundtrack. It is, also, the turning point, as she is pregnant, prompting Ray to assert, "They almost destroyed me. I won't give them a chance to do that to my kid." As if to cement the decision to escape, Ray and Kolya whirl around to the strains of David Peck's "Prove Me Wrong." This was one of several scenes critics pounced upon because of the music. "Framing the two dancers perfectly as they move around a Kirov rehearsal hall, the music they're dancing to is crummy MTV pop stuff, picked with an ear to the sound-track album" said the *Los Angeles Times*. "With ingenious duplicity," said Corliss,

"Hackford has worked in ten new pop tunes, by Phil Collins and Lionel Ritchie, among others, into a ballet film set in the USSR."[84]

"This is Your Day" by Sandy Stewart and Nile Rodgers, disguises Kolya and Darya's covert exit down the fire escape. Ray stays behind to further cover their flight. After a few tense moments they reach the U.S. Embassy compound.

In a year's time, Darya and Raymond are brought together because of a prisoner exchange. The wicked KGB colonel welcomes a Latin spy to the USSR. With Kolya observing, with apparent satisfaction, the couple embraces, with more tears, and finally the voice of Lionel Ritchie sings the title song, "Say You, Say Me." The credits roll to a truth-in-packaging statement, "SONGS ON THE ORIGINAL SOUNDTRACK ALBUM." The closing theme was noticeably absent from the list.

Reviewers almost unanimously agreed that Baryshnikov's interpretation of Petit's ballet was a "bravura performance." After the opening sequence, the film deteriorated into "evil empire" cliches with paper-thin characters. Many objected to the MTVish use of "contemporary music." Andrew Sarris was one of many who thought that the ballet dance "is the stuff of which the highest forms of romantic expression are made, and there is something very interesting going on behind his eyes," but the movie "is simply too silly a piece of trendy calculation to do the job." Moreover, "You can see a condensation of all this crass nonsense on MTV most nights of the week."

"Giggle at the film's naivete, then feast on Misha and dance down the steps," wrote Corliss.[85]

Hackford's portrayal of the Russians was roundly criticized. Libby Slate wrote, "The film is too talky, the heavy-handed dialogue reminiscent of the Cold War films of the 1950s." More in context, Maslin suggested that "the movie's view of the Soviet Union is drab and nasty enough to satisfy the most committed hard-liners." Richard Gehr added an ingredient to that Reagan-era description, saying, "This red-baiting in music-video clothing also includes one of the most brazen soundtrack marketing schemes this month." A number of the name critics concurred.[86]

"Nik's got this little boom box, see, and everytime he flips it on, out pours another bland, yet danceable R&B tune suitable for tapping . . . and purchasing in LP form," Gehr continued. Sterritt wrote, "The soundtrack doesn't help, with grating disco-type music replacing most of the classical score you might expect in a Baryshnikov picture." Ansen accused Hackford of laying on "gobs of bad pop music for the MTV crowd."[87]

Hackford replied to the criticisms. "I put music in my films," he said, "because popular music is important in *my* life and if I'm making contemporary films, why shouldn't it be important to my characters? . . . When they're alone in the dance studio, you expect him to put on Mozart and instead he puts on Lou Reed. I just think the audience is delighted and surprised.''

Expanding his view, the director acknowledged that the use of Collins, Reed, *et al did* make the picture more accessible. ''I make audience films,'' he said, ''and the concept of this film was not to do a ballet picture, although the film opens with an eight-minute ballet and the music is Bach. The rest of the film was designed to be accessible to a much broader audience than normally watches ballet, and to synthesize these two dancers' work into a more contemporary setting.''

More specifically, he added, ''If you were to say 'Mikhail Baryshnikov' or 'Gregory Hines' to a group of high school, or even college, students, there wouldn't be much interest except the few, like the few in society, that love dance. When you incorporate music that is accessible to these people and say *this* music is playing in *this* film and *these* dancers can do it and make it much more accessible to you, you open up an audience . . . I see a lot of young people going to see *White Nights*, which a lot of critics said would never happen.''[88]

The charge that the soundtrack was geared to expand the film's audience and generate album sales is undeniable. The appropriateness of the cuts is another matter. ''Separate Lives,'' as a love theme, is well integrated into the movie. Lou Reed's ''My Love Is Chemical'' fits Hackford's goal. On the album, Hackford explains, ''Hines has lived in the Soviet Union for ten years, away from American popular culture, but Baryshnikov's tapes awaken something within him. He re-experiences his cultural roots, causing him to think about what he has left behind. These songs became a musical bridge, a vehicle by which these two talents communicate, dance, and even escape.''[89]

If this was the goal, the Reed song evokes Hines's character to ask, ''What's that?,'' suggesting that rock is subversive, Kolya drops the subject. After the exchange the only function, a thin one, of the music is to overlay the escape plot. In a contextual framework, Tchaikovsky, Rimsky-Korsakov, and Sergei Rachmaninov, as one reviewer noted, seem more appropriate. The use of the Russian Romantics, of course, would hardly have provided the director with the kind of MTV and CHR exposure desired.

The Atlantic album and the film did benefit from the musical selections. ''Separate Lives'' climbed to the top of the singles chart 30 November and was followed by the Ritchie tune. ''Say You, Say Me'' reached Number 1 Christmas week and stayed for a month. The album was certified platinum in spring 1986 on the strength of the Collins-Martin duet. It went on to pass the two-million-copy sales mark. Motown did not capitalize on the Ritchie song, as *Dancing on the Ceiling* failed to reach the bins until August 1986.

In American and Canadian theaters the film earned $16 million in 1985, adding another $4.8 million the following year. Foreign rentals and ancillary fees finally raised the gross to $42.7 million.

1985: Sweet Little (?) Sixteen

The law of diminishing returns was invoked by the glut of youth films and accompanying soundtracks. The souvenir—take the movie home—factor was considerably reduced by the sheer number of films. It does not appear to be a coincidence that all the successes except one top 1985 album, *Vision Quest*, at double platinum, were showcased by a film with a domestic gross of at least $16 million.

A successful picture was a necessary, but not sufficient, motivator for the gold or platinum designation. *Goonies*, *Fletch*, and *Weird Science* had done little for their musical progeny, for example.

Scout singles and the records that follow them enter the same pipeline as all releases. Singles-oriented CHR stations generally add two or three song titles to a playlist per week. MTV's add-ons consist of five or more. The number of competing videoclips, of course, is smaller than record-oriented films. This is complicated further by the clustering of teen-oriented films from May through September. The result of the overabundance of products, during the summer months, drastically hampers chart performance and sales. For example, *Back To The Future* ended that period with only a gold certification, despite its status as the Number 1 film of the year.

In 1985, *Billboard's* Top 15 soundtrack titles included only three packages released during the school vacation period: *St. Elmo's Fire*, *Back To The Future*, and *A View To Kill*, the James Bond adventure. All had Number 1 singles by such name performers as Huey Lewis and Duran, Duran.

The sheer volume of movie albums underlined the importance of aesthetic quality, or at least name recognition. Madonna's "Crazy For You," and "Gambler," rotated on MTV, did more for the album than the movie. The artist lineup was impressive—Journey, Don Henley, Dion, and Foreigner—even though the cuts were far from exhilarating. Phil Collins's inclusion on the *White Nights* pressing was a definite marketing advantage.

The three coming-of-age scores were generally superior to other generic releases.

For studios, the blueprint indicated that a hit song by a high Q-Profile artist was imperative, especially during the summer. Soundtrack superstars were in short supply. "What I see happening," said Taylor Hackford, "which I think is a little disturbing, is producers going out to buy their way onto the radio."[90] Music publishers and labels capitalized on the situation. Record companies all had B-side material by name performers in their vaults. For the right price, these discarded cuts were available.

Holders of mechanical and performance rights held all the cards, or so it appeared. The volume of material, diluted the overall quality of in-film material and companion recordings. Labels had little incentive for using prime cuts in soundtrack packages. Songs deemed unsuitable for an artist's album frequently showed up as a filler on tracks. Viewers of film, patient enough to sit through credits, were frequently surprised to learn that their favorite artist had contributed to the score.

A large majority of soundtrack albums issued during 1985 failed to break into the Top 50 on the charts. Of the seven films discussed, six arrived in the higher quarter of the LP listings. The James Bond vehicle, with a Number-1 single, topped at Number 63, with *Perfect* peaking at Number 80. *Mad Max—Beyond the Thunderdome*, with Tina Turner's hit, reached Number 68. The remaining titles did not go beyond the halfway mark, although, some had enjoyed decent box office. *Goonies*, *Porky's Revenge*, *Ladyhawke*, *Weird Science*, and others could not transfer theater appeal to record purchases.

In the final analysis, there appeared to be too many teen pictures with too many soundtracks. The increasing number of box office flops correlated with dismal record sales. Only *Vision Quest* managed a two-million-copy album despite poor screen performance.

Movie music, in 1985, surpassed the banner performance of 1984, seven titles, for top-ranked singles. *Vision Quest* ("Crazy For You"), *Breakfast Club* ("Don't You Forget About Me"), *Back To The Future* ("Power of Love"), *White Nights* ("Separate Lives" and "Say You, Say Me"), and title songs "Heaven," "A View To Kill," and "St. Elmo's Fire" produced a total of eight Number 1's. Most became hits after the film's release, except those by name stars like Madonna. Tina Turner's "We Don't Need Another Hero" (*Thunderdome*) flirted with the top spot for several weeks in early September but had the misfortune of competing with Dire Straits ("Money For Nothing") on MTV. With the exception of *White Nights*, the soundtrack albums of 1985 were esthetically inferior to the products of

1983 and 1984. They were one-hit showcases lacking the depth of *Risky Business*, *Eddie and the Cruisers*, or *Footloose*.

Predictably, of the Top-10 albums on the *Billboard* year-end chart, only three were released in 1985. *Breakfast Club* was seventh, with the ninth and tenth spots occupied by *Vision Quest* and *St. Elmo's Fire*.

The music and film industries in 1985 were a disappointment. The record labels could claim the year was a wash in that sales increased a meager 4 percent. The break-even point in dollar values, was reached due to the strength of the compact disc. CD sales jumped, in dollar figures, a wopping 277 percent. Copy shipments, a more precise gauge, showed a minus-4-percent decline. Album sales dipped 18 percent, from 204.6 million in 1984 to 167 million.

MTV, amid some controversy, saw its Nielsen rating reduced from an annual 1.0 in 1983 and 1984 to .8. The summer quarter witnessed a blip of .9. The shrinkage of viewers did not harm the channel's advertising volume, however, as MTV enjoyed a stranglehold on the youth audience.

The movie studios, without a compensatory CD phenomenon, saw box office decline some 7 percent from 1984, a banner year, to $3.75 billion. More significantly, the big losers were the large-budget pictures. Only four releases in ten that cost $14 million or more made money or broke even. The few film people who would discuss the downturn generally pointed to the glut of youth-oriented motion pictures. *Witness* producer Edward S. Feldman observed, "The audience isn't as stupid as some people think. They can only be bludgeoned over the head by the same kind of youth movies so many times, and then they're gonna react."[91]

Directors, producers, and music supervisors in the mid-1980s were confronted with a stark reality, the fickle, swiftly changing musical tastes of under-twenty-five population. Catering to the trendsetters was aesthetically and economically prohibitive. Only Warner and Universal could tap into rosters of sibling branches under the same corporate banner.

Corporations like CBS, which housed Bruce Springsteen, Michael Jackson, and Mick Jagger, were viewed as unapproachable. An insider, discussing the *Mask* soundtrack arrangement with *Premiere*, said, "Universal couldn't make the deal because CBS and little Mr. Yetnikoff (CBS prexy) held everybody up for a fortune."[92] The label reportedly demanded half a million dollars for three Springsteen songs. The CBS Record Group had the artists, but no affiliated film factory. WEA performers were more affordable, as they were part of the Warner Communications family.

The label packaging of artists was a recurring difficulty from the beginning. A filmmaker dependent on a specific artist usually had to take several other acts on the same label; this practice eroded the integrity of the film and choice of labels.

Simpson and Bruckheimer, prior to *Top Gun*, were successful in using predominantly dance selections. (LaBelle was absent from the "A" list, which was comprised of Prince, Springsteen, Loggins, and Jackson. Vintage rock numbers, even in the wake of *American Graffiti* and *The Big Chill*, were relatively inexpensive *if* the studio was flexible. A director wedded to a specific recording could expect to pay dearly for his or her dedication. Music was negotiable, as the buyer had a plethora of catalogue titles to choose from. The seller—publishing houses and record labels—were fairly cooperative, as an oldie might have a second life. (Songs properly placed in a movie *could* enjoy a second life. *Apocalypse Now* rekindled interest in The Doors. *Risky Business*, in hindsight, was a definite bonus for Phil Collins and Bob Seger. "Old Time Rock 'n' Roll" and "In the Air Tonight" were obscure cuts from previously released albums. Owning mechanicals is profitable *only* if a song is in use.)

Studios frequently jacked up prices by insisting on a specific title rather than going for the generic. (A Presley standard is infinitely more costly than a rock-a-billy number by an obscure Sun Records artist.) The balance, ideally, was the territory of the music supervisor and ultimately the director. Rationality, even with period pieces, rarely prevailed, as studio personnel all too frequently insisted on using familiar names and titles. One insider observed that some bought songs forgetting that the audience was barely learning to walk at the time the song was popular. The comment is valid, as most movie-makers are older than the market they are attempting to reach.

For every synergistic success like *White Nights*, label and studio executives could point to numerous failures. Record company greed was frequently cited by movie producers; CBS was a favorite example. The film studios' naivete and hunger for a visible artist, regardless of material, was the music industry's explanation. The basis of synergy, as Danny Goldberg and Al Teller had repeatedly noted, was cooperation. Discussing the success of *Top Gun*, CBS's Teller applauded Paramount, saying, "They weren't looking at music as an add-on, but as something that had to be carefully crafted as the film was put together."[93] Music people wanted to be included in the take-off as well as the landing—successful or otherwise.

The CBS Records president, of course, neglected to mention that Simpson and Bruckheimer, who had a track record exceeding $620 million in grosses from *Flashdance* and *Cop*, could afford to deal with CBS. Producers with smaller budgets could not operate profitably in CBS's rarified economic atmosphere. The marriage of Simpson/Bruckheimer and

CBS, according to Simpson, was occasioned by The Boss. "The first time we heard 'Born in the U.S.A.' on the radio we turned to each other and said 'That's the sound of our movie,' " he said.[94] They failed to get Springsteen but did obtain Kenny Loggins who was hot due to the success of *Footloose* theme.

The prognosis for synergy, by the end of 1985, was mixed. The concept had not been discarded. The process, as discussed in 1984, was hardly operational in most instances. In numerous cases music, even with S&B, was added on in post-production, sometimes, as with *St. Elmo's Fire*, in great haste. The truly synergistic efforts witnessed in marketing *Fever*, *Footloose*, and *Purple Rain* were rarely replicated. John Hughes and Taylor Hackford, at times heavy-handedly, were the few legitimate practitioners of the Goldberg model.

Ironically, a majority of the features released in 1985 were conceived during the *Flashdance* and *Footloose* periods. (The development and production period for a movie averages over eighteen months.) Of course, 1984 had seen the banner $4.3-million industry gross. A good deal of "copy-catism" was in vogue. Becky Shargo's admonition in spring 1985 was relevant: "Movie producers today are trying to get a soundtrack attached to *anything*." The results materialized in the forms of unsold tickets and record returns. Looking back, Irv Ivers, of MGM/UA said, "You need to release the films that have been left behind—good, bad or indifferent."[95]

Notes

1. Quoted in Ed Ochs, "Mining Gold From the Silver Screen," *Billboard*, 2 August 1980, M3.
2. This is the official spin presented by the studio and S/B Productions. Stallone's revisions were unacceptable. During the standoff, Murphy became Paramount's choice. See Maitland McDonagh, "Murphy's 'Cop' A Second Hit For Simpson and Bruckheimer," *Film Journal*, December 1984, 12, 92; "Inside Moves," *Esquire*, January 1985, 112; L. Gruson, "Exit Stallone, Enter Eddie Murphy," *New York Times*, 16 December 1984, 21.
3. Quoted in Richard Corliss, "Street-Smart Cop, Box Office Champ," *Time*, 7 January 1985, 103; David Ansen, "An Officer and a Comedian," *Newsweek*, 3 December 1984, 81.
4. One MCA title rejected was to be a dance hit, Bronski Beat's "Smalltown Boy." Ken Terry, "Beverly Hills Cop' Illustrates Synergy of Film, Record Tie-In," *Variety* 26, 1985, 90.
5. Ibid.
6. David Edelstein, "Murphy's Law," *Village Voice*, 11 December 1984, 66.
7. Kevin Lally, "Breakfast Club," *Film Journal*, March 1985, 38; Michael Sprinkler, "Beverly Hills Cop," *Magill 1984*, 91.

8. Sprinkler, 92; Wendy Weinstein, "Beverly Hills Cop," *Film Journal*, January 1985, 31; Vincent Canby, "Are We Headed for a One-Movie Future?" *New York Times*, 27 January 1985, 46; Ansen, 81; Corliss, 103; David Denby, "Blue Streak," 10 December 1984, 94.

9. Leo Seligsohn, "Beverly Hills Cop," *Newsday*, 5 December 1984, part 2, 57; R. Loynd, "Beverly Hills Cop," *Variety*, 28 November 1984, 19.

10. David Ansen, "The Producer Is King Again," *Newsweek*, 20 May 1985, 89.

11. T. McCarthy, "Heaven Help Us," *Variety*, 6 February 1985, 18; Rex Reed, *New York Post*, 8 February 1985, 27.

12. John Coleman, "Flesh and Blood," *New Statesman*, 25 February 1985, 34.

13. Joseph Gelmis, "Heaven Help Us," *Newsday*, 8 February 1985, 3, sec. 3.

14. Reed, 27.

15. Kevin Lally, "Heaven Help Us," *Film Journal*, March 1985, 40; Alan Karp, "Heaven Help Us," *Boxoffice*, June 1985; Reed, 27; Michael Wilmington, "Heaven Help Us," *Los Angeles Times*, 8 February 1985, 1 (*calendar* section); David Denby, "Moves, Snap, Crackle and Pop," *New York*, 18 February 1985, 96.

16. Janet Maslin, "Heaven Help Us," *New York Times*, 8 February 1985, C8; Jack Kroll, "Brothers and Keepers," *Newsweek*, 11 February 1985, 73; McCarthy, 18.

17. Richard Schickel, *Time*, 14 December 1981, 91; David Ansen, *Newsweek*, 28 December 1981, 65; Michael Dempesy, "Taps," *Film Quarterly*, Spring 1982, 51.

18. "Quest' Helmer Becker To Return" *Variety*, 13 February 1985, 31.

19. Quotes in Bronson, 606.

20. Quoted in Richard Zoglin, "Hollywood Catches the Rock Beat," *Time*, 26 March 1984, 72.

21. Quoted in Amy Paulsen-Nalle, "And the Hits Just Keep Coming," *Premiere*, April 1988, 105.

22. *Billboard*, 16 February 1985, 74.

23. Vincent Canby, "Rites of Youth in 'Vision Quest,' " *New York Times*, 15 February 1985, C8.

24. J. Greenberg, "Vision Quest," *Variety*, 6 February 1985, 19; P.C. Noble, "Vision Quest," *Film in Review*, May 1985, 5–6; David Edelstein, "Greasy Kid Stuff," *Village Voice*, 26 February 1985, 52.

25. Quoted in Jim McCullaugh, "Hackford's Approach to Film is Sound," *Billboard*, 7 December 1985, 40.

26. Quoted in Kate Bales, "The Battle To Make Music Work in Film," *Billboard*, 26 December 1987, 4, 46.

27. Jimmy Summers, "Vision Quest," *Boxoffice*, April 1985, R48; J. Greenberg, "Vision Quest," *Variety*, 6 February 1985, 19; P.C. Noble, "Vision Quest," *Films In Review*, May 1985, 305.

28. Quoted in Julie Richard, "Small, Quiet and Creative," *Boxoffice*, May 1985, 18.

29. David Edelstein, "Greasy Kid Stuff," *Village Voice*, 26 February 1985, 52; David Denby, "Happy Birthday Sweet Sixteen," *New York*, 28 May 1984, 96 98.

30. Quoted in Becky Sue Epstein, "Music Video—The Hot New Way To Sell Hot

New Movies," *Boxoffice*, July 1984, 17; Jim Bessman, "Video Lowdown," *Rock Video*, August 1984, 6.

31. Quoted in Rob Tannenbaum, "Soundtracks Thrived in Summer of '85," *Rolling Stone*, 21 November 1985, 17.

32. Quoted in Fred Bronson, *The Billboard Book of Number One Hits* (revised ed.), (New York: Billboard Books 1988), 607.

33. Jeremy Chase, "About Their Videos: Simple Minds," *Rock Video*, October 1985, 26. Kerr and the band did not agree. In several interviews Kerr admitted that the "song really opened a lot of doors here for us." This was after saying the lyrics were "inane" and the song lacked "soul."

34. Richard Corliss, "Is There Life After Teenpix?" *Time*, 18 February 1985, 90; Louise Stanton, "The Breakfast Club," *Films in Review*, May 1985, 306.

35. Edelstein, "Greasy Kid Stuff"; Corliss; Stanton.

36. Kevin Lally "The Breakfast Club," *Film Journal*, March 1985, 38; Mark Fleishmann, "The Breakfast Club," *Video*, January 1986, 72; David Ansen, "True Confessions," *Newsweek*, 25 February 1985, 85; Corliss; Edelstein.

37. J. Harwood, "The Breakfast Club," *Variety*, 13 February 1985, 19; Lally, 38.

38. Epstein, 12.

39. Quoted in Paul Grein, "Rockbill's 'Synergy' Pays Off," *Billboard*, 17 August 1985, 33.

40. Quoted in Amy Paulson-Nalle, "And the Hits Just Keep Coming," *Premiere*, April 1988, 103, 105.

41. Quoted in Jim McCullaugh, "Hackford's Approach to Film Is Sound," *Billboard*, 7 December 1985, 40.

42. Paulsen-Nalle, 105.

43. Quoted in Tony Scherman, "Ry Cooder's Crossroads Blues," *Rolling Stone* 10 October 1985, 75.

44. Quotes from Esther B. Fein, "Three New Films: From Vision to Reality," *New York Times*, 21 July 1985, 1, 25 (sec. 2); Jack Kroll, "Having the Times of His Life," *Newsweek*, 8 July 1985, 76.

45. Fein, 25.

46. R. Loynd, "Back To the Future," *Variety*, 26 June 1985, 18; Richard Corliss, *Time*, 1 July 1985, 62.

47. Blake Lucas, "Back To the Future," *Magill 1986*, 71.

48. Quotes from "Zemeckis Replaces 'Future' Topliner," *Variety*, 23 January 1985, 7; David Breskin, "Rolling Stone Interview: Steven Spielberg," *Rolling Stone*, 24 October 1985, 102. Lynn Hirschberg offers yet another interpretation: "Some say Zemeckis used him (Stoltz) as a scapegroat in order to reshoot sloppy work, others that Stoltz 'just wasn't any good.' " *Rolling Stone*, 4 July 1985, 25. Casting director Michael Fenton, in retrospect, elaborated, "Eric and Zemeckis knew that the film they were making could be a *good* film, but that it couldn't be as special as it might be. They were both unhappy. Michael J. Fox was simply right for the role, and that's not to say anything negative about Eric." Tom Matthews, "Casting an Eye to the Stars," *Boxoffice*, December 1988, 28–29.

49. Quoted in Jack Kroll, "Having the Time of His Life," *Newsweek*, 8 July 1985, 76.

50. Quotes from Rob Tannenbaum, "Soundtracks Thrived in Summer of '85," *Rolling Stone*, 21 November 1985, 17.

51. Quotes in Bronson (revised ed.), 615.
52. "Pop Picks," *Billboard*, 13 July 1985, 70.
53. Quotes in Steve Pond, "The Box Office Blues," *Rolling Stone*, 13 March 1986, 24; David Edelstein, "Somewhere Over The Rambo," *Rolling Stone*, 2 January 1986, 105.
54. Tannenbaum, 16.
55. Jack Kroll, "Having the Times of His Life," *Newsweek*, 8 July 1985, 76.
56. Steve Gould, "Back To the Future," *Film Journal*, July 1985, 12.
57. David Denby, "Time Warp," *New York*, 15 July 1985, 65.
58. Reviews in *New York Post*, 3 July 1985, 21 and *Los Angeles Times*, 3 July 1985 (Calendar), 2.
59. David Sherritt, "Back To the Future," *Christian Science Monitor*, 3 July 1985, 23; Tom O'Brien, "Summer Encounters," *Commonwealth*, 9 August 1985, 440.
60. Paul Grein, "Chart Beat," *Billboard*, 7 September 1985, 6.
61. Gould, 12; quotes from Alan Karp, "The Summer of '85: Boxoffice Boom or Bust?" *Boxoffice*, October 1985, 8.
62. Janet Maslin, "Tracing the Long Shadow Cast by 'The Big Chill,' " *New York Times*, 14 July 1985, 15 (sec. 2).
63. Quotes from "Top Young Actors Fill 'St. Elmo,' But Casting Them Was Arduous," *Variety*, 26 June 1985, 28.
64. Jeffery Chown, *Hollywood Auteur: Francis Coppola*, (New York: Praeger Publishers 1988), 166.
65. Quoted in Fred Schruers, "Young Guns, or The Western Rides Again" *Premiere*, August 1988, 50.
66. David Blum, "Hollywood's Brat Pack," *New York*, 10 June 1985, 45. Membership lists per writer and spokesperson. Andrew McCarthy, Matt Broderick, Charlie Sheen (Emilio Estevez's brother), Nicholas Cage, Ally Sheedy, Demi Moore, and Molly Ringwald have all been included in discussions.
67. Quotes from Bronson, 616.
68. Jim Bessman, "St. Elmo's Fire," *Video*, June 1986, 103.
69. *Billboard*, 29 June 1985, 66.
70. Quoted in Fred Schruers "Young Guns or the Western Rides Again," *Premiere*, August 1988, 50; Richard Schickel, "Some Sideshows of Summer," *Time*, 1 July 1985, 63.
71. David Denby, "Time Warp," *New York*, 15 July 1985, 66.
72. Janet Maslin, "Tracing the Long Shadow Cast by 'The Big Chill,' " *New York Times*, 14 July 1985, 15 (sec. 2).
73. Jim Bessman, "St. Elmo's Fire," *Video* June 1986, 103.
74. Harwood, "St. Elmo's Fire," *Variety*, 19 June 1985, 25; Janet Maslin, "St. Elmo's Fire," *New York Times*, 28 June 1985, C6; Denby, 66.
75. Jack Kroll, "Hollywood's Lost Lambkins," *Newsweek*, 1 July 1985, 55; Richard Schickel, "St. Elmo's Fire," *Time*, 1 July 1985, 63; Ed Kelleher, "St. Elmo's Fire," *Film Journal*, July 1985, 11.
76. Bessman; Reed.
77. Quoted in Ian Dove, "Soundtracks Score With Rock 'n' Roll," *ASCAP in ACTION*, Spring 1986: 35. One trade listing estimated the gross at $36,754,543.
78. Quoted in Chris Morris, "Early Music-Film Ties Best," *Billboard*, 6 December 1986, 3.

79. Quoted in Richard Harrington, "The Saga of Soundtracks," *Washington Post*, 12 January 1986, K10; Jim McCullaugh "Hackford's Approach to Film Is Sound," *Billboard*, 7 December 1985, 40.
80. Quoted in Bronson, 626.
81. *Billboard*, 19 October 1985, 88.
82. McCarthy, "White Nights," *Variety*, 6 November 1985, 27.
83. Shelia Benson, "White Nights," *Los Angeles Times*, 22 November 1985, 1 (Calendar section).
84. Benson, 1; Richard Corliss, "Dancing Down the Steppes," *Time*, 25 November 1985, 121.
85. Andrew Sarris, "No, but I saw the music video," *Village Voice*, 26 November 1985, 63; Corliss, 121.
86. Libby Slate, "White Nights," *Magill's*, 419; Janet Maslin, "Baryshnikov in 'White Nights,' Tale of Two Defectors," *New York Times*, 22 November 1985, C10; Richard Gehr, "White Nights," *Video*, September 1985, 108.
87. Gehr, 108; David Sterritt "White Nights," *Christian Science Monitor*, 22 November 1985, 31: David Ansen, "Hoofing It to Freedom," *Newsweek*, 18 November 1985, 94.
88. Harrington, K10.
89. Liner notes, *White Nights*, Atlantic Records 812773-1-E 1985.
90. Quoted in Chris Morris, "Early Music-Film Ties Best," *Billboard*, 6 December 1986, 3.
91. Quoted in Steve Pond, "The Box Office Offices," *Rolling Stone*, 13 March 1986, 24.
92. Quoted in Paulsen-Nalle, 104.
93. Quoted in Ken Terry, " 'Top Gun' Soundtrack Duplicates 'Footloose' Pattern in Less Time," *Variety*, 13 August 1986, 108.
94. Quoted in Paul Grein, "Music Means A Lot to 'Cop' Producers," *Billboard*, 27 July 1985, 37.
95. Quoted in Cathleen McGuigan, "Rock Music Goes Hollywood," *Newsweek*, 11 March 1985, 78; Pond.

10

Soundtrack Fever II

All that was missing was the "love theme from Alien"

—Anonymous

As 1986 began, *White Nights* and Sly Stallone's *Rocky IV* gravitated toward platinum certification. The auspicious beginning would prove misleading. Myriad accessible films with attendant albums filled theaters and record bins. A minute percentage of the albums reached the higher rungs of the charts.

Top Gun had been appropriately named, as it dominated the year's box office rentals and soundtrack sales. Simpson and Bruckheimer earned $315 million for Paramount Pictures in the process, adding a third Number-1 title to their album credits. *Flashdance* and *Beverly Hills Cop*, of course, had preceded their film about the antics of naval aviators.

A Little More Travelin' Music . . .

CBS Records president Al Teller, the synergist behind *Footloose*, liked the Simpson & Bruckheimer project, as its aerial sequences had provided considerable "room for music." Some of the most memorable uses of rock in films can be legitimately termed "road" or "traveling" music. The prototype was *Easy Rider*. Wyatt and Billy traverse the nation's concrete arteries allowing The Byrds, The Band, and Steppenwolf to add a significant dimension to the fatal trek. The funeral procession in the *Big Chill*, accompanied by the Stones "You Can't Always Get What You Want," had also supplied a memorable set-up. LaBelle's "Stir It Up" effectively sets the tone as Eddie Murphy cruises down Rodeo Drive in *Beverly Hills*

523

Cop. The key 1980s illustration, perhaps, from NBC's "Miami Vice," a black Ferrari traveling on rain-drenched Miami streets bathed in the gloss of neon signs as Phil Collins's "In The Air Tonight" fills an unspoken void.

Top Gun's soaring F-14 fighters may have lacked the drama of *Miami Vice*, but music opportunities abounded nevertheless. CBS, whose releases in the rock-soundtrack market had been meager, had found an ideal carrier for its multifaceted roster.

Producers Don Simpson and Jerry Bruckheimer, originally enthralled with "Born in The U.S.A.," were faced with a musical genre absent from their previous productions. "We always saw the pilots as rock 'n' roll stars of the sky," said Bruckheimer. This view was reinforced when actual military pilots expressed a preference for Billy Joel and Van Halen. As one co-producer asserted, "That kind of set the tone for the movie right there."[1] (West Coast aviator-cowboys were not mavens of the dance/urban contemporary genre found in *Cop* or *Flashdance*. Had a survey been done, country music may have dominated the poll.)

Teller, delighted to resume working with Paramount, as their previous union moved nine million copies of *Footloose*, recalled that the label "hit the ground running real hard on this one."

"We've been coordinating with Paramount's people on a day-to-day basis for nine months on this project," said marketing director David Gales.

As the film progressed, Giorgio Moroder of *Flashdance*, and Harold Faltermeyer of *Cop* and *Thief of Hearts*, wrote some musical material. Moroder and an assistant engineer on the picture, Tom Whitlock, penned the motion picture's most successful cuts, "Danger Zone" and "Take My Breath Away."

CBS asked its artists to submit songs or interpretations of *a priori* material. Loverboy's "Heaven In Your Eyes" was one of the few accepted. Simpson noted, "Not many of those submissions made it onto the soundtrack."[2]

The final selections were decided partially on aesthetics and territoriality. "Danger Zone" and "Take My Breath Away" were originally given to a Geffen Records AOR group, Berlin. Moroder and Whitlock's first film composition was assigned to Kenny Loggins. Berlin's Terri Nunn noted, "We all liked 'Take My Breath Away' more." One insider suggested that the WCI act received the love theme only because "the right combination" wasn't available at CBS. Teller had told *Variety* the music for *Top Gun* "had to be carefully crafted as the film was put together." The music was tailor-made. The Cruise-McGillis love scene was reshot, according to lyricist Whitlock, "to our song *after* the fact. It wasn't nearly as poetic [so] they went back and shot it to match the song."[3]

Moroder's arrangement also was altered to fit the marketing. "He couldn't be as experimental as he would have liked," recalled Berlin lead singer Nunn. This was synergy at its finest. "You're coordinating," emphasized Gales, "your efforts and trying to create as many impressions as you can on both pieces of product."

The marketing campaign commenced at Paramount's Little Studio 29 April 1986. *Variety's* reviewer was unimpressed with the soundtrack, saying, "It seems there is no experience, from lovemaking to jets taking off, that isn't accompanied by Harold Faltermeyer's soundtrack. Life is given the emotional texture of a three-minute pop song."

Teller, however, felt his goal had been accomplished, saying, "It's extremely important that the music be woven into the film fabric in such a way that, while the viewer is enjoying the film, he or she knows there's some terrific music going on simultaneously."[4]

The label delivered a music trailer to MTV that week. "Danger Zone," the video, featured inner-cuts to Kenny Loggins. It erupted on the music channel's heavy, most cablecast, rotation. The single followed, entering the Hot 100 at number 85 10 May. Throughout, the major markets' program directors, deejays, and record merchandisers were invited to preview screenings.

Memorial Day weekend *Top Gun* opened to lukewarm reviews. The album was properly placed in the record bins, billed as "The Album Loaded With All New Hits." *Billboard* characterized it as containing "a slew of name artists (with) all the ingredients to cross rock, adult contemporary, black and pop radio formats."[5]

The synergism drive was well on schedule. "We established the fact that the Kenny Loggins track is in the movie. And we do radio screenings," related West Coast marketing Vice President Bob Wilcox. "All the movie companies tend to concentrate their (advertising) efforts in the four weeks surrounding the movie. We play off that, to complement our direction with direction."[6]

Teller was satisfied. The motion picture, he recalled, "was doing tremendous box office immediately. So the base audience for this soundtrack album was rapidly escalating from day one." (The instantaneous success of the Loggins single had altered the cluster strategy for *Footloose*. CBS had reasoned, "We'd be better off waiting until a sufficient number of viewers had seen the film and developed familiarity with "Take My Breath Away"), so that when we did release the single, there'd be immediate reaction to it."[7] There was.)

CBS/Record Group deserves the lion's share of the credit. "Berlin got a set fee for doing the song and Columbia pays Geffen (Records) a royalty, which we split 50-50," stated Berlin's manager, Perry Watts-Russell. "I made sure that Columbia sent a couple of hundred albums and singles to Al Coury at Geffen so that he could supply them to his (promotion) troops," he continued. Wilcox stressed that CBS was anxious to assist its corporate arch-rival as "The song is making the *Top Gun* album sell like crazy. So we've handled Berlin no different than we have Kenny Loggins."[8] (Albums, of course, are considerably more profitable than singles.)

The Berlin rendition debuted June 21 at number 96 and soared past "Danger Zone," which had stopped at number 2 26 July, to reach number 1 the week of 13 September 1986.

The film was the proverbial blockbuster, the album went multiplatinum, and home video sales exceeded 600,000. Chronologically, the song begat the father.

Iron Eagle had been another jet-jockey picture with overtly patriotic overtones. The Simpson & Bruckheimer vehicle was a bit more subtle; that is, it had no negative references to President Carter. The lead roles in both aviation sagas were young "hot shots" who violated all the organizational norms.[9] Their economic outcomes would be quite dissimilar, however.

Warnography IA: Iron Eagle

> *I was a teenage Rambo*
> —*Variety*, 1986

John Milius's jingoistic attempt to synthesize John Rambo with the students at Ren McCormack's Beaumont High failed, as *Red Dawn* (1984) proved "too dumb to work as patriotic exhortation and too mawkish to work as blood-and-guts exploitation.[10]

War Games (1983) starring Brat Pack candidate Matthew Broderick, with Ally Sheedy in a supporting role, had partially injected teenagers into the geopolitical scenario of current "Evil Empire" rhetorical climate. For *Iron Eagle*, Milius awkwardly added Conan to the equation. Kevin Elders' screenplay blended the elements which escaped the self-styled "Zen-fascist."

"A sort of Karate Kid-Rambo hybrid," summarized Holly Sklar. Tom Matthews agreed, saying the story attempted "to combine elements from just about every successful film in the past five years with little success. It's a little bit *Rambo*, it's a little bit *Officer and a Gentleman*, it's a little bit John Wayne, and it's a whole lot of silly.''[11] Tom Shale's recycling model was alive and well.

The *Iron Eagle* screenplay was submitted to Joe Wizan. The ex-20th Century Fox president in turn suggested it to Ron Samuels. The television producer, having recently been financed by U.S. Equity Corporation, Texas Oil, and real estate, was seeking a project to be distributed by Tri-Star Pictures, which was savoring its 1985 blockbuster success with *Rambo*.

"I read it the first time without being able to put it down, which for me is a miracle," Samuels recalled. "It was like an old John Wayne western updated and put into jets. It's American, it's patriotic, it's positive, it's saying let's go out there and do something."

Sidney J. Furie of *Lady Sings the Blues* (1972) was retained to direct *Iron Eagle*. Louis Gossett, Jr. was cast to create a similar character as in *Officer and A Gentleman*.

The Israeli Air Force provided the needed hardware. Aerial sequences, including risky dog fights with genuine American built F-16 fighters, were filmed. "We're doing things that have never been done before," Samuels told the *Film Journal*.[12] The production costs reportedly were less than $10 million.

Previous Stallone/Norris films about unauthorized rescue missions where diplomatic and Pentagon personnel feared to tread had made little use of rock music. (One *Missing in Action* episode had, very effectively, used a Saigon bar girl singing, slightly off key, "Don't You Think I'm Sexy.") *Iron Eagle*, with a target audience of young males, evolved a gimmick allowing a profusion of rock 'n' roll during the aerial sequences.

Stephen Powers, Capitol's A&R manager, was the music executive producer and Leslie Morris was music coordinator. "The demographics of the movie and the whole storyline," explained Powers, "dictated to an extent that this should be a hard rock soundtrack."[13] Action movies are primarily aimed at twelve to twenty-four-year-old males who also comprise the substructure of the heavy users of hard/metal/rock.

Powers had arranged for sixteen selections to be used in the film. Half of the choices were by Capitol artists. Notable out-of-house contributors were James Brown doing "There Was A Time," The Spencer Davis Group with "Gimme Some Lovin'," Twisted Sister with "We're Not Gonna Take It," and Kenny Loggins performing "Reggie's Theme." King Kobra's "Iron Eagle (Never Say Die)" was the closing theme. Unfortunately for Capitol, The Spencer Davis Group, James Brown, and Twisted Sister material stood out during the film. "We're Not Gonna Take It" was played twice. Queen and King Kobra were merely musical bookends.

The ten-track package mirrored the Tower roster—specifically, Helix, Jon Butcher Axis, Katrina and the Waves, and King Kobra, with Dion on loan from Warners. (Freddie Mercury of Queen was a Capitol solo artist.) The album's downfall was partially due to a lack of memorable cuts from the movie. For a patron leaving the theater, Twisted Sister's complaint was most likely to linger. "We're Not Gonna Take It" captured the ideological thrust of the film. It was absent from the Capitol release.

The opening musical gambit for the *Iron Eagle* campaign was classic. A month prior to the picture's release date, "One Vision" by Queen surfaced. (The English group was a logical choice as it had name recognition and a title hit from *Flash Gordon* (1980).) The song charted at number 88 the week of 7 December 1985. *Billboard* described it as having a "theme of the universal brotherhood of nations. Sound is ornate melodic metal; movie it accompanies is *Iron Eagle*."[14] In mid-December the cut began its flirtation with AOR, listing around number twenty, where it would stay. The film appeared before the album, thus deviating from the Stigwood marketing formula.

Queen's video was taped while they recorded "One Vision" at Musicland Studios in Munich, Germany. Rudi Dolezal and Hannes Rossoacher incorporated the *Iron Eagle* flavoring by having Queen appear on the console screen of an F-16 flight simulator. "The image," according to a press release, "is a head-and-shoulders photograph of the four band members used to promote Queen's early hit "Bohemian Rhapsody," which transforms into a re-creation of the same shot—10 years to the month after the original." The "Bohemian Rhapsody" bite is believed by many to be the first "concept" video produced. MTV inserted the clip in its medium rotation as the single charted.

Iron Eagle opens with a pair of shiny, silver F-16s streaking across the screen cutting through mounds of fluffy white cloud banks. A symphonic theme underscores their majesty. The mood is invaded by the appearance of five hostile MIG-23s. American jet ace Col. Ted Masters (Tim Thomerson) engages them in combat.

Meanwhile back in the United States—there are many cut-aways in this film—the Masters family is preparing for another day in the suburbs surrounding an Air Force base. The oldest son, Doug (Jason Gedrick), a super military brat, belongs to a teen flying club called the Eagles (hence the film's title), and covertly practices dogfighting on the base's simulator. He zips around the military complex in a red Mustang as "Road of the Gypsy" provides atmosphere.

In a sequence lifted from *Rebel Without A Cause* by way of *Footloose*, Doug is confronted by Knotcher (Michael Bowen), a middle-class version of a biker, who revels in the news that the younger Masters has been rejected by the Air Force Academy. Their hostility is to be resolved by a chicken run. (A Piper Cub versus the bike is the twist.) Despite Knotcher's attempt to sabotage the aircraft, Doug prevails, only to be told that an unidentified, hostile Arab nation has captured the colonel.

In a pivotal set of scenes Doug painfully learns that the United States is no longer the omnipotent power he had believed it to be. The base commander informs him, "There's not much we can do. The suits at the White House have our hands tied . . . we don't even have diplomatic relations."

Under the control of the defense minister (David Suchet) of X Arab country, the detained flier is sentenced to hang in three days. One of the Eagles attempts to reassure Doug that this will not be a repeat of the Iran situation. "Mr. Peanut was in charge then. Now we got this guy who don't take no shit from no gimpy country. Why do you suppose they call him Ronnie Raygun?" The Masters family's appeals to the military are met with, "We're still negotiating." Unpersuaded, Doug formulates a plan. He will rescue the downed officer.

In a lavish, MTVish clubhouse, the Eagles are mobilized to scour the airbase for information and equipment. They visit offices and hangars to the tune of Twisted Sister's "We're Not Gonna Take It." Having accomplished their mission—the KGB wishes for similar results—Doug realizes he needs assistance. He approaches Reserve Colonel Chappy Sinclair (Louis Gossett, Jr.) a comrade of the fallen flier, for help. He agrees. "Something about maniacs messing with good men always puts me off," he explains. Planning for the mission, Chappy blasts a James Brown tune from a well lit Wurlitzer jukebox. Miraculously undetected by the military brass, the duo obtain information, ammunition, and two F-16 fighters for the sortie. When Chappy warns the youth against over confidence, Doug replies, "Maybe I'm not all that ready, but I'm darn proud." They're off.

In scenes that have some stunning aerial photography, the duo nearly immobilizes the hostile nation's defenses. Doug is especially apt at offensive flying (as the boom box blasts away.) Chappy is hit. Turbine failure . . . EJECT reads the ditigal panel. With a Spencer Davis classic filling the cockpit, Doug strikes the headquarters of the captors. The defense minister plans to trap the Americans by releasing Col. Masters on the runway, with snipers at the ready. The defense minister's strategy is foiled and David rescues the Colonel. With his freed father rooting in the back of the jet and rock music blaring, the terrorist kidnapper, an air ace, is shot down. A squadron of F-16 appears in the nick of time to turn back the pursuing Arabs.

At a military hearing Chappy, who had been saved by an Egyptian ship, and Doug are accused of violating "every section of the National Security Act." However, the incident is to be kept quiet. To ensure secrecy, Doug is "confined" to the Air Force Academy.

Returning home, the Masterses and Col. Sinclair are greeted by an honor guard "flown over by special orders of the President." The moral of the story is that properly equipped and motivated military personnel can prevail against all odds. Rambo's famous "Do we get to win this time?" query is answered affirmatively in *Iron Eagle*. The credits crawl to King Kobra's "Iron Eagle (Never Say Die)." Although it is the last musical offering, this could have been the scout product. The tune *did* capture the movie's ideological thrust.

A majority of reviewers saw the project as *Rambo*istic nonsense. *Box-office's* Tom Matthews concluded, "Find an airline that has Rambo as its in-flight movie and go nuts."

"If kids can pull off such a stunt," warned Canby, "what might a bunch of terrorists be able to do?" The other *Times* critic, Janet Maslin, did not treat the movie quite as seriously. She wrote there was "an overabundance of both movie and gung-ho rhetoric" diminishing the film. Still, she contended, these flaws did not "hurt it any with the crowd . . ."[15] Ron Samuels countered, "The only similarity to *Rambo* is that it's one individual going against the odds. This boy does it in an airplane, but it's set up in such a way that is believable. In *Rambo*, as great as the action is, it's not too believable."

Several writers commented on the score. Hoberman characterized the track as "overwhelmingly a series of white bread masculine headbangers with some piquant transformations as a result: Twisted Sister's "We're Not Gonna Take It" becomes a patriotic anthem, Queen's "One Vision" a paean to the new world order . . . but the song this movie really craves is, of course, 'Born in the U.S.A.' You can easily imagine matching explosions to *that* mighty beat."

"Young Gedrick can't quite hit a target unless he's got rock-and-roll playing in the cockpit," noted *Variety*, "That's how you get a music video out of a fighter pilot picture."[16]

Critics have little influence with the Rambo crowd. In a little more than three weeks, *Iron Eagle* grossed more than $18 million. Ron Samuels had prevailed. The soundtrack album appeared two weeks after the film's debut.

Billboard listed the title as a "Top Pop Pick." The selection was described as a "rock/pop grab bag from the current teen action-adventure [and] targetted the young, male audience courted by the film's heroic plotline, prompting an emphasis here on uptemp anthems.'' The review went on to say that the Queen single had stalled, but "even modest box office clout could translate to sales."[17] The album, finally, charted 15 February at number 133, the same week the trade recommended "Iron Eagle". King Kobra's effort stiffed; the film lacked coattails. At the close of February the box office totaled more than $20 million. The singles were gone. The album failed to reach the Top 50 and fell off the rankings in late April without an RIAA certification. Domestic film rentals upon completion of the first run, totaled $23.74 million.

Boudu Sauve des Eaux en Beverly Hills

> *I certainly wouldn't want a movie from one of my old movies.*
> —Paul Mazursky, writer-director

The traffic at the opening days of *Iron Eagle* instilled hope in the film community. In addition, director Paul Mazursky's *Down and Out in Beverly Hills*, a big-event film, had been perceived as a signal for a banner year at the box office. The picture, showing in 800 theaters, earned $13.9 million in its first ten days of exhibition; it had cost $14 million. At Universal City, home of MCA records, there was talk of another *Beverly Hills Cop* phenomenon. The setting for the *Down and Out* Renoir remake, lent itself to such speculation. (Mazursky's career is dotted with recycles of foreign production transposed into contemporary settings.) Public interest in Hollywood remains marketable, as Eddie Murphy confirmed.

Since beginning his show-business career as a stand-up comic in Greenwich Village, Mazursky had moved through several incarnations. He tried television writing. (The pilot for *The Monkees* NBC-TV series was his creation.) At Columbia he co-wrote, with Larry Tucker, and directed *Bob and Carol and Ted and Alice* (1969), which, with a high-production gloss, dealt with mate swapping. The "contemporary" film returned $14.6 million, a figure that endeared Mazursky to the Hollywood community. His second effort, *Alex in Wonderland* (1970), was derisively termed "1 1/2." Andrew Sarris called *Alex* "the director's almost grovelingly humble *hommage* to Federico Fellini's 8 1/2."[18] A decade later Mazursky had attempted to honor Francois Truffaut by transplanting *Jules and Jim* (1961) to America as *Willie and Phil*, which surfaced in 1980 to mixed reviews. Between these films the writer-director had seen a 1932 Jean Renoir adaptation, *Boudu sauve des eaux*. The actual transposition would not occur until after the production of Mazursky's *Moscow on the Hudson* in

1984. Leon Capetanos, the co-writer of *Down and Out*, was also a Renoir enthusiast. Mazursky had mentioned, "It might be interesting to switch *Boudu* to the United States. We decided to poke fun at Beverly Hills, to make fun of my own life, so to speak."[19] This they did, but they changed Renoir's ending.

The *Boudu* screenplay, as presented in the depression-ridden France of the 1930s, possessed a strong tinge of class conflict. In Renoir's depiction, *Boudu* ultimately rejects a bourgeois style of life, and, according to Kauffmann, "flees to resume his unconfined life."[20] Mazursky and Capetanos turn this conclusion around.

For the adaptation, Mazursky recruited three high-profile actors. Nick Nolte was hot, as was Bette Midler. Richard Dreyfuss, a *Graffiti* alumnus, was a gamble. Since *The Goodbye Girl*, which had netted him an Oscar, Dreyfuss had been associated with a series of flops.

Dreyfuss and Midler would act out the roles of *nouveau riche* Beverly Hills inhabitants, the Whitemans. Nolte was the derelict who attempts to end it all in their spacious swimming pool. The "liberal" Whitemans take in the homeless man. After a series of seductions and other manipulations, the Nolte character is confronted. He leaves after the confrontation, only to return later to the now grateful Whitemans. It appears that Jerry Baskin (Nolte) has exorcised the multiplicity of neurotic hangups—anorexia, sexual identity conflict, and a maladjusted canine—that plagued the Beverly Hills residents.

The film, which opened the last day of January, by 19 February was reporting rental revenues of some $22.6 million. At the end of 1986 it would rank as the twelfth highest-grossing film issued during the year. (Self-reflective Hollywood vehicles usually do well.)

Film critics have a tendency to treat adaptations of French films with some kindness. (Wilder's *The Woman in Red* provides an illustration.) Few writers failed to make the comparison. "I'm not about to shed crocodile tears over a supposed Renoir 'masterpiece' being desecrated by a Hollywood vulgarian," wrote Sarris, adding, "He has failed to match Renoir's rigorous tough-mindedness as an artist. Mazursky's ending?" Canby followed the same line writing, "After establishing—with all too much conviction—the monstrously foolish nature of its conspicuously consuming characters, as well as the utterly fatuous lives they lead, Mr. Mazursky draws back, as if afraid to acknowledge the truth of his own observations."

"What we've got here is a Beverly Hills cop-out. Mazursky exploits the myth, but never exposes it," concluded Kopkind. Kauffmann simply noted that the movie vis-à-vis Renoir, was a "subversion of a true work of art cinema."[21]

Pauline Kael, acknowledging the origins of the work, called the picture "preppy and pleasurable in the way that *Moscow on The Hudson* is, and with a modulated visual texture that makes it one of the most sheerly beautiful comedies ever shot." The comparison to *Moscow* is interesting, as its star Robin Williams had acknowledged that "people may have thought the ending broke down and got a little saccharine."[22]

A general consensus emerged that the lead actors had provided above-average to outstanding performances. Canby, in a think piece several months later, commented "The key performance by Richard Dreyfuss is something almost magical."

The music marketing for *Down and Out* was to put it politely, curious and atypical for MCA Records. The clip for Little Richard's "It's a Matter of Time," retitled for video/record consumption as "Great Gosh A' Mighty," was added at MTV three weeks following the film's release. It began in the active column and remained on the music channel for two months. The single entered the *Billboard* chart at number 87 the week of 8 March, some six weeks after the movie's premiere. It would peak at number 42, hardly a hit designation.

The MCA album materialized 15 March as a *Billboard* pick. This was seven weeks after the film's spectacular launch. The trade reviewer made note of the ticket action and Little Richard's role in the movie, saying "This package should spark solid sales despite a relative dearth of new contemporary pop material. The primary lure will be the theme song, Little Richard's 'Great Gosh A' Mighty,' already looming as a single hit, although the inclusion of Randy Newman's ubiquitous 'I Love L.A.' and David Lee Roth's 'California Girls' won't hurt. Second side offers tracks from Andy Summers."[23] Citing the Little Richard "theme" as a "hit" was somewhat disingenous, as the title rested at number 71 its second week on the charts.

MCA Records' experience with soundtrack lends some credibility to the rumor, unconfirmed, that the delay with the album was directly caused by the Talking Heads' refusal to allow "Once in a Lifetime," the opening and closing theme to the movie, to be used on the record. Janet Maslin noted that the classic anthem "wasn't written for the film, but it might as well have been." Several of the LP's selections were strictly of the traveling music variety, including David Lee Roth's cover of "California Girls." A viewer needed to pay close attention to hear the brief bars. To further confuse matters, "Great Gosh" was advertised on the record incorrectly, as the theme is generically listed on the movie's credits as "It's a Matter of Time.'' The title of the song stems from a monologue delivered by The Whiteman's neighbor, Orvis Goodnight (Little Richard), who, when roused in the middle of the night by Beverly Hills cops, said, ''Good gosh a' mighty, I don't get the protection I deserve because I'm black.''

The ''B'' side of the album is comprised of Andy Summers's highly listenable instrumentals. ''Mission Blues'' and the so-called ''Down and Out in Beverly Hills Theme'' are oustanding. This was not one of MCA Records' better soundtrack offerings, which may be explained by the absence of the skillful Kathy Nelson in the film or package credits.

''If it turns out that a director prefers [other label artists], or they work better for the situation,'' commented an MCA executive, ''then we'll go outside. For example, *Beverly Hills Cop* was about half MCA artists and half from other labels.'' The mix was similar for the Mazursky project, following in the footsteps of *Back To The Future*. The problem with *Down and Out* is suggested by the music placement. This is province of the music supervisor or the director. (As *Moscow on the Hudson* illustrated, Mazursky is more of a Spielberg than a Hackford or John Hughes.)

Down and Out demonstrated, once again, the tenuous relationship between the record and film industries. The mere inclusion of a recognizable rocker will not sell the film or the music package. A successful movie *may* generate souvenir sales, assuming the album is available during the film's theater life.

MCA Records, by hitching its fortunes to a hit movie, had little to lose, since public relation is at best unpredictable. Touchstone, with bankable stars, undoubtably employed rockers as insurance.

Nineteen eighty-six had not proved, for merchandisers, to be another 1984, with its ever-expanding soundtrack sales. Structurally, a significant problem was taking hold, the ''Missing-Hit Syndrome.'' The syndrome occurs when the central, infectious song is absent from the soundtrack. For example, The Rolling Stones were notably absent from *The Big Chill* soundtrack and Hackford's Atlantic soundtrack lacked Lionel Ritchie. (Both efforts *did* have compensating material, which aided the multiplatinum status of the albums.) The *Iron Eagle* and *Down and Out* soundtracks hinged on tunes vanished from the product. (It is difficult for a music fan to ''take the movie home'' when the central tune is in another label's stock or catalogue.) One insider said, ''We'll sell all the rights for the right price; if not, well they can always buy the single or the album.''

The *Risky Business* tug-of-war over ''Old Time Rock and Roll'' had demonstrated this phenomenon. Capitol advertised that the film's centerpiece was available on a Bob Seger album. When that failed to stimulate significant sales, a single was released. A Capitol ad read, ''There's only two places your customer can get it. That's the single, or better yet, inside Bob Seger's *Stranger in Town* album.'' Record companies were more than willing to have a film provide exposure for their artists. Aiding a competitor was another matter, however. The CBS Group wisely assisted Berlin, as the band's only hit single was on Columbia, not Geffen, Records. (The band has not repeated its success with *Top Gun*.)

The soundtrack dilemma had slowly begun to take hold in the boardrooms of New York and Los Angeles, but commitments had already been made for the summer season. Anecdotal horror stories abounded, offset by (an increasingly smaller number of) successes. To further muddy the waters, *Rocky IV* had been certified platinum in early February.

What's Rock Got To Do With It

Thanksgiving weekend 1985, the second most profitable of the year, was the target date for the third sequel to Sylvester Stallone's gold-mine film about Rocky Balboa. The marketing drive began early on Memorial Day, with a teaser trailer distributed to some 5,800 theaters during the heavily attended summer months. Afterward, on the basis of call-outs, Stallone had enjoyed a Q-Profile (awareness factor) of 90 percent. Perry Katz, an MGM/UA market researcher, noted that "a studio aims for a 65 percent awareness factor. With 90 percent, we could be talking a *big* opening." The film company had an additional stake in the project, as it was to be the first film to carry the United Artists logo exclusively. Following in the footsteps of Chuck Norris's *MIA* enterprises, *Rocky's* release date was plugged to maximize box office by reaching the MTV crowd.

The result was a gargantuan moneymaker, pulling in $20 million over three days. Two more days saw the amount increase to $31.7 million. ''We're elated—no one could have ever anticipated those numbers,'' noted producer Robert Chartoff.[24] By February 1986 the domestic gross was more than $118 million. A highly successful, textbook case of synergy, the film produced a platinum album the same month.

A bankable star with a blockbuster does not guarantee a gold or a platinum return. *Down and Out* had showcased three name actors. *Back To the Future*, still on many screens as *Rocky IV* began its lucrative run, had surpassed $200 million with only a gold-album certification. Several Sylvester Stallone features with accompanying music packages had stiffed, such as the disappointing collaboration with Dolly Parton in *Rhinestone* (1984).

The *Rocky* series has demonstrated an interesting, if checkered, history in the popular music sphere. The Bill Conti score and theme, ''Gonna Fly

Now,'' climbed to number 1 on the singles chart. The song and score were recycled for the 1979 sequel. Stallone, who had expressed a desire to reach the youth market, needed some contemporary music. Tony Scotti had released some material by Frank Stallone. Director Stallone contacted Scotti. The record executive sent Survivor's *Premonition*. "Sly listened to it and thought the band was great," recalled Scotti Brothers president Johnny Musso. He asked Tony if he thought they could write a song for the movie. A meeting was arranged. "He just said he wanted something with a strong beat. He wanted a contemporary theme, something that would appeal to the rock crowd. That's an audience he felt he didn't have then," said Jim Peterik.[25]

Upon seeing a rough cut of *Rocky III*, Peterik and Frankie Sullivan focused on the phrase "eye of the tiger."

"It was a catch phrase," said Peterik. "Rocky's trainer kept telling him he had to keep the eye of the tiger." It became the theme for subsequent *Rocky* sequels. According to Musso, "Eye of The Tiger" sold five million copies internationally. The Survivor album moved two-and-a-half million copies. Once again, a Rocky Balboa story had created a best-selling record—the single was number 1 for six weeks.

Stallone signed an agreement with Scotti Records for *Rocky IV* and *Cobra*, which was scheduled for a summer 1986 release. The label was anxious to work with the muscular actor, an obvious box office draw.

Stallone had produced some memorable videoclips. Denby wrote, "The famous training sequence in the original *Rocky* may well have been the first rock video—all highlights." Brother Frank's "Far From Over" had been critically cited as the high point of *Staying Alive*. This, of course, was a backhanded compliment. *Rocky IV* would prove to be another film pregnant with rock-video possibilities. This time, however, there would be at least three.

In *Rocky IV*, Survivor's "Eye of The Tiger" accentuates the uplifted boxing glove emboldened in patriotic red, white, and blue. Highlights of previous *Rocky* adventures crosscut. A *Sports Illustrated* cover announces, "Russians Invade U.S." Featured is blond giant Ivan Drago (Dolph Lundgren), the "Siberian Express," who "destroys whatever he hits." Apollo Creed (Carl Weathers) is moved to teach the mechanical Russian the finer points of pugilism American style. After five years of retirement, Creed longs to regain a modicum of his pre-Balboa glory years. Rocky (Sylvester Stallone) is concerned. He warns, "We're changing. We're becoming *regular* people." Unpersuaded, Apollo challenges Drago to an exhibition at MGM's Grand Hotel. Traces of the Joe Louis-Max Schmelling encounter abound. The Las Vegas extravaganza surpasses the pyrotechnics of Leni Riefenstahl's *Triumph der Will* (1935). "The boxers rise and descend via hydraulic stages, there are show girls and chorus girls and laser beams and star filters and spangles and sequins and a pair of almost life-size fighter planes, and roughly 750,000 little American flags being waved by unsportsmanlike American fight planes, and James Brown writhing in the foreground and Russians sneering in the background," described Sheila Benson.[26] The scene provides a natural music trailer for "Living in America" and the movie.

"I cannot be defeated," mumbles Drago, who proceeds to destroy Apollo. Rocky watches the human sacrifice with anger and disgust. He swears vengeance: "If he dies, *he* dies." All of the heart-rending cliches from *Rocky* are reinvented. Adrian Balboa warns, "It's suicide. You can't win." Rocky must go, however, to fight on Christmas Day in wintry Moscow. "And what date better than Christmas Day to underline the high stakes," asked Jack Kroll, "Soviet godlessness versus American piety?"[27] As Balboa drives away in a black Ferrari, a montage-summary of the *Rocky* series flashes to Robert Tepper's "There's No Easy Way Out." The footage is ideal for a trailer or a videoclip. The plane touches down in the icy environs of the Soviet Union to the strains of Survivor's "Burning Heart." Stereotypical KGB types, "official chaperons," stand around menacingly. Rocky is taken, by his request, to a Spartan farm facility which will serve as his training camp.

Drago, conversely, works out in an ultra-high-tech sports laboratory. (If this is reminiscent of *Rocky* it should be. As *Newsweek* wrote: "Intercutting between training camps [its] Yanks versus robot Russky; Rocky chops wood, pulls a sled and runs up snowy slopes; Drago pounds away at computerized machines, is injected with suspicious hypodermics and races on treadmills with electrodes plastered all over his android muscles." As *Vision Quest* had demonstrated, jogging and exercise make for musical opportunities, especially "Burning Heart." Rocky's triumph of the will occurs on a snow-covered mountain peak, arms uplifted as in Philadelphia, as Bill Conti's theme heralds his accomplishment. With the "overcoming-all-odds" motif established, the Drago-Balboa bout is anticlimatic. The outcome, as Schickel noted, is a surprise "only if you have been living in deepest Siberia since 1976."[28] John Cafferty's "Hearts On Fire" closes the film.

The redundant plot, with a Cold War twist, did not detract from the $30-million production. The visuals are engaging. The boxing contests were galas akin to the 1984 Olympics. *Rocky IV*, more than its precursors, was a series of cross-cuts and made for MTV sequences. The only hook is the basic Charles Atlas ideology. "*Rocky IV* establishes both its pop-video aesthetic and its simplistic ideological vision,'' said Floyd. Summers indicated that the film was written and directed "like it was a rock video album. What seems like four-fifths of the movie is taken up with fast-cutting montage sequences that are backed up with loud, tuneless (sic) music."[29]

Although reviewers negatively assessed the pop-video quality of the film most acknowledged its commercial value. Stallone was reaching his target audience and Scotti Brothers Records had ready-made music trailers. These would be employed to market the two products symbiotically.

The marketing campaign was similar to the model employed for *Footloose* and, later, *Top Gun*. The MGM/UA film was the centerpiece, but *Rocky II*, minus a strong rock cut, had pulled relatively modest profits. With $30 million going in, Stallone and backers required at minimum twice that figure to experience "a wash" (break even). The converted, they believed, would buy their admission tickets, and popcorn, to witness another victory for the pugnacious underdog. The synergy drive was aimed at the "rock crowd," not the zenophobes who religiously followed the Golan-Globus school of diplomacy.

In textbook fashion, Scotti Brothers purchased a front-page ad in the music trades expounding, "ROUND 1 SURVIVOR "BURNING HEART" . . . ON YOUR DESK THIS WEEK!,'' 19 October, five weeks prior to *Rocky IV's* release. Program directors, the target of the ad, found that *Billboard's* "pick" reviewer did not share the copy's ardor, writing, "This latest ringside sequel with a Cold-War plot hook . . . burdens the new Survivor main theme, "Burning Heart," with lyrics problems."[30] The soundtrack album debuted in the chart November 16 at a comfortable #147.

"Burning Heart" was the scout, as the ad copy indicated. It entered the singles listing at number 64 the week of 2 November. MTV placed the title in the power slot two weeks later. The week of the opening "Burning Heart" was stationed at number 34 with the album at the halfway mark of number 104. The carrier picture had not yet been shown. After the opening, the album moved up to number 79 and Survivor's entry was in hit contention at number 27.

Following Teller's cluster strategy, James Brown's "Living in America" was issued 7 December appearing at number 91. It placed on the MTV playlist 18 December in the medium catetgory. By year's end all of the Scotti Brothers Records were established and ascending. *The Film Journal* reported, as of 1 January 1986, that *Rocky IV* had grossed $86.5 million. Stallone, statistically, was reaching beyond the usual audience for his endeavors.

As the film was edging the magic $100 million mark, the centerpiece song, "No Easy Way Out," was released the last week of January. Survivor just missed the top of the chart at number 2, 1 February. After twelve weeks the motion picture began to fade into the hereafter of cassette rentals and sales. The clustering continued, however. John Cafferty's "Hearts On Fire" hit the bins 1 March. Of the four releases, it fared poorest. A possible explanation is that the song was not prominant in the movie. The album, by the time of the Cafferty issuance, was platinum.

Song	Peak	Weeks
"Burning Heart"	2	22
"Living in America"	4	19
"No Easy Way Out"	22	16
"Hearts On Fire"	76	6

The Kenny Loggins and Gladys Knight number "Double or Nothing," barely audible in the film, was ignored. CBS had other plans for Loggins, the *Top Gun* project.

9 1/2 Weeks?

> *It's* The Story of O *as it might look if conceived as a two-hour television commercial.*
> —Vincent Canby, film critic

While overshadowed by the braggartish Don Simpson, Adrian Lyne remained *Flashdance's* director of record. The dance film contained Lyne's distinctive television ad touch—commercials like Calvin Klein and Diet Pepsi—full of lightning-flash edits, cut-aways, shadowy images and urban gloss. (Numerous projects arrive for his consideration. He turned down *A Chorus Line* because "It would have been such an obvious movie, another musical.")

A proposal catching his fancy was submitted by Zalman King. The executive producer of *Roadie* (1980) and his wife, Patricia Louisana Knop, had adapted a 1978 novella by Elizabeth McNeil, a pseudonym. In *9 1/2 Weeks* the author is a submissive participant in a sadomasochistic relationship which results in her nervous breakdown. Part of the therapy was the cathartic chronicling of the experience.

As portrayed in the book, Elizabeth is totally compliant. Lyne, accepting the assignment, changed the interaction from "woman as victim" to a situation "where people actually become drunk on each other to the exclusion of the everything else." They, mutually, become overwhelmed by their passion for one another.[31] Had Lyne left Elizabeth as victim the ensuing furor may have been avoided.

Kim Basinger, who had appeared in *The Natural* and *Fool For Love*, was an ideal pick for the female lead. Mickey Rourke was a surprise choice for the male role. (He had gained attention in de Palma's *Body Double* and as Motorcycle Boy in Coppola's *Rumble Fish*.) In mid-April 1984, a cast and crew of sixty gathered in Manhattan for location shots. Three days prior to production Tri-Star had cancelled its participation. Victor Kaufman, the CEO, attributed the pull out to "creative differences with the director as to the direction in which the movie should go." Responding, the director said, "Tri-Star wanted to do a movie about two rare birds of paradise, which I never really understood. I wanted it to have more humanity and be less of an art movie. I wanted it to be something that audiences in Ohio could really see in terms of themselves."[32] Two weeks later, a white knight in the form of Producers Sales Organization took over. PSO became the "money" source for the picture and the sales agent. MGM/UA, "paying a very satisfactory advance," obtained distribution rights.

Production wrapped in New York 10 August, coming in a bit over the $15-million budget. The interaction on the set may have been more compelling than the final product—PSO's Mark Damon characterized it as "a highly charged, emotional situation."[33]

The leads found the experience a strenuous one. Kim Basinger, in a series of interviews, lamented, "I didn't want to do it—nobody wants to be taken that far. I was the sole emotional soul in the entire movie. Every nerve of mine was exposed to cast, crew, everybody."

Mickey Rourke had grievances. "It was such an unlikely part for me to play that the character really interested me. But I can't say I enjoyed doing it," he recalled. "Adrian Lyne is the most meticulous mother . . . I mean God bless him, he's immensely gifted, but he's the most conniving, sneaky, paranoid son of a bitch I ever met." Lyne acknowledged that there were problems, saying "A lot of the turbulence onscreen was real." He praised the actors, especially Basinger, for taking "the truth of their personality and putting it into the character . . . Kim does that as well as anybody."[34] The turbulence on the set would prove minor in contrast to that in the corporate boardroom.

In August 1984 PSO announced that Geffen Records had acquired the soundtrack rights to *9 1/2 Weeks*. The Police's Stewart Copeland was recruited to score the film. (His previous film work was Coppola's *Rumble*

Fish and television's *The Equalizer*.) Lyne told the *Los Angeles Times*, "I feel we've got a hugely commercial movie here."[35]

Months passed and the *New York Times* eventually announced that MGM/UA had withdrawn the title from its 1985 release calendar. Janet Maslin said that the director was "re-editing," but the film "remains very sexually suggestive."[36]

The overzealous editing had created problems for the film's music supervisor. Becky Shargo Mancuso, having survived *Mike's Murder*, complained, "A lot of the scenes that would have had logical places for music have been cut out, so it's hard to say whether we have enough music slots left for an album. Originally, we had at least eight music slots and now we're down to about five, and they're still falling by the wayside." This was a major concern as *Flashdance's* success had hinged on its soundtrack and videos.

In May 1985, Lyne's problems escalated as Geffen Records withdrew from the project. John Kalodner found the film "offensive to women. I don't care if the movie makes $100 million," he said. "I've washed my hands of the whole thing. I think Adrian is very talented and I respect his work, but I just couldn't see having my name on this picture. Some people may find it titilating, but it made me nauseous."[37]

The label's reluctance to become involved with a "sensitive" film in 1985 was understandable. Warner Communications (WCI) in 1976 had become embroiled in a highly publicized dispute with Women Against Violence Against Women (WAVAW) and the National Organization for Women (NOW.). The center of the polemic was The Rolling Stones' *Black and Blue* cover. WAVAW charged that "the implications of the debasing of women are quite obvious." The argument, which raged for several years, was brought to a conclusion by a threatened boycott. David Horowitz, representing the Warners group, issued a statement saying, "WCI is acknowledging that the commercial use of visual and other images that trivialize women victims is irresponsible."[38]

1985 was an inhospitable year for record companies to be challenging conventional wisdom. The Parents Music Resource Center (PMRC), better known as the "Washington Wives," was generating considerable attention by insisting that albums be rated similarly to motion pictures. Unlike many fundamentalist record burners, the PMRC was not to be dismissed. The organization, while small in number, contained the spouses of numerous influential Administration and Senatorial personages.

The Recording Industry Association of America (RIAA), frequently in the vanguard of First-Amendment issues, was caught in a dilemma. The trade association was lobbying for the Morrison bill, which would charge tape hardware and software manufacturers a royalty fee. If passed, the "anticonsumer" legislation would put millions of dollars into the record companies' coffers. Stan Gortikov, RIAA president, walked a tightrope during the summer of 1985. The climate of the time was hardly propitious for a *9 1/2 Weeks* soundtrack.

Producers Sales Organization president Mark Damon defended the work, pointing to test screenings "where 60 percent of the audience felt the picture was excellent or good—and even more women like the picture than men, of those who saw it." He told the *Los Angeles Times* that several other label executives had seen the film and he was on the verge of "closing a deal."[39]

"I wasn't actually offended, but I was a little afraid of it," said Mancuso. "It was a long way from the innocence of *Footloose*. I still have some misgivings about the subject matter. But I really believe in Adrian, who is an immensely talented director." Capitol's Stephen Powers signed on to do the soundtrack.

9 1/2 Weeks curiosity quota, not quite as strong as that of *Apocalypse Now*, was on the rise. Lynn Hirschberg, describing some of the movie's sequences, groused, "You have the makings for great, trashy summer fun. Sadly, sadly, it was not to be."[40] The summer of 1985 was for teenpics, not soft-core S&M.

After an estimated ten rewrites, myriad edits and re-edits, plus $1 million, nearly all of the film's handcuff, bordello, and blindfold scenes were dropped. Other domination material was cut, and even an ad with a blindfold was nixed. The B.D. Fox and Friends marketing agency chose to focus on the universal ingredient. "Sex," asserted Brian Fox, "is something that men and women everywhere have been doing for a long, long time."[41] The distributors definitely were thinking of foreign rentals. At the Cannes Film Festival the theater sheets read, "A smoldering story of passion out of control." A trailer run in Europe stated, "Their love took them beyond desire, beyond passion, beyond obsession." Across the Atlantic, this may have been the case, but in the United States *9 1/2* paled in contrast to *Last Tango in Paris* (1973).

As a *Los Angeles Times* contributor asserted, MGM/UA quietly and "nervously" released the film in five urban markets. "In a business in which talking about the pictures usually is the business, the studio was adamant in refusing to discuss plans for its promotional campaign," wrote Broeske.[42] This was a long-awaited vehicle for reviewers, in light of the "juicy" prepublicity.

Capitol Records' participation in the soundtrack sweepstakes was an anomaly. EMI, the parent company, had indirectly let United Artists have

A Hard Day's Night. *Help* was a Capitol release. Pink Floyd's efforts were distributed by CBS. The landmark *The Harder They Come* (1973) was a Capitol product. ("You know," said Jimmy Cliff, "they didn't even put out a single from that record?" The answering to his rhetorical question was, "It has sold and sold and sold, just by word of mouth."[43]

Entering the Eighties, Capitol enjoyed the top-selling track album with the remake of *The Jazz Singer*. In 1981 *Billboard* ranked the Neil Diamond effort Number 1; it remained at number 5 the following year. The label disappeared from the trade's year-end soundtrack chart until Duran Duran's single theme for *A View to A Kill*.

Geffen Records' retreat from the Lyne project left MGM/UA at a dead end. The ability to reach the youth market hinged on video and audio exposure. Capitol had absorbed United Artist Records—in February 1979. Since *Billboard* began ranking labels on the basis of combined single/album chart performance, Capitol had placed in the top four. There *was* linkage between the two entities, no matter how informal. Capitol had done a credible promotion job with *Teachers*, a MGM/UA title.

For the record label, *9 1/2 Weeks* appeared a very viable option. (The PMRC moved products.) A majority of soundtrack cuts could be used to promote in-house artists. There was, also, the potential bonus of the breakaway feature.

The company cushioned itself by avoiding past mistakes. (Theoretically, "We're Not Gonna Take It" had been tailor-made for a scout video/single for *Iron Eagle*. Atlantic withheld permission. The marginal "One Vision," not one of Queen's better efforts, *did* gain medium exposure. King Kobra, whose play was problematic, was more central to the film, but lacked name recognition. It failed to radio chart, but did show on MTV for several weeks.)

John Taylor, part of the EMI structure, formerly of Duran Duran was assigned the theme. "I Do What I Do," described by *Billboard* as a "post electro-environment theme" aired on MTV three weeks prior to *9 1/2's* release.[44] The single charted at number 73 two weeks after on 8 March 1986.

As Stephen Powers described Capitol's campaign, "We have a very urban pop soundtrack. We have videoclips for the Taylor, Cocker, and Luba singles. For the Cocker song, we have three different versions of the video—the first, which we serviced to all of AOR radio and to cable outlets, has Kim Basinger's tantalizing strip scene, the second combines the movie footage with performance footage of Joe, and has been used a lot by our overseas people, and third is a performance-only clip of Joe

Cocker which went to MTV.'' MTV's Standards and Acquisitions unit was hardly likely to use film material from *9 1/2*.[45]

In *9 1/2*, several plaintive bars of Billie Holiday's ''Strange Fruit'' whisper as a scene of the human congestion in downtown Manhattan flashes. Elizabeth (Kim Basinger) is propelled by the teaming throng. She breaks free, with Luba's ''The Best Is Yet To Come'' accompanying, jaunting puckishly to the Spring Street Galley in the trendy Soho district. Lyne's stylish, Calvin-Klein-activewear approach to urban street scenes is quite apparent.

Elizabeth, a divorcee of three years, is an art dealer. She appears, however, as an innocent, although effective in the New York art world. Despite her chic facade, Elizabeth is awestruck and out of place.

Shopping at a street bazarre, she wanders from stall to stall as a reggae band accompanies dancers. She spies a multicolored French shawl selling for $300 and moves on to a less expensive toy chicken. She is taken with the $30 object, exhibiting a childlike quality. It is here that John (Mickey Rourke) enters her life with the present of the shawl and lunch at an ethnic restaurant. In both instances, she demonstrates a vulnerability to surprises, a trait rare in many residents of Soho.

The impression of Elizabeth's defenselessness is reinforced at John's Jersey Palisades houseboat, when she asks him his occupation. ''I buy and sell money,'' he replies. ''Some people call it arbitrageur.''

''That's a lot of risk taking,'' she answers. The Wall Streeter then points out that she's taking quite a risk going to a remote location with a total stranger. John seems in control, while Elizabeth's fragile. ''Strange Fruit'' reemerges to underscore the mood.

The power relationship is developed when John arranges to leave her hanging on a Coney Island Ferris wheel. The response is feigned anger and a first kiss.

Arriving at her modest apartment, after the small talk is dispensed with, he commands, ''Take off your dress.'' She complies, posing in the figure-silhouetting, refractive glow. She agrees to be blindfolded after he threatens to leave. Being caressed, she indicates fright and excitement. The financier proceeds to run an ice cube over the recesses of her skin. Edelstein's remark, ''a *Last Tango in Paris* for the MTV generation,'' is apt.[46]

John's dominance is further illustrated at his hi-tech, chrome, ultra-modern apartment, which is in stark contrast to Elizabeth's digs. He bestows another gift, an expensive gold watch, with a condition attached— she is to think of them touching. The power of autosuggestion is operative the following day as she commiserates to co-worker and roommate Molly

(Margaret Whitton) about a lack of concentration. She succumbs, in time; watching a slide show of nudes, she masturbating to the rhythms of The Eurythmics' "The City Never Sleeps." Obedience makes pleasure viable. She is afraid of herself, reluctant to take risks. John, and his commands, provide a rationale for the child/woman duality. Her comment, "God, I don't believe this," is a duality of pleasure and disorientation.

The famous food scene, played to the strains of "Bread and Butter," finds Elizabeth sliding to the kitchen floor, eyes closed, being fed everything from luscious strawberries to Vicks 44 to hot peppers. Champagne and honey further kink up the scene.

Her dependency on the relationship heightens. Molly sheepishly announces that she has slept with Elizabeth's ex-husband, to no reaction. Elizabeth is apparently beginning to feel more secure with John. She asks him to meet her friends. He refuses, saying, "The nighttime is ours." He asserts, "I'll take care of you, including cooking, feeding and dressing."

Any misconception about John's submission is quickly put to rest. Elizabeth searches the apartment, discovering pictures of old girlfriends. Unexpectedly, he phones asking, if she's been a bad girl by snooping in the apartment. Her act of rebellion is quickly quelled when John announces, "I'm going to spank you." She protests and is raped. She ultimately "succumbs with pleasure."[47]

The storyline blurs as several sequences, like the boutique and bell-tower incidents, become music placement opportunities, utilizing Lyne's fashion-*noir* techniques, to showcase John Taylor's scout, "I Do What I Do," and Bryan Ferry's "Slave To Love." Ferry's tune seems to fit, as the characters have become more mannequins in an authority interaction.

The undercurrent of the film is only hinted at when Elizabeth follows John to his Wall Street office inquiring if he "always buys lunch for his secretary." This, plus other expressions of jealous sentiments, is quickly overshadowed by a transsexual masquerade which results in a mugging by a gang of gay bashers. In this, the role transfer is the Basinger character, who, grabbing a knife, becomes an Amazon warrior. This character realization is rapidly obscured by a ferocious lovemaking scene in a water-soaked Soho alley.

Unable to find the plot, Lyne resorts to other examples of domination. Elizabeth shoplifts a gold chain and pendant. She and John visit Bloomingdales to try out beds. In full earshot of the prudish salesperson, John urges, "Hold on to the bedboard. Spread your legs for Daddy." John seems to be bent on pushing her into various forms of deviance, such as theft and exhibitionism. (Reportedly several other thematic scenes were cut from the film.)

At this point in the movie, the whip-buying scene is almost laughable. John, quite serious, tries out different models as if he is a connoisseur. The instrument, chosen with such care, then disappears from sight.

The music trailer for video consumption, except MTV, is a sensuous striptease featuring Joe Cocker's "You Can Leave Your Hat On." Toward the conclusion, they run upstairs to the bedroom, where John finally exhibits some emotion, urging, "Take it off." A vague impression is beginning to surface. Both are enjoying the other. Time and mutual experience engender commitment?

John calls, asking Elizabeth to meet him at the Chelsea Hotel in Room 906. The request, "Something I want you to do for me," is repeated. An exotic hooker enters and caresses a blindfolded Elizabeth. John watches. Elizabeth realizes what is happening. John embraces the prostitute. Enraged, Elizabeth lashes out and races into the subway. A denounement is suggested at this point. It is not to be.

The child-woman was content, even as a sex object. The childish part of Elizabeth loved the gifts and the pampering. The sensual aspect of her womanhood was anomic. It was John's affection toward the hooker, not toward Elizabeth, which dissolved her bond.

She ascends into the "pits of depravity," a sex emporium on 42 Street. John follows. Watching an XXX-rated movie, she grabs a male bystander. After a long kiss, she performs the same act with John. This is her act of revenge. Having returned to the gallery, she becomes physically ill, yet she is drawn back to John. As John sleeps, Elizabeth begins packing. Awake, he attempts to reassure her. There *were* other girls, but, "I never felt anything like this before." It is obvious these were the words that should have been spoken weeks ago. She leaves chastened and perhaps stronger from the experience, while John reverts, uttering in the empty room, "Will you please come back by the time I count to fifty . . ."

John, portrayed as a Wall Street wunderkind, proves incapable of playing the risk-taking game in relationships. He is weak and loses. Elizabeth has triumphed, regardless of the price.

This synopsis has glossed over myriad hops, skips, and jumps in the plot. Critics, conversely, had a field day, beginning with the obvious sins of commission: the editing and the cuts.

Writers in the two major media markets led the assault. *Variety* fired first with, the "Filmmakers probably shouldn't have gone ahead with such a picture if they weren't prepared to go all the way and have the guts to really make a film about sexual obsession, ratings be damned." A week prior to the New York opening, Maslin indicated that the film had undergone a year's worth of editing at a cost of $1 million. "What's left after the cuts is frosty and chic and shallow,'' wrote Edelstein. ''Dramatically the film is often laughable.''

''Whoever was responsible for the released film seems to have edited it with a pair of garden shears,'' wrote Canby. Tom Matthews echoed, ''There is no story beyond this oppressive yet mutually enjoyed bonding, there is no plot no structure and precious little to latch onto.''[48]

The *Los Angeles Times* and *Village Voice* took note of some of the material that had ended up on the cutting-room floor. Both pointed to the deviations from the book. Several discarded scenes had Basinger graduating from shoplifting to mugger. The whips and metal material, ideal for some musical material, were scrapped, along with a ''mock-whorehouse'' visual.[49]

Critically, *Flashdance* had enjoyed the dubious distinction of being labelled the first ''99-minute music video.'' Many reviewers perceived *9 1/2 Weeks* as a glitzy follow-up. Lally wrote that the movie was a ''polymorphously perverse self-help video with the same slick urban gloss (minus dancing) of his 1983 smash.''

''Adrian Lyne persists in his flashy, commercial/music video style,'' said McCarthy. ''Lyne merely uses these provocative issues,'' noted Kesten, ''as the framework for a long, glossy music video.'' Edelstein made a positive comparison: ''There have been many *Flashdance* imitations, but only one *Flashdance*, the gorgeously vapid original.''[50]

Basinger and Rourke generally received good notices, with the caveat that there had not been much of a script to work with. The soundtrack, what there was of it, was barely noticed. Canby saw the ''big-beat'' as a centrifugal force that joined the bodies together. Conversely, *Variety* curtly said that the ''collection of pop tunes is mediocre in the extreme.''[51]

''Underneath it all, I didn't want anything to do with book,'' explained Basinger. ''I wanted to come from where I wanted to come from. I don't care where she came from. I'm not a carbon copy of her. I wasn't playing someone's life. Elizabeth was me. I was playing my *own* life.''

This statement appears to be the focus of *9 1/2*. Kim Basinger, a one-time winner of the Junior Miss contest in Athens, Georgia, was a southern belle who had graced commercials for Breck and Ford. One writer characterized the actress as bringing to the screen ''the platitude about Southern women, that below their demure facade is a reservoir of will.'' The image could have come from W. J. Cash's juxtaposition of the lily-pure maid to the hunting goddess.[52] *9 1/2 Weeks*, either by design or chance, in many respects became the exploration of Basinger's psyche interplayed with Lyne's vision.

9 1/2 Weeks is a film easily dismissed as butchered by the temerity of

MGM/UA and Lyne's penchant for the ideal music trailer: Basinger's erotic strip scene to Joe Cocker's "Leave Your Hat On." Almost any plausible thread of a thesis had been lost in gloss, glitter, and Gnosticism. In places, the director makes the thesis take form and then immediately cuts away. A majority of critics were overtly on the mark, suggesting most of the story line censorially was removed. Still, even in the European version, Lyne's ending is almost lifted from the credo of NOW. Women, despite degradation, can survive. John's outcome is that he is overwhelmed and succumbs to the relationship as Elizabeth, in pain, walks away into the ultrasophisticated world. She appears to be more enabled to function in the totally glamorous but exploitative milieu of the hunting goddess.

9 1/2 Weeks opened in sixteen selected theaters the weekend of 21 February. The rentals amounted to a meager $328,000. Its eighth week found it exhibited in thirty-seven theaters. After an eleven-week first run the total gross was $2 million. By year's end, *Variety* estimated its studio return at a little over $2.5 million.

An anxiom in the film industry is that the first three days, usually a weekend, of a movie's run determines its success. All of the prerelease marketing is addressed to getting bodies into the theaters. Preview screenings, scout singles, and videos are designed to reach audiences. Should momentum—word of mouth—occur it behooves the record label to have the soundtrack on the street. With *9 1/2 Weeks* Capitol missed the mark by several weeks. *Billboard* announced the package with a caveat:

> Contemporary pop, rock, and dance tracks skewed to the controversial new film's theme of erotic obsession are well chosen, whether previously issued (Bryan Ferry, Corey Hart, Eurythmics) or newly recorded (Joe Cocker, Devo, Stewart Copeland). Whether the movie's on-screen heat translates to box office sizzle will shape sales, here, though.[53]

John Taylor's "theme" was conspicuously absent, but not from MTV. The music channel added the video 26 February on its power rotation. AM airplay quickly followed. On 8 March it ranked as one of top five add-ons nationally. The video would remain for a two-month stay, immediately followed by the sanitized version of Joe Cocker's "You Can Leave Your Hat On."

The album, finally, charted five weeks after the picture's appearance, at number 170. The video probably helped it more than the film did. The "*Menage-a-Trois* of Hits" visual campaign referring to Taylor, Luba and Cocker, reportedly created some interest. During its fifteen-week stint on the chart, *9 1/2* peaked at number 59, a respectable ranking for a movie earning only $2.5 million in domestic rentals.

Lyne's serendipitous success with *Flashdance*, at the record store, was not to be repeated. Becky Mancuso's lament regarding music placement proved prophetic. The two songs that had survived the Draconian cuts were by non-Capitol artists. The Eurythmics' "This City Never Sleeps" competed with Cocker's "Leave Your Hat On" as the most memorable song from the movie. Ferry's "Slave To Love" came close. Only Cocker and Luba, highlighted in the film, were Tower people. To make the situation more complex, Cocker's "Shelter Me" was scheduled for issuance during the film's first run.

The only musical artifact in the *9 1/2* saga which provided any spin for the movie and record companies was John Taylor's "I Do What I Do," which had a minor impact on the film, because of MTV and AM exposure. The song was on the Hot 100 for three months, peaking at number 23.

Cocker missed CHR play completely. "Leave Your Hat On" was on the AOR ranking beginning 31 May for a period of four weeks. Luba's tune, according to the charts, garnered no airplay. She did surface on MTV for a short stay.

One scribe termed *9 1/2 Weeks* "high-gloss soft porn for yuppies." Lyne's success with *Flashdance* demographically had been widely attributed to the project's appeal to collegiates. John Hughes's draw was to adolescents. High schools were the native turf of a huge portion of filmgoers. In late summer 1985 he brought forth *Weird Science*, a fantasy costing an estimated $15 million. Reportedly, the film broke even. Critics disdained the venture. For the President's Day break, Hughes was back with Molly Ringwald and in the familiar suburban Chicago, secondary school climate.

Pretty in Pink

> *I've never been on a date as an adult.*
> —John Hughes, writer-director-producer

During the final days of filming *Sixteen Candles*, Molly Ringwald introduced John Hughes to an obscure English band, The Psychedelic Furs. She was particularly taken with their *Talk, Talk, Talk* album, which contained "Pretty in Pink." (Molly has a "predisposition toward pink.") Hughes recalled, "I couldn't speak after *Sixteen Candles* was over. I returned to the abandoned house, and they were tearing down [Ringwald's room] and I was just horrified because I wanted to stay there forever." He wrote a script titled after The Furs' album cut the week after *Candles* was finished because, "I so desperately hate to end these movies that the first thing I do when I'm done is write another one. Then I don't feel sad about having to leave and everybody going away."[54] Ringwald, already cast in *The Breakfast Club*, would be in yet a third Hughes project.

To create the proper mood for the project, the material was written to the sounds of The Furs, Lou Reed, and Mott the Hoople. The Beatles' *White Album*, a writer-director favorite, also created the atmosphere.

As Pauline Kael noted, *Pretty in Pink* exhibited "the same basic plot" found in *Candles*. The Ringwald character is a smart-but-poor teenager from the wrong side of the tracks. Andrew McCarthy's "richie" person is upper-crusted, with Don Johnson duds and a BMW. They fall in love only to be confronted by peer and class pressures. Throw in a pink prom dress and the plot is in place. One critic would term it a "Marxist version of *Romeo and Juliet*."[55]

The setting would revisit the affluent Chicago North Shore. "All my references go back there," says Hughes, "and I don't want to abandon them." Many of the outdoor shots occurred in Southern California shopping malls, adding to "an overall vagueness."[56] In the waning days of 1985 even Hughes was under economic constraints.

A&M welcomed Hughes back, as they perceived the filmmaker as "at the cutting edge of what's hip in music." David Anderle supervised the twenty-two-song selection on the film track. The album would feature ten cuts. Four in-house artists would be included. Most notable were Orchestral Maneuvers in the Dark (OMD) and Susan Vega. The title cut by The Psychedelic Furs was obtained from CBS while New Order's "Shell Shock" was owned by Geffen. "Bring on the Dancing Horses" by Echo and The Bunnymen came from the WCI subsidiary, Sire Records. To Hughes and the labels' credit, the artists were not "authoritative" names. "The music in *Pretty in Pink* was not an afterthought," asserted Hughes. "The tracks on this album and in this film are there because Howie Deutch and I believe in the artists."[57]

A&M, under the supervision of Bob Reitman, devised a cluster campaign, issuing "If You Leave" to Top-40 singles stations and AC outlets. New Order's contribution would appear within a week followed by The Furs' title song, which coincided with the film's release date.

An MTV premiere, prerecorded, was also planned. A recycled video of "Bring On the Dancing Horses" was submitted to the music channel.

Nearly two weeks prior to the film's national debut on 872 screens, 15 February, *Billboard* reviewed OMD's "If You Leave" as a pop pick. The writer described the single as "not unlike the Simple Minds hit from the preceding film.''[58] The song by the two-man group, comprised of Paul Humphreys and Andrew McClusky, lacked a companion video. Instead, MTV aired, the week of the movie's release, "Pretty in Pink" by The Psychedelic Furs. The album followed three days later on 1 March 1986.

In the first week of March the film grossed a very respectable $6 million. The Furs' video was in the light rotation and the single was creeping up the CHR chart. The strategy was for the video to scout for the film and the record. The single provided exposure for OMD, highly desirous of an American hit, and the soundtrack.

The rerecorded version of the title track surfaced 12 April at Number 90 while the album comfortably rested at Number 8.

The film, aesthetically, carried the title theme and the rest of the LP. "Pretty in Pink" as an opening and closing hook is not immediately infectious. The song, however, is repeated three times in the film. The prom sequence, particularly the parking-lot close, highlighted the song. "An image of Blane and Andie kissing in front of car headlights is automatically romantic in the finest MTV style," wrote Janet Maslin.[59] The placement was ideal for souvenir shopping.

All Dressed Up With . . .

In *Pretty in Pink* the camera follows a motorized street sweeper as it lumbers through a well kept, aging, working-class neighborhood. Separating the older houses from sterile factories and warehouses are the symbolic railroad tracks. The Psychedelic Furs' title theme accompanies the trek.

Andie Walsh (Molly Ringwald) readies for the day. Clothes will play a major role in the film. She wakes Jake (Harry Dean Stanton), her lethargic father, scolding "Come on, get up; it means a lot to me."

Dressed in Cyndi-Lauperish regalia, she arrives at her suburban high school. She meets the "Duck-man" (Jon Cryer), also clad in Goodwill's finest. The students hurrying by seem to have stepped off a *Miami Vice* set. To underscore the status cleavage, "richie" Bunny Strongly (Kate Vernon), during a lecture on the New Deal, hisses at Andie "Where'd you get your clothes, the five and dime?"

The heroine is able to maintain a strong-willed posture through an after-school job at TRAX record store. Its owner, Iona (Annie Potts), a flakey 1960s Earth Mother, is Andie's only female friend and confidante. Blane McDonough (Andrew McCarthy), a self-described "crown prince," enters Andie's quiescent, well, almost, world. At the record store—a perfect environment for music overlays—he brings up a Steve Lawrence album, asking, "Any good?" The sheepishly executed ploy seems to work. Andie, almost immediately, raises the question of dating a "richie." To further emphasize the concern, she drives by the large estates peopled by the likes of the McDonoughs. The two-different-worlds scenario is established.

Blane arranges a meeting with Andie through the use of a computer—love notes 1986 style. The plot thickens as Duckie declares his everlasting love for Andie. Jake relates the lingering pain created by the desertion of his wife three years earlier. Blane enters the blue-collar section of the school-yard to make a date. At this point the Romeo-and-Juliet aspect of the story is front and center. The reason for the seemingly level-headed Andie's sailing into a sea of social neurosis is never totally explained. The class, peer-group pressure is about to be unleashed. But first, Duckie does his version of the Cruise/Bacon air-guitar lip-sync to Otis Redding's "Try A Little Tenderness." This sequence was more ill-timed than the library romp in *Breakfast Club*. Pauline Kael aptly described this interlude as Duckie's "given junior Pagliacci material—he lip-syncs Otis Redding's 'Try a Little Tenderness,' which doesn't do anything except make us uncomfortable."[60]

Blane arrives at TRAX for the date. The love-sick Duckie lays a guilt trip on Andie, saying, "You can't do this and respect yourself." The rejected suitor is proved partially corect as they go to a "socs" Emperor Party. "Pretty bad" is the mutual judgment. After a sojourn to The Gate, a nitery with rock bands, and a verbal altercation with Duckie, it's time for Andie to go home. Blane and the girl verbally spar until she confesses, "I don't want you to see where I live." No harm done; he invites her to the senior prom.

Jake is waiting up when she arrives. She describes her date, in perfect teen jargon, as "He drives a BMW."

"You like him. He likes you," Jake reassures her. "Take the heat." The world appears through rose-colored glasses to the tune of "Cherish" by The Association. The teens meet in a barn, away from peer pressure. The class distinctions remain the major source of their conversation. Blane provides a sociological insight—"Corporate families replaced royal families. I'm the crown prince . . . I'll just tell them to go to hell." Idealistic naivete. True class consciousness will rapidly enter the picture.

Ringwald's preparations for the prom and the circumstances ensuing from the invitation are remarkably similar to the dilemmas and teen anguish suffered by Tuesday Weld in *Rock, Rock, Rock* (1956). Anticipating the big dance, Andie visits an exclusive dress shop and is immediately humiliated by the snobbish salesperson. Her discomfort is increased upon recognizing Bunny trying on exhorbitantly priced gowns. Blane's absence heightens her anxieties about the dance. She confronts him in the school hallway. Blane insecurely mumbles that he asked somebody else to the prom and forgot about it. In tears, Andie flees the high school.

Apparently steeled by the rejection, she decides to attend the gala. Using a K-Martish dress, along with Iona's old prom gown, Andie designs a stunning outfit. Wearing the Cinderella creation, she tells the startled Jake, "I'm going alone. Walk in, walk out . . . I just want them to know they didn't break me."

Arriving at the posh hotel, as Orchestral Maneuvers in the Dark,'s "If You Leave" is introduced, she begins the long walk to the Grand Ballroom. Uncertainty mounts. Duckie appears appropriately, wearing an elegant tuxedo. He escorts her to the resolution.

In the closing sequence OMD's song replaces Randazzo's "Give Me A Chance." Blane approaches, telling Andie, "I believed in you. I didn't believe in me." The apology is not accepted until Duckie, uncharacteristically, opines, "You're right, he's not like the others." Their reconciliation is overtly predictable.

Fortunately for the movie, most theatergoers were too young to have remembered *Rock, Rock, Rock* during its initial run or on the late shows. Hughes, once again, ended his film on a euphoric note despite the obvious conclusion that the young lovers still had not found that classless "place for us."

Hughes's ability to capture the teen scene, at least to the satisfaction of critics, immunized the director from the usual rough treatment accorded to coming-of-age adventures. One reviewer labelled Hughes "the reigning king of high school reality pictures." The writer/director partially maintained his monarchial status by wisely having *The Breakfast Club* and *Pretty in Pink* released prior to the summer swarm of teen exploiters. "The prolific John Hughes clearly loves writing about teenagers," related Lally, "and it's nice to see that even in a market glutted with teen films, his work still stands apart as something fresh."[61] *Pretty in Pink* was seen by a majority as fitting the description.

The major reviewers warmed up to the movie. *Time's* Corliss was the most enthusiastic, saying, "Any attentive moviegoer can walk into *Pretty in Pink* feeling as old as failure, and—snap—yet younger." Hughes, wrote Stanton, "keeps us feeling we're seeing something real and provides some entertaining characters along the way." The *New Statesman* captured the ethos thus: "The message is that teenage—by a strange chance the age of the most dedicated film audience—is the only real time of life." Harwood added, "In the end, the wrong guy gets the girl, which is a lesson youngsters might as well learn early."[62]

Molly Ringwald won praise from reviewers regardless of their assessment of the movie. *People's* Scott Haller opened with, ''Shining brightly, she unwittingly shames a movie meant to showcase her.'' Ansen agreed, but found the movie ''a gentle and well meaning sketch of teen peer pressures, but its dopey, feel-good ending leaves you suspecting that what you've really been watching is much ado about nothing.''

''Good intentions and fine acting not withstanding, *Pretty in Pink* is all dressed up with nothing to say,'' wrote Ira Robbins.[63]

Howard Deutch, the overseer of the Hughes videoclips and musical trailers, had assumed the director's chair in *Pretty in Pink*. Reviewers portrayed him as an ''actors' director.'' He lets actors, wrote Denby, ''hold onto closeups when he hasn't given them anything to say.'' Corliss perceived him as ''sympathetic to the awkward pauses in teen talk, to the mopery of first love, to the suicidal bravado of words spoken in heat. Like Hughes, he is eager to let his fine young actors strut their stuff.''

''First-time director Howard Deutch gets assured performances from the entire cast,'' wrote Pauline Kael, who added, ''When in doubt, Deutch (whose background is in music videos) goes for close-ups.''[64]

Most critics made note of Deutch's music-trailer experience. The *Village Voice's* Barry Walters suggested that the soundtrack was more profound than the picture. He found the film was a ''smart way to sell albums,'' referring to New Order and The Smiths. Walters asserted, ''Their songs create a world for Andie so much more complex than what she's given on screen that one would be better off buying the album and imagining the film.''[65]

Rolling Stone, with its shrinking review pages, infrequently provides space to soundtrack albums. Its Mark Coleman led with, ''It may appear to be another glorified K-Tel collection, but *Pretty in Pink* sets a new standard for mega-buck pop soundtracks. The music selected actually has something to do with the movie.'' The album, he continued, ''delivers enough angst, fantasy, and heartbreak to keep an alienated teenager company in his or her bedroom for months.'' Psychedelic Furs, OMD, the Smiths, and New Order were applauded for their contributions. Echo and the Bunnymen's ''Bring On the Dancing Horses'' was singled out for ''the sort of quasi-cerebral fantasy troubled teens crave.''[66] Coleman did not object to the exclusion of Redding, the Association and John Lennon's ''Love is Real.''

Georgia Christgau labelled the collection a ''ten-track mixed blessing.''

''Twenty-two songs were used for the movie,'' she wrote, ''obviously stuff like Redding and the Lennon spoof were eliminated from the record to make room for new product, like A&M stablemates Vega and Jesse Jackson. Context is everything, I guess.''[67] Another interpretation might be that Hughes spent the track budget on the title song and turned to David Anderle for other acts.

OMD's scout upon charting, after the film's release, at number 81, peaked at number 4. It enjoyed a three-month stay on the Hot 100. The followup title song spent less time on the chart, falling off after eleven weeks. The A&M album spent a total of twenty-six weeks on the trades listings, eight of them in the Top 10. The package moved 900,000 copies, surpassing *The Breakfast Club*. (As a rule of thumb, any album breaking into the Top 5 with a duration of over three months should attain some RIAA certification.)

Competing with blockbusters like *Top Gun*, *Crocodile Dundee*, *Aliens*, and the fourth *Star Trek* sequel, *Pretty in Pink* finished twenty-second on *Variety's* "Big Rentals of '86" with a studio intake of $16 million. The overall gross was more than $40 million.

Examining release dates and chart action, the pattern is fairly clear. MTV exposure prompted an initial response to the film. A portion of that statistical 68 percent of the music channel's viewers did go and see the Hughes offering. The single did not enter until three weeks after the video's and the film's release. The vinyl product increased in popularity during the theater run. It is difficult to support a notion that a five-year-old album cut by a relatively obscure act as a title song brought much attention to the film. The album was a potpourri, despite Coleman, unless the listener was aware of Hughes's visual connections.

The adage "See the movie, buy the album" was certainly true in 1985 and even more so in 1986. Many issuances, labelled by a *Rolling Stone* writer "calculated snake-oil soundtracks," lacked substance. A successful carrier picture could provide this missing ingredient. The stampede of films, particularly during the summer months, would curtail the ability of any film, except for the few blockbusters, to generate adequate souvenir sales.

William Friedkin's 1973 smash *The Exorcist* showcased an attention-getting theme by Michael Oldfield titled "Tubular Bells." The techno-pop sound did surprisingly well. The single climbed to number 7 on the *Billboard* charts. The album did even better, reaching number 3. The sound was isomorphic to the demonic storyline, and Friedkin returned to syntho-pop in the *Sorcerer* (1977). Across the Atlantic, the chief proponents of this eerie sound were the German group Tangerine Dream. Descriptions of the group vary, but most seem to incorporate terms like "arhythmic, protoplasmic electronics" or "spacey." *Sorceror*, a remake of *Wages of Fear* (1952), bombed, but many remembered the "strange electronic score." The MCA soundtrack offering, never breaking number

150, remained on the trade listing for ten weeks. It enjoyed a longer run than the film.

Michael Mann used the German act for the psycho-drama the *Thief* (1981) starring James Caan. The album earned an eight-week stay on the sales roster. The consensus in the music press viewed the band as having a cult status, except in Hollywood.

Paul Brickman had employed the quartet for the interludes for *Risky Business*. The material was completed in two weeks. (*Risky Business* is easily the most accessible recorded soundtrack made available in the United States.) The group also had made a strong musical contribution to the otherwise disappointing *Vision Quest*. They were excluded, however, from the successful Geffen Records package, which, due to Madonna, exceeded sales of two million. The Brickman-Becker situations were somewhat atypical, but *Legend* would prove unique. Ridley Scott's experience with *Blade Runner* fueled the trade press. *Legend* ranked with *Apocolypse Now* as a $30-million-plus production misadventure. Two location sets had to be rebuilt from the ground up after a fire. The shooting schedule was extended to nearly a year. Tom Cruise remarked, "I'll never want to do another picture like that again." The ensuing cost overruns were monumental. The escalating costs put tremendous pressure on the American distributor, Universal Pictures, to market the project.

Legend opened across in Europe in fall 1985. The medieval fantasy had a running time of 140 minutes and a symphonic score by the multi-Oscar-winning composer Jerry Goldsmith. "It's the best score I've ever done, and people who had heard it felt it was an outstanding score," he said.[68] Universal's market tests suggested that the motion picture dragged. With $30 million at stake, drastic changes were in store for *Legend's* American appearance.

The glossy fairy tale had to be "tightened up," according to Scott, creating an action adventure vehicle. The length was cut to 94 minutes. The edited version found a good deal of the plot missing. "Terry Rawlings' editing," noted *Variety*, "has resulted in a very tight 94-minute running time, leaving audiences no time to ponder the script's inadequacies." Later notices echoed the theme of all style, no substance. Tom Matthews wrote, "A fantastic and other-worldly film like this can only work when all the elements are perfect, and 'Legend' simply has far too many seams showing."[69] The content dissected, executives turned their attention to the score.

Goldsmith, whose credits included *Chinatown*, *Omen*, *Patton* and a hundred others, had composed a "dreamy, bucolic" track celebrating "an enchanged forest with fairies and goblins and unicorns and a sort of Robin

Hood and the Beautiful Princess and good and bad." The scorer spent six months writing the music and constructing the dance sequences. Most of his contributions were to be cut from the movie, including the soundtrack. Goldsmith told the *Washington Post*, "The picture in the United States is coming out with a score by Tangerine Dream. The picture in Europe and the rest of the world is coming out with my score. It came as a total surprise and shock to me.

"Basically," he continued, "from what I've been told, to make it more accessible to teenagers . . . that old story." When asked about the switch, Tangerine Dream's Edgar Froese praised Goldsmith as a "fine composer," adding, "but we're composers ourselves, and don't forget we're also businessmen. So we took it [*Legend*]. Goldsmith definitely tried his best, but the people at Universal didn't like it. That's OK." Philosophically, the ejected composer indicated that the use of Tangerine Dream "seems sort of strange to me."[70]

There was little perplexity associated with the decision. Half of the nation's theatergoers are under twenty years old; a vast majority of them rock listeners. Tangerine Dream, given the texture of *Legend*, seemed ideal. Byran Ferry's "Is Your Love Strong Enough" was added as a title theme. Despite the addition of Ferry and Tangerine Dream and the presence of Tom Cruise in the lead, *Legend* missed its demographic target. *The Film Journal's* Mike McDonagh wrote that the film "falls between two audiences—a little too grotesque for younger children and too simplistic for older ones and adults. Look for a fast fade."[71]

The Ferry tune debuted on MTV a month prior to the movie's U.S. opening 18 April 1986. "Is Your Love Strong Enough?" remained on the music channel for seven weeks.

The album and film hit the streets the same week. *Billboard* greeted the offering with reserve, saying the "package from director Ridley (*Alien*) Scott's fantasy caps a moody Tangerine Dream score with two vocal tracks. Best is Byran Ferry's 'Is Your Love Strong Enough?' already pulled as a single."[72]

Economically, Tangerine Dream's two months of scoring their "best soundtrack" went unrewarded. Moreover, Froese's view of *Legend* as a "great film" was not shared by critics or the public. Its first weekend out the production grossed $4 million in 1,187 theaters, but "not much more was expected."

Legend is one of the films that studio music supervisors prefer to neglect. As soundtrack impressario Taylor Hackford said, "If the studio throws the score out because they want to make something that's a more commercial accommodation, it's probably not going to work."[73] In this instance it failed. Tangerine Dream's 17 May stay on the charts lasted seven weeks, with a high of number 96.

It is debatable if this tactic would have succeeded in previous years, but 1986 was definitely not the year for another "rock-will-carry-the-film" strategy. The market was overwhelmed with "accessing" packages.

In the first week of June, *Billboard* headlined the imminent issuance of seven soundtrack anthologies, with several film-related solo products. Madonna's *True Blue* would include "Live To Tell," a Number 1 single featured in *At Close Range*, a box-office flop starring Sean Penn. "Glory of Love" by Peter Cetera was part of his *Solitude/Solitaire*, a post-Chicago effort. The tune was also scheduled to be the centerpiece of United Artists Records' maiden effort, *Karate Kid Part II*.

The UA resurrection product would appear on the same date as MCA's *Running Scared* and the expected smash from the CBS Group, *Ruthless People*. Sylvester Stallone's *Cobra*, on the heels of *Rocky IV*, aroused high hopes, as did Jim Henson's *Labyrinth* (with David Bowie in the movie and accompanying album.) Of the seven contenders, only one managed to reach gold.

"What Are We Going To Do Now?" Karate Kid II

In 1976 John Avidsen had directed a modest picture, *Rocky*, starring the virtually unknown Sylvester Stallone. The million-dollar project grossed $88.5 million nationally. Eight years later, Avidsen applied the same simplistic formula to *The Karate Kid*. It became a surprise hit: domestic earnings for Columbia Pictures totalled an impressive $41.7 million, based on the portion returned from ticket sales. The *Rocky* formula had repeated its box-office magic. The film's Casablanca soundtrack package, however, scored a disappointing placement of number 114, with a twelve-week chart life.

As *Rocky IV* was igniting the box office, Avidsen reunited the *Karate Kid* ensemble for a sequel. Flashbacks and crosscuts to the original abounded, as in the Stallone effort. (*Part II's* beginning minutes rehashed the first film's first episode.) The locale was shifted from Southern California to the Far East. (The setting was Okinawa, but the movie was actually shot in Hawaii.) The project cost considerably more than the average network movie, $14 million, yet one critic, Richard Strelitz wrote, "it has more in common with the 'made for television' genre than it does with cinema."[74]

Gary LeMel, about to join Warner Brothers, committed the music package to the re-emergent United Artists Records. *Karate Kid Part II* would become UA's re-entry project. Jerry Greenberg, UA president, explained, "Soundtrack albums have become extremely significant and profitable ventures."[75] In post production, Southside Johnny, Carly Simon, The Moody Blues, Mancrab, and The New Edition were signed for the music-store trade.

Peter Cetera, following a bitter disassociation with Chicago, was approached by Greenberg. He was in the throes of completing the *Solitude/Solitaire* album.

"I had the basic concept and a few lines for 'Glory of Love,' " Cetera related. "Initially I played them a more up-tempo song I had, which they liked. But they told me they were looking for a ballad." Having "They Don't Make 'Em Like They Used To" rejected, Chicago's former lead singer sang a few bars from "Glory." "They flipped over it and took me to see the movie," he said. With the aid of his wife, Cetera finished the song.

Warner Brothers Records allowed the song's use in the film and soundtrack, but retained it for Cetera's album.

"When you're dealing with two record companies, usually no one wants to give," said Cetera, "but the Greenbergs were great—and I have to hand it to Warner Bros—they kind of gave in on that one point of it being on the soundtrack."[76] Warner's "largesse" was simply good business; the film provided exposure for a theme song issued by folks in Burbank. A hit single could, marginally, aid Cetera's solo album. There was also the goodwill aspect for LeMel's final Columbia Pictures project. (Subsequent events would prove Warner's tactic to be a wise one.)

The music release schedule was classic LeMel. He reminded *Billboard*, "There's only a short period of time to market between the time the first single comes out and when the movie opens. We always accompany our lead-off records with videos done by major video directors. It must be done right . . . Then it really works."[77]

"The Glory Of Love," the official theme, was a breakout on MTV 21 May and occupied a slot in the station's "active" rotation for nearly three months; the single charted at number 62 in early June. The United Artists soundtrack hit the streets 17 June. Three days prior to the film's debut, Cetera's song was at number 40 and climbing. On 28 June, *Karate Kid Part II* joined *Ruthless People* as a *Billboard* pop pick; "Stand-out contributions by Peter Cetera and Denis DeYoung are good bets for radio, especially adult contemporary format, and compilation offers added depth via covers of 'Rock Around the Clock' and 'Earth Angel' by Paul Rodgers and New Edition respectively."[78]

II starts with appropriate *koto* sounds. A flashback from the original

Karate Kid, a la Rocky IV or a television mini-series, immediately occurs. After nearly eight minutes, the film reintroduces Miyagi (Pat Morita), in tranquil Oriental surroundings, attempting to capture a buzzing insect with chopsticks. The precocious Daniel (Ralph Macchio) interrupts. The karate master proffers the first of myriad homilies dotting the plot: "Man who catch a fly with chopsticks accomplish anything." A few moments later, he says, "No breath, no life." (These little gems of wisdom make up at least half the dialogue in the movie.)

Finally, the story begins to develop as Miyagi is summoned to his native Okinawa, where his father is critically ill. During a protracted discussion, Miyagi explains the reason that he departed the island. It was due to a break with custom. The love of his life, Yukie (Nobu McCarthy), was betrothed to his best friend, Sato (Danny Kamekona). To avoid conflict with tradition and loyalty, he fled, after having made his feelings for Yukie public. Sato lost face. "Never put passion before principle," he explains, "even if you win, you lose." Sato, a successful entrepreneur, seeks vengeance as "in Okinawa honor has no time limit." Daniel volunteers to accompany his teacher to his native little fishing village, which is surrounded by a massive American military installation.

When they land in Japan, the pair's troubles (and the travelogue) begin. When Miyagi's father succumbs, glowing lanterns are floated on a glistening pond as Sato presents a three-day deadline for a fight to the death. Another homily is tossed out: "Never stop war by taking part in one." Another line could easily have been lifted from *Rocky*: "Doesn't matter who's stronger, what matters who's smarter."

Robert M. Kamen's screenplay moves swiftly from violent encounters between Toshio and Daniel to the teenager's awkward attempts at romance with Kumiko. Miyagi's overtures toward Yuki, always in idyllic settings, are equally fumbling. Looking over the moonlit bay, the karate master asks, "Why you never marry?" Answer, "You never come back." During these interludes, Bill Conti's (*Rocky*) score provides the background.

Finally, on a beach date, the younger couple's innocent—very innocent—companionship is underscored by a rock number, "This Is The Time," which is barely audible.

The local 1950s-style sock hop provides a musical opportunity for Paul Young's version of "Rock Around the Clock" and The New Edition's cover of "Earth Angel." Toshio and his gang finally provoke Miyagi into a fracas. They demolish his garden, but he still refuses to fight Sato. At this juncture, it is time for another clumsy romantic scene between the adolescents. Their first abortive attempt at kissing is cut short by the sound of bulldozers.

Sato arrives, leading a construction team to raze the rustic village. The homes, churches, "everything gone." Miyagi agrees to a midnight fight to the finish.

The hour of decision nears just as Daniel is about to be kissed. A storm hits, providing opportunities for individual acts of heroism, including Miyagi's rescue of Sato. All is forgiven between the men.

The presence of loose cannon, Toshio, allows for a *Rocky*esque climax. At a village festival, Sato's wayward nephew grabs Kumiko and challenges Daniel to a fight to the death. The struggle is pure "Italian Stallion," with the karate kid finally prevailing, as in the original movie. Peter Cetera's "Glory of Love" ushers in the credits with another majestic shot of the environment.

The 20 June "overnight" reviews were mixed. Michael Wilmington, in the *Los Angeles Times*, lauded the movie as deserving cheers "without feeling embarrassed." In the other major market, New York, Canby cautioned, "Even as sequels go in this era of movie mega-series, *The Karate Kid Part II* peters out faster than most." The major national news magazines chose to ignore the remake. *Variety* capsulized it as an "over-long, dumb sequel," but added, "Given the lack of terribly strong b.o. (box office) contenders at the moment, familiarity in this case should breed success."[79] That year, in fact, *most* hits fell short of attracting massive audiences. *Poltergeist II* and Stallone's *Cobra* failed to live up to expectations.

Denby, comparing the sequel to the original, noted, "The movie wanders from one soft nothing scene to the next." Addressing exhibitors, Tom Matthews disagreed, finding the film "far surpasses the original in style and genuine emotion."[80]

The film earned $12.7 million in its first week. "It feels great," said executive producer Jerry Weintraub. "I had a sense that it was going to be big, but I thought $9 or $10 million would be fantastic."[81] Weintraub felt even better by the year's end, as the box-office tally reached $113.5 million.

The film's success was not equalled by the album. The title peaked at number 30, staying on the charts seventeen weeks. Sales were less than golden. Cetera's tune outperformed the film anthology, and several observers indicated that the hit single did more for the artist's *Solitude/Solitaire* offering than the UA compilation.

"Glory of Love" reached number 1 status on the singles chart 2 August. The Warners release maintained the position for two weeks.

Jerry Greenberg waxed enthusiastic over *Karate Kid II*. "I think we're already proving ourselves in the business," he said. The reconstructed

United Artists Records chose its debut single from the album. The dance-oriented "Fish for Life" by Mancrab, a Tears For Fears spinoff, was scheduled for a late August release. "As soon as I heard it," noted Greenberg, "I felt it would be great for the movie and knew it would be something we'd want to go for as a single. And it's an excellent way to launch a new act." Gary LeMel had supplied the tune. Issued 23 August, it was described by *Billboard* as "high-stepping motion *a la* Tears For Fears." The record failed to chart, despite a five-week run on MTV's medium rotation.[82]

As "Fish For Life" was being shipped, MCA chose to try its fortunes, again, with New Edition's cover of "Earth Angel." The tune charted 23 August at number 70, surpassing the *Back To the Future* rendition. A third sequel appeared in the summer of 1989.

"And The Meek Shall Inherit . . ." Ruthless People

> *Compassion and Mercy, what the hell is going on over there? I thought you people were ruthless!*
> —Sam Stone, businessman

> *The downside is that you get involved with a really stiff movie and end up on some sort of bastardized compilation soundtrack that never becomes a cohesive piece of work—there's a lot of them around.*
> —Tommy Mottola, manager

Tried and true formulas become normative in the film community. Dale Launer, a novice screenwriter, had penned a Beverly Hills-situated adaption of O. Henry's famous short story "The Ransom of Red Chief." The storyline presented an unscrupulous clothing manufacturer plotting to murder his overindulged wife, an *enfante terrible* despite her age. Before the plan can be implemented, she is kidnapped by two bumbling revenge seekers.

The first draft was given to Jim Abrahams and Jerry and David Zucker, who had co-directed the successful, popular-culture spoof *Airplane* (1980). The trio liked the script, but "when we got the screenplay, Madonna was semi-attached to the script," related Abrahams.[83] The directorial team felt that Madonna was far too attractive to play the obnoxious kidnap victim and convinced her that the role was not in keeping with her image. Bette Midler, enjoying the success of *Down and Out*, was contracted to play yet another Rodeo Drive-Barbara, this time with the temperament of a precocious three-year-old. Danny DeVito, Judge Reinhold, and Helen Slater filled out the cast of principals.

The film began production in early January and wrapped in late March. Touchstone Pictures (*Down and Out*) distributed it.

Ruthless People enjoyed a distinct advantage in the soundtrack sweepstakes, as CBS Records president Walter Yetnikoff was one of the film's executive producers. He brought in Tommy Mottola, Hall and Oates's manager, to supervise the score. The operating budget for the soundtrack was reportedly $1.4 million. Mottola employed Daryl Hall to co-write the theme song with Mick Jagger and The Eurythmics' Dave Stewart. The film package would include a rarity: Bruce Springsteen's "Stand On It," the B-side from his "Glory Days" single, was incorporated into the vinyl. The Boss's biographer, David Marsh, found the tune a "decent cut," but not one of Springsteen's best.[84] Predictably, *Billboard* greeted the ultimate collection by recognizing Yetnikoff's role in the picture, resulting "in a soundtrack featuring the *creme de la creme* of the CBS roster: New tracks by Billy Joel ("Modern Woman") plus selections by Bruce Springsteen, Paul Young, Luther Vandross, Dan Hartman, and Kool & the Gang."[85] CBS's record in the promotion of soundtracks, since *Footloose*, was enviable. With faint praise, executives grudgingly acknowledged that Black Rock's batting average was more than 50 percent. Filmmakers were quick to counter that CBS, given the high rates, only allied itself with "big pictures" like *Rocky IV* and *Top Gun*. (The results on *Cobra* were not in at the time.) One Paramount person suggested that Simpson and Bruckheimer had enjoyed a better percentage than CBS on three different labels. Whatever, Yetnikoff's involvement almost guaranteed a high-power marketing campaign.

CBS commenced its shotgun marketing twenty days prior to the movie's street date. Billy Joel's "Modern Woman" charted at number 54 on 7 June; MTV received Dan Hartman's "Waiting to See You" clip a week later. The album was issued at the same time. AOR stations picked up the Jagger title song as the film debuted. This was a multimedia blitz of unprecedented proportions. Curiously, the Jagger and Joel cuts lacked a video. Hartman failed to chart on AOR and CHR. The Jagger song, of course, had nothing to do with the film. The strategy was an overt deviation from the *Footloose* or *Top Gun* formulas. The film appeared 28 June to generally complimentary reviews.

Once the animation and Mick Jagger's opening theme fade at the film's beginning, Sam Stone (Danny DeVito), a stereotypical garment industry manufacturer, is dining with his not-altogether-devoted mistress, Carol

(Anita Morris): The topic of conversation is a plot to chloroform his heiress spouse and throw her off the Santa Monica pier.

The strategy is disrupted when the Spandex king receives a phone call demanding half a million dollars in ransom for the return of the intended victim.

At this juncture, the O. Henry tale surfaces. Ken (Judge Reinhold) and Sandy Kessler (Helen Slater) transport a person struggling and screaming inside a burlap bag.

Inside the Kessler's modest, working-class bungalow emerges an overweight, foul-mouthed tyrant. Barbara Stone (Bette Midler) has been abducted because her husband is "the Spandex mini-skirt thief" who had defrauded Sandy of her fashion designs. The couple is seeking vengeance, as, "What's the sense of being a decent person when nobody else is?" Barbara's interaction with her captors out-Red Chiefs short story. She's hell on wheels.

The O. Henry theme recedes as Carol, unaware of a real kidnapping, plots with her inept lover Earl (Bill Pullman), to blackmail Sam by videotaping the homicide. Earl inadvertently films the local police chief in a compromising situation. A dizzy number of subthemes begin to unfold, with only occasional cuts to Barbara's basement captivity serving as an anchor.

Sam, delighted with the prospect of Barbara's demise, refuses to cooperate with the increasingly unlikely captors. Ken, working at Crazy Bob's stereo shop, proves to be a paragon of social decency. This portrayal creates the foundation for the conclusion. Mrs. Stone's fascination with workout programs, in keeping with *Vision Quest* and *Rocky IV*, provides abundant musical placement opportunities.

The Spandex king's indifference to the kidnappers' demands concerns the couple. "Let's face it, she's not Mother Teresa," says Ken. "Gandhi would have strangled her." He contacts Sam, offering to reduce the ransom to $50,000. Meanwhile, Barbara exercises to Billy Joel's "Modern Woman."

Believing that Earl has taped Barbara's murder, Carol sends the incriminating visual to the police chief, suggesting that Stone is the culprit.

As Barbara works out, shedding pounds, Ken lowers the return price to $10,000. Sam is furious "You lied to me," he shouts into the receiver, "I dare you to kill her." This attitude rapidly changes when the police accuse Stone of murder.

Attitude adjustment becomes contagious. Barbara struts her new image in the mirror admiring her twenty-pound weight loss, as Jimi Hendrix's "Foxy Lady" is heard. The phantom piece, unlisted, is recognizable, unlike several freeway- and stereo-shop placements. The plot thickens when Mrs. Stone discovers, from her newly adopted friends, "I'm being marked down. I've been kidnapped by K-Mart."

Events finally come to a head, as Sam needs to produce a breathing wife. Conspiring with the Kesslers, Barbara increases the demand to $2.2 million—Sam's total worth. The outcome, with a strained twist, is predictable. The decent people prevail to the accompaniment of Billy Joel's end theme. "The ending, especially, is a cheat," said Wilmington. "It may be the climax everyone expects, but that's exactly what's wrong with it. It's too automatic, and it seems madly illogical, depending on unlikely bursts of brilliance and prowess from people who have previously shown themselves to be absolute dunderheads."[86]

Variety minced few words in hailing the picture as a "hilariously venal comedy," promising to be the box office smash of the summer. *Box Office* and *The Film Journal* concurred. *Newsweek*, with an accompanying Midler profile, concluded, "This boisterous farce merits a case of bubbly." A "rare and old-fashioned pleasure," offered Corliss.[87]

Besides Pauline Kael, most major critics found *Ruthless People* to be essentially uneven. "It's the kind of movie that sounds a lot funnier than it sometimes plays," contended Canby. "*Ruthless People* is profane," added Denby, "but it's also essentially square." John Simon viewed Launer's work as containing "a few jokes amid much desperate huffing and puffing." The *Los Angeles Times* writer found the movie, at its best, "hilarious," and at worst "tasteless and overbroad."[88]

Despite the trades, *Ruthless People* ran into stiff competition. It was nonetheless a success. By 22 July, the film had grossed nearly $30 million. Its year-end totals came to a tidy $71.2 million. The studio return on a cost of $14 million came to $31 million. The box-office volume failed to translate into music sales, however.

The title song fared poorly on AOR and Top-40 charts. On the Album Tracks listing, "Ruthless People" climbed to a high of number 14; the Jagger rendition hit number 51 on the Hot 100. The Billy Joel tune performed better on the singles chart, placing at number 10 for a fifteen-week stay. It is possible to suggest that both offerings, given the artists, would have done as well without a movie.

The album package peaked at number 20, enjoying a four-month chart stay. It was certified gold, hardly an impressive feat. *Ruthless People*, as a microcosm, illustrated a general problem with soundtracks: Song placement, even with the CBS roster and a successful project, required careful crafting.

Ken's stereo-shop scenes were missed musical opportunities. The souvenir strategy, used affectively by Polygram, was sabotaged. *The Gradu-ate, Officer and a Gentleman, Risky Business*, and *The Big Chill* had integrated song selections with memorable segments of their motion pic-tures. In the race to success, studio and record people were now muddying the basic symbiotic interaction between the audio and visual media, however.

The fragmentation and disassociation was apparent on the heels of *Footloose*. By 1985, the decoupling was becoming normative. Steve Pond, reviewing seven track albums, emphasized, "Music should be chosen, not because it's a useful ticket-selling tool, but because it enhances the film. On many of these records, the songs don't belong in the same movie, much less on the same record."[89] By 1986, music integration and place-ment was becoming a lost art. Taylor Hackford's use of rock music in a ballet-oriented picture, deemed inappropriate by some critics, seemed a stroke of genius when compared *Ruthless People*.

As soundtracks proliferated, music placement inversely suffered. Scout products increasingly served as the end or closing themes of a film. The title cut frequently had little, if any, substantive association with the movie's mood or screenplay. Music supervisors were following the LeMel dictum of selecting high Q-Profiles. In *Ruthless People*, the Billy Joel selection fit into several scenes; it was briefly overlayed in one exercise segment.

The failure of placement mirrored the sheer number of artists and songs being diluted by the overuse of rock material.

Running Scared

Appearing in chronological lockstep with *Ruthless People* was the action-comic copshopper *Running Scared* from MGM. The Peter Hyams [*Outland* (1981) and *The Hunter* (1980)], $17-million project, starring Gregory Hines and Billy Crystal, debuted 27 June; MCA Records's release date, paralleling the CBS Group product, was 16 June. The scoring, however, was quite dissimilar. Hyams had commissioned the hottest songwriter in the business to score and arrange the soundtrack.

Rod Temperton was a founding member of and the songwriter for the multinational Heatwave. Three of his compositions had appeared on the GTO debut album, *Too Hot To Handle*. "Boogie Nights" brought him to the attention of Quincy Jones. The superproducer 'wangled" Temperton into contributing to a Michael Jackson album. Three of his songs, including the title cut, appeared on *Off The Wall*. Jackson's CBS package sold nine million copies. "Rock With You" was on the top of the singles chart for a month.

Temperton was invited to contribute to Jackson's next LP, and provided "The Lady In My Life," "Baby Be Mine," *and* "Thriller." This crossover giant would go on to become the best-selling LP in history, at thirty-seven million copies. Signing Temperton for a soundtrack appeared to be a near guarantee for a success. After five months, a film score took shape.

A majority of film and record material was written and arranged by the lyricist; studio musicians were used. Vocalists were recruited from MCA and several competing labels: Michael McDonald was on loan from Warner Brothers; Klymaxx came from Constellation Records. McDonald's "Sweet Freedom" was designated the scout, with a rapid follow-up by Klymaxx. "Man Sized Love" was described as a "good-natured, pop-oriented, Pointers-indebted" dance song,[90] a portrayal frequently applied to Temperton selections.

"Sweet Freedom" appeared on MTV the week of 18 June. At the same time it was found at number 76 on the Hot 100. Seven days later, the album was greeted by *Billboard*: The trade found three potential hit singles. Not on the list was "Man Sized Love" which charted 5 July, the same date as the album. The package would begin its climb to number 172.

The $17-milion, big-screen version of *Hill Street Blues* Hill and Renko with a touch of Alex Foley opens with Fee Waybill's title song and a tourist guide to the grime of Chicago in the throes of winter. Ray Hughes (Gregory Hines) and Danny Costanzo (Billy Crystal) are staking out a punk drug dealer named Snake (Joe Pantolianao). He is their key to nailing the flamboyant Julio Gonzales (Jimmy Smits), who aspires to be "the first Spanish godfather of Chicago." Getting the Colombian is the central thrust of a very traditional, as in *Miami Vice*, plot. The "plot is no more original or eventful than an average police TV show, so it must sink or swim on the moment-by-moment cleverness of the dialogue and behavioral talents of Hines and Crystal," observed McCarthy.[91] The wise-cracking under-cover police duo manage to liven up a number of stock sequences, ranging from Snake's arrest to a confrontation with two ill-prepared, zip-gun-carrying muggers. Hughes rhetorically asks, "Pointing a gun at a police officer. Can we waste them for that?" Having overcome the bad guys, the detectives are moved into the subplot of the death of Danny's Aunt Rose. She leaves him $40,000. He and Ray muse over the possibility of a good life.

Having intimidated Snake into setting up a meeting with Gonzales while wearing a "wire," the pair stumble into a well-set trap and must be rescued by two younger undercover cops, Frank (Steven Bauer) and Tony

(Jonathon Gries). They manage to arrest the Colombian, but six months of undercover work is "blown in two minutes." Captain Logan (Dan Hedaya) is furious and suspends the harried detectives. Dejected, they take a forced vacation in Key West, where life is a party as in *La Dolce Vita*. Going native provides the opportunity for the first of several well-staged music trailers. They bike, skateboard, and roller coast to the strains of "Sweet Freedom." Danny concludes that they "need a crack at the good life." Ray hesitantly concurs.

Returning to Chicago, they apply for short-timer status. Several action packed sequences occur as Ray and Danny unsuccessfully fight with Gonzales. The most striking scene, however cliched, is the frenzied cab-limousine chase over Chicago's 'El' railroad tracks. The duo's visions of a Florida retirement begin to slowly fade, especially when the drug kingpin attempts to have them and their cab crushed in a compactor. The vehicle demolished, they appropriate Gonzales's Mercedes. In a novel twist, this sets up another musical opportunity (for Kim Wilde's "Say You Really Want Me") with inner-cuts to the gritty inner city and breakdancing street corner crowds. The sequence, although obviously made for MTV, is subtly done. The climax, very predictably, occurs at the ultra-modern Illinois State Building. Using the structure's glossy, cavernous expanses, Hyams provides a dynamic setting for the shoot-out. At the close all is well as Hines and Crystal vow to remain in the Windy City to "serve the good people." "Never Too Late To Start" is the end theme.

An almost unanimous reaction to the motion picture was that the plot was thin, but the comedic and sardonic buddies made it worthwhile. "By the movie's close," wrote Benson, "when things have gotten played out and dumb, there is still so much pure, generous joy radiating from this nifty pair that it's impossible to feel shortchanged."

"It is the way Crystal and Hines interact, react, and overact that gives *Running Scared* its special charm," said Granger. Ansen, however, said the two actors "deserve a director more attuned to their charms." In *Boxoffice*, Matthews wrote, "A fine comic pairing highlights this cop movie that may stint on plot, but never on laughs."[92] Three weeks of screenings grossed the adventure film some $23.7 million. Metro Goldwyn Mayer's year-end earnings on it amounted to $16.4 million.

Temperton's dance/urban-contemporary flavoring failed to produce a gold record. The music was well integrated to the film, in sharp contrast to *Ruthless People*, in which most of the music, according to Stephen Holden, "can only be discerned far in the background."[93] "Sweet Free-dom" and "Say You Really Want Me" were strategically situated and fit the flow of the film, although Sheila Benson felt that the entire Key West sequence was "wholly expendable."[94] "Sweet Freedom" peaked in the Top 10, at number 7, enjoying a four-month tenure on the trade list. "Man Sized Love" stalled at number 15 with nearly a three-month chart duration. The album died at number 43, but remained for fifteen weeks, one week less than its CBS counterpart. As a package, *Running Scared* was truer to the movie than most of the summer soundtracks.

Saturday Night Fever, prior to *Thriller*, had been the top-selling album in history. Worldwide, the two-record set had sold twenty-five million copies. In a reactive industry, imitation and cloning are standard practices, and so a son of *Fever* was not far behind. An overabundance of soundtrack products appeared. Paramount's Steve Bedell remarked, "During the days after *Saturday Night Fever* and *Grease*, there were a whole slew of movies out with soundtracks, not all of which were selling. The recording companies were badly hurt. When you end up shipping a million copies but only sell 200,000, that has a tremendously negative effect on record companies. The recording industry had to regroup. They began to realize that not every movie will have a successful soundtrack."[95] The decline in soundtracks was directly attributable to the "Disco Disaster." Merchandisers loudly complained that dance/disco film scores were monopolizing shelf space, with little mainstream rock material being released. Even with more advantageous return policies, the labels were equally unhappy. The top album soundtrack of 1981 was Neil Diamond's *The Jazz Singer*. The remake of the Jolson film had hardly been aimed at the twelve-to-twenty-four audience. *Flashdance* and MTV had somewhat rehabilitated the status of the soundtrack, but memories of Stigwood's *Sergeant Pepper* lingered.

In the spring of 1984, music supervisors and label executives were cautioning against the dangers of market oversaturation, but to no avail. The banner performance in music and movies of 1984, with ten platinum film scores, revived the *Fever* mania. Polygram's Russ Regan, at the time, was a voice crying in the soundtrack wilderness.

Two years later the trade papers abounded with articles concerning imminent soundtrack releases. It was a rare week that *Billboard's* album previews, or "picks," did not contain a movie title. There was an inverse relationship between quantity and sales. By mid-June only two releases showed momentum. *Billboard*, in a special section devoted to the idiom, ran an article by Chris McGowan leading with "Soundtrack Fastlane Already Facing Congestion . . ." The executives interviewed waxed enthusiastic about the prospects for their products. In the section, Regan restated his thesis that albums "are selling very well these days, but right now there's an overabundance of them. It's overkill and I think a lot will fall through the cracks.'' Savoring the success of *Top Gun*, Al Teller agreed, saying ''Since a majority of Hollywood movies these days have soundtrack spinoffs, the competition is tougher than it was three years ago (1983).''[96]

The oversupply position is axiomatic in the record business. As volume increases, many deserving releases do not receive a shot. Lacking a monster marketing campaign, new artists are very likely to fall through the gatekeeping cracks. LeMel's point of having a title song by an immediately recognizable performer partially mitigates against the offering being totally ignored.

''Every picutre is 'unique' is an adage in the film industry. Likewise a soundtrack album. *Auteur* is absent from film anthologies, and only a handful of soundtrack aficionados could look to directorial credits for guidance. The imprimateur of a Hughes, Hackford, or Demme affects a very small group of consumers. Marketing, therefore, is essential, and box office success remains the ideal form of advertising.

Reliance on ticket sales, as the *Big Chill* indicated, was valid. In 1986 the large number of films released diminished the souvenir and word-of-mouth value of motion pictures. Time and the discretionary leisure dollars of the twelve-to-twenty-four-year-olds are finite.

Only three titles topped the singles list in the first half of the year. ''Say You, Say Me'' was a carryover from the preceding year. Prince's ''Kiss'', from the unofficial soundtrack album *Parade* (*ne Under the Cherry Moon*), achieved chart superiority in mid-April for two weeks. Madonna repeated the *Vision Quest* experience with ''Live To Tell,'' written for the Sean Penn showcase *At Close Range*. By the close of July, two singles were moving toward the peak of the Hot 100: Peter Cetera's ''Glory of Love,'' from *Karate Kid Part II*, and Berlin's ''Take My Breath Away,'' a *Top Gun* repeat, reached number 1.

On 13 August an overflow crowd turned out for a National Academy of Recording Arts and Sciences luncheon staged at the Los Angeles Press Club. The widely covered conclave featured Paramount's Steve Bedell and Gary LeMel, now heading Warner Brothers Pictures' music division. The executives were present to quell anxiety about the quantity issue. ''The burning questions I've been asked by reporters in the last three weeks,'' said LeMel, ''are 'Are you experiencing a soundtrack burnout? Are there too many?' '' Bedell answered, ''I have a feeling the backlash is more of a media creation. Obviously, the public has not reacted to it, because they're buying the stuff.'' They *were* purchasing *Top Gun* and *Pretty in Pink*, both Paramount productions. The executive did add, ''It's very important that film companies walk that delicate line of not oversaturating the market-

place.'' The oft-stated criterion should be whether the music ''comple-
ments a scene or advances the story,'' he continued.

LeMel, predictably repeating his favorite thesis, argued that studios
should strive for established, ''automatic at radio and video,'' artists to
record a title song. Not just any name, however, fit the demographic target.
''Is it worthwhile spending the money, which goes into the music budget
and ultimately into the budget of a film, to have a title song to a picture,
which is an adult film for people who are twenty-five and up?'' Answering
the rhetorical question, LeMel said, ''Those people are going to see the
picture anyway. And maybe it could turn those people off by making it
look like a teenage picture, when it's really an adult picture.'' For example,
Rod Stewart's hit from *Legal Eagles*, he claimed, had done little for the
Redford-Winger vehicle.

The pair continued to make the studios' case. ''The film comes first,''
said Bedell, even if the labels believe ''the record is the top priority.''
LeMel was more direct, if possible, saying ''The ultimate goal (for labels)
is to get theater-goers to ''walk right out of the movie theater into the
record store to buy the soundtrack.'' Filmmakers wish to get people into
the theaters. The Warners executives did concede that there were some
'overzealous studio heads, producers, and directors.''[97]

On another occasion, Danny Elfman of Oingo Boingo (*Weird Science*),
was more specific, saying, ''Film people want rock songs, they want pop
songs, they want hits. They know nothing about music, and their tastes
are generally three or four years behind wherever the music scene is.''[98]
That's what music supervisors are for, one could reply.

The musician's argument did have merit. As a totality, many successful
packages, regardless of their title songs, were generically in the dance/
disco motif. ''The Heat Is On'' was as close to rock 'n' roll as the *Beverly
Hills Cop* album would come. Syntho and New Music laced most soundtracks, despite their fade from the charts. Even John Hughes, considered
by many to be one of the three directors with ''ears,'' succumbed to
deadline and cost pressures. Aesthetically, *Risky Business* was one of the
best soundtrack collections of the period, as director Paul Brickman had
chosen the score prior to post-production pressures. The resultant legal
difficulties precluded a deserved platinum record. The movie, of course,
was a money maker.

Danny Goldberg, whose loyalties leaned toward the labels, countered,
''The novelty of a soundtrack has clearly worn off. In the long term, I'm
concerned about a burnout on the part of the consumer. The public tends
to get sick of repetition, and you have to be increasingly discriminating.''

He felt that studios were coming to realize that "when it works big it's great, but when it doesn't it's not worth the money."[99]

Managing Andy Taylor ("Take It Easy" from *American Anthem*), Goldberg repeated a concern for artist placement. "In the wrong situation (film) you can squander a good song, a radio opportunity, and some of the energy and excitement of your artist," he said. John Waite's manager, Steven Machat, echoed this sentiment. "I would never want to get involved in soundtracks unless they buy time (between albums)," he explained. Peter Cetera described the chartbustering "Glory of Love," from *Karate Kid II*, as an interlude between albums. Performers, even those with chart toppers, were unhappy with the constraints of film scores.

Recording artists since The Beatles have grown comfortable with "artistic control." The phrase refers to the performers' ability to dictate everything from album covers to Sunset Strip billboards. Privately, veteran music-industry people are happy to present a dissertation condemning the practice. Still, films have boundaries absent at the labels. Jack-of-all-trades Goldberg aptly outlined the forces at work: "The problem with Hollywood was that people kept talking about films as 'collaborative.' But when it came to music the collaboration was usually already over. Rock stars who lorded over their own turf with absolute power were, in the land of films, treated like high-priced novelty acts, bought for their transient name value alone."[100] Rocker artists were, in fact, frequently recruited for their name recognition at MTV and CHR stations. The result was predictable.

Simple Minds' Jim Kerr was one of the first rockers to go public. He told one writer that "Don't You (Forget About Me)," the theme to *The Breakfast Club*, contained "inane" lyrics. On other occasions he accused Keith Forsey of adding instrumentation. "If we started doing songs like that," he said, "it would be the death of us in the long run. We don't deal in formula music. We're into improvising and doing the unexpected."

Marilyn Martin expressed a very similar view of "Separate Lives." "I have nothing against the song," she told Dennis Hunt. "The only problem is that it's a ballad. I don't want to be classified as a singer who sings these quiet ballads."

Berlin's manager and spokesperson, Watts-Russel, objected, "We don't have anything against ("Take My Breath Away"). It's just that the nature of the song was not representative of the identity of the band."[101]

Simple Minds, Martin, and Berlin's manager all had entered into a Faustian bond. Name recognition and royalties ensued. The price exacted was that AOR broadcasters were not overly impressed with a CHR or, worse yet, an adult contemporary hit.

A cynic may well have retorted, "They cried all the way to the bank."

John Cafferty's reaction, in discussing *Eddie and The Cruisers*, appeared more realistic. He viewed the picture as his group's big break, despite some of the critics. MCA, the most successful of the soundtrack manufacturers, sided with Cafferty. "It gives you a tremendous opportunity to develop careers. We've found it a good way to develop artists," said Larry Solters. Oingo Boingo, according to the executive, was a case in point. "Even though their theme song for *Weird Science* only midcharted, it helped us in exposing them to a national audience,"[102] he said.

Ian Stanley, the Tears for Fears keyboardist and a founder of Mancrab, praised the latter group's participation in *Karate Kid Part II*. "This was a nice break because it is the only medium where you can release a single in America without doing a whole album,"[103] he said. New artists can benefit from a soundtrack date. Mancrab, however, failed to reach the pop/dance charts.

Superstars like Rod Stewart, meanwhile, were averaging about $25,000 for recording a title or scout song for a film. This figure is only seed money. Universal arranged for Stewart to contribute "Love Touch" to *Legal Eagles*. The singer retained single and album rights for Warner Brothers. The advertising campaign extensively utilized the title, including a music video; Universal subsidized the exposure of "Love Touch." Mike Jacobs later observed that the marketing of the movie "helped Stewart more than *Legal Eagles*."[104]

Music publishers, according to most observers, were the major beneficiaries of the sound mania. An ASCAP executive estimated that 20 percent of the agency's most performed titles were in soundtracks. An impressive 62 percent of the licensing firm's standards—golden oldies—were film placements.

By 1986, writers and publishers were lukewarm to mere domestic, first-run box office, as foreign markets, cable pay channels, and syndication all added up to a potential ten-year royalty life. A highly successful song tied to a box office smash could earn an estimated $350,000 its first year, with a potential for an additional $100,000 in future years. (Songs such as "Say You, Say Me" and "Purple Rain" are frequently cited examples.) The key to these numbers resides with the studio and the label. The overabundance of product hampered the achievement of high economic success.

Stand By Me

> *It just shows a good song can last forever.*
> —Ben E. King, artist

Rob Reiner, with *This Is Spinal Tap*, had demonstrated a deft directorial touch. He was no longer just "the meathead." (*The Sure Thing* (1985), hardly a smash, only slightly marred his image.) His follow-up project was a screen adaptation Stephen King's quasi-autobiographical 1982 novella, "The Body." Reiner's expectations for the project were modest. Predicting a small audience, he told screenwriters Ray Gideon and Bruce Evans, "There's no way the picture is going to do business, because no one who went to see *Rambo* will go to see our film."

Reiner auditioned some 300 candidates for the leading roles prior to settling on four relative unknowns—Jerry O'Connell, Corey Feldman, River Phoenix, and Wil Wheaton. Oregon location work commenced in June 1985.

Norman Lear, as he had for *Spinal Tap*, signed the production for Embassy. In the interim, as Reiner was rehearsing the youthful cast, Embassy Communications was corporately absorbed. Columbia Pictures refused to finance *Stand By Me*. Lear intervened with "$8 million and change," and studio agreed to distribute.

The studio, free of expenses, mounted a significant print campaign. "It was a very tough marketing job, a film about four 12-year-old boys with an R rating," recalled marketing president Peter Sealey. The drive relied on "flyers, word-of-mouth and special handling" to reach the potential audience."[105] Rob Reiner, cleverly, captured pre-adolescents in a time frame aimed at the post college-age market.

To recreate the atmosphere of 1959, Reiner incorporated a plethora of music artifacts of the period. The film was set for an early August 1986 screen debut.

The picture begins on a lonely country road, Richard Dreyfuss pondering a newspaper article recounting the violent death of an attorney. A flashback to his childhood begins the action.

Teddy urges "Let's find him, we'll be heroes . . . our picture in the paper." A two-day odyssey is planned to find the remains. Vern, expectedly, forgot the food.

In the process of preparing for a Mark Twainish hike, Gordie Lachance is revealed to be haunted by parental rejection and guilt over his older brother's (Denny) fatal jeep accident. This unresolved inner struggle provides a coordinating theme throughout the journey. In a nightmare, the senior Lachance, at Denny's funeral, says, "It should have been you, Gordon."

Setting out on the quest, the boys accosted by the local ruffians, led by Ace Merrill (Kieffer Sutherland). The town bullies amuse themselves by cruising, blasting rock music, drinking beer, and playing "mailbox baseball."

The narration, a la *Spinal Tap*, interrupts, "The time I was twelve going on thirteen was the first time I saw a dead human being." The scene dissolves into an extended flashback centered in the fictional hamlet of Castle Rock, Oregon, population 1,281—"It was the whole world." As the camera pans Main Street, KLAM-Portland disc jockey Bob Cromier machine guns an intro to Bobby Day's "Rockin Robin." Nestled in a rolling green incline is a tree house containing three preteens playing poker, smoking cigarettes, and exchanging gross-out remarks.

The focus of the trio is Chris Chambers (River Phoenix), the paradoxical "bad kid" with a remarkably keen insight into human foibles. "Does any twelve-year-old talk with such analysis and self-awareness?" asked several reviewers.

Gordie Lachance (Wil Wheaton) is a sensitive introvert, battling internal demons, with hopes of becoming a writer. Teddy DeChamp (Corey Feldman) is a battered child who compensates with bravado and recklessness. Joining them, after characteristically forgetting the club entry signal, is Vern Tessio (Jerry O'Connell) the chubby, overly clumsy, and somewhat dim-witted foil of the others' verbal barbs.

Vern proudly proclaims the whereabouts of Ray Brower. The small town has mounted a highly publicized search for the twelve-year-old. Vern's older brother stumbled across the youngster's body, but can't tell the authorities. He was joyriding in a "borrowed" car.

Escaping their antagonists, the boys begin a thirty-mile march down the railroad tracks, cutting through Oregon's breathtaking forests, singing Johnny Western's "Paladin" theme. Straddling the rail ties, the patter continues. "Finding new and disgusting ways to degrade a friend's mother," the voiceover indicates, "was always held in high regard." Popular culture is intertwined as the foursome address Annette Funicello's developing breasts to "The Book of Love." Moments of insight occur as Gordie describes himself as weird and unworthy. "Yeah," answers the always insightful Chris, "but everybody's weird." During the hike, the "bad kid" continually attempts to bolster Gordie's low self-esteem.

Tiring, they begin to traverse a slim railroad bridge, to make up for lost time, only to be menaced by an oncoming locomotive. Gordie and Vern, naturally, barely reach safety. Teddy concludes it's the "all-time train dodge." The "harrowing" scene is somewhat nonsensical as the engineer had plenty of track in which to slow, or stop, the train.

Settling down for the night, circling a blazing fire, Cokes—product placement—and hamburger meat are consumed topped off by the most satisfying cigarette of the day. The adult ritual is interrupted by coyote howls, interpreted by the easily frightened Vern to be Brower's ghost, a feeling shared by the others.

To calm the situation, Chris prevails upon Gordie for one of his tall tales. "Not one of your horror stories," chides Teddy. Gordie begins the account of "Lardass Hogan," described by the boy as "the greatest vengeance story" or "barf-a-rama." Michael Buckley wrote that "the scene of mass-regurgitation—which might please twelve-year-olds—will probably displease older viewers."

The group evolves into a "pastoral support group, quick to perceive signs of trouble and to lay gentle firm hands on needy shoulders."[106]

The older crowd finally become aware of the Brower corpse. "We're gonna be famous on radio and television shows," says Ace. They obviously have not matured past the pre-junior high schoolers. Driving to the location, they manage to run a logging truck off the road to The Coasters' "Yakety Yak."

Chris's bunch locates the surprisingly well preserved body. For Gordie, the find is cathartic. "When Gordie sees the pale, bloodied corpse of the boy he's never met," writes Denby, "he knows his brother is really dead. And by implication, having confronted this fact, he's free to become a writer, a storyteller."[107] Gordie's denouncement is cut short by Ace and friends. They demand the body. Chris refuses. A knife flashes. Gordie, having quelled the demons, appears with a .45 automatic. "Don't move or I'll kill you!" The younger boys prevail. Satisfied, they leave the remains and anonymously call the authorities.

There is a bittersweet mood to the journey's end. "The boys know that this is their last summer together—that in the fall when they go to junior high (Gordie for college preparatory classes, the others for manual training) they will go separate ways. Their tree house days will be over," wrote Kael. This conclusion, unfortunately, is beclouded by the finale. The film reveals that Chris went on to college and passed the Bar. Mark Fleischman was correct in his contention that the film "blows it only in the denouement, when a grown-up Gordie (Richard Dreyfuss) sentimentalizes about boyhood friendships." At his word processor, the adult Gordie spells out, "I never had any friends later on like the ones I had when I was twelve."

"Jesus, does anyone?" Kael retorted. "Are we supposed to believe that this was the last moment for true friendship? This is like some crazy pedophilic idealization of life before puberty, or perhaps it's just male narcissism about what sensitive boys they were."[108] The credits roll as Ben E. King's title song echoes. The film's finale confuses, but does not remove, the paramount thrust found in *Heaven Help Us* or the prototypical *American Graffiti*.

The comparison to *American Graffiti* only begins with the soundtrack. Richard Dreyfuss's presence aside, the storyline, down to the final coda, deals with a short period of self-revelation and the future dissolution of the peer group. The Lucas film addressed a future of college versus conscription or enlistment. Reiner's treatment centered upon "the class division that asserts itself around puberty—when decisions are made on who prepares for college and who goes to vocational school, who will leave and 'make it' in the world outside the town, and who will remain behind."[109]

Film critics provided a flood of money reviews. Peter Sealey noted, "We knew we had an important film all along [sic]. The number of reviews we got definitely led to two full pages of reviews demanding more space."[110]

The most cited review was Sheila Benson's *Los Angeles Times* piece. Headlined " 'Stand By Me' A Summer Standout," it said, "It's one of those treasures absolutely not to be missed." Columbia's publicity department was ecstatic. National media followed. Many television reviewers raved about the movie.[111]

Television critics, given time constraints, provide a multitude of quotable quotes. *At The Movies* and *Sneak Previews*, with their large audience share, are considered significant exposure vehicles, transcending the print medium. The Corliss, Denby, Ansen, Kael and Knoll analyses, however, are far more enlightening than thirty-second condemnations or recommendations.

The two national newsmagazines produced mixed verdicts. Ansen concluded, "There is more here as well: sweetness of spirit, and comedy that comes from a well remembered vision of the way we were."

"It is," offered Corliss, "a self-conscious elegy to the reckless dreams of youth . . . but *Stand By Me* is a shock. It trumpets its sensitivity while reveling in coarseness." New York critics added more ammunition for the ad drive. Denby, in *New York*, found the movie exhibited "an enchantment almost worthy of Mark Twain. The little pastoral escapade goes further than any of the four expected, but when Reiner works for thrills, he never hypes the action." *National Review's* John Simon, predictably, found the motion picture "pretty nauseating."[112]

The trades, the medium of exposure for theater owners, mostly praised the film. *Variety* said the picture was "sure to generate strong word-of-mouth, but Columbia has a formidable job attracting business considering current b.o. (box office) competition and the film's underserved R-rating, that effectively locks out a sizable chunk of its target audience (sic)." *Stand By Me* was a Yuppie picture, as the statistics would shortly indicate.

Boxoffice, the exhibitors' Bible, proclaimed, "A wonderful little movie about four boys on an unusual quest." *The Film Journal* stated, "This is a film parents and children can truly enjoy together."[113] Reviews do not make a hit movie or musical package, but *Stand By Me* was a success translatable to music sales.

Stand By Me, the soundtrack, surfaced at a very appropriate time, 1986, the year of the recycled artist and sound. The Yuppies had reentered the music milieu through the medium of compact discs (CDs). In 1984, 5.8 million CDs had been sold. In 1986 the figure soared to fifty-three million. In dollars, the leap was from $103.3 million to $930.1 in 1986. The principal demographic players were upscale males in the twenty-five-to-thirty-five-year-old category. As David Wild noted, "Why is it that rock 'n' roll seems to be looking back for its future? One reason, naturally enough is that this sort of nostalgia is good business. In an attempt to target its own Brat Pack demographic—the twenty-five-and-older set with those fresh, young, disposable incomes." The industry was reissuing "replacement CDs" and highlighting artists from previous decades.

The revival year was fueled by CD buyers, but teenagers were willing participants. With the exception of Springsteen, Jackson, Van Halen, and a few others, the megahitters of 1984 were striking out. "Why shouldn't it still be appealing today?" asked RCA's Gregg Geller. "It's not as if pop music has evolved that much in the last twenty years." WMMS-Cleveland's Kid Leo said, "Kids today are more taken with the rock stars of the past than the people who were actually around at that time. They feel as though they missed out on the glory years of rock 'n' roll." Some record company executives lamented the trend. One, Geffen's John Kalodne, said, "I'm in a Catch-22 now. Radio's busy playing all these bands I signed back then, and now I wonder what's going to happen to the next generation of bands."

"Given what's out there," said a Sixties veteran, "The Monkees sound much better today than they did on NBC."[114] Revitalized upscalers and neophyte youngsters fueled the record market of 1986 and created the ideal environment for a golden-oldies soundtrack. The Reiner film, successful despite a generally unenforceable R-rating, showcased ten strong selections from the late 1950s. In the context of 1986, the more theater tickets sold, the greater the number of potential of soundtrack consumers.

Atlantic's reactive campaign produced a gold—502,000 copies—certification. The marketing was hardly synergized. The album appeared prior to the single reissue on 20 September, six weeks after the film's release. MTV added the video, four days later, in the breakout category. The single, "Stand By Me," was reissued in the first week of October. It would remain on the *Billboard* chart for twenty-one weeks, peaking at number 9.

The album/cassette surpassed most soundtracks, climbing to number 31. The "oldies but-goodies" strategy worked. The studio and Lear divided, after exhibitors, an earned $21 million.

A Hard Day's Night In Hell: Sid and Nancy

> *It's true that there's nothing more boring than two junkies in a room watching the telly, and yet . . .*
> —Alex Cox, writer-director

Alex Cox, the Liverpool-born, Oxford-educated director and writer, in the 1950s would have been dubbed an "angry young man." A law school drop-out, he received a Fulbright to study at the UCLA Film School in 1977, the alma mater of Coppola and other recognizable filmmakers. There Cox created a forty-five-minute piece, *Edge City*. The film, described as "politically paranoid" and "thoroughly muddled," suggested Cox's future directions. The resolution of the project was overlayed by Sid Vicious's iconoclastic version of "My Way." (*Edge City* was the progenitor of Cox's "instantaneous cult classic" *Repo Man* (1984).)

Repo Man, Cox's nihilistic commentary on Southern California culture involved troubled teenager Otto Maddox (Emilio Estevez) "fallin' " in with a group of dreaded automobile repossession artists (Cars, as any resident will quickly attest, are the lifeblood of the freeway culture) The "repo men," all named after a brewery, are lead by the bigoted Bud (Harry Dean Stanton). The interaction between Otto and Bud allows for a flood of comments and satires on the foibles of human existence. Bud, accustomed to his unending campaign for Helping Hands Acceptance Co., offers, "An ordinary person spends his life avoiding tense situations. A repo man spends his life getting into them." The sleezy repossessors view ordinary people as loathsome deadbeats especially "Commies and Christians." Injected into the scenario are attractive throwaway lines like "The more you drive, the less intellligent you are," a reference to the populace of Los Angeles.

The thematic undercurrent of the film is bizarre. A lobotomized nuclear scientist (Fox Harris) has driven a copper-colored 1964 Chevy Malibu from a Los Alamos test site to Southern California. Lead by the steel-gloved agent Rogers (Susan Barnes), a crew in Ghostbuster-style outfits is in pursuit of him. A $20,000 reclamation fee is broadcast over the "repo wire"—a Cox version of the Batphone. Otto's punk friends, the repossessors, the "Company" people, and assorted oddballs attempt to corral the auto. Those who have not killed off their competitors assemble at the car lot hoping to take custody of the vehicle and its mysterious contents. A strange glow emanates from the Malibu. Miller (Tracey Walter), an acid burnout with a UFO obsession, is able to get into the car, where Otto joins him. The cargo aboard the Chevy is discovered to be the decomposing remains of radioactive aliens. Appropriately, in a comic twist on *Close Encounters of the Third Kind*, the prized car ascends into the stratosphere as Iggy Pop's theme serenades the credits. Sheila Benson was quite correct in suggesting that the plot was secondary—"style and attitude are all, and *Repo Man* has these in glorious quantity."[115]

Universal City denizens were surprised by the critics' initial reaction to the project. The *Los Angeles Times* characterized the film as "fresh, vinulently funny, with an eye on life that's as offbeat as the early Beatles movies." Comparisons to Beatles flicks and access to teen consciousness did not escape the attention of studio marketing executives. Rex Reed was on the mark, insisting, "Somebody at Universal Pictures has been mesmerized." In July 1984, Cox's debut film opened in selected art houses in "sophisticated cities." The Nickelodeon in Boston drew $270,000 in patrons' funds and $260,000 was spent on the picture at one New York Theater. By November the gross totaled more than $2 million.[116]

Repo Man earned Cox the designation of being a "wry, idiosyncratic filmmaker who could treat even the oddest outcasts of society in universal, human terms." The practitioner of the "humor of alienation," he took dead aim at the obscurantist fare manufactured in Hollywood. "People want to be stroked most of the time," he told Ed Kelleher. "They want to go and see *Flashdance* and feel that life can be perfect. But sometimes, as an alternative to the pablum that television and most films are, people are going to want to see something that says: 'God, you know, life's a really painful thing and it's full of cruelty and things look very bleak, and yet at the same time there is some transcendent thing in there that makes it worth going on living.' "[117]

An important ingredient of the subculture of urban punkdom was music. Cox captured the ambience of the sound. "*Repo Man's* punk quality came from its combination of dreary landscapes and hopped-up characters, its jagged, unpredictable editing rhythms," writes Rafferty, "and its distinctive mood of off-hand nihilism."[118] The sounds of punk were ideal for Cox interface of cinema and music.

Cox's $1.5 million budget did not allow for the use of "name" punkers, assuming any had been available. Legal complications precluded the employment of Sex Pistols' material. Therefore, the director tapped into the esoteric Los Angeles scene to find artists, who were delighted with the attention and exposure.

Repo Man's roster of L.A. punk rockers included The Circle Jerks and The Untouchables. Both appeared briefly in the film. Also on the album tracks were The Plugz, Juicy Bananas, Burning Sensations, Black Flag, and Iggy Pop, the best known of the lineup, doing the title song. (Ex-Pistols guitarist Steve Jones contributed to the song.) Critics did make note of this score, unlike many others.

Rex Reed, in a back-handed compliment, noted the characters were "all so stoned and coked up and trashed out by their punk-rock music and junk food and TV commercials that sometimes they are actually funny in spite of themselves." One writer that felt the soundtrack should do "a lot to convert those unfamiliar with the (musical) delights of American hardcore." Julian Petley went on to single out "the excellent Iggy title track, a new version of Black Flag's 'TV Party,' a great rendering of Jonathon Richman's " 'Pablo Picasso' by the Burning Sensations, and a hilarious acoustic send-up by The Circle Jerks, 'When the Shit Hits the Fan'."[119] Cox's little film, opening originally at eight Los Angeles area theaters, with a three-week gross of $191,733, preached to the converted. It lacked the exposure to legitimate the punk sound.

Repo Man did establish Cox as a minor celebrity in the art-film milieu. Good reviews, however, do not necessarily translate into acceptance in the Hollywood film community. The epithet "*avante garde*" was profanity in some studio boardrooms.

In the glow of the instantaneous cult fame, Cox stayed on in Los Angeles in hopes of landing another film project, but "nothing happened." Migrating to New York City, he collaborated on a screen play with author Abbe Wool. The site of *Love Kills's* germination, literally, was the landmark Chelsea Hotel where "Nauseating Nancy" Spungen, as she was known in the punk milieu, expired.

The original title, changed to *Sid and Nancy* because of "bullshit legalistic reasons," in the writers' terminology, was intended to stress the relationship between Sex Pistols bassist Sid Vicious (*ne* John Simon Ritchie) and American groupie Spungen.

"In a certain romantic sense, to die while you're still in love and still young is okay," asserted Wool. "Nancy was just going to kill herself one way or another. And Sid would have just continued getting f—cked up until he made a fool of himself like Elvis—which is a much more pathetic story."[120]

"*Sid and Nancy* are this great pair of doomed lovers, which is a much more interesting thing to make a film about than The Sex Pistols," offered Cox. "*Sid and Nancy* is much more of a love story, a romance. In love there is so much of tripping your partner out, laying traps for them, and putting them in difficult situations to test them. There's an awful lot of very strange and insane stuff attendant to being in love. Two people who are so much in love," the director felt, "destroy each other." Their violent deaths were the result.

Despite the "punkitude" of the project, Cox was not a participant in the London scene of the mid and late 1970s. "No, I was in Los Angeles [UCLA Film Department] getting suntanned. I used to go to shows a lot, but I was a little bit too old to be part of the scene," he recalled.[121] The material for the script was based on interviews Cox and Wool conducted in London and New York. Leck Kowalski's *D.O.A.* (1981) and Julien Temple's *Great Rock and Roll Swindle* (1980), both Sex Pistols rockumentaries, were consulted. Vicious's parody of Paul Anka's "My Way" in *Swindle* was restaged in the Cox production. With a working script, Cox pitched the project to the American movie community. "The majority," reported Cox, "of studios we approached said 'Nobody wants to see this film. These characters are horrible. They're repulsive and you are happy when they are dead.' Even independents like (Roger) Corman and New World aren't tough enough to do a film like this."[122]

Punk rock in the United States was, at best, a subculture. Reams of copy appeared in the popular and music press describing the weird happenings at CBGB in New York, plus the safety-pin-and-vomit scene in London. The unsigned Sex Pistols were better known in New York and Los Angeles than native recording artists. The "Me Decade" in America had proved inhospitable to the punkers. England's youth, with the class and economic divisions, was more receptive. "Anarchy in the U.K." made sense. By the mid-1980s, punk was assimilated in Britain. "Postcards of punks with great big Mohawks actually outsell postcards of the royal family," noted Cox.[123]

In the United Kingdom, Cox approached videoclip producer Eric Fellner. (The Russell Mulcahy-Fellner "Sri Lanka" videos for Duran Duran, especially "Hungry Like a Wolf," are widely believed to be responsible for the group's popularity in the States.) The videomaker proposed the concept to London-based Zenith Productions. The Central Television (U.K.) subsidiary signed the project. World rights for the production were assigned to the American distributor, Embassy Home Entertainment. Embassy, according to Cox, contributed half of the film's modest $4 million budget.

Filming was scheduled for the fall 1985 in three locations, London, New

York, and Los Angeles. Ten weeks was the time alotted for the shoot. An item requiring attention was the casting of the lead roles. Finding actors with a physical resemblance to the ill-fated duo proved difficult. British stage actor Gary Oldman intrigued Cox, as he possessed "this crocodile grin that goes all the way from one ear to the other. It's just like Sid." Chloe Webb, after several auditions, seemed to fit the character of Nancy. Cox said, "This woman has a quality which fits Nancy. She has a great face, so mobile, changing all the time. I found her attractive in a weird way—not in a conventionally beautiful way, but of like a dangerous way." The director bragged that Gary and Chloe's photos could be confused with the real persons.[124]

Shooting began on schedule in London with the scene depicting the destructive meeting of the star-crossed lovers. The production was done in sequence, working up to the fatal Chelsea days. Interiors of the hotel were shot, but the crew was denied access to the room occupied by Sid and Nancy.

A soundtrack album was preordained. Cox rejected the Sex Pistols' studio recordings found on *Never Mind The Bollocks*, "because those are the official studio versions of those songs, and if you went to see them at a show, they would not sound like that."[125] A search was undertaken for some bootleg tapes of the group. They either didn't fit or clearances couldn't be obtained: "legalistic B.S."

Johnny Lydon, *aka* Johnny Rotten, opposed the project. He was, in fact, threatening a lawsuit to stop the use of Sex Pistols material in the film score. He later withdrew, contending that a suit would only publicize the movie.

Glen Matlock, the Pistols' original bassist, was hired to recreate the punk band's material on screen. Oldman and Drew Schofield, the Johnny Rotten character, provided the vocals. The director argued that this approach "was good for the integrity of the thing, to have them singing and not just the actors miming to somebody else's voice."[126] Clash's Joe Strummer was brought in to do the title theme, "Love Kills," and "Dumdum Club." CBS would release the single in seven- and twelve-inch formats. The Pogues and Pray for Rain contributed to the score. Both were on MCA Records-distributed labels, eliminating buyout costs.

The poorly marketed album emerged on *Billboard's* "recommended" list 20 September 1986. The package was described as the "score for Alex Cox's tragicomic portrait of Sex Pistols' Sid Vicious, boast(ing) fine programmatic songs by Joe Strummer, the Pogues, Circle Jerks, and ex-Pistol Steve Jones. Actor Gary Oldman performs two numbers associated with Vicious."[127]

Fellner produced videos with Strummer and The Pogues. The "Love Kills" music trailer appeared on MTV's breakout rotation 8 October and remained for approximately a month. Strummer would also appear in Cox's post-*Sid and Nancy* project *Straight to Hell*, described as a "hommage" to Sergio Leone of spaghetti western fame.

The film's initial exposure occurred at the Cannes and New York Film Festivals. Following its October appearance, the esoteric offering was booked at "selected" theaters. As a first-run art film, its distribution was limited. The subject matter, quite frankly, created difficulties.

Hollywood money men were correct in their assessment that the Cox film venture was depressing and esoteric. Punk is a footnote in English popular culture, but despite CBGB and several southern California niteries, the punk scene barely took hold in the United States. The Bee Gees' "Night Fever" was more of an anthem for the 1970s than the working-class discontent expressed in "Anarchy in the U.K." or "Seventeen." *Time's* Corliss rejected the film, as had most of the film community, characterizing it as "a 111-minute moral limbo dance." Consequently, he asked, "How low can you go? Underground, if you want, but don't expect anyone to follow you."[128] The *Nation's* Terrence Rafferty described Cox's second feature as "*A Hard Day's Night* in Hell."

The tale begins as a nearly catatonic punk with spiked hair, stares empty-eyed into a void. A commanding voice demands, "Who called 911?" The room comes into focus with uniforms and shadowy figures. A body bag is wheeled into the dark, musty hallway. The punker is lead away. The Chelsea Hotel lobby teams with press people and leather-jacketed youths.

At the police station, the suspect, Sid Vicious (Gary Oldman), is surrounded by detectives in the interrogation room. A cigarette is offered as the center of attention remains transfixed. "Where did you meet her?" the police ask. The tabloid headlines telling of Sid Vicious and Nancy Spungen are revisited. The case histories of Ritchie and Spungen, in factual terms, are bizarre. With Cox's dramatic license, reality and fantasy are blurred even when the outcome is legend. The storyline, as described by Richard Gehr, is simple: "boy meets girl junkie, girl turns boy into junkie, boy junkie kills girl junkie."[129] The episode is hardly this clear-cut.

Johnny Rotten (Andrew Schofield) and Sid are in London kicking out the front window of a Rolls Royce. Tiring, they announce their presence to dominatrix Linda (Anne Lambton) by tossing a brick through her apartment window. Entering, the two Sex Pistols are introduced to Nancy (Chloe Webb), who says "I have all your albums in New York."

"Sex is ugly," snaps Rotten, to which Sid adds, "sex is boring."

The acquaintance resumes as Nancy beats her hands on a concrete wall. She needs a fix. The bassist strikes his head on the brick structure. He gives her money, despite the warning, "Never trust a junkie."

"It's a deft moment, tender and innocent somehow, like a courtship ritual from the Stone Age," stated Edelstein. "From that moment," reasoned Denby, "they are a couple."[130] It is primitive and childlike, while illustrative of the destructive emotions Sid and Nancy act out. The significance of this sidewalk display becomes clearer as the film progresses. Self-flagellation and pain become expressions of need and caring. Joe Strummer's closing theme, "Love Kills," captures this ethos.

After the false start, the pairing occurs at Rotten's apartment. Nancy administers a drug dose to Sid. They make love. "You like me, don't you?" she asks. Responding to her demand for love, he bends to kiss her toes, ripping her black stockings. As Denby wrote, "He became her wretched cavalier; she, his annihilating muse. In their grim way, they fulfilled themselves." Love and heroin are fused. The elements of the coupling lead to a displacement of linear conceptualization.[131]

Reality suspension comes quickly. The Pistols and manager Malcomb McLaren (David Hayman) embark on a promotional cruise on the Thames. The bobbies board the ferry and a riot ensues. Sid and Nancy calmly stroll through the frenzied police action, oblivious to the brutality surrounding them. The couple have become, through bonding emotionally and chemically, other-worldly. Sid's daydreams and fantasies become an integral part of the film's texture. The disengagement is short-lived.

In their habitual quest for drug money, Nancy and Sid squeeze into a telephone booth to "hit" on Mrs. Spungen in Pennsylvania. Nancy, calling her mother, says she's just married: "Send us a wedding present." Her request for $200 is denied. She explodes, destroying the phone booth. One critic interpreted the scene as "a pathetic attempt, on one level to break out of the booth, and on another, to break out of her life's incipient downward spiral."[132]

Another scene is employed to illustrate the downward spiral. Setting up "housekeeping," they toy with dolls. Sid has G.I. Joe and Nancy, Barbie. The washed-out blonde sadly relates that she will never be as pretty, because "Barbie doesn't have bruises" referring to needle marks.

Sid's life is "professionally" out of control. Even Rotten provides Sid with a pair of promo tickets to see a rock star, Rainbow, whom it appears has "cleaned up his act," forsaking drugs and drink.

Vicious's use of the bass comes under attack. McLaren comes to his defense, portraying Sid as a "fabulous disaster. He's a symbolic metaphor! He's the demonic of a nihilistic generation! He's a f—cking star!" The statement is a contradiction. It is not a reaffirmation of the punk ideology of "them against us," rather it embodies Sid versus *all*—including, finally, himself. Nancy recognizes this paradox, insisting, "Sid Vicious *is* The Sex Pistols."

The metaphor is realized on the disastrous American tour. The band's disintegration is briefly shown as they drift from Atlanta through the Lone Star State, finally arriving in San Francisco, where Sid manages to walk through a plate-glass door.

The accident is indicative of the entire misadventure in the U.S. During the cross-country trek, Sid manages to phone Nancy. They reassure each other of "undying love." Nancy returns to servicing a sadomasochistic client. In San Francisco, the Pistols disband, and Sid overdoses on the flight to New York. Recovering in a hospital room from "nervous exhaustion," he is riveted to the television. Romero's *Night of the Living Dead* plays as Nancy arrives. They depart for Paris.

The deterioration continues. Sid vomits on a talent agent who reassures him, "You're going to make someone alotta money, Sidney." The encounter with the music bizzer evokes another hallucinatory fantasy.

The marquee of the world-famous Moulin Rouge flashes on the screen as Sid stands alone, microphone in hand, bathed in spotlight. He begins, slowly, mouthing the words to Paul Anka's "My Life" associated with superstars, Sinatra and Presley, the epitome of punkdom's despised Music Establishment. The lush, off-camera strings continue through the first verse. He segues into his scabrous Pistols sound, with appropriate back beat overwhelming the sweetening. The generic mix suggests "the extent to which Sid Vicious quite contradictorily sought success in the very world punks were attacking: show biz," wrote Viano. "Sid became exactly what he started out rebelling against," said Cox, "aloof and junky rockers who can't perform."[133]

The much maligned music industry is the lovers only, yet diminishing, reality base. McLaren, barely visible in the film, is Vicious's sole source of support. Nancy's interest in Sid originally stemmed from his infamy in the music scene. Their habit is maintained by club gigs. Once the Pistols dissolve, she assumes the role of Sid's manager. Their final days are financed by the abortive Max's Kansas City performances, which net the pair $3,000. Once this tenuous link snaps, their world becomes four walls at the Chelsea with the bed, drugs, and television constructing their shrinking universe.

The flickering television screen provides glimpses into Sid's diminishing capacities. The line of people are seen on the screen in front of the Analytical Laboratories. Sid and Nancy are transported into the vision.

The site is actually a methadone clinic. The caseworker (Sy Richardson) berates the pair's dependency as "smack is the great controller." They, he adds, "could be sellin' healthy anarchy. But as long as you're addicts you'll be full of shit." They are oblivious to these admonitions.

A suicide pact is hinted at in the Manhattan hotel. Nancy relates that all her friends are dead. Sid says, "I couldn't live without you. We'll go together . . ." he assures her.

The depths of the harsh physical and psychic decline is revealed as Nancy accidentally sets fire to the trash-infested room. "They sit catalytically in bed, high on heroin," relates Maslin, "until the orangy light flickering across their faces lets the viewer know the room is on fire."[134] They remain unconcerned until the firemen storm into the room pulling them from the smoke-filled cubicle.

A drug-induced vision places Sid and Nancy in a New York alley, embracing and kissing, as garbage rains down upon them. It is the only "atmosphere in which their love could have flourished," noted Denby. Edelstein offered another view: "There's every reason to believe that Sid and Nancy saw themselves like that at the peak of their druggy bliss—they loved each other, and they *liked* garbage."[135] The reviewers are correct. It was the garbage—drugs—that made the relationship possible. They had little alternative but to use it to further extend the relationship. Nancy tells Sid, "At least you used to be something. I've never been anything." In her despair it is vaguely apparent, even to her, that the pained experience of heroin is what makes the coupling possible. "Drugs are Sid and Nancy's primary means of shared expression," wrote Fenner. "By the end, when lovemaking, music and their sense of adventure have all failed them, drugs become their only real bond."

"It's because there's a third person then," noted Chloe Webb. "It's a triangle. June becomes the mistress."[136]

When the couple has nothing left to lose, the death scene takes place. As with the actual 12 October 1978 assault, Cox's depiction beclouds the event. Nancy lunges at Sid during a quarrel. He is holding a seven-inch knife. They pass out or fall asleep. She rises from the blood-stained bed, staggers to the bathroom, where the body will be found, to examine the wound. The dreamlike sequence leaves unanswered several of the rumors surrounding Nancy's death. Cox flirts with several hypotheses, especially the unfulfilled suicide pact. In a real or imagined visit to Grandma and Grandpa Spungen's home, Sid indicates that he and Nancy would "go out in a blaze of glory." There was also the bedroom exchange. The drug-crazed-frenzy notion is dismissed, as the stomach wound appears to have been an accident although Sid's back is to the camera. Still, the heated verbal exchange did not *seem* provocative enough to trigger the stabbing. Cox *did* say, "I don't know that he was guilty."

Cox and Wool offered the "love-kills" perspective. "All along you're seeing this drug-bucket story of these junkie punks beating up on each other and then all of a sudden," said Wool, "after Sid is arrested for Nancy's murder, he slashes his wrists. There was something so romantic about his not being able to live without her that the story changed into an epic romance with genuine universality to it." Viano concurred, saying, "The romanticizing of their suicides does more than putting love and death on the same level; it focuses a blaze of glory upon self-inflicted death."

"There are no half-measures about nihilism," wrote Albert Camus.[137]

Cox's final sequence appears to emanate from Sid's withdrawal hallucinations in a Manhattan jail cell. The theme mirrors the teenage coffin songs of the early 1960s, in which the protagonists overcome everyday torments in an idyllic afterlife. Edelstein, describing the death scene, suggested that Nancy discovering the "sheets filled with her blood, is strangely sacred. It's like a resurrection, the spirit regarding the body from afar."[138]

Sid is being checked out of the police station by a kindly black desk sergeant. He offers Sid a candy bar as he counts out the $540 from the property envelope. Sid mumbles, he liked to get a pizza and walks out into the bright sun. He manages to come across a pizzeria along a desolate stretch of railiroad tracks and abandoned cars. Devouring the food, he encounters three black youngsters who invite him to breakdance. He does, to the beat from their boombox. A yellow cab pulls up with Nancy in the back seat. "Buoyant and beautifully dressed in white (through most of the film she's worn black), she beckons Sid into the cab and they drive off in an embrace," related Cardullo.[139] In this scene, mostly filmed in slow motion, Sid finally seems at ease as "Pray for Rain" overlays the moody, yet relaxed, "Taxi To Heaven." The coda announces:

> Sid Vicious Died of a Heroin Overdose on February 2nd 1979
> Nancy and Sid R.I.P.

The credits move to Joe Strummers theme, "Love Kills." It is one of a few tunes to be showcased in the film; twenty-five titles are sandwiched into the production. "My Way," originally featured in Julian Temple's *The Great Rock 'n' Roll Swindle*, "Pretty Vacant," and the theme are the most memorable tunes from the film. Two appeared on the thirteen-cut soundtrack album supervised by the able Kathy Nelson.

The album was considerably more accessible than the movie. Most of the razor-sharp Pistols material was absent. None of the *Never Mind the Bollocks* selections are present. The audio package, however, could not escape the intrinsic punk connotations. *Variety's* review, one of the very few it received, praised the anthology as being "emotionally integral" with the carrier. Moreover, the album captured "the anarchic musical energy, defiance and morbid poetry of the punk era that paralleled the life of the doomed, anti-romantic lovers whose story has been elevated by a memorable rock 'n' roll movie."[140] This is precisely the kind of ink MCA Records did not welcome. The film's specialty market was limited, as potential venues indicated. Outside the pockets in New York and Los Angeles the punk label was a marketing negative.

The "little picture" was accorded considerable coverage. Notices appeared in many specialty magazines and journals as well as the familiar publications. On the basis of *Repo Man*, the focus of *Sid and Nancy*, and cult status, Cox was widely interviewed in the trade and alternative press. In the media encounters the director stressed the love story aspect of the project and minimized The Sex Pistols' role.

Reviewers minimized this aspect. *Variety's* Stratton praised the film for bringing "audiences as close as possible to understanding its wayward heroes." Rafferty concurred, writing it was "a rare try to capturing some real rock-and-roll madness on screen." Cox created a "fairly successful evocation of the late—70s punk—subculture," contended Gehr.[141]

Several critics found the project contradictory. "Cox's camera stays just close enough to them to remind us of their humanity, and just far enough away to suggest to us their grotesqueness," concluded Cardullo. "Like a roadside accident," observed another writer, "their story both attracts and repels. We all like blood, guts, gore, drug abuse and death in our movies."[142]

Not all scribes were willing to suspend judgment as to the merits of the film. "The end credits roll, to which Cox thoughtfully added: 'Sid and Nancy—R.I.P.' 'OFF' must have been edited out—to help the film come in at just under 147 hours," wrote Corliss.[143]

In its first week of exhibition, *Sid and Nancy* averaged $36,500 at two theaters. After a month's exposure, rentals totaled $319,296. The first run lasted for nineteen weeks, returning $1.3 million, a respectable amount for a new wave production.

Soho Meets Lunchenback

In 1986, David Byrne, of The Talking Heads, was better known than his music. *Stop Making Sense* (1984), despite a limited run, had returned to

Warner Pictures some $3.4 million on an investment of $800,000 put up by the band and Sire Records. *Down and Out in Beverly Hills* had generated enough interest in "Once in a Lifetime" to prompt a single release. It bubbled in the lower depths of the Hot 100 for a month. A curiosity cult figure, Byrne was a celebrity of sorts. *Weekly World News* provided Byrne with a set of personalities for a proposed film project. One was a lonesome single man who had a neon WIFE WANTED sign on his front lawn. Another was a married couple who hand't directly spoken for some thirty years. Both would appear in Byrne's *True Stories*, a post-modern glimpse of small-town, rural America in the throes of technological turbulence. Byrne's concept was structured in a collaboration with Beth Henley and Stephen Tobolowsky. The Cinematographer was Ed Lachman of *Union City* (1980 and *Desperately Seeking Susan* (1985). Karen Murphy of *This is Spinal Tap*, would co-produce.

Accumulating front money for Byrne's concept proved difficult. Heads' manager, Gary Kurfirst, recalled, "It took us a long time to find the financing. This not your ordinary script. People would read it and look at me and say, 'I know this guy is wonderful, but what is this?' " Warner Records, Sire's distributor, in the wake of *Stop Making Sense* became the major contributor. "Most of the money came from the record company," said Byrne. "We tried numerous independent sources, when the record company said they like the idea of being involved, as far as the money went." Synergism was a definite factor as "they do realize there's some cross-hybridization between the two, one field benefiting the other and all," observed the Heads' leader.[144] Byrne, Kurfirst and Ed Pressman joined with the label in putting together the $5-million production cost. Penguin Books added $200,000 after the editor, Nan Graham, optioned script rights with color stills.

A seven-week location shoot was scheduled in the Dallas area in mid-1985. The director assembled the cast, showing them his drawings and Polaroids to set the visual mood. Musical selections, by the Heads, were played on a small tape deck. "David encouraged us to improvise our own writing. Jo Harvey Allen was going wild, writing speeches all the time," related one staffer. The end product, clearly, was David Byrne's vision, a perception he was more than willing to provide to any media person, print or electronic. He conducted myriad calculated interviews with most of the film magazines and opinion dailies, weeklies, and monthlies. Media relations were as structured as *True Stories*. "Ask him a question and conversation grinds to an awkward halt," noted one New York writer. "You can almost see the gears churning."[145]

During the interview blitz, Byrne provided partial snapshots of the film to publications ranging from the *New York Times* to *Ms*. "This film began, not as one story or script, but with a lot of stories found in various newspaper articles, along with some dramatic visual ideas represented by drawings I made," Byrne told *Ms*. Moreover, "Movies are a combination of sounds and pictures." He told Tom McDonough, "I stay away from loaded subjects. I deal with stuff that's too dumb for people to have bothered to formulate opinions on. I felt that a big part of the movie was a kind of travelogue showing a whole town and how people live, and the more important the story became, the more tangential all the other elements became. So we kind of had to reduce the importance of a story in order for it to seem all right for you to wander off and look at something else for a while," he explained. "It's a G-rated pseudodocumentary." The neophyte director summarized the vehicle as a musical documentary of a mythical Texas community.[146]

Prior to the media visitations, Sire provided radio stations with a preview release of "Wild Wild Life." The song surfaced on AOR and Top-40 outlets 23 August 1986. It charted on the Hot 100 at number 90 two weeks later, when MTV added the title in the power slot. The clip was a perfect blend of film and video in the tradition of the critically acclaimed "One in a Lifetime" and "Burn Down The House." *Billboard* selected the album as a pick because "The Heads perform hard-pumping music from the soundtrack of the David Byrne directed film. Crossmarketing, via film's release and another album of the same songs sung by the actors, will develop big sales."[147] The album appeared at a very respectable number 136 4 October, the film's premiere date at the New York Film Festival. The marketing campaign was a classic illustration of the synergism process. Once again, demonstrating the value of record label as film banker.

True Stories

> Mr. Byrne isn't commending Virgil for its complacency; he's celebrating it as the perfect void.
> —Janet Maslin, *New York Times*

> What is True Stories *if not a parable of creating a community on the road to nowhere?*
> —Richard Corliss, *Time* critic

The post modernesque travelogue begins with a panoramic vision of the wide-skyed Texas plains contrasted with a pre-adolescent innocent skipping along an endless dusty road. A voice-over interrupts with allusions to the evolution of dinosaurs and a PBS-ish fast reprise of Southwestern history. The narrator is David Byrne, cruising along in a bright red Chrysler LeBaron convertible. A micro-chip manufacturer is the economic center of Virgil, Texas (population 40,000). In the high-tech facility, Louis Fyne (John Goodman) is found working in a "clean room." His goal, advertised with a lawn sign, is to meet "someone to share my life." He will be the primary source for this cinematic exercise in pop anthropology. Byrne's running commentary makes the banal profound, or perhaps, banal: "Freeways made this town possible."

The occasion for this visit is Texas's sesquicentennial "Celebration of Specialness." The narrator introduces the town "social" with "real loud music." A local assembly lip-syncs "Wild Wild Life" as the denizens sit motionless, bored—an anomaly?

Sandwiched into the montage is Miss Rolling, The Lazy Lady (Swoosie Kurtz), orchestrating life from a king-sized bed with all of the upper-middle-class electronic toys conceivable. A huge color television is the center of her universe. She is a symbol of bourgeois decadence leading to "mallworld": "Shopping has become the thing that brings people together."

The Rome Front is an expansive, flat-roofed commercial milieu in the middle of nowhere. It allows, Byrne says, for "driving, but not only *that*, but parking."

"They may congregate in malls instead of town halls," contended Corliss, "but by indulging one another's peculiarities, they create a sense of community."[148] This enthographic glimpse at conspicuous consumption is followed by a Celebration Fashion Show emceed by socialite Kate Culver (Annie McEnroe).

On the ramp appear dumpy, ill-shaped, and awkwardly dressed citizens in industrial costumes *á la* Fellini. Modline suits abound as Mrs. Culver, in Miss-America-pageant fashion, serenades the contestants. Louis Fyne spies potential "recruits" for marital bliss.

Brownie's Restaurant is the next stop in Byrne's surgical journey where Louis, continuing his quest, is conversing with the local spinner of very tall tales. Lying Woman's (Jo Harvey Allen) statements are outrageous, beginning with her Darwinian origins—"born with a monkey tail"—to the claim that she wrote "Billie Jean" and "half of Elvis's songs." The lying woman is a curiosity and, perhaps, a symbol of self-delusion.

The theme reappears as Byrne is entertained by the civically prominent Culvers. Earl Culver (Spalding Gray) only speaks to Kay through their precocious children. The community leader lectures the narrator on the decline of free enterprise, employing salad metaphors to illustrate the disintegration. "There's no concept of weekends anymore," relates the electronic tour guide.

The motif of traditional decline becomes more pronounced at Fellowship Hall as the preacher (John Ingle) laments, "Let's look at what's happened to national morals since World War II . . . We lost Vietnam," as pictures of Johnson and Nixon flash on the backdrop screen. "The movies and television are filled with characters I don't even wanna know!" *Dallas* personalities, Mr. T, and an MTV deejay invade the screen. The minister continues, railing against the Trilateral Commission and the deed of "running out of paper towels, toilet paper, and Kleenex at the same time." The assembled choir breaks into a gospel tune, "Puzzling Evidence."

The contradiction again is overlayed by children marching through the sticks and boards of a new, suburban construction site. "I Want a Video" resounds. One resident asks, what good is a field "but to build houses on?"

The narrator launches into a discourse on the glories of metal buildings in the scheme of modern architecture. Texas, he says, possesses the largest number of these sterile prefab edifices.

Miss Rollings is transfixed by the television. Channel-grazing through Remington and other commercials, she settles on a Talking Heads video on MTV. Louis's image interrupts "Wild Wild Life" on the screen: "I'm 6′ 3″ and maintain a very consistent Panda-bear shape. Call 844-WIFE . . . serious inquires only." Lazy Lady responds, inviting the marriage seeker to discuss Country and Western music. "It's the sweetest thing," she says. He previews "People Like Us" *a capella*. "What about my music?" he asks. "It's awful sad" comes the reply.

The eve of the Celebration is at hand, with a salsa band entertaining. Louis "The Bear," feeling rejected, approaches the voodoo shaman Mr. Tucker (Roebuch "Pops" Staples) for a love potion because "matrimony is my life." He is told to "think positive." The Dale Carnegie approach to witchcraft will prevail at the Specialness Festival.

The ritualistically staged parade features the standard artifacts dotting small Main Street celebrations. It's archetypically rural. The lawnmower brigade marches, followed by the Peasant Oaks Majorettes, and the all-too-familiar Shriners in mini-cars and urban low-riders. The emcee greets Grand Marshal Earl Culver with, "Thank you Earl! . . . from all of us . . . and thanks to Anderson autos for the loan of the car . . ." Baby-buggy drivers trail behind. "But there's scarcely a Yuppie (or any Talking Heads constituents) to be seen" notes Hoberman.[149]

A glowing, green festival stage stands silhouetted by a vast blue Texas sky. Byrne says, "Anything you stick in there is just about all there is to look at.''[150] The big show is about to begin, with two auctioneers surrounding a yodeler. Local imitations of the Dallas Cheerleaders continue to be replaced with a Tex-Mex version of "Radio Days."

Louis has center stage to perform with the Country Bachelors. "We don't want justice, we just want someone to love," he laments, "What good is freedom to people like us?" Miss Rollings leaves her satin bed to agree to a marriage—"think positive." They're united in bed. This scene intrinsically suggests that the search for happiness ends in the appliance-dominated materialism of the boudoir.

Departing the mythical Virgil, actually the outskirts of Dallas, Byrne wrestles with neocapitalism. "This is not a rental car. This is privately owned. I really enjoyed forgetting . . ." The Heads' closing vocal says, "We live in the city of dreams/Should we awake and find it gone/Remember this is our favorite town." A credit appears announcing, "Nine songs recorded by The Talking Heads."

Like the group in the 1970s appearing at Gotham's punk Mecca, CBGB, in Brooks-Brothers button-downs, *True Stories*, at minimum, is a postmodern duality. It highlights the foibles and mores of Middle America while satirizing an alternative structure. "*True Stories* coolly presents a set of locations and characters only slightly exaggerated, leaving audiences to interpret Byrne's depiction as condescending or affectionate, biting or bland," observed Bell Meteriau.[151]

Uninhabited, wide-open space surrounding an island of uniform track houses seems surrealistic. A microchip economy supporting fundamentalist values and lifestyles is contradictory. Loud music played to a passive and unresponsive crowd appears strange. The film's narrative structure is without a linear storyline. Fyne's search for marital solace is the sole unifying hook.

The remaining material has the feel of MTV's "Top 20 Countdown." The subjectivism of the motion picture would lead to a miasma of reactions.

Demme's *Stop Making Sense* (1984) had received deserved superlatives, especially from the New York and Los Angeles-based media. The raves made sense as the rockumentary transcended most efforts that had preceded it. *True Stories* defied comparison, although David Lynch's ambiguous *Blue Velvet* was frequently mentioned in the same columns. Lynch's controversial thesis, of course, was that evil lurks behind the facade of Normal Rockwell's America. Critics like Maslin, Corliss, and Edelstein suggested the linkage.[152] Byrne's vision became the focus. *True Stories*, a $5-million picture, received more print coverage than the season's big pictures.

The synergistic campaign—tie-in book, album, and film—along with Byrne's interview blitz succeeded in creating high visibility. The Talking Heads apparently impressed Adelle-Marie Stan, who requested a prepublication copy of the Penguin paperback. " 'Hi, Addie,' he (Byrne) said as I opened the door. No tics or twitches, 'Hi, David,' I responded. 'This is awfully nice of you. I'm looking forward to talking to you later.' He handed me the manila folder that housed the loose pages of his book. 'Likewise,' he said, and was gone."[153] Rarely are journalists afforded such elegant treatment. Even Capitol Records president Joe Smith, while interviewing for *Off The Record*, had cause to complain of the shabby treatment accorded to writers by rock artists of a stature lesser than David Byrne.[154]

Reviewers uniformly praised the casting and Ed Lachman's cinema photography. The focus of attention, however, was the narrator-director. *Time*, with a cover story, dubbed Byrne "rock's renaissance man."

Other writers viewed The Talking Heads as a media creation, and centered their attention on the attitudinal posture of the film. Kroll praised *True Stories* as being Byrne's "funny, worried, loving celebration of a disoriented America."

"Byrne has the joy of a Soho sophisticate discovering that there are other beguiling life forms out there, and *True Stories* communicates that pleasure as ripely as any film made by New Yorkers in Texas since *Bonnie and Clyde*," lauded Corliss. Kauffmann said that *Stories* illustrated "the petty bourgeois customs, the media hype, the bloated vulgarities of American small-town life." However, Byrne "also shows some touches of affection for it all."[155]

The neutrality of the movie bothered several writers. "Is he mocking his small town," asked Ked Toumarkine, "or celebrating the virtues of the highly ordinary?" Denby objected that the motion picture didn't "risk a point of view, so its attitude toward its subjects can be taken as either affectionate or patronizing. The weak-backed jokiness expresses neither anger nor sorrow nor love, just pleasure in its own lightweight chic." Hoberman wrote, "*True Stories* is as blandly positive in its platitudes as *Nashville* was glibly apocalyptic."

"Byrne has love and *hate* for modern technology, and for the quaint and backward way some people live" according to Adam Phillips.[156]

Richard Gold complained, "Byrne is a mite too self-absorbed with his own sense of the absurd," but his review paled when contrasted with others.

Several writers, most notably *Rolling Stone's* Anthony DeCurtis, found Byrne's postmodern neutrality a reverse condescension. "Byrne wants everything to cut both ways: the citizens of Virgil are both wacky and 'normal.' He is the narrator, but he offers little insight," contended DeCurtis. "The result is banal, postmodern slumming that indulges an arty, sentimental curiosity about what the simple folk do." The critic went on to say Byrne sees "these people as too childlike to question, too simple to analyze. Their lives are *beneath* criticism. If they 'don't want freedom' and 'don't want justice,' as the song "People Like Us' states at the film's climax, that's just fine. The film assumes such highfalutin' desires can exist only in the hearts of urban elitists—like David Byrne." Coulson, after toying with *Stories*'s ambiguity, suggested that "Byrne sounds a world from which he and, by implication, *we* are radically detached. And his neutrality masks scorn."[157]

The resultant album, recorded in five days by The Talking Heads, was not a soundtrack *per se*. Instead, the nine selections were covers of songs featured in the film. The two strongest cuts, "Wild, Wild Life" and "City of Dreams," were featured in both media. A second, "legitimate" sound-track was promised.

Film critics, mostly, applauded the music placement in *Stories*. Corliss compared the song usage to that of *A Hard Day's Night* (1964), adding, "It took David Byrne to bring the music back to its roots, to secure it in the mouths and guts of his *True Stories* tellers." Another writer concurred, saying, "All of these scenes have the edge of satire, but the gleeful energy of Byrne's musical score obviates cynical or sinister connotations." Byrne's goal of a "representative sample of all the music you'd hear in that locale" appeared validated . . . at least in the film.[158]

Some journalists, having praised *Stop Making Sense*, wrote that the score "may well appeal more to those who don't know much about Mr. Byrne's music career than those who do," and "The Talking Heads' score is staggeringly mediocre."[159]

Music critic Mark Coleman in *Rolling Stone* lamented, "This is neither Talking Heads' platinum sellout nor their masterpiece. It *is* the looosest and least complex record they've done." A film writer charged that "the amateurs (actors) torpedo what could have been an electrifying sound-track."

"I regret," said David Byrne in typical fashion, "that with *True Stories* we didn't put out a record with the cast singing the songs instead of me. They were written with other voices in mind, and to me the other people, like Pop Staples, did it much better than I did. I regret it never worked out to happen that way."[160] The Talking Heads album would spend over seven months on the charts and certify platinum in the footsteps of *Stop Making Sense*. The merchandising action was welcomed at Sire, since the film's initial run returned to its backers only $1.4 million in fifteen weeks.

Statistically, of the twenty-nine soundtracks to chart in 1986—*Sid and Nancy* and *True Stories* did not—only six broke into the *Billboard* Top 50. Three climbed into the twenty-plus ranking—*Top Gun*, *Pretty in Pink*, and *Ruthless People*. *Top Gun* initially earned a platinum wall decoration. Three others—*Stand By Me*, *Pretty in Pink*, and a disappointing *Ruthless People*—went gold.

The titles with RIAA awards were in *Variety's* annual "Big Rentals" accounting, exhibiting $16 million in studio returns, that is, the highest-grossing twenty-five movies of the year.

Listing as Number-1 songs from 1986 motion pictures were Madonna's "Live To Tell" (*At Close Range*), Peter Cetera's "Glory of Love" (*Karate Kid II*), and *Top Gun's* triple platinum "Take My Breath Away" by Berlin. Two of the titles peaked several months after their film's releases. These year-end figures hardly indicate which medium sells the other. *Stand By Me*, clearly, was a sourvenir anthology. Conversely, *Down and Out in Beverly Hills*, the twelfth-highest gross of the year, only scaled Number 68, moved less than 502,000 copies.

The synergism debate, soon to be rekindled, remained unresolved, but the glaring fact was that the soundtrack momentum, following *Flashdance*, was a downward spiral. Aesthetically, many of the more balanced—music and film—collections became interesting failures, i.e., *9 1/2 Weeks*, *Manhunter*, *Running Scared*, and *Sid and Nancy*.

These results partially can be viewed in ticket and copy sales volumes. The banner year in both industries, 1984, had found the labels shipping 679.8 million pieces net, in contrast to 618.3 million in 1986. Studios estimated 1.03 billion tickets, as opposed to the high of 1.2 billion two years earlier. (Note: copy and ticket returns are a much better gauge of consumer response than dollar volume, as prices fluctuate yearly.) Music and movie grosses would increase in 1987, but the soundtrack market, with a few notable exceptions, would not follow.

Notes

1. Ken Terry, " 'Top Gun' Soundtrack Duplicates 'Footloose' Pattern in Less Time," *Variety*, 13 August 1986, 107-8.
2. Quotes in Chris McGowan, "Soundtrack Fastlane Already Facing Congestion As Labels Strengthen Crossover Links In Marketing Chain," *Billboard*, 21 June 1986, 5-6; Anthony DeCurtis, " 'Top Gun' A Victory For The Marketing Men," *Rolling Stone*, 25 September 1986, 21.
3. Quoted in Bronson, 647.
4. J. Greenberg, "Top Gun," *Variety*, 14 May 1986, 14; Terry, 108.
5. *Billboard*, 31 May 1986, 60.

6. McGowan, 5-4.

7. Terry, 107.

8. Quoted in Steve Gett, "Soundtrack Craze: Mixed Reviews,"· *Billboard*, 23 August 1986, 4, 92.

9. Marcia Pally, "Red Faces," *Film Comment*, January/February 1986, 32-37.

10. Jack Kroll, "Beware the Dogs of August," *Newsweek*, 3 September 1984, 73.

11. Holly Star, "Iron Eagle," *Film Journal*, February 1986, 39; Tom Matthews, "Iron Eagle," *Boxoffice*, April 1986, R42.

12. Quoted in Kevin Lally, "Samuels Launches 'Iron Eagle' First Film for $100 Million Fund," *Film Journal*, January 1986, 18.

13. Quoted in Chris McGowan, "Soundtrack Fastlane Already Facing Congestion . . ." *Billboard*, 21 June 1986, 5-6.

14. *Billboard*, 7 December 1986, 75.

15. Matthews, R42; Vincent Canby, "Don't Mess With Us Celluloid Tigers," *New York Times*, 23 February 1986, 21 (sec. 2); Janet Maslin, "Iron Eagle," *New York Times* 18 January 1986, 15.

16. Lally, 18; J. Hoberman, "Only Make Believe," *Village Voice*, 11 February 1986, 56; J. Harwood, "Iron Eagle," *Variety*, 22 January 1986, 20.

17. *Billboard*, 1 February 1986, 80.

18. Andrew Sarris, "A Bum Rap," *Village Voice*, 4 February 1986, 53.

19. Quoted in Julie Richard, "Down and Out in Beverly Hills: 'A Different View of the Rich,' " *Boxoffice*, 12 February 1986, 12.

20. Stanley Kauffmann, "The Old Order Changeth Not," *New Republic*, 24 February 1986, 25.

21. Sarris, 53; Vincent Canby, "Plenty of Bark But Not Much Bite in 'Beverly Hills,' " *New York Times*, 16 February 1986, 17; Andrew Kopkind, "Down and Out in Beverly Hills, *Nation*, 1 March 1986, 251; Kauffman, 25.

22. Pauline Kael, "White and Gray," *New Yorker*, 10 February 1986, 106; Bill Zehme, "Rolling Stone Interview," *Rolling Stone*, 25 February 1988, 32.

23. *Billboard*, 15 March 1986, 82.

24. Quoted in Pat H. Broeske, "Widespread Appeal of the 'Rocky' Series," *Los Angeles Times*, 27 November 1985, 1; " 'Rocky IV' Shows Its Muscle at Box Office, *Los Angeles Times*, 4 December 1985, 1 (IV).

25. "Releasing the Tiger In Scotti Brothers Records," *Billboard*, 21 January 1984, 513-14; Bronson, 557.

26. Sheila Benson, "Rocky IV," *Los Angeles Times*, 27 November 1985, 1 (Calendar).

27. Jack Kroll, "Socking It To The Russians," *Newsweek*, 9 December 1985, 92.

28. Kroll, 92; Richard Schickel, "Win the Battle, Lose the War," *Time*, 9 December 1985, 110.

29. Nigel Floyd, "Rocky IV," *Monthly Film Bulletin*, February 1986, 48; Jimmy Summers, "Rocky IV," *Boxoffice*, February 1986, R15.

30. *Billboard*, 2 November 1985, 72.

31. Quotes in Roderick Mann, "Director Lyne is Whipping '9 1/2 Weeks' Into Shape," *Los Angeles Times*, 15 July 1984, 18 (Calendar).

32. Quotes in Janet Maslin, " ' 9 1/2 Weeks' Moves to New Company," *New York Times*, 17 May 1985, C8; Janet Maslin, "The Stop-Go Adventure of '9 1/2 Weeks,' " *New York Times*, 15 June 1984, 8 (sec. III).

33. Quoted in Jim Robbins, " '9 1/2 Weeks' Wraps in N.Y. Two Weeks Late; Geffen Gets Track," *Los Angeles Times*, 15 August 1984, 7.

34. Quoted in Hillary Johnson, "Kim Basinger: Nobody's Fool," *Rolling Stone*, 13 February 1986, 70; Lynn Hirschberg, "Summer Dish," *Rolling Stone*, 4 July 1985, 25; Janet Maslin, " '9 1/2 Weeks' Is Ready After Editing," *New York Times*, 14 February 1986, C8.

35. Mann, 18.

36. Maslin, "9 1/2," C8.

37. Quotes in Patrick Goldstein, " '9 1/2 Weeks' Sound Track Too Hot To Handle?" *Los Angeles Times*, 2 June 1985, 59.

38. Quoted in R. Serge Denisoff, *Tarnished Gold: The Record Industry Revisited*, (New Brunswick, N.J.: Transaction Books 1986) 195-96.

39. Goldstein, 59.

40. Hirschberg, 25.

41. Quoted in Pat H. Broeske, "The Cutting Edge," *Los Angeles Times*, 16 February 1985, 22 (*Calendar*).

42. Broeske, 22.

43. Quoted in Jon Bowermaster, "Wonderful World, Beautiful Music," *Premiere* January 1989, 102.

44. *Billboard*, 1 March 1986, 71.

45. Chris McGowan, 5-6.

46. David Edelstein, "Beat Me, Bore Me, But Never Ignore Me," *Village Voice*, 4 March 1986, 56.

47. Kevin Lally, "9 1/2 Weeks," *Film Journal*, March 1986, 13.

48. T. McCarthy, "9 1/2 Weeks," *Variety*, 12 February 1986, 22; Maslin, 1986, C8; Edelstein, 56; Vincent Canby, " '9 1/2 Weeks': A Sexual Journey," *New York Times*, 21 February 1986, C17; Tom Matthews, "9 1/2 Weeks," *Boxoffice*, April 1986, R40.

49. Broeske, 22; Edelstein.

50. Lally, 13; McCarthy, 22; Louis Kesten, "9 1/2 Weeks," *Video*, November 1986, 100; Edelstein, 56.

51. Canby, C17; McCarthy, 22.

52. Johnson, 70; W.J. Cash, *The Mind of the South* (New York: Vintage Books, 1960), 89.

53. *Billboard*, 8 March 1986, 84.

54. Quoted in Molly Ringwald, "An Interview With John Hughes," *Seventeen* March 1986, 228; Thomas O'Connor, "John Hughes: His Movies Speak To Teenagers," *New York Times*, 9 March 1986, 14.

55. Pauline Kael, "The Current Cinema," *New Yorker*, 7 April 1986, 91; David Ansen, "Thrift-Shop Juliet," *Newsweek*, 17 March 1986, 81.

56. David Denby, "Teenage Queen," *New York*, 10 March 1986, 93.

57. John Hughes, liner notes, *Pretty in Pink*, A&M Records SP 3901.

58. *Billboard*, 15 February 1986, 71.

59. Janet Maslin, "John Hughes' 'Pretty in Pink,' " *New York Times*, 28 February 1986, C8.

60. Kael, 91.

61. Kevin Lally, "Pretty in Pink," *Film Journal*, March 1986, 11.

62. Richard Corliss, "Growing Pains," *Time*, 3 March 1986, 83; Louise Stanton, "Pretty in Pink," *Film In Review*, May 1986, 300; Mars-Jones, "Mix and

Match," *New Statesman*, 15 August 1986, 25; J. Harwood, "Pretty in Pink," *Variety*, 12 February 1986, 24.
63. Scott Heller, "Pretty in Pink," *People*, 16 March 1986, 16; Ansen, 81; Ira Robbins, "Pretty in Pink," *Video*, November 1986, 101.
64. Denby; Corliss; Kael.
65. Barry Walters, "See the Album," *Village Voice*, 4 March 1986, 60.
66. Mark Coleman, "Pretty in Pink," *Rolling Stone*, 24 April 1986, 59.
67. Georgia Christgau, "Sweet Little Rock 'n' Roller," *High Fidelity*, June 1986, 63.
68. Quoted in Richard Harrington, "The Saga of the Sound Tracks," *Washington Post*, 12 January 1986, K10.
69. D. Stratton, "Legend," *Variety*, 21 August 1985, 16; Tom Matthews, "Legend," *Boxoffice*, June 1986, R62.
70. Harrington, K10; Steven Smith, "Legend Tangerine Dream Knows The Score," *Los Angeles Times*, 4 July 1986, 11 (sec. VI).
71. Mike McDonagh, "Legend," *Film Journal*, May 1986, 15.
72. *Billboard*, 19 April 1986, 84.
73. Quoted in Harrington, K11.
74. Richard Q. Strelitz, "Karate Kid Part II," *Magill's Cinema Annual 1987*, 250.
75. Quoted in Steve Gett, "UA Issues Debut Single," *Billboard*, 30 August 1986, 25.
76. Quoted in Steve Gett, "Cetera Savors Solo Success of 'Solitude/Solitaire,' " *Billboard*, 30 August 1986, 25.
77. McGowan, "Soundtrack Fastlane," S12.
78. *Billboard*, 28 June 1986, 78.
79. Michael Wilmington, "Let's Hear It For A Winning 'Karate II,' " *Los Angeles Times*, 20 June 1986, 23 (sec. VI); Vincent Canby, "Karate Kid Part II," *New York Times,* 20 June 1986, C17; T. McCarthy, "Karate Kid Part II," *Variety*, 19 June 1986, 19.
80. David Denby, "Don't Go Gentle," 11 August 1986, 61.
81. Quoted in Jack Mathews, " 'Karate' Sequel, Soothes Chop to Producer's Ego," *Los Angeles Times*, 25 June 1986, 1 (sec. VI).
82. Gett, "UA Issues," 25; *Billboard*, 23 August 1986, 73.
83. Quoted in Richard Gold, "Lotsa Rethinking and Recasting Went Into 'Ruthless People' Mix," *Variety*, 2 July 1986.
84. Dave Marsh, *Glory Days*, 164.
85. *Billboard*, 28 June 1986, 78.
86. Michael Wilmington, "Going Full Bore in 'Ruthless,' " *Los Angeles Times*, 27 June 1986, 25.
87. T. McCarthy, "Ruthless People," *Variety*, 25 June 1986, 32; David Ansen, "The Spandex King and the Monster Matron," *Newsweek*, 30 June 1986, 59; Richard Corliss, " 'The Green Laughs of Summer,' " *Time*, 30 June 1986, 87.
88. Pauline Kael, "Toads," *New Yorker*, 14 July 1986, 66; Vincent Canby, "Ruthless People," *New York Times*, 27 June 1986, C2; David Denby, "Noises On," *New York*, 14 July 1986, 55; John Simon, "Ephrontery," *National Review*, 29 August 1986, 46; Wilmington.
89. Steve Pond, "Slack Trax From Hit Flicks," *Rolling Stone*, 9 May 1985, 74.
90. *Billboard*, 5 July 1986, 73.
91. T. McCarthy, "Running Scared," *Variety*, 25 June 1986, 32.

92. Sheila Benson, "Fast Friends 'Running Scared,' " *Los Angeles Times*, 27 June 1986, 1, sec. VI; Robert Granger, "Running Scared," *Film Journal*, July 1986, 17; David Ansen, "One Laugh Ahead of A Bullet," *Newsweek*, 30 June 1986, 60; Tom Matthews, "Running Scared," *Boxoffice*, August 1986, R83.

93. Stephen Holden, "Movie Soundtracks Score in Top 10," *New York Times*, 4 August 1986, C19.

94. Benson, 1.

95. Quoted in Ralph Kisiel, "Soundtrack Fever," *Toledo Blade*, 26 May 1985, 1E.

96. Quoted in Chris McGowan, "Soundtrack Fastlane," S12; Stephen Holden, "Movie Soundtracks Score in Top 10," *New York Times*, 6 August 1986, C19.

97. Luncheon remarks in Steve Gett, "Film Studio Executives Refute Soundtrack Burnout," *Billboard*, 30 August 1986, 92; "Studio Execs Seek Automatic Adds With Title Cuts From Soundtracks," *Variety*, 20 August 1986, 83.

98. Quoted in Ethlie Ann Vare, "Oingo Boingo Aims For The Center," *Billboard*, 10 August 1985, 36.

99. Quoted in Steve Gett, "Soundtrack Craze: Mixed Reviews," *Billboard*, 23 August 1986, 92.

100. Danny Goldberg, "Tracking The Hip Ingredient," *Billboard*, 25 February 1985, 10.

101. Quoted in Dennis Hunt, "Simple Minds Leader & Lyricist Jim Kerr," *Los Angeles Times*, 5 May 1985, 59.

102. Bronson.

103. Gett, 92.

104. Quoted in Steve Gett, "UA Issues Debut Single," 30 August 1986, 25.

105. Quoted in Aljean Harmetz, "How Four Boys in 'Stand By Me' Became A Film Team," *New York Times*, 16 September 1986, C17.

106. Michael Buckley, "Stand By Me," *Film In Review*, November 1986, 16.

107. David Denby, "Roughing It," *New York*, 18 August 1986, 58.

108. Pauline Kael, "The Current Cinema: Ersatz," *New Yorker*, 8 September 1986, 108.

109. Nina Darnton, "Looking Back At Growing Up in the 50's and 60's," *New York Times*, 24 August 1986, 15.

110. Quoted in " 'Stand By Me' Bows Wider Than Planned," *Variety*, 27 August 1986, 4.

111. Sheila Benson, " 'Stand By Me' A Summer Standout," *Los Angeles Times*, 8 August 1986, 1, sec. VI.

112. David Ansen, "Movies Growing Up in the 50's," *Newsweek*, 25 August 1986, 63; Richard Corliss, "No Slumming in Summertime," *Time*, 25 August 1985, 62; Denby, 59; John Simon, "The New Gross," *National Review*, 10 October 1986, 6.

113. J. Galbraith, "Stand By Me," *Variety*, 30 July 1986, 16; Tom Matthews, "Stand By Me," *Boxoffice*, September 1986, R99; Kevin Lally, "Stand By Me," *Film Journal*, September 1986, 41.

114. Quoted in David Wild, "Oops, Wrong Decade," *Rolling Stone*, January 1986, 106.

115. Sheila Benson, "Repo Man," *Los Angeles Times*, 3 May 1984, 3, sec. VI.

116. Quoted in Aljean Harmetz, "Shoestring Movies as an Art," *New York Times*, 28 November 1984, C19.

117. Quoted in Ed Kelleher, "Cox's Dazzling *Sid & Nancy* Explores Punk Romance," *Film Journal*, October/November 1986, 14.
118. Terrence Rafferty, "Sid & Nancy," *Nation*, 1 November 1986, 466.
119. Rex Reed, "Sid and Nancy," *New York Post*, 6 July 1984, 37; Cesar J. Rotondi, "Sid and Nancy," *Films in Review*, October 1984, 497.
120. Quoted in Robert Seidenberg "Out of This World," *Film Comment*, July/August, 1986, 4.
121. Todd McCarthy, "Hard Alex," *Film Comment,* September/October 1986, 37.
122. Quoted in Graham Fuller, "Anarchist in the U.K.," *Village Voice*, 21 October 1986, 58; Todd McCarthy, "Hard Alex," *Film Comment*, September/October 1986, 37; and "Film On Sid Vicious' Fatal Affair Lands At Gold Crest With '1/2 Moon,' " *Variety*, 19 February 1986, 204.
123. McCarthy, 38.
124 Kelleher, 14; and Elliott Murphy, "Love Is Strange," *Rolling Stone*, 4 December 1986, 47.
125. McCarthy, 38.
126. Ibid.
127. *Billboard*, 20 September 1986, 72.
128. Richard Corliss, "Weird Trios and Fun Couples," *Time*, 3 November 1986, 82.
129. Richard Gehr, "Sid and Nancy," *Video*, May 1987, 82.
130. David Edelstein, "Love Kills," *Village Voice*, 21 October 1986, 58; and David Denby, "I Love You, Peggy Sue," *New York*, 20 October 1986.
131. Denby.
132. Jeffrey L. Fenner, "Sid and Nancy," *Magill's Cinema Annual*, 1988.
133. Maurizio Viano, "Sid and Nancy," *Film Quarterly* 40, Spring 1987, 37.
134. Janet Maslin, "Sid and Nancy Re-creates Tale of Punk Romance," *New York Times*, 3 October 1986, C5.
135. Edelstein.
136. Quoted in Murphy, 49.
137. Quoted in Seidenberg, 2; Viano, 37; and Albert Camus, *The Rebel*, (New York: A.A. Knopf), 7.
138. Edelstein, 60. For discussion of Coffin songs as nihilistic rebellion see R. Serge Denisoff, " 'Teen Angel,' Resistance, Rebellion of Death—Revised," *Journal of Popular Culture*, 16 Spring 1983, 116-122.
139. Bert Cardullo, "Sid and Nancy," *Hudson Review*, 40 Spring 1987.
140. "Albums," *Variety*, 1 October 1986, 108.
141. Stratton, 24 and Rafferty, 466; Gehr, 82.
142. Cardullo, 24.
143. Corliss, 82.
144. Adelle-Marie Stan, "Making Sense of Rock's Renaissance Man," *MS*, September 1986, 35.
145. Marie Stan, 36.
146. Quoted in Tom McDonough, "Making Sense of David Byrne," *American Film*, October 1986, 32.
147. "True Stories," *Billboard*, 27 September 1986, F1.
148. Richard Corliss, "Divine Comedy for the '80s," *Time*, 27 October 1986, 81.
149. J. Hoberman, "Avant to Hold Your Hand," *Village Voice*, 14 October 1986, 59.

150. Quoted in Crocker Coulson, "Start Making Sense," *New Republic*, 23 March 1987, 26.
151. Rebecca Bell-Meteriau, "True Stories," *Magills Cinema Annual 1987*, 450.
152. Janet Maslin, "David Byrne in 'Stories,' " *New York Times*, October 1986, 7; Corliss, 80-81; and David Edelstein, "Brains Over Budget," *Rolling Stone*, 18 December 1986, 134.
153. Marie Stan, 40.
154. See Joe Smith, *Off The Record*, (New York: Warner Books: 1988).
155. Jack Kroll, "The Eyes of Virgil Are Upon You.", *Newsweek*, 27 October 1986, 103; Corliss, 80-81; and Stanley Kauffmann, "Lone Stars," *New Republic,* 10 November 1986, 26.
156. Ked Toumarkine, "True Stories," *Film Journal*, October/November 1986, 54-55; J. Hoberman "Avaznt to Hold Your Hand," *Village Voice*, 14 October 1986, 59; and Adam Phillips, "True Stories," *Video*, June 1987, 82, 85.
157. Anthony DeCurtis, "Byrne's 'True Stories' Rings False," *Rolling Stone*, 6 November 1986, 21; and Coulson, 26.
158. Corliss, 80.
159. Maslin, 7.
160. Mark Coleman, "True Stories," *Rolling Stone*, 23 October 1986, 100.

11

Goooood Morning, Vietnam!

> *They sabotaged every effort that we made to
> do the movie accurately. They tried to get all
> of our technical advisors to not work with us.*
> —Douglas Day Stewart, screenwriter,
> *Officer and a Gentleman*

> *. . . it [Platoon] would probably have been
> "Casper Milktoast Goes to Vietnam."*
> —Capt. Dale Dye, USMC, retired,
> film consultant.

Easy Rider had ended with an aerial shot of Wyatt's burning motorbike. The Seventies began as, symbolically, the decade of Woodstock Nation was devoured on the same funeral pyre.

The 5 May 1970 edition of the *Los Angeles Times* headlined: "Troops Kill Four Students in Antiwar Riot at Ohio College." The lead paragraph read:

> KENT, Ohio (UPI)—Four students were shot to death on the Kent State University campus Monday when national guardsmen, believing a sniper had attacked them, fired into a crowd of rioting antiwar protesters.[1]

Crosby, Stills, Nash and Young recorded "Ohio" commemorating the incident: "Tin soldiers and Nixon's coming/We're finally on our own. This summer I hear the drumming/four dead in Ohio. . . ." This remembrance and John Lennon's "Imagine" ushered in the Seventies, which would be characterized by Tom Wolfe and Christopher Lasch as the "Me Decade" and "The Culture of Narcissism," respectively. The premature, drug-related deaths of rock superstars Jimi Hendrix and Janis Joplin further

605

signaled that the counterculture was expiring. If more evidence was required, there was Altamont chronicled in wide-screen color in *Gimme Shelter* (1971). "By now," reported a *Rolling Stone* contributor, "rock was moving away from *making* headlines and toward becoming so much grist for the headline writer's mill."[2]

Halfway through the 1970s, disco was surrounding the rock fortress. Led Zeppelin ruled the roost, joined by an upstart from New Jersey, Bruce Springsteen. "The Boss" proved to be the star that the "Disco Sucks!" advocates were seeking.

Meanwhile, the North Vietnamese military had entered Saigon as Americans hastily climbed aboard helicopters in the evacuation of the U.S. Embassy compound. A few reporters stayed, watching the "Stars and Stripes" lowered as the last evacuees disappeared from sight. Disk jockeys throughout the States, almost spontaneously, aired John Lennon's plaintive lyric: "Imagine there's no country it isn't hard to do/Nothing to kill or die for . . . imagine all the people living life in peace."[3] The song would have provided a perfect "music-over" for those fleeing to Navy carriers in the Pacific.

In the early 1970s, Hollywood had produced a few nostalgic, big-screen, war spectaculars such as *Tora! Tora! Tora!* (1970), *Midway* (1975), and *Patton* (1970), which motivated Richard Nixon to initiate the incursion into Cambodia. (He reportedly had watched the film three times.) All of the movies were throw-backs to the patriotic propaganda films of the war years.

There were two decidedly antimilitary efforts, *M*A*S*H* (1970) and *Catch-22* (1970), which was based on the Joseph Heller classic. These films underlined the folly of war and the ineptitude of commanders who planned and executed policy.

Motion pictures critical of the Vietnam war still were generally unthinkable in Hollywood, until Coppola broke the ice. The *Wall Street Journal* had interviewed several executives two years prior to the release of *Apocalypse Now*. "There was no patriotic fervor connected with that war," observed Sam Z. Arkoff of American International. "For the first time the Vietnam War was being shown every night in living color on television news. There was nothing left for the movies to do." Off the record, another mogul said, "No one will go out of the house to see the Vietnam War on a movie screen. The American people don't want to confront the war yet. Every one of these movies will die." Ted Post, director of *Go Tell the Spartans,* disagreed. "After Watergate we're open to disillusion," he said. "It's safe now to cope with the issues the war raised."[4]

Taking a page from its post-Second-World-War days, Hollywood retreated into the "vet comes home" genre. The basic story line was similar to the *Pride of the Marines* (1945) or *The Men* (1951), in which disabled veterans attempt to cope with their handicaps and adjust to the world. The *Deer Hunter* and *Coming Home,* both debuting in 1978, exhibited conclusions absent from the jingoistic, anti-Axis films.

In *Coming Home,* Luke Martin (Jon Voight) rejects his stint in "Nam." He accepts romantic emotions for the Jane Fonda character. After months of therapy, Martin discovers the death of a Vietnam veteran. In protest, he shackles himself to the gates of a Marine recruit depot, as Steppenwolf's "Born to Be Wild" drones in the background, followed by Jimi Hendrix' "Manic Depression." With this action he prevents others from reporting for duty in Vietnam. His antiwar sentiments increase as the film progresses. In another scene, Luke follows a Marine sergeant at a high school rally, admitting that he killed for his country, but felt guilty because "there's not enough reason." (The blinded Al Schmid (John Garfield) in *Pride of the Marines* (1945) would consider such an action beyond the pale of reason.) The finale further underscores the futility of the war—and perhaps marriage—when Bob Hyde (Bruce Dern), a Marine captain, symbolically discards his dress blues and swims out to sea in a suicidal expiation of guilt and drowns. *New York Times* critic Vincent Canby described *Coming Home* as a story of

> a reviving love affair of a paraplegic Vietnam veteran and the wife of a Marine officer serving in Vietnam, is really about the wife's first fully satisfying orgasm. This she experiences in the company of the paraplegic vet, which may or may not be meant as a kind of irony, but then the Voight character is militantly antiwar (sexy?) and though paralyzed, in touch with himself. The gung-ho husband on the other hand, is full of repressions. He's out of touch—impotent and confused. "Coming Home" is more about Freud, perhaps, than about the war.[5]

The reviewer did not take kindly to the never-released track writing, "The soundtrack is a nonstop collection of yesterday's song hits (Beatles, Rolling Stones and so on), not one of which is allowed to pass without making some drearily obvious or ironic comment on the action on the screen. Mr. Ashby has poured music over the movie like a child with a fondness for maple syrup on his pancakes."[6]

Canby's impressions of the *Coming Home* score were somewhat harsh. Rock is designed to be loud. "This ham-fisted tactic *did,* however, result in a period feel for this erotic/anti-'Nam tract. The ultimate use of rock as sound—right up there with *American Graffiti,*" noted Ehrenstein and Reed.[7] Lesser films emerged with a Vietnam backdrop.

Heroes (1977) led the assault. The erratic melodrama focused on emotionally disturbed Vietnam vet Jack Dunne (Henry Winkler) and Carol Bell (Sally Field), who helps the ex-soldier to work out his psychological troubles. Canby used a picnic analogy to characterize the film. ''Winkler's emotional problems might as easily been blamed on an unhappy Boy Scout picnic where two of his buddies died of ptomaine,'' he wrote. '' 'Heroes' has about as much to say about Vietnam, and its place in American lives, as it has to say about spoiled potato salad—which is nothing.''[8]

Rolling Thunder is a war-related revision of *Death Wish* (1974). Major Charles Rane (William Devane), an ex-POW, comes home to be greeted with cheers and a cash donation from a local San Antonio supermarket, a reward for the eight years he was in North Vietnamese custody. Although a local hero, Rane encounters a devastating domestic situation. As in *Coming Home,* his wife is in love with a friend. The surrogate has, also, stolen the affections of the son the major never knew.

The remainder of the film is essentially a *Death Wish* sequel. Criminals in search of the money awarded to the officer terrorize the Ranes. The intruders kill the unfaithful wife and son. The bad guys torture the Devane character by forcing his right hand into the revolving garbage-disposal unit. Recovering, the avenger finds and destroys his tormentors. *Variety* noted, ''It's bloody, but not bloody, bloody, bloody.''[9]

The first 1978 Vietnam ''in-country'' effort, released 12 January, was *The Boys in Company C.* The movie was a well acted and crafted tale which followed five socially diverse Marines through basic training and Vietnam. They slowly realize that the Southeast Asian adventure is an unwinnable exercise in futility. The action-film with comedic moments, as a *Variety* critic suggested, ''is nowhere near a definitive film about the Vietnam debacle. No geopolitics or other cosmic matters intrude.'' Nearly all reviewers of *Company C* compared the endeavor to older, military-oriented pictures. The plot, wrote Canby, from the boot-camp scenes to the film-ending battle scene, was as ''dramatized in any number of World War II movies.''[10] This effort received the highest praise accorded to Vietnam flicks before the *Deer Hunter.*

Go Tell The Spartans (1978) found itself compared to the WW II films about the Allied Armies. A *Times* writer resurrected the comparison, saying, ''In both its action and its ideology, and in its sentimentality, it could easily be mistaken for a movie about World War II, with the Vietcong substituting for the hateful 'Japs' of yesteryear.''[11] The story is allegorical of the American entrance and withdrawal from war-ravaged 'Nam. Starring Burt Lancaster as Major Asa Barker, the film, adapted from *Incident At Muc Wa,* by novelist Daniel Ford, focuses on American military advisors and Vietnamese troops taking control of a useless outpost. To make the situation more unbearable, Lancaster and his minions discover the compound was the site of an Indochina-War massacre by the previous French occupiers. An attack finds the Americans unceremoniously forced to evacuate. Upon their departure, the squad leaves the native soldiers to fend for themselves.

In many aspects, *Spartans* augured the Waynish plots of the Eighties. It was "a movie that returns us to the normalcy of the war-movie world in which 'we' are still the good guys," wrote one observer. Coppola's project, *Apocalypse Now,* was still in production, thus making the $10-million *Deer Hunter* the biggest Vietnam picture to date.

The Deer Hunter examines three working-class men from a Pennsylvania steel town who go and return from Vietnam. After their traumatic experiences in the American incursion, the trio comes home. Steven (John Savage) is in a wheelchair, having fallen from a helicopter and losing both legs and one arm. The brutality of Vietnam is graphically depicted, as in the powerful Russian-roulette scene.

The picture, however, leaves the viewer confused. Steven is integrated into American society as the conclusion of the story nears. This aspect of the film raises questions such as, "Is Steven free of any guilt or bitterness regarding his experiences of the war?" The singing of "God Bless America," at the "toast to Nick" finale seems to suggest that Steven is coping, or at least accepts his situation. "He is completely in his element," wrote Martin Norden. "When the filmmakers freeze on the glasses raised high to Nick, Steven seems far from a "helpless, dependent victim."[12] Another interpretation was "Though the war *may* have been a mistake, we can still *patriotically* love our country and not be ashamed of having worn her uniform, especially as enlisted men loyal to one another."[13]

Studs Turkel was more direct. "The movie may actually justify to some audiences, especially the young, our adventure in Indochina. They may wonder, if these gooks and slopes are such bastards, why didn't we bomb the bastards back to the Stone Age? Was Curtis LeMay a consultant on this film?" he wrote.[14]

None of the pre-*Apocalypse,* combat-oriented films produced a soundtrack album. *Coming Home* was a natural, as it featured the likes of The Beatles, Stones, Jefferson Airplane, Dylan, Hendrix, and others, but label territorality prevailed.

The Rock 'n' Roll War

As a reaction to a "corrupt American foreign policy" screenwriter John Milius penned *Apocalypse Now,* predicting it would be the "most violent movie ever made. A descent into hell. The loss of all sense of civilization. It's just an evil, dark screenplay."

Milius, then the author of *Jeremiah Johnson* and *The Wind and the Lion,* was hardly an antiwar dove. In fact, he was just the opposite. *Mother Jones* profiled him as "a swaggering militarist who sometimes wears a sombrero and a bandolier of bullets across his chest."[15] An arch-libertarian at heart who had named his son after the John Wayne character in *The Searchers* and called the conservative actor the "Last American," Milius described his political bent as that of a "right-wing anarchist."[16]

The script had been submitted originally to Coppola's production company, American Zoetrope, with Warner Brothers having the distribution rights. The manuscript languished on the director's shelf for nearly eight years until the project was launched.

In the interim Coppola had established a reputation for possessing the Midas Touch. He had co-written the screenplay for *Patton* (1970), earning an Academy Award. Acting as a producer, he had shepherded *American Graffiti* (1973) to the status of a box office smash, with several top-selling soundtracks. Both of these films would have an impact on his later efforts. Colonel Kilgore (Robert Duvall) in *Apocalypse* is a South Asian version of the swaggering Patton. The potential use of 1950s and 1960s rock groups also did not escape Coppola's attention.

Apocalypse would be the producer/director's follow-up to the *Godfather* films. The original *Godfather* cost $6.2 million and returned $86.3 million, a hefty profit margin. The sequel, nearly tripled that.

With three Oscars to his credit, Coppola was clearly in control of his filmmaking destiny. The movie industry adheres to the doctrine of "when you're hot you're hot," and consequently funding was available for any Coppola project. He told *Playboy,* his new project would "be a film about Vietnam, although it won't necessarily be political—it will be about war and the human soul. But it's dangerous, because I'll be venturing into an area that is laden with so many implications that if I select some aspects and ignore others, I may be doing something irresponsible."[17] Hawks *would* consider the movie highly "irresponsible," a sentiment expressed by the Army.

The script, in the Army's view, was "simply a series of some of the worst things, real and imagined, that happened or could have happened during the Vietnam War." The service's memo was terse. "In view of the sick humor or satirical philosophy of the film," co-operation should be withheld.

The military objected to scenes deemed "unrealistic" or "negative." The deadly Huey attack offended military sensibilities, as did the portrayals of officers. The Pentagon was particularly miffed by the drama's order to "terminate with extreme prejudice" the Marlon Brando character, Colonel Kurtz.

Coppola insisted that the film would be made with or without DOD participation. Partially due to the director's status and adamance, DOD was unwilling to cut off negotiations. Hoping to entice Coppola, the department's public affairs office invited the director and co-producer Gray Frederickson to Washington for discussions addressing script changes.

Coppola chose instead to scout production sites in the Far East. He approached the Marcos regime in the Phillipines for assistance in December 1975. The Asian government agreed to provide use of its armed forces and equipment as well as authentic film locations.

Coppola refused to comply with the stipulations laid out by the Pentagon. The director telegrammed Secretary of Defense Donald Rumsfeld, outlined his predicament and requested the same treatment accorded to John Wayne's *Green Berets*. In her diary, Eleanor Coppola wrote, "He really needs a Chinook helicopter to lift the PBR [river patrol boat] into the river for that scene at Village II. The Philippine Air Force has no lifting helicopters. It seems like the Defense Department is exerting a kind of censorship. A film about World War II gets all sorts of cooperation."[18]

Within a week, Rumsfeld wired a reply. He reiterated that the DOD's changes were imperative so that the story "would be of mutual benefit by making the film more *logical* and *factual*."

Coppola ignored further communications from the Defense Department. His rationale was simply that its proposed changes were out of the question, especially in the early portions of the movie, which were already in "the can."

Plagued by the lack of Chinooks, Coppola telegraphed President Jimmy Carter. For the second time the director repeated a need for a copter for one day. He was willing to pay the standard rental fee. He continued seeking a "modicum of cooperation *or* the entire government will appear ridiculous to American and world opinion." Both sides stuck to their positions. Finally, the military disapproved the script and declined to provide any cooperation.

The lack of cooperation reportedly transcended troop and equipment assistance. When a devastating Phillipine typhoon isolated a number of production unit members, Coppola appealed to the U.S. Navy for aid in rescuing, or at least getting supplies to, the stranded, but the Navy apparently refused to "have anything to do with anyone connected with the film."

According to the same source, a CIA "plant" was discovered posing as a military adviser. He was immediately dismissed after having spent several weeks on the jungle set.[19]

From its inception, *Apocalypse Now* received extensive media coverage. The project was hailed as the "Film of the Decade." A rough cut of the endeavor was shown at the Cannes Film Festival and tied for first place. (Works in progress rarely are exhibited, let alone win awards.) Coppola's indecision as to an ending further generated public and media speculation.

The media attention would prove to be a mixed blessing. While keeping public interest alive, the coverage suggested the account of Vietnam involved superhuman insight and promised more than *any* film could possibly deliver. Frank Rich's review in *Time* magazine illustrated the dilemma of high expectations:

> Given his talent for fusing ideas with the diverse demands of big budget entertainment, Coppola was the only real candidate to make the definitive film about Vietnam. *Apocalypse Now* promised to go beyond the narrow scope of *Coming Home,* beyond the wrenching drama of the *Deer Hunter.* These promises, though broken, can still be seen in the film. Like other legendary movie mishaps, from D. W. Griffith's *Intolerance* to Bernardo Bertolucci's *1900,* *Apocalypse Now* is haunted by the ghost of its creator's high ambitions."[20]

In a press handout, Coppola outlined the making of his Vietnam spectacular:

> The process of making the film became very much like the story of the film. I found that many of the ideas and images with which I was working as a film director began to coincide with the realities of my own life, and that I, like Captain Willard, was moving up a river in a faraway jungle, looking for answers and hoping for some kind of catharsis.

The cast and crew were evacuated from their Subic Bay location when Typhoon Olga destroyed sets and equipment valued at $1 million. In a matter of months the stages had to be moved to higher ground due to flooding during the rainy season.

Martin Sheen, who played the central character, was hospitalized, reportedly suffering from heat prostration; the final diagnosis indicated a heart attack. With a sky-rocketing budget and the intervention of Mother Nature, Coppola experienced a "nervous breakdown" which affected his marital and his financial status.[21]

Apocalypse Now started on solid economic ground. The distribution rights, sold to United Artists domestically and to international exhibitors, raised nearly $13 million. The budget for the project was estimated at between $12 and $14 million. Unanticipated events such as the weather, Philippino political graft, poor planning, and the creative capriciousness all contributed to a monumental deficit of $18 million. The original shooting schedule was of five-month's duration. The finished product took more than three years.

Eleanor Coppola had sent an angry Telex to the *Apocalypse* film site. She told her distant husband that he was setting up his own Vietnam with his supply lines of wine and steaks and air conditioners, creating the very situation he went there to expose, that with his staff of hundreds of people carrying out his every request, he was turning into Kurtz—going too far. On another occasion she charged that he would "end up being wiped out financially and owe millions."[22] A year after the release of the film Coppola was "only" $1 million in the red. The couple reconciled.

Apocalypse Now focused on the conflict between traditional values and the "systematized chaos and assault on rationality" found in steaming jungles surrounding devastated villages of Vietnam and also "back in the world." Christopher Sharrett wrote, "The journey into the insanity of war in Southeast Asia exists side-by-side with a journey through American culture."[23] Scriptwriter John Milius described the motif, motivated by the Tet Offensive, as "white Protestant civilization and the inevitable clash of Christianity and civilization with paganism.[24] Willard, the rootless, anomic assassin, would retrace the Conradian pilgrammage (from *Heart of Darkness*) of self-discovery on the Mekong River. Director Coppola captured this quest in metaphorical fashion.

In auteurish fashion, the film, approaching DeMillian proportions, encapsulated the confrontation between the ideational mind set against the emotive sensate mentality: Resolution of sanity in an insane war. Capt. Willard is forced to cope with this dilemma when his commanding general orders the assassination of a highly decorated Special Forces Colonel who has forsaken the linear values of the military and "gone native." Comfortably devouring roast beef and sipping beer, the ranking officer tells Willard, "There is a conflict in every human heart between the rational and irrational. Between good and evil. And good does not always triumph. Sometimes the dark side overcomes what Lincoln called 'the better angels of our nature.' Every man has got a breaking point. You and I have one. Walt Kurtz has reached his. It's very obvious he has gone insane."

Is Kurtz (Marlon Brando) insane, or merely a reflection of the sensate countercultural drifts embracing American society? Willard embarks on his lethal mission confused. Coppola immediately addresses the quandary with a pyrotechnic fantasy bathed in flames, a Dante-esque vision of Hell.

A thick line of coconut trees borders an impenetrable jungle. Colored smoke drifts across the screen, yellow, then violet. "This is the end, my beautiful friend . . ." the plaintive voice of Jim Morrison sings. The "Lizard King" is juxtaposed against the madness of dead civilians, burning villages, and fabricated body counts which is personified by Colonel Kilgore (Robert Duvall) in a helicopter assault on a grass-hutted hamlet. "Shall we dance?" he asks, as a firefight begins to the strains of Wagner's "Ride of the Valkyries." Kilgore's mission was to make the divided, war-torn country "safe for surfing." One writer described the scene:

> The trees waver as if in a light wave or a vision, beautiful and ominous. A helicopter floats by suddenly, the entire jungle bursts into brilliant red flames . . . DISSOLVE.[25]

The face of Willard appears seemingly trapped in a dingy Saigon hotel room. A half-empty bottle of *Martell Cordon Bleu* sits on the bedside table. A .45 Army automatic rests beside it. Both offer escape. The pistol augurs the odyssey General Corman has planned for the shell-shocked intelligence officer.

Willard's trip up-river is an endeavor to rediscover meaning in the midst of alienation and incoherence. The voyage is an exploration of bureaucratic warfare affecting Willard.

Jim Morrison's vocal presence underscores Willard's odyssey to the center of the mind. Discussing Morrison's "Dionysian ecstacy," ex-Door Ray Manzarek explained:

> Dionysus was a Greek god who was the opposite of Apollo. Apollo is the god of order . . . of propriety, of the right stuff. You know, all our missiles, all our rockets that go to moon are called Apollo. America is a very Apollonian country and the Dionysian ecstasy was not a mental order, it was a physical order [sensate]. He would get into the physical and just kind of revel in drunkness, revel in excitement and just being alive, just the spirit of your own body. The road to excess leads to the palace of wisdom, and Jim Morrison was a very excessive person. I think he had to be excessive, he had to take it to extremes, but by being excessive he lived out on the edge for all of us. All of us that are, let's face it, afraid to go out there. It's scary, you're all alone. No rules, no foundation, no mommy, no daddy, no school, no government, no religion. He was out there all alone, all by himself. He was bringing back messages to those afraid to go out there and it was excessive. You know he lived an excessive life but he did it for all of us. You know, I think that kind of talent has to be excessive, that kind of genius has to go out there where we are afraid to go.[26]

Coppola's wife Eleanor wrote, "I think that Francis truly is a visionary, but part of me is filled with anxiety. I feel as though a certain discrimination is missing, that fine discrimination that draws the line between what is visionary and what is madness. I am terrified.''

Usage of ''The End'' reportedly was motivated by a reading of the Morrison biography, *No One Here Gets Out Alive*. Observing the PBR crew, Willard calls them ''rock 'n' rollers with one foot in their graves.'' The Rolling Stones' ''Satisfaction'' segues into his thoughts as a crew member, Lance (Sam Bottoms), waterskis behind the river patrol boat (PBR).

Only ''The End,'' which opens and closes the film, and ''Satisfaction'' are overlayed. Several allusions to rock are included in the dialogue: ''purple haze,'' ''let the good times roll,'' and also ''showtime'' a phrase later popularized in *Miami Vice*.

The film's USO DuLung show, emceed by Bill Graham as the manager of *Playboy au 'go go,* features dancers whirling to the refrains of ''Susie Q.'' The chemically altered G.I.s storm the makeshift stage, recreating a scene from a frenzied Grateful Dead concert. (Graham had told the Coppolas backstage at a Dead ''happening, ''Look at the audience, look at that, the crowd isn't crazy, it's just weaving, everyone is joined together. It's a sociological phenomenon. Somebody ought to study it.''[27] *Apocalypse Now* did investigate the inner workings of the rock-generation psyche.

Analyzing the spectacular, Sharrett wrote, ''The motivations and very metabolisms of the protagonists seem determined by the influence of the music.''[28] Herr extended the Dionysism of Vietnam to Woodstock Nation, writing, ''Out on the street I couldn't tell the Vietnam veterans from the rock and roll veterans. The Sixties had made so many casualties, its war and its music had run off the same circuit for so long, they didn't even have to fuse.''[29]

In the film's much-maligned closing segment, Willard confronts his alter-ego Kurtz in a lotus-land that mirrors the violence of Jonestown. His journey has caused the CIA operative to empathize with the poet warrior: ''No wonder Kurtz put a wee up Command's ass. The war was being run by a bunch of four-star clowns who were going to give the whole circus away.'' Willard murders a complacent Kurtz. The Doors' ''Come on baby take a chance with us . . .'' follows.

The closing credits crawl on the screen. This is generally a signal to leave the theater, but this film's audiences were mesmerized by the deadly light show: a backdrop simulating an LSD experience, utilizing napalm pyrotechnics, strobe effects, and fadeways reminiscent of the festivities at the Fillmore (West).

Using only three songs from the world of rock, all edited, Coppola appears to have captured the ambience of the turbulent Sixties. Scenes of dope-smoking G.I.s mistreating civilians and the mission to "terminate" Kurtz ran afoul of the military image the Pentagon wanted projected. After numerous edits, the picture was released; it had cost $33.8 million.

Coppola previewed the epic for the media 12 May in Hollywood and New York. Elaborate press kits were distributed; the film trade papers covered the event. *Variety* analyzed the offering, saying, "There are no models or miniatures, no tank work, nor process screens for the airborne sequences. The resulting footage outclasses any war pic made to date." The reviewer did express reservations, however, saying the "experience is almost a psychedelic one—unfortunately, it's someone else's psyche, and without a copy of crib notes for the Conrad novel, today's mass audience may be hard put to understand just what is going on, or intended." The conclusion ended on a high note: "It's a complex, demanding, highly intelligent piece of work, coming into a marketplace that does not always embrace those qualities. That doesn't lessen its impact as film or art, but it may give the next filmmaker who plans a $40,000,000 war epic a few second thoughts."[30]

The general public was able to see the controversial movie beginning 15 August 1979. In a month *Apocalypse* netted a disappointing $1.9 million. In overall receipts, the Coppola offering was tenth, competing with *North Dallas Forty, Rocky II, More American Graffiti, The Blues Brothers* and *10*. These films generally are now period pieces, but it has become a rare month that a "pay" cable network does not air Coppola's war classic.

Vincent Canby of the *New York Times* and Andrew Sarris of the *Village Voice,* praised the effort. *Time's* Frank Rich wrote one of the most biting analyses of the picture. "*Apocalypse Now* does remind us that war is hell, but that is not the same thing as confronting the conflicts, agonies and moral chaos of this particular war. Yet, lest we lose our perspective in contemplating this disappointing effort, it should be remembered that the failure of an ambitious $30 million film is not a tragedy. The Viet Nam War was a tragedy. *Apocalypse Now* is but this decade's most extraordinary Hollywood folly," he wrote.[31] Coppola recouped his investment. In 1982 he claimed a $100-million gross. The return to United Artists and Coppola totaled $37.9 million. Until the appearance of *Platoon* and *Full Metal Jacket* some ten years later, *Apocalypse* was the definitive cinematic account of the "dirty little war."

In December 1978, Coppola began putting the film's soundtrack together. "I think it's unique in the sense that it is not only music from the picture, but the soundtrack 'is' the picture: dialog, special effects, narration and music," he reflected. "The purpose and concept of the LP for

Coppola and myself was to recreate the experience of the film on record and I think we have been able to do that," he said.[32]

The two months projected for the work dragged on for six, making the two-record set "maybe the most expensively produced" album in history.

The $15.98 package debuted 5 September 1979 to coincide with the film's release. It was a mix of instrumentals recorded in San Francisco by several members of The Grateful Dead, Phil Lesh, and Mickey Hart, and assorted other musicians, including Randy Hansen. Other cuts contained dialogue and Michael Herr's narrative from the film—"Terminate," "P.B.R.," and "Even The Jungle Wanted Him Dead." The Doors' "The End" opens and closes the album as well as the movie. ("Satisfaction" is absent, due to propriety rights.)

While the original soundtrack missed the album charts, the two main rock numbers revived memories. The album cover of The Rolling Stones' *Hot Rocks* greatest hits offering read "Contains 'Satisfaction'—featured in APOCALYPSE NOW."

"The Doors catalog represents significant sales for us," said Elektra's director of advertising, Dave Cline. Several months after the launch of *Apocalypse Now,* Elektra issued *An American Prayer,* a collection of poems, recorded by the now deceased Morrison. The three remaining Doors were brought in to overdub the recitations. Despite a modest promotional campaign and little airplay, the album fared well in the marketplace, selling more than 200,000 copies.

Claude J. Smith, Jr. wrote that the milieu of the 1980s and the demographic make-up of the theater audience transformed the antiheroes of *Apocalypse Now* and *The Deer Hunter:*

> . . . the age of the typical moviegoer—under twenty-five—makes the antimilitary attitude of the Vietnam generation largely irrelevant today, at least to filmmakers trying to market a mass-media product for a target audience that was fourteen or younger when the war ended. . . . certainly, despair, negativism, and anarchy seem on the way out. Instead, the phenomenal success of *An Officer and a Gentleman* suggests that romance and positivism are in. And, finally, the complex vision of the human condition and of the military evoked in *Apocalypse Now* seems unlikely material for the young mass American audience in 1983, which seems to be increasingly conditioned solely for stories of elemental good and evil.[33]

This analysis was valid. However, it was written before the rise of the Yuppies—upwardly mobile urban professionals—of the *Big Chill* generation. "Madison Avenue rushed to sell to Yuppies," wrote *Newsweek*'s Bill Barol, "whose combination of youth and 'highly disposable income' (translation, nobody was saving a dime) made them dream consumers."[34] Packard's hidden persuaders, or hucksters of hype, focused on this affluent group with technologically sophisticated toys like CDs (compact disks) and BMWs. Radio stations, upon entering the "Re Decade," altered their formats to attract this market, re-airing the "sounds of the Sixties" to coincide with the products being released as CDs. Adolescents comprised the backbone of the theater chains, but *Big Chillers* fleshed out the audience. The success of the recycled *Monkees* series, originally aired in 1966, on MTV was due to its acceptance by ahistorical teens and nostalgia-minded Yuppies.

Top Gun: Take My Breath Away

Top Gun was one of the better examples of 1980s cooperation between the DOD and the film industry, with another player added to the equation: the music world. The Navy saga proved ideal for recruiting and propaganda purposes. It also moved sales of ticket and long-playing soundtrack albums. The vehicle seemed perfect for the Stigwood formula of crosspromotion. The producers, Don Simpson and Jerry Bruckheimer, were veterans in the genre with *Flashdance* and *Beverly Hills Cop* to their credits. These films had platinum soundtracks. The storyline for *Top Gun* greatly appealed to CBS Records. The label's president, Al Teller, observed that the film's aerial segments "leave a lot of room for music."[35] CBS acts were requested to submit material for possible inclusion on a soundtrack. Most were rejected, but nine offerings made the final soundtrack. Berlin, on Geffen Records, performed "Take My Breath Away" for the love scene. The Pentagon, unaware of the musical heavy-hitters involved, was merely delighted with the story line.

Robert B. Sims, the Department of Defense's Assistant Secretary for Public Affairs, said, "In most cases, it is in the best interest of the Government to support a motion picture or television production that portrays the military services in a positive and accurate light, thereby avoiding the distorted images that might be conveyed if a film were made without D.O.D. assistance."[36] Donald Baruch, DOD special assistant for audiovisual media, agreed. The Pentagon, he said, "couldn't buy the sort of publicity films give us."[37] Paramount Pictures' *Top Gun* (1986) was a DOD dream come true in the wake of *Apocalypse Now* and other anti-war films.

Top Gun became the Pentagon's pet film project and received complete cooperation from the Navy. In a *20/20* interview, Capt. Nancy LaLuntas, USMC, DOD, said that *Top Gun* was "an excellent opportunity to tell about the pride and professionalism that goes into becoming a Navy fighter pilot."[38] Described as "a 110-minute commercial for the Navy," the movie inspired Navy recruiting displays outside Chicago and Detroit suburban theaters. Navy officials maintained that *Top Gun* increased public military awareness and also aided in meeting Navy manpower quotas. The *New York Times* fittingly called the film "a live-action recruiting poster."[39]

Top Gun was the top-grossing movie of 1986. The action film was nominated for four Academy Awards, but picked up only one for Best Original Song, "Take My Breath Away." It spawned a record-breaking videocassette and the *Top Gun* LP became the year's bestselling soundtrack.

Top Gun begins where *An Officer and a Gentleman* left off. Zack Mayo (Richard Gere) has just graduated from the Naval Aviation Officers Candidate School. *Top Gun* starts with the selection of Lt. Pete "Maverick" Mitchell (Tom Cruise) and his R.I.O. (Radio Intercept Officer) Lt. Nick "Goose" Bradshaw (Anthony Edwards) as one of six F-14 crews to train at the Navy's elite Fighter Weapons School. Cruise, the co-producers' first choice for the *Top Gun* hero, was initially reluctant to take the role. "An adrenaline-pumping ride in an A-4" in the company of the Navy's aerial demonstration team, the Blue Angels, reportedly caused the actor to join up.[40]

Maverick is driven by the legacy of his father, a fighter pilot whose death in Vietnam is clouded by classified information. A second-generation flying ace, Maverick's character flaw is that he is too independent, too much the rugged individual, breaking the rules by sporting an unorthodox flying style. The plot revolves around these pilots, the Navy's top 1 percent.

An unlikely romance develops between Maverick and Charlotte "Charlie" Blackwood (Kelly McGillis). When the actress, previously in *Reuben, Reuben* and *Witness,* turned down the part of a gymnast as "nobody wants to see me in a leotard," the role was rewritten. "When she became somewhat of an intelligent woman," McGillis said, "I liked the part a lot." Not having done an action film, she wanted to diversify. "That movie to me is not an acting film but an adventure film, which is why I wanted to do it."[41]

Playing "Charlie," a civilian astrophysicist and fight-plan instructor, McGillis is intrigued by Maverick's close encounter with a Soviet-made MIG (her specialty) and falls in love with him. Maverick's navigator and best friend "Goose" is killed in an aerial mishap and the pilot's confidence is nearly destroyed. Predictably, this is the catalyst for a transformation in his character. In a real encounter with the enemy, Maverick, now a team player, finds renewed confidence and blows a few MIGs out of the sky.

The script, written by Jim Cash and Jack Epps, Jr., is filled with World-War-II-movie cliches. It centers on the quest to be the "Top Gun," a high-pressure competition that eventually pales in the face of a real dogfight with enemy MIGs. Forget that the audience has no idea what provoked the climactic confrontation between U.S. planes and the enemy. *Top Gun* is a highly polished film of technical sophistication that follows the lead of MTV and other Bruckheimer/Simpson blockbusters such as *Flashdance* and *Beverly Hills Cop* in combining action and a rock music soundtrack to compensate for a weak plot.

Variety called it "revved-up but empty entertainment," regarding it overdone and tedious: "It seems there is not experience, from lovemaking to jets taking off, that isn't accompanied by Harold Faltermeyer's sound-track. Life is given the emotional texture of a three-minute pop song."[42] The *New York Times* labeled it "a truly absurd movie."[43] Several critics saw the real thrills in the film as the choreographed aerial sequences, which were praised as "some of the best flying footage ever put on film."[44]

Producers Jerry Bruckheimer and Don Simpson got the idea for *Top Gun* from a 1983 *California* magazine article on the Navy Fighter Weapons School entitled "Top Guns." Bruckheimer remarked: "This looks like *Star Wars* on earth."[45] The training school is located at Miramar Naval Air Station near San Diego, where most of the filming for *Top Gun* was done. The school began in 1968 to increase the "kill" ratio of American to North Vietnamese planes. The producers saw "Fightertown U.S.A." as "a very theatrical and dramatic arena."[46]

The producers exemplify the American success story. Concerning *Top Gun,* Bruckheimer said, "It's nice for us to do a story about America's best—the Top Gun pilots are the elite. Aside from being extremely intelli-gent—they're all graduates of excellent colleges—most of them are all-American athletes. Our director, Tony Scott, called them part brain surgeon, part jock."[47]

These all-American flyers, together in a room for an evening's entertain-ment, recreate *Animal House*. As Alexander Cockburn wrote, "These Top Gun pilots, who are the elite of the elite and everyone looks up to them, have this club night and girls from all over Southern California come and it's completely incredible. YOU'VE GOT TO GO TO ANIMAL NIGHT."[48]

Cockburn conducted several interviews at the Miramar Air Base. When an actual pilot at Miramar was asked what it takes to be a Top Gun instructor, he replied, "extremely large penises." After some thought he continued, "You have to be able to fly your plane absolutely perfectly and also think what the other guy is going to do to you and how you can counter. It's like brain time-sharing." The flying ace denied that they were "war mongers" but explained, "On the other hand, we're on a football team that's always practicing, but never gets to play. We work hard to be able to do something we don't want to do. But there is that frustration, because you want to test yourself."[49]

Beneath the thunderous roar of the F-14s there is a sign at Miramar that reads: "The sound of freedom." One navy pilot discussed the context of *Top Gun*, saying, "The intent of the movie is maybe a little bit to take advantage of the newfound—what's the word—patriotism. And that's great. It's good for the Navy. We can't complain about the glamorization. We have an image. I think this is the first place and the only place I'll ever be in the Navy where people ask me for my autograph."[50]

When Bruckheimer and Simpson first approached Pentagon officials, they had only a loose concept for *Top Gun*. Simpson did some quick improvisation: "Jerry (Bruckheimer) kind of gave me a nudge and I got lucky and stood up and pitched them a story which ended up being the movie we made."[51] Pentagon instructions require a written proposal stating story objectives and the benefits to DOD; this provides an excellent opportunity for the Pentagon to be involved in a commercial film project from the start. The equipment needs of *Top Gun* (an aircraft carrier and F-14 Tomcats, for example) made the Navy an indispensible partner. Navy officials became a part of the creative force in the making of *Top Gun*. Simpson remarked, "They'd said no to cooperation over *Officer and a Gentleman*, and it was an enormous success. According to them, the recruiting level in the Navy went up over twenty percent when the movie came out. With *Top Gun*, they'd be in from the start."[52]

DOD's Donald Baruch explained that *Top Gun* "was a very simple project as far as we were concerned." The producers collaborated with Navy people at the Miramar fighter school to develop the script. Baruch called the final product "basically realistic" and said it reflected "a picture of the military and the Navy and the program." *Top Gun* co-writer Jack Epps, Jr., said, "I didn't feel the military pressured me to paint any sort of rosy picture. The only thing they told us was no excessive profanity and no excessive sex. But it's easy to see they're not going to help you if you're painting a negative image of the military."[53]

However, Lt. Col. Sandra Stairs, who was the navy Liaison Officer for *Top Gun*, maintained that military cooperation with commercial film studios was "not a blackmail-type situation." If film producers were not willing to make changes according to Pentagon suggestions, the film was deemed an "unrealistic portrayal" from the Pentagon's point of view. To support something unrealistic, she argued, would be a "disservice to the American public."[54]

Paramount producers made dozens of changes upon Navy insistence. Robert Manning, who initially evaluates commercial film projects for the Navy Department, complained that the opening dogfight segment in *Top Gun* was not to be filmed over land, which, "would have made it over Cuba. We said it had to be over international waters," Manning declared, "and we insisted that the Navy pilots would not fire until they had been fired on."[55] Baruch restated this as an illustration of Navy control over the writing of the script. All that is known of the enemy, he explained, is that they have MIGs. There is no topography in those scenes and it is impossible to say where the planes came from, a tropical country or the frozen North. The scene remains plausible, he went on, in that it could have been an attack like those in the Persian Gulf or the Gulf of Sidra.[56]

Lt. Col. Stairs suggested there were additional script changes. One involved the Maverick character. In the initial version Maverick was too "cocky" and individualistic, not a team player. He would not have made it in the aviation community. For a more "realistic" depiction of an aviation officer, the portrayal was altered so that he eventually overcame this problem.

The Colonel acknowledged certain "artistic license" was granted. Maverick was to fall in love with a naval officer, but there are no women officers at Miramar. The female role was changed, first to an aerobics instructor and finally to an astrophysicist. Stairs said, "We understand Hollywood cannot stick to the dry truth." Though no one like the Kelly McGillis character is at Miramar, it is plausible that specialists like her could be there.

Maverick's navigator, "Goose," was killed in a midair collision in the initial script. Navy officials complained that too many pilots were crashing. The producers changed the midair collision to an actual incident that occurred at Miramar—a spinout in which the copilot was killed while trying to eject.[57]

Top Gun blatantly parades the mythology of American male supremacy. Cruise repeated a conversation with a Miramar pilot: "There are only a few jobs worth having—actor, rock 'n' roll star, president of the United States, and a jet-fighter pilot. Landing on a carrier at night—that's sex in a car wreck."[58] J. Hoberman called this a reformulation of "aggression as sex" taking place in the blending of erotic sexual imagery and combat tactics. The dialogue is filled with double entendres and sexual inuendo—the Cruise and McGillis discussion of thrust ratios, for example. A singles bar is a "target-rich environment." Maverick has "crashed and burned" trying to pick up women. A video-simulated dogfight is enough to jokingly give one pilot "a hard on." In a real encounter with the enemy, victory is portrayed in sexual terms.[59] Both women and war are objects of male conquest.

One reviewer called this motion picture "the most brazenly eroticized recruiting poster in the history of warfare . . . a gleaming techno-dream of clean-limbed young studs blasting evil out of the air.[60] The celebration of the male spirit is so homoerotic, Hoberman writes, that "had Freud lived to see it, he might be excused for thinking *Top Gun* an *avant-garde* representation of Saturday night at the St. Marks Baths."[61] This type of characterization must exist in order for the whole story to be believable. How else could these young pilots justify their enthusiasm for the task of destroying the enemy? To make the narrative plausible, the Pentagon has to expose some of the cruel inconsistencies that are harbored in the military mentality.

The DOD has strict guidelines for determining whether or not the Pentagon will cooperate in the production of a commercial film. "A movie we assist has to be authentic in its portrayal," explained Donald Baruch. "If it portrays actual events and people it has to be authentic. If it's a fictional story it has to be feasible."[62] Considering the content in *Top Gun* and other DOD-approved films, there is some question as to the criteria for "authentic" and "realistic" presentations.

Despite Pentagon directions, Bruckheimer still considered *Top Gun* a "piece of entertainment," a story about "nobility of purpose, how to compete against each other to be the best. It's not jingoistic." Tom Cruise was even more adamant. "This film has nothing to do with *Rambo* or Reagan or war fever," the actor maintained. "I'm not interested in making propaganda films. This is not about the F-14; it's a film about the men who fly the F-14."[63]

Simpson insisted that the film is apolitical. "Notice it's a nameless, faceless enemy," he explained. "If we were making a picture that was militaristic or patriotic in its intent, we would have made them Cubans or Russians . . . We didn't care; it's all a metaphor. We just painted them black—they're like Darth Vader . . . Those black knights in the sky against which he's jousting are merely metaphorical symbols for what's going on inside his own soul."[64]

It is clear from both Manning and Baruch that the decision to avoid naming the enemy came from the Navy, and was not a matter of artistic consideration on the part of the producers. Still, Simpson contended that

Top Gun dealt with reality because it showed death at the training school. It was not a "cartoon movie," he insisted.[65]

The backdrop for this saga of personal gallantry remains the armaments of war. The setting for the movie is the high-tech Eighties. The combat skills and virtues associated with the present are anachronistic. Alexander Cockburn points this out: ". . . *Top Gun* is about character and nobility and heroism, and the fact that these virtues are associated with fighter pilots in *Top Gun* ten years after the United States left Vietnam, in the era of the new patriotism, is entirely besides the point."[66] In one sense, this is a revision of the American past—a fusion of traditional American mythology with the image of high-tech warfare and Vietnam—to justify U.S. involvement there. In the end, as one critic pointed out, *Top Gun* was "simply glamorizing the gathering winds of war."[67]

The real star of *Top Gun* is the sleek, high-tech F-14 that turns warfare into the ultimate video game. Nancy Kolomitz, writing in *Film Journal,* said, "Although Cruise does a fine job . . . the F-14 Tomcat . . . steals the show with an impressive display of 'yanking and banking.' . . . This is some of the best flying footage ever put on film."[68]

The producers' "apparent" naivete about the political nature of the film was challenged by several critics. *New York Times* reviewer Vincent Canby expressed a concern that the film may not be "a dependable inspiration to the youth of the land. There's something awfully foolish about its view of personal as well as international relations." Hoberman called *Top Gun* "state of the art war-nography. It's the sort of suave, go-go propaganda you'd expect to be shown to kamikaze pilots," and concluded with a stern warning: "Make no mistake, draft-age spectator, the target *Top Gun* aims for is you."[69]

Paramount paid substantially for this "piece of entertainment." The Navy sent five separate bills to Paramount Pictures with charges amounting to about $1.2 million for their assistance in the making of *Top Gun*. About $1 million of that figure was for aircraft costs. Several different types of planes were used, with rates ranging from $1,566 per flight hour for a C9B to $7,600 for an F-14.

Aircraft Type	Hourly Rate
F-14A	$7,600.00
CH-53E	$7,371.00
SH-3	$3,220.18
C-1A	$3,787.00
F-5	$4,262.66
A-4	$2,274.43
UH-1	$2,527.00

| HH-46A | $1,772.90 |
| C9B | $1,566.00 |

Paramount was charged for equipment rental and work performed by military personnel. (Navy crews had performed an assortment of tasks, providing logistical and flight-deck support and medical services. Crews installed and removed cameras, did electrical work, operated fork lifts and tow tractors, and participated as extras in the movie.) Paramount also paid for lost or damaged equipment, including $134,930 for an aircraft canopy that was damaged while on loan from the Navy.

The only direct reference to charges for the use of the aircraft carrier The USS Enterprise, is for the period 28 July through 4 August 1985, for which the "STEAMING HOURS" recorded are "NONE." The assumption is that normal military operations were being filmed. Cockburn reported in *American Film* that the Navy charged Paramount $25,000 for an aircraft carrier (which had suddenly changed direction) to resume its original course in order for filmmakers to shoot a specific scene of an F-14 landing in the sunset.[70]

According to a *New York Times* report, an audit of *Top Gun*'s book by Congress's General Accounting Office revealed that the Navy omitted some items. Paramount was not charged for use of five Navy cameras to film scenes from an F-14 aircraft, and for two months of help from a public affairs officers.[71]

All Hands, a Navy publication, reported the premiere of *Top Gun* coincided with celebrations of the seventy-fifth anniversary of naval aviation.[72]

Before the F-14 Tomcats reached the theaters, Paramount Pictures and Columbia Records had already begun an elaborate promotional campaign based on their previous efforts that had produced blockbuster films with successful rock soundtracks: *Flashdance, Footloose,* and *Beverly Hills Cop*. Radio programmers and record retailers and distributors were treated to advance screenings of the film. CBS Records carefully timed the release of a "cluster" of singles and videos, which provided an enormous amount of advance radio and video promotion for the film—what Teller called "a critical mass of airplay."[73] Kenny Loggins' "Danger Zone" was released first. Berlin's "Take My Breath Away" followed; it invoked the image of the Tom Cruise and Kelly McGillis love scenes. Footage from the film was used in the videos for both songs. Even the cover art for the singles was coordinated to strengthen the tie between the music and the film.

The whole effort was one of spin promotion. "When Paramount advertises their movie, there's music on their TV and radio spots, and when we advertise our soundtrack, we're obviously talking about their movie,'' Columbia Records marketing director David Gales explained. "All you can do is expose, and hopefully you're doubling or tripling your impression base."[74]

The domestic box office gross for *Top Gun* was more than $176 million and the film took in more than $300 million worldwide. The *Top Gun* soundtrack topped the *Billboard* charts and was certified double platinum that year. It went on to quadruple platinum.

When *Top Gun* was released on videocassette in March 1987, it debuted at the number 1 spot on *Billboard's* "Top Videocassettes Sales" chart, only the fourth title to do so. The cassette gathered strength from its suggested list price of $26.95, the lowest ever for a major motion picture release. Its performance was likened to that of a hit record, and it set new targets for the industry. "To get those figures in the video industry, it's just like going beyond the moon," said distributor Jim Schwartz."[75]

Paramount was able to offer the *Top Gun* home video at a low price because of a new crosspromotion deal with Pepsi. The arrangement was designed to create close ties between the movie and the product, with in-store promotions and television ads. No money was exchanged in the deal. Instead, in return for putting Pepsi's music-video-style ad on the videocassette, the film studio was compensated with almost $2-million worth of Diet Pepsi television spots flaunting the *Top Gun* video. A commercial during the Grammy Awards launched the campaign.[76]

The *Top Gun* videocassette's record-breaking sales reached 1.9 million copies, surpassing the previous record held by *Indiana Jones and the Temple of Doom,* which sold 1.4 million copies. *Variety's* Tom Bierbaum estimated sales of the cassette (at a wholesale price of $16.17) reached $20.7 million for the 1.9 million copies sold. Subtracting $2 million for marketing and $10 to $11 million for packaging and duplication costs, Paramount reaped profits in the range of $7.7 to $8.7 million.[77]

The Paramount Home Video release became the first major theatrical picture to feature an advertising spot. The movie was preceded by a sixty-second commercial for Diet Pepsi in which a pilot flies upside down to pour the soft drink. In order to film the commercial Pepsi had to get two privately owned jets, which were not F-14s. Lt. Col. Stairs explained that the Pentagon cannot promote commercial products. She added that the DOD refused assistance to a burger chain that wanted to have an F-14 pull up to a drive-thru window and order a hamburger.

"There's no law that says we have to cooperate with Hollywood," said Baruch, "and there's no law that says we can't. But if we can get together with them and make an *accurate* film, it's beneficial for both of us" (emphasis added).[78] So it was with *Top Gun*. The Academy-Award winning *Platoon* was a different story.

Platoon: The Tracks of My Tears

> *In any other war, they would have made movies about us too.* Dateline: Hell!, Dispatch from Dong Ha, *maybe even* A Scrambler to the Front. . . . *But Vietnam is awkward, everybody knows how awkward, and if people don't even want to hear about it, you know they're not going to pay money to sit there in the dark and have it brought up.*
> —Michael Herr, *Dispatches*

Platoon, Oliver Stone's award-winning saga about the Vietnam War, has been compared to Michael Herr's *Dispatches*.[79] Writing in 1968 at the height of the war, Herr could not imagine the American people paying money to relive the United States' longest, costliest, and ugliest war. That is what has happened. "War is theater," Vietnam veteran William Broyles, Jr. wrote in *Esquire,* "and Vietnam had been fought without a third act." At the Vietnam Memorial in Washington, veterans explained, "It was like walking out in the middle of a movie."[80]

Platoon sparked a flurry of controversy. The box office smash is at the center of myriad Vietnam films that have formed a cultural dialogue in the United States about the meaning of the war in Vietnam: Why were we there? Who were we fighting? Why did we lose? The television spinoff, *Tour of Duty,* advertised: "My husband fought over there. I protested back here. It's finally time we talk about it."

The Orion Picture was praised by critics for its authenticity as "a document written in blood that after almost 20 years refuses to dry." Pentagon officials called it an unfair and unrealistic view of the Army, saying, "It had everything that was bad without anything that was good."[81] Despite its low budget ($6.5 million), *Platoon* grossed $150 million. Oliver Stone's personal tribute to fellow veterans was nominated for eight Academy Awards and captured four: Best Picture, Best Sound, Best Film Editing, and Best Director.

> I guess I have always been sheltered and special. I just want to be anonymous. Live up to what Grandpa did in the First War and Dad in the Second. I know this is going to be the war of my generation. (Chris Taylor voice-over from *Platoon*.)

The *Platoon* appearing on screen and videocassette is the product of more than a decade of struggle involving an endless network of people:

directors, producers, actors, Pentagon officials, Hollywood executives, retailers, lawyers, and consumers. The battle began with the personal drama of director-writer Oliver Stone. Stone's early years were fashioned by an on-going conflict with his strict, conservative father, a stockbroker who "always felt it was unseemly to express yourself or show emotion."[82] Oliver measured himself against his father's judgment. At first he saw himself as "an East Coast socioeconomic product" and wanted to break the mold.[83] He dropped out of Yale in 1965 during his freshman year and set out on an adventure to find his manhood. After paying his own way to Saigon, he took a job teaching in a Chinese Catholic school (the Free Pacific Institute) in a Saigon suburb. Reportedly, he played tennis with wealthy French planters, various CIA people, and even General William Westmoreland. That year the first U.S. troops arrived in Vietnam. Stone recalled, "The place was like Dodge City."[84]

Six months later he was working in the engine room of a merchant ship. He sailed home through a hurricane and in 1966 moved to Guadalajara, Mexico to begin working on an autobiographical novel, *Child's Night Dream*. Returning to Yale the following year, he finished his novel while flunking his courses. Publishers were not interested. Heartbroken and convinced his father was right, he opted for total anonymity—he joined the Army:

> They'd cut my hair, and I'd be a number. To me the American involvement was correct. My dad was a Cold Warrior, and I was a Cold-War baby. I knew that Viet Nam was going to be *the* war of my generation, and I didn't want to miss it. I must say, my timing was impeccable."[85]

Specifically, Stone wanted to return to Southeast Asia. "I asked for Vietnam, I asked for 11 Bravo, which is infantry, and they gave it to me," he said. "I felt, like the kid in the movie says, that maybe from down here in the mud I can start up again and be something I can be proud of, without having to fake it, see something I don't yet see, learn something I don't yet know."[86]

Stone spent fifteen months in Vietnam as an infantryman. He was a member of the 2d Platoon of Bravo Company, 3d Battalion, 25th Infantry Division. He served in two other units during his tour of duty, was wounded twice, and was awarded the Bronze Star for bravery.

Alienated and angry, he returned from Vietnam in December 1968. Within a month of his return he was busted for carrying an ounce of marijuana across the U.S.-Mexican border. A call to his father and $2,500 later he was out. "That was my homecoming," he said. "I got a true picture of the States. I hated America. I would have joined the Black Panthers if they'd asked me. I was a radical, ready to kill.''[87] Under the GI Bill he attended the New York University Film School, studying under Martin Scorsese.

In 1976 the screenplay for *Platoon* emerged. ''I wrote the script seven years after I'd come back. It took me that long to come to terms with the reality of what happened there,'' Stone said.[88] Afraid that his own memories would be forgotten, he thought, ''It's (Vietnam) a pocket of our history nobody understands—what it was like over there, how the everyday American, wild, crazy boys from little towns in Ohio, who grew up by the 7-Eleven stores with the souped-up cars and the girls on Friday night, turn into these little monster killers.''[89] The screenplay was turned down by all the major and minor studios. ''They said it was too grim, too down, too realistic,'' Stone explained.[90]

While still peddling the *Platoon* script, the writer received a Best Screenplay Oscar for *Midnight Express,* written in 1978. In the early 1980s, he co-wrote the screenplay for *Conan the Barbarian* with John Milius. Giving up drugs, which he thought were hurting his writing, he wrote the script for *Scarface,* a movie he called ''adieu to cocaine.''[91] His directorial debut came with *The Hand* (1981), a psychological thriller/horror film that he wrote. The critics panned it.

With Brian De Palma's *Scarface* and Michael Cimino's *Year of the Dragon* to his credit, Stone was suspected of being a right-wing macho man. Then in 1986 he received critical acclaim as the writer and director of *Salvador* (1986), which has decidedly leftist leanings. The movie was dedicated to his father, who had died the year before and who would have been irritated by the film's politics.

Producer Arnold Kopelson's claim to fame was that his Inter-Ocean Film Sales helped develop the 1982 hit *Porky's*. A reading of the script for *Platoon* brought him to tears. He had his teenage kids show it to ten friends each. They loved it. ''They said kids today aren't interested in whimsical fluff anymore,'' he explained. ''They want strong subject matter.''[92] His son, a student at Columbia University, spoke of the popularity of a course on Vietnam. That clinched it for Kopelson.

The producer struggled to raise the $6-million project cost, eventually striking a deal with Hemdale Film Corporation, the distributor of *Salvador*. (Several films about Vietnam had acquired financing from foreign sources: *The Deer Hunter, Apocalypse Now, The Boys in Company C,* and *The Killing Fields*.) Ten years after it was written, *Platoon* was independently financed by Hemdale for Orion Pictures distribution. John Daly of Hemdale joked, "We felt we couldn't do any worse than we did with *Salvador*."[93]

Stone's vision of Vietnam was uncompromising. He saw the Vietnam conflict not merely as a struggle between life and death, but one of good versus evil, right versus wrong. "To me Vietnam was very much like *The Iliad*," he explained, "a country beating on foreign shores for 10 years with endless internecine warfare." His impressionistic war film, which Richman called "a movie with more symbolism than an Italian film festival," was a reflection of this view of the war. Stone himself calls it "heightened reality." "I pushed beyond the factual truth to the spiritual . . . no, to a greater truth. This is the spirit of what I saw happening."[94]

Stone approaches all his scripts like a journalist. He was determined that this film be authentic. "I was under an obligation to show it as it was," he said. "If I didn't, I'd be a fraud."[95] *Platoon*, like *Apocalypse*, was filmed on location in the Philippines, an appropriate stand-in for Vietnam, between March and May, monsoon season and summer. The crew arrived as Ferdinand Marcos was leaving and had to work out new deals with the new Philippine command for military equipment.

Dale Dye, former Marine captain and president of Warriors Incorporated, a private military consulting firm, was hired as military adviser for the film. The decorated veteran had fought in several important battles and been wounded three times. His last foreign tour before retirement was with the U.S. Marines in Beirut.

Politically, Dye is a strident anti-Communist. After his retirement from the Marines in 1984, he edited *Soldiers of Fortune* magazine and, according to an account in *Time*, unofficially trained Nicaraguan *contras*. Reportedly, he and Stone had some good-humored political exchange on location, calling each other "John Wayne" and "the Bolshevik."[96]

Dye, affronted by the unrealistic drama and inaccurate detail of *The Deer Hunter* and *Rambo*, had created his consulting firm to present a different point of view, i.e., the human side of those who fought the war. *Platoon* was just such a project. Dye said, "We fought a hell of a war and until now, Hollywood didn't give a damn about getting it right."[97]

The former Marine put the cast through a rigorous two-week boot camp. Striving for authenticity, he tried to recreate the Vietnam war experience for the actors. The idea, Dan Goodgame explained, was for the actors "to experience the fatigue, frayed nerves and fear that preyed on the Viet Nam infantryman and to understand the casual brutality that often emerged."[98] The actors marched through the insect-infested Philippine jungle with full sixty-pound packs and rifles. They climbed and rapelled off cliffs. Special effects, booby traps, and "enemy" ambushes terrorized them. Army rations sustained them and they were denied dry clothing. They dug foxholes to sleep in, and were awakened every two hours for guard duty or sporadically by the blast of grenade simulators. Francesco Quinn, son of Anthony Quinn, who played Rhah in the movie, recalled, "We were issued combat gear and a shovel and told to dig a two-man foxhole. I was in this hole in the ground and scared witless . . . I was up all night, didn't sleep a wink because the bats were flying around and the bugs were eating me alive. Then Captain Dye shot mortar rounds around us. I'll never forget that night!"[99]

Tom Berenger, who played Sergeant Barnes, confirmed the value of the "training," saying, "We didn't even have to act. We were there."[100]

Filming took a demanding nine weeks. Dye commented, "I think that when *Platoon* was finished, everybody felt that they had been through a military tour of duty overseas, even the girls."[101] During the filming the military adviser checked out every detail for authenticity—from Sgt. Barnes's wicked dagger to the proper use of white plastic C-ration spoons. Vietnam vet and co-author of *Vietnam on Trial: Westmoreland vs. CBS* Bob Brewin applauded *Platoon* for "getting the details exactly right. Oliver Stone so meticulously reproduces the look and the lingo of grunts that I can almost smell the jungle. He captures the fear and the desperation of boys fighting only for their lives."[102] After the experience of filming *Platoon,* Charlie Sheen said, "I'd probably be in Canada if there was another Vietnam."[103]

DOD charges to the contrary, Stone insisted that his war film was realistic. Scenes are based on his personal experience or events the writer-director knew to have taken place in Vietnam. Concerning a "search and destroy" segment at a Vietnamese village, Stone maintained, "I wasn't trying to call up My Lai. This is not an academic film. It is based on my experience. We did shoot livestock. We burned hooches. One of my comrades did kill a woman. I did save two girls from being raped and killed. It was madness."[104]

Stone insisted that he was not out to "trash the military," just the "mythologies." Such was the portrayal of the military in *Top Gun* as he saw it—misleading and a false image. "It's very sinister, because it creeps into the national consciousness," he explained. "People start to think of war as not so bad. War becomes a function of hand-eye coordination: you push a computer button and you blow up a Russian MIG."[105] Critics agreed. *Platoon* was not "The Truth," said Ron Rosenbaum, "but it's a better version of the truth than the war-as-video-game version of *Top Gun* or the how-I-beat-the-Soviet-army fantasy of *Rambo.*"[106]

Charlie Sheen plays Stone's alter-ego, Chris Taylor, in this personal war saga. Out of a sense of patriotic duty and a quest for manhood, Taylor drops out of college and enlists in the Army. He leaves his privileged, well-to-do life behind to fight with the poor and uneducated in Vietnam. His moral and psychological journey from an unquestioning patriotism to disillusionment becomes his rite of passage to manhood. The plot of *Platoon* traces this development through a series of clashes with the Vietcong near the Cambodian border in 1967.

Taylor arrives in Vietnam as body bags are returning home. Samuel Barber's "Adagio For Strings," a musical theme that recurs throughout the film, is mixed with the sounds of the military base. Taylor is immediately introduced to combat. During a night ambush a rookie is killed and Taylor, frozen in the face of the enemy, is wounded.

Back at base camp (as "White Rabbit" strains in the distance), he is initiated into the drug-induced comraderie of the "hopheads," led by doubting Sgt. Elias (Willem Dafoe). "Do you believe in this?" Chris asks him. Elias replies, "In '65, yeah, but not now." The "grunts" party to Smokey Robinson's "Tracks of My Tears." This group is contrasted to the beer-drinking, card-playing, "might-is-right," "Okie From Muskogee" rednecks—Sgt. Barnes (Tom Berenger) and his followers. To the "heads," Barnes says, "I don't need this shit to escape reality. I *am* reality." Berenger said this speech "may not be just Barnes's truth, but *the* truth. Certainly war is always gonna be here. . . Perhaps from movies like this people will think twice about doing it . . . When the legislators or the president send people into combat zones like Nicaragua, Central America, which is also jungle, you better make sure you're ready for a five-year war."[107]

The second confrontation with the Vietcong occurs on New Year's Day 1968 when the platoon uncovers a network of underground tunnels. One soldier is blown apart by a booby trap. Another, Manny (Corkey Ford), doesn't answer their calls and is found tied to a tree with his throat slit. These deaths increase fears, frustrations, and anger as the soldiers enter a nearby village, suspecting that the villagers are harboring Vietcong guerillas.

The following scenes are the most powerful in the movie. J. Hoberman said, "Stone's evocation of My Lai is more harrowing than Coppola's, because he leads you step by step into the terrifying breakdown of restraint, the situation unravelling from two points of view. . . . By so deliberately unpacking an atrocity, *Platoon* achieves a timeless quality: This is war."[108] The audience is torn by the experience of American soldiers trying to determine who among the villagers are Vietcong soldiers or sympathizers, and who are innocent farmers.

Chris discovers a woman and her mentally handicapped son hiding in a hole. He goes into a frenzy. A black soldier tries to calm him, saying, "Be cool, be cool, they're scared!" Chris shouts back, "Oh, *they're* scared, huh? What about me?" Taylor fires his automatic rifle at the feet of the child, making him dance. Bunny (Kevin Dillon) mercilessly kills the kid, splattering blood on everyone. He looks at the body only in curiosity to see how easily the skull cracked open and how strange brains look.

Outside, Barnes shoots a woman point-blank because she would not stop screaming. He threatens to kill a small child if the father does not disclose the location of the Vietcong. Elias physically struggles with Barnes over the child.

Chris breaks up a G.I. gang-rape of a young village girl. This emotionally wrenching sequence is intensified by the fact that it is somehow understandable under the circumstances. As *Newsweek*'s reviewers observed, "What's so scary about this scene is that Stone makes you feel how easily, in these chaotic circumstances, one can slide into barbarism."[109]

After the village is destroyed, Elias threatens to press charges against Barnes and the inept Lieutenant Wolfe (Mark Moses). Conflict breaks out in the platoon. Chris is caught in the balance between the two sergeants, who, he says, are "fighting for my soul."

In a third skirmish, Elias goes off alone to cut off enemy ambushers. Running wildly through the jungle, he kills several of them. The mission is a success. Barnes orders Taylor to return to the evacuation area, saying he will find Elias. When they meet, Barnes shoots Elias. He returns to the evacuation area, claiming that he found Elias dead. As the platoon is flown out in helicopters, the men see Elias running, pursued by the Vietcong. He is brutally killed as machine guns roar from the helicopters. Taylor realizes what has happened. He despises Barnes.

The final battle occurs the next night. The Americans, overrun by the Vietcong, are forced to call an air strike on their own base. Military adviser Dale Dye makes an on-screen appearance as the captain who calls in the air strike.

Running and shooting wildly, like Elias in the earlier scene, Chris heroically charges, lobbing a grenade into an enemy foxhole—a repeat of the feat which won Stone a Bronze Star. Though it was dangerous and risky, Stone recalled, "I was pissed off, 'cause I knew the guys that had been killed, and I had been smoking a little dope that morning."[110]

An explosion prevents Barnes from killing Chris. The next morning Chris wanders among the wounded. He finds the sergeant alive, but badly wounded. Instead of getting a medic, Taylor raises his gun and Barnes challenges him, "Do it." Chris fires three rounds. Stone does not really

resolve the controversial question of which sergeant has won in the battle
for his soul? In one respect, Chris is avenging the death of Elias. "You
have to fight evil if you are going to be a good man," said Stone. "That's
why Chris killed Barnes. Because Barnes deserved killing." On the other
hand, Chris acts just like Barnes. "I also wanted to show that Chris came
out of the war stained and soiled," added Stone, as did "all of us, every
vet. I want vets to face up to it and be proud they came back. So what if
there was some bad in us? That's the price you pay. Chris pays a big price.
He becomes a murderer."[111]

Wounded, his tour complete, Chris is airlifted out of the battle zone. He
salutes those remaining. The voice-over presents Stone's reason for the
film:

> We did not fight the enemy. We fought ourselves, and the enemy was in us.
> Those of us who did make it have an obligation to build again, to teach others
> what we know and to try with what's left of our lives to find a goodness and a
> meaning to this life.

The narrative of *Platoon* resembled others from the tradition of war
literature—youthful idealism shattered by bitter knowledge. Stephen
Crane, Norman Mailer, and others have told the same story in different
eras. Fifties war flicks like Anthony Mann's *Men In War* and Samuel
Fuller's *The Steel Helmet* and *Fixed Bayonets* are cinematic examples.
Particularly, Robert Aldrich's *Attack!* (1956) depicted a young man torn
between two officers. As a film, however, the uniqueness of Stone's
creation lies in its almost documentary style of recreating the experience
of soldiers in Vietnam. "It is more than a movie," Steven Spielberg said.
"It's like being in Viet Nam. *Platoon* makes you feel you've been there
and never want to go back." Vietnam was a new kind of war and it
demanded a new kind of war movie. "*Platoon* fits the bill," asserted
Richard Corliss. "It is a huge black slab of remembrance, chiseled in
sorrow and anger—the first Viet Nam Memorial movie."[112]

The film was remarkably successful in demonstrating the kinds of fears
and frustrations that led to the brutality associated with the war. Chris's
letters to his grandmother, however, often diluted the impact of what the
audience had just experienced. These reflections tended to simplify the
complexity of the event.[113]

The DOD refused military cooperation in the making of *Platoon*. Col.
John E. Taylor of the Army's Public Affairs Office defended this decision
in a memo dated 28 June 1984. He wrote:

> We have reviewed the Script, "The Platoon," and have found the Army cannot
> support it as written. In its present form, the script presents an unfair and

unaccurate view of the Army. . . . There are numerous problem areas in the script. They include: the murder and rape of innocent Vietnamese villagers by U.S. soldiers, the coldblooded murder of one U.S. soldier by another, rampant drug use, the stereotyping of black soldiers and the portrayal of the majority of soldiers as illiterate delinquents. The entire script is rife with unrealistic and highly unfavorable depictions of the American soldier.[114]

In a letter dated 5 July 1984, Baruch agreed with Taylor. "In our opinion," he summarized, "the script basically creates an unbalanced portrayal by stereotyping black soldiers, showing rampant drug abuse, illiteracy and concentrating action on brutality . . . Of course, we would be delighted if your company would consider screenplay revisions. A meeting can be arranged to go over the script, if someone wishes to come to Washington."[115]

Baruch said later that the Public Affairs Office "never heard from them again." That comes as no surprise. Jack Anderson and Dale Van Atta of *The Washington Post* were quick to point out that the DOD had objected to "the very features of the movie that eventually drew critical acclaim, led to its commercial success and brought widespread testimony from Vietnam veterans that the story of their war had finally been told as it was."[116]

In the absence of Pentagon support, Dale Dye provided the military expertise and the Philippine Army supplied the military equipment. The president of Warriors Incorporated claims he received calls from public officials trying to dissuade him from working on the film.[117]

Though Dye has military contacts all over the world, working with the Pentagon is cheaper and there are some things that only the Pentagon can supply, i.e., an aircraft carrier or F-14 fighter plane. So a film like *Top Gun* can only be made with Pentagon assistance. Dye said that if *Platoon* had been changed to meet with DOD approval, it would have been "Casper Milktoast Goes to Vietnam."[118]

The battle over *Platoon* raged on. John Podhoretz, writing in the right-wing *Washington Times' Insight* magazine, called it "one of the most repellent movies ever made in this country." The film "blackens the name and belittles the sacrifice of every man and woman who served the United States in the Viet Nam War (including Stone)," he wrote. Some Vietnam veterans were disturbed by Stone's presentation of the war. "He managed to take every cliche—the 'baby killer' and 'dope addict'—that we've lived with for the past 20 years and stick them in *the* movie about Viet Nam," asserted Bob Duncan, who served in Vietnam at the same time as Stone.[119]

David Halberstam, who covered the war for the *New York Times* and wrote a book on the Kennedy and Johnson Administrations, *The Best and the Brightest,* claimed the opposite:

Platoon is the first real Viet Nam film and one of the great war movies of all time. The other Hollywood Viet Nam films have been a rape of history. But *Platoon* is historically and politically accurate. It understands something that the architects of the war never did: how the foliage, the thickness of the jungle, negated U.S. technological superiority. You can see how the forest sucks in American soldiers; they just disappear. I think the film will become an American classic. Thirty years from now, people will think of the Viet Nam War as *Platoon*."[120]

John Wheeler, a veteran who is president of the Center for the Study of the Viet Nam Generation in Washington and chairman of the Viet Nam Memorial Fund, affirmed that

there *were* drug cultures; there *were* green lieutenants. Stone wanted to clean out the festering part of the wound. The next Viet Nam movie may be the one that tells the whole truth: that we were the best-equipped, best-trained army ever fielded, but against a dedicated foe in an impossible terrain. It was a state-of-the-art war on both sides. But *Platoon* is a new statement about Viet Nam veterans. Before, we were either objects of pity or objects that had to be defused to keep us at a distance. *Platoon* makes us real. The Viet Nam Memorial was one gate our country had to pass through; *Platoon* is another. It is part of the healing process. It speaks to our generation. Those guys are us."[121]

The *Platoon* soundtrack was marketed poorly. It had very little new to offer, but still provided an avenue for some spin promotion. Hemdale chairman John Daly praised the "spirit and cooperation of all the various artists' labels" in putting together the *Platoon* soundtrack. He concluded, "I think *Platoon* owes a big part of its success to the music that was used in the film. There's no question about that."[122]

The soundtrack was issued by Atlantic in early March 1987 with little fanfare. The album contained instrumental music from the film. A starting and closing theme, "Adagio for Strings," was performed by the Vancouver Symphony Orchestra. The remaining cuts were vintage period pieces. The film-derived material was an eclectic mix of country—Merle Haggard's "Okie From Muskogee"—to acid—the counterculture staple "White Rabbit." The soul offering was Smokey Robinson's "Tracks of My Tears." In the film the songs are sparsely yet effectively utilized. On the album five filler songs, mostly from the Atlantic vaults, appear. None of these were in the movie.

Three labels sought to capitalize on the critically acclaimed film with reissues of singles: Jefferson Airplane's "White Rabbit" by RCA, Smokey Robinson and the Miracles' "The Tracks of My Tears" (Motown), and Percy Sledge's "When A Man Loves A Woman" from Atlantic. (Sledge's hit was one of the fillers on the *Platoon* track album.)

RCA tied the release of a two-record Jefferson Airplane anthology to the success of the film. The sleeve for the "White Rabbit" single used both the artwork from the *Platoon* and *2400 Fulton Street* LPs. "Because we had worked a long, long time on our Jefferson Airplane anthology," explained Randy Miller, director of product management for RCA, "it makes sense for us to put 'White Rabbit' out and tie it in with 'Platoon.' But we worked such a long time on the anthology album, it's perfect timing. It's a natural."[123] A "White Rabbit" video clip also featured clips from the movie and footage of the Airplane on the Smothers Brothers variety show.

Motown used the "Tracks of My Tears" single from *Platoon* as part of a larger marketing campaign to push Smokey Robinson's new album, *One Heartbeat* and single, "Just to See Her." Executive vice president Skip Miller explained that after seeing the film "we came back and realized how much impact that song really does have in the movie. People walk out of that movie singing that song. So we wanted to get on the bandwagon with that." He continued, "It's just perfect timing that all of it happened. We felt it was necessary to include ["Tracks of My Tears"] because it also helps us from an exposure standpoint with Smokey."[124]

Ironically, Atlantic, the "Platoon" soundtrack label, found additional exposure when Sledge's "When A Man Loves A Woman" drew international attention, topping the U.K. charts more than twenty years after its release.

Lacking the original material of *Top Gun*, the power of Michael Herr's narrative in *Apocalypse Now*, and a crosspromotion drive, the LP did poorly. *Platoon*, the album, stalled at Number 75 on the *Billboard* charts. It stayed for thirteen weeks, spending most of that time in the bottom half of the list.

Full Metal Jacket: Life After 'Platoon'

> *In Vietnam the Wind Doesn't Blow*
> *it Sucks*
> —Warner Bros Pictures

> *I wanted to be the first kid on my block to get a*
> *confirmed kill.*
> —Pvt. Joker, combat correspondent

> *Marines die. That's what we're here for. But*
> *the Marine Corps lives forever, and that*
> *means you live forever.*
> —Gunnery Sergeant Hartman

Following the premiere of *The Shining* (1980), director Stanley Kubrick approached journalist Michael Herr (co-screenwriter of *Apocalypse Now*) with an idea for a Vietnam war movie "with no attitudes about it."[125]

As time passed, Kubrick came across Gustav Hasford's *Short-Timers*, which chronicled the experiences of a Marine correspondent during the Tet Offensive. Like Herr, Hasford had reported events in Vietnam. The title was changed to connote the body-piercing field ammunition employed by combat Marines: *Full Metal Jacket (FMJ)*.

"I reread it almost immediately and I thought," recalled the director, " 'This is very exciting, I better think about it for a few days.' But it was immediately apparent that it was a unique, absolutely wonderful book."[126] Kubrick enlisted Hasford and Herr to collaborate on the screenplay.

Three years of preparation went into the project. Kubrick chose to film the story in London, abandoning the now-familiar jungle scenes from the Phillipines used in *Apocalypse* and *Platoon*. Kubrick, contrasted to Coppola and Stone, had no illusions concerning DOD cooperation. His *Paths of Glory* (1958) and, of course, *Dr. Strangelove* enjoyed few supporters in the Pentagon. However, the British Defense Ministry had no reservations; after all, Vietnam was an American misadventure.

"When you think of Vietnam," said Adam Baldwin, "it's natural to imagine jungles. But this story is about urban warfare. That's why London wasn't such a crazy choice for a location at all." Arliss Howard, the film's Cowboy, concurred, saying, "The script called for scorched ground, a lot of rubble, a defoliated area. That's East London."[127]

In Beckton, near the Thames, an old, bombed-out plant was found. It became the main set. A bonus was that some of the buildings had been designed by a functionalist architect who had worked for the French. "Some of the buildings were absolute carbon copies of the outer industrial areas of Hue," noted Kubrick. "We brought in palm trees from Spain and a hundred thousand plastic tropical plants from Hong Kong. We did little things, details people don't notice right away, that add to the illusion. All in all, a tremendous set dressing and rubble job."[128] As another bonus the site, owned by British Gas, was scheduled for demolition. The production people were allowed to blow up the buildings.

Filming, with a cast of virtual unknowns—except *Vision Quest*'s Matthew Modine—began August 1985 and was completed in September 1986. There were the usual delays attributed to Kubrick's sense of perfection. Technical adviser Lee Ermey was hospitalized for several months after an automobile accident. The actual filming took nine months.

After production, Abigail Mead was retained to score the film. Seven "oldies" were chosen for effect, ranging from Johnny Wright's "Hello Vietnam," a Nashville product, to The Rolling Stones' "Paint It Black."

Kubrick, the perfectionist, has a reputation for choosing attention-getting musical material. (Using "Try a Little Tenderness" along with Vera Lynn's "We'll Meet Again" in *Strangelove* had proved to be a master stroke in juxtaposition. "The Blue Danube Waltz" in *2001* and *Clockwork Orange*'s use of "Singing in the Rain" served similar functions.) The director's use of songs is not complementary, but provides stark contrasts to film action. Kubrick is meticulous in song selection. "We checked through *Billboard*'s list of 'Top 100' hits for each year from 1962 to 1968," he told *Rolling Stone*. "We were looking for interesting material that played well with a scene. We tried a lot of songs. Sometimes the dynamic range of the music was too great, and we couldn't work in dialogue. The music has to come up under speech at some point, and if all you hear is the bass, it's not going to work in the context of the movie."

The use of the Trashmen's "Surfin' Bird" at the close of a battle intrigued many reviewers. "What I love about the music in that scene is that it suggests postcombat euphoria—which you see in the marine's face when he fires at the men running out of the building: he misses the first four, waits a beat, then hits the next two. And that great look on his face, that look of euphoric pleasure and suddenly the music starts and the tanks are rolling and marines are mopping up. The choices weren't arbitrary," said Kubrick.[129]

Full Metal Jacket was distributed by Warner Brothers Pictures, which, beginning with *Clockwork,* had distributed the director's past three efforts.

Marketing *Full Metal Jacket,* in the wake of *Platoon,* was a challenge. Joe Hyams, WB publicity vice president, decided that positive comparisons should be stressed or stated "favorably in the same breath." A handful of critics obliged. The studio public relations were able to round up "The Best War Movie Ever Made" from Toronto's Jan Scott. "The Ultimate Vietnam Movie? Even After 'Platoon'? I'd Say, Yes," contributed the Newhouse chain critic, Richard Freedman. Judith Crist offered "Brilliantly Made. Far Better Than 'Platoon.' "

Most reviewers found the *Platoon* comparison "unfortunate." One said Stone's statement "was ultimately warm and embracing" but *Jacket* "is about as embracing as a full-metal-jacketed bullet in the gut." Another wrote that Kubrick's "vision is, if possible, more terrifying than Stone's because it is without redemption."[130] Janet Maslin contrasted the mood-evoking scores. *Platoon,* she contended, "accompanies its brutal realism with the ennobling sounds of Samuel Barber's 'Adagio for Strings,' but *Jacket* "takes the opposite tack. It scores the sharply poetic imagery to be found here with the most soulless and banal American popular songs imaginable.''[131]

Executives at Orion Pictures, *Platoon*'s distributor, found the comparison campaign ''flattering'', but went on to emphasize that *Full Metal Jacket* had not received media coverage comparable to *Platoon*'s. Charles Glenn, Orion vice president, told *Variety* that Warner Brothers was ''trying to capitalize on the success of *Platoon*.''[132]

Full Metal Jacket begins with a stark scene of seventeen ''maggots,'' Marine recruits, being denuded of their hair, masculinity, and civilian identity with dog clippers. In a matter of seconds these men become lumps of clay to be molded into killing machines by Gunnery Sgt. Hartman (Lee Emery), a sadistic drill instructor.

Hartman uses a form of psycho-terror to resocialize his charges through repeated forms of degradation. ''Everything is made subordinate to 'the corps,' to which end the recruits are humiliated, beaten, exhausted, tricked, lied to, subjected to racial slurs and drilled, constantly drilled, physically and psychologically,'' noted Canby.[133]

For eight weeks the D.I.'s profanity-laden, staccato commands reverberate: ''Move it, move it, move it . . . Private Pyle, Private Pyle . . .'' Pyle (Vincent D'Onofrio), actually Leonard Lawrence, a fat dimwit who somehow got past the ''few good men'' hype, is singled out as an object of Hartman's venom. He is the pivotal character in the Parris Island opening section. Pvt. Joker (Matthew Modine) has the unwanted task of bringing Pyle into Marinehood.

The reprogramming of basic training is starkly demonstrated as the D.I. demands, ''Tonight you will sleep with your rifle. You will give your rifle a girl's name . . . You're married to this weapon of iron and wood and you will be faithful.'' Later, Hartman quizzes the maggots as to the accomplishments of mass-murderer Charles Whitman and assassin Lee Harvey Oswald: ''Where did they learn to shoot? The Marines! You'll be able to do the same thing.''

Christmas is celebrated by a lecture explaining the inevitability of United States domination over the U.S.S.R. ''With God and a few good Marines, we will prevail.'' Why? ''Because we kill everything we see,'' barks the sergeant.

Hartman enrages the company by punishing them for Pyle's transgression—keeping a donut in his footlocker.

In a rare display, as recruits may not speak unless they are spoken to, Pyle confides to Joker, ''Everybody hates me. *I need help*.'' Hartman's relentless screaming and brutalizing continues. Joker senses something is wrong—"Leonard talks to his rifle; he's a section-8." Joker, apparently, is the only grunt to perceive Pyle's psychological deterioration.

The D.I. is pleased with Leonard's marksmanship, the only positive sentiment he demonstrates. Pyle is becoming a mentally ill killer. The sergeant, wrote Corliss, "will shape Pyle into an M-14 with a loaded magazine—a full-metal jacket. Then Pyle, like his sweetheart of a rifle, will go off. The killing machine will be fired too soon. His last smile will be one of emotional vacancy, for he has achieved the purity of madness."[134]

Later, the sergeant's order, "I want that weapon!" provokes a murder/suicide. There is a contradiction as Pyle, now a trained killer (Hartman's definition of a Marine—"What do we do for a living, ladies? Kill, Kill, Kill") is also a maniac. Kubrick's repeated theme of the irreconcilible dilemma of technological sophistication versus Freudian primordial instincts surfaces. In *Jacket,* argued Penelope Gilliatt, "the same primal urge to kill is again turned on the killer, and sophisticated techniques murder the brainwashed technicians as surely as the sophistry peculiar to the Vietnam War killed many Americans' faith that candor held high office."[135]

In the film, Nancy Sinatra's "These Boots Are Made For Walking" introduces the streets of Saigon. Joker's tour as a *Stars & Stripes* correspondent is disrupted by intrusive street hustlers, urchins, and thieves. This is pre-Tet 1968.

Stars & Stripes is portrayed as a propagandistic organ; for example, the briefing officer (John Terry) instructs the staff that "search and destroy" is inoperative and they should use "sweep and clear" instead. Moreover, the magazine runs two basic story angles: "Winning of Hearts and Minds: Grunts Who Give Half Their Pay to Buy Gooks Toothbrushes and Deodorants" and "Winning the War: Kill Ratios."

Photographer Rafterman (Kevyn Major Howard) and Joker are sent to cover Hue. As they move toward the besieged city, a Marine Colonel stops Joker, demanding to know the meaning of the peace button on his coat and "BORN TO KILL" scrawled on his worn helmet. "I think I was trying to suggest the duality of war," replies the combat correspondent.

The press people connect with Cowboy's squad. (He had suffered through Hartman with Joker.)

A television crew arrives to the sounds of The Trashmen's "Surfin' Bird." Of the interviewed squad members, only the All-American Rafterman is gung-ho. Animal Mother (Adam Baldwin), a Ramboesque killing machine, believes America should win the war but, "we're shooting the wrong Gooks." Sarcastically, Eightball (Dorian Harewood) complains that the South Vietnamese "would rather be alive than free, I guess, *poor dumb bastards.*"

"I wanted to meet interesting stimulating people in an ancient culture," concludes Joker, "and kill them."

The patrol is fatally sidetracked by a ghostly sniper who downs Eightball and kills Cowboy. Animal, Joker, and a few others storm the ruins, which are licked by random fires. Joker spots the young female sniper, who is wounded in a blaze of M-14 rounds. Withering at their feet she pleads in broken English, "Shoot me." Hartman's final taunt lingers: "You're not a writer, you're a killer." Joker's .45 explodes. Is there humanity or mercy in murder? "The agonizing scene," emphasized Sheila Benson, "including the sniper's identity, is meant to illuminate the moral dilemma of Vietnam. But the final one does it better: the young Marines, silhouetted against guttering flames, moving forward as they sing "M-I-C-K-E-Y M-O-U-S-E," is Kubrick's vision of a war that leads nowhere but into the pit, fought by boys whose basic innocence has been warped and cynically lost."[136] The Rolling Stone's "Paint It Black" plays over the end credits.

Stanley Kubrick's efforts are unique in filmdom. They have proven worth waiting for. *Dr. Strangelove (Or How I Learned To Stop Worrying And Love The Bomb)* (1964) and *2001: A Space Odyssey* (1968) are considered classics. *A Clockwork Orange* (1971) is a strong contender. Predictably, *Jacket* received considerable critical attention. This was important from a marketing perspective as *Platoon* was widely considered to be the definitive cinematic account of the divisive conflict. The film did "isolate a time, a place, and a disease" called that "dirty-little war," but it also served as "a perfect metaphor for [Kubrick's] overview of the human condition," that of "corruption and dehumanization."[137] At a higher metaphysical level the film, said Penelope Gilliatt *(American Film),* was "about nothing less than the intellect, passions and instincts of humanity . . . Kubrick shows us with droll and pensive zeal that we are totally unsuited to be citizens of this planet."[138] Somewhere between the particular and the more cosmic a consensus emerged that by any standard *Jacket* was "an intense, schematic, superbly made Vietnam War drama that will impress some and confound others."[139] Some felt the movie was more accessible than previous offerings.

The *Los Angeles Times*'s Jack Mathews put some of the reviews in perspective, saying, "Calling a Kubrick movie a failure is like calling Mother Teresa selfish."[140]

Several writers did just that. "Does Kubrick really think we're not callous *enough* about war?" asked Rafferty, "That we'd see it more clearly under anesthesia? By plunging us straight into the living theater of basic training and then, after an abrupt midpicture break, straight into the war itself—each time without bothering to fill in the tiniest detail of his characters' personal histories—Kubrick reduces everything and everyone to the merely functional." Hoberman was even less charitable, accusing Kubrick of "gazing through the wrong end of a telescope from the perspective of *2001*. What fools these insects be?"

"*Full Metal Jacket* seems to have been made with less burning conviction than disciplined revulsion," wrote the *Voice* reviewer. "Joker must be speaking for his creator when, at the end of the film, he proclaims, 'I am in a world of shit, but I am alive and I am not afraid.' "[141]

Warners' limited-run distribution technique was successful. The film had originally premiered in 100 theaters; it opened 26 June in twelve cities on 225 screens, grossing $2.2 million. Three weeks later it was exhibiting in 900 theaters with a gross of $21 million. Theater rentals in North America eventually totalled $22.7 million on a $17-million outlay. Reportedly, Warner Bros. received more than a seven-figure payment for pay-television viewing.

Several reviewers made note of the music. Alexander Walker pointed out that Kubrick had employed "an eclectic mix of music" mixing Nancy Sinatra and Sam the Sham with "The Marine Corps Hymn." "There are moments of ironic detachment, many of them musical (such as the shots of medical helicopters picking up wounded soldiers to the nonsensical 'Surfin' Bird' or of the soldiers singing the Mickey Mouse Club song in the film's final scene) that find a black, chilling humor in the images of death and destruction," he wrote.[142]

Warner Brothers Records issued the soundtrack 21 July 1987 as a souvenir item. It failed to chart. (With the modest exception of *Platoon*, infantry-oriented movies have missed trade listings despite their aesthetic merits.)

The Southeast Asian experience gave birth to different categories of movies: the serious or message film typified by *Apocalypse, Deer Hunter, Coming Home, Platoon* and *Full Metal Jacket,* and the Vietnam-cowboy vehicles popularized by Sylvester Stallone and Chuck Norris.

Good Morning Vietnam, the Mark Johnson-Barry Levinson foray into 'Nam, was a departure from previous movies dealing with the experience. It was a comedy, starring Robin Williams, set in early 1965, when "no one was taking the Vietnam situation very seriously," recalled producer Larry Brezner.

Making Vietnam Safe for Robin Williams

Platoon and *Full Metal Jacket* re-examined "the best and the brightest." *Apocalypse Now* handed down the verdict that the Vietnam intervention was constructed on a foundation of disingenuous falsehoods. Stone, in *Platoon,* portrayed the basics of survival in the jungles of Southeast Asia and the interplay of morality versus survival. While set in Saigon, Kubrick's message was considerably more cosmic, chronicling all war as corruption and dehumanization. *Good Morning Vietnam* was considerably more modest. In the early Forties the OWI had complained bitterly that the armed forces milieu was being exploited as a backdrop for standard storylines. *Good Morning* loosely fit that description as well. "We'd already seen the combat stuff in *Platoon* and *Full Metal Jacket,*" observed Barry Levinson, "so I wanted to give a sense of what it was like in 1965. This movie is on the train tracks heading for the wreck."[143] The director's assessment was qualified by *Good Morning* producer Mark Johnson's argument that the film was difficult to pigeonhole. "Audiences will discover that although it is set against a serious backdrop, it has great humor. I find the coexistence of these two elements in one movie to be very exciting," he said.

Adrian Cronauer had worked with Ben Moses for Armed Forces Radio in 1965. Stateside in the summer of 1978 they hatched a concept which blended *M*A*S*H* with *WKRP in Cincinnati.* "I took the idea to ABC," recalled Moses. "They said they couldn't possibly do anything funny about Vietnam."

Three years later agent Allen Green advised Moses to "write it as a treatment for a movie." The twosome shopped a twenty-page outline in Hollywood, with no avail, until Larry Brezner, the co-producer of *Arthur,* saw it. Brezner, joined by client Robin Williams, sold the concept to Disney Studios.[144]

The film opened in selected markets 23 December 1987 in order to qualify for Oscar nominations. A post-holiday-season national spread was scheduled.

The film commences with Airman Adrian Cronauer arriving in the relatively peaceful Saigon of 1965. In a highly unmilitary uniform, he is driven to the local Armed Forces Vietnam Network (AFVN) outlet. The zany Robin Williams as Cronauer immediately shakes up the station brass. His on-mike persona is irreverent. "On the air he's a rush of energy," wrote a *Variety* reviewer, "perfectly mimicking everyone from Gomer Pyle to Richard Nixon as well as the working grunt in the battlefields, blasting *verbotem* rock 'n' roll over the airwaves while doing James Brown splits in the studio. From the start, the film bowls you over with excitement and for those who can latch on, it's a non-stop ride."[145]

The film was a showcase for Williams's comedic talents. "This is the perfect role for Robin," said Johnson. "When he sat down in the control booth to do the scenes involving Cronauers's broadcasts, we just let the cameras roll. He manages to create something new for every single take." The comedian's dominant role transcends the entire film. The basic plot resides on his confrontations with his superiors, Lt. Steve Hauk (Bruno Kirby) and the overwhelming Sgt. Major Dickerson (J. Y. Walsh), a stereotypical drill instructor. There is considerable dramatic license taken with the Cronauer role. Robin Williams told *Rolling Stone,* "In real life he never did anything outrageous. He did witness a bombing in Saigon. He wanted to report it—he was overruled but he said okay. He didn't want to buck the system, because you can get court-martialed for that shit."[146] The "real" Cronauer agreed. "If I had done some of the things he [Williams] did on the air, I'd probably be in Leavenworth," he said.[147] Walter Cronkite broke the "disinformation" policy of the AFVN on the CBS *Evening News,* a Congressional investigation followed. Defense Secretary Robert McNamera, in May 1967, ruled that "The calculated withholding of unfavorable news stories over Armed Forces Radio is strictly prohibited. His order left standing the AFR directive banning "topical" and "antiwar" songs from its playlists. "In-country" grunts had frequently set up transmitters hidden away in combat zones; these pirate operations were repeatedly abruptly shut down and rapidly replaced by others. (Ironically, the enemy had no reservations or qualms over playing popular rock numbers such as The Animals' "We Gotta Get Otta This Place" or Dylan songs.)

Williams's film infatuation with a young Vietnamese language student causes the disk jockey to teach her English class. "Cat," "dog," and "table" aren't part of the curriculum: The deejay teaches American profane words and phrases. Williams uses the school and his radio shifts to enhance the relationship, which is complicated by Trinh's (Chintara Sukapatana) brother. He proves to be a member of the Vietcong.

The soundtrack fills an important void in the film. *Variety* said, "The constant stream of '50s rhythm-and-blues hits is appealing, but also tends to keep the film rolling over most serious issues. Still, it's one of the more eclectic soundtracks around and part of what makes the film enjoyable."

The trade magazine critic was correct. *Platoon*'s background music was indistinguishable from those of most period pieces. *Full Metal Jacket*'s score, partially composed and performed by Abigail Mead, enhanced the Marine mission—Johnny Wright's "Hello Vietnam" was a perfect juxtaposition in the opening scene. *Good Morning*'s musical overlays would have been significantly improved by an imaginative culling of the *Billboard* charts, and Lenny Kaye's anthology, *Nuggets. Nuggets* included the Amboy Dukes' 1967 version of Joe Williams's "Baby Please Don't Go";

the film employed the version by Them. Martha and the Vandellas was represented by "Nowhere to Run." "I Got You (I Feel Good)" by James Brown is featured. The Beach Boys have two selections on the A&M soundtrack: "I Get Round" and "The Warmth of the Sun." "Sugar and Spice" (The Searchers), "Liar, Liar" (The Castaways), "Game of Love" (Wayne Fontana), "Danger Heartbreak Dead Ahead" (The Marvelles), "California Sun" (The Riveras), and The Vogues' "Five O'Clock World" round out the selections. Adult contemporary (AC) hits from 1965, like "Downtown," "My Girl," "You've Lost that Lovin' Feeling," "I'll Never Find Another You," and "What the World Needs Now" are absent. Actually more artists—Ray Coniff, Percy Faith, Frank Sinatra, and other MORers—are discussed than are actually heard. Louis Armstrong's ballad "What A Wonderful World" was the only AC cut that had any paradoxical connection to the cinematography. The void appears intentional, to further underscore the Philestine playlists at the AFVN station.

Good Morning may have distressed some die-hard West-prelandites, but overall it served as an iconoclastic footnote to the Vietnam misadventure. Even here, Williams's zaniness transcended the escalation taking place "in-country." The traffic-jam segment emphasized the troop movements and allowed the comic to improvise throwaway lines with the soldiers. The reality that many of them would not return is generally avoided.

The end of February 1988 found the Williams vehicle on the top of the box office grosses with $71.4 million. Robin Williams was nominated for an Academy Award (He lost). *Good Morning* had expanded Hollywood's Vietnam horizons. The war has since deteriorated into a mere backdrop for police-action projects, like *Off Limits* and romance tales.[148] The most striking of those was the documentary *Dear America: Letters From Vietnam* (1987) with narration by Tom Berenger, Michael J. Fox, William Defoe, Robin Williams, Sean Penn, and others. The score was filled with Sixties selections and included the unattainable "Born in the U.S.A." sung by Bruce Springsteen. Had a soundtrack in its entirety been issued, the result would have been a near-perfect package, thus improving the fate of infantry-oriented LPs.

Notes

1. "Troops Kill Four Students In Antiwar Riot at Ohio College," *Los Angeles Times,* 5 May 1970, 1.
2. "1970," *Rolling Stone Rock Almanac* (New York: Rolling Stone Press Book, 1983), 167.
3. Maclean Music, Inc., BMI.

4. Quoted in Karl Gottschalk, "After Long Study Movie Makers Find a New War to Fight," *Wall Street Journal*, 1 November 1977, 1, 36.
5. Vincent Canby, "Hollywood Focuses on Vietnam at Last," *New York Times*, 19 February 1978, 1, 13.
6. Vincent Canby, "Detritus of War," *New York Times*, 16 February 1978, C20.
7. David Ehrenstein and Bill Reed, *Rock On Film* (New York: Delilah Books 1982), 134.
8. "Hollywood Focuses," 1; also "Heroes," *Variety*, 2 November 1977, 20.
9. "Rolling Thunder," *Variety*, 5 October 1977, 20.
10. "Hollywood Focuses," and Janet Maslin, "Five in Vietnam," *New York Times*, 30 January 1978, C15.
11. Hilton Kramer, "Go Tell The Spartans," *New York Times*, 21 June, 1978; "Go Tell The Spartans," *Variety*, 14 June 1978.
12. Martin F. Norden, "The Disabled Vietnam Veteran in Hollywood Films," *Journal of Popular Film and Television* Spring 1985, 19.
13. Claude Smith, Jr., "Clean Boys in Bright Uniforms: The Rehabilitation of the U.S. Military in Films Since 1978," *Journal of Popular Film and Television* Winter 1984:147.
14. Studs Terkel, "On Seeing 'The Deer Hunter,' " *Chicago*, May 1979, 210.
15. Deirdre English, "The Dark Heart of Apocalypse Now," *Mother Jones*, September/October 1979, 38.
16. "Joseph McBride," " 'Milius Re-Heats His 'Apocalypse' " *Variety*, 3 September 1975, 5,27.
17. "Playboy Interview: Francis Ford Coppola," *Playboy*, July 1975, 65.
18. Eleanor Coppola, *Notes* (New York: Simon and Schuster 1979), 38.
19. "Word Leaks of Pentagon's Sour View of Coppola's 'Apocalypse,' Deemed 'Anti-U.S.' In Script," *Variety*, 7 July 1976, 1,114. Suid suggested that DOD officials were "willing to take an extra step to avoid a confrontation" with the director. Lawrence Suid, *Guts and Glory: Great American War Movies* (Reading, MA: Addison-Wesley, 1978), 313–17. Conversely, culture writer Maureen Orth reported ". . . the U.S. Department of Defense refused to cooperate with the project in any way." "Watching the 'Apocalypse,' " *Newsweek*, 13 June 1977, 58.
20. Frank Rich, "The Making of a Quagmire," *Time*, 27 August 1979, 55,57.
21. See Richard Grenier, "Coppola's Folly," *Commentary* 68, 4, October 1979, 67.
22. *Notes*, 177.
23. Christopher Sharrett, "Operation Mind Control: *Apocalypse Now* and the Search for Clarity," *Journal of Popular Film and Television* 8:1, Spring 1980, 34–35.
24. Quoted in McBride, 5.
25. English.
26. Quoted in "The Doors: The Fire's Still Burning," MTV Special, 1 July 1984. Also see Albert Goldman, *Freak Show* (N.Y.: Atheneum 1971), 339–45.
27. *Notes*, 279. The similarities between Morrison and Coppola are more than coincidental. Manzarek on CNN's "Day Watch" observed, "When you're looking at a Doors film you're actually looking into 1968."
28. Sharrett, 39.
29. Michael Herr, *Dispatches* (New York: Avon Books 1978), 258.

30. Poll, "Apocalypse Now," *Variety,* 16 May 1979, 20.
31. Rich, 57.
32. Quoted in "Doors Gone, Disks Selling," *Billboard,* 20 October 1979, 10.
33. Smith, 151.
34. Bill Barol, "The Eighties Are Over, *Newsweek,* 4 January 1988, 42.
35. Quoted in Anthony DeCurtis, " 'Top Gun' a Victory for the Marketing Men," *Rolling Stone,* 25 September 1986, 21.
36. Quoted in Richard Halloran, "Guardians of the Screen Image," *New York Times,* 18 August 1986, A12.
37. Quoted in Jacob V. Lamar, Jr., "The Pentagon Goes Hollywood," *Time,* 24 November 1986, 30.
38. ABC News, *20/20,* Stone Phillips, "The Battle to Make 'Platoon,' " 26 March 1987.
39. Jacob V. Lamar, Jr., 30; Vincent Canby, "Vintage Plotting Propels Mach II Planes in 'Top Gun,' " *New York Times,* 8 June 1986, sec. 2, 23.
40. David Ansen, "Cruise Guns for the Top," *Newsweek,* 9 June 1986, 73.
41. Quoted in Dan Yakir, "Kelly McGillis: Earth Angel," *Interview* 17, October 1987, 65.
42. *"Top Gun," Variety,* 14 May 1986, 14.
43. Vincent Canby, "Vintage Plotting," 23.
44. Nancy Kolomitz, *"Top Gun," Film Journal* 89, June 1986, 13. See also David Denby, "Pop Gun," *New York,* 19 May 1986, 102; Vincent Canby, "Vintage Plotting," 23; Lawrence O'Toole, *Maclean's,* 26 May 1986, 57.
45. Quoted in Margot Dougherty, "1 + 1 = $935 Million: Two *Top Gun* Producers See Eye to Eye and Make Back-to-Back Megahits," *LIFE,* 10 April 1987, 98.
46. Quoted in Kevin Lally, "Simpson & Bruckheimer Have High Hopes For Jet Pilot Tale," *Film Journal,* 9 May 1986, 5.
47. Ibid., 5.
48. Alexander Cockburn, "The Selling of the Pentagon?" *American Film,* 11 June 1986, 31.
49. Ibid., 32.
50. Ibid., 32.
51. *20/20* interview.
52. Ibid., 52. In retrospect, some officers wish that the Navy had cooperated in the making of *Officer* because that film also aided recruiting efforts. *Officer* was refused Pentagon assistance because it had too much sex, violence, and profanity. "As soon as we start offending the mothers and fathers in Iowa and Indiana," said Robert Manning, who evaluates commercial films projects for the Navy Department, "we are counterproductive." Quoted in Richard Halloran, "Guardians," A2.
53. Quoted in Joanne Kaufman, "Pentagon Lends a Hand—Sometimes," *Wall Street Journal*, 23 June 1987, 28.
54. Telephone interview with Lt. Col. Sandra Stairs, 20 July 1987.
55. Quoted in Richard Halloran, "Guardians," A12.
56. Telephone interview with Donald Baruch, 17 July 1987.
57. Jacob V. Lamar Jr., "The Pentagon Goes Hollywood," 30.
58. Quoted in Alexander Cockburn, "The Selling of the Pentagon?" 31.
59. J. Hoberman, "Phallus in Wonderland," *Village Voice,* 27 May 1986, 59.
60. David Denby, "Pop Gun," 102–3.

61. J. Hoberman, "Phallus in Wonderland," 52.

62. Quoted in Joanne Kaufman, "Pentagon Lends," 28.

63. *20/20* interview and Alexander Cockburn, 31.

64. Quoted in Kevin Lally, 5.

65. Quoted in Cockburn, 52.

66. Cockburn, 52.

67. Lawrence O'Toole, 57.

68. Nancy Kolomitz, 13.

69. Vincent Canby, 24; J. Hoberman, 59.

70. Cockburn, 52.

71. Richard Halloran, A2.

72. Michael D. P. Flynn, *"Top Gun:* 'It's not just a job . . .' it's a movie!" *All Hands: Magazine of the U.S. Navy* No. 830 (May 1986): 22.

73. Quoted in Anthony DeCurtis, " 'Top Gun' A Victory," 21.

74. Quoted in Chris McGowan, "Soundtrack Fastlane Already Facing Congestion As Labels Strengthen Crossover Links In Marketing Chain," *Billboard,* 21 June 1986, S6.

75. Quoted in Geoff Mayfield, " 'Top Gun' In Fast Takeoff At Retail," *Billboard,* 28 March 1987, 75.

76. See "Do Top Guns Swig Diet Pop?" *Time,* 9 March 1987, 65; Jim McCullaugh, "Price, Pepsi Fuel 'Top Gun' Launch for Paramount Video," *Billboard,* 24 January 1987, 81.

77. See Tom Bierbaum, " 'Top Gun' Cassettes In Record Takeoff: 1,900,000 Units," *Variety,* 4 March 1987, 124.

78. Quoted in Joanne Kaufman, "Pentagon Lends a Hand," 28.

79. Vincent Canby, "Film: The Vietnam War in Stone's 'Platoon'," *New York Times,* 19 December 1986, C12.

80. William Broyles, Jr., "Why Men Love War," *Esquire,* November 1984, 61; Susan Jeffords, "The New Vietnam Films: Is the Movie Over?" *Journal of Popular Film and Television,* 13 Winter 1986, 186.

81. Richard Corliss, "A Document Written in Blood," *Time,* 15 December 1986, 83.

82. Quoted in Fred Schruers, "Soldier's Story," *Rolling Stone,* 29 January 1987, 24.

83. Quoted in Richard Corliss, "Platoon: Viet Nam, the Way It Really Was, on Film," *Time,* 26 January 1987, 59.

84. Quoted in Corliss, "Platoon," 59.

85. Ibid., 60.

86. Quoted in Fred Schruers, "Soldier's Story," 24.

87. Quoted in Corliss, "Platoon," 60.

88. Quoted in David Ansen with Peter McClevey, "A Ferocious Vietnam Elegy," *Newsweek,* 5 January 1987, 57.

89. Quoted in Fred Schruers, "Soldier's Story," 26.

90. Alan Richman, "For His Look Back in Anger at Vietnam, *Platoon*'s Oliver Stone is Bombarded with Oscar Nominations," *People,* 2 March 1987, 87.

91. Quoted in Alan Richman, 88.

92. Quoted in Alex Ben Block, "Getting Respect," *Forbes,* 6 April 1987, 170.

93. Quoted in Alan Richman, 87.

94. Ibid., 85.

95. Quoted in Ansen and McAlevey, 57.
96. Dan Goodgame, "How the War Was Won," *Time,* 26 January 1987, 58.
97. Ibid., 58.
98. Ibid., 58.
99. Quoted in Ansen and McAlevey, 57.
100. Quoted in Goodgame, 58.
101. Quoted in Richman, 85.
102. Bob Brewin, "Hollywood Takes on Vietnam," *Video,* October 1987, 55.
103. Quoted in Richman, 85.
104. Quoted in Michael Norman, " 'Platoon' Grapples With Vietnam," *New York Times,* 21 December 1986, sec. 2, 18.
105. *20/20* interview.
106. Ron Rosenbaum, "The Ultimate Horror Movie," *Mademoiselle,* April 1987, 98. See also Vincent Canby, C12; Michael Norman, 17–18; J. Hoberman, "At War With Ourselves," *Village Voice,* 23 December 1986, 79, 82.
107. Quoted in Fred Schruers, 24.
108. J. Hoberman, 79, 82.
109. Ansen and McClevey, 57.
110. Quoted in Fred Schruers, 53.
111. Quoted in Richard Corliss, "Platoon," 59.
112. Quoted in Richard Corliss, 56, 58.
113. Several reviewers noted this. See Hubert Cohen, rev. of 'Platoon,' *Magill's Cinema Annual 1987: Survey of the Films of 1986* (Englewood Cliffs, N.J.: Salem Press 1987), 358; rev. of "Platoon," *Variety,* 3 December 1986, 19.
114. Quoted in Jack Anderson and Dale Van Atta, "Why the Pentagon Didn't Like 'Platoon,' " *Washington Post,* 30 August 1987, C7.
115. Ibid. The Defense Department keeps a tight line on their story. In an ABC News *20/20* interview, Capt. Nancy LaLuntas, USMC, Department of Defense, used almost the exact words: "It portrayed rampant drug abuse, the stereotypical black soldiers, there were constant brutalities being committed. . . ."
116. Op. cit., Anderson and Van Atta, C7. See also rev. of 'Platoon,' *Variety,* 3 December 1986, 19.
117. *20/20* interview.
118. *Ibid.*
119. Quoted in Richard Corliss, "Platoon," 56, 57.
120. Ibid., 56.
121. Ibid., 57.
122. Quoted in Dave DiMartino, "3 Labels Storm Market With 'Platoon' Songs," *Billboard,* 18 April 1987, 83.
123. Ibid., 83.
124. Ibid., 83.
125. Quoted in Robert Koehler, "Kubrick As Reporter—Distanced Docu-Fiction," *Los Angeles Times,* 5 July 1987, 24.
126. Quoted in Francis X. Clines, "Stanley Kubrick's Vietnam," *New York Times,* 21 June 1987, 14.
127. Quoted in Marc Cooper, "Light at The End of The Tunnel," *American Film* June 1987, 11.
128. Tim Cahill "Rolling Stone Interview" *Rolling Stone,* 27 August 1987, 32.

129. Cahill, 32.
130. Jack Kroll "1968: Kubrick's Vietnam Odyssey," *Newsweek,* 29 June 1987, 64; Sheila Benson, "One Hits Its Target; Another Nearly Does," *Los Angeles Times,* 26 June 1987, 8.
131. Janet Maslin, "Inside The 'Jacket,' " *New York Times,* 5 July 1987, 17.
132. Quoted in Richard Gold, "Warners Drawing On 'Platoon' Comparisons To Plug 'Jacket,' " *Variety,* 8 July 1987, 4.
133. Vincent Canby, "Kubrick's 'Full Metal Jacket' on Vietnam," *New York Times,* 26 June 1987, C3.
134. Richard Corliss, "Welcome to Vietnam, The Movie," *Time* 29 June 1987, 66.
135. Penelope Gilliatt, "Heavy Metal," *American Film,* September 1987, 21.
136. Benson, 8.
137. Corliss, 66; Kroll, 64; Ed Kelleher, "Full Metal Jacket," *Film Journal,* July 1987, 17.
138. Gilliatt, 50.
139. Todd McCarthy, "Full Metal Jacket," *Variety,* 24 June 1987, 12.
140. Jack Mathews, "Always Expecting The Very Best From Stanley Kubrick," *Los Angeles Times,* 7 July 1987, 1 (se. VI).
141. Terrence Rafferty, "Films," *Nation,* 1 August 1987, 98; J. Hoberman, "Dressed to Kill," *Village Voice,* 7 July 1987, 55.
142. Alexander Walker, "Stanley Kubrick's War Realities," *Los Angeles Times,* 21 June 1987, 28.
143. Quoted in Michael Reese, "Black Humor Goes To War," 4 January 1988, 50.
144. Quoted in John Culhane, "Robin Williams Belts Out Verbal Jazz in 'Vietnam,' " *New York Times,* 20 December 1987, 26.
145. "Good Morning, Vietnam," *Variety,* 23 December 1987, 15.
146. "Robin Williams: Rolling Stone Interview" *Rolling Stone,* 25 February 1988, 31.
147. "Robin Owes His Best Role To a Real Deejay—Goooood Morning, Adrian Cronauer," *People,* 22 February 1988, 84.
148. Rod Lurie, "Hollywood Courts Uncle Sam," *Premiere,* September 1989, 37–40.

12

Holy Boxoffice, Batman!

The late Eighties were boom years for studios and labels, fueled by compact-disk sales. The growth, interestingly, neglected to propel soundtrack sales which were flat. Many tried; most failed. Once again filmmakers and those of the record companies were going in separate directions, despite the homilies.

In early 1987 *Dirty Dancing* and its followup package had dominated the record and CD charts. A potential chartbuster like *Light of Day*, starring Michael J. Fox and rocker Joan Jett, with a Springsteen contribution, barely climbed to number 82 on the *Billboard* listing. Steven Spielberg's *An American Tail*, featuring the Linda Ronstadt-James Ingram duet "Somewhere Out There," reached number 42. For soundtrack aficionados, the *Beverly Hills Cop* sequel looked promising.

Cop II "Isn't a Sequel, It's a Heart Attack"

"If at first one succeeds, do it again" is the magic Hollywood formula of the Eighties. Coming-of-age and salt'n'pepper action flicks and sequels have dominated theater screens. The successful followups generate more imitations. Timid studios, almost compulsively, roll the dice one more time.

As crap shooters Don Simpson and Jerry Bruckheimer were hot. In a four-year span "the boys," a studio designation, grossed an estimated $1.4 billion, $500 million of that went into Paramount's corporate coffers. "They're hitting the pulse of the theater audience like no one else," said the president of National Exhibitor. "They've got the best track record in town."[1]

Savoring *Top Gun*'s box office, the duo was pitched a concept for a followup to *Beverly Hills Cop* by Eddie Murphy and his manager, Bob Wachs. "Bob came to us and said, 'What do you think of this,' and we said, 'It's a great idea,' and that's when we jumped and got Larry Ferguson to start writing it," Bruckheimer recalled.[2]

Simpson and Bruckheimer decided to employ *Top Gun*'s Tony Scott to direct, replacing Martin Brest, as he was "dying to work with Eddie Murphy."

Beverly Hills Cop was Murphy's personality vehicle, akin to the Presley offerings in the 1960s. As one scribe suggested, *Beverly Hills Cop II* "is a sign of a career heading down Elvis Presley Boulevard." Simpson, may not have appreciated the comparison, but he acknowledged, "This is an Eddie Murphy movie. You could kill off every character, but you wouldn't have *Beverly Hills Cop* without Eddie." Bruckheimer also saw the project as a Murphy showcase, saying, "It's a continuation of the adventures of Axel Foley [Murphy]." Scott, recalling the original gross of $350 million, told the *Film Journal*, "You always set yourself up to be shot down with a sequel."[3] The director, prophetically, anticipated critical reaction.

Scott reunited the original cast of cops pitted against a trio of villains—Dean Stockwell, Brigitte Nielson, and *Das Boot*'s Jurgen Prochnow.

The $27-million production, scheduled for a pre-Memorial Day debut, was filmed in Southern California with a few location sets in Detroit. The film was brought in at $31 million, due to postproduction outlays. Most of the overage was due to reshooting Murphy's improvised scenes and soundtrack costs.

Cop had enjoyed a $5-million marketing campaign. The sequel was less expensive, but still "high, wide and handsome," according to Simpson. Posters and newspaper ads featured Murphy leaning on a Beverly Hills marker captioned "Back Where He Doesn't Belong." A music trailer was produced with Bob Seger's "Shakedown." MTV aired it simultaneously with the film's national spread in 2,326 media.

With the notable exception of *Top Gun*, supervised by CBS Records, Simpson and Bruckheimer soundtracks have never been marketed synergistically. *Flashdance* lucked out, due to MTV time buys. *Cop* had proved to be a postproduction, clip-and-paste job, with some help from Irving Azoff. The sequel was even more chaotic.

Postproduction for the average film is eight months; *Beverly Hills Cop II* was crammed into a six-week period described by Simpson as "*totally impossible.*"

Kathy Nelson, the MCA vice president who supervised the soundtrack, said, "There was an incredibly short postproduction period, which can make things very difficult. The creative process does not happen overnight, especially when you're dealing with different writers, producers, and artists."[4]

Cop had moved more than 5 million soundtracks. During a prerelease interview, Bruckheimer was asked about the follow-up. "The Pointer Sisters will probably be back," he replied. "We are in the process of putting it together right now, so we don't know absolutely yet who will be on it!"[5]

Glenn Frey, whose "The Heat Is On" was in *Cop*, was pitched the opening song, "Shakedown." He didn't care for the lyrics and in any case contracted laryngitis nine days before the recording session. Irving Azoff, the label's president, recruited Bob Seger, everybody's soundtrack backup. Keeping the chorus "Shakedown, breakdown, you're busted," Seger rewrote the song. It was in the studio four days later.

Nelson scored a coup by having George Michael's (formerly with Wham) first solo cut included on the soundtrack. The song was a marketing plus—more than anyone imagined. Michael's manager was delighted, being aware of the difficulty of having CBS work with another label, as he "felt this as the perfect bridge" between a previous project and the forthcoming *Faith* album. He told a trade reporter, "CBS has a very big investment. He's [Michael] one of its major artists, and it's obviously concerned to make sure his records go out to radio and that his image is out there. CBS was kind enough to allow us to put the song on the MCA soundtrack, but we were always concerned that it had the rights to the single."[6]

On 4 May radio station programmers opened their mail to find advance copies of *Cop II*. The Seger cut received heavy rotation. One hundred thirty-eight Top-40 stations added the single 20 May, its first week out. "Shakedown," beginning its climb to the top of the chart, was easily overwhelmed by the publicity surrounding George Michael's "I Want Your Sex."

The song created a furor in the year of "safe sex." Some stations avoided the title altogether, preferring the "new George Michael song for *Cop II*." WPLJ's (New York) PD Larry Berger was cautious. "I just wasn't comfortable with that record in these times," he said.[7]

CBS, in the process of rush-releasing the single, decided to issue a less attractive, three-version CD to placate programmers.

MTV's standards person—as in censor—demanded three re-edits of the video. The final version had no reference to the motion picture. To stress monogamy, Michael used his girlfriend Kathy Jueng in the clip.

The BBC banned the song from its daytime playlist as the lyric "goes against the grain. It tries to encourage sex."[8]

"All press is good press," to paraphrase George Bernard Shaw, worked. The single was number 3 in the United Kingdom. Across the Atlantic the title reached number 2 and propelled *Faith* into a monster hit.

Cop II premiered 20 May beating the summer glut, on 2,300 screens, the largest exhibition in Paramount history.

The film begins with a jewelry-store heist on Rodeo Drive led by Karla (Brigitte Nielson). The depository is reduced to broken pieces of glass and plastic. The Alphabet Gang has struck again.

Meanwhile, in Detroit, as "Shakedown" accompanies the opening credits, Axel Foley prepares for his high-style undercover gig in Italian suits, $200 ties and a $67,000 red Ferrari which, as Curry observed, "makes Foley look like the star of *Detroit Gigolo*."[9] The undercover assignment is identical to that in the original, except that credit cards have replaced cigarettes. Inspector Todd (Gil Hill) again serves as Foley's nemesis.

Learning that Capt. Bogomil (Ronny Cox) has been wounded, Axel steals away to Tinseltown, where "I'm going deep, deep, deep undercover."

"Better Way" provides the source music for Axel's quick tour of Beverly Hills, where he is reunited with Rosewood (Judge Reinhold) and Taggart (John Ashton). The threesome vow to "solve this." What follows are a series of vignettes unsuccessfully attempting what Don Simpson called "dromedy—part drama, part comedy." Tracking down the Alphabet Gang involves comedic skits, car chases, and a few dramatic moments but none are sustained long enough to develop character or a cohesive storyline. "This is one of the worst scripts ever written for a film budgeted over $1.5 million. Subplots are introduced, and then completely abandoned Clues are introduced with lumbering unsubtlety and then Axel uses these clues with a dexterity that would shame Sherlock Holmes. And the entire crime scenario, as stated, is botched when it's not completely incomprehensible," Matthews asserted.[10]

The Alphabet Gang led, we discover, by gun-runner Maxwell Dent, (Jurgen Prochnow) attempts a heist at the City Deposit building. The plot is foiled, with an ensuing Brinks truck chase and the obligatory police-car pileup.

In pursuit of Dent, Karla, and sub-boss Charlie Cain (Dean Stockwell), the trio arrives at the Playboy Mansion in a cement truck. Even Murphy can't save this sequence.

Foley solves the mystery, realizing that the Alphabet crimes were a cover for Dent to accumulate capital to finance his Latin-American gun-running operation. The *tour de force* is the robbery of Dent's racetrack, during which Karla wastes the gang.

The close is a replay of the original, even to the parting line, "Trust me." James Ingram's "Better Way" accompanies the end credits.

II is "*de ja vu* all over again," as Yogi Berra said. "There is an inherent problem about any sequel that too slavishly duplicates the style and substance of its predecessor," wrote Schickel. "It cannot deliver the delight of discovery that the original provided." Similarly, Maslin wrote that *II* "can't match the first film's novelty, or recapture the excitement of watching a great comic character like Axel Foley as first came to life."[11]

Noting the film's lack of originality, several writers proffered a strictly economic motive for the motion picture. Travers said, "Murphy may still be a sure thing at the box office, but this time he has shortchanged himself and his audience." Another critic found Murphy "strapped to a golden Xerox machine that duplicates setups and box-office receipts."

"*Cop II* is a robotic, hard-sell sequel by folks whose Malibu beach-house-mortgage payment is due," zinged Mike Clark. *Boxoffice's* writer found it "shameless nonsense" and "a coldly calculated money-making machine."[12]

David Denby devoted three pages to discussing the lowest-common-denominator approach in film production as typified by *Cop II*, "arguably the worst movie ever to become a monster hit."[13]

While a majority of critics were either lukewarm or avowedly negative, a few did warm up to *Cop II*. "If you liked *Beverly Hills Cop*, then you will like *II*," Buckley said. *Video's* Ira Robbins wrote, "Given the altogether sorry creative history of cinematic sequels, it's both a surprise and a pleasure to report that *Beverly Hills Cop II* neatly breaks that tradition by improving on the original in virtually every way."[14]

During the film's opening three weeks its box office was $84 million. At the end of 1987, the studio's return was $80 million, some $28 million less than the original.

The soundtrack experienced a similar fate. *Cop II*, fueled by the chart-topping "Shakedown," the Michael controversy, and The Jets' "Cross My Broken Heart," had managed to penetrate the LP Top 10 for twenty-six weeks. The 1985 title had been number 1 for several weeks, with a sixty-two-week chart life. *Cop II* managed a platinum certification.

Cop II was the top-grossing film of 1987, surpassing Oliver Stone's Academy-award-winning *Platoon*. It was one of two platinum soundtracks: *Dirty Dancing* easily outperformed *Cop II* at the music merchandisers.

Lost Boy, Less Than Zero

> *Well, if I bought a soundtrack album, I would*
> *want all the songs that are in the movie to be*

*on the album. If they gave me something ex-
tra, I would thank them.*
—Don Simpson, producer

Director Joel Schumacher (*Car Wash, St. Elmo's Fire*) paired two *Stand By Me* stalwarts—Kiefer Sutherland and Corey Feldman—with would-be Brat Packers for his $18-million "gothic tale of beach-bum town Santa Clara," described by some residents as "the murder capital of the world."

The summer punker vampire comedy, *The Lost Boys*, opened with little fanfare the last day of July 1987.

The tale opens peacefully enough with a shot of the glistening Santa Cruz bay with a female ensemble singing the chorus from "Cry Little Sister:" "Thou shall not want, thou shalt not need . . ."

At the arcade, overlooking the picturesque environ, teenagers mill about as a group of punk bikers are evicted. Opening credits roll with a scan of the burned-out hippies, homeless people, tourists, and assorted weirdos on the boardwalk. A cover of the Doors' "People Are Strange" by Echo and the Bunnymen is overlayed.

Refugees from Phoenix arrive. Lucy (Dianne Wiest) who is fleeing a failed marriage, and her offspring Michael (Jason Patric) and his younger brother Sam (Corey Haim) move in with their creepy, eccentric grandfather. Their host establishes himself as an oddball early by proclaiming, "I just read *TV Guide*; then I don't need a television."

The boys visit the arcade, just in time for Tim Cappello's performance of "I Still Believe." Michael spies Star (Jami Gertz) in the crowd.

Sam visits the comic-book outlet only to encounter the Frog Brothers, Edgar and Alan, played by Feldman and Jamison Newlander. The Ramboesque duo are devoted to the Superman credo while destroying vampires they believe are responsible for the milk-carton missing children.

Mike finally engages Star in conversation, only to be challenged to a motorbike race, *a la Rebel Without a Cause*, with Roger Daltrey's "Don't Let the Sun Go Down On Me" providing background.

The leader of the pack, David (Sutherland), is impressed. Michael is invited to the lair, the ruins of a resort hotel guarded by a huge Jim Morrison poster. David offers, "Drink some of this; be one of us." "Michael," the gang chants as "Cry Little Sister" plays. The seductiveness of evil is presented as the supernatural quartet suggest their powers on a railroad trestle. Michael is merely confused, as is the viewer.

Michael now is prone to sleep all day while eyeing Sam as a potential victim. The aspiring vampire makes an unsuccessful attempt at Sam as Clarence "Frogman" Henry's falsetto echoes "Ain't Got No Home." The family dog intervenes.

"You're a creature of the night," Sam accuses Michael. "Just like in the comic book." The Frog brothers, in combat fatigues, are summoned.

Michael is torn between his family and Star, who beds him. The Frogs urge Sam to "Kill your brother; you'll feel better."

Lucy, who has found a job at the local video store, is dating its proprietor Max (Ed Herrmann), whom the Frogs suspect is the chief vampire. A false start.

Michael is eventually put to the test at a blood-feast when David asserts, "The initiation is over, time to join the club . . . never grow old, Michael, you will never die. *But* you must feed." Michael flees.

The Frog Brothers are still in pursuit. They find the lair. The confrontation is at hand. As the *Post*'s Howe summarized, "They decide to identify and kill the vamp *meister* before Mike becomes a card-carrying neck-nosher. They load up on garlic, holy water and wooden stakes. The sparks will fly. The house will howl. The ending will be happy."[15] Not much has changed since Bram Stoker.

Variety's Todd McCarthy found the quasi-horror picture "blatantly pitched at the lowest common denominator of the adolescent audience, unholy brew qualifies as undoubtedly the dumbest summer release to date."

"Well, you know," replied Jimmy Summers, "it *is* a vampire movie. It's not a science documentary. It's not suppose to be taken seriously."[16] The *Boxoffice* reviewer was supported by most writers. They found the movie to be a mix of comedy with "teen-drama MTV horror," underscored by Michael Chapman's cinematography and a resonant rock score. *People's* Jim Calio wrote, "This is, after all, a summer movie, and if it's nothing to really sink your fangs into, it's often very funny." The flick, according to Ansen, was "no more about real horror than Michael Jackson's 'Thriller' video. It's a sleek, decadent entertainment about the seductions of teenage style."

"It's not timeless," shrugged another critic, "but timely, sardonic and shrewd."[17]

Certainly *Lost Boys* failed to put Christopher Lee out of business. As a production addressing a youth market it appeared to have, partially, succeeded. Arguably, *Boys* was far more entertaining than the slasher, first-seduction teen fare projected during the summer months.

Atlantic Records pursued a traditional MTV strategy. Inxs's "Good Times" debuted 3 June and remained three months in heavy rotation. Three weeks later the .45 charted. The FM listing easily outperformed the Hot 100. By August the single peaked at number 47 while the LP cut showed at a respectable number 3. By the first week of September, "Good

Times" had vanished. No matter, the band's 1987–1988 tour was being planned.

The compilation entered the charts simultaneously with the film's premiere. Starting at number 183, it peaked at number 15.

The standard, ten-song project was half filler. "Ain't Got No Home" was absent. The most memorable cut, "Cry Little Sister" was not highlighted. Indeed, the film version is quite different from the PCV rendition.

The music placement in *Lost Boys* remarkably was superior to most films. The marketing choices were disappointing relying on artist visibility and label affiliation. The album enjoyed a thirty-two week chart tenure, winning gold.

Lost Boys earned $5.2 million in box office action its initial weekend playing 1,027 arenas. The figure was half that of the James Bond vehicle, *Living Daylights*, released the same weekend. By the third week the gross was a tidy $18 million. The teen pic returned to Warner Bros. $14.1 when the rentals were computed.

Cop II and *Lost Boys* found considerable competition in the summer-track sweepstakes: An estimated twenty titles had been scheduled for issuance. Once the hype had cleared, the Ritchie Valens's bio-pic *La Bamba* and the incredible Dirty Dancing joined *Cop II* in the platinum arena.

The euphoria begun in 1984 was ebbing, with dissent on the rise. Studios were increasingly irrate over costs. Labels, absorbing tons of dealer rejects, spoke of the law-of-diminishing returns. "It just makes things worse for everybody by adding one more forgettable soundtrack to a glut in the marketplace," said Joe Regis, "which retailers don't know how to deal with in the first place."[18] Despite the reservations, there was still more product in the pipeline.

Billboard's boxscore for the summer of 1987 was captioned "Movies Hot, Music Not." Steve Gett reported that while summer box office was the highest in history, "*only* two of the top-grossing domestic films were supported by hot soundtrack albums."[19] The writer went on to suggest the other popular films had made money without hot soundtracks. Nonetheless, others were awaiting their spin of the wheel.

*   *   *

It means saying no to your friends and to peer pressure
—Jon Avnet, producer

Reflecting on the pre-safe-sex mores of the Me Generation, Bret Easton Ellis wrote *Less Than Zero*, a graphic novel about affluent Southern

California youth drifting from shining Corvettes to in-crowd clubs, from cocaine to bisexuality. Twentieth Century-Fox optioned the manuscript for $7,500. The studio became excited when the book entered the best-seller lists.

Pulitzer-Prize-winning author Michael Cristofer was commissioned to write the screenplay. He retained Ellis's original thesis, that people can be destroyed by "having everything." 20th Century deemed the script unacceptable, that is, had no commercial potential.

Twentieth Century's production president, Scott Rubin, was determined to adapt the book to the screen. "It came about because we had a real passion for the material," he said. "We thought if we put a story in that would be more compelling and emotional than the story in the book, we would have a shot at catching lightning in a bottle, a chance to do one of those pictures like *The Graduate*, one of those pictures that seem to define a generation."[20]

The project was assigned to *Risky Business* producer Jon Avnet. Predictably, his reaction to the Cristofer script proved negative. "I felt it was so depressing and so degrading," he told the *New York Times*. "A crucial element of the American dream had gone haywire, and you had to put it in recognizable form in a movie, not just shock people." Scripter Harley Peyton was hired to do the rewrite. He later complained, "I did three drafts, and the rules did change daily under my feet."[21]

The final draft was very different. "*Less Than Zero* is a kind of pre-AIDS book," explained Peyton, "so it has a different notion of sexuality than I think you can have now."[22] The conservatively budgeted $8-million production had less than zero to do with the novel or the original screenplay. Instead, the narrative is more of a "just-say-no" commercial, with fortitude and social responsibility—"one thousand points of light"—triumphing over decadent self-indulgence. In a prerelease interview, Avnet stressed the new focus: "It makes a strong statement about friendship and the consequences of certain lifestyles. It accurately portrays a world that exists without, I think, promulgating the lifestyle. Its seductions are presented while ignoring the reality it creates."[23]

The theme of the film is confronting the big myth of doing one's own thing. "People feel," said the producer, "I want to be independent and on my own, yet I still sleep in my parents' home. The drives and aspirations are strong, yet contradicted by dependent behavior. The film also explores an important fact that is difficult to understand: why people want to destroy themselves, what it is about life that makes people want to die. Certainly the hedonist Julian is a memorable character that everyone will feel they know."[24]

The marketing hook for the film was teen idol Andrew McCarthy (*St. Elmo's Fire, Pretty in Pink*) and the conspicuous consumption of the milieu. Young women, noted 20th Century's Scott Rubin, want "to live in a great apartment, have a great boyfriend and wear great clothes."[25] To bridge the gap between opulence and excess, the studio utilized the slogan, "It only looks like a good life."

The film debuted 6 November on 867 screens during a season in which the theater audience is believed older than during the teen-dominated summer months.

Paralleling *St. Elmo's Fire*, the film opens with a high school graduation photo of Blair (Jami Gertz), Clay (Andrew McCarthy), and Julian (Robert Downey, Jr.). The tight-knit trio dissolves as Clay, in keeping with his social class, goes East to college.

He returns to Lotusland with the knowledge that his best friend has bonded with Blair. After a *Cop II* tour of the "in joints," accompanied by opening credits and The Bangles "Hazy Shade of Winter," Clay begins a party crawl, with ever-present background music.

At an opulent Christmas gathering (television monitors cover a wall), Clay encounters Blair, Julian, and a pusher-procurer, Rip, ably acted by James Spader. A poor cover of Kiss's "Rock 'n' Roll All Nite" resonates. Every subsequent party is similarly structured. Each festivity features a new selection plus a vignette. The only tie seems to be Clay's vintage sports car.

As the film, wrote Galbraith, "tracks this angst-ridden trio in a cool, red Corvette convertible between their expensive homes, trendy clubs and other locales, a mood is formed that all is rotten underneath, like a big shiny red apple with a worm in it."[26]

Clay, who appears too preppy-straight for a fast-line life-style, discovers that Blair is a heavy social user. Julian is a dedicated "coke head," $50,000 in debt to Rip. The dealer demands the money or Julian's sexual services.

Why these affluent denizens of West Los Angeles participate in the rites of Dionysus remains muddled. "The movie solemnly inflates these kids' Tragic Dilemma while letting them off the moral hook by blaming their rich, lame parents and the evils of The Scene," Ansen wrote.[27] Julian's familial estrangement nags at him. Blair's father is distant. Clay participates in a "warm" holiday feast *and* he is the nonuser.

On Blair's behest, Clay reluctantly—"Want me to call Betty Ford and get him a room?"—attempts to reach out to Julian, to no avail. Rip and the upper-class derelicts' growing habit accelerate the descent into Dante's Inferno. His pleas for help fall on deaf parental ears.

In the meantime, Clay and Blair resume their relationship, with several gratuitous love scenes. (One occurs in the sports car parked in the middle of the street as bikers race by.) The coupling continues, strengthened by a mutual desire to save their wayward comrade. After Julian has another gutterside bout with drugs, they rescue him. Clay finally knows, "I'll do whatever I can . . . whatever it takes." He confronts Rip. The pusher retorts insightfully, "I'm not the problem, here, Julian is! He's dead. Forget about him."

Drug rehabilitation workers would cringe at the film's moralistic conclusion. Julian, verbally determined to clean up, protests that he must first go to Palm Springs to see the dealer. (As Wilmington asked "Couldn't he have phoned?")[28] Not really, as the denouement takes place in the luxurious retreat and on the road back. The closing scene, as several reviewers were quick to note, could have been scripted by Nancy Reagan's speechwriters.

Clay and Blair pursue their self-destructive pal, managing to free him from Rip's homosexual clients. With a bright future in sight, Julian expires on the road to Los Angeles. Roy Orbison's prophetic and powerful "Life Fades Away" overscores the end credits.

Avnet's attempt to transform Ellis's stream-of-consciousness novel into a structured narrative failed. Individual scenes akin to MTV long-form videos momentarily had appeal, but ninety-eight minutes of disjointed nonstop clips can be disorienting.

"I liked the book, better," is a statement frequently heard as filmgoers exit a theater. Screen adaptations—*The Children's Hour, 9 1/2 Weeks*—frequently sacrifice the original text at the altar of commerciality. 20th Century's tinkering with the Ellis novel was widely publicized. "I'm sure I'll hate whatever anyone does," the author insisted, "but it doesn't matter. I sold it."[29]

A bevy of critics called the film a bastardization of the novel, "a wild, preachy melodrama," or "a shallow swipe at a serious problem."

"Imagine Antonioni making a high school public-service movie and you'll have an inkling of the movie's high-minded silliness." wrote Ansen. "The film script, by Harley Peyton reduces Ellis's sensibilities to those of a public service announcement about drug abuse," noted Haller. "This is *Less Than Zero* as it might be rewritten by Nancy Reagan."

"Where the novel was studiedly amoral, the movie is blatantly moralizing," said Hoberman. "There's too much affect and too little attitude." The *Los Angeles Times* review concluded, "Instead of making this hopped-up 'Just Say No' parable, it's a pity the filmmakers didn't zero in on the novel's true riches: its penetration into a scene and an attitude, its understated morality."[30]

Janet Maslin found herself a lone voice by approving Avnet's alterations. Ellis's material, she said, "would have been paralyzingly downbeat on screen," because "by the time it got to the book's scenes of ultimate depravity—the snuff film watched as casual entertainment, the gang-rape of a twelve-year-old-girl—a faithful film version would have cleared the house." The *New York Times* notice was the only positive piece in newspapers of record. The *Washington Post*'s critic wrote, "Just say no"—to the film.

The antagonists, Robert Downey, Jr. and James Spader, were the only bright spots in Avnet's endeavor. Kemply found that Spader was "easily the most effective member of the cast."[31] "Downey," according to *People*, "survives the script; he threatens to make his outcast character the soul of the movie."[32]

Zero's first weekend, at 867 theaters, grossed $3 million. After a month, the gross was a shade less than $10 million. The studio would eventually receive a rental return of $4.4 million on an $8 million investment.

CBS's marketing of the soundtrack appeared lackluster. In a departure from the *Footloose-Top Gun* strategy, The Bangles' "Hazy Shade of Winter" entered the singles chart at number 73 a week after the film's launch. MTV aired the Bangles video 7 November in a heavy rotation slot. The album was released a month later, 5 December, as the film's box office evaporated. (The Bangles did manage a number 2 single.)

The rock press ignored the package. A *Los Angeles Times* reviewer praised The Bangles and Orbison's "beautiful neo-classic" "Life Fades Away." Waller applauded Public Enemy's "Bring the Noise," L.L. Cool J's "Going Back to Cali," and Aerosmith's cover of "Rockin' Pneumonia."

Conversely, he continued, "Poison and Slayer, respectively, commit the unpardonable sin of rerecording straight-faced renditions of Kiss's 'Rock and Roll All Nite' and Iron Butterfly's 'In-A-Gadda-Da-Vida' (!), and the title track is NOT the Elvis Costello tune from which this multimedia assault springs forth like Minerva from the brow of Jove. Or should that be jive?" The ommission seems curious, as Costello was a CBS artist. The package sold over half-a-million copies.

At the close of 1987, a glaring statistic faced record labels. As video entertainment expanded, or exploded, hit rock soundtracks inversely diminished. The film studios reported a $4.25-billion take in 1987. Only two reached platinum—*Cop II* and *La Bamba*. Two more, *Lost Boys* and *Zero*, were awarded gold plaques. CBS Records' highly publicized synergistic knack had failed with the Jon Avnet production.

Dark clouds do have silver, nay, platinum, linings. A comedy set in the unlikely locale of Saigon, circa 1965, would propel a golden-oldies package up the charts. *Good Morning Vietnam*'s A&M soundtrack contained mostly source material barely recognizable in the Robin Williams spotlighter. Only James Brown's "I Got You" (I Feel Good) and Louis Armstrong's twenty-year-old "What a Wonderful World" enjoyed any prominence. (The latter became a moderate hit in early 1988.) The package's success can be easily attributed to the film and the zany Williams. Nostalgia compilations only work when integrated into films, especially period pieces like *Easy Rider*, *Graffiti*, *Big Chill*, *Stand By Me*, and *Dirty Dancing*. *Diner*, *Heaven Help Us*, and countless others, with superior selections, all expired without notice.

Film analysts had predicted that 1988 would be a banner year. VCR sales, rather than curtailing theater attendance, demonstrably increased interest. The pay-cable channels, HBO, TMC, Showtime, and Cinemax, hyped films with trailers. The record industry, conversely, continued to view the studios as a source of exposure. FM radio, once the labels' white knight, and MTV were brandishing restrictively tight playlists dominated by aging superstars. Film showcasing remained easier than cracking radio or television playlists for new acts. With considerably less fanfare, the quest for synergy went on.

C.R.A.S.H. of Colors

In 1955, Bosley Crowther had labeled *Blackboard Jungle* "social dynamite." Thirty-three years later, *Los Angeles Herald Examiner* reporter John Crust warned that the impending *Colors* would provoke gang violence. He quoted an authority who stated that upon exhibition of the film, Uzi-packing youth would "leave dead bodies from one end of this town [L.A.] to the other."[34]

The depiction of L.A. street gangs and frustrated police officers originated with tabloid headliner Sean Penn. "I'm much more known as Madonna's husband and someone who hits photographers than as an actor," he observed.[35] Dennis Hopper, who "couldn't get hired in Hollywood to direct traffic," reconceptualized the idea for Orion Pictures. The original script had a *Hill Street Blues*-style storyline in which Chicago gangs were dealing a narcotic found in cough syrup. Hopper found the notion of a "major cough-syrup bust" preposterous. He told executives, "Give me a break, man. Make it cocaine, make it real, make it Los Angeles." Their response was, "There are no gangs in Los Angeles." Hopper replied, "This wouldn't even make a bad episode of a television show. Why don't you make it an older cop and younger cop, make 'em white, make it about the L.A. gangs? Make it about real stuff."[36] With a revised script and stars Sean Penn and Robert Duvall, Hopper began a ten-week shoot in East Los Angeles, home to an estimated 70,000 gang members.

The location settings were situated in the San Pedro, Watts, and Boyle Heights districts. The filming was more suspenseful, perhaps, than the film. Academy-award-winning cinematographer Haskell Wexler recalled, "We worked in certain areas in South-Central L.A., where we were told we had to wear flak jackets. There were areas where the police couldn't help us."

"We shot at a project in Watts that even the police won't go into unless there's a body lying there," added the director.[37]

The soundtrack was generally left to Sharon Boyle, Warner Brothers Records music supervisor, as Hopper "wasn't really knowledgeable on the street music art form, but wanted a sense of timing and passage among scenes."[38] A number of rap artists were recruited. Ice-T did the pervasive title rendition. Sean Penn contributed to the film score by persuading John Cougar Mellencamp to allow the use of "Crumlin' Down." The song appeared in the movie, but not the album, which was issued 26 April, two weeks after the film.

Orion Pictures devised a "two-pronged" marketing compaign aimed at young, male action fans, and the older, quality-oriented crowd. Ads appeared, noting Dennis Hopper's *Rider* connection and stressing as well his critically acclaimed performances in *Blue Velvet* (1986) and *River's Edge* (1987). *Colors* was billed as "the first realistic motion picture about the war against street gangs."[39]

Orion coordinated its access to the action-film audience through the Warners soundtrack. Music trailers and spots used Ice-T's "Colors" rap to hype the film with an anti-gang message heard on radio.

The advertising drive was supplemented considerably by the well publicized threat of gang violence surrounding the motion picture. The Joe Crust piece had alarmed some Southern California community leaders. Lynwood's Youth Organized and United for Community Action Network promised a boycott. Los Angeles District Attorney Ira Reinder, conversely, expressed no objections to the "chilling" portrayal.

Curtis Sliwa, with four other Guardian Angels, was arrested picketing Orion Pictures' Manhattan offices. (Protestors had carried signs exclaiming "DEATH FOLLOWS COLORS" and "THE STREETS RUN *BLOODY* SAVE US FROM COLORS.")

In Chicago, Latino aldermen Jesus Garcia and Juan Soliz condemned the movie for glorifying gang violence. Neither had viewed the film. Public reaction, according to *Variety*, resulted in a "box office bonanza, with free publicity paying off to approximately $436,000 in picture's first week at 19 Chicago screens." No incidents were registered in the Windy City as "All the action took place on the screen and at the ticket window."[40]

The *Hollywood Reporter*'s Martin Grove warned, "Controversy typically doesn't help the box office. It could hurt multiplexes where *Colors* is playing next to other movies."[41] Ticket sales would refute this conclusion.

A handful of small California communities actually banned the film and several fistfights were reported in Hollywood.

Hopper protested, "Politicians should be doing something about it [the gang situation] instead of banning movies."[42]

The controversial production debuted 14 April. Following in the tradition of *Blackboard Jungle* (1955), *Colors* opens with the statement that 250 C.R.A.S.H. (Community Resources Against Street Hoodlams) officers are confronted by 70,000 gang-bangers (The outlaw groups accounted for "387 gang-related killings last year," read the closing narration.) To underscore the urgency, a van cruises dark, desolate streets. The occupants pass a joint, digging the rock music blaring from the radio. Spying a figure, one shouts, "Hey, Blood!" A burst from a shotgun explodes. Another drive-by killing has occurred.

The hopeless, Skinnerian maze of stimulus/response continues between the "homeboys," the Cribs and the crimson-attired Bloods.

Attempting unsuccessfully to stem the cycle of mindless slaughter are a band of specially assigned LAPD members.

Bob Hodges (Robert Duvall) and Danny "Pac Man" McGavin (Sean Penn) are the odd-couple inserted into the foray. They are direct opposites. The street-wise Hodges, a year away from retirement, is paired with the impetuous Pac Man, who exhibits an interest in "shooting anything that's black or brown and moves."[43] Hodges is not so concerned with minor "righteous collars." Rather, he attempts to cultivate a rapport with gang members, leading to the "big bust."

The film focuses on the cops' interaction in the context of the deadly war between the gangs. The members are nihilistic "rebels without a context," wrote Benson, who adheres to the belief that "Peace is a dream, reality is a knife." Identity is defined by the blue or red colors symbolic of gang affiliation.[44]

A police sweep places the gang rivals in adjoining jail cells, separated only by steel bars as they exchange threats and profanities. All the while their colors are swaying to the title track: "My colors's my honor . . . Wear the wrong color your life could end . . . ."

The strength of the film, brilliantly captured by Haskell Wexler, is its atmosphere. "The best thing in the picture is Wexler's cinematography," Larner stated, "which shows us an East Los Angeles there is never any need for nonresidents to see." Pauline Kael asserted that the film was "like an art tour of ghettos and barrios, of Watts and Venice and downtown L.A."

"What *Colors* does best is to create a sense of place and a climate of fear, to capture the vivid mark that gang life has left upon the downtown Los Angeles landscape," noted Maslin.[45]

The mood evocation is, essentially, what makes this two-hour production superior to a made-for-television drama. *Colors*, wrote Benson, "shot on weed-choked hills and graffiti-splashed culverts near downtown Los Angeles, gives a thin movie a substance that its screenplay is hard put to support." Moreover, it was a "melodrama in realistic clothing; decent intentions whittled down to soap-opera size by the flatness and predictability of the writing which undercuts much of the care and artistry built around it." Other critics complained about Michael Schiffer's script. Kael objected that the imminent retirement of Hodges is a tip-off: "We wait for the inevitable scene in which he'll be killed. (No, I'm not giving the plot away—unless this is the first movie you've ever seen.)"[46]

Specific sequences do stand out, such as the car chase, the restaurant bust, and the closing reenactment. The rest is painfully predictable, especially to *Hill Street Blues* mavens. "Perhaps we've been spoiled by the economy and precision of *Hill Street Blues*, in which a situation was routinely set up, explored and resolved in thirty minutes, but the dilatory pace of *Colors* is maddening," Biskind wrote. "*Colors* is one of the longest cop dramas in movie history," said Clark, "and all the cliches are packed into the second hour. It fades in the stretch—and so may too many moviegoers."[47]

With reservations, most reviewers liked at least part of the motion picture. David Ansen especially praised the rehabilitated director, saying, "His fusion of sociology and action moviemaking is urgent, honorable, and very scary."[48]

The film, launched in 422 theaters, grossed a respectable $4.7 million the initial weekend. Within a month the gross totaled $30 million from 1,387 screens. By the year's end Orion counted $21.2 million in rentals.

Several explanations were put forth justifying the cop movie's success. Larner contended that the youth market liked the senseless violence, "For more of the youthful audience comes to laugh at movies like *Colors* than to start a shoot-out. The younger generation does not take the American movie product nearly as seriously as critics do."

"Fears that the film would spur mayhem at movie theaters helped *Colors* see green at the box office," offered Spillman.[49]

The film's rap album charted at number 97 14 May 1988 and peaked five weeks later at number 31. It performed strongly on the Urban Contemporary listing, topping off at number 13. The crossover effect, generated by the film, earned Warner Records a gold plaque.

By midyear, *Colors* had the distinction of being the sole carrier film with a successful soundtrack.

Record labels had been growing cautious. Soundtracks were increasingly viewed as exposure vehicles for entry and "cold" artists. As CBS's Michael Dilbeck said, "I think soundtracks are excellent to break new artists, because I look for special voices and find songs for them." Another CBS executive, Jay Landers, found compilations ideal laboratories, "a good vehicle for artists to try material they would not ordinarily use for their own records."[50]

Over at Capitol, soundtracks were viewed as potential reclamation vehicles for older artists. *Dirty Dancing* provided the model: Eric Carman, Bill Medley, and Jennifer Warnes had enjoyed revived careers due to the Vestron production.

Predictably, filmmakers were hardly enthused by these sentiments. Paramount's Steve Bedell reiterated, "I refuse to compromise the integrity of the film, and our directors and producers feel the same way." The studio vice president continued, "We rely on the song and the accompanying video to *help* open our movie." Gary LeMel of Warner Pictures repeated, "We have a much better chance of keeping our picture in theaters when the music is on the tip of everyone's tongue."[51]

The studios clearly wanted chart-bound material by established artists, notably superstars, respected by program directors and MTV's acquisitions committee. New artists and "has beens," according to Bill Graham, were "a one-in-a-thousand shot," a number unlikely to bring confidence and security into studio boardrooms.

Once again the labels and studios had been operating at cross purposes. Moviemakers quickly noted that *Dirty Dancing* and *Colors* sold albums. "Rehearsing low visibility acts in a film," they would say, "does little for the movie." MTV's programming head Abbey Konowitch would counter, "A great film never made a hit out of any song that wasn't one already."[52]

Both media, especially record labels, agreed that a cutback in soundtrack titles seemed desirable. *Married to the Mob*, *Lethal Weapon*, and *Bull Durham* had performed respectably at the box office and had strong musical packages, yet album sales had proved disappointing.

Videos remained the key. "Who benefits more than a movie to have a *major* recording artist interspersed with bits from a movie?" asked LeMel. Capitol's Tim Devine agreed. "Video exposure is very similar to an extended advertising buy," he said.[53] Studios were more than aware of the need for viable music acts to enter the MTV or VH-1 rotation. Disparate goals aside, music video outlets kept the sometimes symbiotic process going.

The irony was in the bottom line. Film company box office receipts soared in the late 1980s. The labels rested on the nostalgic-fed CD market and 1960s superstars. Nonetheless, the music industry still controlled artists and, more important, publishing rights and access to MTV.

The sharply growing number of movies heightened competition within the industry. A hot video, supplemented by a highly rotated song title, was highly desirable.

"When He Pours, He Reigns:" Cocktail

> *It's happy hour all day around here.*
> —Jordon Mooney, *Cocktail*

> *Cocktail becomes the* Saturday Night Fever *of bartending.*
> —Sheila Benson, *Los Angeles Times*

Having written his novel *Cocktail*, Haywood Gould pitched the film treatment to producer Robert W. Cort. Universal Pictures, temporarily, had expressed interest, but Touchstone Pictures' Jeffrey Katzenberg signed it. (Katzenberg had likened the vehicle "to *The Graduate*." Tom Cruise was contracted for $3 million. The entire budget was set at $17 million. Filming began in December 1987; a summer opening was scheduled.

"It's kind of a stern, serious depiction of what the American dream is now," said Tom Cruise of *Cocktail*. Few observers would subscribe to the actor's assessment. "Setting him [Cruise] in a series of 'fabulous' smoke-dense bars from Manhattan to Jamaica where alcohol and wall-to-wall casual sex are the prime ingredients, is hardly in the spirit of the '80s," Benson reported.[54] At best, director's Roger Donaldson (*No Way Out*) vehicle is another Cruise showcase, with the protagonist reprising his *Risky Business* dilemma of choosing between material success and ethical, altruistic behavior. Cruise reenacts the angst (reminiscent of the Joel Goodsen role) in suburban Chicago. In both films, higher education is the key to entry into the world of investment banking. Failing that, human foibles can always be exploited.

Cocktail opened nationally in 1,404 theaters the last weekend of July 1988.

As the film opens, the Starship's "Wild Again" welcomes Brian Flanagan (Tom Cruise) back to civilian life as his Army cohorts drunkenly flag down a Greyhound bus en route to the Big Apple.

Full of dreams "to make a million," the ex-G.I. is ready for Wall Street. The brokers' employment offices, however, are hardly impressed with his resume. "You should go to college," he is repeatedly told. Instead, Brian applies to Doug Coughlin (Byran Brown) for a bartending job.

Passing a trial by fire, Brian learns the techniques of mixing and serving drinks with acrobatics tossed in, to lots of background music. A short stint at CCNY demonstrates that higher ed is not Brian's ticket to the top. Doug, the mixologist-philosopher, presents an alternative: He tells his protegé that barmen are "the aristocrats of the working class . . . you get women and you get the bucks." The two scheme to open a bar, Cocktails and Dreams. The plan fails to materialize when a falling-out sends Brian packing to Jamaica (to the Beach Boys' short "Kokomo" segment.)

Aspiring artist Jordan Mooney (Elizabeth Shue) enters the happy-hour world. (She's ushered in by a barely audible "Don't Worry . . ." The placement did nothing to promote the McFerrin musical homily.) A whirl-wind romance ensues, with a series of scenes in tourist attractions culminating in a breathtaking, waterfall-enhanced love scene. All the while, Jimmy Cliff's "Shelter of Your Love" provides the mood music.

The blissful atmosphere is interrupted with the arrival of Doug with his new bride, a very rich blonde bombshell. He provokes Brian into following his example with a career woman played by Lisa Banes. Jordan observes the pair staggering off into the sunset and leaves. Doug and Brian have apparently completed their game plan, becoming men kept in the lifestyle they most desire. Brian experiences a change of heart—he really loves Jordan—telling his benefactor, "I tried to sell out to you and couldn't close the deal."

The denouement, taken from 1930s romantic melodramas, is predictable. Our hero finds Jordan, only to discover that she is a Park Avenue heiress, and pregnant. Doug was degenerated into a disillusioned, wealthy alcoholic. The glittering Mrs. Couglin attempts to seduce Brian as her husband Doug is successfully commiting suicide. Jordan is reclaimed.

A newly opened Flanagan's bar sports the logo "Cocktails and Dreams." Jordan and Brian are expecting twins. Preston Smith's "Oh, I Love You So," followed by "Wild Again," plays over the closing credits.

Cocktail provided 104 minutes of footage, costing $17 million, of Cruise absorbing gallons of booze with no effect, and challenging the bitch-goddess of economic success. The script, while denouncing materialism at any price, panders to big box office bucks minus any redeeming value. "With just a wisp of a story on which to hang a string of sexy incidents," wrote McCarthy, "the picture delivers the flashy moves expected of this sort of young-man-on-the-rise entertainment, and should pay off accordingly."[55]

Critics, including Roger Ebert, turned an almost unanimous thumbs down on *Cocktail*. *Variety* categorized fifteen of sixteen reviews as "unfavorable."

Beginning alphabetically, David Ansen found the movie "80-proof inanity" and asked, "What were the filmmakers drinking?" Sheila Benson wished that director Donaldson had "a healing case of amnesia."[56]

Several reviewers negatively compared the effort to Stigwood's *Fever*. *Cocktail*, observed Canby was *Saturday Night Fever* "without John Travolta, the Bee-Gees and dancing. It is an inane romantic drama that only a very young, very naive bartender could love."

"This is a low-grade *Saturday Night Fever* with bars subbing for discos," *People* said. The *Film Journal*'s Kolomitz wrote it was "closest in tone to *Saturday Night Fever*, without any of that film's inspiration . . ." Rita Kempley expanded the comparison, writing, "Think of it as *Top Gun* with drink umbrellas, *The Graduate* in night school. This coming-of-age romance-drama has got no swizzle."[57]

Janet Maslin and Sheila Benson, in separate "think" pieces, strongly disputed the 1980s reality link supposedly contained in *Cocktail*. The *New York Times* contributor objected that heavy drinking was not "one of the trappings of 80's-style glamour." Benson wrote, "Body-exchange bar life and killer drinking routines seem a lot less romantic—certainly more fraught with problems—than they did even in the early 1980s. And you treat macho behavior at your peril."[58]

The reviews had no impact on *Cocktail*'s box office. Its first weekend, the film grossed more than $1.7 million. The total take, by the end of August, surpassed $51 million. By the year's end, the Cruise showcase was the sixth-ranked money draw, with $76.2 million. Touchstone Pictures tallied $35 million in its corporate ledger.

Billboard recommended *Cocktail* as containing "superb tracks" by The Beach Boys, Mellencamp, Georgia Satellites, and the Fabulous Thunderbirds.[59] No mention appeared of "Don't Worry Be Happy," the scout single released 30 July. The Beach Boys' "Kokomo" charted at number 96 3 September. Both reached the top of the trade's singles listing.

Cocktail, selling four million copies by mid-1989, defied all of the symbiotic rules. The album and the singles all appeared after the film's release. The hit selections from all the movie were background material. The success of McFerrin's "Don't Worry" remains a mystery; it went on to generate four Grammy Awards the following year. The hit status of "Kokomo" was equally unexpected. Chartmeister Paul Grein said, "If you had said to anyone in the industry that The Beach Boys would have a No. 1 record in 1988, they would have looked at you like you were crazy." Moreover, "If you had said to anyone that The Beach Boys and Brian Wilson would both have projects in 1988 and one would go to No. 1, everyone would have said the record would have been Wilson's."[60] Brian rejoined The Beach Boys due to this breakthrough.

The surfing band parleyed "Kokomo," along with five other film-related songs, into the *Still Cruisin* Capitol package as they worked on an original album. The title song was taken from the score of the $100-million, blockbuster *Lethal Weapon 2*.

To further complicate matters, the lingering song or "love theme" from the film *Cocktail* was Jimmy Cliff's "Shelter of Your Love," absent from the album. As with *The Big Chill*, *Iron Eagle*, and numerous others, the memorable title was excluded. *Cocktail* would be *the* hottest soundtrack of 1988 besides *Dirty Dancing*. The fall season, however, promised an array of soundtracks culled from the rocumentaries: *Imagine*, *U2: Rattle and Hum*, *1969*, *Buster*, starring Phil Collins, and an Elvis fable, *Heartbreak Hotel*.

Heartbreak Hotel

Writer-director Chris Columbus (*Adventures in Babysitting*), a longtime Presley fan, was plagued by an age-old question, "Why did you turn your back on rock 'n' roll? Why did you go to Vegas? Why did you start making those lousy movies?" *Heartbreak Hotel* is a fantasy set in 1972 in which an Ohio youth poses these questions to The King. "I wanted to write a movie that would focus on this idea," Columbus stated, "but *Heartbreak Hotel* is also about isolation. Elvis was an incredibly wealthy person who became isolated by his wealth and status. Similarly the character of Marie Wolfe is also a woman who is isolated—not so much by having too much of everything, but by what is lacking in her life—a husband, a job and a sense of herself. That shared sense of loneliness really fascinated me."[61]

Columbus teamed with *Babysitting* producers Lynda Obst and Debra Hill to create his film fantasy. The most difficult aspect of the production was finding the lead character, Obst said, "I can honestly say that this was the most grueling casting job that I have ever been through, because everyone has an opinion about what Elvis should be like," she added. David Keith, who had appeared in *An Officer and a Gentleman*, was chosen for the Presley part. Tuesday Weld played Marie Wolfe and Columbus's alter-ego role of Johnny Wolfe was given to Charlie Schlatter of *Bright Lights, Big City*.

The filming took place on location in Austin, Texas at the Green Pastures restaurant and Palmer Auditorium. An ad appeared in the *Austin Statesman* asking for extras; the caveat was that the applicants had to dress in 1972 regalia: "Polyester is the fabric of choice. Think hot pants, zipper boots and Army surplus gear."

Lynda Obst marvelled at the turnout. "I could never have gotten these costumes in Los Angeles. What was most amazing is that people didn't rent these outfits, they simply went into their closets and pulled out what they still had on the shelf," she said.

Hoping for a crossover, Touchstone Pictures targeted the end of September as the release date. Their marketing strategy was lifted from the MTV Monkees playbook, that is, appeal to teenagers and older, original Elvis fans. The juxtaposition of David Keith to the adolescent Charlie Schlatter seemed the ideal combination for this crossgenerational mix.

The film's opening narration reads:

IN THE KINGDOM OF ROCK 'N' ROLL, THERE ARE MANY LEGENDS BUT ONLY ONE KING. THIS IS A FABLE ABOUT HIM. THE TIME IS 1972.

The introductory scene is the artificial splendor of the Flamingo Hotel as the King replicates, by the numbers, "All My Trials," followed by the closing "Battle Hymn of The Republic." This is Elvis mired in the glitz and glamor of 1972 Las Vegas.

In contrast, in a small Ohio town, Johnny Wolfe (Schlatter) and the Wolf Pack are auditioning for the "Big Show" with "Soul On Fire." The ensemble is rejected. They are too loud.

Marie invites Johnny and his sister Pam (Angela Goethals) to a drive-in show. "Why do we have to see an Elvis movie when we can see something cool?" protests Johnny. They go to *Loving You*, as Elvis is Marie's escape from the isolation of Taylor, Ohio.

Johnny devises a scheme to kidnap Elvis, using a Gladys Presley look-a-like as the lure and chloroforming the idol. The kidnapping is a success.

Director Columbus, through Johnny, tells the celebrity, "The same people you play for today were scared to death of you in 1956. You *were* a rebel, man, a bad ass, you were *Elvis*."

With the proper musical overlays, Presley begins to solve the Wolfe's family problems, reminding one of *Down and Out in Beverly Hills*. Pam's fear of the dark—"slimy soul suckers"—Johnny's shyness, and Marie's loneliness fade. The house is redecorated in Graceland fashion. (Missed by most critics was a recreation of the restaurant song-and-fight scene taken straight from *Loving You*. Even the antagonist is decked on the jukebox after "Ready Teddy"). Elvis remains skeptical of the 1972 rock scene, referring to contemporary bands as "Satan worshippers."

All is resolved at the Kennedy High Talent Show, billed as "Stars Over Taylor." Elvis sings a duet of "Heartbreak Hotel" with Johnny and his group. The crowd explodes with appreciation.

The farewells follow, with a mutual admiration exchange. "You make me feel like Elvis again."

"Elvis you're still the King," replies John.

Elvis Presley, since *Stage Show*, presented a role conflict. The sexually suggestive stud worshipped his mother, contributed to charity, and sang gospel songs when not being "The Pelvis." A genuine treatment of the American icon, as numerous contradictory biographies illustrate, is difficult at best. Chris Columbus chose one side of the Janus-like character, ignoring the darker angle.

Elvis's greatest sin, in *Heartbreak Hotel* is having left the Sun Record stable, his self-destructive eating and chemical-ingesting habits. What emerges is, as one critic suggested, "sanitized Disneyland."[62]

A majority of reviewers disliked Columbus's fable. *Variety* led with "Even Elvis never made a picture this bad. Writer-director Chris Columbus' weakly conceived fantasy makes the ultimate mockery of the late idol. After initial sampling, b.o. should be nil." Parts of the movie were imitations of Presley exploitation films, and Maslin picked this up, objecting that "they haven't been staged as effectively as they could have been."[63] Michael Wilmington asserted that *Heartbreak Hotel* was "such a bad idea, nothing can rescue it, not even Georges Delerue's music or [David] Keith's impersonation of The King."[64]

Not all the notices were negative. "If you buy the set-up," wrote Tom Green, "*Heartbreak Hotel* goes down real good." *Boxoffice* called the fable "an often colorless and, at times, irresponsibly stupid fable, but it is redeemed by a truly inspired attempt to redeem Presley's legacy."[65]

Opening on 1,338 screens nationally, *Heartbreak Hotel* managed a gross of $2 million. In less than a month, the theater run was complete, with a closing total of $4.9 million.

Georges Delerue's score, including a host of Presley finds, listed at number 176 and faded in two weeks. This time, the film's box office life transcended the album.

Hotel's failure can be attributed to a multitude of factors. Despite the notices, the vehicle is, as Green suggested, a bedtime story with more merit than some big-ticket sellers. The release date, two days after Lennon's *Imagine*, did not help attract filmgoers. *Imagine* garnered *Newsweek* and *Rolling Stone* cover stories. John and Elvis may have proved too much for even the most dedicated nostalgia buff.

The film *1969* joined *Imagine* and *Hotel* that year. Screenwriter Ernest Thompson, *On Golden Pond*, had scripted a semi-autographical look at small-town America in 1969, a time of generational conflict, the antiwar movement, Woodstock, and the Days of Rage. A reflective Thompson had told the *Film Journal*, "I was a 19-year-old boy in 1969 and was faced with many adventures and traumas. It takes place in Maryland, where I was living at the time. I too had an older brother who went to Vietnam. But the movie is about a lot of things. I think, essentially, it's about coming to terms with one's social conscience and I think it was about that time in my life that I decided I'd better develop one."[66]

Peddling his film in 1984, Thompson met with, "Forget about this one, everybody hates it." Complicating the situation, the writer wanted to direct as well. Atlantic Releasing eventually signed the project. "It's still a mystery to me why someone would want to take a chance on a first-time director," said Thompson.[67]

With an allocated $4-million budget and two visible teen stars—Keifer Sutherland (*Lost Boys*) and Robert Downey, Jr. (*Less Than Zero*)—filming began November 1987 in Savannah, Georgia.

The marketing strategy was akin to that of *The Big Chill*. "Theoretically, this could be a movie attractive to a number of different age groups," Thompson indicated. "People in my generation should be interested, because we were all there in 1969, but, for us, it's a double whammy, because the boys in the film are the age that we were 20 years ago, but the parents are our age now—we've become that age. I don't know, maybe our parents will be interested in it, too. I guess it all depends on how they felt back then. Some people don't ever want anything about the '60s again."[68]

The marketing targeted the Big Chillers and the older teen audience, and the film featured a soundtrack loaded with period pieces. Polygram hoped for high souvenir sales in the year of "retro-rock."

In 1968, hundreds of genuine counter-culturites retreated from the hordes of Midwesterners invading the Haight-Ashbury to celebrate a misnamed Summer of Love. The Tet offensive in Vietnam alienated millions, including CBS news anchor Walter Cronkite. Peacemakers like Robert Kennedy and Martin Luther King, Jr. were gunned down. Chicago Mayor Richard Daley and the Democratic political establishment, during the 1968 Democratic Convention, reaffirmed to the young that police brutality and the Vietnam War would continue unfettered. Alienation and frustration spread.

The next year, 1969, had been the year of radicalization. Nonviolence was rejected by some as ineffective. The Days of Rage followed, bifurcating the antiwar movement. Less noticably, bodybags began appearing in middle America.

Ernest Thompson *attempted*, in microcosm, to capture the sociopolitical currents of 1969, the year before the Kent State killing of four students by the National Guard.

In the film, The Animals' "When I was Young" appropriately ushers in 1967, as Scott (Sutherland) and Ralph (Downey) graduate on a flickering home-movie screen. "Nineteen and we owned the world," states the narrative.

The pair go off to Barton State College and return to their patriotic, God-fearing community. "The Sixties hadn't hit yet, and they were almost over in our little town in Maryland," Sutherland narrates. "Nothing much had changed . . . not in my lifetime, anyway."

In Middletown, the viewer is introduced to Scott's family, the confused Jessie (Mariette Hartley), Cliff, played by Bruce Dern, and brother Alden (Christopher Wynne), a Vietnam-bound Marine.

Ralph's liberal mother (Joanna Cassidy) and little sister Beth (Winona Ryder) add spice and distractions to the script. "Thompson should have dispensed with the grown-ups' dysfunctions completely and focused far more on the youngsters," noted Kozak.[69]

The lifestyle dichotomy established, the war issue rapidly surfaces. Scott sees American involvement as "bullshit." His father and Alden recoil; Jessie isn't so sure, but bids the Marine farewell with, "Don't die." (He will.)

Returning to college, Scott applies himself, so as "not to get drafted," as Ralph drifts off, in a drug-induced haze, on the path to flunking out.

The radicalization process continues. Beth, in a high school valedictory address, shocks the crowd by saying, "There's something wrong in America. I don't know what it is. Something's wrong when everybody is mad at everybody else. There's something wrong when we don't understand what our country is doing." Catcalls!

Ralph trips out on acid. Cliff asks, "What's going on?" underscoring the generational cleavage.

Scott begins a summer trek best described as a tourist's visit to Hippie-dom. Ralph finds the draft board is trying to locate him. Alden's listed as an M.I.A.—"They've misplaced your brother."

At this juncture, the well-intentioned Thompson falls into several cliches. Ralph is caught breaking into the Selective Service Office and is jailed. Scott finally loses his virginity to Beth as they plan a prolonged Canadian vacation. Beth, following a symbolic encounter with infantry-men, urges, "Stay with me and fight." Joan Baez's "Amazing Grace" attends Alden's funeral—"the first boy in Culloch County to die in Vietnam." At the funeral, Scott defiantly announces he's off to free the imprisoned Ralph. Most of the mourners trail along. The finale is equiva-lent to the Big Show of other movies. Dern, the epitome of the silent majority, joins in.

As the movie closes, we are told that 357,000 later participated in the March on Washington. The Pretenders' "Windows of the World" provides the closing notes.

The film *1969* resembled an MTV viewer's vision of the troubled 1960s more than its reality. Thompson captured the wane of public support for the Vietnam War, but in a capsulized form. It was oversimplified.

Critics, more con than pro, questioned the authenticity of Thompson's vision of 1969.

"Perhaps 1969—the year, not the movie," Britt noted, "was just too passionate, too visceral a time for movies to capture. This one doesn't even come close." Thompson's state of mind was "not one that anyone else might recognize," wrote Maslin. *Variety* concurred, saying "Affecting memories and good intentions don't always add up to good screen sto-ries."[70]

Kevin Thomas, a supporter, said, "For an older generation, *1969* may seem late in the game and overly familiar. But the film is aimed at those 18 or 19 year olds, just past high school graduation." A *Boxoffice* review summarized, "Thompson ultimately, wants to tell stories too diverse to meld, and winds up with a lot of moments in search of a point."[71]

The vehicle debuted in 520 theaters 18 November, earning $1.7 million. The gross climbed to $3.9 million in a ten-day period.

The Polygram soundtrack barely made the LP charts. It crept on at number 198 17 December and exited six weeks later at its peak, number 186. A souvenir package, including Hendrix, CCR, Cream, The Young-bloods, and Crosby, Stills, Nash & Young, was expected to shine in the mania for classic, "retro-rock" radio.

The soundtrack failed, due to low film traffic and the lack of any identifiable song. (Souvenir albums, again, only function when material is aptly placed in a successful movie.)

Buster

Genesis drummer and successful solo artist Phil Collins enjoyed an acting background. A thirteen-year-old Collins had performed as Artful Dodger in London's New Theatre production of *Oliver*. During the stint, he was also an extra in *A Hard Days Night*. Some twenty years later, *Miami Vice* provided the drummer with the feature role of Phil the Shill. He was an experienced actor by the time director David Green and Hemdale Productions supplied him with a title role as Buster Edwards, England's "Great Train Robber."

Collins wanted his involvement to be predominantly dramatic. The film, set in 1963, was ideal for musical period pieces. The ex-Beatles, Mick Jagger, and others were contracted, "but the lawyers wouldn't let us have it," Collins complained. "Beatles songs were used in *Mask*, so why couldn't we use 'All My Loving' for 30 seconds?"[72]

Collins had arranged for composer Lamont Dozier to contribute to the project. "When I heard 'Two Hearts' and 'Goin' Loco Down in Acapulco,' I fell in love with them," Collins recalled. He wrote the lyrics "from a more British point of view."[73]

Green and Collins began to search for available 1960s material. One song previewed was The Mindbenders' "Groovy Kind of Love." Collins recorded it, in a slow tempo, in half an hour. The cover would reach the top of the charts.

The film debuted 15 August 1988 in London, generating considerable interest. "Groovy" surfaced Stateside 3 September at number 52. *Billboard* reviewed the soundtrack several weeks later, noticing that the filler-laden package contained only three Collins performances and one Four Tops cut. The writer characterized "Groovy" as an "anemic remake" of the Mindbenders' hit, but did praise the Tops for "sounding their best in years on 'Loco In Acapulco'."[74]

Buster's American premiere took place in the last week of November.

The title character Ronald "Buster" Edwards (Phil Collins) is a nondescript, working-class London thief. To the strains of "Be Your Man" he obtains a mourning suit, after demolishing a store front window. He steals everything necessary to maintain a meager life-style, keeping wife June (Julie Edwards) and daughter (Ellen Beaven) relatively free from want.

June, pregnant, dreams of living in a country home where they will not have to hide behind the couch to avoid the landlord monthly. Buster, the dreamer, promises things will improve while planning the big Royal Mail-train robbery. In a riveting segment, with military precision, the gang pulls off the "Biggest Mail Robbery Ever." The loot is a staggering 2.6 million pounds.

The scandal-ridden British government is obsessed with apprehending the robbers. The Edwards family flees to the sun-drenched beaches of Acapulco.

The Four Tops perform Collins' "Goin' Loco in Acapulco."

"I resisted "Loco," said the singer, "because that's in the middle and I didn't want people to hear my voice until the end of the movie. I wanted to just take the acting very seriously."[75]

The Edwards's life in the Mexican resort city is difficult. June is restless and homesick. Taking Nicky, she returns to London. Despite a possible thirty-year prison term, Buster follows, to a preordained fate. "Groovy Kind of Love" underscores the "love at any price" finale. "Would *you* trade a suitcase filled with cash and a life in Acapulco for gray old England and an extended prison sentence?" asked Matthews. The story is based on fact, but the *Boxoffice* reviewer had a point when he noted, "It seemed like a dumb decision to us."[76]

To provide a happy ending Collins, after serving eleven years, becomes a happily married street vendor—with lingering dreams. "Two Hearts (One Mind)" ends this little, ninety-four minute film. (The song would be its second chart topper.)

Buster is a "nice," well-acted love story with an exciting train robbery providing some drama. Reviewers applauded the robbery segment, with scattered praise for Collins and Walters, but American filmgoers apparently were not enthused. The English hit barely grossed $350,000 in its opening ten days, playing 217 theaters. Its five-week run closed with a mere $514,404. The album, then with a three-month chart tenure, easily outlived the motion picture. "Not even MTV could generate much interest in Phil Collins's screen debut," concluded one trade. "This pleasant but forgettable true-life drama barely earned half a million dollars in five weeks."[77]

Another film, *Tequila Sunrise*, opened the first week of December with bankable names like Mel Gibson, Michelle Pfeiffer, and Kurt Russell. The $19-million cop-drug dealer drama grossed more than the combined earnings of Collins, Lennon, U2 and David Keith as Elvis in one weekend. *Sunrise*'s opening box office came to a hefty $12.4 million. By New Year's Day, the thinking-person's *Lethal Weapon* was pushing $32 million.

Capitol released a support single, "Surrender To Me," a duet by Heart's Ann Wilson and Cheap Trick's Robin Zander. The infectious cut premiered at number 80 Christmas Eve. By March it would climb to number 6 on the Hot 100. *Billboard* recommended the package, pointing to the Wilson/ Zander "power ballad" and the "especially powerful" cuts by Duran Duran and The Church.[78] The album, debuting at number 162, crawled to a modest number 101 after a few months.

Aesthetically, the compilation was outstanding, but it sold poorly despite being from a box office hit and despite the efforts of Tim Devine, Capitol's associate A&R director. (In 1988, the label had also struck out with the above-average soundtrack of the successful *Bull Durham*.)

The end of the year also saw the debut of *Beaches*, launched on seven screens and selling only $215,865 worth of tickets.

In 1985 All Girls Productions had been formed with Bette Midler as the "calling card." A bankable presence, she could open studio doors, especially at Touchstone Pictures. (Her *Ruthless People* and *Down and Out* had contributed substantially to the Disney subsidiary's coffers.)

Writer Iris Rainer Dart approached Midler. "I'm writing a book with a part you'd be perfect for" she announced.[79] The book was *Beaches*; the character was the pushy, self-involved singer, C.C. Bloom. The project appealed to Midler's desire to do serious drama like she had in *The Rose*.

Garry Marshall of *Happy Days*, *Laverne and Shirley* and *Mork and Mindy* television fame was hired to direct the $20-million project starring Midler and Barbara Hershey. The singer acted as the producer: "I didn't think it was going to be as much work as it was. Eighteen-hour days, 19 hour days. Singing, dancing, editing soundtrack," she said.[80]

For Midler, playing a singer was second-nature. "It really wasn't what you would call a stretch," she admitted. "The real stretch was the emotion between the two characters—a big range of emotions, a lot of laughter and confrontation with the fact that one of them is going to die."[81]

Music, of course, played a significant role in the film's structure. Marshall credited the co-star, saying, "Bette certainly had a more musical vision of the film than I did."

"I like the musical form a lot. The only people who hate musicals are the studios because they don't know how to make them and they're too expensive and time-consuming," added Midler.[82]

In January, Midler, music supervisor Marc Shaiman, the director, and record producer Arif Mardin began choosing inserts for *Beaches*. Some of the inputs were esoteric like "I've Still Got My Health" from the Broadway show *Sugar Babies*. Bill Hill's 1936 "Glory of Love," redundantly employed in the movie as part of the dramatic close, was suggested by an Alberta Hunter cover. The Drifters' "Under The Boardwalk" and Randy

Newman's "I Think It's Going To Rain Today" were resurrected. The sleeper in the collection was "Wind Beneath My Wings."

Beaches could have been easily classified as a "women's picture." The director, however, thought the tear-jerker had broader appeal. "I think a young guy will like this kind of movie, because he loves it when his girlfriend cries at the end and he gets to console her," said Marshall. "He'll drag his date to the movie, and then get to say [soothingly] 'it's okay, sweetheart,' as she sobs into his arms . . ."[83] Touchstone rejected this somewhat devious approach in its marketing campaign.

Billboard greeted the Divine Miss M's offering with praise. Newman's song was described as "a lovely string-laden version," while "Under the Boardwalk" was called a "languid remake." Shaiman said, "I think the soundtrack contains Bette's best singing." Being the producer of the film, the singer didn't have time for self-analysis rather, "she had to go in and sing the songs," he added.[84] "The Wind Beneath My Wings" was a potential hit, but the reviewers ignored it.

The album hit the merchandising bins 21 January, charting at number 194 the week of the film's national release. The signature single did not surface until early March. "Wind Beneath My Wings" entered the Hot 100 at a lowly number 97.

In the film, while rehearsing "Under The Boardwalk" at the Hollywood Bowl, superstar C.C. Bloom (Midler) receives an urgent letter and races up the California coast to San Francisco. Flashbacks chronicle her three stormy decades of association with aristocratic attorney Hillary Whitney Essex (Barbara Hershey).

The "buddies" first connect in Atlantic City, when the eleven-year-old Hillary is lost. A viper-tongued C.C. rescues her, with a short interlude to audition for a show by singing "Glory of Love." "You're the most fantastic person I've ever met in my entire life," says the overly protected, would-be socialite.

They correspond while pursuing very different career patterns. Hillary graduates from Standford Law School, C.C. does the New York-nitery circuit. (In one club, Hillary shows up.) A cold-water flat becomes home. Still struggling, as a singing messenger, C.C. meets director John Pierce (John Herald). She is cast in his Falcon Player's production. On the basis of the notices, she reaches Broadway.

Hillary and the singer fall out over John's affections. Hillary returns to the Bay Area, marrying stuffed shirt attorney Michael Essex (James Read). John and C.C. follow suit. Their union fails, as C.C. becomes the insufferable "toast of Broadway." Meanwhile, Hillary discovers that Michael is cheating on her. She is pregnant.

C.C., having alienated Hollywood, finds herself in San Francisco. A predictable reunion ensues. All is well until Broadway beckons C.C. back. Hillary's daughter Victoria is born. Hillary is found to have a deteriorating heart. "I Think It's Going to Rain Today" plays as her terminal condition is explored.

The closing forty minutes, an eternity, disposes of the males and focuses on the female-bonding relationship. However, as Denby indicated, "Something silly happens. Having contracted, for plot reasons, a life-threatening disease, Hershey suffers from shortness of breath (for a while, the blundering script is more tersely phrased). She not only suffers beautifully and profitable (teaching Bette Midler to be less *selfish*), she exhibits courage in front of her little daughter. There she sits at her Pacific-coast beach house being resolute and gasping into the sunset. The gasping was the straw that broke the donkey's back."

"Through this (slow, slow) deathwatch," added Kael, "C.C. learns to transcend her self-involvement; she becomes a better person, and—implicitly—a bigger star."[85] Both writers are on the mark, as the resolution is dragged out with numerous near-climaxes. "It seems to have run through several different preliminary endings," noted Maslin. Agreeing Clark stressed that none of "three or four endings" clicked.[86] The most effective moments are the sunset scene and the funeral segment, both accompanied by "Wind Beneath My Wings." These are, unfortunately, overshadowed by the Hollywood Bowl finale of "Glory of Love," accompanied by "every violion in the musician's union."[87]

Variety's McCarthy disagreed. "The tragic climax and its uplifting follow-up will have many viewers in tears, and in boxoffice terms will probably demonstrate once again that a good cry can be as profitable as a good laugh," he wrote.[88]

Midler and Hershey garnered decent notices, but the Dart novel and Mary Agnes Donoghue screen adaptation were blasted. David Noh found the writing "woefully short."

"Implacably terrible," said Denby. "*Beaches* has no outstanding scenes, no highs," wrote Kael, "it just slogs along." Sawahata added the final nail: "The whole story is like *Love Story* rewritten for two women. If this is what women's friendships are about, give me male bonding."[89]

The *Boxoffice* review saw the plot merely as a dramatic device, "just glue to hold the film together between Midler's musical numbers, and while that worked okay in *The Rose*, it doesn't cut the mustard here."

"The score is maudlin, like the movie," concluded Kael. Another negative opinion was expressed in *The Film Journal*: "You get eclectic, unsatisfying snippets of song all too connected [?] to the mountingly dreary plot."[90]

Conversely, specific selections like "I Think It's Going to Rain Today," received praise. "Miss Midler gets to sing a lot," applauded Maslin, "which is a big help."[91]

The music placement in *Beaches* exceeded that of most soundtracks. The semi-backstage format allowed for production numbers like "Boardwalk," "Otto Titsling," and "Glory of Love."

Beaches grossed a paltry $215,865. Within a month, the offering appeared on 809 screens, pulling in $13.2 million. By mid-August 1989 the figure surpassed $56.2 million. The album barely missed the top of the chart, topping off at number 2. It earned a platinum certification, making it the best-selling recorded track since *Cocktail*. *Batman*, however, was about to burst upon the scene.

The Year of The Bat and Slime

> *Movie soundtracks have not proved to be as consistently hot commodities as many expected several years ago when movies like* Flashdance *and* Footloose *seemed to point the way to a new form of movie musical strongly influenced by music videos.*
> —Stephen Holden, *New York Times*

> *If somebody goes to see* Batman, Ghostbusters II *and* Lethal Weapon II, *that might be money they would have used to buy three CDs.*
> —Henry Droz, president of WEA

Back To the Future II, appropriately, had closed Tom Shales's "Re Decade." The "summer of the sequel" swamped venues with retro or classic rock and old-folks' concert tours. The force behind the brand-name loyalty was technology coupled with demographics.

Television, as Peter Travers argued, habituates repeat viewing. "In a sense," he wrote, "these shows [*Cosby, Roseanne*] and others are in the business of spinning off twenty-two sequels a year in the form of episodes. The trick is getting audiences into the habit. Once hooked, they will tolerate astonishing lapses in quality in the name of loyalty. It's originality that breeds contempt; familiarity builds boxoffice."[92]

The summer of 1989 was repleted with reprises of *Star Trek*, *Ghostbusters*, and screen-worn images of Indiana Jones, James Bond, the Karate Kid, and miraculously, Eddie Wilson reuniting with The Cruisers. Hollywood also banked on the nostalgia value of a comic-book staple, Batman, and the firebrand rock-a-billy of the Fifties, Jerry Lee Lewis.

The music industry equally had been looking "back to the future" since 1986 and the so-called CD (compact disk) explosion. CDs revitalized the Yuppie market, enthroning the twenty-five-year-old-plus, upscale male.

In 1986, *Radio and Records* editor Ken Barnes said, "The oldies trend is definitely happening. It's probably the hottest proliferating format right now."[93] It would dominate the airwaves by 1989. Reportedly, 200 of the nation's Album Oriented Rock stations devoted 80 percent of their airtime to classics. "Remakes break across the demographic spectrum," noted radio station Z-100's Steve Kingston. "They're familiar to parents, and they're quality records the kids haven't been exposed to."[94]

Advertisers fueled the return-to-basics format, as it appealed to the magic twenty-five-through-thirty-four-year-old target. Younger listeners, vicariously reliving the Sixties, became subgenerational gravy.

AOR's embrace of "oldies" affected the labels. A "plundering of fossils," according to one A&R person, ensued. Sixties bands were being reunited and contracted to accomodate FM program directors. Cutting-edge new acts were relegated to other media like motion-picture scores. Once again, the goals of the music makers were at odds with those of film creators.

Studio concerns were heightened by myriad sequels and superstar titles scheduled from Memorial Day through Labor Day.

The celluloid pipeline included remakes of *Indiana Jones*, *Star Trek*, *The Karate Kid*, *Delta Force*, *Lethal Weapon*, and *Ghostbusters*, and the eighteenth James Bond action saga. Sylvester Stallone, Clint Eastwood, Michael J. Fox, and other box office draws were sandwiched into the summer timetable. In the midst of heated competition for filmgoers' dollars, any attention-getting device had value.

In three weekends, commencing 16 June with *Ghostbusters II*, five of the anticipated high-profile titles were released. (*Batman* would debut a week later with mega-premieres.) *Karate Kid III* and *Great Balls of Fire* opened 30 June. The Gibson-Glover remake of *Lethal Weapon* and the Bond vehicle followed. All of the contenders took product marketing very seriously.

An estimated $40 to $70 million in advertising and promotion was anticipated for the summer of sequels. Disney Pictures's Bob Levin claimed, "You can afford to spend heavily if your movie has playability and lasts 16 weeks." The largesse, he explained, occurs because "everyone hopes and thinks his movie can be one of the top three."[95] Given the overabundance of productions, there would be some expensive also-rans.

"It was a *tour de force* of publicity campaigns," wrote *People*'s Ralph Novak. "There were a number of ready-made markets with all the sequels."

"The problem is they [the studios] get away from moviemaking—it's advertising," echoed Rita Kempley.[96] Orion had spent $12 million advertising the Jerry Lee Lewis screen biography *Great Balls of Fire*. The *Batman* campaign had begun in January, six months before the film's release. "Its amazing," said Kim Basinger. "This isn't a film, it's an event."[97] Warner Brothers budgeted $10 million for marketing, aided by a massive merchandising campaign. By the film's premiere, some 150 licenses had sold around $200 million in merchandise; $75 million in T-shirts, walking advertisements, moved prior to 23 June. Some observers objected to the "hype," including star Michael Keaton, who called it "unwieldy and getting stupid," but anecodotal material supported the strategy. A New York fast-food worker said, "I couldn't watch everybody wearing these stupid shirts anymore." He went on to see the film.

Indiana Jones's third movie had appeared 24 May with another John Williams symphonic score, a demographic contradiction; the rock heavies had to wait for Columbia's *Ghostbusters II*.

In This Corner the Slime

Sequels are projects with a built-in audience, yet getting *Ghostbusters* back into production involved four years of bruised egos, bickering, and high-level corporate finance.

Britisher David Puttnam, assuming studio control in 1986, was quite cool toward the original *Ghostbusters*. "Frankly, I was surprised by how little respect the first *Ghostbusters* film got," complained director Ivan Reitman. "I feel a little like Rodney Dangerfield."[98]

Puttnam, preferring more cerebral fare, went on to alienate Bill Murray by telling the British-American Chamber of Commerce that the actor "gives nothing back to his art. He's a taker."

When Puttnam left the studio, Dawn Steel was brought in to restore Columbia's profitability. A priority was a *Ghostbusters* follow-up. Considerable ego-massaging was called for. Michael Ovitz of the CAA talent agency, which represented Reitman, Murray, Ackroyd, and Ramis, was consulted.

A luncheon was staged for the stars, Reitman, and other CAA executives. Jimmy's bistro was bedecked in *Ghostbusters* paraphernalia, Bill Murray recalled, "I think walking into the meeting no one really felt we'd make the movie. But in the course of lunch we had so many laughs and so much fun that it became clear we'd really enjoy working together again.'' A year of high pressure deal making followed. Columbia desperately wanted the project, but a reunion of the original cast and director involved megabucks, an estimated $20 million. "We'd much rather pay a piece of the profits than huge salaries," asserted the new studio head.[99] CAA concurred.

As the $30-million production began its thriteen-weeks of filming, the studio and Reitman were nervous about the project. "We're scared," said the director, "because we know that people are going to come to the movie with extraordinarily high expectations . . . that's much more frightening than having an audience come to a brand new movie, not knowing what to expect, and having the chance to be pleasantly surprised. Living up to expectations has kind of frightened all of us." The studio, mired in red ink, was gambling on the sequel. "It's pretty scary," confirmed Steel, "because the summer is so jammed with product. It's a minefield."[100]

Reitman, who gave the Ray Parker, Jr. title song considerable credit for the success of *Ghostbusters* (1984), wanted a similar cushion for the sequel. Peter Afterman shopped the labels for a soundtrack deal, settling on MCA Records. The executives signed in order to get dance-music star Bobby Brown for the theme. Run-D.M.C. was brought in for the title song, but Brown had had a string of top five crossover hits, including "My Prerogative" and "Don't Be Cruel." The flamboyant singer demanded and got a cameo role as the butler in Gracie Mansion. A video of "On Our Own" was produced. Brown also contributed "We're Back" to the film. The remainder of the soundtrack's material came from the MCA roster, including Oingo Boingo, Glenn Frey, Elton John, and J.T. Taylor. The sequel's package was stronger than the original's. Kathy Nelson acted as the music supervisor.

"On Our Own" began climbing the Hot 100 at number 64 a week prior to the movie's debut 16 June. The accompanying package, released to coincide with the premiere, did not chart until July. *Billboard* hailed the endeavor, saying, "Supernatural comedy is already a gold mine at the boxoffice, and there's little reason to believe that sequel's soundtrack won't duplicate the success of the first movie's album."[101] The prediction seemed valid, as most prerelease publicity agreed that "it's hard to see how '*Busters II* could miss."[102] Opening traffic seemed to confirm the projections, as the film grossed $10 million, topping *Indiana Jones*'s opening by $2.1 million. The studio gleefully estimated a weekend take of $28-plus-million, doubling the gross of the first adventure. (It was $29.5 million.)

In the film, five years after the demolition of the Stay-Puff Marshmallow Man and a portion of Manhattan, the ghost fighters have been forcibly retired. Dr. Peter Venkman (Bill Murray) hosts a cable-assess show, *The World of the Psychic*, that features assorted fakes and con men. Spengler (Harold Ramis) is back at Columbia University researching the hypothesis that negative human energy produces psychic phenomena. (This will later be a subplot, of sorts, in the storyline.) Stantz (Ackroyd) and Winston Zeddemore (Ernie Hudson), clad in their old uniforms, entertain at children's birthday parties. In one scene, the pair asks, "Who you gonna call?" "He-Man!" is the retort. All this changes when Dana Barrett, now divorced, (Sigourney Weaver) beckons.

Dana's eight-month old son, is being threatened by another demon, not Gozer but a pale presence, Vigo. This evil seventeenth-century warrior is planning to control the world through Barrett's infant. (If the plot sounds familiar, it should.) Vigo the Carpathian, it appears, controls a red river of slime that runs below the streets of New York City. As Reitman said, "There's lots and lots of slime."

The slime, as Denby argued, seemed "to have been produced by the accumulated bad vibes in New York; it's a river of ill will, a miasma of rudeness and envy, a cloaca of contempt." In order to reduce the Styx-like river into a tranquil "mood slime," the four heroes bring into gigantic portions the Statue of Liberty, *a la* the Marshmallow Man, "to rev up the patriotic good will of the populace, [then] the premise founders and is ignored."[103] Vigo is, naturally, zapped, the infant is saved, and all was well in the Big Apple.

Reviews were decidedly mixed, with a majority in the ambivalent category. "Humanize or sentimentalize them, and you spoil the brew. What the filmmakers have done," Clark contended, "is to soften a mad comic-fantasy into *Four Ghostbusters and a Baby*." Like most critics, *Variety*'s didn't appreciate the script, but said, "The special effects go a long way in camouflaging the thin, overwrought story." Denby asked, "Can anything as flimsy as this material rise off the ground more than once?" Peter Travers wrote, "The sequel is a virtual scene-by-scene rehash of the original, with one crucial difference: The first film was fun; the second isn't. Though the same talent is present . . . no one seems remotely engaged by the material. It's as if the cast had decided to shoot the movie during a stopover between planes." The final assessment was Kevin Lally's: "*Ghostbusters II* misses the first film's spirit, but no words of criticism are likely to scare its fans away."[104]

Bobby Brown's "On Our Own," aided by heavy MTV exposure and the relatively successful film, moved up the charts, eventually resting at number 2 for several weeks. It proved unable to dislodge Richard Marx's "Right Here Waiting," but did rank number 1 on the sales chart for several weeks (The Hot 100 is a mix of sales and airplay).

The album raced to number 14 on 29 July and stalled. By late September it had earned a gold certification, hardly a repeat of its precursor's success.

By September, *Ghostbusters II* had grossed $110.4 million, half the amount earned by its progenitor. Observers speculated that the CAA negotiated "points"—percentages for the film's principals—may "have been so big Columbia Pictures may not even break even on the project." The 1984 production had returned some $130.2 million. The 1989 numbers suggested a 50-percent drop, with a larger cut going to the stars and the director.

The Not So Holy Batman: The Film

> *This isn't a film, it's an event.*
> —Kim Basinger, actress

> Batman's *triumphs are purely a result of ruth-less marketing, a remarkably broad built-in audience, and runaway merchandising oppor-tunities. If blank leader had been projected on its opening weekend, the movie's grosses would've probably still been the same. It may, however, have been more entertaining than the film that was made.*
> —Tom Matthews, *Boxoffice*

June 1938 Action Comics had introduced a comic-book hero appropri-ately named, by Joe Schuster, "Superman." The 10-cent Man of Steel's adventures flew off newsstands. National Comics, the parent company, wasted little time in commissioning a similar caped hero for their *Detective Comics* magazine. Eighteen-year-old Bob Kane received the assignment. "I was looking to create another superhero on the heels of Superman," recalled Kane. "I didn't want to be accused of copying him, so I didn't give [him] any superpowers."[105]

The character was a composite from silent pictures like Douglas Fair-banks, Sr.'s *Mark of Zorro* (1920) and *The Bat Whispers* (1930). In the latter, a master criminal climbs walls wearing a batlike mask and cape. His calling card was a "bat beam."[106] A pulp-magazine character, The Black Bat, may have influenced the dark knight's costume. "The Bat-Man," a dark, urban vigilante, debuted in the May 1939 sixty-four-page issue of *Detective Comics* (#27). *Batman* (#1) appeared in April 1940.

Some forty years later, *Superman-The Movie* had opened. Warner Brothers cashed in. The return of $82.8 million augured a frenzied scurry for movies starring comic-book personages. Trades speculated that Captain America, Spiderman, and Dick Tracy, among others, were destined for big-screen treatment.

Batman, and his sidekick, Robin, having survived psychiatrist Fredric Wertman's charge that the Dynamic Duo comprised "a wish dream of two homosexuals living together" and the 1966 to 1968 BAM!-ZAP!-HOLY CLICHE! television series, were licensed to executive producers Ben Melinker and Michael Uslan October 1979.[107] The twosome pitched the concept to Peter Guber, who, with Jon Peters, presented the Caped Crusader to Superman's studio. Warner's, flush from one superhero hit, signed the project.

Peters reminisced, "People laughed at the idea in the beginning. They thought Batman was just a comic character in tights. . . . I never liked the Batman TV series. I wanted to do a real aggressive picture . . . A great opportunity to have this guy kick some ass."[108]

Once the rights were acquired, conceptual indecision prevailed. Ideas, screenwriters, and directors came and went over a nine-year span. Tom Mankiewics, writer of three James Bond films, did the initial treatment. "I used Superman as the model," he told the *Los Angeles Times*. "At the time, I wanted to do something very dark in tone, but the drafts I did had a lot more fun in them [than I suspect the film] does." The campy adventure notion was dismissed.

A contributor to *Detective Comics*, Steven Englehart, tried another angle. "My first treatment had Robin getting blown away in the first 90 seconds," the writer remembered, "so that every reviewer in the country would begin his review with 'This sure isn't the TV show.' " The script was rejected, but critics did employ Englehart's disclaimer. The treatment lacked "street feeling," indicated co-producer Peters. Several other treatments also did not pass muster.[109]

The galvanizing catalyst for the stagnant project came in the person of Mark Canton, Warner production head. He optioned sophomore scenarist Sam Hamm (*Never Cry Wolf*).

Hamm scrapped the opening childhood-trauma scene, the murder of Thomas and Martha Wayne, choosing flashbacks instead. "You had to wade through 20 years just to get to the first shot of the guy in the costume that we've all come to see," said Hamm.[110]

Influenced by Miller's *Dark Knight*, Hamm penned a script hearkening back to Kane's starting theme. "Here's a millionaire who can have anything he wants, and what he wants is to get dressed up and scare people,'' said the scripter. ''There is a 'Rosebud' aspect [*Citizen Kane*] to his character, and it erupts as 'Batman.' That is the psychological thrust of the plot.''

''I wrote Batman as a psychotic,'' he told *American Film*, ''this guy who's had a terrible crisis of conscience.''[111]

''It wasn't until we got Sam Hamm's script that we found the rough, dark edge we wanted,'' Peters said. ''There's lots of peril in this film and humor, but it's not *Raiders of the Lost Ark* or *Ghostbusters*.''

''Batman is a street hero, a romantic hero,'' expanded Canton.[112]

With a working draft, Peters and Guber now needed a director. Canton suggested Tim Burton, who was working on *Beetlejuice* at the Warner's studio. At the time, Burton's reputation had hinged on *Pee-Wee's Big Adventure*, a $7-million movie with a $40-million gross. Originally, the former Disney animator's view of the Batman had stemmed from the camp television series. He was impressed with Hamm's treatment.

The executive producers felt that hiring Burton was ''risky,'' but a chance worth taking. Studio executives expressed reservations. ''Warner's was a complete, total freak-out, scared to death shooting a $30-million film with a third-time director whose first two films cost about a dollar and a half,'' said Peters.[113] They did approve the choice eventually.

Hamm's storyline appealed to the director, as it stressed ''human issues.''

''Loneliness is a big part of it.'' After the murder of his parents, Batman ''becomes a very lonely, very isolated person . . . I tried to make him as human as possible, a person who has problems,'' Burton explained. ''I wanted to show the fact he is psychotic, but that he is good. If this guy had gotten therapy, he wouldn't have needed to put on a bat suit.''[114] This decision, humanizing the Dark Avenger, would generate a storm of controversy. ''If some guy is 6-foot-5 with gigantic muscles and incredibly handsome, why does he need to put on a batsuit?'' asked Burton. ''Why doesn't he just put on a ski mask and kick the crap out of people?''[115]

The director chose Michael Keaton, his 5'10'' star of *Beetlejuice*, for the lead. Canton's original response was negative. ''You can think of 400 guys before you think of him,'' indicated the production head. ''But it only took me one meeting to get Tim's idea. You don't want Arnold Schwarzenegger in the Batsuit: then there'd be no question who would win the fight with the Joker.'' Burton pressed on, suggesting that the Robin character be eliminated. The studio resisted the idea until it was reminded that the budget could be cut if Robin were eliminated.[116]

Burton sent his *Beetlejuice* star a script. ''I don't know the comic book, the television series, none of that. Never cared about any of it,'' he told

Premiere. Later, "What interested me in the project was what kind of man would do this."[117]

The choice for the villainous Joker was preordained. Creator Bob Kane had even submitted a photograph of Jack Nicholson, from *The Shining*, with white makeup and green hair. The superstar agreed to do the project for scale and points (He will earn, according to insiders, a hefty $60 million). Nicholson's presence reassured the distributor and exhibitors, but not Batmaniacs.

Keaton's selection generated a storm of protest. Newspapers and magazines were flooded with mail from irate fans. "By casting a clown, Warner Brothers and Burton had defecated on the history of Batman," read a letter in the *Los Angeles Times*. Another maven objected, "Treating *Batman* as a comedy is like *The Brady Bunch* going porno." Peters recalled, "Fifty thousand letters of protest arrived at Warner Brothers. A lot of people in the company lobbied against it. One of the most powerful men in Hollywood went as far as to call Steve Ross [WCI chairman] and told him casting Michael was such a horrible idea it would bring Warners to its knees. That the entire studio would crash and burn as a result."[118] Peters attended a convention of "DC fundamentalists," or Batfans, who booed the studio executives. "After all, it's only a movie," quipped Keaton. "I am a little nervous though, about the scene where I fantasize making love to Mary Magdalene"—a reference to the controversial *Last Temptation of Christ*.[119]

Nearly two months into location shooting, at London's Pinewood Studios, the *Wall Street Journal* ran a front page story: "Batman Fans Fear the Joke's On Them In Hollywood Epic." Staffer Kathleen Hughes quoted numerous connoisseurs who objected to Keaton's selection. "If you saw him in an alley wearing a bat suit, you would laugh, not run in fear. Batman should be 6-2, 235 pounds, your classically handsome guy with an imposing, scary image," protested a West Virginia follower. The hard-core fans demanded a Sylvester Stallone, not the 5-foot-10-inch, 160-pound Keaton. "Every [market] analyst I knew sent that to me the day it came out. It just deflated everyone," noted Peters. The controversy was a double-edged sword. Studios usually welcome any sort of publicity, but the devotees were perceived by Warners as the "primary moviegoers," and also "very loyal and affluent."[120] "Damage control" entered Warner's lexicon.

Half-way into the filming, a $400,000, 90-second trailer was cut for a Los Angeles premiere at Bruin Theatre and a nationwide Christmas-season showing.

In Westwood, 400 Batman addicts paid $7 to see the "coming attractions." Many left, satisfied, foregoing the regular feature. One remarked,

"I think comic book fans will like it more than they will [be] upset by it."[121]

"By the start of the year [1989]," Warners' president for worldwide advertising and publicity recalled, "there was a feeding frenzy that we took advantage of, and to a certain extent fueled."[122] Rob Friedman was aware of the "Bat craze" in Britain during 1988 when the television series was rerun. Clothing and other paraphernalia were successfully marketed. A slipover effect took place as East Village skateboarders picked up on the fashion. In January, *Newsweek* ran a feature, with a color photo of Keaton as Batman, leading, "Return to Gotham City" as the sixteen week shoot was ending. The final wrap was 10 March, 1989.

A host of journalists traversed Anton Furst's (*Full Metal Jacket*) gloomy, surrealistic, six-block vision of Bob Kane's "forces of darkness." "The idea for Gotham City was to make the worst aspects of New York City, go back 200 years, and imagine if there was no planning commission," Furst explained. "It makes for a very frightening complex."[123] The sets received almost as much notice as the stars and the youthful director. One visitor dazzled by the Gothic sets was Prince. "I can hear the music," he remarked.

Burton was a fan of the funk-rock star. *Purple Rain* and *1999* were played by the director on the road to the studio. "1999" and "Baby, I'm a Star," from *Rain*, served as temporary music—background noise during shooting—in the rough cuts. "They worked so well that we decided to ask Prince if he would redo them for the picture," Canton recollected. "We flew him to London to take a look at the rushes and he had three ideas right on the spot. The next night he had dinner with Tim and that was that. There was no stopping him. He had a vision for what this music should sound like and, once we heard what he had in mind, we knew he had captured the mood of the film perfectly—dark, edgy and a lot of fun."

Warner Records was delighted with the potential linkage, as Prince's *Lovesexy* had failed to reach the LP Top 10. The label, concerned about oversaturation, delayed another Prince effort until the 1989 holiday season or later. A&R head Michael Ostin said, "All parties had decided that it didn't make sense for Prince to put out 'a Prince Record' for some time . . . Being attached to something with this kind of buzz, that could only be positive right now."[124]

In the midst of the *Lovesexy* tour in Japan, Prince wrote nine songs in three weeks. Burton was amazed at the output, but passed on "Rave to the Joy Fantastic" and "200 Balloons," the B-side to "Batdance." "Partyman" and "Trust" were judged appropriate.

Although hailed as the soundtrack, Prince's *Batman* became an endeavor "inspired" by the motion picture. Of the nine selections, only six are reportedly overlaid in the film.[125] "Batdance," the scout single, "Lemon Crush," and "The Arms of Orion" with Sheena Easton are absent. "The album and the film are two separate works," said Peters, "in two different media, complementing and supporting each other." Prince's created music proved to be central to the music-promotion arm of the *Batman* campaign.

Tim Burton used Danny Elfman for the actual score. The Oingo Boingo leader had contributed to ten film projects, including *Pee Wee's Big Adventure* and *Beetlejuice*. *Batman* posed a creative challenge, as he said, "I had never really done an action adventure before.

"With *Batman*," he added, "I came up with the film's basic theme right after the first screening. I began to lay down musical moods on a keyboard right away, trying my best to capture the color and moods of what I'd seen on screen." The result was a symphonic score exhibiting a "dark, gothic, operatic, romantic and grandiose" feel.[126]

Prince's package would be released 20 June, three days prior to the film's debut, with Elfman's offering scheduled for 8 August. Ostin denied that the staggered dates made the instrumental album merely souvenir fare, explaining, "Unfortunately, they were dubbing the movie up to two weeks ago [early June] so we're really behind on Danny's record in terms of release."[127] "There was a very real time pressure," admitted the scorer. "I only had about six weeks writing time and six weeks of preproduction before the work got underway." Elfman had realized that "an orchestral soundtrack appeals to a limited audience—we're talking 50,000-150,000 copies vs. 3 million-8 million" for Prince. The two simultaneous albums were a breakthrough. "I didn't expect the record company to go for it," sighed Peters.[128]

The *Batman* logo dotted major-market billboards in early spring. May 23 witnessed a $1-million, 90-second time-buy on network and cable television outlets. Then there was silence for several weeks.

"Batdance" premiered on MTV Tuesday 13 June at 8 p.m. *USA Today's* Edna Gundersen, cheerleader qua journalist, had announced it the previous day. A praiseworthy review followed: "The Minneapolis funk meister and master alchemist faces Batman and the Joker into a metaphor for id/superego wrestling matches, then lets the psychodrama unfold at St. Vitus' disco."[129] While not as profound as the hyperbole, the clip did attract the desired viewership.

Rolling Stone and *Premiere* ran cover stories on Michael Keaton. The merchandising campaign operated in overdrive. Warners' Licensing Corporation of America (LCA) had approved some 300 *Batman* items by June;

40,000 T-shirts left J.C. Penney's in May. By September, $75 million in walking billboards had been sold.

The Dark Avenger arrived on 2,194 screens nationwide 23 June as Burton, not so privately, muttered, "By the time it comes out . . . they've gotten all the bubble-gum cards, so they don't know if they should bother to see the movie."[130] The director's anxiety was heightened by remarks following an exclusive showing at Universal City's Registry for junketeering New York scribes. The concensus appeared to be "it's good, but not as good as all the hype."

Advance ticket sales soared, belying some of the concerns. "We sold three-fourths of our tickets to the 10 o'clock Friday night show," reported K.B. Fine Arts Theater in Washington D.C. Cinema 1 in New York sold out its opening five shows.[131]

A banner $13.1 million was spent on Friday to see the collision between Batman and his nemesis the Joker. "The movie begins and ends in darkness," offered Denby. "Here is a grand mock-up of the old comic book metropolis, with gigantic gray towers bunched together, a sunless island city ready to sink, like Atlantis, into nowhere."

"You enter into it as you would a magical forest in a fairy tale, and the deeper you're drawn into it, the more frighteningly vivid it becomes," noted Hinson. Canby added, "Everything seems foreshortened, squeezed, angry and rottened." Canby, joined by other reviewers, connected *Batman*'s atmoshpere to those of Fritz Lang's *Metropolis* (1928) and Ridley Scott's sci/fi *Blade Runner* (1982).[132]

In the film, Furst's darkened, fatalistic backdrop provides the stage for the bizzare psychomachinations of the comic-book rivals.

The antagonistic, Batman-Bruce Wayne (Keaton) and The Joker-Napier (Nicholson), represent the forces of light and darkness. Visually and metaphysically, the reverse is normal. "I made you," monotones Batman, "but you made me first" (referring to Napier's murder of Wayne's parents). The disfigured Napier, now The Joker, is Batman's *doppel ganger* (other side), but the duality is one-sided. The garishly colored and clad Joker is "the world's first fully functioning homicidal artist." Evil as he may be, the Nicholson character appears amusingly modish, bedecked in purple/orange suits, white-faced, green-haired.

The incarnation of evil, the maniacal clown laces cosmetics with chemicals, disfiguring his victims and invading the Gotham City Museum to deface art treasures. He spares only Francis Bacon, and his moll, Alicia (Jerry Hall). A *tour de force* is plotted to paralyze urban dwellers with Smylex gas. The lure is $20 million thrown into the wind.

The white-faced villian is totally evil. Wayne is more complex, bedeviled by inner demons. ("You're not exactly normal, are you?" asks romantic interest Vicki Vale (Kim Basinger). "It's not a normal world," is the answer.) As such, the dark knight is hardly a moralistic counter to The Joker. Their duel, as numerous critics noted, proved a mismatch. "The movie has never shown the complicity between moral opposites that drives the great-villian face offs—even in comic books," wrote Kroll. The Batman character, as written, asserted Corliss, seemed "crushed by the burden of his schizoid eminence." The clash of Titans is one-sided. "They aren't equals," asserted Denby. "That's a big problem." Legions of filmgoers echoed patrons Mary McCormick ("I *loved* Jack Nicholson. I think he should get every acting award there is for this.") and Walchitov Alexis ("If it weren't for Nicholson, it would be no good at all."). Reviewers concurred. "This is a one-man show, and he isn't Batman," concluded Mike Clark.[133]

Notices ranged from the *Washington Post*'s Hinson assertion that the film was "as rich and satisfying as you're likely to see all year" to Canby's dissent, "It's neither funny nor solemn. It has the personality not of a particular movie but of a product, of something arrived at by corporate decision."[134] The majority of reviews sided with Canby, but had little box office impact.

The film grossed $13.1 million its first day, surpassing *Ghostbusters II*'s $10.2-million opener. Filmgoers, by Saturday, had contributed an additional $15.5 million. *Indiana Jones and the Last Crusade*'s record weekend total of $37 million was in jeopardy. *Batman* grossed $40.5 million, $18,455 per screen, its opening four days. Columbia Pictures' survival entry, *Ghostbusters II*, was in danger at the box office. Patrons were calling for the Dark Avenger, not the clumsy, psychodynamic foursome.

Prince's "Batdance" surfaced 13 June on MTV during prime time. The title, absent from the film, became an instant add-on on 130 CHR outlets. The 17 June Hot 100 listed "Batdance" at number 53 with a "hot shot debut."

The funky, dance-music selection clearly benefitted from the video and the unreleased film tie-in.

Warners Records shipped one million copies of the "soundtrack" 20 June. "Prince goes to bat and scores a hit," *USA*'s Gundersen applauded, saying the package was "high-performance funk, bristling with hot-wired guitars, turbo-charged rhythms and a voice that negotiates hairpin turns." Another prerelease review raved, "Holy Moly! Prince hits a commercial goldmine on this nine-song opus inspired by the forthcoming Caped Crusader flick . . . Run to the nearest Bat Cave and throw it in on the CD player." In the sluggish music milieu of 1989, *Billboard*'s enthusiasm was understandable. Tower's Russ Solomon reflected the prevailing mood, when he said, "There's nothing that I can see people waiting in line for."[135] Most merchandisers had shared this sentiment, and *Batman* manifested a welcome surprise. "We ordered light," said a Michigan merchandiser, "but we never even got our whole first shipment." "It's a killer. I imagine Warner Bros is a very happy company," indicated a spokesperson from Tower Records.[136] Numerically, *Batman* sold a million pieces out of the box. "Batdance" recorded gold within a week.

Retailers discounted Prince's role in the package's success. Chuck Papke of Harmony House, remarked "a younger demo is buying the product because it's *Batman*, not because of Prince." At Wherehouse Entertainment, a purchaser admitted, "I'm pleasantly surprised, because Prince's last two or three albums would tail off after two or three weeks or so."[137]

Batman topped the album and CD charts 22 July. It remained for six weeks; the album was film-driven and peaked when box office gross totalled, domestically, $187.5 million.

Elfman's instrumental score charted at number 76 a month later, climbing to number 30 as of 16 September. (The film gross at this juncture amounted to $238.6 million.) The scorer's previous observation was validated: "I realized from the beginning that Prince would get the p.r. But I knew that once the movie opened it would speak for itself."[138] Elfman's orchestration was *the* souvenir package, as only two Prince contributions were audible during the two-hour motion picture.

To further propel the Prince title, hovering at sales of four million copies, Warners issued the "Partyman" video in early September. The package remained in the Top 10, but the mania was dissipating. After considerable corporate game-playing, a *Batman* home video was scheduled 15 November release. Observers estimated that Warners would move eight million cassettes worth an additional $200 million.

Batman dwarfed its highly promoted, and priced, competition. Release dates were altered. Other films lost the battle of print and television publicity.

The summer-vacation months are the most targeted period in filmdom. Film studios perceive the enlarged audience pool during the summer season as able to generate enough box office for a handful of films, at least four, to break $100 million plus gross numbers, the mark of a blockbuster hit. This calculation is valid barring a "must see" offering.

The runaway blockbuster is conventionally viewed by bizzers as stimulating theater attendance, unless a rival film is in a direct booking conflict. Twentieth's Tom Sherak asserted, "Moviegoing is contagious."[139] This

Potential 1989 Summer Hits Cluster	
Release Date	**Title**
24 May	*Indiana Jones and the Last Crusade*
9 June	*Star Trek V*
16 June	*Ghostbusters II*
23 June	*Batman*
30 June	*Great Balls of Fire*
	*Karate Kid III**
7 July	*Lethal Weapon II*
14 July	*License to Kill*
18 August	*Eddie and the Cruisers II*
	(Eddie Lives)

* Originally scheduled for 23 June, postponed due to *Batman*

theorem, perhaps folk saying, had a hollow ring in Columbia Picutres executive suites. Columbia had banked its corporate fortunes on two sequels, *Ghostbusters II* and *Karate Kid III*, spending $15 million for production and $6 million on ads.

Ghostbusters debuted with encouraging numbers. Its first week, it generated more than $44 million at the box office. Then *Batman* entered the fray. *Variety*'s 28 June chart reported a 53-percent decline in *Ghostbusters* receipts. Industry watcher Emmanual Gerard observed that the sequel's domestic rentals were reduced by some $55 to 65 million. "When *Batman* came along it became the hot movie and took the real upside away from *Ghostbusters II*," noted the analyst. "To live in America in 1989 you've got to see *Batman*."[140] *'Busters* lacked this peer driven imperative.

July attendance supported Gerard's estimates. *Ghostbusters II*'s momentum was halted.

Columbia Pictures spokerspersons denied the trade press reports, preferring an upbeat interpretation. "No one can be disappointed with a film that earns over $60 million in film rentals," said Jimmy Spitz. "I hope Ivan Reitman makes *Ghostbusters III*. I'm eagerly awaiting it and I think exhibitors are as well."[141]

Ghostbusters II was in the big-picture arena, earning over the magic $100-million mark. The costs were estimated at more than $30 million, accompanied by a $7- to $15-million marketing budget. The fly in the financial ointment was the Creative Artists deal. Murray, Ackroyd, Ramis and director Reitman were entitled to 60 percent of rental income. "It's hard to see how Columbia will ever make a profit on the remaining 40 percent of revenue," observed the prestigious magazine *American Film*.[142]

Karate Kid III had seemed a sure winner—*Part II* had outperformed the original sleeper by some $15 million. The feature was to hit the streets 23 June in some 1,800 theaters.

MCA Records signed for the soundtrack. The Little River Band's "Listen To Your Heart," the scout single, was slated for 12 June release. The album, advertised as "Music To Your Ears," would emerge two weeks later. The best laid plans failed.

Columbia Pictures postponed the premiere by a week. The "new smash single" plus the vinyl package did not chart. *Variety* labelled the production "an outright flop." *Boxoffice* followed with, "This is an embarrassment of grand proportions." Three months into its initial run, *III* was in the red, with a disappointing $38.8-million gross. "It must not be satisfying an audience," said a New York exhibitor.[143]

Further darkening Columbia's prospects was the $25-million Michael J. Fox-Sean Penn Viet Nam feature, *Casualties of War*, which by early October had been unable to return its costs. The studio's prediction of a 22-percent market share by Labor Day fizzled; it came to a meager 14 percent.

On 27 September 1989, the Sony Corporation announced its $3.4-billion acquisition of Columbia Pictures, including the 49 percent owned by the Coca-Cola Company. A major factor for the takeover, according to Masahiko Goto of New Japan Securities, was to "integrate everything audio and visual," (referring to Sony's 1988 $2 billion purchase of the CBS Record Group.) A prime negotiator in the deal was CAA'a Michael Ovitz, described by a Columbia board member as a "constructive force."[144] Dawn Steel may well have dissented, as Sony immediately bought Guber-Peters Entertainment for $200 million. The *Batman* production firm, especially Peter Guber, was rumored to helm Columbia Pictures. "They need to hire a Guber, and say 'Make us a *Batman*,'" wrote pundit Paul Kagen.[145]

The Killer Dies at the Box Office

"Going in, not too many people said anything," recalled film buyer Bill Thompson, referring to the timing of Orion Pictures' summer contender *Great Balls of Fire*. The Jerry Lee Lewis bio-pic, estimated to cost $20 million, was the studio's highly publicized entry in 1989 sweepstakes. Advertising and marketing were figured to cost between $10 and $14 million. While the cast was still on location in Memphis, *USA Today* reported the saga of the 18-month rise and fall of the frantic rock-a-billy was a film "a great many people are panting to see." (See Chapter 2.)[146]

A 15 January 1989 *New York Times* piece, "Jerry Lee Lewis Can Still Stir Things Up," suggested a built-in controversy, mirroring the *Batman* publicity in the *Wall Street Journal* and *Newsweek*. Of the summer titles, the Orion offering successfully countered its future box office rivals, except *Batman*, for media exposure. Lead Dennis Quaid garnered cover pieces in *USA Today*, *GQ*, *American Film*, and *Premiere*; several Lewis features appeared in *Rolling Stone*.

The obligatory soundtrack was plagued by debate. "At first," Quaid told a reporter, "I wanted to do my own singing. Jerry was dead set against it . . . he even halfway threatened my life. I went and recorded my own version of 'Great Balls of Fire,' doing my own singing and piano playing, and played it for him. He said, 'Son, I didn't know you could do those songs that good,' which made me feel great. At that point, we decided that he'd do half the songs and I'd do half." Director Jim McBride discounted the "cockamamie compromise," suggesting that the star lip-sync. Lewis redid eight of his Sun classics for Polydor. Aspiring rock star Quaid joined The Killer on "Crazy Arms."[147] The *Great Balls* album shipped 20 June, the same date as *Batman*. A month later, the package finally charted at number 76, peaking at a disappointing number 62 12 August. St. Martin's Press reissued Myra Lewis Williams's account upon which the movie was based. Lewis's reaction to the original script was, "LIES, LIES, LIES." To accommodate the subject, alterations were made. Sanitized or not, argued Daven Ansen, the public didn't want Jerry Lee Lewis. Analyst Gerrard said: "Almost everybody said the same thing about it—it was a bad movie."[148]

Critics lambasted the backstage glimpse of The Killer. Word-of-mouth destroyed it and the remake album. George Plasketes observed, "*Great Balls*'s opening-week $3.8 million was pocket change compared to *Batman*'s $100.2 million in ten days. Not that the film would have been more successful during another season."[149] In less than two weeks, box office dropped to $1.1 million. Following a thirty-one-day run, the numbers dipped to $351,011 from 470 theaters. The initial showing barely earned $15 million. Economically, *Great Balls* joined the *Buddy Holly Story* (1978), another biographical fantasy mired in red ink. *La Bamba* had emerged as the *one* rock bio-pic that actually returned its investment.

Warner Brothers's *Lethal Weapon II* did succeed, despite *Batman*, in entering the magic $100-million-plus category. *Billboard* greeted the accompanying soundtrack with glowing terminology: "Smash Mel Gibson-Danny Glover action picture's score should benefit from the box office buzz, but music stands on its own."[150] Two months after the film's debut, it charted at number 164, and lasted only three weeks. The cop-shop adventure lacked record-store coattails.

The summer of 1989 was flat, in terms of music. Ironically, three films with high-ranked soundtracks were perceived as the culprits. "If somebody goes to see 'Batman,' 'Ghostbusters II,' and 'Lethal Weapon II,' that might be money they would have used to buy three CDs," said the president of WCI's music distribution arm, Henry Droz.[151] The argument, reminiscent of the video-arcade crisis of 1981, was somewhat disingenuous, as all of the soundtracks from the high-grossers had charted. *Batman*, with two titles, one with the actual score and one with Prince's input, fed off the movie's $240-million-plus box office. (Several writers have contended, with some validity, that Prince's *Batman* was not up to par with *Purple Rain* and would have suffered the same fate of *Lovesexy* had it not been for Bob Kane's comic-book phenomenon.)

Jeffrey M. Sydney, Polygram's executive producer on *Great Balls Of Fire*, upon looking at that film's soundtrack action, concluded, "With more thoughful use of music in film and better cooperation among all participants in the soundtrack process, we can avoid killing the goose that lays the platinum eggs."

Sydney revived the sourcing argument, suggesting that concepts like synergy beclouded some basic issues. Starting the rock era with *Blackboard Jungle*, music placement has been essential ingredient in promoting the film and its music. As the employment of rock escalated from *The Graduate*, through *Fever*, to *The Big Chill* and onward, songs became identified with films. *The Graduate* evokes "Sounds of Silence." *The Big Chill* is identified with "You Can't Always Get What You Want," and *Fever* with "Stayin' Alive." A record executive adage states, "It's got to be in the grooves." Filmmakers frequently forgot it also has to be on the reel. Music not properly positioned is either intrusive or mere background noise. Sydney further had contended that the studios' musical "promiscuity dilutes the talent pool." The competition for "bankable" rockers only tended to inflate the costs of artists and songs for soundtracks, he claimed. In all, "this musical overkill is in many cases creatively counterproductive for filmmakers and artists alike. In the scramble to put popular music in films," wrote Sydney, "too many filmmakers, artists and record executives seem to forget that the greatest commercial success is based on product that—first and foremost—works creatively."

The core of the problem, suggested Sydney, is structural. Studios and labels have diverse, sometimes conflicting, interests. Studios want all the prerelease publicity possible, preferably with a scout single and video six weeks prior to the film's debut. Record companies, conversely, want to benefit from the movie's box office, publicity, and momentum. This game of "Who goes first?" was to have been resolved by synergy, ideally. In reality, the process rarely was practiced.

The film industry is primarily concerned with doomed scout singles, and much less with albums, as they usually emerge to coincide with the movie's release date. "If a single charts before the movie opens," explained Gary LeMel of Warner Brothers Films, "we have a much better chance of keeping our picture in the theaters, when the music is on the tip of everybody's tongue."[152] Albums, for the labels, are the source of the real money: Every album sold returns to the record company an estimated $2.10 and an additional $1 for compact disks. Consequently, labels see scouts and launch videos as marketing the album.

Labels have a serious concern over release dates, which frequently clash with that of the film's producer. Columbia Records allowed Paramount and MCA Records to use George Michael's "I Want Your Sex," as his *Faith* album was not scheduled for several months. If the soundtrack selection had garnered attention, which it did, the CBS single would be issued. Warner Brothers Records used a similar tactic with Peter Cetera's "Glory of Love" and UA's *Karate Kid Part II*.

Another difficulty has been the labels' desire to use soundtracks to expose new or lesser-known acts. (MCA has used Elfman's Oingo Boingo in numerous film scores.) The studios want high-profile superstars. The trade-off frequently has been a two-hit album or cassette with filler by unknowns. *American Gigolo* contained two rock-disco selections, "Call Me"and"Love and Passion"; the remaining material was Giorgio Moroder instrumentals. Prince's nine-cut *Batman* album had only two songs recognizable in the movie. (Only six minutes in the film were devoted to the funkmeister.)

A "Commentary" piece in *Billboard* was an endorsement of synergy when it was operational. The writer wisely recognized that in most cases it was not. "If we focus only on our successes," he contended, "we run the risk of lulling ourselves into a dangerous complacency. In fact, there are real and growing problems that threaten the continued success of the soundtrack phenomenon."[153]

The lip service to synergy was finally questioned; however, mythology dies hard in Hollywood. The failures, a multitude, were overshadowed by the success of *Top Gun*, *Dirty Dancing*, and *Batman* in corporate consciousness.

The 1989 finger-pointing of film and record executives became somewhat one-sided as the record industry had found that their celluloid counterparts had been gaining ground. (An alternative perspective, voiced privately, was that the movies had gotten better and the music industry was living off the CD replacement phenomenon.) Studios with record affiliations and labels that own filmmaking organizations couldn't care less, as profits go into the same conglomerate. As of the turn of the deacde, the balance of power may be shifting. There is an adage not lost to many of the players, "Don't get mad, get even." Although the industry remains a jungle, some artistic high points occasionally emerge.

Notes

1. Quoted in Ronald Grove, "You Don't Know Them—But They Know Movie-goers," *Business Week*, 25 May 1987, 166.
2. Quoted in Susan Royal, "The Making of *Beverly Hills Cop II*," *American Premier*, (1987), 19.
3. David Handleman, "Free Eddie Murphy," *Rolling Stone*, 2 August 1987, 27; Tony Schwartz, "The Emotion of Triumph," *Premiere*, July/August 1987, 56; quoted in Jack Curry, "Murphy Shoots for Another Hit," *USA Today*, 20 May 1987, 2D; and Kevin Lally, "Another Blockbuster For Tony Scott," *Film Journal*, June 1987, 6.
4. Quoted in Steve Gett, "MCA's 'Cop 2' Turns Up Heat," *Billboard*, 16 May 1987, 24.
5. Royal, 19.
6. Quoted in Steve Gett, "Michael Fires Off 'Cop' Hit," *Billboard*, 30 May 1987, 32.
7. Quoted in Kim Freeman, "Michael's 'Sex' Forces Lyrics Issue," *Billboard*, 30 May 1987, 13.
8. Peter Jones, "BBC Doesn't Want 'Sex' Single," *Billboard*, 6 June 1987, 100.
9. Jack Curry, "Murphy Shoots For Another Hit," *USA Today*, 20 May 1987, 1D.
10. Tom Matthews, "Beverly Hills Cop II," *Boxoffice*, July 1987, R61.
11. Richard Schickel, "Din Among The Sheltering Palms," *Time*, 1 June 1987, 73; Janet Maslin, "Murphy in Cop II," *New York Times*, 20 May 1987, C28.
12. Peter Travers, "Beverly Hills Cop II," *People*, 25 May 1987, 10; Stanley Kauffmann, "Comedians Better and The Same," *New Republic*, 29 June 1987, 25; Mike Clark, " 'Cop II' is Just a Cop-out," *USA Today*, 20 May 1987, 1D; Matthews, R61.
13. David Denby, "Bewitched, Bored and Bewildered," *New York*, 22 June 1987, 72.
14. Michael Buckley, "Beverly Hills Cop II," *Film In Review*, August/September 1987, 422; Ira Robbins, "Beverly Hills Cop II," *Video*, April 1988, 63.
15. Desson Howe, " 'Lost Boys' Loses Nerve, Then Verve," *Washington Post*, 31 July 1987.
16. Todd McCarthy, "The Lost Boys," *Variety*, 22 July 1987, 12; Jimmy Summers, "The Lost Boys," *Boxoffice*, October 1987, R912.
17. Jim Calio, "The Lost Boys," *People*, 17 August 1987, 10; David Ansen, "From California, Vampires with Cheekbones," *Newsweek*, 3 August 1987, 67.

18. Quoted in Jim Bessman, "The Soundtrack Craze Grows Up . . .", *Billboard*, 12 November 1988, V8.
19. Steve Gett, "Movies Hot, Music Not," *Billboard*, 3 October 1987, 7.
20. Quoted in Karen Back, " 'Less Than Zero' Is Adding Up to a Movie," *New York Times*, 30 August 1987, 14.
21. Quoted in Aljean Harmetz, "Sanitizing a Novel for the Screen," *New York Times*, 18 November 1987, C25.
22. Harmetz, C25.
23. Back, 14.
24. Quoted in Myron Meisel, "Fox *Less Than Zero* Takes Youth To Extreme," *Film Journal*, October 1987, 10.
25. Harmetz, C25.
26. J. Galbraith, "Less Than Zero," *Variety*, 11 November 1987, 13.
27. David Ansen, "Down and Out in Gucci and Gomorrah," *Newsweek*, 16 November 1987, 14.
28. Michael Wilmington, " 'Less Than Zero' Adds Up to a Feverish Nullity," *Los Angeles Times*, 6 November 1987, 16, (VI).
29. Back, 14.
30. Ansen, 14; Scott Haller, "Less Than Zero," *People*, 14 December 1987, 14; J. Hoberman, "Party Animals Welcome To L.A.," *Village Voice*, 17 November 1987, 67; Wilmington, 16.
31. Janet Maslin, "Less Than Zero," *New York Times*, 6 November 1987, C23; Rita Empley, " 'Zero': Paying Through The Nose," *Washington Post*, 6 November 1987.
32. Haller, 14.
33. Don Waller, "Rock, Rap and Remakes," *Los Angeles Times*, 13 December 1987, 109.
34. Quoted in Montgomery Brower, "Gang Violence: Color It Real," *People*, 27 April 1988, 42.
35. Quoted in James Kaplan, "The Bad Boys of 'Colors'," *Premiere*, April 1988, 40.
36. Quoted in Bill Kelley, "True Colors," *American Film*, March 1988, 21.
37. Quoted in "When Wexler's Not On The Spot, He's A Choosy Cinematographer," *Variety*, 10 February 1988, 19; and Kelley, 21.
38. Quoted in Jim Bessman, "The Soundtrack Craze Grows Up," *Billboard*, 12 November 1988, V-8.
39. Richard Gold, "Orion Pushing Hopper's 'Colors' As A 'Different' Action Film," *Variety*, 13 April 1988, 5.
40. "Protests & Cancellations Attend Opening Of Gang Film 'Colors'," *Variety*, 20 April 1988, 26.
41. Quoted in Susan Spillman, "Gang Fears May Dull 'Colors' Box Office," *USA Today*, 4 April 1988, 1D.
42. "Gangs: Will Life Imitate a Movie?" *Newsweek*, 25 April 1988, 25.
43. Peter Biskind, "Colors," *The Nation*, 30 April 1988, 620.
44. Sheila Benson, "Complexity & Content Washed Out of 'Colors,' " *Los Angeles Times*, 15 April 1988, 1, 13 (Sec. VI).
45. Jeremy Larner, "A Movie of Violence," *Dissent*, Fall 1988, 491; Pauline Kael, "Art Tour," *New Yorker*, 2 May 1988, 86; and Janet Maslin, "Police vs. Street Gangs in Hopper's 'Colors,' " *New York Times*, 15 April 1988, C4.

46. Benson, 1; and Kael, 86.
47. Biskind, 620; and Mike Clark, "The Impact of 'Colors' Fades," 15 April 1988, 5D.
48. David Ansen, "War On The Mean Streets," *Newsweek*, 18 April 1988, F3.
49. Larner, 491; and Susan Spillman, "Gambles and 'toons Pay Off at Theaters," *USA Today*, 16 December 1988, 2D.
50. Quoted in Jean Rosenbluth, "Soundtracks: No Other Vehicle Packs the Sheer Liftoff Power to Boost Talent Old & New Into Higher Orbit," *Billboard*, 16 July 1988, S1, S9.
51. Quoted in Jim Bessman, "The Soundtrack Craze Grows Up," *Billboard*, 12 November 1988, V4, V8.
52. Bessman, V4.
53. Jean Rosenbluth, "Soundtrack Specialists: Maximizing Cross-Market Connections," *Billboard*, 16 July 1988, S4.
54. Quoted in Lynn Hirschoberg, "A Conversation with Tom Cruise," *Rolling Stone*, 11 August 1988, 46; Sheila Benson, "Tepid 'Cocktail' For Two Flashy Performers," *Los Angeles Times*, 29 July 1988, 14.
55. Todd McCarthy, "Cocktail," *Variety*, 27 July 1988, 16.
56. David Ansen, "Cruise Takes a Dive in Booze," *Newsweek*, 8 August 1988, 67; Benson, 15.
57. Vincent Canby, "Mixing and Matching In The Singles-Bar Life," *New York Times*, 29 July 1988, C6; Peter Travers, "Cocktail," *People*, 8 August 1988, 10; Nancy Kolomitz, "Cocktail," *Film Journal*, August 1988, 21; Rita Kempley, "Drinking Problem," *Washington Post*, 29 July 1988, B-F.
58. Janet Maslin, "When a Movie Serves a Mickey," *New York Times*, 14 August 1988, 14; Sheila Benson, "Drinking, Sexism and Boxoffice Woes," *Los Angeles Times*, 14 August 1988, 28.
59. *Billboard*, 30 July 1988, 66.
60. Quoted in Jefferson Graham, "Beach Boys Hit a No. 1 Grove," *USA Today*, 28 October 1988, 80.
61. Quoted in Scott Immergut, "Heartbreak Hotel," *Premiere*, November 1988, 66.
62. "Heartbreak Hotel," *Variety*, 28 September 1988, 14.
63. *Variety*, 14; Janet Maslin, "Winning Elvis's Heart (And the Rest of Him)," *New York Times*, 30 September 1988, C18.
64. Michael Wilmington, "A Lot of Vacancies in 'Heartbreak Hotel,'" *Los Angeles Times*, 30 September 1988, 10 sec. VI.
65. Tom Green, "'Hotel': For Those Who Love Elvis Tender," *USA Today*, 30 September 1988, 8D; Jim Kozak, "Heartbreak Hotel," *Boxoffice*, December 1988, R105.
66. Quoted in Ed Kelleher, "Atlantic's *1969* Relives a Controversial Time," *Film Journal*, September/October 1988, 8.
67. Kelleher, 8.
68. Kelleher, 102. Also see Leonard Klady, "'1969': A Look at Coming of Age in Turbulent Times," *Los Angeles Times*, 28 February 1988, 28–29.
69. Jim Kozak, "1969," *Boxoffice*, January 1989, R17.
70. Donna Britt, "'1969' Takes a Look at the Way It Wasn't," *USA Today*, 22 November 1988, 4D; Janet Maslin, "Two Families Seek Peace With Honor, in

'1969,' " *New York Times*, 18 November 1988, C10; "1969," *Variety*, 23 November 1988, 14.

71. Kevin Thomas, "Movie Reviews," *Los Angeles Times*, 18 November 1988, 12; Kozak, R17.
72. Quoted in Jeannie Williams, " 'Around The World' to the Auction Block," *USA Today*, 7 December 1988, 2D.
73. Quoted in "About That Groovy 'Buster' Sound Track," *USA Today*, 25 November 1988, 5D.
74. *Billboard*, 24 September 1988, 88.
75. Quoted in "About That," 5D.
76. Tom Matthews, "Buster," *Boxoffice*, February 1989, 7.
77. Matthews, R7.
78. *Billboard*.
79. Quoted in Susan Spillman, "Midler and Company Hit the 'Beaches,' " *USA Today*, 5 January 1989, 2D.
80. Quoted in Lawrence Van Gelder, "At The Movies," *New York Times*, 16 December 1988, C12.
81. Gelder, C12.
82. Quoted in Kevin Lally, "Midler Returns to Music, Drama, As Marshall Directs *Beaches*," *Film Journal*, January 1988, 8; Spillman, 2D.
83. Tom Matthews, "On 'Beaches,' " *Boxoffice*, February 1989, 8.
84. *Billboard*, 17 December 1988, 56; quoted in Stephen Holden, "The Pop Life," *New York Times*, 21 December 1988, C28.
85. David Denby, "Washed Up," *New York Times*, 16 January 1989, 58; Pauline Kael, "Fogged In," *New Yorker*, 23 January 1989, 91.
86. Janet Maslin, "A Friendship On and Off the Rocks," *New York Times*, 21 December 1988, C28; Mike Clark, "Bette Runs Aground in Rocky 'Beaches,' " *USA Today*, 21 December 1988, 5D.
87. David Noh, "Beaches," *Film Journal*, January 1989, 23.
88. Todd McCarthy, "Beaches," *Variety*, 21 December 1988, 12.
89. Noh, 23; Denby; 58; Kael, 91; Lesa Sawahata, "Beaches," *Boxoffice*, February 1989, R3.
90. Sawahata, R3; Kael, 92; Noh, 23.
91. Maslin, C28.
92. Peter Travers, "Oh, No, Not Again," *Rolling Stone*, 10 August 1989, 31.
93. Quoted in Kurt Loder, "Radio Gets a Blast From The Past," *Rolling Stone*, 14 August 1986, 9.
94. Quoted in David Handelman, "The Same Old Songs," *Rolling Stone*, 26 January 1989, 11.
95. Quoted in Aljean Harmetz, "Boom Summer for Film Sequels," *New York Times*, 3 May 1989, C19.
96. Quoted in Dylan Jones, "Even Discerning Critics Found Something to Love," *USA Today*, 23 August 1989, 4D.
97. Quoted in Susan Spillman, "This isn't a Film, It's an Event," *USA Today*, 19 June 1989, 1D.
98. Quoted in Susan Spillman, "Box Office Nears $1 B at Halfway Mark," *USA Today*, 14 July 1989, 2D.
99. Quoted in Patrick Goldstein, "The Return of the Money Making Slime," *Rolling Stone*, 1 June 1989, 96.

100. Goldstein, 56.

101. *Billboard*, 1 July 1989, 74.

102. See Peter Travers, "The Gold Rush," *Rolling Stone*, 15 June 1989, 74.

103. David Denby, "A Bat Out of Hell," *New York*, 17 July 1989, 46; quoted in Tom Matthews, "It's Slime Time Again," *Boxoffice*, July 1989, 13; Goldstein, 54.

104. Mike Clark, "A So-So Return to the Scene of the Slime," *USA Today*, 16 June 1989, 1D; "Ghostbusters II," *Variety*, 21 June 1989, 24; Denby, 46; Peter Travers, "Oh, No, Not Again," *Rolling Stone*, 10 August 1989, 31; Kevin Lally, "Ghostbusters II," *Film Journal*, August 1989, 11.

105. Quoted in Jack Mathews, "Batman, the Gamble," *Los Angeles Times*, 18 June 1989, 16 (*Calendar*).

106. *The Bat Whispers* (1930) was a remake of the 1926 silent-screen adaptation of the Mary Roberts Rinehart and Avery Hopwood stage play, *The Bat*. The villain was described as a "mysterious criminal who dressed like a bat, and whose sign was the shadow of a bat projected from the front of an electric flashlight." "The Bat," *Variety*, 17 March 1926; also see Mordaunt Hall, "The Screen," *New York Times*, 16 January 1931, 27.

107. The 120-episode, two-year ABC-TV series generated a sizable $150 million in merchandising, a fact not lost on Warner Brothers Pictures.

108. Quotes in Susan Spillman, "This Isn't," 2D; Matthews, 17; Bill Barol, "Batmania," *Newsweek*, 26 June 1989, 71.

109. Mathews, 17–18.

110. Quoted in Richard Corliss, "The Caped Crusader Flies Again," *Time*, 19 June 1989, 60.

111. Quoted in Hiliary de Vries, " 'Batman' Battles for Big Money," *New York Times*, 5 February 1989, 11; Howard A. Rodman, "They Shoot Comic Books Don't They?" *American Film*, May 1989, 38.

112. de Vries, 11; Mathews, 18.

113. Corliss, 61.

114. Barol, 72; Mathews, 18.

115. Quoted in Jack Kroll, "Return to Gotham City," *Newsweek*, 23 January 1989, 68.

116. Quoted in Terri Minsky, "Bat Guy," *Premiere*, July 1989, 51.

117. Minsky, 50; Kroll, 68.

118. Quoted in Bill Zehme, "Batman: As the Comic Classic Becomes A Movie, Its Star Contemplates Life in the Bat Lane," *Rolling Stone*, 29 June 1989, 41.

119. Corliss, 62.

120. Kathleen A. Hughes, "Batman Fans Fear the Joke's on Them In *Hollywood Epic*," *Wall Street Journal*, 29 November 1988, A1; Barol, 72; Mathews, 16.

121. Mathews, 16.

122. Barol, 73.

123. Quoted in de Vries: 19; "Holy Cape, Batman, What A Costume," *Life*, Spring 1989, 86.

124. Quoted in Michael Goldberg, "Prince Scores Batman Film," *Rolling Stone*, 29 June 1989, 21; also Melinda Newman, "Holy Soundtracks, Batman! There's Two!" *Billboard*, 24 June 1989, 4, 97.

125. The label-supplied figure may be correct; however, most critics recall *two*

scenes with a Prince overlay. Estimates have been that four to six minutes of Prince material is heard during the two-hour saga.

126. Quoted in Jefferson Graham, "Elfman's Music sets the Mood," *USA Today*, 29 June 1989, 6D.

127. Newman, 97.

128. Newman, 97.

129. Edna Gunderson, "Prince Goes Batty in Latest Video," *USA Today*, 14 June 1989, 1D.

130. "1989," *Premiere*, November 1989, 104.

131. Quoted in Anne Ayers, " 'Batman' Fever Thermometer: Superhot," *USA Today*, 22 June 1989, 1D.

132. David Denby, "A Bat Out of Hell," *New York* 17 July 1989, 45; Hal Hinson, " 'Batman,' with Dark Grandeur," *Washington Post*, 23 June 1989, F1; Vincent Canby, "Nicholson and Keaton Do Battle in 'Batman,' " *New York Times*, 23 June 1989, C12.

133. Jack Kroll, "The Joker Is Wild, But Batman Carries the Night," *Newsweek*, 26 June 1989, 73; Richard Corliss, "Murk in the Myth," *Time*, 19 June 1989, 61; Denby.

134. Ayers, 1D.

135. Edna Gundersen, "Prince's Batman' LP: Gotham as Funkytown," *USA Today*, 19 June 1989, 1D; *Billboard*, 24 June 1989, 84; Jeffrey Ressner, "Summer's Hot Music Forecast," *Rolling Stone*, 29 June 1989, 17.

136. " 'Batman' Does Right Thing," *Billboard*, 22 July 1989, 82.

137. Ibid, 82.

138. Quoted in Jefferson Graham, "Elfman's Music Sets the Mood," *USA Today*, 29 June 1989, 6D.

139. Quoted in Aljean Harmetz, "Boom Summer for Film Sequels," *New York Times*, 3 May 1989, C19.

140. Quoted in Richard Gold, "Summer Sequels' Fading B.O. Belies 'Blockbusters' Status: Current Boom May Be Peaking," *Variety*, 26 July 1989, 4.

141. Gold, 4.

142. Betsy Sharkey, "The Return of the Return of the Summer Sequels," *American Film*, June 1989, 41.

143. Gold, 4; Tom Matthews, "The Karate Kid III," *Boxoffice*, September 1989, R9.

144. Quoted in John Schwartz, "Japan Goes Hollywood," *Newsweek*, 9 October 1989, 65.

145. Quoted in Shelley Liles-Morris, "Sony Likely to Tap Guber," *USA Today*, 28 September 1989, 7B.

146. Michael St. Gerard, "Quaid Fires Up For Lewis Film," *USA Today*, 9 November 1988, 2D.

147. Quoted in Robert Palmer, "Simmer Down, Son," *American Film*, June 1989, 29.

148. Quoted in Gold, 4.

149. George Plasketes, "Great Balls of Fire!" *PMS*, 13, no. 3 (Fall 1989), 75–80.

150. *Billboard*, 1 July 1989, 74.

151. Quoted in "Soft Music Retail Bix Has Trade Worried," *Billboard*, 5 August 1989, 87.

152. Quoted in Jean Rosenbluth, "Southtrack Specialists: Maximizing Cross-Market Connections," *Billboard*, 16 July 1988, 5–9.
153. Quotes from Jeffrey M. Sydney, "How To Keep Laying Platinum Eggs: Putting Soundtracks On A Second Basis," *Billboard*, 14 February 1987, 9.

13

On the Cutting Room Floor: Epilogue

"Rockumentaries," as rock documentaries have been called, constitute the only accurate portrayal of artists "doing their own thing" prior to the advent of music television in 1981. Before MTV, the motion picture provided a realistic image of rock fans attending a concert. As Parales and Romanowski observed, "The best known and most important rock movies are the rock documentaries."[1] As with most generalizations, the statement is a bit strong, but Mick Jagger and The Stones, The Beatles, and other luminaries were far more accessible in theaters than on commercial television.

American Bandstand, unfortunately, set the television standard in mid-1957. Artists were paid scale and forced to lip-sync their latest releases. The appearances were labelled promotional. Clark's legacy to rock television was pitifully low wages, banal camera work, and censorship. *Bandstand* did generate record sales and prompt some concert attendance, however. Still, the fare emanating from Philadelphia on weekday afternoons barely captured the essence of rock music.

Surprisingly, no one in Hollywood stumbled onto the idea of filming a rock concert during the 1950s. Technologically, remotes were difficult but possible. A filmmaker could easily have bussed in thousands of teens to see Elvis, Ricky, or whomever on a studio lot.

A.I.P. gets the credit for the first rock-concert film. On 28 October 1964, the first "Teenage Awards Music International" (T.A.M.I.) show was staged at the Santa Monica Civic Auditorium. Jan and Dean hosted the ninety-minute extravaganza. The participants constituted an impressive lineup: The Rolling Stones, Gerry and The Pacemakers, and Billy J. Kramer represented the British Invasion. Along with Jan and Dean, The Beach Boys recreated the Malibu surfin' sound. Leslie Gore's feminist plaint, "You Don't Own Me," was included. A star-studded roster of black artists, past and present, received equal billing. Chuck Berry, Bo Diddley, and James Brown shone along with Motowners like The Supremes, Smokey Robinson and The Miracles, and the irrepressible Marvin Gaye. *The T.A.M.I. Show* was the first rockumentary, and many critics consider it the best.[2]

T.A.M.I., like many others, is basically a cult film. Its cinematic quality is akin to an early 1950s kinescope—grainy, using a stationary camera. Only dedicated mavens are willing to sit through the one and one-half-hour showing. There was no soundtrack. *The Big T.N.T. Show* followed in 1965; the two were condensed into a ninety-minute videotape called *That Was Rock* in 1986.

The three major rock festivals in the late Sixties were recorded on film. The Monterey International Pop Festival marked the beginning of the rock-festival era. A Los Angeles concert promoter, Alan Pariser, had formed the idea for the festival in fall 1966. "I started thinking about how they had jazz festivals but there was no forum for rock and roll," he explained later, "and I thought that it would be great to have a festival up in Monterey that would be the Monterey Pop Festival, instead of the Monterey Jazz Festival. It was very plain to me that rock and roll was what was happening in the world at that time. It was the music of the people."[3]

Rock stars were immediately involved in staging the event. John Phillips of the Mamas and the Papas and Lou Adler, then president of Dunhill Records, became co-directors. They lined up a "board of governors" including Mick Jagger, Paul McCartney, Paul Simon, Donovan, Brian Wilson, and Smokey Robinson as well as record industry executives. A number of lesser-known acts were invited to the festival, including the Jimi Hendrix Experience and The Who. The non-profit event began on 16 June 1967 and ran for three days before an overcapacity crowd of 10,000. Admission prices for each show ranged from $3.00 to $6.50.

Spectacular performances were turned in by Janis Joplin, The Who, Jimi Hendrix, Otis Redding, and Ravi Shankar, all of whom received their initial, national exposure at the festival. Numbered among the others who performed were The Grateful Dead, The Byrds, Jefferson Airplane, Canned Heat, Buffalo Springfield, Country Joe and The Fish, The Steve Miller Band, Simon and Garfunkel, and The Mamas and The Papas. Monterey Pop awakened record company executives to the new rock culture. "It shook the business," said Capitol's Joe Smith, adding:

> The fact that all these musicians got together and played off each other and talked to each other—you knew that there was a community of music and people

that were making a definite break from what was. You knew the music and the music business had inexorably changed. Monterey was the catalyst. Shortly thereafter, radio changed and record companies' attitudes changed. You said, 'Wow, this is what people are going to buy and listen to.'[4]

Performers at Monterey were courted and offered enormous contracts by executives who were anxious to capitalize on the new youth market. Janis Joplin and Jimi Hendrix were introduced to the world and furious bidding took place to sign them (Warner and Columbia won).

Filmmaker D. A. Pennebaker and his crew canned hours of footage from the festival, which was shot in 16mm and then blown up for 35mm distribution in theaters. (Pennebaker's experimentation with the *cinema verite* style of filming rock concerts had been seen earlier in *Don't Look Back*, a chronicle of Bob Dylan's 1965 tour of Great Britain. The ninety-six-minute documentary included concert vignettes and revealing, behind-the-scenes, black-and-white footage. Though it is considered a classic in the genre,[5] it did not have a mass release.)

Monterey Pop also did not enjoy a general release in 1969, though it received favorable notices. *Variety* called it a "top documentary that records, comments on and reveals pop music in action as well as subtly noting its effects and appeal to evolving youth and elders alike." Richard Schickel considered it "one of the truly invaluable artifacts of our era," but noted the limitations of *cinema verite* and the failure of Pennebaker "to probe into the spirit animating both the festival itself and pop music in general."[6]

According to a report in the first issue of *Rolling Stone*, the festival would have ended up in the red had it not been for a deal Adler inked with ABC for the television and film rights. As a result, the festival turned a profit of about $200,000, which was destined for charity.[7] The commercial potential of festivals and succeeding film documentaries was not lost upon many industry people or concert promoters.

The Woodstock Music and Art Fair, held 15, 16, and 17 August 1969 in Bethel, New York, was the apex of the rock festivals. The three days of peace, love, and music generated an ethos, a mythology, which lent support to the most ardent proponents of the dawning of a new community as well as to its many opponents.

Not even the most optimistic promoter could have imagined the phenomenal-sized crowd that attended. Because 186,000 tickets had been sold, Woodstock Ventures expected 200,000 people at most. As *Rolling Stone* commented, "No one was prepared for what happened and no one could have been."[8] Lines of cars stretched for twenty miles from the fair; the fences surrounding the Yasgur farm collapsed, allowing thousands of gate crashers to mingle with those who had paid their $18 for the three days. On the second day, it was announced to the crowd that this was to be a "free concert."

After the festival, the Woodstock promoters claimed to be $1.3 million in the red.[9] The alleged losses could partially be attributed to the fact that only one customer in ten had actually paid admission, and partially to the phenomenal fees and services rendered to the entertainers. As Robert Santelli observed, however, "Those who were clever enough realized that the interest the media had generated over Woodstock would guarantee that enough money would be made from the movie and albums to at least wipe out the figures in the loss column.[10] Two months before the festival, Woodstock Ventures had signed a deal with filmmakers Michael Wadleigh and Bob Maurice to film the event. Wadleigh and Maurice were responsible for production costs and finding a distributor; Woodstock Ventures was to share in a percentage of the film's profits. After struggling for some time, Wadleigh settled (for a paltry, $100,000 production budget) with Warner Brothers.

To ease the financial straits of Woodstock Ventures, the family of promoter Billy Roberts assumed the debt in full. One of the stipulations in the arrangement was that "Woodstock Ventures enter into an immediate agreement with Warner Bros. Pictures in order to recoup a portion of the loss," Robert Stephen Spitz reported in his chronicle of the festival. "Warner's received exclusive distribution rights to the Woodstock film in return for a flat sum of $1 million plus a fractional participation in the net box office receipts. It was a wretched deal for Woodstock Ventures, considering they had a finished product that was rumored to be 'dynamite' and fifty percent of all profits going into the negotiating meeting."[11]

Directed by Michael Wadleigh and produced by Bob Maurice, the film opened in March 1970 with admission prices around $5. Executives had correctly assumed that the audience would treat the film as a concert and not object to the high ticket price.[12] *Film Quarterly* reviewers disagreed: "Since the peacefulness of Woodstock already seems ancient history, *FQ* will wait to comment on the film—as we did with *Cleopatra*—until it can be seen at less outrageous prices."[13] Wadleigh's visual effects (split screens, superimpositions, and double framing), scenes and interviews with the crowd, as well as spectacular concert footage, made the documentary something special.

The film was greeted with critical acclaim. *Variety* called it "an absolute triumph in the marriage of cinematic technology to reality." *Sight and Sound* considered the Warner Brothers release "a revolutionary hybrid of commercial and underground cinema.'' Canby thought it was ''somewhat less extraordinary than the event it preserves—that is, in comparison with a documentary that transforms its subject into cinematic art that is its own justification.''[14] *Woodstock* became a stunning financial success, earning $16.4 million in rentals for Warners. Worldwide box office gross exceeded $50 million by January 1979.

The soundtrack album was issued *prior* to the film. Since the studio and Atlantic are subsidiaries of WCI, the release strategy worked well. The three-record set was the biggest package released by Atlantic Records, with the highest list price, $14.98. It became one of the company's most successful albums, selling more than two million copies that year and continuing with a long shelf-life. (A follow-up, *Woodstock II*, released in 1971, was certified platinum.)

Attempts to restage Woodstock were unsuccessful. In 1979, promoters of Woodstock II had anticipated a ten-year reunion that would include a seventy-two-hour concert, a film, a CBS album, two books, and a magazine special. ''T-shirts, vinyl jackets, ashtrays, crayons and anything else the great American public will buy will follow later,'' a Woodstock II marketing consultant, Bennett Sims said.[15] Instead, the promoters spent a quarter-of-a-million dollars just trying to find a site in New York State to host the festival. Local townspeople carried bad memories of the 1969 invasion and were strongly outspoken against a rerun. Woodstock II, ''The Second Gathering,'' failed for lack of a site.

Plans for a Woodstock sequel in 1989 also flopped. Promoters Tom Roberts and Joel Rosenman could not arrange the planned four-day, global festival, combining concert performances in Moscow, Washington, D.C., and Europe. The two sold the rights to the Woodstock logo, music, and videos to Warner Communications in order to recoup costs. Warner *did* sell 250,000 copies of the Woodstock records, but ended up cancelling plans for another documentary, as well as a theatrical rerelease of the *Woodstock* film in conjunction with a special concert tour. Warner Home Video reissued the feature film on videocassette as the centerpiece of a seventeen-title compilation of rockumentaries and videoclips called *Sound Investments*. MTV and VH-1 gave extensive promotion throughout summer 1989, including music clips from the film and a two-hour broadcast of previously unseen footage from the festival.[16]

The triumph of *Woodstock* stood in stark contrast to *Gimme Shelter*, also released in 1970. Canby called the cinematic record of The Rolling Stones' American tour ''one of the most unpleasant, bleak, depressing movies I've ever encountered.''[17]

In December 1969, *Rolling Stone* ran a banner headline proclaiming

"FREE ROLLING STONES: IT'S GOING TO HAPPEN!" After a series of planning mishaps, the event took place at Altamont Speedway, a dusty, auto-race track near Livermore, where 300,000 people came out to hear The Grateful Dead, Jefferson Airplane, and The Stones. In contrast to Woodstock, Santelli pointed out, "The Altamont stage was a war zone, a place to avoid if possible."[18] During the chaotic afternoon, a young black man, Meredith Hunter, was stabbed to death by one of the Hell's Angels who had been hired to keep order at the affair. In all, four persons died, and a number of injuries and discomforts were endured. Even performer Marty Balin of The Jefferson Airplane was felled by a Hell's Angel. After describing the tragic events at the concert, Jay Cocks concluded, "It was hard to believe that Woodstock had taken place back East just four months before."[19]

Ironically, the entire event had been staged to allow The Rolling Stones' management to film a *Woodstock*-like movie. The film, *Gimme Shelter*, including the murder scene, was released a year later. The headline of the underground San Francisco paper *Good Times* summed up the general reaction to Altamont: "Mick Jagger Used Us For Dupes," a quote attributed to a member of Hell's Angels. It could have been said by any one of those who went to Altamont in search of another Woodstock "weekend of love."

Filmmakers David and Albert Maysles had been contracted to shoot The Rolling Stones' Madison Square Garden concerts. The deal was later extended to others on the last leg of the 1969 American tour, including the free concert at Altamont. Profits from the film, The Stones announced, would go to charity. (A small gesture, considering the tour grossed an estimated $1.5 million.)

Previously, the Maysles brothers had produced a television special on The Beatles and worked at the Monterey Festival. They were best known for *Salesman*, a 1968 feature film *Time* called "one of the most moving and accomplished examples of *cinema verite* so far."[20] (*Cinema verite*, or direct cinema, the term the Maysles brothers use to describe their documentary filmmaking, is a process in which the filmmaker, "rather than creating (or reconstructing) events, attempts to situate himself in the midst of them." The anticipated result is a "real-life drama" determined by the nature of the event.[21])

Gimme Shelter, which included sequences from the Madison Square Garden and Altamont concerts, raised questions about the authenticity of the filmmakers' approach. Scenes of Rolling Stone band members reviewing footage of the murder at Altamont create a "film within a film." After seeing it once, Jagger asks, "Can you run that for me again?" David

Maysles obliges, this time in slow motion, with freeze-frames allowing the filmmaker to point out every detail of the crime. Critics charged that the filmmakers had exploited and sensationalized the violence at Altamont. "What might have been a straight concert film is, instead, a carefully structured little horror movie," wrote Canby. Jay Cocks concurred, writing, "Without the tragic murder, *Gimme Shelter* would be another not particularly revealing *cinema verite* essay about the personalities that shape pop culture."[22] In response, David Maysles argued that the film was not a "contrived attempt to take the talent of the Stones and then structure events or a movie around it in some kind of fake way. The life of the tour, which is what the film represents, is a natural happening . . . [the film] raises a lot of questions about what America is all about, but in a way that's not a lecture or anything of that sort."[23] Brother Albert, however, commented, "I think we would have been disappointed if everything had stopped just at Madison Square Garden."[24]

Gimme Shelter did not fare well at the box office, due in part to a limited distribution. A live-concert album recorded at Madison Square Garden, *Get yer Ya-Ya's Out!*, was released in October 1970. It was certified gold.

In 1968, The Beatles had agreed to produce a documentary film of the group making of an album, topped with a live performance, as a substitute for another tour. Behind McCartney's impetus, the project was originally titled *Get Back*, an attempt to return to their roots and hold the band together. Filming began in January 1969 under the direction of Michael Lindsay-Hogg. The project dragged along in a tense atmosphere of personal resentment and bickering as the group was on the verge of their breakup. "Instead of a film about the making of an album, it was a portrait of the dissolution of a group," wrote biographers.[25] More than thirty hours of music and ninety-six hours of film were recorded. By the time it was over, the band's hostilities were in the open and the project went on the shelf. "Nobody could look at it," Lennon said. "I really couldn't stand it."[26]

Phil Spector, who had produced Lennon's single "Instant Karma," was brought in to complete the album. In the remix, Spector added the female choruses and lush orchestrations that characterized his trademark "wall of sound." McCartney was furious, especially at the producer's treatment of "The Long and Winding Road," but found there was nothing he could do about it.

Let It Be, a United Artists picture, premiered in May 1970. The most memorable moment from the eighty-eight-minute film chronicling the studio sessions was a performance on the roof of the Apple Records office in London. Amid the continuous quarreling in the basement studio, director Michael Lindsay-Hogg had suggested the rooftop concert. "You had a sense of a rare and odd occasion, that you were actually at a Beatles concert with nobody up there except yourself," the director said.[27] The lunchtime performance drew a large crowd and eventually police responded to a noise complaint. The officers politely ordered the group to stop playing. Lennon parted with his characteristic wit: "I'd like to say thank you very much on behalf of the group and myself and I hope we passed the audition."

Though the movie drew very few to theaters, the recordsetting LP sold 3.7 million copies in just over two weeks. It won the 1970 Grammy Award for Best Original Score written for a Motion Picture. "Let It Be" captured an Oscar for Best Original Song/Score for a Film.

A host of rockumentaries were made during the Seventies and Eighties. The majority were not box office sensations or chartbusters. Most were not seen outside of the art-house and collegiate circuits. (For example, Neil Young's *Rust Never Sleeps* would receive more exposure on the USA Network's *Night Flight* than in movie theaters.) Record companies often financed the films for their soundtracks. Album sales generally outpaced box office figures. Led Zeppelin's *The Song Remains The Same* (1976) was a box office flop, but the soundtrack rapidly climbed to Number 2 and achieved multi-platinum stature. *Rust Never Sleeps* (1979) experienced a similar fate while reaching Number 9 on the LP chart. U2's *Rattle and Hum* (1988) equally enjoyed the peak of *Billboard*'s "Top Pop Albums," but the rockumentary was an economic disappointment.

These numbers indicate that wedding a concert audio to a rockumentary is generally a risky gamble. Beginning with *Woodstock*, the albums promoted the movies. Only a handful of rock documentaries since *T.A.M.I.—Woodstock*, *The Last Waltz*, and *Stop Making Sense*—have generated enough theater traffic for record labels to rely on the souvenir power of these vehicles, as a concert-film soundtrack is little more than a glorified "live" package.

The key to a successful concert film, besides the rock group featured, has been to recreate the experience of the live performance in this altogether different medium. Generally, directors have met the challenge with performance footage and crowd shots combined with backstage incidents and interviews, which give the viewer an additional perspective on the event. Most of the concert films, however, simply came off as self-glorifying profiles.

A few of the more memorable rockumentaries of the Seventies were *Jimi Plays Berkeley*, *Elvis on Tour*, the last concert at the *Fillmore* (west), Alice Cooper's United Kingdom tour entitled *Welcome to My Nightmare*, and Led Zeppelin's *The Song Remains the Same*, filmed at Madison

Square Garden and the West Coast. (The latter included "concept" material, which now dominates music videos, and was designated platinum four weeks after its release.) "*The Song Remains the Same* is a movie to listen to Led Zeppelin by," wrote a *Times* critic, "if you want to listen to Led Zeppelin. If you don't, there's no point going."[28] The movie flopped, though it became a cult attraction at midnight showings.

The Concert for Bangladesh (1972) documented the 1 August 1971 performance at Madison Square Garden to raise money for the United Nations Children's Fund, designated for the refugee children of Bangladesh. Former Beatle George Harrison organized the event; participants included Harrison, Leon Russell, Bob Dylan, Billy Preston, Ringo Starr, and Ravi Shankar.

Released in December 1971, the triple-disc soundtrack made an impressive debut at Number 5 on the U.S. charts, in spite of a $12.98 list price. Within weeks it had sold 900,000 copies globally. At the end of 1972, sales reached an estimated three million. The United Nations Children's Fund received $5 on each copy sold and $243,418 from the concert. The album captured a 1972 Grammy Award for Album of the Year.

Unfortunately, the Twentieth Century Fox picture did not reach theaters until spring 1972. Unable to capitalize on the initial explosion in record sales, the film did nothing at the box office. Reviews were scarce. On the occasion of the film's opening, a *New York Times* writer looked at rock-festival films as sociological barometers. In comparison to *Woodstock* and *Gimme Shelter*, *The Concert for Bangladesh* reflected "a disheartening social and political vacuum," he suggested. "Evidently reluctant to mingle with Causes, shy of overloading the concert with social dimensions, the filmmakers have ended up with a tight-corseted film which, alas, reflects only too well the mood of the moment. Late sixties energy has faded into early seventies lethargy."[29]

Of greater significance was Martin Scorsese's filming of The Band's farewell concert in San Francisco Thanksgiving 1976. The group decided to do the final concert and invite famous friends to participate as a way of "saying goodbye to the road" after sixteen years of traveling and performing. As the invitation list grew so did the idea—from a home movie to a full-length feature film. "We just didn't know the next time when people like this were gonna get together, for whatever reason," band member and the film's producer, Robbie Robertson, said. "I was a little nervous about letting it slip by."[30] Also, Robertson thought rock music on film was terrible. "That's another reason to do this," he said. "I watched music on television and in movies, and I asked myself, 'Is this the line of work I'm in?' Because if it is, I find it embarrassing, obnoxious and very poorly done—so less than listening to music in my imagination."[31]

Scorsese, who was an editor for *Woodstock* and had produced *Mean Streets*, was his choice for a director. He decided to abandon the hand-held-camera, *cinema verite* approach of previous rockumentaries and brought in instead a Hollywood crew of professionals. The Band's final show featured a number of guest performers, including Ronnie Hawkins, Bob Dylan, Neil Young, Eric Clapton, Van Morrison, Joni Mitchell, Muddy Waters, and others. Concert footage was mixed with interviews the director did with band members, discussing the group's history and feelings about this final, live performance.

Scorsese's film took a year of late nights and $1.5 million to produce. It opened in theaters in April 1978. Critics were not impressed. The *Times*' Maslin considered it "a great lost opportunity. There is a dazzling array of talent on display here, and the film surely has its memorable moments. But it articulates so little of the end-of-an-era feeling it hints at . . . that it's impossible to view 'The Last Waltz' as anything but an also-ran."[32]

The three-record album also received poor reviews. "A classic recording of a classic pseudoevent, *The Last Waltz* poses as a document of rock history in the making," said *Rolling Stone*. "But no new standards are set, few old standards are met, and future challenges are never raised. What we have here is a glittering but empty rite of passage."[33]

The last rockumentary of the Seventies was The Who's *The Kids Are Alright*, released in June 1979. The album was really a greatest-hits collection. Fans bought the LP, which achieved platinum status that year, but were not interested in the film.

There were also a host of rockumentaries in the Eighties, most of which generated little in terms of record sales, box office receipts, and critical attention. *D.O.A.* (1980) and *Urgh!—A Music War* (1981) treated the Punk scene. *Bongo Man* (1982) and *Heartland Reggae* (1980) featured reggae groups. *No Nukes* (1980) showcased a number of performers protesting the use of nuclear power. Footage was taken primarily from five concerts of the same name at Madison Square Garden and an outdoor rally at Battery Park in September 1979. Artists included Jackson Browne, John Hall, James Taylor, Carly Simon, The Doobie Brothers, Bonnie Raitt, Crosby, Stills and Nash, and, most notably, Bruce Springsteen, in his movie debut. The Asylum LP was certified gold. Other rockumentaries of note were *This is Elvis* (1981); a Monty Python-hosted affair, *The Secret Policeman's Other Ball* (1982), which featured Pete Townshend, Sting, and others; *Let's Spend the Night Together*, a chronicle of The Stones' 1981 tour released in 1983; and Chuck Berry's *Hail! Hail! Rock'n'Roll* (1987). Talking Heads' *Stop Making Sense* and U2's *Rattle and Hum* deserve some attention.

Stop Making Sense

Jonathan Demme, a New World Pictures-Roger Corman alumnus, had enjoyed several critically noteworthy pictures. *Handle With Care*, originally *Citizen's Band*, and the wistful *Melvin and Howard* were Demme projects. In 1978, Demme had seen the New Wave band Talking Heads in a Central Park, daytime, open-air concert. They became his "all-time favorite rock group." He attended their Los Angeles Greek Theatre concert during the 1983 *Speaking in Tongues* tour: The event spawned a cult film.

Demme was in postproduction with the Goldie Hawn feature *Swing Shift*. Due to the demands of Hawn, the director's cut was altered substantially by the studio; to enhance the star, significant re-shooting and editing was done. During this period, Demme began to conceptualize a "performance," as opposed to "concert" motion picture. He told the *Film Journal*, "I didn't want to do a film *about* a Talking Heads concert. I wanted it to be a performance film, for better or worse." His film, he told the *Voice*, would portray "what it's like to rock through a Talking Heads concert."[34]

Through a mutual friend, Gary Goetzman, the director met with David Byrne. "I told them it was an incredibly cinematic show already, and the way to see it to best advantage was to make it into a film . . . I told them I wouldn't do it with a lot of quick cuts, which seem to be so popular these days, but rather with long takes. And I didn't want to go the route of constant cutaways to the audience . . . that all sounded good to them. It appealed to their sense of craftsmanship," he explained.[35]

The shooting would be done at the Hollywood Pantages 17, 18, and 19 December. Jordon Cronenweth of *Blade Runner* would shoot the highly structured script. Demme said, "We were constantly writing photographic scripts for how we were going to shoot the film and rewriting and rewriting them. So by the time we got down to the actual shooting, I knew what I wanted to catch and I had communicated that to the camera people. None of us think that we missed a thing." The sound would be a twenty-four-track, digitally produced recording, creating a "perfect balance in Dolby stereo, and lyrics come across as clearly as imaginable." Pauline Kael wrote, "The sound seems better than live sound; it is better—it has been filtered and mixed and fussed over, so that it achieves ideal clarity."[36]

The three concerts were edited down to eighty-eight minutes. The cinematography was stunning. Six locked-in cameras, a Panaglide, and a hand-held camera were used. "It was an attempt to give a roving best seat in the house to the audience," said Demme, "and to hang with what seems to be most exciting at that moment as opposed to jumping around and trying to create an unnecessary artificial energy through editing."[37]

Talking Heads was able to raise $800,000 for the project. The record rights were the band's. Sire Records would release the material. The independent project was marketed and distributed by Warner Brothers Records.

A scout single did not materialize, as the New Wave group was an AOR phenomenon. "Fans are probably a bit older and more upscale than is the rock norm," one critic politely said. Another writer labeled The Heads as "the intellectual's rock group," a sure kiss of death in many circles.[38]

The Talking Heads rockumentary surfaced as the San Francisco Film Festival finale at the 1,560-capacity Castro Theatre. The 24 April debut was followed a day later with a Warners press showing. Jack McDonough, *Billboard*'s Bay City writer, waxed enthusiastic, suggesting that the film made the viewer feel "like a welcome loiterer on stage as the band blazes through its set."

"The band is seen and heard to good advantage here, and their fans should be generally pleased," concurred McCarthy.[39]

Film Comment's Michael Sragow did a three-page piece on the project. He characterized the movie as "an exhilarating experience—almost a call to rock 'n' roll faith." In a not-so-subtle reference, he reminded corporate readers, "The movie is now ready for release."[40] Warner Pictures partially on the basis of these reviews, decided to market the product.

A *Variety* writer, after the April Burbank showing, cautioned that *Stop Making Sense*'s "potential in theatrical release is highly questionable; music pictures toplining groups much more popular than the Heads have made little impact at the b.o. [boxoffice] . . . Highly selective openings in carefully chosen theatres, tied in with concurrent release of a live album, would seem the best way to go, and good response should be found down the line in cable and vidcassette markets" suggested the writer.[41]

Warners, having signed the film, followed this advice. To its credit, the studio knew it would be issuing a "cult film" from the outset. The action would be at the audio and video outlets. Inner-conglomerate cooperation, in this case, was essential, as the movie was marketed to sell the album. The record package appeared the week of 15 September. Full page ads announced:

> Special Limited Edition Package Includes 20-Page Booklet Featuring Photos and Drawings by David Byrne from Stage Production Storyboards

The tape sticker read, "This cassette features extended versions of six songs and a different mix of 'Slippery People'." While spotlighting *Woman in Red*, *Billboard* reviewed the Heads album, noting that the duplication of previously released material might undercut its appeal. "Modern Heads music has certainly changed since their inception as art school primitives, and now sustains remarkable polish. Lavish package also merits the higher $9.98 tag," the piece continued.[42] Late September found the LP on the trade charts, hovering around Number 80: It remained for a surprising forty-seven weeks. The videoclip of "Once In a Life Time" hit MTV's heavy rotation at the same time and stayed for the rest of 1984.

Stop Making Sense, a phrase from "Girlfriend is Better," begins with a shot of David Byrne's white sneakers moving toward a microphone. A boombox accompanies the Talking Head vocalist through "Psycho Killer." The stark stage underscores the lyric. This will be the first of sixteen songs performed throughout. Bassist Tina Weymouth enters to collaborate on "Heaven." As the song is played, stagehands set up the drum platform for Chris Franz. 'Swamp" follows. The congregation of group members goes on through the numbers until all are present.

The band's expansion adds more power and intensity to the performances. Diverse sounds, vocals with myriad styles—New Music, calypso, Third World, gospel, and New Age—coalesce into a chant, or dirge-like crescendo. The full power of Talkings Heads is felt in "What A Day Was," "Girlfriend" and, climatically, Rev. Al Green's "Take Me to the River," during which the audience is finally seen.

Throughout, Byrne dominates with his gestures, jerks, strawman postures, and chickenlike head throbs. In one number he resorts to a controlled, seemingly effortless version of Chuck Berry's famous duckwalk. A fitting description of Byrne was provided by Pauline Kael: "David Byrne dances in the guise of a revved-up catatonic; he's an idea man, an aesthetician who works in the modernist mode of scary, catatonic irony. That's what he emanates." Another characterization could well be "Pee-wee Herman on Thorazine." Byrne's carefully measured performance is contrasted to his body language and the demeanor of the other Talking Heads. The band—particularly backup vocalists Lynn Mabry and Edna Holt and percussionist Steve Scales, the cheerleader—heightens the lyrical dualism.

The cinematography is stellar. Backstage scenes, interviews, and crowd shots are notably absent. It is only in the anticlimactic closing number that audience cuts are used.

Byrne is the focus of the feature. Only once does he relinquish the leadership role. Tina Weymouth does "Tom Tom Club" during which Byrne changes into The Big Suit—a Frankensteinish zoot suit—to contrast with his previous rumpled-Yuppie uniform.

The cinematography seems to challenge the Heads personae, working in tandem with the group; the frames, lighting, and backdrops highlight, then begin to compete for the viewers' attention. This isn't Demme's intention, but the visual assault goes beyond normal enhancement. (The lack of backstage footage and crowd shots, however commendable, may partially account for the stress on the visual.)

Cronenweth's montage of techniques, Byrne's choice of colors, and MTV-style editing rivet the viewer to the stage. The film begins with an impressionistic feel, "rich with deep, oily sheen and shadow," and moves to stark, black-and-white contrasts. The "Once in a Lifetime" segment, the video from the film, is bathed in red as smoke drifts slowly to a single spotlight. The chorus is repeated with a sinister feel. The next song is immersed in darkness—black shadows on the lightened backdrop.

As the music intensifies, the sensory juxtaposition heightens. Words and split-screen photos appear on the backdrop. "There's considerable artifice, as gorgeously effective lighting schemes alternate with slides of such things as dogs' paws and buzzwords in block letters . . ." writes Schruers.[43] "Making Flippy Floppy" and "Top Tom Club" are as close to the Fillmore of 1966 as the performance will come. The subtle sights compete with, if not surpass, some of the sounds.

Stop was a definite contribution to the filmography of concerts; the film garnered rave reviews. "Demme's camera is always in the right place, and for the right length of time," wrote Ansen, "unlike, say, Hal Ashby's Rolling Stones movie, 'Let's Spend the Night Together,' which seemed to watch the show through the wrong end of the telescope."[44]

The highly praised film made little if any attempt to reach out to the unconverted. Demme's highly commendable and innovative direction could not undo the inbreeding of the performance. Concertgoers have a vested interest in the performance; theatregoers may exhibit less commitment. Byrne does not introduce any of the songs, an unfortunate but common practice. He utters two sentences, "I got a tape I want to play" in the opening and, toward the end, "I'd like to introduce the band by name." (Preaching to the converted has been a Heads trademark. The practice has equally rendered the talented group inaccessible to many rock fans.)

Plaudits were lavished upon the motion picture. With the exception of John Simon, the vast majority of critics waxed enthusiastic over Demme's project. On the East Coast, David Denby termed the film "superb" and ended by writing that the picture "should reach a wider audience than ever before without giving up any of its startling individuality."

"The movie audience will recognize their [Talking Heads] happiness as its own," concluded Ansen. In a five-column piece, Pauline Kael found the motion picture "a dose of happiness from beginning to end." *Rolling Stone* concluded it was "the most innovative and captivating concert film in a long time." MTV staffer and author Michael Shore wrote a summary, adulation piece for *Stop*. He asserted "Talking Heads is the best American rock band of the past decade or so, and this tape captures them at the peak of their form at L.A.'s Pantages Theater during their 1984 US tour. Their awesome set was shot with more elegant care and beauty than we'd seen in any rock film since Martin Scorcese's *The Last Waltz*."[45]

The reviewers focused upon two aspects of the vehicle for praise. The film was "thrilling testimony to Demme's and the Heads' audiovisual virtuosity and empathy," David Byrne was singled out as the catalyst; "He commands the stage by his hollow-eyed, frosty verve," said Kael. "Watching him," wrote Denby, "I thought of great professional entertainers like Astaire or Tommy Tune, who gauge their effects modestly and in relation to the results they want to achieve." Ansen called Byrne "a star of near-maniacal intensity." The hosannas continued.

Demme's cinematography deservedly received raves. The film, argued Maslin, "owed very little to the rock film-making formulas of the past. It may well help inspire those of the future." Schruers found an "eloquent simplicity in the structure of the show."[46] All of the applause would not translate into box office, the bottom line, however.

The superlatives heaped upon *Stop* generally reflected the ethos of film criticism and its readers. The Talking Heads have a celebral quality missing from most rock groups. The art-school, American version, roots of the band are missing in many heavy-metallers and punks. (The Velvet Underground, adopted by Andy Warhol, had enjoyed a similar status in the 1960s. Both acts were/are the darlings of the media intelligensia. It is not a mere coincidence that both emerged from the club scene of New York's Max's Kansas City or CBGB. The success of New York bands west of the Hudson can charitably be counted on the fingers of one hand. Money reviews are only as good as the number of people that see them.)

Rockers rarely read reviews, especially as most appear in the specialty and trade press. *Rolling Stone* reviewed the movie. Robert Palmer did a piece for the *New York Times* music section. These columns may have stirred some interest, but, as the *Variety* writer noted, the financial viability of the effort lay in record and cassette sales and rentals.

Criticisms of the concert footage were few. One writer complained that the film lacked "the all-stops-out abandon" of some Heads performances. Another objected to the editing, a common flaw in this genre, saying "one can see rapidly alternating movements in one song where Byrne's shirt is buttoned up to the neck, then unbuttoned, then buttoned again."[47] The most voracious attack on the film and critics came from *National Review*'s John Simon.

Simon, admitting a dislike for rock 'n' roll, described *Stop* as "mind-starving and ear-blasting." Another target of his rage was fellow writer Pauline Kael. Among other things, he objected, "We live in a wonderful age in which such drivel passes for criticism." Other critics were "happy hysterics." Rock fans, not heavy readers of the *National Review* and the critic's obscurantist prose, were not affected. *Vogue* magazine's Tracy Young, noting Simon's early departure from the *Stop* screening, wrote, "so they can't be all bad."⁴⁸

The most pervasive objection was the absence of audience cutaways. McDonough noted, "Even the best concert films are hard-pressed to command full attention to nothing but ninety minutes of straight stage performance."

"Were it not for the audience response at the ends of numbers," *Variety* noted, "one might forget this is a live show."⁴⁹ Others merely commented on this usual technique. The director merely replied, "I hope I was right."

At year's end, Talking Heads had enjoyed an eleven-week run on MTV and a fourteen-week stay on the *Billboard* album chart. The box office from a nine-week theater tenure in six theaters was only $745,743. The motion picture, as *Variety* had predicted, "was one of the better performance projects but entirely a cult film." Hoberman had been correct when he wrote "Even if it doesn't broaden the band's base, it ought to drive true believers wild."⁵⁰

U2: Rattle and Hum

The career of the Irish rock band U2 is comparable to that of Bruce Springsteen. The Boss had been recording for seven years before he landed his first Number 1 album, *The River*, in 1980. Beginning that year, U2's first four albums failed to crack the Top 10 despite critical acclaim and a substantial global following. Their breakthrough LP came in 1987. *The Joshua Tree* debuted at Number 7 and sold more than fourteen million copies globally. U2 became the first group to have an album debut in the Top 10 without having charted that high with a previous release. The band captured Grammys for Best Rock Performance by a Duo or Group and Album of the Year, a considerable achievement considering their competition included the likes of Michael Jackson, Whitney Houston, and Prince.

It was during *The Joshua Tree* tour in the U.S. that the decision was made to produce a film chronicling the event. The 1987 tour, which grossed $40 million, gave U2 its long-awaited superstar status. (During the previous two years, the group had been approached by numerous filmmakers with scripts, but nothing had appealed to them.) The idea was to satisfy U2's now-enormous audience without spending three years on the road. Band members wanted a film in the tradition of their favorites, *Gimme Shelter*, *The Last Waltz*, and *Stop Making Sense*.

U2's video producer, Michael Hamlyn, was selected as producer. Band members met with several directors before choosing Phil Joanou, a graduate of USC's famed film school. Joanou's slim credits included two television episodes of Steven Spielberg's *Amazing Stories* and the feature film *Three O'Clock High*. The director was a die-hard U2 fan. When he heard about the project, he arranged an introduction through a mutual friend and flew from Los Angeles to Connecticut at his own expense to sell himself to the band. U2 liked him immediately. The band financed the project themselves after studios balked at the estimated $5-million production costs.

A basis for the movie was found in U2's own search for a musical foundation. "The music of U2 is in space somewhere," lead singer and lyricist Bono told Bob Dylan. "There is no particular musical roots or heritage for us. In Ireland there is a tradition, but we've never plugged into it." Dylan suggested that U2 "reach back into music."[51] The project was conceived as an exploration of the American musical culture that forged rock music. As the U2 tour crossed the country, the band stopped off at various historic locations to pay tribute to great musicians who had influenced them.

The film opens with a U2 cover of The Beatles' "Helter Skelter." Dylan sings on "Love Rescue Me" and plays the organ on a Bo Diddley-sounding "Hawkmoon 269." U2 also performs Dylan's "All Along the Watchtower" in concert. Hendrix's "Star-Spangled Banner" introduces a live version of U2's "Bullet in the Sky." Blues guitarist B.B. King shares the stage with the group on "When Love Comes to Town." The band offers "Angel of Harlem" as a tribute to Billie Holiday and enlists a Harlem gospel choir in a passionate version of "I Still Haven't Found What I'm Looking For." Nonconcert highlights include a private tour of Graceland and a recording session at the famed Sun Studios in Memphis, where owner Sam Phillips and Elvis hammered out the rock-a-billy sound.

Joanou designed the film in thirds. One part included black-and-white, 35mm concert footage from two Denver-area, indoor performances. A second part consisted of black-and-white documentary footage and scenes from a Los Angeles recording session, shot with 16mm, hand-held cameras. A third section, of outdoor shows in Tempe, Arizona, was shot in color (at great expense because of the lighting specifications.) Joanou filmed the Tempe concert with twelve cameras, a helicopter, and a 120-member crew. "It's like *Apocalypse Now*, without so many helicopters," said Bono.[52] The first two-thirds of the film mix the black-and-white concert vignettes with the nonconcert footage. Then the film bursts into spectacular color for the final scenes of a U2 stadium concert. The effect elicited criticism of the band's self-claimed importance. When the tour ended in December 1987, the director had filmed 150 hours of documentary footage along with the concert film. After months of editing, he and a crew flew to Dublin and shot additional footage, in 16mm, of the band recording in an empty factory.

The film's double-disc soundtrack was a collection of live and studio recordings that included original U2 material, cover versions, and collaborations. "The live portion of the album is not what you'd expect," said soundtrack producer Jimmy Iovine. "There are different arrangements, new songs and a flow to it. It's not the greatest hits cut live—it's a real album."[53] Eight songs performed in the movie were not included on the soundtrack album, while three songs on the record were not in the film.

Despite U2's intentions, the film turned their journey into the American musical past into a cinematic statement of self-proclaimed importance. Critics were disappointed. "Designed as a look at U2 as the band encountered America during the *Joshua Tree* tour, Phil Joanou's movie plays like a homage to U2's importance, from the backstage scene in which B.B. King tells Bono how heavy his lyrics are to the lovingly photographed concert footage," Steve Pond wrote in *Rolling Stone*. He correctly observed that film critics missed the band's intention and "painted a similarly unflattering portrait of U2 as a humorless, self-satisfied band, trying to boost its own image by aligning itself with the giants of American roots music."[54] *Film Comment*, for example, said, "No concert film has shown more care or concentrated imagination. It's not Joanou's fault his subject is the world's most pompous rock band."[55]

The soundtrack received similar notices. With *Rattle and Hum*, U2 had aimed at a musical versatility beyond the homespun abilities of the hard-rock-oriented band. "But for all its excitement," wrote Anthony DeCurtis, "*Rattle and Hum* seems a tad calculated in its supposed spontaneity. . . . The album ably demonstrates U2's force but devotes too little attention to the band's vision."[56] *Times'* critic Jon Parales was particularly disappointed with the U2 offering, writing:

> From the beginning, U2 has had an unguarded quality, a sense of urgency and vulnerability that it maintained even as its audience grew into the millions. But that urgency has curdled on *Rattle and Hum*, where U2 insists that clumsy

attempts at interpreting other people's music are as important as the real thing. What comes across in song after song is sincere egomania.[57]

U2 discovered that, unlike in the recording studio, where producer and artist often collaborate on the final product, in filmmaking artistic control is in the hands of the director. During the filming of *Rattle*, Joanou told *Rolling Stone*, "I always felt that this is as much their movie as it is mine. This is a movie made by myself *and* U2. If they don't like something, it will be out. I will fight for what I believe in tooth and nail, but if Bono says, 'I hate that shot of me,' it will go out."[58] Rhetoric and reality are seldom the same in the entertainment business, and U2 told a different story. "He says all the time, 'Oh, you know, I'm collaborating and making this film with you.' But he's not, really," Bono said. "He's making the film he wants to make, because as long as he can keep coming up with good reasons for doing things, nobody can say no. We can't just come up with an answer like, 'We don't like it.' He's having his way all the way."[59] The band was more than disappointed with the final product. "He double-crossed us, the bastard," said U2 band member the Edge. "The only important thing about this film is that we've survived it."[60] Only later did the director admit, "The movie was meant to be a fairly serious depiction of their music, as opposed to a light one. I have footage that could have changed that, but my plan was to do an aggressive, grab-people-by-the-throat-and-shake-them kind of movie rather than a romp through America with U2. A romp with U2 wasn't something I could swallow, so I went for an overly serious, pretentious look at U2. That's a fair criticism, but what the hell?"[61]

The whole *Rattle and Hum* project included the concert film, a double album, and an illustrated, souvenir book. The movie was released with a major push from Paramount and lavish premieres in Madrid, Dublin, London, New York, and Los Angeles. On its 4 November opening weekend, the U2 film captured $3.8 million at 1,400 theaters in three days. Box office attendance fell dramatically afterwards. By Thanksgiving weekend, *Rattle and Hum* had earned only $8.3 million in the United States. Exhibitors dropped it for Christmas features like Bill Murray's *Scrooged*. By 7 December, U2 was no longer listed on *Variety*'s Top 50 chart. Simultaneously, the soundtrack was enjoying its fifth consecutive week dominating the trade rankings. (U2 fans were content to own *Rattle and Hum*'s cassette or CD.) The story was the same in the international market. "It's not doing too well anywhere," a Paramount executive said. "Kids want to go to a concert, not a film of a concert."[62]

Box office figures were disappointing, but hardly surprising, considering those of previous concert films. In its short theatrical run *Rattle* grossed less than $9 million; Paramount earned only $4.1 million in domestic rentals. A spokesperson from the distributor called it a "disappointment."[63] An ABC television special on the making of *Rattle and Hum* was never aired. *Rattle* was rushed onto videocassette to recoup losses. Listed at $24.95, it appeared in mid-February 1989 just three and a half months after its theatrical opening.

Soundtrack sales compensated for the film's poor showing. The album went double platinum in Britain on advance sales alone. (It was the fastest-selling LP in British record history.) In textbook fashion, Island Records issued the scout single "Desire," a 1990s version of "Who Do You Love," six weeks prior to the film. It charted at Number 50. MTV received a video the last week of October. At Number 14, *U2: Rattle and Hum* had the highest chart debut for a double album since *Stevie Wonder's Original Musiquarium I* had hit the charts at Number 5 in 1982. The album quickly moved to the top of *Billboard*'s pop-album chart, becoming the first double album to reach Number 1 since Springsteen's *The River* in 1980. The soundtrack LP eventually sold more than five million copies and spawned two hit singles.

Warner Brothers Pictures' music head, Gary LeMel, attributed U2's disappointing run to overexposure. MTV, Cinemax, and other cable channels regularly present live concerts. The ensemble's 1987 tour, from which the film footage emanated, was still fresh in the minds of many fans. Those who missed seeing the band in person, according to LeMel, were awaiting the video. The Warner executive was depressed by U2's box office, as it provided ammunition for studios to reject rock-oriented pictures. "I felt," he professed, "that if ever a concert movie was going to happen, this was the one, coming exactly the right moment in time for the group."[64]

Super Fine and Super Bad: Blaxploitation Films

Hollywood had neglected the growing black audience in the 1950s and early 1960s. After the NAACP had threatened legal and economic measures against the film industry in 1963, more blacks began to appear in minor parts in features and television shows, playing cops, civil servants, students, and workers. The box office success of Sydney Poitier in the late Sixties drew the attention of Hollywood filmmakers. (In 1967 Poitier was among the top five box office draws.) Further, it was estimated that year that although blacks represented only 15 percent of the U.S. population, they accounted for about 30 percent of theatrical audiences in urban centers.[65]

Film studios began to court the urban black market with what has been dubbed the "Superspade" caricature.[66] Former Cleveland Browns football star Jim Brown, Ossie Davis, and Raymond St. Jacques pioneered the new black image of the aggressive, urban black male. As St. Jacques said of one film, "Artistically it was a fake, but the 'brothers' loved it because I kicked hell out of a white man."[67]

In the early Seventies, a host of "blaxploitation" films, as they have been called, were produced for the black audience, with the hope of also reaching a broader market, in some cases. With whites vacating the cities, Hollywood executives sought to lure black audiences into large, downtown theaters with films featuring black heroes and heroines. White roles were simply converted into black ones. The blaxploitation pics were "products of the same Hollywood minds that made millions of dollars while excluding blacks from the industry," a *Times* report asserted in 1972. "Now they've discovered a latter-day vein of gold to rip off."[68]

Hollywood's full-scale exploitation of the black market included black westerns, horror films, dramas, documentaries, bio-pics, detective stories, and social films. In 1972, one quarter of the film industry's annual output, about 200 films a year, were black-oriented. Several scored big at the box office, outpacing the white films of the time. Rather than spawning cultural or cinematic innovations, however, these movies were simply reworkings of traditional American film genres, now with black casts. In 1972 *Newsweek* reported, "The furious action on celluloid is pointed toward the triumph of black good over white evil; audiences are whooping it up with such glee that projectionists must jack up the volume during the climaxes, and theater owners are counting more dollars than they've handled in years."[69]

The first of the "Superspade" pics was a 1971 independent production by Melvin Van Peebles. In 1968, Van Peebles had become the first black to direct a feature film that was commercially released in the U.S. (although it was a French film). After years of bitter struggle for artistic and financial control of his pictures, Van Peebles vowed to "get the Man's foot out of all our black asses" by producing a film "about a brother *getting* the Man's foot out of his ass."[70] *Sweet Sweetback's Baadasssss Song* was released in 1971. Van Peebles had worked completely outside the established film industry. He not only wrote the screenplay and composed the music, but produced, directed, and played the lead role. The multitalented filmmaker personally raised the $500,000 production costs and chose Cinemation Industries, a firm noted for dealing with exploitation movies, to distribute the film. Van Peebles previewed the film to pimps and hairdressers in Harlem instead of to New York film critics. The picture, about a black professional stud, generated both controversy and earnings. It grossed an astonishing $11 million.

Just a few months after *Sweet Sweetback's Baadasssss Song* reached theaters, MGM's *Shaft* opened and quickly became a spectacular box office success. Within a year of its release, *Shaft* earned more than nine times its $1.2 million production cost.

The film was directed by Gordon Parks, an internationally known photographer, composer, and writer. Parks became the first black American to direct a feature at a major U.S. studio. Newcomer Richard Roundtree starred as John Shaft, hailed by MGM promotion as "a new James Bond." Shaft was a hard-nosed, urban detective hired by a Harlem underworld boss to find his daughter, who had been kidnapped by the Mafia. Shaft is one mean dude. He delivers the girl to the Harlem chief and half the East Coast mob to his friend, a white police lieutenant. The film was filmed in New York, in the Times Square area, in January 1971.

Shaft opened 2 July 1971 and received mostly favorable notices. *Variety* called Roundtree's debut a "smash." *Time* said, "*Shaft* is a fast-moving pleasure. Director Gordon Parks keeps things going at such a headlong pace that the movie hardly pauses for breath." *Newsweek*, however, considered the camera work "surprisingly insipid," and the script "laboriously slow." Canby said it was "not a great film, but it's very entertaining." A black critic, Clayton Riley, panned the movie in a *Times* review, calling it an artistic and technical "disaster . . . that lacks both style and substance." Riley was most disturbed by the film's portrayal of contemporary black America. *Shaft*, he wrote, "is a Xerox copy of all the fraudulence America can construct in its mania for hero worship, or *white* anti-hero worship." Most black critics, however, agreed with Parks that the movie was "a Saturday night fun picture which people go to see becaues they want to see the black guy winning."[71] Reportedly, 90 percent of the audiences were black.[72]

The soundtrack became the fastest-selling album in Stax Records' history. Released in August 1971, it topped the pop, R&B, and jazz charts. Isaac Hayes won a Grammy for Best Original Score. The double album was certified platinum that year. "Theme from *Shaft*" reached Number 1 on 20 November, selling over 1 million copies. It became the third Number 1 single to receive an Oscar for Best Song.

Based on the original's success, two sequels followed. *Shaft's Big Score* grossed $10 million in 1972. *Shaft in Africa*, however, flopped the following year.

Parks's son, Gordon, Jr., directed *Superfly*, a 1972 Warner Brothers release. (The title was a reference to the ghetto term for cocaine.) Produced for less than $1 million, the film starred Ron O'Neal as Youngblood Priest, a black street-hustler and cocaine dealer who decides he wants to make one last sale and then get out of the business. His suppliers, corrupt white cops, are not ready to let him go. Priest engineers an escape that outwits The Man.

Showing no confidence, Warner Brothers opened *Superfly* with little promotion. Most critics panned the picture. *Time* deemed *Superfly* "remarkably exploitative and inept." *Variety* predicted it would drown in the flood of blaxploitation films "with no cast names to lure and word-of-mouth certain to hurt." The reviewer concluded, "An ultra-fast sell-and-pull-out approach will be necessary to make anything off this one." A *Times* reviewer gave it a qualified "very good movie."[73]

The critics did not understand the black audience. Word-of-mouth turned *Superfly* into a surprise hit. "People are flocking to see the sympathetic story of a Black man who makes a small fortune selling drugs and gets out of the business, triumphant and unpunished by the law," reported the *Times*. "The story fulfills a deep-seated fantasy for many people, especially Blacks, who dream of beating the Establishment."[74] *Superfly*'s gross topped $11 million; Warner Brothers grabbed $6.4 million in domestic rentals.

Curtis Mayfield had composed the score for *Superfly*. By November 1972, the album had sold 1.4 million copies and the film had grossed more than $10 million. The soundtrack was eventually certified double platinum. Two Top-10 singles, "Freddie's Dead" and "Superfly," each sold a million copies.

While these pictures provided opportunities for blacks in film production, the major studios reaped most of the profits. *Superfly*'s financial backers received a portion of the receipts from distributor Warner Brothers, but the film company made the sequel without the financiers of the original. Several blacks involved in the first production, including Gordon Parks, Jr., were excluded from the 1973 sequel. Ron O'Neal filled in as director and revived his role in *Superfly T.N.T.*.

The blaxploitation films quickly ran their course. As black actor Calvin Lockhart had warned in 1972, "Unless black films explore other areas of black experience, black films will wind up on the shelf and eventually stop." The prediction came true. Unable to generate financing from the black community, black filmmakers had to rely on traditional Hollywood. Blaxploitation pics seldom got beyond exploitive sex and violence. "They want s— and we're giving them s—," one racist studio executive reportedly said.[75] The blaxploitation pics dried up. The second *Shaft* sequel,

Shaft in Africa, and Warner's *Superfly T.N.T.* (both 1973) were both disappointments at the box office.

An independent production, *The Harder They Come* (1973), deserves some attention as the first full-fledged Jamaican feature film. Perry Penzell directed and co-wrote the screenplay. Reggae musician Jimmy Cliff turned out a fine performance as Ivan, an ambitious Jamaican musician. Ivan pens a potential hit, the title song, but refuses to sign away the rights for a mere $20. In financial desperation, he turns to the underworld of drug trafficking and ends up caught between the mob and the police (for killing a cop). His notoriety as a murderer spawns the success of his record, which tops the Kingston charts. The story ends tragically with his death.

The film never benefitted from a general release, but attracted a cult following at midnight showings in the United States. Critical notices were positive, especially regarding the invigorating use of reggae music in the movie. "Fast, tough, sinuous, with a score of Jamaican reggae that jauntily accentuates its vigor, this saga of the career of a small-time pot pusher and pop star is a kind of Caribbean *Threepenny Opera*," said *Time*. *The Nation* called it "an excitingly violent, deeply appealing picture; it is also a disturbing study of a post-colonial society in ruins." Pauline Kael wrote, "The film itself is a mess, but the music is redeeming, and Jimmy Cliff's joy in music, along with the whole culture's, stays with you."

"*The Harder They Come* has more guts, wit, humor and sheer exuberance than most movies you'll see in any one year of movie-going," raved Canby in the *Times*. "A lot of this—though not all—has to do with the superb music."[76]

Rock Biographies

Major film studios produced several pictures that brought the lives of rock 'n' roll legends to the screen. In 1978, disc jockey Alan Freed had received treatment in *American Hot Wax*, as did The Beatles in *I Wanna Hold Your Hand*, The Band and company in *The Last Waltz*. In addition, Columbia Pictures released *The Buddy Holly Story* that year. "Films like these . . . are better admired for their innocence and simplicity than faulted for their lack of sophistication," Maslin wrote about musical bio-pics (in a review of *La Bamba*). "They are made in the same eager, admiring spirit that marked their heroes' or heroines' love of popular music. At their best, they bring that music to life all over again."[77]

Robert Gittler's screenplay for *The Buddy Holly Story* followed the life of the legendary rock singer who died tragically at age twenty-two in a 1959 plane crash that also claimed the lives of The Big Bopper and Ritchie

Valens. The story, which traces Holly's rise from obscurity in Lubbock, Texas, to national recognition, "embraces all the romantic cliches of showbiz success sagas," one critic pointed out.[78] Holly's small-town girlfriend is left behind; he surmounts early rejection, leaves his original band behind, and goes on to make rock 'n' roll history. The film does, however, capture the trials of rock and the recording industry in the 1950s, as well as the fusion of black and white musicial cultures. "When the hero leads an infectious jam session at Harlem's Apollo Theater, the walls of cultural segregation almost tangibly tumble down," noted a *Time* critic.[79] Not surprisingly, the film's musical sequences were its best moments.

The film's star, Gary Busey, had previously appeared in *The Last American Hero, A Star is Born*, and, with Dustin Hoffman, in *Straight Time*. The actor also had earlier played the drummer in Holly's band, The Crickets, in an abandoned production about the rock singer called *Not Fade Away*. The project had been aborted when it was discovered that the producer did not have full legal clearance. A casting agent, however, remembered Busey.[80]

The producers decided not to use a score of Holly's original songs, but recorded all the music live on twenty-four tracks, with Busey and The Crickets (played by Don Stroud and Charles Martin Smith).

Like Holly, Busey had been born in Texas. He grew up listening to rock and was familiar with Holly's music. Busey had enjoyed a parallel career as a drummer. Under the name Teddy Jack Eddy, he had played with friends Leon Russell, Willie Nelson, and Kris Kristofferson. For the Holly role, he worked on his guitar playing and developed his own fiery renditions of Holly's hits, "Peggy Sue," "That'll Be the Day," "Oh Boy," and "Not Fade Away," among others.

While the film received favorable reviews—*Variety* called it "first-rate filmmaking"—Busey's performance stole the show. Canby said, "The movie isn't great but Mr. Busey's performance . . . is tremendous, full of drive, eccentric life and the sort of idiosyncracy that creates a screen personality the public will remember." *Newsweek* said Busey did "a brilliant job of acting."[81] Columbia earned $6.4 million in domestic rentals. Soundtrack sales were disappointing.

La Bamba

America's growing Mexican-American population, like the African-American, was for a long time ignored by Hollywood. Spanish-dubbed or subtitled prints made for Latin American or European markets were typically made available in the United States weeks or even months after their initial runs. (Selected pictures *were* distributed simultaneously in Anglo and Chicano markets. Universal released Spanish and English versions when the studio reissued *E.T.: The Extraterrestrial* in 1985. In 1986, Universal distributed, nationwide, twenty-five Spanish-dubbed prints of Spielberg's *An American Tail*. The Spanish-language prints nearly doubled the national per-screen average take. The film studio could only find one Hispanic exhibitor in Los Angeles, but overflow crowds generated the second-highest gross of any theater in the country showing the film.)

Surveys put the Mexican-American population at twenty-five million in 1987. It was estimated that Hispanics attended movie theaters 30 to 40 percent more than Anglo-Americans.[82] That year, a Spanish-subtitled version of Warner's *Over the Top* earned more than $70,000 in two Los Angeles theaters, accounting for 17 percent of the total box office gross in southern California. The Spanish version, however, failed elsewhere in the country. Spanish-language versions of MGM's *Running Scared* had grossed $500,000 nationally in 1987. Despite the obvious potential, Hollywood had yet to score with a film directed at the Chicano audience. With extensive bilingual screenings and media campaigns, Columbia was the first major film company to aggressively court the Mexican-American population. "If we can establish it as an ongoing market, it will be a great asset to us," Columbia Pictures president David Picker said. "One reason we are doing 'La Bamba' at all is that we have a market that has never been addressed with the care and attention it deserves."[83]

Chicano screenwriter-director Luis Valdez and his brother Daniel developed the idea for *La Bamba*. Valdez had been previously known for *Zoot Suit*, a stark play based on the infamous "Sleepy Lagoon" murder of 1942, in which a Chicano boy was killed in a gang fight and seventeen Mexican-American gang members were found guilty in the racist trial that followed. The play, which included Big-Band and Latin music, had been a hit at the Aquarius Theater in Los Angeles, where it earned $3.5 million in nine months in 1978. Its West Coast success, however, would not be repeated on Broadway. While most Los Angeles critics raved about it, New York notices labeled it "overblown and undernourished." One reviewer said that *Zoot Suit* had "its heart in the right place and its foot firmly lodged in its mouth."[84] Attempts to draw a large Hispanic audience were unsuccessful and the play closed after only fifty-eight performances. Despite the East Coast failure, *Zoot Suit* certified Valdez as the first Chicano to have a Broadway production.

In 1981, Universal had released a film version of the stage production, shot at the Aquarius Theater in two weeks on a $3-million budget. The picture fared well in Los Angeles, but flopped in nationwide distribution.

Canby panned the film, calling it "a holy mess of a movie, full of earnest, serious intentions and virtually no achievements."[85]

It was while they were on Broadway that Valdez and his brother conceived the idea for a movie about Ritchie Valens. Daniel tracked down Valens's family and took the project to Taylor Hackford, who had his own production company, New Visions. Hackford purchased the rights to the story from the Valenzuela family. Luis was asked to write the script, and after reading it Taylor hired him to direct. The film was shot in a forty-seven-day period in summer 1986 in various locations in California, including Valens's hometown, Pacoima. Production costs totalled a mere $6.5 million at a time when the average "big picture" was estimated at $19 million.

La Bamba is a Chicano version of the classic American dream—the Horatio Alger, rags-to-riches ideal. The screenplay traces Valens's life from laboring in the orchards of the San Fernando Valley to touring the country as a rock star. Valdez's screenplay was largely autobiographical, in that Valens's rise to stardom paralleled in many ways the screenwriter's own rise from San Fernando Valley farmworker to Hollywood filmmaker. His aim was to unravel the myth about Hispanic Americans. Hackford agreed. "It's the first truly positive film about the Hispanic-American experience to come out of Hollywood," he said.[86]

As early as preproduction, Hackford and screenwriter/director Valdez were convinced that the film should be released in both English and Spanish. They also thought that music would be the key to the film's success. Columbia's domestic-marketing campaign revealed both the studio's cross-cultural aims and the crucial role of the music in marketing the film:

1. To create a groundswell of positive word-of-mouth and to generate prerelease awareness among the target audience of people aged 12-49 through an extensive national screening program and publicity/promotion activitites;

2. to fully exploit the music as the key crossover element through the single and soundtrack release plan, the music-video, the MTV Premiere Party and the use of an outside music marketing consultant to maximize cross-promotion at the retail level;

3. To support the day-and-date release of Spanish-dubbed and subtitled versions of the film with a parallel publicity/promotion/advertising effort in the Hispanic community;

4. To support the wide release of 1000+ prints with an aggressive advertising campaign encompassing two national sneak previews running one Friday and one Saturday night in the two weeks prior to opening day, 7/24.[87]

Columbia began screening a final print to audiences in April 1987. Marketers were convinced they had "a classic audience picture with the potential to cross over age, language and cultural barriers."[88]

The imaginative promotional and advertising campaign, which cost nearly $6 million, addressed both the Spanish and the English movie and music press. Columbia spent more than $250,000 on Spanish-language promotion. Three demographic sectors were targeted: Yuppies, teens, and Hispanics.

The Valens docudrama was pitched at the Baby Boomers through television spots, on shows like *Late Night with David Letterman*, and fourteen magazines, including *Glamour*, *People*, and *Life*. The print campaign was coordinated with the release of the single.

To reach the under-twenty-five audience, ads were purchased on daytime soap operas, which have a large youth audience during the summer months. Cable spots included the USA Network, *Night Tracks*, a TBS weekend late-nighter, and MTV. A fifty-five-minute video featured trailers and clips aimed at "places like MTV, HBO and local shows," according to Tom Andrews at Columbia Pictures.[89]

Advertising time was also bought on the two Spanish-language television networks, Univision and Telemundo. A Coca-Cola (Columbia Pictures' parent company) tie-in included a bilingual campaign in all media, point-of-purchase materials in retail stores, and a sweepstakes promotion.

Ritchie Valens (real name Richard Valenzuela) was the first Mexican-American to crack the charts in the first decade of rock. Valens, however, was not exactly a rock sensation in the late Fifties. His first disc, "Come On, Let's Go," peaked at Number 42 on 24 November 1958 and sold 750,000 copies. It was followed by his only million-selling single, "Donna," named for his girlfriend Donna Ludwig. "Donna" stalled posthumously at Number 2 on 23 February 1959. Its B side, "La Bamba," which had peaked at Number 22 on 2 February, was based on a traditional Mexican folk song (the title meaning "wedding song"). Valens's version became the first rock song with a Latin sound and Spanish lyrics.

Valens was a prototype of assimilation. The young rock 'n' roller was a third-generation Mexican-American who spoke English, not Spanish, and had never seen Mexico. The film portrays Valens's success as the result of natural talent and hard, honest work. On the way to the top of the charts, the singer discovers his Mexican heritage. Valdez struggled to create a dramatic element for *La Bamba*. The film's cliches—Valens's Anglo girlfriend, a jealous, older half-brother with a drinking problem, success coming to a nice boy from a poor Chicano family—were real enough, but Valens's brief and not-all-that-senational career did not provide an enormous amount of material for the screenwriter. As *Time* reviewer Richard Corliss said, Valens' "music is surely worth remembering; his life is hardly worth dramatizing."[90]

Warner executives decided to use a Chicano band from southern California to revitalize Valens's music. The members of Los Lobos had grown up in the Chicano neighborhoods of East Los Angeles, where they fused traditional Mexican music and American rock 'n' roll. The group, whose name means "the wolves," had been playing clubs in the Los Angeles area for nine years before the *La Bamba* project. Los Lobos' versions of Valens's songs were chosen over the originals. Valens's original producer, Bob Keane was not happy with the decision. "I think [using them] was a mistake because I think the people are ultimately going to want to hear the real Ritchie Valens," he said. To that end, Keane issued a 7-inch and a 12-inch single, "La Bamba '87," on his Del-Fi label, "utilizing Valens' original vocal in a contemporary setting." Valens's three original albums were also reissued by distributor Rhino Records. Label executives had pointed to the success of *The Buddy Holly Story* in generating sales of Buddy Holly reissues for MCA. Warner Brothers, however, saw the film as strategic to Los Lobos' career. "We needed a vehicle to break the group," said one executive, "and it ended up that 'La Bamba' came along."[91] The choice proved a good one, as the soundtrack sold more than 2.5 million copies and spawned a Number-1 single.

Six of the eight Los Lobos tracks on the album were remakes of Valens songs. Each of the four remaining cuts were done by different artists. Brian Stetzer, who appeared in the film as Eddie Cochran, performed "Summertime Blues." Marshall Crenshaw played "Crying, Waiting, Hoping." Howard Huntsberry did a striking impression of Jackie Wilson singing "Lonely Teardrops," and Bo Diddley did a remake of his own "Who Do You Love."

CBS and Warners utilized a Stigwood-type marketing approach for *La Bamba*. "The first step . . . was to coordinate the single and soundtrack with the film's release, so the song would have impact on radio and television via the video," a Columbia Pictures executive Tom Andrews said.[92] The Los Lobos single "La Bamba" had an early June release about six weeks before the film's opening. It topped the *Billboard* charts for three weeks beginning 29 August 1987. MTV began rotating the video for "La Bamba" 24 June. The clip featured Los Lobos and scenes from the movie. The soundtrack came out 30 June 1987 and reached Number 1 29 July. The single's sleeve and the album's cover both carried the same artwork as the movie campaign. "The record's successful and widespread airplay gave Columbia what was, in effect, free advertising, especially because its title and the film's title were identical," noted *Billboard*.[93]

Columbia and Warner Brothers coordinated screenings for record industry people, the music press, distributors, sales representatives, and disc jockeys. Benefit premieres were shown in major markets, with proceeds marked for community organizations. The film's 17 July Los Angeles premiere party was filmed for an MTV special that aired on 19 and 23 July, the latter date being the eve of the film's national opening. Live performances by Los Lobos, Brian Stetzer, Marshall Crenshaw, Bo Diddley, and Howard Huntsberry were featured, along with interviews with Lou Diamond Phillips, who played Valens, and Gary Busey.

La Bamba opened nationwide 24 July on over 1,000 screens. Three different versions were employed: English, Spanish, and English with Spanish subtitles. Spanish versions were shown in seventy-seven theaters, earning an average of $5,004 as compared with a $4,086 average for the 1,174 English-language versions. On its first weekend, the film earned a respectable $5.5 million; the Spanish-language showings constituted ten percent of the box office gross. The Hispanic population added more than $2.6 million to the 1987 box office gross. *La Bamba* was among the top-ten-grossing pictures released in the summer of 1987.[94] By August it had grossed $21 million in domestic rentals; eventually the total reached $54 million. The film marketing had worked well, as the picture returned to New Visions and Columbia $23.9 million.

The movie received moderate notices. "Mr. Valdez gives 'La Bamba' enough warmth to make up for its conventionality, as well as a strong feeling for Valens's Chicano roots," Maslin wrote in the *Times*. *Variety* gave a favorable review, noting outstanding individual performances and the Los Lobos covers of Valens's songs. "Culturally, film is somewhat provocative for its presentation of Ritchie's denial of his roots and total buy-in to the American dream," the reviewer said. "Film could have benefited from increased attention to Ritchie's subjective view of things." *Rolling Stone* disliked the movie but gave a favorable review of the soundtrack, saying, "If Valens's life is treated in storybook terms, his music comes across with all the momentum and feeling it embodied nearly three decades ago." Pauline Kael was not impressed at all. "Even with the music, this is a feeble, lachrymose piece of filmmaking," she wrote.[95]

The crosscultural success of *La Bamba* was not lost on Hollywood executives. "What they hear in the Latin beat of 'La Bamba' is the sound of money," a *Newsweek* writer chimed in. "The Hispanic population is expected to reach 30 million by 1990—that's a lot of popcorn." Columbia president David Picker anticipated that *La Bamba* would "change the way we market, the content of movies, the use of Hispanic stories and actors. We'd be fools not to take advantage of what we've learned."[96] Although Universal *did* open Cheech Marin's *Born in East L.A.* in August 1987 with Spanish subtitles, and several independent productions featured Hispanic themes and actors, the Columbia executive's prediction and Valdez' dream have not come to pass. "I understand that show business is a business, but it seems to me there is a social responsibility no matter how much money is being made," said Valdez. " 'La Bamba' has proven that audiences will respond to the simple, honest truth about people, and if Hollywood has the decency and courage to represent Hispanics as human beings, there is a profit to be made."[97]

Imagine: John Lennon

On 15 August 1988 *People* magazine initiated a two-part series excerpted from Albert Goldman's soon-to-be-published unauthorized biography, *The Lives of John Lennon*. Goldman's penchant for demystifying rock legends regardless of the facts, as in *Elvis*, was maliciously applied to the martyred ex-Beatle. Among the author's allegations were charges of homosexuality, heroin abuse, responsibility for Stu Sutcliffe's death, and tenure as a Howard Hughes-like, reclusive househusband. *Rolling Stone*, *Newsweek*, and a host of reviewers devoted gallons of ink to refuting Goldman's bill of particulars.[98]

Into this polemic climate entered the 103-minute documentary *Imagine: John Lennon*. Appropriately, the film's beginning is overlaid by Lennon saying, "I was always a rebel . . . but on the other hand, I wanted to be loved and accepted by all facets of society and not be just a loud mouth, lunatic, poet, musician. But I cannot be what I am not . . . I'm not going to change the way I look or the way I feel to conform to anything." What was promised was John Lennon's story. In the context of 1988 and Goldman's character assassination, this cinematic statement seemed to be a rebuttal to the 719-page volume.

Coincidentally, perhaps, the film had been commissioned by Yoko Ono in 1986. She had contacted producer David Wolper, of *This Is Elvis* and *Roots*, indicating that the "time was right to make the film."[99] He called director Andrew Solt, also *This Is Elvis*. "Andrew's enthusiasm helped convince me, as did my sons, who are Beatles fans," said the sixty-year-old filmmaker. "I told Yoko I'd do it on one condition, that we be given complete creative control." The widow agreed, as she did not want to be seen as "a shadow cast on the portrait." Several months later, two air-freight packages containing 200 hours of film footage appeared at Wolper's office. "I don't think there has ever been anybody that there was more personal footage of," the producer said. "It's mind-boggling. The camera recorded it all. You're seeing the real person live out his life in front of you. He's telling his own life in his own words and music with pictures to back it up."[100]

While screening the material, executives discovered lapses, which the surviving ex-Beatles, mostly, filled with session material and outtakes from *Let It Be*. Production began on the $7-million project in February 1987, some sixteen months before Goldman's publication date. Wolper was satisfied, telling an interviewer, "I have a feeling that John was writing his own biography through his music, whether he knew it or not."[101]

The rock bio-pic contained thirty-six titles, which were reduced to twenty-one on the two-record album. Two previously unreleased selections, "Real Love" and a rehearsal version of "Imagine," were introduced. The remaining material was vintage Beatles and Lennon solos.

Journalists insisted that *Imagine* refuted *Lives*. The film, wrote Edna Gunderson, "may prove to be the most effective antidote to Goldman's venom. It depicts Lennon as a complex, gifted artist who both relished and reviled his own stardom."

"This documentary is not dedicated to those who'd like to see author Albert Goldman rot in hell for his biography," wrote Travers in *People*, "but it might as well have been." *Variety* noted, "It all comes at a time when Albert Goldman's unflattering biography has laid Lennon's life bare—and raised controversy that will no doubt benefit 'Imagine' at the b.o."[102]

The Warner Brothers Pictures/Capitol media blitz began prior to the film's premiere on 561 screens the first week of October. The record label issued the twenty-one song package 4 October along with MacMillan's 250,000-copy issuance of *Imagine*, a photo-filled, coffee-table book. *Cinemax* played the 1969 "Live Peace in Toronto" concert during the month. MTV and its sister channel, VH-1, ran Lennon specials. A seven-page advertising supplement was inserted in major-market newspapers. In a fitting move, Barbara Nessim's Lennon lithograph appeared on the cover of *Rolling Stone*.

Reviews were above average. *Boxoffice*'s Jim Kuzak concluded a glowing assessment with, "If people aren't sick to death of the Lennon media blitz by this film's premiere, look for it to become one of the most popular non-concert documentaries ever made."[103] The conventional wisdom had *Imagine* as a cross-pollinated smash prior to its release.

By 19 October, *Imagine* had grossed almost $2.5 million at 561 theaters after a ten-day showing. By the end of October it was rapidly fading. The studio's take, according to 1988 numbers, was a disappointing $1.5 million.

The soundtrack, outliving the feature's box office life, earned a gold record from RIAA. This unexpectedly small showing was surprising, as other Beatle/Lennon anthologies had done well—perhaps, for *Imagine*, too well: Fans of the Liverpudlians' collective and solo efforts would find most of the *Imagine* titles already in their record libraries. (CDs replacement action only accelerated the focus on *The Beatles Greatest Hits*.) The album had depended on strong box office, but the traffic was absent. *Imagine* would join Dylan's *Don't Look Back* as a critically acclaimed box office disaster. In order to recoup losses, *Imagine* was rushed onto videocassette appearing in April 1989.

With the notable exception of *La Bamba*, the films discussed in this chapter did not have large mass appeal. Most of the rockumentaries were limited to cult followings, although many of their soundtracks did well in terms of unit sales. In retrospect, pictures aimed at minority groups were fashionable, and perhaps timely, but they never established a lasting trend in Hollywood.

Notes

1. *The Rolling Stone Encyclopedia of Rock & Roll*, Jon Pareles and Patricia Romanowski, ed., (New York: Rolling Stone Press/Summit Books 1983), 188.
2. Ehrenstein and Reed, 77.
3. Quoted in Michael Goldberg, "Monterey Pop: The Dawning of an Age," *Rolling Stone*, 4 June 1987, 116.
4. *Ibid.*, 120.
5. See Greil Marcus, "Rock Films," in *The Rolling Stone Illustrated History of Rock & Roll*, ed. Jim Miller (New York: Random House/Rolling Stone Press Book 1976, 1980), 390-400.
6. *Variety*, 18 September 1968, 28; Richard Schickel, "When Cinema Shouldn't Be Verite," *Life*, 7 February 1969, 10.
7. See Michael Lydon, "The High Cost of Music and Love: Where's the Money From Monterey?" *Rolling Stone*, 9 November 1967, 1.
8. Greil Marcus, "The Woodstock Festival," *Rolling Stone*, 20 September 1969, 17.
9. Robert Santelli, *Aquarius Rising: The Rock Festival Years* (Dell Publishing, a Delta Book 1980), 149. See also John Roberts, Joel Rosenman, and Robert Pilpel, *Young Men with Unlimited Capitol* (New York: Harcourt Brace Jovanovich 1974).
10. *Ibid.*
11. Robert Stephen Spitz, *Barefoot in Babylon: The Creation of the Woodstock Music Festival, 1969* (New York: The Viking Press 1979), 488.
12. Santelli, 150.
13. "Woodstock," *Film Quarterly* 23:4, Summer 1970, 61.

14. *Variety*, 1 April 1970, 14; David Pire, "Woodstock and Monterey Pop," *Sight and Sound* 39:3, Summer 1970, 159; Vincent Canby, "Screen: Woodstock Ecstasy Caught on Film," *New York Times*, 27 March 1970, 22.
15. Quoted in "A Woodstock II?" *Newsweek*, 16 July 1979, 12.
16. See John Schwartz with Peter McKillop, "Woodstock '89: A Bad Trip," *Newsweek*, 21 August 1989, 42. The six other titles from the *Sound Investments* collection were *AC/DC: Let There Be Rock*, *Bring on the Night*, *Divine Madness*, *Jimi Hendrix*, *The Song Remains the Same*, and *True Stories*. Music videoclips included, among others, *Blondie: Eat to the Beat*, *The Doors: A Tribute to Jim Morrison*, *Paul Simon in Concert*, and *Joni Mitchell: Shadows and Light*.
17. Vincent Canby, "Making Murder Pay?," *New York Times*, 13 December 1970, 3, sec. 2. See also Stanley Booth, "Altamont Remembered," *Rolling Stone*, 9 September 1984, 25-28, 52-54. A fuller account is found in Booth, *Dance with the Devil: The Rolling Stones and Their Times* (New York: Random House 1984); Jonathan Eisen, *Altamont: Death of Innocence in the Woodstock Nation*, (New York: Avon 1970).
18. Santelli, 185.
19. Jay Cocks, "Apocalypse '69," *Time*, 14 December 1970, 101.
20. "The Drawbacks of Reality," *Time*, 7 March 1969, 83.
21. Joel Haycock, "Gimme Shelter," *Film Quarterly* 24:4, Summer 1971, 58.
22. Vincent Canby, "Making Murder Pay?" *New York Times*, 13 December 1970, 45, sec. 2; Cocks, "Apocalypse," 101.
23. Haycock, 59-60.
24. *Ibid.*, 60.
25. Peter Brown and Steven Gaines, *The Love You Make: An Insider's Story of The Beatles* (New York: McGraw-Hill 1983), 376.
26. *Ibid.*, 327.
27. Quoted in "The Beatles: The Roof of Apple Records' London," *Rolling Stone*, 4 June 1987, 59-60.
28. Richard Eder, "Screen: Song 'Remains the Same,' " *New York Times*, 21 October 1976, 45.
29. Foster Hirsch, "Where Have All the Woodstock Flowers Gone?" *New York Times*, 16 April 1972, 11, sec. 2.
30. Quoted in Chris Hodenfield, "The Last Waltz," *Rolling Stone* 1 June 1978, 48.
31. *Ibid.*, 48.
32. Janet Maslin, "Film: Scorsese and the Band," *New York Times*, 26 April 1978, C15. See also Dave Marsh, "Schlock Around the Clock," in *Fortunate Son* (New York: Random House 1985), 151-62.
33. Jim Miller, "The Band's Last Supper," *Rolling Stone*, 1 June 1978, 56.
34. Quoted in Wendy Weinstein, "Filling the Big Screen with Talking Heads," *Film Journal*, November 1984, 105; J. Hoberman, "That Sirkian," *Village Voice* 23 October 1984, 60.
35. Quoted in Michael Sragow, "Heads Will Roll," *Film Comment*, May/June 1984, 20.
36. Pauline Kael, "The Current Cinema: Three Cheers," *New Yorker*, 26 November 1984, 113.
37. Quoted in Weinstein, 14.

38. "Cart," "Stop Making Sense," *Variety*, 25 April 1984, 22; John Simon, "Automata," *National Review*, 28 December 1984, 47.
39. Jack McDonough, "Talking Heads Captured Lovingly," *Billboard*, 2 June 1984, 43; "Cart," 22.
40. Sragow, 19.
41. "Cart," 22.
42. "Pop," *Billboard*, 15 September 1984, 63.
43. Fred Schruers, "Heads play from Heart in New Film," *Rolling Stone*, 25 October 1984, 53.
44. David Ansen, "Once in a Lifetime," *Newsweek*, 22 October 1984, 101.
45. Denby, *New York*, 5 November 1984, 68; Ansen, 101; Kael, 114; Schruers, 53; Shore, 422.
46. *Ibid*.; Hoberman, 58.
47. "Cart," 22; McDonough, 43.
48. Simon, 48.
49. McDonough, 43; "Cart," 22.
50. Hoberman, 66, 124.
51. Quoted in Jay Cocks, "U2 Explores America," *Time*, 21 November 1988, 146.
52. Quoted in Steve Pond, "U2 On Location," *Rolling Stone*, 11 February 1988, 89.
53. Quoted in Jeffrey Ressner, "U2 Soundtrack Album Set," *Rolling Stone*, 8 September 1988, 26.
54. Steve Pond, "Now What?" *Rolling Stone*, 9 March 1989, 54.
55. Armond White, "U2: 'Rattle and Ho-Hum," *Film Comment* 24 November-December 1988, 36.
56. Anthony DeCurtis, "U2's American Curtain Call," *Rolling Stone*, 17 November 1988, 150.
57. Jon Pareles, "When Self-Importance Interferes With the Music," *New York Times*, 16 October 1988, 31, sec. 2.
58. Quoted in Steve Pond, "U2 On Location," 90.
59. Quoted in David Rensin, "U2: Band of Gold," *Premiere* November 1988, 52.
60. Quoted in Ted Mico, "Hating U2," *Spin*, January 1989, 36-37.
61. Quoted in Steve Pond, "Now What?" 58.
62. Quoted in Jeffrey Ressner, "Bono Less than Boffo at Box Office," *Rolling Stone*, 12 January 1989, 16.
63. Quoted in Susan Linfield, "From Screen To Store, In a Hurry," *New York Times*, 26 February 1989, 36, sec. 2.
64. Quoted in Dave DiMartino, "Music Films: Not Quite Boffo at Box Office," *Billboard*, 3 December 1988, 4, 64.
65. See Daniel J. Leab, *From Sambo to SUPERSPADE: The Black Experience in Motion Pictures*, (Boston: Houghton Mifflin 1975), 233-34.
66. *Ibid*., 234.
67. *Ibid*., 239.
68. Clayton Riley, " 'Shaft Can do Everything—I Can Do Nothing'," *New York Times*, 13 August 1972, 9, sec. 2.
69. Charles Michener, "Black Movies," *Newsweek*, 23 October 1972, 74.
70. Quoted in Charles Michener, "Black Movies," *Newsweek*, 23 October 1972, 74.

71. *Variety*, 16 June 1971, 15; Jay Cocks, "Summers Coolers," *Time*, 26 July 1971, 51; S. K. Oberbeck, "Black Eye," *Newsweek*, 19 July 1971, 80; Vincent Canby, " 'Shaft'—At Last, a Good Saturday Night Movie," *New York Times*, 11 July 1971, 1, sec. 2; Clayton Riley, "A Black Movie for White Audiences?" *New York Times*, 25 July 1971, 13, sec. 2; Parks quoted in Leab, 252.
72. See "Aiming Shafts at A Critic of 'Shaft,' " *New York Times*, 22 August 1971, 8, sec. 2. See also Leab, 249.
73. Jay Cocks, "Racial Slur," *Time*, 11 September 1972, 78; *Variety*, 2 August 1972, 18; Roger Greenspun, "The Screen: 'Super Fly,' " *New York Times*, 5 August 1972, 14.
74. Maurice Peterson, "Ron Was Too Light for 'Shaft,' But . . . ," *New York Times*, 17 September 1972, 11, sec. 2.
75. Quoted in Michener, "Black Movies," 80.
76. Jay Cocks, "Ha'penny Opera," *Time*, 19 February 1973, 64; Robert Hatch, "Films," *The Nation*, 4 March 1973, 316; Pauline Kael, "The Current Cinema: The Riddles of Pop," *New Yorker*, 24 February 1973, 121; Vincent Canby, "Films That Refuse To Fade Away," *New York Times*, 14 July 1974, 11, sec. 2.
77. Janet Maslin, "Film: 'La Bamba,' a Musical Biography," *New York Times*, 24 July 1987, C4.
78. Frank Rich, "Memory Lanes," *Time*, 24 July 1978, 58.
79. *Ibid*.
80. Janet Maslin, "Folksiness Is Gary Busey's Film Career," *New York Times*, 23 July 1978, 34.
81. *Variety*, 17 May 1978, 54; Vincent Canby, "It Isn't Always the Star Who Carries the Film," *New York Times*, 30 July 1978, 13, sec. 2; David Ansen, "Buddy Rides Again," *Newsweek*, 26 June 1978, 79.
82. See Jennifer Foote, "Hispanic Hollywood," *Newsweek*, 17 August 1987, 66; Katherine Moore, "From Out of Left Field," *Film Journal*, February-March 1988, 52.
83. Quoted in Victor Valle, "Ritchie Valens Film Boosts Prospects of Dubbing, Subtitles," *Los Angeles-Times*, 24 July 1987, 18, sec. 6.
84. Richard Eder, "Theater: 'Zoot Suit,' Chicano Music-Drama," *New York Times*, 26 March 1979, C13; Walter Kerr, " 'Zoot Suit' Loses Its Way in Bloodless Rhetoric," *New York Times*, 1 April 1979, B1.
85. Vincent Canby, "The Screen: 'Zoot Suit,' Filmed From the Stage," *New York Times*, 22 January 1982, C10.
86. Quoted in John Stark, "A Bright New Diamond Brings a Fading Legend to Life in *La Bamba*," *People*, 17 August 1987, 60.
87. Katherine A. Moore, "*La Bamba*: Tapping The Hispanic Market," *Film Journal*, February-March 1988, 45.
88. *Ibid*.
89. Quoted in Dave D. Martino, "Valens Bounces Back On Chart," *Billboard*, 1 August 1987, 6.
90. Richard Corliss, "Rock Fable or Teen Ballad?" *Time*, 17 August 1987, 62.
91. Quotes in Dave DiMartino, 80.
92. *Ibid.*, 6.
93. Geraldine Fabrikant, "Advertising: Campaign Propels 'La Bamba,' " *Billboard*, 13 August 1987, D19.

94. See Susan Spillman, " 'La Bamba' Rocks into the Top 5," *USA Today*, 28 July 1987, 1D.

95. Janet Maslin, "Film: 'La Bamba,' A Musical Biography," *New York Times*, 24 July 1987, C4; *Variety*, 20 May 1987, 20; Anthony DeCurtis, "Flawed 'La Bamba,' " *Rolling Stone*, 13 August 1987, 13; Pauline Kael, "The Current Cinema: Siblings and Cyborgs," *The New Yorker*, 19 August 1987, 71.

96. Foote, "Hispanic Hollywood," 66-67.

97. *Ibid.*, 67.

98. See David Fricke and Jeffery Ressner, "Imaginary Lennon," *Rolling Stone*, 20 October 1988, 42-44, 48, 52, 93; David Gates, "Lennon: The Battle Over His Memory," *Newsweek*, 17 October 1988, 64-73.

99. Quoted in Barbara Miller, "Rare Scenes of Life With Lennon Featured in a New Film," *Los Angeles Times*, 5 October 1988, sec. 8, 7.

100. Quoted in Phoebe Hoban, "Lennon Remembered," *Premiere,* November 1988, 64.

101. Miller, 7.

102. Edna Gunderson and Tom Green, " 'Imagine': Antidote to Harsh Bio," *USA Today*, 7 October 1988, 2D; Pat Travers, "Imagine: John Lennon," *People*, 10 October 1988, 22; *Variety*, 28 September 1988, 16.

103. Jim Kuzak, "Imagine: John Lennon," *Boxoffice*, December 1988: R101-02.

Bibliographical Notes

Rock, Rock, Rock 1956 was the first soundtrack in the genre. It generated little, if any, press coverage. Some three-and-a-half decades later soundtracks *do* attract attention, especially in trade publications such as *Billboard* and *Variety*. Academic observers of the phenomenon have been relatively late in entering this subject area.

Without listing all of the sources used in this volume (See End Notes), we did find the following books and articles to be particularly useful. No doubt some titles have been overlooked, a failing we immediately apologize for.

Philip Jenkinson and Alan Warner's *Celluloid Rock: Twenty Years of Movie Rock* (1974) and David Ehrenstein and Bill Reed's *Rock on Film* (1982) are the two, and only, non-coffee-table books on the subject. These efforts exhibit one major shortcoming: They incorrectly assume that the reader is familiar with the movies discussed, although most of them are gathering dust in studio vaults or warehouses. Many of the 1950s rock films are unavailable on video cassette, including the Katzman and Corman productions. *Blackboard Jungle*, shown sparsely on Ted Turner's TNT at inconvenient times—as of this writing—cannot be purchased or rented. Mike Shore's *Music Video* (1987), as of 1986, does a nice job of listing and reviewing those rockumentaries and showcasers that are available on cassette.

A highly welcome and valuable addition to the rock-film literature surfaced late in 1988. Thomas Doherty's *Teenagers and Teenpics: The Juvenilization of American Movies in the 1950s* is a study of Hollywood studios' attempt to combat television through so-called youth-exploitation productions, including showcasers and personality pics. This highly readable book also raises some interesting questions regarding the popularization of rock in America.

In the arena of war movies, Allen L. Woll's *The Hollywood Musical Goes to War* (1983) is one of the few volumes that addresses this topic. Lawrence Suid's *Guts and Glory: Great American War Movies* (1978), while not concerned with soundtracks, provides invaluable background information.

There are some good introductory articles on the rock soundtrack which, however cryptic, do shed some light on the phenomenon. Richard Staehling's "From Rock Around The Clock To The Trip: The Truth About Teen Movies (1969)" in *Rolling Stone* (December 1969) presents a nice commentary, especially on the Fifties. Mitchell Cohen's *Phonograph Record Magazine* (1976), provides a critical history of films entitled "Rockcinema: The First 21 Years, 1955-1976." A more worthwhile account is John Blair's "Early Rock Cinema 1956-1960" in *Goldmine* (September 1979). Blair, a collector, has some valuable insights; unfortunately, several of his loose citations are impossible to verify. Greil Marcus's "Rock Films" contribution to *The Rolling Stone Illustrated History of Rock 'n' Roll* (1981) is helpful. A filmologist's view is presented in Barry K. Grant's "The Classic Hollywood Musical and the 'Problem' of Rock 'n' Roll" in the *Journal of Popular Film and Television* (Winter 1986).

Interest in the genre grew in 1988. Gary Burn's "Film and Popular Music" in *Film and the Arts in Symbiosis* (1988) treats the intersection between the two media. Alexander Doty wrestles with the synergy issue quite well in "Music Sells Movies: (Re) New (ed) Conservatism in Film Marketing" in *Wide Angle* (1988). Armond White's "Hell of a Note: Rock's Rebellion" in *Film Comment* (1988) and Gillian G. Gaar's "Rock Soundtracks" in *Goldmine* (1989) sort of reinvent the wheel, but are good places to start.

Beginning in 1978, *Billboard* commenced, unpredictably, publishing special suppliments on soundtracks. Some are quite good. The problem is finding them. A few, as in 1984 and 1987, appear in year-end summary issues. Some surface in the summer months without a discernable pattern.

Sporadic articles of value have emerged since *Saturday Night Fever*. Of interest to those concerned with marketing processes are Mark Hunter's "Hitching Discs to Flick" in *Mother Jones* (May 1981); Debby Miller's "Rock is Money to Hollywood Ears" in *Rolling Stone* (October 1983), Peter Occhiogrosso's "Reelin' and Rockin' " in *American Film* (April 1984), and the highly insightful analysis provided by Jeffery M. Sydney in the 14 February 1987 issue of *Billboard* entitled "Putting Soundtracks on a Sound Basis." These pieces are thematic.

Specific motion pictures can be investigated by consulting *Film and Literature* and the *Music Index*. These should not, however, be viewed as the ultimate in bibliographical material. *F&L*, for example, omits such important sources as *The Hollywood Reporter*, *Premiere*, the *Los Angeles Times*, and *The Washington Post*. *American Film* is a must.

The Music Index is flawed, but it is the only tool available. Barry Lazell's, et al, *Rock Movers and Shakers* (1989) lists nearly 1,000 rock artists with a chronology of their activities, including soundtrack contributions. Cross-tabulating Lazell's dates with publications frequently proves fruitful.

Two encyclopedias are available: Jan Stacy and Ryder Syvertsen's *Rockin' Reels: An Illustrated History of Rock & Roll Movies*, and Linda J. Sandahl's *Encyclopedia of Rock Music on Film*. Both list credits and song titles along with brief plot synopses. Neither is exhaustive in coverage. Rob Burt's *Rock and Roll: The Movies* is primarily an illustrated history.

Index